Großes EURO Wörterbuch

WIRTSCHAFT

Deutsch, Englisch, Französisch, Italienisch, Spanisch

Buch und Zeit Verlagsgesellschaft mbH · Köln

Vorwort

Im Zeichen eines neuen, vereinigten Europa gewinnt die Beherrschung von Fremdsprachen im Wirtschaftsstudium und im Beruf immer mehr an Bedeutung. Die zunehmende Vernetzung und internationale Zusammenarbeit gerade auf wirtschaftlichem Gebiet machen es erforderlich, das vorliegende mehrsprachige Wörterbuch als kompetentes, zuverlässiges Nachschlagewerk zur Seite zu haben.

Rund 20.000 Stichwörter mit 80.000 Übersetzungen vermitteln die gängigsten Fachbegriffe aus dem Wirtschaftsleben in den fünf wichtigsten europäischen Sprachen: Deutsch, Englisch, Französisch, Italienisch und Spanisch. Der alphabetische Aufbau ermöglicht den schnellen Zugriff auf ein bestimmtes Stichwort und seine Übersetzungen – gleich in welcher der genannten Sprachen das Stichwort steht.

Somit ist dieser umfassende internationale Wirtschafts-Wortschatz unentbehrlich für alle Bereiche des modernen Wirtschaftslebens.

Abkürzungen:

D = Deutsch
E = Englisch
F = Französisch
I = Italienisch
Es = Spanisch
f = feminin
m = maskulin
n = Neutrum
pl = Plural

	D	E	F	I	Es
abaratamiento (Es)	Verbilligung f	cheapening	réduction du prix f	ribasso m	—
abastecedor (Es)	Zulieferer m	supplier	sous-traitant m	fornitore m	—
abastecimiento (Es)	Versorgung f	supply	approvisionne-ment m	approvvigiona-mento m	—
abastecimiento energético (Es)	Energieversorgung f	energy supply	approvisionnement en énergie f	approvvigionamento d'energia m	—
abatement of an action (E)	Verfahrens-einstellung f	—	arrêt d'une procédure m	sospensione del procedimento f	sobreseimiento del proceso m
ab Bahnhof (D)	—	ex rail/free on rail	départ gare	franco stazione	puesto en estación
Abbau (D)	—	reduction/lay off	réduction f/ diminution f	riduzione f/ diminuzione f	reducción f/ disminución f
abbonamento (I)	Abonnement n	subscription	abonnement m	—	suscripción f
abbonato (I)	Abonnent m	subscriber	abonné m	—	suscriptor m
abbuono (I)	Bonifikation f	bonus	bonification f	—	bonificación f
ABC-Analyse (D)	—	ABC analysis	analyse ABC f	analisi ABC f	análisis ABC m
ABC analysis (E)	ABC-Analyse f	—	analyse ABC f	analisi ABC f	análisis ABC m
Abfall (D)	—	waste	déchet m	rifiuti m pl	desechos m pl
Abfallbeseitigung (D)	—	waste disposal ·	élimination de déchets f	smaltimento dei rifiuti m	evacuación de residuos f
Abfallbörse (D)	—	recycling exchange	bourse de recyclage f	borsa dei rifiuti f	bolsa de reciclaje f
Abfallexperte (D)	—	expert on waste products	expert de déchets m	esperto dei rifiuti m	experto de productos residuales m
Abfallwirtschaft (D)	—	waste management	industrie de déchets f	industria dei rifiuti f	industria de desperdicios f
Abfertigung (D)	—	dispatch/clearance	expédition f/expédition en douane f	spedizione f/ sdoganamento m	despacho m/des-pacho de aduana m
Abfindung (D)	—	indemnity/ compensation	indemnité f/ compensation f	indennità f/ compensazione f	indemnización f/ compensación f
Abfindungsangebot (D)	—	compensation offer	offre d'indemnité f	offerta d'indennità f	oferta de indemnización f
Abgabe (D)	—	tax/duty	taxe f	imposta f/dazio m	impuesto m/ arancel m
abgabenfrei (D)	—	tax-free/duty-free	exempt de taxes	esente da contributi	exento de impuestos/ exento de derechos
abgabenpflichtig (D)	—	liable to tax	soumis à l'impôt	soggetto a contributi	sujeto a impuestos
Abgrenzung (D)	—	demarcation	délimitation f	delimitazione f	delimitación f
Abgrenzungsposten (D)	—	deferred item	comptes transitoires m pl	ratei e risconti m pl	cuentas de orden f pl
abholbereit (D)	—	ready for collection	disponible	pronto per il ritiro	listo para la recogida
abilità nel trattare (I)	Verhandlungs-geschick n	negotiation skills	habileté en matière de négociation f	—	tino de negociar m
ability (E)	Fähigkeit f	—	capacité f	capacità f	capacidad f
abitazione (I)	Wohnung f	apartment	appartement m	—	vivienda f
ab Kai (D)	—	ex quay/f.a.s.	départ quai	franco banchina	ex muelle
Abkommen (D)	—	agreement	accord m	accordo m	acuerdo m
Abladegewicht (D)	—	shipping (delivered) weight	poids au déchargement m	peso di scarico m	peso de descarga m
Ablage (D)	—	file	collection des dossiers f	archivio m	archivo m
Ablauffrist (D)	—	time limit	délai m	termine di scadenza m	vencimiento m
Ablauforganisation (D)	—	scheduling organization	organisation fonction-nelle de l'entreprise f	organizzazione del lavoro f	organización funcional f
Ablehnung (D)	—	refusal/rejection	refus m/rejet m	rifiuto m/rigetto m	recusación f/repulsa f
abliefern (D)	—	hand over	livrer	consegnare	entregar
ablösen (D)	—	redeem	amortir	rimborsare	sustituir/amortizar
Ablösesumme (D)	—	redemption sum	montant de rachat m	importo di rimborso m	suma de amortización f
Ablösungs-finanzierung (D)	—	redemption financing	financement du rachat m	finanziamento del rimborso m	financiamiento de amortización m
Abnahme (D)	—	acceptance/decrease	réception f/ réduction f	accettazione f/ riduzione f	aceptación f/ disminución f

	D	E	F	I	Es
Abnahmemenge (D)	—	purchased quantity	quantité commercialisée f	quantità d'acqusto f	cantidad de compra f
Abnahmepflicht (D)	—	obligation to accept delivery	obligation d'acceptation de la marchandise f	obbligo di accettare la consegna m	obligación de recepción f
Abnehmer (D)	—	buyer/purchaser/customer	acheteur m	acquirente m/cliente m	tomador m
Abnehmerland (D)	—	buyer country	pays acheteur m	paese acquirente m	país comprador m
Abnutzung (D)	—	wear and tear	dépréciation f	usura f	desgaste m
abogado (Es)	Rechtsanwalt m	lawyer	avocat m	avvocato m	—
abonar en cuenta (Es)	gutschreiben	credit	créditer	accreditare	—
abondance de matières premières (F)	Rohstoffreichtum m	abundancy of raw materials	—	ricchezza di materie prime f	abundancia en materias primas f
abonné (F)	Abonnent m	subscriber	—	abbonato m	suscriptor m
Abonnement (D)	—	subscription	abonnement m	abbonamento m	suscripción f
abonnement (F)	Abonnement n	subscription	—	abbonamento m	suscripción f
Abonnent (D)	—	subscriber	abonné m	abbonato m	suscriptor m
abono (Es)	Gutschrift f	credit	crédit m	accredito m	—
Abrechnung (D)	—	settlement of accounts	règlement m	liquidazione f	liquidación f
Abrechnungstag (D)	—	settling day	jour de la liquidation m	giorno di liquidazione m	fecha de liquidación f
Abrechnungs-verfahren (D)	—	settling procedure	méthode de l'apurement des comptes	metodo di liquidazione m	operaciones de descuento f pl
Abrechnungs-zeitraum (D)	—	accounting period	période comptable f	periodo di liquidazione m	período contable m
Abreisedatum (D)	—	date of departure	date de départ f	data di partenza f	fecha de partida f
a breve scadenza (I)	kurzfristig	short-term	à court terme	—	a corto plazo
abroad (E)	im Ausland	—	à l'étranger	all'estero	en el extranjero
Abruf (D)	—	call	appel m	richiesta f	reclamación de la entrega de un pedido f
Absage (D)	—	refusal	refus m	risposta negativa f	negativa f
Absatz (D)	—	sale/distribution	volume des ventes m	vendita f	cifra de ventas f
Absatzanalyse (D)	—	sales analysis	analyse de la distribution f	analisi di mercato f	análisis de venta m
Absatzchance (D)	—	sales prospects	possibilités de réussite des ventes f pl	prospettive di smercio f pl	posibilidades de venta f pl
Absatzfinanzierung (D)	—	sales financing	financement des ventes m	finanziamento delle vendite m	financiación de las ventas f
Absatzförderung (D)	—	sales promotion	promotion des ventes f	promozione dello smercio f	promoción comercial f
Absatzkrise (D)	—	sales crisis	crise de vente f	crisi di mercato f	crisis en la venta f
Absatzorganisation (D)	—	sales organization	organisation de vente f	organizzazione di vendita f	organización de ventas f
Absatzplanung (D)	—	sales planning	planning de la distribution m	pianificazione delle vendite f	planificación de ventas f
Absatzpolitik (D)	—	marketing policy	politique de vente f	politica di vendita f	política de ventas f
Absatzsegment (D)	—	sales segment	segment de vente m	segmento di vendita m	segmento de venta m
Absatzstatistik (D)	—	sales statistics	statistique de la vente f	statistica delle vendite f	estadística de ventas f
Absatzstrategie (D)	—	sales strategy	stratégie de vente f	strategia di vendita f	estrategia de ventas f
Absatzweg (D)	—	channel of distribution	canal de distribution m	via della distribuzione f	medio de venta f
Absatzwirtschaft (D)	—	marketing	commercialisation f	marketing m	economía de distribución f
Absatzziel (D)	—	sales target	objectif de vente m	obbiettivo di vendita m	fin de venta m
ab Schiff (D)	—	ex ship	départ navire	franco bordo	ex vapor
Abschlag (D)	—	reduction	déduction f	detrazione f	descuento m

	D	E	F	I	Es
Abschlagszahlung (D)	—	partial payment/ payment on account	premier verse- ment *m*/acompte *m*	pagamento a rate *m*/ pagamento in acconto *m*	pago parcial *m*/ pago a cuenta *m*
Abschluß (D)	—	conclusion	conclusion *f*	stipulazione *f*	contratación *f*/ conclusión *f*/cierre *m*
Abschlußprüfer (D)	—	auditor	vérificateur des comptes *m*	revisore *m*	revisor contable *m*
Abschlußprüfung (D)	—	audit	vérification des comptes *m*	revisione *f*	revisión contable *f*
Abschlußtechnik (D)	—	finishing technique	technique de conclusion *f*	metodo di chiusura *m*	técnica de conclusión *f*
Abschöpfungs- system (D)	—	absorption system	système d'absorption *m*	regime di prelievo *m*	sistema de gravámenes *m*
Abschreibung (D)	—	depreciation	amortissement *m*	ammortamento *m*	amortización *f*
Abschreibungs- fonds (D)	—	depreciation fund	fonds d'amortissement *m*	fondo ammortamenti *m*	fondo amortización *m*
Abschreibungs- gesellschaft (D)	—	project write-off company	société d'amortissement *f*	società di ammortamento *f*	sociedad de amortización *f*
Abschreibungs- objekt (D)	—	object of depreciation	objet d'amortissement *m*	oggetto da ammortizzare *m*	objeto de amortización *m*
Abschrift (D)	—	copy	copie *f*	copia *f*	copia *f*
Abschwung (D)	—	down-swing	dépression *f*	regresso *m*	baja *f*
Absender (D)	—	sender	envoyeur *m*	mittente *m*	remitente *m*
Absendung (D)	—	dispatch	expédition *f*	spedizione *f*	expedición *f*
absent (E)	abwesend	—	absent	assente	ausente
absent (F)	abwesend	absent	—	assente	ausente
absolutamente confidential (Es)	streng vertraulich	strictly confidential	strictement confidentiel	strettamente confidenziale	—
absorción (Es)	Absorption *f*	absorption	absorption *f*	assorbimento *m*	—
Absorption (D)	—	absorption	absorption *f*	assorbimento *m*	absorción *f*
absorption (E)	Absorption *f*	—	absorption *f*	assorbimento *m*	absorción *f*
absorption (F)	Absorption *f*	absorption	—	assorbimento *m*	absorción *f*
absorption system (E)	Abschöpfungs- system *n*	—	système d'absorption *m*	regime di prelievo *m*	sistema de gravámenes *m*
Abstand (D)	—	distance	distance *f*	distanza *f*	distancia *f*
Abteilung (D)	—	division/department	service *m*	reparto *m*	sección *f*
Abteilungsleiter (D)	—	head of department	chef de service *m*	capo reparto *m*	jefe de sección *m*
Abteilungs- organisation (D)	—	department organization	organisation du service *f*	organizzazione reparto *f*	organización de sección *f*
Abtretung (D)	—	assignment	cession *f*	cessione *f*	cesión *f*
Abtretungsvertrag (D)	—	contract of assignment	contrat de cession *m*	contratto di cessione *m*	contrato de cesión *m*
abuso del computer (I)	Computer- kriminalität *f*	computer criminality	délits informatiques *m pl*	—	delincuencia informática *f*
abuso di fiducia (I)	Veruntreuung *f*	misappropriation	détournement *m*	—	malversación *f*
Abwärtstrend (D)	—	downward trend	baisse *f*	tendenza al ribasso *f*	tendencia bajista *f*
Abwasser (D)	—	waste water	eaux résiduelles *f pl*	acque di scarico *f pl*	aguas residuales *f pl*
Abwasserkosten (D)	—	sewage disposal costs	coûts de traitement des eaux usées *m pl*	costi per le acque di scarico *m pl*	gastos para aguas residuales *m pl*
Abwasserreinigung (D)	—	purification of sewage	clarification des eaux usées *f*	depurazione delle acque di scarico *f*	depuración de las aguas residuales *f*
Abweichung (D)	—	deviation	divergence *f*	deviazione *f*	diferencia *f*
Abwerbung (D)	—	pirating	débauchage *m*	accaparramento *m*	sonsacamiento *m*
ab Werk (D)	—	ex works	départ usine	franco fabbrica	ex fábrica
Abwertung (D)	—	devaluation	dévaluation *f*	svalutazione *f*	devaluación *f*
abwesend (D)	—	absent	absent	assente	ausente
Abwickler (D)	—	liquidator	liquidateur *m*	liquidatore *m*	liquidador *m*
Abwicklung (D)	—	settlement	exécution *f*	esecuzione *f*	ejecución *f*
Abwicklungskonto (D)	—	settlement account	compte de liquidation *m*	conto di liquidazione *f*	cuenta de liquidación *f*
abzahlen (D)	—	pay off	régler par compte	pagare a rate	pagar por cuotas

	D	E	F	I	Es
Abzahlung (D)	—	repayment	remboursement *m*	rimborso *m*	reintegro *m*/ pago a plazos *m*
Abzahlungs- geschäft (D)	—	hire purchase transaction	achat à tempérament *m*	operazione con pagamento a rate *f*	venta a plazos *f*
Abzinsung (D)	—	discounting	déduction des intérêts non courus *f*	deduzione di interessi *f*	deducción de intere- ses no acumulados *f*
Abzug (D)	—	deduction/discount	diminution *f*/ escompte *m*	detrazione *f*/ sconto *m*	deducción *f*/ descuento *m*
academia (Es)	Akademie *f*	academy	académie *f*	accademia *f*	—
académie (F)	Akademie *f*	academy	—	accademia *f*	academia *f*
academy (E)	Akademie *f*	—	académie *f*	accademia *f*	academia *f*
a cargo de (Es)	zu Lasten	chargeable to	à la charge de	a carico di	—
a carico di (I)	zu Lasten	chargeable to	à la charge de	—	a cargo de
accademia (I)	Akademie *f*	academy	académie *f*	—	academia *f*
accantonamento (I)	Rückstellung *f*	reserves	provision pour pertes et charges *f*	—	reserva *f*
accaparramento (I)	Abwerbung *f*	pirating	débauchage *m*	—	sonsacamiento *m*
acceleration principle (E)	Akzelerations- prinzip *n*	—	principe d'accélération *m*	principio di accelerazione *m*	principio de aceleración *m*
accelerato (I)	beschleunigt	speedy	accéléré	—	acelerado
accéléré (F)	beschleunigt	speedy	—	accelerato	acelerado
accensione di un mutuo (I)	Geldaufnahme *f*	raising of money	emprunt *m*	—	dinero tomado a préstamo *m*
acceptable (E)	akzeptabel	—	acceptable	accettabile	aceptable
acceptable (F)	akzeptabel	acceptable	—	accettabile	aceptable
acceptable risk (E)	Restrisiko *n*	—	risque acceptable *m*	rischio rimanente *m*	riesgo aceptable *m*
acceptance[1] (E)	Annahme *f*	—	acceptation *f*	accettazione *f*	aceptación *f*
acceptance[2] (E)	Abnahme *f*	—	réception *f*	accettazione *f*	aceptación *f*/ disminución *f*
acceptance credit[1] (E)	Wechselkredit *m*	—	crédit d'escompte *m*	credito cambiario *m*	crédito cambiario *m*
acceptance credit[2] (E)	Akzeptkredit *m*	—	crédit par traites acceptées *m*	credito d'accettazione *m*	crédito de aceptación *m*
acceptation (F)	Annahme *f*	acceptance	—	accettazione *f*	aceptación *f*
acceptation de prendre le risque en charge (F)	Deckungszusage *f*	confirmation of cover	—	impegno di copertura *m*	nota de cobertura *f*
accepted bill (E)	Akzept *n*	—	traite acceptée *f*	accettazione *f*	aceptación *f*
accertamento tributario (I)	Steuerveranlagung *f*	tax assessment	taxation fiscale *f*	—	tasación de los impuestos *f*
acceso (Es)	Zugang *m*	access	entrée *f*	accesso *m*	—
access (E)	Zugang *m*	—	entrée *f*	accesso *m*	acceso *m*
accesso (I)	Zugang *m*	access	entrée *f*	—	acceso *m*
accesso al mercato (I)	Marktzutritt *m*	access to the market	accès au marché *m*	—	acceso al mercado *m*
accettabile (I)	akzeptabel	acceptable	acceptable	—	aceptable
accettazione[1] (I)	Akzept *n*	accepted bill	traite acceptée *f*	—	aceptación *f*
accettazione[2] (I)	Annahme *f*	acceptance	acceptation *f*	—	aceptación *f*
accettazione[3] (I)	Abnahme *f*	acceptance	réception *f*	—	aceptación *f*
accident du travail (F)	Arbeitsunfall *m*	industrial injury	—	infortunio sul posto di lavoro *m*	accidente profesional *m*
accidente profesional (Es)	Arbeitsunfall *m*	industrial injury	accident du travail *m*	infortunio sul posto di lavoro *m*	—
acción (Es)	Aktie *f*	share	action *f*	azione *f*	—
acción al portador (Es)	Inhaberaktie *f*	bearer share	action au porteur *f*	azione al portatore *f*	—
acción de impugnación (Es)	Anfechtungsklage *f*	action for avoidance	action en annulation *f*	azione di impugnazione *f*	—
acciones[1] (Es)	Aktien *pl*	shares	actions *f pl*	azioni *f*	—
acciones[2] (Es)	Aktionen *pl*	actions	actions *f pl*	azioni *f pl*	—
acción especial (Es)	Sonderaktion *f*	special action	action spéciale *f*	azione speciale *f*	—
accionista (Es)	Aktionär *m*	shareholder	actionnaire *m*	azionista *m*	—
acción nominal (Es)	Namensaktie *f*	registered share	action nominative *f*	azione nominativa *f*	—

	D	E	F	I	Es
acción ordinaria (Es)	Stammaktie f	ordinary share	action ordinaire f	azione ordinaria f	—
acción preferente (Es)	Vorzugsaktie f	preference share	action privilégiée f	azione privilegiata f	—
accollamento (I)	Überwälzung f	passing on	répercussion f	—	traslación f
accommodating (E)	kulant	—	arrangement	corrente	de fácil avenencia
accommodation (E)	Kulanz f	—	souplesse en affaires f	correntezza f	facilidad en los negocios f
accompanying documents (E)	Begleitpapiere pl	—	pièces accompagnant l'envoi f pl	bolle di accompagnamento f pl	documentos adjuntos m pl
accoppiamento a reazione (I)	Rückkopplung f	feedback	accouplement réactif m	—	reacoplamiento m
accord¹ (F)	Abkommen n	agreement	—	accordo m	acuerdo m
accord² (F)	Zustimmung f	consent	—	consenso m	consentimiento m
accord de compensation de devises (F)	Devisenausgleichsabkommen n	foreign exchange offset agreement	—	accordo di clearing valutario m	acuerdo de compensación de divisas m
accord de contrôle (F)	Beherrschungsvertrag m	control agreement	—	contratto di controllo m	contrato de dominación m
accord de payement (F)	Zahlungsabkommen n	payments arrangement	—	accordo di pagamento m	acuerdo de pagos m
accord de salaires (F)	Lohnvereinbarung f	wage agreement	—	accordo salariale m	pacto salarial m
accord douanier (F)	Zollabkommen n	customs convention	—	accordo sulle tariffe doganali m	convenio aduanero m
accord monétaire (F)	Währungsabkommen n	currency agreement	—	accordo monetario m	acuerdo monetario m
accordo (I)	Abkommen n	agreement	accord m	—	acuerdo m
accordo di clearing valutario (I)	Devisenausgleichsabkommen n	foreign exchange offset agreement	accord de compensation de devises m	—	acuerdo de compensación de divisas m
accordo di pagamento (I)	Zahlungsabkommen n	payments arrangement	accord de payement m	—	acuerdo de pagos m
accordo monetario (I)	Währungsabkommen n	currency agreement	accord monétaire m	—	acuerdo monetario m
accordo salariale (I)	Lohnvereinbarung f	wage agreement	accord de salaires m	—	pacto salarial m
accordo speciale (I)	Sondervereinbarung f	special agreement	accord particulier m	—	acuerdo especial m
accordo sui prezzi (I)	Preisabsprache f	price fixing	accord sur les prix m	—	acuerdo de precios m
accordo sulle materie prime (I)	Rohstoffabkommen n	International Commodity Agreements	accord sur les matières premières m	—	acuerdo de materias primas m
accordo sulle tariffe doganali (I)	Zollabkommen n	customs convention	accord douanier m	—	convenio aduanero m
accord particulier (F)	Sondervereinbarung f	special agreement	—	accordo speciale m	acuerdo especial m
accords généraux de crédit (F)	allgemeine Kreditvereinbarungen pl	general borrowing agreements	—	condizioni generali di credito f pl	acuerdos generales de crédito m pl
accord sur les matières premières (F)	Rohstoffabkommen n	International Commodity Agreements	—	accordo sulle materie prime m	acuerdo de materias primas m
accord sur les prix (F)	Preisabsprache f	price fixing	—	accordo sui prezzi m	acuerdo de precios m
account (E)	Konto n	—	compte m	conto m	cuenta f
account book (E)	Kontobuch n	—	livre de compte m	libro dei conti m	libro de cuentas m
account books (E)	Geschäftsbücher pl	—	livres de commerce m pl	libri contabili m pl	libros de contabilidad m pl
account holder (E)	Kontoinhaber m	—	titulaire d'un compte m	titolare del conto m	titular de una cuenta m
accounting (E)	Buchhaltung f	—	comptabilité f	contabilità f	contabilidad f
accounting period (E)	Abrechnungszeitraum m	—	période comptable f	periodo di liquidazione m	período contable m
accounting system (E)	Rechnungswesen n	—	comptabilité f	ragioneria f	contabilidad f
account number (E)	Kontonummer f	—	numéro de compte m	numero di conto m	número de cuenta m
accouplement réactif (F)	Rückkopplung f	feedback	—	accoppiamento a reazione m	reacoplamiento m
accredit (E)	akkreditieren	—	accréditer	accreditare	acreditar
accreditare¹ (I)	akkreditieren	accredit	accréditer	—	acreditar
accreditare² (I)	gutschreiben	credit	créditer	—	abonar en cuenta
accréditer (F)	akkreditieren	accredit	—	accreditare	acreditar

	D	E	F	I	Es
accréditif (F)	Akkreditiv *n*	letter of credit	—	credito documentario *m*	crédito documentario *m*
accréditif bancaire (F)	Bankakkreditiv *n*	bank letter of credit	—	lettera di credito *f*	carta de crédito bancaria *f*
accréditif irrévocable (F)	unwiderrufliches Akkreditiv *n*	irrevocable letter of credit	—	apertura di credito *f* documentario irrevocabile	crédito documentario irrevocable *m*
accréditif payable en espèce (F)	Barakkreditiv	cash letter of credit	—	apertura di credito documentario semplice *f*	crédito simple *m*
accredito (I)	Gutschrift *f*	credit	crédit *m*	—	abono *m*
accreedor (Es)	Gläubiger *m*	creditor	créancier *m*	creditore *m*	—
accroissement constant (F)	lineares Wachstum *n*	linear growth	—	crescita lineare *f*	crecimiento lineal *m*
accroissement de la population (F)	Bevölkerungs-wachstum *m*	increase in population	—	incremento demografico *m*	crecimiento demográfico *m*
accroissement de valeur (F)	Wertzuwachs *m*	appreciation	—	incremento di valore *m*	plusvalía *f*
accumulation (E)	Akkumulation *f*	—	accumulation *f*	accumulazione *f*	acumulación *f*
accumulation (F)	Akkumulation *f*	accumulation	accumulation	accumulazione *f*	acumulación *f*
accumulazione (I)	Akkumulation *f*	accumulation	accumulation *f*	—	acumulación *f*
accusé de réception (F)	Empfangs-bestätigung *f*	acknowledgement of receipt	—	ricevuta *f*	recibo *m*
aceite usado (Es)	Altöl *n*	waste oil	huile usée *m*	olio usato *m*	—
acelerado (Es)	beschleunigt	speedy	accéléré	accelerato	—
aceptable (Es)	akzeptabel	acceptable	acceptable	accettabile	—
aceptación[1] (Es)	Akzept *n*	accepted bill	traite acceptée *f*	accettazione *f*	—
aceptación[2] (Es)	Annahme *f*	acceptance	acceptation *f*	accettazione *f*	—
aceptación[3] (Es)	Abnahme *f*	acceptance	réception *f*	accettazione *f*	—
achat[1] (F)	Kauf *m*	purchase	—	acquisto *m*	compra *f*
achat[2] (F)	Einkauf *m*	purchase	—	acquisto *m*	compra *f*
achat à crédit[1] (F)	Kreditgeschäft *n*	credit business	—	operazione di credito *f*	operaciones de crédito *f pl*
achat à crédit[2] (F)	Kreditkauf *m*	credit purchase	—	acquisto a credito *m*	compra de crédito *f*
achat à l'éssai (F)	Kauf auf Probe *m*	sale on approval	—	acquisto a titolo di prova *m*	compra a prueba *f*
achat à tempérament[1] (F)	Teilzahlungs-geschäft *n*	partial payment transaction	—	vendita a rate *f*	operación a plazo *f*
achat à tempérament[2] (F)	Ratenkauf *m*	hire-purchase transaction	—	acquisto a rate *m*	compra a plazo *f*
achat à tempérament[3] (F)	Abzahlungs-geschäft *n*	hire purchase transaction	—	operazione con pagamento a rate *f*	venta a plazos *f*
achat à terme (F)	Zielkauf *m*	purchase on credit	—	acquisto a termine *m*	compra a plazos *m*
achat de remplacement (F)	Ersatzkauf *m*	substitute purchase	—	acquisto di compensazione *m*	compra de sustitución *f*
achat de soutien (F)	Stützungskauf *m*	support buying	—	acquisto di sostegno *m*	compra para sostener precios *f*
achat d'impulsion (F)	Impulskauf *m*	impulse buying	—	acquisto impulsivo *m*	compra espóntánea *f*
achat d'une quantité minimum (F)	Mindestabnahme *f*	minimum purchase	—	quantitativo minimo di fornitura *m*	recogida mínima *f*
achat intermédiaire (F)	Zwischenabnahme *f*	intermediate purchase	—	acquisto intermediario *m*	compra intermediaria *f*
achats d'intervention (F)	Interventionskäufe *pl*	intervention buying	—	acquisti d'intervento *m pl*	compras de intervención *f pl*
achats spéculatifs (F)	Meinungskäufe *pl*	speculative buying	—	acquisti speculativi *m pl*	compras especulativas *f pl*
acheter (F)	kaufen	buy	—	acquistare	comprar
acheteur[1] (F)	Abnehmer *m*	buyer/purchaser/customer	—	acquirente *m/* cliente *m*	tomador *m*
acheteur[2] (F)	Einkäufer *m*	buyer	—	acquirente *m*	comprador *m*
acheteur[3] (F)	Besteller *m*	customer	—	committente *m*	demandante *m*
acheteur[4] (F)	Käufer *m*	purchaser	—	acquirente *m*	adquirente *m*

	D	E	F	I	Es
acheteur en gros (F)	Großabnehmer *m*	bulk buyer	—	acquirente all'ingrosso *m*	comprador al por mayor *m*
achèvement (F)	Fertigstellung *f*	completion	—	completamento *m*	terminación total *f*
Ackerbau (D)	—	agriculture	agriculture *f*	agricoltura *f*	agricultura *f*
acknowledgement of a debt (E)	Schuldanerkennung *f*	—	reconnaissance de dette *f*	riconoscimento del debito *m*	reconocimiento de la deuda *m*
acknowledgement of receipt (E)	Empfangs-bestätigung *f*	—	accusé de réception *m*	ricevuta *f*	recibo *m*
a comisión (Es)	auf Provisionsbasis	on a commission basis	à la commission	a provvigione	—
acompte[1] (F)	Rate *f*	instalment/rate	—	rata *f*	plazo *m*
acompte[2] (F)	Anzahlung *f*	deposit	—	pagamento in acconto *m*	pago a cuenta *m*
acompte provisionnel sur l'imposition (F)	Steuer-vorauszahlung *f*	advanced payment of taxes	—	pagamento anticipato delle imposte *m*	impuestos adelantados *m pl*
a-conto-Zahlung (D)	—	payment on account	payement acompte *m*	pagamento a conto *m*	pago a cuenta *m*
à convenance (F)	auf Abruf	on call	—	su richiesta	a requerimiento
a corto plazo (Es)	kurzfristig	short-term	à court terme	a breve scadenza	—
à court terme (F)	kurzfristig	short-term	—	a breve scadenza	a corto plazo
acque di scarico (I)	Abwasser *n*	waste water	eaux résiduelles *f pl*	—	aguas residuales *f pl*
acque territoriali (I)	Küstengewässer *n*	coastal waters	eaux côtières *f pl*	—	zona costera *f*
acquirente[1] (I)	Einkäufer *m*	buyer	acheteur *m*	—	comprador *m*
acquirente[2] (I)	Abnehmer *m*	buyer/purchaser/customer	acheteur *m*	—	tomador *m*
acquirente[3] (I)	Käufer *m*	purchaser	acheteur *m*	—	adquirente *m*
acquirente all'ingrosso (I)	Großabnehmer *m*	bulk buyer	acheteur en gros *m*	—	comprador al por mayor *m*
acquirente finale (I)	Endabnehmer *m*	ultimate buyer	preneur final *m*	—	comprador final *m*
acquisition[1] (E)	Anschaffung *f*	—	acquisition *f*	acquisto *m*	adquisición *f*
acquisition[2] (E)	Aquisition *f*	—	acquisition *f*	acquisizione *f*	adquisición *f*
acquisition[1] (F)	Aquisition *f*	acquisition	—	acquisizione *f*	adquisición *f*
acquisition[2] (F)	Anschaffung *f*	acquisition	—	acquisto *m*	adquisición *f*
acquisition value (E)	Anschaffungswert *m*	—	valeur d'acquisition *f*	valore d'acquisto *m*	valor de adquisición *m*
acquisizione (I)	Aquisition *f*	acquisition	acquisition *f*	—	adquisición *f*
acquistare (I)	einkaufen	buy	acheter	—	comprar
acquistare (I)	kaufen	buy	acheter	—	comprar
acquisti d'intervento (I)	Interventionskäufe *pl*	intervention buying	achats d'intervention *m pl*	—	compras de intervención *f pl*
acquisti speculativi (I)	Meinungskäufe *pl*	speculative buying	achats spéculatifs *m pl*	—	compras especulativas *f pl*
acquisto[1] (I)	Einkauf *m*	purchase	achat *m*	—	compra *f*
acquisto[2] (I)	Anschaffung *f*	acquisition	acquisition *f*	—	adquisición *f*
acquisto[3] (I)	Kauf *m*	purchase	achat *m*	—	compra *f*
acquisto a credito (I)	Kreditkauf *m*	credit purchase	achat à crédit *m*	—	compra de crédito *f*
acquisto a rate (I)	Ratenkauf *m*	hire-purchase transaction	achat à tempérament *m*	—	compra a plazo *f*
acquisto a termine (I)	Zielkauf *m*	purchase on credit	achat à terme *m*	—	compra a plazos *m*
acquisto a titolo di prova (I)	Kauf auf Probe *m*	sale on approval	achat à l'éssai *m*	—	compra a prueba *f*
acquisto di compensazione (I)	Ersatzkauf *m*	substitute purchase	achat de remplacement *m*	—	compra de sustitución *f*
acquisto di sostegno (I)	Stützungskauf *m*	support buying	achat de soutien *m*	—	compra para sostener precios *f*
acquisto di un'azienda (I)	Geschäfts-übernahme *f*	business acquisition	reprise d'une affaire *f*	—	adquisición de una empresa *f*
acquisto impulsivo (I)	Impulskauf *m*	impulse buying	achat d'impulsion *m*	—	compra espontánea *f*
acquisto intermediario (I)	Zwischenabnahme *f*	intermediate purchase	achat intermédiaire *m*	—	compra intermediaria *f*
acquit d'entrée (F)	Zolleinfuhrschein *m*	bill of entry	—	bolletta d'entrata *f*	certificado de aduana *m*

	D	E	F	I	Es
acquit de transit (F)	Durchgangsschein *m*	transit certificate	—	bolletta di transito *f*	pasavante *m*
acquittement (F)	Erfüllung *f*	compliance	—	adempimento *m*	cumplimiento *m*
acreditar (Es)	akkreditieren	accredit	acccréditer	accreditare	—
acreedor (Es)	Kreditor *pl*	creditor	créditeur *m*	creditore *m*	—
acreedor de la quiebra (Es)	Konkursgläubiger *m*	bankrupt's creditor	créancier de la faillite *m*	creditore della massa fallimentare *m*	—
acte administratif (F)	Verwaltungsakt *m*	administrative act	—	atto amministrativo *m*	acto administrativo *m*
acte de société (F)	Gesellschafts-vertrag *m*	shareholder's agreement	—	contratto di società *m*	contrato social *m*
acte juridique (F)	Rechtsgeschäft *n*	legal transaction	—	negozio giuridico *m*	negocio jurídico *m*
actif¹ (F)	erwerbstätig	gainfully employed	—	attivo	activo
actif² (F)	Aktivbestand *m*	assets	—	effetivo *m*	activo disponible *m*
action (F)	Aktie *f*	share	—	azione *f*	acción *f*
action au porteur (F)	Inhaberaktie *f*	bearer share	—	azione al portatore *f*	acción al portador *f*
action de presse (F)	Presseaktion *f*	press campaign	—	azione stampa *f*	campaña de prensa *f*
action en annulation (F)	Anfechtungsklage *f*	action for avoidance	—	azione di impugnazione *f*	acción de impugnación *f*
action en dommages-intérêts (F)	Schadens-ersatzklage *f*	action for damages	—	azione di risarcimen-to danni *f*	demanda de daños y perjuicios *f*
action en justice (F)	Klage *f*	legal action	—	citazione in giudizio *f*	demanda *f*
action for avoidance (E)	Anfechtungsklage *f*	—	action en annulation *f*	azione di impugnazione *f*	acción de impugnación *f*
action for damages (E)	Schadens-ersatzklage *f*	—	action en dommages-intérêts *f*	azione di risarcimen-to danni *f*	demanda de daños y perjuicios *f*
actionnaire (F)	Aktionär *m*	shareholder	—	azionista *m*	accionista *m*
action nominative (F)	Namensaktie *f*	registered shares	—	azione nominativa *f*	acción nominal *f*
action ordinaire (F)	Stammaktie *f*	ordinary shares	—	azione ordinaria *f*	acción ordinaria *f*
action parameter (E)	Aktionsparameter *m*	—	paramètre d'action *m*	parametro d'azione *m*	parámetro de acción *m*
action privilégiée (F)	Vorzugsaktie *f*	preference share	—	azione privilegiata *f*	acción preferente *f*
actions (E)	Aktionen *pl*	—	actions *f pl*	azioni *f pl*	acciones *f pl*
actions¹ (F)	Aktien *pl*	shares	—	azioni *f pl*	acciones *f pl*
actions² (F)	Aktionen *pl*	actions	—	azioni *f pl*	acciones *f pl*
action spéciale (F)	Sonderaktion *f*	special action	—	azione speciale *f*	acción especial *f*
action successorale (F)	Erbstreit *m*	dispute concerning an inheritance	—	causa ereditaria *f*	litigio hereditario *m*
active balance (E)	Aktivsaldo *m*	—	solde créditeur *m*	saldo attivo *m*	saldo activo *m*
active partner (E)	aktiver Teilhaber *m*	—	associé prenant part à la gestion *m*	socio attivo *m*	socio activo *m*
actividad del Estado (Es)	Staatstätigkeit *f*	state activity	activité de l'Etat *f*	attività pubblica *f*	—
activité de l'Etat (F)	Staatstätigkeit *f*	state activity	—	attività pubblica *f*	actividad del Estado *f*
activité professionnelle (F)	Gewerbe *n*	trade/industry/craft	—	commercio *m*/indu-stria *f*/artigianato *m*	industria *f*/comer-cio *m*/artesanía *f*
activity rate (E)	Erwerbsquote *f*	—	proportion de la population active *f*	quota della popolazione attiva *f*	proporción de la población activa *f*
activo¹ (Es)	Aktiva *pl*	assets	masse active *f*	attivo *m*	—
activo² (Es)	erwerbstätig	gainfully employed	actif	attivo	—
activo disponible (Es)	Aktivbestand *m*	assets	actif *m*	effettivo *m*	—
activo efectivo (Es)	Barvermögen *n*	cash assets	valeurs réalisables à court terme ou disponibles *f pl*	patrimonio in contanti *m*	—
activo exterior (Es)	Auslandsvermögen *n*	foreign assets	avoirs à l'étranger *m pl*	patrimonio estero *m*	—
activo fijo (Es)	Anlagevermögen *n*	fixed assets	valeurs immobilisées *f pl*	attivo fisso *m*	—
activo inmobiliario (Es)	Realvermögen *n*	real wealth	patrimoine réel *m*	patrimonio reale *m*	—
activo monetario (Es)	Geldvermögen *n*	financial assets	moyens financiers *m pl*	patrimonio monetario *m*	—
acto administrativo (Es)	Verwaltungsakt *m*	administrative act	acte administratif *m*	atto amministrativo *m*	—
actual costs (E)	Istkosten *pl*	—	coûts réels *m pl*	costi effettivi *m pl*	gastos efectivos *m pl*

	D	E	F	I	Es
actual figures (E)	Istzahlen *pl*	—	résultats effectifs *m pl*	dati effettivi *m pl*	cifras efectivas *f pl*
actual wage (E)	Effektivlohn *m*	—	salaire effectif *m*	salario effettivo *m*	salario efectivo *m*
acuerdo (Es)	Abkommen *n*	agreement	accord *m*	accordo *m*	—
acuerdo de apertura (Es)	Eröffnungs-beschluß *m*	order opening a trial	arrêt de mise en accusation *m*	decreto di citazione in giudizio *m*	—
acuerdo de compensación de divisas (Es)	Devisenausgleichs-abkommen *n*	foreign exchange offset agreement	accord de compensation de devises *m*	accordo di clearing valutario *m*	—
acuerdo de materias primas (Es)	Rohstoffabkommen *n*	International Commodity Agreements	accord sur les matières premières *m*	accordo sulle materie prime *m*	—
acuerdo de pagos (Es)	Zahlungs-abkommen *n*	payments arrangement	accord de payement *m*	accordo di pagamento *m*	—
acuerdo de precios (Es)	Preisabsprache *f*	price fixing	accord sur les prix *m*	accordo sui prezzi *m*	—
acuerdo especial (Es)	Sondervereinbarung *f*	special agreement	accord particulier *m*	accordo speciale *m*	—
acuerdo monetario (Es)	Währungs-abkommen *n*	currency agreement	accord monétaire *m*	accordo monetario *m*	—
acuerdos generales de crédito (Es)	allgemeine Kreditver-einbarungen *pl*	general borrowing agreements	accords généraux de crédit *f pl*	condizioni generali di credito *f pl*	—
acumulación (Es)	Akkumulation *f*	accumulation	accumulation *f*	accumulazione *f*	—
acuse de recibo (Es)	Rückschein *m*	advice of delivery	avis de réception *m*	ricevuta di ritorno *f*	—
ad alta incidenza di capitale (I)	kapitalintensiv	capital-intensive	avec grande intensité de capital	—	con gran intensidad de capital
ad alta incidenza di lavoro (I)	arbeitsintensiv	labour-intensive	déterminé par le facteur main-d'œuvre	—	con gran intensidad de mano de obra
ad alta incidenza salariale (I)	lohnintensiv	wage-intensive	déterminé par le facteur salaire	—	con gran intensidad de costos salariales
adaptación (Es)	Anpassung *f*	adaptation	adaptation *f*	adattamento *m/* adeguamento *m*	
adaptation (E)	Anpassung *f*	—	adaptation *f*	adattamento *m/* adeguamento *m*	adaptación *f/*ajuste *m*
adaptation (F)	Anpassung *f*	adaptation	—	adattamento *m/* adeguamento *m*	adaptación *f/*ajuste *m*
adattamento (I)	Anpassung *f*	adaptation	adaptation *f*	—	adaptación *f/*ajuste *m*
add (E)	addieren	—	additionner	addizionare	sumar
addebitare (I)	belasten	load/charge	débiter	—	cargar/adeudar
addebito¹ (I)	Belastung *f*	load	charge *f*	—	gravamen *m*
addebito² (I)	Lastschrift *f*	debit note	note de débit *f*	—	cargo en cuenta *m*
addestramento dei venditori (I)	Verkäuferschulung *f*	sales training	formation des vendeurs *f*	—	formación de los vendedores *f*
addieren (D)	—	add	additionner	addizionare	sumar
adding mistake (E)	Additionsfehler *m*	—	erreur d'addition *f*	errore di addizione *m*	error de adición *m*
Addition (D)	—	addition	addition *f*	addizione *f*	adición *f*
addition (E)	Addition *f*	—	addition *f*	addizione *f*	adición *f*
addition (F)	Addition *f*	addition	—	addizione *f*	adición *f*
additional burden (E)	Mehrbelastung *f*	—	surcharge *f*	onere supplementare *m*	carga suplementaria *f*
additional delivery (E)	Mehrlieferung *f*	—	livraison supplémentaire *f*	fornitura supplementare *f*	exceso *m*
additional freight charges (E)	Frachtzuschlag *m*	—	supplément de fret *m*	supplemento di nolo *m*	sobreporte *m*
additional payment of taxes (E)	Steuernachzahlung *f*	—	payement d'un rappel d'impôt *m*	pagamento arretrato delle imposte *m*	pago de impuestos atrasados *m*
additional period (E)	Nachfrist *f*	—	prolongation *f*	termine supplementare *m*	plazo de gracia *m*
additional sale (E)	Zusatzverkauf *m*	—	vente additionnelle *f*	vendita complementare *f*	venta adicional *f*
additional work (E)	Mehrarbeit *f*	—	travail supplémentaire *m*	lavoro supplementare *m*	trabajo extraordinario *m*
additionner (F)	addieren	add	—	addizionare	sumar
Additionsfehler (D)	—	adding mistake	erreur d'addition *f*	errore di addizione *m*	error de adición *m*
addizionare (I)	addieren	add	additionner	—	sumar

	D	E	F	I	Es
addizione (I)	Addition *f*	addition	addition *f*	—	adición *f*
address¹ (E)	Anschrift *f*	—	adresse *f*	indirizzo *m*	dirección *f*
address² (E)	adressieren	—	adresser	indirizzare	dirigir
address³ (E)	Adresse *f*	—	adresse *f*	indirizzo *m*	dirección *f*
addressee (E)	Adressat *m*	—	destinataire *m*	destinatario *m*	destinatario *m*
adelanto (Es)	Vorauszahlung *f*	payment in advance	payement anticipé *m*	pagamento anticipato *m*	—
adempimento (I)	Erfüllung *f*	compliance	acquittement *m*	—	cumplimiento *m*
adición (Es)	Addition *f*	addition	addition *f*	addizione *f*	—
adjoint (F)	Stellvertreter *m*	deputy	—	sostituto *m*	sustituto *m*
adjudicated bankrupt (E)	Gemeinschuldner *m*	—	failli *m*	debitore fallito *m*	deudor común *m*
adjustment costs (E)	Anpassungskosten *pl*	—	coûts d'adaptation *m pl*	costi d'adattamento *m pl*	gastos de readaptación *m pl*
adjustment lag (E)	Anpassungs- verzögerung *f*	—	retard d'adaptation *m*	ritardo d'adattamento *m*	retraso de adaptación *m*
administered prices (E)	administrierte Preise *pl*	—	prix administrés *m pl*	prezzi amministrati *m pl*	precios administrados *m pl*
administración (Es)	Verwaltung *f*	administration	administration *f*	amministrazione *f*	—
administración de almacén (Es)	Lagerverwaltung *f*	stockkeeping	entreposage *m*	amministrazione del magazzino *f*	—
administración de hacienda (Es)	Steuerbehörden *pl*	tax authority	administration des contributions *f*	autorità fiscali *f pl*	—
administración del proyecto (Es)	Projekt- Management *n*	project management	gestion d'un projet *f*	management di progetto *m*	—
administración de una cuenta (Es)	Kontoführung *f*	keeping of an account	tenue de compte *f*	tenuta di un conto *f*	—
administración forzosa (Es)	Zwangsverwaltung *f*	receivership	séquestre judiciare *m*	amministrazione giudiziaria *f*	—
administrador (Es)	Verwalter *m*	administrator	administrateur *m*	amministratore *m*	—
administrador de la herencia (Es)	Nachlaßverwalter *m*	administrator of the deceased's estate	administrateur de la succession *m*	amministratore dell'eredità *m*	—
administrateur (F)	Verwalter *m*	administrator	—	amministratore *m*	administrador *m*
administrateur de la succession (F)	Nachlaßverwalter *m*	administrator of the deceased's estate	—	amministratore dell'eredità *m*	administrador de la herencia *m*
Administration (D)	—	administration	administration *f*	amministrazione *f*	administración *f*
administration (E)	Verwaltung *f*	—	administration *f*	amministrazione *f*	administración *f*
administration (F)	Verwaltung *f*	administration	—	amministrazione *f*	administración *f*
administration des contributions (F)	Steuerbehörden *pl*	tax authority	—	autorità fiscali *f pl*	administración de hacienda *f*
administration fee (E)	Bußgeld *n*	—	amende *f*	pena pecuniaria *f*	multa *f*
administration of justice (E)	Rechtsprechung *f*	—	jurisprudence *f*	giurisprudenza *f*	jurisprudencia *f*
administration of prices (E)	Preislenkung *f*	—	réglementation des prix *f*	gestione dei prezzi *f*	reglamentación de precios *f*
administrative act (E)	Verwaltungsakt *m*	—	acte administratif *m*	atto amministrativo *m*	acto administrativo *m*
administrator (E)	Verwalter *m*	—	administrateur *m*	amministratore *m*	administrador *m*
administrator in bankruptcy proceedings (E)	Konkursverwalter *m*	—	liquidateur de la faillite *m*	curatore fallimentare *m*	síndico de quiebra *m*
administrator of the deceased's estate (E)	Nachlaßverwalter *m*	—	administrateur de la succession *m*	amministratore dell'eredità *m*	administrador de la herencia *m*
administrierte Preise (D)	—	administered prices	prix administrés *m pl*	prezzi amministrati *m pl*	precios administrados *m pl*
admisión (Es)	Zulassung *f*	admission	admission *f*	ammissione *f*	—
admission (E)	Zulassung *f*	—	admission *f*	ammissione *f*	admisión *f*
admission (F)	Zulassung *f*	admission	—	ammissione *f*	admisión *f*
admission ticket (E)	Eintrittskarte *f*	—	billet *m*	biglietto d'ingresso *m*	entrada *f*
(ad)monición (Es)	Mahnung *f*	demand for payment	mise en demeure *f*	sollecito *m*	—
adorno del escaparate (Es)	Schaufenster- dekoration *f*	window dressing	décoration de vitrine *f*	allestimento di vetrina *m*	—
adquirente (Es)	Käufer *m*	purchaser	acheteur *m*	acquirente *m*	—

	D	E	F	I	Es
adquisición¹ (Es)	Aquisition f	acquisition	acquisition f	acquisizione f	—
adquisición² (Es)	Anschaffung f	acquisition	acquisition f	acquisto m	—
adquisición de una empresa (Es)	Geschäfts-übernahme f	business acquisition	reprise d'une affaire f	acquisto di un'azienda m	—
Adressat (D)	—	addressee	destinataire m	destinatario m	destinatario m
Adresse (D)	—	address	adresse f	indirizzo m	dirección f
adresse¹ (F)	Anschrift f	address	—	indirizzo m	dirección f
adresse² (F)	Adresse f	address	—	indirizzo m	dirección f
adresse de la maison (F)	Firmenanschrift f	company address	—	indirizzo della ditta m	dirección de la empresa f
adresser (F)	adressieren	address	—	indirizzare	dirigir
adressieren (D)	—	address	adresser	indirizzare	dirigir
aduana (Es)	Zoll m	customs	douane f	dogana f	—
aduana aparte (Es)	unverzollt	duty unpaid	non dédouané	non sdoganato	—
aduana proteccionista (Es)	Schutzzoll m	protective duty	droit de protection m	dazio protettivo m	—
aduanas ad valorem (Es)	Wertzoll m	ad valorem duty	taxe de douane ad valorem f	dazio ad valorem m	—
aduanas preferenciales (Es)	Präferenzzoll m	preferential duty	taxe préférentielle de douane f	dazio preferenziale m	—
aduanas uniformes (Es)	Einheitszoll m	uniform duty	droit unique m	dazio unitario m	—
ad valorem duty (E)	Wertzoll m	—	taxe de douane ad valorem f	dazio ad valorem m	aduanas ad valorem f pl
advance (E)	Vorschuß m	—	avance f	anticipo m	anticipo m
advanced payment of taxes (E)	Steuer-vorauszahlung f	—	acompte provisionnel sur l'imposition m	pagamento anticipato delle imposte m	impuestos adelantados m pl
advantage (E)	Vorteil m	—	avantage m	vantaggio m	ventaja f
advertisement¹ (E)	Anzeige f	—	annonce f	inserzione f	anuncio m
advertisement² (E)	Zeitungsanzeige f	—	annonce de journal f	inserzione sul giornale f	anuncio de prensa m
advertisement of a vacancy (E)	Stellen-ausschreibung f	—	mise au concours d'une place f	bando di concorso per impiegati m	convocatoria de oposiciones f
advertisement under a box number (E)	Chiffre-Anzeige f	—	annonce chiffrée f	inserzione in cifra f	anuncio codificado m
advertising (E)	Reklame f	—	publicité f	réclame f	publicidad f
advertising activity (E)	Werbeaktion f	—	campagne publicitaire f	azione pubblicitaria f	campaña publicitaria f
advertising agency (E)	Werbeagentur f	—	agence de publicité f	agenzia pubblicitaria f	agencia publicitaria f
advertising aids (E)	Werbemittel n	—	moyen publicitaire m	mezzo pubblicitario m	medio publicitario m
advertising bill (E)	Aktionsplakat n	—	affiche d'action f	manifesto promozionale m	cartel de acción m
advertising budget (E)	Werbebudget n	—	budget de publicité m	budget pubblicitario m	presupuesto publicitario m
advertising campaign (E)	Werbekampagne f	—	campagne publicitaire f	campagna pubblicitaria f	campaña publicitaria f
advertising control (E)	Werbeerfolgs-kontrolle f	—	contrôle du résultat de la publicité m	controllo del succes-so pubblicitario m	análisis del resultado publicitario m
advertising copy (E)	Werbetext m	—	texte publicitaire m	testo pubblicitario m	texto publicitario m
advertising expert (E)	Werbefachmann m	—	technicien publicitaire m	esperto di pubblicità m	perito publicitario m
advertising film (E)	Werbefilm m	—	film publicitaire m	film pubblicitario m	película promocional f
advertising frequency (E)	Werbefrequenz f	—	fréquence publicitaire f	frequenza della pubblicità f	frecuencia publicitaria f
advertising gift (E)	Werbegeschenk n	—	cadeau publicitaire m	omaggio pubblicitario m	regalo publicitario m
advertising letter (E)	Werbebrief m	—	lettre publicitaire f	lettera pubblicitaria f	circular de publicidad f
advertising media (E)	Werbemedien pl	—	médias publicitaires m pl	mezzi pubblicitari m pl	medios de publicidad m pl
advertising medium (E)	Werbeträger m	—	support publicitaire m	veicolo pubblicitario m	medio de publicidad m

	D	E	F	I	Es
advertising objectives (E)	Werbeziele pl	—	objectifs publicitaires m pl	obiettivi pubblicitari m pl	objetivos de la publicidad m pl
advertising spot (E)	Werbespot m	—	spot publicitaire m	spot pubblicitario m	spot publicitario m
advice¹ (E)	Beratung f	—	consultation f	consulenza f	asoramiento m
advice² (E)	Avis m	—	avis m	avviso m	aviso m
advice of delivery (E)	Rückschein m	—	avis de réception m	ricevuta di ritorno f	acuse de recibo m
adviser (E)	Berater m	—	conseiller m	consulente m	asesor m
affaire (F)	Geschäft n	business	—	negozio m	negocio m
affaire au comptant (F)	Tagesgeschäft n	day-to-day operations	—	contratto a contanti m	operación al contado f
affaire couplée (F)	Kopplungsgeschäft n	tie-in transaction	—	operazione abbinata f	negocio acoplado m
affaire de compensation (F)	Kompensations- geschäft n	barter transaction	—	operazione di compensazione f	operacion de compensación f
affaire déficitaire (F)	Verlustgeschäft n	losing business	—	affare in perdita m	venta con pérdida f
affaire d'exportation (F)	Exportgeschäft n	export business	—	operazione d'esportazione f	operación de exportación f
affaire d'immobilière (F)	Immobiliengeschäft n	property transactions	—	operazione immobiliare f	negocio de inmuebles m
affaire en commission (F)	Kommissions- geschäft n	commission business	—	operazione di commissione f	operación de comisión f
affaire spéculative (F)	Spekulations- geschäft n	speculative operations	—	operazione speculativa f	operación de especulación f
affare con l'estero (I)	Auslandsgeschäft n	foreign business	opération avec l'étranger f	—	negocio de exporta- ción o importación m
affare in perdita (I)	Verlustgeschäft n	losing business	affaire déficitaire f	—	venta con pérdida f
affectation (F)	Zuwendung f	bestowal	—	assegnazione f	gratificación f
affermato (I)	behauptet	maintained	affirmé	—	sostenido
affichage des prix (F)	Preisauszeichnung f	pricemarking	—	indicazione del prezzo f	indicación de precios f
affiche (F)	Plakat n	poster	—	manifesto m	cartel m
affiche d'action (F)	Aktionsplakat n	advertising bill	—	manifesto promozionale m	cartel de acción m
affidabile (I)	zuverlässig	reliable	de confiance	—	de confianza
affiliated company (E)	Schwester- gesellschaft f	—	société affiliée f	consorella f	compañía asociada f
affirmé (F)	behauptet	maintained	—	affermato	sostenido
affluent society (E)	Wohlstands- gesellschaft f	—	société de bien-être f	società del benessere f	sociedad de bienestar f
affrancare (I)	frankieren	prepay the postage	affranchir	—	franquear
affranchir (F)	frankieren	prepay the postage	—	affrancare	franquear
affrètement (F)	Verfrachtung f	carriage of goods by sea	—	trasporto marittimo m	expedición f
after-sale service (E)	Kundendienst m	—	service après-vente m	servizio d'assistenza m	servicio posventa m
after treatment (E)	Nachbereitung f	—	remise en ordre f	rielaborazione f	tratamiento ulterior m
against cash (E)	gegen Barzahlung	—	au comptant	contro pagamento in contanti	al contado
against letter of credit (E)	gegen Akkreditiv	—	contre accréditif	contro lettera di credito	con crédito documentario
age group (E)	Altersgruppe f	—	groupe d'âge m	gruppo d'età m	grupo según la edad m
age limit (E)	Altersgrenze f	—	limite d'âge f	limite d'età m	limite de edad m
agence¹ (F)	Zweigstelle f	branch	—	agenzia f	filial f
agence² (F)	Agentur f	agency	—	agenzia f	agencia f
agence³ (F)	Geschäftsstelle f	office	—	ufficio m	oficina f
agence⁴ (F)	Filiale f	branch	—	filiale f	filial f
agence à l'étranger (F)	Auslandsvertretung f	agency abroad	—	rappresentanza estera f	representación en el exterior f
agence de publicité (F)	Werbeagentur f	advertising agency	—	agenzia pubblicitaria f	agencia publicitaria f
agence de renseignements (F)	Auskunftei f	information bureau	—	agenzia d'informazioni f	oficina de información f

	D	E	F	I	Es
agence de voyages (F)	Reisebüro n	travel agency	—	ufficio viaggi m	agencia de viajes f
agence exclusive (F)	Alleinvertretung f	sole agency	—	rappresentanza esclusiva f	representación exclusiva f
agencia (Es)	Agentur f	agency	agence f	agenzia f	—
agencia de viajes (Es)	Reisebüro n	travel agency	agence de voyages f	ufficio viaggi m	—
agencia laboral (Es)	Arbeitsvermittlung f	employment agency	bureau de placement m	ufficio di collocamento m	—
agencia publicitaria (Es)	Werbeagentur f	advertising agency	agence de publicité f	agenzia pubblicitaria f	—
agency (E)	Agentur f	—	agence f	agenzia f	agencia f
agency abroad (E)	Auslandsvertretung f	—	agence à l'étranger f	rappresentanza estera f	representación en el exterior f
Agent (D)	—	agent	agent m	agente m	agente m
agent (E)	Agent m	—	agent m	agente m	agente m
agent (F)	Agent m	agent	—	agente m	agente m
agent d'assurance (F)	Versicherungs-agent m	insurance agent	—	agente d'assicurazione m	agente de seguros m
agente (Es)	Agent m	agent	agent m	agente m	—
agente (I)	Agent m	agent	agent m	—	agente m
agente cambio y bolsa (Es)	Kursmakler m	stock broker	courtier en bourse m	agente di borsa m	—
agente d'assicurazione (I)	Versicherungs-agent m	insurance agent	agent d'assurance m	—	agente de seguros m
agente de inmuebles (Es)	Immobilienmakler m	estate agent	courtier en affaires immoblières m	agente immobiliare m	—
agente de seguros (Es)	Versicherungs-agent m	insurance agent	agent d'assurance m	agente d'assicurazione m	—
agente di borsa (I)	Kursmakler m	stock broker	courtier en bourse m	—	agente cambio y bolsa m
agente di cambio (I)	Börsenmakler m	stock broker	courtier en bourse m	—	corredor de bolsa m
agente di zona (I)	Gebietsvertreter m	area representative	représentant régional m	—	representante regional m
agente immobiliare (I)	Immobilienmakler m	estate agent	courtier en affaires immoblières m	—	agente de inmuebles m
agente marittimo (I)	Schiffsmakler m	shipbroker	courtier maritime m	—	corredor marítimo m
agente regional (Es)	Bezirksvertreter m	local agent	agent local m	rappresentante di zona m	—
agent exclusif (F)	Alleinvertreter m	sole agent	—	rappresentante esclusivo m	representante exclusivo m
agent général (F)	Generalvertreter m	general agent	—	rappresentante generale m	representante general m
agent local (F)	Bezirksvertreter m	local agent	—	rappresentante di zona m	agente regional m
Agentur (D)	—	agency	agence f	agenzia f	agencia f
agenzia[1] (I)	Zweigstelle f	branch	agence f	—	filial f
agenzia[2] (I)	Agentur f	agency	agence f	—	agencia f
agenzia d'informazioni (I)	Auskunftei f	information bureau	agence de renseignements f	—	oficina de información f
agenzia pubblicitaria (I)	Werbeagentur f	advertising agency	agence de publicité f	—	agencia publicitaria f
agevolazione sugli interessi (I)	Zinserleichterung f	reduction of interest	minoration de l'intérêt m	—	reducción de intereses f
aggio[1] (I)	Aufgeld n	agio	prime f	—	agio m
aggio[2] (I)	Agio n	agio	agio m	—	agio m
aggiunta[1] (I)	Zugabe f	extra	prime f	—	suplemento m
aggiunta[2] (I)	Aufschlag m	surcharge	hausse f	—	recargo m
Agglomeration (D)	—	agglomeration	agglomération f	agglomerazione f	aglomeración f
agglomeration (E)	Agglomeration f	—	agglomération f	agglomerazione f	aglomeración f
agglomération (F)	Agglomeration f	agglomeration	—	agglomerazione f	aglomeración f
agglomerazione (I)	Agglomeration f	agglomeration	agglomération f	—	aglomeración f
Agio (D)	—	agio	agio m	aggio m	agio m
agio (F)	Agio n	agio	—	aggio m	agio m

	D	E	F	I	Es
agio¹ (E)	Aufgeld n	—	prime f	aggio m	agio m
agio² (E)	Agio n	—	agio m	aggio m	agio m
agio¹ (Es)	Agio n	agio	agio m	aggio m	—
agio² (Es)	Aufgeld n	agio	prime f	aggio m	—
a giro di posta (I)	postwendend	by return of post	par retour du courrier	—	a vuelta de correo
aglomeración (Es)	Agglomeration f	agglomeration	agglomération f	agglomerazione f	—
Agrarbetrieb (D)	—	agricultural enterprise	entreprise agricole f	azienda agricola f	empresa agrícola f
Agrarerzeugnis (D)	—	agricultural product	produit agricole m	prodotto agricolo m	producto agrícola m
Agrarexport (D)	—	farm exports	exportation de produits agricoles f	esportazione agricola f	exportación agrícola f
Agrargüter (D)	—	agricultural goods	produits agricoles m pl	beni agricoli m pl	bienes agrícolas m pl
Agrarimport (D)	—	farm imports	importation de produits agricoles f	importazione agricola f	importación agrícola f
Agrarkrise (D)	—	agricultural crisis	crise de l'agriculture f	crisi agricola f	crisis agrícola f
Agrarmarkt (D)	—	agricultural market	marché agricole m	mercato agrario m	mercado agrícola m
Agrarmarkt-ordnung (D)	—	agricultural market organization	organisation des marchés agricoles f	regolamento del mercato agrario m	reglamentación del mercado agrícola f
Agrarpolitik (D)	—	agricultural policy	politique agricole f	politica agraria f	política agrícola f
Agrarpreis (D)	—	prices of farm products	prix agricole m	prezzo agrario m	precio agrícola m
Agrarprodukt (D)	—	farm product	produit agricole m	prodotto agricolo m	producto agrario m
Agrarstaat (D)	—	agricultural state	état agricole m	paese agrario m	estado agrario m
Agrarstatistik (D)	—	agricultural statistics	statistique agricole f	statistica agraria f	estadística agrícola f
Agrarstruktur (D)	—	agricultural structure	structure agraire f	struttura agraria f	estructura agraria f
Agrarsubventionen (D)	—	agricultural subsidies	subvèntions de l'agriculture f pl	sovvenzioni agrarie f pl	subvención a la agricultura f
Agrarüberschüsse (D)	—	agricultural surpluses	excédents agricoles m pl	eccedenze agricole f pl	excedentes agrícolas m pl
Agrarunion (D)	—	agricultural union	union agricole f	unione agraria f	unión agrícola f
Agrarwirtschaft (D)	—	farming	économie agricole f	economia agraria f	economía agraria f
agreement (E)	Abkommen n	—	accord m	accordo m	acuerdo m
agricoltura (I)	Ackerbau m	agriculture	agriculture f	—	agricultura f
agricultura (Es)	Ackerbau m	agriculture	agriculture f	agricoltura f	—
agricultural crisis (E)	Agrarkrise f	—	crise de l'agriculture f	crisi agricola f	crisis agrícola f
agricultural enterprise (E)	Agrarbetrieb m	—	entreprise agricole f	azienda agricola f	empresa agrícola f
agricultural goods (E)	Agrargüter pl	—	produits agricoles m pl	beni agricoli m pl	bienes agrícolas m pl
agricultural market (E)	Agrarmarkt m	—	marché agricole m	mercato agrario m	mercado agrícola m
agricultural market organization (E)	Agrarmarktordnung f	—	organisation des marchés agricoles f	regolamento del mercato agrario m	reglamentación del mercado agrícola f
agricultural policy (E)	Agrarpolitik f	—	politique agricole f	politica agraria f	política agrícola f
agricultural produce (E)	Agrarerzeugnis n	—	produit agricole m	prodotto agricolo m	producto agrícola m
agricultural state (E)	Agrarstaat m	—	état agricole m	paese agrario m	estado agrario m
agricultural statistics (E)	Agrarstatistik f	—	statistique agricole f	statistica agraria f	estadística agrícola f
agricultural structure (E)	Agrarstruktur f	—	structure agraire f	struttura agraria f	estructura agraria f
agricultural subsidies (E)	Agrarsubventionen pl	—	subventions de l'agriculture f pl	sovvenzioni agrarie f pl	subvención a la agricultura f
agricultural surpluses (E)	Agrarüberschüsse pl	—	excédents agricoles m pl	eccedenze agricole f pl	excedentes agrícolas m pl
agricultural union (E)	Agrarunion f	—	union agricole f	unione agraria f	unión agrícola f
agriculture (E)	Ackerbau m	—	agriculture f	agricoltura f	agricultura f
agriculture (F)	Ackerbau m	agriculture	—	agricoltura f	agricultura f
aguas residuales (Es)	Abwasser n	waste water	eaux résiduelles f pl	acque di scarico f pl	—
ahorro¹ (Es)	Sparen n	saving	épargne f	risparmio m	—

	D	E	F	I	Es
ahorro² (Es)	Ersparnis f	savings	épargne f	risparmio m	—
ahorro forzoso (Es)	Zwangssparen n	compulsory saving	épargne forcée f	risparmio coatto m	—
aide (F)	Aushilfe f	auxiliary worker	—	aiuto m	ayudante m
aide au développement (F)	Entwicklungshilfe f	development aid	—	aiuto ai paesi in via di sviluppo m	ayuda al desarrollo f
aide financière (F)	Kapitalhilfe f	capital aid	—	aiuto finanziario m	ayuda financiera f
aide financière à l'exportation (F)	Außenhandels-finanzierung f	foreign trade financing	—	finanziamento del commercio estero m	financiación del comercio exterior f
aide sociale (F)	Sozialhilfe f	public assistance	—	assistenza sociale f	ayuda social f
air carrier (E)	Luftfrachtführer m	—	voiturier aérien m	vettore aereo m	transportista m
air freight (E)	Luftfracht f	—	fret aérien m	nolo aereo m	flete aéreo m
air freight traffic (E)	Luftfrachtverkehr m	—	transport aérien des marchandises m	traffico aereo commerciale m	tráfico de flete aéreo m
air mail (E)	Luftpost f	—	par avion	posta aerea f	correo aéreo m
air route (E)	Luftweg m	—	voie aérienne f	via aerea f	vía aérea f
airway bill (E)	Luftfrachtbrief m	—	lettre de transport aérien f	lettera di trasporto aereo f	transporte aéreo m
aiuto (I)	Aushilfe f	auxiliary worker	aide m	—	ayudante m
aiuto ai paesi in via di sviluppo (I)	Entwicklungshilfe f	development aid	aide au développement f	—	ayuda al desarrollo f
aiuto all'esportazione (I)	Exporthilfe f	export subsidy	subvention à l'exportatiion f	—	ayuda a la exportación f
aiuto finanziario (I)	Kapitalhilfe f	capital aid	aide financière f	—	ayuda financiera f
ajournement (F)	Vertagung f	postponement	—	rinvio m	aplazamiento m/ suspensión f
ajuste financiero (Es)	Finanzausgleich m	financial equalization	compensation financière f	compensazione finanziaria f	—
ajuste presupuestario (Es)	Planrevision f	budget adjustment	révision des coûts marginaux f	revisione del piano f	—
Akademie (D)	—	academy	académie f	accademia f	academia f
Akkord (D)	—	piece work	convention de salaire à la tâche f	cottimo m	destajo m
Akkordarbeit (D)	—	piecework	travail à la tâche m	lavora a cottimo m	trabajo a destajo m
Akkordlohn (D)	—	piece work wages	salaire à la pièce m	retribuzione per il lavoro a cottimo f	salario a destajo m
Akkordsystem (D)	—	piece work system	système du travail aux pièces m	sistema del lavoro a cottimo m	régimen de trabajo a destajo m
akkreditieren (D)	—	accredit	accréditer	accreditare	acreditar
Akkreditiv (D)	—	letter of credit	accréditif m	credito documentario m	crédito documentario m
Akkreditiv-abwicklung (D)	—	settlement by letter of credit	exécution par crédit documentaire f	procedura del credito documentario f	ejecución por crédito documentario f
Akkreditiv-eröffnung (D)	—	opening of a letter of credit	ouverture d'un accréditif f	apertura del credito documentario f	apertura de un crédito documentario f
Akkreditivklausel (D)	—	letter of credit clause	clause de payement par accréditif f	clausola del credito documentario f	cláusula de crédito documentario f
Akkreditivsumme (D)	—	amount of the letter of credit	montant de l'accréditif m	importo del credito documentario m	suma del crédito documentario f
Akkreditivzahlung (D)	—	payment by letter of credit	payement par accréditif m	pagamento contro credito documentario m	pago por crédito documentario m
Akkumulation (D)	—	accumulation	accumulation f	accumulazione f	acumulación f
Akte (D)	—	file	dossier m	pratica f	documento m
Aktenablage (D)	—	filing	archives f pl	archivio delle pratiche m	archivo m
Aktennotiz (D)	—	memorandum	note f	annotazione f	nota f
Aktie (D)	—	share	action f	azione f	acción f
Aktienausgabe (D)	—	share issue	émission d'actions f	emissione di azioni f	emisión de acciones f
Aktienbestand (D)	—	shareholding	portefeuille d'actions m	portafoglio di azioni m	cartera de acciones f
Aktiendepot (D)	—	share deposit	dépôt d'actions m	deposito di azioni m	depósito de acciones m

	D	E	F	I	Es
Aktienemision (D)	—	share issue	émission d'actions f	emissione di azioni f	emisión de acciones f
Aktiengesellschaft (D)	—	joint stock company	société anonyme f	società per azioni f	sociedad anónima f
Aktiengesetz (D)	—	Companies Act	loi sur les sociétés par actions f	legge sulle società per azioni f	ley sobre sociedades anónimas f
Aktienhandel (D)	—	dealing in shares	négociation des actions f	commercio azionario m	contratación de acciones f
Aktienindex (D)	—	share index	indice du cours des actions m	indice azionario m	índice de cotización de acciones m
Aktienkapital (D)	—	share capital	fonds social m	capitale azionario m	capital en acciones m
Aktienkurs (D)	—	share price	cours des actions m	corso delle azioni m	cotización de las acciones f
Aktienmehrheit (D)	—	majority of shares	majorité d'actions f	maggioranza delle azioni f	mayoría de acciones f
Aktiennotierung (D)	—	share quotation	cotation des actions f	quotazione delle azioni f	cotización de acciones f
Aktienpaket (D)	—	block of shares	paquet d'actions m	pacchetto delle azioni m	paquete de acciones m
Aktienrecht (D)	—	company law	loi sur les sociétés anonymes f pl	diritto azionario m	derecho de sociedades anónimas m
Aktionär (D)	—	shareholder	actionnaire m	azionista m	accionista m
Aktionen (D)	—	actions	actions f pl	azioni f pl	acciones f pl
Aktionsfeld (D)	—	field of action	champ d'action m	campo d'azione m	campo de acción m
Aktionsparameter (D)	—	action parameter	paramètre d'action m	parametro d'azione m	parámetro de acción m
Aktionsplakat (D)	—	advertising bill	affiche d'action f	manifesto promozionale m	cartel de acción m
Aktiva (D)	—	assets	masse active f	attivo m	activo m
Aktivbestand (D)	—	assets	actif m	effettivo m	activo disponible m
aktiver Teilhaber (D)	—	active partner	associé prênant part à la gestion m	socio attivo m	socio activo m
Aktivgeschäft (D)	—	credit transaction	opération active f	operazione attiva f	operaciones activas f pl
Aktivsaldo (D)	—	active balance	solde créditeur m	saldo attivo m	saldo activo m
Akzelerationsprinzip (D)	—	acceleration principle	principe d'accélération m	principio di accelerazione m	principio de aceleración m
Akzept (D)	—	accepted bill	traite acceptée f	accettazione f	aceptación f
akzeptabel (D)	—	acceptable	acceptable	accettabile	aceptable
Akzepteinlösung (D)	—	honouring of an acceptance	honner la traite acceptée	pagamento di un effetto m	descuento de una letra aceptada m
Akzeptkredit (D)	—	acceptance credit	crédit par traites acceptées m	credito d'accettazione m	crédito de aceptación m
a la atención (Es)	zu treuen Händen	for safekeeping	remettre en mains sûres	alla particolare attenzione	—
à la charge de (F)	zu Lasten	chargeable to	—	a carico di	a cargo de
à la commission (F)	auf Provisionsbasis	on a commission basis	—	a provvigione	a comisión
a largo plazo (Es)	langfristig	long-term	à long terme	a lunga scadenza	—
alarma de smog (Es)	Smogalarm m	smog warning	alerte au smog f	allarme smog m	—
a la vista (Es)	auf Sicht	at sight	à vue	a vista	—
alcance publicitario (Es)	Werbereichweite f	scope of advertising effect	zone de rayonnement de la publicité f	raggio d'azione della pubblicità m	—
alcista (Es)	Haussier m	bull	haussier m	speculatore al rialzo m	—
al contado (Es)	gegen Barzahlung	against cash	au comptant	contro pagamento in contanti	—
al contado contra documentos (Es)	Dokumente gegen Zahlung pl	documents against payments	documents contre payement m pl	pagamento contro documenti m	—
alerte au smog (F)	Smogalarm m	smog warning	—	allarme smog m	alarma de smog f
à l'essai (F)	auf Probe	on trial	—	in prova	a prueba
à l'étranger (F)	im Ausland	abroad	—	all'estero	en el extranjero
aliénation (F)	Veräußerung f	sale/alienation	—	alienazione f	enajenación f
alienazione (I)	Veräußerung f	sale/aleination	aliénation f	—	enajenación f

	D	E	F	I	Es
Alkoholsteuer (D)	—	tax on alcohol	impôt sur l'alcool *m*	imposta sugli alcolici *f*	impuesto sobre el alcohol *m*
alla particolare attenzione (I)	zu treuen Händen	for safekeeping	remettre en mains sûres	—	a la atención
allarme smog (I)	Smogalarm *m*	smog warning	alerte au smog *f*	—	alarma de smog *f*
allegato (I)	Anlage *f*	enclosure	pièce jointe *f*	—	anexo *m*
Alleininhaber (D)	—	sole owner	seul propriétaire *m*	titolare unico *m*	propietario exclusivo *m*
Alleinvertreter (D)	—	sole agent	agent exclusive *m*	rappresentante esclusivo *m*	representante exclusivo *m*
Alleinvertretung (D)	—	sole agency	agence exclusive *f*	rappresentanza esclusiva *f*	representación exclusiva *f*
Alleinvertretungs-recht (D)	—	sole and exclusive agency right	droit exclusif de représentation *m*	diritto di rappresen-tanza esclusiva *m*	derecho de representación exclusiva *m*
Alleinvertrieb (D)	—	exclusive distribution	vente exclusive *f*	vendita esclusiva *f*	distribución exclusiva *f*
all'estero (I)	im Ausland	abroad	à l'étranger	—	en el extranjero
allestimento di vetrina (I)	Schaufenster-dekoration *f*	window dressing	décoration de vitrine *f*	—	adorno del escaparate *m*
allgemeine Geschäfts-bedingungen (D)	—	general terms of contract	conditions générales de contrat *f pl*	condizioni generali di contratto *f pl*	condiciones generales de contrato *f pl*
allgemeine Kredit-vereinbarungen (D)	—	general borrowing agreements	accords généraux de crédit *f pl*	condizioni generali di credito *f pl*	acuerdos generales de crédito *m pl*
Allgemeinwohl (D)	—	public wellfare	bien général *m*	benestare pubblico *m*	bienestar público *m*
allocation[1] (E)	Allokation *f*	—	allocation *f*	allocazione *f*	alocación *f*
allocation[2] (E)	Zuteilung *f*	—	répartition *f*	attribuzione *f*/ ripartizione *f*	asignación *f*
allocation[1] (F)	Zuschuß *m*	allowance	—	sovvenzione *f*	subvención *f*
allocation[2] (F)	Allokation *f*	allocation	—	allocazione *f*	alocación *f*
allocazione (I)	Allokation *f*	allocation	allocation *f*	—	alocación *f*
Allokation (D)	—	allocation	allocation *f*	allocazione *f*	alocación *f*
allowance (E)	Zuschuß *m*	—	allocation *f*	sovvenzione *f*	subvención *f*
allowance for expenses (E)	Spesenpauschale *f*	—	forfait de frais *m*	forfait di spese *m*	suma global de gastos *f*
allowance per kilometre (E)	Kilometergeld *n*	—	indemnité par kilomètre *f*	indennità per chilometro *f*	kilometraje *m*
all-risks-clause (E)	all-risks-Klausel *f*	—	clause d'assurance (contre) tous (les) risques *f*	clausola tutti i rischi *f*	cláusula a todo riesgo *f*
all-risks-Klausel (D)	—	all-risks-clause	clause d'assurance (contre) tous (les) risques *f*	clausola tutti i rischi *f*	cláusula a todo riesgo *f*
almacén[1] (Es)	Lager *n*	warehouse	magasin *m*	magazzino *m*	—
almacén[2] (Es)	Lagerraum *m*	storage space	halle de dépôt *f*	magazzino *m*	—
almacenaje[1] (Es)	Lagerung *f*	storage	stockage *m*	magazzinaggio *m*	—
almacenaje[2] (Es)	Lagerhaltung *f*	stockkeeping	entreposage *m*	magazzinaggio *m*	—
almacenamiento (Es)	Einlagerung *f*	storage	entreposage *m*	immagazzina-mento *m*	—
almacén de entregas (Es)	Auslieferungslager *n*	distribution centre	entrepôt de distribution *m*	deposito di consegna *m*	—
al mejor cambio[1] (Es)	bestens	at best	au mieux	ottimo	—
al mejor cambio[2] (Es)	billigst	at best price	au meilleur prix	al prezzo più basso	—
al netto degli influssi stagionali (I)	saisonbereinigt	seasonally adjusted	corrigé du mouvement saisonnier	—	desestacionalizado
alocación (Es)	Allokation *f*	allocation	allocation *f*	allocazione *f*	—
à long terme (F)	langfristig	long-term	—	a lunga scadenza	a largo plazo
al più presto possibile (I)	schnellstmöglich	as quickly as possible	le plus vite possible	—	tan rápido como sea posible
al prezzo più basso (I)	billigst	at best price	au meilleur prix	—	al mejor cambio
alquiler (Es)	Miete *f*	rent	location *f*	canone di locazione *m*	—

	D	E	F	I	Es
alquiler de almacenaje (Es)	Lagermiete f	warehouse rent	location d'une surface pour magasinage f	spese di magazzinaggio f pl	—
Alta Autoridad (Es)	hohe Behörde f	high authority	haute autorité f	alta autorità f	—
alta autorità (I)	hohe Behörde f	high authority	haute autorité f	—	Alta Autoridad f
alta congiuntura (I)	Hochkonjunktur f	boom	haute conjoncture f	—	alta coyuntura f
alta coyuntura (Es)	Hochkonjunktur f	boom	haute conjoncture f	alta congiuntura f	—
alta dirección (Es)	Management n	management	management m	management m	—
alternativa (Es)	Alternative f	alternative	alternative f	alternativa f	—
alternativa (I)	Alternative f	alternative	alternative f	—	alternativa f
Alternative (D)	—	alternative	alternative f	alternativa f	alternativa f
alternative (E)	Alternative f	—	alternative f	alternativa f	alternativa f
alternative (F)	Alternative f	alternative	—	alternativa f	alternativa f
alternative planning (E)	Alternativplanung f	—	planification alternative f	pianificazione alternativa f	planificación alternativa f
Alternativkosten (D)	—	opportunity costs	coûts alternatifs m pl	costi alternativi m pl	coste alternativo m
Alternativplanung (D)	—	alternative planning	planification alternative f	pianificazione alternativa f	planificación alternativa f
Altersgrenze (D)	—	age limit	limite d'âge f	limite d'età m	limite de edad m
Altersgruppe (D)	—	age group	groupe d'âge m	gruppo d'età m	grupo según la edad m
Altersversicherung (D)	—	old age insurance	assurance-vieillesse f	assicurazione per la vecchiaia f	seguro de vejez m
Altersversorgung (D)	—	provision for old age	prévoyance vieillesse f	previdenza per la vecchiaia f	previsión para la vejez f
alto directivo (Es)	Manager m	manager	manager m	manager m	—
Altöl (D)	—	waste oil	huile usée f	olio usato m	aceite usado m
Altölbeseitigung (D)	—	disposal of waste oil	élimination d'huile usée f	smaltimento dell'olio usato m	eliminación de petróleo usado f
a lunga scadenza (I)	langfristig	long-term	à long terme	—	a largo plazo
alza (Es)	Hausse f	boom	hausse f	rialzo m	—
alza de las cotizaciones (Es)	Kurssteigerung f	price advance	hausse f	aumento dei corsi m	—
a macchina (I)	maschinell	by machine	mécanique	—	a máquina
a máquina (Es)	maschinell	by machine	mécanique	a macchina	—
ambiente de trabajo (Es)	Betriebsklima n	working conditions and human relations	climat social m	atmosfera di lavoro f	—
ambulantes Gewerbe (D)	—	itinerant trade	commerce ambulant m	commercio ambulante m	comercio ambulante m
a media scadenza (I)	mittelfristig	medium-term	à moyen terme	—	a medio plazo
a medio plazo (Es)	mittelfristig	medium-term	à moyen terme	a media scadenza	—
amélioration du rendement (F)	Leistungs-steigerung f	increase in efficiency	—	aumento della produttività m	incremento del rendimiento m
aménagement des espaces (F)	Raumordnung f	regional policy	—	ordinamento territoriale m	ordenación del territorio f
aménagement régional (F)	Regionalplanung f	regional planning	—	pianificazione regionale f	planificación regional f
amende¹ (F)	Bußgeld n	administration fee	—	pena pecuniaria f	multa f
amende² (F)	Geldbuße f	fine	—	pena pecuniaria f	multa f
amendement d'une loi (F)	Gesetzesänderung f	amendment of a law	—	emendamento di legge m	enmienda de la ley f
amendment of a law (E)	Gesetzesänderung f	—	amendement d'une loi m	emendamento di legge m	enmienda de la ley f
amendment of the statutes (E)	Satzungsänderung f	—	modification des statuts f	modificazione dello statuto f	modificación de los estatutos f
amministratore¹ (I)	Geschäftsführer m	manager	gérant d'une affaire m	—	gerente m
amministratore² (I)	Verwalter m	administrator	administrateur m	—	administrador m
amministratore dell'eredità (I)	Nachlaßverwalter m	administrator of the deceased's estate	administrateur de la succession m	—	administrador de la herencia m
amministrazione¹ (I)	Geschäftsführung f	management	gestion f	—	gestión f
amministrazione² (I)	Verwaltung f	administration	administration f	—	administración f

	D	E	F	I	Es
amministrazione del magazzino (I)	Lagerverwaltung f	stockkeeping	entreposage m	—	administración de almacén f
amministrazione giudiziaria (I)	Zwangsverwaltung f	receivership	séquestre judiciare m	—	administración forzosa f
ammissione (I)	Zulassung f	admission	admission f	—	admisión f
ammontare della fattura (I)	Rechnungsbetrag m	amount of invoice	montant de la facture m	—	importe de la factura m
ammortamenti straordinari (I)	Sonder-abschreibungen pl	special depreciation	amortissement extraordinaire m	—	amortización extraordinaria f
ammortamento¹ (I)	Tilgung f	redemption	amortissement m	—	amortización f
ammortamento² (I)	Amortisation f	amortization	amortissement m	—	amortización f
ammortamento³ (I)	Abschreibung f	depreciation	amortissement m	—	amortización f
ammortamento decrescente (I)	degressive Abschreibung f	declining-balance depreciation	amortissement dégressif m	—	amortización decreciente f
ammortamento lineare (I)	lineare Abschreibung f	linear depreciation	amortissement constant m	—	amortización constante f
ammortamento progressivo (I)	progressive Abschreibung f	progressive depreciation	amortissement progressif m	—	amortización progresiva f
amortir (F)	ablösen	redeem	—	rimborsare	amortizar
Amortisation (D)	—	amortization	amortissement m	ammortamento m	amortización f
amortissement¹ (F)	Abschreibung f	depreciation	—	ammortamento m	amortización f
amortissement² (F)	Tilgung f	redemption	—	ammortamento m	amortización f
amortissement³ (F)	Amortisation f	amortization	—	ammortamento m	amortizacion constante f
amortissement constant (F)	lineare Abschreibung f	linear depreciation	—	ammortamento lineare m	depreciación proporcional f
amortissement dégressif (F)	degressive Abschreibung f	declining-balance depreciation	—	ammortamento decrescente m	amortización decreciente f
amortissement extraordinaire (F)	Sonder-abschreibungen pl	special depreciation	—	deduzione per usura f	amortización extraordinaria f
amortissement progressif (F)	progressive Abschreibung f	progressive depreciation	—	ammortamento progressivo m	amortización progresiva f
amortización¹ (Es)	Abschreibung f	depreciation	amortissement m	ammortamento m	—
amortización² (Es)	Amortisation f	amortization	amortissement m	ammortamento m	—
amortización³ (Es)	Tilgung f	redemption	amortissement m	ammortamento m	—
amortización constante (Es)	lineare Abschreibung f	linear depreciation	amortissement constant m	ammortamento lineare m	—
amortización decreciente (Es)	degressive Abschreibung f	declining-balance depreciation	amortissement dégressif m	ammortamento decrescente m	—
amortización extraordinaria (Es)	Sonder-abschreibungen f	special depreciation	amortissement extraordinaire m	ammortamenti straordinari m pl	—
amortización progresiva (Es)	progressive Abschreibung f	progressive depreciation	amortissement progressif m	ammortamento progressivo m	—
amortizar (Es)	ablösen	redeem	amortir	rimborsare	—
amortization (E)	Amortisation f	—	amortissement m	ammortamento m	amortización f
amount (E)	Betrag m	—	montant m	importo m	suma f
amount of invoice (E)	Rechnungsbetrag m	—	montant de la facture m	ammontare della fattura m	importe de la factura m
amount of money (E)	Geldbetrag m	—	somme d'argent f	somma di denaro f	suma de dinero f
amount of the letter of credit (E)	Akkreditivsumme f	—	montant de l'accréditif m	importo del credito documentario m	suma del crédito documentario f
à moyen terme (F)	mittelfristig	medium-term	—	a media scadenza	a medio plazo
ampliación de la capacidad (Es)	Kapazitäts-ausweitung f	increase in capacity	extension de la capacité f	ampliamento delle capacità m	—
ampliamento delle capacità (I)	Kapazitäts-ausweitung f	increase in capacity	extension de la capacité f	—	ampliación de la capacidad f
Amt (D)	—	office	bureau m	ufficio m	cargo m
analisi ABC (I)	ABC-Analyse f	ABC analysis	analyse ABC f	—	análisis ABC m
analisi aziendale (I)	Betriebsanalyse f	operation analysis	situation analytique de l'exploitation f	—	análisis de la empresa m
analisi congiunturale (I)	Konjunkturanalyse f	economic analysis	analyse de la conjoncture f	—	análisis de la situación económica m

	D	E	F	I	Es
analisi costi-benefici (I)	Kosten-Nutzen-Analyse *f*	cost-benefit analysis	analyse du ratio coût à profit *f*	—	análisis de coste-beneficio *m*
analisi del fabbisogno (I)	Bedarfsanalyse *f*	analysis of requirements	analyse des besoins *m*	—	análisis de las necesidades *m*
analisi dell'assortimento (I)	Sortimentsanalyse *f*	analysis of assortment	analyse d'assortiment *f*	—	análisis del surtido *m*
analisi delle tendenze (I)	Trendanalyse *f*	trend analysis	analyse de la tendence générale *f*	—	análisis de tendencia *m*
analisi delle vendite (I)	Verkaufsanalyse *f*	sales analysis	analyse des ventes *f*	—	análisis de las ventas *m*
analisi del potere d'acquisto (I)	Kaufkraftanalyse *f*	spending capacity analysis	analyse du pouvoir d'achat *f*	—	análisis del poder adquisitivo *m*
analisi di bilancio (I)	Bilanzanalyse *f*	balance analysis	analyse du bilan *f*	—	análisis de balance *m*
analisi di categoria (I)	Branchenanalyse *f*	trade analysis	analyse des branches *f*	—	análisis del ramo *m*
analisi di mercato[1] (I)	Absatzanalyse *f*	sales analysis	analyse de la distribution *f*	—	análisis de venta *m*
analisi di mercato[2] (I)	Marktuntersuchung *f*	market survey	étude de marché *f*	—	estudio del mercado *m*
analisi di mercato[3] (I)	Marktanalyse *f*	market analysis	analyse du marché *f*	—	análisis de mercado *m*
analisi di sistema (I)	Systemanalyse *f*	systems analysis	analyse du système *f*	—	análisis de los sistemas *m*
analisi economica (I)	Wirtschaftsanalyse *f*	economic analysis	analyse de l'économie *f*	—	análisis económico *m*
analisi input-output (I)	Input-Output-Analyse *f*	input-output analysis	tableau économique input-output *m*	—	análisis de input-output *m*
análisis ABC (Es)	ABC-Analyse *f*	ABC analysis	analyse ABC *f*	analisi ABC *f*	—
análisis de balance (Es)	Bilanzanalyse *f*	balance analysis	analyse du bilan *f*	analisi di bilancio *f*	—
análisis de coste-beneficio (Es)	Kosten-Nutzen-Analyse *f*	cost-benefit analysis	analyse du ratio coût à profit *f*	analisi costi-benefici *f*	—
análisis de costes (Es)	Kostenanalyse *f*	cost analysis	analyse des coûts *f*	analisi dei costi *f*	—
análisis de flujos monetarios (Es)	Finanzierungsrechnung *f*	flow-of-funds analysis	analyse des flux monétaires *f*	calcolo di finanziamento *m*	—
análisis de input-output (Es)	Input-Output-Analyse *f*	input-output analysis	tableau économique input-output *m*	analisi input-output *f*	—
análisis de la empresa (Es)	Betriebsanalyse *f*	operation analysis	situation analytique de l'expoitation *f*	analisi aziendale *f*	—
análisis de la situación económica (Es)	Konjunkturanalyse *f*	economic analysis	analyse de la conjoncture *f*	analisi congiunturale *f*	—
análisis de las necesidades (Es)	Bedarfsanalyse *f*	analysis of requirements	analyse des besoins *m*	analisi del fabbisogno *f*	—
análisis de las ventas (Es)	Verkaufsanalyse *f*	sales analysis	analyse des ventes *f*	analisi delle vendite *f*	—
análisis de los sistemas (Es)	Systemanalyse *f*	systems analysis	analyse du système *f*	analisi di sistema *f*	—
análisis del poder adquisitivo (Es)	Kaufkraftanalyse *f*	spending capacity analysis	analyse du pouvoir d'achat *f*	analisi del potere d'acquisto *f*	—
análisis del ramo (Es)	Branchenanalyse *f*	trade analysis	analyse des branches *f*	analisi di categoria *f*	—
análisis del resultado publicitario (Es)	Werbeerfolgskontrolle *f*	advertising control	contrôle du résultat de la publicité *m*	controllo del successo pubblicitario *m*	—
análisis del surtido (Es)	Sortimentsanalyse *f*	analysis of assortment	analyse d'assortiment *f*	analisi dell'assortimento *f*	—
análisis de mercado (Es)	Marktanalyse *f*	market analysis	analyse du marché *f*	analisi di mercato *f*	—
análisis de tendencia (Es)	Trendanalyse *f*	trend analysis	analyse de la tendence générale *f*	analisi delle tendenze *f*	—
análisis de venta (Es)	Absatzanalyse *f*	sales analysis	analyse de la distribution *f*	analisi di mercato *f*	—
análisis económico (Es)	Wirtschaftsanalyse *f*	economic analysis	analyse de l'économie *f*	analisi economica *f*	—
analisi sul tempo impiegato (I)	Zeitstudie *f*	time study	étude des temps *f*	—	estudio de tiempo *m*
analyse ABC (F)	ABC-Analyse *f*	ABC analysis	—	analisi ABC *f*	análisis ABC *m*

animation d'innovation

	D	E	F	I	Es
analyse d'assortiment (F)	Sortimentsanalyse f	analysis of assortment	—	analisi dell'assortimento f	análisis del surtido m
analyse de la conjoncture (F)	Konjunkturanalyse f	economic analysis	—	analisi congiunturale f	análisis de la situación económica m
analyse de la distribution (F)	Absatzanalyse f	sales analysis	—	analisi di mercato f	análisis de venta m
analyse de la tendance générale (F)	Trendanalyse f	trend analysis	—	analisi delle tendenze f	análisis de tendencia m
analyse de l'économie (F)	Wirtschaftsanalyse f	economic analysis	—	analisi economica f	análisis económico m
analyse des besoins (F)	Bedarfsanalyse f	analysis of requirements	—	analisi del fabbisogno f	análisis de las necesidades f
analyse des branches (F)	Branchenanalyse f	trade analysis	—	analisi di categoria f	análisis del ramo m
analyse des flux monétaires (F)	Finanzierungs-rechnung f	flow-of-funds analysis	—	calcolo di finanziamento m	análisis de flujos monetarios
analyse des ventes (F)	Verkaufsanalyse f	sales analysis	—	analisi delle vendite f	análisis de las ventas m
analyse du bilan (F)	Bilanzanalyse f	balance analysis	—	analisi di bilancio f	análisis de balance m
analyse du marché (F)	Marktanalyse f	market analysis	—	analisi di mercato f	análisis de mercado m
analyse du pouvoir d'achat (F)	Kaufkraftanalyse f	spending capacity analysis	—	analisi del potere d'acquisto f	análisis del poder adquisitivo m
analyse du ratio coût à profit (F)	Kosten-Nutzen-Analyse f	cost-benefit analysis	—	analisi costi-benefici f	análisis de coste-beneficio m
analyse du système (F)	Systemanalyse f	systems analysis	—	analisi di sistema f	análisis de los sistemas m
analysis of assortment (E)	Sortimentsanalyse f	—	analyse d'assortiment f	analisi dell'assortimento f	análisis del surtido m
analysis of requirements (E)	Bedarfsanalyse f	—	analyse des besoins f	analisi del fabbisogno f	análisis de las necesidades m
Anbau-beschränkung (D)	—	restriction on cultivation	limitation des cultures f	restrizione di coltivazione f	limitación de cultivos f
Anbaufläche (D)	—	area under cultivation	surface plantée f	area coltivata f	superficie agrícola utilizada f
anbieten (D)	—	offer	offrir	offrire	ofrecer
ancillary costs (E)	Nebenkosten pl	—	coûts accessoires m pl	costi accessori m pl	gastos adicionales m pl
ancillary wage costs (E)	Lohnnebenkosten pl	—	charges salariales annexes f pl	costi complementari del lavoro m pl	cargas salariales accesorias f pl
andamento dell'economia (I)	Wirtschaftsverlauf m	course of the economic evolution	évolution économique f	—	evolución económica f
Anderkonto (D)	—	fiduciary account	compte de tiers m	conto per terzi m	cuenta fiduciaria de un abogado f
anexo (Es)	Anlage f	enclosure	pièce jointe f	allegato m	—
Anfangsbestand (D)	—	opening inventory	stock initial m	scorte iniziali f pl	existencias iniciales f pl
Anfangsgehalt (D)	—	starting salary	salaire initial m	stipendio iniziale m	salario inicial m
Anfangskapital (D)	—	opening capital	capital initial m	capitale iniziale m	capital inicial m
Anfechtungsklage (D)	—	action for avoidance	action en annulation f	azione di impugnazione f	acción de impugnación f
Anforderungs-merkmal (D)	—	requirement characteristics	caractéristique d'exigences f	caratteristica richiesta f	característica de requisitos f
Anfrage (D)	—	inquiry	demande f	richiesta f	demanda f
Anführer (D)	—	leader	chef m	leader m	líder m
Angebot (D)	—	offer	proposition f	offerta f	propuesta f/oferta f
Angebotsüberhang (D)	—	excess of supply over demand	excès de l'offre m	eccedenza d'offerta f	exceso de oferta m
angelernt (D)	—	semi-skilled	semi-qualifié	semi-qualificato	semicualificado
Angestellten-versicherung (D)	—	Salaried Employees' Pension Insurance	assurance invalidité-vieillesse des employés f	assicurazione degli impiegati f	seguro de empleados m
Angestellter (D)	—	employee	employé m	impiegato m	empleado m
animation d'innovation (F)	Innovationsschub m	technology push	—	spinta innovativa f	empuje innovador m

	D	E	F	I	Es
aniversario de la empresa (Es)	Geschäftsjubiläum *n*	jubilee	anniversaire de l'entreprise *m*	anniversario aziendale *m*	—
Ankauf (D)	—	purchase	achat *m*	acquisto *m*	compra *f*
Ankaufgarantie (D)	—	purchase guarantee	garantie d'achat *f*	garanzia d'acquisto *f*	garantía de compra *f*
Ankunftsdatum (D)	—	date of arrival	date d'arrivée *f*	data d'arrivo *f*	fecha de llegada *f*
Anlage (D)	—	enclosure/investment	pièce jointe *f*/ investissement *m*	allegato *m*/ investimento *m*	anexo *m*/ inversión *f*
Anlagegüter (D)	—	capital goods	valeur immobilisée *f*	beni d'investimento *m pl*	bienes de inversión *m pl*
Anlageinvestition (D)	—	investment in fixed assets	investissement productif *m*	investimento fisso *m*	inversión fija *f*
Anlagepapiere (D)	—	investment securities	valeurs de placement *f pl*	titoli d'investimento *m pl*	valores de inversión *m pl*
Anlagevermögen (D)	—	fixed assets	valeurs immobilisées *f pl*	attivo fisso *m*	activo fijo *m*
Anlaufperiode (D)	—	initial period	période de mise en marche *f*	periodo iniziale *m*	período de puesta en marcha *m*
Anleihe (D)	—	loan	emprunt *m*	prestito *m*	empréstito *m*
Anleitung (D)	—	instructions	instruction *f*	istruzione *f*	instrucción *f*
Anmeldefrist (D)	—	time for application	délai de déclaration *m*	termine di denuncia *m*	plazo de solicitud *m*
Anmeldung (D)	—	registration/ declaration	inscription *f*/ déclaration *f*	avviso *m*/ dichiarazione *f*	solicitud *f*/ declaración *f*
Annahme (D)	—	acceptance	acceptation *f*	accettazione *f*	aceptación *f*
Annahme- verweigerung (D)	—	refusal of delivery	refus d'acceptation *m*	rifiuto d'accettazione *m*	rehuso de aceptación *m*
année civile (F)	Kalenderjahr *n*	calendar year	—	anno solare *m*	año civil *m*
année de base (F)	Basisjahr *n*	base year	—	anno di base *m*	año básico *m*
anniversaire (F)	Geburtstag *m*	birthday	—	compleanno *m*	cumpleaños *m*
anniversaire de l'entreprise (F)	Geschäftsjubiläum *n*	jubilee	—	anniversario aziendale *m*	aniversario de la empresa *m*
anniversario aziendale (I)	Geschäftsjubiläum *n*	jubilee	anniversaire de l'entreprise *m*	—	aniversario de la empresa *m*
anno d'esercizio (I)	Rechnungsjahr *n*	financial year	exercice comptable *m*	—	ejercicio *m*
anno di base (I)	Basisjahr *n*	base year	année de base *f*	—	año básico *m*
anno finanziario (I)	Haushaltsjahr *n*	financial year	exercice budgétaire *m*	—	ejercicio *m*
annonce (F)	Anzeige *f*	advertisement	—	inserzione *f*	anuncio *m*
annonce chiffrée (F)	Chiffre-Anzeige *f*	advertisement under a box number	—	inserzione in cifra *f*	anuncio codificado *m*
annonce de journal (F)	Zeitungsanzeige *f*	advertisement	—	inserzione sul giornale *f*	anuncio de prensa *m*
annonce d'emploi (F)	Stellenanzeige *f*	position offered	—	inserzione d'impiego *f*	anuncio de empleo *m*
annonce de visiteurs (F)	Besuchsanmeldung *f*	announcement of a visitor	—	avviso di visita *m*	anuncio de visita *m*
anno solare (I)	Kalenderjahr *n*	calendar year	année civile *f*	—	año civil *m*
annotazione[1] (I)	Aktennotiz *f*	memorandum	note *f*	—	nota *f*
annotazione[2] (I)	Vermerk *m*	note	remarque *f*	—	nota *f*
annotazione[3] (I)	Notiz *f*	note	note *f*	—	noticia *f*
announcement of a visitor (E)	Besuchsanmeldung *f*	—	annonce de visiteurs *f*	avviso di visita *m*	anuncio de visita *m*
annual (E)	jährlich	—	annuel	annuale	anual
annual accounts (E)	Jahresabschluß *m*	—	clôture annuelle des comptes *f*	chiusura d'esercizio *f*	cierre de cuentas *m*
Annual Economic Report (E)	Jahreswirtschafts- bericht *m*	—	compte rendu d'activité économique annuel *m*	relazione generale sulla situazione economica *f*	informe económico anual *m*
annual holiday (E)	Betriebsferien *pl*	—	clôture annuelle de l'établissement *f*	ferie aziendali *f pl*	vacaciones de la empresa *f pl*
annual holidays (E)	Urlaub *m*	—	congé *m*/ vacances *f pl*	ferie *f pl*/ vacanze *f pl*	vacaciones *f pl*
annual hours of work (E)	Jahresarbeitszeit *f*	—	temps de travail annuel *m*	orario di lavoro annuale *m*	jornada anual *f*
annual income (E)	Jahreseinkommen *n*	—	revenu annuel *m*	reddito annuale *m*	renta anual *f*

	D	E	F	I	Es
annual meeting of shareholders (E)	Jahreshauptversammlung f	—	assemblée générale annuelle f	assemblea generale annuale f	junta general anual f
annual need (E)	Jahresbedarf m	—	besoin annuel m	bisogno annuale m	necesidad anual f
annual profit (E)	Jahresgewinn m	—	bénéfice annuel m	utile dell'anno m	beneficio del ejercicio m
annual surplus (E)	Jahresüberschuß m	—	excédent annuel m	surplus dell'anno m	superávit del ejercicio m
annuale (I)	jährlich	annual	annuel	—	anual
annualità (I)	Annuität f	annuity	annuité f	—	anualidad f
annuel (F)	jährlich	annual	—	annuale	anual
Annuität (D)	—	annuity	annuité f	annualità f	anualidad f
Annuitätendarlehen (D)	—	annuity loan	prêt amortissable par annuités m	prestito rimborsabile in annualità m	empréstito sin vencimiento m
annuité (F)	Annuität f	annuity	—	annualità f	anualidad f
annuity[1] (E)	Rente f	—	rente f/ pension de vieillesse f	rendita f/ pensione f	renta f/ pensión f
annuity[2] (E)	Annuität f	—	annuité f	annualità f	anualidad f
annuity bonds (E)	Rentenanleihe f	—	effet public m	prestito a reddito fisso m	empréstito por anualidades m
annuity loan (E)	Annuitätendarlehen n	—	prêt amortissable par annuités m	prestito rimborsabile in annualità m	empréstito por anualidades m
annul (E)	annullieren	—	annuler	annullare	anular
annulation (F)	Stornierung f	cancellation	—	storno m	cancelación f/ anulación f/ contrapartida f
annuler[1] (F)	annullieren	annul	—	annullare	anular
annuler[2] (F)	löschen	cancel	—	cancellare	cancelar
annullare (I)	annullieren	annul	annuler	—	anular
annullieren (D)	—	annul	annuler	annullare	anular
año básico (Es)	Basisjahr n	base year	année de base f	anno di base m	—
año civil (Es)	Kalenderjahr n	calendar year	année civile f	anno solare m	—
Anordnung (D)	—	order	ordre m	ordine m	orden f
Anpassung (D)	—	adaption	adaptation f	adattamento m	adaptación f
Anpassungskosten (D)	—	adjustment costs	coûts d'adaptation m pl	costi d'adattamento m pl	gastos readaptación m pl
Anpassungsverzögerung (D)	—	adjustment lag	retard d'adaptation m	ritardo d'adattamento m	retraso de adaptación m
Anrede (D)	—	form of address	début de lettre m	titolo m	tratamiento m
Anreiz (D)	—	incentive	incitation f	incentivo m	incentivo m
Anreizsystem (D)	—	incentive system	système d'incitation m	sistema d'incentivo m	sistema de incentivos m
Anrufbeantworter (D)	—	answering machine	répondeur automatique m	segreteria telefonica f	contestador de llamadas m
Anschaffung (D)	—	acquisition	acquisition f	acquisto m	adquisición f
Anschaffungskosten (D)	—	purchase costs	frais d'acquisition m pl	costi d'acquisto m pl	coste de adquisición m
Anschaffungswert (D)	—	acquisition value	valeur d'acquisition f	valore d'acquisto m	valor de adquisición m
Anschlußfinanzierung (D)	—	follow-up financing	financement successif m	finanziamento successivo m	financiación sucesiva f
Anschrift (D)	—	address	adresse f	indirizzo m	dirección f
Ansichtssendung (D)	—	consignment on approval	envoi à condition m	campione per esame m	envío para inspección m
Anspruch (D)	—	claim	prétention f	pretesa f	reivindicación f
anstehen (D)	—	be due	être échu	essere scaduto	estar pendiente
anstellen (D)	—	employ	employer	impiegare	emplear
Anstellung (D)	—	employment	emploi m	impiego m	empleo m
answering machine (E)	Anrufbeantworter m	—	répondeur automatique m	segreteria telefonica f	contestador de llamadas m
Anteilnahme (D)	—	sympathy	participation f	interesse m	participación f

	D	E	F	I	Es
anticipazioni (I)	Lombardgeschäft *n*	lending on securities	prêt sur gage *m*	—	operaciones de pignoración *f pl*
anticipo (Es)	Vorschuß *m*	advance	avance *f*	anticipo *m*	—
anticipo (I)	Vorschuß *m*	advance	avance *f*	—	anticipo *m*
antidated cheque (E)	vordatierter Scheck *m*	—	chèque antidaté *m*	assegno antidatato *m*	cheque de fecha adelantada *m*
Antrag (D)	—	application	demande *f*	domanda *f*	solicitud *f*
Antragsformular (D)	—	application form	formulaire de demande *m*	modulo di domanda *m*	formulario de solicitud *m*
Antwort (D)	—	reply	réponse *f*	risposta *f*	respuesta *f*
anual (Es)	jährlich	annual	annuel	annuale	—
anualidad (Es)	Annuität *f*	annuity	annuité *f*	annualità *f*	—
anular (Es)	annullieren	annul	annuler	annullare	—
anuncio (Es)	Anzeige *f*	advertisement	annonce *f*	inserzione *f*	—
anuncio codificado (Es)	Chiffre-Anzeige *f*	advertisement under a box number	annonce chiffrée *f*	inserzione in cifra *f*	—
anuncio de empleo (Es)	Stellenanzeige *f*	position offered	annonce d'emploi *f*	inserzione d'impiego *f*	—
anuncio de prensa (Es)	Zeitungsanzeige *f*	advertisement	annonce de journal *f*	inserzione sul giornale *f*	—
anuncio de visita (Es)	Besuchsanmeldung *f*	announcement of a visitor	annonce de visiteurs *f*	avviso di visita *m*	—
Anwalt (D)	—	lawyer	avocat *m*	avvocato *m*	abogado *m*
Anwaltskanzlei (D)	—	lawyer's office	cabinet d'avocat *m*	studio d'avvocato *m*	bufete de abogado *m*
Anwartschaft (D)	—	candidature	candidature *f*	candidatura *f*	expectativa de un futuro pago *f*
Anweisung (D)	—	transfer	mandat *m*	ordine di pagamento *m*	transferencia *f*
Anwerbung (D)	—	recruitment	recrutement *m*	reclutamento *m*	contratación *f*
Anzahlung (D)	—	deposit	acompte *m*	pagamento in acconto *m*	pago a cuenta *m*
Anzeige (D)	—	advertisement	annonce *f*	inserzione *f*	anuncio *m*
Anzeigenformat (D)	—	size of an advertisement	format de l'annonce *m*	formato dell'inserzione *m*	tamaño del anuncio *m*
Anzeigengestaltung (D)	—	lay-out of an advertisement	arrangement de l'annonce *m*	tipo d'inserzione *m*	estructuración del anuncio *f*
Anzeigenplazierung (D)	—	placing of an advertisement	disposition de l'annonce *f*	collocamento dell'inserzione *m*	colocación del anuncio *f*
Anzeigenschaltung (D)	—	insertion of an advertisement	placement de l'annonce *m*	posizionamento dell'inserzione *m*	inserción del anuncio *f*
Anzeigenwerbung (D)	—	newspaper and magazine advertising	publicité par la presse *f*	pubblicità per inserzione *f*	publicidad por anuncios *f*
Anzeigenwirkung (D)	—	effectiveness of an advertisement	effet de l'annonce *m*	effetto dell'inserzione *m*	efectividad del anuncio *f*
apartado postal (Es)	Postfach *n*	post office box	boîte postale *f*	casella postale *f*	—
apartment (E)	Wohnung *f*	—	appartement *m*	abitazione *f*	vivienda *f*
apertura del credito documentario (I)	Akkreditiveröffnung *f*	opening of a letter of credit	ouverture d'un accréditif *f*	—	apertura de un crédito documentario *f*
apertura de los establecimientos (Es)	Geschäftseröffnung *f*	opening of a business	ouverture d'une affaire *f*	apertura di un negozio *f*	—
apertura del testamento (I)	Testamentseröffnung *f*	opening of the will	ouverture du testament *f*	—	apertura de testamento *f*
apertura de testamento (Es)	Testamentseröffnung *f*	opening of the will	ouverture du testament *f*	apertura del testamento *f*	—
apertura de una cuenta (Es)	Kontoeröffnung *f*	opening of an account	ouverture de compte *f*	apertura di un conto *f*	—
apertura de un crédito documentario (Es)	Akkreditiveröffnung *f*	opening of a letter of credit	ouverture d'un accréditif *f*	apertura del credito documentario *f*	—
apertura di credito documentario (I)	Dokumentenakkreditiv *n*	documentary letter of credit	crédit documentaire *m*	—	crédito documentario *m*
apertura di credito documentario irrevocabile (I)	unwiderrufliches Akkreditiv *n*	irrevocable letter of credit	accréditif irrévocable *m*	—	crédito documentario irrevocable *m*

	D	E	F	I	Es
apertura di credito documentario semplice (I)	Barakkreditiv	cash letter of credit	accréditif payable en espèce *m*	—	crédito simple *m*
apertura di mercato (I)	Markteintritt *m*	entry into the market	entrée dans le marché *f*	—	entrada en el mercado *f*
apertura di un conto (I)	Kontoeröffnung *f*	opening of an account	ouverture d'un compte *f*	—	apertura de una cuenta *f*
apertura di un negozio (I)	Geschäftseröffnung *f*	opening of a business	ouverture d'une affaire *f*	—	apertura de los establecimientos *f*
aplazamiento¹ (Es)	Aufschiebung *f*	postponement	remise *f*	rinvio *m*	—
aplazamiento² (Es)	Vertagung *f*	postponement	ajournement *m*	rinvio *m*	—
aplazamiento de gastos (Es)	Ausgaben-verzögerung *f*	expenditure delay	dépenses retardées *f pl*	dilazione delle spese *f*	—
aplicación de la garantía (Es)	Garantieleistung *f*	guarantee	fourniture sous garantie *f*	prestazione di garanzia *f*	—
aplicación de los resultatdos (Es)	Gewinnverwendung *f*	appropriation of net income	utilisation des bénéfices *f*	impiego dell'utile *m*	—
apoderado especial (Es)	Handlungsbevoll-mächtigter *m*	commercial agent	personne ayant le pouvoir commercial *f*	mandatario commerciale *m*	—
apoderado general (Es)	Prokurist *m*	"Prokurist" (authorized clerk)	fondé de procuration *f*	procuratore *m*	—
apoderamiento (Es)	Bevollmächtigung *f*	authorization	pouvoir *m*	autorizzazione *f*	—
aportación de cobertura (Es)	Deckungsbeitrag *m*	contribution margin	proportion de garantie *f*	contributo per copertura *m*	—
appalto (I)	Ausschreibung *f*	tender	soumission *f*	—	concurso-subasta *m*
appareil à dicter (F)	Diktiergerät *n*	dictaphone	—	dittafono *m*	máquina de dictar *f*
appareil automatique (F)	Automat *m*	vending machine	—	distributore automatico *m*	distribuidor automático *m*
appareil téléphonique (F)	Fernsprecher *m*	telephone	—	telefono *m*	teléfono *m*
appartamento in condominio (I)	Eigentumswohnung *f*	freehold flat	logement en propriété *m*	—	piso en propiedad *m*
appartement (F)	Wohnung *f*	apartment	—	abitazione *f*	vivienda *f*
appeal court (E)	Berufungsgericht *n*	—	tribunal d'appel *m*	corte d'appello *f*	tribunal de apelación *m*
appel (F)	Abruf *m*	call	—	richiesta *f*	reclamación de la entrega de un pedido *f*
applicant (E)	Bewerber *m*	—	candidat *m*	aspirante *m*	aspirante *m*
application¹ (E)	Bewerbung *f*	—	candidature *f*	domanda d'impiego *f*	candidatura *f*
application² (E)	Antrag *m*	—	demande *f*	domanda *f*	solicitud *f*
application documents (E)	Bewerbungs-unterlagen *pl*	—	dossier de candidature *m*	documenti della domanda d'impiego *m pl*	documentos de solicitud *m pl*
application form (E)	Antragsformular *n*	—	formulaire de demande *m*	modulo di domanda *m*	formulario de solicitud *m*
appointment (E)	Ernennung *f*	—	nomination *f*	nomina *f*	nombramiento *m*
appointment for a meeting (E)	Gesprächstermin *m*	—	date de conversation *f*	appuntamento per un colloquio *m*	fecha de cita *f*
apport personnel (F)	Privateinlagen *pl*	private contribution	—	depositi privati *m pl*	depósitos privados *m pl*
apport social (F)	Stammeinlage *f*	initial contribution	—	quota sociale *f*	capital suscrito *m*
appreciation (E)	Wertzuwachs *m*	—	accroissement de valeur *m*	incremento di valore *m*	plusvalía *f*
apprendistato (I)	Ausbildung *f*	apprenticeship	apprentissage *m*	—	aprendizaje *m*
apprendistato di commercio (I)	kaufmännische Lehre *f*	commercial apprenticeship	apprentissage commercial *m*	—	aprendizaje comercial *m*
apprenti (F)	Trainee *m*	trainee	—	trainee *m*	entrenamiento
apprenticeship (E)	Ausbildung *f*	—	apprentissage *m*	apprendistato *m*	aprendizaje *m*
apprentissage (F)	Ausbildung *f*	apprenticeship	—	apprendistato *m*	aprendizaje *m*
apprentissage commercial (F)	kaufmännische Lehre *f*	commercial apprenticeship	—	apprendistato di commercio *m*	aprendizaje comercial *m*
appropriation of income (E)	Einkommens-verwendung *f*	—	utilisation du revenu *f*	impiego dei redditi *m*	distribución de la renta *f*

	D	E	F	I	Es
appropriation of net income (E)	Gewinnverwendung f	—	utilisation des bénéfices f	impiego dell'utile m	aplicación de los resultados f
appropriazione indebita (I)	Unterschlagung f	embezzlement	détournement m	—	defraudación f
approvisionnement (F)	Versorgung f	supply	—	approvvigionamento m	abastecimiento m
approvisionnement de matières premières (F)	Rohstoffversorgung f	provisioning with raw materials	—	approvvigionamento di materie prime m	aprovisionamiento de materias primas m
approvisionnement en énergie (F)	Energieversorgung f	energy supply	—	approvvigionamento d'energia m	abastecimiento energético m
approvvigionamento (I)	Versorgung f	supply	approvisionnement m	—	abastecimiento m
approvvigionamento d'energia (I)	Energieversorgung f	energy supply	approvisionnement en énergie m	—	abastecimiento energético m
approvvigionamento di materie prime (I)	Rohstoffversorgung f	provisioning with raw materials	approvisionnement de matières premières m	—	aprovisionamiento de materias primas m
appuntamento di presentazione (I)	Vorstellungstermin m	date of interview	rendez-vous de présentation m	—	fecha de entrevista personal f
appuntamento per un colloquio (I)	Gesprächstermin m	appointment for a meeting	date de conversation f	—	fecha de cita f
aprendizaje (Es)	Ausbildung f	apprenticeship	apprentissage m	apprendistato m	—
aprendizaje comercial (Es)	kaufmännische Lehre f	commercial apprenticeship	apprentissage commercial m	apprendistato di commercio m	—
après avoir réçu la facture (F)	nach Erhalt der Rechnung	on receipt of the invoice	—	a ricevimento della fattura	después de haber recibo la factura
aprovisionamiento de materias primas (Es)	Rohstoffversorgung f	provisioning with raw materials	approvisionnement de matières premières m	approvvigionamento di materie prime m	—
a provvigione (I)	auf Provisionsbasis	on a commission basis	à la commission	—	a comisión
a prueba (Es)	auf Probe	on trial	à l'essai	in prova	—
a prueba de crisis (Es)	krisenfest	slump-proof	insensible aux influences de la crise économique	resistente alle crisi	—
Aquisition (D)	—	acquisition	acquisition f	acquisizione f	adquisición f
arancel aduanero cuantitativo (Es)	Mengenzoll m	specific duty	droit de douane par quantité m	dazio di quantità m	—
arancel de importación (Es)	Einfuhrzoll m	import duty	droit d'entrée m	dazio d'importazione m	—
Arbeit (D)	—	work	travail m	lavoro m	trabajo m
Arbeiter (D)	—	worker	travailleur m	operaio m	trabajador m
Arbeiterklasse (D)	—	working class	classe ouvrière f	classe degli operai f	clase obrera f
Arbeitgeber (D)	—	employer	employeur m	datore di lavoro m	patrón m
Arbeitnehmer (D)	—	employee	salarié m	prestatore d'opera m	empleado m
Arbeitnehmer-beteiligung (D)	—	worker participation	participation du personnel f	partecipazione dei prestatori d'opera f	participación de los empleados f
Arbeitsanfall (D)	—	volume of work	travail à exécuter m	volume di lavoro m	volumen de trabajo m
Arbeitsbewertung (D)	—	job evaluation	qualification du travail f	valutazione del lavoro f	evaluación del trabajo f
Arbeitserlaubnis (D)	—	work permit	permis de travail m	permesso di lavoro m	permiso de trabajo m
Arbeitsertrag (D)	—	work performed	rendement du travail m	rendimento del lavoro m	rendimiento del trabajo m
Arbeitsessen (D)	—	working lunch	déjeuner de travail m	pranzo di lavoro m	comida de trabajo f
arbeitsintensiv (D)	—	labour-intensive	déterminé par le facteur main-d'œuvre	ad alta incidenza di lavoro	con gran intensidad de mano de obra
Arbeitsleistung (D)	—	productivity	rendement m	produttività f	productividad f
Arbeitslosen-unterstützung (D)	—	unemployment benefits	indemnité de chômage f	sussidio di disoccupazione m	prestaciones por desempleo f pl
Arbeitslosigkeit (D)	—	unemployment	chômage m	disoccupazione f	desempleo m
Arbeitsmarkt (D)	—	labour market	marché du travail m	mercato del lavoro m	mercado laboral m
Arbeitsnachfrage (D)	—	job demand	demande d'emploi f	domanda di lavoro f	demanda de trabajo f
Arbeitsnachweis (D)	—	employment vacancies	emploi vacant m	informazioni sui posti vacanti f pl	servicio de colocación f
Arbeitsnorm (D)	—	fair labour standards	norme de travail f	norma di lavoro f	norma de producción f

	D	E	F	I	Es
Arbeitsplatz (D)	—	place of employment	poste de travail *m*	posto di lavoro *m*	puesto de trabajo *m*
Arbeitsplatzwechsel (D)	—	change of employment	changement d'emploi *m*	cambiamento del posto di lavoro *m*	cambio de puesto *m*
Arbeitspsychologie (D)	—	industrial psychology	psychologie de travail *f*	psicologia del lavoro *f*	psicología laboral *f*
Arbeitsraum (D)	—	workroom	lieu de travail *m*	locale di lavoro *m*	sala de trabajo *f*
Arbeitsrecht (D)	—	labour law	législation industrielle *f*	diritto di lavoro *m*	derecho laboral *m*
Arbeitsrhythmus (D)	—	work rhythm	rythme de travail *m*	ritmo di lavoro *m*	ritmo de trabajo *m*
Arbeitsschutz (D)	—	employment protection	protection sociale du travail *f*	tutela del lavoro *f*	protección del trabajo *f*
Arbeitssicherheit (D)	—	safety at work	sécurité du travail *f*	sicurezza del lavoro *f*	seguridad del trabajo *f*
Arbeitstag (D)	—	working day	jour de travail *m*	giorno lavorativo *m*	día laboral *m*
Arbeitstechnik (D)	—	working technique	technique de travail *f*	tecnica lavorativa *f*	técnica del trabajo *f*
Arbeitsteilung (D)	—	division of labour	division du travail *f*	divisione del lavoro *f*	división del trabajo *f*
Arbeitsunfall (D)	—	industrial injury	accident du travail *m*	infortunio sul posto di lavoro *m*	accidente profesional *m*
Arbeitsverhältnis (D)	—	employee-employer relationship	rapport de travail *m*	rapporto di lavoro *m*	relación laboral *f*
Arbeitsverhältnis auf Probe (D)	—	employee-employer relationship on a trial basis	contrat de travail convenu à l'essai *m*	rapporto di lavoro in prova *m*	relación laboral a prueba *f*
Arbeitsvermittlung (D)	—	employment agency	bureau de placement *m*	ufficio di collocamento *m*	agencia laboral *f*
Arbeitsvertrag (D)	—	contract of employment	contrat de travail *m*	contratto di lavoro *m*	contrato laboral *m*
Arbeitsvorbereitung (D)	—	job preparation	préparation du travail *f*	preparazione del lavoro *f*	preparación laboral *f*
Arbeitswoche (D)	—	working week	semaine de travail *f*	settimana lavorativa *f*	semana laboral *f*
Arbeitszeit (D)	—	working hours	heures de travail *f pl*	orario di lavoro *m*	jornada laboral *f*
Arbeits-zufriedenheit (D)	—	job satisfaction	satisfaction de travail *f*	soddisfazione del lavoro *f*	satisfacción en el trabajo *f*
Arbitrage (D)	—	arbitration	arbitrage *m*	arbitraggio *m*	arbitraje *m*
arbitrage (F)	Arbitrage *f*	arbitration	—	arbitraggio *m*	arbitraje *m*
arbitrage sur les devises (F)	Devisenarbitrage *f*	exchange arbitrage	—	arbitraggio valutario *m*	arbitraje de divisas *m*
arbitraggio (I)	Arbitrage *f*	arbitration	arbitrage *m*	—	arbitraje *m*
arbitraggio valutario (I)	Devisenarbitrage *f*	exchange arbitrage	arbitrage sur les devises *m*	—	arbitraje de divisas *m*
arbitraje (Es)	Arbitrage *f*	arbitration	arbitrage *m*	arbitraggio *m*	—
arbitraje de divisas (Es)	Devisenarbitrage *f*	exchange arbitrage	arbitrage sur les devises *m*	arbitraggio valutario *m*	—
arbitration (E)	Arbitrage *f*	—	arbitrage *m*	arbitraggio *m*	arbitraje *m*
Archiv (D)	—	archives	archives *f pl*	archivio *m*	archivo *m*
archives (E)	Archiv *n*	—	archives *f pl*	archivio *m*	archivo *m*
archives[1] (F)	Aktenablage *f*	filing	—	archivio delle pratiche *m*	archivo *m*
archives[2] (F)	Archiv *n*	archives	—	archivio *m*	archivo *m*
archivio[1] (I)	Archiv *n*	archives	archives *f pl*	—	archivo *m*
archivio[2] (I)	Ablage *f*	file	collection des dossiers *f*	—	archivo *m*
archivio delle pratiche (I)	Aktenablage *f*	filing	archives *f pl*	—	archivo *m*
archivo[1] (Es)	Archiv *n*	archives	archives *f pl*	archivio *m*	—
archivo[2] (Es)	Aktenablage *f*	filing	archives *f pl*	archivio delle pratiche *m*	—
archivo[3] (Es)	Ablage *f*	file	collection des dossiers *f*	archivio *m*	—
archivo de datos (Es)	Datei *f*	file	fichier de données *m*	file *m*	—
area coltivata (I)	Anbaufläche *f*	area under cultivation	surface plantée *f*	—	superficie agrícola utilizada *f*

	D	E	F	I	Es
area doganale di confine (I)	Zollgrenzgebiet *n*	customs frontier district	territoire de surveillance douanière *m*	—	territorio aduanero fronterizo *m*
area edificabile (I)	Bauland *n*	building land	espace à bâtir *m*	—	terreno edificable *m*
área monetaria (Es)	Währungsgebiet *n*	currency area	zone monétaire *f*	area monetaria *f*	—
area monetaria (I)	Währungsgebiet *n*	currency area	zone monétaire *f*	—	área monetaria *f*
area representative (E)	Gebietsvertreter *m*	—	représentant régional *m*	agente di zona *m*	representante regional *m*
area sales manager (E)	Gebietsverkaufs- leiter *m*	—	chef de vente régionale *m*	direttore di vendita regionale *m*	jefe de venta regional *m*
area under cultivation (E)	Anbaufläche *f*	—	surface plantée *f*	area coltivata *f*	superficie agrícola utilizada *f*
a requerimiento (Es)	auf Abruf	on call	à convenance	su richiesta	—
argent[1] (F)	Silber *n*	silver	—	argento *m*	plata *f*
argent[2] (F)	Geld *n*	money	—	denaro *m*	dinero *m*/efectivo *m*
argent au jour le jour (F)	Tagesgeld *n*	day-to-day money	—	prestito giornaliero *m*	dinero de día a día *m*
argent bon marché (F)	billiges Geld *n*	easy money	—	crediti agevolati *m pl*	dinero barato *m*
argent comptant (F)	Bargeld *n*	cash	—	denaro contante *m*	dinero efectivo *m*
argent immobilisé (F)	Festgeld *n*	fixed deposit	—	denaro vincolato *m*	depósito a plazo *m*
argento (I)	Silber *n*	silver	argent *m*	—	plata *f*
argomentazione (I)	Argumentation *f*	argumentation	argumentation *f*	—	argumentación *f*
argumentación (Es)	Argumentation *f*	argumentation	argumentation *f*	argomentazione *f*	—
Argumentation (D)	—	argumentation	argumentation *f*	argomentazione *f*	argumentación *f*
argumentation (E)	Argumentation *f*	—	argumentation *f*	argomentazione *f*	argumentación *f*
argumentation (F)	Argumentation *f*	argumentation	—	argomentazione *f*	argumentación *f*
Argumentations- stärke (D)	—	talent for argumentation	capacité d'argumentation *f*	forza d'argomentazione *f*	fuerza de argumentación *f*
a ricevimento della fattura (I)	nach Erhalt der Rechnung	on receipt of the invoice	après avoir réçu la facture	—	después de haber recibido la factura
armador (Es)	Reeder *m*	shipowner	armateur *m*	armatore *m*	—
armateur (F)	Reeder *m*	shipowner	—	armatore *m*	armador *m*
armatore (I)	Reeder *m*	shipowner	armateur *m*	—	armador *m*
armonizado a nivel comunitario (Es)	EG-einheitlich	standardized within the European Community	uniforme au niveau communautaire	uniforme all'interno della CEE	—
arrangeant (F)	kulant	accommodating	—	corrente	de fácil avenencia
arrangement de l'annonce (F)	Anzeigengestaltung *f*	lay-out of an advertisement	—	tipo d'inserzione *m*	estructuración del anuncio *f*
arrangement forcé (F)	Zwangsvergleich *m*	compulsory settlement	—	concordato fallimentare *m*	convenio forzoso *m*
arranging for a credit (E)	Kreditvermittlung *f*	—	médiation du crédit *f*	intermediazione di crediti *f*	mediación de créditos *f*
arrears (E)	Rückstand *m*	—	arriéré *m*	arretrato *m*	pago atrasado *m*/ atraso *m*
arrendamiento (Es)	Mietzins *m*	rent	prix de location *m*	canone di locazione *m*	—
arrendatante financiero (Es)	Leasing-Nehmer *m*	lessee	preneur de leasing *m*	utente del leasing *m*	—
arrendatario financiero (Es)	Leasing-Geber *m*	lessor	donneur de leasing *m*	concedente del leasing *m*	—
arrêt de mise en accusation (F)	Eröffnungs- beschluß *m*	order opening a trial	—	decreto di citazione in giudizio *m*	acuerdo de apertura *m*
arrêt d'une procédure (F)	Verfahrens- einstellung *f*	abatement of an action	—	sospensione del procedimento *f*	sobreseimiento del proceso *m*
arretrato (I)	Rückstand *m*	arrears	arriéré *m*	—	pago atrasado *m*/ atraso *m*
arriéré (F)	Rückstand *m*	arrears	—	arretrato *m*	pago atrasado *m*/ atraso *m*
arriéré de payement (F)	Zahlungsrückstand *m*	payment in arrears	—	morosità di pagamento *f*	pago atrasado *m*
arriesgado (Es)	riskant	risky	risqué	rischioso	—
arrival of goods (E)	Wareneingang *m*	—	entrée de marchandises *f*	entrata merci *f*	entrada de mercancías *f*

	D	E	F	I	Es
art de vendre (F)	Verkaufstechnik f	sales technique	—	tecnica di vendita f	técnica de venta f
art director (E)	Art-director m	—	directeur artistique m	art director m	director artístico m
art director (I)	Art-director m	art director	directeur artistique m	—	director artístico m
Art-director (D)	—	art director	directeur artistique m	art director m	director artístico m
artesanía (Es)	Handwerk n	craft trade	artisanat m	artigianato m	—
article de mode (F)	Modeartikel m	fashion article	—	articolo di moda m	artículos de moda m pl
articolo di marca (I)	Markenartikel m	brandname article	produit de marque m	—	artículo de marca m
articolo di moda (I)	Modeartikel m	fashion article	article de mode m	—	artículos de moda m pl
artículo fundamental (Es)	Stapelware f	staple commodities	produit de stockage m	merce immagazzinata f	—
artículos de moda (Es)	Modeartikel m	fashion article	article de mode m	articolo di moda m	—
artigianato (I)	Handwerk n	craft trade	artisanat m	—	artesanía f
artisanat (F)	Handwerk n	craft trade	—	artigianato m	artesanía f
as agreed (E)	vereinbarungsgemäß	—	comme convenu	come convenuto	según lo acordado
ascendente (Es)	steigend	rising	croissant(e)	in aumento	—
ascenso (Es)	Beförderung f	promotion	nomination f	promozione f	—
asegurado (Es)	Versicherungs- nehmer m	insured person	souscripteur d'une assurance m	assicurato m	—
asesor (Es)	Berater m	adviser	conseiller m	consulente m	—
asesor de marketing (Es)	Marketingberater m	marketing consultant	conseiller de marketing m	consulente di marketing m	—
asesor fiscal (Es)	Steuerberater m	tax adviser	conseiller fiscal m	consulente fiscale m	—
asiento en otra cuenta (Es)	Umbuchung f	transfer of an entry	jeu d'écritures m	giro di partite m	—
asignación (Es)	Zuteilung f	allocation	répartition f	attribuzione f/ ripartizione f	—
asked price (E)	Briefkurs m	—	cours de vente m	prezzo d'offerta m	cotización ofrecida f
asociación[1] (Es)	Verband m	association	association f	associazione f	—
asociación[2] (Es)	Verein m	association	association f	associazione f	—
asociación con un fin determinado (Es)	Zweckverband m	special purpose association	association à but déterminé f	consorzio intercomunale m	—
asociación económica (Es)	Wirtschafts- verband m	trade association	association économique f	associazione economica f	—
asociación empresarial (Es)	Unternehmer- verband m	employers' association	association des chefs d'entreprise f	unione degli imprenditori f	—
asoramiento (Es)	Beratung f	advice	consultation f	consulenza f	—
aspirante (Es)	Bewerber m	applicant	candidat m	aspirante m	—
aspirante (I)	Bewerber m	applicant	candidat m	—	aspirante m
as quickly as possible (E)	schnellstmöglich	—	le plus vite possible	al più presto possibile	tan rápido como sea posible
assainissement (F)	Sanierung f	urban renewal	—	risanamento m	saneamiento m
assegnazione (I)	Zuwendung f	bestowal	affectation f	—	gratificación f
assegno (I)	Scheck m	cheque	chèque m	—	cheque m
assegno all'ordine (I)	Orderscheck m	order cheque	chèque à ordre m	—	cheque a la orden m
assegno al portatore[1] (I)	Inhaberscheck m	cheque payable to bearer	chèque au porteur m	—	cheque al portador m
assegno al portatore[2] (I)	Überbringerscheck m	bearer cheque	chèque au porteur m	—	cheque al portador m
assegno antidatato (I)	vordatierter Scheck m	antedated cheque	chèque antidaté m	—	cheque de fecha adelantada m
assegno circolare (I)	Barscheck m	open cheque	chèque non barré m	—	cheque de caja m
assegno falsificato (I)	gefälschter Scheck m	forged cheque	chèque maquillé m	—	cheque falsificado m
assegno in bianco (I)	Blankoscheck m	blank cheque	chèque en blanc m	—	cheque en blanco m
assegno postale (I)	Postscheck m	postal giro	chèque postal m	—	cheque postal m
assegno sbarrato[1] (I)	gekreuzter Scheck m	crossed cheque	chèque barré m	—	cheque cruzado m
assegno sbarrato[2] (I)	Verrechnungs- scheck m	crossed cheque	chèque à porter en compte m	—	cheque cruzado m
assegno turistico (I)	Reisescheck m	traveller's cheque	chèque de voyage m	—	cheque de viaje m

	D	E	F	I	Es
Assekuranz (D)	—	assurance	assurance f	assicurazione f	seguro m
assemblea dei soci (I)	Gesellschafter-versammlung f	meeting of shareholders	réunion des associés f	—	junta social f
assemblea generale annuale (I)	Jahreshaupt-versammlung f	annual meeting of shareholders	assemblée générale annuelle f	—	junta general anual f
assemblée des créanciers (F)	Gläubiger-versammlung f	creditors' meeting	—	riunione dei creditori f	junta de acreedores f
assemblée générale annuelle (F)	Jahreshaupt-versammlung f	annual meeting	—	assemblea generale annuale f	junta general anual f
assente (I)	abwesend	absent	absent	—	ausente
assets¹ (E)	Aktivbestand m	—	actif m	effettivo m	activo disponible m
assets² (E)	Aktiva pl	—	masse active f	attivo m	activo m
assets value (E)	Substanzwert m	—	valeur de remplacement f	valore sostanziale m	valor sustancial m
assicurato (I)	Versicherungs-nehmer m	insured person	souscripteur d'une assurance f	—	asegurado m
assicuratore diretto (I)	Erstversicherer m	direct insurer	assureur direct m	—	primer asegurador m
assicurazione¹ (I)	Assekuranz f	assurance	assurance f	—	seguro m
assicurazione² (I)	Versicherung f	insurance	assurance f	—	seguro m
assicurazione autoveicoli (I)	Kraftfahrzeug-versicherung f	motor insurance	assurance responsabilité civile automobile f	—	seguro de automóviles m
assicurazione contro il furto (I)	Diebstahl-versicherung f	theft insurance	assurance contre le vol f	—	seguro contra el robo m
assicurazione contro il furto con scasso (I)	Einbruch-versicherung f	housebreaking insurance	assurance contre le vol avec effraction f	—	seguro contra robo con fractura m
assicurazione contro incendi (I)	Feuerversicherung f	fire insurance	assurance contre l'incendie f	—	seguro contra incendios m
assicurazione contro infortuni (I)	Unfallversicherung f	personal accident insurance	assurance accidents corporels f	—	seguro de accidentes m
assicurazione contro le malattie (I)	Kranken-versicherung f	health insurance	assurance maladie f	—	seguro de enfermedad m
assicurazione corpi del ramo trasporto (I)	Kaskoversicherung f	comprehensive insurance	assurance tous risques f	—	seguro de casco m
assicurazione degli impiegati (I)	Angestellten-versicherung f	Salaried Employees' Pension Insurance	assurance invalidité-vieillesse des employés f	—	seguro de empleados m
assicurazione dei crediti (I)	Kreditversicherung f	credit insurance	assurance crédit f	—	seguro crediticio m
assicurazione dei fabbricati (I)	Gebäude-versicherung f	insurance on buildings	assurance des bâtiments f	—	seguro inmobiliario m
assicurazione dei trasporti (I)	Transport-versicherung f	transportation insurance	assurance transports f	—	seguro de transporte m
assicurazione del bagaglio (I)	Reisegepäck-versicherung f	baggage insurance	assurance des bagages f	—	seguro de equipajes m
assicurazione della responsabilità civile (I)	Haftpflicht-versicherung f	third party liability insurance	assurance respon-sabilité civile f	—	seguro de respon-sabilidad civil m
assicurazione delle macchine (I)	Maschinen-versicherung f	machine insurance	assurance des machines f	—	seguro de maquinaria m
assicurazione di cose (I)	Sachversicherung f	property insurance	assurance de choses f	—	seguro de cosas m
assicurazione di persone (I)	Personen-versicherung f	insurance of persons	assurance des personnes f	—	seguro personal m
assicurazione invali-dità e vecchiaia (I)	Rentenversicherung f	old-age pension insurance	assurance sociale in-validité-vieillesse f	—	seguro de pensiones m
assicurazione per la vecchiaia (I)	Altersversicherung f	old age insurance	assurance-vieillesse f	—	seguro de vejez m
assicurazione privata (I)	Privatversicherung f	private insurance	assurance privée f	—	seguro privado m
assicurazione recessione viaggio (I)	Reiserücktritts-versicherung f	travel cancellation insurance	assurance de résilia-tion du voyage f	—	seguro de rescisión del viaje m
assicurazione rischio-vita (I)	Risiko-Lebens-versicherung f	term life insurance	assurance-vie temporaire f	—	seguro de vida temporal m
assicurazione sulla vita (I)	Lebens-versicherung f	life insurance	assurance vie f	—	seguro de vida m
assignee (E)	Zessionar m	—	cessionnaire m	cessionario m	cesionario m

	D	E	F	I	Es
assignment (E)	Abtretung *f*	—	cession *f*	cessione *f*	cesión *f*
assignor (E)	Zedent *m*	—	cédant *m*	cedente *m*	cedente *m*
assistenza sociale (I)	Sozialhilfe *f*	public assistance	aide sociale *f*	—	ayuda social *f*
association¹ (E)	Verband *m*	—	association *f*	associazione *f*	asociación *f*
association² (E)	Verein *m*	—	association *f*	associazione *f*	asociación *f*
association¹ (F)	Verein *m*	association	—	associazione *f*	asociación *f*
association² (F)	Verband *m*	association	—	associazione *f*	asociación *f*
association à but déterminé (F)	Zweckverband *m*	special purpose association	—	consorzio intercomunale *m*	asociación con un fin determinado *f*
association commerciale en participation (F)	stille Gesellschaft *f*	dormant partnership	—	associazione in partecipazione *f*	sociedad en participación *f*
association des chefs d'entreprise (F)	Unternehmer-verband *m*	employers' association	—	unione degli imprenditori *f*	asociación empresarial *f*
association économique (F)	Wirtschafts-verband *m*	trade association	—	associazione economica *f*	asociación económica *f*
associazione¹ (I)	Verein *m*	association	association *f*	—	asociación *f*
associazione² (I)	Sozietät *f*	partnership	groupe de sociétaires *m*	—	sociedad *f*
associazione³ (I)	Verband *m*	association	association *f*	—	asociación *f*
associazione di categoria (I)	Berufs-genossenschaft *f*	professional association	association profes-sionnelle d'assurance accident *f*	—	mutua profesional *f*
associazione economica (I)	Wirtschafts-verband *m*	trade association	association économique *f*	—	asociación económica *f*
associazione in partecipazione (I)	stille Gesellschaft *f*	dormant partnership	association commer-ciale en participation *f*	—	sociedad en participación *f*
associé¹ (F)	Gesellschafter *m*	partner	—	socio *m*	socio *m*
associé² (F)	Geschäftspartner *m*	business partner	—	partner commerciale *m*	socio *m*
associé prenant part à la gestion (F)	aktiver Teilhaber *m*	active partner	—	socio attivo *m*	socio activo *m*
assorbimento (I)	Absorption *f*	absorption	absorption *f*	—	absorción *f*
assortiment (F)	Sortiment *n*	assortment	—	assortimento *m*	surtido *m*
assortimento (I)	Sortiment *n*	assortment	assortiment *m*	—	surtido *m*
assortment (E)	Sortiment *n*	—	assortiment *m*	assortimento *m*	surtido *m*
assortment policy (E)	Sortimentspolitik *f*	—	politique d'assortiment *f*	politica dell'assortimento *f*	política de surtido *f*
assortment structuring (E)	Sortiments-gestaltung *f*	—	structure d'assortiment *f*	composizione dell'assortimento *f*	configuración del surtido *f*
assujettissement obligatoire à l'assurance (F)	Versicherungs-pflicht *f*	liability to insure	—	obbligo d'assicurazione *m*	obligatoriedad del seguro *f*
assurance (E)	Assekuranz *f*	—	assurance *f*	assicurazione *f*	seguro *m*
assurance¹ (F)	Versicherung *f*	insurance	—	assicurazione *f*	seguro *m*
assurance² (F)	Assekuranz *f*	assurance	—	assicurazione *f*	seguro *m*
assurance accidents corporels (F)	Unfallversicherung *f*	personal accident insurance	—	assicurazione contro infortuni *f*	seguro de accidentes *m*
assurance contre le vol (F)	Diebstahl-versicherung *f*	theft insurance	—	assicurazione contro il furto *f*	seguro contra el robo *m*
assurance contre le vol avec effraction (F)	Einbruch-versicherung *f*	housebreaking insurance	—	assicurazione contro il furto con scasso *f*	seguro contra robo con fractura *m*
assurance contre l'incendie (F)	Feuerversicherung *f*	fire insurance	—	assicurazione contro incendi *f*	seguro contra incendios *m*
assurance crédit (F)	Kreditversicherung *f*	credit insurance	—	assicurazione dei crediti *f*	seguro crediticio *m*
assurance de choses (F)	Sachversicherung *f*	property insurance	—	assicurazione di cose *f*	seguro de cosas *m*
assurance de résilia-tion du voyage (F)	Reiserücktritts-versicherung *f*	travel cancellation insurance	—	assicurazione recessione viaggio *f*	seguro de rescisión del viaje *m*
assurance des bagages (F)	Reisegepäck-versicherung *f*	baggage insurance	—	assicurazione del bagaglio *f*	seguro de equipajes *m*
assurance des bâtiments (F)	Gebäude-versicherung *f*	insurance on buildings	—	assicurazione dei fabbricati *f*	seguro inmobiliario *m*

	D	E	F	I	Es
assurance des machines (F)	Maschinen-versicherung *f*	machine insurance	—	assicurazione delle macchine *f*	seguro de maquinaria *m*
assurance des personnes (F)	Personen-versicherung *f*	insurance of persons	—	assicurazione di persone *f*	seguro personal *m*
assurance invalidité-vieillesse des employés (F)	Angestellten-versicherung *f*	Salaried Employees' Pension Insurance	—	assicurazione degli impiegati *f*	seguro de empleados *m*
assurance maladie (F)	Kranken-versicherung *f*	health insurance	—	assicurazione contro le malattie *f*	seguro de enfermedad *m*
assurance mutuelle (F)	Versicherung auf Gegenseitigkeit *f*	mutual insurance	—	mutua assicurazione *f*	caja de socorros mutuos *f*
assurance privée (F)	Privatversicherung *f*	private insurance	—	assicurazione privata *f*	seguro privado *m*
assurance responsa-bilité civile (F)	Haftpflicht-versicherung *f*	third party liability insurance	—	assicurazione della responsabilità civile *f*	seguro de respon-sabilidad civil *m*
assurance responsabilité civile automobile (F)	Kraftfahrzeug-versicherung *f*	motor insurance	—	assicurazione autoveicoli *f*	seguro de automóviles *m*
assurance sociale (F)	Sozialversicherung *f*	social security	—	previdenza sociale *f*	seguro social *m*
assurance sociale invalidité-vieillesse (F)	Rentenversicherung *f*	old-age pension insurance	—	assicurazione invali-dità e vecchiaia *f*	seguro de pensiones *m*
assurance tous risques (F)	Kaskoversicherung *f*	comprehensive insurance	—	assicurazione ramo trasporto *f*	seguro de casco *m*
assurance transports (F)	Transport-versicherung *f*	transportation insurance	—	assicurazione dei trasporti *f*	seguro de transporte *m*
assurance vie (F)	Lebensversicherung *f*	life insurance	—	assicurazione sulla vita *f*	seguro de vida *m*
assurance-vieillesse (F)	Altersversicherung *f*	old age pension	—	assicurazione per *f* la vecchiaia	seguro de vejez *m*
assurance-vie temporaire (F)	Risiko-Lebens-versicherung *f*	term life insurance	—	assicurazione rischio-vita *f*	seguro de vida temporal *m*
assureur direct (F)	Erstversicherer *m*	direct insurer	—	assicuratore diretto *m*	primer asegurador *m*
asta (I)	Auktion *f*	auction	vente à l'enchère *f*	—	subasta *f*
asta giudiziaria (I)	Zwangs-versteigerung *f*	sale by court order	vente de biens par justice *f*	—	subasta forzosa *f*
at best (E)	bestens	—	au mieux	ottimo	al mejor cambio
at best price (E)	billigst	—	au meilleur prix	al prezzo più basso	al mejor cambio
a título de pago¹ (Es)	zahlungshalber	on account of payment	à titre de payement	a titolo di pagamento	—
a título de pago² (Es)	zahlungsstatt	in lieu of payment	à titre de payement	a titolo di pagamento	—
a titolo di pagamento¹ (I)	zahlungshalber	on account of payment	pour raison de payement	—	a título de pago
a titolo di pagamento² (I)	zahlungsstatt	in lieu of payment	à titre de payement	—	a título de pago
à titre de payement (F)	zahlungsstatt	in lieu of payment	—	a titolo di pagamento	a título de pago
à titre gracieux (F)	unentgeltlich	free of charge	—	gratuito	gratuito
atmósfera (Es)	Atmosphäre *f*	atmosphere	atmosphère *f*	atmosfera *f*	—
atmosfera (I)	Atmosphäre *f*	atmosphere	atmosphère *f*	—	atmósfera *f*
atmosfera di lavoro (I)	Betriebsklima *n*	working conditions and human relations	climat social *m*	—	ambiente de trabajo *m*
Atmosphäre (D)	—	atmosphere	atmosphère *f*	atmosfera *f*	atmósfera *f*
atmosphere (E)	Atmosphäre *f*	—	atmosphère *f*	atmosfera *f*	atmósfera *f*
atmosphère (F)	Atmosphäre *f*	atmosphere	—	atmosfera *f*	atmósfera *f*
Atomkraftwerk (D)	—	nuclear power plant	centrale nucléaire *f*	centrale nucleare *f*	central nuclear *f*
at sight (E)	auf Sicht	—	à vue	a vista	a la vista
attachment of earnings (E)	Lohnpfändung *f*	—	saisie-arrêt sur le salaire *f*	pignoramento del salario *m*	embargo de salario *m*
atteggiamento razionale (I)	Rationalverhalten *n*	rational behaviour	comportement rationnel *m*	—	comportamiento racional *m*
attività pubblica (I)	Staatstätigkeit *f*	state activity	activité de l'Etat *f*	—	actividad del Estado *f*
attivo¹ (I)	Haben *n*	credit side	avoir *m*	—	haber *m*
attivo² (I)	Aktiva *pl*	assets	masse active *f*	—	activo *m*
attivo³ (I)	erwerbstätig	gainfully employed	actif	—	activo

	D	E	F	I	Es
attivo fisso (I)	Anlagevermögen *n*	fixed assets	valeurs immobilisées *f pl*	—	activo fijo *m*
atto amministrativo (I)	Verwaltungsakt *m*	administrative act	acte administratif *m*	—	acto administrativo *m*
attribuzione (I)	Zuteilung *f*	allocation	répartition *f*	—	asignación *f*
au comptant (F)	gegen Barzahlung	against cash	—	contro pagamento in contanti	al contado
au pair (F)	pari	at par	—	pari	a la par
auction¹ (E)	Versteigerung *f*	—	vente à l'enchère *f*	vendita all'asta *f*	subasta *f*
auction² (E)	Auktion *f*	—	vente à l'enchère *f*	asta *f*	subasta *f*
auction fees (E)	Auktionsgebühr *f*	—	droits de vente aux enchères *m pl*	diritto d'asta *m*	gastos de subasta *m pl*
audit¹ (E)	Abschlußprüfung *f*	—	vérification des comptes *f*	revisione *f*	revisión contable *f*
audit² (E)	Revision *f*	—	vérification *f*	revisione *f*	revisión *f*
auditing (E)	Wirtschaftsprüfung *f*	—	contrôle de la gestion et des comptes *m*	revisione *f*	revisoría *f*
auditor¹ (E)	Abschlußprüfer *m*	—	vérificateur des comptes *m*	revisore *m*	revisor contable *m*
auditor² (E)	Betriebsprüfer *m*	—	expert-comptable *m*	revisore aziendale *m*	contador público *m*
auditor³ (E)	Wirtschaftsprüfer *m*	—	expert comptable économique et financier *m*	revisore dei conti *m*	revisor de cuentas *m*/ experto contable *m*
auditor⁴ (E)	Rechnungsprüfer *m*	—	commissaire aux comptes *m*	revisore dei conti *m*	revisor contable *m*
auf Abruf (D)	—	on call	à convenance	su richiesta	a requerimiento
Aufbauphase (D)	—	development phase	phase d'organisation *f*	fase di costruzione *f*	fase de desarrollo *f*
aufbereiten (D)	—	process/prepare	élaborer/traiter	elaborare/lavorare	elaborar/tratar
Aufbewahrungspflicht (D)	—	obligation to preserve records	obligation de conservation *f*	obbligo di conservazione *m*	deber de conservación *m*
Aufenthaltserlaubnis (D)	—	residence permit	autorisation de séjour *f*	permesso di soggiorno *m*	permiso de residencia *m*
Aufgeld (D)	—	agio	prime *f*	aggio *m*	agio *m*
Aufkleber (D)	—	sticker	étiquette *f*	etichetta adesiva *f*	pegatina *f*
auf Kommissionsbasis (D)	—	on a commission basis	en commission	in base commissionaria	en comisión
auf Lager (D)	—	in stock	en stock	in magazzino	en almacén
auf Lager haben (D)	—	have in stock	avoir en stock	avere in magazzino	tener en almacén
Auflösung (D)	—	dissolution	liquidation *f*	scioglimento *m*	disolución *f*
Aufrechnung (D)	—	set-off	compensation *f*	compensazione *f*	compensación *f*
auf Probe (D)	—	on trial	à l'essai	in prova	a prueba
auf Provisionsbasis (D)	—	on a commission basis	à la commission	a provvigione	a comisión
Aufschiebung (D)	—	postponement	remise *f*	rinvio *m*	aplazamiento *m*
Aufschlag (D)	—	surcharge	hausse *f*	aggiunta *f*	recargo *m*
Aufsicht (D)	—	supervision	surveillance *f*	sorveglianza *f*	inspección *f*
auf Sicht (D)	—	at sight	à vue	a vista	a la vista
Aufsichtspflicht (D)	—	duty of supervision	obligation de surveillance *f*	obbligo di sorveglianza *m*	obligación de vigilancia *f*
Aufsichtsrat (D)	—	supervisory board	conseil de surveillance *m*	consiglio di sorveglianza *m*	consejo de vigilancia *m*
Aufsichtsratsvorsitzender (D)	—	chairman of the supervisory board	président du conseil de surveillance *m*	presidente del consiglio di sorveglianza *m*	presidente del consejo de vigilancia *m*
Aufstiegsmöglichkeit (D)	—	promotion possibility	perspectives de promotion *f pl*	possibilità di carriera *f*	posibilidades de ascenso *f pl*
Auftrag (D)	—	order	commande *f*	ordine *m*	pedido *m*
Auftraggeber (D)	—	client	commettant *m*	committente *m*	mandante *m*
Auftragsabwicklung (D)	—	execution of the order	exécution d'une commande *f*	esecuzione ordini *f*	ejecución de pedidos *f*
Auftragsbearbeitung (D)	—	order processing	réalisation d'une commande *f*	esecuzione ordini *f*	tramitación de pedidos *f*
Auftragsbestätigung (D)	—	confirmation of order	confirmation de commande *f*	conferma d'ordine *f*	confirmación de pedido *f*

	D	E	F	I	Es
Auftragserteilung (D)	—	placing of an order	passation d'une commande f	ordinazione f	otorgamiento de un pedido m
Auftragsnummer (D)	—	order number	numéro de commande m	numero d'ordine m	número de pedido m
Auftragsplanung (D)	—	order scheduling	planification des commandes f	pianificazione degli ordini f	planificación de la ejecución de pedidos f
Aufwand (D)	—	expenditure	dépenses f pl	spese f pl	gastos m pl
Aufwandsfaktor (D)	—	expenditure factor	facteur des frais m	fattore spese m	factor de gastos m
Aufwands-minimierung (D)	—	expenditure minimization	minimiser les frais	riduzione delle spese f	minimación de gastos f
Aufwärtstrend (D)	—	upward trend	mouvement ascendant m	tendenza al rialzo f	tendencia alcista f
Aufwendung (D)	—	expenditure	dépenses f pl	spese f pl	gastos m pl
Aufwertung (D)	—	revaluation	revalorisation f	rivalutazione f	revalorización f
augmentation de capital (F)	Kapitalerhöhung f	increase of the share capital	—	aumento del capitale m	aumento de capital m
augmentation des prix (F)	Preiserhöhung f	price increase	—	rialzo dei prezzi m	aumento de precios m
augmentation du chiffre d'affaires (F)	Umsatzanstieg m	turnover increase	—	aumento del fatturato m	aumento del volumen de facturación m
augmentation du revenu (F)	Einkommens-erhöhung f	rise in income	—	aumento del reddito m	aumento de salario m
augmentation du salaire (F)	Lohnerhöhung f	increase in wages	—	aumento salariale m	aumento de salario m
augmentation du traitement (F)	Gehaltserhöhung f	increase in salary	—	aumento dello stipendio m	aumento de sueldo m
auguri (I)	Glückwunsch m	congratulations	félicitations f pl	—	felicitaciones f pl
Auktion (D)	—	auction	vente à l'enchère f	asta f	subasta f
Auktionsgebühr (D)	—	auction fees	droits de vente aux enchères m pl	diritto d'asta m	gastos de subasta m pl
au meilleur prix (F)	billigst	at best price	—	al prezzo più basso	al mejor cambio
aumento de capital (Es)	Kapitalerhöhung f	increase of the share capital	augmentation de capital f	aumento del capitale m	—
aumento dei corsi (I)	Kurssteigerung f	price advance	hausse f	—	alza de las cotizaciones f
aumento dei prezzi (I)	Preissteigerung f	price increase	hausse des prix f	—	aumento de precios m
aumento del capitale (I)	Kapitalerhöhung f	increase of the share capital	augmentation de capital f	—	aumento de capital m
aumento del fatturato (I)	Umsatzanstieg m	turnover increase	augmentation du chiffre d'affaires f	—	aumento del volumen de facturación m
aumento delle imposte (I)	Steuererhöhung f	increase of taxes	relèvement des impôts m	—	aumento de los impuestos m
aumento dello stipendio (I)	Gehaltserhöhung f	increase in salary	augmentation du traitement f	—	aumento de sueldo m
aumento de los impuestos (Es)	Steuererhöhung f	increase of taxes	relèvement des impôts m	aumento delle imposte m	—
aumento del prezzo (I)	Preisanstieg m	price rise	hausse des prix f	—	aumento de precios m
aumento del reddito (I)	Einkommens-erhöhung f	rise in income	augmentation du revenu f	—	aumento de salario m
aumento del volumen de facturación (Es)	Umsatzanstieg m	turnover increase	augmentation du chiffre d'affaires f	aumento del fatturato m	—
aumento de precios¹ (Es)	Preiserhöhung f	price increase	augmentation des prix f	rialzo dei prezzi m	—
aumento de precios² (Es)	Preissteigerung f	price increase	hausse des prix f	aumento dei prezzi m	—
aumento de precios³ (Es)	Preisanstieg m	price rise	hausse des prix f	aumento del prezzo m	—
aumento de salario¹ (Es)	Lohnerhöhung f	increase in wages	augmentation du salaire f	aumento salariale m	—
aumento de salario² (Es)	Einkommens-erhöhung f	rise in income	augmentation du revenu f	aumento del reddito m	—
aumento de sueldo (Es)	Gehaltserhöhung f	increase in salary	augmentation du traitement f	aumento dello stipendio m	—

	D	E	F	I	Es
aumento della produttività (I)	Leistungs-steigerung *f*	increase in efficiency	amélioration du rendement *f*	—	incremento del rendimiento *m*
aumento salariale (I)	Lohnerhöhung *f*	increase in wages	augmentation du salaire *f*	—	aumento de salario *m*
au mieux (F)	bestens	at best	—	ottimo	al mejor cambio
Ausbilder (D)	—	trainer	instructeur *m*	istruttore *m*	instructor *m*
Ausbildung (D)	—	apprenticeship	apprentissage *m*	apprendistato *m*	aprendizaje *m*
ausente (Es)	abwesend	absent	absent	assente	—
Ausfallbürgschaft (D)	—	deficiency guarantee	garantie de bonne fin *f*	fideiussione d'indennità *f*	fianza con beneficio de excusión *f*
Ausfallquote (D)	—	default rate	ratio de perte *m*	tasso di perdita *m*	cuota de pérdida *f*
Ausfallrisiko (D)	—	default risk	risque de perte *m*	rischio di perdita *m*	riesgo de pérdida *m*
Ausfuhr (D)	—	export	exportation *f*	esportazione *f*	exportación *f*
Ausfuhrabfertigung (D)	—	customs clearance of exports	formalités en douane à l'exportation *f pl*	sdoganamento delle esportazioni *m*	despacho de exportación *m*
Ausfuhr-beschränkung (D)	—	export restriction	contingentement de l'exportation *m*	restrizione delle esportazioni *f*	restricción a la exportación *f*
Ausfuhr-bestimmungen (D)	—	export regulations	dispositions d'exportation *f pl*	disposizioni per le esportazioni *f pl*	reglamento de exportación *m*
Ausfuhr-finanzierung (D)	—	export financing	financement de l'exportation *m*	finanziamento delle esportazioni *m*	financiación de la exportación *f*
Ausfuhrförderung (D)	—	measures to encourage exports	encouragement à l'exportation *m*	promozione delle esportazioni *f*	fomento de la exportación *m*
Ausfuhr-genehmigung (D)	—	export licence	autorisation d'exportation *f*	autorizzazione per le esportazioni *f*	licencia de exportación *f*
Ausfuhrpapiere (D)	—	export documents	documents d'exportation *m pl*	documenti d'esportazione *m pl*	documentos de exportación *m pl*
Ausfuhrzoll (D)	—	export duty	taxe de sortie *f*	dazio sull'esportazione *m*	derechos de exportación *m pl*
Ausgaben (D)	—	expenses	dépenses *f pl*	spese *f pl*	gastos *m pl*
Ausgabenkontrolle (D)	—	expenditure control	contrôle des dépenses *m*	controllo delle spese *m*	control de gastos *m*
Ausgabensenkung (D)	—	drop in expenditure	diminution des dépenses *f*	riduzione delle spese *f*	reducción de gastos *f*
Ausgaben-verzögerung (D)	—	expenditure delay	dépenses retardées *f pl*	dilazione delle spese *f*	aplazamiento de gastos *m*
Ausgleichsfonds (D)	—	compensation fund	fonds de compensation *m*	fondo di compensazione *m*	fondo de compensación *m*
Ausgleichszahlung (D)	—	compensation payment	payement pour solde de compte *m*	conguaglio *m*	pago de compensación *m*
Aushilfe (D)	—	auxiliary worker	aide *m*	aiuto *m*	ayudante *m*
ausiliario (I)	Erfüllungsgehilfe *m*	vicarious agent	auxiliaire d'exécution *m*	—	auxiliar *m*
Auskunft (D)	—	information	renseignement *m*	informazione *f*	información *f*
Auskunftei (D)	—	information bureau	agence de renseignements *f*	agenzia d'informazioni *f*	oficina de información *f*
Auslage (D)	—	display	étalage *f*	vetrina *f*	vitrina *f*
Ausländer (D)	—	foreigner	étranger *m*	straniero *m*	extranjero *m*
ausländische Arbeitnehmer (D)	—	foreign worker	travailleur étranger *m*	prestatori d'opera stranieri *m pl*	trabajadores extranjeros *m*
Auslandsanleihe (D)	—	foreign bond	emprunt extérieur *m*	prestito estero *m*	empréstito exterior *m*
Auslandsgeschäft (D)	—	foreign business	opération avec l'étranger *f*	affare con l'estero *m*	negocio de exporta-ción o importación *m*
Auslandskapital (D)	—	foreign capital	capital étranger *m*	capitale estero *m*	capital extranjero *m*
Auslandskonto (D)	—	foreign account	compte d'étranger *m*	conto estero *m*	cuenta exterior *f*
Auslandskunde (D)	—	foreign customer	client étranger *m*	cliente estero *m*	cliente extranjero *m*
Auslandsmärkte (D)	—	foreign markets	marchés extérieurs *m pl*	mercati esteri *m pl*	mercado exterior *m*
Auslandsnachfrage (D)	—	foreign demand	demande en provenance de l'étranger *f*	domanda estera *f*	demanda exterior *m*
Auslands-niederlassung (D)	—	branch abroad	succursale à l'étranger *f*	succursale estera *f*	filial en el exterior *m*

	D	E	F	I	Es
Auslandsschulden (D)	—	foreign debts	dettes à l'étranger *f pl*	debiti con l'estero *m pl*	deudas exteriores *f pl*
Auslandsvermögen (D)	—	foreign assets	avoirs à l'étranger *m pl*	patrimonio estero *m*	activo exterior *m*
Auslands-vertretung (D)	—	agency abroad	agence à l'étranger *f*	rappresentanza estera *f*	representación en el exterior *f*
Auslandswechsel (D)	—	foreign bill of exchange	traite tirée sur l'étranger *f*	cambiale estera *f*	letra sobre el exterior *f*
Auslastungsgrad (D)	—	capacity utilisation rate	dégré de saturation *m*	grado di sfruttamento *m*	tasa de utilización *f*
Auslieferungslager (D)	—	distribution centre	entrepôt de distribution *m*	deposito di consegna *m*	almacén de entregas *m*
Ausnutzungsgrad (D)	—	utilization rate	taux d'utilisation *m*	grado di utilizzazione *m*	grado de utilización *m*
Ausschreibung (D)	—	tender	soumission *f*	appalto *m*	concurso-subasta *m*
Außendienst (D)	—	field work	service extérieur *m*	servizio esterno *m*	servicio exterior *m*
Außendienst-mitarbeiter (D)	—	field staff	personnel du service extérieur *m*	collaboratore del servizio esterno *m*	colaborador en el servicio exterior *m*
Außenhandel (D)	—	foreign trade	commerce extérieur *m*	commercio estero *m*	comercio exterior *m*
Außenhandels-defizit (D)	—	trade deficit	déficit de la balance du commerce extérieur *m*	deficit del commercio estero *m*	déficit del comercio exterior *m*
Außenhandels-finanzierung (D)	—	foreign trade financing	aide financière à l'exportation *m*	finanziamento del commercio estero *m*	financiación del comercio exterior *f*
Außenhandels-freiheit (D)	—	free trade	libre-échange *m*	libertà di commercio estero *f*	librecambio *m*
Außenhandels-kammer (D)	—	chamber of foreign trade	chambre du commerce extérieur *f*	camera di commercio estero *f*	cámara del comercio exterior *f*
Außenhandels-monopol (D)	—	foreign trade monopoly	monopole du commerce extérieur *m*	monopolio del commercio estero *m*	monopolio del comercio exterior *m*
Außenhandels-politik (D)	—	foreign trade policy	politique de commerce extérieur *f*	politica del commercio estero *f*	política comercial exterior *f*
Außenstände (D)	—	outstanding debts	dettes actives *f pl*	debiti insoluti *m pl*	cobros pendientes *m pl*
Außenwerbung (D)	—	outdoor publicity	publicité extérieure *f*	pubblicità all'aperto *f*	publicidad al aire libre *f*
außergerichtlich (D)	—	extrajudicial	extrajudiciaire	extragiudiziale	extrajudicial
außergewöhnliche Belastung (D)	—	extraordinary expenses	charges exceptionnelles *f pl*	oneri straordinari *m pl*	carga extraordinaria *f*
Aussperrung (D)	—	lockout	lock-out *m*	serrata *f*	cierre patronal *m*
Aussteller (D)	—	exhibitor	exposant *m*	espositore *m*	expositor *m*
Ausstellung (D)	—	exhibition	exposition *f*	esposizione *f*	exhibición *f*
Ausverkauf (D)	—	clearance sale	soldes *m pl*	svendita *f*	liquidación *f*
Auszahlung (D)	—	paying out	payement *m*	pagamento *m*	pago *m*
autenticazione (I)	Beglaubigung *f*	authentication	certification *f*	—	legalización *f*
auteur de la procuration (F)	Vollmachtgeber *m*	grantor of power of attorney	—	mandante *m*	poderdante *m*
authenticated copy (E)	beglaubigte Abschrift *f*	—	copie certifiée *f*	copia autenticata *f*	copia legalizada *f*
authentication (E)	Beglaubigung *f*	—	certification *f*	autenticazione *f*	legalización *f*
authoritarian (E)	autoritär	—	autoritaire	autoritario	autoritario
authority (E)	Behörde *f*	—	autorité *f*	autorità *f*	autoridad *f*
authority to sign (E)	Zeichnungs-berechtigung *f*	—	autorisation de signer *f*	diritto di firma *m*	facultad de firma *f*
authorization¹ (E)	Bevollmächtigung *f*	—	pouvoir *m*	autorizzazione *f*	apoderamiento *m*
authorization² (E)	Befugnis *f*	—	pouvoir *m*	prerogativa *f*	autorización *f*
authorization to receive (E)	Empfangs-berechtigung *f*	—	autorité pour recevoir *f*	autorizzazione di ricezione *f*	autorización de recibimiento *f*
authorized to represent (E)	Vertretungs-berechtigung *f*	—	autorisation de représentation *f*	autorizzazione alla rappresentanza *f*	derecho de representación *m*
authorized to under-take the collection (E)	inkassoberechtigt	—	autorisé à l'encaissement	autorizzato all'incasso	autorizado al encobro

	D	E	F	I	Es
autofinancement¹ (F)	Selbstfinanzierung f	self-financing	—	autofinanziamento m	autofinanciación f
autofinancement² (F)	Eigenfinanzierung f	self-financing	—	autofinanziamento m	financiación propia f
autofinanciación (Es)	Selbstfinanzierung f	self-financing	autofinancement m	autofinanziamento m	—
autofinanziamento¹ (I)	Selbstfinanzierung f	self-financing	autofinancement m	—	autofinanciación f
autofinanziamento² (I)	Eigenfinanzierung f	self-financing	autofinancement m	—	financiación propia f
Automat (D)	—	vending machine	appareil automatique m	distributore automatico m	distribuidor automático m
Automatenverkauf (D)	—	automatic vending	vente par distributeur automatique f	vendita per distributori automatici f	venta por distribuidores automáticos f
automatic vending (E)	Automatenverkauf m	—	vente par distributeur automatique f	vendita per distributori automatici f	venta por distribuidores automáticos f
Automation (D)	—	automation	automation f	automazione f	automatización f
automation (F)	Automation f	automation	—	automazione f	automatización f
automation¹ (E)	Automatisierung f	—	automatisation f	automatizzazione f	automatización f
automation² (E)	Automation f	—	automation f	automazione f	automatización f
automatisation (F)	Automatisierung f	automation	—	automatizzazione f	automatización f
Automatisierung (D)	—	automation	automatisation f	automatizzazione f	automatización f
automatización¹ (Es)	Automation f	automation	automation f	automazione f	—
automatización² (Es)	Automatisierung f	automation	automatisation f	automatizzazione f	—
automatizzazione (I)	Automatisierung f	automation	automatisation f	—	automatización f
automazione (I)	Automation f	automation	automation f	—	automatización f
automobile (I)	Kraftfahrzeug n	motor vehicle	véhicule à moteur m	—	automóvil m
automobile usata (I)	Gebrauchtwagen m	used car	voiture d'occasion f	—	coche de segunda mano m
automóvil (Es)	Kraftfahrzeug n	motor vehicle	véhicule à moteur m	automobile f	—
autonomía (Es)	Autonomie f	autonomy	autonomie f	autonomia f	—
autonomia (I)	Autonomie f	autonomy	autonomie f	—	autonomía f
Autonomie (D)	—	autonomy	autonomie f	autonomia f	autonomía f
autonomie (F)	Autonomie f	autonomy	—	autonomia f	autonomía f
autonomie d'administration (F)	Verwaltungshoheit f	power of administration	—	sovranità amministrativa f	soberanía administrativa f
autonomy (E)	Autonomie f	—	autonomie f	autonomia f	autonomía f
autoridad (Es)	Behörde f	authority	autorité f	autorità f	—
autoridad monetaria (Es)	Währungsbehörde f	monetary authority	autorité monétaire f	autorità monetaria f	—
autorisation (F)	Genehmigung f	permission	—	autorizzazione f	autorización f
autorisation de change (F)	Devisen-genehmigung f	foreign exchange authorization	—	autorizzazione valutaria f	certificado de divisas m
autorisation de représentation (F)	Vertretungs-berechtigung f	authorization to represent	—	autorizzazione alla rappresentanza f	derecho de representación m
autorisation de séjour (F)	Aufenthalts-erlaubnis f	residence permit	—	permesso di soggiorno m	permiso de residencia m
autorisation de signer (F)	Zeichnungs-berechtigung f	authority to sign	—	diritto di firma m	facultad de firma f
autorisation d'exportation (F)	Ausfuhr-genehmigung f	export licence	—	autorizzazione per le esportazioni f	licencia de exportación f
autorisation d'importation (F)	Einfuhr-genehmigung f	import licence	—	permesso d'importazione m	permiso de importación m
autorisé à l'encaissement (F)	inkassoberechtigt	authorized to under-take the collection	—	autorizzato all'incasso	autorizado al encobro
autorità (I)	Behörde f	authority	autorité f	—	autoridad f
autorità antimonopoli (I)	Kartellbehörde f	cartel authority	office de surveillance des cartels et ententes m	—	oficina de cártels f
autorità fiscali (I)	Steuerbehörden pl	tax authority	administration des contributions f	—	administración de hacienda f
autoritaire (F)	autoritär	authoritarian	—	autoritario	autoritario
autorità monetaria (I)	Währungsbehörde f	monetary authority	autorité monétaire f	—	autoridad monetaria f
autoritär (D)	—	authoritarian	autoritaire	autoritario	autoritario
autoritario (Es)	autoritär	authoritarian	autoritaire	autoritario	—

	D	E	F	I	Es
autoritario (I)	autoritär	authoritarian	autoritaire	—	autoritario
autorité (F)	Behörde f	authority	—	autorità f	autoridad f
autorité monétaire (F)	Währungsbehörde f	monetary authority	—	autorità monetaria f	autoridad monetaria f
autorité pour recevoir (F)	Empfangs-berechtigung f	authorization to receive	—	autorizzazione a ricevere f	autorización de recibimiento f
autorización¹ (Es)	Genehmigung f	permission	autorisation f	autorizzazione f	—
autorización² (Es)	Befugnis f	authorization	pouvoir m	prerogativa f	—
autorización de funcionamiento (Es)	Betriebserlaubnis f	operating permit	droit d'exploitation m	autorizzazione per l'esercizio f	—
autorización de recibimiento (Es)	Empfangs-berechtigung f	authorization to receive	autorité pour recevoir f	autorizzazione a ricevere f	—
autorizado al encobro (Es)	inkassoberechtigt	authorized to under-take the collection	autorisé à l'encaissement	autorizzato all'incasso	—
autorizzato all'incasso (I)	inkassoberechtigt	authorized to under-take the collection	autorisé à l'encaissement	—	autorizado al encobro
autorizzazione¹ (I)	Bevollmächtigung f	authorization	pouvoir m	—	apoderamiento m
autorizzazione² (I)	Genehmigung f	permission	autorisation f	—	autorización f
autorizzazione³ (I)	Vollmacht f	full power/ power of attorney	plein pouvoir m/ mandat m	—	poder m/ autorización f
autorizzazione alla rappresentanza (I)	Vertretungs-berechtigung f	authorization to represent	autorisation de représentation f	—	derecho de representación m
autorizzazione di ricezione (I)	Empfangs-berechtigung f	authorization to receive	autorité pour recevoir f	—	autorización de recibimiento f
autorizzazione per l'esercizio (I)	Betriebserlaubnis f	operating permit	droit d'exploitation m	—	autorización de funcionamiento f
autorizzazione per le esportazioni (I)	Ausfuhr-genehmigung f	export licence	autorisation d'exportation f	—	licencia de exportación f
autorizzazione valutaria (I)	Devisen-genehmigung f	foreign exchange authorization	autorisation de change f	—	certificado de divisas m
autoservicio (Es)	Selbstbedienung f	self-service	self-service m	self service m	—
autumn fair (E)	Herbstmesse f	—	foire d'automne f	fiera autunnale f	feria de otoño f
auxiliary worker (E)	Aushilfe f	—	aide m	aiuto m	ayudante m
Aval (D)	—	guarantee of a bill	aval m	avallo m	aval m
aval (Es)	Aval m	guarantee of a bill	aval m	avallo m	—
aval (F)	Aval m	guarantee of a bill	—	avallo m	aval m
Avalkredit (D)	—	credit by way of bank guarantee	crédit d'escompte sur traite avalisée m	credito d'avallo m	crédito de aval m
avallo (I)	Aval m	guarantee of a bill	aval m	—	aval m
avance (F)	Vorschuß m	advance	—	anticipo m	anticipo m
avance sur compte courant (F)	Überziehungs-kredit m	credit by way of overdraft	—	credito allo scoperto m	crédito en descubierto m
avance sur marchandises (F)	Warenkredit m	trade credit	—	credito su merci m	crédito comercial m
avantage (F)	Vorteil m	advantage benefit	—	vantaggio m	ventaja f
avantage de concurrence (F)	Wettbewerbs-vorteil m	competitive advantage	—	vantaggio concorrenziale m	ventaja de competencia f
avantage de coût (F)	Kostenvorteil m	cost advantage	—	vantaggio di costo m	ventaja de costes f
avaria (I)	Havarie f	damage by sea	avarie f	—	avería f
avarie (F)	Havarie f	damage by sea	—	avaria f	avería f
avec grande intensité de capital (F)	kapitalintensiv	capital-intensive	—	ad alta incidenza di capitale	con gran intensidad de capital
average (E)	Durchschnitt m	—	moyenne f	media f	promedio m
average costs (E)	Durchschnitts-kosten pl	—	coût moyen m	costi medi m pl	gastos medios m pl
avere in magazzino (I)	auf Lager haben	have in stock	avoir en stock	—	tener en almacén
avería (Es)	Havarie f	damage by sea	avarie f	avaria f	—
Avis (D)	—	advice	avis m	avviso m	aviso m
avis¹ (F)	Nachricht f	news	—	notizia f	noticia f
avis² (F)	Avis m	advice	—	avviso m	aviso m
avis de chargement (F)	Ladeschein m	bill of lading	—	bolletta di carico f	póliza de carga f
avis de crédit (F)	Gutschriftsanzeige f	credit advice	—	nota di accredito f	aviso de abono m

	D	E	F	I	Es
avis de réception (F)	Rückschein *m*	advice of delivery	—	ricevuta di ritorno *f*	acuse de recibo *m*
avis d'imposition (F)	Steuerbescheid *m*	notice of assessment	—	cartella delle imposte *f*	liquidación de impuestos *f*
aviso¹ (Es)	Avis *m*	advice	avis *m*	avviso *m*	—
aviso² (Es)	Mitteilung *f*	information	notification *f*	comunicazione *f*	—
aviso bancario (Es)	Bankavis *m*	bank notification	confirmation banquaire *f*	avviso bancario *m*	—
aviso de abono (Es)	Gutschriftsanzeige *f*	credit advice	avis de crédit *m*	nota di accredito *f*	—
aviso de siniestro (Es)	Schadensmeldung *f*	notification of damage	déclaration du sinistre *f*	avviso di danni *m*	—
aviso de vicios (Es)	Mängelanzeige *f*	notice of defect	notification d'un	denuncia dei vizi *f* vice *f*	—
a vista (I)	auf Sicht	at sight	à vue	—	a la vista
avocat (F)	Rechtsanwalt *m*	lawyer	—	avvocato *m*	abogado *m*
avoir¹ (F)	Haben *n*	credit side	—	attivo *m*	haber *m*
avoir² (F)	Guthaben *n*	money owed	—	saldo attivo *m*	haber *m*
avoir en stock (F)	auf Lager haben	have in stock	—	avere in magazzino	tener en almacén
avoir net (F)	Reinvermögen *n*	net assets	—	patrimonio netto *m*	patrimonio neto *m*
avoirs à l'étranger (F)	Auslandsvermögen *n*	foreign assets	—	patrimonio estero *m*	activo exterior *m*
à vue¹ (F)	auf Sicht	at sight	—	a vista	a la vista
à vue² (F)	zur Ansicht	on approval	—	in visione	para examen
a vuelta de correo (Es)	postwendend	by return of post	par retour du courrier	a giro di posta	—
avviso¹ (I)	Avis *m*	advice	avis *m*	—	aviso *m*
avviso² (I)	Anmeldung *f*	registration	inscription *f*	—	solicitud *f*
avviso bancario (I)	Bankavis *m*	bank notification	confirmation bancaire *f*	—	aviso bancario *m*
avviso di danni (I)	Schadensmeldung *f*	notification of damage	déclaration du sinistre *f*	—	aviso de siniestro *m*
avviso di visita (I)	Besuchsanmeldung *f*	announcement of a visitor	annonce des visiteurs *f*	—	anuncio de visita *m*
avvocato (I)	Rechtsanwalt *m*	lawyer	avocat *m*	—	abogado *m*
ayuda a la exportación (Es)	Exporthilfe *f*	export subsidy	subvention à l'exportatiin *f*	aiuto all'esportazione *m*	—
ayuda al desarrollo (Es)	Entwicklungshilfe *f*	development aid	aide au développement *f*	aiuto ai paesi in via di sviluppo *m*	—
ayuda financiera (Es)	Kapitalhilfe *f*	capital aid	aide financière *f*	aiuto finanziario *m*	—
ayudante (Es)	Aushilfe *f*	auxiliary worker	aide *m*	aiuto *m*	—
ayuda social (Es)	Sozialhilfe *f*	public assistance	aide sociale *f*	assistenza sociale *f*	—
azienda (I)	Betrieb *m*	factory	usine *f*	—	fábrica *f*
azienda agricola (I)	Agrarbetrieb *m*	agricultural enterprise	entreprise agricole *f*	—	empresa agrícola *f*
azienda commerciale (I)	gewerblicher Betrieb *m*	industrial undertaking	établissement commercial	—	empresa industrial *f*
azienda di grande dimensione (I)	Großbetrieb *m*	large-scale operation	grande exploitation *f*	—	gran explotación *f*
azienda industriale (I)	Industriebetrieb *m*	industrial enterprise	entreprise industrielle *f*	—	establecimiento industrial *m*
aziende pubbliche (I)	öffentliche Betriebe *pl*	public sector industrial enterprises	entreprises *pl* publiques *f*	—	empresa pública *f*
aziende statali (I)	staatliche Betriebe *pl*	state-owned enterprise	entreprise publique *f*	—	empresas públicas *f pl*
azione (I)	Aktie *f*	share	action *f*	—	acción *f*
azione al portatore (I)	Inhaberaktie *f*	bearer share	action au porteur *f*	—	acción al portador *f*
azione di impugnazione (I)	Anfechtungsklage *f*	action for avoidance	action en annulation *f*	—	acción de impugnación *f*
azione di risarcimento danni (I)	Schadensersatz- klage *f*	action for damages	action en dommages-intérêts *f*	—	demanda de daños y perjuicios *f*
azione nominativa (I)	Namensaktie *f*	registered shares	action nominative *f*	—	acción nominal *f*
azione ordinaria (I)	Stammaktie *f*	ordinary shares	action ordinaire *f*	—	acción ordinaria *f*
azione privilegiata (I)	Vorzugsaktie *f*	preference share	action privilégiée *f*	—	acción preferente *f*
azione pubblicitaria (I)	Werbeaktion *f*	advertising activity	campagne publicitaire *f*	—	campaña publicitaria *f*

	D	E	F	I	Es
azione speciale (I)	Sonderaktion *f*	special action	action spéciale *f*	—	acción especial *f*
azione stampa (I)	Presseaktion *f*	press campaign	action de presse *f*	—	campaña de prensa *f*
azioni¹ (I)	Aktionen *pl*	actions	actions *f pl*	—	acciones *f pl*
azioni² (I)	Aktien *pl*	shares	actions *f pl*	—	acciones *f pl*
azionista (I)	Aktionär *m*	shareholder	actionnaire *m*	—	accionista *m*
baby bonds (E)	Baby-Bonds *pl*	—	bons de petite valeur nominale *m pl*	baby bonds *m pl*	bonos de pequeño valor nominal *m pl*
baby bonds (I)	Baby-Bonds *pl*	baby bonds	bons de petite valeur nominale *m pl*	—	bonos de pequeño valor nominal *m pl*
Baby-Bonds (D)	—	baby bonds	bons de petite valeur nominale *m pl*	baby bonds *m pl*	bonos de pequeño valor nominal *m pl*
Bagatellschaden (D)	—	minimal damage	dommage mineur *m*	danno piccolo *m*	siniestro leve *m*
baggage insurance (E)	Reisegepäck-versicherung *f*	—	assurance des bagages *f*	assicurazione del bagaglio *f*	seguro de equipajes *m*
Bahnfracht (D)	—	rail freight	fret par rail *m*	nolo ferroviario *m*	transporte ferroviario *m*
bail (E)	Haftkaution *f*	—	caution pour être mis en liberté *f*	cauzione per la scarcerazione *f*	fianza de puesta en libertad *f*
bailiff (E)	Gerichtsvollzieher *m*	—	huissier de justice *m*	ufficiale giudiziario *m*	ejecutor judicial *m*
bailleur de fonds (F)	Geldgeber *m*	financial backer	—	finanziatore *m*	prestamista *m*
baisse (F)	Abwärtstrend *m*	downward trend	—	tendenza al ribasso *f*	tendencia bajista *f*
baisse de l'offre d'emploi (F)	Beschäftigungs-rückgang *m*	drop in employment	—	calo dell'occupazione *m*	descenso del empleo *m*
baisse des prix (F)	Preissenkung *f*	price reduction	—	riduzione dei prezzi *f*	reducción de precios *f*
baisse sur les cours (F)	Kursverlust *m*	loss in exchange	—	perdita sul cambio *f*	pérdida en bolsa *f*
baja (Es)	Abschwung *m*	down-swing	dépression *f*	regresso *m*	—
balance¹ (E)	Gleichgewicht *n*	—	équilibre *m*	equilibrio *m*	equilibrio *m*
balance² (E)	Saldo *m*	—	solde *m*	saldo *m*	saldo *m*
balance (Es)	Bilanz *f*	balance sheet	bilan *m*	bilancio *m*	—
balance analysis (E)	Bilanzanalyse *f*	—	analyse du bilan *f*	analisi di bilancio *f*	análisis de balance *m*
balance consolidado (Es)	konsolidierte Bilanz *f*	consolidated balance sheet	bilan consolidé *m*	bilancio consolidato *m*	—
balance del consorcio (Es)	Konzernbilanz *f*	balance sheet of a group	bilan consolidé d'un groupement de sociétés *m*	bilancio del gruppo *m*	—
balance del presupuesto (Es)	Budgetausgleich *m*	balancing of the budget	équilibrage du budget *m*	pareggio di bilancio *m*	—
balance des opéra-tions courantes (F)	Leistungsbilanz *f*	balance of goods and services	—	bilancia delle partite correnti *f*	balanza por cuenta corriente *f*
balance des opéra-tions en capital (F)	Kapitalbilanz *f*	balance of capital transactions	—	bilancia dei capitali *f*	balanza de capitales *f*
balance des opérations en marchandises (F)	Handelsbilanz *f*	balance of trade	—	bilancia commerciale *f*	balanza comercial *f*
balance des payements (F)	Zahlungsbilanz *f*	balance of payments	—	bilancia dei pagamenti *f*	balanza de pagos *f*
balance des paye-ments déficitaire (F)	Zahlungsbilanz-defizit *n*	deficit in the balance of payments	—	disavanzo della bilan-cia dei pagamenti *m*	déficit en la balanza de pagos *m*
balance des paye-ments équilibrée (F)	Zahlungsbilanz-gleichgewicht *n*	equilibrium of the balance of payments	—	equilibrio della bilan-cia dei pagamenti *m*	balanza de pagos equilibrada *f*
balance des paye-ments excédentaire (F)	Zahlungsbilanz-überschuß *m*	surplus in the balance of payments	—	eccedenza della bilan-cia dei pagamenti *f*	superávit en la balanza de pagos *m*
balance d'or et de devises (F)	Gold- und Devisenbilanz *f*	foreign exchange and gold balance	—	bilancia dell'oro e delle divise *f*	balanza de oro y divisas *f*
balance final (Es)	Schlußbilanz *f*	closing balance	bilan de clôture *m*	bilancio consuntivo *m*	—
balance impositivo (Es)	Steuerbilanz *f*	tax balance-sheet	bilan fiscal *m*	bilancio fiscale *m*	—
balance inicial (Es)	Eröffnungsbilanz *f*	opening balance sheet	bilan d'ouverture *m*	bilancio d'apertura *m*	—
balance intermedio (Es)	Zwischenbilanz *f*	interim balance sheet	bilan intermédiaire *m*	bilancio provvisorio *m*	—
balance of capital transactions (E)	Kapitalbilanz *f*	—	balance des opéra-tions en capital *f*	bilancia dei capitali *f*	balanza de capitales *f*

	D	E	F	I	Es
balance of goods and services (E)	Leistungsbilanz f	—	balance des opérations courantes f	bilancia delle partite correnti f	balanza de cuentas f
balance of payments (E)	Zahlungsbilanz f	—	balance des payements f	bilancia dei pagamenti f	blanza de pagos f
balance of payments policy (E)	Zahlungsbilanzpolitik f	—	politique en matière de la balance des payements f	politica della bilancia dei pagamenti f	política en materia de balanza de pagos f
balance of trade (E)	Handelsbilanz f	—	balance des opérations en marchandises f	bilancia commerciale f	balanza comercial f
balance policy (E)	Bilanzpolitik f	—	politique du bilan f	politica di bilancio f	política en materia de balanzas f
balance sheet (E)	Bilanz f	—	bilan m	bilancio m	balance m
balance sheet of a group (E)	Konzernbilanz f	—	bilan consolidé d'un groupement de sociétés m	bilancio del gruppo m	balance del consorcio m
balance transparency (E)	Bilanzklarheit f	—	clarté du bilan f	trasparenza di bilancio f	claridad del balance f
balancing of the budget (E)	Budgetausgleich m	—	équilibrage du budget m	pareggio di bilancio m	balance del presupuesto m
balanza comercial (Es)	Handelsbilanz f	balance of trade	balance des opérations en marchandises f	bilancia commerciale f	—
balanza de capitales (Es)	Kapitalbilanz f	balance of capital transactions	balance des opérations en capital f	bilancia dei capitali f	—
balanza de divisas (Es)	Devisenbilanz f	foreign exchange balance	compte de devises m	bilancia delle divise f	—
balanza de oro y divisas (Es)	Gold- und Devisenbilanz f	foreign exchange and gold balance	balance d'or et de devises f	bilancia dell'oro e delle divise f	—
balanza de pagos (Es)	Zahlungsbilanz f	balance of payments	balance des payements f	bilancia dei pagamenti f	—
balanza de pagos equilibrada (Es)	Zahlungsbilanzgleichgewicht n	equilibrium of the balance of payments	balance des payements équilibrée f	equilibrio della bilancia dei pagamenti m	—
balanza por cuenta corriente (Es)	Leistungsbilanz f	balance of goods and services	balance des opérations courantes f	bilancia delle partite correnti f	—
Banca Centrale[1] (I)	Zentralbank f	central bank	banque centrale f	—	banco emisor m
Banca Centrale[2] (I)	Staatsbank f	state bank	banque nationale f	—	banco del Estado m
banca commerciale (I)	Handelsbank f	merchant bank	banque de commerce f	—	banco comercial m
banca d'emissione (I)	Notenbank f	central bank	banque d'émission f	—	banco emisor m
banca dati (I)	Datenbank f	data bank	banque de données f	—	banco de datos m
banca di credito (I)	Kreditbank f	commercial bank	banque de crédit f	—	banco de crédito m
banca d'investimento (I)	Investmentbank f	investment bank	banque d'investissement f	—	banco de inversiones m
banca di preferenza (I)	Hausbank f	company's bank	banque habituelle f	—	banco particular m
banca ipotecaria (I)	Hypothekenbank f	mortgage bank	banque hypothécaire f	—	banco hipotecario m
Banca Mondiale (I)	Weltbank f	World Bank	banque mondiale f	—	Banco Mundial m
banca regionale (I)	Regionalbank f	regional bank	banque régionale f	—	banco regional m
bancarotta (I)	Bankrott m	bankruptcy	banqueroute f	—	quiebra f
bancarotta fraudolenta (I)	betrügerischer Bankrott m	fraudulent bankruptcy	banqueroute frauduleuse f	—	quiebra fraudulenta f
banchiere (I)	Bankier m	banker	banquier m	—	banquero m
banco comercial (Es)	Handelsbank f	merchant bank	banque de commerce f	banca commerciale f	—
banco de crédito (Es)	Kreditbank f	commercial bank	banque de crédit f	banca di credito f	—
banco de datos (Es)	Datenbank f	data bank	banque de données f	banca dati f	—
banco de giros (Es)	Girobank f	clearing bank	banque de dépôts et de virements f	banca fungente da stanza di compensazione f	—
banco de inversiones (Es)	Investmentbank f	investment bank	banque d'investissement f	banca d'investimento f	—
banco del Estado (Es)	Staatsbank f	state bank	banque nationale f	Banca Centrale f	—
banco emisor[1] (Es)	Notenbank f	central bank	banque d'émission f	banca d'emissione f	—
banco emisor[2] (Es)	Zentralbank f	central bank	banque centrale f	Banca Centrale f	—

	D	E	F	I	Es
banco hipotecario (Es)	Hypothekenbank *f*	mortgage bank	banque hypothécaire *f*	banca ipotecaria *f*	—
bancomat (I)	Bankomat *m*	cash dispenser	billetterie *m*	—	cajero automático *m*
Banco Mundial (Es)	Weltbank *f*	World Bank	banque mondiale *f*	Banca Mondiale *f*	—
banconota (I)	Banknote *f*	bank-note	billet de banque *m*	—	billete de banco *m*
banconote (I)	Papiergeld *n*	paper money	monnaie de papier *f*	—	papel-moneda *m*
banco particular (Es)	Hausbank *f*	company's bank	banque habituelle *f*	banca di preferenza *f*	—
banco regional (Es)	Regionalbank *f*	regional bank	banque régionale *f*	banca regionale *f*	—
Bandbreite (D)	—	margin	marge *f*	margine *m*	margen de fluctuación *f*
bande étiquette (F)	Streifband *f*	postal wrapper	—	fascia *f*	precinto *m*
bando di concorso per impiegati (I)	Stellenausschreibung *f*	advertisement of a vacancy	mise au concours d'une place *f*	—	convocatoria de oposiciones *f*
bank account (E)	Bankkonto *n*	—	compte en banque *m*	conto bancario *m*	cuenta bancaria *f*
Bankakkreditiv (D)	—	bank letter of credit	accréditif bancaire *m*	lettera di credito *f*	carta de crédito bancaria *f*
Bankavis (D)	—	bank notification	confirmation bancaire *f*	avviso bancario *m*	aviso bancario *m*
bank charges[1] (E)	Kontogebühren *pl*	—	frais de tenue de compte *m pl*	diritti di conto *m pl*	gastos de administración de una cuenta *m pl*
bank charges[2] (E)	Bankspesen *pl*	—	frais de banque *m pl*	commissioni bancarie *f pl*	gastos bancarios *m pl*
Bankenaufsicht (D)	—	public supervision of banking	contrôle des banques *m*	commissione bancaria *f*	supervisión bancaria *f*
Bankenkonsortium (D)	—	banking syndicate	consortium des banques *m*	consorzio bancario *m*	consorcio bancario *m*
banker (E)	Bankier *m*	—	banquier *m*	banchiere *m*	banquero *m*
banker's duty of secrecy (E)	Bankgeheimnis *n*	—	secret bancaire *m*	segreto bancario *m*	secreto bancario *m*
Bankgarantie (D)	—	bank guarantee	garantie de banque *f*	garanzia bancaria *f*	garantía bancaria *f*
Bankgeheimnis (D)	—	banker's duty of secrecy	secret bancaire *m*	segreto bancario *m*	secreto bancario *m*
bank guarantee (E)	Bankgarantie *f*	—	garantie de banque *f*	garanzia bancaria *f*	garantía bancaria *f*
Bankier (D)	—	banker	banquier *m*	banchiere *m*	banquero *m*
banking syndicate (E)	Bankenkonsortium *n*	—	consortium des banques *m*	consorzio bancario *m*	consorcio bancario *m*
Bankkonto (D)	—	bank account	compte en banque *m*	conto bancario *m*	cuenta bancaria *f*
bank letter of credit (E)	Bankakkreditiv *n*	—	accréditif bancaire *m*	lettera di credito *f*	carta de crédito bancaria *f*
Banknote (D)	—	bank-note	billet de banque *m*	banconota *f*	billete de banco *m*
bank-note (E)	Banknote *f*	—	billet de banque *m*	banconota *f*	billete de banco *m*
bank notification (E)	Bankavis *m*	—	confirmation bancaire *f*	avviso bancario *m*	aviso bancario *m*
Bankomat (D)	—	cash dispenser	billetterie *m*	bancomat *m*	cajero automático *m*
Bankrott (D)	—	bankruptcy	banqueroute *f*	bancarotta *f*	quiebra *f*
bankruptcy[1] (E)	Konkurs *m*	—	faillite *f*	fallimento *m*	quiebra *f*
bankruptcy[2] (E)	Bankrott *m*	—	banqueroute *f*	bancarotta *f*	quiebra *f*
Bankruptcy Act (E)	Konkursordnung *f*	—	régime juridique de la faillite *m*	legge fallimentare *f*	ley de las quiebras *f*
bankruptcy court (E)	Konkursgericht *n*	—	tribunal de la faillite *m*	tribunale fallimentare *m*	tribunal de quiebras *m*
bankruptcy petition (E)	Konkursantrag *m*	—	demande en déclaration de faillite *f*	domanda di dichiarazione del fallimento *f*	petición de quiebra *f*
bankrupt's creditor (E)	Konkursgläubiger *m*	—	créancier de la faillite *m*	creditore della massa fallimentare *m*	acreedor de la quiebra *m*
bankrupt's estate (E)	Konkursmasse *f*	—	masse de la faillite *f*	massa fallimentare *f*	masa de la quiebra *f*
Bankspesen (D)	—	bank charges	frais de banque *m pl*	commissioni bancarie *f pl*	gastos bancarios *m pl*
bank transfer (E)	Banküberweisung *f*	—	virement bancaire *m*	rimessa bancaria *f*	transferencia bancaria *f*
Banküberweisung (D)	—	bank transfer	virement bancaire *m*	rimessa bancaria *f*	transferencia bancaria *f*

base de capital

	D	E	F	I	Es
ban on advertising[1] (E)	Werbeverbot n	—	défense de publicité f	divieto di pubblicità m	prohibición de publicidad f
ban on advertising[2] (E)	Werbeverbot	—	défense de publicité f	divieto dei pubblicità m	prohibición de publicidad f
banque centrale (F)	Zentralbank f	central bank	—	Banca Centrale f	banco emisor m
banque centrale de virement (F)	Girozentrale f	central giro institution	—	stanza centrale di compensazione f	central de giros f
banque de commerce (F)	Handelsbank f	merchant bank	—	banca commerciale f	banco comercial m
banque de crédit (F)	Kreditbank f	commercial bank	—	banca di credito f	banco de crédito m
banque de données (F)	Datenbank f	data bank	—	banca dati f	banco de datos m
banque d'émission (F)	Notenbank f	central bank	—	banca d'emissione f	banco emisor m
banque d'investissement (F)	Investmentbank f	investment bank	—	banca d'investimento f	banco de inversiones m
banque habituelle (F)	Hausbank f	company's bank	—	banca di preferenza f	banco particular m
banque hypothécaire (F)	Hypothekenbank f	mortgage bank	—	banca ipotecaria f	banco hipotecario m
banque mondiale (F)	Weltbank f	World Bank	—	Banca Mondiale f	Banco Mundial m
banque nationale (F)	Staatsbank f	state bank	—	Banca Centrale f	banco del Estado m
banque régionale (F)	Regionalbank f	regional bank	—	banca regionale f	banco regional m
banquero (Es)	Bankier m	banker	banquier m	banchiere m	—
banqueroute (F)	Bankrott m	bankruptcy	—	bancarotta f	quiebra f
banqueroute frauduleuse (F)	betrügerischer Bankrott m	fraudulent bankruptcy	—	bancarotta fraudolenta f	quiebra fraudulenta f
banquier (F)	Bankier m	banker	—	banchiere m	banquero m
bar (D)	—	cash	comptant	in contanti	al contado
Barakkreditiv (D)	—	cash letter of credit	accréditif payable en espèce m	apertura di credito documentario semplice f	crédito simple m
Bargeld (D)	—	cash	argent comptant m	denaro contante m	dinero efectivo m
Bargeldbestand (D)	—	cash in hand	espèces en caisse f pl	denaro contante in cassa m	saldo en efectivo m
bargeldlos (D)	—	non-cash	par virement	mediante assegno	por transferencia
Barkredit (D)	—	cash credit	crédit de caisse m	credito per cassa m	crédito en efectivo m
barometer of public opinion (E)	Stimmungs-barometer n	—	baromètre de la tendance m	barometro economico m	barómetro de la opinión pública m
baromètre de la tendance (F)	Stimmungs-barometer n	barometer of public opinion	—	barometro economico m	barómetro de la opinión pública m
barómetro de la opinión pública (Es)	Stimmungs-barometer n	barometer of public opinion	baromètre de la tendance m	barometro economico m	—
barometro economico (I)	Stimmungs-barometer n	barometer of public opinion	baromètre de la tendance m	—	barómetro de la opinión pública m
Barrengold (D)	—	gold in bars	or en lingot m	oro in lingotti m	oro en barras m
Barscheck (D)	—	open cheque	chèque non barré m	assegno circolare m	cheque de caja m
barter transaction (E)	Kompensations-geschäft n	—	affaire de compensation f	operazione di compensazione f	operacion de compensación f
Barvermögen (D)	—	cash assets	valeurs réalisables à court terme ou disponibles f pl	patrimonio in contanti m	activo efectivo m
Barzahlung (D)	—	cash payment	payement comptant m	pagamento in contanti m	pago al contado m
Barzahlungskonto (D)	—	cash discount	escompte de caisse m	sconto per paga-mento in contanti m	descuento de pago al contado f
Barzahlungs-nachlaß (D)	—	discount for cash payment	remise pour paye-ment au comptant f	sconto per pagamen-to in contanti m	descuento por pago al contado m
Barzahlungsrabatt (D)	—	cash discount	remise pour paye-ment comptant f	ribasso per pagamen-to in contanti m	descuento por pago al contado m
base (E)	Basis f	—	base f	base f	base f
base (Es)	Basis f	base	base f	base f	—
base (F)	Basis f	base	—	base f	base f
base (I)	Basis f	base	base f	—	base f
base de capital (Es)	Kapitalbasis f	capital base	base de capital f	base di capitale f	—

	D	E	F	I	Es
base de capital (F)	Kapitalbasis *f*	capital base	—	base di capitale *f*	base de capital *f*
base di capitale (I)	Kapitalbasis *f*	capital base	base de capital *f*	—	base de capital *f*
base period (E)	Basisperiode *f*	—	période de base *f*	periodo di base *m*	período básico *m*
base year (E)	Basisjahr *n*	—	année de base *f*	anno di base *m*	año básico *m*
basic income (E)	Basiseinkommen *n*	—	revenu de base *m*	introiti base *m pl*	salario base *m*
basic information (E)	Basisinformation *f*	—	information de base *f*	informazione base *f*	información básica *f*
basic knowledge (E)	Grundkenntnisse *pl*	—	connaissances fondamentales *f pl*	cognizioni elementari *f pl*	conocimientos básicos *m pl*
basic pension (E)	Grundrente *f*	—	pension de base *f*	pensione base *f*	pensión básica *f*
basic salary (E)	Grundgehalt *n*	—	traitement de base *m*	stipendio base *m*	salario base *m*
basic wage (E)	Basislohn *m*	—	salaire de référence *m*	salario base *m*	sueldo base *m*
Basis (D)	—	base	base *f*	base *f*	base *f*
Basiseinkommen (D)	—	basic income	revenu de base *m*	introiti base *m pl*	salario base *m*
Basisinformation (D)	—	basic information	information de base *f*	informazione base *f*	información básica *f*
Basisjahr (D)	—	base year	année de base *f*	anno di base *m*	año básico *m*
Basislohn (D)	—	basic wage	salaire de référence *m*	salario base *m*	sueldo base *m*
Basisperiode (D)	—	base period	période de base *f*	periodo di base *m*	período básico *m*
basura de embalaje (Es)	Verpackungsmüll *m*	packing waste	déchets d'emballage *m pl*	rifiuti da imballaggi *m pl*	—
basura especial (Es)	Sondermüll *m*	special refuse	détritus spéciaux *m pl*	rifiuti speciali *m pl*	—
Bau (D)	—	construction	construction *f*	costruzione *f*	construcción *f*
Baufinanzierung (D)	—	construction financing	financement à la construction *m*	finanziamento di costruzione *m*	financiación de la construcción *f*
Bauindustrie (D)	—	construction industry	industrie de sous-traitance du bâtiment *f*	industria edile *f*	industria de la construcción *f*
Bauinvestitionen (D)	—	structural investments	investissements à la construction *m pl*	investimenti edili *m pl*	inversión inmobiliaria *f*
Baukredit (D)	—	building loan	crédit à la construction *m*	credito edilizio *m*	crédito para la construcción *f*
Bauland (D)	—	building land	espace à bâtir *m*	area edificabile *f*	terreno edificable *m*
Bauwirtschaft (D)	—	building and construction industry	(industrie du) bâtiment *f*	edilizia *f*	ramo de la construcción *m*
Beamter (D)	—	official	fonctionnaire *m*	funzionario *m*	funcionario *m*
Beanstandung (D)	—	objection	objection *f*	reclamo *m*	queja *f*
bear sale (E)	Leerverkauf *m*	—	vente à découvert *f*	vendita allo scoperto *f*	venta al descubierto *f*
bearer (E)	Überbringer *m*	—	porteur *m*	portatore *m*	portador *m*
bearer cheque (E)	überbringerscheck *m*	—	chèque au porteur *m*	assegno al portatore *m*	cheque al portador *m*
bearer instrument (E)	Inhaberpapier *n*	—	titre souscrit au porteur *m*	titolo al portatore *m*	título al portador *m*
bearer share (E)	Inhaberaktie *f*	—	action au porteur *f*	azione al portatore *f*	acción al portador *f*
Bedarf (D)	—	need/demand	besoin *m*/demande *f*	fabbisogno *m*/domanda *f*	necesidades *f pl*/demanda *f*
Bedarfsanalyse (D)	—	analysis of requirements	analyse des besoins *m*	analisi del fabbisogno *f*	análisis de las necesidades *m*
Bedarfsfaktoren (D)	—	requirement factors	éléments pouvant influencer la demande *m pl*	fattori del fabbisogno *m pl*	factores determinantes de las necesidades *m pl*
Bedarfs-schwankung (D)	—	fluctuations in requirements	oscillations de demande *f pl*	oscillazioni del fabbisogno *f pl*	fluctuación de las necesidades *f*
Bedienungsgeld (D)	—	tip	pourboire *m*	diritto di servizio *m*	propina *f*
Bedingung (D)	—	condition	condition *f*	condizione *f*	condición *f*
be due (E)	anstehen	—	être échnu	essere scaduto	estar pendiente
Bedürfnis (D)	—	need	besoin *m*	bisogno *m*	necesidad *f*
Bedürfnis-befriedigung (D)	—	satisfaction of needs	satisfaction des besoins *f*	soddisfazione dei bisogni *f*	satisfacción de las necesidades *f*
beeidigte Erklärung (D)	—	sworn statement	déclaration sous serment *f*	dichiarazione giurata *f*	declaración jurada *f*
beeinflußbar (D)	—	be influenced	influençable	influenzabile	sugestionable

	D	E	F	I	Es
Beförderung (D)	—	promotion/transport	nomination f/ transport m	promozione f/ trasporto m	ascenso m/ transporte m
Beförderungs-bedingungen (D)	—	terms of conveyance	conditions de transport f pl	condizioni di trasporto f pl	condiciones de transporte f pl
Beförderungs-geschäfte (D)	—	transport services	transports m pl	operazioni di trasporto f pl	negocios de transporte m pl
before hours dealing (E)	Vorbörse f	—	marché avant le marché officiel m	mercato preborsistico m	operaciones antes de la apertura de la bolsa f pl
Befragung (D)	—	poll	enquête f	interrogazione f	encuesta f
Befugnis (D)	—	authorization	pouvoir m	prerogativa f	autorización f
beglaubigte Abschrift (D)	—	authenticated copy	copie certifiée f	copia autenticata f	copia legalizada f
Beglaubigung (D)	—	authentication	certification f	autenticazione f	legalización f
Begleitpapiere (D)	—	accompanying documents	pièces accompa-gnant l'envoi f pl	bolle di accom-pagnamento f pl	documentos adjuntos m pl
Begrüßung (D)	—	salutation	salutations f pl	saluto m	saludo m
Begünstigter (D)	—	beneficiary	bénéficiaire m	beneficiario m	favorecido m
Behälterverkehr (D)	—	container transport	transport utilisant des containers m	trasporto container m	transportación en contenedores f
behauptet (D)	—	maintained	affirmé	affermato	sostenido
Beherrschungs-vertrag (D)	—	control agreement	accord de contrôle m	contratto di controllo m	contrato de dominación m
Behörde (D)	—	authority	autorité f	autorità f	autoridad f
Beilage (D)	—	supplement	encart non broché à la revue m	inserto m	suplemento m
be influenced (E)	beeinflußbar	—	influençable	influenzabile	sugestionable
Beiträge (D)	—	contributions	participations f pl	contributi m pl	contribuciones f pl
belasten (D)	—	load/charge	débiter	addebitare	cargar/adeudar
Belastung (D)	—	load	charge f	addebito m	gravamen m
Beleg (D)	—	voucher	justificatif m	quietanza f	justificativo m
Belegschaft (D)	—	staff	personnel m	maestranza f	plantilla f
Beleihungswert (D)	—	sum as security for a loan	montant de la garantie m	valore finanziabile m	valor para préstamos m
Belieferungspflicht (D)	—	duty to supply	obligation de livraison f	obbligo di fornitura m	obligación de suministro f
bene economico (I)	Wirtschaftsgut n	economic good	bien économique m	—	bien económico m
bénéfice (F)	Gewinn m	profit/surplus	—	utile m	beneficio m/ superávit m
bénéfice annuel (F)	Jahresgewinn m	annual profit	—	utile dell'anno m	beneficio del ejercicio m
bénéfice brut¹ (F)	Handelsspanne f	trading margin	—	margine commerciale m	margen comercial f
bénéfice brut² (F)	Rohgewinn m	gross profit on sales	—	utile lordo m	ganancia bruta f
bénéfice comptable (F)	Buchgewinn m	book profit	—	utile contabile m	beneficio contable m
bénéfice d'exploitation (F)	Unternehmens-gewinn m	profit of the enterprise	—	utile d'impresa m	beneficio empresarial m
bénéfice net (F)	Reingewinn m	net profit	—	utile netto m	ganancia neta f
bénéficiaire (F)	Begünstigter m	beneficiary	—	beneficiario m	favorecido m
bénéficiaire d'un crédit (F)	Kreditnehmer m	borrower	—	beneficiario del credito m	prestatario m
bénéficiaire du payement (F)	Zahlungs-berechtigter m	beneficiary of payment	—	beneficiario del pagamento m	beneficiario del pago m
beneficial to the environment (E)	umweltfreundlich	—	favorable à l'environnement	ecologico	no contaminante
beneficiario¹ (I)	Begünstigter m	beneficiary	bénéficiaire m	—	favorecido m
beneficiario² (I)	Remittent m	payee	remettant m	—	remitente m
beneficiario del credito (I)	Kreditnehmer m	borrower	bénéficiaire d'un crédit m	—	prestatario m
beneficiario del pagamento (I)	Zahlungs-berechtigter m	beneficiary of payment	bénéficiaire du payement m	—	beneficiario del pago m
beneficiario del pago (Es)	Zahlungs-berechtigter m	beneficiary of payment	bénéficiaire du payement m	beneficiario del pagamento m	—

	D	E	F	I	Es
beneficiary (E)	Begünstigter *m*	—	bénéficiaire *m*	beneficiario *m*	favorecido *m*
beneficiary of payment (E)	Zahlungs-berechtigter *m*	—	bénéficiaire du payement *m*	beneficiario del pagamento *m*	beneficiario del pago *m*
beneficio¹ (Es)	Gewinn *m*	profit/surplus	bénéfice *m*	utile *m*	—
beneficio² (Es)	Erlös *m*	proceeds	produit des ventes *m*	ricavo *m*	—
beneficio³ (Es)	Profit *m*	profit	profit *m*	profitto *m*	—
beneficio contable (Es)	Buchgewinn *m*	book profit	bénéfice comptable *m*	utile contabile *m*	—
beneficio del ejercicio (Es)	Jahresgewinn *m*	annual profit	bénéfice annuel *m*	utile dell'anno *m*	—
beneficio de racionalización (Es)	Rationalisierungs-gewinn *m*	rationalization profit	profit de rationalisation *m*	profitto di razionalizzazione *m*	—
beneficio empresarial (Es)	Unternehmens-gewinn *m*	profit of the enterprise	bénéfice d'exploitation *m*	utile d'impresa *m*	—
beneficio simulado (Es)	Scheingewinn *m*	fictitious profit	gain fictif *m*	utile fittizio *m*	—
benessere (I)	Wohlstand *m*	prosperity	prospérité *f*	—	bienestar *m*
benestare pubblico (I)	Allgemeinwohl *n*	public welfare	bien général *m*	—	bienestar público *m*
beni (I)	Güter *pl*	goods	biens *m pl*	—	bienes *m pl*
beni agricoli (I)	Agrargüter *pl*	agricultural goods	produits agricoles *m pl*	—	bienes agrícolas *m pl*
beni collettivi (I)	Kollektivgüter *pl*	collective goods	biens collectifs *m pl*	—	bienes sociales *m pl*
beni complementari (I)	komplementäre Güter *pl*	complementary goods	produits de complément *m pl*	—	bienes com-plementarios *m pl*
beni di consumo (I)	Konsumgüter *pl*	consumer goods	biens de consommation *m pl*	—	bienes de consumo *m pl*
beni di consumo durevoli (I)	Gebrauchsgüter *pl*	durable consumer goods	biens d'utilisation courante *m pl*	—	bienes de consumo duradero *m pl*
beni di investimento (I)	Investitionsgüter *pl*	capital goods	biens d'investissement *m pl*	—	bienes de inversión *m pl*
beni d'investimento (I)	Anlagegüter *pl*	capital goods	valeur immoblisée *f*	—	bienes de inversión *m pl*
beni di lusso (I)	Luxusgüter *pl*	luxury goods	produits de luxe *m pl*	—	bienes de lujo *m pl*
beni di massa (I)	Massengüter *pl*	bulk goods	marchandises en vrac *f pl*	—	productos a granel *m pl*
beni in conto deposito (I)	Kommissionsgüter *pl*	goods for sale on commission	marchandises en commission *f pl*	—	mercancías en comisión *f pl*
beni inferiori (I)	inferiore Güter *pl*	inferior goods	biens inférieurs *m pl*	—	bienes inferiores *m pl*
beni mobili (I)	bewegliche Güter	movable goods	biens meubles *m pl*	—	bienes muebles *m pl*
beni non durevoli (I)	Verbrauchsgüter *pl*	consumer goods	biens de consommation *m pl*	—	bienes de consumo *m pl*
beni pubblici (I)	öffentliche Güter *pl*	public goods	biens publics *m pl*	—	bienes públicos *m pl*
Benzin (D)	—	petrol	essence *f*	benzina *f*	gasolina *f*
benzina (I)	Benzin *n*	petrol	essence *f*	—	gasolina *f*
Benzingutscheine (D)	—	petrol voucher	bon d'essence *m*	coupons *m pl*	bono de gasolina *m*
Berater (D)	—	adviser	conseiller *m*	consulente *m*	asesor *m*
Beratung (D)	—	advice	consultation *f*	consulenza *f*	asesoramiento *m*
Berechnung (D)	—	computation	calcul *m*	calcolo *m*	calculación *f*
Bereitstellungs-kosten (D)	—	commitment fee	coûts administratifs *m pl*	spese di stanziamento *f pl*	gastos fijos *m pl*
Bereitstellungs-zinsen (D)	—	commitment interests	intérêts de disponibilité *m pl*	interessi per lo stanziamento *m pl*	interés de disponibilidad *m*
Bergbau (D)	—	mining	industrie extractive *f*	industria mineraria *f*	minería *f*
Bergung (D)	—	salvage	sauvetage *m*	ricupero *m*	salvamento *m*
Berichterstattung (D)	—	reporting	compte rendu *m*	relazione *f*	reportaje *m*
Berichtigung (D)	—	correction	rectification *f*	correzione *f*	rectificación *f*
Berichtspflicht (D)	—	obligation to report	obligation d'information *f*	obbligo di relazione *m*	obligación de información *f*
Beruf (D)	—	profession	profession *f*	professione *f*	profesión *f*
Berufsausbildung (D)	—	professional training	formation professionelle *f*	formazione professionale *f*	formación profesional *f*
Berufsgeheimnis (D)	—	professional secret	secret professionnel *m*	segreto professionale *m*	secreto profesional *m*

	D	E	F	I	Es
Berufsrisiko (D)	—	occupational hazard	risque professionnel *m*	rischio professionale *m*	riesgo profesional *m*
Berufungsgericht (D)	—	appeal court	tribunal d'appel *m*	corte d'appello *f*	tribunal de apelación *m*
Beschädigung (D)	—	damage	endommagement *m*	danno *m*	deterioración *f*
Beschäftigung (D)	—	employment	occupation *f*	occupazione *f*	ocupación *f*
Beschäftigungsgrad (D)	—	level of employment	taux d'emploi *m*	tasso d'occupazione *m*	grado de empleo *m*
Beschäftigungspolitik (D)	—	employment policy	politique d'emploi *f*	politica d'occupazione *f*	política de empleo *f*
Beschäftigungsrückgang (D)	—	drop in employment	baisse de l'offre d'emploi *f*	calo dell'occupazione *m*	descenso del empleo *m*
Beschäftigungstheorie (D)	—	employment theory	théorie d'emploi *f*	teoria dell'occupazione *f*	teoría del empleo *f*
Beschlagnahme (D)	—	confiscation	saisie *f*	sequestro *m*	confiscación *f*
beschleunigt (D)	—	speedy	accéléré	accelerato	acelerado
Beschluß (D)	—	decision	décision *f*	delibera *f*	decisión *f*
Beschwerde (D)	—	complaint	réclamation *f*	protesta *f*	recurso *m*
Besitz (D)	—	possession	possession *f*	possesso *m*	posesión *f*
Besitzeinkommen (D)	—	unearned income	revenu du patrimoine *m*	reddito da possesso *m*	renta de la propiedad *f*
Besitzgesellschaft (D)	—	controlling company	société contrôleuse *f*	società finanziaria *f*	sociedad controladora *f*
besoin[1] (F)	Bedarf *m*	need/demand	—	fabbisogno *m*/ domanda *f*	necesidades *f pl*/ demanda *f*
besoin[2] (F)	Bedürfnis *n*	need	—	bisogno *m*	necesidad *f*
besoin annuel (F)	Jahresbedarf *m*	annual need	—	bisogno annuale *m*	necesidad anual *f*
besoin d'information (F)	Informationsbedarf *m*	requirement of information	—	bisogno d'informazioni *m*	necesidad de información *f*
besoin en capital (F)	Kapitalbedarf *m*	capital requirements	—	domanda di capitale *f*	necesidad de capital *f*
besoin individuel (F)	Individualbedürfnis *n*	individual need	—	fabbisogno individuale *m*	necesidades individuales *f pl*
Besoldung (D)	—	pay	rétribution *f*	retribuzione *f*	sueldo *m*
Besprechung (D)	—	discussion	conférence *f*	colloquio *m*	conferencia *f*
Besprechungstermin (D)	—	meeting date	date de la conférence *f*	termine del colloquio *m*	fecha de conferencia *f*
Bestandsgröße (D)	—	stock variable	stock variable *m*	entità dell'inventario *f*	magnitud *f*
Bestandskonto (D)	—	real account	compte d'existences *m*	conto merci *m*	cuenta de existencias *f*
Bestätigung (D)	—	confirmation	confirmation *f*	conferma *f*	confirmación *f*
Bestechung (D)	—	bribe	corruption *f*	corruzione *f*	soborno *f*
Bestelldaten (D)	—	details of order	références de commande *f pl*	dati delle ordinazioni *m pl*	datos de pedido *m pl*
Besteller (D)	—	customer	acheteur *m*	committente *m*	demandante *m*
Bestellformular (D)	—	order form	bon de commande *m*	modulo d'ordinazione *m*	formulario de pedido *m*
Bestellmenge (D)	—	ordered quantity	quantité commandée *f*	quantità d'ordinazione *f*	cantidad pedida *f*
Bestellschein (D)	—	order form	bulletin de commande *m*	bolletta d'ordinazione *f*	hoja de pedido *f*
Bestellung (D)	—	order	commande *f*	ordinazione *f*	pedido *m*
bestens (D)	—	at best	au mieux	ottimo	al mejor cambio
Bestensorder (D)	—	order at best	ordre non limité *m*	ordine al miglior corso *m*	orden al mejor cambio posible *f*
beste Qualität (D)	—	first class quality	première qualité *f*	qualità ottima *f*	primera calidad *f*
Bestimmungsbahnhof (D)	—	station of destination	gare destinataire *f*	stazione di destinazione *f*	estación de destino *f*
Bestimmungsort (D)	—	place of destination	lieu de destination *m*	luogo di destinazione *m*	lugar de destino *m*
bestowal (E)	Zuwendung *f*	—	affectation *f*	assegnazione *f*	gratificación *f*
Besuchsanmeldung (D)	—	announcement of a visitor	annonce de visiteurs *f*	avviso di visita *m*	anuncio de visita *m*

	D	E	F	I	Es
Beteiligung (D)	—	participation	participation f	partecipazione f	participación f
Betrag (D)	—	amount	montant m	importo m	suma f
Betrieb (D)	—	factory	usine f	azienda f	fábrica f
Betriebsanalyse (D)	—	operation analysis	situation analytique de l'exploitation f	analisi aziendale f	análisis de la empresa m
Betriebsausgaben (D)	—	(current) operational expenses	charges d'exploitation f pl	spese aziendali f pl	gastos de explotación m pl
Betriebsausweis (D)	—	staff identification card	pièce d'identité de l'entreprise f	tessera aziendale f	carné de empresa f
Betriebserlaubnis (D)	—	operating permit	droit d'exploitation m	autorizzazione per l'esercizio f	autorización de funcionamiento f
Betriebsferien (D)	—	annual holiday	clôture annuelle de l'établissement f	ferie aziendali f pl	vacaciones de la empresa f pl
Betriebsgeheimnis (D)	—	trade secret	secret d'exploitation m	segreto aziendale m	secreto empresarial m
Betriebs- gesellschaft (D)	—	operating company	entreprise d'exploitation f	società d'esercizio f	empresa de explotación f
Betriebsgröße (D)	—	size of the company	dimension de l'entreprise f	dimensione dell'azienda f	tamaño de la explotación m
Betriebskapital (D)	—	working capital	capital de roulement m	capitale d'esercizio m	capital de explotación m
Betriebsklima (D)	—	working conditions and human relations	climat social m	atmosfera di lavoro f	ambiente de trabajo m
Betriebskosten (D)	—	operating costs	charges d'exploitation f pl	spese d'esercizio f pl	gastos de explotación m pl
Betriebsprüfer (D)	—	auditor	expert-comptable m	revisore aziendale m	contador público m
Betriebsprüfung (D)	—	investigation by the tax authorities	vérification des livres de l'entreprise f	revisione aziendale f	inspección de la explotación f
Betriebsspionage (D)	—	industrial espionage	espionnage dans l'entreprise	spionaggio aziendale m	espionaje industrial m
Betriebsstatistik (D)	—	operational statistics	statistique commerciale et industrielle f	statistica aziendale f	estadística de la empresa f
Betriebswirtschafts- lehre (D)	—	business administration	(science de la) gestion industrielle et commerciale f	economia aziendale f	teoría de la empresa f
Betrug (D)	—	fraud	fraude f	frode f	fraude m
betrügerischer Bankrott (D)	—	fraudulent bankruptcy	banqueroute frauduleuse f	bancarotta fraudolenta f	quiebra fraudulenta f
Bevölkerung (D)	—	population	population f	popolazione f	población f
Bevölkerungsdichte (D)	—	density of population	densité da la population f	densità di popolazione f	densidad de la población f
Bevölkerungspolitik (D)	—	population policy	politique démographi- que populationniste f	politica demografica f	política demográfica f
Bevölkerungs- statistik (D)	—	population statistics	statistique démographique f	statistica demografica f	estadística de población f
Bevölkerungs- struktur (D)	—	population structure	structure démographique f	struttura demografica f	estructura demográfica f
Bevölkerungs- wachstum (D)	—	increase in population	accroissement de la population m	incremento demografico m	crecimiento vegetativo m
Bevollmächtigung (D)	—	authorization	pouvoir m	autorizzazione f	apoderamiento m
bewegliche Güter (D)	—	movable goods	biens meubles m pl	beni mobili m pl	bienes muebles m pl
Beweis (D)	—	proof	preuve f	prova f	prueba f
Beweislast (D)	—	burden of proof	charge de la preuve f	onere di prova m	carga de la prueba f
Bewerber (D)	—	applicant	candidat m	aspirante m	aspirante m
Bewerbung (D)	—	application	candidature f	domanda d'impiego f	candidatura f
Bewerbungs- schreiben (D)	—	letter of application	lettre de demande d'emploi f	domanda d'impiego f	carta de solicitud f
Bewerbungs- unterlagen (D)	—	application documents	dossier de candidature m	documenti della domanda d'impiego m pl	documentos de solicitud m pl
Bewertung (D)	—	valuation	valorisation f	valutazione f	valoración f
Bewirtung (D)	—	hospitality/ catering	hospitalité f/ accueil m	ospitalità f/ servizio m	hospedaje m/ atenciones f pl

	D	E	F	I	Es
bezahlter Urlaub (D)	—	paid vacation	congé payé *m*	ferie pagate *f pl*	vacaciones con goce de sueldo *f pl*
Bezirksvertreter (D)	—	local agent	agent local *m*	rappresentante di zona *m*	agente regional *m*
Bezogener (D)	—	drawee	tiré *m*	trattario *m*	librado *m*
Bezug (D)	—	reference	référence *f*	riferimento *m*	referencia *f*
Bezüge (D)	—	earnings	émoluments *m pl*	entrate *f pl*	retribuciones *f pl*
bezugnehmend (D)	—	referring to	se référant (à)	con riferimento a	con referencia a
Bezugskosten (D)	—	purchasing costs	coûts d'acquisition *m pl*	prezzo d'acquisto *m*	gastos de adquisición *m pl*
Bezugsquelle (D)	—	source of supply	source d'approvisionnement *f*	fonte d'acquisto *f*	fuente de suministro *f*
bien económico (Es)	Wirtschaftsgut *n*	economic good	bien économique *m*	bene economico *m*	—
bien économique (F)	Wirtschaftsgut *n*	economic good	—	bene economico *m*	bien económico *m*
bienes (Es)	Güter *pl*	goods	biens *m pl*	beni *m pl*	—
bienes agrícolas (Es)	Agrargüter *pl*	agricultural goods	produits agricoles *m pl*	beni agricoli *m pl*	—
bienes complementarios (Es)	komplementäre Güter *pl*	complementary goods	produits de complément *m pl*	beni complementari *m pl*	—
bienes de consumo[1] (Es)	Konsumgüter *pl*	consumer goods	biens de consommation *m pl*	beni di consumo *m pl*	—
bienes de consumo[2] (Es)	Verbrauchsgüter *pl*	consumer goods	biens de consommation *m pl*	beni non durevoli *m pl*	—
bienes de consumo duradero (Es)	Gebrauchsgüter *pl*	durable consumer goods	biens d'utilisation courante *m pl*	beni di consumo durevoli *m pl*	—
bienes de inversión[1] (Es)	Investitionsgüter *pl*	capital goods	biens d'investissement *m pl*	beni di investimento *m pl*	—
bienes de inversión[2] (Es)	Anlagegüter *pl*	capital goods	valeur immobilisée *f*	beni d'investimento *m pl*	—
bienes de lujo (Es)	Luxusgüter *pl*	luxury goods	produits de luxe *m pl*	beni di lusso *m pl*	—
bienes inferiores (Es)	inferiore Güter *pl*	inferior goods	biens inférieurs *m pl*	beni inferiori *m pl*	—
bienes muebles (Es)	bewegliche Güter	movable goods	biens meubles *m pl*	beni mobili *m pl*	—
bienes públicos (Es)	öffentliche Güter *pl*	public goods	biens publics *m pl*	beni pubblici *m pl*	—
bienes sociales (Es)	Kollektivgüter *pl*	collective goods	biens collectifs *m pl*	beni collettivi *m pl*	—
bienestar (Es)	Wohlstand *m*	prosperity	prospérité *f*	benessere *m*	—
bienestar público (Es)	Allgemeinwohl *n*	public welfare	bien général *m*	benestare pubblico *m*	—
bien général (F)	Allgemeinwohl *n*	public welfare	—	benestare pubblico *m*	bienestar público *m*
bien immobilier (F)	Immobilie *f*	item of real estate	—	immobile *m*	inmueble *m*
biens (F)	Güter *pl*	goods	—	beni *m pl*	bienes *m pl*
biens collectifs (F)	Kollektivgüter *pl*	collective goods	—	beni collettivi *m pl*	bienes sociales *m pl*
biens corporels (F)	Sachvermögen *n*	material assets	—	capitale reale *m*	patrimonio real *m*
biens corporels immobilisés (F)	Realkapital *n*	real capital	—	capitale reale *m*	capital real *m*
biens de consommation[1] (F)	Verbrauchsgüter *pl*	consumer goods	—	beni non durevoli *m pl*	bienes de consumo *m pl*
biens de consommation[2] (F)	Konsumgüter *pl*	consumer goods	—	beni di consumo *m pl*	bienes de consumo *m pl*
biens d'investissement (F)	Investitionsgüter *pl*	capital goods	—	beni di investimento *m pl*	bienes de inversión *m pl*
biens d'utilisation courante (F)	Gebrauchsgüter *pl*	durable consumer goods	—	beni di consumo durevoli *m pl*	bienes de consumo duradero *m pl*
biens inférieurs (F)	inferiore Güter *pl*	inferior goods	—	beni inferiori *m pl*	bienes inferiores *m pl*
biens meubles (F)	bewegliche Güter	movable goods	—	beni mobili *m pl*	bienes muebles *m pl*
biens publics (F)	öffentliche Güter *pl*	public goods	—	beni pubblici *m pl*	bienes públicos *m pl*
bien transporté (F)	Speditionsgut *n*	forwarding merchandise	—	merce spedita *f*	mercancía transportada *f*
Bietungsgarantie (D)	—	tender guarantee	cautionnement provisoire *m*	garanzia d'offerta *f*	caución de licitación *f*
biglietto di andata e ritorno (I)	Rückfahrkarte *f*	return ticket	billet d'aller et retour *m*	—	billete de ida y vuelta *m*
biglietto d'ingresso (I)	Eintrittskarte *f*	admission ticket	billet *m*	—	entrada *f*

	D	E	F	I	Es
biglietto gratuito (I)	Freikarte f	free ticket	billet de faveur m	—	entrada gratuita f
bilan (F)	Bilanz f	balance sheet	—	bilancio m	balance m
bilancia commerciale (I)	Handelsbilanz f	balance of trade	balance des opérations en marchandises f	—	balanza comercial f
bilancia dei capitali (I)	Kapitalbilanz f	balance of capital transactions	balance des opérations en capital f	—	balanza de capitales f
bilancia dei pagamenti (I)	Zahlungsbilanz f	balance of payments	balance des payements f	—	balanza de pagos f
bilancia delle divise (I)	Devisenbilanz f	foreign exchange balance	compte de devises m	—	balanza de divisas f
bilancia delle partite correnti (I)	Leistungsbilanz f	balance of goods and services	balance des opérations courantes f	—	balanza por cuenta corriente f
bilancia dell'oro e delle divise (I)	Gold- und Devisenbilanz f	foreign exchange and gold balance	balance d'or et de devises f	—	balanza de oro y divisas f
bilancia per corrispondenza (I)	Briefwaage f	letter scales	pèse-lettres f	—	pesacartas m
bilancio[1] (I)	Bilanz f	balance sheet	bilan m	—	balance m
bilancio[2] (I)	Budget n/Etat m	budget	budget m	—	presupuesto m
bilancio consolidato (I)	konsolidierte Bilanz f	consolidated balance sheet	bilan consolidé m	—	balance consolidado m
bilancio consuntivo (I)	Schlußbilanz f	closing balance	bilan de clôture m	—	balance final m
bilancio d'apertura (I)	Eröffnungsbilanz f	opening balance sheet	bilan d'ouverture m	—	balance inicial m
bilancio del gruppo (I)	Konzernbilanz f	balance sheet of a group	bilan consolidé d'un groupement de sociétés m	—	balance del consorcio m
bilancio fiscale (I)	Steuerbilanz f	tax balance sheet	bilan fiscal m	—	balance impositivo m
bilancio parziale (I)	Teilbilanz f	partial balance sheet	bilan partiel m	—	balance parcial m
bilancio preventivo (I)	Haushaltsplan m	budget	budget m	—	presupuesto m
bilancio provvisorio (I)	Zwischenbilanz f	interim balance sheet	bilan intermédiaire m	—	balance intermedio m
bilan consolidé (F)	konsolidierte Bilanz f	consolidated balance sheet	—	bilancio consolidato m	balance consolidado m
bilan consolidé d'un groupement de sociétés (F)	Konzernbilanz f	balance sheet of a group	—	bilancio del gruppo m	balance del consorcio m
bilan de clôture (F)	Schlußbilanz f	closing balance	—	bilancio consuntivo m	balance final m
bilan d'ouverture (F)	Eröffnungsbilanz f	opening balance sheet	—	bilancio d'apertura m	balance inicial m
bilan fiscal (F)	Steuerbilanz f	tax balance sheet	—	bilancio fiscale m	balance impositivo m
bilan intermédiaire (F)	Zwischenbilanz f	interim balance sheet	—	bilancio provvisorio m	balance intermedio m
Bilanz (D)	—	balance sheet	bilan m	bilancio m	balance m
Bilanzanalyse (D)	—	balance analysis	analyse du bilan f	analisi di bilancio f	análisis de balance m
Bilanzklarheit (D)	—	balance transparency	clarté du bilan f	trasparenza di bilancio f	claridad del balance f
Bilanzkontinuität (D)	—	formal identity	identité des bilans successifs f	continuità di bilancio f	identidad de los balances sucesivos f
Bilanzpolitik (D)	—	balance policy	politique du bilan f	politica di bilancio f	política en materia de balanzas f
Bilanzwahrheit (D)	—	truth in the balance sheet	sincérité du bilan f	chiarezza di bilancio f	sinceridad del balance f
bilateral (D)	—	bilateral	bilatéral	bilaterale	bilateral
bilateral (E)	bilateral	—	bilatéral	bilaterale	bilateral
bilateral (Es)	bilateral	bilateral	bilatéral	bilaterale	—
bilatéral (F)	bilateral	bilateral	—	bilaterale	bilateral
bilaterale (I)	bilateral	bilateral	bilatéral	—	bilateral
Bildschirm (D)	—	screen	écran m	video m	pantalla f
Bildschirmarbeit (D)	—	screen work	travail à l'écran	lavoro video m	trabajo de pantalla m
Bildschirm-arbeitsplatz (D)	—	screen job	poste de travail à l'écran m	posto di lavoro video m	puesto de trabajo de pantalla m
Bildschirmtext (D)	—	videotext	videotex international m	videotex, Btx m	teletexto m
Bildung (D)	—	education	formation f	formazione f	educación f

	D	E	F	I	Es
bill of entry (E)	Zolleinfuhrschein *m*	—	acquit d'entrée *m*	bolletta d'entrata *f*	certificado de aduana *m*
bill of exchange (E)	Wechsel *m*	—	lettre de charge *f*	cambiale *f*	letra de cambio *f*
billet (F)	Eintrittskarte *f*	admission ticket	—	biglietto d'ingresso *m*	entrada *f*
billet d'aller et retour (F)	Rückfahrkarte *f*	return ticket	—	biglietto di andata e ritorno *m*	billete de ida y vuelta *m*
billet de banque (F)	Banknote *f*	bank-note	—	banconota *f*	billete de banco *m*
billet de créance (F)	Schuldschein *m*	certificate of indebtedness	—	certificato di debito *m*	pagaré *m*
billet de faveur (F)	Freikarte *f*	free ticket	—	biglietto gratuito *m*	entrada gratuita *f*
billete de banco (Es)	Banknote *f*	bank-note	billet de banque *m*	banconota *f*	—
billete de ida y vuelta (Es)	Rückfahrkarte *f*	return ticket	billet d'aller et retour *m*	biglietto di andata e ritorno *m*	—
billetterie (F)	Bankomat *m*	cash dispenser	—	bancomat *m*	cajero automático *m*
billiges Geld (D)	—	easy money	argent à bon marché *m*	crediti agevolati *m pl*	dinero barato *m*
billigst (D)	—	at best price	au meilleur prix	al prezzo più basso	al mejor cambio
bill of lading[1] (E)	Ladeschein *m*	—	avis de chargement *m*	bolletta di carico *f*	póliza de carga *f*
bill of lading[2] (E)	Seefrachtbrief *m*	—	connaissement maritime *m*	polizza di carico *f*	póliza *f*
bill of lading[3] (E)	Konnossement *n*	—	connaissement *m*	polizza di carico *f*	conocimiento *m*
bill of loading (E)	Ladeschein *m*	—	avis de chargement *m*	bolletta di carico *f*	póliza de carga *f*
binnen (D)	—	within	dans le délai de	entro	en el término de
Binnenhandel (D)	—	domestic trade	commerce intérieur *m*	commercio nazionale *m*	comercio interior *m*
Binnenmarkt (D)	—	home market	marché national *m*	mercato nazionale *m*	mercado interior *m*
Binnenschiffahrt (D)	—	inland navigation	navigation fluviale *f*	navigazione interna *f*	navegación fluvial *f*
Binnenwirtschaft (D)	—	domestic economy	économie nationale *f*	economia nazionale *f*	economía interior *f*
birthday (E)	Geburtstag *m*	—	anniversaire *m*	compleanno *m*	cumpleaños *m*
birth rate (E)	Geburtenrate *f*	—	taux de natalité *m*	tasso di natalità *m*	tasa de natalidad *f*
bisogno (I)	Bedürfnis *n*	need	besoin *m*	—	necesidad *f*
bisogno annuale (I)	Jahresbedarf *m*	annual need	besoin annuel *m*	—	necesidad anual *f*
bisogno d'informazioni (I)	Informationsbedarf *m*	requirement of information	besoin d'information *m*	—	necesidad de información *f*
black market (E)	Schwarzmarkt *m*	—	marché noir *m*	mercato nero *m*	mercado negro *m*
blank cheque (E)	Blankoscheck *m*	—	chèque en blanc *m*	assegno in bianco *m*	cheque en blanco *m*
blank form (E)	Blankoformular *n*	—	imprimé en blanc *m*	modulo in bianco *m*	formulario en blanco *m*
Blankoformular (D)	—	blank form	imprimé en blanc *m*	modulo in bianco *m*	formulario en blanco *m*
Blankokredit (D)	—	open credit	crédit en compte courant *m*	credito scoperto *m*	crédito en blanco *m*
Blankoscheck (D)	—	blank cheque	chèque en blanc *m*	assegno in bianco *m*	cheque en blanco *m*
Blankounterschrift (D)	—	blank signature	signature en blanc *f*	firma in bianco *f*	firma en blanco *f*
Blankoverkauf (D)	—	short sale	vente à découvert *f*	vendita allo scoperto *f*	venta al descubierto *f*
blank signature (E)	Blankounterschrift *f*	—	signature en blanc *f*	firma in bianco *f*	firma en blanco *f*
blocage de livraisons (F)	Liefersperre *f*	delivery ban	—	blocco delle forniture *m*	embargo *m*
blocage des prix (F)	Preisstopp *m*	price stop	—	blocco dei prezzi *m*	limitación de precios *f*
blocage des salaires (F)	Lohnstopp *m*	wage freeze	—	blocco dei salari *m*	congelación salarial *f*
bloccaggio (I)	Blockade *f*	blockade	blocus *m*	—	bloqueo *m*
blocco d'assegno (I)	Schecksperrung *f*	stopping payment of cheque	opposition au payement d'un chèque *f*	—	bloqueo de un cheque *m*
blocco dei prezzi (I)	Preisstopp *m*	price stop	blocage des prix *m*	—	limitación de precios *f*
blocco dei salari (I)	Lohnstopp *m*	wage freeze	blocage des salaires *m*	—	congelación salarial *f*

	D	E	F	I	Es
blocco delle forniture (I)	Liefersperre f	delivery ban	blocage de livraisons m	—	embargo m
blocco marittimo (I)	Seeblockade f	naval blockade	blocus maritime m	—	bloqueo marítimo m
Blockade (D)	—	blockade	blocus m	bloccaggio m	bloqueo m
hlockade (E)	Blockade f	—	blocus m	bloccaggio m	bloqueo m
blocked account¹ (E)	Sperrkonto n	—	compte bloqué m	conto vincolato m	fondos bloqueados m pl
blocked account² (E)	gesperrtes Konto n	—	compte bloqué m	conto bloccato m	cuenta congelada f
blocking minority (E)	Sperrminorität f	—	minorité suffisante pour bloquer qch. f	sindacato di blocco m	minoría de bloqueo f
block of shares (E)	Aktienpaket n	—	paquet d'actions m	pacchetto delle azioni m	paquete de acciones m
blocus (F)	Blockade f	blockade	—	bloccaggio m	bloqueo m
blocus maritime (F)	Seeblockade f	naval blockade	—	blocco marittimo m	bloqueo marítimo m
bloqueo (Es)	Blockade f	blockade	blocus m	bloccaggio m	—
bloqueo de un cheque (Es)	Schecksperrung f	stopping payment of cheque	opposition au payement d'un chèque f	blocco d'assegno m	—
bloqueo marítimo (Es)	Seeblockade f	naval blockade	blocus maritime m	blocco marittimo m	—
board (E)	Vorstand m	—	comité directeur m	consiglio di amministrazione m	consejo de dirección m
board of directors (E)	Direktion f	—	direction f	direzione f	junta directiva f
Boden (D)	—	ground/soil	sol m/terrain m	terra f/suolo m	suelo m/terreno m
Bodenpolitik (D)	—	land policy	politique de la terre f	politica del suolo f	política del suelo f
Bodenpreis (D)	—	land price	prix du terrain m	prezzo del suolo m	precio del suelo m
Bodenreform (D)	—	land reform	réforme agraire f	riforma agraria f	reforma agraria f
bogus firm (E)	Scheinfirma f	—	raison sociale imaginaire f	pseudoditta f	casa ficticia f
boicot (Es)	Boykott m	boycott	boycottage m	boicottaggio m	—
boicot económico (Es)	Wirtschaftsboykott m	economic boycott	boycottage économique m	boicottaggio economico m	—
boicottaggio (I)	Boykott m	boycott	boycottage m	—	boicot m
boicottaggio economico (I)	Wirtschaftsboykott m	economic boycott	boycottage économique m	—	boicot económico m
boîte aux lettres (F)	Briefkasten m	mail box	—	cassetta postale f	buzón m
boîte postale (F)	Postfach n	post office box	—	casella postale f	apartado postal m
boletín de cambios (Es)	Kurszettel m	stock exchange list	bulletin des cours m	listino di borsa m	—
bolle di accompagnamento (I)	Begleitpapiere pl	accompanying documents	pièces accompagnant l'envoi f pl	—	documentos adjuntos m pl
bolletta d'entrata (I)	Zolleinfuhrschein m	bill of entry	acquit d'entrée m	—	certificado de aduana m
bolletta di carico (I)	Ladeschein m	bill of lading	avis de chargement m	—	póliza de carga f
bolletta di consegna (I)	Lieferschein m	delivery note	bulletin de livraison m	—	recibo de entrega m
bolletta di transito (I)	Durchgangsschein m	transit certificate	acquit de transit m	—	pasavante m
bollette doganali (I)	Einfuhrpapiere pl	import documents	documents d'importation m pl	—	documentos de importación m pl
bolletta d'ordinazione (I)	Bestellschein m	order form	bulletin de commande m	—	hoja de pedido f
bolsa (Es)	Börse f	(stock) exchange	bourse f	borsa f	—
Bolsa de divisas (Es)	Devisenbörse f	foreign exchange market	bourse de devises f	borsa valutaria f	—
bolsa de mercancías (Es)	Warenbörse f	commodity exchange	bourse de marchandises f	borsa merci f	—
bolsa de mercancías a plazo (Es)	Warenterminbörse f	commodity forward exchange	bourse d'opérations à livrer f	borsa merci a termine f	—
bolsa de reciclaje (Es)	Abfallbörse f	recycling exchange	bourse de recyclage f	borsa dei rifiuti f	—
Bolsa de valores (Es)	Effektenbörse f	stock exchange	bourse des titres et valeurs mobilières f	borsa valori f	—
bolsa de valores a término (Es)	Terminbörse f	futures market	bourse à terme f	mercato a termine m	—

	D	E	F	I	Es
Bon (D)	—	voucher	bon *m*	buono *m*	bono *m*
bon (F)	Bon *m*	voucher	—	buono *m*	bono *m*
bona fide (E)	gutgläubig	—	de bonne foi	di buona fede	de buena fe
bon de commande (F)	Bestellformular *n*	order form	—	modulo d'ordinazione *m*	formulario de pedido *m*
bon d'essence (F)	Benzingutscheine *pl*	petrol voucher	—	coupons *m pl*	bono de gasolina *m*
bond market (E)	Rentenmarkt *m*	—	marché des effets publics *m*	mercato dei titoli a reddito fisso *m*	mercado de títulos de renta fija *m*
bonds (E)	Rentenpapiere *pl*	—	titres de rente *m pl*	titoli a reddito fisso *m pl*	títulos de renta fija *m pl*
bonificación (Es)	Bonifikation *f*	bonus	bonification *f*	abbuono *m*	—
bonification¹ (F)	Bonus *m*	bonus	—	premio *m*	gratificación *f*
bonification² (F)	Bonifikation *f*	bonus	—	abbuono *m*	bonificación *f*
bonifico postale (I)	Postüberweisung *f*	postal remittance	virement postal *m*	—	giro postal *m*
bonifico telegrafico (I)	Kabelüberweisung *f*	cable transfer	virement par câble *m*	—	giro telegráfico *m*
Bonifikation (D)	—	bonus	bonification *f*	abbuono *m*	bonificación *f*
Bonität (D)	—	solvency	solvabilité *f*	solvibilità *f*	solvencia *f*
bono (Es)	Bon *m*	voucher	bon *m*	buono *m*	—
bono de gasolina (Es)	Benzingutscheine *pl*	petrol voucher	bon d'essence *m*	coupons *m pl*	—
bonos de pequeño valor nominal (Es)	Baby-Bonds *pl*	baby bonds	bons de petite valeur nominale *m pl*	baby bonds *m pl*	—
bons de petite valeur nominale (F)	Baby-Bonds *pl*	baby bonds	—	baby bonds *m pl*	bonos de pequeño valor nominal *m pl*
Bonus (D)	—	bonus	bonification *f*	premio *m*	gratificación *f*
bonus¹ (E)	Bonifikation *f*	—	bonification *f*	abbuono *m*	bonificación *f*
bonus² (E)	Bonus *m*	—	bonification *f*	premio *m*	gratificación *f*
bonus³ (E)	Prämie *f*	—	prime *f*	premio *m*	gratificación *f*/prima *f*
bonus⁴ (E)	Gratifikation *f*	—	gratification *f*	gratificazione *f*	gratificación *f*
bonus system (E)	Prämiensystem *n*	—	système de primes *m*	sistema dei premi *m*	sistema de primas *m*
bookkeeper (E)	Buchhalter *m*	—	comptable *m*	ragioniere *m*	tenedor de libros *m*
bookkeeping (E)	Buchführung *f*	—	comptabilité *f*	contabilità *f*	contabilidad *f*
bookkeeping error (E)	Buchungsfehler *m*	—	erreur de comptabilité *f*	errore di contabilità *m*	error contable *m*
book profit (E)	Buchgewinn *m*	—	bénéfice comptable *m*	utile contabile *m*	beneficio contable *m*
book value (E)	Buchwert *m*	—	valeur comptable *f*	valore contabile *m*	valor contable *m*
boom¹ (E)	Hausse *f*	—	hausse *f*	rialzo *m*	alza *f*
boom² (E)	Hochkonjunktur *f*	—	haute conjoncture *f*	alta congiuntura *f*	alta coyuntura *f*
boom de inversión (Es)	Investitionsboom *m*	investment boom	boom d'investissement *m*	boom d'investimento *m*	—
boom d'investimento (I)	Investitionsboom *m*	investment boom	boom d'investissement *m*	—	boom de inversión *m*
boom d'investissement (F)	Investitionsboom *m*	investment boom	—	boom d'investimento *m*	boom de inversión *m*
boomerang effect (E)	Bumerang-Effekt *m*	—	effet boomerang *m*	effetto bumerang *m*	efecto bumerán *m*
border control (E)	Grenzkontrolle *f*	—	contrôle à la frontière *m*	controllo alla frontiera *m*	control fronterizo *m*
borrower (E)	Kreditnehmer *m*	—	bénéficiaire d'un crédit *m*	beneficiario del credito *m*	prestatario *m*
borrowing limit (E)	Kreditlimit *n*	—	plafond du crédit alloué *m*	limite di credito *m*	límite de crédito *m*
borsa (I)	Börse *f*	(stock) exchange	bourse *f*	—	bolsa *f*
borsa dei rifiuti (I)	Abfallbörse *f*	recycling exchange	bourse de recyclage *f*	—	bolsa de reciclaje *f*
borsa merci (I)	Warenbörse *f*	commodity exchange	bourse de marchandises *f*	—	bolsa de mercancías *f*
borsa merci a termine (I)	Warenterminbörse *f*	commodity forward exchange	bourse d'opérations à livrer *f*	—	bolsa de mercancías a plazo *f*
borsa valori¹ (I)	Wertpapierbörse *f*	securities market	bourse des titres et valeurs *f*	—	mercado de valores *m*
borsa valori² (I)	Effektenbörse *f*	stock exchange	bourse des titres et valeurs mobilières *f*	—	bolsa de valores *f*

	D	E	F	I	Es
borsa valutaria (I)	Devisenbörse f	foreign exchange market	bourse de devises f	—	bolsa de divisas f
Börse (D)	—	(stock) exchange	bourse f	borsa f	bolsa f
Börsengeschäfte (D)	—	stock market transactions	opérations de bourse f pl	operazioni di borsa f pl	operación bursátil f
Börsenhandel (D)	—	stock exchange transactions	transactions boursiaires f pl	commercio in borsa m	negociación bursátil f
Börsenindex (D)	—	stock exchange index	indice des cours des actions m	indice delle quotazioni m	índice bursátil m
Börsenkrach (D)	—	stockmarket crash	débâcle boursière f	crollo di borsa m	caída en picado de la bolsa f
Börsenkurs (D)	—	quotation on the stock exchange	cours de bourse m pl	corso di borsa m	cotización en bolsa f
Börsenmakler (D)	—	stockbroker	courtier en bourse m	agente di cambio f	corredor de bolsa m
Börsennotierung (D)	—	quotation on the stock exchange	cotation des cours en bourse f	quotazione di borsa f	cotización de bolsa f
Börsenplatz (D)	—	stock exchange centre	place boursière f	piazza f	plaza bursátil f
Börsentag (D)	—	market day	jour de bourse m	giorno di borsa m	sesión bursátil f
Börsenumsatzsteuer (D)	—	stock exchange turnover tax	droit de transaction sur les opérations boursières m	imposta sulle operazioni di borsa f	impuesto de negociación bursátil m
bosquejo (Es)	Konzept n	concept	brouillon m	piano m	—
bottleneck in capacity (E)	Kapazitätsengpaß m	—	goulot d'étranglement de capacité m	strettoia di capacità f	escasez de capacidad f
bourse (F)	Börse f	(stock) exchange	—	borsa f	bolsa f
bourse à terme (F)	Terminbörse f	futures market	—	mercato a termine m	bolsa de valores a término f
bourse de devises (F)	Devisenbörse f	foreign exchange market	—	borsa valutaria f	bolsa de divisas f
bourse de marchandises (F)	Warenbörse f	commodity exchange	—	borsa merci f	bolsa de mercancías f
bourse de recyclage (F)	Abfallbörse f	recycling exchange	—	borsa dei rifiuti f	bolsa de reciclaje f
bourse des titres et valeurs (F)	Wertpapierbörse f	securities market	—	borsa valori f	mercado de valores m
bourse des titres et valeurs mobilières (F)	Effektenbörse f	stock exchange	—	borsa valori f	bolsa de valores f
bourse d'opérations à livrer (F)	Warenterminbörse f	commodity forward exchange	—	borsa merci a termine f	bolsa de mercancías f
box (E)	Kiste f	—	caisse f	cassa f	caja f
boycott (E)	Boykott m	—	boycottage m	boicottaggio m	boicot m
boycottage (F)	Boykott m	boycott	—	boicottaggio m	boicot m
boycottage économique (F)	Wirtschaftsboykott m	economic boycott	—	boicottaggio economico m	boicot económico m
Boykott (D)	—	boycott	boycottage m	boicottaggio m	boicot m
branch¹ (E)	Filiale f	—	agence f	filiale f	filial f
branch² (E)	Zweigstelle f	—	agence f	agenzia f	filial f
branch abroad (E)	Auslandsniederlassung f	—	succursale à l'étranger f	succursale estera f	filial en el exterior m
branch business (E)	Zweigbetrieb m	—	établissement secondaire m	filiale f	sucursal f
branch manager (E)	Filialleiter m	—	directeur d'agence m	direttore della filiale m	jefe de sucursal m
branch network (E)	Filialnetz n	—	réseau de succursales m	rete delle filiali f	red de sucursales f
branch office (E)	Zweigniederlassung f	—	succursale f	succursale f	filial f
Branche (D)	—	line of business	branche f	categoria f	ramo m
branche (F)	Branche f	line of business	—	categoria f	ramo m
Branchenanalyse (D)	—	trade analysis	analyse des branches f	analisi di categoria f	análisis del ramo m
Branchenstatistik (D)	—	trade statistics	statistique sur les différentes branches économiques f	statistica di categoria f	estadística del ramo f

	D	E	F	I	Es
Branchenstruktur (D)	—	trade structure	structure de la branche f	struttura di categoria f	estructura del ramo f
Branchenvergleich (D)	—	trade comparison	comparaison des différentes branches f	comparazione delle categorie f	comparación de ramos f
brandname article (E)	Markenartikel m	—	produit de marque m	articolo di marca m	artículo de marca m
Brandschutz (D)	—	protection against fire	protection contre l'incendie f	protezione antincendio f	protección contra incendios f
Brandversicherung (D)	—	fire insurance	assurance contre l'incendie f	assicurazione contro incendio f	seguro contra incencios f
Braunkohle (D)	—	brown coal	lignite m	lignite f	lignito m
break-even point¹ (E)	Gewinnschwelle f	—	seuil de rentabilité m	soglia dell'utile f	umbral de la rentabilidad m
break-even point² (E)	Rentabilitätschwelle f	—	seuil de rentabilité m	soglia di redditività f	límite inferior de rentabilidad m
brevet d'invention (F)	Patent n	patent	—	brevetto m	patente f
brevet européen (F)	Europapatent n	European patent	—	brevetto europeo m	patente europea f
brevetto¹ (I)	Patent n	patent	brevet d'invention m	—	patente f
brevetto² (I)	Patenturkunde f	patent document	certificat d'attestation du brevet d'invention m	—	patente f
brevetto europeo (I)	Europapatent n	European patent	brevet européen m	—	patente europea f
bribe (E)	Bestechung f	—	corruption f	corruzione f	soborno f
bridging loan (E)	Überbrückungs-kredit m	—	crédit transitoire m	credito ponte m	crédito transitorio m
Brief (D)	—	letter	lettre f	lettera f	carta f
Briefkasten (D)	—	mail box	boîte aux lettres f	cassetta postale f	buzón m
Briefkastenfirma (D)	—	bubble company	entreprise fantôme f	società bucalettere f	empresa ficticia f
Briefkopf (D)	—	letterhead	en-tête m	intestazione f	encabezamiento m
Briefkurs (D)	—	ask(ed) price	cours de vente m	prezzo d'offerta m	cotización ofrecida f
Briefmarke (D)	—	stamp	timbre-poste m	francobollo m	sello m
Briefträger (D)	—	postman	facteur m	portalettere m	cartero m
Briefumschlag (D)	—	envelope	enveloppe de lettre f	busta f	sobre m
Briefwaage (D)	—	letter scales	pèse-lettres m	bilancia per corrispondenza f	pesacartas m
brochure (E)	Broschüre f	—	prospectus m	depliant m	folleto m
broken period interest (E)	Stückzinsen f	—	intérêts courus m pl	interessi maturati m pl	intereses por fracción de período m pl
Broker (D)	—	broker	courtier m	broker m	corredor de bolsa m
broker¹ (E)	Makler m	—	courtier m	mediatore m	corredor m
broker² (E)	Broker m	—	courtier m	broker m	corredor de bolsa m
broker (I)	Broker m	broker	courtier m	—	corredor de bolsa m
brokerage (E)	Courtage f	—	courtage m	courtage f	corretaje m
Broschüre (D)	—	brochure	prospectus m	depliant m	folleto m
brouillon (F)	Konzept n	concept	—	piano m	bisquejo m
brown coal (E)	Braunkohle f	—	lignite m	lignite f	lignito m
Bruchteil (D)	—	fraction	fraction f	frazione f	parte fraccionaria f
Bruchteils-eigentümer (D)	—	co-owner	copropriétaire d'une quote-part m	comproprietario di quota ideale m	copropietario de bienes indivisos m
Bruttoeinkommen (D)	—	gross income	revenu brut m	reddito lordo m	ingreso bruto m
Bruttoinlands-produkt (D)	—	gross domestic product	produit intérieur brut m	prodotto interno lordo m	producto interior bruto m
Bruttolohn (D)	—	gross pay	salaire brut m	salario lordo m	salario bruto m
Bruttopreis (D)	—	gross price	prix brut m	prezzo lordo m	precio bruto m
Bruttoproduktion (D)	—	gross production	production brute f	produzione lorda f	producción bruta f
Bruttoregistertonne (D)	—	gross register(ed) ton	tonneau de jauge brut m	tonnellata di stazza lorda f	tonelada de registro bruto f
Bruttosozialprodukt (D)	—	gross national product	produit national brut m	prodotto nazionale lordo m	producto nacional bruto m
bubble company (E)	Briefkastenfirma f	—	entreprise fantôme f	società bucalettere f	empresa ficticia f
Buchführung (D)	—	bookkeeping	comptabilité f	contabilità f	contabilidad f

	D	E	F	I	Es
Buchgeld (D)	—	money in account	monnaie de crédit f	moneta bancaria f	dinero bancario m
Buchgewinn (D)	—	book profit	bénéfice comptable m	utile contabile m	beneficio contable m
Buchhalter (D)	—	bookkeeper	comptable m	ragioniere m	tenedor de libros m
Buchhaltung (D)	—	accounting	comptabilité f	contabilità f	contabilidad f
Buchungsfehler (D)	—	bookkeeping error	erreur de comptabilité f	errore di contabilità m	error contable m
Buchwert (D)	—	book value	valeur comptable f	valore contabile m	valor contable m
Budget (D)	—	budget	budget m	bilancio m	presupuesto m
budget¹ (E)	Haushaltsplan m	—	budget m	bilancio preventivo m	presupuesto m
budget² (E)	Haushalt m	—	budget m	bilancio m	presupuesto m
budget³ (E)	Budget n/Etat m	—	budget m	bilancio m	presupuesto m
budget¹ (F)	Haushaltsplan m	budget	—	bilancio preventivo m	presupuesto m
budget² (F)	Budget n/Etat m	budget	—	bilancio m	presupuesto m
budget³ (F)	Haushalt m	budget	—	bilancio m	presupuesto m
budget adjustment (E)	Planrevision f	—	révision des coûts marginaux f	revisione del piano f	ajuste presupuestario m
budgetary control (E)	Finanzkontrolle f	—	contrôle de financement m	controllo finanziario m	control financiero m
budgetary deficit (E)	Haushaltsdefizit n	—	déficit budgétaire m	deficit del bilancio m	déficit presupuestario m
budgetary planning (E)	Budgetplanung f	—	planification du budget f	programmazione del bilancio f	planificación del presupuesto m
Budgetausgleich (D)	—	balancing of the budget	équilibrage du budget m	pareggio di bilancio m	balance del presupuesto m
budget control (E)	Budgetkontrolle f	—	contrôle du budget m	controllo del bilancio m	control del presupuesto m
budget de publicité (F)	Werbebudget n	advertising budget	—	budget pubblicitario m	presupuesto publicitario m
budgeted costs (E)	Sollkosten pl	—	coûts ex ante m pl	costi calcolati m pl	gastos precalculados m pl
Budgetgrundsätze (D)	—	budget principles	principes budgétaires	principi di bilancio m pl	principios presupuestarios m pl
Budgetierung (D)	—	budgeting	établissement du budget m	compilazione del bilancio f	establecimiento del presupuesto m
budgeting (E)	Budgetierung f	—	établissement du budget m	compilazione del bilancio f	establecimiento del presupuesto m
Budgetkontrolle (D)	—	budget control	contrôle du budget m	controllo del bilancio m	control del presupuesto m
Budgetplanung (D)	—	budgetary planning	planification du budget f	programmazione del bilancio f	planificación del presupuesto f
budget principles (E)	Budgetgrundsätze f	—	principes budgétaires	principi di bilancio m pl	principios presupuestarios m pl
budget pubblicitario (I)	Werbebudget n	advertising budget	budget de publicité m	—	presupuesto publicitario m
buena reputación (Es)	Seriosität f	seriousness	caractère sérieux m	serietà f	—
bufete de abogado (Es)	Anwaltskanzlei f	lawyer's office	cabinet d'avocat m	studio d'avvocato m	—
building and construction industry (E)	Bauwirtschaft f	—	(industrie du) bâtiment f	edilizia f	ramo de la construcción m
building land (E)	Bauland n	—	espace à bâtir m	area edificabile f	terreno edificable m
building loan (E)	Baukredit m	—	crédit à la construction m	credito edilizio m	crédito para la construcción f
bulk buyer (E)	Großabnehmer m	—	acheteur en gros m	acquirente all'ingrosso m	comprador al por mayor m
bulk goods (E)	Massengüter pl	—	marchandises en vrac f pl	beni di massa m pl	productos a granel m pl
bull (E)	Haussier m	—	haussier m	speculatore al rialzo m	alcista m
bulletin de commande (F)	Bestellschein m	order form	—	bolletta d'ordinazione f	hoja de pedido f
bulletin de livraison (F)	Lieferschein m	delivery note	—	bolletta di consegna f	recibo de entrega m
bulletin des cours (F)	Kurszettel m	stock exchange list	—	listino di borsa m	boletín de bolsa m

	D	E	F	I	Es
bulto (Es)	Paket *n*	parcel	colis *m*	pacco *m*	—
Bumerang-Effekt (D)	—	boomerang effect	effet boomerang *m*	effetto bumerang *m*	efecto bumerán *m*
buono (I)	Bon *m*	voucher	bon *m*	—	bono *m*
burden of proof (E)	Beweislast *f*	—	charge de la preuve *f*	onere di prova *m*	carga de la prueba *f*
bureau¹ (F)	Schreibtisch *m*	desk	—	scrivania *f*	escritorio *m*
bureau² (F)	Amt	office	—	ufficio *m*	cargo *m*
bureaucracy (E)	Bürokratie *f*	—	bureaucratie *f*	burocrazia *f*	burocracia *f*
bureaucratie (F)	Bürokratie *f*	bureaucracy	—	burocrazia *f*	burocracia *f*
bureaucratie communautaire (F)	EG-Bürokratie *f*	burocracy inside the European Communities	—	burocrazia CEE *f*	burocracia comunitaria *f*
bureau de chèques postaux (F)	Postscheckamt *n*	postal giro centre	—	ufficio dei conti correnti postali *m*	oficina de cheques postales *f*
bureau de déclaration de résidence (F)	Einwohner-meldeamt *n*	residents' registration office	—	ufficio anagrafe *m*	oficina del censo *f*
bureau de douane (F)	Zollstelle *f*	customs office	—	posto di dogana *m*	oficina de aduanas *f*
bureau de la paye (F)	Lohnbüro *n*	pay office	—	ufficio paga *m*	departamento de nóminas *m*
bureau de marketing (F)	Marketingabteilung *f*	marketing department	—	reparto marketing *m*	departamento de mercadeo *m*
bureau de placement (F)	Arbeitsvermittlung *f*	employment agency	—	ufficio di collocamento *m*	agencia laboral *f*
bureau de poste (F)	Postamt *n*	post office	—	ufficio postale *m*	correos *m pl*
bureau du personnel (F)	Personalbüro *n*	personnel office	—	ufficio del personale *m*	oficina de personal *f*
bureau juridique (F)	Rechtsabteilung *f*	legal department	—	ufficio legale *m*	sección jurídica *f*
Bürge (D)	—	guarantor	garant *m*	fideiussore *m*	fiador *m*
Bürgschaft (D)	—	guarantee	caution *f*	fideiussione *f*	fianza *f*
Bürgschaftskredit (D)	—	credit by way of bank guarantee	crédit cautionné *m*	credito di fideiussione *m*	crédito de garantía *m*
burocracia (Es)	Bürokratie *f*	bureaucracy	bureaucratie *f*	burocrazia *f*	—
burocrazia (I)	Bürokratie *f*	bureaucracy	bureaucratie *f*	—	burocracia *f*
Bürokratie (D)	—	bureaucracy	bureaucratie *f*	burocrazia *f*	burocracia *f*
business (E)	Geschäft *n*	—	affaire *f*	negozio *m*	negocio *m*
business acquisition (E)	Geschäfts-übernahme *f*	—	reprise d'une affaire *f*	acquisto di un'azienda *m*	adquisición de una empresa *f*
business administration (E)	Betriebswirtschafts-lehre *f*	—	(science de la) gestion industrielle et commerciale *f*	economia aziendale *f*	teoría de la empresa *f*
business concentration (E)	Unternehmens-konzentration *f*	—	concentration d'entreprises *f*	pool d'imprese *m*	concentración de empresas *f*
business concept (E)	Unternehmens-konzept *n*	—	stratégie de l'entreprise *f*	piano imprenditoriale *m*	concepto comercial *m*
business connections¹ (E)	Geschäfts-beziehung *f*	—	relations d'affaires *f pl*	rapporti d'affari *m pl*	relaciones comerciales *f pl*
business connections² (E)	Geschäfts-verbindung *f*	—	relation d'affaires *f*	relazione d'affari *f*	relación comercial *f*
business cycle¹ (E)	Konjunktur *f*	—	conjoncture *f*	congiuntura *f*	conyuntura *f*
business cycle² (E)	Konjunkturzyklus *m*	—	cycle conjoncturel *m*	ciclo congiunturale *m*	ciclo económico *m*
business friend (E)	Geschäftsfreund *m*	—	correspondant *m*	partner d'affari *m*	corresponsal *m*
business hours (E)	Geschäftszeit *f*	—	heures d'ouverture *f pl*	orario d'apertura *m*	horas de despacho *f pl*
business papers (E)	Geschäftspapiere *pl*	—	papiers d'affaires *m pl*	documenti commerciali *m pl*	documentos comerciales *m pl*
business partner (E)	Geschäftspartner *m*	—	associé *m*	partner commerciale *m*	socio *m*
business practice (E)	Handelsbrauch *m*	—	usage commercial *m*	usanza commerciale *f*	uso comercial *m*
business premises (E)	Geschäftsräume *pl*	—	local à usage commercial *m*	locali commerciali *m pl*	local comercial *m*
business report (E)	Geschäftsbericht *m*	—	rapport de gestion *m*	relazione sull'esercizio commerciale *f*	informe *m*

	D	E	F	I	Es
business secret (E)	Geschäfts-geheimnis n	—	secret d'affaires m	segreto commerciale m	secreto comercial m
business year (E)	Wirtschaftsjahr n	—	exercice comptable m	esercizio m	ejercicio m
businessman (E)	Kaufmann m	—	négociant m	commerciante m	comerciante m
businessmen (E)	Kaufleute pl	—	commerçants m pl	commercianti m pl	comerciantes m pl
Bußgeld (D)	—	administration fee	amende f	pena pecuniaria f	multa f
busta¹ (I)	Briefumschlag m	envelope	enveloppe de lettre f	—	sobre m
busta² (I)	Kuvert n	envelope	enveloppe f	—	sobre m
but (F)	Ziel n	objective	—	obiettivo m	objetivo m
buy (E)	(ein-)kaufen	—	acheter	acquistare	comprar
buyer¹ (E)	Abnehmer m	—	acheteur m	acquirente m	tomador m
buyer² (E)	Einkäufer m	—	acheteur m	acquirente m/ cliente m	comprador m
buyer country (E)	Abnehmerland n	—	pays acheteur m	paese acquirente m	país comprador m
buyer's commission (E)	Käuferprovision f	—	commission d'acheteur f	provvigione dell'acquirente f	comisión al comprador f
buyer's market (E)	Käufermarkt m	—	marché d'acheteurs m	mercato favorevole all'acquirente m	mercado favorable al comprador m
buying motive (E)	Kaufanlaß m	—	motif d'achat m	motivo d'acquisto m	motivo de compra m
buying intention (E)	Kaufbereitschaft f	—	propension à l'achat f	propensione all'acquisto f	disposición a comprar f
buzón (Es)	Briefkasten m	mail box	boîte aux lettres f	cassetta postale f	—
by express (mail) (E)	per Express	—	par exprès	per espresso	por expreso
by lorry (E)	per Lastkraftwagen	—	par camion	per autocarro	por camión
by machine (E)	maschinell	—	mécanique	a macchina	a máquina
by order (E)	im Auftrag	—	par ordre	per ordine	por poder
by procuration (E)	per procura	—	par procuration	per procura	por poder
by-product (E)	Nebenprodukt n	—	produit dérivé m	prodotto secondario m	producto accesorio m
by registered post (E)	per Einschreiben	—	sous pli recommandé	per raccomandata	certificado
by return of post (E)	postwendend	—	par retour du courrier	a giro di posta	a vuelta de correo
cabinet d'avocat (F)	Anwaltskanzlei f	lawyer's office	—	studio d'avvocato m	bufete de abogado m
cablegram (E)	Kabeltelegramm n	—	câblogramme m	cablogramma m	cablegrama f
cablegrama (Es)	Kabeltelegramm n	cablegramm	câblogramme m	cablogramma m	—
cable television (E)	Kabelfernsehen n	—	télévision par câble f	televisione via cavo f	televisión por cable f
cable transfer (E)	Kabelüberweisung f	—	virement par câble m	bonifico telegrafico m	giro telegráfico m
cablogramma (I)	Kabeltelegramm n	cablogramm	câblogramme m	—	cablegrama f
câblogramme (F)	Kabeltelegramm n	cablegram	—	cablogramma m	cablegrama f
cachet (F)	Gage f	salary	—	onorario m	remuneración f
cachet de la poste (F)	Poststempel m	postmark	—	timbro postale m	matasellos m
cadaster (E)	Kataster m	—	cadastre m	catasto m	catastro m
cadastre (F)	Kataster m	cadaster	—	catasto m	catastro m
cadeau publicitaire (F)	Werbegeschenk n	advertising gift	—	omaggio pubblicitario m	regalo publicitario m
cadre (F)	Führungsperson f	executive	—	dirigente m	ejecutivo m
caduta dei prezzi (I)	Preisverfall m	decline in prices	chute des prix f	—	caída de precios f
caída de los cambios (Es)	Kurs-zusammbruch m	collapse of prices	chute des cours f	crollo delle quotazioni m	—
caída de precios (Es)	Preisverfall m	decline in prices	chute des prix f	caduta dei prezzi f	—
caída en picado de la bolsa (Es)	Börsenkrach m	stockmarket crash	débâcle boursière f	crollo di borsa m	—
caisse (F)	Kiste f	box	—	cassa f	caja f
caissier (F)	Kassierer m	cashier	—	cassiere m	cajero m
caja (Es)	Kiste f	box	caisse f	cassa f	—
caja de ahorros (Es)	Sparkasse f	savings bank	institut bancaire d'épargne m	cassa di risparmio f	—
caja de seguridad (Es)	Safe m	safe	coffre-fort m	cassetta di sicurezza f	—

	D	E	F	I	Es
caja de socorros mutuos (Es)	Versicherung auf Gegenseitigkeit *f*	mutual insurance	assurance mutuelle *f*	mutua assicurazione *f*	—
caja fuerte (Es)	Tresor *m*	safe	coffre-fort *m*	cassaforte *f*	—
cajero (Es)	Kassierer *m*	cashier	caissier *m*	cassiere *m*	—
cajero automático (Es)	Bankomat *m*	cash dispenser	billetterie *m*	bancomat *m*	—
calcolatore (I)	Rechner *m*	computer/calculator	ordinateur *m*/ calculateur de poche *m*	—	ordenador *m*/ calculadora de bolsillo *f*
calcolazione (I)	Kalkulation *f*	calculation	calcul *m*	—	calculación *f*
calcolo (I)	Berechnung *f*	computation	calcul *m*	—	calculación *f*
calcolo degli interessi (I)	Zinsberechnung *f*	calculating the interest	calcul des intérêts *m*	—	cálculo de intereses *m*
calcolo dei costi pianificati (I)	Plankosten- rechnung *f*	calculation of the budget costs	calcul de l'écart sur cadence de fabrication *m*	—	cálculo de costes normalizados *m*
calcolo del contributo per copertura (I)	Deckungsbeitrags- rechnung *f*	contribution costing	calcul de la propor- tion de garantie *m*	—	factura de aportación de fondos *f*
calcolo della liquidità (I)	Liquiditätsrechnung *f*	liquidity calculation	compte de liquidité *m*	—	cálculo de liquidez *m*
calcolo della probabilità (I)	Wahrscheinlichkeits- rechnung *f*	calculation of probabilities	calcul des probabilités *m*	—	cálculo de probabilidades *m*
calcolo del patrimonio (I)	Vermögens- rechnung *f*	capital account	calcul du patrimoine *m*	—	cálculo del valor neto *m*
calcolo di finanziamento (I)	Finanzierungs- rechnung *f*	flow-of-funds analysis	analyse des flux monétaires *f*	—	análisis de flujos monetarios *m*
calcolo pianificato (I)	Plankalkulation *f*	target calculation	calcul des coûts prévisionnels *m*	—	cálculo de los objetivos *m*
calcolo preventivo (I)	Vorkalkulation *f*	estimation of cost	calcul des coûts a priori *m*	—	cálculo provisional *m*
calcul[1] (F)	Kalkulation *f*	calculation	—	calcolazione *f*	calculación *f*
calcul[2] (F)	Berechnung *f*	computation	—	calcolo *m*	calculación *f*
calculación[1] (Es)	Berechnung *f*	computation	calcul *m*	calcolo *m*	—
calculación[2] (Es)	Kalkulation *f*	calculation	calcul *m*	calcolazione *f*	—
calculating the interest (E)	Zinsberechnung *f*	—	calcul des intérêts *m*	calcolo degli interessi *m*	cálculo de intereses *m*
calculation (E)	Kalkulation *f*	—	calcul *m*	calcolazione *f*	calculación *f*
calculation of probabilities (E)	Wahrscheinlichkeits- rechnung *f*	—	calcul des probabilités *m*	calcolo della probabilità *m*	cálculo de probabilidades *m*
calculation of the budget costs (E)	Plankosten- rechnung *f*	—	calcul de l'écart sur cadence de fabrication *m*	calcolo dei costi pianificati *m*	cálculo de costes normalizados *m*
cálculo de costes a posteriori (Es)	Nachkalkulation *f*	historical costing	calcul des coûts a posteriori *m*	computisteria *f*	—
calcul de la proportion de garantie (F)	Deckungsbeitrags- rechnung *f*	contribution costing	—	calcolo del contributo per copertura *m*	factura de aportación de fondos *f*
calcul de l'écart sur cadence de fabrication (F)	Plankosten- rechnung *f*	calculation of the budget costs	—	calcolo dei costi pianificati *m*	cálculo de costes normalizados *m*
calcul des coûts a posteriori (F)	Nachkalkulation *f*	historical costing	—	computisteria *f*	cálculo de costes a posteriori *m*
calcul des coûts a priori (F)	Vorkalkulation *f*	estimation of cost	—	calcolo preventivo *m*	cálculo provisional *m*
calcul des coûts prévisionnels (F)	Plankalkulation *f*	target calculation	—	calcolo pianificato *m*	cálculo de los objetivos *m*
calcul des intérêts[1] (F)	Zinsberechnung *f*	calculating the interest	—	calcolo degli interessi *m*	cálculo de intereses *m*
calcul des intérêts[2] (F)	Zinsrechnung *f*	interest account	—	conteggio degli interessi *m*	cómputo de intereses *m*
calcul des probabilités (F)	Wahrscheinlichkeits- rechnung *f*	calculation of probabilities	—	calcolo della probabilità *m*	cálculo de probabilidades *m*
calcul du patrimoine (F)	Vermögens- rechnung *f*	capital account	—	calcolo del patrimonio *m*	cálculo del valor neto *m*
calculation unit (E)	Recheneinheit *f*	—	unité de calcul *f*	unità di conteggio *f*	unidad de cuenta *f*
cálculo de costes normalizados (Es)	Plankostenrechnung *f*	calculation of the budget costs	calcul de l'écart sur cadence de fabrication *m*	calcolo dei costi pianificati *m*	—

	D	E	F	I	Es
cálculo de intereses (Es)	Zinsberechnung f	calculating the interest	calcul des intérêts m	calcolo degli interessi m	—
cálculo de liquidez (Es)	Liquiditätsrechnung f	liquidity calculation	compte de liquidité m	calcolo della liquidità m	—
cálculo de los costes marginales (Es)	Grenzkosten-rechnung f	marginal costing	détermination du coût marginal f	conto dei costi limite m	—
cálculo de los objetivos (Es)	Plankalkulation f	target calculation	calcul des coûts prévisionnels m	calcolo pianificato m	—
cálculo del valor neto (Es)	Vermögens-rechnung f	capital account	calcul du patrimoine m	calcolo del patrimonio m	—
cálculo de probabilidades (Es)	Wahrscheinlichkeits-rechnung f	calculation of probabilities	calcul des probabilités m	calcolo della probabilità m	—
cálculo provisional (Es)	Vorkalkulation f	estimation of cost	calcul des coûts a priori m	calcolo preventivo m	—
calendar year (E)	Kalenderjahr n	—	année civile f	anno solare m	año civil m
calidad (Es)	Qualität f	quality	qualité f	qualità f	—
calidad del agua potable (Es)	Trinkwasserqualität f	drinking water quality	qualité de l'eau potable f	qualità dell'acqua potabile f	—
calidad de vida (Es)	Lebensqualität f	quality of life	qualité de la vie f	qualità di vita f	—
calidades aseguradas (Es)	zugesicherte Eigenschaften pl	warranted characteristics	qualité promise f	caratteristiche promesse f pl	—
call (E)	Abruf m	—	appel m	richiesta f	reclamación de la entrega de un pedido f
callable (E)	kündbar	—	résiliable/ remboursable	risolubile/redimibile	revocable/rescindible
calle (Es)	Straße f	street/road	rue f/route f	via f/strada f	—
calo del fatturato (I)	Umsatzrückgang m	decrease of turnover	recul du chiffre d'affaires m	—	disminución de la cifra de facturación f
calo dell'occupazione (I)	Beschäftigungs-rückgang m	drop in employment	baisse de l'offre d'emploi f	—	descenso del empleo m
cámara de artesanía (Es)	Handwerkskammer f	chamber of handicrafts	chambre artisanale f	camera dell'artigianato f	—
cámara de comercio (Es)	Handelskammer f	Chamber of Commerce	chambre de commerce f	camera di commercio f	—
cámara de industria y comercio (Es)	Industrie- und Handelskammer f	Chamber of Industry and Commerce	chambre de com-merce et d'industrie f	camera di commercio e industria f	—
cámara del comercio exterior (Es)	Außenhandels-kammer f	chamber of foreign trade	chambre du com-merce extérieur f	camera di commercio estero f	—
cambiale (I)	Wechsel f	bill of exchange	lettre de change f	—	letra de cambio f
cambiale commerciale (I)	Warenwechsel m	commercial bill	traite commerciale f	—	letra comercial f
cambiale domiciliata (I)	Domizilwechsel m	domiciliary bill	effet domicilier m	—	letra domiciliada f
cambiale estera (I)	Auslandswechsel n	foreign bill of exchange	traite tirée sur l'étranger f	—	letra sobre el exterior f
cambiamenti strutturali (I)	Strukturwandel m	structural change	changement dans les structures m	—	cambio de estructuras m
cambiamento dell'abitazione (I)	Wohnungs-wechsel m	change of residence	transfert de résidence m	—	cambio de vivienda m
cambiamento del posto di lavoro (I)	Arbeitsplatz-wechsel m	change of employment	changement d'emploi m	—	cambio de puesto m
cambi fissi (I)	feste Wechselkurse pl	fixed exchange rates	taux de change fixe m	—	tipos de cambio fijos m pl
cambi multipli (I)	gespaltene Wechselkurse pl	two-tier exchange rate	cours du change multiple m	—	tipo de cambio múltiple m
cambio[1] (Es)	Umtausch m	exchange	échange m	cambio m	—
cambio[2] (Es)	Tausch m	exchange/barter	échange m/troc m	scambio m/baratto m	—
cambio[1] (I)	Wechselkurs m	exchange rate	cours du change m	—	tipo de cambio m
cambio[2] (I)	Umtausch m	exchange	échange m	—	cambio m/ conversión f
cambio a término (Es)	Terminkurs m	forward price	cours de bourse à terme m	corso a termine m	—
cambio de divisas (Es)	Devisenkurs m	foreign exchange rate	taux de change m	cambio delle divise m	—

	D	E	F	I	Es
cambio de empleo (Es)	Stellungswechsel *m*	change of employment	changement d'emploi *m*	cambiamento del posto di lavoro *m*	—
cambio de estructuras (Es)	Strukturwandel *m*	structural change	changement dans les structures *m*	cambiamenti strutturali *m pl*	—
cambio del equipo de obreros (Es)	Schichtwechsel *m*	change of shift	relève d'équipe *f*	cambio di turno *m*	—
cambio delle divise (I)	Devisenkurs *m*	foreign exchange rate	taux de change *m*	—	cambio de divisas *m*
cambio del personale (I)	Personalwechsel *m*	staff changes	mouvements dans le personnel *m pl*	—	cambio de personal *m*
cambio de personal (Es)	Personalwechsel *m*	staff changes	mouvements dans le personnel *m pl*	cambio del personale *m*	—
cambio de puesto (Es)	Arbeitsplatzwechsel *m*	change of employment	changement d'emploi *m*	cambiamento del posto di lavoro *m*	—
cambio de vivienda (Es)	Wohnungswechsel *m*	change of residence	transfert de résidence *m*	cambiamento dell'abitazione *m*	—
cambio di turno (I)	Schichtwechsel *m*	change of shift	relève d'équipe *f*	—	cambio del equipo de obreros *m*
cambio en el poder adquisitivo (Es)	Kaufkraftänderung *f*	changes in purchasing power	modification du pouvoir d'achat *f*	mutamento del potere d'acquisto *m*	—
cambio flessibile (I)	flexibler Wechselkurs *m*	flexible exchange rate	taux de change flottant *m*	—	tipo flotante de cambio *m*
cambio reale (I)	Mengennotierung *f*	fixed exchange	cotation de quantité *f*	—	cotización real *f*
cambio unitario (I)	Einheitskurs *m*	spot price	cours unique *m*	—	cotización única *f*
cambio valuta (I)	Sortenhandel *m*	dealing in foreign notes and coins	commerce de change *m*	—	operación de moneda extranjera *f*
camera d'albergo (I)	Hotelzimmer *n*	hotel room	chambre d'hôtel *f*	—	habitación de hotel *f*
camera dell'artigianato (I)	Handwerkskammer *f*	chamber of handicrafts	chambre artisanale *f*	—	cámara de artesanía *f*
camera di commercio (I)	Handelskammer *f*	Chamber of Commerce	chambre de commerce *f*	—	cámara de comercio *f*
camera di commercio e industria (I)	Industrie- und Handelskammer *f*	Chamber of Industry and Commerce	chambre de commerce et d'industrie *f*	—	cámara de industria y comercio *f*
camera di commercio estero (I)	Außenhandelskammer *f*	chamber of foreign trade	chambre du commerce extérieur *f*	—	cámara del comercio exterior *f*
camionnage (F)	Rollgeld *n*	haulage	—	spese di trasporto *f pl*	derechos de acarreo *m pl*
campagna (I)	Kampagne *f*	campaign	campagne *f*	—	campaña *f*
campagna di vendita (I)	Verkaufskampagne *f*	sales campaign	campagne de vente *f*	—	campaña de venta *f*
campagna pubblicitaria (I)	Werbekampagne *f*	advertising campaign	campagne publicitaire *f*	—	campaña publicitaria *f*
campagne (F)	Kampagne *f*	campaign	—	campagna *f*	campaña *f*
campagne de vente (F)	Verkaufskampagne *f*	sales campaign	—	campagna di vendita *f*	campaña de venta *f*
campagne publicitaire[1] (F)	Werbekampagne *f*	advertising campaign	—	campagna pubblicitaria *f*	campaña publicitaria *f*
campagne publicitaire[2] (F)	Werbeaktion *f*	advertising activity	—	azione pubblicitaria *f*	campaña publicitaria *f*
campaign (E)	Kampagne *f*	—	campagne *f*	campagna *f*	campaña *f*
campaña (Es)	Kampagne *f*	campaign	campagne *f*	campagna *f*	—
campaña de prensa (Es)	Presseaktion *f*	press campaign	action de presse *f*	azione stampa *f*	—
campaña de venta (Es)	Verkaufskampagne *f*	sales campaign	campagne de vente *f*	campagna di vendita *f*	—
campaña publicitaria[1] (Es)	Werbekampagne *f*	advertising campaign	campagne publicitaire *f*	campagna pubblicitaria *f*	—
campaña publicitaria[2] (Es)	Werbeaktion *f*	advertising activity	campagne publicitaire *f*	azione pubblicitaria *f*	—
campione[1] (I)	Muster *n*	sample/pattern	échantillon *m*/ dessin *m*	—	muestra *f*/dibujo *m*
campione[2] (I)	(Waren-)Probe *f*	sample	échantillon *m*	—	muestra *f*
campione di merce (I)	Warenprobe *f*	sample	échantillon *m*	—	muestra de mercancía *f*
campione per esame (I)	Ansichtssendung *f*	consignment on approval	envoi à condition *m*	—	envío para inspección *m*
campione senza valore (I)	Muster ohne Wert *n*	sample, no commercial value	échantillon sans valeur *m*	—	muestra sin valor *f*

	D	E	F	I	Es
campioni (I)	Stichproben *pl*	random test	sondage *m*	—	prueba por sondeo *f*
campo d'azione[1] (I)	Tätigkeitsfeld *n*	field of activity	champ d'acitivité *m*	—	campo de actividad *m*
campo d'azione[2] (I)	Aktionsfeld *n*	field of action	champ d'action *m*	—	campo de acción *m*
campo de acción (Es)	Aktionsfeld *n*	field of action	champ d'action *m*	campo d'azione *m*	—
campo de actividad (Es)	Tätigkeitsfeld *n*	field of activity	champ d'acitivité *m*	campo d'azione *m*	—
canal de distribution[1] (F)	Vertriebsweg *m*	distribution channel	—	rete di distribuzione *f*	circuito de distribución *m*
canal de distribution[2] (F)	Absatzweg *m*	channel of distribution	—	via della distribuzione *f*	medio de venta *m*
cancel (E)	löschen	—	annuler	cancellare	cancelar
cancelación (Es)	Stornierung *f*	cancellation	annulation *f*	storno *m*	—
cancelar (Es)	löschen	cancel	annuler	cancellare	—
cancellare (I)	löschen	cancel	annuler	—	cancelar
cancellation (E)	Stornierung *f*	—	annulation *f*	storno *m*	cancelación *f*/ anulación *f*/ contrapartida *f*
candidat (F)	Bewerber *m*	applicant	—	aspirante *m*	aspirante *m*
candidatura (Es)	Bewerbung *f*	application	candidature *f*	domanda d'impiego *f*	—
candidatura (I)	Anwartschaft *f*	candidature	candidature *f*	—	expectativa de un futuro pago *f*
candidature (E)	Anwartschaft *f*	—	candidature *f*	candidatura *f*	expectativa de un futuro pago *f*
candidature[1] (F)	Anwartschaft *f*	candidature	—	candidatura *f*	expectativa de un futuro pago *f*
candidature[2] (F)	Bewerbung *f*	application	—	domanda d'impiego *f*	candidatura *f*
canone di locazione[1] (I)	Miete *f*	rent	location *f*	—	alquiler *m*
canone di locazione[2] (I)	Mietzins *m*	rent	prix de location *m*	—	arrendamiento *m*
cantidad (Es)	Menge *f*	quantity	quantité *f*	quantità *f*	—
cantidad de compra (Es)	Abnahmemenge *f*	purchased quantity	quantité commercialisée *f*	quantità d'acquisto *f*	—
cantidad mínima[1] (Es)	Mindestmenge *f*	minimum quantity	quantité minimum *f*	quantitativo minimo *m*	—
cantidad mínima[2] (Es)	Mindesthöhe *f*	minimum amount	montant minimum *m*	importo minimo *m*	—
cantidad mínima de pedido (Es)	Mindestbestell- menge *f*	minimum quantity order	quantité commandée minimum *f*	quantitativo minimo di ordine *m*	—
cantidad pedida (Es)	Bestellmenge *f*	ordering quantity	quantité commandée *f*	quantità d'ordinazione *f*	—
cantidad producida[1] (Es)	Fördermenge *f*	output	quantité extraite *f*	quantitativo d'estrazione *m*	—
cantidad producida[2] (Es)	Fertigungsmenge *f*	manufactured quantity	quantité fabriquée *f*	quantitativo di produzione *m*	—
capability of asserting one's rights (E)	Durchsetzungs- vermögen *n*	—	capacité de se faire valoir *f*	capacità di imporsi *f*	capacidad de imponerse *f*
capability to establish public relations (E)	Kontaktfähigkeit *f*	—	capacité d'entrer en contact *f*	comunicativa *f*	capacidad de anudar contactos *f*
capability to innovate (E)	Innovationsfähigkeit *f*	—	capacité d'innovation *f*	capacità innovativa *f*	capacidad de innovación *f*
capable de jouir des droits (F)	rechtsfähig	capable of acting in law	—	avendo capacità giuridica	jurídicamente capaz
capable of acting in law (E)	rechtsfähig	—	capable de jouir des droits	avendo capacità giuridica	jurídicamente capaz
capacidad[1] (Es)	Fähigkeit *f*	ability	capacité *f*	capacità *f*	—
capacidad[2] (Es)	Kapazität *f*	capacity	capacité *f*	capacità *f*	—
capacidad[3] (Es)	Leistung *f*	performance	prestation *f*	capacità *f*	—
capacidad de almacenaje (Es)	Lagerkapazität *f*	storage capacity	capacité de stockage *f*	capacità di magazzino *f*	—
capacidad de anudar contactos (Es)	Kontaktfähigkeit *f*	capability to estab- lish public relations	capacité d'entrer en contact *f*	comunicativa *f*	—
capacidad de entrega (Es)	Lieferkapazität *f*	delivery capacity	capacité de livraison *f*	capacità di fornitura *f*	—
capacidad de imponerse (Es)	Durchsetzungs- vermögen *n*	capability of asserting one's right	capacité de se faire valoir *f*	capacità di imporsi *f*	—

capital aid

	D	E	F	I	Es
capacidad de innovación (Es)	Innovationsfähigkeit *f*	capability to innovate	capacité d'innovation *f*	capacità innovativa *f*	—
capacidad de memoria (Es)	Speicherkapazität *f*	storage capacity	capacité de mémoire *f*	capacità di memoria *f*	—
capacidad de producción (Es)	Produktionskapazität *f*	production capacity	capacité de production *f*	capacità produttiva *f*	—
capacidad jurídica (Es)	Rechtsfähigkeit *f*	legal capacity	capacité de jouissance des droits *f*	capacità giuridica *f*	—
capacidad negocial (Es)	Geschäftsfähigkeit *f*	capacity to enter into legal transactions	capacité d'accomplir des actes juridiques *f*	capacità di agire *f*	—
capacidad productiva (Es)	Leistungsfähigkeit *f*	efficiency	efficience *f*	efficienza *f*	—
capacità[1] (I)	Fähigkeit *f*	ability	capacité *f*	—	capacidad *f*
capacità[2] (I)	Kapazität *f*	capacity	capacité *f*	—	capacidad *f*
capacità[3] (I)	Leistung *f*	performance	rendement *m*	—	rendimiento *m*
capacità di agire (I)	Geschäftsfähigkeit *f*	capacity to enter into legal transactions	capacité d'accomplir des actes juridiques *f*	—	capacidad negocial *f*
capacità di credito (I)	Kreditfähigkeit *f*	financial standing	solvabilité *f*	—	crédito *m*
capacità di fornitura (I)	Lieferkapazität *f*	delivery capacity	capacité de livraison *f*	—	capacidad de entrega *f*
capacità di imposizione (I)	Durchsetzungsvermögen *n*	capability of asserting one's rights	capacité de se faire valoir *f*	—	capacidad de imponerse *f*
capacità di magazzino (I)	Lagerkapazität *f*	storage capacity	capacité de stockage *f*	—	capacidad de almacenaje *f*
capacità eccessiva (I)	Überkapazität *f*	overcapacity	surcapacité *f*	—	supercapacidad *f*
capacità giuridica (I)	Rechtsfähigkeit *f*	legal capacity	capacité de jouissance des droits *f*	—	capacidad jurídica *f*
capacità innovativa (I)	Innovationsfähigkeit *f*	capability to innovate	capacité d'innovation *f*	—	capacidad de innovación *f*
capacità produttiva (I)	Produktionskapazität *f*	production capacity	capacité de production *f*	—	capacidad de producción *f*
capacité[1] (F)	Fähigkeit *f*	ability	—	capacità *f*	capacidad *f*
capacité[2] (F)	Kapazität *f*	capacity	—	capacità *f*	capacidad *f*
capacité d'accomplir des actes juridiques (F)	Geschäftsfähigkeit *f*	capacity to enter into legal transactions	—	capacità di agire *f*	capacidad negocial *f*
capacité d'argumentation (F)	Argumentationsstärke *f*	talent for argumentation	—	forza d'argomentazione *f*	fuerza de argumentación *f*
capacité de jouissance des droits (F)	Rechtsfähigkeit *f*	legal capacity	—	capacità giuridica *f*	capacidad jurídica *f*
capacité de livraison (F)	Lieferkapazität *f*	delivery capacity	—	capacità di fornitura *f*	capacidad de entrega *f*
capacité d'entrer en contact (F)	Kontaktfähigkeit *f*	capability to establish public relations	—	comunicativa *f*	capacidad de anudar contactos *f*
capacité de production (F)	Produktionskapazität *f*	production capacity	—	capacità produttiva *f*	capacidad de producción *f*
capacité de se faire valoir (F)	Durchsetzungsvermögen *n*	capability of asserting one's rights	—	capacità di imporsi *f*	capacidad de imponerse *f*
capacité de stockage (F)	Lagerkapazität *f*	storage capacity	—	capacità di magazzino *f*	capacidad de almacenaje *f*
capacité d'innovation (F)	Innovationsfähigkeit *f*	capability to innovate	—	capacità innovativa *f*	capacidad de innovación *f*
capacity (E)	Kapazität *f*	—	capacité *f*	capacità *f*	capacidad *f*
capacity to enter into legal transactions (E)	Geschäftsfähigkeit *f*	—	capacité d'accomplir des actes juridiques *f*	capacità di agire *f*	capacidad negocial *f*
capacity utilisation rate (E)	Auslastungsgrad *m*	—	dégré de saturation *m*	grado di sfruttamento *m*	tasa de utilización *f*
capa del ozono (Es)	Ozonschicht *f*	ozone layer	ozonosphère *f*	strato d'ozono *m*	—
capital (E)	Kapital *n*	—	capital *m*	capitale *m*	capital *m*
capital (Es)	Kapital *n*	capital	capital *m*	capitale *m*	—
capital (F)	Kapital *n*	capital	—	capitale *m*	capital *m*
capital account (E)	Vermögensrechnung *f*	—	calcul du patrimoine *m*	calcolo del patrimonio *m*	cálculo del valor neto *m*
capital aid (E)	Kapitalhilfe *f*	—	aide financière *f*	aiuto finanziario *m*	ayuda financiera *f*

	D	E	F	I	Es
capital a largo plazo (Es)	langfristiges Kapital *n*	long-term capital	capital à long terme *m*	capitale a lungo termine *m*	—
capital à long terme (F)	langfristiges Kapital *n*	long-term capital	—	capitale a lungo termine *m*	capital a largo plazo *m*
capital base (E)	Kapitalbasis *f*	—	base de capital *f*	base di capitale *f*	base de capital *f*
capital circulante (Es)	Umlaufvermögen *n*	current assets/ floating assets	capital de roulement *m*	patrimonio circolante *m*	—
capital de explotación (Es)	Betriebskapital *n*	working capital	capital de roulement *m*	capitale d'esercizio *m*	—
capital de roulement¹ (F)	Umlaufvermögen *n*	current assets/ floating assets	—	patrimonio circolante *m*	capital circulante *m*
capital de roulement² (F)	Betriebskapital *n*	working capital	—	capitale d'esercizio *m*	capital de explotación *m*
capitale (I)	Kapital *n*	capital	capital *m*	—	capital *m*
capitale a lungo termine (I)	langfristiges Kapital *n*	long-term capital	capital à long terme *m*	—	capital a largo plazo *m*
capitale azionario (I)	Aktienkapital *n*	share capital	fonds social *m*	—	capital en acciones *m*
capitale d'esercizio (I)	Betriebskapital *n*	working capital	capital de roulement *m*	—	capital de explotación *m*
capitale estero (I)	Auslandskapital *n*	foreign capital	capital étranger *m*	—	capital extranjero *m*
capitale infruttifero (I)	totes Kapital *n*	unproductive capital	capital improductif *m*	—	capital improductivo *m*
capitale iniziale (I)	Anfangskapital *n*	opening capital	capital initial *m*	—	capital inicial *m*
capitale minimo (I)	Mindestkapital *n*	minimum capital	capital minimum *m*	—	capital mínimo *m*
capital en acciones (Es)	Aktienkapital *n*	share capital	fonds social *m*	capitale azionario *m*	—
capitale proprio (I)	Eigenkapital *n*	equity capital	capital propre *m*	—	capital propio *m*
capitale reale¹ (I)	Sachvermögen *n*	material assets	biens corporels *m pl*	—	patrimonio real *m*
capitale reale² (I)	Realkapital *n*	real capital	biens corporels immobilisés *m pl*	—	capital real *m*
capitale sociale¹ (I)	Stammkapital *n*	share capital/ nominal capital	capital social *m*	—	capital social *m*
capitale sociale² (I)	Grundkapital *n*	share capital	capital initial *m*	—	capital social *m*
capital étranger (F)	Auslandskapital *n*	foreign capital	—	capitale estero *m*	capital extranjero *m*
capitale versato (I)	eingezahltes Kapital *n*	paid-up capital	capital versé *m*	—	capitial desembolsado *m*
capital export (E)	Kapitalexport *m*	—	exportation de capitaux *f*	esportazione di capitale *f*	exportación de capital *f*
capital extranjero (Es)	Auslandskapital *n*	foreign capital	capital étranger *m*	capitale estero *m*	—
capital formation (E)	Vermögensbildung *f*	—	formation de capital *f*	formazione del patrimonio *f*	formación de capital *f*
capital goods¹ (E)	Investitionsgüter *pl*	—	biens d'investisse- ment *m pl*	beni di investimento *m pl*	bienes de inversión *m pl*
capital goods² (E)	Anlagegüter *pl*	—	valeur immobilisée *f*	beni d'investimento *m pl*	bienes de inversión *m pl*
capital import (E)	Kapitalimport *m*	—	importation de capitaux *f*	importazione di capitali *f*	importación de capital *f*
capital improductif (F)	totes Kapital *n*	unproductive capital	—	capitale infruttifero *m*	capital improductivo *m*
capital improductivo (Es)	totes Kapital *n*	unproductive capital	capital improductif *m*	capitale infruttifero *m*	—
capital inicial (Es)	Anfangskapital *n*	opening capital	capital initial *m*	capitale iniziale *m*	—
capital initial¹ (F)	Grundkapital *n*	share capital	—	capitale sociale *m*	capital social *m*
capital initial² (F)	Anfangskapital *n*	opening capital	—	capitale iniziale *m*	capital inicial *m*
capital-intensive (E)	kapitalintensiv	—	avec grande intensité de capital	ad alta incidenza di capitale	con gran intensidad de capital
capital investment (E)	Kapitalanlage *f*	—	investissement de capitaux *m*	investimento di capitale *m*	inversión de capital *f*
capitalisation (F)	Kapitalisierung *f*	capitalization	—	capitalizzazione *f*	capitalización *f*
capitalism (E)	Kapitalismus *m*	—	capitalisme *m*	capitalismo *m*	capitalismo *m*
capitalisme (F)	Kapitalismus *m*	capitalism	—	capitalismo *m*	capitalismo *m*
capitalismo (Es)	Kapitalismus *m*	capitalism	capitalisme *m*	capitalismo *m*	—
capitalismo (I)	Kapitalismus *m*	capitalism	capitalisme *m*	—	capitalismo *m*

	D	E	F	I	Es
capitalización (Es)	Kapitalisierung f	capitalization	capitalisation f	capitalizzazione f	—
capitalization (E)	Kapitalisierung f	—	capitalisation f	capitalizzazione f	capitalización f
capitalized value (E)	Ertragswert m	—	valeur d'une chose mesurée à son rendement f	valore del reddito m	valor de rendimiento m
capitalizzazione (I)	Kapitalisierung f	capitalization	capitalisation f	—	capitalización f
capital market (E)	Kapitalmarkt m	—	marché des capitaux m	mercato finanziario m	mercado financiero m
capital mínimo (Es)	Mindestkapital n	minimum capital	capital minimum m	capitale minimo m	—
capital minimum (F)	Mindestkapital n	minimum capital	—	capitale minimo m	capital mínimo m
capital productif (F)	Produktivvermögen n	productive property	—	patrimonio produttivo m	patrimonio productivo m
capital propio (Es)	Eigenkapital n	equity capital	capital propre m	capitale proprio m	—
capital propre (F)	Eigenkapital n	equity capital	—	capitale proprio m	capital propio m
capital real (Es)	Realkapital n	real capital	biens corporels immobilisés m pl	capitale reale m	—
capital requirements (E)	Kapitalbedarf m	—	besoin en capital m	domanda di capitale m	necesidad de capital f
capital resources (E)	Kapitalausstattung f	—	dotation en capital f	dotazione di capitale f	dotación de capital f
capital social (F)	Stammkapital n	share capital/ nominal capital	—	capitale sociale m	capital social m
capital social¹ (Es)	Stammkapital n	share capital/ nominal capital	capital social m	capitale sociale m	—
capital social² (Es)	Grundkapital n	share capital	capital initial m	capitale sociale m	—
capital stock (E)	Kapitalstock m	—	réserve de capital f	riserva di capitale f	fondo de capital m
capital suscrito¹ (Es)	eingezahltes Kapital n	paid-up capital	capital versé m	capitale versato m	—
capital suscrito² (Es)	Stammeinlage f	initial contribution	apport social m	quota sociale f	—
capital theory (E)	Kapitaltheorie f	—	théorie du capital f	teoria del capitale f	teoría financiera f
capital transactions (E)	Kapitalverkehr m	—	mouvement des capitaux m	movimento dei capitali m	circulación de capitales f
capital turnover (E)	Kapitalumschlag m	—	roulement des capitaux m	rotazione del capitale f	rotación del capital f
capital value (E)	Kapitalwert m	—	valeur en capital f	valore del capitale m	valor capitalizado m
capital versé (F)	eingezahltes Kapital n	paid-up capital	—	capitale versato m	capital desembolsado m
capo (I)	Chef m	head	chef m	—	jefe m
Capodanno (I)	Neujahr n	New Year	nouvel an m	—	(día de) Año Nuevo m
capo reparto (I)	Abteilungsleiter m	head of department	chef de service m	—	jefe de sección m
capo reparto personale (I)	Personalleiter m	staff manager	chef du personnel m	—	jefe de personal m
capo reparto spedizioni (I)	Versandleiter m	manager of shipping department	chef du service des expéditions m	—	jefe del departamento de expedición m
caractère sérieux (F)	Seriosität f	seriousness	—	serietà f	buena reputación f
característica (Es)	Marke f	mark	marque f	marca f	—
característica de requisitos (Es)	Anforderungs- merkmal n	requirement characteristics	caractéristique d'exigences f	caratteristica richiesta f	—
caractéristique d'exigences (F)	Anforderungs- merkmal n	requirement characteristics	—	caratteristica richiesta f	característica de requisitos f
carat (E)	Karat n	—	carat m	carato m	quilate m
carat (F)	Karat n	carat	—	carato m	quilate m
carato (I)	Karat n	carat	carat m	—	quilate m
caratteristica richiesta (I)	Anforderungs- merkmal n	requirement characteristics	caractéristique d'exigences f	—	característica de requisitos f
caratteristiche promesse (I)	zugesicherte Eigenschaften pl	warranted characteristics	qualité promise f	—	calidades aseguradas f pl
carbone fossile (I)	Steinkohle f	hard coal	houille f	—	hulla f
carburant (F)	Treibstoff m	fuel	—	carburante m	combustible m
carburante (I)	Treibstoff m	fuel	carburant m	—	combustible m
card-index (E)	Kartei f	—	cartothèque	schedario m	fichero m
carga (Es)	Fracht f	freight	fret m	nolo m	—

	D	E	F	I	Es
carga colectiva (Es)	Sammelladung f	collective consignment	envoi par groupage m	carico a collettame m	—
carga de la prueba (Es)	Beweislast f	burden of proof	charge de la preuve f	onere di prova m	—
carga de un vagón (Es)	Wagenladung f	lorryload	charge de voiture f	carico di autocarro m	—
carga extraordinaria (Es)	außergewöhnliche Belastung f	extraordinary expenses	charges exceptionnelles f pl	oneri straordinari m pl	—
carga por expreso (Es)	Expressgut n	express goods	colis express m	merce spedita per espresso f	—
cargar (Es)	belasten	load/charge	débiter	addebitare	—
cargas salariales accesorias (Es)	Lohnnebenkosten pl	ancillary wage costs	charges salariales annexes f pl	costi complementari del lavoro m pl	—
carga suplementaria (Es)	Mehrbelastung f	additional burden	surcharge f	onere supplementare m	—
cargo (E)	Frachtgut n	—	marchandise à transporter f	merce di trasporto f	mercancías en pequeña velocidad f pl
cargo (Es)	Amt n	office	bureau m	ufficio m	—
cargo en cuenta (Es)	Lastschrift f	debit note	note de débit f	addebito m	—
caricare (I)	verladen	load	charger	—	expedir
carico a collettame (I)	Sammelladung f	collective consignment	envoi par groupage m	—	carga colectiva f
carico di autocarro (I)	Wagenladung f	lorryload	charge de voiture f	—	carga de un vagón f
carico pesante (I)	Schwergut n	heavy freight	produit pondéreux m	—	mercancía pesada f
carné de empresa (Es)	Betriebsausweis m	staff identification card	pièce d'identité de l'entreprise f	tessera aziendale f	—
carné de identidad (Es)	Personalausweis m	identity card	pièce d'identité f	carta d'identità f	—
carnet de chèques (F)	Scheckheft n	cheque book	—	carnet degli assegni m	libreta de cheques f
carnet degli assegni (I)	Scheckheft n	cheque book	carnet de chèques m	—	libreta de cheques f
carriage of goods (E)	Güterbeförderung f	—	transport de marchandises m	trasporto di merci m	transporte de mercancías m
carriage of goods by sea (E)	Verfrachtung f	—	affrètement m	trasporto marittimo m	expedición f
carriage of passengers (E)	Personenbeförderung f	—	transport de personnes m	trasporto di persone m	transporte de personas m
carrier (E)	Frachtführer m	—	transporteur m	vettore m	transportista m
carta (Es)	Brief m	letter	lettre f	lettera f	—
carta (ad)monitoria (Es)	Mahnbrief m	reminder	lettre d'avertissement f	lettera di sollecito f	—
carta assegni (I)	Scheckkarte f	cheque card	carte d'identité eurochèque f	—	tarjeta de cheques f
carta certificada (Es)	Einschreibebrief m	registered letter	lettre recommandée f	lettera raccomandata f	—
carta certificada con talón de recibo (Es)	Einschreiben-Rückschein m	recorded registered letter (with advice)	lettre recommandée avec avis de réception f	lettera raccomandata con ricevuta di ritorno f	—
carta de agradecimiento (Es)	Dankschreiben n	letter of thanks	lettre de remerciement f	lettera di ringraziamento f	—
carta de confirmación (Es)	Schlußbrief m	letter of confirmation	lettre de confirmation des conditions f	lettera di conferma f	—
carta de crédito (Es)	Kreditbrief m	letter of credit	lettre de crédit f	lettera di credito f	—
carta de crédito bancaria (Es)	Bankakkreditiv n	bank letter of credit	accréditif bancaire m	lettera di credito bancario f	—
carta de crédito comercial (Es)	Handelskreditbrief m	commercial letter of credit	lettre de crédit commercial f	lettera di credito commerciale f	—
carta de pago (Es)	Zahlkarte f	money order	mandat-carte m	modulo di versamento m	—
carta de porte (Es)	Frachtbrief m	consignment note	lettre de voiture f	lettera di vettura f	—
carta de recomendación (Es)	Empfehlungsschreiben n	letter of recommendation	lettre de recommandation f	lettera di raccomandazione f	—
carta de solicitud (Es)	Bewerbungsschreiben n	letter of application	lettre de demande d'emploi f	domanda d'impiego f	—
carta di credito (I)	Kreditkarte f	credit card	carte accréditive f	—	tarjeta de crédito f
carta d'identità (I)	Personalausweis m	identity card	pièce d'identité f	—	carné de identidad m

	D	E	F	I	Es
carta urgente (Es)	Eilbrief *m*	express letter	lettre par exprès *f*	lettera espresso *f*	—
carte accréditive (F)	Kreditkarte *f*	credit card	—	carta di credito *f*	tarjeta de crédito *f*
carte de garantie (F)	Garantiekarte *f*	certificate of warranty	—	certificato di garanzia *m*	tarjeta de garantía *f*
carte d'identité eurochèque (F)	Scheckkarte *f*	cheque card	—	carta assegni *f*	tarjeta de cheques *f*
cartel (E)	Kartell *n*	—	cartel *m*	cartello *m*	cártel *m*
cartel (Es)	Plakat *n*	poster	affiche *f*	manifesto *m*	—
cartel (F)	Kartell *n*	cartel	—	cartello *m*	cártel *m*
cártel (Es)	Kartell *n*	cartel	cartel *m*	cartello *m*	—
cartel authority (E)	Kartellbehörde *f*	—	office de surveillance des cartels et ententes *m*	autorità antimonopoli *f pl*	oficina de cártels *f*
cartel de acción (Es)	Aktionsplakat *n*	advertising bill	affiche d'action *f*	manifesto promozionale *m*	—
cartel formation (E)	Kartellbildung *f*	—	cartellisation *f*	costituzione di cartelli *f*	formación de carteles *f*
cartella campioni (I)	Mustermappe *f*	sample bag	dossier à échantillons *m*	—	muestrario *m*
cartella delle imposte (I)	Steuerbescheid *m*	notice of assessment	avis d'imposition *m*	—	liquidación de impuestos *f*
Cartel Law (E)	Kartellgesetz *n*	—	loi sur les cartels *f*	legge sui cartelli *f*	ley relativa a los cártels *f*
cartellisation (F)	Kartellbildung *f*	cartel formation	—	costituzione di cartelli *f*	formación de carteles *f*
cartello (I)	Kartell *n*	cartel	cartel *m*	—	cártel *m*
carte postale (F)	Postkarte *f*	postcard	—	cartolina postale *f*	tarjeta postal *f*
cartera (Es)	Portfolio *n*	portfolio	portefeuille *m*	portafoglio *m*	—
cartera de acciones (Es)	Aktienbestand *m*	shareholding	portefeuille d'actions *m*	portafoglio di azioni *m*	—
cartero (Es)	Postbote *m*	postman	facteur *m*	portalettere *m*	—
cartolina postale (I)	Postkarte *f*	postcard	carte postale *f*	—	tarjeta postal *f*
cartothèque (F)	Kartei *f*	card-index	—	schedario *m*	fichero *m*
casa editrice (I)	Verlag *m*	publishing house	maison d'édition *f*	—	editorial *f*
casa ficticia (Es)	Scheinfirma *f*	bogus firm	raison sociale imaginaire *f*	pseudoditta *f*	—
casa madre[1] (I)	Mutterhaus *n*	mother house	maison mère *f*	—	casa matriz *f*
casa madre[2] (I)	Stammhaus *n*	parent company	maison mère *f*	—	casa matriz *f*
casa matriz[1] (Es)	Stammhaus *n*	parent company	maison mère *f*	casa madre *f*	—
casa matriz[2] (Es)	Mutterhaus *n*	mother house	maison mère *f*	casa madre *f*	—
casella postale (I)	Postfach *n*	post office box	boîte postale *f*	—	apartado postal *m*
cash[1] (E)	Bargeld *n*	—	argent comptant *m*	denaro contante *m*	dinero efectivo *m*
cash[2] (E)	bar	—	comptant	in contanti	al contado
cash-and-carry clause (E)	Cash-and-carry-Klausel *f*	—	clause de prix sur place comptant *f*	clausola cash-and-carry *f*	cláusula page y llévatelo *f*
Cash-and-carry-Klausel (D)	—	cash-and-carry clause	clause de prix sur place comptant *f*	clausola cash-and-carry *f*	cláusula page y llévatelo *f*
cash assets (E)	Barvermögen *n*	—	valeurs réalisables à court terme ou disponibles *f pl*	patrimonio in contanti *m*	activo efectivo *m*
cash book (E)	Kassenbuch *n*	—	compte de caisse *m*	libro di cassa *m*	libro de caja *m*
cash credit (E)	Barkredit *m*	—	crédit de caisse *m*	credito per cassa *m*	crédito en efectivo *m*
cash discount[1] (E)	Barzahlungsrabatt *m*	—	remise pour payement comptant *f*	ribasso per pagamento in contanti *m*	descuento por pago al contado *m*
cash discount[2] (E)	Barzahlungskonto *n*	—	escompte de caisse *m*	sconto per pagamento in contanti *m*	descuento de pago al contado *m*
cash dispenser (E)	Bankomat *m*	—	billetterie *m*	bancomat *m*	cajero automático *m*
cash forecasting plan (E)	Liquiditätsplan *m*	—	plan de liquidité *m*	piano della liquidità *m*	plan de liquidez *m*
cashier (E)	Kassierer *m*	—	caissier *m*	cassiere *m*	cajero *m*
cash in hand (E)	Bargeldbestand *m*	—	espèces en caisse *f pl*	denaro contante in cassa *m*	saldo en efectivo *m*

	D	E	F	I	Es
cash letter of credit (E)	Barakkreditiv	—	accréditif payable en espèce *m*	apertura di credito documentario semplice *f*	crédito simple *m*
cash on delivery[1] (E)	Nachnahme *f*	—	remboursement *m*	contrassegno *m*	reembolso *m*
cash on delivery[2] (E)	gegen Nachnahme	—	contre remboursement	contro assegno	contra rembolso
cash on delivery[3] (E)	Zahlung per Nachnahme *f*	—	payement contre remboursement *m*	pagamento contro assegno *m*	pago contra reembolso *m*
cash on delivery[4] (E)	Lieferung gegen Nachnahme *f*	—	livraison contre remboursement *f*	consegna contro assegno *f*	entrega contra reembolso *f*
cash payment (E)	Barzahlung *f*	—	payement comptant *m*	pagamento in contanti *m*	pago al contado *m*
caso di sinistro (I)	Versicherungsfall *m*	event insured against	sinistre *m*	—	situación de siniestro *f*
cassa (I)	Kiste *f*	box	caisse *f*	—	caja *f*
cassa continua (I)	Nachttresor *m*	night safe	dépôt de nuit *m*	—	depósito de noche *m*
cassa di risparmio (I)	Sparkasse *f*	savings bank	institut bancaire d'épargne *m*	—	caja de ahorros *f*
cassaforte (I)	Tresor *m*	safe	coffre-fort *m*	—	caja fuerte *f*
cassetta di sicurezza (I)	Safe *m*	safe	coffre-fort *m*	—	caja de seguridad *f*
cassetta postale (I)	Briefkasten *m*	mail box	boîte aux lettres *f*	—	buzón *m*
cassiere (I)	Kassierer *m*	cashier	caissier *m*	—	cajero *m*
catalizador (Es)	Katalysator *m*	catalytic converter	catalyseur *m*	catalizzatore *m*	—
catalizzatore (I)	Katalysator *m*	catalytic converter	catalyseur *m*	—	catalizador *m*
catálogo (Es)	Katalog *m*	catalogue	catalogue *m*	catalogo *m*	—
catalogo (I)	Katalog *m*	catalogue	catalogue *m*	—	catálogo *m*
catalogue (E)	Katalog *m*	—	catalogue *m*	catalogo *m*	catálogo *m*
catalogue (F)	Katalog *m*	catalogue	—	catalogo *m*	catálogo *m*
catalyseur (F)	Katalysator *m*	catalytic converter	—	catalizzatore *m*	catalizador *m*
catalytic converter (E)	Katalysator *m*	—	catalyseur *m*	catalizzatore *m*	catalizador *m*
catasto (I)	Kataster *m*	cadaster	cadastre *m*	—	catastro *m*
catastro (Es)	Kataster *m*	cadaster	cadastre *m*	catasto *m*	—
categoria[1] (I)	Sorte *f*	variety/foreign notes and coins	genre *m*/devises *f pl*	—	especie *f*/calidad *f*/ marca *f*/moneda extranjera *f*
categoria[2] (I)	Branche *f*	line of business	branche *f*	—	ramo *m*
categoria commerciale (I)	Handelsklasse *f*	grade	catégorie de produits *f*	—	clase *f*
categoría de calidad (Es)	Güteklasse *f*	grade	catégorie de qualité *f*	qualità *f*	—
categoría de mercancías (Es)	Warenart *f*	class of goods	catégorie de marchandise *f*	tipo di merce *m*	—
catégorie de marchandise (F)	Warenart *f*	class of goods	—	tipo di merce *m*	categoría de mercancías *f*
catégorie de produits (F)	Handelsklasse *f*	grade	—	categoria commerciale *f*	clase *f*
catégorie de qualité (F)	Güteklasse *f*	grade	—	qualità *f*	categoría de calidad *f*
category of goods (E)	Gütergruppe *f*	—	groupe de marchandises *m*	gruppo di merci *m*	grupo de mercancías *m*
caución (Es)	Kaution *f*	security/bond	caution *f*	cauzione *f*	—
caución de licitación (Es)	Bietungsgarantie *f*	tender guarantee	cautionnement provisoire *m*	garanzia d'offerta *f*	—
causa (I)	Rechtsstreit *m*	legal action	litige *m*	—	conflicto jurídico *m*
causa ereditaria (I)	Erbstreit *m*	dispute concerning an inheritance	action successorale *f*	—	litigio hereditario *m*
causing environmental damage (E)	umweltschädlich	—	nuisible à l'environnement	inquinante	contaminante
caution[1] (F)	Bürgschaft *f*	guarantee	—	fideiussione *f*	fianza *f*
caution[2] (F)	Kaution *f*	security/bond	—	cauzione *f*	caución *f*/garantía *f*
caution de garantie (F)	Gewährleistungs- garantie *f*	guarantee for proper execution	—	garanzia di esecuzione *f*	fianza de contratista *f*

	D	E	F	I	Es
cautionnement provisoire (F)	Bietungsgarantie *f*	tender guarantee	—	garanzia d'offerta *f*	caución de licitación *f*
caution pour être mis en liberté (F)	Haftkaution *f*	bail	—	cauzione per la scarcerazione *f*	fianza de puesta en libertad *f*
cauzione (I)	Kaution *f*	security/bond	caution *f*	—	caución *f*/garantía *f*
cauzione per la scarcerazione (I)	Haftkaution *f*	bail	caution pour être mis en liberté *f*	—	fianza de puesta en libertad *f*
cédant (F)	Zedent *m*	assignor	—	cedente *m*	cedente *m*
cedente (Es)	Zedent *m*	assignor	cédant *m*	cedente *m*	—
cedente (I)	Zedent *m*	assignor	cédant *m*	—	cedente *m*
cedola (I)	Coupon *m*	coupon	coupon *m*	—	cupón *m*
cédula hipotecaria (Es)	Pfandbrief *m*	mortgage bond	obligation hypothécaire *f*	titolo ipotecario *m*	—
ceiling (E)	Plafond *m*	—	plafond *m*	plafond *m*	límite máximo *m*
censimento (I)	Volkszählung *f*	census of population	recensement démographique *m*	—	censo *m*
censo (Es)	Volkszählung *f*	census of population	recensement démographique *m*	censimento *m*	—
census of population (E)	Volkszählung *f*	—	recensement démographique *m*	censimento *m*	censo *m*
central bank[1] (E)	Zentralbank *f*	—	banque centrale *f*	Banca Centrale *f*	banco emisor *m*
central bank[2] (E)	Notenbank *f*	—	banque d'émission *f*	banca d'emissione *f*	banco emisor *m*
Central Bank Council (E)	Zentralbankrat *m*	—	Conseil de la Banque Centrale *m*	consiglio superiore della Banca Centrale *m*	Consejo del Banco Central *m*
central de giros (Es)	Girozentrale *f*	central giro institution	banque centrale de virement *f*	stanza centrale di compensazione *f*	—
centrale nucléaire (F)	Atomkraftwerk *n*	nuclear power plant	—	centrale nucleare *f*	central nuclear *f*
centrale nucleare (I)	Atomkraftwerk *n*	nuclear power plant	centrale nucléaire *f*	—	central nuclear *f*
central giro institution (E)	Girozentrale *f*	—	banque centrale de virement *f*	stanza centrale di compensazione *f*	central de giros *f*
central interurbana (Es)	Fernmeldeamt *n*	telephone exchange	service de télécommunication *m*	ufficio telecomunicazioni *m*	—
centralisation (F)	Zentralisierung *f*	centralization	—	centralizzazione *f*	centralización *f*
centralización (Es)	Zentralisierung *f*	centralization	centralisation *f*	centralizzazione *f*	—
centralization (E)	Zentralisierung *f*	—	centralisation *f*	centralizzazione *f*	centralización *f*
centralizzazione (I)	Zentralisierung *f*	centralization	centralisation *f*	—	centralización *f*
centrally controlled economy (E)	zentrale Planwirtschaft *f*	—	économie planifiée centrale *f*	economia pianificata *f*	economía planificada central *f*
central nuclear (Es)	Atomkraftwerk *n*	nuclear power plant	centrale nucléaire *f*	centrale nucleare *f*	—
central rate (E)	Leitkurs *m*	—	taux central *m*	parità centrale *f*	tipo pivote *m*
central unit (E)	Zentraleinheit *f*	—	unité centrale *f*	unità centrale *f*	unidad central *f*
centre commercial (F)	Shopping Center *n*	shopping centre	—	centro commerciale *m*	centro comercial *m*
centre de calcul (F)	Rechenzentrum *n*	computer centre	—	centro da computer *m*	centro de computación *m*
centro comercial (Es)	Shopping Center *n*	shopping centre	centre commercial *m*	centro commerciale *m*	—
centro commerciale (I)	Shopping Center *n*	shopping centre	centre commercial *m*	—	centro comercial *m*
centro da computer (I)	Rechenzentrum *n*	computer centre	centre de calcul *m*	—	centro de computación *m*
centro de computación (Es)	Rechenzentrum *n*	computer centre	centre de calcul *m*	centro da computer *m*	—
certificado[1] (Es)	per Einschreiben	by registered post	sous pli recommandé	per raccomandata	—
certificado[2] (Es)	Zertifikat *n*	certificate	certificat *m*	certificato *m*	—
certificado[3] (Es)	Einschreiben *n*	Registered	en recommandé	raccomandata *f*	—
certificado de aduana (Es)	Zolleinfuhrschein *m*	bill of entry	acquit d'entrée *m*	bolletta d'entrata *m*	—
certificado de avería (Es)	Havariezertifikat *n*	survey/ damage report	certificat d'avarie *m*	certificato d'avaria *m*	—
certificado de divisas (Es)	Devisen- genehmigung *f*	foreign exchange authorization	autorisation de change *f*	autorizzazione valutaria *f*	—

certificado de escuela

	D	E	F	I	Es
certificado de escuela (Es)	Zeugnis n	school report	certificat scolaire m	pagella f	—
certificado de origen (Es)	Ursprungszeugnis n	certificate of origin	certificat d'origine m	certificato d'origine m	—
certificado de participación (Es)	Investmentzertifikat n	investment certificate	certificat émis par un fonds commun de placement m	certificato d'investimento m	—
certificado de sanidad (Es)	Gesundheitszeugnis n	health certificate	certificat de santé m	certificato sanitario m	—
certificado policial (Es)	polizeiliches Führungszeugnis n	police certificate of good conduct	certificat de bonnes vie et mœurs m	certificato di buona condotta m	—
certificado provisional (Es)	Zwischenzeugnis n	interim report	certificat provisoire m	certificato provvisorio m	—
certificat (F)	Zertifikat n	certificate	—	certificato m	certificado m
certificat d'attestation du brevet d'invention (F)	Patenturkunde f	patent document	—	brevetto m	patente f
certificat d'avarie (F)	Havariezertifikat n	survey/ damage report	—	certificato d'avaria m	certificado de avería m
certificat de bonnes vie et mœurs (F)	polizeiliches Führungszeugnis n	police certificate of good conduct	—	certificato di buona condotta m	certificado policial m
certificat de dépôt (F)	Lagerschein m	warehouse warrant	—	ricevuta di deposito f	resguardo de almacén m
certificat de santé (F)	Gesundheitszeugnis n	health certificate	—	certificato sanitario m	certificado de sanidad m
certificat d'origine (F)	Ursprungszeugnis n	certificate of origin	—	certificato d'origine m	certificado de origen m
certificate (E)	Zertifikat n	—	certificat m	certificato m	certificado m
certificat émis par un fonds commun de placement (F)	Investmentzertifikat n	investment certificate	—	certificato d'investimento m	certificado de participación m
certificate of indebtedness (E)	Schuldschein m	—	billet de créance m	certificato di debito m	pagaré m
certificate of origin (E)	Ursprungszeugnis n	—	certificat d'origine m	certificato d'origine m	certificado de origen m
certificate of warranty (E)	Garantiekarte f	—	carte de garantie f	certificato di garanzia m	tarjeta de garantía f
certification (F)	Beglaubigung f	authentication	—	autenticazione f	legalización f
certificato (I)	Zertifikat n	certificate	certificat m	—	certificado m
certificato d'avaria (I)	Havariezertifikat n	survey/ damage report	certificat d'avarie m	—	certificado de avería m
certificato di buona condotta (I)	polizeiliches Führungszeugnis n	police certificate of good conduct	certificat de bonnes vie et mœurs m	—	certificado policial m
certificato di debito (I)	Schuldschein m	certificate of indebtedness	billet de créance m	—	pagaré m
certificato di garanzia (I)	Garantiekarte f	certificate of warranty	carte de garantie f	—	tarjeta de garantía f
certificato d'investimento (I)	Investmentzertifikat n	investment certificate	certificat émis par un fonds commun de placement m	—	certificado de participación m
certificato d'origine (I)	Ursprungszeugnis n	certificate of origin	certificat d'origine m	—	certificado de origen m
certificato provvisorio (I)	Zwischenzeugnis n	interim report	certificat provisoire m	—	certificado provisional m
certificato sanitario (I)	Gesundheitszeugnis n	health certificate	certificat de santé m	—	certificado de sanidad m
certificat provisoire (F)	Zwischenzeugnis n	interim report	—	certificato provvisorio m	certificado provisional m
certificat scolaire (F)	Zeugnis n	school report	—	pagella f	certificado de escuela m
cesión (Es)	Abtretung f	assignment	cession f	cessione f	—
cesionario (Es)	Zessionar m	assignee	cessionnaire m	cessionario m	—
cesión en bloque (Es)	Globalzession f	global assignment	cession globale f	cessione globale f	—
cessation of payments (E)	Zahlungseinstellung f	—	suspension de payement f	cessazione dei pagamenti f	suspensión de pagos f
cessazione dei pagamenti (I)	Zahlungseinstellung f	cessation of payments	suspension de payement f	—	suspensión de pagos f

	D	E	F	I	Es
cession (F)	Abtretung f	assignment	—	cessione f	cesión f
cessionario (I)	Zessionar m	assignee	cessionnaire m	—	cesionario m
cessione (I)	Abtretung f	assignment	cession f	—	cesión f
cessione globale (I)	Globalzession f	global assignment	cession globale f	—	cesión en bloque f
cession globale (F)	Globalzession f	global assignment	—	cessione globale f	cesión en bloque f
cessionnaire (F)	Zessionar m	assignee	—	cessionario m	cesionario m
ceto medio (I)	Mittelstand m	middle class(es)	classe moyenne f	—	clase media f
chairman of the board (E)	Vorstands-vorsitzender m	—	président du comité de direction m	presidente del consiglio di amministrazione m	presidente del consejo m
chairman of the supervisory board (E)	Aufsichtsrats-vorsitzender m	—	président du conseil de surveillance m	presidente del consiglio di sorveglianza m	presidente del consejo de vigilancia m
chairmanship (E)	Vorsitz m	—	présidence f	presidenza f	presidencia f
Chamber of Commerce (E)	Handelskammer f	—	chambre de commerce f	camera di commercio f	cámara de comercio f
chamber of foreign trade (E)	Außenhandels-kammer f	—	chambre du commerce extérieur f	camera di commer-cio estero f	cámara del comercio exterior f
chamber of handicrafts (E)	Handwerkskammer f	—	chambre artisanale f	camera dell'artigianato f	cámara de artesanía f
Chamber of Industry and Commerce (E)	Industrie- und Han-delskammer f	—	chambre de commer-ce et d'industrie f	camera di commercio e industria f	cámara de industria y comercio f
chambre artisanale (F)	Handwerkskammer f	chamber of handicrafts	—	camera dell'artigianato f	cámara de artesanía f
chambre de commerce (F)	Handelskammer f	Chamber of Commerce	—	camera di commercio f	cámara de comercio f
chambre de commerce et d'industrie (F)	Industrie- und Han-delskammer f	Chamber of Industry and Commerce	—	camera di commercio e industria f	cámara de industria y comercio f
chambre du commerce extérieur (F)	Außenhandels-kammer f	chamber of foreign trade	—	camera di commercio estero f	cámara del comercio exterior f
champ d'acitivité (F)	Tätigkeitsfeld n	field of activity	—	campo d'azione m	campo de actividad m
champ d'action (F)	Aktionsfeld n	field of action	—	campo d'azione m	campo de acción m
changement dans les structures (F)	Strukturwandel m	structural change	—	cambiamenti strutturali m pl	cambio de estructuras m
changement d'emploi¹ (F)	Stellungswechsel m	change of employment	—	cambiamento del posto di lavoro m	cambio de empleo m
changement d'emploi² (F)	Arbeitsplatz-wechsel m	change of employment	—	cambiamento del posto di lavoro m	cambio de puesto m
change of employment¹ (E)	Arbeitsplatz-wechsel m	—	changement d'emploi m	cambiamento del posto di lavoro m	cambio de puesto m
change of employment² (E)	Stellungswechsel m	—	changement d'emploi m	cambiamento del posto di lavoro m	cambio de empleo m
change of residence¹ (E)	Umzug m	—	déménagement m	trasferimento m	mudanza f
change of residence² (E)	Wohnungswechsel m	—	transfert de résidence m	cambiamento dell'abitazione m	cambio de vivienda m
change of shift (E)	Schichtwechsel m	—	relève d'équipe f	cambio di turno m	cambio del equipo de obreros m
changes in purchasing power (E)	Kaufkraftänderung f	—	modification du pou-voir d'achat f	mutamento del po-tere d'acquisto m	cambio en el poder adquisitivo m
channel of distribution (E)	Absatzweg m	—	canal de distribution m	via della distribuzione f	medio de venta f
charge (F)	Belastung f	load	—	addebito m	gravamen m
chargeable to (E)	zu Lasten	—	à la charge de	a carico di	a cargo de
charge de la preuve (F)	Beweislast f	burden of proof	—	onere di prova f	carga de la prueba f
charge de voiture (F)	Wagenladung f	lorryload	—	carico di autocarro m	carga de un vagón f
charge levied (E)	Umlage f	—	répartition f	ripartizione f	reparto m
charge primaire (F)	Primäraufwand m	primary expenses	—	spese primarie f pl	gastos directos m pl
charger (F)	verladen	load	—	caricare	expedir
charges d'exploitation¹ (F)	Betriebsausgaben f	(current) operational expenses	—	spese aziendali f pl	gastos de explotación m pl
charges d'exploitation² (F)	Betriebskosten pl	operating costs	—	spese d'esercizio f pl	gastos de explotación m pl

	D	E	F	I	Es
charges exceptionnelles (F)	außergewöhnliche Belastung *f*	extraordinary expenses	—	oneri straordinari *m pl*	carga extraordinaria *f*
charges salariales annexes (F)	Lohnnebenkosten *pl*	ancillary wage costs	—	costi complementari del lavoro *m pl*	cargas salariales accesorias *f pl*
charter flight (E)	Charterflug *m*	—	vol charter *m*	volo charter *m*	vuelo fletado *m*
Charterflug (D)	—	charter flight	vol charter *m*	volo charter *m*	vuelo fletado *m*
charter party (E)	Chartervertrag *m*	—	contrat d'affrètement *m*	contratto di noleggio *m*	contrato de fletamento *m*
Chartervertrag (D)	—	charter party	contrat d'affrètement *m*	contratto di noleggio *m*	contrato de fletamento *m*
cheapening (E)	Verbilligung *f*	—	réduction du prix *f*	ribasso *m*	abaratamiento *m*
checklist (E)	Checkliste *f*	—	liste de contrôle *f*	lista di controllo *f*	lista de control *f*
Checkliste (D)	—	checklist	liste de contrôle *f*	lista di controllo *f*	lista de control *f*
Chef (D)	—	head	chef *m*	capo *m*	jefe *m*
chef¹ (F)	Chef *m*	head	—	capo *m*	jefe *m*
chef² (F)	Anführer *m*	leader	—	leader *m*	líder *m*
chef de service (F)	Abteilungsleiter *m*	head of department	—	capo reparto *m*	jefe de sección *m*
chef de vente régionale (F)	Gebietsverkaufs-leiter *m*	area sales manager	—	direttore di vendita regionale *m*	jefe de venta regional *m*
chef du personnel (F)	Personalleiter *m*	staff manager	—	capo reparto personale *m*	jefe de personal *m*
chef du service des expéditions (F)	Versandleiter *m*	manager of shipping department	—	capo reparto spedizioni *m*	jefe del departamento de expedición *m*
Chemie (D)	—	chemistry	chimie *f*	chimica *f*	química *f*
chemistry (E)	Chemie *f*	—	chimie *f*	chimica *f*	química *f*
cheque (Es)	Scheck *m*	cheque	chèque *m*	assegno *m*	—
chèque (F)	Scheck *m*	cheque	—	assegno *m*	cheque *m*
cheque (E)	Scheck *m*	—	chèque *m*	assegno *m*	cheque *m*
cheque a la orden (Es)	Orderscheck *m*	order cheque	chèque à ordre *m*	assegno all'ordine *m*	—
cheque al portador¹ (Es)	Inhaberscheck *m*	cheque payable to bearer	chèque au porteur *m*	assegno al portatore *m*	—
cheque al portador² (Es)	Überbringerscheck *m*	bearer cheque	chèque au porteur *m*	assegno al portatore *m*	—
chèque à ordre (F)	Orderscheck *m*	order cheque	—	assegno all'ordine *m*	cheque a la orden *m*
chèque à porter en compte (F)	Verrechnungs-scheck *m*	crossed cheque	—	assegno sbarrato *m*	cheque cruzado *m*
chèque antidaté (F)	vordatierter Scheck *m*	antedated cheque	—	assegno antidatato *m*	cheque de fecha adelantada *m*
chèque au porteur¹ (F)	Überbringerscheck *m*	bearer cheque	—	assegno al portatore *m*	cheque al portador *m*
chèque au porteur² (F)	Inhaberscheck *m*	cheque payable to bearer	—	assegno al portatore *m*	cheque al portador *m*
chèque barré (F)	gekreuzter Scheck *m*	crossed cheque	—	assegno sbarrato *m*	cheque cruzado *m*
cheque book¹ (E)	Scheckbuch *n*	—	livre d'enregistre-ment des chèques *m*	libretto degli assegni *m*	libro de cheques *m*
cheque book² (E)	Scheckheft *n*	—	carnet de chèques *m*	carnet degli assegni *m*	libreta de cheques *f*
cheque card (E)	Scheckkarte *f*	—	carte d'identité eurochèque *f*	carta assegni *f*	tarjeta de cheques *f*
cheque cruzado¹ (Es)	gekreuzter Scheck *m*	crossed cheque	chèque barré *m*	assegno sbarrato *m*	—
cheque cruzado² (Es)	Verrechnungs-scheck *m*	crossed cheque	chèque à porter en compte *m*	assegno sbarrato *m*	—
cheque de caja (Es)	Barscheck *m*	open cheque	chèque non barré *m*	assegno circolare *m*	—
cheque de fecha adelantada (Es)	vordatierter Scheck *m*	antedated cheque	chèque antitdaté *m*	assegno antidatato *m*	—
cheque de viaje (Es)	Reisescheck *m*	traveller's cheque	chèque de voyage *m*	assegno turistico *m*	—
chèque de voyage (F)	Reisescheck *m*	traveller's cheque	—	assegno turistico *m*	cheque de viaje *m*
chèque en blanc (F)	Blankoscheck *m*	blank cheque	—	assegno in bianco *m*	cheque en blanco *m*
cheque en blanco (Es)	Blankoscheck *m*	blank cheque	chèque en blanc *m*	assegno in bianco *m*	—
cheque falsificado (Es)	gefälschter Scheck *m*	forged cheque	chèque maquillé *m*	assegno falsificato *m*	—

	D	E	F	I	Es
cheque fraud (E)	Scheckbetrug *m*	—	irrégularité en matière de chèque *f*	emissione di assegno a vuoto *f*	falsificación de cheques *f*
chèque maquillé (F)	gefälschter Scheck *m*	forged cheque	—	assegno falsificato *m*	cheque falsificado *m*
chèque non barré (F)	Barscheck *m*	open cheque	—	assegno circolare *m*	cheque de caja *m*
cheque payable to bearer (E)	Inhaberscheck *m*	—	chèque au porteur *m*	assegno al portatore *m*	cheque al portador *m*
cheque postal (Es)	Postscheck *m*	postal giro	chèque postal *m*	assegno postale *m*	—
chèque postal (F)	Postscheck *m*	postal giro	—	assegno postale *m*	cheque postal *m*
chiarezza di bilancio (I)	Bilanzwahrheit *f*	truth in the balance sheet	sincérité du bilan *f*	—	sinceridad del balance *f*
Chiffre-Anzeige (D)	—	advertisement under a box number	annonce chiffrée *f*	inserzione in cifra *f*	anuncio codificado *m*
chiffre d'affaires (F)	Umsatz *m*	turnover	—	fatturato *m*	volumen de ventas *m*
chiffre d'affaires minimum (F)	Mindestumsatz *m*	minimum turnover	—	fatturato minimo *m*	cifra de venta mínima *f*
chiffre d'affaires net (F)	Nettoumsatz *m*	net turnover	—	fatturato netto *m*	ventas netas *f pl*
chiffres prévisionnels (F)	Sollzahlen *pl*	target figures	—	cifre calcolate *f pl*	cifras estimadas *f pl*
chiffres rouges (F)	rote Zahlen *pl*	(in) the red	—	conti in rosso *m pl*	cifras rojas *f pl*
chimica (I)	Chemie *f*	chemistry	chimie *f*	—	química *f*
chimie (F)	Chemie *f*	chemistry	—	chimica *f*	química *f*
chi si assume i costi (I)	Kostenträger *m*	unit assuming cost	poste de production absorbant des coûts *m*	—	que sufraga los costes
chiusura d'esercizio (I)	Jahresabschluß *m*	annual accounts	clôture annuelle des comptes *f*	—	cierre de cuentos *m*
choice of location (E)	Standortwahl *f*	—	choix du lieu d'implantation *m*	scelta dell'ubicazione *f*	elección de la ubicación *f*
choix du lieu d'implantation (F)	Standortwahl *f*	choice of location	—	scelta dell'ubicazione *f*	elección de la ubicación *f*
chômage (F)	Arbeitslosigkeit *f*	unemployment	—	disoccupazione *f*	desempleo *m*
chômage saisonnier (F)	saisonale Arbeitslosigkeit *f*	seasonal unemployment	—	disoccupazione stagionale *f*	paro estacional *m*
chômage structurel (F)	strukturelle Arbeitslosigkeit *f*	structural unemployment	—	disoccupazione strutturale *f*	paro estructural *m*
Christmas (E)	Weihnachten *n*	—	Noël *m*	Natale *m*	Navidad *f*
chute des cours (F)	Kurs-zusammenbruch *m*	collapse of prices	—	crollo delle quotazioni *m*	caída de los cambios *f*
chute des prix (F)	Preisverfall *m*	decline in prices	—	caduta dei prezzi *f*	caída de precios *f*
cibernética (Es)	Kybernetik *f*	cybernetics	cybernétique *f*	cibernetica *f*	—
cibernetica (I)	Kybernetik *f*	cybernetics	cybernétique *f*	—	cibernética *f*
ciclo (Es)	Zyklus *m*	cycle	cycle *m*	ciclo *m*	—
ciclo (I)	Zyklus *m*	cycle	cycle *m*	—	ciclo *m*
ciclo congiunturale (I)	Konjunkturzyklus *m*	business cycle	cycle conjoncturel *m*	—	ciclo económico *m*
ciclo de vida (Es)	Lebenszyklus *m*	life cycle	cycle de vie *m*	ciclo di vita *m*	—
ciclo di magazzinaggio (I)	Lagerzyklus *m*	stock cycle	cycle de stockage *m*	—	período de almacenaje *m*
ciclo di vita (I)	Lebenszyklus *m*	life cycle	cycle de vie *m*	—	ciclo de vida *m*
ciclo económico (Es)	Konjunkturzyklus *m*	business cycle	cycle conjoncturel *m*	ciclo congiunturale *m*	—
ciencias económicas[1] (Es)	Wirtschafts-wissenschaften *pl*	economics	sciences économiques *f pl*	scienze economiche *f pl*	—
ciencias económicas[2] (Es)	Volks-wirtschaftslehre *f*	economics	économie politique *f*	economia politica *f*	—
cierre de cuentas (Es)	Jahresabschluß *m*	annual accounts	clôture annuelle des comptes *f*	chiusura d'esercizio *f*	—
cierre patronal (Es)	Aussperrung *f*	lockout	lock-out *m*	serrata *f*	—
cifra de venta mínima (Es)	Mindestumsatz *m*	minimum turnover	chiffre d'affaires minimum *m*	fatturato minimo *m*	—
cifra de ventas (Es)	Absatz *m*	sale/distribution	volume des ventes *m*	vendita *f*	—
cifras efectivas (Es)	Istzahlen *pl*	actual figures	résultats effectifs *m pl*	dati effettivi *m pl*	—

	D	E	F	I	Es
cifras estimadas (Es)	Sollzahlen *pl*	target figures	chiffres prévisionnels *m pl*	cifre calcolate *f pl*	—
cifras índice (Es)	Kennziffern *pl*	code numbers	indice *m*	cifre d'identificazione *f pl*	—
cifras rojas (Es)	rote Zahlen *pl*	(in) the red	chiffres en déficit *m*	conti in rosso *m pl*	—
cifre calcolate (I)	Sollzahlen *pl*	target figures	chiffres prévisionnels *m pl*	—	cifras estimadas *f pl*
cifre d'identificazione (I)	Kennziffern *pl*	code numbers	indice *m*	—	cifras índice *f pl*
circolare (I)	Rundschreiben *n*	circular (letter)	lettre circulaire *f*	—	circular *m*
circolazione delle banconote (I)	Notenumlauf *m*	notes in circulation	circulation fiduciaire *f*	—	circulación fiduciaria *f*
circolazione delle merci (I)	Handelsverkehr *m*	commercial intercourse	échanges commerciaux *m pl*	—	comercio *m*
circolazione di denaro (I)	Geldumlauf *m*	circulation of money	circulation monétaire *f*	—	circulación monetaria *f*
circuit économique (F)	Wirtschafts-kreislauf *m*	economic cycle	—	circuito economico *m*	circuito económico *m*
circuito de distribución (Es)	Vertriebsweg *m*	distribution channel	canal de distribution *m*	rete di distribuzione *f*	—
circuito económico (Es)	Wirtschafts-kreislauf *m*	economic cycle	circuit économique *m*	circuito economico *m*	—
circuito economico (I)	Wirtschafts-kreislauf *m*	economic cycle	circuit économique *m*	—	circuito económico *m*
circulación[1] (Es)	Straßenverkehr *m*	road traffic	trafic routier *m*	traffico stradale *m*	—
circulación[2] (Es)	Verkehr *m*	traffic	circulation *f*	traffico *m*	—
circulación de capitales (Es)	Kapitalverkehr *m*	capital transactions	mouvement des capitaux *m*	movimento dei capitali *m*	—
circulación fiduciaria (Es)	Notenumlauf *m*	notes in circulation	circulation fiduciaire *f*	circolazione delle banconote *f*	—
circulación monetaria (Es)	Geldumlauf *m*	circulation of money	circulation monétaire *f*	circolazione di denaro *f*	—
circular (Es)	Rundschreiben *n*	circular (letter)	lettre circulaire *f*	circolare *f*	—
circular de publicidad (Es)	Werbebrief *m*	advertising letter	lettre publicitaire *f*	lettera pubblicitaria *f*	—
circular (letter) (E)	Rundschreiben *n*	—	lettre circulaire *f*	circolare *f*	circular *m*
circulation (F)	Verkehr *m*	traffic	—	traffico *m*	circulación *f*
circulation fiduciaire (F)	Notenumlauf *m*	notes in circulation	—	circolazione delle banconote *f*	circulación fiduciaria *f*
circulation monétaire (F)	Geldumlauf *m*	circulation of money	—	circolazione di denaro *f*	circulación monetaria *f*
circulation of money (E)	Geldumlauf *m*	—	circulation monétaire *f*	circolazione di denaro *f*	circulación monetaria *f*
citación (Es)	Ladung *f*	summons to appear	citation *f*	citazione *f*	—
citation (F)	Ladung *f*	summons to appear	—	citazione *f*	citación *f*
citazione (I)	Ladung *f*	summons to appear	citation *f*	—	citación *f*
citazione in giudizio (I)	Klage *f*	legal action	action en justice *f*	—	demanda *f*
claim (E)	Anspruch *m*	—	prétention *f*	pretesa *f*	reivindicación *f*
claim for damages[1] (E)	Schadensforderung *f*	—	prétention à dommages-intérêts *f*	credito da danni *m*	pretensión de indemnización *f*
claim for damages[2] (E)	Schadenersatz-ansprüche *pl*	—	droit à l'indemnité *m*	diritti al risarcimento danni *m pl*	derecho a indemnización por daños y perjuicios *m*
claim to subsequent delivery (E)	Nachlieferungs-anspruch *m*	—	droit à livraison complémentaire *m*	diritto alla fornitura supplementare *m*	derecho de suminis-tro adicional *m*
claridad del balance (Es)	Bilanzklarheit *f*	balance transparency	clarté du bilan *f*	trasparenza di bilancio *f*	—
clarification des eaux usées (F)	Abwasserreinigung *f*	purification of sewage	—	depurazione delle acque di scarico *f*	depuración de las aguas residuales *f*
clarté du bilan (F)	Bilanzklarheit *f*	balance transparency	—	trasparenza di bilancio *f*	claridad del balance *f*
clase (Es)	Handelsklasse *f*	grade	catégorie de produits *f*	categoria commerciale *f*	—
clase media (Es)	Mittelstand *m*	middle class(es)	classe moyenne *f*	ceto medio *m*	—

cláusula comercial

	D	E	F	I	Es
clase obrera (Es)	Arbeiterklasse *f*	working class	classe ouvrière *f*	classe degli operai *f*	—
clases de costes (Es)	Kostenarten *pl*	cost types	coûts par nature *m pl*	tipi di costi *m pl*	—
classe degli operai (I)	Arbeiterklasse *f*	working class	classe ouvrière *f*	—	clase obrera *f*
classe moyenne (F)	Mittelstand *m*	middle class(es)	—	ceto medio *m*	clase media *f*
classe ouvrière (F)	Arbeiterklasse *f*	working class	—	classe degli operai *f*	clase obrera *f*
class of goods (E)	Warenart *f*	—	catégorie de marchandise *f*	tipo di merce *m*	categoría de mercancías *f*
clause (E)	Klausel *f*	—	clause *f*	clausola *f*	cláusula *f*
clause (F)	Klausel *f*	clause	—	clausola *f*	cláusula *f*
clause commerciale (F)	Handelsklausel *f*	trade terms	—	clausola commerciale *f*	cláusula comercial *f*
clause d'assurance (contre) tous (les) risques (F)	all-risks-Klausel *f*	all-risks clause	—	clausola tutti i rischi *f*	cláusula a todo riesgo *f*
clause de la nation la plus favorisée (F)	Meistbegünstigungs-klausel *f*	most-favoured nation clause	—	clausola della nazione più favorita *f*	cláusula de la nación más favorecida *f*
clause de livraison (F)	Lieferklausel *f*	delivery clause	—	clausola di fornitura *f*	cláusula de entrega *f pl*
clause de payement par accréditif (F)	Akkreditivklausel *f*	letter of credit clause	—	clausola del credito documentario *f*	cláusula de crédito documentario *f*
clause de prix sur place comptant (F)	Cash-and-carry-Klausel *f*	cash-and-carry clause	—	clausola cash-and-carry *f*	cláusula page y llévatelo *f*
clause de résolution du contrat (F)	Rücktrittsklausel *f*	escape clause	—	clausola di recesso *f*	cláusula de arrepentimiento *f*
clause de révocation (F)	Widerrufsklausel *f*	revocation clause	—	clausola di revoca *f*	cláusula revocatoria *f*
clause de stabilité (F)	Wertsicherungs-klausel *f*	stable value clause	—	clausola di garanzia monetaria *f*	cláusula de índice variable *f*
clause de transit (F)	Transitklausel *f*	transit clause	—	clausola di transito *f*	cláusula de tránsito *f*
clause d'indexation (F)	Indexklausel *f*	index clause	—	clausola dell'indice *f*	cláusula de índice variable *f*
clause dollar (F)	Dollarklausel *f*	dollar clause	—	clausola dollaro *f*	cláusula dólar *f*
clause monétaire (F)	Währungsklausel *f*	currency clause	—	clausola monetaria *f*	cláusula monetaria *f*
clausola (I)	Klausel *f*	clause	clause *f*	—	cláusula *f*
clausola cash-and-carry (I)	Cash-and-carry-Klausel *f*	cash-and-carry clause	clause de prix sur place comptant *f*	—	cláusula page y llévatelo *f*
clausola commerciale (I)	Handelsklausel *f*	trade terms	clause commerciale *f*	—	cláusula comercial *f*
clausola del credito documentario (I)	Akkreditivklausel *f*	letter of credit clause	clause de payement par accréditif *f*	—	cláusula de crédito documentario *f*
clausola della nazione più favorita (I)	Meistbegünstigungs-klausel *f*	most-favoured nation clause	clause de la nation la plus favorisée *f*	—	cláusula de la nación más favorecida *f*
clausola dell'indice (I)	Indexklausel *f*	index clause	clause d'indexation *f*	—	cláusula de índice variable *f*
clausola di fornitura (I)	Lieferklausel *f*	delivery clause	clause de livraison *f*	—	cláusula de entrega *f pl*
clausola di garanzia monetaria (I)	Wertsicherungs-klausel *f*	stable value clause	clause de stabilité *f*	—	cláusula de índice variable *f*
clausola di recesso (I)	Rücktrittsklausel *f*	escape clause	clause de résolution du contrat *f*	—	cláusula de arrepentimiento *f*
clausola di revoca (I)	Widerrufsklausel *f*	revocation clause	clause de révocation *f*	—	cláusula revocatoria *f*
clausola di transito (I)	Transitklausel *f*	transit clause	clause de transit *f*	—	cláusula de tránsito *f*
clausola dollaro (I)	Dollarklausel *f*	dollar clause	clause dollar *f*	—	cláusula dólar *f*
clausola monetaria (I)	Währungsklausel *f*	currency clause	clause monétaire *f*	—	cláusula monetaria *f*
clausola tutti i rischi (I)	all-risks-Klausel *f*	all-risks clause	clause d'assurance (contre) tous (les) risques *f*	—	cláusula a todo riesgo *f*
cláusula (Es)	Klausel *f*	clause	clause *f*	clausola *f*	—
cláusula a todo riesgo (Es)	all-risks-Klausel *f*	all-risks clause	clause d'assurance (contre) tous (les) risques *f*	clausola tutti i rischi *f*	—
cláusula comercial (Es)	Handelsklausel *f*	trade terms	clause commerciale *f*	clausola commerciale *f*	—

	D	E	F	I	Es
cláusula de arrepentimiento (Es)	Rücktrittsklausel *f*	escape clause	clause de résolution du contrat *f*	clausola di recesso *f*	—
cláusula de crédito documentario (Es)	Akkreditivklausel *f*	letter of credit clause	clause de payement par accréditif *f*	clausola del credito documentario *f*	—
cláusula de entrega (Es)	Lieferklausel *f*	delivery clause	clause de livraison *f*	clausola di fornitura *f*	—
cláusula de índice variable[1] (Es)	Indexklausel *f*	index clause	clause d'indexation *f*	clausola dell'indice *f*	—
cláusula de índice variable[2] (Es)	Wertsicherungsklausel *f*	stable value clause	clause de stabilité *f*	clausola di garanzia monetaria *f*	—
cláusula de la nación más favorecida (Es)	Meistbegünstigungsklausel *f*	most-favoured nation clause	clause de la nation la plus favorisée *f*	clausola della nazione più favorita *f*	—
cláusula de tránsito (Es)	Transitklausel *f*	transit clause	clause de transit *f*	clausola di transito *f*	—
cláusula dólar (Es)	Dollarklausel *f*	dollar clause	clause dollar *f*	clausola dollaro *f*	—
cláusula monetaria (Es)	Währungsklausel *f*	currency clause	clause monétaire *f*	clausola monetaria *f*	—
cláusula page y llévatelo (Es)	Cash-and-carry-Klausel *f*	cash-and-carry clause	clause de prix sur place comptant *f*	clausola cash-and-carry *f*	—
cláusula revocatoria (Es)	Widerrufsklausel *f*	revocation clause	clause de révocation *f*	clausola di revoca *f*	—
clavier (F)	Tastatur *f*	keyboard	—	tastiera *f*	teclado *m*
clearance sale[1] (E)	Räumungsverkauf *m*	—	liquidation des stocks *f*	liquidazione totale *f*	venta total *f*
clearance sale[2] (E)	Ausverkauf *m*	—	soldes *m pl*	svendita *f*	liquidación *f*
clearing unit (E)	Verrechnungseinheit *f*	—	unité de compte *f*	unità di compensazione *f*	unidad de compensación *f*
client (E)	Auftraggeber *m*	—	commettant *m*	committente *m*	mandante *m*
client (F)	Kunde *m*	customer	—	cliente *m*	cliente *m*
client étranger (F)	Auslandskunde *f*	foreign customer	—	cliente estero *m*	cliente extranjero *m*
client habituel (F)	Stammkunde *f*	regular customer	—	cliente fisso *m*	cliente habitual *m*
cliente (Es)	Kunde *m*	customer	client *m*	cliente *m*	—
cliente (I)	Kunde *m*	customer	client *m*	—	cliente *m*
cliente estero (I)	Auslandskunde *f*	foreign customer	client étranger *m*	—	cliente extranjero *m*
cliente extranjero (Es)	Auslandskunde *f*	foreign customer	client étranger *m*	cliente estero *m*	—
cliente fisso (I)	Stammkunde *f*	regular customer	client habituel *m*	—	cliente habitual *m*
cliente habitual (Es)	Stammkunde *f*	regular customer	client habituel *m*	cliente fisso *m*	—
clientela[1] (Es)	Klientel *f*	clientele	clients *m pl*	clientela *f*	—
clientela[2] (Es)	Kundenkreis *m*	clientele	clientèle *f*	clientela *f*	—
clientela[1] (I)	Klientel *f*	clientele	clients *m pl*	—	clientela *f*
clientela[2] (I)	Kundenkreis *m*	clientele	clientèle *f*	—	clientela *f*
clientela fija (Es)	Kundenstamm *m*	regular customers	clients en portefeuille *m pl*	clientela fissa *f*	—
clientela fissa (I)	Kundenstamm *m*	regular customers	clients en portefeuille *m pl*	—	clientela fija *f*
clientele[1] (E)	Klientel *f*	—	clients *m pl*	clientela *f*	clientela *f*
clientele[2] (E)	Kundschaft *f*	—	clientèle *f*	clientela *f*	clientela *f*
clientele[3] (E)	Kundenkreis *m*	—	clientèle *f*	clientela *f*	clientela *f*
clientèle[1] (F)	Kundschaft *f*	clientele	—	clientela *f*	clientela *f*
clientèle[2] (F)	Kundenkreis *m*	clientele	—	clientela *f*	clientela *f*
clients (F)	Klientel *f*	clientele	—	clientela *f*	clientela *f*
clients en portefeuille (F)	Kundenstamm *m*	regular customers	—	clientela fissa *f*	clientela fija *f*
climat social (F)	Betriebsklima *n*	working conditions and human relations	—	atmosfera di lavoro *f*	ambiente de trabajo *m*
closing balance (E)	Schlußbilanz *f*	—	bilan de clôture *m*	bilancio consuntivo *m*	balance final *m*/ balanza de saldos definitivos *f*
closing price (E)	Schlußkurs *m*	—	dernier cours *m*	quotazione di chiusura *f*	cotización final *f*
clôture annuelle de l'établissement (F)	Betriebsferien *pl*	annual holiday	—	ferie aziendali *f pl*	vacaciones de la empresa *f pl*

	D	E	F	I	Es
clôture annuelle des comptes (F)	Jahresabschluß m	annual accounts	—	chiusura d'esercizio f	cierre de cuentas m
Club (D)	—	club	club m	club m	club m
club (E)	Club m	—	club m	club m	club m
club (Es)	Club m	club	club m	club m	—
club (F)	Club m	club	—	club m	club m
club (I)	Club m	club	club m	—	club m
coastal waters (E)	Küstengewässer n	—	eaux côtières f pl	acque territoriali f pl	zona costera f
cobertura (Es)	Deckung f	cover	couverture f	copertura f	—
cobertura de seguro (Es)	Versicherungs-schutz m	insurance cover	couverture de l'assurana f	copertura assicurativa f	—
cobros pendientes (Es)	Außenstände pl	outstanding debts	dettes actives f pl	debiti insoluti m pl	—
coche de alquiler (Es)	Leihwagen m	hired car	voiture de location f	vettura da noleggio f	—
coche de empresa (Es)	Firmenwagen m	company car	voiture appartenant à l'entreprise f	vettura aziendale f	—
coche de segunda mano (Es)	Gebrauchtwagen m	used car	voiuture d'occasion f	automobile usata f	—
coche de servicio (Es)	Dienstwagen m	official car	voiture de service f	vettura di servizio f	—
cociente (Es)	Quotient m	quotient	quotient m	quoziente m	—
Code (D)	—	code	code m	codice m	código m
code (F)	Code m	code	—	codice m	código m
code[1] (E)	Code m	—	code m	codice m	código m
code[2] (E)	codieren	—	coder	codificare	codificar
code de commerce (F)	Handelsgesetzbuch n	Commercial Code	—	codice commerciale m	código mercantil m
code de l'artisanat (F)	Handwerksordnung f	Handicrafts Regulation Act	—	codice dell'artigianato m	reglamento del artesanado m
code numbers[1] (E)	Kennziffern pl	—	indice m	cifre d'identificazione f pl	cifras índice f pl
code numbers[2] (E)	Kennzahlen pl	—	numéros de référence m pl	numeri d'identificazione m pl	números índice m pl
code postal (F)	Postleitzahl f	postal code	—	codice d'avviamento postale m	código postal m
coder (F)	codieren	code	—	codificare	codificar
co-determination of labour (E)	Mitbestimmung f	—	cogestion f	cogestione f	cogestión f
codeword (E)	Codewort n	—	mot de code m	parola di codice f	palabra de clave f
Codewort (D)	—	codeword	mot de code m	parola di codice f	palabra de clave f
codice (I)	Code m	code	code m	—	código m
codice commerciale (I)	Handelsgesetzbuch n	Commercial Code	code de commerce m	—	código mercantil m
codice d'avviamento postale (I)	Postleitzahl f	postal code	code postal m	—	código postal m
codice dell'artigianato (I)	Handwerksordnung f	Handicrafts Regulation Act	code de l'artisanat m	—	reglamento del artesanado m
codieren (D)	—	code	coder	codificare	codificar
codificar (Es)	codieren	code	coder	codificare	—
codificare (I)	codieren	code	coder	—	codificar
código (Es)	Code m	code	code m	codice m	—
código mercantil (Es)	Handelsgesetzbuch n	Commercial Code	code de commerce m	codice commerciale m	—
código postal (Es)	Postleitzahl f	postal code	code postal m	codice d'avviamento postale m	—
coffre-fort[1] (F)	Safe m	safe	—	cassetta di sicurezza f	caja de seguridad f
coffre-fort[2] (F)	Tresor m	safe	—	cassaforte f	caja fuerte f
cogestión (Es)	Mitbestimmung f	co-determination of labour	cogestion f	cogestione f	—
cogestion (F)	Mitbestimmung f	co-determination of labour	—	cogestione f	cogestión f
cogestione (I)	Mitbestimmung f	co-determination of labour	cogestion f	—	cogestión f
cognizioni elementari (I)	Grundkenntnisse pl	basic knowledge	connaissances fondamentales f pl	—	conocimientos básicos m pl

	D	E	F	I	Es
cognizioni professionali (I)	Fachwissen *n*	professional knowledge	connaissances professionnelles *f pl*	—	conocimientos especializados *m pl*
coin (E)	Münze *f*	—	monnaie *f*	moneta *f*	moneda *f*
colaboración (Es)	Mitarbeit *f*	collaboration	collaboration *f*	collaborazione *f*	—
colaborador en el servicio exterior (Es)	Außendienstmitarbeiter *m*	field staff	personnel du service extérieur *m*	collaboratore del servizio esterno *m*	—
cold storage lorry (E)	Kühlwagen *m*	—	wagon frigorifique *m*	vagone frigorifero *m*	vagón frigorífico *m*
colectivismo (Es)	Kollektivismus *m*	collectivism	collectivisme *m*	collettivismo *m*	—
colectivo (Es)	Kollektiv *n*	collective	collectif *m*	collettivo *m*	—
colis¹ (F)	Paket *n*	parcel	—	pacco *m*	bulto *m*
colis² (F)	Frachtstücke *pl*	packages	—	colli *m pl*	fardo *m*
colis de détail (F)	Stückgut *n*	mixed cargo	—	collettame *m*	fardos *m pl*
colis exprès (F)	Eilpaket *n*	express parcel	—	pacco espresso *m*	paquete urgente *m*
colis express (F)	Expressgut *n*	express goods	—	merce spedita per espresso *f*	carga por expreso *f*
collaboration (E)	Mitarbeit *f*	—	collaboration *f*	collaborazione *f*	colaboración *f*
collaboration¹ (F)	Zusammenarbeit *f*	cooperation	—	collaborazione *f*	cooperación *f*
collaboration² (F)	Mitarbeit *f*	collaboration	—	collaborazione *f*	colaboración *f*
collaboratore del servizio esterno (I)	Außendienstmitarbeiter *m*	field staff	personnel du service extérieur *m*	—	colaborador en el servicio exterior *m*
collaborazione¹ (I)	Zusammenarbeit *f*	cooperation	collaboration *f*	—	cooperación *f*
collaborazione² (I)	Mitarbeit *f*	collaboration	collaboration *f*	—	colaboración *f*
collapse of prices (E)	Kurszusammenbruch *m*	—	chute des cours *f*	crollo delle quotazioni *m*	caída de los cambios *f*
collectif (F)	Kollektiv *n*	collective	—	collettivo *m*	colectivo *m*
collection (E)	Inkasso *n*	—	recouvrement *m*	incasso *m*	encobro *m*
collection des dossiers (F)	Ablage *f*	file	—	archivio *m*	archivo *m*
collective (E)	Kollektiv *n*	—	collectif *m*	collettivo *m*	colectivo *m*
collective advertisement (E)	Sammelwerbung *f*	—	publicité groupée *f*	pubblicità collettiva *f*	publicidad colectiva *f*
collective agreement (E)	Tarifvertrag *m*	—	convention collective *f*	contratto salariale *m*	contrato colectivo *m*
collective consignment (E)	Sammelladung *f*	—	envoi par groupage *m*	carico a collettame *m*	carga colectiva *f*
collective goods (E)	Kollektivgüter *pl*	—	biens collectifs *m pl*	beni collettivi *m pl*	bienes sociales *m pl*
collective property (E)	Gemeinschaftseigentum *n*	—	propriété collective *f*	proprietà comunitaria *f*	propiedad colectiva *f*
collective transport (E)	Sammeltransport *m*	—	transport de groupage *m*	trasporto a collettame *m*	transporte colectivo *m*
collectivism (E)	Kollektivismus *m*	—	collectivisme *m*	collettivismo *m*	colectivismo *m*
collectivisme (F)	Kollektivismus *m*	collectivism	—	collettivismo *m*	colectivismo *m*
collectivité (F)	Körperschaft *f*	corporation	—	ente *m*	corporación *f*
collegamento telex (I)	Telexanschluß *m*	telex connection	communication de télex *f*	—	comunicación de télex *f*
collettame (I)	Stückgut *n*	mixed cargo	colis de détail *m*	—	fardos *m pl*
collettivismo (I)	Kollektivismus *m*	collectivism	collectivisme *m*	—	colectivismo *m*
collettivo (I)	Kollektiv *n*	collective	collectif *m*	—	colectivo *m*
colli (I)	Frachtstücke *pl*	packages	colis *m*	—	fardo *m*
collocamento¹ (I)	Plazierung *f*	placing	placement *m*	—	colocación *f*
collocamento² (I)	Placierung *f*	placement	placement *m*	—	colocación
collocamento dell'inserzione (I)	Anzeigenplazierung *f*	placing of an advertisement	disposition de l'annonce *f*	—	colocación del anuncio *f*
collocare (I)	plazieren	place	placer	—	colocar
colloquio¹ (I)	Besprechung *f*	discussion	conférence *f*	—	conferencia *f*
colloquio² (I)	Unterredung *f*	discussion	entretien *m*	—	conversación *f*
colloquio di vendita (I)	Verkaufsgespräch *n*	sales talk	conversation de vente *f*	—	conversación de venta *f*
colloquio personale (I)	persönliches Gespräch *n*	personal conversation	conversation personnelle *f*	—	conversación personal *f*

	D	E	F	I	Es
colocación¹ (Es)	Plazierung f	placing	placement m	collocamento m	—
colocación² (Es)	Placierung f	placement	placement m	collocamento m	—
colocación del anuncio (Es)	Anzeigenplazierung f	placing of an advertisement	disposition de l'annonce f	collocamento dell'inserzione m	—
colocar¹ (Es)	plazieren	place	placer	collocare	—
colocar² (Es)	placieren	place	placer	collocare	—
colposo (I)	schuldhaft	culpable	coupable	—	culpable
comanditario (Es)	Kommanditist m	limited partner	commanditaire m	socio accomandante m	—
combatting rising costs (E)	Kostendämpfung f	—	réduction des coûts f	contenimento dei costi m	disminución de costes f
combustible (Es)	Treibstoff m	fuel	carburant m	carburante m	—
combustión (Es)	Verbrennung f	incineration	combustion f	combustione f	—
combustion (F)	Verbrennung f	incineration	—	combustione f	combustión f
combustione (I)	Verbrennung f	incineration	combustion f	—	combustión f
come convenuto (I)	vereinbarungsgemäß	as agreed	comme convenu	—	según lo acordado
comerciable (Es)	marktfähig	marketable	vendable	smerciabile	—
comercialización de las materias primas (Es)	Rohstoff-vermarktung f	raw materials marketing	commercialisation des matières premières f	smercio delle materie prime m	—
comercialización directa (Es)	Direct-Marketing n	direct marketing	stratégie des ventes directes f	marketing in prima persona m	—
comercializar (Es)	vermarkten	market	commercialiser	lanciare sul mercato	—
comerciante¹ (Es)	Händler m	trader	commerçant m	commerciante m	—
comerciante² (Es)	Kaufmann m	businessman	négociant m	commerciante m	—
comerciante particular (Es)	Einzelhandels-kaufmann m	retail merchant	détaillant m	commerciante al dettaglio m	—
comerciantes (Es)	Kaufleute pl	businessmen	commerçants m pl	commercianti m pl	—
comercio¹ (Es)	Handel m	trade	commerce m	commercio m	—
comercio² (Es)	Handelsverkehr m	commercial intercourse	échanges commerciaux m pl	circolazione delle merci f	—
comercio³ (Es)	Kommerz m	commerce	commerce m	commercio m	—
comercio al por menor (Es)	Einzelhandel m	retail trade	commerce de détail m	commercio al dettaglio m	—
comercio ambulante (Es)	ambulantes Gewerbe n	itinerant trade	commerce ambulant m	commercio ambulante m	—
comercio de comisión (Es)	Kommissionshandel	commission trade	commissionnage m	commercio di commissione m	—
comercio de exportación (Es)	Exporthandel m	export trade	commerce d'exportation m	esportazioni f pl	—
comercio de importación (Es)	Importhandel m	import trade	commerce d'importation m	commercio delle importazioni m	—
comercio de tránsito (Es)	Transithandel m	transit trade	commerce de transit m	commercio di transito m	—
comercio de ultramar (Es)	Überseehandel m	overseas trade	commerce d'outre-mer m	commercio d'oltremare m	—
comercio este-oeste (Es)	Ost-West-Handel m	East-West trade	commerce Est-Ouest m	scambio est-ovest m	—
comercio exterior (Es)	Außenhandel m	foreign trade	commerce extérieur m	commercio estero m	—
comercio interior (Es)	Binnenhandel m	domestic trade	commerce intérieur m	commercio nazionale m	—
comercio internacional (Es)	Welthandel m	world trade	commerce mondial m	commercio mondiale m	—
comercio mayorista (Es)	Großhandel m	wholesale trade	commerce de gros m	commercio all'ingrosso m	—
comida de trabajo (Es)	Arbeitsessen n	working lunch	déjeuner de travail m	pranzo di lavoro m	—
comisión¹ (Es)	Kommission f	commission	commission f	commissione f	—
comisión² (Es)	Provision f	commission	commission f	provvigione f	—
comisión al comprador (Es)	Käuferprovision f	buyer's commission	commission d'acheteur f	provvigione dell'acquirente f	—

	D	E	F	I	Es
comisión de apertura de crédito (Es)	Kreditprovision f	credit commission	frais de commissions d'ouverture de crédit m pl	provvigione di credito f	—
comisión de garantía (Es)	Delkredereprovision f	del credere commission	commission ducroire f	provvigione dello star del credere f	—
comisionista (Es)	Kommissionär m	commission agent	commissionnaire m	commissionario m	—
comisión sobre la cifra de ventas (Es)	Umsatzprovision f	commission on turnover	commission sur le chiffre d'affaires f	provvigione sul fatturato f	—
comisión sobre la venta (Es)	Verkäuferprovision f	sales commission	commission sur les ventes f	provvigione del venditore f	—
comité directeur (F)	Vorstand m	board	—	consiglio di amministrazione m	consejo de dirección m
commande¹ (F)	Bestellung f	order	—	ordinazione f	pedido m
commande² (F)	Auftrag m	order	—	ordine m	pedido m
commande consécutive (F)	Folgeauftrag m	follow-up order	—	ordine successivo m	orden sucesivo m
commande d'exportation (F)	Exportauftrag m	export order	—	ordine d'esportazione m	pedido destinado a la exportación m
commande directe (F)	Direktbestellung f	direct ordering	—	ordinazione diretta f	pedido directo m
commande préalable (F)	Vorbestellung f	reservation	—	ordinazione anticipata f	pedidio anticipado m
commanditaire (F)	Kommanditist m	limited partner	—	socio accomandante m	comanditario m
commandité (F)	Komplementär m	general partner	—	socio accomandatario m	socio colectivo m
comme convenu (F)	vereinbarungsgemäß	as agreed	—	come convenuto	según lo acordado
comment (E)	Stellungnahme f	—	prise de position f	presa di posizione f	dictamen m
commentaire de presse (F)	Pressemitteilung f	press release	—	comunicazione stampa f	remitido a la prensa m
commerçant (F)	Händler m	trader	—	commerciante m	comerciante m
commerçant détaillant (F)	Einzelhändler m	retailer	—	dettagliante m	minorista m
commerçants (F)	Kaufleute pl	businessmen	—	commercianti m pl	comerciantes m pl
commerce (E)	Kommerz m	—	commerce m	commercio m	comercio m
commerce¹ (F)	Kommerz m	commerce	—	commercio m	comercio m
commerce² (F)	Handel m	trade	—	commercio m	comercio m
commerce ambulant (F)	ambulantes Gewerbe n	itinerant trade	—	commercio ambulante m	comercio ambulante m
commerce de change (F)	Sortenhandel m	dealing in foreign notes and coins	—	cambio valuta m	operación de moneda extranjera f
commerce de détail (F)	Einzelhandel m	retail trade	—	commercio al dettaglio m	comercio al por menor m
commerce de gros (F)	Großhandel m	wholesale trade	—	commercio all'ingrosso m	comercio mayorista m
commerce des valeurs mobilières (F)	Effektengeschäft n	securities business	—	operazione su titoli f	operación de valores f
commerce de transit (F)	Transithandel m	transit trade	—	commercio di transito m	comercio de tránsito m
commerce de vente au détail par correspondance (F)	Versandhandel m	mail order business	—	vendita per corrispondenza f	venta por correspondencia f
commerce d'exportation (F)	Exporthandel m	export trade	—	esportazioni f pl	comercio de exportación m
commerce d'importation (F)	Importhandel m	import trade	—	commercio delle importazioni m	comercio de importación m
commerce d'opérations à terme (F)	Warenterminhandel m	commodity forward dealing	—	operazioni a termine su merci f pl	tráfico de futuro m
commerce d'outre-mer (F)	Überseehandel m	overseas trade	—	commercio d'oltremare m	comercio de ultramar m
commerce Est-Ouest (F)	Ost-West-Handel m	East-West trade	—	scambio est-ovest m	comercio este-oeste m
commerce extérieur (F)	Außenhandel m	foreign trade	—	commercio estero m	comercio exterior m
commerce intérieur (F)	Binnenhandel m	domestic trade	—	commercio nazionale m	comercio interior m
commerce libre (F)	Freihandel m	free trade	—	scambio libero m	librecambio m

	D	E	F	I	Es
commerce mondial (F)	Welthandel *m*	world trade	—	commercio mondiale *m*	comercio internacional *m*
commercial agency (E)	Handelsvertretung *f*	—	représentation commerciale *f*	rappresentanza commerciale *f*	representación comercial *f*
commercial agent[1] (E)	Handlungsbevollmächtigter *m*	—	personne ayant le pouvoir commercial *f*	mandatario commerciale *m*	apoderado especial *m*
commercial agent[2] (E)	Handelsvertreter *m*	—	représentant de commerce *m*	rappresentante commerciale *m*	representante comercial *m*
commercial apprenticeship (E)	kaufmännische Lehre *f*	—	apprentissage commercial *m*	apprendistato di commercio *m*	aprendizaje comercial *m*
commercial bank (E)	Kreditbank *f*	—	banque de crédit *f*	banca di credito *f*	banco de crédito *m*
commercial bill (E)	Warenwechsel *m*	—	traite commerciale *f*	cambiale commerciale *f*	letra comercial *f*
Commercial Code (E)	Handelsgesetzbuch *n*	—	code de commerce *m*	codice commerciale *m*	código mercantil *m*
commercial intercourse (E)	Handelsverkehr *m*	—	échanges commerciaux *m pl*	circolazione delle merci *f*	comercio *m*
commercial letter of credit (E)	Handelskreditbrief *m*	—	lettre de crédit commercial *f*	lettera di credito commerciale *f*	carta de crédito comercial *f*
commercialisation (F)	Absatzwirtschaft *f*	marketing	—	marketing *m*	economía de distribución *f*
commercialisation des matières premières (F)	Rohstoffvermarktung *f*	raw materials marketing	—	smercio delle materie prime *m*	comercialización de las materias primas *f*
commercialiser (F)	vermarkten	market	—	lanciare sul mercato	comercializar
commercial policy (E)	Handelspolitik *f*	—	politique commerciale *f*	politica commerciale *f*	política comercial *f*
commercial register (E)	Handelsregister *n*	—	registre du commerce *m*	registro commerciale *m*	registro mercantil *m*
commerciante[1] (I)	Kaufmann *m*	businessman	négociant *m*	—	comerciante *m*
commerciante[2] (I)	Händler *m*	trader	commerçant *m*	—	comerciante *m*
commerciante al dettaglio (I)	Einzelhandelskaufmann *m*	retail merchant	détaillant *m*	—	comerciante particular *m*
commercianti (I)	Kaufleute *pl*	businessmen	commerçants *m pl*	—	comerciantes *m pl*
commercio[1] (I)	Handel *m*	trade	commerce *m*	—	comercio *m*
commercio[2] (I)	Gewerbe *n*	trade/industry/craft	activité professionnelle *f*/ industrie *f*/artisanat *m*	—	industria *f*/ comercio *m*/ artesanía *f*
commercio[3] (I)	Kommerz *m*	commerce	commerce *m*	—	comercio *m*
commercio al dettaglio (I)	Einzelhandel *m*	retail trade	commerce de détail *m*	—	comercio al por menor *m*
commercio all'ingrosso (I)	Großhandel *m*	wholesale trade	commerce de gros *m*	—	comercio mayorista *m*
commercio ambulante (I)	ambulantes Gewerbe *n*	itinerant trade	commerce ambulant *m*	—	comercio ambulante *m*
commercio azionario (I)	Aktienhandel *m*	dealing in shares	négociation des actions *f*	—	contratación de acciones *f*
commercio dei cambi (I)	Devisenverkehr *m*	foreign exchange dealings	mouvement des devises *m*	—	tráfico de divisas *m*
commercio delle divise (I)	Devisenhandel *m*	foreign exchange dealings	marché des changes *m*	—	operaciones de divisas *f pl*
commercio delle importazioni (I)	Importhandel *m*	import trade	commerce d'importation *m*	—	comercio de importación *m*
commercio di commissione (I)	Kommissionshandel	commission trade	commissionnage *m*	—	comercio de comisión *m*
commercio di transito (I)	Transithandel *m*	transit trade	commerce de transit *m*	—	comercio de tránsito *m*
commercio d'oltremare (I)	Überseehandel *m*	overseas trade	commerce d'outre-mer *m*	—	comercio de ultramar *m*
commercio estero (I)	Außenhandel *m*	foreign trade	commerce extérieur *m*	—	comercio exterior *m*
commercio in borsa (I)	Börsenhandel *m*	stock exchange transactions	transactions boursiaires *f pl*	—	negociación bursátil *f*
commercio mondiale (I)	Welthandel *m*	world trade	commerce mondial *m*	—	comercio internacional *m*
commercio nazionale (I)	Binnenhandel *m*	domestic trade	commerce intérieur *m*	—	comercio interior *m*

	D	E	F	I	Es
commettant (F)	Auftraggeber *m*	client	—	committente *m*	mandante *m*
commissaire aux comptes (F)	Rechnungsprüfer *m*	auditor	—	revisore dei conti *m*	revisor contable *m*
commission¹ (E)	Kommission *f*	—	commission *f*	commissione *f*	comisión *f*
commission² (E)	Provision *f*	—	commission *f*	provvigione *f*	comisión *f*
commission¹ (F)	Provision *f*	commission	—	provvigione *f*	comisión *f*
commission² (F)	Kommission *f*	commission	—	commissione *f*	comisión *f*
commission agent (E)	Kommissionär *m*	—	commissionnaire *m*	commissionario *m*	comisionista *m*
commissionario (I)	Kommissionär *m*	commission agent	commissionnaire *m*	—	comisionista *m*
commission business (E)	Kommissionsgeschäft *n*	—	affaire en commission	operazione di commissione *f*	operación de comisión *f*
commission d'acheteur (F)	Käuferprovision *f*	buyer's commission	—	provvigione dell'acquirente *f*	comisión al comprador *f*
commission ducroire (F)	Delkredereprovision *f*	del credere commission	—	provvigione dello star del credere *f*	comisión de garantía *f*
commissione (I)	Kommission *f*	commission	commission *f*	—	comisión *f*
commissione bancaria (I)	Bankenaufsicht *f*	public supervision of banking	contrôle des banques *m*	—	supervisión bancaria *f*
commission guarantee (E)	Provisionsgarantie *f*	—	garantie de commission *f*	garanzia di provvigione *f*	garantía de comisión *f*
commissioni bancarie (I)	Bankspesen *pl*	bank charges	frais de banque *m pl*	—	gastos bancarios *m pl*
commissionnage¹ (F)	Kommissionshandel	commission trade	—	commercio di commissione *m*	comercio de comisión *m*
commissionnaire² (F)	Kommissionär *m*	commission agent	—	commissionario *m*	comisionista *m*
commissionnaire de transport (F)	Spediteur *m*	forwarder	—	spedizioniere *m*	expeditor *m*
commission on turnover (E)	Umsatzprovision *f*	—	commission sur le chiffre d'affaires *f*	provvigione sul fatturato *f*	comisión sobre la cifra de ventas *f*
commission payment (E)	Provisionszahlung *f*	—	payement de commission *m*	pagamento di provvigione *m*	pago de comisión *m*
commission sur le chiffre d'affaires (F)	Umsatzprovision *f*	commission on turnover	—	provvigione sul fatturato *f*	comisión sobre la cifra de ventas *f*
commission sur les ventes (F)	Verkäuferprovision *f*	sales commission	—	provvigione del venditore *f*	comisión sobre la venta *f*
commission trade (E)	Kommissionshandel	—	commissionnage *m*	commercio di commissione *m*	comercio de comisión *m*
commitment fee (E)	Bereitstellungskosten *pl*	—	coûts administratifs *m pl*	spese di stanziamento *f pl*	gastos fijos *m pl*
commitment interests (E)	Bereitstellungszinsen *f*	—	intérêts de disponibilité *m pl*	interessi per lo stanziamento *m pl*	interés de disponibilidad *m*
committente¹ (I)	Besteller *m*	customer	acheteur *m*	—	demandante *m*
committente² (I)	Auftraggeber *m*	client	commettant *m*	—	mandante *m*
commodity exchange (E)	Warenbörse *f*	—	bourse de marchandises *f*	borsa merci *f*	bolsa de mercancías *f*
commodity forward dealing (E)	Warenterminhandel *m*	—	commerce d'opérations à terme *m*	operazioni a termine su merci *f pl*	tráfico de futuro *m*
commodity forward exchange (E)	Warenterminbörse *f*	—	bourse d'opérations à livrer *f*	borsa merci a termine *f*	bolsa de mercancías a plazo *f*
commodity forward transaction (E)	Warentermingeschäft *n*	—	opération de livraison à terme *f*	operazione a termine su merci *f*	operación a plazo de mercancías *f*
commodity market (E)	Rohstoffmarkt *m*	—	marchés des matières premières *m*	mercato delle materie prime *m*	mercado de materias primas *m*
common business-oriented language (E)	Programmiersprache *f*	—	langage de programmation *m*	linguaggio di programmazione *m*	lenguaje de programación *m*
common market (E)	gemeinsamer Markt *m*	—	marché commun *m*	mercato comune *m*	mercado común *m*
communauté économique (F)	Wirtschaftsgemeinschaft *f*	economic community	—	comunità economica *f*	comunidad económica *f*
Communauté Européenne (F)	Europäische Gemeinschaft, EG *f*	European Community	—	Comunità Europea CEE *f*	Comunidad Europea, C.E. *f*
commune¹ (F)	Kommune *f*	municipality	—	comune *m*	municipalidad *f*
commune² (F)	Gemeinde *f*	community	—	comune *m*	comunidad *f*

	D	E	F	I	Es
communication de télex (F)	Telexanschluß *m*	telex connection	—	collegamento telex *m*	comunicación de télex *f*
community (E)	Gemeinde *f*	—	commune *f*	comune *m*	comunidad *f*
community of heirs (E)	Erbengemeinschaft *f*	—	communauté d'héritiers *f*	comunità degli eredi *f*	comunidad sucesoria *f*
compagnia armatoriale (I)	Reederei *f*	shipping company	société d'armateurs *f*	—	compañía naviera *f*
compagnia di assicurazione (I)	Versicherungsgesellschaft *f*	insurance company	société d'assurance *f*	—	sociedad de seguros *f*
compañía asociada (Es)	Schwestergesellschaft *f*	affiliated company	société affiliée *f*	consorella *f*	—
compañía distribuidora (Es)	Vertriebsfirma *f*	distributor	distributeur *m*	ditta di distribuzione *f*	—
compañía naviera (Es)	Reederei *f*	shipping company	société d'armateurs *f*	compagnia armatoriale *f*	—
Companies Act (E)	Aktiengesetz *n*	—	loi sur les sociétés par actions *f*	legge sulle società per azioni *f*	ley sobre sociedades anónimas *f*
company (E)	Firma *f*	—	entreprise *f*	impresa *f*	empresa *f*
company account (E)	Firmenkonto *n*	—	compte de maison *m*	conto intestato ad una ditta *m*	cuenta de la empresa *f*
company address (E)	Firmenanschrift *f*	—	adresse de la maison *f*	indirizzo della ditta *m*	dirección de la empresa *f*
company car (E)	Firmenwagen *m*	—	voiture appartenant à l'entreprise *f*	vettura aziendale *f*	coche de empresa *m*
company law (E)	Aktienrecht *n*	—	loi sur les sociétés anonymes *f pl*	diritto azionario *m*	derecho de sociedades anónimas *m*
company limited by shares (E)	Kapitalgesellschaft *f*	—	société de capitaux *f*	società di capitale *f*	sociedad capitalista *f*
company name (E)	Firmenname *m*	—	nom de la maison *m*	denominazione *f*/ ragione sociale *f*	razón social *f*
company objective (E)	Unternehmensziel *n*	—	objectif de l'entreprise *m*	obiettivo imprenditoriale *m*	objetivo empresarial *m*
company's bank (E)	Hausbank *f*	—	banque habituelle *f*	banca di preferenza *f*	banco particular *m*
company's name plate (E)	Firmenschild *n*	—	enseigne commerciale *f*	insegna dell'impresa *f*	letrero de establecimiento *m*
comparación (Es)	Vergleich *m*	comparison	comparaison *f*	confronto *m*	—
comparación de las cotizaciones (Es)	Kursvergleich *m*	comparison of prices	comparaison des cours *f*	confronto dei corsi *m*	—
comparación de ramos (Es)	Branchenvergleich *m*	trade comparison	comparaison des différentes branches *f*	comparazione delle categorie *f*	—
comparación entre los resultados efectivos y las previsiones (Es)	Soll/Ist-Vergleich *m*	comparison of estimates with results	comparaison entre les résultats effectifs et les prévisions *f*	confronto costi calcolati/costi reali *m*	—
comparaison (F)	Vergleich *m*	comparison	—	confronto *m*	comparación *f*
comparaison des cours (F)	Kursvergleich *m*	comparison of prices	—	confronto dei corsi *m*	comparación de las cotizaciones *f*
comparaison des différentes branches (F)	Branchenvergleich *m*	trade comparison	—	comparazione delle categorie *f*	comparación de ramos *f*
comparaison entre les résultats effectifs et les prévisions (F)	Soll/Ist-Vergleich *m*	comparison of estimates with results	—	confronto costi calcolati/costi reali *m*	comparación entre los resultados efectivos y las previsiones *f*
comparative advertising (E)	vergleichende Werbung *f*	—	publicité comparative *f*	pubblicità comparativa *f*	publicidad comparativa *f*
comparazione delle categorie (I)	Branchenvergleich *m*	trade comparison	comparaison des différentes branches *f*	—	comparación de ramos *f*
comparison (E)	Vergleich *m*	—	comparaison *f*	confronto *m*	comparación *f*
comparison of estimates with results (E)	Soll/Ist-Vergleich *m*	—	comparaison entre les résultats effectifs et les prévisions *f*	confronto costi calcolati/costi reali *m*	comparación entre los resultados efectivos y las previsiones *f*
comparison of prices (E)	Kursvergleich *m*	—	comparaison des cours *f*	confronto dei corsi *m*	comparación de las cotizaciones *f*
compensación¹ (Es)	Verrechnung *f*	compensation	compensation *f*	compensazione *f*	—
compensación² (Es)	Kompensation *f*	compensation	compensation *f*	compensazione *f*	—
compensación³ (Es)	Aufrechnung *f*	set-off	compensation *f*	compensazione *f*	—
compensation¹ (E)	Kompensation *f*	—	compensation *f*	compensazione *f*	compensación *f*

	D	E	F	I	Es
compensation² (E)	Entschädigung f	—	indemnité f	indennità f	indemnización f
compensation³ (E)	Verrechnung f	—	compensation f	compensazione f	compensación f
compensation¹ (F)	Verrechnung f	compensation	—	compensazione f	compensación f
compensation² (F)	Aufrechnung f	set-off	—	compensazione f	compensación f
compensation³ (F)	Kompensation f	compensation	—	compensazione f	compensación f
compensation financière (F)	Finanzausgleich m	financial equalization	—	compensazione finanziaria f	ajuste financiero m
compensation for loss suffered (E)	Schadensersatz m	—	dommages-intérêts m pl	risarcimento danni m	indemnización f
compensation fund (E)	Ausgleichsfonds m	—	fonds de compensation m	fondo di compensazione m	fondo de compensación m
compensation offer (E)	Abfindungsangebot n	—	offre d'indemnité f	offerta d'indennità f	oferta de indemnización f
compensation payment (E)	Ausgleichszahlung f	—	payement pour solde de compte m	conguaglio m	pago de compensación m
compensazione¹ (I)	Verrechnung f	compensation	compensation f	—	compensación f
compensazione² (I)	Kompensation f	compensation	compensation f	—	compensación f
compensazione³ (I)	Aufrechnung f	set-off	compensation f	—	compensación f
compensazione finanziaria (I)	Finanzausgleich m	financial equalization	compensation financière f	—	ajuste financiero m
compenso straordinario (I)	Sondervergütung f	special remuneration	rémunération spéciale f	—	gratificación f
competence (E)	Kompetenz f	—	compétence f	competenza f	competencia f
compétence¹ (F)	Kompetenz f	competence	—	competenza f	competencia f
compétence² (F)	Sachkenntnis f	know-how	—	competenza f	conocimiento de causa m
compétence législative (F)	Gesetzgebungshoheit f	legislative sovereignty	—	sovranità legislativa f	soberanía legislativa f
competencia¹ (Es)	Konkurrenz f	competition	concurrence f	concorrenza f	—
competencia² (Es)	Kompetenz f	competence	compétence f	competenza f	—
competencia³ (Es)	Wettbewerb m	competition	compétition f	concorrenza f	—
competencia de precios (Es)	Preiswettbewerb m	competition in prices	concurrence des prix f	competizione dei prezzi f	—
competencia desleal (Es)	unlauterer Wettbewerb m	unfair competition	concurrence déloyale f	concorrenza sleale f	—
competencia viable (Es)	funktionsfähiger Wettbewerb m	workable competition	concurrence viable f	concorrenza perfetta f	—
competenza¹ (I)	Sachkenntnis f	know-how	compétence f	—	conocimiento de causa m
competenza² (I)	Kompetenz f	competence	compétence f	—	competencia f
competición de vendedores (Es)	Verkäuferwettbewerb m	sellers competition	compétition des vendeurs f	concorrenza dei venditori f	—
competidor (Es)	Konkurrent m	competitor	concurrent m	concorrente m	—
competing firm (E)	Konkurrenzfirma f	—	maison concurrente f	ditta concorrente f	empresa competidora f
compétition (F)	Wettbewerb m	competition	—	concorrenza f	competencia f
competition¹ (E)	Wettbewerb m	—	compétition f	concorrenza f	competencia f
competition² (E)	Konkurrenz f	—	concurrence f	concorrenza f	competencia f
compétition des vendeurs (F)	Verkäuferwettbewerb m	sellers competition	—	concorrenza dei venditori f	competición de vendedores f
competition in prices (E)	Preiswettbewerb m	—	concurrence des prix f	competizione dei prezzi f	competencia de precios f
competition policy (E)	Wettbewerbspolitik f	—	politique de concurrence f	politica concorrenziale f	política de competencia f
competitive advantage (E)	Wettbewerbsvorteil m	—	avantage de concurrence m	vantaggio concorrenziale m	ventaja de competencia f
competitiveness (E)	Wettbewerbsfähigkeit f	—	compétitivité f	competitività f	competitividad f
competitive situation (E)	Konkurrenzsituation f	—	situation de concurrence f	situazione concorrenziale f	situación de competencia f
competitividad (Es)	Wettbewerbsfähigkeit f	competitiveness	compétitivité f	competitività f	—

	D	E	F	I	Es
competitività (I)	Wettbewerbs-fähigkeit f	competitiveness	compétitivité f	—	competitividad f
compétitivité (F)	Wettbewerbs-fähigkeit f	competitiveness	—	competitività f	competitividad f
competitor[1] (E)	Konkurrent m	—	concurrent m	concorrente m	competidor m
competitor[2] (E)	Mitbewerber m	—	concurrent m	competitore m	contendiente m
competitore (I)	Mitbewerber m	competitor	concurrent m	—	contendiente m
competizione dei prezzi (I)	Preiswettbewerb m	competition in prices	concurrence des prix f	—	competencia de precios f
compettive undertaking (E)	Konkurrenz-unternehmen n	—	entreprise concurrente f	impresa concorrente f	empresa competitoria f
compilazione del bilancio (I)	Budgetierung f	budgeting	établissement du budget m	—	establecimiento del presupuesto m
complaint[1] (E)	Reklamation f	—	réclamation f	reclamo m	reclamación f
complaint[2] (E)	Beschwerde f	—	réclamation f	protesta f	recurso m
compleanno (I)	Geburtstag m	birthday	anniversaire m	—	cumpleaños m
complementary goods (E)	komplementäre Güter pl	—	produits de complément m pl	beni complementari m pl	bienes com-plementarios m pl
completamento (I)	Fertigstellung f	completion	achèvement m	—	terminación total f
completion (E)	Fertigstellung f	—	achèvement m	completamento m	terminación total f
compliance (E)	Erfüllung f	—	acquittement m	adempimento m	cumplimiento m
componenti essenziali (I)	wesentliche Bestandteile pl	integral parts	parties constitutives essentielles f pl	—	partes integrantes esencial f pl
comportamiento de compra (Es)	Kaufverhalten n	purchase pattern	comportement d'achat m	filosofia d'acquisto f	—
comportamiento racional (Es)	Rationalverhalten n	rational behaviour	comportement rationnel m	atteggiamento razionale m	—
comportement d'achat (F)	Kaufverhalten n	purchase pattern	—	filosofia d'acquisto f	comportamiento de compra m
comportement rationnel (F)	Rationalverhalten n	rational behaviour	—	atteggiamento razionale m	comportamiento racional m
composition proceedings (E)	Vergleichsverfahren n	—	procédure de conciliation f	procedura di concordato f	procedimiento conciliatorio m
composizione dell'assortimento (I)	Sortiments-gestaltung f	assortment structuring	structure du sortiment f	—	configuración del surtido f
compound interest (E)	Zinseszins m	—	intérêt composé m	interessi composti m pl	interés compuesto m
compra[1] (Es)	Ankauf m	purchase	achat m	acquisto m	—
compra[2] (Es)	Einkauf m	purchase	achat m	acquisto m	—
compra[3] (Es)	Kauf m	purchase	achat m	acquisto m	—
compra a plazo (Es)	Ratenkauf m	hire-purchase transaction	achat à tempérament m	acquisto a rate m	—
compra a plazos (Es)	Zielkauf m	purchase on credit	achat à terme m	acquisto a termine m	—
compra a prueba (Es)	Kauf auf Probe m	sale on approval	achat à l'éssai m	acquisto a titolo di prova m	—
compra de crédito (Es)	Kreditkauf m	credit purchase	achat à crédit m	acquisto a credito m	—
compra de sustitución (Es)	Ersatzkauf m	substitute purchase	achat de remplacement m	acquisto di compensazione m	—
comprador (Es)	Einkäufer m	buyer	acheteur m	acquirente m	—
comprador al por mayor (Es)	Großabnehmer m	bulk buyer	acheteur en gros m	acquirente all'ingrosso m	—
comprador final (Es)	Endabnehmer m	ultimate buyer	preneur final m	acquirente finale m	—
compra espontánea (Es)	Impulskauf m	impulse buying	achat d'impulsion m	acquisto impulsivo m	—
compra intermediaria (Es)	Zwischenabnahme f	intermediate purchase	achat intermédiaire m	acquisto intermediario m	—
compra para sostener precios (Es)	Stützungskauf m	support buying	achat de soutien m	acquisto di sostegno m	—
comprar[1] (Es)	einkaufen	buy	acheter	acquistare	—
comprar[2] (Es)	kaufen	buy	acheter	acquistare	—
compras de intervención (Es)	Interventionskäufe pl	intervention buying	achats d'intervention m pl	acquisti d'intervento m pl	—
compras de sostén (Es)	Kurspflege f	price nursing	soutien des cours m	sostegno dei corsi m	—

	D	E	F	I	Es
compras especulativas (Es)	Meinungskäufe pl	speculative buying	achats spéculatifs m pl	acquisti speculativi m pl	—
comprehensive insurance (E)	Kaskoversicherung f	—	assurance tous risques f	assicurazione corpi del ramo trasporto f	seguro de casco m
compromiso (Es)	Engagement n	engagement/ commitment	engagement m	impegno m	—
comproprietà (I)	Miteigentum n	co-ownership	copropriété f	—	copropiedad f
comproprietario di quota ideale (I)	Bruchteils-eigentümer m	co-owner	copropriétaire d'une quote-part m	—	copropietario de bienes indivisos m
comptabilisation économique (F)	Wirtschafts-rechnung f	economic account	—	conto economico m	contabilización económica f
comptabilité¹ (F)	Rechnungswesen n	accounting system	—	ragioneria f	contabilidad f
comptabilité² (F)	Buchhaltung f	accounting	—	contabilità f	contabilidad f
comptabilité³ (F)	Buchführung f	bookkeeping	—	contabilità f	contabilidad f
comptabilité en partie double (F)	doppelte Buchführung f	double entry bookkeeping	—	contabilità a partita doppia f	contabilidad por doble partida f
comptabilité financière (F)	Finanzbuchhaltung f	financial accounting	—	contabilità finanziaria f	contabilidad financiera f
comptabilité national (F)	Volkswirtschaftliche Gesamtrechnung f	national accounting	—	contabilità nazionale f	contabilidad nacional f
comptable (F)	Buchhalter m	bookkeeper	—	ragioniere m	tenedor de libros m
comptant¹ (F)	bar	cash	—	in contanti	al contado
comptant² (F)	in bar	in cash	—	in contanti	en efectivo
compte (F)	Konto n	account	—	conto m	cuenta f
compte anonyme (F)	Nummernkonto n	numbered account	—	conto cifrato m	cuenta cifrada f
compte bloqué¹ (F)	Sperrkonto n	blocked account	—	conto vincolato m	fondos bloqueados m pl
compte bloqué² (F)	gesperrtes Konto n	blocked account	—	conto bloccato m	cuenta congelada f
compte chèque postal (F)	Postscheckkonto n	(postal) giro account	—	conto corrente postale m	cuenta corriente postal f
compte courant¹ (F)	laufende Rechnung f	current account	—	conto corrente m	cuenta corriente f
compte courant² (F)	Kontokorrent n	account current	—	conto corrente m	cuenta corriente f
compte de caisse (F)	Kassenbuch n	cash book	—	libro di cassa m	libro de caja m
compte de dépôt à terme (F)	Festgeldkonto n	time deposit account	—	deposito vincolato m	cuenta a plazo f
compte de devises (F)	Devisenbilanz f	foreign exchange balance	—	bilancia delle divise f	balanza de divisas f
compte de domicilia-tion du salaire (F)	Gehaltskonto n	salary account	—	conto stipendi m	cuenta de salario f
compte de frais par secteurs (F)	Kostenstelle f	departmental expense account	—	posizione costi f	posición de costes f
compte de liquidation (F)	Abwicklungskonto n	settlement account	—	conto di liquidazione f	cuenta de liquidación f
compte de liquidité (F)	Liquiditätsrechnung f	liquidity calculation	—	calcolo della liquidità m	cálculo de liquidez m
compte de maison (F)	Firmenkonto n	company account	—	conto intestato ad una ditta m	cuenta de la empresa f
compte de pertes et profits (F)	Gewinn- und Verlustrechnung f	profit and loss account	—	conto profitti e perdite m	cuenta de pérdidas y ganancias f
compte de résultats (F)	Erfolgskonto n	profit account	—	conto profitti m	cuenta de beneficios y pérdidas f
compte de tiers (F)	Anderkonto n	fiduciary account	—	conto per terzi m	cuenta fiduciaria de un abogado f
compte d'étranger (F)	Auslandskonto n	foreign account	—	conto estero m	cuenta exterior m
compte d'existences (F)	Bestandskonto n	real account	—	conto merci m	cuenta de existencias f
compte en banque (F)	Bankkonto n	bank account	—	conto bancario m	cuenta bancaria f
compte en monnaies étrangères (F)	Währungskonto n	foreign currency account	—	conto in valuta m	cuenta de moneda extranjera f
compte privé (F)	Privatkonto n	private account	—	conto privato m	cuenta particular f
compte provisoire (F)	Zwischenkonto n	interim account	—	conto transitorio m	cuenta provisional f
compter des intérêts (F)	verzinsen	pay interest	—	pagare interessi	pagar interés
compte rendu (F)	Berichterstattung f	reporting	—	relazione f	reportaje m

	D	E	F	I	Es
compte rendu d'activité économique annuel (F)	Jahreswirtschafts-bericht *m*	Annual Economic Report	—	relazione generale sulla situazione economica *f*	informe económico anual *m*
comptes-transitoires (F)	Abgrenzungs-posten *m*	deferred item	—	ratei e risconti *m pl*	cuentas de orden *f pl*
compte tenu en compte courant (F)	Kontokorrentkonto *n*	current account	—	conto corrente *m*	cuenta corriente *f*
compte trimestriel (F)	Quartalsrechnung *f*	quarterly invoice	—	conto trimestrale *m*	cuenta trimestral *f*
compulsory consolidation of farmland (E)	Flurbereinigung *f*	—	remembrement parcellaire *m*	ricomposizione fondiaria *f*	concentración par celaria *f*
compulsory saving (E)	Zwangssparen *n*	—	épargne forcée *f*	risparmio coatto *m*	ahorro forzoso *m*
compulsory settlement (E)	Zwangsvergleich *m*	—	arrangement forcé *m*	concordato fallimentare *m*	convenio forzoso *m*
computation (E)	Berechnung *f*	—	calcul *m*	calcolo *m*	calculación *f*
Computer (D)	—	computer	ordinateur *m*	computer *m*	ordenador *m*
computer¹ (E)	Rechner *m*	—	ordinateur *m*/ calculateur de poche *m*	calcolatore *m*	ordenador *m*/ calculadora de bolsillo *f*
computer² (E)	Computer *m*	—	ordinateur *m*	computer *m*	ordenador *m*
computer (I)	Computer *m*	computer	ordinateur *m*	—	ordenador *m*
computer-aided information system (E)	computergestützes Informationssystem *n*	—	système d'informa-tion assisté par ordinateur *m*	sistema di informazione computerizzato *m*	sistema de información asistido por ordenador *m*
computer centre (E)	Rechenzentrum *n*	—	centre de calcul *m*	centro da computer *m*	centro de computación *m*
computer criminality (E)	Computer-kriminalität *f*	—	délits informatiques *m pl*	abuso del computer *m*	delincuencia informática *f*
Computereinsatz (D)	—	use of computers	emploi d'ordinateurs *m*	impiego di computer *m*	utilización de ordenadores *f*
computergestützes Informations-system (D)	—	computer-aided information system	système d'informa-tion assisté par ordinateur *m*	sistema di informazione computerizzato *m*	sistema de información asistido por ordenador *m*
Computer-kriminalität (D)	—	computer criminality	délits informatiques *m pl*	abuso del computer *m*	delincuencia informática *f*
Computertechnik (D)	—	computer technology	technique informatique *f*	tecnica dei computer *f*	técnica informática *f*
computer technology (E)	Computertechnik *f*	—	technique informatique *f*	tecnica dei computer *f*	técnica informática *f*
computisteria (I)	Nachkalkulation *f*	historical costing	calcul des coûts a posteriori *m*	—	cálculo de costes a posteriori *m*
cómputo de intereses (Es)	Zinsrechnung *f*	interest account	calcul des intérêts *m*	conteggio degli interessi *m*	—
comune¹ (I)	Gemeinde *f*	community	commune *f*	—	comunidad *f*
comune² (I)	Kommune *f*	municipality	commune *f*	—	municipalidad *f*
comunicación de télex (Es)	Telexanschluß *m*	telex connection	communication de télex *f*	collegamento telex *m*	—
comunicaciones (Es)	Wegenetz *n*	road network	voirie *f*	rete stradale *f*	—
comunicativa (I)	Kontaktfähigkeit *f*	capability to establish public relations	capacité d'entrer en contact *f*	—	capacidad de anudar contactos *f*
comunicazione (I)	Mitteilung *f*	information	notification *f*	—	aviso *m*
comunicazione stampa (I)	Pressemitteilung *f*	press release	commentaire de presse *m*	—	remitido a la prensa *m*
comunidad (Es)	Gemeinde *f*	community	commune *f*	comune *m*	—
comunidad económica (Es)	Wirtschafts-gemeinschaft *f*	economic community	communauté économique *f*	comunità economica *f*	—
Comunidad Europea (Es)	Europäische Gemeinschaft, EG *f*	European Community	Communauté Européenne, EC *f*	Comunità Europea CEE *f*	—
comunidad sucesoria (Es)	Erbengemeinschaft *f*	community of heirs	communauté d'héritiers *f*	comunità degli eredi *f*	—
comunità degli eredi (I)	Erbengemeinschaft *f*	community of heirs	communauté d'héritiers *f*	—	comunidad sucesoria *f*
comunità economica (I)	Wirtschafts-gemeinschaft *f*	economic community	communauté économique *f*	—	comunidad económica *f*
Comunità Europea (I)	Europäische Gemeinschaft, EG *f*	European Community	Communauté Européenne, EC *f*	—	Comunidad Europea, C.E. *f*

	D	E	F	I	Es
concédant de licence (F)	Lizenzgeber m	licenser	—	concedente di licenza m	licitador m
concedente del leasing (I)	Leasing-Geber m	lessor	donneur de leasing m	—	arrendatario financiero m
concedente di licenza (I)	Lizenzgeber m	licenser	concédant de licence m	—	licitador m
concentración (Es)	Konzentration f	concentration	concentration f	concentrazione f	—
concentración de empresas (Es)	Unternehmens-konzentration f	business concentration	concentration d'entreprises f	pool d'imprese m	—
concentración económica (Es)	Wirtschafts-konzentration f	economic concentration	concentration économique f	concentrazione economica f	—
concentración parcelaria (Es)	Flurbereinigung f	compulsory consolidation of farmland	remembrement parcellaire m	ricomposizione fondiaria f	—
concentration (F)	Konzentration f	concentration	—	concentrazione f	concentración f
concentration (E)	Konzentration f	—	concentration f	concentrazione f	concentración f
concentration d'entreprises (F)	Unternehmens-konzentration f	business concentration	—	pool d'imprese m	concentración de empresas f
concentration économique (F)	Wirtschafts-konzentration f	economic concentration	—	concentrazione economica f	concentración económica f
concentrazione (I)	Konzentration f	concentration	concentration f	—	concentración f
concentrazione economica (I)	Wirtschafts-konzentration f	economic concentration	concentration économique f	—	concentración económica f
concepción (Es)	Konzeption f	conception	conception f	concezione f	—
concepción de venta (Es)	Verkaufskonzeption f	sales conception	conception de vente f	concezione di vendita f	—
concepción general (Es)	Gesamtkonzeption f	overall conception	conception générale f	concezione universale f	—
concept (E)	Konzept n	—	brouillon m	piano m	bosquejo m
conception (E)	Konzeption f	—	conception f	concezione f	concepción f
conception (F)	Konzeption f	conception	—	concezione f	concepción f
conceptional thinking (E)	konzeptionelles Denken n	—	penser conceptionnel m	mentalità concezionale f	pensar concepcional m
conception de vente (F)	Verkaufskonzeption f	sales conception	—	concezione di vendita f	concepción de venta f
conception générale (F)	Gesamtkonzeption f	overall conception	—	concezione universale f	concepción general f
concepto comercial (Es)	Unternehmens-konzept n	business concept	stratégie de l'entreprise f	piano imprenditoriale m	—
concesión (Es)	Konzession f	licence	concession f	concessione f	—
concesionario (Es)	Franchisenehmer m	concessionary	concessionaire m	concessionarion m	—
concesionary (E)	Franchisenehmer m	—	concessionaire m	concessionario m	concesionario m
concesión de un plazo (Es)	Fristgewährung f	granting a respite	octroi d'un délai m	concessione di un termine f	—
concession (F)	Konzession f	licence	—	concessione f	concesión f
concessionario (I)	Franchise-nehmer m	concessionary	concessionaire m	—	concesionario m
concessionario di licenza (I)	Lizenznehmer m	licensee	preneur d'une licence m	—	licenciado m
concessione (I)	Konzession f	licence	concession f	—	concesión f
concessione di un termine (I)	Fristgewährung f	granting a respite	octroi d'un délai m	—	concesión de un plazo f
concessionnaire (F)	Franchisenehmer m	concessionary	—	concessionario m	concesionario m
concezione (I)	Konzeption f	conception	conception f	—	concepción f
concezione di vendita (I)	Verkaufskonzeption f	sales conception	conception de vente f	—	concepción de venta f
concezione universale (I)	Gesamtkonzeption f	overall conception	conception générale f	—	concepción general f
conclusion (E)	Abschluß m	—	conclusion f	stipulazione f	contratación f/ conclusión f/cierre m
conclusion (F)	Abschluß m	conclusion	—	stipulazione f	contratación f/ conclusión f/cierre m
conclusion d'une affaire (F)	Geschäftsabschluß m	conclusion of a deal	—	conclusione di un affare f	conclusión de un negocio f/cierre de cuentas m

	D	E	F	I	Es
conclusión de la venta (Es)	Verkaufsabschluß m	sales contract	contrat de vente m	conclusione di vendita f	—
conclusión de un contrato (Es)	Vertragsabschluß m	conclusion of a contract	conclusion du contrat f	stipulazione del contratto f	—
conclusión de un negocio (Es)	Geschäftsabschluß m	conclusion of a deal	conclusion d'une affaire f	conclusione di un affare f	—
conclusion du contrat (F)	Vertragsabschluß m	conclusion of a contract	—	stipulazione del contratto f	conclusión de un contrato f
conclusion du marché (F)	Kaufabschluß m	conclusion of a sales contract	—	conclusione d'acquisto f	convenio de compra m
conclusione d'acquisto (I)	Kaufabschluß m	conclusion of a sales contract	conclusion du marché f	—	convenio de compra m
conclusione di un affare (I)	Geschäftsabschluß m	conclusion of a deal	conclusion d'une affaire f	—	conclusión de un negocio f
conclusione di vendita (I)	Verkaufsabschluß m	sales contract	contract de vente m	—	conclusión de la venta f
conclusion of a contract (E)	Vertragsabschluß m	—	conclusion du contrat f	stipulazione del contratto f	conclusión de un contrato f
conclusion of a deal (E)	Geschäftsabschluß m	—	conclusion d'une affaire f	conclusione di un affare f	conclusión de un negocio f/cierre de cuentas m
conclusion of a sales contract (E)	Kaufabschluß m	—	conclusion du marché f	conclusione d'acquisto f	convenio de compra m
concordato fallimentare (I)	Zwangsvergleich m	compulsory settlement	arrangement forcé m	—	convenio forzoso m
concorrente (I)	Konkurrent m	competitor	concurrent m	—	competidor m
concorrenza[1] (I)	Wettbewerb m	competition	compétition f	—	competencia f
concorrenza[2] (I)	Konkurrenz f	competition	concurrence f	—	competencia f
concorrenza dei venditori (I)	Verkäuferwettbewerb m	sellers competition	compétition des vendeurs f	—	competición de vendedores f
concorrenza sleale (I)	unlauterer Wettbewerb m	unfair competition	concurrence déloyale f	—	competencia desleal f
con crédito documentario (Es)	gegen Akkreditiv	against letter of credit	contre accréditif	contro lettera di credito	—
concurrence (F)	Konkurrenz f	competition	—	concorrenza f	competencia f
concurrence déloyale (F)	unlauterer Wettbewerb m	unfair competition	—	concorrenza sleale f	competencia desleal f
concurrence des prix (F)	Preiswettbewerb m	competition in prices	—	competizione dei prezzi f	competencia de precios f
concurrent (E)	Zug um Zug	—	de point en point	contestualmente	punto por punto
concurrent[1] (F)	Konkurrent m	competitor	—	concorrente m	competidor m
concurrent[2] (F)	Mitbewerber m	competitor	—	competitore m	contendiente m
concurso-subasta (Es)	Ausschreibung f	tender	soumission f	appalto m	—
condición (Es)	Bedingung f	condition	condition f	condizione f	—
condiciones comerciales (Es)	Handelsbedingungen pl	trading conditions	conditions commerciales f pl	condizioni commerciali f pl	—
condiciones contractuales (Es)	Vertragsbedingung f	term of contract	condition du contrat f	condizione del contratto f	—
condiciones de compra (Es)	Einkaufsbedingungen pl	purchasing terms	conditions d'achat f pl	condizioni d'acquisto f pl	—
condiciones de pago (Es)	Zahlungsbedingung f	terms of payment	conditions de payement f pl	condizione di pagamento f	—
condiciones de suministro (Es)	Lieferbedingungen pl	terms of delivery	conditions de livraison f pl	condizioni di consegna f pl	—
condiciones de transporte (Es)	Beförderungsbedingungen f	terms of conveyance	conditions de transport f pl	condizioni di trasporto f pl	—
condiciones del mercado (Es)	Marktlage f	state of the market	situation du marché f	situazione di mercato f	—
condiciones generales de contrato (Es)	allgemeine Geschäftsbedingungen pl	general terms	conditions générales de contract f pl	condizioni generali di contratto f pl	—
condición previa (Es)	Voraussetzung f	precondition	condition préalable f	presupposto m	—
condition[1] (E)	Bedingung f	—	condition f	condizione f	condición f
condition[1] (F)	Kondition f	condition	—	condizione f	condición f
condition[2] (E)	Kondition f	—	condition f	condizione f	condición f

	D	E	F	I	Es
condition² (F)	Bedingung f	condition	—	condizione f	condición f
condition du contrat (F)	Vertragsbedingung f	term of contract	—	condizione del contratto f	condiciones contractuales f pl
condition préalable (F)	Voraussetzung f	precondition	—	presupposto m	condición previa f
conditions commerciales (F)	Handelsbedingungen pl	trading conditions	—	condizioni commerciali f pl	condiciones comerciales f pl
conditions d'achat (F)	Einkaufsbedingungen pl	purchasing terms	—	condizioni d'acquisto f pl	condiciones de compra f pl
conditions de livraison (F)	Lieferbedingungen pl	terms of delivery	—	condizioni di consegna f pl	condiciones de suminstro pl
conditions de payement (F)	Zahlungsbedingung f	terms of payment	—	condizione di pagamento f	condiciones de pago f pl
conditions de transport (F)	Beförderungsbedingungen f	terms of conveyance	—	condizioni di trasporto f pl	condiciones de transporte f pl
conditions générales de contract (F)	allgemeine Geschäftsbedingungen pl	general terms	—	condizioni generali di contratto f pl	condiciones generales de contrato f pl
condizione¹ (I)	Kondition f	condition	condition f	—	condición f
condizione² (I)	Bedingung f	condition	condition f	—	condición f
condizione del contratto (I)	Vertragsbedingung f	term of contract	condition du contrat f	—	condiciones contractuales f pl
condizione di pagamento (I)	Zahlungsbedingung f	terms of payment	conditions de payement f pl	—	condiciones de pago f pl
condizioni commerciali (I)	Handelsbedingungen pl	trading conditions	conditions commerciales f pl	—	condiciones comerciales f pl
condizioni d'acquisto (I)	Einkaufsbedingungen pl	purchasing terms	conditions d'achat f pl	—	condiciones de compra f pl
condizioni di consegna (I)	Lieferbedingungen pl	terms of delivery	conditions de livraison f pl	—	condiciones de suminstro f pl
condizioni di trasporto (I)	Beförderungsbedingungen f	terms of conveyance	conditions de transport f pl	—	condiciones de transporte f pl
condizioni generali di contratto (I)	allgemeine Geschäftsbedingungen pl	general terms	conditions générales de contract f pl	—	condiciones generales de contrato f pl
condizioni generali di credito (I)	allgemeine Kreditvereinbarungen pl	general borrowing agreements	accords généraux de crédit f pl	—	acuerdos generales de crédito m pl
con effetto retroattivo (I)	rückwirkend	retrospective	rétroactif	—	retroactivo
con falta de objetividad (Es)	unsachgemäß	improper	non adéquat	non idoneo	—
conference (E)	Konferenz f	—	conférence f	conferenza f	conferencia f
conférence¹ (F)	Konferenz f	conference	—	conferenza f	conferencia f
conférence² (F)	Besprechung f	discussion	—	colloquio m	conferencia f
conférence de presse (F)	Pressekonferenz f	press conference	—	conferenza stampa f	rueda de prensa f
Conférence des Nations Unies sur le Commerce et le Développement (F)	Welthandelskonferenz f	United Nations Conference on Trade and Development	—	Comitato delle Nazioni Unite per il commercio e lo sviluppo m	Conferencia de las Naciones Unidas sobre el Comercio y el Desarrollo f
conference room¹ (E)	Sitzungszimmer n	—	salle de réunion f	sala riunioni f	sala de conferencia f
conference room² (E)	Konferenzraum m	—	salle de conférences f	sala conferenze f	sala de conferencia f
conferencia¹ (Es)	Besprechung f	discussion	conférence f	colloquio m	—
conferencia² (Es)	Konferenz f	conference	conférence f	conferenza f	—
Conferencia de las Naciones Unidas sobre el Comercio y el Desarrollo (Es)	Welthandelskonferenz f	United Nations Conference on Trade and Development	Conférence des Nations Unies sur le Commerce et le Développement	Comitato delle Nazioni Unite per il commercio e lo sviluppo m	—
conferencia de representantes (Es)	Vertretertagung f	sales meeting	réunion de représentants f	convegno dei rappresentanti m	—
Conferencia Internacional de Materias Primas (Es)	internationale Rohstoff-Konferenz f	International Resources Conference	Conférence Internationale des Matières Premières f	Conferenza Internazionale sulle Materie Prime f	—
conferencia telefónica (Es)	Telefongespräch n	telephone conversation	conversation téléphonique f	telefonata f	—
conferenza (I)	Konferenz f	conference	conférence f	—	conferencia f
conferenza stampa (I)	Pressekonferenz f	press conference	conférence de presse f	—	rueda de prensa f

	D	E	F	I	Es
conferma[1] (I)	Zusage f	promise	promesse f	—	promesa f
conferma[2] (I)	Bestätigung f	confirmation	confirmation f	—	confirmación f
conferma della prenotazione (I)	Reservierungs-bestätigung f	reservation confirmation	confirmation de réservation f	—	confirmación de la reservación f
conferma di pagamento (I)	Zahlungs-bestätigung f	receipt for payment	confirmation de payement f	—	confirmación de pago f
conferma d'ordine (I)	Auftragsbestätigung f	confirmation of order	confirmation de commande f	—	confirmación de pedido f
confezione campione (I)	Probepackung f	trial package	échantillon m	—	muestra f
confidencial (Es)	vertraulich	confidential	confidentiel	confidenziale	—
confidential (E)	vertraulich	—	confidentiel	confidenziale	confidencial
confidential relationship (E)	Vertrauens-verhältnis n	—	rapport de confiance m	rapporto di fiducia m	relación de confianza f
confidentiality (E)	Diskretion f	—	discrétion f	discrezione f	discreción f
confidentiel (F)	vertraulich	confidential	—	confidenziale	confidencial
confidenziale (I)	vertraulich	confidential	confidentiel	—	confidencial
configuración del surtido (Es)	Sortiments-gestaltung f	assortment structuring	structure du sortiment f	composizione dell'assortimento f	—
confine doganale (I)	Zollgrenze f	customs frontier	frontière douanière f	—	frontera aduanera f
confirmación (Es)	Bestätigung f	confirmation	confirmation f	conferma f	—
confirmación de la reservación (Es)	Reservierungs-bestätigung f	reservation confirmation	confirmation de réservation f	conferma della prenotazione f	—
confirmación de pago (Es)	Zahlungs-bestätigung f	receipt for payment	confirmation de payement f	conferma di pagamento f	—
confirmación de pedido (Es)	Auftragsbestätigung f	confirmation of order	confirmation de commande f	conferma d'ordine f	—
confirmation (E)	Bestätigung f	—	confirmation f	conferma f	confirmación f
confirmation (F)	Bestätigung f	confirmation	—	conferma f	confirmación f
confirmation bancaire (F)	Bankavis m	bank notification	—	avviso bancario m	aviso bancario m
confirmation de commande (F)	Auftragsbestätigung f	confirmation of order	—	conferma d'ordine f	confirmación de pedido f
confirmation de payement (F)	Zahlungs-bestätigung f	receipt for payment	—	conferma di pagamento f	confirmación de pago f
confirmation de réservation (F)	Reservierungs-bestätigung f	reservation confirmation	—	conferma della prenotazione f	confirmación de la reservación f
confirmation of cover (E)	Deckungszusage f	—	acceptation de prendre le risque en charge f	impegno di copertura m	nota de cobertura f
confirmation of order (E)	Auftragsbestätigung f	—	confirmation de commande f	conferma d'ordine f	confirmación de pedido f
confiscación (Es)	Beschlagnahme f	confiscation	saisie f	sequestro m	—
confiscation (E)	Beschlagnahme f	—	saisie f	sequestro m	confiscación f
conflicting goals (E)	Zielkonflikt m	—	conflit d'objectifs m	incompatibilità degli obiettivi f	conflicto de objectivos m
conflicto de objectivos (Es)	Zielkonflikt m	conflicting goals	conflit d'objectifs m	incompatibilità degli obiettivi f	—
conflicto jurídico (Es)	Rechtsstreit m	legal action	litige m	causa f	—
conflit d'objectifs (F)	Zielkonflikt m	conflicting goals	—	incompatibilità degli obiettivi f	conflicto de objectivos m
conforme al mercado (Es)	marktkonform	in conformity with market conditions	conforme au marché	conforme al mercato	—
conforme al mercato (I)	marktkonform	in conformity with market conditions	conforme au marché	—	conforme al mercado
conforme au marché (F)	marktkonform	in conformity with market conditions	—	conforme al mercato	conforme al mercado
confronto (I)	Vergleich m	comparison	comparaison f	—	comparación f
confronto costi calcolati/costi reali (I)	Soll/Ist-Vergleich m	comparison of estimates with results	comparaison entre les résultats effectifs et les prévisions f	—	comparación entre los resultados efectivos y las previsiones f
confronto dei corsi (I)	Kursvergleich m	comparison of prices	comparaison des cours f	—	comparación de las cotizaciones f

	D	E	F	I	Es
congé (F)	Urlaub *m*	annual holidays/ vacation	—	ferie *f pl*/vacanze *f pl*	vacaciones *f pl*/ vacaciones colectivas de la empresa *f pl*
congelación salarial (Es)	Lohnstopp *m*	wage freeze	blocage des salaires *m*	blocco dei salari *m*	—
congé non payé (F)	unbezahlter Urlaub *m*	unpaid vacation	—	ferie non pagate *f pl*	vacaciones no pagadas *f pl*
congé payé (F)	bezahlter Urlaub *m*	paid vacation	.	ferie pagate *f pl*	vacaciones con goce de sueldo *f pl*
congiuntura (I)	Konjunktur *f*	business cycle	conjuncture *f*	—	conyuntura *f*
congiuntura quantitativa (I)	Mengenkonjunktur *f*	quantitative boom	conjoncture de quantité *f*	—	coyuntura cuantitativa *f*
con gran intensidad de capital (Es)	kapitalintensiv	capital-intensive	avec grande intensité de capital	ad alta incidenza di capitale	—
con gran intensidad de costos salariales (Es)	lohnintensiv	wage-intensive	déterminé par le facteur salaire	ad alta incidenza salariale	—
con gran intensidad de mano de obra (Es)	arbeitsintensiv	labour-intensive	déterminé par le facteur main-d'œuvre	ad alta incidenza di lavoro	—
congratulations (E)	Glückwunsch *m*	—	félicitations *f pl*	auguri *m pl*	felicitaciones *f pl*
congrès (F)	Tagung *f*	meeting	—	convegno *m*	reunión *f*
conguaglio (I)	Ausgleichszahlung *f*	compensation payment	payement pour solde de compte *m*	—	pago de compensación *m*
conjecture (E)	Mutmaßung *f*	—	présomption *f*	presunzione *f*	suposición *f*
conjoncture (F)	Konjunktur *f*	business cycle	—	congiuntura *f*	conyuntura *f*
conjoncture de quantité (F)	Mengenkonjunktur *f*	quantitative boom		congiuntura quantitativa *f*	coyuntura cuantitativa *f*
connaissances fondamentales (F)	Grundkenntnisse *pl*	basic knowledge	—	cognizioni elementari *f pl*	conocimientos básicos *m pl*
connaissances professionnelles (F)	Fachwissen *n*	professional knowledge	—	cognizioni professionali *f pl*	conocimientos especializados *m pl*
connaissement (F)	Konnossement *n*	bill of lading	—	polizza di carico *f*	conocimiento *m*
connaissement maritime (F)	Seefrachtbrief *m*	bill of lading	—	polizza di carico *f*	póliza *f*
connoisseur's price (E)	Liebhaberpreis *m*	—	prix d'amateur *m*	prezzo d'affezione *m*	precio afectivo *m*
conocimiento (Es)	Konnossement *n*	bill of lading	connaissement *m*	polizza di carico *f*	—
conocimiento de causa (Es)	Sachkenntnis *f*	know-how	compétence *f*	competenza *f*	—
conocimientos básicos (Es)	Grundkenntnisse *pl*	basic knowledge	connaissances fondamentales *f pl*	cognizioni elementari *f pl* -	—
conocimientos especializados (Es)	Fachwissen *n*	professional knowledge	connaissances professionnelles *f pl*	cognizioni professionali *f pl*	—
con referencia a (Es)	bezugnehmend	referring to	se référant (à)	con riferimento a	—
con riferimento a (I)	bezugnehmend	referring to	se référant (à)	—	con referencia a
con rispetto dell'ambiente (I)	umweltbewußt	environmental by aware	conscient de la réalité écologique	—	consciente del medio ambiente
conscient de la réalité écologique (F)	umweltbewußt	environmental-conscious	—	con rispetto dell'ambiente	consciente del medio ambiente
consciente del medio ambiente (Es)	umweltbewußt	environmental-conscious	conscient de la réalité écologique	con rispetto dell'ambiente	—
consegna (I)	Übergabe *f*	delivery	remise *f*	—	entrega *f*
consegna contro assegno (I)	Lieferung gegen Nachnahme *f*	cash on delivery	livraison contre remboursement *f*	—	entrega contra reembolso *f*
consegna immediata (I)	sofortige Lieferung *f*	immediate delivery	livraison immédiate *f*	—	entrega inmediata *f*
consegna per espresso (I)	Eilzustellung *f*	express delivery	remise par exprès *f*	—	entrega urgente *f*
consegnare (I)	abliefern	hand over	livrer	—	entregar
Conseil de la Banque Centrale (F)	Zentralbankrat *m*	Central Bank Council	—	consiglio superiore della Banca Centrale *m*	Consejo del Banco Central *m*
conseil de surveillance (F)	Aufsichtsrat *m*	supervisory board	—	consiglio di sorveglianza *m*	consejo de vigilancia *m*
conseiller (F)	Berater *m*	adviser	—	consulente *m*	asesor *m*
conseiller de marketing (F)	Marketingberater *m*	marketing consultant	—	consulente di marketing *m*	asesor de marketing *m*

	D	E	F	I	Es
conseiller fiscal (F)	Steuerberater *m*	tax adviser	—	consulente fiscale *m*	asesor fiscal *m*
consejero directivo (Es)	Vorstandsmitglied *n*	member of the managing board	membre du comité de direction *m*	membro del consiglio di amministrazione *m*	—
consejo de dirección (Es)	Vorstand *m*	board	comité directeur *m*	consiglio di amministrazione *m*	—
Consejo del Banco Central (Es)	Zentralbankrat *m*	Central Bank Council	Conseil de la Banque Centrale *m*	consiglio superiore della Banca Centrale *m*	—
consejo de vigilancia (Es)	Aufsichtsrat *m*	supervisory board	conseil de surveillance *m*	consiglio di sorveglianza *m*	—
consenso¹ (I)	Einwilligung *f*	consent	consentement *m*	—	consentimiento *m*
consenso² (I)	Zustimmung *f*	consent	accord *m*	—	consentimiento *m*
consenso di credito (I)	Kreditzusage *f*	promise of credit	promesse de crédit *f*	—	promesa de créditos *f*
consent¹ (E)	Einwilligung *f*	—	consentement *m*	consenso *m*	consentimiento *m*
consent² (E)	Zustimmung *f*	—	accord *m*	consenso *m*	consentimiento *m*
consentement (F)	Einwilligung *f*	consent	—	consenso *m*	consentimiento *m*
consentimiento¹ (Es)	Zustimmung *f*	consent	accord *m*	consenso *m*	—
consentimiento² (Es)	Einwilligung *f*	consent	consentement *m*	consenso *m*	—
consequential damages (E)	Folgeschäden *pl*	—	dommage consécutif *m*	danni indiretti *m pl*	daño consecuencial *m*
conservación de la sustancia (Es)	Substanzerhaltung *f*	maintaining the real value	maintien de la substance *m*	mantenimento della sostanza *m*	—
conservation du sevret (F)	Geheimhaltung *f*	maintenance of secrecy	—	segretezza *f*	mantenimiento del secreto *m*
conservative estimate (E)	vorsichtige Schätzung *f*	—	évaluation approximative *f*	valutazione approssimativa *f*	evaluación aproximativa *f*
consiglio di amministrazione (I)	Vorstand *m*	board	comité directeur *m*	—	consejo de dirección *m*
consiglio di sorveglianza (I)	Aufsichtsrat *m*	supervisory board	conseil de surveillance *m*	—	consejo de vigilancia *m*
consiglio superiore della Banca Centrale (I)	Zentralbankrat *m*	Central Bank Council	Conseil de la Banque Centrale *m*	—	Consejo del Banco Central *m*
consignment (E)	Sendung *f*	—	envoi *m*	spedizione *f*	envío *m*
consignment note (E)	Frachtbrief *m*	—	lettre de voiture *f*	lettera di vettura *f*	carta de porte *f*
consignment of goods (E)	Warensendung *f*	—	expédition de marchandises *f*	spedizione di merci *f*	envío de mercancías *m*
consignment on approval (E)	Ansichtssendung *f*	—	envoi à condition *m*	campione per esame *m*	envío para inspección *m*
consignment with value declared (E)	Wertsendung *f*	—	envoi avec valeur déclarée *m*	spedizione con valore dichiarato *f*	envío con valor declarado *m*
consolato (I)	Konsulat *n*	consulate	consulat *m*	—	consulado *m*
console (I)	Konsul *m*	consul	consul *m*	—	cónsul *m*
console onorario (I)	Wahlkonsul *m*	honorary consul	consul honoraire *m*	—	cónsul honorario *m*
consolidación (Es)	Konsolidierung *f*	consolidation	consolidation *f*	consolidamento *m*	—
consolidamento (I)	Konsolidierung *f*	consolidation	consolidation *f*	—	consolidación *f*
consolidated balance sheet (E)	konsolidierte Bilanz *f*	—	bilan consolidé *m*	bilancio consolidato *m*	balance consolidado *m*
consolidation (E)	Konsolidierung *f*	—	consolidation *f*	consolidamento *m*	consolidación *f*
consolidation (F)	Konsolidierung *f*	consolidation	—	consolidamento *m*	consolidación *f*
consommateur¹ (F)	Verbraucher *m*	consumer	—	consumatore *m*	consumidor *m*
consommateur² (F)	Konsument *m*	consumer	—	consumatore *m*	consumidor *m*
consommateur final (F)	Endverbraucher *m*	ultimate consumer	—	consumatore finale *m*	consumidor final *m*
consommation (F)	Konsum *m*, Verbrauch *m*	consumption	—	consumo *m*	consumo *m*
consommation personnelle (F)	Eigenverbrauch *m*	personal consumption	—	consumo proprio *m*	consumo propio *m*
consommer (F)	verbrauchen	consume	—	consumare	consumir
consorcio¹ (Es)	Konsortium *n*	consortium	consortium *m*	consorzio *m*	—
consorcio² (Es)	Konzern *m*	group/combine	groupe industriel *m*	gruppo *m*	—
consorcio bancario (Es)	Bankenkonsortium *n*	banking syndicate	consortium des banques *m*	consorzio bancario *m*	—

	D	E	F	I	Es
consorella (I)	Schwester-gesellschaft f	affiliated company	société affiliée f	—	compañía asociada f
consortium (E)	Konsortium n	—	consortium m	consorzio m	consorcio m
consortium (F)	Konsortium n	consortium	—	consorzio m	consorcio m
consortium des banques (F)	Bankenkonsortium n	banking syndicate	—	consorzio bancario m	consorcio bancario m
consorzio (I)	Konsortium n	consortium	consortium m	—	consorcio m
consorzio bancario (I)	Bankenkonsortium n	banking syndicate	consortium des banques m	—	consorcio bancario m
consorzio intercomunale (I)	Zweckverband m	special purpose association	association à but déterminé f	—	asociación con un fin determinado f
constitution (F)	Gründung f	formation	—	costituzione f	fundación f
constitution de capital par apport de tiers (F)	Fremdfinanzierung f	debt financing	—	finanziamento passivo m	financiación externa f
construcción (Es)	Bau m	construction	construction f	costruzione f	—
construcción de viviendas (Es)	Wohnungsbau m	housing construction	construction de logements f	edilizia abitativa f	—
construction (E)	Bau m	—	construction f	costruzione f	construcción f
construction (F)	Bau m	construction	—	costruzione f	construcción f
construction de logements (F)	Wohnungsbau m	housing construction	—	edilizia abitativa f	construcción de viviendas f
construction financiation (E)	Baufinanzierung f	—	financement à la construction m	finanziamento di costruzione m	financiación de la construcción f
construction industry (E)	Bauindustrie f	—	industrie de sous-traitance du bâtiment f	industria edile f	industria de la construcción f
consuetudine di pagamento (I)	Zahlungs-gewohnheit f	practice of payment	habitude de payement f	—	práctica de pago f
consul (E)	Konsul m	—	consul m	console m	cónsul m
cónsul (Es)	Konsul m	consul	consul m	console m	—
consul (F)	Konsul m	consul	—	console m	cónsul m
consulado (Es)	Konsulat n	consulate	consulat m	consolato m	—
consulat (F)	Konsulat n	consulate	—	consolato m	consulado m
consulate (E)	Konsulat n	—	consulat m	consolato m	consulado m
consulente (I)	Berater m	adviser	conseiller m	—	asesor m
consulente di marketing (I)	Marketingberater m	marketing consultant	conseiller de marketing m	—	asesor de marketing m
consulente fiscale (I)	Steuerberater m	tax adviser	conseiller fiscal m	—	asesor fiscal m
consulente legale (I)	Syndikus	legal adviser	syndic m	—	síndico m
consulenza (I)	Beratung f	advice	consultation f	—	asesoramiento m
consul honoraire (F)	Wahlkonsul m	honorary consul	—	console onorario m	cónsul honorario m
cónsul honorario (Es)	Wahlkonsul m	honorary consul	consul honoraire m	console onorario m	—
consultation (F)	Beratung f	advice	—	consulenza f	asesoramiento m
consumare (I)	verbrauchen	consume	consommer	—	consumir
consumatore (I)	Verbraucher m	consumer	consommateur m	—	consumidor m
consumatore finale (I)	Endverbraucher m	ultimate consumer	consommateur final m	—	consumidor final m
consume (E)	verbrauchen	—	consommer	consumare	consumir
consumer (E)	Verbraucher m	—	consommateur m	consumatore m	consumidor m
consumer credit (E)	Konsumkredit m	—	crédit à la consommation m	credito al consumatore m	crédito de consumo m
consumer goods[1] (E)	Verbrauchsgüter pl	—	biens de consommation m pl	beni non durevoli m pl	bienes de consumo m pl
consumer goods[2] (E)	Konsumgüter pl	—	biens de consommation m pl	beni di consumo m pl	bienes de consumo m pl
consumer goods industry (E)	Konsumgüter-industrie f	—	industrie des biens de consommation f	industria dei beni di consumo f	industria de bienes de consumo f
consumer information (E)	Verbraucher-information f	—	information des consommateurs f	informazione per i consumatori f	información de consumidores f
consumer market (E)	Verbrauchermarkt m	—	marché des consommateurs m	ipermercato m	mercado favorable al consumidor m

	D	E	F	I	Es
consumer protection (E)	Verbraucherschutz *m*	—	protection des consommateurs *f*	tutela dei consumatori *f*	protección de los consumidores *f*
consumer protection organization (E)	Verbraucher-organisation *f*	—	organisation des consommateurs *f*	organizzazione dei consumatori *f*	organización de defensa del consumidor *f*
consumer's information (E)	Konsumenten-information *f*	—	information des consommateurs *f*	informazione per i consumatori *f*	información a los comsumidores *f*
consumidor (Es)	Verbraucher *m*	consumer	consommateur *m*	consumatore *m*	—
consumidor final (Es)	Endverbraucher *m*	ultimate consumer	consommateur final *m*	consumatore finale *m*	—
consumir (Es)	verbrauchen	consume	consommer	consumare	—
consumo (Es)	Konsum *m*, Verbrauch *m*	consumption	consommation *f*	consumo *m*	—
consumo (I)	Konsum *m*, Verbrauch *m*	consumption	consommation *f*	—	consumo *m*
consumo propio (Es)	Eigenverbrauch *m*	personal consumption	consommation personnelle *f*	consumo proprio *m*	—
consumo proprio (I)	Eigenverbrauch *m*	personal consumption	consommation personnelle *f*	—	consumo propio *m*
consumption (E)	Konsum *m*, Verbrauch *m*	—	consommation *f*	consumo *m*	consumo *m*
consumption (E)	Konsumstruktur *f*	—	structure de consommation	struttura del consumo *f*	estructura del consumo *f*
contabilidad[1] (Es)	Buchführung *f*	bookkeeping	comptabilité *f*	contabilità *f*	—
contabilidad[2] (Es)	Buchhaltung *f*	accounting	comptabilité *f*	contabilità *f*	—
contabilidad[3] (Es)	Rechnungs-wesen *n*	accounting system	comptabilité *f*	ragioneria *f*	—
contabilidad financiera (Es)	Finanzbuchhaltung *f*	financial accounting	comptabilité financière *f*	contabilità finanziaria *f*	—
contabilidad nacional (Es)	Volkswirtschaftliche Gesamtrechnung *f*	national accounting	comptabilité nationale *f*	contabilità nazionale *f*	—
contabilidad por doble partida (Es)	doppelte Buchführung *f*	double entry bookkeeping	comptabilité en partie double *f*	contabilità a partita doppia *f*	—
contabilità[1] (I)	Buchhaltung *f*	accounting	comptabilité *f*	—	contabilidad *f*
contabilità[2] (I)	Buchführung *f*	bookkeeping	comptabilité *f*	—	contabilidad *f*
contabilità a partita doppia (I)	doppelte Buchführung *f*	double entry bookkeeping	comptabilité en partie double *f*	—	contabilidad por doble partida *f*
contabilità finanziaria (I)	Finanzbuchhaltung *f*	financial accounting	comptabilité financière *f*	—	contabilidad financiera *f*
contabilità nazionale (I)	Volkswirtschaftliche Gesamtrechnung *f*	national accounting	comptabilité nationale *f*	—	contabilidad nacional *f*
contabilización económica (Es)	Wirtschafts-rechnung *f*	economic account	comptabilisation économique *f*	conto economico *m*	—
contador público (Es)	Betriebsprüfer *m*	auditor	expert-comptable *m*	revisore aziendale *m*	—
Container (D)	—	container	container *m*	container *m*	contenedor *m*
container (E)	Container *m*	—	container *m*	container *m*	contenedor *m*
container (F)	Container *m*	container	—	container *m*	contenedor *m*
container (I)	Container *m*	container	container *m*	—	contenedor *m*
container di grande dimensione (I)	Großcontainer *m*	large container	conteneur à grand volume *m*	—	gran contenedor *m*
container transport (E)	Behälterverkehr *m*	—	transport utilisant des containers *m*	trasporto container *m*	transportación en contenedores *f*
contaminación (Es)	Kontamination *f*	contamination	contamination *f*	contaminazione *f*	—
contaminación del agua (Es)	Wasser-verschmutzung *f*	water pollution	contamination des eaux *f*	inquinamento delle acque *m*	—
contaminación del medio ambiente (Es)	Umwelt-verschmutzung *f*	environmental pollution	pollution de l'environnement *f*	inquinamento dell'ambiente *m*	—
contaminante (Es)	umweltschädlich	causing environ-mental damage	nuisible à l'environnement	inquinante	—
contamination (E)	Kontamination *f*	—	contamination *f*	contaminazione *f*	contaminación *f*
contamination (F)	Kontamination *f*	contamination	—	contaminazione *f*	contaminación *f*
contamination des eaux (F)	Wasser-verschmutzung *f*	water pollution	—	inquinamento delle acque *m*	contaminación del agua *f*
contaminazione (I)	Kontamination *f*	contamination	contamination *f*	—	contaminación *f*

	D	E	F	I	Es
conteggio degli interessi (I)	Zinsrechnung f	interest account	calcul des intérêts m	—	cómputo de intereses m
conteggio dei costi di viaggio (I)	Reisekosten-abrechnung f	travel expense accounting	règlement des frais de voyage m	—	liquidación de los gastos de viaje f
conteggio delle provvigioni (I)	Provisions-abrechnung f	statement of a commission	liquidation des commissions f	—	liquidación de la comisión f
conteggio delle spese (I)	Spesenabrechung f	statement of expenses	décompte des frais m	—	liquidación de gastos f
contendiente (Es)	Mitbewerber m	competitor	concurrent m	competitore m	—
contenedor (Es)	Container m	container	container m	container m	—
conteneur à grand volume (F)	Großcontainer m	large container	—	container di grande dimensione m	gran contenedor m
contenimento dei costi (I)	Kostendämpfung f	combatting rising costs	réduction des coûts f	—	disminución de costes f
contestador de llamadas (Es)	Anrufbeantworter m	answering machine	répondeur automatique m	segreteria telefonica f	—
contestualmente (I)	Zug um Zug	concurrent	de point en point	—	punto por punto
conti in nero (I)	schwarze Zahlen pl	surplus	excédent m	—	superávit m
conti in rosso (I)	rote Zahlen pl	(in) the red	chiffres en déficit m	—	cifras rojas f pl
contingent (F)	Kontingent n	quota	—	contingente m	contingente m
contingentación (Es)	Kontingentierung f	fixing of a quota	contingentement m	contingentamento m	—
contingentamento (I)	Kontingentierung f	fixing of a quota	contingentement m	—	contingentación f
contingent de marchandises (F)	Mengenkontingent n	quantity quota	—	contingente di quantità m	contingente cuantitativo m
contingent d'importation (F)	Importquote f	import quota	—	quota d'importazione f	cuota de importación f
contingente (Es)	Kontingent n	quota	contingent m	contingente m	—
contingente (I)	Kontingent n	quota	contingent m	—	contingente m
contingente cuantitativo (Es)	Mengenkontingent n	quantity quota	contingent de marchandises m	contingente di quantità m	—
contingente d'esportazione (I)	Exportquote f	export quota	quota d'exportation m	—	cupo de exportación m
contingente di quantità (I)	Mengenkontingent n	quantity quota	contingent de marchandises m	—	contingente cuantitativo m
contingentement (F)	Kontingentierung f	fixing of a quota	—	contingentamento m	contingentación f
contingentement de l'exportation (F)	Ausfuhr-beschränkung f	export restriction	—	restrizione delle esportazioni f	restricción a la exportación f
continuità di bilancio (I)	Bilanzkontinuität f	formal identity	identité des bilans successifs f	—	identidad de los balances sucsivos f
conto (I)	Konto n	account	compte m	—	cuenta f
conto aperto (I)	offene Rechnung f	unsettled account	facture pas encore payée f	—	factura pendiente f
conto bancario (I)	Bankkonto n	bank account	compte en banque m	—	cuenta bancaria f
conto bloccato (I)	gesperrtes Konto n	blocked account	compte bloqué m	—	cuenta congelada f
conto cifrato (I)	Nummernkonto n	numbered account	compte anonyme m	—	cuenta cifrada f
conto corrente[1] (I)	Kontokorrent n	current account	compte courant m	—	cuenta corriente f
conto corrente[2] (I)	laufende Rechnung f	current account	compte courant m	—	cuenta corriente f
conto corrente[3] (I)	Kontokorrentkonto n	current account	compte tenu en compte courant m	—	cuenta corriente f
conto corrente postale (I)	Postscheckkonto n	(postal) giro account	compte chèque postal m	—	cuenta corriente postal f
conto dei costi limite (I)	Grenzkosten-rechnung f	marginal costing	détermination du coût marginal f	—	cálculo de los costes marginales m
conto di liquidazione (I)	Abwicklungskonto n	settlement account	compte de liquidation m	—	cuenta de liquidación f
conto economico[1] (I)	Ertragsrechnung f	profit and loss account	solde net de l'exploitation m	—	cuenta de ganancias f pl
conto economico[2] (I)	Wirtschaftsrechnung f	economic account	comptabilisation économique f	—	contabilización económica f
conto estero (I)	Auslandskonto n	foreign account	compte d'étranger m	—	cuenta exterior m
conto intestato ad una ditta (I)	Firmenkonto n	foreign company account	compte de maison m	—	cuenta de la empresa f

	D	E	F	I	Es
conto in valuta (I)	Währungskonto *n*	currency account	compte en monnaies étrangères *m*	—	cuenta de moneda extranjera *f*
contol de planificación (Es)	Planungskontrolle *f*	planning control	contrôle de la planification *f*	controllo della programmazione *m*	—
conto merci (I)	Bestandskonto *n*	real account	compte d'existences *m*	—	cuenta de existencias *f*
conto per terzi (I)	Anderkonto *n*	fiduciary account	compte de tiers *m*	—	cuenta fiduciaria de un abogado *f*
conto privato (I)	Privatkonto *n*	private account	compte privé *m*	—	cuenta particular *f*
conto profitti (I)	Erfolgskonto *n*	profit account	compte de résultats *m*	—	cuenta de beneficios y pérdidas *f*
conto profitti e perdite (I)	Gewinn- und Verlustrechnung *f*	profit and loss account	compte de pertes et profits *m*	—	cuenta de pérdidas y ganancias *f*
conto stipendi (I)	Gehaltskonto *n*	salary account	compte de domiciliation du salaire *m*	—	cuenta de salario *f*
conto transitorio (I)	Zwischenkonto *n*	interim account	compte provisoire *m*	—	cuenta provisional *f*
conto trimestrale (I)	Quartalsrechnung *f*	quarterly invoice	compte trimestriel *m*	—	cuenta trimestral *f*
conto vincolato (I)	Sperrkonto *n*	blocked account	compte bloqué *m*	—	fondos bloqueados *m pl*
contrabando (Es)	Schmuggel *m*	smuggling	contrebande *f*	contrabbando *m*	—
contrabbando (I)	Schmuggel *m*	smuggling	contrebande *f*	—	contrabando *m*
contract¹ (E)	Vertrag *m*	—	contrat *m*/traité *m*/ accord *m*	contratto *m*	contrato *m*/tratado *m*/ acuerdo *m*
contract² (E)	Kontrakt *m*	—	contrat *m*	contratto *m*	contrato *m*
contract for work and services (E)	Werkvertrag *m*	—	contrat de louage d'ouvrage et d'industrie *m*	contratto d'appalto *m*	contrato de obra *m*
contract of assignment (E)	Abtretungsvertrag *m*	—	contrat de cession *m*	contratto di cessione *m*	contrato de cesión *m*
contract of employment (E)	Arbeitsvertrag *m*	—	contrat de travail *m*	contratto di lavoro *m*	contrato laboral *m*
contract of sale (E)	Kaufvertrag *m*	—	contrat de vente *m*	contratto di compravendita *m*	contrato de compraventa *m*
contract period (E)	Vertragsdauer *f*	—	durée du contrat *f*	durata del contratto *f*	duración del contrato *f*
contract services (E)	Auftragswesen *n*	—	services commandes *m pl*	settore ordini *m*	servicio de pedidos *m*
contractual penalty (E)	Konventionalstrafe *f*	—	pénalité *f*	penalità convenzionale *f*	pena convencional *f*
contrafirma (Es)	Gegenzeichnung *f*	countersignature	contreseing *m*	controfirma *f*	—
contraire à la loi (F)	ungesetzlich	illegal	—	illegale	ilegal
contra rembolso (Es)	gegen Nachnahme	cash on delivery	contre remboursement	contro assegno	—
contrassegno (I)	Nachnahme *f*	cash on delivery	remboursement *m*	—	reembolso *m*
contrastar (Es)	eichen	gauge	jauger	tarare	—
contrat¹ (F)	Vertrag *m*	contract/treaty	—	contratto *m*	contrato *m*/ tratado *m*
contrat² (F)	Kontrakt *m*	contract	—	contratto *m*	contrato *m*
contrata (Es)	Liefervertrag *m*	supply contract	contrat de fourniture *m*	contratto di consegna *m*	—
contrat à terme (F)	Terminkontrakt *m*	forward contract	—	contratto a termine *m*	contrato de entrega futura *m*
contratación¹ (Es)	Anwerbung *f*	recruitment	recrutement *m*	reclutamento *m*	—
contratación² (Es)	Abschluß *m*	conclusion	conclusion *f*	stipulazione *f*	—
contratación de acciones (Es)	Aktienhandel *m*	dealing in shares	négociation des actions *f*	commercio azionario *m*	—
contrat d'affrètement¹ (F)	Chartervertrag *m*	charter party	—	contratto di noleggio *m*	contrato de fletamento *m*
contrat d'affrètement² (F)	Frachtvertrag *m*	freight contract	—	contratto di trasporto *m*	contrato de transporte *m*
contrat d'assurance (F)	Versicherungsvertrag *m*	insurance contract	—	contratto d'assicurazione *m*	contrato de seguro *m*
contrat de cession (F)	Abtretungsvertrag *m*	contract of assignment	—	contratto di cessione *m*	contrato de cesión *m*

	D	E	F	I	Es
contrat de concession de licence (F)	Lizenzvertrag *m*	licence agreement	—	contratto di licenza *m*	contrato de licencia *m*
contrat de fourniture (F)	Liefervertrag *m*	supply contract	—	contratto di consegna *m*	contrata *f*
contrat de leasing (F)	Leasing-Vertrag *m*	leasing contract	—	contratto leasing *m*	contrato de arrendamiento financiero *m*
contrat de louage d'ouvrage et d'industrie (F)	Werkvertrag *m*	contract for work and services	—	contratto d'appalto *m*	contrato de obra *m*
contrat de travail (F)	Arbeitsvertrag *m*	contract of employment	—	contratto di lavoro *m*	contrato laboral *m*
contrat de travail convenu à l'essai (F)	Arbeitsverhältnis auf Probe *n*	employee-employer relationship on a trial basis	—	rapporto di lavoro in prova *m*	relación laboral a prueba *f*
contrat de vente¹ (F)	Kaufvertrag *m*	contract of sale	—	contratto di compravendita *m*	contrato de compraventa *m*
contrat de vente² (F)	Verkaufsabschluß *m*	sales contract	—	conclusione di vendita *f*	conclusión de la venta *f*
contrato¹ (Es)	Kontrakt *m*	contract	contrat *m*	contratto *m*	—
contrato² (Es)	Vertrag *m*	contract	contrat *m*	contratto *m*	—
contrato colectivo (Es)	Tarifvertrag *m*	collective agreement	convention collective *f*	contratto salariale *m*	—
contrato de arrendamiento financiero (Es)	Leasing-Vertrag *m*	leasing contract	contrat de leasing *m*	contratto leasing *m*	—
contrato de cesión (Es)	Abtretungsvertrag *m*	contract of assignment	contrat de cession *m*	contratto di cessione *m*	—
contrato de compraventa (Es)	Kaufvertrag *m*	contract of sale	contrat de vente *m*	contratto di compravendita *m*	—
contrato de dominación (Es)	Beherrschungsvertrag *m*	control agreement	accord de contrôle *m*	contratto di controllo *m*	—
contrato de entrega futura (Es)	Terminkontrakt *m*	forward contract	contrat à terme *m*	contratto a termine *m*	—
contrato de fletamento (Es)	Chartervertrag *m*	charter party	contrat d'affrètement *m*	contratto di noleggio *m*	—
contrato de licencia (Es)	Lizenzvertrag *m*	licence agreement	contrat de concession de licence *m*	contratto di licenza *m*	—
contrato de obra (Es)	Werkvertrag *m*	contract for work and services	contrat de louage d'ouvrage et d'industrie *m*	contratto d'appalto *m*	—
contrato de seguro¹ (Es)	Versicherungsvertrag *m*	insurance contract	contrat d'assurance *m*	contratto d'assicurazione *m*	—
contrato de seguro² (Es)	Versicherungsschutz *m*	insurance cover	couverture de l'assurance *f*	copertura assicurativa *f*	—
contrato de transporte (Es)	Frachtvertrag *m*	freight contract	contrat d'affrètement *m*	contratto di trasporto *m*	—
contrato laboral (Es)	Arbeitsvertrag *m*	contract of employment	contrat de travail *m*	contratto di lavoro *m*	—
contrato social (Es)	Gesellschaftsvertrag *m*	shareholder's agreement/partnership agreement	acte de société *m*	contratto di società *m*	—
contratto¹ (I)	Kontrakt *m*	contract	contrat *m*	—	contrato *m*
contratto² (I)	Vertrag *m*	contract/treaty	contrat *m*/traité *m*/accord *m*	—	contrato *m*/tratado *m*
contratto a contanti (I)	Tagesgeschäft *n*	day-to-day operations	affaire au comptant *f*	—	operación al contado *f*
contratto a termine (I)	Terminkontrakt *m*	forward contract	contrat à terme *m*	—	contrato de entrega futura *m*
contratto d'appalto (I)	Werkvertrag *m*	contract for work and services	contrat de louage d'ouvrage et d'industrie *m*	—	contrato de obra *m*
contratto d'assicurazione (I)	Versicherungsvertrag *m*	insurance contract	contrat d'assurance *m*	—	contrato de seguro *m*
contratto di cessione (I)	Abtretungsvertrag *m*	contract of assignment	contrat de cession *m*	—	contrato de cesión *m*
contratto di compravendita (I)	Kaufvertrag *m*	contract of sale	contrat de vente *m*	—	contrato de compraventa *m*
contratto di consegna (I)	Liefervertrag *m*	supply contract	contrat de fourniture *m*	—	contrata *f*

	D	E	F	I	Es
contratto di controllo (I)	Beherrschungs-vertrag *m*	control agreement	accord de contrôle *m*	—	contrato de dominación *m*
contratto di lavoro (I)	Arbeitsvertrag *m*	contract of employment	contrat de travail *m*	—	contrato laboral *m*
contratto di licenza (I)	Lizenzvertrag *m*	licence agreement	contrat de concession de licence *m*	—	contrato de licencia *m*
contratto di noleggio (I)	Chartervertrag *m*	charter party	contrat d'affrètement *m*	—	contrato de fletamento *m*
contratto di società (I)	Gesellschafts-vertrag *m*	shareholder's agreement/partnership agreement	acte de société *m*	—	contrato social *m*
contratto di trasporto (I)	Frachtvertrag *m*	freight contract	contrat d'affrètement *m*	—	contrato de transporte *m*
contratto leasing (I)	Leasing-Vertrag *m*	leasing contract	contrat de leasing *m*	—	contrato de arrenda-miento financiero *m*
contratto salariale (I)	Tarifvertrag *m*	collective agreement	convention collective *f*	—	contrato colectivo *m*
contravalor (Es)	Gegenwert *m*	equivalent	contre-valeur *f*	controvalore *m*	—
contre accréditif (F)	gegen Akkreditiv	against letter of credit	—	contro lettera di credito	con crédito documentario
contrebande (F)	Schmuggel *m*	smuggling	—	contrabbando *m*	contrabando *m*
contre remboursement (F)	gegen Nachnahme	cash on delivery	—	contro assegno	contra rembolso
contreseing (F)	Gegenzeichnung *f*	countersignature	—	controfirma *f*	contrafirma *f*
contre-valeur (F)	Gegenwert *m*	equivalent	—	controvalore *m*	contravalor *m*
contribuable (F)	Steuerzahler *m*	taxpayer	—	contribuente *m*	contribuyente *m*
contribuciones (Es)	Beiträge *pl*	contributions	participations *f pl*	contributi *m pl*	—
contribuente (I)	Steuerzahler *m*	taxpayer	contribuable *m*	—	contribuyente *m*
contributi (I)	Beiträge *pl*	contributions	participations *f pl*	—	contribuciones *f pl*
contribution costing (E)	Deckungsbeitrags-rechnung *f*	—	calcul de la proportion de garantie *m*	calcolo del contri-buto per copertura *m*	factura de aportación de fondos *f*
contribution margin (E)	Deckungsbeitrag *m*	—	proportion de garantie *f*	contributo per copertura *m*	aportación de cobertura *f*
contributions (E)	Beiträge *pl*	—	participations *f pl*	contributi *m pl*	contribuciones *f pl*
contributo per copertura (I)	Deckungsbeitrag *m*	contribution margin	proportion de garantie *f*	—	aportación de cobertura *f*
contribuyente (Es)	Steuerzahler *m*	taxpayer	contribuable *m*	contribuente *m*	—
contro assegno (I)	gegen Nachnahme	cash on delivery	contre remboursement	—	contra rembolso
controfirma (I)	Gegenzeichnung *f*	countersignature	contreseing *m*	—	contrafirma *f*
control[1] (E)	Kontrolle *f*	—	contrôle *m*	controllo *m*	control *m*
control[2] (E)	Steuerung *f*	—	contrôle *f*	controllo *m*	control *m*
control[1] (Es)	Kontrolle *f*	control	contrôle *m*	controllo *m*	—
control[2] (Es)	Steuerung *f*	control	contrôle *f*	controllo *m*	—
control agreement (E)	Beherrschungs-vertrag *m*	—	accord de contrôle *m*	contratto di controllo *m*	contrato de dominación *m*
control de divisas[1] (Es)	Devisenkontrolle *f*	foreign exchange control	contrôle des changes *m*	controllo delle divise *m*	—
control de divisas[2] (Es)	Devisenbewirt-schaftung *f*	foreign exchange control	contrôle des devises *m*	controllo valutario *m*	—
control de eficiencia (Es)	Effizienzkontrolle *f*	efficiency control	contrôle de l'efficience *m*	controllo d'efficienza *m*	—
control de fusiones (Es)	Fusionskontrolle *f*	merger control	contrôle de fusion *m*	controllo delle fusioni *m*	—
control de gastos (Es)	Ausgabenkontrolle *f*	expenditure control	contrôle des dépenses *m*	controllo delle spese *m*	—
control de las inversiones (Es)	Investitionskontrolle *f*	investment control	contrôle d'investissement *m*	controllo degli investimenti *m*	—
control del presupuesto (Es)	Budgetkontrolle *f*	budget control	contrôle du budget *m*	controllo del bilancio *m*	—
control del sistema (Es)	Systemsteuerung *f*	system control	contrôle du système *m*	controllo del sistema *m*	—
control de precios (Es)	Preiskontrolle *f*	price control	contrôle des prix *m*	controllo dei prezzi *m*	—

	D	E	F	I	Es
control de producción (Es)	Produktions-kontrolle *f*	production control	contrôle de la production *m*	controllo della produzione *m*	—
contrôle¹ (F)	Kontrolle *f*	control	—	controllo *m*	control *m*
contrôle² (F)	Steuerung *f*	control	—	controllo *m*	control *m*
contrôle à la frontière (F)	Grenzkontrolle *f*	border control	—	controllo alla frontiera *m*	control fronterizo *m*
contrôle de financement (F)	Finanzkontrolle *f*	budgetary control	—	controllo finanziario *m*	control financiero *m*
contrôle de fusion (F)	Fusionskontrolle *f*	merger control	—	controllo delle fusioni *m*	control de fusiones *m*
contrôle de la gestion et des comptes (F)	Wirtschaftsprüfung *f*	auditing	—	revisione *f*	revisoría *f*
contrôle de la planification (F)	Planungskontrolle *f*	planning control	—	controllo della programmazione *m*	contol de planificación *m*
contrôle de la production (F)	Produktions-kontrolle *f*	production control	—	controllo della produzione *m*	control de producción *m*
contrôle de la qualité (F)	Qualitätskontrolle *f*	quality control	—	controllo di qualità *m*	verificación de la calidad *f*
contrôle de l'efficience (F)	Effizienzkontrolle *f*	efficiency control	—	controllo d'efficienza *m*	control de eficiencia *m*
contrôle des banques (F)	Bankenaufsicht *f*	public supervision of banking	—	commissione bancaria *f*	supervisión bancaria *f*
contrôle des changes (F)	Devisenkontrolle *f*	foreign exchange control	—	controllo delle divise *m*	control de divisas *m*
contrôle des dépenses (F)	Ausgabenkontrolle *f*	expenditure control	—	controllo delle spese *m*	control de gastos *m*
contrôle des devises (F)	Devisen-bewirtschaftung *f*	foreign exchange control	—	controllo valutario *m*	control de divisas *m*
contrôle des livres comptables (F)	Einsichtnahme *f*	inspection	—	presa visione *f*	inspección *f*
contrôle des prix (F)	Preiskontrolle *f*	price control	—	controllo dei prezzi *m*	control de precios *m*
contrôle d'investissement (F)	Investitionskontrolle *f*	investment control	—	controllo degli investimenti *m*	control de las inversiones *m*
contrôle du budget (F)	Budgetkontrolle *f*	budget control	—	controllo del bilancio *m*	control del presupuesto *m*
contrôle du résultat de la publicité (F)	Werbeerfolgs-kontrolle *f*	advertising control	—	controllo del succes-so pubblicitario *m*	análisis del resultado publicitario *m*
contrôle du système (F)	Systemsteuerung *f*	system control	—	controllo del sistema *m*	control del sistema *m*
contrôle final (F)	Endkontrolle *f*	final control	—	controllo finale *m*	control final *m*
contro lettera di credito (I)	gegen Akkreditiv	against letter of credit	contre accréditif	—	con crédito documentario
control final (Es)	Endkontrolle *f*	final control	contrôle final *m*	controllo finale *m*	—
control financiero (Es)	Finanzkontrolle *f*	budgetary control	contrôle de financement *m*	controllo finanziario *m*	—
control fronterizo (Es)	Grenzkontrolle *f*	border control	contrôle à la frontière *m*	controllo alla frontiera *m*	—
controlled economy (E)	Dirigismus *m*	—	dirigisme *m*	dirigismo *m*	dirigismo *m*
controlling company¹ (E)	herrschendes Unternehmen *n*	—	entreprise dirigeante *f*	impresa controllante *f*	empresa dominante *f*
controlling company² (E)	Besitzgesellschaft *f*	—	société contrôleuse *f*	società finanziaria *f*	sociedad controladora *f*
controllo¹ (I)	Steuerung *f*	control	contrôle *m*	—	control *m*
controllo² (I)	Kontrolle *f*	control	contrôle *m*	—	control *m*
controllo³ (I)	Prüfung *f*	inspection/examination	vérification *f*/ examen *m*	—	verificación *f*/ examen *m*
controllo alla frontiera (I)	Grenzkontrolle *f*	border control	contrôle à la frontière *m*	—	control fronterizo *m*
controllo d'efficienza (I)	Effizienzkontrolle *f*	efficiency control	contrôle de l'efficience *m*	—	control de eficiencia *m*
controllo degli investimenti (I)	Investitions-kontrolle *f*	investment control	contrôle d'investissement *m*	—	control de las inversiones *m*
controllo dei prezzi (I)	Preiskontrolle *f*	price control	contrôle des prix *m*	—	control de precios *m*
controllo del bilancio (I)	Budgetkontrolle *f*	budget control	contrôle du budget *m*	—	control del presupuesto *m*

	D	E	F	I	Es
controllo della produzione (I)	Produktions-kontrolle f	production control	contrôle de la production m	—	control de producción m
controllo della programmazione (I)	Planungskontrolle f	planning control	contrôle de la planification f	—	contol de planificación m
controllo delle divise (I)	Devisenkontrolle f	foreign exchange control	contrôle des changes m	—	control de divisas m
controllo delle fusioni (I)	Fusionskontrolle f	merger control	contrôle de fusion m	—	control de fusiones m
controllo delle spese (I)	Ausgabenkontrolle f	expenditure control	contrôle des dépenses m	—	control de gastos m
controllo del sistema (I)	Systemsteuerung f	system control	contrôle du système m	—	control del sistema m
controllo del successo pubblicitario (I)	Werbeerfolgs-kontrolle f	advertising control	contrôle du résultat de la publicité m	—	análisis del resultado publicitario m
controllo di qualità (I)	Qualitätskontrolle f	quality control	contrôle de la qualité m	—	verificación de la calidad f
controllo finale (I)	Endkontrolle f	final control	contrôle final m	—	control final m
controllo finanziario (I)	Finanzkontrolle f	budgetary control	contrôle de financement m	—	control financiero m
controllo globale (I)	Globalsteuerung f	global control	régulation globale f	—	regulación global f
controllo valutario (I)	Devisenbewirt-schaftung f	foreign exchange control	contrôle des devises m	—	control de divisas m
contro pagamento in contanti (I)	gegen Barzahlung	against cash	au comptant	—	al contado
controvalore (I)	Gegenwert m	equivalent	contre-valeur f	—	contravalor m
convegno (I)	Tagung f	meeting	congrès m	—	reunión f
convegno dei rappresentanti (I)	Vertretertagung f	sales meeting	réunion de représentants f	—	conferencia de representantes f
convenio aduanero (Es)	Zollabkommen n	customs convention	accord douanier m	accordo sulle tariffe doganali m	—
convenio de compra (Es)	Kaufabschluß m	conclusion of a sales contract	conclusion du marché f	conclusione d'acquisto f	—
convenio forzoso (Es)	Zwangsvergleich m	compulsory settlement	arrangement forcé m	concordato fallimentare m	—
convention collective (F)	Tarifvertrag m	collective agreement	—	contratto salariale m	contrato colectivo m
convention de salaire à la tâche (F)	Akkord m	piece work	—	cottimo m	destajo m
conversación (Es)	Unterredung f	discussion	entretien m	colloquio m	—
conversación de venta (Es)	Verkaufsgespräch n	sales talk	conversation de vente f	colloquio di vendita m	—
conversación personal (Es)	persönliches Gespräch n	personal conversation	conversation personnelle f	colloquio personale m	—
conversation de vente (F)	Verkaufsgespräch n	sales talk	—	colloquio di vendita m	conversación de venta f
conversation personnelle (F)	persönliches Gespräch n	personal conversation	—	colloquio personale m	conversación personal f
conversation téléphonique (F)	Telefongespräch n	telephone conversation	—	telefonata f	conferencia telefónica f
convertibile (I)	konvertibel	convertible	convertible	—	convertible
convertibilidad (Es)	Konvertibilität f	convertibility	convertibilité f	convertibilità f	—
convertibilità (I)	Konvertibilität f	convertibility	convertibilité f	—	convertibilidad f
convertibilité (F)	Konvertibilität f	convertibility	—	convertibilità f	convertibilidad f
convertibility (E)	Konvertibilität f	—	convertibilité f	convertibilità f	convertibilidad f
convertible (E)	konvertibel	—	convertible	convertibile	convertible
convertible (Es)	konvertibel	convertible	convertible	convertibile	—
convertible (F)	konvertibel	convertible	—	convertibile	convertible
convertible bonds (E)	Wandelschuld-verschreibung f	—	obligation convertible f	obbligazione convertibile f	obligaciones convertibles f pl
convocatoria de oposiciones (Es)	Stellen-ausschreibung f	advertisement of a vacancy	mise au concours d'une place f	bando di concorso per impiegati m	—
conyuntura (Es)	Konjunktur f	business cycle	conjoncture f	congiuntura f	—
cooperación[1] (Es)	Kooperation f	cooperation	coopération f	cooperazione f	—

	D	E	F	I	Es
cooperación² (Es)	Zusammenarbeit f	cooperation	collaboration f	collaborazione f	—
coopératif (F)	kooperativ	cooperative	—	cooperativo	cooperativo
cooperation¹ (E)	Zusammenarbeit f	—	collaboration f	collaborazione f	cooperación f
cooperation² (E)	Kooperation f	—	coopération f	cooperazione f	cooperación f
coopération (F)	Kooperation f	cooperation	—	cooperazione f	cooperación f
cooperativa (I)	Genossenschaft f	co-operative	société coopérative f	—	sociedad cooperativa f
cooperativa de producción (Es)	Produktions-genossenschaft f	producer cooperative	société coopérative de production f	cooperativa di produzione f	—
cooperativa di produzione (I)	Produktions-genossenschaft f	producer cooperative	société coopérative de production f	—	cooperativa de producción f
cooperative (E)	kooperativ	—	coopératif	cooperativo	cooperativo
co-operative (E)	Genossenschaft f	—	société coopérative f	cooperativa f	sociedad cooperativa f
cooperativo (Es)	kooperativ	cooperative	coopératif	cooperativo	—
cooperativo (I)	kooperativ	cooperative	coopératif	—	cooperativo
cooperazione (I)	Kooperation f	cooperation	coopération f	—	cooperación f
coordinación (Es)	Koordination f	coordination	coordination f	coordinazione f	—
coordination (E)	Koordination f	—	coordination f	coordinazione f	coordinación f
coordination (F)	Koordination f	coordination	—	coordinazione f	coordinación f
coordinazione (I)	Koordination f	coordination	coordination f	—	coordinación f
co-owner (E)	Bruchteils-eigentümer m	—	copropriétaire d'une quote-part m	comproprietario di quota ideale m	copropietario de bienes indivisos m
co-ownership (E)	Miteigentum n	—	copropriété f	comproprietà f	copropiedad f
copertura (I)	Deckung f	cover	couverture f	—	cobertura f
copertura assicurativa (I)	Versicherungs-schutz m	insurance cover	couverture de l'assurance f	—	cobertura de seguro f
copia¹ (Es)	Abschrift f	copy	copie f	copia f	—
copia² (Es)	Kopie f	copy	copie f	copia f	—
copia¹ (I)	Abschrift f	copy	copie f	—	copia f
copia² (I)	Kopie f	copy	copie f	—	copia f
copia autenticata (I)	beglaubigte Abschrift f	authenticated copy	copie certifiée f	—	copia legalizada f
copia legalizada (Es)	beglaubigte Abschrift f	authenticated copy	copie certifiée f	copia autenticata f	—
copialettere (I)	Fotokopierer m	photocopier	photocopieur m	—	fotocopiadora f
copie¹ (F)	Kopie f	copy	—	copia f	copia f
copie² (F)	Abschrift f	copy	—	copia f	copia f
copie certifiée (F)	beglaubigte Abschrift f	authenticated copy	—	copia autenticata f	copia legalizada f
coproducción (Es)	Koppel-produktion f	tied production	production couplée f	produzione abbinata f	—
copropiedad (Es)	Miteigentum n	co-ownership	copropriété f	comproprietà f	—
copropietario de bienes indivisos (Es)	Bruchteils-eigentümer m	co-owner	copropriétaire d'une quote-part m	comproprietario di quota ideale m	—
copropriétaire d'une quote-part (F)	Bruchteils-eigentümer m	co-owner	—	comproprietario di quota ideale m	copropietario de bienes indivisos m
copropriété (F)	Miteigentum n	co-ownership	—	comproprietà f	copropiedad f
copy¹ (E)	Abschrift f	—	copie f	copia f	copia f
copy² (E)	Kopie f	—	copie f	copia f	copia f
copyright (E)	Urheberrecht n	—	droit d'auteur m	diritto d'autore m	derecho del autor m
corpo (I)	Kasko m	comprehensive	sur corps	—	de casco
corporación (Es)	Körperschaft f	corporation	collectivité f	ente m	—
corporate strategy (E)	Unternehmens-strategie f	—	stratégie de l'entreprise f	strategia imprenditoriale f	estrategia empresarial f
corporation (E)	Körperschaft f	—	collectivité f	ente m	corporación f
corporation stock (E)	Kommunal-obligation f	—	obligation communale f	obbligazioni comunali f pl	obligación comunal f
corporation tax (E)	Körperschaftsteuer f	—	taxe sur les sociétés f	imposta sul reddito delle società f	impuesto de corporaciones m

	D	E	F	I	Es
corps de sécurité d'entreprise (F)	Werkschutz m	works protection force	—	servizio di sorveglianza aziendale m	policía de la empresa f
correct (E)	korrigieren	—	corriger	correggere	corrigir
correct (F)	ordnungsgemäß	orderly/duly	—	regolare	debidamente
correction (E)	Berichtigung f	—	rectification f	correzione f	rectificación f
corredor (Es)	Makler m	broker	courtier m	mediatore m	—
corredor de bolsa[1] (Es)	Börsenmakler m	stockbroker	courtier en bourse m	agente di cambio m	—
corredor de bolsa[2] (Es)	Broker m	broker	courtier m	broker m	—
corredor de següros (Es)	Versicherungsmakler m	insurance broker	courtier en assurance m	mediatore d'assicurazione m	—
corredor marítimo (Es)	Schiffsmakler m	shipbroker	courtier maritime m	agente marittimo m	—
correggere (I)	korrigieren	correct	corriger	—	corrigir
correlación (Es)	Korrelation f	correlation	corrélation f	correlazione f	—
correlation (E)	Korrelation f	—	corrélation f	correlazione f	correlación f
corrélation (F)	Korrelation f	correlation	—	correlazione f	correlación f
correlazione (I)	Korrelation f	correlation	corrélation f	—	correlación f
corrente (I)	kulant	accommodating	arrangeant	—	de fácil avenencia
correntezza (I)	Kulanz f	accommodation	souplesse en affaires f	—	facilidad en los negocios f
correo aéreo (Es)	Luftpost f	air mail	par avion	posta aerea f	—
correos (Es)	Postamt n	post office	bureau de poste m	ufficio postale m	—
correspondant (F)	Geschäftsfreund m	business friend	—	partner d'affari m	corresponsal m
corresponsal (Es)	Geschäftsfreund m	business friend	correspondant m	partner d'affari m	—
corretaje (Es)	Courtage f	brokerage	courtage m	courtage f	—
correzione (I)	Berichtigung f	correction	rectification f	—	rectificación f
corriere (I)	Eilbote m	express messenger	facteur spécial m	—	expreso m
corrigé du mouvement saisonnier (F)	saisonbereinigt	seasonally adjusted	—	al netto degli influssi stagionali	desestacionalizado
corriger (F)	korrigieren	correct	—	correggere	corrigir
corrigir (Es)	korrigieren	correct	corriger	correggere	—
corruption (F)	Bestechung f	bribe	—	corruzione f	soborno f
corruzione (I)	Bestechung f	bribe	corruption f	—	soborno f
corso (I)	Kurs m	exchange rate	cours (du change) m	—	cotización f/tipo de cambio m
corso a pronti (I)	Kassakurs m	spot price	cours au comptant m	—	cotización al contado f
corso a termine (I)	Terminkurs m	forward price	cours de bourse à terme m	—	cambio a término m
corso dei cambi (I)	Sortenkurs m	rate for foreign notes and coins	cours des monnaies étrangères m	—	tipo de cambio de billetes y monedas extranjeras m
corso delle azioni (I)	Aktienkurs m	share price	cours des actions m	—	cotización de las acciones f
corso di borsa (I)	Börsenkurs m	quotation on the stock exchange	cours de bourse m pl	—	cotización en bolsa f
corso di cambio (I)	Umrechnungskurs m	rate of conversion	cours de conversion m	—	tasa de cambio f
corso massimo (I)	Höchstkurs m	highest rate	cours le plus haut m	—	cotización máxima f
corso minimo (I)	Niedrigstkurs m	floor price	cours le plus bas m	—	cotización mínima f
corte d'appello (I)	Berufungsgericht n	appeal court	tribunal d'appel m	—	tribunal de apelación m
Corte di Giustizia Europea (I)	Europäischer Gerichtshof m	European Court	Cour de Justice Européenne f	—	Tribunal de Justicia de las Comunidades Europeas m
cost (E)	Selbstkosten pl	—	coût de revient m	spese vive f pl	costes propios m pl
cost accounting system (E)	Kostenrechnungssystem n	—	méthode de calcul des coûts f	sistema dei costi m	sistema de costes m
cost advantage (E)	Kostenvorteil m	—	avantage de coût m	vantaggio di costo m	ventaja de costes f
cost allocation (E)	Kostenverrechnung f	—	répartition des frais f	ripartizione dei costi f	repartición de costes f

	D	E	F	I	Es
cost analysis (E)	Kostenanalyse f	—	analyse des coûts f	analisi dei costi f	análisis de costes m
costas (Es)	Verfahrenskosten pl	costs of the proceedings	frais de procédure m pl	spese del procedimento f pl	—
cost-benefit analysis (E)	Kosten-Nutzen-Analyse f	—	analyse du ratio coût à profit f	analisi costi-benefici f	análisis de coste-beneficio m
cost degression (E)	Kostendegression f	—	dégressivité des coûts f	riduzione dei costi f	reducción de costes f
coste alternativo (Es)	Alternativkosten pl	opportunity costs	coûts alternatifs m pl	costi alternativi m pl	—
coste de adquisición (Es)	Anschaffungs-kosten pl	purchase costs	frais d'acquisition m pl	costi d'acquisto m pl	—
coste de material (Es)	Materialaufwand m	material expenditure	dépenses en matériel f pl	spese materiale f pl	—
coste de salarios (Es)	Lohnkosten pl	cost of wages	coût du travail m	costo del lavoro m	—
coste directo (Es)	direkte Kosten pl	direct cost	coûts directs m pl	costi diretti m pl	—
coste por unidad (Es)	Stückkosten pl	costs per unit	coût unitaire de production m	costi unitari m pl	—
cost escalation (E)	Kostenexplosion f	—	explosion des coûts f	esplosione dei costi f	incremento desmesu-rado de los costes m
costes de apelación al crédito (Es)	Kreditbeschaffungs-kosten pl	cost of borrowing	coûts d'obtention de crédits m pl	spese d'approvvi-gionamento di credito f pl	—
costes propios (Es)	Selbstkosten pl	cost	coût de revient m	spese vive f pl	—
costi (I)	Kosten pl	costs	coût m	—	gastos m pl
costi accessori (I)	Nebenkosten pl	ancillary costs	coûts accessoires m pl	—	gastos adicionales m pl
costi alternativi (I)	Alternativkosten pl	opportunity costs	coûts alternatifs m pl	—	coste alternativo m
costi calcolati (I)	Sollkosten pl	budgeted costs	coûts ex ante m pl	—	gastos precalculados m pl
costi complementari del lavoro (I)	Lohnnebenkosten pl	ancillary wage costs	charges salariales annexes f pl	—	cargas salariales accesorias f pl
costi comuni (I)	Gemeinkosten pl	overhead expenses	coûts indirects m pl	—	gastos generales m pl
costi d'acquisto (I)	Anschaffungs-kosten pl	purchase costs	frais d'acquisition m pl	—	coste de adquisición m
costi d'adattamento (I)	Anpassungskosten pl	adjustment costs	coûts d'adaptation m pl	—	gastos readaptación m pl
costi d'informazione (I)	Informationskosten pl	information costs	coûts d'information m pl	—	gastos de información m pl
costi della costituzione (I)	Gründungskosten pl	organization costs	frais de fondation m pl	—	gastos de fundación m pl
costi del materiale (I)	Materialkosten pl	material costs	frais coûts de matériel m pl	—	gastos de material m pl/coste de material m
costi di caricamento (I)	Verladekosten pl	loading charges	coût du chargement m	—	gastos de carga m pl
costi di produzione (I)	Herstellungskosten pl	production costs	frais de fabrication m pl	—	costo de la producción m
costi diretti (I)	direkte Kosten pl	direct cost	coûts directs m pl	—	coste directo m
costi di riproduzione (I)	Reproduktions-kosten pl	reproduction cost	coût de reproduction m	—	gastos de reproducción m pl
costi di risanamento (I)	Sanierungskosten pl	renewal costs	coûts d'assainissent m pl	—	gastos de saneamien-to m pl/gastos de rehabilitación m pl
costi di sviluppo (I)	Entwicklungs-kosten pl	development costs	coûts de développement m pl	—	gastos de desarrollo m pl
costi di viaggio (I)	Reisekosten pl	travelling expenses	frais de voyage m pl	—	gastos de viaje m pl
costi effettivi (I)	Istkosten pl	actual costs	coûts réels m pl	—	gastos efectivos m pl
costi fissi (I)	Fixkosten pl	fixed costs	coûts fixes m pl	—	gastos fijos m pl
costi fissi di utilizzo (I)	Nutzkosten pl	utility costs	coûts fixes utiles m pl	—	gastos fijos de utilización m pl
costi medi (I)	Durchschnitts-kosten pl	average costs	coût moyenne m	—	gastos medios m pl
costi per le acque di scarico (I)	Abwasserkosten pl	sewage disposal costs	coûts de traitement des eaux usées m pl	—	gastos para aguas residuales m pl
costi produttivi (I)	Produktionskosten pl	cost of production	coût de production m	—	gastos de producción m pl

	D	E	F	I	Es
costi sociali (I)	Sozialkosten *pl*	social insurance costs	coûts sociaux *m pl*	—	costo social *m/* cargas sociales *f pl*
costi totali (I)	Gesamtkosten *pl*	total costs	coût total *m*	—	gastos generales *m pl*
costituzione di cartelli (I)	Kartellbildung *f*	cartel formation	cartellisation *f*	—	formación de carteles *f*
costituzione di un lavoro indipendente (I)	Existenzgründung *f*	setting up of new business	fondation d'existence *f*	—	fundación de existencia *f*
costituzione di un sindacato (I)	Syndizierung *f*	syndication	syndication *f*	—	sindicación *f*
costituzione nuova (I)	Neugründung *f*	new foundation	création d'une nouvelle société *f*	—	fundación nueva *f*
costi unitari (I)	Stückkosten *pl*	costs per unit	coût unitaire de production *m*	—	coste por unidad *m*
costi variabili (I)	variable Kosten *pl*	variable costs	coûts variables *m pl*	—	gastos variables *m pl*
costituzione (I)	Gründung *f*	formation	constitution *f*	—	fundación *f*
costo de la producción (Es)	Herstellungskosten *pl*	production costs	frais de fabrication *m pl*	costi di produzione *m pl*	—
costo del lavoro (I)	Lohnkosten *pl*	cost of wages	coût du travail *m*	—	coste de salarios *m*
cost of borrowing (E)	Kreditbeschaffungs-kosten *pl*	—	coûts d'obtention de crédits *m pl*	spese d'approvvi-gionamento di credito *f pl*	costes de apelación al crédito *m pl*
cost of production (E)	Produktionskosten *pl*	—	coût de production *m*	costi produttivi *m pl*	gastos de producción *m pl*
cost of wages (E)	Lohnkosten *pl*	—	coût du travail *m*	costo del lavoro *m*	coste de salarios *m*
costo social (Es)	Sozialkosten *pl*	social insurance costs	coûts sociaux *m pl/* charges sociales *f pl*	costi sociali *m pl*	—
cost price[1] (E)	Selbstkostenpreis *m*	—	prix coûtant *m*	prezzo di costo *m*	precio de coste *m*
cost price[2] (E)	Einstandspreis *m*	—	prix coûtant *m*	prezzo di costo *m*	precio de coste *m*
cost reduction (E)	Kostensenkung *f*	—	diminution des coûts *f*	ribasso dei costi *m*	reducción de coste *f*
costruzione (I)	Bau *m*	construction	construction *f*	—	construcción *f*
costs (E)	Kosten *pl*	—	coût *m*	costi *m pl*	gastos *m pl*
cost schedule (E)	Kostenplan *m*	—	planning des coûts *m*	piano dei costi *m*	planilla de costas *f*
costs of the proceedings (E)	Verfahrenskosten *pl*	—	frais de procédure *m pl*	spese del procedimento *f pl*	costas *f pl*
costs per unit (E)	Stückkosten *pl*	—	coût unitaire de production *m*	costi unitari *m pl*	coste por unidad *m*
cost types (E)	Kostenarten *pl*	—	coûts par nature *m pl*	tipi di costi *m pl*	clases de costes *f pl*
cotation[1] (F)	Kursnotierung *f*	quotation of prices	—	quotazione dei corsi *f*	cotización *m*
cotation[2] (F)	Notierung *f*	quotation	—	quotazione *f*	cotización *f*
cotation de quantité (F)	Mengennotierung *f*	fixed exchange	—	cambio reale *m*	cotización real *f*
cotation des actions (F)	Aktiennotierung *f*	share quotation	—	quotazione delle azioni *f*	cotización de acciones *f*
cotation des cours en bourse (F)	Börsennotierung *f*	quotation on the stock exchange	—	quotazione di borsa *f*	cotización de bolsa *f*
cotation des prix (F)	Preisnotierung *f*	prices quoted	—	quotazione dei prezzi *f*	cotización de precios *f*
cotización[1] (Es)	Kurs *m*	exchange rate	cours (du change) *m*	corso *m*	—
cotización[2] (Es)	Kursnotierung *f*	quotation of prices	cotation *f*	quotazione dei corsi *f*	—
cotización[3] (Es)	Notierung *f*	quotation	cotation *f*	quotazione *f*	—
cotización al contado (Es)	Kassakurs *m*	spot price	cours au comptant *m*	corso a pronti *m*	—
cotización de acciones (Es)	Aktiennotierung *f*	share quotation	cotation des actions *f*	quotazione delle azioni *f*	—
cotización de bolsa (Es)	Börsennotierung *f*	quotation on the stock exchange	cotation des cours en bourse *f*	quotazione di borsa *f*	—
cotización de las acciones (Es)	Aktienkurs *m*	share price	cours des actions *m*	corso delle azioni *m*	—
cotización de precios (Es)	Preisnotierung *f*	prices quoted	cotation des prix *f*	quotazione dei prezzi *f*	—
cotización demandada (Es)	Geldkurs *m*	demand price	cours de la demande *m*	prezzo di domanda *m*	—

	D	E	F	I	Es
cotización en bolsa (Es)	Börsenkurs *m*	quotation on the stock exchange	cours de bourse *m pl*	corso di borsa *m*	—
cotización final (Es)	Schlußkurs *m*	closing price	dernier cours *m*	quotazione di chiusura *f*	—
cotización máxima (Es)	Höchstkurs *m*	highest rate	cours le plus haut *m*	corso massimo *m*	—
cotización mínima (Es)	Niedrigstkurs *m*	floor price	cours le plus bas *m*	corso minimo *m*	—
cotización ofrecida (Es)	Briefkurs *m*	ask price	cours de vente *m*	prezzo d'offerta *m*	—
cotización real (Es)	Mengennotierung *f*	fixed exchange	cotation de quantité *f*	cambio reale *m*	—
cotización única (Es)	Einheitskurs *m*	spot price	cours unique *m*	cambio unitario *m*	—
cottimo (I)	Akkord *m*	piece work	convention de salaire à la tâche *f*	—	destajo *m*
counter entry (E)	Storno *n*	—	écriture de contre-passation *f*	storno *m*	extorno *m*
countersignature (E)	Gegenzeichnung *f*	—	contreseing *m*	controfirma *f*	contrafirma *f*
country of origin[1] (E)	Herkunftsland *n*	—	pays de provenance *m*	paese d'origine *m*	país de origen *m*
country of origin[2] (E)	Ursprungsland *n*	—	pays d'origine *m*	paese d'origine *m*	país de origen *m*
country of purchase (E)	Einkaufsland *n*	—	pays où l'on achète *m*	paese acquirente *m*	país de compra *m*
coupable (F)	schuldhaft	culpable	—	colposo	culpable
Coupon (D)	—	coupon	coupon *m*	cedola *f*	cupón *m*
coupon (E)	Coupon *m*	—	coupon *m*	cedola *f*	cupón *m*
coupon (F)	Coupon *m*	coupon	—	cedola *f*	cupón *m*
coupons (I)	Benzingutscheine *pl*	petrol voucher	bon d'essence *m*	—	bono de gasolina *m*
Cour de Justice Européenne (F)	Europäischer Gerichtshof *m*	European Court	—	Corte di Giustizia Europea *f*	Tribunal de Justicia de la Comunidad Europea *m*
cours (F)	Kurs *m*	exchange rate	—	corso *m*/cambio *m*	cotización *f*/tipo de cambio *m*
cours au comptant (F)	Kassakurs *m*	spot price	—	corso a pronti *m*	cotización al contado *f*
cours de bourse (F)	Börsenkurs *m*	quotation on the stock exchange	—	corso di borsa *m*	cotización en bolsa *f*
cours de bourse à terme (F)	Terminkurs *m*	forward price	—	corso a termine *m*	cambio a término *m*
cours de conversion (F)	Umrechnungskurs *m*	rate of conversion	—	corso di cambio *m*	tasa de cambio *f*
cours de la demande (F)	Geldkurs *m*	demand price	—	prezzo di domanda *m*	cotización demandada *f*/precio ofrecido *m*
cours d'émission (F)	Emissionskurs *m*	price of issue	—	prezzo d'emissione *m*	tipo de emisión *m*
cours des actions (F)	Aktienkurs *m*	share price	—	corso delle azioni *m*	cotización de las acciones *f*
cours des monnaies étrangères (F)	Sortenkurs *m*	rate for foreign notes and coins	—	corso dei cambi *m*	tipo de cambio de billetes y monedas extranjeras *m*
cours de vente (F)	Briefkurs *m*	ask price	—	prezzo d'offerta *m*	cotización ofrecida *f*
cours du change (F)	Wechselkurs *m*	exchange rate	—	cambio *m*	tipo de cambio *m*
cours du change multiple (F)	gespaltene Wechselkurse *pl*	two-tier exchange rate	—	cambi multipli *m pl*	tipo de cambio múltiple *m*
course des prix et des salaires (F)	Lohn-Preis-Spirale *f*	wage-price spiral	—	spirale prezzi-salari *f*	espiral salarios-precios *m*
course of the economic evolution (E)	Wirtschaftsverlauf *m*	—	évolution économique *f*	andamento dell'economia *m*	evolución económica *f*
cours le plus bas (F)	Niedrigstkurs *m*	floor price	—	corso minimo *m*	cotización mínima *f*
cours le plus haut (F)	Höchstkurs *m*	highest rate	—	corso massimo *m*	cotización máxima *f*
cours unique (F)	Einheitskurs *m*	spot price	—	cambio unitario *m*	cotización única *f*
court of arbitration (E)	Schiedsgericht *n*	—	tribunal d'arbitrage *m*	tribunale arbitrale *m*	tribunal arbitral *m*
Courtage (D)	—	brokerage	courtage *m*	courtage *f*	corretaje *m*
courtage (F)	Courtage *f*	brokerage	—	courtage *f*	corretaje *m*
courtage (I)	Courtage *f*	brokerage	courtage *m*	—	corretaje *m*
courtier[1] (F)	Broker *m*	broker	—	broker *m*	corredor de bolsa *m*
courtier[2] (F)	Makler *m*	broker	—	mediatore *m*	corredor *m*

	D	E	F	I	Es
courtier en affaires immobilières (F)	Immobilienmakler *m*	estate agent	—	agente immobiliare *m*	agente de inmuebles *m*
courtier en assurance (F)	Versicherungs-makler *m*	insurance broker	—	mediatore d'assicurazione *m*	corredor de seguros *m*
courtier en bourse¹ (F)	Börsenmakler *m*	stockbroker	—	agente di cambio *m*	corredor de bolsa *m*
courtier en bourse² (F)	Kursmakler *m*	stock broker/ exchange broker	—	agente di borsa *m*	agente cambio y bolsa *m*/corredor de cambios *m*
courtier maritime (F)	Schiffsmakler *m*	shipbroker	—	agente marittimo *m*	corredor marítimo *m*
coût (F)	Kosten *pl*	costs	—	costi *m pl*	gastos *m pl*
coût de production (F)	Produktionskosten *pl*	cost of production	—	costi produttivi *m pl*	gastos de producción *m pl*
coût de reproduction (F)	Reproduktions-kosten *pl*	reproduction cost	—	costi di riproduzione *m pl*	gastos de reproducción *m pl*
coût de revient (F)	Selbstkosten *pl*	cost	—	spese vive *f pl*	costes propios *m pl*
coût du chargement (F)	Verladekosten *pl*	loading charges	—	costi di caricamento *m pl*	gastos de carga *m pl*
coût du travail (F)	Lohnkosten *pl*	cost of wages	—	costo del lavoro *m*	coste de salarios *m*
coût du voyage (F)	Fahrgeld *n*	fare	—	spese di trasferta *f pl*	precio de la travesía *m*
coût moyen (F)	Durchschnitts-kosten *pl*	average costs	—	costi medi *m pl*	gastos medios *m pl*
coûts accessoires (F)	Nebenkosten *pl*	ancillary costs	—	costi accessori *m pl*	gastos adicionales *m pl*
coûts administratifs (F)	Bereitstellungs-kosten *pl*	commitment fee	—	spese di stanziamento *f pl*	gastos fijos *m pl*
coûts alternatifs (F)	Alternativkosten *pl*	opportunity costs	—	costi alternativi *m pl*	coste alternativo *m*
coûts d'acquisition (F)	Bezugskosten *pl*	purchasing costs	—	prezzo d'acquisto *m*	gastos de adquisición *m pl*
coûts d'adaptation (F)	Anpassungskosten *pl*	adjustment costs	—	costi d'adattamento *m pl*	gastos readaptación *m pl*
coûts d'assainissement (F)	Sanierungskosten *pl*	renewal costs/ construction costs	—	costi di risanamento *m pl*	gastos de saneamien-to *m pl*/gastos de rehabilitación *m pl*
coûts de déchargement (F)	Entladungskosten *pl*	discharging expenses	—	spese di scaricamento *f pl*	gastos de descargo *m pl*
coûts de développement (F)	Entwicklungs-kosten *pl*	development costs	—	costi di sviluppo *m pl*	gastos de desarrollo *m pl*
coûts de nuitée (F)	Übernachtungs-kosten *pl*	overnight expenses	—	spese di pernottamento *f pl*	gastos de alojamiento *m pl*
coûts de traitement des eaux usées (F)	Abwasserkosten *pl*	sewage disposal costs	—	costi per le acque di scarico *m pl*	gastos para aguas residuales *m pl*
coûts d'information (F)	Informations-kosten *pl*	information costs	—	costi d'informazione *m pl*	gastos de información *m pl*
coûts directs (F)	direkte Kosten *pl*	direct costs	—	costi diretti *m pl*	coste directo *m*
coûts d'obtention de crédits (F)	Kreditbeschaffungs-kosten *pl*	cost of borrowing	—	spese d'approvvi-gionamento di credito *f pl*	costes de apelación al crédito *m pl*
coûts ex ante (F)	Sollkosten *pl*	budgeted costs	—	costi calcolati *m pl*	gastos precalculados *m pl*
coûts fixes (F)	Fixkosten *pl*	fixed costs	—	costi fissi *m pl*	gastos fijos *m pl*
coûts fixes utiles (F)	Nutzkosten *pl*	utility costs	—	costi fissi di utilizzo *m pl*	gastos fijos de utilización *m pl*
coûts indirects (F)	Gemeinkosten *pl*	overhead expenses	—	costi comuni *m pl*	gastos generales *m pl*
coûts par nature (F)	Kostenarten *pl*	cost types	—	tipi di costi *m pl*	clases de costes *f pl*
coûts réels (F)	Istkosten *pl*	actual costs	—	costi effettivi *m pl*	gastos efectivos *m pl*
coûts sociaux (F)	Sozialkosten *pl*	social insurance costs	—	costi sociali *m pl*	costo social *m*/cargas sociales *f pl*
coûts variables (F)	variable Kosten *pl*	variable costs	—	costi variabili *m pl*	gastos variables *m pl*
coût total (F)	Gesamtkosten *pl*	total costs	—	costi totali *m pl*	gastos generales *m pl*
coût unitaire de production (F)	Stückkosten *pl*	costs per unit	—	costi unitari *m pl*	coste por unidad *m*
couverture (F)	Deckung *f*	cover	—	copertura *f*	cobertura *f*
couverture de l'assurance (F)	Versicherungs-schutz *m*	insurance cover	—⁸	copertura assicurativa *f*	cobertura de seguro *f*

	D	E	F	I	Es
cover (E)	Deckung f	—	couverture f	copertura f	cobertura f
coyuntura cuantitativa (Es)	Mengenkonjunktur f	quantitative boom	conjoncture de quantité f	congiuntura quantitativa f	—
craft trade (E)	Handwerk n	—	artisanat m	artigianato m	artesanía f
creación de dinero (Es)	Geldschöpfung f	money creation	création de trésorerie f	creazione di denaro f	—
creación de riqueza (Es)	Wertschöpfung f	value added	création de valeurs f	valore aggiunto m	—
créance douteuse (F)	zweifelhafte Forderung f	doubtful account	—	credito dubbio m	créditos dudosos m pl
créancier (F)	Gläubiger m	creditor	—	creditore m	accreedor m
créancier de la faillite (F)	Konkursgläubiger m	bankrupt's creditor	—	creditore della massa fallimentare m	acreedor de la quiebra m
créatif (F)	kreativ	creative	—	creativo	creativo
création de dinero (Es)	Geldschöpfung f	money creation	création de trésorerie f	creazione di denaro f	—
création de trésorerie (F)	Geldschöpfung f	money creation	—	creazione di denaro f	creación de dinero f
création de valeurs (F)	Wertschöpfung f	value added	—	valore aggiunto m	creación de riqueza f
création d'une nouvelle société (F)	Neugründung f	new foundation	—	costituzione nuova f	fundación nueva f
creative (E)	kreativ	—	créatif	creativo	creativo
creative thinking (E)	kreatives Denken n	—	créativité conceptionnelle f	mentalità creativa f	creatividad concepcional f
creatividad concepcional (Es)	kreatives Denken n	creative thinking	créativité conceptionnelle f	mentalità creativa f	—
créativité conceptionnelle (F)	kreatives Denken n	creative thinking	—	mentalità creativa f	creatividad concepcional f
creativo (Es)	kreativ	creative	créatif	creativo	—
creativo (I)	kreativ	creative	créatif	—	creativo
creazione del prodotto (I)	Produktgestaltung f	product design	présentation d'un produit f	—	diseño del producto m
creazione di denaro (I)	Geldschöpfung f	money creation	création de trésorerie f	—	creación de dinero f
crecimiento (Es)	Wachstum n	growth	croissance f	crescita f	—
crecimiento cero (Es)	Nullwachstum n	zero growth	croissance zéro m	crescita zero f	—
crecimiento económico (Es)	Wirtschaftswachstum n	economic growth	croissance économique f	crescita economica f	—
crecimiento lineal (Es)	lineares Wachstum n	linear growth	accroissement constant m	crescita lineare f	—
crecimiento vegetativo (Es)	Bevölkerungswachstum m	increase in population	accroissement de la population m	incremento demografico m	—
credit¹ (E)	gutschreiben	—	créditer	accreditare	abonar en cuenta
credit² (E)	Gutschrift f	—	crédit m	accredito m	abono m
credit³ (E)	Kredit m	—	crédit m	credito m	crédito m
crédit¹ (F)	Kredit m	credit	—	credito m	crédito m
crédit² (F)	Gutschrift f	credit	—	accredito m	abono m
crédit à court terme (F)	kurzfristiger Kredit m	short-term credit	—	credito a breve scadenza m	crédito a corto plazo m
credit advice (E)	Gutschriftsanzeige f	—	avis de crédit m	nota di accredito f	aviso de abono m
credit against securities (E)	Lombardkredit m	—	crédit garanti par nantissement m	credito su pegno m	crédito pignoraticio m
crédit à la consommation (F)	Konsumkredit m	consumer credit	—	credito al consumatore m	crédito de consumo m
crédit à la construction (F)	Baukredit m	building loan	—	credito edilizio m	crédito para la construcción f
crédit à long terme (F)	langfristiger Kredit m	long-term credit	—	credito a lunga scadenza m	crédito a largo plazo m
crédit à moyen terme (F)	mittelfristiger Kredit m	medium-term credit	—	credito a media scadenza m	crédito a medio plazo m
crédit-bail (F)	Leasing n	leasing	—	leasing m	leasing m
credit business (E)	Kreditgeschäft n	—	achat à crédit m	operazione di credito f	operaciones de crédito f pl

	D	E	F	I	Es
credit by way of bank guarantee[1] (E)	Bürgschaftskredit m	—	crédit cautionné m	credito di fideiussione m	crédito de garantía m
credit by way of bank guarantee[2] (E)	Avalkredit m	—	crédit d'escompte sur traite avalisée m	credito d'avallo m	crédito de aval m
credit by way of overdraft (E)	Überziehungskredit m	—	avance sur compte courant f	credito allo scoperto m	crédito en descubierto m
credit card (E)	Kreditkarte f	—	carte accréditive f	carta di credito f	tarjeta de crédito f
crédit cautionné (F)	Bürgschaftskredit m	credit by way of bank guarantee	—	credito di fideiussione m	crédito de garantía m
credit commission (E)	Kreditprovision f	—	frais de commissions d'ouverture de crédit m pl	provvigione di credito f	comisión de apertura de crédito f
crédit de caisse (F)	Barkredit m	cash credit	—	credito per cassa m	crédito en efectivo m
crédit de fournisseurs (F)	Lieferantenkredit m	supplier's credit	—	credito al fornitore m	crédito comercial m
crédit d'escompte (F)	Wechselkredit m	acceptance credit	—	credito cambiario m	crédito cambiario m
crédit d'escompte sur traite avalisée (F)	Avalkredit m	credit by way of bank guarantee	—	credito d'avallo m	crédito de aval m
crédit d'investissement (F)	Investitionskredit m	investment credit	—	credito d'investimento m	crédito de inversión m
crédit documentaire (F)	Dokumentenakkreditiv n	documentary letter of credit	—	apertura di credito documentario f	crédito documentario m
crédit documentaire confirmé (F)	Rembourskredit m	documentary acceptance credit	—	credito di rimborso m	crédito de reembolso m
crédit en compte courant[1] (F)	Kontokorrentkredit m	current account credit	—	credito in conto corrente m	crédito en cuenta corriente m
crédit en compte courant[2] (F)	Blankokredit m	open credit	—	credito scoperto m	crédito en blanco m
créditer (F)	gutschreiben	credit	—	accreditare	abonar en cuenta
créditeur (F)	Kreditor m	creditor	—	creditore m	acreedor m
crédit garanti par nantissement (F)	Lombardkredit m	credit against securities	—	credito su pegno m	crédito pignoraticio m
crediti agevolati (I)	billiges Geld n	easy money	argent à bon marché m	—	dinero barato m
credit institution (E)	Kreditinstitut n	—	établissement de crédit m	istituto di credito m	instituto de crédito m
credit insurance (E)	Kreditversicherung f	—	assurance crédit f	assicurazione dei crediti f	seguro crediticio m
credit interest (E)	Habenzinsen pl	—	intérêts créditeur m	interessi creditori m pl	intereses acreedores m pl
crediti stand-by (I)	Stand-by-Kredite pl	stand-by credits	crédit stand-by m	—	créditos stand-by m pl
credit line (E)	Kreditlinie f	—	plafond du crédit accordé m	linea creditizia f	línea de crédito f
credit margin (E)	Kreditrahmen m	—	marge de crédit accordé f	plafond di credito m	margen de crédito m
crédito[1] (Es)	Kreditfähigkeit f	financial standing	solvabilité f	capacità di credito f	—
crédito[2] (Es)	Kreditwürdigkeit f	creditworthiness	solvabilité f	essere degno di credito	—
crédito[3] (Es)	Kredit m	credit	crédit m	credito m	—
credito (I)	Kredit m	credit	crédit m	—	crédito m
credito a breve scadenza (I)	kurzfristiger Kredit m	short-term credit	crédit à court terme m	—	crédito a corto plazo m
crédito a corto plazo (Es)	kurzfristiger Kredit m	short-term credit	crédit à court terme m	credito a breve scadenza m	—
crédito a largo plazo (Es)	langfristiger Kredit m	long-term credit	crédit à long terme m	credito a lunga scadenza m	—
credito a lunga scadenza (I)	langfristiger Kredit m	long-term credit	crédit à long terme m	—	crédito a largo plazo m
credito a media scadenza (I)	mittelfristiger Kredit m	medium-term credit	crédit à moyen terme m	—	crédito a medio plazo m
crédito a medio plazo (Es)	mittelfristiger Kredit m	medium-term credit	crédit à moyen terme m	credito a media scadenza m	—
credito al consumatore (I)	Konsumkredit m	consumer credit	crédit à la consommation m	—	crédito de consumo m

	D	E	F	I	Es
credito al fornitore (I)	Lieferantenkredit *m*	supplier's credit	crédit de fournisseurs *m*	—	crédito comercial *m*
credito allo scoperto (I)	Überziehungskredit *m*	credit by way of overdraft	avance sur compte courant *f*	—	crédito en descubierto *m*
credito al personale (I)	Personalkredit *m*	personal loan	crédit personnel *m*	—	crédito personal *m*
crédito cambiario (Es)	Wechselkredit *m*	acceptance credit	crédit d'escompte *m*	credito cambiario *m*	—
crédito cambiario (I)	Wechselkredit *m*	acceptance credit	crédit d'escompte *m*	—	crédito cambiario *m*
crédito comercial[1] (Es)	Warenkredit *m*	trade credit	avance sur marchandises *f*	credito su merci *m*	—
crédito comercial[2] (Es)	Lieferantenkredit *m*	supplier's credit	crédit de fournisseurs *m*	credito al fornitore *m*	—
credito d'accettazione (I)	Akzeptkredit *m*	acceptance credit	crédit par traites acceptées *m*	—	crédito de aceptación *m*
credito da danni (I)	Schadensforderung *f*	claim for damages	prétention à dommages-intérêts *f*	—	pretensión de indemnización *f*
credito d'avallo (I)	Avalkredit *m*	credit by way of bank guarantee	crédit d'escompte sur traite avalisée *m*	—	crédito de aval *m*
crédito de aceptación (Es)	Akzeptkredit *m*	acceptance credit	crédit par traites acceptées *m*	credito d'accettazione *m*	—
crédito de aval (Es)	Avalkredit *m*	credit by way of bank guarantee	crédit d'escompte sur traite avalisée *m*	credito d'avallo *m*	—
crédito de consumo (Es)	Konsumkredit *m*	consumer credit	crédit à la consommation *m*	credito al consumatore *m*	—
crédito de garantía (Es)	Bürgschaftskredit *m*	credit by way of bank guarantee	crédit cautionné *m*	credito di fideiussione *m*	—
crédito de inversión (Es)	Investitionskredit *m*	investment credit	crédit d'investissement *m*	credito d'investimento *m*	—
crédito de reembolso (Es)	Rembourskredit *m*	documentary acceptance credit	crédit documentaire confirmé *m*	credito di rimborso *m*	—
credito di fideiussione (I)	Bürgschaftskredit *m*	credit by way of bank guarantee	crédit cautionné *m*	—	crédito de garantía *m*
credito d'investimento (I)	Investitionskredit *m*	investment credit	crédit d'investissement *m*	—	crédito de inversión *m*
credito di rimborso (I)	Rembourskredit *m*	documentary acceptance credit	crédit documentaire confirmé *m*	—	crédito de reembolso *m*
crédito documentario[1] (Es)	Akkreditiv *n*	letter of credit	accréditif *m*	credito documentario *m*	—
crédito documentario[2] (Es)	Dokumenten-akkreditiv *n*	documentary letter of credit	crédit documentaire *m*	apertura di credito documentario *f*	—
crédito documentario (I)	Akkreditiv *n*	letter of credit	accréditif *m*	—	crédito documentario *m*
crédito documentario irrevocable (Es)	unwiderrufliches Akkreditiv *n*	irrevocable letter of credit	accréditif irrévocable *m*	apertura di credito documentario irrevocabile *f*	—
credito dubbio (I)	zweifelhafte Forderung *f*	doubtful account	créance douteuse *f*	—	créditos dudosos *m pl*
credito edilizio (I)	Baukredit *m*	building loan	crédit à la construction *m*	—	crédito para la construcción *m*
crédito en blanco (Es)	Blankokredit *m*	open credit	crédit en compte courant *m*	credito scoperto *m*	—
crédito en cuenta corriente (Es)	Kontokorrent-kredit *m*	current account credit	crédit en compte courant *m*	credito in conto corrente *m*	—
crédito en descubierto (Es)	Überziehungs-kredit *m*	credit by way of overdraft	avance sur compte courant *f*	credito allo scoperto *m*	—
crédito en efectivo (Es)	Barkredit *m*	cash credit	crédit de caisse *m*	credito per cassa *m*	—
credito in conto corrente (I)	Kontokorrentkredit *m*	current account credit	crédit en compte courant *m*	—	crédito en cuenta corriente *m*
crédito para la construcción (Es)	Baukredit *m*	building loan	crédit à la construction *m*	credito edilizio *m*	—
crédito per cassa (I)	Barkredit *m*	cash credit	crédit de caisse *m*	—	crédito en efectivo *m*
crédito personal (Es)	Personalkredit *m*	personal loan	crédit personnel *m*	credito al personale *m*	—
crédito pignoraticio (Es)	Lombardkredit *m*	credit against securities	crédit garanti par nantissement *m*	credito su pegno *m*	—
credito ponte (I)	Überbrückungs-kredit *m*	bridging loan	crédit transitoire *m*	—	crédito transitorio *m*
creditor[1] (E)	Gläubiger *m*	—	créancier *m*	creditore *m*	accreedor *m*

	D	E	F	I	Es
creditor² (E)	Kreditor *m*	—	créditeur *m*	creditore *m*	accreedor *m*
creditore¹ (I)	Gläubiger *m*	creditor	créancier *m*	—	accreedor *m*
creditore² (I)	Kreditor *m*	creditor	créditeur *m*	—	accreedor *m*
crédito real (Es)	Realkredit *m*	credit secured by real property	crédit sur gage mobilier *m*	credito reale *m*	—
credito reale (I)	Realkredit *m*	credit secured by real property	crédit sur gage mobilier *m*	—	crédito real *m*
creditore della massa fallimentare (I)	Konkursgläubiger *m*	bankrupt's creditor	créancier de la faillite *m*	—	accreedor de la quiebra *m*
crédito roll over (Es)	Roll-over-Kredit *m*	roll-over credit	crédit roll-over *m*	credito roll-over *m*	—
credito roll-over (I)	Roll-over-Kredit *m*	roll-over credit	crédit roll-over *m*	—	crédito roll over *m*
crédito rotativo (Es)	Revolving-Kredit *m*	revolving credit	crédit rotatif *m*	credito rotativo *m*	—
credito rotativo (I)	Revolving-Kredit *m*	revolving credit	crédit rotatif *m*	—	crédito rotativo *m*
credito scoperto (I)	Blankokredit *m*	open credit	crédit en compte courant *m*	—	crédito en blanco *m*
crédito simple (Es)	Barakkreditiv	cash letter of credit	accréditif payable en espèce *m*	apertura di credito documentario semplice *f*	—
credito su merci (I)	Warenkredit *m*	trade credit	avance sur marchandises *f*	—	crédito comercial *m*
credito su pegno (I)	Lombardkredit *m*	credit against securities	crédit garanti par nantissement *m*	—	crédito pignoraticio *m*
crédito transitorio (Es)	Überbrückungs-kredit *m*	bridging loan	crédit transitoire *m*	credito ponte *m*	—
creditors' meeting (E)	Gläubiger-versammlung *f*	—	assemblée des créanciers *f*	riunione dei creditori *f*	junta de acreedores *f*
créditos dudosos (Es)	zweifelhafte Forderung *f*	doubtful account	créance douteuse *f*	credito dubbio *m*	—
créditos stand-by (Es)	Stand-by-Kredite *pl*	stand-by credits	crédit stand-by *m*	crediti stand-by *m pl*	—
crédit par traites acceptées (F)	Akzeptkredit *m*	acceptance credit	—	credito d'accettazione *m*	crédito de aceptación *m*
crédit personnel (F)	Personalkredit *m*	personal loan	—	credito al personale *m*	crédito personal *m*
credit policy (E)	Kreditpolitik *f*	—	politique favorisant le crédit *f*	politica creditizia *f*	política de crédito *f*
credit purchase (E)	Kreditkauf *m*	—	achat à crédit *m*	acquisto a credito *m*	compra de crédito *f*
credit restriction (E)	Kreditrestriktion *f*	—	restriction du crédit *f*	restrizione creditizia *f*	restricción de créditos *f*
crédit roll-over (F)	Roll-over-Kredit *m*	roll-over credit	—	credito roll-over *m*	crédito roll over *m*
crédit rotatif (F)	Revolving-Kredit *m*	revolving credit	—	credito rotativo *m*	crédito rotativo *m*
credit secured by real property (E)	Realkredit *m*	—	crédit sur gage mobilier *m*	credito reale *m*	crédito real *m*
credit side (E)	Haben *n*	—	avoir *m*	attivo *m*	haber *m*
crédit stand-by (F)	Stand-by-Kredite *pl*	stand-by credits	—	crediti stand-by *m pl*	créditos stand-by *m pl*
crédit sur gage mobilier (F)	Realkredit *m*	credit secured by real property	—	credito reale *m*	crédito real *m*
credit transaction (E)	Aktivgeschäft *n*	—	opération active *f*	operazione attiva *f*	operaciones activas *f pl*
credit transfer (E)	Giro *n*	—	virement *m*	giro *m*	giro *m*
crédit transitoire (F)	Überbrückungs-kredit *m*	bridging loan	—	credito ponte *m*	crédito transitorio *m*
creditworthiness (E)	Kreditwürdigkeit *f*	—	solvabilité *f*	essere degno di credito	crédito *m*
creditworthy (E)	kreditwürdig	—	solvable	degno di credito	solvente
creeping inflation (E)	schleichende Inflation *f*	—	inflation rampante *f*	inflazione strisciante *f*	inflación latente *f*
créneau du marché (F)	Marktlücke *f*	market gap	—	lacuna di mercato *f*	sector del mercado no abarcado por la oferta *m*
crescita (I)	Wachstum *n*	growth	croissance *f*	—	crecimiento *m*
crescita economica (I)	Wirtschaftswachs-tum *n*	economic growth	croissance économique *f*	—	crecimiento económico *m*
crescita lineare (I)	lineares Wachstum *n*	linear growth	accroissement linéaire *m*	—	crecimiento lineal *m*

	D	E	F	I	Es
crescita zero (I)	Nullwachstum *n*	zero growth	croissance zéro *f*	—	crecimiento cero *m*
cría de animales (Es)	Tierzucht *f*	livestock breeding	élevage *m*	zootecnia *f*	—
criminal (Es)	straffällig	liable to prosecution	encourir une peine	passibile di pena	—
criminalidad económica[1] (Es)	Wirtschafts-kriminalität *f*	white-collar crime	délinquence économique *f*	criminalità economica *f*	—
criminalidad económica[2] (Es)	White-collar-Kriminalität *f*	white-collar delinquency	délinquence économique *f*	criminalità dei colletti bianchi *f*	—
criminalità dei colletti bianchi (I)	White-collar-Kriminalität *f*	white-collar delinquency	délinquence économique *f*	—	criminalidad económica *f*
criminalità economica (I)	Wirtschafts-kriminalität *f*	white-collar crime	délinquence économique *f*	—	criminalidad económica *f*
crise (F)	Krise *f*	crisis	—	crisi *f*	crisis *f*
crise de l'agriculture (F)	Agrarkrise *f*	agricultural crisis	—	crisi agricola *f*	crisis agrícola *f*
crise de l'énergie (F)	Energiekrise *f*	energy crisis	—	crisi energetica *f*	crisis energética *f*
crise de vente (F)	Absatzkrise *f*	sales crisis	—	crisi di mercato *f*	crisis en la venta *f*
crise économique (F)	Wirtschaftskrise *f*	economic crisis	—	crisi economica *f*	crisis económica *f*
crise économique mondiale (F)	Weltwirtschaftskrise *f*	worldwide economic crisis	—	crisi dell'economia mondiale *f*	crisis económica internacional *f*
crisi (I)	Krise *f*	crisis	crise *f*	—	crisis *f*
crisi agricola (I)	Agrarkrise *f*	agricultural crisis	crise de l'agriculture *f*	—	crisis agrícola *f*
crisi dell'economia mondiale (I)	Weltwirtschaftskrise *f*	worldwide economic crisis	crise économique mondiale *f*	—	crisis económica internacional *f*
crisi di mercato (I)	Absatzkrise *f*	sales crisis	crise de vente *f*	—	crisis en la venta *f*
crisi economica (I)	Wirtschaftskrise *f*	economic crisis	crise économique *f*	—	crisis económica *f*
crisi energetica (I)	Energiekrise *f*	energy crisis	crise de l'énergie *f*	—	crisis energética *f*
crisis (E)	Krise *f*	—	crise *f*	crisi *f*	crisis *f*
crisis (Es)	Krise *f*	crisis	crise *f*	crisi *f*	—
crisis agrícola (Es)	Agrarkrise *f*	agricultural crisis	crise de l'agriculture *f*	crisi agricola *f*	—
crisis económica (Es)	Wirtschaftskrise *f*	economic crisis	crise économique *f*	crisi economica *f*	—
crisis económica internacional (Es)	Weltwirtschaftskrise *f*	worldwide economic crisis	crise économique mondiale *f*	crisi dell'economia mondiale *f*	—
crisis energética (Es)	Energiekrise *f*	energy crisis	crise de l'énergie *f*	crisi energetica *f*	—
crisis en la venta (Es)	Absatzkrise *f*	sales crisis	crise de vente *f*	crisi di mercato *f*	—
croissance (F)	Wachstum *n*	growth	—	crescita *f*	crecimiento *m*
croissance économique (F)	Wirtschafts-wachstum *n*	economic growth	—	crescita economica *f*	crecimiento económico *m*
croissance zéro (F)	Nullwachstum *n*	zero growth	—	crescita zero *f*	crecimiento cero *m*
croissant (F)	steigend	rising	—	in aumento	ascendente
crollo delle quotazioni (I)	Kurszusammen-bruch *m*	collapse of prices	chute des cours *f*	—	caída de los cambios *f*
crollo di borsa (I)	Börsenkrach *m*	stockmarket crash	débâcle boursière *f*	—	caída en picado de la bolsa *f*
crollo finanziario (I)	finanzieller Zusammenbruch *m*	financial failure	débâcle financière *f*	—	derrumbamiento financiero *m*
crossed cheque[1] (E)	gekreuzter Scheck *m*	—	chèque barré *m*	assegno sbarrato *m*	cheque cruzado *m*
crossed cheque[2] (E)	Verrechnungs-scheck *m*	—	chèque à porter en compte *m*	assegno sbarrato *m*	cheque cruzado *m*
crude oil (E)	Rohöl *n*	—	pétrole brut *m*	petrolio greggio *m*	crudo *m*
crude oil price (E)	Rohölpreis *m*	—	prix du pétrole brut *m*	prezzo del petrolio greggio *m*	precio del crudo *m*
crudo[1] (Es)	Rohöl *n*	crude oil	pétrole brut *m*	petrolio greggio *m*	—
crudo[2] (Es)	Erdöl *n*	mineral oil	pétrole *m*	petrolio *m*	—
cuadro (Es)	Schaubild *n*	graph	graphique *m*	diagramma *m*	—
cualificación (Es)	Qualifikation *f*	qualification	qualification *f*	qualificazione *f*	—
cualitativo (Es)	qualitativ	qualitative	qualitatif	qualitativo	—
cuantitativo (Es)	quantitativ	quantitative	quantitatif	quantitativo	—
cuenta (Es)	Konto *n*	account	compte *m*	conto *m*	—
cuenta a plazo (Es)	Festgeldkonto *n*	time deposit account	compte de dépôt à terme *m*	deposito vincolato *m*	—

	D	E	F	I	Es
cuenta bancaria (Es)	Bankkonto n	bank account	compte en banque m	conto bancario m	—
cuenta cifrada (Es)	Nummernkonto n	numbered account	compte anonyme m	conto cifrato m	—
cuenta congelada (Es)	gesperrtes Konto n	blocked account	compte bloqué m	conto bloccato m	—
cuenta corriente[1] (Es)	laufende Rechnung f	account current	compte courant m	conto corrente m	—
cuenta corriente[2] (Es)	Kontokorrent n	account current	compte courant m	conto corrente m	—
cuenta corriente[3] (Es)	Kontokorrentkonto n	current account	compte tenu en compte courant m	conto corrente m	—
cuenta corriente postal (Es)	Postscheckkonto n	(postal) giro account	compte chèque postal m	conto corrente postale m	—
cuenta de beneficios y pérdidas (Es)	Erfolgskonto n	profit account	compte de résultats m	conto profitti m	—
cuenta de existencias (Es)	Bestandskonto n	real account	compte d'existences m	conto merci m	—
cuenta de ganancias (Es)	Ertragsrechnung f	profit and loss account	solde net de l'exploitation m	conto economico m	—
cuenta de la empresa (Es)	Firmenkonto n	company account	compte de maison m	conto intestato ad una ditta m	—
cuenta de liquidación (Es)	Abwicklungskonto n	settlement account	compte de liquidation m	conto di liquidazione f	—
cuenta de moneda extranjera (Es)	Währungskonto n	foreign currency account	compte en monnaies étrangères m	conto in valuta m	—
cuenta de pérdidas y ganancias (Es)	Gewinn- und Verlustrechnung f	profit and loss account	compte de pertes et profits m	conto profitti e perdite m	—
cuenta de salario (Es)	Gehaltskonto n	salary account	compte de domiciliation du salaire m	conto stipendi m	—
cuenta exterior (Es)	Auslandskonto n	foreign account	compte d'étranger m	conto estero m	—
cuenta fiduciaria de un abogado (Es)	Anderkonto n	fiduciary account	compte de tiers m	conto per terzi m	—
cuenta particular (Es)	Privatkonto n	private account	compte privé m	conto privato m	—
cuenta provisional (Es)	Zwischenkonto n	interim account	compte provisoire m	conto transitorio m	—
cuenta trimestral (Es)	Quartalsrechnung f	quarterly invoice	compte trimestriel m	conto trimestrale m	—
cuentas de orden (Es)	Abgrenzungsposten m	deferred item	comptes transitoires m pl	ratei e risconti m pl	—
cuestionario (Es)	Fragebogen m	questionnaire	questionnaire m	questionario m	—
culpable (E)	schuldhaft	—	coupable	colposo	culpable
culpable (Es)	schuldhaft	culpable	coupable	colposo	—
cultura empresarial (Es)	Unternehmenskultur f	entrepreneurial culture	culture de l'entreprise f	cultura imprenditoriale f	—
cultura imprenditoriale (I)	Unternehmenskultur f	entrepreneurial culture	culture de l'entreprise f	—	cultura empresarial f
culture de l'entreprise (F)	Unternehmenskultur f	entrepreneurial culture	—	cultura imprenditoriale f	cultura empresarial f
cumpleaños (Es)	Geburtstag m	birthday	anniversaire m	compleanno m	—
cumplimiento (Es)	Erfüllung f	compliance	acquittement m	adempimento m	—
cuota (Es)	Quote f	quota	quota m	quota f	—
cuota del mercado (Es)	Marktanteil m	market share	participation au marché f	quota di mercato f	—
cuota de ahorro (Es)	Sparquote f	savings ratio	quote-part de revenu réservée à des fins d'épargne f	quota di risparmio f	—
cuota de importación (Es)	Importquote f	import quota	contingent d'importation m	quota d'importazione f	—
cuota de pérdida (Es)	Ausfallquote f	default rate	ratio de perte m	tasso di perdita m	—
cuota de producción (Es)	Förderquote f	production quota	quote-part de production f	quota d'estrazione f	—
cupo de exportación (Es)	Exportquote f	export quota	quota d'exportation m	contingente d'esportazione m	—
cupón (Es)	Coupon m	coupon	coupon m	cedola f	—
curatore fallimentare (I)	Konkursverwalter m	administrator in bankruptcy proceedings	liquidateur de la faillite m	—	síndico de quiebra m
currency (E)	Währung f	—	monnaie f	valuta f/moneta f	moneda f
currency agreement (E)	Währungsabkommen n	—	accord monétaire m	accordo monetario m	acuerdo monetario m

	D	E	F	I	Es
currency area (E)	Währungsgebiet n	—	zone monétaire f	area monetaria f	área monetaria f
currency clause (E)	Währungsklausel f	—	clause monétaire f	clausola monetaria f	cláusula monetaria f
currency risk (E)	Währungsrisiko n	—	risque de change m	rischio monetario m	riesgo monetario m
currency snake (E)	Währungsschlange f	—	serpent monétaire m	serpente monetario m	serpiente monetaria f
currency zone (E)	Währungszone f	—	zone monétaire f	zona monetaria f	zona monetaria f
current account[1] (E)	laufende Rechnung f	—	compte courant m	conto corrente m	cuenta corriente f
current account[2] (E)	Kontokorrentkonto n	—	compte tenu en compte courant m	conto corrente m	cuenta corriente f
current account credit (E)	Kontokorrentkredit m	—	crédit en compte courant m	credito in conto corrente m	crédito en cuenta corriente m
current account (E)	Kontokorrent n	—	compte courant m	conto corrente m	cuenta corriente f
current assets (E)	Umlaufvermögen n	—	capital de roulement m	patrimonio circolante m	capital circulante m
current market value (E)	Zeitwert m	—	valeur à une certaine date f	valore corrente m	valor actual m
(current) operational expenses (E)	Betriebsausgaben f	—	charges d'exploitation f pl	spese aziendali f pl	gastos de explotación m pl
current value (E)	Tageswert m	—	valeur du jour f	valore del giorno m	valor del día m
curriculum vitae (E)	Lebenslauf m	—	curriculum vitae m	curriculum vitae m	curriculum vitae m
curriculum vitae (Es)	Lebenslauf m	curriculum vitae	curriculum vitae m	curriculum vitae m	—
curriculum vitae (F)	Lebenslauf m	curriculum vitae	—	curriculum vitae m	curriculum vitae m
curriculum vitae (I)	Lebenslauf m	curriculum vitae	curriculum vitae m	—	curriculum vitae m
curriculum vitae écrit à la main (F)	handgeschriebener Lebenslauf m	hand-written curriculum vitae	—	curriculum vitae scritto a mano m	curriculum vitae escrito a mano m
curriculum vitae escrito a mano (Es)	handgeschriebener Lebenslauf m	hand-written curriculum vitae	curriculum vitae écrit à la main m	curriculum vitae scritto a mano m	—
curriculum vitae scritto a mano (I)	handgeschriebener Lebenslauf m	hand-written curriculum vitae	curriculum vitae écrit à la main m	—	curriculum vitae escrito a mano m
custodia (Es)	Verwahrung f	custody	dépôt m	custodia f	—
custodia (I)	Verwahrung f	custody	dépôt m	—	custodia f/ incautación f
custodia de valores (Es)	Depotgeschäft n	deposit banking	garde des titres f	operazione di deposito f	—
custody (E)	Verwahrung f	—	dépôt m	custodia f	custodia f/ incautación f
customer[1] (E)	Kunde m	—	client m	cliente m	cliente m
customer[2] (E)	Besteller m	—	acheteur m	committente m	demandante m
customer magazine (E)	Kundenzeitschrift f	—	journal destiné à la clientèle m	periodico per i clienti m	revista para los clientes f
customer's reference number (E)	Kundennummer f	—	numéro de référence du client m	numero di cliente m	número del cliente m
customer survey (E)	Kundenbefragung f	—	enquête parmi les clients f	intervista ai clienti f	encuesta entre los clientes f
customs (E)	Zoll m	—	douane f/droit de douane m	dogana f/dazio m	aduana f/arancel m
customs application (E)	Zollantrag m	—	demande de dédouanement f	domanda di sdoganamento f	solicitud de aduana f
customs clearance of exports (E)	Ausfuhrabfertigung f	—	formalités en douane à l'exportation f pl	sdoganamento delle esportazioni m	despacho de exportación m
customs convention (E)	Zollabkommen n	—	accord douanier m	accordo sulle tariffe doganali m	convenio aduanero m
customs declaration[1] (E)	Zollerklärung f	—	déclaration en douane f	dichiarazione doganale f	declaración arancelaria f
customs declaration[2] (E)	Zollanmeldung f	—	déclaration en douane f	dichiarazione doganale f	declaración arancelaria f
customs documents (E)	Zollpapiere pl	—	documents douaniers m pl	documenti doganali m pl	documentos aduaneros m pl
customs drawback (E)	Rückzoll m	—	ristourne des droits de douane f	restituzione di dazi f	drawback m
customs duties (E)	Zollgebühren pl	—	droit de douane m	diritti doganali m pl	derechos arancelarios m pl
customs formalities (E)	Zollformalität f	—	formalité douanières f	formalità doganale f	formalidades aduaneras f pl

	D	E	F	I	Es
customs frontier (E)	Zollgrenze f	—	frontière douanière f	confine doganale m	frontera aduanera f
customs frontier district (E)	Zollgrenzgebiet n	—	territoire de surveillance douanière m	area doganale di confine f	territorio aduanero fronterizo m
customs invoice (E)	Zollfaktura f	—	facture douanière f	fattura doganale f	factura arancelaria f
customs office (E)	Zollstelle f	—	bureau de douane m	posto di dogana m	oficina de aduanas f
customs procedure (E)	Zollverkehr m	—	régime douanier m	procedure doganali f pl	régimen aduanero de mercancías m
(customs) procedure (E)	Verfahren n	—	méthode f/ procédure f	procedimento m/ procedura f	proceso m/ procedimiento m
customs seal (E)	Zollverschluß m	—	fermeture douanière f	sigillo doganale m	precinto aduanero m
customs tariff (E)	Zolltarif m	—	tarif des douanes m	tariffa doganale f	tarifa arancelaria f
customs territory (E)	Zollgebiet n	—	territoire douanier m	territorio doganale m	distrito aduanero m
customs union (E)	Zollunion f	—	union douanière f	unione doganale f	unión aduanera f
customs warehouse procedure (E)	Zollagerung f	—	dépôt en entrepôt sous douane m	immagazzinamento doganale m	depósito de aduana m
cybernetics (E)	Kybernetik f	—	cybernétique f	cibernetica f	cibernética f
cybernétique (F)	Kybernetik f	cybernetics	—	cibernetica f	cibernética f
cycle (E)	Zyklus m	—	cycle m	ciclo m	ciclo m
cycle (F)	Zyklus m	cycle	—	ciclo m	ciclo m
cycle conjoncturel (F)	Konjunkturzyklus m	business cycle	—	ciclo congiunturale m	ciclo económico m
cycle de stockage (F)	Lagerzyklus m	stock cycle	—	ciclo di magazzinaggio m	período de almacenaje m
cycle de vie (F)	Lebenszyklus m	life cycle	—	ciclo di vita m	ciclo de vida m
d'accord avec (F)	im Einvernehmen mit	in agreement with	—	d'accordo con	de conformidad con
d'accordo con (I)	im Einvernehmen mit	in agreement with	d'accord avec	—	de conformidad con
Dachgesellschaft (D)	—	holding company	société holding f	società finanziaria f	sociedad holding f
daily (E)	täglich	—	quotidien	giornaliero	diario
damage¹ (E)	Schaden m	—	dommage m	danno m	daño m
damage² (E)	Beschädigung f	—	endommagement m	danno m	deterioración f
damage by sea (E)	Havarie f	—	avarie f	avaria f	avería m
damage caused by water (E)	Wasserschaden m	—	dommage causé par l'eau m	danno dovuto all'acqua m	daño causado por el agua m
damage in transit (E)	Transportschaden m	—	dommage au cours d'un transport m	danno di trasporto m	daño de transporte m
Damnum (D)	—	damnum	perte f	perdita f	pérdida f
damnum (E)	Damnum n	—	perte f	perdita f	pérdida f
danger (E)	Gefahr f	—	danger m	pericolo m	peligro m
danger (F)	Gefahr f	danger	—	pericolo m	peligro m
danger money (E)	Gefahrenzulage f	—	prime de danger f	premio di rischio m	incremento por peligrosidad m
Dankschreiben (D)	—	letter of thanks	lettre de remerciement f	lettera di ringraziamento f	carta de agradecimiento f
danni indiretti (I)	Folgeschäden pl	consequential damages	dommage consécutif m	—	daño consecuencial m
danno¹ (I)	Beschädigung f	damage	endommagement m	—	deterioración f
danno² (I)	Schaden m	damage	dommage m	—	daño m
danno di trasporto (I)	Transportschaden m	damage in transit	dommage au cours d'un transport m	—	daño de transporte m
danno dovuto all'acqua (I)	Wasserschaden m	damage caused by water	dommage causé par l'eau m	—	daño causado por el agua m
danno immateriale (I)	immaterieller Schaden m	non-material damage	dommage immatériel m	—	daño inmaterial m
danno piccolo (I)	Bagatellschaden m	minimal damage	dommage mineur m	—	siniestro leve m
danno totale (I)	Totalschaden m	total loss	dommage total m	—	daño total m
daño (Es)	Schaden m	damage	dommage m	danno m	—
daño causado por el agua (Es)	Wasserschaden m	damage caused by water	dommage causé par l'eau m	danno dovuto all'acqua m	—
daño consecuencial (Es)	Folgeschäden pl	consequential damages	dommage consécutif m	danni indiretti m pl	—

	D	E	F	I	Es
daño de transporte (Es)	Transportschaden m	damage in transit	dommage au cours d'un transport m	danno di trasporto m	—
daño inmaterial (Es)	immaterieller Schaden m	non-material damage	dommage immatériel m	danno immateriale m	—
daño total (Es)	Totalschaden m	total loss	dommage total m	danno totale m	—
dans le délai de (F)	binnen	within	—	entro	en el término de
dans les délais[1] (F)	termingerecht	on schedule	—	puntuale	en la fecha fijada
dans les délais[2] (F)	fristgerecht	timely	—	entro il termine convenuto	dentro del plazo fijado
Darlehen (D)	—	loan	prêt m	mutuo m	préstamo m
data (E)	Daten f	—	données f pl	dati m pl	datos m pl
data (I)	Datum n	date	date f	—	fecha f
data bank (E)	Datenbank f	—	banque de données f	banca dati f	banco de datos m
data collection (E)	Datenerfassung f	—	saisie des données informatiques f	raccolta dati f	recogida de datos f
data d'arrivo (I)	Ankunftsdatum n	date of arrival	date d'arrivée f	—	fecha de llegada f
data di nascita (I)	Geburtsdatum n	date of birth	date de naissance f	—	fecha de nacimiento f
data di partenza (I)	Abreisedatum n	date of departure	date de départ f	—	fecha de partida f
data di scadenza (I)	Verfallsdatum n	expiry date	date d'échéance f	—	fecha de vencimiento f
data flow chart (E)	Datenflußplan m	—	organigramme de flux des données m	diagramma flusso dati m	organigrama de flujo de datos m
data medium (E)	Datenträger m	—	porteur des données m	supporto dati m	medio de datos m
data processing[1] (E)	Datenverarbeitung f	—	traitement des information m	elaborazione dati f	procesamiento de datos m
data processing[2] (E)	Informatik f	—	informatique f	informatica f	informática f
data processing system (E)	Datenverarbeitungs-anlage f	—	installation de traite-ment électronique des informations f	elaboratore elettronico di dati m	ordenador m
data protection (E)	Datensicherung f	—	protection de données f	protezione dei dati f	protección de datos f
Data Protection Act (E)	Datenschutzgesetz n	—	loi sur l'informatique f	legge sulla tutela dei dati f	ley de protección de datos f
data securing (E)	Datenschutz m	—	sauvegarde des données f	tutela dei dati f	protección de los datos f
data transmission (E)	Datenübertragung f	—	transmission de dates f	trasmissione dati f	transmisión de datos f
date (E)	Datum n	—	date f	data f	fecha f
date (F)	Datum n	date	—	data f	fecha f
date d'arrivée (F)	Ankunftsdatum n	date of arrival	—	data d'arrivo f	fecha de llegada f
date d'échéance (F)	Verfallsdatum n	expiry date	—	data di scadenza f	fecha de vencimiento f
date de conversation (F)	Gesprächstermin m	appointment for a meeting	—	appuntamento per un colloquio m	fecha de cita f
date de départ (F)	Abreisedatum n	date of departure	—	data di partenza f	fecha de partida f
date de la conférence (F)	Besprechungs-termin m	meeting date	—	termine del colloquio m	fecha de conferencia f
date de naissance (F)	Geburtsdatum n	date of birth	—	data di nascita f	fecha de nacimiento f
date limite (F)	Termin m	deadline	—	termine m	fecha f/cita f
date of arrival (E)	Ankunftsdatum n	—	date d'arrivée f	data d'arrivo f	fecha de llegada f
date of birth (E)	Geburtsdatum n	—	date de naissance f	data di nascita f	fecha de nacimiento f
date of delivery (E)	Liefertermin m	—	délai de livraison m	termine di consegna m	plazo de entrega m
date of departure (E)	Abreisedatum n	—	date de départ f	data di partenza f	fecha de partida f
date of interview (E)	Vorstellungstermin m	—	rendez-vous de présentation m	appuntamento di presentazione m	fecha de entrevista personal f
date of payment (E)	Zahlungstermin m	—	terme du payement m	termine di pagamento m	plazo de pago m
Datei (D)	—	file	fichier de données m	file m	archivo de datos m
Daten (D)	—	data	données f pl	dati m pl	datos m pl
Datenbank (D)	—	data bank	banque de données f	banca dati f	banco de datos m

	D	E	F	I	Es
Datenerfassung (D)	—	data collection	saisie des données informatiques *f*	raccolta dati *f*	recogida de datos *f*
Datenfern-übertragung (D)	—	remote of data transmission	télétransmission des données informatiques *f*	teletrasmissione dati *f*	transmisión de datos *f*
Datenflußplan (D)	—	data flow chart	organigramme de flux des données *m*	diagramma flusso dati *m*	organigrama de flujo de datos *m*
Datenschutz (D)	—	data securing	sauvegarde des données *f*	tutela dei dati *f*	protección de los datos *f*
Datenschutzgesetz (D)	—	Data Protection Act	loi sur l'informatique *f*	legge sulla tutela dei dati *f*	ley de protección de datos *f*
Datensicherung (D)	—	data protection	protection de données *f*	protezione dei dati *f*	protección de datos *f*
Datenträger (D)	—	data medium	porteur des données *m*	supporto dati *m*	medio de datos *m*
Datentypistin (D)	—	terminal operator	perforatrice *f*	dattilografa *f*	perforadora *f*
Datenübertragung (D)	—	data transmission	transmission de données *f*	trasmissione dati *f*	transmisión de datos *f*
Datenverarbeitung (D)	—	data processing	traitement des information *m*	elaborazione dati *f*	procesamiento de datos *m*
Datenverarbeitungs-anlage (D)	—	data processing system	installation de traitement électronique des informations *f*	elaboratore elettronico di dati *m*	ordenador *m*
dati (I)	Daten *f*	data	données *f pl*	—	datos *m pl*
dati delle ordinazioni (I)	Bestelldaten *pl*	details of order	références de commande *f pl*	—	datos de pedido *m pl*
dati di mercato (I)	Marktdaten *pl*	market details	données sur le marché *f pl*	—	datos del mercado *m pl*
dati effettivi (I)	Istzahlen *pl*	actual figures	résultats effectifs *m pl*	—	cifras efectivas *f pl*
datore di lavoro (I)	Arbeitgeber *m*	employer	employeur *m*	—	patrón *m*
datos (Es)	Daten *f*	data	données *f pl*	dati *m pl*	—
datos del mercado (Es)	Marktdaten *pl*	market details	données sur le marché *f pl*	dati di mercato *m pl*	—
datos de pedido (Es)	Bestelldaten *pl*	details of order	références de commande *f pl*	dati delle ordinazioni *m pl*	—
datos personales (Es)	Personalien *pl*	personal data	identité *f*	generalità *f pl*	—
dattilografa (I)	Datentypistin *f*	terminal operator	perforatrice *f*	—	perforadora *f*
Datum (D)	—	date	date *f*	data *f*	fecha *f*
Dauerauftrag (D)	—	standing order	ordre régulier *m*	ordine permanente *m*	órden permanente *f*
Dauerschuld-verschreibung (D)	—	unredeemable bond	obligation perpétuelle *f*	obbligazione perpetua *f*	obligación perpetua *f*
day of expiry (E)	Verfalltag *m*	—	jour de l'échéance *m*	giorno di scadenza *m*	día de vencimiento *m*
day-to-day money (E)	Tagesgeld *n*	—	argent au jour le jour *m*	prestito giornaliero *m*	dinero de día a día *m*
day-to-day operations (E)	Tagesgeschäft *n*	—	affaire au comptant *f*	contratto a contanti *m*	operación al contado *f*
dazio ad valorem (I)	Wertzoll *m*	ad valorem duty	taxe de douane ad valorem *f*	—	aduanas ad valorem *f pl*
dazio d'importazione (I)	Einfuhrzoll *m*	import duty	droit d'entrée *m*	—	arancel de importación *m*
dazio di quantità (I)	Mengenzoll *m*	specific duty	droit de douane par quantité *m*	—	arancel aduanero cuantitativo *m*
dazio preferenziale (I)	Präferenzzoll *m*	preferential duty	taxe préférentielle de douane *f*	—	aduanas preferenciales *f pl*
dazio proibitivo (I)	Prohibitivzoll *m*	prohibitive duty	droit prohibitif *m*	—	derechos prohibitivos *m pl*
dazio protettivo (I)	Schutzzoll *m*	protective duty	droit de protection *m*	—	aduana proteccionista *f*
dazio sull'esportazione (I)	Ausfuhrzoll *m*	export duty	taxe de sortie *f*	—	derechos de exportación *m pl*
dazio unitario (I)	Einheitszoll *m*	uniform duty	droit unique *m*	—	aduanas uniformes *f pl*
deadline (E)	Termin *m*	—	date limite *f*	termine *m*	fecha *f*/cita *f*

	D	E	F	I	Es
dealing in foreign notes and coins (E)	Sortenhandel *m*	—	commerce de change *m*	cambio valuta *m*	operación de moneda extranjera *f*
dealing in shares (E)	Aktienhandel *m*	—	négociation des actions *f*	commercio azionario *m*	contratación acciones *f*
débâcle boursière (F)	Börsenkrach *m*	stockmarket crash	—	crollo di borsa *m*	caída en picado de la bolsa *f*
débâcle fiancière (F)	Finanzdebakel *n*	financial debacle	—	dissesto finanziario *m*	descalabro financiero *m*
débâcle financière (F)	finanzieller Zusammenbruch *m*	financial failure	—	crollo finanziario *m*	derrumbamiento financiero *m*
débauchage (F)	Abwerbung *f*	pirating	—	accaparramento *m*	sonsacamiento *m*
debe (Es)	Soll *m*	debit/target	doit *m*	passivo *m*	—
debenture loan (E)	Obligationsanleihe *f*	—	emprunt obligataire *m*	prestito obbligazionario *m*	empréstito sobre obligaciones *f*
debenture stock (E)	Schuldverschreibung *f*	—	obligation *f*	obbligazione *f*	obligación *f*
deber de conservación (Es)	Aufbewahrungspflicht *f*	obligation to preserve records	obligation de conservation *f*	obbligo di custodia *m*	—
debidamente (Es)	ordnungsgemäß	orderly	correct(e)	regolare	—
debit (E)	Soll *m*	—	doit *m*	passivo *m*	debe m
débiter (F)	belasten	load/charge	—	addebitare	cargar/adeudar
débiteur¹ (F)	Schuldner *m*	debtor	—	debitore *m*	deudor *m*/responsable *m*/obligado *m*
débiteur² (F)	Debitor *m*	debtors	—	debitore *m*	deudor *m*
debiti (I)	Schulden *pl*	debts	dettes *f pl*	—	deudas *f pl*
debiti con l'estero (I)	Auslandsschulden *pl*	foreign debts	dettes à l'étranger *f pl*	—	deudas exteriores *f pl*
debiti insoluti (I)	Außenstände *pl*	outstanding debts	dettes actives *f pl*	—	cobros pendientes *m pl*
debit note (E)	Lastschrift *f*	—	note de débit *f*	addebito *m*	cargo en cuenta *m*
debito (I)	Schuld *f*	debt	dette *f*	—	deuda *f*/crédito pasivo *m*
debito fondiario (I)	Grundschuld *f*	mortgage	dette foncière *f*	—	hipoteca *f*
debito pubblico (I)	Staatsverschuldung *f*	state indebtedness	endettement de l'Etat *m*	—	endeudamiento público *m*
Debitor (D)	—	debtors	débiteur *m*	debitore *m*	deudor *m*
debitore¹ (I)	Schuldner *m*	debtor	débiteur *m*	—	deudor *m*/responsable *m*/obligado *m*
debitore² (I)	Debitor *m*	debtors	débiteur *m*	—	deudor *m*
debitore fallito (I)	Gemeinschuldner *m*	adjudicated bankrupt	failli *m*	—	deudor común *m*
de bonne foi (F)	gutgläubig	bona fide	—	di buona fede	de buena fe
debt financing (E)	Fremdfinanzierung *f*	—	constitution de capital par apport de tiers *f*	finanziamento passivo *m*	financiación externa *f*
debtor (E)	Schuldner *m*	—	débiteur *m*	debitore *m*	deudor *m*/responsable *m*/obligado *m*
debtor countries (E)	Schuldnerländer *pl*	—	pays débiteurs *m pl*	paesi debitori *m pl*	países deudores *m pl*
debtor interest rates (E)	Sollzinsen *pl*	—	intérêt débiteur *m*	interessi debitori *m pl*	intereses deudores *m pl*
debtors (E)	Debitor *m*	—	débiteur *m*	debitore *m*	deudor *m*
debt ratio (E)	Verschuldungsgrad *m*	—	niveau de l'endettement *m*	tasso d'indebitamento *m*	grado de endeudamiento *m*
debts (E)	Schulden *pl*	—	dettes *f pl*	debiti *m pl*	deudas *f pl*
debt service (E)	Schuldendienst *m*	—	service de la dette *m*	servizio dei debiti *m*	servicio de la deuda *m*
début de lettre (F)	Anrede *f*	form of address	—	titolo *m*	tratamiento *m*
de buena fe (Es)	gutgläubig	bona fide	de bonne foi	di buona fede	—
décalage entre les prix et les salaires (F)	Lohnlag *m*	wage lag	—	lag salariale *m*	diferencial entre precios y salarios *m*
de casco (Es)	Kasko *m*	comprehensive	sur corps	corpo *m*	—
deceit (E)	Täuschung *f*	—	tromperie *f*	inganno *m*	engaño *m*
décentralisation (F)	Dezentralisierung *f*	decentralization	—	decentralizzazione *f*	descentralización *f*
decentralization (E)	Dezentralisierung *f*	—	décentralisation *f*	decentralizzazione *f*	descentralización *f*

	D	E	F	I	Es
decentralizzazione (I)	Dezentralisierung *f*	decentralization	décentralisation *f*	—	descentralización *f*
décharge (F)	Entlastung *f*	discharge	—	sgravio *m*	desgravamen *m*
déchet[1] (F)	Abfall *m*	waste	—	rifiuti *m pl*	desechos *m pl*
déchet[2] (F)	Rückstände *pl*	residues	—	residui m p	residuos *m pl*
déchets d'emballage (F)	Verpackungsmüll *m*	packing waste	—	rifiuti da imballaggi *m pl*	basura de embalaje *f*
decision (E)	Beschluß *m*	—	décision *f*	delibera *f*	decisión *f*
decisión (Es)	Beschluß *m*	decision	décision *f*	delibera *f*	—
décision (F)	Beschluß *m*	decision	—	delibera *f*	decisión *f*
décision d'acheter (F)	Kaufentscheidung *f*	decision to purchase	—	decisione d'acquisto *f*	decisión de compra *f*
decisión de compra (Es)	Kaufentscheidung *f*	decision to purchase	décision d'acheter *f*	decisione d'acquisto *f*	—
décision de l'implantation (F)	Standortentscheidung *f*	location decision	—	determinazione dell'ubicazione *f*	decisión de ubicación *f*
decisión de ubicación (Es)	Standortentscheidung *f*	location decision	décision de l'implantation *f*	determinazione dell'ubicazione *f*	—
decisione d'acquisto (I)	Kaufentscheidung *f*	decision to purchase	décision d'acheter *f*	—	decisión de compra *f*
decision to purchase (E)	Kaufentscheidung *f*	—	décision d'acheter *f*	decisione d'acquisto *f*	decisión de compra *f*
Deckung (D)	—	cover	couverture *f*	copertura *f*	cobertura *f*
Deckungsbeitrag (D)	—	contribution margin	proportion de garantie *f*	contributo per copertura *m*	aportación de cobertura *f*
Deckungsbeitragsrechnung (D)	—	contribution costing	calcul de la proportion de garantie *m*	calcolo del contributo per copertura *m*	factura de aportación de cobertura *f*
Deckungszusage (D)	—	confirmation of cover	acceptation de prendre le risque en charge *f*	impegno di copertura *m*	nota de cobertura *f*
declaración a efectos fiscales (Es)	Steuererklärung *f*	tax return	déclaration d'impôts *f*	dichiarazione dei redditi *f*	—
declaración arancelaria[1] (Es)	Zollerklärung *f*	customs declaration	déclaration en douane *f*	dichiarazione doganale *f*	—
declaración arancelaria[2] (Es)	Zollanmeldung *f*	customs declaration	déclaration en douane *f*	dichiarazione doganale *f*	—
declaración bajo juramento (Es)	eidesstattliche Erklärung *f*	declaration in lieu of an oath	déclaration formelle sans prestation de serment *f*	dichiarazione sostitutiva del giuramento *f*	—
declaración de importación (Es)	Einfuhrerklärung *f*	import declaration	déclaration d'entrée *f*	dichiarazione doganale *f*	—
declaración de la renta (Es)	Einkommenserklärung *f*	income declaration	déclaration du revenue *f*	dichiarazione del reddito *f*	—
declaración de la voluntad (Es)	Willenserklärung *f*	declaration of intent	déclaration de volonté *f*	dichiarazione di volontà *f*	—
declaración jurada (Es)	beeidigte Erklärung *f*	sworn statement	déclaration sous serment *f*	dichiarazione giurata *f*	—
declarar (Es)	deklarieren	declare	déclarer	dichiarare	—
déclaration d'entrée (F)	Einfuhrerklärung *f*	import declaration	—	dichiarazione doganale *f*	declaración de importación *f*
déclaration de volonté (F)	Willenserklärung *f*	declaration of intent	—	dichiarazione di volontà *f*	declaración de la voluntad *f*
déclaration d'impôts (F)	Steuererklärung *f*	tax return	—	dichiarazione dei redditi *f*	declaración a efectos fiscales *f*
déclaration du revenue (F)	Einkommenserklärung *f*	income declaration	—	dichiarazione del reddito *f*	declaración de la renta *f*
déclaration du sinistre (F)	Schadensmeldung *f*	notification of damage	—	avviso di danni *m*	aviso de siniestro *m*
déclaration en douane[1] (F)	Zollanmeldung *f*	customs declaration	—	dichiarazione doganale *f*	declaración arancelaria *f*
déclaration en douane[2] (F)	Zollerklärung *f*	customs declaration	—	dichiarazione doganale *f*	declaración arancelaria *f*
déclaration formelle sans prestation de serment (F)	eidesstattliche Erklärung *f*	declaration in lieu of an oath	—	dichiarazione sostitutiva del giuramento *f*	declaración bajo juramento *f*
declaration in lieu of an oath (E)	eidesstattliche Erklärung *f*	—	déclaration formelle sans prestation de serment *f*	dichiarazione sostitutiva del giuramento *f*	declaración bajo juramento *f*

	D	E	F	I	Es
declaration of intent (E)	Willenserklärung f	—	déclaration de volonté f	dichiarazione di volontà f	declaración de la voluntad f
déclaration sous serment (F)	beeidigte Erklärung f	sworn statement	—	dichiarazione giurata f	declaración jurada f
declare (E)	deklarieren	—	déclarer	dichiarare	declarar
déclarer (F)	deklarieren	declare	—	dichiarare	declarar
decline in prices (E)	Preisverfall m	—	chute des prix f	caduta dei prezzi f	caída de precios f
declining-balance depreciation (E)	degressive Abschreibung f	—	amortissement dégressif m	ammortamento decrescente m	amortización decreciente f
decode (E)	decodieren	—	décoder	decodificare	decodificar
décoder (F)	decodieren	decode	—	decodificare	decodificar
decodieren (D)	—	decode	décoder	decodificare	decodificar
decodificar (Es)	decodieren	decode	décoder	decodificare	—
decodificare (I)	decodieren	decode	décoder	—	decodificar
décompte des frais (F)	Spesenabrechnung f	statement of expenses	—	conteggio delle spese m	liquidación de gastos f
de confiance (F)	zuverlässig	reliable	—	affidabile	de confianza
de confianza (Es)	zuverlässig	reliable	de confiance	affidabile	—
de conformidad con (Es)	im Einvernehmen mit	in agreement with	d'accord avec	d'accordo con	—
décoration de vitrine (F)	Schaufenster-dekoration f	window dressing	—	allestimento di vetrina m	adorno del escaparate m
découvert de compte (F)	Kontoüberziehung f	overdraft of an account	—	scoperto di conto m	descubierto m
decrease in demand (E)	Nachfragerückgang m	—	recul de la demande m	flessione della domanda f	disminución en la demanda f
decrease in value (E)	Wertminderung f	—	diminution de la valeur f	riduzione di valore f	depreciación f
decrease of turnover (E)	Umsatzrückgang m	—	recul du chiffre d'affaires m	calo del fatturato m	disminución de la cifra de facturación f
decree (E)	Verordnung f	—	décret m	regolamento m	ordenanza f
décret (F)	Verordnung f	decree	—	regolamento m	ordenanza f
decreto di citazione in giudizio (I)	Eröffnungs-beschluß m	order opening a trial	arrêt de mise en accusation m	—	acuerdo de apertura m
de derecho público (Es)	öffentlich-rechtlich	under public law	de droit public	di diritto pubblico	—
dédouané (F)	verzollt	duty paid	—	sdoganato	pagado
de droit public (F)	öffentlich-rechtlich	under public law	—	di diritto pubblico	de derecho público
deducción (Es)	Abzug m	deduction/discount	diminution f/ escompte m	detrazione f/ sconto m	—
deducción de intereses no acumulados (Es)	Abzinsung f	discounting	déduction des in-térêts non courus f	deduzione di interessi f	—
deducción del descuento (Es)	Skontoabzug m	discount deduction	déduction de l'escompte f	detrazione di sconto f	—
deducción de porte (Es)	Portoabzug m	postage deduction	déduction de port f	detrazione porto f	—
deduction (E)	Abzug m	—	diminution f/ escompte m	detrazione f/ sconto m	deducción f/ descuento m
déduction (F)	Abschlag m	reduction	—	detrazione f	descuento m
déduction de l'escompte (F)	Skontoabzug m	discount deduction	—	detrazione di sconto f	deducción del descuento f
déduction de port (F)	Portoabzug m	postage deduction	—	detrazione porto f	deducción de porte f
déduction des intérêts non courus (F)	Abzinsung f	discounting	—	deduzione di interessi f	deducción de intere-ses no acumulados f
deduzione di interessi (I)	Abzinsung f	discounting	déduction des intérêts non courus f	—	deducción de intere-ses no acumulados f
de facil avenencia (Es)	kulant	accommodating	arrangeant	corrente	—
default interest (E)	Verzugszinsen pl	—	intérêts moratoires m pl	interessi di mora m pl	intereses de demora m pl
default rate (E)	Ausfallquote f	—	ratio de perte m	tasso di perdita m	cuota de pérdida f
default risk (E)	Ausfallrisiko n	—	risque de perte m	rischio di perdita m	riesgo de pérdida m
défaut (F)	Mangel m	defect	—	vizio m	defecto m
defect (E)	Mangel m	—	défaut m	vizio m	defecto m/vicio m

	D	E	F	I	Es
defective (E)	fehlerhaft	—	défectueux	difettoso	defectuoso
defecto (Es)	Mangel *m*	defect	défaut *m*	vizio *m*	—
défectueux (F)	fehlerhaft	defective	—	difettoso	defectuoso
defectuoso (Es)	fehlerhaft	defective	défectueux	difettoso	—
défense de publicité (F)	Werbeverbot *n*	ban on advertising	—	divieto di pubblicità *m*	prohibición de publicidad *f*
deferred item (E)	Abgrenzungs- posten *m*	—	comptes transitoires *m pl*	ratei e risconti *m pl*	cuentas de orden *f pl*
défiant toute concurrence (F)	konkurrenzlos	without competition	—	senza concorrenza	sin competencia
deficiency guarantee (E)	Ausfallbürgschaft *f*	—	garantie de bonne fin *f*	fideiussione d'indennità *f*	fianza con beneficio de excusión *f*
déficit budgétaire (F)	Haushaltsdefizit *n*	budgetary deficit	—	deficit del bilancio *m*	déficit presupuestario *m*
déficit de la balance du commerce extérieur (F)	Außenhandels- defizit *n*	trade deficit	—	deficit del commercio estero *m*	déficit del comercio exterior *m*
deficit del bilancio (I)	Haushaltsdefizit *n*	budgetary deficit	déficit budgétaire *m*	—	déficit presupuestario *m*
déficit del comercio exterior (Es)	Außenhandels- defizit *n*	trade deficit	déficit de la balance du commerce extérieur *m*	deficit del commercio estero *m*	—
deficit del commercio estero (I)	Außenhandels- defizit *n*	trade deficit	déficit de la balance du commerce extérieur *m*	—	déficit del comercio exterior *m*
déficit en la balanza de pagos (Es)	Zahlungsbilanz- defizit *n*	deficit in the balance of payments	balance des paye- ments déficitaire *f*	disavanzo della bilancia dei pagamenti *m*	—
deficit financing (E)	Defizitfinanzierung *f*	—	financement du déficit *m*	finanziamento del deficit *m*	financiación del déficit *f*
deficit in the balance of payments (E)	Zahlungsbilanz- defizit *n*	—	balance des paye- ments déficitaire *f*	disavanzo della bilan- cia dei pagamenti *m*	déficit en la balanza de pagos *m*
déficit presupuestario (Es)	Haushaltsdefizit *n*	budgetary deficit	déficit budgétaire *m*	deficit del bilancio *m*	—
Defizitfinanzierung (D)	—	deficit financing	financement du déficit *m*	finanziamento del deficit *m*	financiación del déficit *f*
deflación (Es)	Deflation *f*	deflation	déflation *f*	deflazione *f*	—
Deflation (D)	—	deflation	déflation *f*	deflazione *f*	deflación *f*
deflation (E)	Deflation *f*	—	déflation *f*	deflazione *f*	deflación *f*
déflation (F)	Deflation *f*	deflation	—	deflazione *f*	deflación *f*
deflazione (I)	Deflation *f*	deflation	déflation *f*	—	deflación *f*
deflusso di divise (I)	Devisenabfluß *m*	foreign exchange outflow	sortie de devises *f*	—	drenaje de divisas *m*
defraudación[1] (Es)	Unterschlagung *f*	embezzlement	détournement *m*	appropriazione indebita *f*	—
defraudación[2] (Es)	Hinterziehung *f*	evasion of taxes	fraude fiscale *f*	evasione *f*	—
defraudación fiscal (Es)	Steuerhinterziehung *f*	tax evasion	dissimulation en matière fiscale *f*	evasione fiscale *f*	—
degno di credito (I)	kreditwürdig	creditworthy	solvable	—	solvente
dégré de saturation (F)	Auslastungsgrad *m*	capacity utilisation rate	—	grado di sfruttamento *m*	tasa de utilización *f*
degressive Abschreibung (D)	—	declining-balance depreciation	amortissement dégressif *m*	ammortamento decrescente *m*	amortización decreciente *f*
dégressivité des coûts (F)	Kostendegression *f*	cost degression	—	riduzione dei costi *f*	reducción de costes *f*
déjeuner de travail (F)	Arbeitsessen *n*	working lunch	—	pranzo di lavoro *m*	comida de trabajo *f*
deklarieren (D)	—	declare	déclarer	dichiarare	declarar
délai[1] (F)	Frist *f*	period	—	termine *m*	plazo *m*
délai[2] (F)	Ablauffrist *f*	time limit	—	termine di scadenza *m*	vencimiento *m*
délai de carence (F)	Karenzzeit *f*	qualifying period	—	periodo d'attesa *m*	período carencial *m*
délai de déclaration (F)	Anmeldefrist *f*	time for application	—	termine di denuncia *m*	plazo de solicitud *m*
délai d'engagement sur le taux d'intérêt accordé (F)	Zinsbindungsfrist *f*	lock-down period for interest rates	—	scadenza degli interessi vincolati *f*	plazo de vinculación al tipo de interés pactado *m*

	D	E	F	I	Es
délai de livraison¹ (F)	Lieferfrist f	time for delivery	—	termine di consegna m	plazo de entrega m
délai de livraison² (F)	Liefertermin m	date of delivery	—	termine di consegna m	plazo de entrega m
délai de payement¹ (F)	Zahlungsziel n	period for payment	—	termine di pagamento m	plazo de pago m
délai de payement² (F)	Zahlungsfrist f	terms of payment	—	scadenza di pagamento m	plazo de pago m
délai de préavis (F)	Kündigungsfrist f	period of notice	—	termine di preavviso per la disdetta m	plazo de preaviso m
délai de protection (F)	Schutzfrist f	term of protection	—	durata della protezione f	plazo de protección m
delay¹ (E)	Verzug m	—	demeure f	mora f	retraso m/demora f
delay² (E)	Verspätung f	—	retard m	ritardo m	retraso m
delay in delivery¹ (E)	Lieferverzug m	—	demeure du fournisseur f	mora nella consegna f	demora en la entrega f
delay in delivery² (E)	Lieferungs- verzögerung f	—	retard dans la livraison m	ritardo della consegna m	demora en la entrega f
delcrédere (Es)	Delkredere n	del credere	ducroire m	star del credere m	—
del credere (E)	Delkredere n	—	ducroire m	star del credere m	delcrédere m
del credere commission (E)	Delkredereprovision f	—	commission ducroire f	provvigione dello star del credere f	comisión de garantía f
delegación (Es)	Delegation f	delegation	délégation f	delegazione f	—
delegar (Es)	delegieren	delegate	déléguer	delegare	—
delegare (I)	delegieren	delegate	déléguer	—	delegar
delegate (E)	delegieren	—	déléguer	delegare	delegar
Delegation (D)	—	delegation	délégation f	delegazione f	delegación f
delegation (E)	Delegation f	—	délégation f	delegazione f	delegación f
délégation (F)	Delegation f	delegation	—	delegazione f	delegación f
delegazione (I)	Delegation f	delegation	délégation f	—	delegación f
delegieren (D)	—	delegate	déléguer	delegare	delegar
déléguer (F)	delegieren	delegate	—	delegare	delegar
de l'Etat (F)	staatlich	state	—	statale	estatal
delibera (I)	Beschluß m	decision	décision f	—	decisión f
delimitación (Es)	Abgrenzung f	demarcation	délimitation f	delimitazione f	—
délimitation (F)	Abgrenzung f	demarcation	—	delimitazione f	delimitación f
delimitazione (I)	Abgrenzung f	demarcation	délimitation f	—	delimitación f
delincuencia informática (Es)	Computer- kriminalität f	computer criminality	délits informatiques m pl	abuso del computer m	—
délinquance économique¹ (F)	White-collar- Kriminalität f	white-collar delinquency	—	criminalità dei colletti bianchi f	criminalidad económica f
délinquence économique² (F)	Wirtschafts- kriminalität f	white-collar crime	—	criminalità economica f	criminalidad económica f
délits informatiques (F)	Computer- kriminalität f	computer criminality	—	abuso del computer m	delincuencia informática f
deliverable (E)	lieferbar	—	livrable	disponibile	suministrable
delivery¹ (E)	Zustellung f	—	remise f	notifica f/recapito m	envío m
delivery² (E)	Übergabe f	—	remise f	consegna f	entrega f
delivery³ (E)	Lieferung f	—	livraison f	fornitura f/consegna f	suministro m
delivery ban (E)	Liefersperre f	—	blocage de livraisons m	blocco delle forniture m	embargo m
delivery capacity (E)	Lieferkapazität f	—	capacité de livraison f	capacità di fornitura f	capacidad de entrega f
delivery clause (E)	Lieferklausel f	—	clause de livraison f	clausola di fornitura f	cláusulas comerciales f pl
delivery note (E)	Lieferschein m	—	bulletin de livraison m	bolletta di consegna f	recibo de entrega m
delivery programme (E)	Lieferprogramm n	—	programme de livraison m	programma di fornitura m	programa de entrega m
Delkredere (D)	—	del credere	ducroire m	star del credere m	delcrédere m
Delkredere- provision (D)	—	del credere commission	commission ducroire f	provvigione dello star del credere f	comisión de garantía f

	D	E	F	I	Es
demand (E)	Nachfrage f	—	demande f	domanda f	demanda f
demanda¹ (Es)	Klage f	legal action	action en justice f	citazione in giudizio f	—
demanda² (Es)	Anfrage f	inquiry	demande f	richiesta f	—
demanda³ (Es)	Nachfrage f	demand	demande f	domanda f	—
demanda de daños y perjuicios (Es)	Schadensersatz-klage f	action for damages	action en dommages-intérêts f	azione di risarcimento danni f	—
demanda de trabajo (Es)	Arbeitsnachfrage f	job demand	demande d'emploi f	domanda di lavoro f	—
demanda exterior (Es)	Auslandsnachfrage f	foreign demand	demande en prove-nance de l'étranger f	domanda estera f	—
demanda interior (Es)	Inlandsnachfrage f	home demand	demande intérieure f	domanda interna f	—
demanda monetaria (Es)	Geldnachfrage f	demand for money	demande sur le marché monétaire f	domanda di denaro f	—
demandante (Es)	Besteller m	customer	acheteur m	committente m	—
demande¹ (F)	Nachfrage f	demand	—	domanda f	demanda f
demande² (F)	Anfrage f	inquiry	—	richiesta f	demanda f
demande³ (F)	Antrag m	application	—	domanda f	solicitud f
demande de dédouanement (F)	Zollantrag m	customs application	—	domanda di sdoganamento f	solicitud de aduana f
demande d'emploi¹ (F)	Stellengesuch n	situation wanted/application for a job	—	domanda d'impiego f	solicitud de colocación f
demande d'emploi² (F)	Arbeitsnachfrage f	job demand	—	domanda di lavoro f	demanda de trabajo f
demande en déclara-tion de faillite (F)	Konkursantrag m	bankruptcy petition	—	domanda di dichiara-zione del fallimento f	petición de quiebra f
demande en prove-nance de l'étranger (F)	Auslandsnachfrage f	foreign demand	—	domanda estera f	demanda exterior m
demande intérieure (F)	Inlandsnachfrage f	home demand	—	domanda interna f	demanda interior f
demande sur le marché monétaire (F)	Geldnachfrage f	demand for money	—	domanda di denaro	demanda monetaria f
demand for money (E)	Geldnachfrage f	—	demande sur le marché monétaire f	domanda di denaro	demanda monetaria f
demand for payment (E)	Mahnung f	—	mise en demeure f	sollecito m	(ad)monición f
demand price (E)	Geldkurs m	—	cours de la demande m	prezzo di domanda m	cotización demandada f/precio ofrecido m
demarcation (E)	Abgrenzung f	—	délimitation f	delimitazione f	delimitación f
déménagement (F)	Umzug m	change of residence/parade/demonstration	—	trasferimento m	mudanza f/desfile m/manifestación f
demeure (F)	Verzug m	delay	—	mora f	retraso m/demora f
demeure du débiteur (F)	Zahlungsverzug m	failure to pay on due date	—	morosità di pagamento f	retraso en el pago m
demeure du fournisseur (F)	Lieferverzug m	delay in delivery	—	mora nella consegna f	demora en la entrega f
démission (F)	Rücktritt m	resignation	—	dimissioni f pl	dimisión f
demografía (Es)	Demographie f	demography	démographie f	demografia f	—
demografia (I)	Demographie f	demography	démographie f	—	demografía f
Demographie (D)	—	demography	démographie f	demografia f	demografía f
démographie (F)	Demographie f	demography	—	demografia f	demografía f
demography (E)	Demographie f	—	démographie f	demografia f	demografía f
demora en el pago (Es)	Zahlungs-verzögerung f	delay in payment	retard dans le payement m	ritardo del pagamento m	—
demora en la entrega¹ (Es)	Lieferverzug m	delay in delivery	demeure du fournisseur f	mora nella consegna f	—
demora en la entrega² (Es)	Lieferungs-verzögerung f	delay in delivery	retard dans la livraison m	ritardo della consegna m	—
demoscopia (Es)	Demoskopie f	public opinion research	sondage de l'opinion publique m	demoscopia f	—
demoscopia (I)	Demoskopie f	public opinion research	sondage de l'opinion publique m	—	demoscopia f
Demoskopie (D)	—	public opinion research	sondage de l'opinion publique m	demoscopia f	demoscopia f
denaro (I)	Geld n	money	argent m	—	dinero m/efectivo m

	D	E	F	I	Es
denaro contante (I)	Bargeld *n*	cash	argent comptant *m*	—	dinero efectivo *m*
denaro contante in cassa (I)	Bargeldbestand *m*	cash in hand	espèces en caisse *f pl*	—	saldo en efectivo *m*
denaro vincolato (I)	Festgeld *n*	fixed deposit	argent immobilisé *m*	—	depósito a plazo *m*
dénationalisation (F)	Reprivatisierung *f*	reversion to private ownership	—	riprivatizzazione *f*	desnacionalización *f*
denationalization (E)	Privatisierung *f*	—	privatisation *f*	privatizzazione *f*	privatización *f*
denominazione (I)	Firmenname *m*	company name	nom de la maison *m*	—	razón social *f*
dénoncer (F)	kündigen	terminate	—	disdire	denunciar
densidad de la población (Es)	Bevölkerungsdichte *f*	density of population	densité de la population *f*	densità di popolazione *f*	—
densità di popolazione (I)	Bevölkerungsdichte *f*	density of population	densité de la population *f*	—	densidad de la población *f*
densité de la population (F)	Bevölkerungsdichte *f*	density of population	—	densità di popolazione *f*	densidad de la población *f*
density of population (E)	Bevölkerungsdichte *f*	—	densité de la population *f*	densità di popolazione *f*	densidad de la población *f*
dentro del plazo fijado (Es)	fristgerecht	timely	dans les délais	entro il termine convenuto	—
denuncia dei vizi (I)	Mängelanzeige *f*	notice of defect	notification d'un vice *f*	—	aviso de vicios *m*
denunciar (Es)	kündigen	terminate	dénoncer	disdire	—
denutrizione (I)	Unterernährung *f*	malnutrition	sous-alimentation *f*	—	subalimentación *f*
departamento de expedición (Es)	Versandabteilung *f*	dispatch department	service des expéditions *m*	reparto spedizioni *m*	—
departamento de exportación (Es)	Exportabteilung *f*	export department	service d'exportation *m*	reparto esportazioni *m*	—
departamento de mercadeo (Es)	Marketingabteilung *f*	marketing department	bureau de marketing *m*	reparto marketing *m*	—
departamento de nóminas (Es)	Lohnbüro *n*	pay office	bureau de la paye *m*	ufficio paga *m*	—
departamento técnico (Es)	technische Abteilung *f*	engineering department	service technique *m*	reparto tecnico *m*	—
départ gare (F)	ab Bahnhof	ex rail/free on rail	—	franco stazione	puesto en estación
departmental expense account (E)	Kostenstelle *f*	—	compte de frais par secteur *m*	posizione costi *f*	posición de costes *f*
department organization (E)	Abteilungs-organisation *f*	—	organisation du service *f*	organizzazione reparto *f*	organización de sección *f*
department store (E)	Waren-, Kaufhaus *n*	—	grand magasin *m*	grande magazzino *m*	gran almacén *m*
départ navire (F)	ab Schiff	ex ship	—	franco bordo	ex vapor
départ quai (F)	ab Kai	ex quay	—	franco banchina	ex muelle
départ usine (F)	ab Werk	ex works	—	franco fabbrica	ex fábrica
depending on the cyclical trend (E)	konjunkturanfällig	—	sensible aux oscillations de la conjoncture	soggetto ad influssi congiunturali	sensible a las fluctuaciones coyunturales
dépenses[1] (F)	Aufwand *m*	expenditure	—	spese *f pl*	gastos *m pl*
dépenses[2] (F)	Aufwendung *f*	expenditure	—	spese *f pl*	gasto *m*
dépenses[3] (F)	Ausgaben *pl*	expenses	—	spese *f pl*	gastos *m pl*
dépense spéciale (F)	Sonderausgaben *pl*	special expenses	—	spese straordinarie *f pl*	gastos extraordinarios *m pl*
dépenses en matériels (F)	Materialaufwand *m*	material expenditure	—	spese materiale *f pl*	coste de material *m*
dépenses publiques[1] (F)	Staatsausgaben *pl*	public spending	—	spese pubbliche *f pl*	gastos públicos *m pl*
dépenses publiques[2] (F)	öffentliche Ausgaben *pl*	public spending	—	spesa pubblica *f*	gastos públicos *m pl*
dépenses retardées (F)	Ausgaben-verzögerung *f*	expenditure delay	—	dilazione delle spese *f*	aplazamiento de gastos *m*
deperibile (I)	verderblich	perishable	périssable	—	perecedero
depliant (I)	Broschüre *f*	brochure	prospectus *m*	—	folleto *m*
de point en point (F)	Zug um Zug	concurrent	—	contestualmente	punto por punto
dépollution (F)	Entsorgung *f*	waste disposal	—	smaltimento *m*	eliminación *f*

depreciation

	D	E	F	I	Es
deposit¹ (E)	Einlagen pl	—	dépôt m	depositi bancari m pl	depósitos bancarios m pl
deposit² (E)	Anzahlung f	—	acompte m	pagamento in acconto m	pago a cuenta m
deposit³ (E)	Depot n	—	dépôt m	deposito m	depósito m
deposit⁴ (E)	Hinterlegung f	—	dépôt m	deposito m	depósito m
depositi bancari (I)	Einlagen pl	deposit	dépôt m	—	depósitos bancarios m pl
deposit banking (E)	Depotgeschäft n	—	garde des titres f	operazione di deposito f	custodia de valores f
depositi di risparmio (I)	Spareinlagen pl	savings deposits	dépôt d'épargne m	—	imposiciones de ahorro f pl
depósitio de acciones (Es)	Aktiendepot n	share deposit	dépôt d'actions m	deposito di azioni m	—
depositi privati (I)	Privateinlagen pl	private contribution	apport personnel m	—	depósitos privados m pl
depósito¹ (Es)	Depot n	deposit	dépôt m	deposito m	—
depósito² (Es)	Hinterlegung f	deposit	dépôt m	deposito m	—
deposito¹ (I)	Hinterlegung f	deposit	dépôt m	—	depósito m
deposito² (I)	Depot n	deposit	dépôt m	—	depósito m
depósito a plazo (Es)	Festgeld n	fixed deposit	argent immobilisé m	denaro vincolato m	—
depósito de aduana (Es)	Zollagerung f	customs warehouse procedure	dépôt en entrepôt sous douane m	immagazzinamento doganale m	—
depósito de importación (Es)	Importdepot n	import deposit	dépôt d'importation m	deposito d'importazione m	—
depósito de mercancías (Es)	Warenlager n	stock room	stock de marchandises m	magazzino m	—
depósito de noche (Es)	Nachttresor m	night safe	dépôt de nuit m	cassa continua f	—
deposito di azioni (I)	Aktiendepot n	share deposit	dépôt d'actions m	—	depósitio de acciones m
deposito di consegna (I)	Auslieferungslager n	distribution centre	entrepôt de distribution m	—	almacén de entregas m
deposito d'importazione (I)	Importdepot n	import deposit	dépôt d'importation m	—	depósito de importación m
deposito vincolato (I)	Festgeldkonto n	time deposit account	compte de dépôt à terme m	—	cuenta a plazo f
depósitos bancarios (Es)	Einlagen pl	deposit	dépôt m	depositi bancari m pl	—
depósitos privados (Es)	Privateinlagen pl	private contribution	apport personnel m	depositi privati m pl	—
deposit transactions passive (E)	Passivgeschäft n	—	opération passive f	operazione passiva f	operación pasiva f
Depot (D)	—	deposit	dépôt m	deposito m	depósito m
dépôt¹ (F)	Depot n	deposit	—	deposito m	depósito m
dépôt² (F)	Einlagen pl	deposit/ contributed capital	—	depositi bancari m pl	depósitos bancarios m pl
dépôt³ (F)	Hinterlegung f	deposit	—	deposito m	depósito m
dépôt⁴ (F)	Verwahrung f	custody	—	custodia f	custodia f/ incautación f
dépôt d'actions (F)	Aktiendepot n	share deposit	—	deposito di azioni m	depósito de acciones m
dépôt de nuit (F)	Nachttresor m	night safe	—	cassa continua f	depósito de noche m
dépôt d'épargne (F)	Spareinlagen pl	savings deposits	—	depositi di risparmio m pl	imposiciones de ahorro f pl
dépôt d'importation (F)	Importdepot n	import deposit	—	deposito d'importazione m	depósito de importación m
dépôt en entrepôt sous douane (F)	Zollagerung f	customs warehouse procedure	—	immagazzinamento doganale m	depósito de aduana m
Depotgeschäft (D)	—	deposit banking	garde des titres f	operazione di deposito f	custodia de valores f
depreciación¹ (Es)	Wertminderung f	decrease in value	diminution de la valeur f	riduzione di valore f	—
depreciación² (Es)	Wertverfall m	loss of value	dévalorisation f	deprezzamento m	—
depreciation (E)	Abschreibung f	—	amortissement m	ammortamento m	amortización f

	D	E	F	I	Es
dépréciation (F)	Abnutzung f	wear and tear	—	usura f	desgaste m
depreciation fund (E)	Abschreibungs-fonds m	—	fonds d'amortissement m	fondo ammortamenti m	fondo amortización m
de première qualité (F)	erstklassig	first class	—	di prima categoria	de primera calidad
depresión (Es)	Depression f	depression	dépression f	depressione f	—
Depression (D)	—	depression	dépression f	depressione f	depresión f
depression (E)	Depression f	—	dépression f	depressione f	depresión f
dépression[1] (F)	Abschwung m	down-swing	—	regresso m	baja f
dépression[2] (F)	Depression f	depression	—	depressione f	depresión f
depressione (I)	Depression f	depression	dépression f	—	depresión f
deprezzamento (I)	Wertverfall m	loss of value	dévalorisation f	—	depreciación f
de primera calidad (Es)	erstklassig	first class	de première qualité	di prima categoria	—
depuración de las aguas residuales (Es)	Abwasserreinigung f	purification of sewage	clarification des eaux usées f	depurazione delle acque di scarico f	—
depurazione delle acque di scarico (I)	Abwasserreinigung f	purification of sewage	clarification des eaux usées f	—	depuración de las aguas residuales f
deputy (E)	Stellvertreter m	—	adjoint m	sostituto m	sustituto m
derecho[1] (Es)	Recht n	law	droit m	diritto m	—
derecho[2] (Es)	Gebühr f	fee	taxe f	tassa f	—
derecho a indemnización por daños y perjuicios (Es)	Schadenersatz-ansprüche pl	claim for damages	droit à l'indemnité m	diritti al risarcimento danni m pl	—
derecho a voto (Es)	Stimmrecht n	right to vote	droit de vote m	diritto al voto m	—
derecho de devolución (Es)	Rückgaberecht n	right of redemption	droit à restitution m	diritto alla restituzione m	—
derecho de garantía real (Es)	Pfandrecht n	pledge	droit de gage m	diritto di pegno m	—
derecho de la competencia (Es)	Wettbewerbsrecht n	law on competition	législation en matière de concurrence commerciale m	diritto della concorrenza m	—
derecho del autor (Es)	Urheberrecht n	copyright	droit d'auteur m	diritto d'autore m	—
derecho de licencia (Es)	Lizenzgebühr f	royalty	taxe d'exploitation de licence f	tassa di licenza f	—
derecho de preferencia (Es)	Vorkaufsrecht n	preemption right	droit de préemption m	diritto di prelazione m	—
derecho de representación (Es)	Vertretungs-berechtigung f	authorized to represent	autorisation de représentation f	autorizzazione alla rappresentanza f	—
derecho de representación exclusiva (Es)	Alleinvertretungs-recht n	sole and exclusive agency right	droit exclusif de représentation m	diritto di rappresen-tanza esclusiva m	—
derecho de revocación (Es)	Widerrufsrecht n	right of revocation	droit de révocation m	diritto di revoca m	—
derecho de socieda-des anónimas (Es)	Aktienrecht n	company law	loi sur les sociétés anonymes f pl	diritto azionario m	—
derecho de suministro adicional (Es)	Nachlieferungs-anspruch m	claim to subsequent delivery	droit à livraison complémentaire m	diritto alla fornitura supplementare m	—
derecho de tránsito (Es)	Transitzoll m	transit duty	droit de transit m	diritti di transito m pl	—
derecho económico (Es)	Wirtschaftsrecht n	economic law	législation économique f	diritto economico m	—
derecho laboral (Es)	Arbeitsrecht n	labour law	législation industrielle f	diritto di lavoro m	—
derecho minoritario (Es)	Minoritätsrecht n	minority right	droit de minorité m	diritto delle minoranze m	—
derecho pesquero (Es)	Fischereirecht n	fishing rights	droit de pêche m	diritto della pesca m	—
derecho preferente (Es)	Vorrecht n	privilege	prérogative f	privilegio m	—
derecho real (Es)	dingliches Recht n	real right	droit réel m	diritto reale m	—
derechos arancelarios (Es)	Zollgebühren pl	customs duties	droit de douane m	diritti doganali m pl	—
derechos de acarreo (Es)	Rollgeld n	haulage	camionnage m	spese di trasporto f pl	—
derechos de carga (Es)	Ladegebühren pl	loading charges	taxe de chargement f	spese di carico f pl	—
derechos de exportación (Es)	Ausfuhrzoll m	export duty	taxe de sortie f	dazio sull'esportazione m	—
derechos de giro (Es)	Ziehungsrechte pl	drawing rights	droits de tirage m pl	diritti di prelievo m pl	—

	D	E	F	I	Es
derechos de giro especial (Es)	Sonderziehungsrechte *pl*	special drawing rights	droits de tirage spécial *m pl*	diritti speciali di prelievo *m pl*	—
derechos de soberanía nacional (Es)	nationale Souveränitätsrechte *pl*	national sovereignty rights	droits de souveraineté nationale *m pl*	diritti di sovranità nazionale *m pl*	—
derechos de timbre (Es)	Stempelgebühr *f*	stamp duty	droit de timbre *m*	tassa di bollo *f*	—
derechos portuarios (Es)	Hafengebühren *pl*	harbour dues	droits de port *m pl*	diritti di porto *m pl*	—
derechos prohibitivos (Es)	Prohibitivzoll *m*	prohibitive duty	droit prohibitif *m*	dazio proibitivo *m*	—
deregolazione (I)	Deregulierung *f*	deregulation	dérégularisation *f*	—	deregulación *f*
deregulación (Es)	Deregulierung *f*	deregulation	dérégularisation *f*	deregolazione *f*	—
dérégularisation (F)	Deregulierung *f*	deregulation	—	deregolazione *f*	deregulación *f*
deregulation (E)	Deregulierung *f*	—	dérégularisation *f*	deregolazione *f*	deregulación *f*
Deregulierung (D)	—	deregulation	dérégularisation *f*	deregolazione *f*	deregulación *f*
dernier cours (F)	Schlußkurs *m*	closing price	—	quotazione di chiusura *f*	cotización final *f*
déroulement de la fabrication (F)	Fertigungsprozess *m*	production procedure	—	processo produttivo *m*	proceso de producción *m*
derrumbamiento financiero (Es)	finanzieller Zusammenbruch *m*	financial failure	débâcle financière *f*	crollo finanziario *m*	—
desalojamiento (Es)	Räumung *f*	evacuation	évacuation *f*	evacuazione *f*	—
desarrollo (Es)	Entwicklung *f*	development	développement *m*	sviluppo *m*	—
désavantage (F)	Nachteil *m*	disadvantage	—	svantaggio *m*	desventaja *f*
descalabro financiero (Es)	Finanzdebakel *n*	financial debacle	débâcle fiancière *f*	dissesto finanziario *m*	—
descenso del empleo (Es)	Beschäftigungsrückgang *m*	drop in employment	baisse de l'offre d'emploi *f*	calo dell'occupazione *m*	—
descentralización (Es)	Dezentralisierung *f*	decentralization	décentralisation *f*	decentralizzazione *f*	—
descripción del puesto de trabajo (Es)	Stellenbeschreibung *f*	job description	description de l'emploi *f*	descrizione d'impiego *f*	—
description de l'emploi (F)	Stellenbeschreibung *f*	job description	—	descrizione d'impiego *f*	descripción del puesto de trabajo *f*
descrizione d'impiego (I)	Stellenbeschreibung *f*	job description	description de l'emploi *f*	—	descripción del puesto de trabajo *f*
descubierto (Es)	Kontoüberziehung *f*	overdraft of an account	découvert de compte *m*	scoperto di conto *m*	—
descuendo por pago al contado[1] (Es)	Barzahlungsnachlaß *m*	discount for cash payment	remise pour payement au comptant *f*	sconto per pagamento in contanti *m*	—
descuendo por pago al contado[2] (Es)	Barzahlungsrabatt *m*	cash discount	remise pour payement comptant *f*	ribasso per pagamento in contanti *m*	—
descuento[1] (Es)	Skonto *n*	discount	escompte *m*	sconto *m*	—
descuento[2] (Es)	Diskont *m*	discount	escompte *m*	sconto *m*	—
descuento[3] (Es)	Abschlag *m*	reduction	déduction *f*	detrazione *f*	—
descuento[4] (Es)	Preisabzug *m*	price deduction	réduction de prix *f*	riduzione del prezzo *f*	—
descuento de pago al contado (Es)	Barzahlungskonto *n*	cash discount	escompte de caisse *m*	sconto per pagamento in contanti *m*	—
descuento de suscripción (Es)	Vorbestellrabatt *m*	discount on advance orders	escompte de suscription *m*	ribasso per ordinazioni anticipate *m*	—
descuento de una letra aceptada (Es)	Akzepteinlösung *f*	honouring of an acceptance	honorer la traite acceptée	pagamento di un effetto *m*	—
descuento suplementario (Es)	Sonderrabatt *m*	special discount	ristourne exceptionnelle *f*	ribasso speciale *m*	—
descuido (Es)	Fahrlässigkeit *f*	negligence	négligence *f*	negligenza *f*	—
desechos (Es)	Abfall *m*	waste	déchet *m*	rifiuti *m pl*	—
desempleo (Es)	Arbeitslosigkeit *f*	unemployment	chômage *m*	disoccupazione *f*	—
desestacionalizado (Es)	saisonbereinigt	seasonally adjusted	corrigé du mouvement saisonnier	al netto degli influssi stagionali	—
desgaste (Es)	Abnutzung *f*	wear and tear	dépréciation *f*	usura *f*	—
desgravamen (Es)	Entlastung *f*	discharge	décharge *f*	sgravio *m*	—
Design (D)	—	design	design *m*	design *m*	diseño *m*
design (E)	Design *n*	—	design *m*	design *m*	diseño *m*
design (F)	Design *n*	design	—	design *m*	diseño *m*

	D	E	F	I	Es
design (I)	Design *n*	design	design *m*	—	diseño *m*
desk (E)	Schreibtisch *m*	—	bureau *m*	scrivania *f*	escritorio *m*
desnacionalización (Es)	Reprivatisierung *f*	reversion to private ownership	dénationalisation *f*	riprivatizzazione *f*	—
despacho (Es)	Abfertigung *f*	dispatch	expédition *f*	spedizione *f*	—
despacho de exportación (Es)	Ausfuhrabfertigung *f*	customs clearance of exports	formalités en douane à l'exportation *f pl*	sdoganamento delle esportazioni *m*	—
despido (Es)	Entlassung *f*	dismissal	licenciement *m*	licenziamento *m*	—
después de haber recibo la factura (Es)	nach Erhalt der Rechnung	on receipt of the invoice	après avoir reçu la facture	a ricevimento della fattura	—
destajo (Es)	Akkord *m*	piece work	convention de salaire à la tâche *f*	cottimo *m*	—
destinataire[1] (F)	Empfänger *m*	receiver	—	destinatario *m*	destinatario *m*
destinataire[2] (F)	Adressat *m*	addressee	—	destinatario *m*	destinatario *m*
destinatario[1] (Es)	Empfänger *m*	receiver	destinataire *m*	destinatario *m*	—
destinatario[2] (Es)	Adressat *m*	addressee	destinataire *m*	destinatario *m*	—
destinatario[1] (I)	Adressat *m*	addressee	destinataire *m*	—	destinatario *m*
destinatario[2] (I)	Empfänger *m*	receiver	destinataire *m*	—	destinatario *m*
desventaja (Es)	Nachteil *m*	disadvantage	désavantage *m*	svantaggio *m*	—
desviación standard (Es)	Standard-abweichung *f*	standard deviation	déviation standard *f*	scarto tipo *m*	—
détaillant (F)	Einzelhandels-kaufmann *m*	retail merchant	—	commerciante al dettaglio *m*	comerciante particular *m*
details of order (E)	Bestelldaten *pl*	—	références de commande *f pl*	dati delle ordinazioni *m pl*	datos de pedido *m pl*
deterioración (Es)	Beschädigung *f*	damage	endommagement *m*	danno *m*	—
détermination des cours (F)	Kursfestsetzung *f*	fixing of prices	—	fissazione dei corsi *f*	fijación de los cambios *f*
détermination du coût marginal (F)	Grenzkosten-rechnung *f*	marginal costing	—	conto dei costi limite *m*	cálculo de los costes marginales *m*
determinazione dell'ubicazione (I)	Standort-entscheidung *f*	location decision	décision de l'implantation *f*	—	decisión de ubicación *f*
déterminé par le fac-teur main-d'oeuvre (F)	arbeitsintensiv	labour-intensive	—	ad alta incidenza di lavoro	con gran intensidad de mano de obra
déterminé par le facteur salaire (F)	lohnintensiv	wage-intensive	—	ad alta incidenza salariale	con gran intensidad de costos salariales
détournement[1] (F)	Veruntreuung *f*	misappropriation	—	abuso di fiducia *m*	malversación *f*
détournement[2] (F)	Unterschlagung *f*	embezzlement	—	appropriazione indebita *f*	defraudación *f*
detracción privada (Es)	Privatentnahmen *pl*	personal withdrawals	prélèvement personnel *m*	prelevamento a titolo personale *m*	—
detrazione[1] (I)	Abschlag *m*	reduction	déduction *f*	—	descuento *m*
detrazione[2] (I)	Abzug *m*	deduction/discount	diminution *f*/ escompte *m*	—	deducción *f*/ descuento *m*
detrazione di sconto (I)	Skontoabzug *m*	discount deduction	déduction de l'escompte *f*	—	deducción del descuento *f*
detrazione porto (I)	Portoabzug *m*	postage deduction	déduction de port *f*	—	deducción de porte *f*
détritus spéciaux (F)	Sondermüll *m*	special refuse	—	rifiuti speciali *m pl*	basura especial *f*
dettagliante (I)	Einzelhändler *m*	retailer	commerçant détaillant *m*	—	minorista *m*
dettato (I)	Diktat *n*	dictation	dictée *f*	—	dictado *m*
dette (F)	Schuld *f*	debt	—	debito *m*	deuda *f*
dette foncière (F)	Grundschuld *f*	mortgage	—	debito fondiario *m*	hipoteca *f*
dettes (F)	Schulden *pl*	debts	—	debiti *m pl*	deudas *f pl*
dettes actives (F)	Außenstände *pl*	outstanding debts	—	crediti *m pl*	cobros pendientes *m pl*
dettes à l'étranger (F)	Auslandsschulden *pl*	foreign debts	—	debiti con l'estero *m pl*	deudas exteriores *f pl*
deuda (Es)	Schuld *f*	debt	dette *f*	debito *m*	—
deuda neta (Es)	Nettoverschuldung *f*	net indebtedness	endettement net *m*	indebitamento netto *m*	—
deudas (Es)[2]	Schulden *pl*	debts	dettes *f pl*	debiti *m pl*	—

	D	E	F	I	Es
deudas exteriores (Es)	Auslandsschulden *pl*	foreign debts	dettes à l'étranger *f pl*	debiti con l'estero *m pl*	—
deudor¹ (Es)	Debitor *m*	debtors	débiteur *m*	debitore *m*	—
deudor² (Es)	Schuldner *m*	debtor	débiteur *m*	debitore *m*	—
deudor común (Es)	Gemeinschuldner *m*	adjudicated bankrupt	failli *m*	debitore fallito *m*	—
Deutsche Industrie-Norm (D)	—	German Industrial Standards	norme industrielle allemande *f*	norma tedesca di normalizzazione *f*	norma industrial alemana *f*
dévalorisation (F)	Wertverfall *m*	loss of value	—	deprezzamento *m*	depreciación *f*
devaluación (Es)	Abwertung *f*	devaluation	dévaluation *f*	svalutazione *f*	—
devaluation (E)	Abwertung *f*	—	dévaluation *f*	svalutazione *f*	devaluación *f*
dévaluation (F)	Abwertung *f*	devaluation	—	svalutazione *f*	devaluación *f*
development (E)	Entwicklung *f*	—	développement *m*	sviluppo *m*	desarrollo *m*
development aid (E)	Entwicklungshilfe *f*	—	aide au développement *f*	aiuto ai paesi in via di sviluppo *m*	ayuda al desarrollo *f*
development costs (E)	Entwicklungs-kosten *pl*	—	coûts de développement *m pl*	costi di sviluppo *m pl*	gastos de desarrollo *m pl*
development phase (E)	Aufbauphase *f*	—	phase d'organisation *f*	fase di costruzione *f*	fase de desarrollo *f*
développement (F)	Entwicklung *f*	development	—	sviluppo *m*	desarrollo *m*
deviación de dimensión (Es)	Größenabweichung *f*	deviation from size	déviation de dimension *f*	differenza di dimensione *f*	—
deviation (E)	Abweichung *f*	—	divergence *f*	deviazione *f*	diferencia *f*
déviation de dimension (F)	Größenabweichung *f*	deviation from size	—	differenza di dimensione *f*	deviación de dimensión *f*
deviation from quality (E)	Qualitäts-abweichung *f*	—	écart qualitatif *m*	differenza di qualità *f*	diferencia de calidad *f*
deviation from size (E)	Größenabweichung *f*	—	déviation de dimension *f*	differenza di dimensione *f*	deviación de dimensión *f*
déviation standard (F)	Standard-abweichung *f*	standard deviation	—	scarto tipo *m*	desviación standard *f*
deviazione (I)	Abweichung *f*	deviation	divergence *f*	—	diferencia *f*
devis (F)	Voranschlag *m*	estimate	—	preventivo *m*	presupuesto *m*
Devisen (D)	—	foreign exchange	devises *f pl*	divise *f pl*	divisas *f pl*
Devisenabfluß (D)	—	foreign exchange outflow	sortie de devises *f*	deflusso di divise *m*	drenaje de divisas *m*
Devisenarbitrage (D)	—	exchange arbitrage	arbitrage sur les devises *m*	arbitraggio valutario *m*	arbitraje de divisas *m*
Devisenausgleichs-abkommen (D)	—	foreign exchange offset agreement	accord de compen-sation de devises *m*	accordo di clearing valutario *m*	acuerdo de compen-sación de divisas *m*
Devisen-bewirtschaftung (D)	—	foreign exchange control	contrôle des devises *m*	controllo valutario *m*	control de divisas *m*
Devisenbilanz (D)	—	foreign exchange balance	compte de devises *m*	bilancia delle divise *f*	balanza de divisas *f*
Devisenbörse (D)	—	foreign exchange market	bourse de devises *f*	borsa valutaria *f*	bolsa de divisas *f*
Devisen-genehmigung (D)	—	foreign exchange authorization	autorisation de change *f*	autorizzazione valutaria *f*	certificado de divisas *m*
Devisenhandel (D)	—	foreign exchange dealings	marché des changes *m*	commercio delle divise *m*	operaciones de divisas *f pl*
Deviseninländer (D)	—	resident	résident *m*	persona residente *f*	residente *m*
Devisenkontrolle (D)	—	foreign exchange control	contrôle des changes *m*	controllo delle divise *m*	control de divisas *m*
Devisenkurs (D)	—	foreign exchange rate	taux de change *m*	cambio delle divise *m*	cambio *m*
Devisenmarkt (D)	—	foreign exchange market	marché des changes *m*	mercato valutario *m*	mercado de divisas *m*
Devisen-termingeschäft (D)	—	forward exchange dealings	opérations à terme sur les changes *f pl*	operazione valutaria a termine *f*	transacciones a tér-mino en divisas *f pl*
Devisenverkehr (D)	—	foreign exchange dealings	mouvement des devises *m*	commercio dei cambi *m*	tráfico de divisas *m*
devises (F)	Devisen *pl*	foreign exchange	—	divise *f pl*	divisas *f pl*
devis estimatif des frais (F)	Kostenvoranschlag *m*	estimate of cost	—	preventivo dei costi *m*	presupuesto de coste *m*
devolución (Es)	Rücksendung *f*	return	renvoi *m*	rispedizione *f*	—

	D	E	F	I	Es
Dezentralisierung (D)	—	decentralization	décentralisation *f*	decentralizzazione *f*	descentralización *f*
(día de) Año Nuevo (Es)	Neujahr *n*	New Year	Nouvel An *m*	Capodanno *m*	—
día de pago (Es)	Zahltag *m*	payday	jour de paye *m*	giorno di paga *m*	—
día de vencimiento (Es)	Verfalltag *m*	day of expiry	jour de l'échéance *m*	giorno di scadenza *m*	—
día laboral (Es)	Arbeitstag *m*	working day	jour de travail *m*	giorno lavorativo *m*	—
diagram (E)	Diagramm *n*	—	diagramme *m*	diagramma *m*	diagrama *m*
diagrama (Es)	Diagramm *n*	diagram	diagramme *m*	diagramma *m*	—
Diagramm (D)	—	diagram	diagramme *m*	diagramma *m*	diagrama *m*
diagramma¹ (I)	Diagramm *n*	diagram	diagramme *m*	—	diagrama *m*
diagramma² (I)	Schaubild *n*	graph	graphique *m*	—	cuadro *m*
diagramma flusso dati (I)	Datenflußplan *m*	data flow chart	organigramme de flux des données *m*	—	organigrama de flujo de datos *m*
diagramme (F)	Diagramm *n*	diagram	—	diagramma *m*	diagrama *m*
Diaprojektor (D)	—	slide projector	projecteur pour diapositives *m*	proiettore per diapositive *m*	projector de diapositivas *m*
diario (Es)	täglich	daily	quotidien	giornaliero	—
di buona fede (I)	gutgläubig	bona fide	de bonne foi	—	de buena fe
dichiarare (I)	deklarieren	declare	déclarer	—	declarar
dichiarazione dei redditi (I)	Steuererklärung *f*	tax return	déclaration d'impôts *f*	—	declaración a efectos fiscales *f*
dichiarazione del reddito (I)	Einkommens- erklärung *f*	income declaration	déclaration du revenu *f*	—	declaración de la renta *f*
dichiarazione di volontà (I)	Willenserklärung *f*	declaration of intent	déclaration de volonté *f*	—	declaración de la voluntad *f*
dichiarazione doganale¹ (I)	Zollerklärung *f*	customs declaration	déclaration en douane *f*	—	declaración arancelaria *f*
dichiarazione doganale² (I)	Zollanmeldung *f*	customs declaration	déclaration en douane *f*	—	declaración arancelaria *f*
dichiarazione doganale³ (I)	Einfuhrerklärung *f*	import declaration	déclaration d'entrée *f*	—	declaración de importación *f*
dichiarazione giurata (I)	beeidigte Erklärung *f*	sworn statement	déclaration sous serment *f*	—	declaración jurada *f*
dichiarazione sostitutiva del giuramento (I)	eidesstattliche Erklärung *f*	declaration in lieu of an oath	déclaration formelle sans prestation de serment *f*	—	declaración bajo juramento *f*
dictado (Es)	Diktat *n*	dictation	dictée *f*	dettato *m*	—
dictamen (Es)	Stellungnahme *f*	comment	prise de position *f*	presa di posizione *f*	—
dictamen pericial (Es)	Expertise *f*	expert opinion	expertise *f*	perizia *f*	—
dictaphone (E)	Diktiergerät *n*	—	appareil à dicter *m*	dittafono *m*	máquina de dictar *f*
dictation (E)	Diktat *n*	—	dictée *f*	dettato *m*	dictado *m*
dictée (F)	Diktat *n*	dictation	—	dettato *m*	dictado *m*
di diritto pubblico (I)	öffentlich-rechtlich	under public law	de droit public	—	de derecho público
Diebstahl (D)	—	theft	vol *m*	furto *m*	robo *m*
Diebstahl- versicherung (D)	—	theft insurance	assurance contre le vol *f*	assicurazione contro il furto *f*	seguro contra el robo *m*
Dienst (D)	—	service	service *m*	servizio *m*	servicio *m*
Dienstgeheimnis (D)	—	official secret	secret de service *m*	segreto d'ufficio *m*	secreto profesional *m*
Dienstleistung (D)	—	service	prestation de service *f*	servizio *m*	prestación de servicio *m*
Dienstwagen (D)	—	official car	voiture de service *f*	vettura di servizio *f*	coche de servicio *m*
diferencia (Es)	Abweichung *f*	deviation	divergence *f*	deviazione *f*	—
diferenciación de los precios (Es)	Preisdifferenzierung *f*	price differentiation	différenciation de prix *f*	differenziazione dei prezzi *f*	—
diferencia de calidad (Es)	Qualitäts abweichung *f*	deviation from quality	écart qualitatif *f*	differenza di qualità *f*	—
diferencia de precios (Es)	Preisunterschied *m*	price difference	écart de prix *m*	differenza dei prezzi *f*	—
diferencia entre los tipos de interés (Es)	Zinsgefälle *n*	margin between interest rates	disparité des niveaux d'intérêts *f*	differenza dei tassi d'interesse *f*	—

	D	E	F	I	Es
diferencial entre precios y salarios (Es)	Lohnlag *m*	wage lag	décalage entre les prix et les salaires *m*	lag salariale *m*	—
difesa dei corsi (I)	Kursstützung *f*	price support	soutiens des cours *m*	—	sostén de las cotizaciones *m*
difettoso (I)	fehlerhaft	defective	défectueux	—	defectuoso
différenciation de prix (F)	Preisdifferenzierung *f*	price differentiation	—	differenziazione dei prezzi *f*	diferenciación de los precios *f*
differenza dei prezzi (I)	Preisunterschied *m*	price difference	écart de prix *m*	—	diferencia de precios *f*
differenza dei tassi d'interesse (I)	Zinsgefälle *n*	margin between interest rates	disparité des niveaux d'intérêts *f*	—	diferencia entre los tipos de interés *f*
differenza di dimensione (I)	Größenabweichung *f*	deviation from size	déviation de dimension *f*	—	deviación de dimensión *f*
differenza di qualità (I)	Qualitäts-abweichung *f*	deviation from quality	écart qualitatif *m*	—	diferencia de calidad *f*
differenziato (I)	gestaffelt	graduated	progressif	—	escalonado
differenziazione dei prezzi (I)	Preisdifferenzierung *f*	price differentiation	différenciation de prix *f*	—	diferenciación de los precios *f*
difficoltà di pagamento (I)	Zahlungs-schwierigkeit *f*	financial difficulties	difficultés financières *f pl*	—	dificultades de pago *f pl*
dificultades de pago (Es)	Zahlungs-schwierigkeit *f*	financial difficulties	difficultés financières *f pl*	difficoltà di pagamento *f*	—
difficultés financières (F)	Zahlungs-schwierigkeit *f*	financial difficulties	—	difficoltà di pagamento *f*	dificultades de pago *f pl*
Diktat (D)	—	dictation	dictée *f*	dettato *m*	dictado *m*
Diktatzeichen (D)	—	reference	références *f pl*	sigla *f*	referencias *f pl*
Diktiergerät (D)	—	dictaphone	appareil à dicter *m*	dittafono *m*	máquina de dictar *f*
dilatory (E)	säumig	—	retardataire	moroso	moroso
dilazione (I)	Stundung *f*	respite	prorogation *f*	—	moratoria *f*
dilazione del pagamento (I)	Zahlungsaufschub *m*	extension of time for payment	sursis de payement *m*	—	pago aplazado *m*
dilazione delle spese (I)	Ausgaben-verzögerung *f*	expenditure delay	dépenses retardées *f pl*	—	aplazamiento de gastos *m*
dimensión de la empresa (Es)	Unternehmens-größe *f*	size of the company	dimension de l'entreprise *f*	dimensione dell'impresa *f*	—
dimension de l'entreprise[1] (F)	Unternehmens-größe *f*	size of the company	—	dimensione dell'impresa *f*	dimensión de la empresa *f*
dimension de l'entreprise[2] (F)	Betriebsgröße *f*	size of the company	—	dimensione dell'azienda *f*	tamaño de la explotación *m*
dimensione dell'azienda (I)	Betriebsgröße *f*	size of the company	dimension de l'entreprise *f*	—	tamaño de la explotación *m*
dimensione dell'impresa (I)	Unternehmens-größe *f*	size of the company	dimension de l'entreprise *f*	—	dimensión de la empresa *f*
diminution[1] (F)	Minderung *f*	reduction	—	riduzione *f*	reducción *f*
diminution[2] (F)	Abzug *m*	deduction/discount	—	detrazione *f*/sconto *m*	deducción *f*/descuento *m*
diminution de la valeur (F)	Wertminderung *f*	decrease in value	—	riduzione di valore *f*	depreciación *f*
diminution des coûts (F)	Kostensenkung *f*	cost reduction	—	ribasso dei costi *m*	reducción de coste *f*
diminution des dépenses (F)	Ausgabensenkung *f*	drop in expenditure	—	riduzione delle spese *f*	reducción de gastos *f*
diminution du capital (F)	Kapitalherabsetzung *f*	reduction of capital	—	riduzione del capitale *f*	reducción de capital *f*
diminution du taux de l'intérêt (F)	Zinssenkung *f*	reduction of interest	—	riduzione degli interessi *f*	reducción del tipo de interés *f*
diminuzione dei costi (I)	Kostenminimierung *f*	minimization of costs	minimalisation des coûts *f*	—	minimación de gastos *f*
dimisión (Es)	Rücktritt *m*	resignation	démission *f*	dimissioni *f pl*	—
dimissioni (I)	Rücktritt *m*	resignation	démission *f*	—	dimisión *f*
dinero (Es)	Geld *n*	money	argent *m*	denaro *m*	—
dinero bancario (Es)	Buchgeld *n*	money in account	monnaie de crédit *f*	moneta bancaria *f*	—
dinero barato (Es)	billiges Geld *n*	easy money	argent à bon marché *m*	crediti agevolati *m pl*	—

	D	E	F	I	Es
dinero de día a día (Es)	Tagesgeld *n*	day-to-day money	argent au jour le jour *m*	prestito giornaliero *m*	—
dinero efectivo (Es)	Bargeld *n*	cash	argent comptant *m*	denaro contante *m*	—
dinero metálico (Es)	Hartgeld *n*	specie	pièce de monnaie *f*	moneta metallica *f*	—
dinero tomado a préstamo (Es)	Geldaufnahme *f*	raising of money	emprunt *m*	accensione di un mutuo *f*	—
dingliche Sicherung (D)	—	real security	sécurité réelle *f*	garanzia reale *f*	garantía real *f*
dingliches Recht (D)	—	real right	droit réel *m*	diritto reale *m*	derecho real *m*
dipendente (I)	Untergebener *m*	subordinate	subalterne *m*	—	subordinado *m*
Diplom (D)	—	diploma	diplôme *m*	diploma *m*	diploma *m*
diploma (E)	Diplom *n*	—	diplôme *m*	diploma *m*	diploma *m*
diploma (Es)	Diplom *n*	diploma	diplôme *m*	diploma *m*	—
diploma (I)	Diplom *n*	diploma	diplôme *m*	—	diploma *m*
diplôme (F)	Diplom *n*	diploma	—	diploma *m*	diploma *m*
di prima categoria (I)	erstklassig	first class	de première qualité	—	de primera calidad
dirección¹ (Es)	Anschrift *f*	address	adresse *f*	indirizzo *m*	—
dirección² (Es)	Geschäftsleitung *f*	management	direction commerciale *f*	direzione *f*	—
dirección³ (Es)	Adresse *f*	address	adresse *f*	indirizzo *m*	—
dirección⁴ (Es)	Leitung *f*	management	direction *f*	direzione *f*	—
dirección de inversiones (Es)	Investitionslenkung *f*	investment control	politique d'investissement *f*	politica d'investimento *f*	—
dirección de la empresa¹ (Es)	Firmenanschrift *f*	company address	adresse de la maison *f*	indirizzo della ditta *m*	—
dirección de la empresa² (Es)	Unternehmens-leitung *f*	executive management	direction de l'entreprise *f*	direzione dell'impresa *f*	—
dirección de personal (Es)	Personalführung *f*	personnel management	direction du personnel *f*	gestione del personale *f*	—
direct cost (E)	direkte Kosten *pl*	—	coûts directs *m pl*	costi diretti *m pl*	coste directo *m*
direct selling (E)	Direktverkauf *m*	—	vente directe *f*	vendita diretta *f*	venta directa *f*
direct taxes (E)	direkte Steuern *pl*	—	impôts directs *m pl*	imposte dirette *f pl*	impuestos directos *m pl*
directeur (F)	Direktor *m*	director	—	direttore *m*	director *m*
directeur artistique (F)	Art-director *m*	art director	—	art director *m*	director artístico *m*
directeur d'agence (F)	Filialleiter *m*	branch manager	—	direttore della filiale *m*	jefe de sucursal *m*
directeur général (F)	Generaldirektor *m*	director managing	—	direttore generale *m*	director general *m*
direct insurer (E)	Erstversicherer *m*	—	assureur direct *m*	assicuratore diretto *m*	primer asegurador *m*
direct investments (E)	Direktinvestitionen *pl*	—	investissements directs *m pl*	investimenti diretti *m pl*	inversiones directas *f pl*
direction¹ (F)	Führung *f*	management	—	gestione *f*	gestión *f*
direction² (F)	Direktion *f*	board of directors	—	direzione *f*	junta directiva *f*
direction³ (F)	Leitung *f*	management	—	direzione *f*	dirección *f*
direction commerciale (F)	Geschäftsleitung *f*	management	—	direzione *f*	dirección *f*
direction de l'entreprise (F)	Unternehmens-leitung *f*	executive management	—	direzione dell'impresa *f*	dirección de la empresa *f*
direction du personnel (F)	Personalführung *f*	personnel management	—	gestione del personale *f*	dirección de personal *f*
Direct-Marketing (D)	—	direct marketing	stratégie des ventes directes *f*	marketing in prima persona *m*	comercialización directa *f*
direct marketing (E)	Direct-Marketing *n*	—	stratégie des ventes directes *f*	marketing in prima persona *m*	comercialización directa *f*
direct means of advertising (E)	Direktwerbemittel *n*	—	moyens publicitaires directs *m pl*	mezzo pubblicitario diretto *m*	medios publicitarios directos *m pl*
director (E)	Direktor *m*	—	directeur *m*	direttore *m*	director *m*
director (Es)	Direktor *m*	director	directeur *m*	direttore *m*	—
director artístico (Es)	Art-director *m*	art director	directeur artistique *m*	art director *m*	—
direct ordering (E)	Direktbestellung *f*	—	commande directe *f*	ordinazione diretta *f*	pedido directo *m*
director general (E)	Generaldirektor *m*	—	directeur général *m*	direttore generale *m*	director general *m*

	D	E	F	I	Es
director general (Es)	Generaldirektor m	director general	directeur général m	direttore generale m	—
Direktbestellung (D)	—	direct ordering	commande directe f	ordinazione diretta f	pedido directo m
direkte Kosten (D)	—	direct cost	coûts directs m pl	costi diretti m pl	coste directo m
direkte Steuern (D)	—	direct taxes	impôts directs m pl	imposte dirette f pl	impuestos directos m pl
Direktinvestitionen (D)	—	direct investments	investissements directs m pl	investimenti diretti m pl	inversiones directas f pl
Direktion (D)	—	board of directors	direction f	direzione f	junta directiva f
Direktor (D)	—	director	directeur m	direttore m	director m
Direktverkauf (D)	—	direct selling	vente directe f	vendita diretta f	venta directa f
Direktwerbemittel (D)	—	direct means of advertising	moyens publicitaires directs m pl	mezzo pubblicitario diretto m	medios publicitarios directos m pl
direttore (I)	Direktor m	director	directeur m	—	director m
direttore della filiale (I)	Filialleiter m	branch manager	directeur d'agence m	—	jefe de sucursal m
direttore di vendita regionale (I)	Gebietsverkaufs-leiter m	area sales manager	chef de vente régionale m	—	jefe de venta regional m
direttore generale (I)	Generaldirektor m	director managing	directeur général m	—	director general m
direzione¹ (I)	Leitung f	management	direction f	—	dirección f
direzione² (I)	Geschäftsleitung f	management	direction commerciale f	—	dirección f
direzione³ (I)	Direktion f	board of directors	direction f	—	junta directiva f
direzione dell'impresa (I)	Unternehmens-leitung f	executive management	direction de l'entreprise f	—	dirección de la empresa f
dirigente (I)	Führungsperson f	executive	cadre m	—	ejecutivo m
dirigir (Es)	adressieren	address	adresser	indirizzare	—
dirigisme (F)	Dirigismus m	controlled economy	—	dirigismo m	dirigismo m
dirigismo (Es)	Dirigismus m	controlled economy	dirigisme m	dirigismo m	—
dirigismo (I)	Dirigismus m	controlled economy	dirigisme m	—	dirigismo m
Dirigismus (D)	—	controlled economy	dirigisme m	dirigismo m	dirigismo m
diritti al risarcimento danni (I)	Schadenersatz-ansprüche m pl	claim for damages	droit à l'indemnité m	—	derecho a indemniza-ción por daños y perjuicios m
diritti di conto (I)	Kontogebühren pl	bank charges	frais de tenue de compte m pl	—	gastos de administración de una cuenta m pl
diritti di porto (I)	Hafengebühren pl	harbour dues	droits de ports m pl	—	derechos portuarios m pl
diritti di prelievo (I)	Ziehungsrechte pl	drawing rights	droits de tirage m pl	—	derechos de giro m pl
diritti di sovranità nazionale (I)	nationale Souveräni-tätsrechte pl	national sovereignty rights	droits de souveraine-té nationale m pl	—	derechos de sobe-ranía nacional m pl
diritti di transito (I)	Transitzoll m	transit duty	droit de transit m	—	derecho de tránsito m
diritti doganali (I)	Zollgebühren pl	customs duties	droit de douane m	—	derechos arancelarios m pl
diritti speciali di prelievo (I)	Sonderziehungs-rechte pl	special drawing rights	droits de tirage spécial m pl	—	derechos de giro especial m pl
diritto (I)	Recht n	law	droit m	—	derecho m
diritto alla fornitura supplementare (I)	Nachlieferungs-anspruch m	claim to subsequent delivery	droit à livraison complémentaire m	—	derecho de suminis-tro adicional m
diritto alla restituzione (I)	Rückgaberecht n	right of redemption	droit à restitution m	—	derecho de devolución m
diritto al voto (I)	Stimmrecht n	right to vote	droit de vote m	—	derecho a voto m
diritto azionario (I)	Aktienrecht n	company law	loi sur les sociétés anonymes f pl	—	derecho de socieda-des anónimas m
diritto d'asta (I)	Auktionsgebühr f	auction fees	droits de vente aux enchères m pl	—	gastos de subasta m pl
diritto d'autore (I)	Urheberrecht n	copyright	droit d'auteur m	—	derecho del autor m
diritto della concorrenza (I)	Wettbewerbsrecht n	law on competition	législation en matière de concurrence commerciale f	—	derecho de la competencia m
diritto della pesca (I)	Fischereirecht n	fishing rights	droit de pêche m	—	derecho pesquero m
diritto delle minoranze (I)	Minoritätsrecht n	minority right	droit de minorité m	—	derecho minoritario m

	D	E	F	I	Es
diritto di firma (I)	Zeichnungs-berechtigung f	authority to sign	autorisation de signer f	—	facultad de firma f
diritto di lavoro (I)	Arbeitsrecht n	labour law	législation industrielle f	—	derecho laboral m
diritto di pegno (I)	Pfandrecht n	pledge	droit de gage m	—	derecho de garantía real m
diritto di prelazione (I)	Vorkaufsrecht n	preemption right	droit de préemption m	—	derecho de preferencia m
diritto di rappresen-tanza esclusiva (I)	Alleinvertretungs-recht n	sole and exclusive agency right	droit exclusif de représentation m	—	derecho de representación exclusiva m
diritto di revoca (I)	Widerrufsrecht n	right of revocation	droit de révocation m	—	derecho de revocación m
diritto di servizio (I)	Bedienungsgeld n	tip	pourboire m	—	propina f
diritto di sovranità (I)	Hoheitsrecht n	sovereign right	droit de souveraineté m	—	soberanía f
diritto economico (I)	Wirtschaftsrecht n	economic law	législation économique f	—	derecho económico m
diritto reale (I)	dingliches Recht n	real right	droit réel m	—	derecho real m
disability for work (E)	Erwerbsunfähigkeit f	—	incapacité d'exercer toute activité professionnelle f	inabilità al lavoro f	incapacidad profesional f
disadvantage (E)	Nachteil m	—	désavantage m	svantaggio m	desventaja f
disaggio (I)	Disagio n	disagio	disagio m	—	disagio m
Disagio (D)	—	disagio	disagio m	disaggio m	disagio m
disagio (E)	Disagio n	—	disagio m	disaggio m	disagio m
disagio (Es)	Disagio n	disagio	disagio m	disaggio m	—
disagio (F)	Disagio n	disagio	—	disaggio m	disagio m
disavanzo della bilan-cia dei pagamenti (I)	Zahlungsbilanz-defizit n	deficit in the balance of payments	balance des paye-ments déficitaire f	—	déficit en la balanza de pagos m
discharge (E)	Entlastung f	—	décharge f	sgravio m	desgravamen m
discharging expenses[1] (E)	Löschgebühren pl	—	droit de déchargement m	spese di scarico f pl	gastos de descarga m pl
discharging expenses[2] (E)	Entladungskosten pl	—	coûts de déchargement m pl	spese di scaricamento f pl	gastos de descargo m pl
dischetto (I)	Diskette f	disk	disquette f	—	diskette f
disclosure (E)	Offenlegung f	—	révélation des derniers bilans du postulant d'un prêt f	pubblicità del bilancio f	publicidad para fines de inspección f
discount[1] (E)	Skonto n	—	escompte m	sconto m	descuento m
discount[2] (E)	Diskont m	—	escompte m	sconto m	descuento m
discount[3] (E)	Rabatt m	—	remise f	ribasso m	rebaja f
discount deduction (E)	Skontoabzug m	—	déduction de l'escompte f	detrazione di sconto f	deducción del descuento f
discount for cash payment (E)	Barzahlungs-nachlaß m	—	remise pour paye-ment au comptant f	sconto per paga-mento in contanti m	descuento por pago al contado m
discounting (E)	Abzinsung f	—	déduction des intérêts non courus f	deduzione di interessi f	deducción de intere-ses no acumulados f
discount on advance orders (E)	Vorbestellrabatt m	—	escompte de suscription m	ribasso per ordina-zioni anticipate m	descuento de suscripción m
discount policy (E)	Diskontpolitik f	—	politique d'escompte f	politica di sconto f	política de descuento f
discount rate (E)	Diskontsatz m	—	taux d'escompte m	saggio di sconto m	tasa de descuento f
discreción (Es)	Diskretion f	confidentiality	discrétion f	discrezione f	—
discrétion (F)	Diskretion f	confidentiality	—	discrezione f	discreción f
discrétion professionnelle (F)	Schweigepflicht f	professional discretion	—	obbligo del segreto professionale m	secreto profesional m
discrezione (I)	Diskretion f	confidentiality	discrétion f	—	discreción f
discriminación (Es)	Diskriminierung f	discrimination	discrimination f	discriminazione f	—
discrimination (E)	Diskriminierung f	—	discrimination f	discriminazione f	discriminación f
discrimination (F)	Diskriminierung f	discrimination	—	discriminazione f	discriminación f
discriminazione (I)	Diskriminierung f	discrimination	discrimination f	—	discriminación f
discussion[1] (E)	Besprechung f	—	conférence f	colloquio m	conferencia f

	D	E	F	I	Es
discussion² (E)	Unterredung f	—	entretien m	colloquio m	conversación f
disdetta (I)	Kündigung f	notice of termination	résiliation f	—	rescisión f
disdire (I)	kündigen	terminate/give notice	dénoncer/résilier	—	denunciar/dar aviso de despido
diseño (Es)	Design n	design	design m	design m	—
diseño del producto (Es)	Produktgestaltung f	product design	présentation d'un produit f	creazione del prodotto f	—
disk (E)	Diskette f	—	disquette f	dischetto m	diskette f
Diskette (D)	—	disk	disquette f	dischetto m	diskette f
diskette (Es)	Diskette f	disk	disquette f	dischetto m	—
Diskont (D)	—	discount	escompte m	sconto m	descuento m
Diskontpolitik (D)	—	discount policy	politique d'escompte f	politica di sconto f	política de descuento f
Diskontsatz (D)	—	discount rate	taux d'escompte m	saggio di sconto m	tasa de descuento f
Diskretion (D)	—	confidentiality	discrétion f	discrezione f	discreción f
Diskriminierung (D)	—	discrimination	discrimination f	discriminazione f	discriminación f
disminución de costes (Es)	Kostendämpfung f	combatting rising costs	réduction des coûts f	contenimento dei costi m	—
disminución de la cifra de facturación (Es)	Umsatzrückgang m	decrease of turnover	recul du chiffre d'affaires m	calo del fatturato m	—
disminución en la demanda (Es)	Nachfrage-rückgang m	decrease in demand	recul de la demande m	flessione della domanda f	—
dismissal (E)	Entlassung f	—	licenciement m	licenziamento m	despido m
disoccupazione (I)	Arbeitslosigkeit f	unemployment	chômage m	—	desempleo m
disoccupazione stagionale (I)	saisonale Arbeitslosigkeit f	seasonal unemployment	chômage saisonnier m	—	paro estacional m
disoccupazione strutturale (I)	strukturelle Arbeitslosigkeit f	structural unemployment	chômage structurel m	—	paro estructural m
disolución (Es)	Auflösung f	dissolution	liquidation f	scioglimento m	—
disparité des niveaux d'intérêts (F)	Zinsgefälle n	margin between interest rates	—	differenza dei tassi d'interesse f	diferencia entre los tipos de interés f
dispatch¹ (E)	Abfertigung f	—	expédition f	spedizione f	despacho m
dispatch² (E)	Absendung f	—	expédition f	spedizione f	expedición f
dispatch³ (E)	Versand m	—	expédition f	spedizione f	envío m
dispatch department (E)	Versandabteilung f	—	service des expéditions m	reparto spedizioni m	departamento de expedición m
dispensé de l'impôt (F)	steuerfrei	tax-free	—	esente da imposte	libre de impuesto
display (E)	Auslage f	—	étalage m	vetrina f	vitrina f
disponibile (I)	lieferbar	deliverable	livrable	—	suministrable
disponible (F)	abholbereit	ready for collection	—	pronto per il ritiro	listo para la recogida
disposable income (E)	verfügbares Einkommen n	—	revenu disponible m	introito disponibile m	ingresos disponibles m pl
disposal¹ (E)	Disposition f	—	disposition f	disposizione f	disposición f
disposal² (E)	Verfügung f	—	disposition f/acte de disposition m	disposizione f/ ordinanza f	disposición f/ decreto m
disposal of waste oil (E)	Altölbeseitigung f	—	élimination d'huile usée f	smaltimento dell'olio usato m	eliminación de petróleo usado f
disposición¹ (Es)	Verfügung f	disposal/order	disposition f/acte de disposition m	disposizione f/ ordinanza f	—
disposición² (Es)	Disposition f	disposal	disposition f	disposizione f	—
disposición a comprar (Es)	Kaufbereitschaft f	buying intention	propension à l'achat f	propensione all'acquisto f	—
Disposition (D)	—	disposal	disposition f	disposizione f	disposición f
disposition¹ (F)	Verfügung f	disposal/order	—	disposizione f/ ordinanza f	disposición f/ decreto m
disposition² (F)	Disposition f	disposal	—	disposizione f	disposición f
disposition de l'annonce (F)	Anzeigenplazierung f	placing of an advertisement	—	collocamento dell'inserzione m	colocación del anuncio f
dispositions d'exportation (F)	Ausfuhr-bestimmungen pl	export regulations	—	disposizioni per le esportazioni f pl	reglamento de exportación m
disposizione¹ (I)	Disposition f	disposal	disposition f	—	disposición f

	D	E	F	I	Es
disposizione² (I)	Verfügung f	disposal/order	disposition f/acte de disposition m	—	disposición f/ decreto m
disposizioni per le esportazioni (I)	Ausfuhr-bestimmungen pl	export regulations	dispositions d'exportation f pl	—	reglamiento de exportación m
dispute concerning an inheritance (E)	Erbstreit m	—	action successorale f	causa ereditaria f	litigio hereditario m
disquette (F)	Diskette f	disk	—	dischetto m	diskette f
dissesto finanziario (I)	Finanzdebakel n	financial debacle	débâcle fiancière f	—	descalabro financiero m
dissimulation en matière fiscale (F)	Steuerhinterziehung f	tax evasion	—	evasione fiscale f	defraudación fiscal f
dissolution (E)	Auflösung f	—	liquidation f	scioglimento m	disolución f
distance (E)	Abstand m	—	distance f	distanza f	distancia f
distance (F)	Abstand m	distance	—	distanza f	distancia f
distancia (Es)	Abstand m	distance	distance f	distanza f	—
distanza (I)	Abstand m	distance	distance f	—	distancia f
distribución¹ (Es)	Vertrieb m	distribution	distribution f	distribuzione f	—
distribución² (Es)	Verteilung f	distribution	distribution f	distribuzione f	—
distribución de beneficios (Es)	Gewinn-ausschüttung f	distribution of profits	distribution de bénéfices f	ripartizione dell'utile f	—
distribución de la renta¹ (Es)	Einkommens-verteilung f	distribution of income	distribution du revenu f	distribuzione dei redditi f	—
distribución de la renta² (Es)	Einkommens-verwendung f	appropriation of income	utilisation du revenu f	impiego dei redditi m	—
distribución exclusiva (Es)	Alleinvertrieb m	exclusive distribution	vente exclusive f	vendita esclusiva f	—
distribuidor automático¹ (Es)	Automat m	vending machine	appareil automatique m	distributore automatico m	—
distribuidor automático² (Es)	Verkaufsautomat m	vending machine	distributeur automatique m	distributore automatico m	—
distributeur (F)	Vertriebsfirma f	distributor	—	ditta di distribuzione f	compañía distribuidora f
distributeur automatique (F)	Verkaufsautomat m	vending machine	—	distributore automatico m	distribuidor automático m
Distribution (D)	—	distribution	distribution f	distribuzione f	distribución f
distribution¹ (E)	Vertrieb m	—	distribution f	distribuzione f	distribución f
distribution² (E)	Verteilung f	—	distribution f	distribuzione f	distribución f
distribution³ (E)	Distribution f	—	distribution f	distribuzione f	distribución f
distribution¹ (F)	Vertrieb m	distribution	—	distribuzione f	distribución f
distribution² (F)	Distribution f	distribution	—	distribuzione f	distribución f
distribution³ (F)	Verteilung f	distribution	—	distribuzione f	distribución f
distribution centre (E)	Auslieferungslager n	—	entrepôt de distribution m	deposito di consegna m	almacén de entregas m
distribution channel (E)	Vertriebsweg m	—	canal de distribution m	rete di distribuzione f	circuito de distribución f
distribution de bénéfices (F)	Gewinn-ausschüttung f	distribution of profits	—	ripartizione dell'utile f	distribución de beneficios f
distribution du revenu (F)	Einkommens-verteilung f	distribution of income	—	distribuzione dei redditi f	distribución de la renta f
distribution of income (E)	Einkommens-verteilung f	—	distribution du revenu f	distribuzione dei redditi f	distribución de la renta f
distribution of profits¹ (E)	Gewinnverteilung f	—	répartition des bénéfices f	ripartizione dell'utile f	reparto de beneficios m
distribution of profits² (E)	Gewinn-ausschüttung f	—	distribution de bénéfices f	ripartizione dell'utile f	distribución de beneficios f
distribution of wealth (E)	Vermögens-verteilung f	—	repartition du patrimoine f	ripartizione del patrimonio f	reparto de la riqueza m
distribution policy (E)	Verteilungspolitik f	—	politique de répartition f	politica della distribuzione f	política de distribución f
distributor (E)	Vertriebsfirma f	—	distributeur m	ditta di distribuzione f	compañía distribuidora f
distributore automatico¹ (I)	Automat m	vending machine	appareil automatique m	—	distribuidor automático m

	D	E	F	I	Es
distributore automatico² (I)	Verkaufsautomat *m*	vending machine	distributeur automatique *m*	—	distribuidor automático *m*
distribuzione¹ (I)	Verteilung *f*	distribution	distribution *f*	—	distribución *f*
distribuzione² (I)	Vertrieb *m*	distribution	distribution *f*	—	distribución *f*
distribuzione dei redditi (I)	Einkommens- verteilung *f*	distribution of income	distribution du revenu *f*	—	distribución de la renta *f*
distrito aduanero (Es)	Zollgebiet *n*	customs territory	territoire douanier *m*	territorio doganale *m*	—
ditta concorrente (I)	Konkurrenzfirma *f*	competing firm	maison concurrente *f*	—	empresa competidora *f*
ditta di distribuzione (I)	Vertriebsfirma *f*	distributor	distributeur *m*	—	compañía distribuidora *f*
dittafono (I)	Diktiergerät *n*	dictaphone	appareil à dicter *m*	—	máquina de dictar *f*
divergence (F)	Abweichung *f*	deviation	—	deviazione *f*	diferencia *f*
diversificación (Es)	Diversifikation *f*	diversification	diversification *f*	diversificazione *f*	—
diversification (E)	Diversifikation *f*	—	diversification *f*	diversificazione *f*	diversificación *f*
diversification (F)	Diversifikation *f*	diversification	—	diversificazione *f*	diversificación *f*
diversificazione (I)	Diversifikation *f*	diversification	diversification *f*	—	diversificación *f*
Diversifikation (D)	—	diversification	diversification *f*	diversificazione *f*	diversificación *f*
dividend (E)	Dividende *f*	—	dividende *m*	dividendo *m*	dividendo *m*
dividend-bearing shares (E)	Dividendenpapiere *pl*	—	titre donnant droit à des dividendes *m*	titoli a reddito variabile *m pl*	títulos de renta variable *m pl*
Dividende (D)	—	dividend	dividende *m*	dividendo *m*	dividendo *m*
dividende (F)	Dividende *f*	dividend	—	dividendo *m*	dividendo *m*
Dividendenpapiere (D)	—	dividend-bearing shares	titre donnant droit à des dividendes *m*	titoli a reddito variabile *m pl*	títulos de renta variable *m pl*
dividendo (Es)	Dividende *f*	dividend	dividende *m*	dividendo *m*	—
dividendo (I)	Dividende *f*	dividend	dividende *m*	—	dividendo *m*
divieto di concorrenza (I)	Wettbewerbsverbot *n*	prohibition of competition	interdiction en ma- tière de concurrence *f*	—	prohibición de competencia *f*
divieto di pubblicità (I)	Werbeverbot *n*	ban on advertising	défense de publicité *f*	—	prohibición de publicidad *f*
divisas (Es)	Devisen *pl*	foreign exchange	devises *f pl*	divise *f pl*	—
divise (I)	Devisen *pl*	foreign exchange	devises *f pl*	—	divisas *f pl*
division (E)	Abteilung *f*	—	service *m*	reparto *m*	sección *f*
división del trabajo (Es)	Arbeitsteilung *f*	division of labour	division du travail *f*	divisione del lavoro *f*	—
division du travail (F)	Arbeitsteilung *f*	division of labour	—	divisione del lavoro *f*	división del trabajo *f*
divisione del lavoro (I)	Arbeitsteilung *f*	division of labour	division du travail *f*	—	división del trabajo *f*
division of labour (E)	Arbeitsteilung *f*	—	division du travail *f*	divisione del lavoro *f*	división del trabajo *f*
document¹ (E)	Urkunde *f*	—	document *m*	documento *m*	documento *m*
document² (E)	Dokument *n*	—	document *m*	documento *m*	documento *m*
document¹ (F)	Dokument *n*	document	—	documento *m*	documento *m*
document² (F)	Urkunde *f*	document	—	documento *m*	documento *m*
documentary acceptance credit (E)	Rembourskredit *m*	—	crédit documentaire confirmé *m*	credito di rimborso *m*	crédito de reembolso *m*
documentary letter of credit (E)	Dokumenten- akkreditiv *n*	—	crédit documentaire *m*	apertura di credito documentario *f*	crédito documentario *m*
documenti commerciali (I)	Geschäftspapiere *pl*	business papers	papiers d'affaires *m pl*	—	documentos comerciales *m pl*
documenti della domanda d'impiego (I)	Bewerbungs- unterlagen *pl*	application documents	dossier de candidature *m*	—	documentos de solicitud *m pl*
documenti d'esportazione (I)	Ausfuhrpapiere *pl*	export documents	documents d'exportation *m pl*	—	documentos de exportación *m pl*
documenti di trasporto (I)	Transportpapiere *pl*	documents covering transportation	documents de transport *m pl*	—	documentos de transporte *m pl*
documenti doganali (I)	Zollpapiere *pl*	customs documents	documents douaniers *m pl*	—	documentos aduaneros *m pl*
documento¹ (Es)	Urkunde *f*	document	document *m*	documento *m*	—
documento² (Es)	Dokument *n*	document	document *m*	documento *m*	—
documento³ (Es)	Akte *f*	file	dossier *m*	pratica *f*	—
documento¹ (I)	Urkunde *f*	document	document *m*	—	documento *m*

	D	E	F	I	Es
documento² (I)	Dokument n	document	document m	—	documento m
documento di spedizione (I)	Versanddokument n	shipping document	documents d'expédition m pl	—	documentos de expedición m pl
documentos adjuntos (Es)	Begleitpapiere pl	accompanying documents	pièces accompagnant l'envoi f pl	bolle di accompagnamento f pl	—
documentos aduaneros (Es)	Zollpapiere pl	customs documents	documents douaniers m pl	documenti doganali m pl	—
documentos comerciales (Es)	Geschäftspapiere pl	business papers	papiers d'affaires m pl	documenti commerciali m pl	—
documentos de expedición (Es)	Versanddokument n	shipping document	documents d'expédition m pl	documento di spedizione m	—
documentos de exportación (Es)	Ausfuhrpapiere pl	export documents	documents d'exportation m pl	documenti d'esportazione m pl	—
documentos de importación (Es)	Einfuhrpapiere pl	import documents	documents d'importation m pl	bollette doganali f pl	—
documentos de solicitud (Es)	Bewerbungsunterlagen pl	application documents	dossier de candidature m	documenti della domanda d'impiego m pl	—
documentos de transporte (Es)	Transportpapiere pl	documents covering transportation	documents de transport m pl	documenti di trasporto m pl	—
documents against payments (E)	Dokumente gegen Zahlung pl	—	documents contre payement m pl	pagamento contro documenti m	al contado contra documentos
documents contre payement (F)	Dokumente gegen Zahlung pl	documents against payments	—	pagamento contro documenti m	al contado contra documentos
documents covering transportation (E)	Transportpapiere pl	—	documents de transport m pl	documenti di trasporto m pl	documentos de transporte m pl
documents de transport (F)	Transportpapiere pl	documents covering transportation	—	documenti di trasporto m pl	documentos de transporte m pl
documents d'expédition (F)	Versanddokument n	shipping document	—	documento di spedizione m	documentos de expedición m pl
documents d'exportation (F)	Ausfuhrpapiere pl	export documents	—	documenti d'esportazione m pl	documentos de exportación m pl
documents d'importation (F)	Einfuhrpapiere pl	import documents	—	bollette doganali f pl	documentos de importación m pl
documents douaniers (F)	Zollpapiere pl	customs documents	—	documenti doganali m pl	documentos aduaneros m pl
dogana (I)	Zoll m	customs/customs duty	douane f/droit de douane m	—	aduana f/arancel m
doit (F)	Soll m	debit/target/quota	—	passivo m	debe m
Dokument (D)	—	document	document m	documento m	documento m
Dokumente gegen Zahlung (D)	—	documents against payments	documents contre payement m pl	pagamento contro documenti m	al contado contra documentos
Dokumentenakkreditiv (D)	—	documentary letter of credit	crédit documentaire m	apertura di credito documentario f	crédito documentario m
dollar clause (E)	Dollarklausel f	—	clause dollar f	clausola dollaro f	cláusula dólar f
Dollarklausel (D)	—	dollar clause	clause dollar f	clausola dollaro f	cláusula dólar f
Dolmetscher (D)	—	interpreter	interprète m	interprete m	intérprete m
domanda¹ (I)	Antrag m	application	demande f	—	solicitud f
domanda² (I)	Nachfrage f	demand	demande f	—	demanda f
domanda di capitale (I)	Kapitalbedarf m	capital requirements	besoin en capital m	—	necesidad de capital f
domanda di denaro (I)	Geldnachfrage f	demand for money	demande sur le marché monétaire f	—	demanda monetaria f
domanda di dichiarazione del fallimento (I)	Konkursantrag m	bankruptcy petition	demande en déclaration de faillite f	—	petición de quiebra f
domanda di lavoro (I)	Arbeitsnachfrage f	job demand	demande d'emploi f	—	demanda de trabajo f
domanda d'impiego¹ (I)	Bewerbungsschreiben n	letter of application	lettre de demande d'emploi f	—	carta de solicitud f
domanda d'impiego² (I)	Bewerbung f	application	candidature f	—	candidatura f
domanda d'impiego³ (I)	Stellengesuch n	situation wanted/application for a job	demande d'emploi f	—	solicitud de colocación f
domanda di sdoganamento (I)	Zollantrag m	customs application	demande de dédouanement f	—	solicitud de aduana f
domanda estera (I)	Auslandsnachfrage f	foreign demand	demande en provenance de l'étranger f	—	demanda exterior m
domanda interna (I)	Inlandsnachfrage f	home demand	demande intérieure f	—	demanda interior f

	D	E	F	I	Es
domestic customs territory (E)	Zollinland *n*	—	territoire douanier national *m*	territorio doganale nazionale *m*	territorio aduanero interior *m*
domestic economy (E)	Binnenwirtschaft *f*	—	économie nationale *f*	economia nazionale *f*	economía interior *f*
domestic establishment (E)	Inlandsniederlassung *f*	—	succursale à l'intérieur *f*	succursale nazionale *f*	sucursal en el interior *f*
domestic trade (E)	Binnenhandel *m*	—	commerce intérieur *m*	commercio nazionale *m*	comercio interior *m*
domicile of the company (E)	Firmensitz *m*	—	siège social *m*	sede *f*	sede social *f*
domiciliary bill (E)	Domizilwechsel *m*	—	effet domicilier *m*	cambiale domiciliata *f*	letra domiciliada *f*
Domizilwechsel (D)	—	domiciliary bill	effet domicilier *m*	cambiale domiciliata *f*	letra domiciliada *f*
dommage (F)	Schaden *m*	damage	—	danno *m*	daño *m*
dommage au cours d'un transport (F)	Transportschaden *m*	damage in transit	—	danno di trasporto *m*	daño de transporte *m*
dommage causé par l'eau (F)	Wasserschaden *m*	damage caused by water	—	danno dovuto all'acqua *m*	daño causado por el agua *m*
dommage consécutif (F)	Folgeschäden *pl*	consequential damages	—	danni indiretti *m pl*	daño consecuencial *m*
dommage immatériel (F)	immaterieller Schaden *m*	non-material damage	—	danno immateriale *m*	daño inmaterial *m*
dommage mineur (F)	Bagatellschaden *m*	minimal damage	—	danno piccolo *m*	siniestro leve *m*
dommages-intérêts (F)	Schadensersatz *m*	compensation for loss suffered	—	risarcimento danni *m*	indemnización *f*
dommage total (F)	Totalschaden *m*	total loss	—	danno totale *m*	daño total *m*
donación (Es)	Schenkung *f*	donation	donation *f*	donazione *f*	—
donation (E)	Schenkung *f*	—	donation *f*	donazione *f*	donación *f*
donation (F)	Schenkung *f*	donation	—	donazione *f*	donación *f*
donazione (I)	Schenkung *f*	donation	donation *f*	—	donación *f*
données (F)	Daten *f*	data	—	dati *m pl*	datos *m pl*
données sur le marché (F)	Marktdaten *pl*	market details	—	dati di mercato *m pl*	datos del mercado *m pl*
donneur de leasing (F)	Leasing-Geber *m*	lessor	—	concedente del leasing *m*	arrendatario financiero *m*
doppelte Buchführung (D)	—	double entry bookkeeping	comptabilité en partie double *f*	contabilità a partita doppia *f*	contabilidad por doble partida *f*
dormant partnership (E)	stille Gesellschaft *f*	—	association commerciale en participation *f*	associazione in partecipazione *f*	sociedad en participación *f*
dossier (F)	Akte *f*	file	—	pratica *f*	documento *m*
dossier à échantillons (F)	Mustermappe *f*	sample bag	—	cartella campioni *f*	muestrario *m*
dossier de candidature (F)	Bewerbungsunterlagen *pl*	application documents	—	documenti della domanda d'impiego *m pl*	documentos de solicitud *m pl*
dotación (Es)	Dotierung *f*	endowment	dotation *f*	dotazione *f*	—
dotación en capital (F)	Kapitalausstattung *f*	capital resources	—	dotazione di capitale *f*	dotación de capital *f*
dotation (F)	Dotierung *f*	endowment	—	dotazione *f*	dotación *f*
dotation de capital (Es)	Kapitalausstattung *f*	capital resources	dotation en capital *f*	dotazione di capitale *f*	—
dotazione (I)	Dotierung *f*	endowment	dotation *f*	—	dotación *f*
dotazione di capitale (I)	Kapitalausstattung *f*	capital resources	dotation en capital *f*	—	dotación de capital *f*
Dotierung (D)	—	endowment	dotation *f*	dotazione *f*	dotación *f*
douane (F)	Zoll *m*	customs/ customs duty	—	dogana *f*/dazio *m*	aduana *f*/arancel *m*
double entry bookkeeping (E)	doppelte Buchführung *f*	—	comptabilité en partie double *f*	contabilità a partita doppia *f*	contabilidad por doble partida *f*
doubtful account (E)	zweifelhafte Forderung *f*	—	créance douteuse *f*	credito dubbio *m*	créditos dudosos *m pl*
Dow-Jones-Index (D)	—	Dow-Jones Industrial Average	indice Dow-Jones *m*	indice Dow-Jones *m*	Indice Dow Jones *m*
Dow-Jones Industrial Average (E)	Dow-Jones-Index *m*	—	indice Dow-Jones *m*	indice Dow-Jones *m*	Indice Dow Jones *m*
down-swing (E)	Abschwung *m*	—	dépression *f*	regresso *m*	baja *f*
downward trend (E)	Abwärtstrend *m*	—	baisse *f*	tendenza al ribasso *f*	tendencia bajista *f*

	D	E	F	I	Es
draft (E)	Entwurf *m*	—	projet *m*	progetto *m*	proyecto *m*
drawback (Es)	Rückzoll *m*	customs drawback	ristourne des droits de douane *f*	restituzione di dazi *f*	—
drawee (E)	Bezogener *m*	—	tiré *m*	trattario *m*	librado *m*
drawing rights (E)	Ziehungsrechte *pl*	—	droits de tirage *m pl*	diritti di prelievo *m pl*	derechos de giro *m pl*
Dreiecksgeschäft (D)	—	triangular transaction	opération commerciale triangulaire *f*	operazione triangolare *f*	operación triangular *f*
Dreimonatspapier (D)	—	three months papers	titre à trois mois *m*	titolo trimestrale *m*	títulos a tres meses *m*
drenaje de divisas (Es)	Devisenabfluß *m*	foreign exchange outflow	sortie de devises *f*	deflusso di divise *m*	—
Drittländer (D)	—	third countries	pays tiers *m pl*	paesi terzi *m pl*	terceros países *m pl*
droit (F)	Recht *n*	law	—	diritto *m*	derecho *m*
droit à l'indemnité (F)	Schadenersatzansprüche *pl*	claim for damages	—	diritti al risarcimento danni *m pl*	derecho a indemnización por daños y perjuicios *m*
droit à livraison complémentaire (F)	Nachlieferungsanspruch *m*	claim to subsequent delivery	—	diritto alla fornitura supplementare *m*	derecho de suministro adicional *m*
droit à restitution (F)	Rückgaberecht *n*	right of redemption	—	diritto alla restituzione *m*	derecho de devolución *m*
droit d'auteur (F)	Urheberrecht *n*	copyright	—	diritto d'autore *m*	derecho del autor *m*
droit de déchargement (F)	Löschgebühren *pl*	discharging expenses	—	spese di scarico *f pl*	gastos de descarga *m pl*
droit de douane (F)	Zollgebühren *pl*	customs duties	—	diritti doganali *m pl*	derechos arancelarios *m pl*
droit de douane par quantité (F)	Mengenzoll *m*	specific duty	—	dazio di quantità *m*	arancel aduanero cuantitativo *m*
droit de gage (F)	Pfandrecht *n*	pledge	—	diritto di pegno *m*	derecho de garantía real *m*
droit de minorité (F)	Minoritätsrecht *n*	minority right	—	diritto delle minoranze *m*	derecho minoritario *m*
droit d'entrée (F)	Einfuhrzoll *m*	import duty	—	dazio d'importazione *m*	arancel de importación *m*
droit de pêche (F)	Fischereirecht *n*	fishing rights	—	diritto della pesca *m*	derecho pesquero *m*
droit de préemption (F)	Vorkaufsrecht *n*	preemption right	—	diritto di prelazione *m*	derecho de preferencia *m*
droit de protection (F)	Schutzzoll *m*	protective duty	—	dazio protettivo *m*	aduana proteccionista *f*
droit de révocation (F)	Widerrufsrecht *n*	right of revocation	—	diritto di revoca *m*	derecho de revocación *m*
droit de souveraineté (F)	Hoheitsrecht *n*	sovereign right	—	diritto di sovranità *m*	soberanía *f*
droit de timbre (F)	Stempelgebühr *f*	stamp duty	—	tassa di bollo *f*	derechos de timbre *m pl*
droit de transaction sur les opérations boursières (F)	Börsenumsatzsteuer *f*	stock exchange turnover tax	—	imposta sulle operazioni di borsa *f*	impuesto de negociación bursátil *m*
droit de transit (F)	Transitzoll *m*	transit duty	—	diritti di transito *m pl*	derecho de tránsito *m*
droit de vote (F)	Stimmrecht *n*	right to vote	—	diritto al voto *m*	derecho a voto *m*
droit exclusif de représentation (F)	Alleinvertretungsrecht *n*	sole and exclusive agency right	—	diritto di rappresentanza esclusiva *m*	derecho de representación exclusiva *m*
droit d'exploitation (F)	Betriebserlaubnis *f*	operating permit	—	autorizzazione per l'esercizio *f*	autorización de funcionamiento *f*
droit prohibitif (F)	Prohibitivzoll *m*	prohibitive duty	—	dazio proibitivo *m*	derechos prohibitivos *m pl*
droit réel (F)	dingliches Recht *n*	real right	—	diritto reale *m*	derecho real *m*
droits de ports (F)	Hafengebühren *pl*	harbour dues	—	diritti di porto *m pl*	derechos portuarios *m pl*
droits de souveraineté nationale (F)	nationale Souveränitätsrechte *pl*	national sovereignty rights	—	diritti di sovranità nazionale *m pl*	derechos de soberanía nacional *m pl*
droits de tirage (F)	Ziehungsrechte *pl*	drawing rights	—	diritti di prelievo *m pl*	derechos de giro *m pl*
droits de tirage spécial (F)	Sonderziehungsrechte *pl*	special drawing rights	—	diritti speciali di prelievo *m pl*	derechos de giro especial *m pl*
droits de vente aux enchères (F)	Auktionsgebühr *f*	auction fees	—	diritto d'asta *m*	gastos de subasta *m pl*

	D	E	F	I	Es
droit unique (F)	Einheitszoll *m*	uniform duty	—	dazio unitario *m*	aduanas uniformes *f pl*
drop in employment (E)	Beschäftigungs-rückgang *m*	—	baisse de l'offre d'emploi *f*	calo dell'occupazione *m*	descenso del empleo *m*
drop in expenditure (E)	Ausgabensenkung *f*	—	diminution des dépenses *f*	riduzione delle spese *f*	reducción de gastos *f*
Drucker (D)	—	printer	imprimante *f*	stampante *f*	impresora *f*
Drucksache (D)	—	printed matter	imprimé *m*	stampa *f*	impreso *m*
dualism (E)	Dualismus *m*	—	dualisme *m*	dualismo *m*	dualismo *m*
dualisme (F)	Dualismus *m*	dualism	—	dualismo *m*	dualismo *m*
dualismo (Es)	Dualismus *m*	dualism	dualisme *m*	dualismo *m*	—
dualismo (I)	Dualismus *m*	dualism	dualisme *m*	—	dualismo *m*
Dualismus (D)	—	dualism	dualisme *m*	dualismo *m*	dualismo *m*
ducroire (F)	Delkredere *n*	del credere	—	star del credere *m*	delcrédere *m*
due payment reserved (E)	Eingang vorbehalten	—	sauf bonne fin	salvo buon fine	salvo buen cobro *m*
duplicado de la carta de porte (Es)	Frachtbriefdoppel *n*	duplicate consignment note	duplicata de la lettre de voiture *m*	duplicato della lettera di vettura *m*	
duplicata de la lettre de voiture (F)	Frachtbriefdoppel *n*	duplicate consignment note	—	duplicato della lettera di vettura *m*	duplicado de la carta de porte *m*
duplicate consignment note (E)	Frachtbriefdoppel *n*	—	duplicata de la lettre de voiture *m*	duplicato della lettera di vettura *m*	duplicado de la carta de porte *m*
duplicato della lettera di vettura (I)	Frachtbriefdoppel *n*	duplicate consignment note	duplicata de la lettre de voiture *m*	—	duplicado de la carta de porte *m*
durable consumer goods (E)	Gebrauchsgüter *pl*	—	biens d'utilisation courante *m pl*	beni di consumo durevoli *m pl*	bienes de consumo duradero *m pl*
duración del contrato (Es)	Vertragsdauer *f*	contract period	durée du contrat *f*	durata del contratto *f*	—
duración mínima (Es)	Mindestdauer *f*	minimum length/ minimum duration	durée minimum *f*	durata minima *f*	—
durata del contratto (I)	Vertragsdauer *f*	contract period	durée du contrat *f*	—	duración del contrato *f*
durata del finanziamento (I)	Finanzierungsdauer *f*	period of financing	durée du financement *f*	—	período de financiación *m* ‹
durata della protezione (I)	Schutzfrist *f*	term of protection	délai de protection *m*	—	plazo de protección *m*
durata minima (I)	Mindestdauer *f*	minimum length/ minimum duration	durée minimum *f*	—	duración mínima *m*/ plazo mínimo *m*
durata probabile della vita (I)	Lebenserwartung *f*	expectation of life	espérance de vie *f*	—	expectativa de vida *f*
duration of credit (E)	Kreditlaufzeit *f*	—	durée de l'allocation de crédit *f*	scadenza del credito *f*	período concesional de un crédito *m*
Durchführung (D)	—	realization	réalisation *f*	esecuzione *f*	ejecución *m*
Durchgangsschein (D)	—	transit certificate	acquit de transit *m*	bolletta di transito *f*	pasavante *m*
Durchschnitt (D)	—	average	moyenne *f*	media *f*	promedio *m*
Durchschnitts-kosten (D)	—	average costs	coût moyen *m*	costi medi *m pl*	gastos medios *m pl*
Durchsetzungs-vermögen (D)	—	capability of asserting one's right	capacité de se faire valoir *f*	capacità di imposizione *f*	capacidad de imponerse *f*
durée (F)	Laufzeit *f*	term	—	scadenza *f*/durata *f*	plazo de vencimiento *m*
durée de l'allocation de crédit (F)	Kreditlaufzeit *f*	duration of credit	—	scadenza del credito *f*	período concesional de un crédito *m*
durée du contrat (F)	Vertragsdauer *f*	contract period	—	durata del contratto *f*	duración del contrato *f*
durée du financement (F)	Finanzierungsdauer *f*	period of financing	—	durata del finanziamento *f*	período de financiación *m*
durée minimum (F)	Mindestdauer *f*	minimum length/ minimum duration	—	durata minima *f*	duración mínima *f*/ plazo mínimo *m*
durée restante (F)	Restlaufzeit *f*	residual time to maturity	—	scadenza residua *f*	plazo de vencimiento restante *m*
duty in kind (E)	Naturalabgabe *f*	—	taxe acquittée en nature *f*	imposta in natura *f*	impuesto en especie *m*
duty of supervision (E)	Aufsichtspflicht *f*	—	obligation de surveillance *f*	obbligo di sorveglianza *m*	obligación de vigilancia *f*

	D	E	F	I	Es
duty paid (E)	verzollt	—	dédouané	sdoganato	pagado
duty to supply (E)	Belieferungspflicht f	—	obligation de livraison f	obbligo di fornitura m	obligación de suministro f
duty unpaid (E)	unverzollt	—	non dédouané	non sdoganato	aduana aparte
earning capacity (E)	Ertragskraft f	—	force productive f	redditività f	rentabilidad f
earnings (E)	Bezüge pl	—	émoluments m pl	entrate f pl	retribuciones f pl
earning situation (E)	Ertragslage f	—	niveau du rendement m	situazione economica f	situación del beneficio f
East-West trade (E)	Ost-West-Handel m		commerce Est-Ouest m	scambio est-ovest m	comercio este-oeste m
easy money (E)	billiges Geld n	—	argent bon marché m	crediti agevolati m pl	dinero barato m
eaux côtières (F)	Küstengewässer n	coastal waters	—	acque territoriali f pl	zona costera f
eaux résiduelles (F)	Abwasser n	waste water	—	acque di scarico f pl	aguas residuales f pl
écart de prix (F)	Preisunterschied m	price difference	—	differenza dei prezzi f	diferencia de precios f
écart qualitatif (F)	Qualitäts- abweichung f	deviation from quality	—	differenza di qualità f	diferencia de calidad f
eccedenza (I)	Überschuß m	excess	excédent m	—	excedente m
eccedenza commerciale (I)	Handelsüberschuß m	trade surplus	excédent commercial m	—	excedente comercial m
eccedenza della bilan- cia dei pagamenti (I)	Zahlungsbilanz- überschuß m	surplus in the balance of payments	balance des paye- ments excédentaire f	—	superávit en la balanza de pagos m
eccedenza delle esportazioni (I)	Exportüberschuß m	export surplus	excédent d'exportation m	—	excedente de exportación m
eccedenza di liquidità (I)	Liquiditäts- überschuß m	excess liquidity	excédent de liquidité m	—	exceso de liquidez m
eccedenza d'offerta (I)	Angebotsüberhang m	excess of supply over demand	excès de l'offre m	—	exceso de oferta m
eccedenze agricole (I)	Agrarüberschüsse pl	agricultural surpluses	excédents agricoles m pl	—	excedentes agrícolas m pl
eccessivo (I)	übermäßig	excessive	excessif	—	excesivo
échange¹ (F)	Umtausch m	exchange	—	cambio m	cambio m/ conversión f
échange² (F)	Tausch m	exchange/barter	—	scambio m/baratto m	cambio m/ trueque m
échanges commerciaux¹ (F)	Handelsverkehr m	commercial intercourse	—	circolazione delle merci f	comercio m
échanges commerciaux² (F)	Warenaustausch m	exchange of goods	—	scambio merci m	intercambio de mercancías m
échantillon¹ (F)	Probepackung f	trial package	—	confezione campione f	muestra f
échantillon² (F)	Muster n	sample/pattern	—	campione m/ disegno m	muestra f/dibujo m
échantillon³ (F)	Warenprobe f	sample	—	campione di merce m	muestra de mercancía f
échantillon sans valeur (F)	Muster ohne Wert n	sample, no commercial value	—	campione senza valore m	muestra sin valor f
école (F)	Schule f	school	—	scuola f	escuela f
ecología (Es)	Ökologie f	ecology	écologie f	ecologia f	—
ecologia (I)	Ökologie f	ecology	écologie f	—	ecología f
ecologico (I)	umweltfreundlich	beneficial to the environment	favorable à l'environnement	—	no contaminante
écologie (F)	Ökologie f	ecology	—	ecologia f	ecología f
ecology (E)	Ökologie f	—	écologie f	ecologia f	ecología f
economía¹ (Es)	Wirtschaft f	economy	économie f	economia f	—
economía² (Es)	Ökonomie f	economy	économie f	economia f	—
economia¹ (I)	Wirtschaft f	economy	économie f	—	economía f
economia² (I)	Ökonomie f	economy	économie f	—	economía f
economía agraria (Es)	Agrarwirtschaft f	farming	économie agricole f	economia agraria f	—
economia agraria (I)	Agrarwirtschaft f	farming	économie agricole f	—	economía agraria f
economia aziendale (I)	Betriebs- wirtschaftslehre f	business administration	(science de la) gestion industrielle et commerciale f	—	teoría de la empresa f

economic expert

	D	E	F	I	Es
economía de distribución (Es)	Absatzwirtschaft f	marketing	commercialisation f	marketing m	—
economía de mercado (Es)	Marktwirtschaft f	market economy	économie de marché f	economia di mercato f	—
economía de mercado social (Es)	soziale Marktwirtschaft f	social market economy	économie sociale du marché f	economia sociale di mercato f	—
economia di mercato (I)	Marktwirtschaft f	market economy	économie de marché f	—	economía de mercado f
economía doméstica[1] (Es)	privater Haushalt m	private household	ménage privé m	famiglia f	—
economía doméstica[2] (Es)	Haushalt m	private household/budget	ménage de particuliers m/budget m	economia domestica f/bilancio m	—
economia domestica (I)	Haushalt m	private household/budget	ménage de particuliers m/budget m	—	economía doméstica f/presupuesto m
economia forestale (I)	Forstwirtschaft f	forestry	économie forestière f	—	silvicultura f
economía interior (Es)	Binnenwirtschaft f	domestic economy	économie nationale f	economia nazionale f	—
economía internacional (Es)	Weltwirtschaft f	world economy	économie mondiale f	economia mondiale f	—
economia mondiale (I)	Weltwirtschaft f	world economy	économie mondiale f	—	economía internacional f
economía nacional[1] (Es)	Nationalökonomie f	economics	économie nationale f	economia nazionale f	—
economía nacional[2] (Es)	Volkswirtschaft f	national economy	économie nationale f	economia politica f	—
economia nazionale[1] (I)	Nationalökonomie f	economics	économie nationale f	—	economía nacional f
economia nazionale[2] (I)	Binnenwirtschaft f	domestic economy	économie nationale f	—	economía interior f
economía planificada (Es)	Planwirtschaft f	planned economy	économie planifiée f	economia pianificata f	—
economía planificada central (Es)	zentrale Planwirtschaft f	centrally controlled economy	économie planifiée centrale f	economia pianificata f	—
economia pianificata[1] (I)	zentrale Planwirtschaft f	centrally controlled economy	économie planifiée centrale f	—	economía planificada central f
economia pianificata[2] (I)	Planwirtschaft f	planned economy	économie planifiée f	—	economía planificada f
economia politica[1] (I)	Volkswirtschaft f	national economy	économie nationale f	—	economía nacional f
economia politica[2] (I)	Volkswirtschaftslehre f	economics	économie politique f	—	ciencias económicas f pl
economía privada (Es)	Privatwirtschaft f	private sector of the economy	économie privée f	economia privata f	—
economia privata (I)	Privatwirtschaft f	private sector of the economy	économie privée f	—	economía privada f
economia pubblica (I)	öffentliche Wirtschaft f	public sector of the economy	économie publique f	—	economía pública f
economía pública (Es)	öffentliche Wirtschaft f	public sector of the economy	économie publique f	economia pubblica f	—
economia sociale di mercato (I)	soziale Marktwirtschaft f	social market economy	économie sociale de marché f	—	economía de mercado social f
economic account (E)	Wirtschaftsrechnung f	—	comptabilisation économique f	conto economico m	contabilización económica f
economic analysis[1] (E)	Konjunkturanalyse f	—	analyse de la conjoncture f	analisi congiunturale f	análisis de la situación económica m
economic analysis[2] (E)	Wirtschaftsanalyse f	—	analyse de l'économie f	analisi economica f	análisis económico m
economic boycott (E)	Wirtschaftsboykott m	—	boycottage économique m	boicottaggio economico m	boicot económico m
economic community (E)	Wirtschaftsgemeinschaft f	—	communauté économique f	comunità economica f	comunidad económica f
economic concentration (E)	Wirtschaftskonzentration f	—	concentration économique f	concentrazione economica f	concentración económica f
economic crisis (E)	Wirtschaftskrise f	—	crise économique f	crisi economica f	crisis económica f
economic cycle (E)	Wirtschaftskreislauf m	—	circuit économique m	circuito economico m	circuito económico m
economic efficiency (E)	Wirtschaftlichkeit f	—	rentabilité f	economicità f	rentabilidad f
economic expert (E)	Wirtschaftsexperte m	—	expert économique m	esperto in materia economica m	economista m

	D	E	F	I	Es
economic geography (E)	Wirtschafts- geographie f	—	géographie économique f	geografia economica f	geografía económica f
economic good (E)	Wirtschaftsgut n	—	bien économique m	bene economico m	bien económico m
economic growth (E)	Wirtschafts- wachstum n	—	croissance économique f	crescita economica f	crecimiento económico m
economic history (E)	Wirtschafts- geschichte f	—	histoire économique f	storia economica f	historia económica f
economic integration (E)	wirtschaftliche Integration f	—	intégration économique f	integrazione economica f	integración económica f
economicità (I)	Wirtschaftlichkeit f	economic efficiency	rentabilité f	—	rentabilidad f
economic law (E)	Wirtschaftsrecht n	—	législation économique f	diritto economico m	derecho económico m
economic order (E)	Wirtschaftsordnung f	—	ordre économique m	ordinamento economico m	orden económico m
economic plan (E)	Wirtschaftsplan m	—	plan économique m	piano economico m	plan económico m
economic policy[1] (E)	Konjunkturpolitik f	—	politique de conjoncture f	politica congiunturale f	política de coyuntura f
economic policy[2] (E)	Wirtschaftspolitik f	—	politique économique f	politica economica f	política económica f
economics[1] (E)	Wirtschaftswissen- schaften pl	—	sciences économiques f pl	scienze economiche f pl	ciencias económicas f pl
economics[2] (E)	Nationalökonomie f	—	économie nationale f	economia nazionale f	economía nacional f
economics[3] (E)	Volkswirtschafts- lehre f	—	économie politique f	economia politica f	ciencias económicas f pl
economic structure (E)	Wirtschaftsstruktur f	—	structure économique f	struttura economica f	estructura económica f
economic theory (E)	Wirtschaftstheorie f	—	théorie économique f	teoria dell'economia f	teoría económica f
economic trend (E)	Konjunktur- entwicklung f	—	évolution de la conjoncture f	sviluppo congiunturale m	evolución de la coyuntura f
economic union (E)	Wirtschaftsunion f	—	union économique f	unione economica f	unión económica f
economic upturn (E)	Konjunkturbelebung f	—	relance économique f	ripresa congiunturale f	recuperación coyuntural f
economic use (E)	wirtschaftliche Nutzung m	—	utilisation économique f	utilizzo economico m	utilización económica f
economic war (E)	Wirtschaftskrieg m	—	guerre économique f	guerra economica f	guerra económica f
économie[1] (F)	Wirtschaft f	economy	—	economia f	economía f
économie[2] (F)	Ökonomie f	economy	—	economia f	economía f
économie agricole (F)	Agrarwirtschaft f	farming	—	economia agraria f	economía agraria f
économie de marché (F)	Marktwirtschaft f	market economy	—	economia di mercato f	economía de mercado f
économie forestière (F)	Forstwirtschaft f	forestry	—	economia forestale f	silvicultura f
économie mondiale (F)	Weltwirtschaft f	world economy	—	economia mondiale f	economía internacional f
économie nationale[1] (F)	Binnenwirtschaft f	domestic economy	—	economia nazionale f	economía interior f
économie nationale[2] (F)	Volkswirtschaft f	national economy	—	economia politica f	economía nacional f
économie nationale[3] (F)	Nationalökonomie f	economics	—	economia nazionale f	economía nacional f
économie planifiée (F)	Planwirtschaft f	planned economy	—	economia pianificata f	economía planificada f
économie planifiée centrale (F)	zentrale Planwirtschaft f	centrally controlled economy	—	economia pianificata f	economía planificada central f
économie politique (F)	Volkswirtschafts- lehre f	economics	—	economia politica f	ciencias económicas f pl
économie privée (F)	Privatwirtschaft f	private sector of the economy	—	economia privata f	economía privada f
économie publique (F)	öffentliche Wirtschaft f	public sector of the economy	—	economia pubblica f	economía pública f
économie sociale du marché (F)	soziale Marktwirtschaft f	social market economy	—	economia sociale di mercato f	economía de mercado social f
economista (Es)	Wirtschaftsexperte m	economic expert	expert économique m	esperto in materia economica m	—
economy[1] (E)	Ökonomie f	—	économie f	economia f	economía f
economy[2] (E)	Wirtschaft f	—	économie f	economia f	economía f
écran (F)	Bildschirm m	screen	—	video m	pantalla f

	D	E	F	I	Es
écriture de contre-passation (F)	Storno *n*	counter entry	—	storno *m*	extorno *m*
edilizia (I)	Bauwirtschaft *f*	building and construction industry	(industrie du) bâtiment *f*	—	ramo de la construcción *m*
edilizia abitativa (I)	Wohnungsbau *m*	housing construction	construction de logements *f*	—	construcción de viviendas *f*
éditeur (F)	Verleger *m*	publisher	—	editore *m*	editor *m*
editor (Es)	Verleger *m*	publisher	éditeur *m*	editore *m*	—
editore (I)	Verleger *m*	publisher	éditeur *m*	—	editor *m*
editorial (Es)	Verlag *m*	publishing house	maison d'édition *f*	casa editrice *f*	—
educación (Es)	Bildung *f*	education	formation *f*	formazione *f*	—
education (E)	Bildung *f*	—	formation *f*	formazione *f*	educación *f*
efectividad del anuncio (Es)	Anzeigenwirkung *f*	effectiveness of an advertisement	effet de l'annonce *m*	effetto dell'inserzione *m*	—
efecto bumerán (Es)	Bumerang-Effekt *m*	boomerang effect	effet boomerang *m*	effetto bumerang *m*	—
efecto invernadero (Es)	Treibhauseffekt *m*	global warming	effet de serre *m*	effetto serra *m*	—
efectos (Es)	Effekten *f*	securities	valeurs mobilières *f pl*	titoli *m pl*	—
efecto snob (Es)	Snob-Effekt *m*	snob effect	effet snob *m*	effetto snob *m*	—
effectif (F)	Aktivbestand *m*	assets	—	effettivo *m*	activo disponible *m*
effectif du personnel (F)	Personalsituation *f*	personnel situation	—	situazione occupazionale *f*	situación de personal *f*
effective (E)	in Kraft	—	en vigueur	in vigore	en vigor
effective interest (E)	Effektivzins *m*	—	intérêt effectif *m*	tasso d'interesse effettivo *m*	intereses reales *m pl*
effective interest yield (E)	Effektivverzinsung *f*	—	taux effectif (de l'intérêt) *f*	interessi effettivi *m pl*	interés efectivo *m*
effectiveness of an advertisement (E)	Anzeigenwirkung *f*	—	effet de l'annonce *m*	effetto dell'inserzione *m*	efectividad del anuncio *f*
Effekten (D)	—	securities	valeurs mobilières *f pl*	titoli *m pl*	efectos *m pl*
Effektenbörse (D)	—	stock exchange	bourse des titres et valeurs mobilières *f*	borsa valori *f*	Bolsa de valores *f*
Effektengeschäft (D)	—	securities business	commerce des valeurs mobilières *m*	operazione su titoli *f*	operación de valores *f*
effektive Verschuldung (D)	—	real indebtedness	endettement effectif *m*	indebitamento effettivo *m*	endeudamiento efectivo *m*
Effektivlohn (D)	—	actual wage	salaire effectif *m*	salario effettivo *m*	salario efectivo *m*
Effektivverzinsung (D)	—	effective interest yield	taux effectif (de l'intérêt) *m*	interessi effettivi *m pl*	interés efectivo *m*
Effektivzins (D)	—	effective interest	intérêt effectif *m*	tasso d'interesse effettivo *m*	intereses reales *m pl*
effet boomerang (F)	Bumerang-Effekt *m*	boomerang effect	—	effetto bumerang *m*	efecto bumerán *m*
effet de l'annonce (F)	Anzeigenwirkung *f*	effectiveness of an advertisement	—	effetto dell'inserzione *m*	efectividad del anuncio *f*
effet de serre (F)	Treibhauseffekt *m*	global warming	—	effetto serra *m*	efecto invernadero *m*
effet domicilier (F)	Domizilwechsel *m*	domiciliary bill	—	cambiale domiciliata *f*	letra domiciliada *f*
effet public (F)	Rentenanleihe *f*	annuity bonds	—	prestito a reddito fisso *m*	empréstito por anualidades *m*
effet snob (F)	Snob-Effekt *m*	snob effect	—	effetto snob *m*	efecto snob *m*
effettivo (I)	Aktivbestand *m*	assets	actif *m*	—	activo disponible *m*
effetto bumerang (I)	Bumerang-Effekt *m*	boomerang effect	effet boomerang *m*	—	efecto bumerán *m*
effetto dell'inserzione (I)	Anzeigenwirkung *f*	effectiveness of an advertisement	effet de l'annonce *m*	—	efectividad del anuncio *f*
effetto serra (I)	Treibhauseffekt *m*	global warming	effet de serre *m*	—	efecto invernadero *m*
effetto snob (I)	Snob-Effekt *m*	snob effect	effet snob *m*	—	efecto snob *m*
efficience[1] (F)	Effizienz *f*	efficiency	—	efficienza *f*	eficiencia *f*
efficience[2] (F)	Leistungsfähigkeit *f*	efficiency	—	efficienza *f*	capacidad productiva *f*
efficiency[1] (E)	Effizienz *f*	—	efficience *f*	efficienza *f*	eficiencia *f*
efficiency[2] (E)	Leistungsfähigkeit *f*	—	efficience *f*	efficienza *f*	capacidad productiva *f*

	D	E	F	I	Es
efficiency control (E)	Effizienzkontrolle f	—	contrôle de l'efficience m	controllo d'efficienza m	control de eficiencia m
efficienza[1] (I)	Leistungsfähigkeit f	efficiency	efficience f	—	capacidad productiva f
efficienza[2] (I)	Effizienz f	efficiency	efficience f	—	eficiencia f
Effizienz (D)	—	efficiency	efficience f	efficienza f	eficiencia f
Effizienzkontrolle (D)	—	efficiency control	contrôle de l'efficience m	controllo d'efficienza m	control de eficiencia m
eficiencia (Es)	Effizienz f	efficiency	efficience f	efficienza f	—
eichen (D)	—	gauge	jauger	tarare	contrastar
eidesstattliche Erklärung (D)	—	declaration in lieu of an oath	déclaration formelle sans prestation de serment f	dichiarazione sostitutiva del giuramento f	declaración bajo juramento f
Eigenfinanzierung (D)	—	self-financing	autofinancement m	autofinanziamento m	financiación propia f
Eigenkapital (D)	—	equity capital	capital propre m	capitale proprio m	capital propio m
Eigentum (D)	—	property	propriété f	proprietà f	propiedad f
Eigentums-verhältnisse (D)	—	property relations	régime de la propriété m	rapporti di proprietà m pl	régimen de tenencia m
Eigentums-wohnung (D)	—	freehold flat	logement en propriété m	appartamento in condominio m	piso en propiedad m
Eigenverbrauch (D)	—	personal consumption	consommation personnelle f	consumo proprio m	consumo propio m
Eilbote (D)	—	express messenger	facteur spécial m	corriere m	expreso m
Eilbrief (D)	—	express letter	lettre par exprès f	lettera espresso f	carta urgente f
Eilgut (D)	—	goods sent by express	marchandise en grande vitesse f	merce a grande velocità f	mercancía en gran velocidad f
Eilpaket (D)	—	express parcel	colis exprès m	pacco espresso m	paquete urgente m
Eilzustellung (D)	—	express delivery	remise par exprès f	consegna per espresso f	entrega urgente f
Einarbeitung (D)	—	vocational adjustment	entraînement m	periodo d'adattamento m	entrenamiento m
Einbruch-versicherung (D)	—	housebreaking insurance	assurance contre le vol avec effraction f	assicurazione contro il furto con scasso f	seguro contra robo con fractura m
Einflußbereich (D)	—	sphere of influence	sphère d'influence f	sfera d'influenza f	esfera de influencia f
Einfuhr (D)	—	import	importation f	importazione f	importación f
Einfuhrabgabe (D)	—	import duties	taxe à l'importation f	tassa d'importazione f	tasa a la importación f
Einfuhr-beschränkung (D)	—	import restriction	limitation des importations f	restrizione d'importazione f	restricción a la importación f
Einfuhrerklärung (D)	—	import declaration	déclaration d'entrée f	dichiarazione doganale f	declaración de importación f
Einfuhr-genehmigung (D)	—	import licence	autorisation d'importation f	permesso d'importazione m	permiso de importación m
Einfuhrpapiere (D)	—	import documents	documents d'importation m pl	bollette doganali f pl	documentos de importación m pl
Einführungsrabatt (D)	—	introductory discount	rabais d'introduction m	sconto di lancio m	rebaja de lanzamiento f
Einfuhrzoll (D)	—	import duty	droit d'entrée m	dazio d'importazione m	arancel de importación m
Eingang vorbehalten (D)	—	due payment reserved	sauf bonne fin	salvo buon fine	salvo buen cobro m
eingezahltes Kapital (D)	—	paid-up capital	capital versé m	capitale versato m	capitial desembolsado m
Einheitskurs (D)	—	spot price	cours unique m	cambio unitario m	cotización única f
Einheitspreis (D)	—	uniform price	prix unique m	prezzo unitario m	precio único m
Einheitstarif (D)	—	uniform tariff	tarif standard m	tariffa unitaria f	tarifa única f
Einheitswährung (D)	—	uniform currency	monométallisme m	moneta unitaria f	moneda única f
Einheitszoll (D)	—	uniform duty	droit unique m	dazio unitario m	aduanas uniformes f pl
Einkauf (D)	—	purchase	achat m	acquisto m	compra f
einkaufen (D)	—	buy	acheter	acquistare	comprar
Einkäufer (D)	—	buyer	acheteur m	acquirente m	comprador m

	D	E	F	I	Es
Einkaufs-bedingungen (D)	—	purchasing terms	conditions d'achat *f pl*	condizioni d'acquisto *f pl*	condiciones de compra *f pl*
Einkaufsland (D)	—	country of purchase	pays où l'on achète *m*	paese acquirente *m*	país de compra *m*
Einkaufspreis (D)	—	purchase price	prix d'achat *m*	prezzo d'acquisto *m*	precio de compra *m*
Einkommen (D)	—	income	revenu *m*	reddito *m*	ingresos *m pl*/renta *f*
Einkommens-erhöhung (D)	—	rise in income	augmentation du revenu *f*	aumento del reddito *m*	aumento de salario *m*
Einkommens-erklärung (D)	—	income declaration	déclaration du revenu *f*	dichiarazione del reddito *f*	declaración de la renta *f*
Einkommensteuer (D)	—	income tax	impôt sur le revenu *m*	imposta sui redditi *f*	impuesto sobre la renta de las personas físicas *m*
Einkommens-umverteilung (D)	—	redistribution of income	redistribution des revenus *f*	ridistribuzione dei redditi *f*	redistribución de la renta *f*
Einkommens-verteilung (D)	—	distribution of income	distribution du revenu *f*	distribuzione dei redditi *f*	distribución de la renta *f*
Einkommens-verwendung (D)	—	appropriation of income	utilisation du revenu *f*	impiego dei redditi *m*	distribución de la renta *f*
einladen (D)	—	invite	inviter	invitare	invitar
Einlagen (D)	—	deposit	dépôt *m*	depositi bancari *m pl*	depósitos bancarios *m pl*
Einlagerung (D)	—	storage	entreposage *m*	immagazzinamento *m*	almacenamiento *m*
Einlösung (D)	—	payment	payement *m*	pagamento *m*	pago *m*
Einnahmen (D)	—	receipts	revenu *m*	entrate *f pl*	ingresos *m pl*
Einschreibebrief (D)	—	registered letter	lettre recommandée *f*	lettera raccomandata *f*	carta certificada *f*
Einschreiben (D)	—	Registered	en recommandé	raccomandata *f*	certificado *m*
Einschreiben-Rückschein (D)	—	Recorded delivery letter (with advice)	lettre recommandée avec avis de réception *f*	lettera raccomandata con ricevuta di ritorno *f*	carta certificada con talón de recibo *f*
Einsichtnahme (D)	—	inspection	contrôle des livres comptables *m*	presa visione *f*	inspección *f*
Einstandspreis (D)	—	cost price	prix coûtant *m*	prezzo di costo *m*	precio de coste *m*
einstweilig (D)	—	temporary	provisoire	temporaneo	provisional
einstweilige Verfügung (D)	—	temporary injunction	ordonnance sur référé civil *f*	provvedimento temporaneo *m*	interdicto provisorio *m*
Eintrittskarte (D)	—	admission ticket	billet *m*	biglietto d'ingresso *m*	entrada *f*
Einwilligung (D)	—	consent	consentement *m*	consenso *m*	consentimiento *m*
Einwohner-meldeamt (D)	—	residents' registration office	bureau de déclaration de résidence *m*	ufficio anagrafe *m*	oficina del censo *f*
Einzelhandel (D)	—	retail trade	commerce de détail *m*	commercio al dettaglio *m*	comercio al por menor *m*
Einzelhandels-kaufmann (D)	—	retail merchant	détaillant *m*	commerciante al dettaglio *m*	comerciante particular *m*
Einzelhandels-spanne (D)	—	retail price margin	marge de détail *f*	margine del commercio al dettaglio *m*	margen del comercio al por menor *m*
Einzelhändler (D)	—	retailer	commerçant détaillant *m*	dettagliante *m*	minorista *m*
Eisenbahntarif (D)	—	railway tariff	tarif ferroviaire *m*	tariffa ferroviaria *f*	tarifa ferroviaria *f*
ejecución[1] (Es)	Vollstreckung *f*	enforcement	exécution *f*	esecuzione *f*	—
ejecución[2] (Es)	Durchführung *f*	realization	réalisation *f*	esecuzione *f*	—
ejecución[3] (Es)	Abwicklung *f*	settlement/liquidation	exécution *f*/liquidation *f*	esecuzione *f*	—
ejecución de pedidos (Es)	Auftragsabwicklung *f*	execution of the order	exécution d'une commande *f*	esecuzione ordini *f*	—
ejecución forzosa (Es)	Zwangs-vollstreckung *f*	judicial execution	exécution forcée *f*	esecuzione forzata *f*	—
ejecución por crédito documentario (Es)	Akkreditiv-abwicklung *f*	settlement by letter of credit	exécution par crédit documentaire *f*	procedura del credito documentario *f*	—
ejecutivo (Es)	Führungsperson *f*	executive	cadre *m*	dirigente *m*	—
ejecutor judicial (Es)	Gerichtsvollzieher *m*	bailiff	huissier de justice *m*	ufficiale giudiziario *m*	—
ejercicio[1] (Es)	Wirtschaftsjahr *n*	business year	exercice comptable *m*	esercizio *m*	—

	D	E	F	I	Es
ejercicio² (Es)	Rechnungsjahr *n*	financial year	exercice comptable *m*	anno d'esercizio *m*	—
ejercicio³ (Es)	Haushaltsjahr *n*	financial year	exercice budgétaire *m*	anno finanziario *m*	—
ejercicio⁴ (Es)	Geschäftsjahr *n*	financial year	exercice commerciale *m*	esercizio commerciale *m*	—
elaboración ulterior (Es)	Weiterverarbeitung *f*	further processing	transformation complémentaire *f*	trasformazione *f*	—
elaborar (Es)	aufbereiten	process/prepare	élaborer/traiter	elaborare/lavorare	—
elaborare (I)	aufbereiten	process/prepare	élaborer/traiter	—	elaborar/tratar
élaboration de texte (F)	Textverarbeitung *f*	word processing	—	elaborazione testi *f*	tratamiento de textos *m*
elaboratore elettronico di dati (I)	Datenverarbeitungs-anlage *f*	data processing system	installation de traite-ment électronique des informations *f*	—	ordenador *m*
elaborazione dati (I)	Datenverarbeitung *f*	data processing	traitement des information *m*	—	procesamiento de datos *m*
elaborazione testi (I)	Textverarbeitung *f*	word processing	élaboration de texte *f*	—	tratamiento de textos *m*
élaborer (F)	aufbereiten	process/prepare	—	elaborare/lavorare	elaborar/tratar
elección de la ubicación (Es)	Standortwahl *f*	choice of location	choix du lieu d'implantation *m*	scelta dell'ubicazione *f*	—
electric power (E)	Strom *m*	—	énergie électrique *f*	energia elettrica *f*	energía *f*
electronic (E)	elektronisch	—	électronique	elettronico	electrónico
electrónica (Es)	Elektronik *f*	electronics	électronique *f*	elettronica *f*	—
electrónico (Es)	elektronisch	electronic	électronique	elettronico	—
electronics (E)	Elektronik *f*	—	électronique *f*	elettronica *f*	electrónica *f*
électronique¹ (F)	Elektronik *f*	electronics	—	elettronica *f*	electrónica *f*
électronique² (F)	elektronisch	electronic	—	elettronico	electrónico
Elektronik (D)	—	electronics	électronique *f*	elettronica *f*	electrónica *f*
elektronisch (D)	—	electronic	électronique	elettronico	electrónico
élément polluant (F)	Schadstoff *m*	pollutants	—	sostanza nociva *f*	substancia nociva *f*
éléments pouvant influencer la demande (F)	Bedarfsfaktoren *pl*	requirements factors	—	fattori del fabbisogno *m pl*	factores determinantes de las necesidades *m pl*
elettronica (I)	Elektronik *f*	electronics	électronique *f*	—	electrónica *f*
elettronico (I)	elektronisch	electronic	électronique	—	electrónico
élevage (F)	Tierzucht *f*	livestock breeding	—	zootecnia *f*	cría de animales *f*
eliminación (Es)	Entsorgung *f*	waste disposal	dépollution *f*	smaltimento *m*	—
eliminación de petróleo usado (Es)	Altölbeseitigung *f*	disposal of waste oil	élimination d'huile usée *f*	smaltimento dell'olio usato *m*	—
élimination de déchets (F)	Abfallbeseitigung *f*	waste disposal	—	smaltimento dei rifiuti *m*	evacuación de residuos *f*
élimination du pétrole usé (F)	Altölbeseitigung *f*	disposal of waste oil	—	smaltimento dell'olio usato *m*	eliminación de petróleo usado *f*
elocuencia (Es)	Redegewandtheit *f*	eloquence	élocution aisée *f*	eloquenza *f*	—
élocution aisée (F)	Redegewandtheit *f*	eloquence	—	eloquenza *f*	elocuencia *f*
eloquence (E)	Redegewandtheit *f*	—	élocution aisée *f*	eloquenza *f*	elocuencia *f*
eloquenza (I)	Redegewandtheit *f*	eloquence	élocution aisée *f*	—	elocuencia *f*
embalaje (Es)	Verpackung	packing	emballage *m*	imballaggio *m*	—
embalaje marítimo (Es)	seemäßige Verpackung *f*	seaproof packing	emballage maritime *m*	imballaggio marittimo *m*	—
emballage (F)	Verpackung	packing	—	imballaggio *m*	embalaje *m*
emballage maritime (F)	seemäßige Verpackung *f*	seaproof packing	—	imballaggio marittimo *m*	embalaje marítimo *m*
Embargo (D)	—	embargo	embargo *m*	embargo *m*	embargo *m*
embargo (E)	Embargo *n*	—	embargo *m*	embargo *m*	embargo *m*
embargo¹ (Es)	Embargo *n*	embargo	embargo *m*	embargo *m*	—
embargo² (Es)	Liefersperre *f*	delivery ban	blocage de livraisons *m*	blocco delle forniture *m*	—
embargo (F)	Embargo *n*	embargo	—	embargo *m*	embargo *m*
embargo (I)	Embargo *n*	embargo	embargo *m*	—	embargo *m*

	D	E	F	I	Es
embargo comercial (Es)	Handelsembargo *n*	trade embargo	embargo commercial *m*	embargo commerciale *m*	—
embargo commercial (F)	Handelsembargo *n*	trade embargo	—	embargo commerciale *m*	embargo comercial *m*
embargo commerciale (I)	Handelsembargo *n*	trade embargo	embargo commercial *m*	—	embargo comercial *m*
embargo de salario (Es)	Lohnpfändung *f*	attachment of earnings	saisie-arrêt sur le salaire *f*	pignoramento del salario *m*	—
embarque (Es)	Verschiffung *f*	shipment	embarquement *m*	imbarco *m*	—
embarquement (F)	Verschiffung *f*	shipment	—	imbarco *m*	embarque *m*
embezzlement (E)	Unterschlagung *f*	—	détournement *m*	appropriazione indebita *f*	defraudación *f*
emblema comercial (Es)	Markenzeichen *n*	trademark	marque déposée *f*	marchio *m*	
emendamento di legge (I)	Gesetzesänderung *f*	amendment of a law	amendement d'une loi *m*	—	enmienda de la ley *f*
emisión (Es)	Emission *f*	issue	émission *f*	emissione *f*	—
emisión de acciones (Es)	Aktienemission *f*	share issue	émission d'actions *f*	emissione di azioni *f*	—
emisión parcial (Es)	Tranche *f*	tranche	tranche *f*	tranche *f*	—
Emission (D)	—	issue	émission *f*	emissione *f*	emisión *f*
émission (F)	Emission *f*	issue	—	emissione *f*	emisión *f*
émission d'actions (F)	Aktienemission *f*	share issue	—	emissione di azioni *f*	emisión de acciones *f*
émission publicitaire télévisée (F)	Fernsehwerbung *f*	television advertising	—	pubblicità televisiva *f*	publicidad televisiva *f*
emissione (I)	Emission *f*	issue	émission *f*	—	emisión *f*
emissione di assegno a vuoto (I)	Scheckbetrug *m*	cheque fraud	irrégularité en matière de chèque *f*	—	falsificación de cheques *f*
emissione di azioni (I)	Aktienemission *f*	share issue	émission d'actions *f*	—	emisión de acciones *f*
emissione di tratte incrociate (I)	Wechselreiterei *f*	kiteflying	tirage d'une traite de cavalerie *m*	—	libramiento de letras cruzadas *m*
Emissions-begrenzung (D)	—	issuing restriction	limitation d'émission *f*	limitazione d'emissione *f*	limitación de emisiones *f*
Emissionsgeschäft (D)	—	investment business	opération succédant à une émission *f*	operazione d'emissione *f*	operación de emisión *f*
Emissionskurs (D)	—	price of issue	cours d'émission *m*	prezzo d'emissione *m*	tipo de emisión *m*
émoluments (F)	Bezüge *pl*	earnings	—	entrate *f pl*	retribuciones *f pl*
empaque (Es)	Verpackungs-material *n*	packing material	matériel d'emballage *m*	materiale d'imballaggio *m*	—
Empfänger (D)	—	receiver	destinataire *m*	destinatario *m*	destinatario *m*
Empfangs-berechtigung (D)	—	authorization to receive	autorité pour recevoir *f*	autorizzazione di ricezione *f*	autorización de recibimiento *f*
Empfangs-bestätigung (D)	—	acknowledgement of receipt	accusé de réception *m*	ricevuta *f*	recibo *m*
Empfehlung (D)	—	recommendation	recommandation *f*	raccomandazione *f*	recomendación *f*
Empfehlungs-schreiben (D)	—	letter of recommendation	lettre de recommandation *f*	lettera di raccomandazione *f*	carta de recomendación *f*
empirical market research (E)	empirische Marktforschung *f*	—	étude de marché empirique *f*	ricerca di mercato empirica *f*	estudio del mercado empírico *m*
empirische Marktforschung (D)	—	empirical market research	étude de marché empirique *f*	ricerca di mercato empirica *f*	estudio del mercado empírico *m*
empleado¹ (Es)	Arbeitnehmer *m*	employee	salarié *m*	prestatore d'opera *m*	—
empleado² (Es)	Angestellter *m*	employee	employé *m*	impiegato *m*	—
emplear (Es)	anstellen	employ	employer	impiegare	—
empleo¹ (Es)	Stellung *f*	position	position *f*	posizione *f*	—
empleo² (Es)	Anstellung *f*	employment	emploi *m*	impiego *m*	—
empleo parcial (Es)	Teilzeit-beschäftigung *f*	part-time employment	emploi à temps partiel *m*	occupazione part-time *f*	—
empleo total (Es)	Vollbeschäftigung *f*	full employment	plein emploi *m*	piena occupazione *f*	—
emploi (F)	Anstellung *f*	employment	—	impiego *m*	empleo *m*
emploi à temps partiel (F)	Teilzeit-beschäftigung *f*	part-time employment	—	occupazione part-time *f*	empleo parcial *m*

	D	E	F	I	Es
emploi d'ordinateurs (F)	Computereinsatz *m*	use of a computer	—	impiego di computer *m*	utilización de ordenadores *f*
emploi vacant (F)	Arbeitsnachweis *m*	employment vacancies	—	informazioni sui posti vacanti *f pl*	servicio de colocación *m*
employ (E)	anstellen	—	employer	impiegare	emplear
employé (F)	Angestellte *pl*	employee	—	impiegati *m pl*	empleado *m*
employee[1] (E)	Arbeitnehmer *m*	—	salarié *m*	prestatore d'opera *m*	empleado *m*
employee[2] (E)	Angestellter *m*	—	employé *m*	impiegato *m*	empleado *m*
employee-employer relationship (E)	Arbeitsverhältnis *n*	—	rapport de travail *m*	rapporto di lavoro *m*	relación laboral *f*
employee-employer relationship on a trial basis (E)	Arbeitsverhältnis auf Probe *n*	—	contrat de travail convenu à l'essai *m*	rapporto di lavoro in prova *m*	relación laboral a prueba *f*
employer (E)	Arbeitgeber *m*	—	employeur *m*	datore di lavoro *m*	patrón *m*
employer (F)	anstellen	employ	—	impiegare	emplear
employers' association (E)	Unternehmer- verband *m*	—	association des chefs d'entreprise *f*	unione degli imprenditori *f*	asociación empresarial *f*
employeur (F)	Arbeitgeber *m*	employer	—	datore di lavoro *m*	patrón *m*
employment[1] (E)	Anstellung *f*	—	emploi *m*	impiego *m*	empleo *m*
employment[2] (E)	Beschäftigung *f*	—	occupation *f*	occupazione *f*	ocupación *f*
employment agency (E)	Arbeitsvermittlung *f*	—	bureau de placement *m*	ufficio di collocamento *m*	agencia laboral *f*
employment policy (E)	Beschäftigungs- politik *f*	—	politique d'emploi *f*	politica d'occupazione *f*	política de empleo *f*
employment protection (E)	Arbeitsschutz *m*	—	protection sociale du travail *f*	tutela del lavoro *f*	protección del trabajo *f*
employment theory (E)	Beschäftigungs- theorie *f*	—	théorie d'emploi *f*	teoria dell'occupazione *f*	teoría del empleo *f*
employment vacancies (E)	Arbeitsnachweis *m*	—	emploi vacant *m*	informazioni sui posti vacanti *f pl*	servicio de colocación *m*
empresa (Es)	Firma *f*	company	entreprise *f*	impresa *f*	—
empresa agrícola (Es)	Agrarbetrieb *m*	agricultural enterprise	entreprise agricole *f*	azienda agricola *f*	—
empresa competidora (Es)	Konkurrenzfirma *f*	competing firm	maison concurrente *f*	ditta concorrente *f*	—
empresa competitoria (Es)	Konkurrenz- unternehmen *n*	competitive undertaking	entreprise concurrente *f*	impresa concorrente *f*	—
empresa de beneficio común (Es)	gemeinnütziges Unternehmen *n*	public institution	entreprise d'utilité publique *f*	impresa di utilità pubblica *f*	—
empresa de explotación (Es)	Betriebsgesellschaft *f*	operating company	entreprise d'exploitation *f*	società d'esercizio *f*	—
empresa dominante (Es)	herrschendes Unternehmen *n*	controlling company	entreprise dirigeante *f*	impresa controllante *f*	—
empresa estatal (Es)	Regiebetrieb *m*	publicly owned enterprise	établissement en régie *m*	gestione in economia *f*	—
empresa ficticia (Es)	Briefkastenfirma *f*	bubble company	entreprise fantôme *f*	società bucalettere *f*	—
empresa industrial (Es)	gewerblicher Betrieb *m*	industrial undertaking	établissement commercial *m*	azienda com- merciale *f*/azienda industriale *f*	—
empresa multinacional (Es)	multinationale Unternehmen *n*	multinational enterprise	entreprises multinationales *f pl*	imprese multinazionali *f pl*	—
empresa pública[1] (Es)	öffentliche Betriebe *pl*	public sector industrial enterpises	entreprises publiques *f pl*	aziende pubbliche *f pl*	—
empresa pública[2] (Es)	öffentliche Unternehmen *n*	public enterprises	entreprises publiques *f pl*	imprese pubbliche *f pl*	—
empresario[1] (Es)	Unternehmer *m*	entrepreneur	entrepreneur *m*	imprenditore *m*	—
empresario[2] (Es)	Unternehmen *n*	enterprise	entreprise *f*	impresa *f*	—
empresas públicas (Es)	staatliche Betriebe *pl*	state-owned enterprise	entreprise publique *f*	aziende statali *f pl*	—
empréstito (Es)	Anleihe *f*	loan	emprunt *m*	prestito *m*	—
empréstito estatal (Es)	Staatsanleihen *pl*	government loan	emprunt d'Etat *m*	titoli pubblici *m pl*	—
empréstito exterior (Es)	Auslandsanleihe *f*	foreign bond	emprunt extérieur *m*	prestito estero *m*	—
empréstito municipal (Es)	Kommunalanleihen *pl*	local authorities loan	emprunt communal *m*	prestiti comunali *m pl*	—

	D	E	F	I	Es
empréstito por anualidades¹ (Es)	Rentenanleihe f	annuity bonds	effet public m	prestito a reddito fisso m	—
empréstito por anualidades² (Es)	Annuitätendarlehen n	annuity loan	prêt amortissable par annuités m	prestito rimborsabile in annualità m	—
empréstito sobre obligaciones (Es)	Obligationsanleihe f	debenture loan	emprunt obligataire m	prestito obbligazionario m	—
emprunt¹ (F)	Anleihe f	loan	—	prestito m	empréstito m
emprunt² (F)	Geldaufnahme f	raising of money	—	accensione di un mutuo f	dinero tomado a préstamo m
emprunt communal (F)	Kommunalanleihen pl	local authorities loan	—	prestiti comunali m pl	empréstito municipal m
emprunt d'Etat (F)	Staatsanleihen pl	government loan	—	titoli pubblici m pl	empréstito estatal m
emprunt extérieur (F)	Auslandsanleihe f	foreign bond	—	prestito estero m	empréstito exterior m
emprunt obligataire (F)	Obligationsanleihe f	debenture loan	—	prestito obbligazionario m	empréstito sobre obligaciones m
empuje innovador (Es)	Innovationsschub m	technology push	animation d'innovation f	spinta innovativa f	—
enajenación (Es)	Veräußerung f	sale/alienation	aliénation f	alienazione f	—
en almacén (Es)	auf Lager	in stock	en stock	in magazzino	—
encabezamiento (Es)	Briefkopf m	letterhead	en-tête m	intestazione f	—
encarecimiento (Es)	Verteuerung f	rise in price	enchérissement m	rincaro m	—
encart non broché à la revue (F)	Beilage f	supplement	—	inserto m	suplemento m
enchérissement (F)	Verteuerung f	rise in price	—	rincaro m	encarecimiento m
enclosure (E)	Anlage f	—	pièce jointe f	allegato m	anexo m
encobro (Es)	Inkasso n	collection	recouvrement m	incasso m	—
en comisión (Es)	auf Kommissionsbasis	on a commission basis	en commission	in base commissionaria	—
en commission (F)	auf Kommissionsbasis	on a commission basis	—	in base commissionaria	en comisión
encouragement à l'exportation (F)	Ausfuhrförderung f	measures to encourage exports	—	promozione delle esportazioni f	fomento de la exportació m
encouragement à la vente (F)	Verkaufsförderung f	sales promotion	—	promozione di vendita f	promoción de las ventas f
encourir une peine (F)	straffällig	liable to prosecution	—	passibile di pena	criminal
encuesta (Es)	Befragung f	poll	enquête f	interrogazione f	—
encuesta entre los clientes (Es)	Kundenbefragung f	customer survey	enquête parmi les clients f	intervista ai clienti f	—
encuesta por muestreo (Es)	Stichproben-erhebung f	sample survey	enquête par sondage f	prelievo di campioni m	—
en deux exemplaires (F)	in zweifacher Ausfertigung	in duplicate	—	in due copie	por duplicado
en la fecha fijada (Es)	termingerecht	on schedule	dans les délais	puntuale	—
Endabnehmer (D)	—	ultimate buyer	preneur final m	acquirente finale m	comprador final m
endettement (F)	Verschuldung f	indebtedness	—	indebitamento m	endeudamiento m
endettement de l'Etat (F)	Staatsverschuldung f	state indebtedness	—	debito pubblico m	endeudamiento público m
endettement effectif (F)	effektive Verschuldung f	real indebtedness	—	indebitamento effettivo m	endeudamiento efectivo m
endettement net (F)	Nettoverschuldung f	net indebtedness	—	indebitamento netto m	deuda neta m
endeudamiento (Es)	Verschuldung f	indebtedness	endettement m	indebitamento m	—
endeudamiento efectivo (Es)	effektive Verschuldung f	real indebtedness	endettement effectif m	indebitamento effettivo m	—
endeudamiento público (Es)	Staatsverschuldung f	state indebtedness	endettement de l'Etat m	debito pubblico m	—
Endkontrolle (D)	—	final control	contrôle final m	controllo finale m	control final m
end of a quarter (E)	Quartalsende n	—	fin de trimestre f	fine trimestre f	final del trimestre m
end of the month (E)	Ultimo n	—	fin de mois f	fine mese m	fin de mes m
endommagement (F)	Beschädigung f	damage	—	danno m	deterioración f
endoso (Es)	Indossament n	endorsement	endossement m	girata f	—
endossement (F)	Indossament n	endorsement	—	girata f	endoso m

	D	E	F	I	Es
endowment (E)	Dotierung *f*	—	dotation *f*	dotazione *f*	dotación *f*
Endprodukt (D)	—	finished product	produit final *m*	prodotto finito *m*	producto final *m*
Endverbraucher (D)	—	ultimate consumer	consommateur final *m*	consumatore *m*	consumidor final *m*
en efectivo (Es)	in bar	in cash	comptant	in contanti	—
en el extranjero (Es)	im Ausland	abroad	à l'étranger	all'estero	—
en el término de (Es)	binnen	within	dans le délai de	entro	—
energía (Es)	Strom *m*	electric power	énergie électrique *f*	enrgia elettrica *f*	—
energia elettrica (I)	Strom *m*	electric power	énergie électrique *f*	—	energía *f*
energía eólica (Es)	Windenergie *f*	eolian energy	énergie éolienne *f*	energia eolica *f*	—
energia eolica (I)	Windenergie *f*	eolian energy	énergie éolienne *f*	—	energía eólica *f*
energía nuclear (Es)	Kernenergie *f*	nuclear energy	énergie nucléaire *f*	energia nucleare *f*	—
energia nucleare (I)	Kernenergie *f*	nuclear energy	énergie nucléaire *f*	—	energía nuclear *f*
energía primaria (Es)	Primärenergie *f*	primary energy	énergie primaire *f*	energia primaria *f*	—
energia primaria (I)	Primärenergie *f*	primary energy	énergie primaire *f*	—	energía primaria *f*
energia secondaria (I)	Sekundärenergie *f*	secondary energy	énergie secondaire *f*	—	energía secundaria *f*
energía secundaria (Es)	Sekundärenergie *f*	secondary energy	énergie secondaire *f*	energia secondaria *f*	—
énergie électrique (F)	Strom *m*	electric power	—	energia elettrica *f*	energía *f*
énergie éolienne (F)	Windenergie *f*	eolian energy	—	energia eolica *f*	energía eólica *f*
Energiekrise (D)	—	energy crisis	crise de l'énergie *f*	crisi energetica *f*	crisis energética *f*
énergie nucléaire (F)	Kernenergie *f*	nuclear energy	—	energia nucleare *f*	energía nuclear *f*
énergie primaire (F)	Primärenergie *f*	primary energy	—	energia primaria *f*	energía primaria *f*
énergie secondaire (F)	Sekundärenergie *f*	secondary energy	—	energia secondaria *f*	energía secundaria *f*
Energieversorgung (D)	—	energy supply	approvisionnement en énergie *m*	approvvigionamento d'energia *m*	abastecimiento energético *m*
energy crisis (E)	Energiekrise *f*	—	crise de l'énergie *f*	crisi energetica *f*	crisis energética *f*
energy supply (E)	Energieversorgung *f*	—	approvisionnement en énergie *m*	approvvigionamento d'energia *m*	abastecimiento energético *m*
enforcement (E)	Vollstreckung *f*	—	exécution *f*	esecuzione *f*	ejecución *f*
Engagement (D)	—	engagement/commitment	engagement *m*	impegno *m*/assunzione *f*	compromiso *m*
engagement (E)	Engagement *n*	—	engagement *m*	impegno *m*/assunzione *f*	compromiso *m*
engagement¹ (F)	Engagement *n*	engagement/commitment	—	impegno *m*/assunzione *f*	compromiso *m*
engagement² (F)	Obligo *n*	liability	—	obbligo *m*	obligación *f*
engagement de garantie (F)	Garantieverpflichtung *f*	guarantee obligation	—	obbligo di garanzia *m*	obligación de garantía *f*
engaño¹ (Es)	Schwindel *m*	swindle	tromperie *f*	truffa *f*	—
engaño² (Es)	Täuschung *f*	deceit	tromperie *f*	inganno *m*	—
engineer (E)	Ingenieur *m*	—	ingénieur *m*	ingegnere *m*	ingeniero *m*
engineering department (E)	technische Abteilung *f*	—	service technique *m*	reparto tecnico *m*	departamento técnico *m*
enmienda de la ley (Es)	Gesetzesänderung *f*	amendment of a law	amendement d'une loi *m*	emendamento di legge *m*	
en nombre propio (Es)	im eigenen Namen	in one's own name	en nom propre	per nome proprio	—
en nom propre (F)	im eigenen Namen	in one's own name	—	per nome proprio	en nombre propio
en particular (Es)	im einzelnen	in particular	en particulier	in dettaglio	—
en particulier (F)	im einzelnen	in particular	—	in dettaglio	en particular
en recommandé (F)	Einschreiben *n*	Registered	—	raccomandata *f*	certificado *m*
enquête¹ (F)	Interview *n*	interview	—	intervista *f*	entrevista *f*
enquête² (F)	Befragung *f*	poll	—	interrogazione *f*	encuesta *f*
enquête par sondage (F)	Stichprobenerhebung *f*	sample survey	—	prelievo di campioni *m*	encuesta por muestreo *f*
enquête parmi les clients (F)	Kundenbefragung *f*	customer survey	—	intervista ai clienti *f*	encuesta entre los clientes *f*
ensayo (Es)	Probe *f*	trial/sample	essai *m*/échantillon *m*	prova *f*/campione *m*	—

	D	E	F	I	Es
enseigne commerciale (F)	Firmenschild *n*	company's name plate	—	insegna dell'impresa *f*	letrero de establecimiento *m*
en stock (F)	auf Lager	in stock	—	in magazzino	en almacén
ente (I)	Körperschaft *f*	corporation	collectivité *f*	—	corporación *f*
Enteignung (D)	—	expropriation	expropriation *f*	espropriazione *f*	expropiación *f*
enterprise (E)	Unternehmen *n*	—	entreprise *f*	impresa *f*	empresario *m*
en-tête (F)	Briefkopf *m*	letterhead	—	intestazione *f*	encabezamiento *m*
entità (I)	Umfang *m*	volume	volume *m*	—	volumen *m*/ dimensión *f*
entità dell'inventario (I)	Bestandsgröße *f*	stock variable	stock variable *m*	—	magnitud *f*
Entladungskosten (D)	—	discharging expenses	coûts de déchargement *m pl*	spese di scaricamento *f pl*	gastos de descargo *m pl*
Entlassung (D)	—	dismissal	licenciement *m*	licenziamento *m*	despido *m*
Entlastung (D)	—	discharge	décharge *f*	sgravio *m*	desgravamen *m*
entrada (Es)	Eintrittskarte *f*	admission ticket	billet *m*	biglietto d'ingresso *m*	—
entrada de mercancías (Es)	Wareneingang *m*	arrival of goods	entrée de marchandises *f*	entrata merci *f*	—
entrada en el mercado (Es)	Markteintritt *m*	entry into the market	entrée dans le marché *f*	apertura di mercato *f*	—
entrada gratuita (Es)	Freikarte *f*	free ticket	billet de faveur *m*	biglietto gratuito *m*	—
entraînement (F)	Einarbeitung *f*	vocational adjustment	—	periodo d'adattamento *m*	entrenamiento *m*
entrata merci (I)	Wareneingang *m*	arrival of goods	entrée de marchandises *f*	—	entrada de mercancías *f*
entrate¹ (I)	Bezüge *pl*	earnings	émoluments *m pl*	—	retribuciones *f pl*
entrate² (I)	Einnahmen *pl*	receipts	revenu *m*	—	ingresos *m pl*
entrate pubbliche¹ (I)	Staatseinnahmen *pl*	public revenue	recettes de l'Etat *f pl*	—	ingresos del Estado *m pl*
entrate pubbliche² (I)	öffentliche Einnahmen *pl*	public revenues	recettes publiques *f pl*	—	ingresos públicos *m pl*
entrée¹ (F)	Input *m*	input	—	input *m*	insumo *m*
entrée² (F)	Zugang *m*	access	—	accesso *m*	acceso *m*
entrée dans le marché (F)	Markteintritt *m*	entry into the market	—	apertura di mercato *f*	entrada en el mercado *f*
entrée de marchandises (F)	Wareneingang *m*	arrival of goods	—	entrata merci *f*	entrada de mercancías *f*
entrega (Es)	Übergabe *f*	delivery	remise *f*	consegna *f*	—
entrega contra reembolso (Es)	Lieferung gegen Nachnahme *f*	cash on delivery	livraison contre remboursement *f*	consegna contro assegno *f*	—
entrega de reposición (Es)	Ersatzlieferung *f*	substitute delivery	livraison de remplacement *f*	fornitura di compensazione *f*	—
entrega inmediata (Es)	sofortige Lieferung *f*	immediate delivery	livraison immédiate *f*	consegna immediata *f*	—
entrega parcial (Es)	Teillieferung *f*	partial delivery	livraison partielle *f*	fornitura parziale *f*	—
entregar (Es)	abliefern	hand over	livrer	consegnare	—
entrega urgente (Es)	Eilzustellung *f*	express delivery	remise par exprès *f*	consegna per espresso *f*	—
entrenamiento¹ (Es)	Einarbeitung *f*	vocational adjustment	entraînement *m*	periodo d'adattamento *m*	—
entrenamiento² (Es)	Trainee *m*	trainee	apprenti *m*	trainee *m*	—
entreposage¹ (F)	Lagerverwaltung *f*	stockkeeping	—	amministrazione del magazzino *f*	administración de almacén *f*
entreposage² (F)	Lagerhaltung *f*	stockkeeping	—	magazzinaggio *m*	almacenaje *m*
entreposage³ (F)	Einlagerung *f*	storage	—	immagazzinamento *m*	almacenamiento *m*
entrepôt de distribution (F)	Auslieferungslager *n*	distribution centre	—	deposito di consegna *m*	almacén de entregas *m*
entrepreneur (E)	Unternehmer *m*	—	entrepreneur *m*	imprenditore *m*	empresario *m*
entrepreneur (F)	Unternehmer *m*	entrepreneur	—	imprenditore *m*	empresario *m*
entrepreneur débutant (F)	Jungunternehmer *m*	young businessman	—	imprenditore giovane *m*	joven empresario *m*

	D	E	F	I	Es
entrepreneurial culture (E)	Unternehmenskultur *f*	—	culture de l'entreprise *f*	cultura imprenditoriale *f*	cultura empresarial *f*
entrepreneurial income (E)	Unternehmerlohn *m*	—	rémunération de l'entrepreneur *f*	retribuzione dell'imprenditore *f*	remuneración del empresario *f*
entreprise[1] (F)	Firma *f*	company	—	impresa *f*	empresa *f*
entreprise[2] (F)	Unternehmen *n*	enterprise	—	impresa *f*	empresario *m*
entreprise agricole (F)	Agrarbetrieb *m*	agricultural enterprise	—	azienda agricola *f*	empresa agrícola *f*
entreprise concurrente (F)	Konkurrenzunternehmen *n*	competitive undertaking	—	impresa concorrente *f*	empresa competitiva *f*
entreprise d'exploitation (F)	Betriebsgesellschaft *f*	operating company	—	società d'esercizio *f*	empresa de explotación *f*
entreprise d'utilité publique (F)	gemeinnütziges Unternehmen *n*	public institution	—	impresa di utilità pubblica *f*	empresa de beneficio común *f*
entreprise dirigeante (F)	herrschendes Unternehmen *n*	controlling company	—	impresa controllante *f*	empresa dominante *f*
entreprise fantôme (F)	Briefkastenfirma *f*	bubble company	—	società bucalettere *f*	empresa ficticia *f*
entreprise industrielle (F)	Industriebetrieb *m*	industrial enterprise	—	azienda industriale *f*	establecimiento industrial *m*
entreprise publique (F)	staatliche Betriebe *pl*	state-owned enterprises	—	aziende statali *f pl*	empresas públicas *f pl*
entreprises multinationales (F)	multinationale Unternehmen *n*	multinational enterprises	—	imprese multinazionali *f pl*	empresa multinacional *f*
entreprises publiques[1] (F)	öffentliche Betriebe *pl*	public sector industrial enterprises	—	aziende pubbliche *f pl*	empresa pública *f*
entreprises publiques[2] (F)	öffentliche Unternehmen *n*	public enterprise	—	imprese pubbliche *f pl*	empresa pública *f*
entretien (F)	Unterredung *f*	discussion	—	colloquio *m*	conversación *f*
entrevista (Es)	Interview *n*	interview	enquête *f*	intervista *f*	—
entro (I)	binnen	within	dans le délai de	—	en el término de
entro il termine convenuto (I)	fristgerecht	timely	dans les délais	—	dentro del plazo fijado
entry into the market (E)	Markteintritt *m*	—	entrée dans le marché *f*	apertura di mercato *f*	entrada en el mercado *f*
Entschädigung (D)	—	compensation/ indemnification	indemnité *f*	indennità *f*	indemnización *f*/pago de compensación *m*
Entsorgung (D)	—	waste disposal	dépollution *f*	smaltimento *m*	eliminación *f*
Entwicklung (D)	—	development	développement *m*	sviluppo *m*	desarrollo *m*
Entwicklungshilfe (D)	—	development aid	aide au développement *f*	aiuto ai paesi in via di sviluppo *m*	ayuda al desarrollo *f*
Entwicklungskosten (D)	—	development costs	coûts de développement *m pl*	costi di sviluppo *m pl*	gastos de desarrollo *m pl*
Entwurf (D)	—	draft	projet *m*	progetto *m*	proyecto *m*
envelope[1] (E)	Briefumschlag *m*	—	enveloppe de lettre *f*	busta *f*	sobre *m*
envelope[2] (E)	Kuvert *n*	—	enveloppe *f*	busta *f*	sobre *m*
enveloppe (F)	Kuvert *n*	envelope	—	busta *f*	sobre *m*
enveloppe de lettre (F)	Briefumschlag *m*	envelope	—	busta *f*	sobre *m*
en vigor (Es)	in Kraft	effective/in force	en vigueur	in vigore	—
en vigueur (F)	in Kraft	effective/in force	—	in vigore	en vigor
envío[1] (Es)	Zustellung *f*	delivery	remise *f*	notifica *f*/recapito *m*	—
envío[2] (Es)	Versand *m*	dispatch	expédition *f*	spedizione *f*	—
envío[3] (Es)	Sendung *f*	consignment	envoi *m*	spedizione *f*	—
envío con valor declarado (Es)	Wertsendung *f*	consignment with value declared	envoi avec valeur déclarée *m*	spedizione con valore dichiarato *f*	—
envío de mercancías (Es)	Warensendung *f*	consignment of goods	expédition de marchandises *f*	spedizione di merci *f*	—
envío de muestras (Es)	Mustersendung *f*	sample consignment	envoi d'échantillons *m*	spedizione di campioni *f*	—
envío de prueba (Es)	Probelieferung *f*	trial shipment	livraison à titre d'essai *f*	fornitura a titolo di prova *f*	—
envío incompleto (Es)	Minderlieferung *f*	short delivery	livraison en quantité inférieure *f*	fornitura ridotta *f*	—
envío para inspección (Es)	Ansichtssendung *f*	consignment on approval	envoi à condition *m*	campione per esame *m*	—

	D	E	F	I	Es
envío perdido (Es)	verlorengegangene Sendung f	lost shipment	envoi perdu m	spedizione andata persa f	—
envío postal colectivo (Es)	Postwurfsendung f	printed papers or samples of merchandise posted in bulk	envoi publicitaire collectif f	spedizione postale cumulativa di stampati f	—
environmental pollution (E)	Umweltverschmutzung f	—	pollution de l'environnement f	inquinamento dell'ambiente m	contaminación del medio ambiente f
environmentally aware (E)	umweltbewußt	—	conscient de la réalité écologique	con rispetto dell'ambiente	consciente del medio ambiente
envoi (F)	Sendung f	consignment	—	spedizione f	envío m
envoi à condition (F)	Ansichtssendung f	consignment on approval	—	campione per esame m	envío para inspección m
envoi avec valeur déclarée (F)	Wertsendung f	consignment with value declared	—	spedizione con valore dichiarato f	envío con valor declarado m
envoi d'échantillons (F)	Mustersendung f	sample consignment	—	spedizione di campioni f	envío de muestras m
envoi par groupage (F)	Sammelladung f	collective consignment	—	carico a collettame m	carga colectiva f
envoi perdu (F)	verlorengegangene Sendung f	lost shipment	—	spedizione andata persa f	envío perdido m
envoi publicitaire collectif (F)	Postwurfsendung f	printed papers or samples of merchandise posted in bulk	—	spedizione postale cumulativa di stampati f	envío postal colectivo m
eolian energy (E)	Windenergie f	—	énergie éolienne f	energia eolica f	energía eólica f
épargne (F)	Ersparnis f	savings	—	risparmio m	ahorro m
épargne forcée (F)	Zwangssparen n	compulsory saving	—	risparmio coatto m	ahorro forzoso m
équilibrage du budget (F)	Budgetausgleich m	balancing of the budget	—	pareggio di bilancio m	balance del presupuesto m
équilibre (F)	Gleichgewicht n	balance	—	equilibrio m	equilibrio m
equilibrio (Es)	Gleichgewicht n	balance	équilibre m	equilibrio m	—
equilibrio (I)	Gleichgewicht n	balance	équilibre m	—	equilibrio m
equilibrio della bilancia dei pagamenti (I)	Zahlungsbilanzgleichgewicht n	equilibrium of the balance of payments	balance des payements équilibrée f	—	balanza de pagos equilibrada f
equilibrium of the balance of payments (E)	Zahlungsbilanzgleichgewicht n	—	balance des payements équilibrée f	equilibrio della bilancia dei pagamenti m	balanza de pagos equilibrada f
equilibrium price (E)	Gleichgewichtspreis m	—	prix équilibré m	prezzo d'equilibrio m	precio de equilibrio m
équipe de nuit (F)	Nachtschicht f	night shift	—	turno notturno m	turno de noche m
équipe de vente (F)	Verkaufsstab m	sales staff	—	staff di venditori m	equipo de venta m
équipe¹ (F)	Team n	team	—	équipe f	equipo m
équipe² (F)	Mannschaft f	team/crew	—	équipe f/ equipaggio m	equipo m/ tripulación f
équipe¹ (I)	Mannschaft f	team/crew	équipe f/équipage m	—	equipo m/ tripulación f
équipe² (I)	Team n	team	équipe f	—	equipo m
equipo¹ (Es)	Mannschaft f	team/crew	équipe f/équipage m	équipe f/equipaggio m	—
equipo² (Es)	Team n	team	équipe f	équipe f	—
equipo de venta (Es)	Verkaufsstab m	sales staff	équipe de vente f	staff di venditori m	—
equity capital (E)	Eigenkapital n	—	capital propre m	capitale proprio m	capital propio m
equivalent (E)	Gegenwert m	—	contre-valeur f	controvalore m	contravalor m
Erben (D)	—	heirs	héritiers m pl	eredi m pl	heredero m
Erbengemeinschaft (D)	—	community of heirs	communaute d'héritiers f	comunità degli eredi f	comunidad sucesoria f
Erbschaft (D)	—	inheritance	héritage m	eredità f	herencia f
Erbschaftsteuer (D)	—	inheritance tax	impôt sur les successions m	imposta di successione f	impuesto sobre sucesiones m
Erbstreit (D)	—	dispute concerning an inheritance	action successorale f	causa ereditaria f	litigio hereditario m
Erdgas (D)	—	natural gas	gaz naturel m	gas naturale m	gas natural m
Erdöl (D)	—	mineral oil	pétrole m	petrolio m	crudo m
eredi (I)	Erben pl	heirs	héritiers m pl	—	heredero m
eredità (I)	Erbschaft f	inheritance	héritage m	—	herencia f

	D	E	F	I	Es
Erfolgskonto (D)	—	profit account	compte de résultats *m*	conto profitti *m*	cuenta de beneficios y pérdidas *f*
erfolgsorientiert (D)	—	success-oriented	orienté vers le succès	orientato al successo	orientado hacia el éxito
Erfüllung (D)	—	compliance	acquittement *m*	adempimento *m*	cumplimiento *m*
Ergebnis (D)	—	result	résultat *m*	risultato *m*	resultado *m*
erkennen (D)	—	recognize	reconnaître	riconoscere	reconocer
Erklärung (D)	—	explanation/ declaration	explication *f*/ déclaration *f*	spiegazione *f*/ dichiarazione *f*	explicación *f*/ declaración *f*
Erlaubnis (D)	—	permission	permission *f*	permesso *m*	permiso *m*
Erlös (D)	—	proceeds	produit des ventes *m*	ricavo *m*	beneficio *m*
ermäßigte Tarife (D)	—	reduced tariffs	tarifs réduits *m pl*	tariffe ridotte *f pl*	tarifas reducidas *f pl*
Ermäßigung (D)	—	reduction	réduction *f*	riduzione *f*	reducción *f*
Ernennung (D)	—	apointment	nomination *f*	nomina *f*	nombramiento *m*
Eröffnungsbeschluß (D)	—	order opening a trial	arrêt de mise en accusation *m*	decreto di citazione in giudizio *m*	acuerdo de apertura *m*
Eröffnungsbilanz (D)	—	opening balance sheet	bilan d'ouverture *m*	bilancio d'apertura *m*	balance inicial *m*
erreur d'addition (F)	Additionsfehler *m*	adding mistake	—	errore di addizione *m*	error de adición *m*
erreur de calcul (F)	Rechenfehler *m*	miscalculation	—	errore di calcolo *m*	error de cálculo *m*
erreur de comptabilité (F)	Buchungsfehler *m*	bookkeeping error	—	errore di contabilità *m*	error contable *m*
erreur de droit (F)	Rechtsirrtum *m*	mistake of law	—	errore di diritto *m*	error de derecho *m*
erreur de transcription (F)	Übertragungsfehler *m*	transcription error	—	errore di trascrizione *m*	error de transcripción *m*
error (Es)	Fehler *m*	mistake	faute *f*	errore *m*	—
error contable (Es)	Buchungsfehler *m*	bookkeeping error	erreur de comptabilité *f*	errore di contabilità *m*	—
error de adición (Es)	Additionsfehler *m*	adding mistake	erreur d'addition *f*	errore di addizione *m*	—
error de cálculo (Es)	Rechenfehler *m*	miscalculation	erreur de calcul *f*	errore di calcolo *m*	—
error de derecho (Es)	Rechtsirrtum *m*	mistake of law	erreur de droit *m*	errore di diritto *m*	—
error de transcripción (Es)	Übertragungsfehler *m*	transcription error	erreur de transcription *f*	errore di trascrizione *m*	
errore (I)	Fehler *m*	mistake	faute *f*	—	error *m*
errore di addizione (I)	Additionsfehler *m*	adding mistake	erreur d'addition *f*	—	error de adición *m*
errore di calcolo (I)	Rechenfehler *m*	miscalculation	erreur de calcul *f*	—	error de cálculo *m*
errore di contabilità (I)	Buchungsfehler *m*	bookkeeping error	erreur de comptabilité *f*	—	error contable *m*
errore di diritto (I)	Rechtsirrtum *m*	mistake of law	erreur de droit *m*	—	error de derecho *m*
errore di trascrizione (I)	Übertragungsfehler *m*	transcription error	erreur de transcription *f*	—	error de transcripción *m*
errors excepted (E)	Irrtum vorbehalten	—	sauf erreur	salvo errore	salvo error
Ersatzkauf (D)	—	substitute purchase	achat de remplacement *m*	acquisto di compensazione *m*	compra de sustitución *f*
Ersatzlieferung (D)	—	substitute delivery	livraison de remplacement *f*	fornitura di compensazione *f*	entrega de reposición *f*
Ersatzteil (D)	—	spare part	pièce de rechange *f*	pezzo di ricambio *m*	pieza de recambio *f*
Ersparnis (D)	—	savings	épargne *f*	risparmio *m*	ahorro *m*
erstklassig (D)	—	first class	de première qualité	di prima categoria	de primera calidad
Erstversicherer (D)	—	direct insurer	assureur direct *m*	assicuratore diretto *m*	primer asegurador *m*
Ertrag (D)	—	income/earnings	rendement *m*/ revenu *m*	reddito *m*/ rendimento *m*	rendimiento *m*/renta *f*
Ertragsbeteiligung (D)	—	participation in profits	participation aux bénéfices *f*	partecipazione al reddito *f*	participación en los resultados *f*
Ertragsfaktor (D)	—	income factor	facteur productif *m*	fattore reddito *m*	factor de beneficio *m*
Ertragskraft (D)	—	earning capacity	force productive *f*	redditività *f*	rentabilidad *f*
Ertragslage (D)	—	earning situation	niveau du rendement *m*	situazione economica *f*	situación del beneficio *f*
Ertragsrechnung (D)	—	profit and loss account	solde net de l'exploitation *m*	conto economico *m*	cuenta de ganancias *f pl*

	D	E	F	I	Es
Ertragsteuer (D)	—	tax on income	impôt assis sur le produit *m*	imposta cedolare *f*/ imposta sul reddito *f*	impuesto sobre beneficios *m*
Ertragswert (D)	—	capitalized value	valeur d'une chose *m*ésurée à son rendement *f*	valore del reddito *m*	valor del rendimiento *m*
Erwerbsperson (D)	—	gainfully employed person	personne active *f*	persona attiva *f*	persona en activo *f*
Erwerbsquote (D)	—	activity rate	proportion de la population active *f*	quota della popolazione attiva *f*	proporción de la población activa *f*
erwerbstätig (D)	—	gainfully employed	actif	attivo	activo
Erwerbstätiger (D)	—	gainfully employed person	personne ayant un emploi *f*	persona attiva *f*	persona activa *f*
Erwerbsunfähigkeit (D)	—	disability for work	incapacité d'exercer toute activité professionnelle *f*	inabilità al lavoro *f*	incapacidad profesional *f*
Erzeuger (D)	—	manufacturer	producteur *m*	produttore *m*	productor *m*
Erzeugerpreis (D)	—	producer price	prix à la production *m*	prezzo di fabbrica *m*	precio de producción *m*
Erzeugerpreisindex (D)	—	producer price index	indice des prix à la production *m*	indice dei prezzi di fabbrica *m*	índice de precios de producción *m*
Erzeugnis (D)	—	product	produit *m*	prodotto *m*	producto *m*
esame (I)	Examen *n*	examination	examen *m*	—	examen *m*
escalonado (Es)	gestaffelt	graduated	progressif	differenziato	—
escaparate (Es)	Schaufenster *n*	shop-window	vitrine *f*	vetrina *f*	—
escape clause (E)	Rücktrittsklausel *f*	—	clause de résolution du contrat *f*	clausola di recesso *f*	cláusula de arrepentimiento *f*
escasez (Es)	Knappheit *f*	shortage	rareté *f*	scarsità *f*	—
escasez de capacidad (Es)	Kapazitätsengpaß *m*	bottleneck in capacity	goulot d'étranglement de capacité *m*	strettoia di capacità *f*	—
escasez de materias primas (Es)	Rohstoffknappheit *f*	raw materials shortage	pénurie de matières premières *f*	scarsità di materie prime *f*	—
escasez de mercancías (Es)	Warenknappheit *f*	shortage of goods	pénurie de marchandises *f*	scarsità di merci *f*	—
escaso (Es)	knapp	scarce	rare	scarso	—
escompte[1] (F)	Diskont *m*	discount	—	sconto *m*	descuento *m*
escompte[2] (F)	Skonto *n*	discount	—	sconto *m*	descuento *m*
escompte de caisse (F)	Barzahlungskonto *n*	cash discount	—	sconto per pagamento in contanti *m*	descuento de pago al contado *m*
escompte de suscription (F)	Vorbestellrabatt *m*	discount on advance orders	—	ribasso per ordinazioni anticipate *m*	descuento de suscripción *m*
escritorio (Es)	Schreibtisch *m*	desk	bureau *m*	scrivania *f*	—
escuela (Es)	Schule *f*	school	école *f*	scuola *f*	—
esecuzione[1] (I)	Vollstreckung *f*	enforcement	exécution *f*	—	ejecución *f*
esecuzione[2] (I)	Durchführung *f*	realization	réalisation *f*	—	ejecución *f*
esecuzione[3] (I)	Abwicklung *f*	settlement/liquidation	exécution *f*/ liquidation *f*	—	ejecución *f*
esecuzione forzata (I)	Zwangsvollstreckung *f*	judicial execution	exécution forcée *f*	—	ejecución forzosa *f*
esecuzione ordini[1] (I)	Auftragsabwicklung *f*	execution of the order	exécution d'une commande *f*	—	ejecución de pedidos *f*
esecuzione ordini[2] (I)	Auftragsbearbeitung *f*	order processing	réalisation d'une commande *f*	—	tramitación de pedidos *f*
esente da contributi (I)	abgabenfrei	tax-free/duty-free	exempt de taxes	—	exento de impuestos/ exento de derechos
esente da imposte (I)	steuerfrei	tax-free	dispensé de l'impôt	—	libre de impuesto
esente da vizi (I)	mangelfrei	free of defects	sans défaut	—	sin vicios
esercizio (I)	Wirtschaftsjahr *n*	business year	exercice comptable *m*	—	ejercicio *m*
esercizio commerciale (I)	Geschäftsjahr *n*	financial year	exercice commercial *m*	—	ejercicio *m*
esfera de influencia (Es)	Einflußbereich *m*	sphere of influence	sphère d'influence *f*	sfera d'influenza *f*	—
esistenza (I)	Existenz *f*	existence	existence *f*	—	existencia *f*
espace à bâtir (F)	Bauland *n*	building land	—	area edificabile *f*	terreno edificable *m*

	D	E	F	I	Es
espansione (I)	Expansion f	expansion	expansion f	—	expansión f
espansivo (I)	expansiv	expansive	tendant à l'expansion	—	expansivo
espanso (I)	Schaumstoff m	foam material	mousse synthétique f	—	espumaso plástico m
espèces en caisse (F)	Bargeldbestand m	cash in hand	—	denaro contante in cassa m	saldo en efectivo m
especialización (Es)	Spezialisierung f	specialization	spécialisation f	specializzazione f	—
especie (Es)	Sorte f	variety/foreign notes and coins	genre m/devises f pl	categoria f	—
especificación (Es)	Spezifikation f	specification	spécification f	specificazione f	—
especulación (Es)	Spekulation f	speculation	spéculation f	speculazione f	—
espérance de vie (F)	Lebenserwartung f	expectation of life	—	durata probabile della vita f	expectativa de vida f
esperto dei rifiuti (I)	Abfallexperte m	expert on waste products	expert en déchets m	—	experto de productos residuales m
esperto di pubblicità (I)	Werbefachmann m	advertising expert	technicien publicitaire m	—	perito publicitario m
esperto in materia economica (I)	Wirtschaftsexperte m	economic expert	expert économique m	—	economista m
esperto in materia monetaria (I)	Währungsexperte m	monetary expert	expert monétaire m	—	experto en materia monetaria m
espionage (E)	Spionage f	—	espionnage m	spionaggio m	espionaje m
espionaje (Es)	Spionage f	espionage	espionnage m	spionaggio m	—
espionaje industrial[1] (Es)	Werkspionage f	industrial espionage	espionnage industriel m	spionaggio aziendale m	—
espionaje industrial[2] (Es)	Industriespionage f	industrial espionage	espionnage industriel m	spionaggio industriale m	—
espionnage (F)	Spionage f	espionage	—	spionaggio m	espionaje m
espionnage industriel[1] (F)	Werkspionage f	industrial espionage	—	spionaggio aziendale m	espionaje industrial m
espionnage industriel[2] (F)	Industriespionage f	industrial espionage	—	spionaggio industriale m	espionaje industrial m
espiral inflacionista (Es)	Inflationsspirale f	inflationary spiral	spirale inflationniste f	spirale inflazionistica f	—
espiral salarios-precios (Es)	Lohn-Preis-Spirale f	wage-price spiral	course des prix et des salaires f	spirale prezzi-salari f	—
esplosione (I)	Explosion f	explosion	explosion f	—	explosión f
esplosione dei costi (I)	Kostenexplosion f	cost escalation	explosion des coûts f	—	incremento desmesurado de los costes m
esportazione (I)	Export m	export	exportation f	—	exportación f
esportazione agricola (I)	Agrarexport m	farm exports	exportation de produits agricoles f	—	exportación agrícola f
esportazione di capitale (I)	Kapitalexport m	capital export	exportation de capitaux f	—	exportación de capital f
esportazioni (I)	Exporthandel m	export trade	commerce d'exportation m	—	comercio de exportación m
espositore (I)	Aussteller m	exhibitor/issuer/drawer	exposant m/émetteur m/tireur m	—	expositor m/emisor m/librador m
esposizione (I)	Ausstellung f	exhibition/making out/issue	exposition f/émission f	—	exhibición f/facturación f
esposizione specializzata (I)	Fachausstellung f	trade fair	exposition spécialisée f	—	exposición especializada f
espropriazione (I)	Enteignung f	expropriation	expropriation f	—	expropiación f
espumoso plástico (Es)	Schaumstoff m	foam material	mousse synthétique f	espanso m	—
essayer (F)	probieren	try	—	provare	probar
essence (F)	Benzin n	petrol	—	benzina f	gasolina f
essere degno di credito (I)	Kreditwürdigkeit f	creditworthiness	solvabilité f	—	crédito m
estabilidad (Es)	Stabilität f	stability	stabilité f	stabilità f	—
estabilidad de precios (Es)	Preisstabilität f	stability of prices	stabilité des prix f	stabilità dei prezzi f	—
estabilidad monetaria (Es)	Geldwertstabilität f	stability of the value of money	stabilité monétaire f	stabilità monetaria f	—
estabilización (Es)	Stabilisierung f	stabilization	stabilisation f	stabilizzazione f	—

	D	E	F	I	Es
establecimiento del presupuesto (Es)	Budgetierung f	budgeting	établissement du budget m	compilazione del bilancio f	—
establecimiento industrial (Es)	Industriebetrieb m	industrial enterprise	entreprise industrielle f	azienda industriale f	—
establishment (E)	Niederlassung f	—	succursale f	succursale f	sucursal f
estación de destino (Es)	Bestimmungsbahnhof m	station of destination	gare destinataire f	stazione di destinazione f	—
estación satélite (Es)	Satellitenstation f	space station	station de satellite f	stazione satellite f	—
estadías (Es)	Liegetage pl	lay days	staries f pl	stallie f pl	—
estadística (Es)	Statistik f	statistics	statistique f	statistica f	—
estadística agrícola (Es)	Agrarstatistik f	agricultural statistics	statistique agricole f	statistica agraria f	—
estadística de la empresa (Es)	Betriebsstatistik f	operational statistics	statistique commerciale et industrielle f	statistica aziendale f	—
estadística de población (Es)	Bevölkerungsstatistik f	population statistics	statistique démographique f	statistica demografica f	—
estadística de ventas (Es)	Absatzstatistik f	sales statistics	statistique de la vente f	statistica delle vendite f	—
estadística del ramo (Es)	Branchenstatistik f	trade statistics	statistique sur les différentes branches économiques f	statistica di categoria f	—
estadística económica (Es)	Wirtschaftsstatistik f	housekeeping account	statistique économique f	statistica economica f	—
estado (Es)	Staat m	state	Etat m	stato m	—
estado agrario (Es)	Agrarstaat m	agricultural state	état agricole m	paese agrario m	—
estado de bienestar (Es)	Wohlfahrtsstaat m	welfare state	Etat social m	stato assistenziale m	—
estado del mercado (Es)	Marktsituation f	market situation	situation du marché f	situazione di mercato f	—
Estado social (Es)	Sozialstaat m	social state based on the rule of law	Etat social m	stato sociale m	—
estancamiento (Es)	Stagnation f	stagnation	stagnation f	stagnazione f	—
estándar (Es)	Standard m	standard	standard m	standard m	—
estandardizado (Es)	standardisiert	standardized	standardisé	standardizzato	—
estanflación (Es)	Stagflation f	stagflation	stagflation f	stagflazione f	—
estar pendiente (Es)	anstehen	be due	être échnu	essere scaduto	—
estatal (Es)	staatlich	state	de l'Etat	statale	—
estate agent (E)	Immobilienmakler m	—	courtier en affaires immobilières m	agente immobiliare m	agente de inmuebles m
estatuto (Es)	Satzung f	statutes	statut m	statuto m	—
esterno (I)	extern	external	extérieur	—	externo
estilo de compra (Es)	Käuferstil m	style of the purchaser	style des acheteurs m	stile dell'acquirente m	—
estimación (Es)	Schätzwert m	estimated value	valeur d'estimation f	valore stimato m	—
estimate (E)	Voranschlag m	—	devis m	preventivo m	presupuesto m
estimated value¹ (E)	Schätzwert m	—	valeur d'estimation f	valore stimato m	estimación f
estimated value² (E)	Taxwert m	—	valeur de taxation f	valore stimato m	valor de tasación m
estimate of cost (E)	Kostenvoranschlag m	—	devis estimatif des frais m	preventivo dei costi m	presupuesto de coste m
estimation of cost (E)	Vorkalkulation f	—	calcul des coûts a priori m	calcolo preventivo m	cálculo provisional m
estímulo a la inversión (Es)	Investitionsförderung f	investment promotion	promotion de l'investissement	promozione degli investimenti f	—
estrategia (Es)	Strategie f	strategy	stratégie f	strategia f	—
estrategia de personal (Es)	Personalstrategie f	personnel strategy	stratégie en matière de personnel f	strategia occupazionale f	—
estrategia de ventas (Es)	Absatzstrategie f	sales strategy	stratégie de vente f	strategia di vendita f	—
estrategia empresarial (Es)	Unternehmensstrategie f	corporate strategy	stratégie de l'entreprise f	strategia imprenditoriale f	—
estratégico (Es)	strategisch	strategic	stratégique	strategico	
estratto conto (I)	Kontoauszug m	statement of account	extrait de compte m	—	extracto de cuenta m
estrés (Es)	Stress m	stress	stress m	stress m	—

	D	E	F	I	Es
estructura (Es)	Struktur *f*	structure	structure *f*	struttura *f*	—
estructura agraria (Es)	Agrarstruktur *f*	agricultural structure	structure agraire *f*	struttura agraria *f*	—
estructuración del anuncio (Es)	Anzeigengestaltung *f*	lay-out of an advertisement	arrangement de l'annonce *m*	tipo d'inserzione *m*	—
estructuración del texto (Es)	Textgestaltung *f*	text configuration	structure du texte *f*	redazione del testo *f*	—
estructura de distribución (Es)	Vertriebsstruktur *f*	structure of distribution	structure de distribution *f*	struttura della distribuzione *f*	—
estructura del consumo (Es)	Konsumstruktur *f*	consumption structure	structure de consommation	struttura del consumo *f*	—
estructura del ramo (Es)	Branchenstruktur *f*	trade structure	structure de la branche *f*	struttura di categoria *f*	—
estructura demográfica (Es)	Bevölkerungs- struktur *f*	population structure	structure démographique *f*	struttura demografica *f*	—
estructura económica (Es)	Wirtschaftsstruktur *f*	economic structure	structure économique *f*	struttura economica *f*	—
estructura territorial (Es)	Raumstruktur *f*	spatial structure	structure des espaces *f*	struttura territoriale *f*	—
estudio del mercado[1] (Es)	Marktforschung *f*	market research	étude de marché *f*	ricerca di mercato *f*	—
estudio del mercado[2] (Es)	Marktuntersuchung *f*	market survey	étude du marché *f*	analisi di mercato *f*	—
estudio del mercado empírico (Es)	empirische Marktforschung *f*	empirical market research	étude de marché empirique *f*	ricerca di mercato empirica *f*	—
estudio de tiempo (Es)	Zeitstudie *f*	time study	étude des temps *f*	analisi sul tempo impiegato *f*	—
établissement de crédit (F)	Kreditinstitut *n*	credit institution	—	istituto di credito *m*	instituto de crédito *m*
établissement du budget (F)	Budgetierung *f*	budgeting	—	compilazione del bilancio *f*	establecimiento del presupuesto *m*
établissement d'une facture (F)	Rechnungsstellung *f*	invoicing	—	fatturazione *f*	facturación *f*
établissement en régie (F)	Regiebetrieb *m*	publicly owned enterprise	—	gestione in economia *f*	empresa estatal *f*
établissement industriel (F)	gewerblicher Betrieb *m*	industrial undertaking	—	azienda commerciale, azienda industriale *f*	empresa industrial *f*
établissement secondaire (F)	Zweigbetrieb *m*	branch business	—	filiale *f*	sucursal *f*
étalage (F)	Auslage *f*	display	—	vetrina *f*	vitrina *f*
étalon or (F)	Goldstandard *m*	gold standard	—	gold standard *m*	patrón-oro *m*
Etat (D)	—	budget	budget *m*	bilancio *m*	presupuesto *m*
état[1] (F)	Status *m*	status	—	stato *m*	status *m*
état[2] (F)	Staat *m*	state	—	stato *m*	estado *m*
état agricole (F)	Agrarstaat *m*	agricultural state	—	paese agrario *m*	estado agrario *m*
état social[1] (F)	Sozialstaat *m*	social state based on the rule of law	—	stato sociale *m*	estado social *m*
état social[2] (F)	Wohlfahrtsstaat *m*	welfare state	—	stato assistenziale *m*	estado de bienestar *m*
etichetta adesiva (I)	Aufkleber *m*	sticker	étiquette *f*	—	pegatina *f*
etichetta (I)	Etikett *n*	label	étiquette *f*	—	etiqueta *f*
Etikett (D)	—	label	étiquette *f*	etichetta *f*	etiqueta *f*
etiqueta (Es)	Etikett *n*	label	étiquette *f*	etichetta *f*	—
étiquette[1] (F)	Etikett *n*	label	—	etichetta *f*	etiqueta *f*
étiquette[2] (F)	Aufkleber *m*	sticker	—	etichetta adesiva *f*	pegatina *f*
étranger (F)	Ausländer *m*	foreigner	—	straniero *m*	extranjero *m*
être échu (F)	anstehen	be due	—	essere scaduto	estar pendiente
étude (F)	Untersuchung *f*	examination	—	indagine *f*	inspección *f*
étude de marché empirique (F)	empirische Marktforschung *f*	empirical market research	—	ricerca di mercato empirica *f*	estudio del mercado empírico *m*
étude de marché (F)	Marktbeobachtung *f*	observation of markets	—	sondaggio del mercato *m*	observación del mercado *f*
étude des temps (F)	Zeitstudie *f*	time study	—	analisi sul tempo impiegato *f*	estudio de tiempo *m*

	D	E	F	I	Es
étude du marché (F)	Marktuntersuchung *f*	market survey	—	analisi di mercato *f*	estudio del mercado *m*
euroassegno (I)	Euroscheck *m*	Eurocheque	eurochèque *m*	—	eurocheque *m*
eurobon (F)	Eurobond *m*	Eurobond	—	eurobond *m*	euroemisión *f*
Eurobond (D)	—	Eurobond	eurobon *m*	eurobond *m*	euroemisión *f*
Eurobond (E)	Eurobond *m*	—	eurobon *m*	eurobond *m*	euroemisión *f*
eurobond (I)	Eurobond *m*	Eurobond	eurobon *m*	—	euroemisión *f*
Eurobrand (E)	Euro-Markenzeichen *n*	—	euromarque *f*	euromarchio *m*	euromarca *f*
Eurocheque (E)	Euroscheck *m*	—	eurochèque *m*	euroassegno *m*	eurocheque *m*
eurocheque (Es)	Euroscheck *m*	Eurocheque	eurochèque *m*	euroassegno *m*	—
eurochèque (F)	Euroscheck *m*	Eurocheque	—	euroassegno *m*	eurocheque *m*
Eurocredit (E)	Euro-Kredit *m*	—	eurocrédit *m*	eurocredito *m*	eurocrédito *m*
eurocrédit (F)	Euro-Kredit *m*	Eurocredit	—	eurocredito *m*	eurocrédito *m*
eurocrédito (Es)	Euro-Kredit *m*	Eurocredit	eurocrédit *m*	eurocredito *m*	—
eurocredito (I)	Euro-Kredit *m*	Eurocredit	eurocrédit *m*	—	eurocrédito *m*
Eurocurrency (E)	Eurogeld *n*	—	eurodevises *f pl*	euromoneta *f*	eurodinero *m*
eurodevises (F)	Eurogeld *n*	Eurocurrency	—	euromoneta *f*	eurodinero *m*
eurodinero (Es)	Eurogeld *n*	Eurocurrency	eurodevises *f pl*	euromoneta *f*	—
eurodólar (Es)	Euro-Dollar *m*	Eurodollar	eurodollar *m*	eurodollaro *m*	—
Euro-Dollar (D)	—	Eurodollar	eurodollar *m*	eurodollaro *m*	eurodólar *m*
Eurodollar (E)	Euro-Dollar *m*	—	eurodollar *m*	eurodollaro *m*	eurodólar *m*
eurodollar (F)	Euro-Dollar *m*	Eurodollar	—	eurodollaro *m*	eurodólar *m*
eurodollaro (I)	Euro-Dollar *m*	Eurodollar	eurodollar *m*	—	eurodólar *m*
euroemisión (Es)	Eurobond *m*	Eurobond	eurobon *m*	eurobond *m*	—
Eurogeld (D)	—	Eurocurrency	eurodevises *f pl*	euromoneta *f*	eurodinero *m*
Euro-Kredit (D)	—	Eurocredit	eurocrédit *m*	eurocredito *m*	eurocrédito *m*
euromarca (Es)	Euro-Markenzeichen *n*	Eurobrand	euromarque *f*	euromarchio *m*	—
euromarché (F)	Euromarkt *m*	Euromarket	—	euromercato *m*	euromercado *m*
euromarchio (I)	Euro-Markenzeichen *n*	Eurobrand	euromarque *f*	—	euromarca *f*
Euro-Markenzeichen (D)	—	Eurobrand	euromarque *f*	euromarchio *m*	euromarca *f*
Euromarket (E)	Euromarkt *m*	—	euromarché *m*	euromercato *m*	euromercado *m*
Euromarkt (D)	—	Euromarket	euromarché *m*	euromercato *m*	euromercado *m*
euromarque (F)	Euro-Markenzeichen *n*	Eurobrand	—	euromarchio *m*	euromarca *f*
euromercado (Es)	Euromarkt *m*	Euromarket	euromarché *m*	euromercato *m*	—
euromercato (I)	Euromarkt *m*	Euromarket	euromarché *m*	—	euromercado *m*
euromoneta (I)	Eurogeld *n*	Eurocurrency	eurodevises *f pl*	—	eurodinero *m*
Euronorm (D)	—	Eurostandard	euronorme *f*	euronorma *f*	euronorma *f*
euronorma (Es)	Euronorm *f*	Eurostandard	euronorme *f*	euronorma *f*	euronorma *f*
euronorma (I)	Euronorm *f*	Eurostandard	euronorme *f*	—	euronorma *f*
euronorme (F)	Euronorm *f*	Eurostandard	—	euronorma *f*	euronorma *f*
Europäische Gemeinschaft (D)	—	European Community	Communauté Européenne *f*	Comunità Europea *f*	Comunidad Europea *f*
Europäischer Gerichtshof (D)	—	European Court	Cour de Justice Européenne *f*	Corte di Giustizia Europea *f*	Tribunal de Justicia de las Comunidades Europeas *m*
Europäischer-Binnenmarkt (D)	—	Internal Market of the European Community	Marché Intérieur de la Communauté Européenne *m*	mercato unico *m*	Mercado Unico *m*
Europäisches Parlament (D)	—	European Parliament	Parlement européen *m*	Parlamento Europeo *m*	Parlamento Europeo *m*
Europäisches Patentamt (D)	—	European Patent Office	Office Européen de Brevets *f*	Ufficio Europeo Brevetti *m*	Oficina Europea de Patentes *f*
Europäische Währungseinheit (D)	—	European Currency Unit	unité de compte européenne *f*	unità monetaria europea *f*	unidad monetaria europea *f*

	D	E	F	I	Es
Europäische Zahlungsunion (D)	—	European Payments Union	union européenne des payements f	Unione Europea dei Pagamenti f	Unión Europea de Pagos f
Europäisches Währungssystem (D)	—	European Monetary System	Système Monétaire Européen m	Sistema Monetario Europeo m	Sistema Monetario Europeo m
europaleta (Es)	Euro-Palette f	Europallet	europalette f	europaletta f	—
europaletta (I)	Euro-Palette f	Europallet	europalette f	—	europaleta f
Euro-Palette (D)	—	Europallet	europalette f	europaletta f	europaleta f
europalette (F)	Euro-Palette f	Europallet	—	europaletta f	europaleta f
Europallet (E)	Euro-Palette f	—	europalette f	europaletta f	europaleta f
Europapatent (D)	—	European patent	brevet européen m	brevetto europeo m	patente europea f
European Communities (E)	Europäische Gemeinschaft f	—	Communauté Européenne f	Comunità Europea f	Comunidad Europea f
European Court (E)	Europäischer Gerichtshof m	—	Cour de Justice Européenne f	Corte di Giustizia Europea f	Tribunal de Justicia de las Comunidades Europeas m
European Currency Unit (E)	Europäische Währungseinheit f	—	unité de compte européenne f	unità monetaria europea f	unidad monetaria europea f
European Monetary System (E)	Europäisches Währungssystem n	—	Système Monétaire Européen m	Sistema Monetario Europeo m	Sistema Monetario Europeo m
European Parliament (E)	Europäisches Parlament n	—	Parlement européen m	Parlamento Europeo m	Parlamento Europeo m
European patent (E)	Europapatent n	—	brevet européen m	brevetto europeo m	patente europea f
European Patent Office (E)	Europäisches Patentamt n	—	Office Européen de Brevets f	Ufficio Europeo Brevetti m	Oficina Europea de Patentes f
European Payments Union (E)	Europäische Zahlungsunion f	—	union européenne des payements f	Unione Europea dei Pagamenti f	Unión Europea de Pagos f
Euroscheck (D)	—	Eurocheque	eurochèque m	euroassegno m	eurocheque m
Eurostandard (E)	Euronorm f	—	euronorme f	euronorma f	euronorma f
evacuación de residuos (Es)	Abfallbeseitigung f	waste disposal	élimination de déchets f	smaltimento dei rifiuti m	—
evacuation (E)	Räumung f	—	évacuation f	evacuazione f	desalojamiento m
évacuation (F)	Räumung f	evacuation	—	evacuazione f	desalojamiento m
evacuazione (I)	Räumung f	evacuation	évacuation f	—	desalojamiento m
evaluación aproximativa (Es)	vorsichtige Schätzung f	conservative estimate	évaluation approximative f	valutazione approssimativa f	—
evaluación del trabajo (Es)	Arbeitsbewertung f	job evaluation	qualification du travail f	valutazione del lavoro f	—
évaluation approximative (F)	vorsichtige Schätzung f	conservative estimate	—	valutazione approssimativa f	evaluación aproximativa f
évasion des capitaux (F)	Kapitalflucht f	flight of capital	—	fuga dei capitali f	fuga de capital f
evasione (I)	Hinterziehung f	evasion of taxes	fraude fiscale f	—	defraudación f
evasione fiscale (I)	Steuerhinterziehung f	tax evasion	dissimulation en matière fiscale f	—	defraudación fiscal f
evasion of taxes (E)	Hinterziehung f	—	fraude fiscale f	evasione f	defraudación f
event insured against (E)	Versicherungsfall m	—	sinistre m	caso di sinistro m	situación de siniestro f
evolución de la coyuntura (Es)	Konjunktur-entwicklung f	economic trend	évolution de la conjoncture f	sviluppo congiunturale m	—
evolución del volumen de facturación (Es)	Umsatzentwicklung f	turnover trend	évolution du chiffre d'affaires f	sviluppo del fatturato m	—
evolución económica (Es)	Wirtschaftsverlauf m	course of the economic evolution	évolution économique f	andamento dell'economia f	—
évolution de la conjoncture (F)	Konjunktur-entwicklung f	economic trend	—	sviluppo congiunturale m	evolución de la coyuntura f
évolution du chiffre d'affaires (F)	Umsatzentwicklung f	turnover trend	—	sviluppo del fatturato m	evolución del volumen de facturación f
évolution économique (F)	Wirtschaftsverlauf m	course of the economic evolution	—	andamento dell'economia m	evolución económica f
Examen (D)	—	examination	examen m	esame m	examen m
examen (Es)	Examen n	examination	examen m	esame m	—
examen (F)	Examen n	examination	—	esame m	examen m

	D	E	F	I	Es
examinación del mercado (Es)	Markttest *m*	market test	test du marché *m*	test di mercato *m*	—
examination¹ (E)	Untersuchung *f*	—	étude *f*	indagine *f*	inspección *f*
examination² (E)	Examen *n*	—	examen *m*	esame *m*	examen *m*
excédent¹ (F)	schwarze Zahlen *pl*	surplus	—	conti in nero *m pl*	superávit *m*
excédent² (F)	Überschuß *m*	excess	—	eccedenza *f*	excedente *m*
excédent annuel (F)	Jahresüberschuß *m*	annual surplus	—	surplus dell'anno *m*	superávit del ejercicio *m*
excédent commercial (F)	Handelsüberschuß *m*	trade surplus	—	eccedenza commerciale *f*	excedente comercial *m*
excédent de liquidité (F)	Liquiditäts-überschuß *m*	excess liquidity	—	eccedenza di liquidità *f*	exceso de liquidez *m*
excédent d'exportation (F)	Exportüberschuß *m*	export surplus	—	eccedenza delle esportazioni *f*	excedente de exportación *m*
excedente (Es)	Überschuß *m*	excess	excédent *m*	eccedenza *f*	—
excedente comercial (Es)	Handelsüberschuß *m*	trade surplus	excédent commercial *m*	eccedenza commerciale *f*	—
excedente de exportación (Es)	Exportüberschuß *m*	export surplus	excédent d'exportation *m*	eccedenza delle esportazioni *f*	—
excedentes agrícolas (Es)	Agrarüberschüsse *pl*	agricultural surpluses	excédents agricoles *m pl*	eccedenze agricole *f pl*	—
excédents agricoles (F)	Agrarüberschüsse *pl*	agricultural surpluses	—	eccedenze agricole *f pl*	excedentes agrícolas *m pl*
excès de l'offre (F)	Angebotsüberhang *m*	excess of supply over demand	—	eccedenza d'offerta *f*	exceso de oferta *m*
excesivo (Es)	übermäßig	excessive	excessif	eccessivo	—
exceso (Es)	Mehrlieferung *f*	additional delivery	livraison supplémentaire *f*	fornitura supplementare *f*	—
exceso de deudas (Es)	Überschuldung *f*	excessive indebtedness	surendettement *m*	indebitamento eccessivo *m*	—
exceso de empleo (Es)	Überbeschäftigung *f*	overcharge	surchargement *m*	occupazione eccedente *f*	—
exceso de liquidez (Es)	Liquiditäts-überschuß *m*	excess liquidity	excédent de liquidité *m*	eccedenza di liquidità *f*	—
exceso de oferta (Es)	Angebotsüberhang *m*	excess of supply over demand	excès de l'offre *m*	eccedenza d'offerta *f*	—
excess (E)	Überschuß *m*	—	excédent *m*	eccedenza *f*	excedente *m*
excessif (F)	übermäßig	excessive	—	eccessivo	excesivo
excessive (E)	übermäßig	—	excessif	eccessivo	excesivo
excessive indebtedness (E)	Überschuldung *f*	—	surendettement *m*	indebitamento eccessivo *m*	exceso de deudas *m*
excess liquidity (E)	Liquiditäts-überschuß *m*	—	excédent de liquidité *m*	eccedenza di liquidità *f*	exceso de liquidez *m*
excess of supply over demand (E)	Angebotsüberhang *m*	—	excès de l'offre *m*	eccedenza d'offerta *f*	exceso de oferta *m*
excess weight (E)	Übergewicht *n*	—	surcharge *f*	sovrappeso *m*	sobrepeso *m*
exchange¹ (E)	Tausch *m*	—	échange *m*/troc *m*	scambio *m*/baratto *m*	cambio *m*/ trueque *m*
exchange² (E)	Umtausch *m*	—	échange *m*	cambio *m*	cambio *m*/ conversión *f*
exchange arbitrage (E)	Devisenarbitrage *f*	—	arbitrage sur les devises *m*	arbitraggio valutario *m*	arbitraje de divisas *m*
exchange of goods (E)	Warenaustausch *m*	—	échanges commerciaux *m pl*	scambio merci *m*	intercambio de mercancías *m*
exchange rate¹ (E)	Kurs *m*	—	cours (du change) *m*	corso *m*/cambio *m*	cotización *f*/ tipo de cambio *m*
exchange rate² (E)	Wechselkurs *m*	—	cours du change *m*	cambio *m*	tipo de cambio *m*
exchangeable container (E)	Wechselbehälter *m*	—	conteneur interchangeable *m*	contenitore sostituibile *m*	contenedores intercambiables *m pl*
exclave aduanero (Es)	Zollausschluß *m*	territory inside political but outside customs frontier	territoire considéré hors frontière douanière nationale *m*	zona franca *f*	—
exclusive distribution (E)	Alleinvertrieb *m*	—	vente exclusive *f*	vendita esclusiva *f*	distribución exclusiva *f*

	D	E	F	I	Es
exclusivité territoriale (F)	Gebietsschutz m	territory protection	—	tutela territoriale f	protección territorial f
exécution¹ (F)	Abwicklung f	settlement/liquidation	—	esecuzione f	ejecución f
exécution² (F)	Vollstreckung f	enforcement	—	esecuzione f	ejecución f
exécution d'une commande (F)	Auftragsabwicklung f	execution of the order	—	esecuzione ordini f	ejecución de pedidos f
exécution forcée (F)	Zwangs-vollstreckung f	judicial execution	—	esecuzione forzata f	ejecución forzosa f
execution of the order (E)	Auftragsabwicklung f	—	exécution d'une commande f	esecuzione ordini f	ejecución de pedidos f
exécution par crédit documentaire (F)	Akkreditiv-abwicklung f	settlement by letter of credit	—	procedura del credito documentario f	ejecución por crédito documentario f
executive (E)	Führungsperson f	—	cadre m	dirigente m	ejecutivo m
executive level (E)	Führungsebene f	—	niveau de gestion m	quadri dirigenti m	nivel de dirección m
executive management (E)	Unternehmens-leitung f	—	direction de l'entreprise f	direzione dell'impresa f	dirección de la empresa f
exempt de frais de transport (F)	frachtfrei	freight paid	—	franco di nolo	franco de porte
exempt de taxes (F)	abgabenfrei	tax-free/duty-free	—	esente da contributi	exento de derechos
exento de impuestos (Es)	abgabenfrei	tax-free	exempt de taxes	esente da contributi	—
exercice budgétaire (F)	Haushaltsjahr n	financial year	—	anno finanziario m	ejercicio m
exercice commercial (F)	Geschäftsjahr n	financial year	—	esercizio commerciale m	ejercicio m
exercice comptable¹ (F)	Wirtschaftsjahr n	business year	—	esercizio m	ejercicio m
exercice comptable² (F)	Rechnungsjahr n	financial year	—	anno d'esercizio m	ejercicio m
ex fábrica (Es)	ab Werk	ex works	départ usine	franco fabbrica	—
exhibición (Es)	Ausstellung f	exhibition	exposition f	esposizione f	—
exhibition (E)	Ausstellung f	—	exposition f	esposizione f	exhibición f
exhibitor (E)	Aussteller m	—	exposant m	espositore m	expositor m
existence (E)	Existenz f	—	existence f	esistenza f	existencia f
existence (F)	Existenz f	existence	—	esistenza f	existencia f
existencia (Es)	Existenz f	existence	existence f	esistenza f	—
existencias¹ (Es)	Reserve f	reserve stock/reserves	stocks de réserve m pl/réserve f	scorte f pl/riserva f	—
existencias² (Es)	Vorrat m	stock	stock m	scorte f pl	—
existencias de mercancías (Es)	Warenbestand m	stock	stock de marchandises m	scorte merci f pl	—
existencias iniciales (Es)	Anfangsbestand m	opening inventory	stock initial m	scorte iniziali f pl	—
Existenz (D)	—	existence	existence f	esistenza f	existencia f
Existenzgründung (D)	—	setting up of new business	fondation d'existence f	costituzione di un lavoro indipendente f	fundación de existencia f
Existenzminimum (D)	—	subsistence minimum	minimum vital m	minimo di esistenza m	mínimo vital m
ex muelle (Es)	ab Kai	ex quay	départ quai	franco banchina	—
exorbitant rent (E)	Mietwucher m	—	hausse illicite des loyers f	strozzinaggio sui canoni di locazione m	usura arrendaticia f
Expansion (D)	—	expansion	expansion f	espansione f	expansión f
expansion (E)	Expansion f	—	expansion f	espansione f	expansión f
expansión (Es)	Expansion f	expansion	expansion f	espansione f	—
expansion (F)	Expansion f	expansion	—	espansione f	expansión f
expansiv (D)	—	expansive	tendant à l'expansion	espansivo	expansivo
expansive (E)	expansiv	—	tendant à l'expansion	espansivo	expansivo
expansivo (Es)	expansiv	expansive	tendant à l'expansion	espansivo	—
expectation of life (E)	Lebenserwartung f	—	espérance de vie f	durata probabile della vita f	expectativa de vida f
expectativa de un futuro pago (Es)	Anwartschaft f	candidature	candidature f	candidatura f	—
expectativa de vida (Es)	Lebenserwartung f	expectation of life	espérance de vie f	durata probabile della vita f	—

	D	E	F	I	Es
expedición¹ (Es)	Verfrachtung f	carriage of goods by sea	affrètement m	trasporto marittimo m	—
expedición² (Es)	Absendung f	dispatch	expédition f	spedizione f	—
expedir¹ (Es)	verladen	load	charger	caricare	—
expedir² (Es)	verfrachten	freight/ship	fréter/embarquer	imbarcare	—
expéditeur (F)	Absender m	sender	—	mittente m	remitente m
expédition¹ (F)	Abfertigung f	dispatch/clearance	—	spedizione f/ sdoganamento m	despacho m/despacho de aduana m
expédition² (F)	Absendung f	dispatch	—	spedizione f	expedición f
expédition³ (F)	Versand m	dispatch	—	spedizione f	envío m
expédition de marchandises (F)	Warensendung f	consignment of goods	—	spedizione di merci f	envío de mercancías m
expéditions de détail (F)	Stückgutverkehr m	general cargo trade	—	trasporto di collettame m	tráfico de mercancías en bultos sueltos m
expeditor (Es)	Spediteur m	forwarder	commissionnaire de transport m	spedizioniere m	—
expenditure¹ (E)	Aufwand m	—	charge f	spese f pl	gastos m pl
expenditure² (E)	Aufwendung f	—	dépenses f pl	spese f pl	gasto m
expenditure control (E)	Ausgabenkontrolle f	—	contrôle des dépenses m	controllo delle spese m	control de gastos m
expenditure delay (E)	Ausgabenverzögerung f	—	dépenses retardées f pl	dilazione delle spese f	aplazamiento de gastos m
expenditure factor (E)	Aufwandsfaktor m	—	facteur des frais m	fattore spese m	factor de gastos m
expenditure minimization (E)	Aufwandsminimierung f	—	minimiser les frais	riduzione delle spese f	minimación de gastos f
expenditure of time (E)	Zeitaufwand m	—	temps passé m	tempo impiegato m	tiempo consagrado m
expenses¹ (E)	Spesen pl	—	frais m pl	spese f pl	gastos m pl
expenses² (E)	Ausgaben pl	—	dépenses f pl	spese f pl	gastos m pl
expert-comptable (F)	Betriebsprüfer m	auditor	—	revisore aziendale m	contador público m
expert comptable économique et financier (F)	Wirtschaftsprüfer m	auditor	—	revisore dei conti m	revisor de cuentas m/ experto contable m
expert de déchets (F)	Abfallexperte m	expert on waste products	—	esperto dei rifiuti m	experto de productos residuales m
expert économique (F)	Wirtschaftsexperte m	economic expert	—	esperto in materia economica m	economista m
expert monétaire (F)	Währungsexperte m	monetary expert	—	esperto in materia monetaria m	experto en materia monetaria m
experto de productos residuales (Es)	Abfallexperte m	expert on waste products	expert en déchets m	esperto dei rifiuti m	—
experto en materia monetaria (Es)	Währungsexperte m	monetary expert	expert monétaire m	esperto in materia monetaria m	—
expert on waste products (E)	Abfallexperte m	—	expert en déchets m	esperto dei rifiuti m	experto de productos residuales m
expert opinion (E)	Expertise f	—	expertise f	perizia f	dictamen pericial m
Expertise (D)	—	expert opinion	expertise f	perizia f	dictamen pericial m
expertise (F)	Expertise f	expert opinion	—	perizia f	dictamen pericial m
expiry date (E)	Verfallsdatum n	—	date d'échéance f	data di scadenza f	fecha de vencimiento f
explanation (E)	Erklärung f	—	explication f/ déclaration f	spiegazione f/ dichiarazione f	explicación f/ declaración f
explicación (Es)	Erklärung f	explanation/ declaration	explication f/ déclaration f	spiegazione f/ dichiarazione f	—
explication (F)	Erklärung f	explanation/ declaration	—	spiegazione f/ dichiarazione f	explicación f/ declaración f
exploitation abusive (F)	Raubbau m	ruinous exploitation	—	sfruttamento abusivo m	explotación abusiva f
Explosion (D)	—	explosion	explosion f	esplosione f	explosión f
explosion (E)	Explosion f	—	explosion f	esplosione f	explosión f
explosión (Es)	Explosion f	explosion	explosion f	esplosione f	—
explosion (F)	Explosion f	explosion	—	esplosione f	explosión f

	D	E	F	I	Es
explosion des coûts (F)	Kostenexplosion *f*	cost escalation	—	esplosione dei costi *f*	incremento desmesurado de los costes *m*
explotación abusiva (Es)	Raubbau *m*	ruinous exploitation	exploitation abusive *f*	sfruttamento abusivo *m*	—
Export (D)	—	export	exportation *f*	esportazione *f*	exportación *f*
export (E)	Ausfuhr *f*	—	exportation *f*	esportazione *f*	exportación *f*
Exportabteilung (D)	—	export department	service d'exportation *m*	reparto esportazioni *m*	departamento de exportación *m*
exportación (Es)	Ausfuhr *f*	export	exportation *f*	esportazione *f*	—
exportación agrícola (Es)	Agrarexport *m*	farm exports	exportation de produits agricoles *f*	esportazione agricola *f*	—
exportación de capital (Es)	Kapitalexport *m*	capital export	exportation de capitaux *f*	esportazione di capitale *f*	—
exportation (F)	Ausfuhr *f*	export	—	esportazione *f*	exportación *f*
exportation de capitaux (F)	Kapitalexport *m*	capital export	—	esportazione di capitale *f*	exportación de capital *f*
exportation de produits agricoles (F)	Agrarexport *m*	farm exports	—	esportazione agricola *f*	exportación agrícola *f*
Exportauftrag (D)	—	export order	commande d'exportation *f*	ordine d'esportazione *m*	pedido destinado a la exportación *m*
export business (E)	Exportgeschäft *n*	—	affaire d'exportation *f*	operazione d'esportazione *f*	operación de exportación *f*
export department (E)	Exportabteilung *f*	—	service d'exportation *m*	reparto esportazioni *m*	departamento de exportación *m*
export documents (E)	Ausfuhrpapiere *pl*	—	documents d'exportation *m pl*	documenti d'esportazione *m pl*	documentos de exportación *m pl*
export duty (E)	Ausfuhrzoll *m*	—	taxe de sortie *f*	dazio sull'esportazione *m*	derechos de exportación *m pl*
export factoring (E)	Export-Factoring *n*	—	factoring d'exportation *m*	factoring delle esportazioni *m*	facturing de exportación *m*
Export-Factoring (D)	—	export factoring	factoring d'exportation *m*	factoring delle esportazioni *m*	facturing de exportación *m*
export financing (E)	Ausfuhrfinanzierung *f*	—	financement de l'exportation *m*	finanziamento delle esportazioni *m*	financiación de la exportación *f*
Exportfinanzierung (D)	—	financing of exports	financement d'opération d'exportation *m*	finanziamento delle esportazioni *m*	financiación de exportación *f*
Exportgeschäft (D)	—	export business	affaire d'exportation *f*	operazione d'esportazione *f*	operación de exportación *f*
Exporthandel (D)	—	export trade	commerce d'exportation *m*	esportazioni *f pl*	comercio de exportación *m*
Exporthilfe (D)	—	export subsidy	subvention à l'exportatoin *f*	aiuto all'esportazione *m*	ayuda a la exportación *f*
export licence (E)	Ausfuhrgenehmigung *f*	—	autorisation d'exportation *f*	autorizzazione per le esportazioni *f*	licencia de exportación *f*
export market (E)	Exportmarkt *m*	—	marché d'exportation *m*	mercato delle esportazioni *m*	mercado de exportación *m*
Exportmarkt (D)	—	export market	marché d'exportation *m*	mercato delle esportazioni *m*	mercado de exportación *m*
export order (E)	Exportauftrag *m*	—	commande d'exportation *f*	ordine d'esportazione *m*	pedido destinado a la exportación *m*
Exportpreisliste (D)	—	export price list	liste des prix à l'exportation *f*	listino prezzi delle esportazioni *m*	lista de precios de exportación *f*
export price list (E)	Exportpreisliste *f*	—	liste des prix à l'exportation *f*	listino prezzi delle esportazioni *m*	lista de precios de exportación *f*
export quota (E)	Exportquote *f*	—	quota d'exportation *m*	contingente d'esportazione *m*	cupo de exportación *m*
Exportquote (D)	—	export quota	quota d'exportation *m*	contingente d'esportazione *m*	cupo de exportación *m*
export regulations (E)	Ausfuhrbestimmungen *pl*	—	dispositions d'exportation *f pl*	disposizioni per le esportazioni *f pl*	reglamiento de exportación *m*
export restriction (E)	Ausfuhrbeschränkung *f*	—	contingentement de l'exportation *m*	restrizione delle esportazioni *f*	restricción a la exportación *f*
export subsidy (E)	Exporthilfe *f*	—	subvention à l'exportation *f*	aiuto all'esportazione *m*	ayuda a la exportación *f*
export surplus (E)	Exportüberschuß *m*	—	excédent d'exportation *m*	eccedenza delle esportazioni *f*	excedente de exportación *m*

	D	E	F	I	Es
export trade (E)	Exporthandel *m*	—	commerce d'exportation *m*	esportazioni *f pl*	comercio de exportación *m*
Exportüberschuß (D)	—	export surplus	excédent d'exportation *m*	eccedenza delle esportazioni *f*	excedente de exportación *m*
exposant (F)	Aussteller *m*	exhibitor	—	espositore *m*	expositor *m*
exposición especializada (Es)	Fachausstellung *f*	trade fair	exposition spécialisée *f*	esposizione specializzata *f*	—
exposition (F)	Ausstellung *f*	exhibition	—	esposizione *f*	exhibición *f*
exposition spéciliée (F)	Fachausstellung *f*	trade fair	—	esposizione specializzata *f*	exposición especializada *f*
expositor (Es)	Aussteller *m*	exhibitor	exposant *m*	espositore *m*	—
expreso (Es)	Eilbote *m*	express messenger	facteur spécial *m*	corriere *m*	—
express delivery (E)	Eilzustellung *f*	—	remise par exprès *f*	consegna per espresso *f*	entrega urgente *f*
express goods (E)	Expressgut *n*	—	colis express *m*	merce spedita per espresso *f*	carga por expreso *f*
express letter (E)	Eilbrief *m*	—	lettre par exprès *f*	lettera espresso *f*	carta urgente *f*
express messenger (E)	Eilbote *m*	—	facteur spécial *m*	corriere *m*	expreso *m*
express parcel (E)	Eilpaket *n*	—	colis exprès *m*	pacco espresso *m*	paquete urgente *m*
Expressgut (D)	—	express goods	colis express *m*	merce spedita per espresso *f*	carga por expreso *f*
expropiación (Es)	Enteignung *f*	expropriation	expropriation *f*	espropriazione *f*	—
expropriation (E)	Enteignung *f*	—	expropriation *f*	espropriazione *f*	expropiación *f*
expropriation (F)	Enteignung *f*	expropriation	—	espropriazione *f*	expropiación *f*
ex quay (E)	ab Kai	—	départ quai	franco banchina	ex muelle
ex rail (E)	ab Bahnhof	—	départ gare	franco stazione	puesto en estación
ex ship (E)	ab Schiff	—	départ navire	franco bordo	ex vapor
extension[1] (E)	Prolongation *f*	—	prolongation *f*	proroga *f*	prolongación *f*
extension[2] (E)	Verlängerung *f*	—	prolongation *f*	prolungamento *m*	prórroga *f*
extension de la capacité (F)	Kapazitätsausweitung *f*	increase in capacity	—	ampliamento delle capacità *m*	ampliación de la capacidad *f*
extension of time for payment (E)	Zahlungsaufschub *m*	—	sursis de payement *m*	dilazione del pagamento *f*	pago aplazado *m*
extérieur (F)	extern	external	—	esterno	externo
extern (D)	—	external	extérieur	esterno	externo
external (E)	extern	—	extérieur	esterno	externo
externo[1] (Es)	extern	external	extérieur	esterno	—
extorno[2] (Es)	Storno *n*	counter entry	écriture de contre-passation *f*	storno *m*	—
extra (E)	Zugabe *f*	—	prime *f*	aggiunta *f*	suplemento *m*
extra charge (E)	Zuschlag *m*	—	supplément *m*	supplemento *m*	suplemento *m*
extraction de matières premières (F)	Rohstoffgewinnung *f*	raw material production	—	produzione delle materie prime *f*	producción de materias primas *f*
extracto de cuenta (Es)	Kontoauszug *m*	statement of account	extrait de compte *m*	estratto conto *m*	—
extragiudiziale (I)	außergerichtlich	extrajudicial	extrajudiciaire	—	extrajudicial
extrait de compte (F)	Kontoauszug *m*	statement of account	—	estratto conto *m*	extracto de cuenta *m*
extrajudiciaire (F)	außergerichtlich	extrajudicial	—	extragiudiziale	extrajudicial
extrajudicial (E)	außergerichtlich	—	extrajudiciaire	extragiudiziale	extrajudicial
extrajudicial (Es)	außergerichtlich	extrajudicial	extrajudiciaire	extragiudiziale	—
extranjero (Es)	Ausländer *m*	foreigner	étranger *m*	straniero *m*	—
extraordinary expenses (E)	außergewöhnliche Belastung *f*	—	charges exceptionnelles *f pl*	oneri straordinari *m pl*	carga extraordinaria *f*
ex vapor (Es)	ab Schiff	ex ship	départ navire	franco bordo	—
ex works (E)	ab Werk	—	départ usine	franco fabbrica	ex fábrica
fabbisogno (I)	Bedarf *m*	need/demand	besoin *m*/demande *f*	—	necesidades *f*/demanda *f*
fabbisogno individuale (I)	Individualbedürfnis *n*	individual need	besoin individuel *m*	—	necesidades individuales *f pl*
fabbricazione di massa (I)	Massenfertigung *f*	mass production	production en série *f*	—	fabricación en masa *f*

	D	E	F	I	Es
fábrica (Es)	Betrieb *m*	factory	usine *f*	azienda *f*	—
fabricación en masa (Es)	Massenfertigung *f*	mass production	production en série *f*	fabbricazione di massa *f*	—
fabricación especial (Es)	Sonderanfertigung *f*	manufacture to customer's specifications	fabrication spéciale *f*	produzione fuori serie *f*	—
fabricant (F)	Hersteller *m*	producer	—	produttore *m*	fabricante *m*
fabricante (Es)	Hersteller *m*	producer	fabricant *m*	produttore *m*	
fabrication en série (F)	Serienfertigung *f*	series production	—	produzione in serie *f*	producción en serie *f*
fabrication spéciale (F)	Sonderanfertigung *f*	manufacture to customer's specifications	—	produzione fuori serie *f*	fabricación especial *f*
Fachausstellung (D)	—	trade fair	exposition spécialisée *f*	esposizione specializzata *f*	exposición especializada *f*
Fachbuch (D)	—	technical book	livre technique *m*	libro specializzato *m*	libro técnico *m*
Fachwissen (D)	—	professional knowledge	connaissances professionnelles *f pl*	cognizioni professionali *f pl*	conocimientos especializados *m pl*
facilidad en lo negocios (Es)	Kulanz *f*	accommodation	souplesse en affaires *f*	correntezza *f*	—
facteur (F)	Postbote m	postman	—	portalettere m	cartero *m*
facteur des frais (F)	Aufwandsfaktor *m*	expenditure factor		fattore spese *m*	factor de gastos *m*
facteur productif (F)	Ertragsfaktor *m*	income factor	—	fattore reddito *m*	factor de beneficio *m*
facteurs de production (F)	Produktions-faktoren *pl*	factors of production	—	fattori di produzione *m pl*	factores de producción *m pl*
facteurs dépendant du lieu d'implantation (F)	Standortfaktoren *pl*	location factors	—	fattori d'ubicazione *m pl*	factores de ubicación *m pl*
facteur spécial (F)	Eilbote *m*	express messenger	—	corriere *m*	expreso
factor de beneficio (Es)	Ertragsfaktor *m*	income factor	facteur productif *m*	fattore reddito *m*	—
factor de gastos (Es)	Aufwandsfaktor *m*	expenditure factor	facteur des frais *m*	fattore spese *m*	—
factores de producción (Es)	Produktions-faktoren *pl*	factors of production	facteurs de production *m pl*	fattori di produzione *m pl*	—
factores determinantes de las necesidades (Es)	Bedarfsfaktoren *pl*	requirement factors	éléments pouvant influencer la demande *m pl*	fattori del fabbisogno *m pl*	—
factores de ubicación (Es)	Standortfaktoren *pl*	location factors	facteurs dépendant du lieu d'implantation *m pl*	fattori d'ubicazione *m pl*	—
factoring d'exportation (F)	Export-Factoring *n*	export factoring	—	factoring delle esportazioni *m*	facturing de exportación *m*
factoring delle esportazioni (I)	Export-Factoring *n*	export factoring	factoring d'exportation *m*	—	facturing de exportación *m*
factors of production (E)	Produktions-faktoren *pl*	—	facteurs de production *m pl*	fattori di produzione *m pl*	factores de producción *m pl*
factory (E)	Betrieb *m*	—	usine *f*	azienda *f*	fábrica *f*
factura¹ (Es)	Rechnung *f*	invoice	facture *f*	fattura *f*	—
factura² (Es)	Faktura *f*	invoice	facture *f*	fattura *f*	—
factura arancelaria (Es)	Zollfaktura *f*	customs invoice	facture douanière *f*	fattura doganale *f*	—
facturación¹ (Es)	Rechnungsstellung *f*	invoicing	établissement d'une facture *m*	fatturazione *f*	—
facturación² (Es)	Fakturierung *f*	making out an invoice	facturation *f*	fatturazione *f*	—
factura de aportación de fondos (Es)	Deckungsbeitrags-rechnung *f*	contribution costing	calcul de la propor-tion de garantie *m*	calcolo del contributo per copertura *m*	—
factura ficticia (Es)	fingierte Rechnung *f*	fictitious invoice	facture simulée *f*	fattura fittizia *f*	—
factura pendiente (Es)	offene Rechnung *f*	unsettled account	facture pas encore payée *f*	conto aperto *m*	—
factura proforma (Es)	Proforma-Rechnung *f*	pro forma invoice	facture pro forma *f*	fattura pro forma *f*	—
facturation (F)	Fakturierung *f*	making out an invoice	—	fatturazione *f*	facturación *f*
facture¹ (F)	Faktura *f*	invoice	—	fattura *f*	factura *f*
facture² (F)	Rechnung *f*	invoice	—	fattura *f*	factura *f*
facture douanière (F)	Zollfaktura *f*	customs invoice	—	fattura doganale *f*	factura arancelaria *f*
facture pas encore payée (F)	offene Rechnung *f*	unsettled account	—	conto aperto *m*	factura pendiente *f*

	D	E	F	I	Es
facture pro forma (F)	Proforma-Rechnung *f*	pro forma invoice	—	fattura pro forma *f*	factura proforma *f*
facture simulée (F)	fingierte Rechnung *f*	fictitious invoice	—	fattura fittizia *f*	factura ficticia *f*
facturing de exportación (Es)	Export-Factoring *n*	export factoring	factoring d'exportation *m*	factoring delle esportazioni *m*	—
facultad de firma (Es)	Zeichnungsberechtigung *f*	authority to sign	autorisation de signer *f*	diritto di firma *m*	—
Fähigkeit (D)	—	ability	capacité *f*	capacità *f*	capacidad *f*
Fahrgeld (D)	—	fare	coût du voyage *m*	spese di trasferta *f pl*	precio de la travesía *m*
Fahrlässigkeit (D)	—	negligence	négligence *f*	negligenza *f*	descuido *m*
failli (F)	Gemeinschuldner *m*	adjudicated bankrupt	—	debitore fallito *m*	deudor común *m*
faillite (F)	Konkurs *m*	bankruptcy	—	fallimento *m*	quiebra *f*
failure to pay on due date (E)	Zahlungsverzug *m*	—	demeure du débiteur *f*	morosità di pagamento *f*	retraso en el pago *m*
fair (E)	Messe *f*	—	foire *f*	fiera *f*	feria *f*
faire la queue (F)	Schlange stehen	queue up	—	fare la coda	hacer la cola
faire un prélèvement à découvert (F)	überziehen	overdraw	—	mandare allo scoperto	sobrepasar
fair labour standards (E)	Arbeitsnorm *f*	—	norme de travail *f*	norma di lavoro *f*	norma de producción *f*
Faktura (D)	—	invoice	facture *f*	fattura *f*	factura *f*
Fakturierung (D)	—	making out an invoice	facturation *f*	fatturazione *f*	facturación *f*
fallimento (I)	Konkurs *m*	bankruptcy	faillite *f*	—	quiebra *f*
falsificación de cheques (Es)	Scheckbetrug *m*	cheque fraud	irrégularité en matière de chèque *f*	emissione di assegno a vuoto *f*	—
falta de liquidez (Es)	Illiquidität *f*	illiquidity	manque de trésorerie *f*	illiquidità *f*	—
falta de personal (Es)	Personalmangel *m*	shortage of staff	manque de personnel *m*	mancanza di personale *f*	—
famiglia (I)	privater Haushalt *m*	private household	ménage privé *m*	—	economía doméstica *f*
fardeau inacceptable (F)	unzumutbare Belastung *f*	unacceptable hardship	—	onere inammissibile *m*	carga no exigible *f*
fardo (Es)	Frachtstücke *pl*	packages	colis *m*	colli *m pl*	—
fardos (Es)	Stückgut *n*	mixed cargo	colis de détail *m*	collettame *m*	—
fare (E)	Fahrgeld *n*	—	coût du voyage *m*	spese di trasferta *f pl*	precio de la travesía *m*
fare la coda (I)	Schlange stehen	queue up	faire la queue	—	hacer la cola
farm exports (E)	Agrarexport *m*	—	exportation de produits agricoles *f*	esportazione agricola *f*	exportación agrícola *f*
farm imports (E)	Agrarimport *m*	—	importation de produits agricoles *f*	importazione agricola *f*	importación agrícola *f*
farming (E)	Agrarwirtschaft *f*	—	économie agricole *f*	economia agraria *f*	economía agraria *f*
farm produce (E)	Agrarprodukt *n*	—	produit agricole *m*	prodotto agricolo *m*	producto agrario *m*
fascia (I)	Streifband *f*	postal wrapper	bande étiquette *f*	—	precinto *m*
fase de desarrollo (Es)	Aufbauphase *f*	development phase	phase d'organisation *f*	fase di costruzione *f*	—
fase di costruzione (I)	Aufbauphase *f*	development phase	phase d'organisation *f*	—	fase de desarrollo *f*
fashion article (E)	Modeartikel *m*	—	article de mode *m*	articolo di moda *m*	artículos de moda *m pl*
fashion fair (E)	Modemesse *f*	—	foire de la mode *f*	fiera della moda *f*	feria de moda *f*
fattore reddito (I)	Ertragsfaktor *m*	income factor	facteur productif *m*	—	factor de beneficio *m*
fattore spese (I)	Aufwandsfaktor *m*	expenditure factor	facteur des frais *m*	—	factor de gastos *m*
fattori del fabbisogno (I)	Bedarfsfaktoren *pl*	requirement factors	éléments pouvant influencer la demande *m pl*	—	factores determinantes de las necesidades *m pl*
fattori di produzione (I)	Produktionsfaktoren *pl*	factors of production	facteurs de production *m pl*	—	factores de producción *m pl*
fattori d'ubicazione (I)	Standortfaktoren *pl*	location factors	facteurs dépendant du lieu d'implantation *m pl*	—	factores de ubicación *m pl*

	D	E	F	I	Es
fattura¹ (I)	Rechnung f	invoice	facture f	—	factura f
fattura² (I)	Faktura f	invoice	facture f	—	factura f
fattura doganale (I)	Zollfaktura f	customs invoice	facture douanière f	—	factura arancelaria f
fattura fittizia (I)	fingierte Rechnung f	fictitious invoice	facture simulée f	—	factura ficticia f
fattura pro forma (I)	Proforma-Rechnung f	pro forma invoice	facture pro forma f	—	factura proforma f
fatturato (I)	Umsatz m	turnover	chiffre d'affaires m	—	volumen de ventas m
fatturato minimo (I)	Mindestumsatz m	minimum turnover	chiffre d'affaires minimum m	—	cifra de venta mínima f
fatturato netto (I)	Nettoumsatz m	net turnover	chiffre d'affaires net m	—	ventas netas f pl
fatturazione¹ (I)	Fakturierung f	making out an invoice	facturation f	—	facturación f
fatturazione² (I)	Rechnungsstellung f	invoicing	établissement d'une facture m	—	facturación f
faute (F)	Fehler m	mistake	—	errore m	error m
faute non intentionnelle (F)	Fahrlässigkeit f	negligence	—	negligenza f	descuido m
favorable à l'environnement (F)	umweltfreundlich	beneficial to the environment	—	ecologico	no contaminante
favorecido (Es)	Begünstigter m	beneficiary	bénéficiaire m	beneficiario m	—
fecha¹ (Es)	Datum n	date	date f	data f	—
fecha² (Es)	Termin m	deadline	date limite f	termine m	—
fecha de cita (Es)	Gesprächstermin m	appointment for a meeting	date de conversation f	appuntamento per un colloquio m	—
fecha de conferencia (Es)	Besprechungs- termin m	meeting date	date de la conférence f	termine del colloquio m	—
fecha de entrevista personal (Es)	Vorstellungstermin m	date of interview	rendez-vous de présentation m	appuntamento di presentazione m	—
fecha de liquidación (Es)	Abrechnungstag m	settling day	jour de la liquidation m	giorno di liquidazione m	—
fecha de llegada (Es)	Ankunftsdatum n	date of arrival	date d'arrivée f	data d'arrivo f	—
fecha de nacimiento (Es)	Geburtsdatum n	date of birth	date de naissance f	data di nascita f	—
fecha de partida (Es)	Abreisedatum n	date of departure	date de départ f	data di partenza f	—
fecha de vencimiento (Es)	Verfallsdatum n	expiry date	date d'échéance f	data di scadenza f	—
fee (E)	Gebühr f	—	taxe f	tassa f	derecho m
Feedback (D)	—	feedback	feed-back m	feedback m	repercusión f
feed-back (F)	Feedback n	feedback	—	feedback m	repercusión f
feedback (I)	Feedback n	feedback	feed-back m	—	repercusión f
feedback¹ (E)	Feedback n	—	feed-back m	feedback m	repercusión f
feedback² (E)	Rückkopplung f	—	accouplement réactif m	accoppiamento a reazione m	reacoplamiento m
Fehler (D)	—	mistake	faute f	errore m	error m
fehlerhaft (D)	—	defective	défectueux	difettoso	defectuoso
Fehlerprotokoll (D)	—	record of errors	protocole d'erreurs m	protocollo errori m	protocolo de errores m
Fehlinvestition (D)	—	misconceived capital projects	mauvais investissement m	investimento sbagliato m	inversión equivocada f
Feingehalt (D)	—	fine gold content	titre m	titolo m	ley f
Feingewicht (D)	—	weight of fine gold	poids de métal fin m	peso fino m	peso fino m
felicitaciónes (Es)	Glückwunsch m	congratulations	félicitations f	auguri m pl	—
félicitations (F)	Glückwunsch m	congratulations	—	auguri m pl	felicitaciónes f
feria (Es)	Messe f	fair	foire f	fiera f	—
feria comercial (Es)	Handelsmesse f	trade fair	foire commerciale f	fiera commerciale f	—
feria de moda (Es)	Modemesse f	fashion fair	foire de la mode f	fiera della moda f	—
feria de muestras (Es)	Mustermesse f	trade fair	foire d'échantillons f	fiera campionaria f	—
feria de otoño (Es)	Herbstmesse f	autumn fair	foire d'automne f	fiera autunnale f	—
ferie (I)	Urlaub m	annual holidays/ vacation	congé m/ vacances f pl	—	vacaciones f pl/ vacaciones colectivas de la empresa f pl

	D	E	F	I	Es
ferie aziendali (I)	Betriebsferien *pl*	annual holiday	clôture annuelle de l'établissement *f*	—	vacaciones de la empresa *f pl*
ferie non pagate (I)	unbezahlter Urlaub *m*	unpaid vacation	congé non payé *m*	—	vacaciones no pagadas *f pl*
ferie pagate (I)	bezahlter Urlaub *m*	paid vacation	congé payé *m*	—	vacaciones con goce de sueldo *f pl*
fermeture douanière (F)	Zollverschluß *m*	customs seal	—	sigillo doganale *m*	precinto aduanero *m*
fermo posta (I)	postlagernd	poste restante	poste restante	—	lista de correos *m*
Fernmeldeamt (D)	—	telephone exchange	service de télécommunication *m*	ufficio telecomunicazioni *m*	central interurbana *f*
Fernschreiber (D)	—	teleprinter	téléimprimeur *m*	telescrivente *m*	télex *m*
Fernsehwerbung (D)	—	television advertising	émission publicitaire télévisée *f*	pubblicità televisiva *f*	publicidad televisiva *f*
Fernsprecher (D)	—	telephone	appareil téléphonique *m*	telefono *m*	teléfono *m*
Fernverkehr (D)	—	long distance traffic	trafic sur longues distances *m*	traffico a grande distanza *m*	transporte a distancia *m*
Fertigprodukt (D)	—	finished product	produit fini *m*	prodotto finito *m*	producto acabado *m*
Fertigstellung (D)	—	completion	achèvement *m*	completamento *m*	terminación total *f*
Fertigungsmenge (D)	—	manufactured quantity	quantité fabriquée *f*	quantitativo di produzione *m*	cantidad producida *f*
Fertigungs-programm (D)	—	production programme	programme de fabrication *m*	programma di produzione *m*	programa de producción *m*
Fertigungsprozeß (D)	—	production procedure	déroulement de la fabrication *m*	processo produttivo *m*	proceso de producción *m*
Fertigungs-verfahren (D)	—	production process	méthode de production *f*	procedimento produttivo *m*	procedimiento de fabricación *m*
feste Wechselkurse (D)	—	fixed exchange rates	taux de change fixe *m*	cambi fissi *m pl*	tipos de cambio fijos *m pl*
Festeinkommen (D)	—	fixed income	revenu fixe *m*	reddito fisso *m*	salario fijo *m*
fester Zins (D)	—	fixed interest rate	intérêt fixe *m*	tasso d'interesse fisso *m*	interés fijo *m*
Festgeld (D)	—	fixed deposit	argent immobilisé *m*	denaro vincolato *m*	depósito a plazo *m*
Festgeldkonto (D)	—	time deposit account	compte de dépôt à terme *m*	deposito vincolato *m*	cuenta a plazo *f*
Festpreis (D)	—	fixed price	prix fixe *m*	prezzo fisso *m*	precio fijo *m*
Feuerversicherung (D)	—	fire insurance	assurance contre l'incendie *f*	assicurazione contro incendi *f*	seguro contra incendios *m*
feuille publicitaire (F)	Prospekt *m*	leaflet/prospectus	—	prospetto *m*	prospecto *m*/ folleto *m*
fiador (Es)	Bürge *m*	guarantor	garant *m*	fideiussore *m*	—
fianza (Es)	Bürgschaft *f*	guarantee	caution *f*	fideiussione *f*	—
fianza con beneficio de excusión (Es)	Ausfallbürgschaft *f*	deficiency guarantee	garantie de bonne fin *f*	fideiussione d'indennità *f*	—
fianza de contratista (Es)	Gewährleistungs-garantie *f*	guarantee for proper execution	caution de garantie *f*	garanzia di esecuzione *f*	—
fianza de puesta en libertad (Es)	Haftkaution *f*	bail	caution pour être mis en liberté *f*	cauzione per la scarcerazione *f*	—
ficha (Es)	Karteikarte *f*	index card	fiche *f*	scheda *f*	—
fiche (F)	Karteikarte *f*	index card	—	scheda *f*	ficha *f*
fichero (Es)	Kartei *f*	card-index	cartothèque	schedario *m*	—
fichier de données (F)	Datei *f*	file	—	file *m*	archivo de datos *m*
fictitious invoice (E)	fingierte Rechnung *f*	—	facture simulée *f*	fattura fittizia *f*	factura ficticia *f*
fictitious prices (E)	Mondpreise *pl*	—	prix fictifs *m pl*	prezzi alle stelle *m pl*	precios ficticios *m pl*
fictitious profit (E)	Scheingewinn *m*	—	gain fictif *m*	utile fittizio *m*	beneficio simulado *m*
fictitious transaction (E)	Scheingeschäft *n*	—	opération simulée *f*	negozio simulato *m*	operación ficticia *f*
fideiussione (I)	Bürgschaft *f*	guarantee	caution *f*	—	fianza *f*
fideiussione d'indennità (I)	Ausfallbürgschaft *f*	deficiency guarantee	garantie de bonne fin *f*	—	fianza con beneficio de excusión *f*
fideiussore (I)	Bürge *m*	guarantor	garant *m*	—	fiador *m*
fiduciary account (E)	Anderkonto *n*	—	compte de tiers *m*	conto per terzi *m*	cuenta fiduciaria de un abogado *f*

	D	E	F	I	Es
field of action (E)	Aktionsfeld n	—	champ d'action m	campo d'azione m	campo de acción m
field of activity (E)	Tätigkeitsfeld n	—	champ d'acitivité m	campo d'azione m	campo de actividad m
field of the economy (E)	Wirtschaftszweig m	—	secteur économique m	settore economico m	ramo económico m
field staff (E)	Außendienst-mitarbeiter m	—	personnel du service extérieur m	collaboratore del servizio esterno m	colaborador en el servicio exterior m
field work (E)	Außendienst m	—	service extérieur m	servizio esterno m	servicio exterior m
fiera (I)	Messe f	fair	foire f	—	feria f
fiera autunnale (I)	Herbstmesse f	autumn fair	foire d'automne f	—	feria de otoño f
fiera campionaria (I)	Mustermesse f	trade fair	foire d'échantillons f	—	feria de muestras f
fiera commerciale (I)	Handelsmesse f	trade fair	foire commerciale f	—	feria comercial f
fiera della moda (I)	Modemesse f	fashion fair	foire de la mode f	—	feria de moda f
fijación de los cambios (Es)	Kursfestsetzung f	fixing of prices	détermination des cours f	fissazione dei corsi f	—
fijo (Es)	Fixum n	fixed sum	somme fixe f	somma fissa f	—
fijo anual (Es)	Jahresfixum n	fixed annual salary	fixe annuel m	fisso annuale m	—
file¹ (E)	Datei f	—	fichier de données m	file m	archivo de datos m
file² (E)	Akte f	—	dossier m	pratica f	documento m
file³ (E)	Ablage f	—	collection des dossiers f	archivio m	archivo m
file (I)	Datei f	file	fichier de données m	—	archivo de datos m
filial¹ (Es)	Zweigstelle f	branch	agence f	agenzia f	—
filial² (Es)	Filiale f	branch	agence f	filiale f	—
filial³ (Es)	Zweigniederlassung f	branch office	succursale f	succursale f	—
filial⁴ (Es)	Tochtergesellschaft f	subsidiary	société filiale f	società affiliata f	—
Filiale (D)	—	branch	agence f	filiale f	filial f
filiale¹ (I)	Zweigbetrieb m	branch business	établissement secondaire m	—	sucursal f
filiale² (I)	Filiale f	branch	agence f	—	filial f
filial en el exterior (Es)	Auslands-niederlassung f	branch abroad	succursale à l'étranger f	succursale estera f	—
Filialleiter (D)	—	branch manager	directeur d'agence m	direttore della filiale m	jefe de sucursal m
Filialnetz (D)	—	branch network	réseau de succursales m	rete delle filiali f	red de sucursales f
filing (E)	Aktenablage f	—	archives f pl	archivio delle pratiche m	archivo m
film pubblicitario (I)	Werbefilm m	advertising film	film publicitaire m	—	película promocional f
film publicitaire (F)	Werbefilm m	advertising film	—	film pubblicitario m	película promocional f
filosofia d'acquisto (I)	Kaufverhalten n	purchase pattern	comportement d'achat m	—	comportamiento de compra m
fils du partenaire (F)	Junior-Partner m	junior partner	—	junior partner m	socio menor m
final control (E)	Endkontrolle f	—	contrôle final m	controllo finale m	control final m
final del trimestre (Es)	Quartalsende n	end of a quarter	fin de trimestre f	fine trimestre f	—
financement (F)	Finanzierung f	financing	—	finanziamento m	financiación f
financement à la construction (F)	Baufinanzierung f	construction financing	—	finanziamento di costruzione m	financiación de la construcción f
financement de la vente à crédit (F)	Konsum-finanzierung f	financing of consumption	—	finanziamento del consumo m	financiación del consumo f
financement de l'exportation (F)	Ausfuhrfinanzierung f	export financing	—	finanziamento delle esportazioni m	financiación de la exportación f
financement des ventes (F)	Absatzfinanzierung f	sales financing	—	finanziamento delle vendite m	financiación de las ventas f
financement d'opéra-tion d'exportation (F)	Exportfinanzierung f	financing of exports	—	finanziamento delle esportazioni m	financiación de exportación f
financement du déficit (F)	Defizitfinanzierung f	deficit financing	—	finanziamento del deficit m	financiación del déficit m
financement du rachat (F)	Ablösungs-finanzierung f	redemption financing	—	finanziamento del rimborso m	financiamiento de amortización m

	D	E	F	I	Es
financement sans recours (F)	Forfaitierung f	non-recourse financing	—	forfetizzazione f	financiación sin recurso f
financement successif (F)	Anschlußfinanzierung f	follow-up financing	—	finanziamento successivo m	financiación sucesiva f
finances (E)	Finanzen pl	—	finances f pl	finanze f pl	finanzas f pl
finances (F)	Finanzen pl	finances	—	finanze f pl	finanzas f pl
financiación (Es)	Finanzierung f	financing	financement m	finanziamento m	—
financiación de exportación (Es)	Exportfinanzierung f	financing of exports	financement d'opération d'exportation m	finanziamento delle esportazioni m	—
financiación de la construcción (Es)	Baufinanzierung f	construction financing	financement à la construction m	finanziamento di costruzione m	—
financiación de la exportación (Es)	Ausfuhrfinanzierung f	export financing	financement de l'exportation m	finanziamento delle esportazioni m	—
financiación de las ventas (Es)	Absatzfinanzierung f	sales financing	financement des ventes m	finanziamento delle vendite m	—
financiación del comercio exterior (Es)	Außenhandelsfinanzierung f	foreign trade financing	aide financière à l'exportation m	finanziamento del commercio estero m	—
financiación del consumo (Es)	Konsumfinanzierung f	financing of consumption	financement de la vente à crédit m	finanziamento del consumo m	—
financiación del déficit (Es)	Defizitfinanzierung f	deficit financing	financement du déficit m	finanziamento del deficit m	—
financiación externa (Es)	Fremdfinanzierung f	debt financing	constitution de capital par apport de tiers f	finanziamento passivo m	—
financiación propia (Es)	Eigenfinanzierung f	self-financing	autofinancement m	autofinanziamento m	—
financiación sin recurso (Es)	Forfaitierung f	non-recourse financing	financement sans recours m	forfetizzazione f	—
financiación sucesiva (Es)	Anschlußfinanzierung f	follow-up financing	financement successif m	finanziamento successivo m	—
financial accounting (E)	Finanzbuchhaltung f	—	comptabilité financière f	contabilità finanziaria f	contabilidad financiera f
financial assets (E)	Geldvermögen n	—	moyens financiers m	patrimonio monetario m	activo monetario m
financial backer (E)	Geldgeber m	—	bailleur de fonds m	finanziatore m	prestamista m
financial debacle (E)	Finanzdebakel n	—	débâcle fiancière f	dissesto finanziario m	descalabro financiero m
financial difficulties (E)	Zahlungsschwierigkeit f	—	difficultés financières f pl	difficoltà di pagamento f	dificultades de pago f pl
financial equalization (E)	Finanzausgleich m	—	compensation financière f	compensazione finanziaria f	ajuste financiero m
financial failure (E)	finanzieller Zusammenbruch m	—	débâcle financière f	crollo finanziario m	derrumbamiento financiero m
financial plan (E)	Finanzplan m	—	plan financier m	piano finanziario m	presupuesto m
financial report (E)	Finanzbericht m	—	rapport financier m	relazione finanziaria f	informe financiero m
financial situation (E)	Vermögensverhältnisse pl	—	situation financière f	situazione patrimoniale f	situación económica f
financial sovereignty (E)	Finanzhoheit f	—	souveraineté en matière budgétaire f	sovranità finanziaria f	soberanía financiera f
financial standing (E)	Kreditfähigkeit f	—	solvabilité f	capacità di credito f	crédito m
financial year[1] (E)	Geschäftsjahr n	—	exercice commercial m	esercizio commerciale m	ejercicio m
financial year[2] (E)	Rechnungsjahr n	—	exercice comptable m	anno d'esercizio m	ejercicio m
financial year[3] (E)	Haushaltsjahr n	—	exercice budgétaire m	anno finanziario m	ejercicio m
financiamiento de amortización (Es)	Ablösungsfinanzierung f	redemption financing	financement du rachat m	finanziamento del rimborso m	—
financing (E)	Finanzierung f	—	financement m	finanziamento m	financiación f
financing of consumption (E)	Konsumfinanzierung f	—	financement de la vente à crédit m	finanziamento del consumo m	financiación del consumo f
financing of exports (E)	Exportfinanzierung f	—	financement d'opération d'exportation m	finanziamento delle esportazioni m	financiación de exportación f
Finanzamt (D)	—	inland revenue office	service de contributions m	ufficio delle imposte m	Hacienda f
finanzas (Es)	Finanzen pl	finances	finances f pl	finanze f pl	—
Finanzausgleich (D)	—	financial equalization	compensation financière f	compensazione finanziaria f	ajuste financiero m

	D	E	F	I	Es
Finanzbericht (D)	—	financial report	rapport financier *m*	relazione finanziaria *f*	informe financiero *m*
Finanzbuchhaltung (D)	—	financial accounting	comptabilité financière *f*	contabilità finanziaria *f*	contabilidad financiera *f*
Finanzdebakel (D)	—	financial debacle	débâcle fiancière *f*	dissesto finanziario *m*	descalabro financiero *m*
finanze (I)	Finanzen *pl*	finances	finances *f pl*	—	finanzas *f pl*
Finanzen (D)	—	finances	finances *f pl*	finanze *f pl*	finanzas *f pl*
Finanzhoheit (D)	—	financial sovereignty	souveraineté en matière budgétaire *f*	sovranità finanziaria *f*	soberanía financiera *f*
finanziamento (I)	Finanzierung *f*	financing	financement *m*	—	financiación *f*
finanziamento del commercio estero (I)	Außenhandels-finanzierung *f*	foreign trade financing	aide financière à l'exportation *m*	—	financiación del comercio exterior *f*
finanziamento del consumo (I)	Konsum-finanzierung *f*	financing of consumption	financement de la vente à crédit *m*	—	financiación del consumo *f*
finanziamento del deficit (I)	Defizitfinanzierung *f*	deficit financing	financement du déficit *m*	—	financiación del déficit *f*
finanziamento delle esportazioni (I)	Exportfinanzierung *f*	financing of exports	financement d'opéra-tion d'exportation *m*	—	financiación de exportación *f*
finanziamento delle esportazioni (I)	Ausfuhrfinanzierung *f*	export financing	financement de l'exportation *m*	—	financiación de la exportación *f*
finanziamento delle vendite (I)	Absatzfinanzierung *f*	sales financing	financement des ventes *m*	—	financiación de las ventas *f*
finanziamento del rimborso (I)	Ablösungs-finanzierung *f*	redemption financing	financement du rachat *m*	—	financiamiento de amortización *m*
finanziamento di costruzione (I)	Baufinanzierung *f*	construction financing	financement à la construction *m*	—	financiación de la construcción *f*
finanziamento passivo (I)	Fremdfinanzierung *f*	debt financing	constitution de capital par apport de tiers *f*	—	financiación externa *f*
finanziamento successivo (I)	Anschluß-finanzierung *f*	follow-up financing	financement successif *m*	—	financiación sucesiva *f*
finanziatore (I)	Geldgeber *m*	financial backer	bailleur de fonds *m*	—	prestamista *m*
finanzieller Zusammenbruch (D)	—	financial failure	débâcle financière *f*	crollo finanziario *m*	derrumbamiento financiero *m*
Finanzierung (D)	—	financing	financement *m*	finanziamento *m*	financiación *f*
Finanzierungsdauer (D)	—	period of financing	durée du financement *f*	durata del finanziamento *f*	período de financiación *m*
Finanzierungs-rechnung (D)	—	flow-of-funds analysis	analyse des flux monétaires *f*	calcolo di finanziamento *m*	análisis de flujos monetarios *m*
Finanzkontrolle (D)	—	budgetary control	contrôle de financement *m*	controllo finanziario *m*	control financiero *m*
Finanzministerium (D)	—	Ministry of Finance	ministère des finances *m*	ministero delle Finanze *m*	Hacienda *f*
Finanzmonopol (D)	—	fiscal monopoly	monopole fiscal *m*	monopolio fiscale *m*	monopolio financiero *m*
Finanzplan (D)	—	financial plan	plan financier *m*	piano finanziario *m*	presupuesto *m*
Finanzpolitik (D)	—	fiscal policy	politique financière *f*	politica finanziaria *f*	política financiera *f*
fin de mes (Es)	Ultimo *n*	end of the month	fin de mois *f*	fine mese *m*	—
fin de mois (F)	Ultimo *n*	end of the month	—	fine mese *m*	fin de mes *m*
fin de trimestre (F)	Quartalsende *n*	end of a quarter	—	fine trimestre *f*	final del trimestre *m*
fin de venta (Es)	Absatzziel *n*	sales target	objectif de vente *m*	obbiettivo di vendita *m*	—
fine¹ (E)	Geldbuße *f*	—	amende *f*	pena pecuniaria *f*	multa *f*
fine² (E)	Geldstrafe *f*	—	peine pécuniaire *f*	multa *f*	multa *f*
fine gold content (E)	Feingehalt *m*	—	titre *m*	titolo *m*	ley *f*
fine mese (I)	Ultimo *n*	end of the month	fin de mois *f*	—	fin de mes *m*
fine trimestre (I)	Quartalsende *n*	end of a quarter	fin de trimestre *f*	—	final del trimestre *m*
fingierte Rechnung (D)	—	fictitious invoice	facture simulée *f*	fattura fittizia *f*	factura ficticia *f*
finished product¹ (E)	Fertigprodukt *n*	—	produit fini *m*	prodotto finito *m*	producto acabado *m*
finished product² (E)	Endprodukt *n*	—	produit final *m*	prodotto finito *m*	producto final *m*
finishing technique (E)	Abschlußtechnik *f*	—	technique de conclusion *f*	metodo di chiusura *m*	técnica de conclusión *f*
fire insurance (E)	Feuerversicherung *f*	—	assurance contre l'incendie *f*	assicurazione contro incendi *f*	seguro contra incendios *m*

	D	E	F	I	Es
Firma (D)	—	company	entreprise f	impresa f	empresa f
firma (Es)	Unterschrift f	signature	signature f	firma f	—
firma (I)	Unterschrift f	signature	signature f	—	firma f
firma en blanco (Es)	Blankounterschrift f	blank signature	signature en blanc f	firma in bianco f	—
firma in bianco (I)	Blankounterschrift f	blank signature	signature en blanc f	—	firma en blanco f
firmare (I)	unterschreiben	sign	signer	—	signar
Firmenanschrift (D)	—	company address	adresse de la maison f	indirizzo della ditta m	dirección de la empresa f
Firmenkonto (D)	—	company account	compte de maison m	conto intestato ad una ditta m	cuenta de la empresa f
Firmenname (D)	—	company name	nom de la maison m	denominazione f/ ragione sociale f	razón social f
Firmenschild (D)	—	company's name plate	enseigne commerciale f	insegna dell'impresa f	letrero de establecimiento m
Firmensitz (D)	—	domicile of the company	siège social m	sede f	sede social f
Firmenwagen (D)	—	company car	voiture appartenant à l'entreprise f	vettura aziendale f	coche de empresa m
Firmenwert (D)	—	goodwill	valeur commerciale f	goodwill m	fondo de comercio m
first class (E)	erstklassig	—	de première qualité	di prima categoria	de primera calidad
first class quality (E)	beste Qualität	—	première qualité f	qualità ottima f	primera calidad f
fiscal fraud (E)	Steuerbetrug m	—	fraude fiscale f	frode fiscale f	fraude fiscal m
fiscal monopoly (E)	Finanzmonopol n	—	monopole fiscal m	monopolio fiscale m	monopolio financiero m
fiscal policy (E)	Finanzpolitik f	—	politique financière f	politica finanziaria f	política financiera f
fiscal policy (E)	Steuerpolitik f	—	politique fiscale f	politica fiscale f	política fiscal f
Fischerei (D)	—	fishing	pêcherie f	pesca f	pesca f
Fischereirecht (D)	—	fishing rights	droit de pêche m	diritto della pesca m	derecho pesquero m
fishing (E)	Fischerei f	—	pêcherie f	pesca f	pesca f
fishing rights (E)	Fischereirecht n	—	droit de pêche m	diritto della pesca m	derecho pesquero m
fissazione dei corsi (I)	Kursfestsetzung f	fixing of prices	détermination des cours f	—	fijación de los cambios f
fisso annuale (I)	Jahresfixum n	fixed annual salary	fixe annuel m	—	fijo anual m
fixe annuel (F)	Jahresfixum n	fixed annual salary	—	fisso annuale m	fijo anual m
fixed annual salary (E)	Jahresfixum n	—	fixe annuel m	fisso annuale m	fijo anual m
fixed assets[1] (E)	Sachanlagen pl	—	immobilisations corporelles f pl	immobilizzazioni f pl	inmuebles y utillaje m pl
fixed assets[2] (E)	Anlagevermögen n	—	valeurs immobilisées f pl	attivo fisso m	activo fijo m
fixed costs (E)	Fixkosten pl	—	coûts fixes m pl	costi fissi m pl	gastos fijos m pl
fixed deposit (E)	Festgeld n	—	argent immobilisé m	denaro vincolato m	depósito a plazo m
fixed exchange (E)	Mengennotierung f	—	cotation de quantité f	cambio reale m	cotización real f
fixed exchange rates (E)	feste Wechselkurse pl	—	taux de change fixe m	cambi fissi m pl	tipos de cambio fijos m pl
fixed income (E)	Festeinkommen n	—	revenu fixe m	reddito fisso m	salario fijo m
fixed interest rate (E)	fester Zins m	—	intérêt fixe m	tasso d'interesse fisso m	interés fijo m
fixed price (E)	Festpreis m	—	prix fixe m	prezzo fisso m	precio fijo m
fixed sum (E)	Fixum n	—	somme fixe f	somma fissa f	fijo m
fixing of a quota (E)	Kontingentierung f	—	contingentement m	contingentamento m	contingentación f
fixing of prices (E)	Kursfestsetzung f	—	détermination des cours f	fissazione dei corsi f	fijación de los cambios f
Fixkosten (D)	—	fixed costs	coûts fixes m pl	costi fissi m pl	gastos fijos m pl
Fixum (D)	—	fixed sum	somme fixe f	somma fissa f	fijo m
flaconnage non consigné (F)	Einwegflasche f	one-way bottle	—	bottiglia a perdere f	botella de un solo uso f
flat rate amount (E)	Pauschalbetrag m	—	somme forfaitaire f	somma forfettaria f	suma global f
flessione della domanda (I)	Nachfragerückgang m	decrease in demand	recul de la demande m	—	disminución en la demanda f
flete aéreo (Es)	Luftfracht f	air freight	fret aérien m	nolo aereo m	—

	D	E	F	I	Es
flete pagado (Es)	Fracht bezahlt	freight paid	fret payé	nolo pagato	—
flexible exchange rate (E)	flexibler Wechselkurs m	—	taux de change flottant m	cambio flessibile m	tipo flotante de cambio m
flexibler Wechselkurs (D)	—	flexible exchange rate	taux de change flottant m	cambio flessibile m	tipo flotante de cambio m
flight of capital (E)	Kapitalflucht f	—	évasion des capitaux f	fuga dei capitali f	fuga de capital f
Floating (D)	—	floating	système des changes flottants m	floating m	flotación f
floating (E)	Floating n	—	système des changes flottants m	floating m	flotación f
floating (I)	Floating n	floating	système des changes flottants m	—	flotación f
floor price (E)	Niedrigstkurs m	—	cours le plus bas m	corso minimo m	cotización mínima f
flotación (Es)	Floating n	floating	système des changes flottants m	floating m	—
flow-of-funds analysis (E)	Finanzierungs-rechnung f	—	analyse des flux monétaires f	calcolo di finanziamento m	análisis de flujos monetarios m
fluctuación (Es)	Fluktuation f	fluctuation	fluctuation f	fluttuazione f	—
fluctuación de las necesidades (Es)	Bedarfsschwankung f	fluctuations in requirements	oscillations de demande f pl	oscillazioni del fabbisogno f pl	—
fluctuaciones en la producción (Es)	Produktions-schwankung f	fluctuations in production	fluctuation de la production f pl	oscillazione della produzione f	—
fluctuation (E)	Fluktuation f	—	fluctuation f	fluttuazione f	fluctuación f
fluctuation (F)	Fluktuation f	fluctuation	—	fluttuazione f	fluctuación f
fluctuation de la production (F)	Produktions-schwankung f	fluctuations in production	—	oscillazione della produzione f	fluctuaciones en la producción f pl
fluctuation des prix (F)	Preisschwankung f	price fluctuation	—	fluttuazione dei prezzi f	oscilación de precios f
fluctuations in production (E)	Produktions-schwankung f	—	fluctuation de la production f pl	oscillazione della produzione f	fluctuaciones en la producción f pl
fluctuations in requirements (E)	Bedarfsschwankung f	—	oscillations de demande f pl	oscillazioni del fabbisogno f pl	fluctuación de las necesidades f
Fluktuation (D)	—	fluctuation	fluctuation f	fluttuazione f	fluctuación f
Flurbereinigung (D)	—	compulsory consoli-dation of farmland	remembrement parcellaire m	ricomposizione fondiaria f	concentración parcelaria f
fluttuazione (I)	Fluktuation f	fluctuation	fluctuation f	—	fluctuación f
fluttuazione dei prezzi (I)	Preisschwankung f	price fluctuation	fluctuation des prix f	—	oscilación de precios f
foam material (E)	Schaumstoff m	—	mousse synthétique f	espanso m	espumoso plástico m
foire (F)	Messe f	fair	—	fiera f	feria f
foire commerciale (F)	Handelsmesse f	trade fair	—	fiera commerciale f	feria comercial f
foire d'automne (F)	Herbstmesse f	autumn fair	—	fiera autunnale f	feria de otoño f
foire d'échantillons (F)	Mustermesse f	trade fair	—	fiera campionaria f	feria de muestras f
foire de la mode (F)	Modemesse f	fashion fair	—	fiera della moda f	feria de moda f
Folgeauftrag (D)	—	follow-up order	commande consécutive f	ordine successivo m	orden sucesivo f
Folgeschäden (D)	—	consequential damages	dommage consécutif m	danni indiretti m pl	daño consecuencial m
folleto (Es)	Broschüre f	brochure	prospectus m	depliant m	—
follow-up financing (E)	Anschluß-finanzierung f	—	financement successif m	finanziamento successivo m	financiación sucesiva f
follow-up order (E)	Folgeauftrag m	—	commande consécutive f	ordine successivo m	orden sucesivo f
fomento de la exportació (Es)	Ausfuhrförderung f	measures to encourage exports	encouragement à l'exportation m	promozione delle esportazioni f	—
fonctionnaire (F)	Beamter m	official	—	funzionario m	funcionario m
fondation (F)	Stiftung f	foundation	—	fondazione f	fundación f
fondation d'existence (F)	Existenzgründung f	setting up of new business	—	costituzione di un lavoro indipendente f	fundación de existencia f
fondazione (I)	Stiftung f	foundation	fondation f	—	fundación f
fondé de procuration (F)	Prokurist m	"Prokurist" (authorized clerk)	—	procuratore m	apoderado general m

	D	E	F	I	Es
fondo (Es)	Fonds *m*	fund	fonds *m pl*	fondo *m*	—
fondo (I)	Fonds *m*	fund	fonds *m pl*	—	fondo *m*
fondo ammortamenti (I)	Abschreibungs-fonds *m*	depreciation fund	fonds d'amortissement *m*	—	fondo amortización *m*
fondo amortización (Es)	Abschreibungs-fonds *m*	depreciation fund	fonds d'amortissement *m*	fondo ammortamenti *m*	—
fondo de bonos (Es)	Rentenfonds *m*	pension fund	fonds d'Etat *m*/ effets publics *m pl*	fondo obbligazionario *m*	—
fondo de capital (Es)	Kapitalstock *m*	capital stock	réserve de capital *f*	riserva di capitale *f*	—
fondo de comercio (Es)	Firmenwert *m*	goodwill	valeur commerciale *f*	goodwill *m*	—
fondo de compensación (Es)	Ausgleichsfonds *m*	compensation fund	fonds de compensation *m*	fondo di compensazione *m*	—
fondo de inversión mobiliaria (Es)	Wertpapierfonds *m*	securities fund	fonds de valeurs mobilières *m*	fondo titoli *m*	—
fondo de inversiones (Es)	Investmentfonds *m*	unit trust	fonds commun de placement *m*	fondo d'investimento *m*	—
fondo de reserva (Es)	Reservefonds *m*	reserve fund	fonds de réserve *m*	fondo di riserva *m*	—
fondo di compensazione (I)	Ausgleichsfonds *m*	compensation fund	fonds de compensation *m*	—	fondo de compensación *m*
fondo d'investimento (I)	Investmentfonds *m*	unit trust	fonds commun de placement *m*	—	fondo de inversiones *m*
fondo di riserva (I)	Reservefonds *m*	reserve fund	fonds de réserve *m*	—	fondo de reserva *m*
fondo immobiliare (I)	Immobilienfonds *m*	real estate fund	fonds immobilier *m*	—	fondo inmobiliario *f*
fondo inmobiliario (Es)	Immobilienfonds *m*	real estate fund	fonds immobilier *m*	fondo immobiliare *m*	—
fondo obbligazionario (I)	Rentenfonds *m*	pension fund	fonds d'Etat *m*/ effets publics *m pl*	—	fondo de bonos *m*
fondos bloqueados (Es)	Sperrkonto *n*	blocked account	compte bloqué *m*	conto vincolato *m*	—
fondo titoli (I)	Wertpapierfonds *m*	securities fund	fonds de valeurs mobilières *m*	—	fondo de inversión mobiliaria *m*
Fonds (D)	—	fund	fonds *m pl*	fondo *m*	fondo *m*
fonds (F)	Fonds *m*	fund	—	fondo *m*	fondo *m*
fonds commun de placement (F)	Investmentfonds *m*	unit trust	—	fondo d'investimento *m*	fondo de inversiones *m*
fonds d'amortissement (F)	Abschreibungs-fonds *m*	depreciation fund	—	fondo ammortamenti *m*	fondo amortización *m*
fonds de compensation (F)	Ausgleichsfonds *m*	compensation fund	—	fondo di compensazione *m*	fondo de compensación *m*
fonds de réserve (F)	Reservefonds *m*	reserve fund	—	fondo di riserva *m*	fondo de reserva *m*
fonds d'Etat (F)	Rentenfonds *m*	pension fund	—	fondo obbligazionario *m*	fondo de bonos *m*
fonds de valeurs mobilières (F)	Wertpapierfonds *m*	securities fund	—	fondo titoli *m*	fondo de inversión mobiliaria *m*
fonds immobilier (F)	Immobilienfonds *m*	real estate fund	—	fondo immobiliare *m*	fondo inmobiliario *f*
fonds social (F)	Aktienkapital *n*	share capital	—	capitale azionario *m*	capital en acciones *m*
fonte d'acquisto (I)	Bezugsquelle *f*	source of supply	source d'approvi-sionnement *f*	—	fuente de suministro *f*
for account of a third party (E)	für fremde Rechnung	—	pour compte de tiers	per conto terzi	por cuenta ajena
forced sale (E)	Zwangsverkauf *m*	—	vente forcée *f*	vendita giudiziaria *f*	venta forzada *f*
force productive (F)	Ertragskraft *f*	earning capacity	—	redditività *f*	rentabilidad *f*
forces du marché (F)	Marktkräfte *pl*	market forces	—	forze di mercato *f pl*	fuerzas del mercado *f pl*
Förderlimit (D)	—	production limit	limite de production *f*	limite d'estrazione *m*	limite de producción *m*
Fördermenge (D)	—	output	quantité extraite *f*	quantitativo d'estrazione *m*	cantidad producida *f*
Förderquote (D)	—	production quota	quote-part de production *f*	quota d'estrazione *f*	cuota de producción *f*
forecast(ing) (E)	Prognose *f*	—	perspective *f*	prognosi *f*	pronóstico *m*
forecasting techniques (E)	Prognosetechnik *f*	—	technique de pronostic *f*	tecnica della prognosi *f*	técnica de pronóstico *f*
foreign account (E)	Auslandskonto *n*	—	compte d'étranger *m*	conto estero *m*	cuenta exterior *m*

	D	E	F	I	Es
foreign assets (E)	Auslandsvermögen *n*	—	avoirs à l'étranger *m pl*	patrimonio estero *m*	activo exterior *m*
foreign bill of exchange (E)	Auslandswechsel *n*	—	traite tirée sur l'étranger *f*	cambiale estera *f*	letra sobre el exterior *f*
foreign bond (E)	Auslandsanleihe *f*	—	emprunt extérieur *m*	prestito estero *m*	empréstito exterior *m*
foreign business (E)	Auslandsgeschäft *n*	—	opération avec l'étranger *f*	affare con l'estero *m*	negocio de exporta- ción o importación *m*
foreign capital (E)	Auslandskapital *n*	—	capital étranger *m*	capitale estero *m*	capital extranjero *m*
foreign currency account (E)	Währungskonto *n*	—	compte en monnaies étrangères *m*	conto in valuta *m*	cuenta de moneda extranjera *f*
foreign customer (E)	Auslandskunde *f*	—	client étranger *m*	cliente estero *m*	cliente extranjero *m*
foreign customs territory (E)	Zollausland *n*	—	territoire hors du con- trôle de la douane *m*	territorio doganale estero *m*	territorio aduanero exterior *m*
foreign debts (E)	Auslandsschulden *pl*	—	dettes à l'étranger *f pl*	debiti con l'estero *m pl*	deudas exteriores *f pl*
foreign demand (E)	Auslandsnachfrage *f*	—	demande en prove- nance de l'étranger *f*	domanda estera *f*	demanda exterior *f*
foreigner (E)	Ausländer *m*	—	étranger *m*	straniero *m*	extranjero *m*
foreign exchange and gold balance (E)	Gold- und Devisenbilanz *f*	—	balance d'or et de devises *f*	bilancia dell'oro e delle divise *f*	balanza de oro y divisas *f*
foreign exchange authorization (E)	Devisen- genehmigung *f*	—	autorisation de change *f*	autorizzazione valutaria *f*	certificado de divisas *m*
foreign exchange balance (E)	Devisenbilanz *f*	—	compte de devises *m*	bilancia delle divise *f*	balanza de divisas *f*
foreign exchange control[1] (E)	Devisenkontrolle *f*	—	contrôle des changes *m*	controllo delle divise *m*	control de divisas *m*
foreign exchange control[2] (E)	Devisen- bewirtschaftung *f*	—	contrôle des devises *m*	controllo valutario *m*	control de divisas *m*
foreign exchange dealings[1] (E)	Devisenhandel *m*	—	marché des changes *m*	commercio delle divise *m*	operaciones de divisas *f pl*
foreign exchange dealings[2] (E)	Devisenverkehr *m*	—	mouvement des devises *m*	commercio dei cambi *m*	tráfico de divisas *m*
foreign exchange market[1] (E)	Devisenmarkt *m*	—	marché des changes *m*	mercato valutario *m*	mercado de divisas *m*
foreign exchange market[2] (E)	Devisenbörse *f*	—	bourse de devises *f*	borsa valutaria *f*	Bolsa de divisas *f*
foreign exchange offset agreement (E)	Devisenausgleichs- abkommen *n*	—	accord de compensa- tion de devises *m*	accordo di clearing valutario *m*	acuerdo de compen- sación de divisas *m*
foreign exchange outflow (E)	Devisenabfluß *m*	—	sortie de devises *f*	deflusso di divise *m*	drenaje de divisas *m*
foreign exchange rate (E)	Devisenkurs *m*	—	taux de change *m*	cambio delle divise *m*	cambio *m*
foreign exchange[1] (E)	Devisen *pl*	—	devises *f pl*	divise *f pl*	divisas *f pl*
foreign exchange[2] (E)	Valuta *f*	—	monnaie étrangère *f*	valuta *f*/divise *f pl*	moneda extranjera *f*/ divisas *f pl*/valuta *f*
foreign markets (E)	Auslandsmärkte *pl*	—	marchés extérieurs *m pl*	mercati esteri *m pl*	mercado exterior *m*
foreign trade (E)	Außenhandel *m*	—	commerce extérieur *m*	commercio estero *m*	comercio exterior *m*
foreign trade financing (E)	Außenhandels- finanzierung *f*	—	aide financière à l'exportation *m*	finanziamento del commercio estero *m*	financiación del comercio exterior *f*
foreign trade monopoly (E)	Außenhandels- monopol *n*	—	monopole du commerce extérieur *m*	monopolio del commercio estero *m*	monopolio del comercio exterior *m*
foreign trade policy (E)	Außenhandelspolitik *f*	—	politique de commerce extérieur *f*	politica del commercio estero *f*	politica comercial exterior *f*
foreign worker (E)	ausländische Arbeitnehmer *m*	—	travailleur étranger *m*	prestatori d'opera stranieri *m pl*	trabajadores extranjeros *m*
forestry (E)	Forstwirtschaft *f*	—	économie forestière *f*	economia forestale *f*	silvicultura *f*
forfait de frais (F)	Spesenpauschale *f*	allowance for expenses	—	forfait di spese *m*	suma global de gastos *f*
forfait di spese (I)	Spesenpauschale *f*	allowance for expenses	forfait de frais *m*	—	suma global de gastos *f*
Forfaitierung (D)	—	non-recourse financing	financement sans recours *m*	forfetizzazione *f*	financiación sin recurso *f*
forfetizzazione (I)	Forfaitierung *f*	non-recourse financing	financement sans recours *m*	—	financiación sin recurso *f*

	D	E	F	I	Es
forged cheque (E)	gefälschter Scheck *m*	—	chèque maquillé *m*	assegno falsificato *m*	cheque falsificado *m*
form (E)	Formular *n*	—	formulaire *m*	modulo *m*	formulario *m*
formación de capital (Es)	Vermögensbildung *f*	capital formation	formation de capital *f*	formazione del patrimonio *f*	—
formación de carteles (Es)	Kartellbildung *f*	cartel formation	cartellisation *f*	costituzione di cartelli *f*	—
formación de los vendedores (Es)	Verkäuferschulung *f*	sales training	formation des vendeurs *f*	addestramento dei venditori *m*	—
formación de precios (Es)	Preisbildung *f*	formation of prices	formation des prix *f*	formazione dei prezzi *f*	—
formación de stocks (Es)	Vorratshaltung *f*	stockpiling	stockage *m*	gestione delle scorte *f*	—
formación profesional (Es)	Berufsausbildung *f*	professional training	formation professionelle *f*	formazione professionale *f*	—
forma de envío (Es)	Versandform *f*	manner of delivery	forme d'expéditoin *f*	tipo di spedizione *m*	—
forma de organización (Es)	Organisationsform *f*	pattern of organization	forme de l'organisation *f*	forma di organizzazione *f*	—
forma de organización empresarial (Es)	Unternehmensform *f*	form of business	forme de l'entreprise *f*	forma d'impresa *f*	—
forma de pago (Es)	Zahlungsform *f*	payment system	forme de payement *f*	tipo di pagamento *m*	—
forma d'impresa (I)	Unternehmensform *f*	form of business	forme de l'entreprise *f*	—	forma de organización empresarial *f*
forma di organizzazione (I)	Organisationsform *f*	pattern of organization	forme de l'organisation *f*	—	forma de organización *f*
forma escrita (Es)	Schriftform *f*	written form	forme par écrit *f*	forma scritta *f*	—
forma giuridica (I)	Rechtsform *f*	legal form	forme juridique *f*	—	forma jurídica *f*
forma jurídica (Es)	Rechtsform *f*	legal form	forme juridique *f*	forma giuridica *f*	—
forma scritta (I)	Schriftform *f*	written form	forme par écrit *f*	—	forma escrita *f*
formalidades aduaneras (Es)	Zollformalität *f*	customs formalities	formalité douanière *f*	formalità doganale *f*	—
formal identity (E)	Bilanzkontinuität *f*	—	identité des bilans successifs *f*	continuità di bilancio *f*	identidad de los balances sucsivos *f*
formalità doganale (I)	Zollformalität *f*	customs formalities	formalité douanière *f*	—	formalidades aduaneras *f pl*
formalité douanière (F)	Zollformalität *f*	customs formalities	—	formalità doganale *f*	formalidades aduaneras *f pl*
formalités en douane à l'exportation (F)	Ausfuhrabfertigung *f*	customs clearance of exports	—	sdoganamento delle esportazioni *m*	despacho de exportación *m*
formas del mercado (Es)	Marktformen *pl*	types of markets	formes du marché *f pl*	tipi di mercato *m pl*	—
format de l'annonce (F)	Anzeigenformat *n*	size of an advertisement	—	formato dell'inserzione *m*	tamaño del anuncio *m*
formatieren (D)	—	format	formatiser	formattare	formatizar
formation (E)	Gründung *f*	—	constitution *f*	costituzione *f*	fundación *f*
formation (F)	Bildung *f*	education	—	formazione *f*	educación *f*
formation de capital (F)	Vermögensbildung *f*	capital formation	—	formazione del patrimonio *f*	formación de capital *f*
formation des prix (F)	Preisbildung *f*	formation of prices	—	formazione dei prezzi *f*	formación de precios *f*
formation des vendeurs (F)	Verkäuferschulung *f*	sales training	—	addestramento dei venditori *m*	formación de los vendedores *f*
formation of prices (E)	Preisbildung *f*	—	formation des prix *f*	formazione dei prezzi *f*	formación de precios *f*
formation plan (E)	Gründungsplanung *f*	—	planification de fondation *f*	progettazione della costituzione *f*	planificación de la fundación *f*
formation professionelle (F)	Berufsausbildung *f*	professional training	—	formazione professionale *f*	formación profesional *f*
formation report (E)	Gründungsbericht *m*	—	procès-verbal de fondation *m*	relazione di costituzione *f*	informe de los fundadores *m*
formatiser (F)	formatieren	formatting	—	formattare	formatizar
formatizar (Es)	formatieren	formatting	formatiser	formattare	—
formato dell'inserzione (I)	Anzeigenformat *n*	size of an advertisement	format de l'annonce *m*	—	tamaño del anuncio *m*
formattare (I)	formatieren	format	formatiser	—	formatizar

	D	E	F	I	Es
formatting (E)	formatieren	—	formatiser	formattare	formatizar
formazione (I)	Bildung *f*	education	formation *f*	—	educación *f*
formazione dei prezzi (I)	Preisbildung *f*	formation of prices	formation des prix *f*	—	formación de precios *f*
formazione del patrimonio (I)	Vermögensbildung *f*	capital formation	formation de capital *f*	—	formación de capital *f*
formazione professionale (I)	Berufsausbildung *f*	professional training	formation professionelle *f*	—	formación profesional *f*
forme de l'entreprise (F)	Unternehmensform *f*	form of business	—	forma d'impresa *f*	forma de organización empresarial *f*
forme de l'organisation (F)	Organisationsform *f*	pattern of organization	—	forma di organizzazione *f*	forma de organización *f*
forme de payement (F)	Zahlungsform *f*	payment system	—	tipo di pagamento *m*	forma de pago *f*
forme d'expédition (F)	Versandform *f*	manner of delivery	—	tipo di spedizione *m*	forma de envío *f*
forme juridique (F)	Rechtsform *f*	legal form	—	forma giuridica *f*	forma jurídica *f*
forme par écrit (F)	Schriftform *f*	written form	—	forma scritta *f*	forma escrita *f*
formes du marché (F)	Marktformen *pl*	types of markets	—	tipi di mercato *m pl*	formas del mercado *f*
form of address (E)	Anrede *f*	—	début de lettre *m*	titolo *m*	tratamiento *m*
form of business (E)	Unternehmensform *f*	—	forme de l'entreprise *f*	forma d'impresa *f*	forma de organización empresarial *f*
formulaire (F)	Formular *n*	form	—	modulo *m*	formulario *m*
formulaire de demande (F)	Antragsformular *n*	application form	—	modulo di domanda *m*	formulario de solicitud *m*
Formular (D)	—	form	formulaire *m*	modulo *m*	formulario *m*
formulario (Es)	Formular *n*	form	formulaire *m*	modulo *m*	—
formulario de pedido (Es)	Bestellformular *n*	order form	bon de commande *m*	modulo d'ordinazione *m*	—
formulario de solicitud (Es)	Antragsformular *n*	application form	formulaire de demande *m*	modulo di domanda *m*	—
formulario en blanco (Es)	Blankoformular *n*	blank form	imprimé en blanc *m*	modulo in bianco *m*	—
fornitore¹ (I)	Lieferant *m*	supplier	fournisseur *m*	—	suministrador *m*
fornitore² (I)	Zulieferer *m*	supplier	sous-traitant *m*	—	abastecedor *m*
fornitura³ (I)	Lieferung *f*	delivery	livraison *f*	—	suministro *m*
fornitura a titolo di prova (I)	Probelieferung *f*	trial shipment	livraison à titre d'essai *f*	—	envío de prueba *m*
fornitura completa (I)	Gesamtlieferung *f*	total delivery	livraison totale *f*	—	suministro total *f*
fornitura di compensazione (I)	Ersatzlieferung *f*	substitute delivery	livraison de remplacement *f*	—	entrega de reposición *f*
fornitura parziale (I)	Teillieferung *f*	partial delivery	livraison partielle *f*	—	entrega parcial *f*
fornitura ridotta (I)	Minderlieferung *f*	short delivery	livraison en quantité inférieure *f*	—	envío incompleto *m*
fornitura supplementare (I)	Mehrlieferung *f*	additional delivery	livraison supplémentaire *f*	—	exceso *m*
foro competente (I)	Gerichtsstand *m*	jurisdiction	juridiction compétente *f*	—	tribunal competente *m*
for one's own account (E)	für eigene Rechnung	—	pour son propre compte	per conto proprio	por cuenta propia
for safekeeping (E)	zu treuen Händen	—	remettre en mains sûres	alla particolare attenzione	a la atención de
Forschung (D)	—	research	recherche *f*	ricerca *f*	investigación *f*
Forstwirtschaft (D)	—	forestry	économie forestière *f*	economia forestale *f*	silvicultura *f*
fortnight (E)	vierzehn Tage	—	quinze jours	quindici giorni	quince días *m pl*
forward contract (E)	Terminkontrakt *m*	—	contrat à terme *m*	contratto a termine *m*	contrato de entrega futura *m*
forwarder (E)	Spediteur *m*	—	commissionnaire de transport *m*	spedizioniere *m*	expeditor *m*
forward exchange dealings (E)	Devisentermingeschäft *n*	—	opérations à terme sur les changes *f pl*	operazione valutaria a termine *f*	transacciones a término en divisas *f pl*
forwarding instruction (E)	Versandvorschrift *f*	—	prescriptions concernant l'expédition *f pl*	prescrizione per la spedizione *f*	instrucción para el envío *f*
forwarding merchandise (E)	Speditionsgut *n*	—	bien transporté *m*	merce spedita *f*	mercancía transportada *f*

	D	E	F	I	Es
forward price (E)	Terminkurs *m*	—	cours de bourse à terme *m*	corso a termine *m*	cambio a término *m*
forza d'argomentazione (I)	Argumentations-stärke *f*	talent for argumentation	capacité d'argumentation *f*	—	fuerza de argumentación *f*
forze di mercato (I)	Marktkräfte *pl*	market forces	forces du marché	—	fuerzas del mercado *f pl*
fosfato (Es)	Phosphat *n*	phosphate	phosphate *m*	fosfato *m*	—
fosfato (I)	Phosphat *n*	phosphate	phosphate *m*	—	fosfato *m*
fotocopia (Es)	Fotokopie *f*	photocopy	photocopie *f*	fotocopia *f*	—
fotocopia (I)	Fotokopie *f*	photocopy	photocopie *f*	—	fotocopia *f*
fotocopiadora (Es)	Fotokopierer *m*	photocopier	photocopieur *m*	copialettere *m*	—
Fotokopie (D)	—	photocopy	photocopie *f*	fotocopia *f*	fotocopia *f*
Fotokopierer (D)	—	photocopier	photocopieur *m*	copialettere *m*	fotocopiadora *f*
foundation (E)	Stiftung *f*	—	fondation *f*	fondazione *f*	fundación *f*
fournisseur (F)	Lieferant *m*	supplier	—	fornitore *m*	suministrador *m*
fourniture sous garantie (F)	Garantieleistung *f*	guarantee	—	prestazione di garanzia *f*	aplicación de la garantía *f*
Fracht (D)	—	freight	fret *m*	nolo *m*	carga *f*
Fracht bezahlt (D)	—	freight paid	fret payé	nolo pagato	flete pagado
Frachtbrief (D)	—	consignment note	lettre de voiture *f*	lettera di vettura *f*	carta de porte *f*
Frachtbriefdoppel (D)	—	duplicate consignment note	duplicata de la lettre de voiture *f*	duplicato della lettera di vettura *m*	duplicado de la carta de porte *m*
frachtfrei (D)	—	freight paid	exempt de frais de transport	franco di nolo	franco de porte
Frachtführer (D)	—	carrier	transporteur *m*	vettore *m*	transportista *m*
Frachtgut (D)	—	cargo	marchandise à transporter *f*	merce di trasporto *f*	mercancías en pequeña velocidad *f pl*
Frachtkosten (D)	—	freight charges	frais de transport *m pl*	spese di trasporto *f pl*	gastos de transporte *m pl*
Frachtrate (D)	—	(freight) rate	taux de fret *m*	tariffa di nolo *f*	tipo de flete *m*
Frachtstücke (D)	—	packages	colis *m*	colli *m pl*	fardo *m*
Frachtvertrag (D)	—	freight contract	contrat d'affrètement *m*	contratto di trasporto *m*	contrato de transporte *m*
Frachtzuschlag (D)	—	additional freight charges	supplément de fret *m*	supplemento di nolo *m*	sobreporte *m*
fraction (E)	Bruchteil *m*	—	fraction *f*	frazione *f*	parte fraccionaria *f*
fraction (F)	Bruchteil *m*	fraction	—	frazione *f*	parte fraccionaria *f*
Fragebogen (D)	—	questionnaire	questionnaire *m*	questionario *m*	cuestionario *m*
frais (F)	Spesen *pl*	expenses	—	spese *f pl*	gastos *m pl*
frais d'acquisition (F)	Anschaffungs-kosten *pl*	purchase costs	—	costi d'acquisto *m pl*	coste de adquisición *m*
frais de banque (F)	Bankspesen *pl*	bank charges	—	commissioni bancarie *f pl*	gastos bancarios *m pl*
frais de commissions d'ouverture de crédit (F)	Kreditprovision *f*	credit commission	—	provvigione di credito *f*	comisión de apertura de crédito *f*
frais de fabrication (F)	Herstellungskosten *pl*	production costs	—	costi di produzione *m pl*	costo de la producción *m*
frais de fondation (F)	Gründungskosten *pl*	organization costs	—	costi della costituzione *m pl*	gastos de fundación *m pl*
frais de matériel (F)	Materialkosten *pl*	material costs	—	costi del materiale *m pl*	gastos de material *m pl*/coste de material *m*
frais de procédure (F)	Verfahrenskosten *pl*	costs of the proceedings	—	spese del procedimento *f pl*	costas *f pl*
frais de tenue de compte (F)	Kontogebühren *pl*	bank charges	—	diritti di conto *m pl*	gastos de administración de una cuenta *m pl*
frais de transport (F)	Frachtkosten *pl*	freight charges	—	spese di trasporto *f pl*	gastos de transporte *m pl*
frais de voyage[1] (F)	Reisespesen *pl*	travelling expenses	—	spese di viaggio *f pl*	gastos de viaje *m pl*
frais de voyage[2] (F)	Reisekosten *pl*	travelling expenses	—	costi di viaggio *m pl*	gastos de viaje *m pl*
frais judiciaires taxables exposés (F)	Gerichtskosten *pl*	legal costs	—	spese giudiziarie *f pl*	gastos judiciales *m pl*

	D	E	F	I	Es
Franchise (D)	—	franchise	franchise *f*	franchise *m*	franquicia *f*
franchise (E)	Franchise *f*	—	franchise *f*	franchise *m*	franquicia *f*
franchise (F)	Franchise *f*	franchise	—	franchise *m*	franquicia *f*
franchise (I)	Franchise *f*	franchise	franchise *f*	—	franquicia *f*
Franchisenehmer (D)	—	concessionary	concessionnaire *m*	concessionario *m*	concesionario *m*
Franchising (D)	—	franchising	franchising *m*	franchising *m*	franquicia *f*
franchising (E)	Franchising *n*	—	franchising *m*	franchising *m*	franquicia *f*
franchising (F)	Franchising *n*	franchising	—	franchising *m*	franquicia *f*
franchising (I)	Franchising *n*	franchising	franchising *m*	—	franquicia *f*
franco (Es)	frei Hafen	free port	franco port	franco porto	—
franco a bordo (I)	frei Schiff	free on board	franco sur navire	—	franco vapor
franco almacén (Es)	frei Lager	free warehouse	franco entrepôt	franco magazzino	—
franco banchina (I)	ab Kai	ex quay	départ quai	—	ex muelle
francobollo (I)	Briefmarke *f*	stamp	timbre-poste *m*	—	sello *m*
franco bordo (I)	ab Schiff	ex ship	départ navire	—	ex vapor
franco confine (I)	frei Grenze	free frontier	franco frontière	—	franco frontera
franco de port (F)	portofrei	post-free	—	franco di porto	porte pagado
franco de porte (Es)	frachtfrei	freight paid	exempt de frais de transport	franco di nolo	—
franco di nolo (I)	frachtfrei	freight paid	exempt de frais de transport	—	franco de porte
franco di porto (I)	portofrei	post-free	franco de port	—	porte pagado
franco domicile (F)	frei Haus	free domicile	—	franco domicilio	franco domicilio
franco domicilio (Es)	frei Haus	free domicile	franco domicile	franco domicilio	—
franco domicilio (I)	frei Haus	free domicile	franco domicile	—	franco domicilio
franco en gare (F)	frei Station	free station	—	franco stazione	franco estación
franco entrepôt (F)	frei Lager	free warehouse	—	franco magazzino	franco almacén
franco estación (Es)	frei Station	free station	franco en gare	franco stazione	—
franco fabbrica (I)	ab Werk	ex works	départ usine	—	ex fábrica
franco frontera (Es)	frei Grenze	free frontier	franco frontière	franco confine	—
franco frontière (F)	frei Grenze	free frontier	—	franco confine	franco frontera
franco magazzino (I)	frei Lager	free warehouse	franco entrepôt	—	franco almacén
franco port (F)	frei Hafen	free port	—	franco porto	franco
franco porto (I)	frei Hafen	free port	franco port	—	franco
franco stazione¹ (I)	frei Station	free station	franco en gare	—	franco estación
franco stazione² (I)	ab Bahnhof	ex rail/free on rail	départ gare	—	puesto en estación
franco sur navire (F)	frei Schiff	free on board	—	franco a bordo	franco vapor
franco sur wagon (F)	frei Waggon	free on rail	—	franco vagone	franco vagón
franco vagón (Es)	frei Waggon	free on rail	franco sur wagon	franco vagone	—
franco vagone (I)	frei Waggon	free on rail	franco sur wagon	—	franco vagón
franco vapor (Es)	frei Schiff	free on board	franco sur navire	franco a bordo	—
frankieren (D)	—	prepay the postage	affranchir	affrancare	franquear
franquear (Es)	frankieren	prepay the postage	affranchir	affrancare	—
franquicia¹ (Es)	Franchising *n*	franchising	franchising *m*	franchising *m*	—
franquicia² (Es)	Franchise *f*	franchise	franchise *f*	franchise *m*	—
fraud (E)	Betrug *m*	—	fraude *f*	frode *f*	fraude *m*
fraude (Es)	Betrug *m*	fraud	fraude *f*	frode *f*	—
fraude (F)	Betrug *m*	fraud	—	frode *f*	fraude *m*
fraude fiscal (Es)	Steuerbetrug *m*	fiscal fraud	fraude fiscale *f*	frode fiscale *f*	—
fraude fiscale¹ (F)	Steuerbetrug *m*	fiscal fraud	—	frode fiscale *f*	fraude fiscal *m*
fraude fiscale² (F)	Hinterziehung *f*	evasion of taxes	—	evasione *f*	defraudación *f*
fraudulent bankruptcy (E)	betrügerischer Bankrott *m*	—	banqueroute frauduleuse *f*	bancarotta fraudolenta *f*	quiebra frandulenta *f*
frazione (I)	Bruchteil *m*	fraction	fraction *f*	—	parte fraccionaria *f*

	D	E	F	I	Es
frecuencia de transbordo (Es)	Umschlags-häufigkeit f	transshipment frequencies	fréquence de transbordement f	velocità di rotazione f	—
frecuencia publicitaria (Es)	Werbefrequenz f	advertising frequency	fréquence publicitaire f	frequenza della pubblicità f	—
free domicile (E)	frei Haus	—	franco domicile	franco domicilio	franco domicilio
freedom of association (E)	Koalitionsfreiheit f	—	liberté d'association f	libertà di coalizione f	libertad de coalición f
freedom of consumption (E)	Konsumfreiheit f	—	liberté de consommation f	libertà di consumo f	libertad de consumo f
freedom of contract (E)	Vertragsfreiheit f	—	liberté de contracter f	libertà contrattuale f	libertad contractual f
freedom of trade (E)	Gewerbefreiheit f	—	liberté des professions industrielles et commerciales f	libertà d'industria f	libertad de industria f
free frontier (E)	frei Grenze	—	franco frontière	franco confine	franco frontera
freehold flat (E)	Eigentumswohnung f	—	logement en propriété m	appartamento in condominio m	piso en propiedad m
free movement of capital (E)	freier Kapitalverkehr m	—	libre circulation des capitaux f	libera circolazione dei capitali f	libre circulación de capitales
free of charge (E)	kostenlos	—	gratuit	gratuito	libre de gastos
free of charge (E)	unentgeltlich	—	à titre gracieux	gratuito	gratuito
free of defects (E)	mangelfrei	—	sans défaut	esente da vizi	sin vicios
free of phosphate (E)	phosphatfrei	—	sans phosphate	privo di fosfato	sin fosfato
free on board (E)	frei Schiff	—	franco sur navire	franco a bordo	franco vapor
free on rail (E)	frei Waggon	—	franco sur wagon	franco vagone	franco vagón
free port[1] (E)	frei Hafen	—	franco port	franco porto	franco
free port[2] (E)	Freihafen m	—	port franc m	porto franco m	puerto franco m
free station (E)	frei Station	—	franco en gare	franco stazione	franco estación
free ticket (E)	Freikarte f	—	billet de faveur m	biglietto gratuito m	entrada gratuita f
free trade[1] (E)	Freihandel m	—	commerce libre m	scambio libero m	librecambio m
free trade[2] (E)	Außenhandels-freiheit f	—	libre-échange m	libertà di commercio estero f	librecambio m
free trade area (E)	Freihandelszone f	—	zone de libre-échange f	zona di libero scambio f	zona de librecambio f
free warehouse (E)	frei Lager	—	franco entrepôt	franco magazzino	franco almacén
Freiberufler (D)	—	selfemployed person	personne exerçant une profession libérale f	libero professionista m	profesional m
freibleibend (D)	—	subject to confirmation	sans engagement	senza impegno	no vinculante
freier Kapitalverkehr (D)	—	free movement of capital	libre circulation des capitaux f	libera circolazione dei capitali f	libre circulación de capitales
freight[1] (E)	Fracht f	—	fret m	nolo m	carga f
freight[2] (E)	verfrachten	—	fréter/embarquer	imbarcare	expedir/fletar
freight[3] (E)	Ladung f	—	charge f	carico m	carga f
freight charges (E)	Frachtkosten pl	—	frais de transport m pl	spese di trasporto f pl	gastos de transporte m pl
freight contract (E)	Frachtvertrag m	—	contrat d'affrètement m	contratto di trasporto m	contrato de transporte m
freight paid[1] (E)	Fracht bezahlt	—	fret payé	nolo pagato	flete pagado
freight paid[2] (E)	frachtfrei	—	exempt de frais de transport	franco di nolo	franco de porte
(freight) rate (E)	Frachtrate f	—	taux de fret m	tariffa di nolo f	tipo de flete m
frei Grenze (D)	—	free frontier	franco frontière	franco confine	franco frontera
frei Hafen (D)	—	free port	franco port	franco porto	franco
Freihafen (D)	—	free port	port franc m	porto franco m	puerto franco m
Freihandel (D)	—	free trade	commerce libre m	scambio libero m	librecambio m
Freihandelszone (D)	—	free trade area	zone de libre-échange f	zona di libero scambio f	zona de librecambio f
frei Haus (D)	—	free domicile	franco domicile	franco domicilio	franco domicilio
Freikarte (D)	—	free ticket	billet de faveur m	biglietto gratuito m	entrada gratuita f
frei Lager (D)	—	free warehouse	franco entrepôt	franco magazzino	franco almacén

	D	E	F	I	Es
frei Schiff (D)	—	free on board	franco sur navire	franco a bordo	franco vapor
frei Station (D)	—	free station	franco en gare	franco stazione	franco estación
frei Waggon (D)	—	free on rail	franco sur wagon	franco vagone	franco vagón
Fremdfinanzierung (D)	—	debt financing	constitution de capital par apport de tiers f	finanziamento passivo m	financiación externa f
fréquence de transbordement (F)	Umschlags-häufigkeit f	transshipment frequencies	—	velocità di rotazione f	frecuencia de transbordo f
fréquence publicitaire (F)	Werbefrequenz f	advertising frequency	—	frequenza della pubblicità f	frecuencia publicitaria f
frequenza della pubblicità (I)	Werbefrequenz f	advertising frequency	fréquence publicitaire f	—	frecuencia publicitaria f
fret (F)	Fracht f	freight	—	nolo m	carga f
fret aérien (F)	Luftfracht f	air freight	—	nolo aereo m	flete aéreo m
fréter (F)	verfrachten	freight/to ship	—	imbarcare	expedir/fletar
fret par rail (F)	Bahnfracht f	rail freight	—	nolo ferroviario m	transporte ferroviario m
fret payé (F)	Fracht bezahlt	freight paid	—	nolo pagato	flete pagado
Frist (D)	—	period	délai m	termine m	plazo m
fristgerecht (D)	—	timely	dans les délais	entro il termine convenuto	dentro del plazo fijado
Fristgewährung (D)	—	granting a respite	octroi d'un délai m	concessione di un termine f	concesión de un plazo f
fristlos (D)	—	without prior notice	sans délai	senza preavviso	sin plazo
frode (I)	Betrug m	fraud	fraude f	—	fraude m
frode fiscale (I)	Steuerbetrug m	fiscal fraud	fraude fiscale f	—	fraude fiscal m
frontera aduanera (Es)	Zollgrenze f	customs frontier	frontière douanière f	confine doganale m	—
frontière douanière nationale (F)	Zollgrenze f	customs frontier	—	confine doganale m	frontera aduanera f
fuel (E)	Treibstoff m	—	carburant m	carburante m	combustible m
fuente de suministro (Es)	Bezugsquelle f	source of supply	source d'approvisionnement f	fonte d'acquisto f	—
fuerza de argumentación (Es)	Argumentations-stärke f	talent for argumentation	capacité d'argumentation f	forza d'argomentazione f	—
fuerzas del mercado (Es)	Marktkräfte pl	market forces	forces du marché	forze di mercato f pl	—
fuga de capital (Es)	Kapitalflucht f	flight of capital	évasion des capitaux f	fuga dei capitali f	—
fuga dei capitali (I)	Kapitalflucht f	flight of capital	évasion des capitaux f	—	fuga de capital f
Führung (D)	—	management	direction f	gestione f	gestión f
Führungsebene (D)	—	executive level	niveau de gestion m	quadri dirigenti m	nivel de dirección m
Führungsperson (D)	—	executive	cadre m	dirigente m	ejecutivo m
full employment (E)	Vollbeschäftigung f	—	plein emploi m	piena occupazione f	empleo total m
full power (E)	Vollmacht f	—	plein pouvoir m/ mandat m	autorizzazione f/ procura f	poder m/ autorización f/ escritura de poder f
funcionario (Es)	Beamter m	official	fonctionnaire m	funzionario m	—
fund (E)	Fonds m	—	fonds m pl	fondo m	fondo m
fundación¹ (Es)	Stiftung f	foundation	fondation f	fondazione f	—
fundación² (Es)	Gründung f	formation	constitution f	costituzione f	—
fundación de existencia (Es)	Existenzgründung f	setting up of new business	fondation d'existence f	costituzione di un lavoro indipendente f	—
fundación nueva (Es)	Neugründung f	new foundation	création d'une nouvelle société f	costituzione nuova f	—
fungibilidad (Es)	Fungibilität f	fungibility	qualité fongible f d'un bien	fungibilità f	—
fungibilità (I)	Fungibilität f	fungibility	qualité fongible f d'un bien f	—	fungibilidad f
Fungibilität (D)	—	fungibility	qualité fongible f d'un bien f	fungibilità f	fungibilidad f
fungibility (E)	Fungibilität f	—	qualité fongible f d'un bien f	fungibilità f	fungibilidad f

	D	E	F	I	Es
Funkspruch (D)	—	radio message	message par radio *m*	radiotelefonata *f*	mensaje radiado *m*
funzionario (I)	Beamter *m*	official	fonctionnaire *m*	—	funcionario *m*
für eigene Rechnung (D)	—	for one's own account	pour son propre compte	per conto proprio	por cuenta propia
für fremde Rechnung (D)	—	for account of a third party	pour compte de tiers	per conto terzi	por cuenta ajena
further processing (E)	Weiterverarbeitung *f*	—	transformation complémentaire *f*	trasformazione *f*	elaboración ulterior *f*
furto (I)	Diebstahl *m*	theft	vol *m*	—	robo *m*
fusée (F)	Rakete *f*	rocket	—	missile *m*	cohete *m*
Fusion (D)	—	fusion	fusion *f*	fusione *f*	fusión *f*
fusion (E)	Fusion *f*	—	fusion *f*	fusione *f*	fusión *f*
fusión¹ (Es)	Fusion *f*	fusion	fusion *f*	fusione *f*	—
fusión² (Es)	Verschmelzung *f*	merger	fusion *f*	fusione *f*	—
fusion¹ (F)	Verschmelzung *f*	merger	—	fusione *f*	fusión *f*
fusion² (F)	Fusion *f*	fusion	—	fusione *f*	fusión *f*
fusión de empresas (Es)	Unternehmens-fusion *f*	merger of companies	fusion de sociétés *f*	fusione d'imprese *f*	—
fusion de sociétés (F)	Unternehmens-fusion *f*	merger of companies	—	fusione d'imprese *f*	fusión de empresas *f*
fusione¹ (I)	Fusion *f*	fusion	fusion *f*	—	fusión *f*
fusione² (I)	Verschmelzung *f*	merger	fusion *f*	—	fusión *f*
fusione d'imprese (I)	Unternehmens-fusion *f*	merger of companies	fusion de sociétés *f*	—	fusión de empresas *f*
Fusionskontrolle (D)	—	merger control	contrôle de fusion *m*	controllo delle fusioni *m*	control de fusiones *m*
future prospects (E)	Zukunftschance *f*	—	perspectives d'avenir *f pl*	prospettiva *f*	posibilidades futuras *f pl*
futures market (E)	Terminbörse *f*	—	bourse à terme *f*	mercato a termine *m*	bolsa de valores a término *f*
Gage (D)	—	salary	cachet *m*	onorario *m*	remuneración *f*
gain fictif (F)	Scheingewinn *m*	fictitious profit	—	utile fittizio *m*	beneficio simulado *m*
gainfully employed (E)	erwerbstätig	—	actif	attivo	activo
gainfully employed person¹ (E)	Erwerbstätiger *m*	—	personne ayant un emploi *f*	persona attiva *f*	persona activa *f*
gainfully employed person² (E)	Erwerbsperson *f*	—	personne active *f*	persona attiva *f*	persona en activo *f*
galloping inflation (E)	galoppierende Inflation *f*	—	inflation galopante *f*	inflazione galoppante *f*	inflación galopante *f*
galoppierende Inflation (D)	—	galloping inflation	inflation galopante *f*	inflazione galoppante *f*	inflación galopante *f*
gama de productos (Es)	Produktpalette *f*	range of products	gamme des produits *f*	gamma dei prodotti *f*	—
gamma dei prodotti (I)	Produktpalette *f*	range of products	gamme des produits *f*	—	gama de productos *f*
gamme (F)	Produktions-programm *n*	production programme	—	programma di produzione *m*	programa de producción *m*
gamme des produits (F)	Produktpalette *f*	range of products	—	gamma dei prodotti *f*	gama de productos *f*
ganancia bruta (Es)	Rohgewinn *m*	gross profit on sales	bénéfice brut *m*	utile lordo *m*	—
ganancia neta (Es)	Reingewinn *m*	net profit	bénéfice net *m*	utile netto *m*	—
ganancias de capital (Es)	Kapitaleinkommen *n*	unearned income	revenu du capital *m*	reddito del capitale *m*	—
garant (F)	Bürge *m*	guarantor	—	fideiussore *m*	fiador *m*
garantía¹ (Es)	Garantie *f*	warranty	garantie *f*	garanzia *f*	—
garantía² (Es)	Gewährleistung *f*	warranty	prestation de garantie *f*	garanzia *f*	—
garantía bancaria (Es)	Bankgarantie *f*	bank guarantee	garantie de banque *f*	garanzia bancaria *f*	—
garantía de comisión (Es)	Provisionsgarantie *f*	commission guarantee	garantie de commission *f*	garanzia di provvigione *f*	—
garantía de compra (Es)	Ankaufgarantie *f*	purchase guarantee	garantie d'achat *f*	garanzia d'acquisto *f*	—

	D	E	F	I	Es
garantía de la calidad (Es)	Qualitätssicherung f	quality assurance	garantie de la qualité f	garanzia di qualità f	—
garantía real (Es)	dingliche Sicherung f	real security	sécurité réelle f	garanzia reale f	—
Garantie (D)	—	warranty	garantie f	garanzia f	garantía f
garantie (F)	Garantie f	warranty	—	garanzia f	garantía f
garantie d'achat (F)	Ankaufgarantie f	purchase guarantee	—	garanzia d'acquisto f	garantía de compra f
garantie de banque (F)	Bankgarantie f	bank guarantee	—	garanzia bancaria f	garantía bancaria f
garantie de bonne fin (F)	Ausfallbürgschaft f	deficiency guarantee	—	fideiussione d'indennità f	fianza con beneficio de excusión f
garantie de commission (F)	Provisionsgarantie f	commission guarantee	—	garanzia di provvigione f	garantía de comisión f
garantie de la qualité (F)	Qualitätssicherung f	quality assurance	—	garanzia di qualità f	garantía de la calidad f
garantie des crénciers (F)	Gläubigerschutz m	protection of creditors	—	tutela del creditore f	protección de los acreedores f
Garantiekarte (D)	—	certificate of warranty	carte de garantie f	certificato di garanzia m	tarjeta de garantía f
Garantieleistung (D)	—	guarantee	fourniture sous garantie f	prestazione di garanzia f	aplicación de la garantía f
Garantie-verpflichtung (D)	—	guarantee obligation	engagement de garantie m	obbligo di garanzia m	obligación de garantía f
garanzia¹ (I)	Gewährleistung f	warranty	prestation de garantie f	—	garantía f
garanzia² (I)	Garantie f	warranty	garantie f	—	garantía f
garanzia bancaria (I)	Bankgarantie f	bank guarantee	garantie de banque f	—	garantía bancaria f
garanzia d'acqusto (I)	Ankaufgarantie f	purchase guarantee	garantie d'achat f	—	garantía de compra f
garanzia di esecuzione (I)	Gewährleistungs-garantie f	guarantee for proper execution	caution de garantie f	—	fianza de contratista f
garanzia di provvigione (I)	Provisionsgarantie f	commission guarantee	garantie de commission f	—	garantía de comisión f
garanzia di qualità (I)	Qualitätssicherung f	quality assurance	garantie de la qualité f	—	garantía de la calidad f
garanzia d'offerta (I)	Bietungsgarantie f	tender guarantee	cautionnement provisiore m	—	caución de licitación f
garanzia reale (I)	dingliche Sicherung f	real security	sécurité réelle f	—	garantía real f
garde des titres (F)	Depotgeschäft n	deposit banking	— deposito f	operazione di	custodia de valores f
gare destinataire (F)	Bestimmungs-bahnhof m	station of destination	—	stazione di destinazione f	estación de destino f
garzone (I)	Geselle m	journeyman	ouvrier artisan m	—	oficial m
gas natural (Es)	Erdgas n	natural gas	gaz naturel m	gas naturale m	—
gas naturale (I)	Erdgas n	natural gas	gaz naturel m	—	gas natural m
gasolina (Es)	Benzin n	petrol	essence f	benzina f	—
gasot (Es)	Aufwendung f	expenditure	dépenses f pl	spese f pl	—
gastos¹ (Es)	Kosten pl	costs	coût m	costi m pl	—
gastos² (Es)	Ausgaben pl	expenses	dépenses f pl	spese f pl	—
gastos³ (Es)	Aufwand m	expenditure	charge f	spese f pl	—
gastos⁴ (Es)	Spesen pl	expenses	frais m pl	spese f pl	—
gastos adicionales (Es)	Nebenkosten pl	ancillary costs	coûts accessoires m pl	costi accessori m pl	—
gastos bancarios (Es)	Bankspesen pl	bank charges	frais de banque m pl	commissioni bancarie f pl	—
gastos de administra-ción de una cuenta (Es)	Kontogebühren pl	bank charges	frais de tenue de compte m pl	diritti di conto m pl	—
gastos de adquisición (Es)	Bezugskosten pl	purchasing costs	coûts d'acquisition m pl	prezzo d'acquisto m	—
gastos de alojamiento (Es)	Übernachtungs-kosten pl	overnight expenses	coûts de nuitée m pl	spese di pernottamento f pl	—
gastos de carga (Es)	Verladekosten pl	loading charges	coût du chargement m	costi di caricamento m pl	—
gastos de desarrollo (Es)	Entwicklungs-kosten pl	development costs	coûts de développement m pl	costi di sviluppo m pl	—

Gebietsvertreter

	D	E	F	I	Es
gastos de descarga[1] (Es)	Löschgebühren *pl*	discharging expenses	droit de déchargement *m*	spese di scarico *f pl*	—
gastos de descargo[2] (Es)	Entladungskosten *pl*	discharging expenses	coûts de déchargement *m pl*	spese di scaricamento *f pl*	—
gastos de explotación[1] (Es)	Betriebsausgaben *f*	(current) operational expenses	charges d'exploitación *f pl*	spese aziendali *f pl*	—
gastos de explotación[2] (Es)	Betriebskosten *pl*	operating costs	charges d'exploitation *f pl*	spese d'esercizio *f pl*	—
gastos de fundación (Es)	Gründungskosten *pl*	organization costs	frais de fondation *m pl*	costi della costituzione *m pl*	—
gastos de información (Es)	Informations-kosten *pl*	information costs	coûts d'information *m pl*	costi d'informazione *m pl*	—
gastos de material (Es)	Materialkosten *pl*	material costs	frais de matériel *m pl*	costi del materiale *m pl*	—
gastos de producción (Es)	Produktionskosten *pl*	cost of production	coût de production *m*	costi produttivi *m pl*	—
gastos de readaptación (Es)	Anpassungskosten *pl*	adjustment costs	coûts d'adaptation *m pl*	costi d'adattamento *m pl*	—
gastos de reproducción (Es)	Reproduktions-kosten *pl*	reproduction cost	coût de reproduction *m*	costi di riproduzione *m pl*	—
gastos de saneamiento (Es)	Sanierungskosten *pl*	renewal costs	coûts d'assainisse-ment *m pl*	costi di risanamento *m pl*	—
gastos de subasta (Es)	Auktionsgebühr *f*	auction fees	droits de vente aux enchères *m pl*	diritto d'asta *m*	—
gastos de transporte (Es)	Frachtkosten *pl*	freight charges	frais de transport *m pl*	spese di trasporto *f pl*	—
gastos de utilización de capital (Es)	Kapitalnutzungs-kosten *pl*	costs of the utilization of capital	coûts d'utilisation de capital *m pl*	costo del capitale *m*	—
gastos de viaje (Es)	Reisespesen *pl*	travelling expenses	frais de voyage *m pl*	spese di viaggio *f pl*	—
gastos directos (Es)	Primäraufwand *m*	primary expenses	charge primaire *f*	spese primarie *f pl*	—
gastos efectivos (Es)	Istkosten *pl*	actual costs	coûts réels *m pl*	costi effettivi *m pl*	—
gastos extraordinarios (Es)	Sonderausgaben *pl*	special expenses	dépense spéciale *f*	spese straordinarie *f pl*	—
gastos fijos[1] (Es)	Fixkosten *pl*	fixed costs	coûts fixes *m pl*	costi fissi *m pl*	—
gastos fijos[2] (Es)	Bereitstellungs-kosten *pl*	commitment fee	coûts administratifs *m pl*	spese di stanziamento *f pl*	—
gastos fijos de utilización (Es)	Nutzkosten *pl*	utility costs	coûts fixes utiles *m pl*	costi fissi di utilizzo *m pl*	—
gastos generales[1] (Es)	Gesamtkosten *pl*	total costs	coût total *m*	costi totali *m pl*	—
gastos generales[2] (Es)	Gemeinkosten *pl*	overhead expenses	coûts indirects *m pl*	costi comuni *m pl*	—
gastos judiciales (Es)	Gerichtskosten *pl*	legal costs	frais judiciaires tax-ables exposés *m pl*	spese giudiziarie *f pl*	—
gastos medios (Es)	Durchschnitts-kosten *pl*	average costs	coût moyen *m*	costi medi *m pl*	—
gastos para aguas residuales (Es)	Abwasserkosten *pl*	sewage disposal costs	coûts de traitement des eaux usées *m pl*	costi per le acque di scarico *m pl*	—
gastos precalculados (Es)	Sollkosten *pl*	budgeted costs	coûts ex ante *m pl*	costi calcolati *m pl*	—
gastos públicos[1] (Es)	Staatsausgaben *pl*	public spending	dépenses publiques *f pl*	spese pubbliche *f pl*	—
gastos públicos[2] (Es)	öffentliche Ausgaben *pl*	public spending	dépenses publiques *f pl*	spesa pubblica *f*	—
gastos variables (Es)	variable Kosten *pl*	variable costs	coûts variables *m pl*	costi variabili *m pl*	—
gauge (E)	eichen	—	jauger	tarare	contrastar
gaz naturel (F)	Erdgas *n*	natural gas	—	gas naturale *m*	gas natural *m*
Gebäude-versicherung (D)	—	insurance on buildings	assurance des bâtiments *f*	assicurazione dei fabbricati *f*	seguro inmobiliario *m*
Gebietshoheit (D)	—	territorial jurisdiction	souveraineté territoriale *f*	sovranità territoriale *f*	soberanía territorial *f*
Gebietsschutz (D)	—	territory protection	exclusivité territoriale *f*	tutela territoriale *f*	protección territorial *f*
Gebiets-verkaufsleiter (D)	—	area sales manager	chef de vente régionale *m*	direttore di vendita regionale *m*	jefe de venta regional *m*
Gebietsvertreter (D)	—	area representative	représentant régional *m*	agente di zona *m*	representante regional *m*

	D	E	F	I	Es
Gebrauch (D)	—	use	utilisation f	uso m	uso m
Gebrauchsgüter (D)	—	durable consumer goods	biens d'utilisation courante m pl	beni di consumo durevoli m pl	bienes de consumo duradero m pl
Gebrauchtwagen (D)	—	used car	voiture d'occasion f	automobile usata f	coche de segunda mano m
Gebühr (D)	—	fee	taxe f	tassa f	derecho m
Geburtenrate (D)	—	birth rate	taux de natalité m	tasso di natalità m	tasa de natalidad f
Geburtsdatum (D)	—	date of birth	date de naissance f	data di nascita f	fecha de nacimiento f
Geburtsort (D)	—	place of birth	lieu de naissance m	luogo di nascita m	lugar de nacimiento m
Geburtstag (D)	—	birthday	anniversaire m	compleanno m	día de nacimiento m
Gefahr (D)	—	danger	danger m	pericolo m	peligro m
Gefahrenzulage (D)	—	danger money	prime de danger f	premio di rischio m	incremento por peligrosidad m
gefälschter Scheck (D)	—	forged cheque	chèque maquillé m	assegno falsificato m	cheque falsificado m
gegen Akkreditiv (D)	—	against letter of credit	contre accréditif	contro lettera di credito	con crédito documentario
gegen Barzahlung (D)	—	against cash	au comptant	contro pagamento in contanti	al contado
gegen Nachnahme (D)	—	cash on delivery	contre remboursement	contro assegno	contra rembolso
Gegenwert (D)	—	equivalent	contre-valeur f	controvalore m	contravalor m
Gegenzeichnung (D)	—	countersignature	contreseing m	controfirma f	contrafirma f
Gehalt (D)	—	salary	traitement m	stipendio m	sueldo m
Gehaltserhöhung (D)	—	increase in salary	augmentation du traitement f	aumento dello stipendio m	aumento de sueldo m
Gehaltskonto (D)	—	salary account	compte de domiciliation du salaire m	conto stipendi m	cuenta de salario f
geheim (D)	—	secret	secret	segreto	secreto
Geheimhaltung (D)	—	maintenance of secrecy	conservation du secret f	segretezza f	mantenimiento del secreto m
Geheimnis (D)	—	secret	secret m	segreto m	secreto m
gekreuzter Scheck (D)	—	crossed cheque	chèque barré m	assegno sbarrato m	cheque cruzado m
Geld (D)	—	money	argent m	denaro m	dinero m/efectivo m
Geldaufnahme (D)	—	raising of money	emprunt m	accensione di un mutuo f	dinero tomado a préstamo m
Geldbetrag (D)	—	amount of money	somme d'argent f	somma di denaro f	suma de dinero f
Geldbuße (D)	—	fine	amende f	pena pecuniaria f	multa f
Geldgeber (D)	—	financial backer	bailleur de fonds m	finanziatore m	prestamista m
Geldkurs (D)	—	demand price	cours de la demande m	prezzo di domanda m	cotización demanda-da f/precio ofrecido m
Geldmarkt (D)	—	money market	marché monétaire m	mercato monetario m	mercado monetario m
Geldmenge (D)	—	money supply	quantité de monnaie en circulation f	massa monetaria f	volumen monetario m
Geldnachfrage (D)	—	demand for money	demande sur le marché monétaire f	domanda di denaro f	demanda monetaria f
Geldpolitik (D)	—	monetary policy	politique monétaire f	politica monetaria f	política monetaria f
Geldschöpfung (D)	—	money creation	création de trésorerie f	creazione di denaro f	creación de dinero f
Geldstrafe (D)	—	fine	peine pécuniaire f	multa f	multa f
Geldtheorie (D)	—	monetary theory	théorie monétaire f	teoria del denaro f	teoría monetaria f
Geldumlauf (D)	—	circulation of money	circulation monétaire f	circolazione di denaro f	circulación monetaria f
Geldverknappung (D)	—	monetary restriction	pénurie d'argent f	riduzione del denaro f	restricción monetaria f
Geldvermögen (D)	—	financial assets	moyens financiers m	patrimonio monetario m	activo monetario m
Geldvolumen (D)	—	volume of money	masse monétaire f	volume monetario m	volumen monetario m
Geldwert (D)	—	value of money	valeur de l'argent f	valore monetario m	valor monetario m
Geldwertstabilität (D)	—	stability of the value of money	stabilité monétaire f	stabilità monetaria f	estabilidad monetaria f
Gemeinde (D)	—	community	commune f	comune m	comunidad f
Gemeineigentum (D)	—	public property	propriété publique f	proprietà collettiva f	propiedad común m

	D	E	F	I	Es
Gemeinkosten (D)	—	overhead expenses	coûts indirects *m pl*	costi comuni *m pl*	gastos generales *m pl*
gemeinnütziges Unternehmen (D)	—	public institution	entreprise d'utilité publique *f*	impresa di utilità pubblica *f*	empresa de beneficio común *f*
gemeinsamer Markt (D)	—	common market	marché commun *m*	mercato comune *m*	mercado común *m*
Gemeinschafts-eigentum (D)	—	collective property	propriété collective *f*	proprietà collettiva *f*	propiedad colectiva *f*
Gemeinschafts-werbung (D)	—	joint publicity	publicité collective *f*	pubblicità collettiva *f*	publicidad colectiva *f*
Gemeinschuldner (D)	—	adjudicated bankrupt	failli *m*	debitore fallito *m*	deudor común *m*
Genehmigung (D)	—	permission	autorisation *f*	autorizzazione *f*	autorización *f*
general agent (E)	Generalvertreter *m*	—	agent général *m*	rappresentante generale *m*	representante general *m*
general borrowing agreements (E)	allgemeine Kredit-vereinbarungen *f pl*	—	accords généraux de crédit *f pl*	condizioni generali di credito *f pl*	acuerdos generales de crédito *m pl*
general cargo trade (E)	Stückgutverkehr *m*	—	expéditions de détail *f*	trasporto di collettame *m*	tráfico de mercancías en bultos sueltos *m*
general director (E)	Generaldirektor *m*	—	directeur général *m*	direttore generale *m*	director general *m*
Generaldirektor (D)	—	director general	directeur général *m*	direttore generale *m*	director general *m*
generalità (I)	Personalien *pl*	personal data	identité *f*	—	datos personales *m pl*
general partner (E)	Komplementär *m*	—	commandité *m*	socio accomandatario *m*	socio colectivo *m*
general power (E)	Generalvollmacht *f*	—	pouvoir général *m*	procura generale *f*	poder general *m*
Generalstreik (D)	—	general strike	grève générale *f*	sciopero generale *m*	huelga general *f*
general strike (E)	Generalstreik *m*	—	grève générale *f*	sciopero generale *m*	huelga general *f*
general terms (E)	allgemeine Geschäfts-bedingungen *f pl*	—	conditions générales de contrat *f pl*	condizioni generali di contratto *f pl*	condiciones generales de contrato *f pl*
Generalpolice (D)	—	floating policy	police d'abonnement *f*	polizza generale *f*	póliza global *f*
Generalvertreter (D)	—	general agent	agent général *m*	rappresentante generale *m*	representante general *m*
Generalvollmacht (D)	—	general power	pouvoir général *m*	procura generale *f*	poder general *m*
generic product (E)	No-name-Produkt *n*	—	produit sans nom *m*	prodotto senza nome *m*	producto genérico *m*
genormt (D)	—	standardized	normalisé	standardizzato	normalizado
Genossenschaft (D)	—	co-operative	société coopérative *f*	cooperativa *f*	sociedad cooperativa *f*
genre (F)	Sorte *f*	variety	—	categoria *f*	especie *f*
geografía económica (Es)	Wirtschafts-geographie *f*	economic geography	géographie économique *f*	geografia economica *f*	—
geografia economica (I)	Wirtschafts-geographie *f*	economic geography	géographie économique *f*	—	geografía económica *f*
géographie économique (F)	Wirtschafts-geographie *f*	economic geography	—	geografia economica *f*	geografía económica *f*
gérant d'une affaire (F)	Geschäftsführer *m*	manager	—	amministratore *m*	gerente *m*
gerarchia (I)	Hierarchie *f*	hierarchy	hiérarchie *f*	—	jerarquía *f*
gerechtfertigt (D)	—	justified	justifié	giustificato	justificado
gerente (Es)	Geschäftsführer *m*	manager	gérant d'une affaire *m*	amministratore *m*	—
gerichtlich (D)	—	judicial	judiciaire	giudiziario	judicial
Gerichtskosten (D)	—	legal costs	frais judiciaires tax-ables exposés *m pl*	spese giudiziarie *f pl*	gastos judiciales *m pl*
Gerichtsstand (D)	—	jurisdiction	juridiction compétente *f*	foro competente *m*	tribunal competente *m*
Gerichtsvollzieher (D)	—	bailiff	huissier de justice *m*	ufficiale giudiziario *m*	ejecutor judicial *m*
German Industrial Standards (E)	Deutsche Industrie-Norm *f*	—	norme industrielle allemande *f*	norma tedesca di normalizzazione *f*	norma industrial alemana *f*
Gesamtkonzeption (D)	—	overall conception	conception générale *f*	concezione universale *f*	concepción general *f*
Gesamtkosten (D)	—	total costs	coût total *m*	costi totali *m pl*	gastos generales *m pl*
Gesamtlieferung (D)	—	total delivery	livraison totale *f*	fornitura completa *f*	suministro total *f*
Gesamtsumme (D)	—	total amount	montant total *m*	importo totale *m*	suma total *f*
Geschäft (D)	—	business	affaire *f*	negozio *m*	negocio *m*
Geschäftsabschluß (D)	—	conclusion of a deal	conclusion d'une affaire *f*	conclusione di un affare *f*	conclusión de un negocio *f*
Geschäftsanteil (D)	—	share	part sociale *f*	quota sociale *f*	participación *f*

	D	E	F	I	Es
Geschäftsbericht (D)	—	business report	rapport de gestion *m*	relazione sull'esercizio commerciale *f*	informe *m*
Geschäftsbeziehung (D)	—	business connections	relations d'affaires *f pl*	rapporti d'affari *m pl*	relaciones comerciales *f pl*
Geschäftsbücher (D)	—	account books	livres de commerce *m pl*	libri contabili *m pl*	libros de contabilidad *m pl*
Geschäftseröffnung (D)	—	opening of a business	ouverture d'une affaire *f*	apertura di un negozio *f*	apertura de los establecimientos *f*
Geschäftsfähigkeit (D)	—	capacity to enter into legal transactions	capacité d'accomplir des actes juridiques *f*	capacità di agire *f*	capacidad negocial *f*
Geschäftsfreund (D)	—	business friend	correspondant *m*	partner d'affari *m*	corresponsal *m*
Geschäftsführer (D)	—	manager	gérant d'une affaire *m*	amministratore *m*	gerente *m*
Geschäftsführung (D)	—	management	gestion *f*	amministrazione *f*	gestión *f*
Geschäftsgeheimnis (D)	—	business secret	secret d'affaires *m*	segreto commerciale *m*	secreto comercial *m*
Geschäftsjahr (D)	—	financial year	exercice commercial *m*	esercizio commerciale *m*	ejercicio *m*
Geschäftsjubiläum (D)	—	jubilee	anniversaire de l'entreprise *m*	anniversario aziendale *m*	aniversario de la empresa *m*
Geschäftsleitung (D)	—	management	direction commerciale *f*	direzione *f*	dirección *f*
Geschäftspapiere (D)	—	business papers	papiers d'affaires *m pl*	documenti commerciali *m pl*	documentos comerciales *m pl*
Geschäftspartner (D)	—	business partner	associé *m*	partner commerciale *m*	socio *m*
Geschäftsräume (D)	—	business premises	local à usage commercial *m*	locali commerciali *m pl*	local comercial *m*
Geschäftsstelle (D)	—	office	agence *f*	ufficio *m*	oficina *f*
Geschäfts- übernahme (D)	—	business acquisition	reprise d'une affaire *f*	acquisto di un'azienda *m*	adquisición de una empresa *f*
Geschäfts- verbindung (D)	—	business relation	relation d'affaires *f*	relazione d'affari *f*	relación comercial *f*
Geschäftswert (D)	—	goodwill	valeur commerciale *f*	valore d'avviamento *m*	valor comercial *m*
Geschäftszeit (D)	—	business hours	heures d'ouverture *f pl*	orario d'apertura *m*	hora de despacho *f pl*
Geselle (D)	—	journeyman	ouvrier artisan *m*	garzone *m*	oficial *m*
Gesellschafter (D)	—	partner	associé *m*	socio *m*	socio *m*
Gesellschafter- versammlung (D)	—	meeting of shareholders	réunion des associés *f*	assemblea dei soci *f*	junta social *f*
Gesellschaft mit be- schränkter Haftung (D)	—	limited liability company	société à responsa- bilité limitée *f*	società a responsa- bilità limitata *f*	sociedad de responsa- bilidad limitada *f*
Gesellschafts- vermögen (D)	—	partnership assets	patrimoine social *m*	patrimonio sociale *m*	patrimonio social *m*
Gesellschafts- vertrag (D)	—	shareholder's agreement/partner- ship agreement	acte de société *m*	contratto di società *m*	contrato social *m*
Gesetz (D)	—	law	loi *f*	legge *f*	ley *f*
Gesetzesänderung (D)	—	amendment of a law	amendement d'une loi *m*	emendamento di legge *m*	enmienda de la ley *f*
Gesetzgebungs- hoheit (D)	—	legislative sovereignty	compétence législative *f*	sovranità legislativa *f*	soberanía legislativa *f*
gesetzliches Zahlungsmittel (D)	—	legal tender	monnaie légale *f*	mezzo di pagamento legale *m*	medio legal de pago *m*
gespaltene Wechselkurse (D)	—	two-tier exchange rate	cours du change multiple *m*	cambi multipli *m pl*	tipo de cambio múltiple *m*
gesperrtes Konto (D)	—	blocked account	compte bloqué *m*	conto bloccato *m*	cuenta congelada *f*
Gesprächstermin (D)	—	appointment for a meeting	date de conversation *f*	appuntamento per un colloquio *m*	fecha de cita *f*
gestaffelt (D)	—	graduated	progressif	differenziato	escalonado
gestión[1] (Es)	Geschäftsführung *f*	management	gestion *f*	amministrazione *f*	—
gestión[2] (Es)	Führung *f*	management	direction *f*	gestione *f*	—
gestion (F)	Geschäftsführung *f*	management	—	amministrazione *f*	gestión *f*
gestion d'un projet (F)	Projekt- Management *n*	project management	—	management di progetto *m*	administración del proyecto *f*

	D	E	F	I	Es
gestione (I)	Führung f	management	direction f	—	gestión m
gestione dei prezzi (I)	Preislenkung f	administration of prices	réglementation des prix f	—	reglamentación de precios f
gestione del personale (I)	Personalführung f	personnel management	direction du personnel f	—	dirección de personal m
gestione delle scorte (I)	Vorratshaltung f	stockpiling	stockage m	—	formación de stocks f
gestione in economia (I)	Regiebetrieb m	publicly owned enterprise	établissement en régie m	—	empresa estatal f
Gesundheitswesen (D)	—	public health	santé publique f	sanità f	sanidad f
Gesundheits-zeugnis (D)	—	health certificate	certificat de santé m	certificato sanitario m	certificado de sanidad m
Gewährleistung (D)	—	warranty	prestation de garantie f	garanzia f	garantía f
Gewährleistungs-garantie (D)	—	guarantee for proper execution	caution de garantie f	garanzia di esecuzione f	fianza de contratista f
Gewährleistungs-haftung (D)	—	liability for breach of warranty	responsabilité en matière de garantie f	responsabilità di garanzia f	responsabilidad de garantía f
Gewerbe (D)	—	trade/industry/craft	activité profession-nelle f/industrie f/ artisanat m	commercio m/ industria f/ artigianato m	industria f/ comercio m/ artesanía f
Gewerbefreiheit (D)	—	freedom of trade	liberté des profes-sions industrielles et commerciales f	libertà d'industria economica f	libertad de industria f
Gewerbesteuer (D)	—	trade tax	impôt sur les béné-fices des professions industrielles et commerciales m	imposta industriale f	impuesto industrial m
gewerblicher Betrieb (D)	—	industrial undertaking	établissement com-mercial m/établisse-ment industriel m	azienda commerciale/ azienda industriale f	empresa industrial f
Gewerkschaften (D)	—	trade union	syndicat m	sindacati m pl	sindicato m
Gewicht (D)	—	weight	poids m	peso m	peso m
Gewinn (D)	—	profit surplus	bénéfice m	utile m	beneficio m/ superávit m
Gewinnabführung (D)	—	transfer of profit	transfert du bénéfice m	trasferimento dell'utile m	tranferencia de beneficios f
Gewinnaufschlag (D)	—	profit mark-up	majoration de bénéfice f	maggiorazione dell'utile f	margen de benificio f
Gewinn-ausschüttung (D)	—	distribution of profits	distribution de bénéfices f	ripartizione dell'utile f	distribución de beneficios f
Gewinnbeteiligung (D)	—	participation in profits	participation auxbénéfices f	partecipazione all'utile f	participación en los beneficios f
Gewinnmarge (D)	—	profit margin	marge bénéficiaire f	margine dell'utile m	margen de beneficios f
Gewinn-maximierung (D)	—	maximization of profits	maximisation du gain f	massimizzazione dell'utile f	maximación de los beneficios f
Gewinnschwelle (D)	—	break-even point	seuil de rentabilité m	soglia dell'utile f	umbral de la rentabilidad m
Gewinnspanne (D)	—	margin of profit	marge de bénéfice f	margine dell'utile m	margen de beneficios f
Gewinn- und Verlustrechnung (D)	—	profit and loss account	compte de pertes et profits m	conto profitti e perdite m	cuenta de pérdidas y ganancias f
Gewinnverteilung (D)	—	distribution of profits	répartition des bénéfices f	ripartizione dell'utile f	reparto de beneficios m
Gewinnverwendung (D)	—	appropriation of net income	utilisation des bénéfices f	impiego dell'utile m	aplicación de los resultatods f
gift tax (E)	Schenkungssteuer f	—	impôt sur les donations m	imposta sulle donazioni f	impuesto sobre donaciones m
gioco di strategia imprenditoriale (I)	Planspiel n	management games	jeu d'entreprise m	—	juego de ensayo m
giornaliero (I)	täglich	daily	quotidien	—	diario
giorno di borsa (I)	Börsentag m	market day	jour de bourse m	—	sesión bursátil f
giorno di liquidazione (I)	Abrechnungstag m	settling day	jour de la liquidation m	—	fecha de liquidación f
giorno di paga (I)	Zahltag m	payday	jour de paye m	—	día de pago m
giorno di scadenza (I)	Verfalltag m	day of expiry	jour de l'échéance m	—	día de vencimiento m

	D	E	F	I	Es
giorno lavorativo (I)	Arbeitstag *m*	working day	jour de travail *m*	—	día laboral *m*
girata (I)	Indossament *n*	endorsement	endossement *m*	—	endoso *m*
Giro (D)	—	credit transfer	virement *m*	giro *m*	giro *m*
giro (Es)	Giro *n*	credit transfer	virement *m*	giro *m*	—
giro (I)	Giro *n*	credit transfer	virement *m*	—	giro *m*
giro di partite (I)	Umbuchung *f*	transfer of an entry	jeu d'écritures *m*	—	asiento en otra cuenta *m*
giro postal¹ (Es)	Postgiro *n*	postal giro	virement postal *m*	postagiro *m*	—
giro postal² (Es)	Postüberweisung *f*	postal remittance	virement postal *m*	bonifico postale *m*	—
giro telegráfico (Es)	Kabelüberweisung *f*	cable transfer	virement par câble *m*	bonifico telegrafico *m*	—
Girozentrale (D)	—	central giro institution	banque centrale de virement *f*	stanza centrale di compensazione *f*	central de giros *f*
giudice (I)	Richter *m*	judge	juge *m*	—	juez *m*
giudiziario (I)	gerichtlich	judicial	judiciaire	—	judicial
giurisprudenza (I)	Rechtsprechung *f*	administration of justice	jurisprudence *f*	—	jurisprudencia *f*
giustificato (I)	gerechtfertigt	justified	justifié	—	justificado
Gläubiger (D)	—	creditor	créancier *m*	creditore *m*	accreedor *m*
Gläubigerschutz (D)	—	protection of creditors	garantie des crénciers *f*	tutela del creditore *f*	protección de los acreedores *f*
Gläubiger-versammlung (D)	—	creditors' meeting	assemblée des créanciers *f*	riunione dei creditori *f*	junta de acreedores *f*
Gleichgewicht (D)	—	balance	équilibre *m*	equilibrio *m*	equilibrio *m*
Gleichgewichtspreis (D)	—	equilibrium price	prix équilibré *m*	prezzo d'equilibrio *m*	precio de equilibrio *m*
global assignment (E)	Globalzession *f*	—	cession globale *f*	cessione globale *f*	cesión en bloque *f*
global control (E)	Globalsteuerung *f*	—	régulation globale *f*	controllo globale *m*	regulación golbal *f*
Globalsteuerung (D)	—	global control	régulation globale *f*	controllo globale *m*	regulación global *f*
global warming (E)	Treibhauseffekt *m*	—	effet de serre *m*	effetto serra *m*	efecto invernadero *m*
Globalzession (D)	—	global assignment	cession globale *f*	cessione globale *f*	cesión en bloque *f*
Glückwunsch (D)	—	congratulations	félicitations *f pl*	auguri *m pl*	felicitación *f*
gobierno (Es)	Regierung *f*	government/Ministry	gouvernement *m*	governo *m*	—
Gold (D)	—	gold	or *m*	oro *m*	oro *m*
gold (E)	Gold *n*	—	or *m*	oro *m*	oro *m*
gold bar (E)	Goldbarren *m*	—	lingot d'ór *m*	lingotto d'oro *m*	lingote de oro *m*
Goldbarren (D)	—	gold bar	lingot d'ór *m*	lingotto d'oro *m*	lingote de oro *m*
gold currency (E)	Goldwährung *f*	—	monnaie à couverture or *f*	valuta aurea *f*	moneda oro *f*
gold in bars (E)	Barrengold *n*	—	or en lingot *m*	oro in lingotti *m*	oro en barras *m*
gold market (E)	Goldmarkt *m*	—	marché de l'ór *m*	mercato dell'oro *m*	mercado del oro *m*
Goldmarkt (D)	—	gold market	marché de l'ór *m*	mercato dell'oro *m*	mercado del oro *m*
Goldmine (D)	—	goldmine	mine d'or *f*	miniera d'oro *f*	mina de oro *f*
goldmine (E)	Goldmine *f*	—	mine d'or *f*	miniera d'oro *f*	mina de oro *f*
Goldparität (D)	—	gold parity	parité de l'or *f*	parità aurea *f*	paridad-oro *f*
gold parity (E)	Goldparität *f*	—	parité de l'or *f*	parità aurea *f*	paridad-oro *f*
Goldpreis (D)	—	gold price	prix de l'ór *m*	prezzo dell'oro *m*	precio del oro *m*
gold price (E)	Goldpreis *m*	—	prix de l'ór *m*	prezzo dell'oro *m*	precio del oro *m*
gold standard (E)	Goldstandard *m*	—	étalon or *m*	gold standard *m*	patrón-oro *m*
Goldstandard (D)	—	gold standard	étalon or *m*	gold standard *m*	patrón-oro *m*
gold standard (I)	Goldstandard *m*	gold standard	étalon or *m*	—	patrón-oro *m*
Gold- und Devisenbilanz (D)	—	foreign exchange and gold balance	balance d'or et de devises *f*	bilancia dell'oro e delle divise *f*	balanza de oro y divisas *f*
Goldwährung (D)	—	gold currency	monnaie à couverture or *f*	valuta aurea *f*	moneda oro *f*
goods¹ (E)	Ware *f*	—	marchandise *f*	merce *f*	mercancía *f*
goods² (E)	Güter *pl*	—	biens *m pl*	beni *m pl*	bienes *m pl*
goods for sale on commission (E)	Kommissionsgüter *pl*	—	marchandises en commssion *f pl*	beni in conto deposito *m pl*	mercancías en comisión *f pl*

gratuito

	D	E	F	I	Es
goods sent by express (E)	Eilgut *n*	—	marchandise en grande vitesse *f*	merce a grande velocità *f*	mercancía en gran velocidad *f*
goodwill¹ (E)	Firmenwert *m*	—	valeur commerciale *f*	goodwill *m*	fondo de comercio *m*
goodwill² (E)	Geschäftswert *m*	—	valeur commerciale *f*	valore d'avviamento *m*	valor comercial *m*
goodwill (I)	Firmenwert *m*	goodwill	valeur commerciale *f*	—	fondo de comercio *m*
goulot d'étranglement de capacité (F)	Kapazitätsengpaß *m*	bottleneck in capacity	—	strettoia di capacità *f*	escasez de capacidad *f*
goulot d'étranglement dans la trésorerie (F)	Liquiditätsengpaß *m*	liquidity squeeze	—	strettoia di liquidità *f*	restricción de la liquidez *f*
gouvernement (F)	Regierung *f*	government/Ministry	—	governo *m*	gobierno *m*
government (E)	Regierung *f*	—	gouvernement *m*	governo *m*	gobierno *m*
government grant (E)	Staatszuschuß *m*	—	subvention de l'Etat *f*	sovvenzione pubblica *f*	subvenciones del Estado *f pl*
government loan (E)	Staatsanleihen *pl*	—	emprunt d'Etat *m*	titoli pubblici *m pl*	empréstito estatal *m*
governo (I)	Regierung *f*	government/Ministry	gouvernement *m*	—	gobierno *m*
grade¹ (E)	Handelsklasse *f*	—	catégorie de produits *f*	categoria commerciale *f*	clase *f*
grade² (E)	Güteklasse *f*	—	catégorie de qualité *f*	qualità *f*	categoría de calidad *f*
grado de empleo (Es)	Beschäftigungsgrad *m*	level of employment	taux d'emploi *m*	tasso d'occupazione *m*	—
grado de endeudamiento (Es)	Verschuldungsgrad *m*	debt ratio	niveau de l'endettement *m*	tasso d'indebitamento *m*	—
grado de utilización (Es)	Ausnutzungsgrad *m*	utilization rate	taux d'utilisation *m*	grado di utilizzazione *m*	—
grado di sfruttamento (I)	Auslastungsgrad *m*	capacity utilization rate	dégré de saturation *m*	—	tasa de utilización *f*
grado di utilizzazione (I)	Ausnutzungsgrad *m*	utilization rate	taux d'utilisation *m*	—	grado de utilización *m*
graduated (E)	gestaffelt	—	progressif	differenziato	escalonado
graduated price (E)	Staffelpreis *m*	—	prix échelonné *m*	prezzo differenziato *m*	precios escalonados *m pl*
graduated tariff (E)	Staffeltarif *m*	—	tarif échelonné *m*	tariffa differenziata *f*	tarifa diferencial *f*
gran almacén (Es)	Waren-, Kaufhaus *n*	department store	grand magasin *m*	grande magazzino *m*	—
gran contenedor (Es)	Großcontainer *m*	large container	conteneur à grand volume *m*	container di grande dimensione *m*	—
grande exploitation (F)	Großbetrieb *m*	large-scale operation	—	azienda di grande dimensione *f*	gran explotación *f*
grande magazzino (I)	Waren-, Kaufhaus *n*	department store	grand magasin *m*	—	gran almacén *m*
grand magasin (F)	Kaufhaus *n*	department store	—	grande magazzino *m*	gran almacén *m*
grand marché (F)	Großmarkt *m*	wholesale market	—	mercato all'ingrosso *m*	mercado central *m*
gran explotación (Es)	Großbetrieb *m*	large-scale operation	grande exploitation *f*	azienda di grande dimensione *f*	—
granting a respite (E)	Fristgewährung *f*	—	octroi d'un délai *m*	concessione di un termine *f*	concesión de un plazo *f*
grantor of a power of attorney (E)	Vollmachtgeber *m*	—	auteur de la procuration *m*	mandante *m*	poderdante *m*
graph (E)	Schaubild *n*	—	graphique *m*	diagramma *m*	cuadro *m*
graphique (F)	Schaubild *n*	graph	—	diagramma *m*	cuadro *m*
gratificación¹ (Es)	Prämie *f*	bonus/premium	prime *f*	premio *m*	—
gratificación² (Es)	Gratifikation *f*	bonus	gratification *f*	gratificazione *f*	—
gratificación³ (Es)	Bonus *m*	bonus	bonification *f*	premio *m*	—
gratificación⁴ (Es)	Zuwendung *f*	bestowal	affectation *f*	assegnazione *f*	—
gratificación⁵ (Es)	Sondervergütung *f*	special remuneration	rémunération spéciale *f*	compenso straordinario *m*	—
gratification (F)	Gratifikation *f*	bonus	—	gratificazione *f*	gratificación *f*
gratificazione (I)	Gratifikation *f*	bonus	gratification *f*	—	gratificación *f*
Gratifikation (D)	—	bonus	gratification *f*	gratificazione *f*	gratificación *f*
gratuit (F)	kostenlos	free of charge	—	gratuito	libre de gastos
gratuito (Es)	unentgeltlich	free of charge	à titre gracieux	gratuito	—
gratuito¹ (I)	kostenlos	free of charge	gratuit	—	libre de gastos

	D	E	F	I	Es
gratuito² (I)	unentgeltlich	free of charge	à titre gracieux	—	gratuito
Grauer Markt (D)	—	grey market	marché gris *m*	mercato grigio *m*	mercado gris *m*
gravamen (Es)	Belastung *f*	load	charge *f*	addebito *m*	—
Grenzkonrolle (D)	—	border control	contrôle à la frontière *m*	controllo alla frontiera *m*	control fronterizo *m*
Grenzkosten- rechnung (D)	—	marginal costing	détermination du coût marginal *f*	conto dei costi limite *m*	cálculo de los costes marginales *m*
Grenzwert (D)	—	limiting value	valeur marginale *f*	valore limite *m*	valor límite *m*
grève (F)	Streik *m*	strike	—	sciopero *m*	huelga *f*
grève générale (F)	Generalstreik *m*	general strike	—	sciopero generale *m*	huelga general *f*
grey market (E)	Grauer Markt *m*	—	marché gris *m*	mercato grigio *m*	mercado gris *m*
Großabnehmer (D)	—	bulk buyer	acheteur en gros *m*	acquirente all'ingrosso *m*	comprador al por mayor *m*
Großauftrag (D)	—	large-scale order	grosse commande *f*	ordine di grandi quantità *m*	importante pedido *m*
Großbetrieb (D)	—	large-scale operation	grande exploitation *f*	azienda di grande dimensione *f*	gran explotación *f*
Großcontainer (D)	—	large container	conteneur à grand volume *m*	container di grande dimensione *m*	gran contenedor *m*
gross domestic product (E)	Bruttoinlands- produkt *n*	—	produit intérieur brut *m*	prodotto interno lordo *m*	producto interior bruto *m*
grosse commande (F)	Großauftrag *m*	large-scale order	—	ordine di grandi quantità *m*	importante pedido *m*
Größenabweichung (D)	—	deviation from size	déviation de dimension *f*	differenza di dimensione *f*	deviación de dimensión *f*
Großhandel (D)	—	wholesale trade	commerce de gros *m*	commercio all'ingrosso *m*	comercio mayorista *m*
Großhandelspreis (D)	—	wholesale prices	prix de gros *m*	prezzo all'ingrosso *m*	precio mayorista *m*
gross income (E)	Bruttoeinkommen *n*	—	revenu brut *m*	reddito lordo *m*	ingreso bruto *m*
Grossist (D)	—	wholesaler	grossiste *m*	grossista *m*	mayorista *m*
grossista (I)	Grossist *m*	wholesaler	grossiste *m*	—	mayorista *m*
grossiste (F)	Grossist *m*	wholesaler	—	grossista *m*	mayorista *m*
Großmarkt (D)	—	wholesale market	grand marché *m*	mercato all'ingrosso *m*	mercado central *m*
gross national product (E)	Bruttosozialprodukt *n*	—	produit national brut *m*	prodotto nazionale lordo *m*	producto nacional bruto *m*
gross pay (E)	Bruttolohn *m*	—	salaire brut *m*	salario lordo *m*	salario bruto *m*
gross price (E)	Bruttopreis *m*	—	prix brut *m*	prezzo lordo *m*	precio bruto *m*
gross proceeds (E)	Rohertrag *m*	—	produit brut *m*	reddito lordo *m*	producto bruto *m*
gross production (E)	Bruttoproduktion *f*	—	production brut *f*	produzione lorda *f*	producción bruta *m*
gross profit on sales (E)	Rohgewinn *m*	—	bénéfice brut *m*	utile lordo *m*	ganancia bruta *f*
gross register(ed) ton (E)	Bruttoregistertonne *f*	—	tonneau de jauge brut *m*	tonnellata di stazza lorda *f*	tonelada de registro bruto *f*
ground (E)	Boden *m*	—	sol *m*/terrain *m*	terra *f*/suolo *m*	suelo *m*/terreno *m*
group (E)	Konzern *m*	—	groupe industriel *m*	gruppo *m*	consorcio *m*
groupe de marchandises¹ (F)	Warengruppe *f*	product line	—	gruppo merci *m*	grupo de mercancías *m*
groupe de marchandises² (F)	Gütergruppe *f*	category of goods	—	gruppo di merci *m*	grupo de mercancías *m*
groupe de sociétaires (F)	Sozietät *f*	partnership	—	associazione *f*	sociedad *f*
groupe destinataire (F)	Zielgruppe *f*	target group	—	gruppo di riferimento *m*	grupo destinatario *m*
groupe d'âge (F)	Altersgruppe *f*	age group	—	gruppo d'età *m*	grupo según la edad *m*
groupe d'intérêts (F)	Interessengruppe *f*	interest group	—	gruppo d'interesse *m*	grupo de presión *m*
groupe industriel (F)	Konzern *m*	group/combine	—	gruppo *m*	consorcio *m*
groupe multinational (F)	multinationaler Konzern *m*	multinational group	—	gruppo multinazionale *m*	grupo multinacional *m*
growth (E)	Wachstum *n*	—	croissance *f*	crescita *f*	crecimiento *m*
growth impulse (E)	Wachstumsimpuls *m*	—	stimulation de l'accroissement *f*	impulso di crescita *m*	impulso de crecimiento *m*

	D	E	F	I	Es
growth policy (E)	Wachstumspolitik f	—	politique d'accroissement f	politica di crescita f	política de crecimiento económico f
Grundgehalt (D)	—	basic salary	traitement de base m	stipendio base m	salario base m
Grundkapital (D)	—	share capital	capital initial m	capitale sociale m	capital social m
Grundkenntnisse (D)	—	basic knowledge	connaissances fondamentales f pl	cognizioni elementari f pl	conocimientos básicos m pl
Grundrente (D)	—	basic pension	pension de base f	pensione base f	pensión básica f
Grundschuld (D)	—	mortgage	dette foncière f	debito fondiario m	hipoteca f
Grundstück (D)	—	real estate	terrain m	terreno m	terreno m
Gründung (D)	—	formation	constitution f	costituzione f	fundación f
Gründungsbericht (D)	—	formation report	procès-verbal de fondation m	relazione di costituzione f	informe de los fundadores m
Gründungskosten (D)	—	organization costs	frais de fondation m pl	costi della costituzione m pl	gastos de fundación m pl
Gründungsplanung (D)	—	formation plan	planification de fondation f	progettazione della costituzione f	planificación de la fundación f
grupo de mercancías[1] (Es)	Warengruppe f	product line	groupe de marchandises m	gruppo merci m	—
grupo de mercancías[2] (Es)	Gütergruppe f	category of goods	groupe de marchandises m	gruppo di merci m	—
grupo de presión[1] (Es)	Lobby f	lobbying group	lobby m	lobby m	—
grupo de presión[2] (Es)	Interessengruppe f	interest group	groupe d'intérêts m	gruppo d'interesse m	—
grupo destinatario (Es)	Zielgruppe f	target group	groupe destinataire m	gruppo di riferimento m	—
grupo multinacional (Es)	multinationaler Konzern m	multinational group	groupe multinational m	gruppo multinazionale m	—
grupo según la edad (Es)	Altersgruppe f	age group	groupe d'âge m	gruppo d'età m	—
gruppo (I)	Konzern m	group/combine	groupe industriel m	—	consorcio m
gruppo d'età (I)	Altersgruppe f	age group	groupe d'âge m	—	grupo según la edad m
gruppo d'interesse (I)	Interessengruppe f	interest group	groupe d'intérêts m	—	grupo de presión m
gruppo di merci (I)	Gütergruppe f	category of goods	groupe de marchandises m	—	grupo de mercancías m
gruppo di riferimento (I)	Zielgruppe f	target group	groupe destinataire m	—	grupo destinatario m
gruppo merci (I)	Warengruppe f	product line	groupe de marchandises m	—	grupo de mercancías m
gruppo multinazionale (I)	multinationaler Konzern m	multinational group	groupe multinational m	—	grupo multinacional m
guarantee[1] (E)	Garantieleistung f	—	fourniture sous garantie f	prestazione di garanzia f	aplicación de la garantía f
guarantee[2] (E)	Bürgschaft f	—	caution f	fideiussione f	fianza f
guarantee for proper execution (E)	Gewährleistungsgarantie f	—	caution de garantie f	garanzia di esecuzione f	fianza de contratista f
guarantee obligation (E)	Garantieverpflichtung f	—	engagement de garantie m	obbligo di garanzia m	obligación de garantía f
guarantee of a bill (E)	Aval m	—	aval m	avallo m	aval m
guarantor (E)	Bürge m	—	garant m	fideiussore m	fiador m
guerra comercial (Es)	Handelskrieg m	trade war	guerre commerciale f	guerra commerciale f	—
guerra commerciale (I)	Handelskrieg m	trade war	guerre commerciale f	—	guerra comercial f
guerra económica (Es)	Wirtschaftskrieg m	economic war	guerre économique f	guerra economica f	—
guerra economica (I)	Wirtschaftskrieg m	economic war	guerre économique f	—	guerra económica f
guerre commerciale (F)	Handelskrieg m	trade war	—	guerra commerciale f	guerra comercial f
guerre économique (F)	Wirtschaftskrieg m	economic war	—	guerra economica f	guerra económica f
guide price (E)	Orientierungspreis m	—	prix d'orientation m	prezzo d'orientamento m	precio de orientación m
günstigstes Angebot (D)	—	most favourable offer	offre favorable f	offerta vantaggiosa f	oferta favorable f
Güteklasse (D)	—	grade	catégorie de qualité f	qualità f	categoría de calidad f
Güter (D)	—	goods	biens m pl	beni m pl	bienes m pl
Güterbeförderung (D)	—	carriage of goods	transport de marchandises m	trasporto di merci m	transporte de mercancías m

	D	E	F	I	Es
Gütergruppe (D)	—	category of goods	groupe de marchandises *m*	gruppo di merci *m*	grupo de mercancías *m*
Gütertarif (D)	—	trade tariff	tarif marchandises *m*	tariffa merci *f*	tarifa de transporte *f*
gutgläubig (D)	—	bona fide	de bonne foi	di buona fede	de buena fe
Guthaben (D)	—	money owed	avoir *m*	saldo attivo *m*	haber *m*
gutschreiben (D)	—	credit	créditer	accreditare	abonar en cuenta
Gutschrift (D)	—	credit	crédit *m*	accredito *m*	abono *m*
Gutschriftsanzeige (D)	—	credit advice	avis de crédit *m*	nota di accredito *f*	aviso de abono *m*
Haben (D)	—	credit side	avoir *m*	attivo m	haber m
Habenzinsen (D)	—	credit interest	intérêts créditeur *m*	interessi creditori *m pl*	intereses acreedores *m pl*
haber¹ (Es)	Haben *n*	credit side	avoir *m*	attivo *m*	—
haber² (Es)	Guthaben *n*	money owed	avoir *m*	saldo attivo *m*	—
haber social repartible (Es)	Liquidationserlös *m*	remaining assets after liquidation	produit de la liquidation *m*	ricavo della liquidazione *m*	—
habileté en matière de négociations (F)	Verhandlungs- geschick *n*	negotiation skills	—	abilità nel trattare *f*	tino de negociar *m*
habitude de payement (F)	Zahlungs- gewohnheit *f*	practice of payment	—	consuetudine di pagamento *f*	práctica de pago *f*
hacer la cola (Es)	Schlange stehen	queue up	faire la queue	fare la coda	—
hacer quincalla (Es)	verschrotten	scrap	mettre à la ferraille	ridurre a rottame	—
Hacienda¹ (Es)	Finanzamt *n*	inland revenue office	service de contributions *m*	ufficio delle imposte *m*	—
Hacienda² (Es)	Finanzministerium *n*	Ministry of Finance	ministère des finances *m*	ministero delle Finanze *m*	—
Hafen (D)	—	port	port *m*	porto *m*	puerto *m*
Hafengebühren (D)	—	harbour dues	droits de ports *m pl*	diritti di porto *m pl*	derechos portuarios *m pl*
Haftkaution (D)	—	bail	caution pour être mis en liberté *f*	cauzione per la scarcerazione *f*	fianza de puesta en libertad *f*
Haftpflicht- versicherung (D)	—	third party liability insurance	assurance responsa- bilité civile *f*	assicurazione della responsabilità civile *f*	seguro de responsa- bilidad civil *m*
Haftung (D)	—	liability	responsabilité *f*	responsabilità *f*	responsabilidad *f*
Halberzeugnis (D)	—	semi-finished good	produit demi-fini *m*	prodotto semifinito *m*	producto semielaborado *m*
halbjährlich (D)	—	half-yearly	semestriel	semestrale	semestral
half-yearly (E)	halbjährlich	—	semestriel	semestrale	semestral
halle de dépôt (F)	Lagerraum *m*	storage space	—	magazzino *m*	almacén *m*
hand over (E)	abliefern	—	livrer	consegnare	entregar
Handarbeit (D)	—	manual work	travail manuel *m*	lavoro manuale *m*	trabajo a mano *m*
Handbuch (D)	—	manual	manuel *m*	manuale *m*	manual *m*
Handel (D)	—	trade	commerce *m*	commercio *m*	comercio *m*
Handelsbank (D)	—	merchant bank	banque de commerce *f*	banca commerciale *f*	banco comercial *m*
Handels- bedingungen (D)		trading conditions	conditions commerciales *f pl*	condizioni commerciali *f pl*	condiciones comerciales *f pl*
Handels- beschränkungen (D)	—	trade restrictions	restrictions au commerce *f pl*	restrizioni commerciali *f pl*	restricciones commerciales *f pl*
Handels- beziehungen (D)		trade relations	relations commerciales *f pl*	rapporti commerciali *m pl*	relaciones comerciales *f pl*
Handelsbilanz (D)	—	balance of trade	balance des opérations en marchandises *f*	bilancia commerciale *f*	balanza comercial *f*
Handelsbrauch (D)	—	business practice	usage commercial *m*	usanza commerciale *f*	uso comercial *m*
Handelsembargo (D)	—	trade embargo	embargo commercial *m*	embargo commerciale *m*	embargo comercial *m*
Handelsfaktura (D)	—	commercial invoice	facture commerciale *f*	fattura commerciale *f*	factura comercial *f*
Handelsgesellschaft (D)	—	trading company	société commerciale *f*	società commerciale *f*	sociedad comercial *f*
Handelsgesetzbuch (D)	—	Commercial Code	code de commerce *m*	codice commerciale *m*	código mercantil *m*
Handelskammer (D)	—	Chamber of Commerce	chambre de commerce *f*	camera di commercio *f*	cámara de comercio *f*

	D	E	F	I	Es
Handelsklasse (D)	—	grade	catégorie de produits *f*	categoria commerciale *f*	clase *f*
Handelsklausel (D)	—	trade terms	clause commerciale *f*	clausola commerciale *f*	cláusula comercial *f*
Handelskreditbrief (D)	—	commercial letter of credit	lettre de crédit commercial *f*	lettera di credito commerciale *f*	carta de crédito comercial *f*
Handelskrieg (D)	—	trade war	guerre commerciale *f*	guerra commerciale *f*	guerra comercial *f*
Handelsmesse (D)	—	trade fair	foire commerciale *f*	fiera commerciale *f*	feria comercial *f*
Handelsmission (D)	—	trade mission	mission commerciale *f*	missione commerciale *f*	misión comercial *f*
Handelspartner (D)	—	trading partner	partenaire commercial *m*	partner commerciale *m*	socio comercial *m*
Handelsplatz (D)	—	trade centre	place marchande *f*	piazza commerciale *f*	plaza comercial *f*
Handelspolitik (D)	—	commercial policy	politique commerciale *f*	politica commerciale *f*	política comercial *f*
Handelsregister (D)	—	commercial register	registre du commerce *m*	registro commerciale *m*	registro mercantil *m*
Handelsspanne (D)	—	trading margin	bénéfice brut *m*	margine commerciale *m*	margen comercial *f*
Handelsüberschuß (D)	—	trade surplus	excédent commercial *m*	eccedenza commerciale *f*	excedente comercial *m*
Handelsusancen (D)	—	trade practice	usages commerciaux *m pl*	usanze commerciali *f pl*	usos comerciales *m pl*
Handelsverkehr (D)	—	commercial intercourse	échanges commerciaux *m pl*	circolazione delle merci *f*	comercio *m*
Handelsvertreter (D)	—	commercial agent	représentant de commerce *m*	rappresentante commerciale *m*	representante comercial *m*
Handelsvertretung (D)	—	commercial agency	représentation commerciale *f*	rappresentanza commerciale *f*	representación comercial *f*
handgeschriebener Lebenslauf (D)	—	hand-written curriculum vitae	curriculum vitae écrit à la main *m*	curriculum vitae scritto a mano *m*	curriculum vitae escrito a mano *m*
Handicrafts Regulation Act (E)	Handwerksordnung *f*	—	code de l'artisanat *m*	codice dell'artigianato *m*	reglamento del artesanado *m*
Händler (D)	—	trader	commerçant *m*	commerciante *m*	comerciante *m*
Handlungs-bevollmächtigter (D)	—	commercial agent	personne ayant le pouvoir commercial *f*	mandatario commerciale *m*	apoderado especial *m*
Handwerk (D)	—	craft trade	artisanat *m*	artigianato *m*	artesanía *f*
Handwerkskammer (D)	—	chamber of handicrafts	chambre artisanale *f*	camera dell'artigianato *f*	cámara de artesanía *f*
Handwerksordnung (D)	—	Handicrafts Regulation Act	code de l'artisanat *m*	codice dell'artigianato *m*	reglamento del artesanado *m*
handwork (E)	Handarbeit *f*	—	travail manuel *m*	lavoro manuale *m*	trabajo a mano *m*
hand-written curriculum vitae (E)	handgeschriebener Lebenslauf *m*	—	curriculum vitae écrit à la main *m*	curriculum vitae scritto a mano *m*	curriculum vitae escrito a mano *m*
harbour dues (E)	Hafengebühren *pl*	—	droits de port *m pl*	diritti di porto *m pl*	derechos portuarios *m pl*
hard coal (E)	Steinkohle *f*	—	houille *f*	carbone fossile *m*	hulla *f*
hard currency (E)	harte Währung *f*	—	monnaie solide *f*	moneta forte *f*	moneda dura *f*
harte Währung (D)	—	hard currency	monnaie solide *f*	moneta forte *f*	moneda dura *f*
Hartgeld (D)	—	specie	pièce de monnaie *f*	moneta metallica *f*	dinero metálico *m*
haulage (E)	Rollgeld *n*	—	camionnage *m*	spese di trasporto *f pl*	derechos de acarreo *m pl*
Hauptspeicher (D)	—	main memory	mémoire principale *f*	memoria principale *f*	memoria principal *f*
Hausbank (D)	—	company's bank	banque habituelle *f*	banca di preferenza *f*	banco particular *m*
Hausbesitzer (D)	—	home property owner	propriétaire d'immeuble *m*	possessore di casa *m*	propietario de una casa *m*
Hauseigentümer (D)	—	owner of a house	propriétaire d'une maison *m*	proprietario di casa *m*	propietario de una casa *m*
Haushalt (D)	—	budget	budget *m*	bilancio *m*	presupuesto *m*
Haushaltsdefizit (D)	—	budgetary deficit	déficit budgétaire *m*	deficit del bilancio *m*	déficit presupuestario *m*
Haushaltsjahr (D)	—	financial year	exercice budgétaire *m*	anno finanziario *m*	ejercicio *m*
Haushaltsplan (D)	—	budget	budget *m*	bilancio preventivo *m*	presupuesto *m*

	D	E	F	I	Es
Hausse (D)	—	boom	hausse f	rialzo m	alza f
hausse¹ (F)	Hausse f	boom	—	rialzo m	alza f
hausse² (F)	Kurssteigerung f	price advance	—	aumento dei corsi m	alza de las cotizaciones f
hausse³ (F)	Aufschlag m	surcharge	—	aggiunta f	recargo m
hausse (I)	Hausse f	boom	hausse f	—	alza f
hausse des prix (F)	Preissteigerung f	price increase	—	aumento dei prezzi m	aumento de precios m
hausse illicite des loyers (F)	Mietwucher m	exorbitant rent	—	strozzinaggio sui canoni di locazione m	usura arrendaticia f
Haussier (D)	—	bull	haussier m	speculatore al rialzo m	alcista m
haussier (F)	Haussier m	bull	—	speculatore al rialzo m	alcista m
haussier (I)	Haussier m	bull	haussier m	—	alcista m
haute autorité (F)	hohe Behörde f	high authority	—	alta autorità f	Alta Autoridad f
haute conjoncture (F)	Hochkonjunktur f	boom	—	alta congiuntura f	alta coyuntura f
Havarie (D)	—	damage by sea	avarie f	avaria f	avería m
Havariezertifikat (D)	—	damage report	certificat d'avarie m	certificato d'avaria m	certificado de avería m
have in stock (E)	auf Lager haben	—	avoir en stock	avere in magazzino	tener en almacén
head (E)	Chef m	—	chef m	capo m	jefe m
head of department (E)	Abteilungsleiter m	—	chef de service m	capo reparto m	jefe de sección m
health certificate (E)	Gesundheitszeugnis n	—	certificat de santé m	certificato sanitario m	certificado de sanidad m
health insurance (E)	Krankenversicherung f	—	assurance maladie f	assicurazione contro le malattie f	seguro de enfermedad m
heavy freight (E)	Schwergut n	—	produit pondéreux m	carico pesante m	mercancía pesada f
heavy metal (E)	Schwermetall n	—	métal lourd m	metallo pesante m	metal pesado m
hebdomadaire (F)	wöchentlich	weekly	—	settimanale	semanal
hecho a medida (Es)	maßgefertigt	manufactured to measure	travaillé sur mesure	prodotto su misura	—
Heimarbeit (D)	—	homework	travail à domicile m	lavoro a domicilio m	trabajo a domicilio m
heirs (E)	Erben pl	—	héritiers m pl	eredi m pl	heredero m
Herbstmesse (D)	—	autumn fair	foire d'automne f	fiera autunnale f	feria de otoño f
heredero (Es)	Erben pl	heirs	héritiers m pl	eredi m pl	—
herencia (Es)	Erbschaft f	inheritance	héritage m	eredità f	—
héritage (F)	Erbschaft f	inheritance	—	eredità f	herencia f
héritiers (F)	Erben pl	heirs	—	eredi m pl	heredero m
Herkunftsland (D)	—	country of origin	pays de provenance m	paese d'origine m	país de origen m
herrschendes Unternehmen (D)	—	controlling company	entreprise dirigeante f	impresa controllante f	empresa dominante f
Herstellen-oder-zukaufen (D)	—	produce or buy in addition	produire ou acheter additionnellement	produrre o comprare in aggiunta	producir o comprar adicionalmente
Hersteller (D)	—	producer	fabricant m	produttore m	fabricante m
Herstellungskosten (D)	—	production costs	frais de fabrication m	costi di produzione m pl	costo de la producción m
Herstellungswert (D)	—	production value	prix de revient m	valore di produzione m	valor de fabricación m
heures d'ouverture (F)	Geschäftszeit f	business hours	—	orario d'apertura m	hora de despacho f pl
heures de travail (F)	Arbeitszeit f	working hours	—	orario di lavoro m	jornada laboral f
heure supplémentaire (F)	Überstunde f	overtime	—	ora straordinaria f	hora extraordinaria f
hidden reserves (E)	stille Reserve f	—	réserve cachée f	riserva occulta f	reserva tácita f
Hierarchie (D)	—	hierarchy	hiérarchie f	gerarchia f	jerarquía f
hiérarchie (F)	Hierarchie f	hierarchy	—	gerarchia f	jerarquía f
hierarchy (E)	Hierarchie f	—	hiérarchie f	gerarchia f	jerarquía f
high authority (E)	hohe Behörde f	—	haute autorité f	alta autorità f	Alta Autoridad f
highest rate (E)	Höchstkurs m	—	cours le plus haut m	corso massimo m	cotización máxima f
Hinterlegung (D)	—	deposit	dépôt m	deposito m	depósito m
Hinterziehung (D)	—	evasion of taxes	fraude fiscale f	evasione f	defraudación f

	D	E	F	I	Es
hiperinflación (Es)	Hyperinflation f	hyperinflation	hyperinflation f	iperinflazione f	—
hipoteca¹ (Es)	Hypothek f	mortgage	hypothéque f	ipoteca f	—
hipoteca² (Es)	Grundschuld f	mortgage	dette foncière f	debito fondiario m	—
hipótesis (Es)	Hypothese f	hypothesis	hypothèse f	ipotesi f	—
hired car (E)	Leihwagen m	—	voiture de location f	vettura da noleggio f	coche de alquiler m
hire purchase transaction (E)	Abzahlungsgeschäft n	—	achat à tempérament m	operazione con pagamento a rate f	venta a plazos f
hire-purchase transaction (E)	Ratenkauf m	—	achat à tempérament m	acquisto a rate m	compra a plazo f
hiring of personnel (E)	Personalwerbung f	—	recrutement de personnel m	reclutazione di personale f	reclutamiento de personal m
histoire économique (F)	Wirtschafts-geschichte f	economic history	—	storia economica f	historia económica f
historia económica (Es)	Wirtschafts-geschichte f	economic history	histoire économique f	storia economica f	—
historical costing (E)	Nachkalkulation f	—	calcul des coûts a posteriori m	computisteria f	cálculo de costes a posteriori m
Hochkonjunktur (D)	—	boom	haute conjoncture f	alta congiuntura f	alta coyuntura f
Höchstkurs (D)	—	highest rate	cours le plus haut m	corso massimo m	cotización máxima f
Höchstpreis (D)	—	top price	prix plafond m	prezzo massimo m	precio máximo m
hohe Behörde (D)	—	high authority	haute autorité f	alta autorità f	Alta Autoridad f
Hoheitsrecht (D)	—	sovereign right	droit de souveraineté m	diritto di sovranità m	soberanía f
hoja de pedido (Es)	Bestellschein m	order form	bulletin de commande m	bolletta d'ordinazione f	—
holding company (E)	Dachgesellschaft f	—	société holding f	società finanziaria f	sociedad holding f
holiday allowance (E)	Urlaubsgeld n	—	prime de vacances f	indennità di ferie f	retribución por vacaciones f
home demand (E)	Inlandsnachfrage f	—	demande intérieure f	domanda interna f	demanda interior f
home market (E)	Binnenmarkt m	—	marché national m	mercato nazionale m	mercado interior m
home property owner (E)	Hausbesitzer m	—	propriétaire d'immeuble m	possessore di casa m	propietario de una casa m
homework (E)	Heimarbeit f	—	travail à domicile m	lavoro a domicilio m	trabajo a domicilio m
homogeneidad (Es)	Homogenität f	homogeneity	homogénéité f	omogeneità f	—
homogeneity (E)	Homogenität f	—	homogénéité f	omogeneità f	homogeneidad f
homogénéité (F)	Homogenität f	homogeneity	—	omogeneità f	homogeneidad f
Homogenität (D)	—	homogeneity	homogénéité f	omogeneità f	homogeneidad f
honoraires (F)	Honorar n	professional fee	—	onorario m	honorario m
Honorar (D)	—	professional fee	honoraires m pl	onorario m	honorario m
honorario (Es)	Honorar n	professional fee	honoraires m pl	onorario m	—
honorary consul (E)	Wahlkonsul m	—	consul honoraire m	console onorario m	cónsul honorario m
honorer la traite acceptée (F)	Akzepteinlösung f	honouring of an acceptance	—	pagamento di un effetto m	descuento de una letra aceptada m
honouring of an acceptance (E)	Akzepteinlösung f	—	honorer la traite acceptée	pagamento di un effetto m	descuento de una letra aceptada m
hora de despacho (Es)	Geschäftszeit f	business hours	heures d'ouverture f pl	orario d'apertura m	—
hora extraordinaria (Es)	Überstunde f	overtime	heure supplémentaire f	ora straordinaria f	—
hospedaje (Es)	Bewirtung f	hospitality/catering	hospitalité f/accueil m	ospitalità f/servizio m	—
hospitalité (F)	Bewirtung f	hospitality/catering	—	ospitalità f/servizio m	hospedaje m/ atenciones f pl
hospitality (E)	Bewirtung f	—	hospitalité f/accueil m	ospitalità f/servizio m	hospedaje m/ atenciones f pl
houille (F)	Steinkohle f	hard coal	—	carbone fossile m	hulla f
hourly wage (E)	Stundenlohn m	—	salaire horaire m	salario ad ora m	salario-hora m
housebreaking insurance (E)	Einbruch-versicherung f	—	assurance contre le vol avec effraction f	assicurazione contro il furto con scasso f	seguro contra robo con fractura m
housekeeping account (E)	Wirtschaftsstatistik f	—	statistique économique f	statistica economica f	estadística económica f

	D	E	F	I	Es
housing construction (E)	Wohnungsbau m	—	construction de logements f	edilizia abitativa f	construcción de viviendas f
Huckepackverkehr (D)	—	piggyback service	transport pick-a-back m	trasporto strada-rotaia m	transporte combinado ferrocarril-carretera m
Huckepackwerbung (D)	—	piggyback advertisement	publicité pick-a-back f	pubblicità per il trasporto strada-rotaia f	publicidad combinada ferrocarril-carretera f
huelga (Es)	Streik m	strike	grève f	sciopero m	—
huelga general (Es)	Generalstreik m	general strike	grève générale f	sciopero generale m	—
huile usée (F)	Altöl n	waste oil	—	olio usato m	aceite usado m
huissier de justice (F)	Gerichtsvollzieher m	bailiff	—	ufficiale giudiziario m	ejecutor judicial m
hulla (Es)	Steinkohle f	hard coal	houille f	carbone fossile m	—
Hyperinflation (D)	—	hyperinflation	hyperinflation f	iperinflazione f	hiperinflación f
hyperinflation (E)	Hyperinflation f	—	hyperinflation f	iperinflazione f	hiperinflación f
hyperinflation (F)	Hyperinflation f	hyperinflation	—	iperinflazione f	hiperinflación f
Hypothek (D)	—	mortgage	hypothéque f	ipoteca f	hipoteca f
Hypothekenbank (D)	—	mortgage bank	banque hypothécaire f	banca ipotecaria f	banco hipotecario m
hypothéque (F)	Hypothek f	mortgage	—	ipoteca f	hipoteca f
Hypothese (D)	—	hypothesis	hypothèse f	ipotesi f	hipótesis f
hypothèse (F)	Hypothese f	hypothesis	—	ipotesi f	hipótesis f
hypothesis (E)	Hypothese f	—	hypothèse f	ipotesi f	hipótesis f
idea (E)	Idee f	—	idée f	idea f	idea f
idea (Es)	Idee f	idea	idée f	idea f	—
idea (I)	Idee f	idea	idée f	—	idea f
Idee (D)	—	idea	idée f	idea f	idea f
idée (F)	Idee f	idea	—	idea f	idea f
identidad de los balances sucsivos (Es)	Bilanzkontinuität f	formal identity	identité des bilans successifs f	continuità di bilancio f	—
identité (F)	Personalien pl	personal data	—	generalità f pl	datos personales m pl
identité des bilans successifs (F)	Bilanzkontinuität f	formal identity	—	continuità di bilancio f	identidad de los balances sucsivos f
identity card (E)	Personalausweis m	—	pièce d'identité f	carta d'identità f	carné de identidad m
ilegal (Es)	ungesetzlich	illegal	contraire à la loi	illegale	—
illegal (E)	ungesetzlich	—	contraire à la loi	illegale	ilegal
illegale (I)	ungesetzlich	illegal	contraire à la loi	—	ilegal
illicit trade (E)	Schwarzhandel m	—	commerce clandestin m	commercio abusivo m	comercio clandestino m
illicit work (E)	Schwarzarbeit f	—	travail noir m	lavoro abusivo m	trabajo clandestino m
illiquidità (I)	Illiquidität f	illiquidity	manque de trésorerie f	—	falta de liquidez f
Illiquidität (D)	—	illiquidity	manque de trésorerie f	illiquidità f	falta de liquidez f
illiquidity (E)	Illiquidität f	—	manque de trésorerie f	illiquidità f	falta de liquidez f
Image (D)	—	image	image f	immagine f	imagen f
image (E)	Image n	—	image f	immagine f	imagen f
image (F)	Image n	image	—	immagine f	imagen f
imagen (Es)	Image n	image	image f	immagine f	—
im Auftrag (D)	—	by order	par ordre	per ordine	por poder
im Ausland (D)	—	abroad	à l'étranger	all'estero	en el extranjero
imballaggio (I)	Verpackung	packing	emballage m	—	embalaje m
imballaggio marittimo (I)	seemäßige Verpackung f	seaproof packing	emballage maritime m	—	embalaje marítimo m
imbarcare (I)	verfrachten	freight/ship	fréter/embarquer	—	expedir/fletar
imbarco (I)	Verschiffung f	shipment	embarquement m	—	embarque m
im eigenen Namen (D)	—	in one's own name	en nom propre	per nome proprio	en nombre propio
im Einvernehmen mit (D)	—	in agreement with	d'accord avec	d'accordo con	de conformidad con
im einzelnen (D)	—	in particular	en particulier	in dettaglio	en particular
imitación (Es)	Imitation f	imitation	imitation f	imitazione f	—
Imitation (D)	—	imitation	imitation f	imitazione f	imitación f

	D	E	F	I	Es
imitation (E)	Imitation f	—	imitation f	imitazione f	imitación f
imitation (F)	Imitation f	imitation	—	imitazione f	imitación f
imitazione (I)	Imitation f	imitation	imitation f	—	imitación f
immagazzinamento (I)	Einlagerung f	storage	entreposage m	—	almacenamiento m
immagazzinamento doganale (I)	Zollagerung f	customs warehouse storage	dépôt en entrepôt sous douane m	—	depósito de aduana m
immagine (I)	Image n	image	image f	—	imagen f
immaterieller Schaden (D)	—	non-material damage	dommage immatériel m	danno immateriale m	daño inmaterial m
immediate delivery (E)	sofortige Lieferung f	—	livraison immédiate f	consegna immediata f	entrega inmediata f
immediate(ly) (E)	umgehend	—	immédiatement	immediatamente	inmediatamente
immédiatement (F)	umgehend	immediate(ly)	—	immediatamente	inmediatamente
immediate payment (E)	sofortige Zahlung f	—	payement immédiat m	pagamento immediato m	pago inmediato m
immediato (I)	umgehend	immediate(ly)	immédiatement	—	inmediatamente
immobile (I)	Immobilie f	item of real estate	bien immobilier m	—	inmueble m
Immobilie (D)	—	item of real estate	bien immobilier m	immobile m	inmueble m
Immobilienfonds (D)	—	real estate fund	fonds immobilier m	fondo immobiliare m	fondo inmobiliario f
Immobiliengeschäft (D)	—	property transactions	affaire immobilière f	operazione immobiliare f	negocio de inmuebles m
Immobilien-Leasing (D)	—	leasing of real estate	leasing de biens immobiliers m	leasing immobiliare m	leasing de inmuebles m
Immobilienmakler (D)	—	estate agent	courtier en affaires immobilières m	agente immobiliare m	agente de inmuebles m
immobilisations corporelles (F)	Sachanlagen pl	fixed assets	—	immobilizzazioni f pl	inmuebles y utillaje m pl
immobilizzazioni (I)	Sachanlagen pl	fixed assets	immobilisations corporelles f pl	—	inmuebles y utillaje m pl
impegno (I)	Engagement n	engagement/ commitment	engagement m	—	compromiso m
impegno di copertura (I)	Deckungszusage f	confirmation of cover	acceptation de prendre le risque en charge f	—	nota de cobertura f
impersonal taxes (E)	Realsteuern pl	—	impôt réel m	imposte reali f pl	impuestos reales m pl
impianti di produzione (I)	Produktionsanlagen pl	production facilities	installations industrielles f pl	—	instalaciones de producción f pl
impianto industriale (I)	Industrieanlage f	industrial plant	installation industrielle f	—	planta industrial f
impiegare (I)	anstellen	employ	employer	—	emplear
impiegati (I)	Angestellter m	employee	employé m pl	—	empleado m
impiego (I)	Anstellung f	employment	emploi m	—	empleo m
impiego dei redditi (I)	Einkommensverwendung f	appropriation of income	utilisation du revenu f	—	distribución de la renta f
impiego dell'utile (I)	Gewinnverwendung f	appropriation of net income	utilisation des bénéfices f	—	aplicación de los resultatods f
impiego di computer (I)	Computereinsatz m	use of a computer	emploi d'ordinateurs m	—	utilización de ordenadores f
Import (D)	—	import	importation f	importazione f	importación f
import[1] (E)	Einfuhr f	—	importation f	importazione f	importación f
import[2] (E)	Import m	—	importation f	importazione f	importación f
importación[1] (Es)	Import m	import	importation f	importazione f	—
importación[2] (Es)	Einfuhr f	import	importation f	importazione f	—
importación agrícola (Es)	Agrarimport m	farm imports	importation de produits agricoles f	importazione agricola f	—
importación de capital (Es)	Kapitalimport m	capital import	importation de capitaux f	importazione di capitali f	—
importante (Es)	relevant	relevant	significatif	rilevante	—
importante pedido (Es)	Großauftrag m	large-scale order	grosse commande f	ordine di grandi quantità m	—
importation[1] (F)	Einfuhr f	import	—	importazione f	importación f
importation[2] (F)	Import m	import	—	importazione f	importación f

	D	E	F	I	Es
importation de capitaux (F)	Kapitalimport *m*	capital import	—	importazione di capitali *f*	importación de capital *f*
importation de l'inflation (F)	Inflationsimport *m*	import of inflation	—	importazione di inflazione *f*	inflación importada *f*
importation de produits agricoles (F)	Agrarimport *m*	farm imports	—	importazione agricola *f*	importación agrícola *f*
importazione¹ (I)	Import *m*	import	importation *f*	—	importación *f*
importazione² (I)	Einfuhr *f*	import	importation *f*	—	importación *f*
importazione agricola (I)	Agrarimport *m*	farm imports	importation de produits agricoles *f*	—	importación agrícola *f*
importazione di capitali (I)	Kapitalimport *m*	capital import	importation de capitaux *f*	—	importación de capital *f*
importazione di inflazione (I)	Inflationsimport *m*	import of inflation	importation de l'inflation *f*	—	inflación importada *f*
import declaration (E)	Einfuhrerklärung *f*	—	déclaration d'entrée *f*	dichiarazione doganale *f*	declaración de importación *f*
import deposit (E)	Importdepot *n*	—	dépôt d'importation *m*	deposito d'importazione *m*	depósito de importación *m*
Importdepot (D)	—	import deposit	dépôt d'importation *m*	deposito d'importazione *m*	depósito de importación *m*
import documents (E)	Einfuhrpapiere *pl*	—	documents d'importation *m pl*	bollette doganali *f pl*	documentos de importación *m pl*
import duties (E)	Einfuhrabgabe *f*	—	taxe à l'importation *f*	tassa d'importazione *f*	tasa a la importación *f*
import duty (E)	Einfuhrzoll *m*	—	droit d'entrée *m*	dazio d'importazione *m*	arancel de importación *m*
importe de la factura (Es)	Rechnungsbetrag *m*	amount of invoice	montant de la facture *m*	ammontare della fattura *m*	—
imported inflation (E)	importierte Inflation *f*	—	inflation importée *f*	inflazione importata *f*	inflación importada *f*
Importhandel (D)	—	import trade	commerce d'importation *m*	commercio delle importazioni *m*	comercio de importación *m*
importierte Inflation (D)	—	imported inflation	inflation importée *f*	inflazione importata *f*	inflación importada *f*
import licence (E)	Einfuhrgenehmigung *f*	—	autorisation d'importation *f*	permesso d'importazione *m*	permiso de importación *m*
importo (I)	Betrag *m*	amount	montant *m*	—	suma *f*
importo del credito documentario (I)	Akkreditivsumme *f*	amount of the letter of credit	montant de l'accréditif *m*	—	suma del crédito documentario *f*
importo della fattura (I)	Rechnungssumme *f*	invoice amount	montant de la facture *m*	—	suma de la factura *f*
importo di rimborso (I)	Ablösesumme *f*	redemption sum	montant de rachat *m*	—	suma de amortización *f*
import of inflation (E)	Inflationsimport *m*	—	importation de l'inflation *f*	importazione di inflazione *f*	inflación importada *f*
importo minimo (I)	Mindesthöhe *f*	minimum amount	montant minimum *m*	—	cantidad mínima *f*
importo nominale (I)	Nominalbetrag *m*	nominal amount	montant nominal *m*	—	montante nominal *m*
importo nominale minimo (I)	Mindestnennbetrag *m*	minimum nominal amount	montant nominal minimum *m*	—	valor nominal mínimo *m*
importo totale (I)	Gesamtsumme *f*	total amout	montant total *m*	—	suma total *f*
Importquote (D)	—	import quota	contingent d'importation *m*	quota d'importazione *f*	cuota de importación *f*
import quota (E)	Importquote *f*	—	contingent d'importation *m*	quota d'importazione *f*	cuota de importación *f*
import restriction (E)	Einfuhrbeschränkung *f*	—	limitation des importations *f*	restrizione d'importazione *f*	restricción a la importación *f*
import trade (E)	Importhandel *m*	—	commerce d'importation *m*	commercio delle importazioni *m*	comercio de importación *m*
imposiciones de ahorro (Es)	Spareinlagen *pl*	savings deposits	dépôt d'épargne *m*	depositi di risparmio *m pl*	—
imposición separada e igual de los cónyuges (Es)	Splitting *n*	splitting	péréquation fiscale des revenus des deux époux *f*	splittaggio *m*	—
imposta¹ (I)	Abgabe *f*	tax/duty	taxe *f*	—	impuesto *m*/arancel *m*
imposta² (I)	Steuer *f*	tax	impôt *m*	—	impuesto *m*
imposta cedolare (I)	Ertragsteuer *f*	tax on income	impôt assis sur le produit *m*	—	impuesto sobre beneficios *m*

	D	E	F	I	Es
imposta di successione (I)	Erbschaftsteuer f	inheritance tax	impôt sur les successions m	—	impuesto sobre sucesiones m
imposta generale sulle entrate (I)	Umsatzsteuer f	turnover tax	impôt sur le chiffre d'affaires m	—	impuesto sobre el volumen de ventas m
imposta industriale (I)	Gewerbesteuer f	trade tax	patente f	—	impuesto industrial m
imposta in natura (I)	Naturalabgabe f	duty in kind	taxe acquittée en nature f	—	impuesto en especie m
imposta sugli alcolici (I)	Alkoholsteuer f	tax on alcohol	impôt sur l'alcool m	—	impuesto sobre el alcohol m
imposta sugli investimenti (I)	Investitionssteuer f	investment tax	impôt sur les investissements m	—	impuesto sobre las inversiones m
imposta sugli olii minerali (I)	Mineralölsteuer f	mineral oil tax	taxe sur les carburants f	—	impuesto sobre la gasolina m
imposta sui consumi di lusso (I)	Luxussteuer f	luxury tax	taxe de luxe f	—	impuesto de lujo m
imposta sui redditi (I)	Einkommensteuer f	income tax	impôt sur le revenu m	—	impuesto sobre la renta de las personas físicas m
imposta sui salari (I)	Lohnsteuer f	wages tax	impôt sur les traitements et salaires m	—	impuesto sobre los rendimientos del trabajo personal f
imposta sul fatturato d'acquisto (I)	Vorsteuer f	input tax	impôt perçu en amont m	—	impuesto sobre el valor añadido deducible m
imposta sul reddito delle società (I)	Körperschaftsteuer f	corporation tax	taxe sur les sociétés f	—	impuesto de corporaciones m
imposta sul valore aggiunto (I)	Mehrwertsteuer f	value-added tax	taxe à la valeur ajoutée f	—	impuesto sobre el valor añadido m
imposta sulla circolazione degli autoveicoli (I)	Kraftfahrzeugsteuer f	motor vehicle tax	taxe sur les véhicules à moteur f	—	impuesto sobre vehículos m
imposta sulla rendita del capitale (I)	Kapitalertragsteuer f	tax on investment income	impôt sur le revenue du capital m	—	impuesto sobre la renta del capital m
imposta sulle donazioni (I)	Schenkungssteuer f	gift tax	impôt sur les donations m	—	impuesto sobre donaciones m
imposta sulle operazioni di borsa (I)	Börsen-umsatzsteuer f	stock exchange turnover tax	droit de transaction sur les opérations boursières f	—	impuesto de negociación bursátil m
imposte dirette (I)	direkte Steuern pl	direct taxes	impôts directs m pl	—	impuestos directos m pl
imposte indirette (I)	indirekte Steuern pl	indirect taxes	impôts indirects m	—	impuestos indirectos m pl
imposte reali (I)	Realsteuern pl	impersonal taxes	impôt réel m	—	impuestos reales m pl
impôt (F)	Steuer f	tax	—	imposta f	impuesto m
impôt assis sur le produit (F)	Ertragsteuer f	tax on income	—	imposta cedolare f/ imposta sul reddito f	impuesto sobre beneficios m
impôt perçu en amont (F)	Vorsteuer f	input tax	—	imposta sul fatturato d'acquisto f	impuesto sobre el valor añadido deducible m
impôt réel (F)	Realsteuern pl	impersonal taxes	—	imposte reali f pl	impuestos reales m pl
impôts directs (F)	direkte Steuern pl	direct taxes	—	imposte dirette f pl	impuestos directos m pl
impôts indirects (F)	indirekte Steuern pl	indirect taxes	—	imposte indirette f pl	impuestos indirectos m pl
impôt sur l'alcool (F)	Alkoholsteuer f	tax on alcohol	—	imposta sugli alcolici f	impuesto sobre el alcohol m
impôt sur le chiffre d'affaires (F)	Umsatzsteuer f	turnover tax	—	imposta generale sulle entrate f	impuesto sobre el volumen de ventas m
impôt sur le revenu (F)	Einkommensteuer f	income tax	—	imposta sui redditi f	impuesto sobre la renta de las personas físicas m
impôt sur le revenu du capital (F)	Kapitalertragsteuer f	tax on investment income	—	imposta sulla rendita del capitale f	impuesto sobre la renta del capital m
impôt sur les donations (F)	Schenkungssteuer f	gift tax	—	imposta sulle donazioni f	impuesto sobre donaciones m
impôt sur les investissements (F)	Investitionssteuer f	investment tax	—	imposta sugli investimenti f	impuesto sobre las inversiones m

	D	E	F	I	Es
impôt sur les successions (F)	Erbschaftsteuer f	inheritance tax	—	imposta di successione f	impuesto sobre sucesiones m
impôt sur les traitements et salaires (F)	Lohnsteuer f	wages tax	—	imposta sui salari f	impuesto sobre los rendimientos del trabajo personal f
im Preis inbegriffen (D)	—	included in the price	inclus dans le prix	incluso nel prezzo	incluido
imprenditore (I)	Unternehmer m	entrepreneur	entrepreneur m	—	empresario m
imprenditore giovane (I)	Jungunternehmer m	young businessman	entrepreneur débutant m	—	joven empresario m
impresa (I)	Unternehmen n	enterprise	entreprise f	—	empresario m
impresa concorrente (I)	Konkurrenz-unternehmen n	competitive undertaking	entreprise concurrente f	—	empresa competitoria f
impresa controllante (I)	herrschendes Unternehmen n	controlling company	entreprise dirigeante f	—	empresa dominante f
impresa di utilità pubblica (I)	gemeinnütziges Unternehmen n	public institution	entreprise d'utilité publique f	—	empresa de beneficio común f
imprese multinazionali (I)	multinationale Unternehmen n	multinational enterprise	entreprises multinationales	—	empresa multinacional f
imprese pubbliche (I)	öffentliche Unternehmen n	public enterprise	entreprises publiques f	—	empresa pública f
impresión offset (Es)	Offsetdruck m	offset (printing)	offset m	stampa offset f	—
impreso[1] (Es)	Drucksache f	printed matter	imprimé m	stampa f	—
impreso[2] (Es)	Vordruck m	printed form	imprimé m	modulo m	—
impresora (Es)	Drucker m	printer	imprimante f	stampante f	—
impresora laser (Es)	Laserdrucker m	laser printer	imprimante au laser f	stampante laser f	—
Impressum (D)	—	imprint	mention des responsables de l'édition f	impressum m	pie de imprenta m
impressum (I)	Impressum n	imprint	mention des responsables de l'édition f	—	pie de imprenta m
imprimante (F)	Drucker m	printer	—	stampante f	impresora f
imprimante au laser (F)	Laserdrucker m	laser printer	—	stampante laser f	impresora laser m
imprimé[1] (F)	Vordruck m	printed form	—	modulo m	impreso m
imprimé[2] (F)	Drucksache f	printed matter	—	stampa f	impreso m
imprimé en blanc (F)	Blankoformular n	blank form	—	modulo in bianco m	formulario en blanco m
imprint (E)	Impressum n	—	mention des responsables de l'édition f	impressum m	pie de imprenta m
improper (E)	unsachgemäß	—	non adéquat	non idoneo	con falta de objetividad
impuesto[1] (Es)	Steuer f	tax	impôt m	imposta f	—
impuesto[2] (Es)	Abgabe f	tax/duty	taxe f	imposta f/dazio m	—
impuesto de corporaciones (Es)	Körperschaftsteuer f	corporation tax	taxe sur les sociétés f	imposta sul reddito delle società f	—
impuesto de lujo (Es)	Luxussteuer f	luxury tax	taxe de luxe f	imposta sui consumi di lusso f	—
impuesto de negociación bursátil (Es)	Börsenumsatzsteuer f	stock exchange turnover tax	droit de transaction sur les opérations boursières m	imposta sulle operazioni di borsa f	—
impuesto en especie (Es)	Naturalabgabe f	duty in kind	taxe acquittée en nature f	imposta in natura f	—
impuesto industrial (Es)	Gewerbesteuer f	trade tax	patente f	imposta industriale f	—
impuestos adelantados (Es)	Steuer-vorauszahlung f	advanced payment of taxes	acompte provisionnel sur l'imposition m	pagamento anticipato delle imposte m	—
impuestos directos (Es)	direkte Steuern pl	direct taxes	impôts directs m pl	imposte dirette f pl	—
impuestos indirectos (Es)	indirekte Steuern pl	indirect taxes	impôts indirects m	imposte indirette f pl	—
impuesto sobre beneficios (Es)	Ertragsteuer f	tax on income	impôt assis sur le produit m	imposta cedolare f/ imposta sul reddito f	—
impuesto sobre donaciones (Es)	Schenkungssteuer f	gift tax	impôt sur les donations m	imposta sulle donazioni f	—
impuesto sobre el alcohol (Es)	Alkoholsteuer f	tax on alcohol	impôt sur l'alcool m	imposta sugli alcolici f	—

	D	E	F	I	Es
impuesto sobre el valor añadido (Es)	Mehrwertsteuer f	value-added tax	taxe à la valeur ajoutée f	imposta sul valore aggiunto f	—
impuesto sobre el valor añadido deducible (Es)	Vorsteuer f	input tax	impôt perçu en amont m	imposta sul fatturato d'acquisto f	—
impuesto sobre el volumen de ventas (Es)	Umsatzsteuer f	turnover tax	impôt sur le chiffre d'affaires m	imposta generale sulle entrate f	—
impuesto sobre la gasolina (Es)	Mineralölsteuer f	mineral oil tax	taxe sur les carburants f	imposta sugli olii minerali f	—
impuesto sobre la renta de las personas físicas (Es)	Einkommensteuer f	income tax	impôt sur le revenu m	imposta sui redditi f	—
impuesto sobre la renta del capital (Es)	Kapitalertragsteuer f	tax on investment income	impôt sur le revenu du capital m	imposta sulla rendita del capitale f	—
impuesto sobre las inversiones (Es)	Investitionssteuer f	investment tax	impôt sur les investissements m	imposta sugli investimenti f	—
impuesto sobre los rendimientos del trabajo personal (Es)	Lohnsteuer f	wages tax	impôt sur les traitements et salaires m	imposta sui salari f	—
impuesto sobre sucesiones (Es)	Erbschaftsteuer f	inheritance tax	impôt sur les successions m	imposta di successione f	—
impuesto sobre vehículos (Es)	Kraftfahrzeugsteuer f	motor vehicle tax	taxe sur les véhicules à moteur f	imposta sulla circolazione degli autoveicoli f	—
impuestos reales (Es)	Realsteuern pl	impersonal taxes	impôt réel m	imposte reali f pl	—
impulse buying (E)	Impulskauf m	—	achat d'impulsion m	acquisto impulsivo m	compra espontánea f
Impulskauf (D)	—	impulse buying	achat d'impulsion m	acquisto impulsivo m	compra espontánea f
impulso de crecimiento (Es)	Wachstumsimpuls m	growth impulse	stimulation de l'accroissement f	impulso di crescita m	—
impulso di crescita (I)	Wachstumsimpuls m	growth impulse	stimulation de l'accroissement f	—	impulso de crecimiento m
inabilità al lavoro (I)	Erwerbsunfähigkeit f	disability for work	incapacité d'exercer toute activité professionnelle f	—	incapacidad profesional f
inadempienza (I)	Nichterfüllung f	non-performance	inexécution f	—	incumplimiento m
in agreement with (E)	im Einvernehmen mit	—	d'accord avec	d'accordo con	de conformidad con
in aumento (I)	steigend	rising	croissant(e)	—	ascendente
in bar (D)	—	in cash	comptant	in contanti	en efectivo
in base commissionaria (I)	auf Kommissionsbasis	on a commission basis	en commission	—	en comisión
incapacidad profesional (Es)	Erwerbsunfähigkeit f	disability for work	incapacité d'exercer toute activité professionnelle f	inabilità al lavoro f	—
incapacité d'exercer toute activité professionnelle (F)	Erwerbsunfähigkeit f	disability for work	—	inabilità al lavoro f	incapacidad profesional f
in cash (E)	in bar	—	comptant	in contanti	en efectivo
incasso (I)	Inkasso n	collection	recouvrement m	—	encobro m
incentive (E)	Anreiz m	—	incitation f	incentivo m	incentivo m
incentive system (E)	Anreizsystem n	—	système d'incitation m	sistema d'incentivo m	sistema de incentivos m
incentivo (Es)	Anreiz m	incentive	incitation f	incentivo m	—
incentivo (I)	Anreiz m	incentive	incitation f	—	incentivo m
inchiesta tributaria (I)	Steuerfahndung f	investigation into suspected tax offences	recherche de la fraude fiscale f	—	investigación tributaria f
incineration (E)	Verbrennung f	—	combustion f	combustione f	combustión f
incitation (F)	Anreiz m	incentive	—	incentivo m	incentivo m
included in the price (E)	im Preis inbegriffen	—	inclus dans le prix	incluso nel prezzo	incluido
incluido (Es)	im Preis inbegriffen	included in the price	inclus dans le prix	incluso nel prezzo	—
inclus dans le prix (F)	im Preis inbegriffen	included in the price	—	incluso nel prezzo	incluido
inclusive (E)	inklusiv	—	inclusivement	incluso	incluso
inclusivement (F)	inklusiv	inclusive	—	incluso	incluso
incluso (Es)	inklusiv	inclusive	inclusivement	incluso	—
incluso (I)	inklusiv	inclusive	inclusivement	—	incluso

	D	E	F	I	Es
incluso nel prezzo (I)	im Preis inbegriffen	included in the price	inclus dans le prix	—	incluido
income[1] (E)	Einkommen n	—	revenu m	reddito m	ingresos m pl/renta f
income[2] (E)	Ertrag m	—	rendement m/ revenu m	reddito m/ rendimento m	rendimiento m/ renta f
income declaration (E)	Einkommens- erklärung f	—	déclaration du revenu f	dichiarazione del reddito f	declaración de la renta f
income factor (E)	Ertragsfaktor m	—	facteur productif m	fattore reddito m	factor de beneficio m
income from capital (E)	Kapitalertrag m	—	produit du capital m	rendita del capitale f	rendimiento del capital m
income tax (E)	Einkommensteuer f	—	impôt sur le revenu m	imposta sui redditi f	impuesto sobre la renta de las personas físicas m
incompatibilità degli obiettivi (I)	Zielkonflikt m	conflicting goals	conflit d'objectifs m	—	conflicto de objectivos m
incomplet (F)	unvollständig	incomplete	—	incompleto	incompleto
incomplete (E)	unvollständig	—	incomplet	incompleto	incompleto
incompleto (Es)	unvollständig	incomplete	incomplet	incompleto	—
incompleto (I)	unvollständig	incomplete	incomplet	—	incompleto
in conformity with market conditions (E)	marktkonform	—	conforme au marché	conforme al mercato	conforme al mercado
in contanti[1] (I)	bar	cash	comptant	—	al contado
in contanti[2] (I)	in bar	in cash	comptant	—	en efectivo
increase (E)	Zulage f	—	prime f/complément de salaire m	premio m/indennità f	suplemento m/plus m
increase in capacity (E)	Kapazitäts- ausweitung f	—	extension de la capacité f	ampliamento delle capacità m	ampliación de la capacidad f
increase in efficiency (E)	Leistungssteigerung f	—	amélioration du rendement f	aumento della produttività m	incremento del rendimiento m
increase in population (E)	Bevölkerungs- wachstum m	—	accroissement de la population m	incremento demografico m	crecimiento vegetativo m
increase in salary (E)	Gehaltserhöhung f	—	augmentation du traitement f	aumento dello stipendio m	aumento de sueldo m
increase in wages (E)	Lohnerhöhung f	—	augmentation du salaire f	aumento salariale m	aumento de salario m
increase of taxes (E)	Steuererhöhung f	—	relèvement des impôts m	aumento delle imposte m	aumento de los impuestos m
increase of the share capital (E)	Kapitalerhöhung f	—	augmentation de capital f	aumento del capitale m	aumento de capital m
incremento del rendimiento (Es)	Leistungs- steigerung f	increase in efficiency	amélioration du rendement f	aumento della produttività m	—
incremento demografico (I)	Bevölkerungs- wachstum m	increase in population	accroissement de la population m	—	crecimiento vegetativo m
incremento desmesu- rado de los costes (Es)	Kostenexplosion f	cost escalation	explosion des coûts f	esplosione dei costi f	—
incremento di valore (I)	Wertzuwachs m	appreciation	accroissement de valeur m	—	plusvalía f
incremento por peligrosidad (Es)	Gefahrenzulage f	danger money	prime de danger f	premio di rischio m	—
incumplimiento (Es)	Nichterfüllung f	non-performance	inexécution f	inadempienza f	—
indagine[1] (I)	Nachforschung f	investigation	recherche f	—	pesquisas f pl
indagine[2] (I)	Untersuchung f	examination	étude f	—	inspección f
indebitamento (I)	Verschuldung f	indebtedness	endettement m	—	endeudamiento m
indebitamento eccessivo (I)	Überschuldung f	excessive indebtedness	surendettement m	—	exceso de deudas m
indebitamento effettivo (I)	effektive Verschuldung f	real indebtedness	endettement effectif m	—	endeudamiento efectivo m
indebitamento netto (I)	Nettoverschuldung f	net indebtedness	endettement net m	—	deuda neta m
indebtedness (E)	Verschuldung f	—	endettement m	indebitamento m	endeudamiento m
indemnité[1] (F)	Abfindung f	indemnity/ compensation	—	indennità f/ compensazione f	indemnización f/ compensación f
indemnité[2] (F)	Entschädigung f	compensation/ indemnification	—	indennità f	indemnización f/pago de compensación m
indemnité de chômage (F)	Arbeitslosen- unterstützung f	unemployment benefit	—	sussidio di disoccupazione m	prestaciones por desempleo m

	D	E	F	I	Es
indemnité en capital (F)	Kapitalabfindung *f*	lump sum settlement	—	indennità in capitale *f*	indemnización en capital *f*
indemnité par kilomètre (F)	Kilometergeld *n*	allowance per kilometre	—	indennità per chilometro *f*	kilometraje *m*
indemnity (E)	Abfindung *f*	—	indemnité *f*/ compensation *f*	indennità *f*/ compensazione *f*	indemnización *f*/ compensación *f*
indemnización¹ (Es)	Schadensersatz *m*	compensation for loss suffered	dommages-intérêts *m pl*	risarcimento danni *m*	—
indemnización² (Es)	Abfindung *f*	indemnity/ compensation	indemnité *f*/ compensation *f*	indennità *f*/ compensazione *f*	—
indemnización³ (Es)	Entschädigung *f*	compensation/ indemnification	indemnité *f*	indennità *f*	—
indemnización en capital (Es)	Kapitalabfindung *f*	lump sum settlement	indemnité en capital *f*	indennità in capitale *f*	—
indennità¹ (I)	Entschädigung *f*	compensation/ indemnification	indemnité *f*	—	indemnización *f*/pago de compensación *m*
indennità² (I)	Abfindung *f*	indemnity/ compensation	indemnité *f*/ compensation *f*	—	indemnización *f*/ compensación *f*
indennità di ferie (I)	Urlaubsgeld *n*	holiday allowance	prime de vacances *f*	—	retribución por vacaciones *f*
indennità in capitale (I)	Kapitalabfindung *f*	lump sum settlement	indemnité en capital *f*	—	indemnización de capital *f*
indennità per chilometro (I)	Kilometergeld *n*	allowance per kilometre	indemnité par kilomètre *f*	—	kilometraje *m*
indépendance (F)	Unabhängigkeit *f*	independence	—	indipendenza *f*	independencia *f*
indépendant (F)	selbständig	independent	—	indipendente	independiente/no asalariado/autónomo
independence (E)	Unabhängigkeit *f*	—	indépendance *f*	indipendenza *f*	independencia *f*
independencia (Es)	Unabhängigkeit *f*	independence	indépendance *f*	indipendenza *f*	—
independent (E)	selbständig	—	indépendant	indipendente	independiente/no asalariado/autónomo
independiente (Es)	selbständig	independent	indépendant	indipendente	—
in dettaglio (I)	im einzelnen	in particular	en particulier	—	en particular
Index (D)	—	index	indice *m*	indice *m*	índice *m*
index (E)	Index *m*	—	indice *m*	indice *m*	índice *m*
indexation (F)	Indizierung *f*	putting on the index	—	indicizzazione *f*	indiciación *f*
index card (E)	Karteikarte *f*	—	fiche *f*	scheda *f*	ficha *f*
index clause (E)	Indexklausel *f*	—	clause d'indexation *f*	clausola dell'indice *f*	cláusula de índice variable *f*
Indexklausel (D)	—	index clause	clause d'indexation *f*	clausola dell'indice *f*	cláusula de índice variable *f*
index-linked wages (E)	Indexlohn *m*	—	salaire indexé *m*	salario indicizzato *m*	salario-índice *m*
Indexlohn (D)	—	index-linked wages	salaire indexé *m*	salario indicizzato *m*	salario-índice *m*
indicación de cantidades (Es)	Mengenangabe *f*	indication of quantity	indication de la quantité *f*	indicazione della quantità *f*	—
indicación de precios (Es)	Preisauszeichnung *f*	pricemarking	affichage des prix *f*	indicazione del prezzo *f*	—
indication de la quantité (F)	Mengenangabe *f*	indication of quantity	—	indicazione della quantità *f*	indicación de cantidades *f*
indication of quantity (E)	Mengenangabe *f*	—	indication de la quantité *f*	indicazione della quantità *f*	indicación de cantidades *f*
indicazione del prezzo (I)	Preisauszeichnung *f*	pricemarking	affichage des prix *f*	—	indicación de precios *f*
indicazione della quantità (I)	Mengenangabe *f*	indication of quantity	indication de la quantité *f*	—	indicación de cantidades *f*
índice (Es)	Index *m*	index	indice *m*	indice *m*	—
indice¹ (F)	Index *m*	index	—	indice *m*	índice *m*
indice² (F)	Kennziffern *pl*	code numbers	—	cifre d'identificazione *f pl*	cifras índice *f pl*
indice (I)	Index *m*	index	indice *m*	—	índice *m*
indice azionario (I)	Aktienindex *m*	share index	indice du cours des actions *m*	—	índice de cotización de acciones *m*
índice bursátil (Es)	Börsenindex *m*	stock exchange index	indice des cours des actions *m*	indice delle quotazioni *m*	—

	D	E	F	I	Es
índice de cotización de acciones (Es)	Aktienindex *m*	share index	indice du cours des actions *m*	indice azionario *m*	—
índice de precios (Es)	Preisindex *m*	price index	indice des prix *m*	indice dei prezzi *m*	—
índice de precios de producción (Es)	Erzeugerpreisindex *m*	producer price index	indice des prix à la production *m*	indice dei prezzi di fabbrica *m*	—
indice dei prezzi (I)	Preisindex *m*	price index	indice des prix *m*	—	ínidce de precios *m*
indice dei prezzi di fabbrica (I)	Erzeugerpreisindex *m*	producer price index	indice des prix à la production *m*	—	índice de precios de producción *m*
indice delle quotazioni (I)	Börsenindex *m*	stock exchange index	indice des cours des actions *m*	—	índice bursátil *m*
indice des cours des actions (F)	Börsenindex *m*	stock exchange index	—	indice delle quotazioni *m*	índice bursátil *m*
indice des prix (F)	Preisindex *m*	price index	—	indice dei prezzi *m*	ínidce de precios *m*
indice des prix à la production (F)	Erzeugerpreisindex *m*	producer price index	—	indice dei prezzi di fabbrica *m*	índice de precios de producción *m*
Indice Dow Jones (Es)	Dow-Jones-Index *m*	Dow-Jones Industrial Average	indice Dow-Jones *m*	indice Dow-Jones *m*	—
indice Dow-Jones (F)	Dow-Jones-Index *m*	Dow-Jones Industrial Average	—	indice Dow-Jones *m*	Indice Dow Jones *m*
indice Dow-Jones (I)	Dow-Jones-Index *m*	Dow-Jones Industrial Average	indice Dow-Jones *m*	—	Indice Dow Jones *m*
indice du cours des actions (F)	Aktienindex *m*	share index	—	indice azionario *m*	índice de cotización de acciones *m*
indiciación (Es)	Indizierung *f*	putting on the index	indexation *f*	indicizzazione *f*	—
indicizzazione (I)	Indizierung *f*	putting on the index	indexation *f*	—	indiciación *f*
indipendente (I)	selbständig	independent	indépendant	—	independiente/no asalariado/autónomo
indipendenza (I)	Unabhängigkeit *f*	independence	indépendance *f*	—	independencia *f*
indirect taxes (E)	indirekte Steuern *pl*	—	impôts indirects *m*	imposte indirette *f pl*	impuestos indirectos *m pl*
indirekte Steuern (D)	—	indirect taxes	impôts indirects *m*	imposte indirette *f pl*	impuestos indirectos *m pl*
indirizzare (I)	adressieren	address	adresser	—	dirigir
indirizzo (I)	Adresse *f*	address	adresse *f*	—	dirección *f*
indirizzo della ditta (I)	Firmenanschrift *f*	company address	adresse de la maison *f*	—	dirección de la empresa *f*
Individualbedürfnis (D)	—	individual need	besoin individuel *m*	fabbisogno individuale *m*	necesidades individuales *f pl*
Indizierung (D)	—	putting on the index	indexation *f*	indicizzazione *f*	indiciación *f*
indorsement (E)	Indossament *n*	—	endossement *m*	girata *f*	endoso *m*
Indossament (D)	—	indorsement	endossement *m*	girata *f*	endoso *m*
in due copie (I)	in zweifacher Ausfertigung	in duplicate	en deux exemplaires	—	por duplicado
in duplicate (E)	in zweifacher Ausfertigung	—	en deux exemplaires	in due copie	por duplicado
industria (Es)	Gewerbe *n*	trade/industry/craft	activité profession-nelle *f*/industrie *f*/artisanat *m*	commercio *m*/industria *f*/artigianato *m*	—
industria de bienes de consumo (Es)	Konsumgüter-industrie *f*	consumer goods industry	industrie des biens de consommation *f*	industria dei beni di consumo *f*	—
industria de bienes de producción (Es)	Produktionsgüter-Industrie *f*	producer goods industry	industrie des biens de production *f*	industria dei beni strumentali *f*	—
industria de desperdicios (Es)	Abfallwirtschaft *f*	waste management	industrie de déchets *f*	industria dei rifiuti *f*	—
industria dei beni di consumo (I)	Konsumgüter-industrie *f*	consumer goods industry	industrie des biens de consommation *f*	—	industria de bienes de consumo *f*
industria dei beni strumentali (I)	Produktionsgüter-Industrie *f*	producer goods industry	industrie des biens de production *f*	—	industria de bienes de producción *f*
industria dei rifiuti (I)	Abfallwirtschaft *f*	waste management	industrie de déchets *f*	—	industria de desperdicios *f*
industria de la construcción (Es)	Bauindustrie *f*	construction industry	industrie de sous-traitance du bâtiment *f*	industria edile *f*	—
industria di trasformazione (I)	verarbeitende Industrie *f*	manufacturing industry	industrie transformatrice *f*	—	industria transformadora *f*

	D	E	F	I	Es
industria edile (I)	Bauindustrie *f*	construction industry	industrie de sous-traitance du bâtiment *f*	—	industria de la construcción *f*
industrial area (E)	Industriegebiet *n*	—	région industrielle *f*	zona industriale *f*	región industrial *f*
industrial bonds (E)	Industrie-obligationen *pl*	—	obligations de l'industrie *f pl*	obbligazioni industriali *f pl*	obligaciónes industriales *f pl*
industrial enterprise (E)	Industriebetrieb *m*	—	entreprise industrielle *f*	azienda industriale *f*	establecimiento industrial *m*
industrial espionage[1] (E)	Industriespionage *f*	—	espionnage industriel *m*	spionaggio industriale *m*	espionaje industrial *m*
industrial espionage[2] (E)	Werkspionage *f*	—	espionnage industriel *m*	spionaggio aziendale *m*	espionaje industrial *m*
industrial espionage[3] (E)	Betriebsspionage *f*	—	espionnage dans l'entreprise	spionaggio aziendale *m*	espionaje industrial *m*
industrial injury (E)	Arbeitsunfall *m*	—	accident du travail *m*	infortunio sul posto di lavoro *m*	accidente profesional *m*
industrial plant (E)	Industrieanlage *f*	—	installation industrielle *f*	impianto industriale *m*	planta industrial *f*
industrial psychology (E)	Arbeitspsychologie *f*	—	psychologie de travail *f*	psicologia del lavoro *f*	psicología laboral *f*
industrial undertaking (E)	Industrie-unternehmen *n*	—	entreprise industrielle *f*	impresa industriale *f*	empresa industrial *f*
industria minera (Es)	Montanindustrie *f*	mining industry	industrie minière *f*	industria mineraria e siderurgica *f*	—
industria mineraria (I)	Bergbau *m*	mining	industrie extractive *f*	—	minería *f*
industria mineraria e siderurgica (I)	Montanindustrie *f*	mining industry	industrie minière *f*	—	industria minera *f*
industria transformadora (Es)	verarbeitende Industrie *f*	manufacturing industry	industrie transformatrice *f*	industria di trasformazione *f*	—
Industrieanlage (D)	—	industrial plant	installation industrielle *f*	impianto industriale *m*	planta industrial *f*
Industriebetrieb (D)	—	industrial enterprise	entreprise industrielle *f*	azienda industriale *f*	establecimiento industrial *m*
industrie de déchets (F)	Abfallwirtschaft *f*	waste management	—	industria dei rifiuti *f*	industria de desperdicios *f*
industrie des biens de consommation (F)	Konsumgüter-industrie *f*	consumer goods industry	—	industria dei beni di consumo *f*	industria de bienes de consumo *f*
industrie des biens de production (F)	Produktionsgüter-Industrie *f*	producer goods industry	—	industria dei beni strumentali *f*	industria de bienes de producción *f*
industrie de sous-traitance du bâtiment (F)	Bauindustrie *f*	construction industry	—	industria edile *f*	industria de la construcción *f*
(industrie du) bâtiment (F)	Bauwirtschaft *f*	building and construction industry	—	edilizia *f*	ramo de la construcción *m*
industrie extractive (F)	Bergbau *m*	mining	—	industria mineraria *f*	minería *f*
Industriegebiet (D)	—	industrial area	région industrielle *f*	zona industriale *f*	región industrial *f*
industrie minière (F)	Montanindustrie *f*	mining industry	—	industria mineraria e siderurgica *f*	industria minera *f*
Industrieobligation (D)	—	industrial bond	obligation de l'industrie *f pl*	obbligazioni industriali *f pl*	obligaciones industriales *f pl*
Industriespionage (D)	—	industrial espionage	espionnage industriel *m*	spionaggio industriale *m*	espionaje industrial *m*
industrie transformatrice (F)	verarbeitende Industrie *f*	manufacturing industry	—	industria di trasformazione *f*	industria transformadora *f*
Industrie- und Handelskammer (D)	—	Chamber of Industry and Commerce	chambre de commerce et d'industrie *f*	camera di commercio e industria *f*	cámara de industria y comercio *f*
inexécution (F)	Nichterfüllung *f*	non-performance	—	inadempienza *f*	incumplimiento *m*
inferiore Güter (D)	—	inferior goods	biens inférieurs *m pl*	beni inferiori *m pl*	bienes inferiores *m pl*
inferior goods (E)	inferiore Güter *pl*	—	biens inférieurs *m pl*	beni inferiori *m pl*	bienes inferiores *m pl*
inflación (Es)	Inflation *f*	inflation	inflation *f*	inflazione *f*	—
inflación galopante (Es)	galoppierende Inflation *f*	galloping inflation	inflation galopante *f*	inflazione galoppante *f*	—
inflación importada[1] (Es)	Inflationsimport *m*	import of inflation	importation de l'inflation *f*	importazione di inflazione *f*	—
inflación importada[2] (Es)	importierte Inflation *f*	imported inflation	inflation importée *f*	inflazione importata *f*	—

	D	E	F	I	Es
inflación latente (Es)	schleichende Inflation f	creeping inflation	inflation rampante f	inflazione strisciante f	—
Inflation (D)	—	inflation	inflation f	inflazione f	inflación f
inflation (E)	Inflation f	—	inflation f	inflazione f	inflación f
inflation (F)	Inflation f	inflation	—	inflazione f	inflación f
inflationary spiral (E)	Inflationsspirale f	—	spirale inflationniste f	spirale inflazionistica f	espiral inflacionista m
inflationary theory (E)	Inflationstheorie f	—	théorie d'inflation f	teoria dell'inflazione f	teoría inflacionista f
inflation galopante (F)	galoppierende Inflation f	galloping inflation	—	inflazione galoppante f	inflación galopante f
inflation importée (F)	importierte Inflation f	imported inflation	—	inflazione importata f	inflación importada f
inflation rampante (F)	schleichende Inflation f	creeping inflation	—	inflazione strisciante f	inflación latente f
Inflationsimport (D)	—	import of inflation	importation de l'inflation f	importazione di inflazione f	inflación importada f
Inflationsrate (D)	—	rate of inflation	taux d'inflation m	tasso d'inflazione m	tasa de inflación f
Inflationsspirale (D)	—	inflationary spiral	spirale inflationniste f	spirale inflazionistica f	espiral inflacionista m
Inflationstheorie (D)	—	inflationary theory	théorie d'inflation f	teoria dell'inflazione f	teoría inflacionista f
inflazione (I)	Inflation f	inflation	inflation f	—	inflación f
inflazione galoppante (I)	galoppierende Inflation f	galloping inflation	inflation galopante f	—	inflación galopante f
inflazione importata (I)	importierte Inflation f	imported inflation	inflation importée f	—	inflación importada f
inflazione strisciante (I)	schleichende Inflation f	creeping inflation	inflation rampante f	—	inflación latente f
influençable (F)	beeinflußbar	be influenced	—	influenzabile	sugestionable
influenzabile (I)	beeinflußbar	be influenced	influençable	—	sugestionable
información¹ (Es)	Information f	information	information f	informazione f	—
información² (Es)	Auskunft f	information	renseignement m	informazione f	—
información a los comsumidores (Es)	Konsumenten-information f	consumer information	information des consommateurs f	informazione per i consumatori f	—
información básica (Es)	Basisinformation f	basic information	information de base f	informazione base f	—
información de consumidores (Es)	Verbraucher-information f	consumer information	information des consommateurs f	informazione per i consumatori f	—
información de sí mismo (Es)	Selbstauskunft f	voluntary disclosure	renseignement fourni par l'intéressé lui-même m	informazione volontaria f	—
informaciones privilegiadas (Es)	Insider-Informationen pl	insider information	informations d'initiés f pl	informazioni per gli addetti al lavoro f pl	—
informática (Es)	Informatik f	data processing	informatique f	informatica f	—
informatica (I)	Informatik f	data processing	informatique f	—	informática f
Informatik (D)	—	data processing	informatique f	informatica f	informática f
Information (D)	—	information	information f	informazione f	información f
information¹ (E)	Auskunft f	—	renseignement m	informazione f	información f
information² (E)	Mitteilung f	—	notification f	comunicazione f	aviso m
information³ (E)	Information f	—	information f	informazione f	información f
information (F)	Information f	information	—	informazione f	información f
information bureau (E)	Auskunftei f	—	agence de renseignements f	agenzia d'informazioni f	oficina de información f
information costs (E)	Informations-kosten pl	—	coûts d'information m pl	costi d'informazione m pl	gastos de información m pl
information de base (F)	Basisinformation f	basic information	—	informazione base f	información básica f
information des consommateurs¹ (F)	Konsumenten-information f	consumer information	—	informazione per i consumatori f	información a los comsumidores f
information des consommateurs² (F)	Verbraucher-information f	consumer information	—	informazione per i consumatori f	información de consumidores f
informations d'initiés (F)	Insider-Informationen pl	insider information	—	informazioni per gli addetti al lavoro f pl	informaciones privilegiadas f pl
Informationsbedarf (D)	—	requirement of information	besoin d'information m	bisogno d'informazioni m	necesidad de información f
Informationskosten (D)	—	information costs	coûts d'information m pl	costi d'informazione m pl	gastos de información m pl

	D	E	F	I	Es
Informationssystem (D)	—	information system	système d'information *m*	sistema d'informazione *m*	sistema de información *m*
Informations-technologie (D)	—	information technology	technologie d'information *f*	tecnologia d'informazione *f*	tecnología de información *f*
Informationstheorie (D)	—	information theory	théorie d'information *f*	teoria dell'informazione *f*	teoría de la información *f*
information system (E)	Informationssystem *n*	—	système d'information *m*	sistema d'informazione *m*	sistema de información *m*
information technology (E)	Informations-technologie *f*	—	technologie d'information *f*	tecnologia d'informazione *f*	tecnología de información *f*
information theory (E)	Informationstheorie *f*	—	théorie d'information *f*	teoria dell'informazione *f*	teoría de la información *f*
informatique (F)	Informatik *f*	data processing	—	informatica *f*	informática *f*
informazione[1] (I)	Information *f*	information	information *f*	—	información *f*
informazione[2] (I)	Auskunft *f*	information	renseignement *m*	—	información *f*
informazione per i consumatori (I)	Konsumenten-information *f*	consumer's information	information des consommateurs *f*	—	información a los comsumidores *f*
informazione base (I)	Basisinformation *f*	basic information	information de base *f*	—	información básica *f*
informazione per i consumatori (I)	Verbraucher-information *f*	consumer information	information des consommateurs *f*	—	información de consumidores *f*
informazione volontaria (I)	Selbstauskunft *f*	voluntary disclosure	renseignement fourni par l'intéressé lui-même *m*	—	información de sí mismo *f*
informazioni per gli addetti al lavoro (I)	Insider-Informationen *pl*	insider information	informations d'initiés *f pl*	—	informaciones privilegiadas *f pl*
informazioni sui posti vacanti (I)	Arbeitsnachweis *m*	employment vacancies	emploi vacant *m*	—	servicio de colocación *m*
informe[1] (Es)	Geschäftsbericht *m*	business report	rapport de gestion *m*	relazione sull'esercizio commerciale *f*	—
informe[2] (Es)	Report *m*	report	rapport *m*	rapporto *m*	—
informe de los fundadores (Es)	Gründungsbericht *m*	formation report	procès-verbal de fondation *m*	relazione di costituzione *f*	—
informe de venta (Es)	Verkaufsbericht *m*	sales report	rapport de vente *m*	rapporto sulle vendite *m*	—
informe económico anual (Es)	Jahreswirtschafts-bericht *m*	Annual Economic Report	compte rendu d'activité économique annuel *m*	relazione generale sulla situazione economica *f*	—
informe financiero (Es)	Finanzbericht *m*	financial report	rapport financier *m*	relazione finanziaria *f*	—
infortunio sul posto di lavoro (I)	Arbeitsunfall *m*	industrial injury	accident du travail *m*	—	accidente profesional *m*
infraestructura (Es)	Infrastruktur *f*	infrastructure	infrastructure *f*	infrastruttura *f*	—
infraseguro (Es)	Unterversicherung *f*	underinsurance	insuffisance d'assurance *f*	sottassicurazione *f*	—
infrastructural measures (E)	Infrastruktur-maßnahmen *f*	—	mesures pour l'amélioration de l'infrastructure *f pl*	misure per l'infrastruttura *f pl*	medidas de infraestructura *f pl*
infrastructure (E)	Infrastruktur *f*	—	infrastructure *f*	infrastruttura *f*	infraestructura *f*
infrastructure (F)	Infrastruktur *f*	infrastructure	—	infrastruttura *f*	infraestructura *f*
Infrastruktur (D)	—	infrastructure	infrastructure *f*	infrastruttura *f*	infraestructura *f*
Infrastruktur-maßnahmen (D)	—	infrastructural measures	mesures pour l'amélioration de l'infrastructure *f pl*	misure per l'infrastruttura *f pl*	medidas de infraestructura *f pl*
infrastruttura (I)	Infrastruktur *f*	infrastructure	infrastructure *f*	—	infraestructura *f*
inganno (I)	Täuschung *f*	deceit	tromperie *f*	—	engaño *m*
ingegnere (I)	Ingenieur *m*	engineer	ingénieur *m*	—	ingeniero *m*
ingeniero (Es)	Ingenieur *m*	engineer	ingénieur *m*	ingegnere *m*	—
Ingenieur (D)	—	engineer	ingénieur *m*	ingegnere *m*	ingeniero *m*
ingénieur (F)	Ingenieur *m*	engineer	—	ingegnere *m*	ingeniero *m*
ingiunzione di pagamento (I)	Zahlungsbefehl *m*	order for payment	ordre de payement *m*	—	mandamiento de pago *m*
ingreso bruto (Es)	Bruttoeinkommen *n*	gross income	revenu brut *m*	reddito lordo *m*	—
ingreso neto (Es)	Nettoeinkommen *n*	net income	revenu net *m*	reddito netto *m*	—
ingreso real (Es)	Realeinkommen *n*	real income	revenu réel *m*	reddito reale *m*	—

	D	E	F	I	Es
ingresos[1] (Es)	Einnahmen *pl*	receipts	revenu *m*	entrate *f pl*	—
ingresos[2] (Es)	Einkommen *n*	income	revenu *m*	reddito *m*	—
ingresos del Estado (Es)	Staatseinnahmen *pl*	public revenue	recettes de l'Etat *f pl*	entrate pubbliche *f pl*	—
ingresos disponibles (Es)	verfügbares Einkommen *n*	disposable income	revenu disponible *m*	introito disponibile *m*	—
ingresos nominales (Es)	Nominaleinkommen *n*	nominal income	revenu nominal *m*	reddito nominale *m*	—
ingresos públicos (Es)	öffentliche Einnahmen *pl*	public revenues	recettes publiques *f pl*	entrate pubbliche *f pl*	—
Inhaber (D)	—	proprietor	propriétaire *m*	proprietario *m*	propietario *m*
Inhaberaktie (D)	—	bearer shares	action au porteur *f*	azione al portatore *f*	acción al portador *f*
Inhaberpapier (D)	—	bearer instrument	titre souscrit au porteur *m*	titolo al portatore *m*	título al portador *m*
Inhaberscheck (D)	—	cheque payable to bearer	chèque au porteur *m*	assegno al portatore *m*	cheque al portador *m*
inheritance (E)	Erbschaft *f*	—	héritage *m*	eredità *f*	herencia *f*
inheritance tax (E)	Erbschaftsteuer *f*	—	impôt sur les successions *m*	imposta di successione *f*	impuesto sobre sucesiones *m*
initial contribution (E)	Stammeinlage *f*	—	apport social *m*	quota sociale *f*	capital suscrito *m*
initial period (E)	Anlaufperiode *f*	—	période de mise en marche *f*	periodo iniziale *m*	período de puesta en marcha *m*
Inkasso (D)	—	collection	recouvrement *m*	incasso *m*	encobro *m*
inkassoberechtigt (D)	—	authorized to undertake the collection	autorisé à l'encaissement	autorizzato all'incasso	autorizado al encobro
inklusiv (D)	—	inclusive	inclusivement	incluso	incluso
in Kraft (D)	—	effective/in force	en vigueur	in vigore	en vigor
inland navigation (E)	Binnenschiffahrt *f*	—	navigation fluviale *f*	navigazione interna *f*	navegación fluvial *f*
inland revenue office (E)	Finanzamt *n*	—	service de contributions *m*	ufficio delle imposte *m*	Hacienda *f*
Inländer (D)	—	national resident	national *m*	persona residente *f*	residente *m*
Inlandsnachfrage (D)	—	home demand	demande intérieure *f*	domanda interna *f*	demanda interior *f*
Inlands-niederlassung (D)	—	domestic establishment	succursale à l'intérieur *f*	succursale nazionale *f*	sucursal en el interior *f*
in lieu of payment (E)	zahlungsstatt	—	à titre de payement	a titolo di pagamento	a título de pago
in magazzino (I)	auf Lager	in stock	en stock	—	en almacén
inmediatamente (Es)	umgehend	immediate(ly)	immédiatement	immediatamente	—
inmueble (Es)	Immobilie *f*	item of real estate	bien immobilier *m*	immobile *m*	—
inmuebles y utillaje (Es)	Sachanlagen *pl*	fixed assets	immobilisations corporelles *f pl*	immobilizzazioni *f pl*	—
innovación (Es)	Innovation *f*	innovation	innovation *f*	innovazione *f*	—
Innovation (D)	—	innovation	innovation *f*	innovazione *f*	innovación *f*
innovation (E)	Innovation *f*	—	innovation *f*	innovazione *f*	innovación *f*
innovation (F)	Innovation *f*	innovation	—	innovazione *f*	innovación *f*
Innovationsfähigkeit (D)	—	capability to innovate	capacité d'innovation *f*	capacità innovativa *f*	capacidad de innovación *f*
Innovationsschub (D)	—	technology push	animation d'innovation *f*	spinta innovativa *f*	empuje innovador *m*
innovazione (I)	Innovation *f*	innovation	innovation *f*	—	innovación *f*
in one's own name (E)	im eigenen Namen	—	en nom propre	per nome proprio	en nombre propio
in particular (E)	im einzelnen	—	en particulier	in dettaglio	en particular
in plico a parte (I)	mit getrennter Post	under separate cover	sous pli séparé	—	por correo aparte
in prova (I)	auf Probe	on trial	à l'essai	—	a prueba
Input (D)	—	input	entrée *f*	input *m*	insumo *m*
input (E)	Input *m*	—	entrée *f*	input *m*	insumo *m*
input (I)	Input *m*	input	entrée *f*	—	insumo *m*
input tax (E)	Vorsteuer *f*	—	impôt perçu en amont *m*	imposta sul fatturato d'acquisto *f*	impuesto sobre el valor añadido deducible *m*
Input-Output-Analyse (D)	—	input-output analysis	tableau économique input-output *m*	analisi input-output *f*	análisis de input-output *m*

	D	E	F	I	Es
input-output analysis (E)	Input-Output-Analyse f	—	tableau économique input-output m	analisi input-output f	análisis de input-output m
inquilino (Es)	Mieter m	tenant	locataire m	locatario m	—
inquinamento dell'ambiente (I)	Umweltverschmutzung f	environmental damage	pollution de l'environnement f	—	contaminación del medio ambiente f
inquinamento delle acque (I)	Wasserverschmutzung f	water pollution	contamination des eaux f	—	contaminación del agua f
inquinante (I)	umweltschädlich	causing pollution	nuisible à l'environnement	—	contaminante
inquiry (E)	Anfrage f	—	demande f	richiesta f	demanda f
inscription (F)	Anmeldung f	registration/declaration	—	avviso m/dichiarazione f	solicitud f/declaración f
insécurité (F)	Unsicherheit f	uncertainty	—	insicurezza f	inseguridad f
insegna dell'impresa (I)	Firmenschild n	company's name plate	enseigne commerciale f	—	letrero de establecimiento m
inseguridad (Es)	Unsicherheit f	uncertainty	insécurité f	insicurezza f	—
insensible aux influences de la crise économique (F)	krisenfest	slump-proof	—	resistente alle crisi	a prueba de crisis
inserción del anuncio (Es)	Anzeigenschaltung f	insertion of an advertisement	placement de l'annonce m	posizionamento dell'inserzione m	—
insertion of an advertisement (E)	Anzeigenschaltung f	—	placement de l'annonce m	posizionamento dell'inserzione m	inserción del anuncio f
inserto (I)	Beilage f	supplement	encart non broché à la revue m	—	suplemento m
inserzione (I)	Anzeige f	advertisement	annonce f	—	anuncio m
inserzione d'impiego (I)	Stellenanzeige f	position offered	annonce d'emploi f	—	anuncio de empleo m
inserzione in cifra (I)	Chiffre-Anzeige f	advertisement under a box number	annonce chiffrée f	—	anuncio codificado m
inserzione sul giornale (I)	Zeitungsanzeige f	advertisement	annonce de journal f	—	anuncio de prensa m
insicurezza (I)	Unsicherheit f	uncertainty	insécurité f	—	inseguridad f
insider information (E)	Insider-Informationen pl	—	informations d'initiés f pl	informazioni per gli addetti al lavoro f pl	informaciones privilegiadas f pl
Insider-Informationen (D)	—	insider information	informations d'initiés f pl	informazioni per gli addetti al lavoro f pl	informaciones privilegiadas f pl
insolvabilité[1] (F)	Insolvenz f	insolvency	—	insolvenza f	insolvencia f
insolvabilité[2] (F)	Zahlungsunfähigkeit f	insolvency	—	insolvenza f	insolvencia f
insolvencia[1] (Es)	Zahlungsunfähigkeit f	insolvency	insolvabilité f	insolvenza f	—
insolvencia[2] (Es)	Insolvenz f	insolvency	insolvabilité f	insolvenza f	—
insolvency[1] (E)	Insolvenz f	—	insolvabilité f	insolvenza f	insolvencia f
insolvency[2] (E)	Zahlungsunfähigkeit f	—	insolvabilité f	insolvenza f	insolvencia f
Insolvenz (D)	—	insolvency	insolvabilité f	insolvenza f	insolvencia f
insolvenza[1] (I)	Insolvenz f	insolvency	insolvabilité f	—	insolvencia f
insolvenza[2] (I)	Zahlungsunfähigkeit f	insolvency	insolvabilité f	—	insolvencia f
inspección de la explotación (Es)	Betriebsprüfung f	investigation by the tax authorities	vérification des livres de l'entreprise f	revisione aziendale f	—
inspección[1] (Es)	Aufsicht f	supervision	surveillance f	sorveglianza f	—
inspección[2] (Es)	Untersuchung f	examination	étude f	indagine f	—
inspección[3] (Es)	Einsichtnahme f	inspection	contrôle des livres comptables m	presa visione f	—
inspection[1] (E)	Prüfung f	—	vérification f/examen m	controllo m/esame m	verificación f/examen m
inspection[2] (E)	Einsichtnahme f	—	contrôle des livres comptables m	presa visione f	inspección f
instalaciones de producción (Es)	Produktionsanlagen pl	production facilities	installations industrielles f pl	impianti di produzione m pl	—
installation (E)	Montage f	—	montage m	montaggio m	montaje m
installation de traitement électronique des informations (F)	Datenverarbeitungsanlage f	data processing system	—	elaboratore elettronico di dati m	ordenador m
installation industrielle (F)	Industrieanlage f	industrial plant	—	impianto industriale m	planta industrial f

	D	E	F	I	Es
installations industrielles (F)	Produktions-anlagen *pl*	production facilities	—	impianti di produzione *m pl*	instalaciones de producción *f pl*
instalment (E)	Rate *f*	—	acompte *m*	rata *f*	plazo *m*
instalment sale transaction (E)	Ratengeschäft *n*	—	vente à tempérament *f*	vendita a rate *f*	venta a plazo *f*
instance (E)	Instanz *f*	—	instance *f*	istanza *f*	instancia *f*
instance (F)	Instanz *f*	instance	—	istanza *f*	instancia *f*
instancia (Es)	Instanz *f*	instance	instance *f*	istanza *f*	—
Instanz (D)	—	instance	instance *f*	istanza *f*	instancia *f*
institución de prevision (Es)	Versorgungs-einrichtung *f*	pension scheme	institution de retraite *f*	istituto previdenziale *m*	—
institut bancaire d'épargne (F)	Sparkasse *f*	savings bank	—	cassa di risparmio *f*	caja de ahorros *f*
institut d'études de marché (F)	Marktforschungs-institut *n*	market research institute	—	istituto della ricerca di mercato *m*	instituto de investiga-ción del mercado *m*
institution de retraite (F)	Versorgungs-einrichtung *f*	pension scheme	—	istituto previdenziale *m*	institución de previsión *f*
instituto de crédito (Es)	Kreditinstitut *n*	credit institution	établissement de crédit *m*	istituto di credito *m*	—
instituto de investiga-ción del mercado (Es)	Marktforschungs-institut *n*	market research institute	institut d'études de marché *m*	istituto della ricerca di mercato *m*	—
in stock (E)	auf Lager	—	en stock	in magazzino	en almacén
instrucción (Es)	Anleitung *f*	instructions	instruction *f*	istruzione *f*	—
instrucción de reparación (Es)	Reparaturanleitung *f*	repair instructions	instruction de réparation *f*	istruzione per la riparazione *f*	—
instrucción para el envío (Es)	Versandvorschrift *f*	forwarding instruction	prescriptions concer-nant l'expédition *f pl*	prescrizione per la spedizione *f*	—
instructeur (F)	Ausbilder *m*	trainer	—	istruttore *m*	instructor *m*
instruction (F)	Anleitung *f*	instructions	—	istruzione *f*	instrucción *f*
instruction de réparation (F)	Reparaturanleitung *f*	repair instructions	—	istruzione per la riparazione *f*	instrucción de reparación *m*
instructions (E)	Anleitung *f*	—	instruction *f*	istruzione *f*	instrucción *f*
instructor (Es)	Ausbilder *m*	trainer	instructeur *m*	istruttore *m*	—
Instrument (D)	—	instrument	instrument *m*	strumento *m*	instrumento *m*
instrument (E)	Instrument *n*	—	instrument *m*	strumento *m*	instrumento *m*
instrument (F)	Instrument *n*	instrument	—	strumento *m*	instrumento *m*
instrumento *m*	Instrument *n*	instrument	instrument *m*	strumento *m*	—
instrumentos de medida (Es)	Meßgeräte *pl*	measuring instruments	instrument de mesure *m*	strumenti di misura *m*	—
instruments (made out) to order (E)	Orderpapier *n*	—	papier à ordre *m*	titolo all'ordine *m*	título a la orden *m*
insuffisance d'assurance (F)	Unterversicherung *f*	underinsurance	—	sottassicurazione *f*	infraseguro *m*
insumo (Es)	Input *m*	input	entrée *f*	input *m*	—
insurance (E)	Versicherung *f*	—	assurance *f*	assicurazione *f*	seguro *m*
insurance agent (E)	Versicherungs-agent *m*	—	agent d'assurance *m*	agente d'assicurazione *m*	agente de seguros *m*
insurance broker (E)	Versicherungs-makler *m*	—	courtier en assurance *m*	mediatore d'assicurazione *m*	corredor de seguros *m*
insurance company (E)	Versicherungs-gesellschaft *f*	—	société d'assurance *f*	compagnia di assicurazione *f*	sociedad de seguros *f*
insurance contract (E)	Versicherungs-vertrag *m*	—	contrat d'assurance *m*	contratto d'assicurazione *m*	contrato de seguro *m*
insurance cover (E)	Versicherungs-schutz *m*	—	couverture de l'assurance *f*	copertura assicurativa *f*	cobertura de seguro *f*
insurance of persons (E)	Personen-versicherung *f*	—	assurance des personnes *f*	assicurazione di persone *f*	seguro personal *m*
insurance on buildings (E)	Gebäude-versicherung *f*	—	assurance des bâtiments *f*	assicurazione dei fabbricati *f*	seguro inmobiliario *m*
insurance policy (E)	Versicherungspolice *f*	—	police d'assurance *f*	polizza d'assicurazione *f*	seguro *m*
insurance premium (E)	Versicherungs-prämie *f*	—	prime d'assurance *f*	premio d'assicurazione *m*	prima de seguro *f*

	D	E	F	I	Es
insurance sum (E)	Versicherungssumme f	—	montant de l'assurance m	somma assicurata f	suma asegurada f
insured letter (E)	Wertbrief m	—	lettre avec valeur déclarée f	lettera con valore dichiarato f	letra con valor declarado f
insured person (E)	Versicherungsnehmer m	—	souscripteur d'une assurance m	assicurato m	asegurado m
integración (Es)	Integration f	integration	intégration f	integrazione f	—
integración económica (Es)	wirtschaftliche Integration f	economic integration	intégration économique f	integrazione economica f	—
integral part (E)	wesentliche Bestandteile pl	—	parties constitutives essentielles f pl	componenti essenziali f pl	partes integrantes esencial f pl
Integration (D)	—	integration	intégration f	integrazione f	integración f
integration (E)	Integration f	—	intégration f	integrazione f	integración f
intégration (F)	Integration f	integration	—	integrazione f	integración f
intégration économique (F)	wirtschaftliche Integration f	economic integration	—	integrazione economica f	integración económica f
integrazione (I)	Integration f	integration	intégration f	—	integración f
integrazione economica (I)	wirtschaftliche Integration f	economic integration	intégration économique f	—	integración económica f
interbank rate (E)	Interbankrate f	—	taux interbancaire m	tasso interbancario m	tipo interbancario m
Interbankrate (D)	—	interbank rate	taux interbancaire m	tasso interbancario m	tipo interbancario m
intercambio de mercancías (Es)	Warenaustausch m	exchange of goods	échanges commerciaux m pl	scambio merci m	—
interchangeable (F)	substituierbar	replaceable	—	sostituibile	sustituible
interdépendance (F)	Interdependenz f	interdependence	—	interdipendenza f	interdependencia f
interdependence (E)	Interdependenz f	—	interdépendance f	interdipendenza f	interdependencia f
interdependencia (Es)	Interdependenz f	interdependence	interdépendance f	interdipendenza f	—
Interdependenz (D)	—	interdependence	interdépendance f	interdipendenza f	interdependencia f
interdiction en matière de concurrence (F)	Wettbewerbsverbot n	prohibition of competition	—	divieto di concorrenza m	prohibición de competencia f
interdicto provisorio (Es)	einstweilige Verfügung f	temporary injunction	ordonnance sur référé civil f	provvedimento temporaneo m	—
interdipendenza (I)	Interdependenz f	interdependence	interdépendance f	—	interdependencia f
interés[1] (Es)	Zins m	interest	intérêt m	interessi m pl	—
interés[2] (Es)	Interesse n	interest	intérêt m	interesse m	—
interesado (Es)	Interessent m	person interested	intéressé m	interessato m	—
interés compuesto (Es)	Zinseszins m	compound interest	intérêt composé m	interessi composti m pl	—
interés de disponibilidad (Es)	Bereitstellungszinsen pl	commitment interests	intérêts de disponibilité m pl	interessi per lo stanziamento m pl	—
interés efectivo (Es)	Effektivverzinsung f	effective interest yield	taux effectif (de l'intérêt) m	interessi effettivi m pl	—
intereses acreedores (Es)	Habenzinsen pl	credit interest	intérêts créditeur m	interessi creditori m pl	—
intereses de demora (Es)	Verzugszinsen pl	default interest	intérêts moratoires m pl	interessi di mora m pl	—
intereses deudores (Es)	Sollzinsen pl	debtor interest rates	intérêt débiteur m	interessi debitori m pl	—
intereses por fracción de período (Es)	Stückzinsen f	broken period interest	intérêts courus m pl	interessi maturati m pl	—
intereses reales (Es)	Effektivzins m	effective interest	intérêt effectif m	tasso d'interesse effettivo m	—
interés fijo (Es)	fester Zins m	fixed interest rate	intérêt fixe m	tasso d'interesse fisso m	—
interés real (Es)	Realzins m	real (rate of) interest	rendement réel m	tasso d'interesse reale m	—
interessato (I)	Interessent m	person interested	intéressé m	—	interesado m
Interesse (D)	—	interest	intérêt m	interesse m	interés m
intéressé (F)	Interessent m	person interested	—	interessato m	interesado m
interesse[1] (I)	Anteilnahme f	sympathy	participation f	—	participación f
interesse[2] (I)	Interesse n	interest	intérêt m	—	interés m
interesse del capitale (I)	Kapitalzins m	interest on capital	intérêt du capital m	—	renta del capital f

	D	E	F	I	Es
Interessengruppe (D)	—	interest group	groupe d'intérêts *m*	gruppo d'interesse *m*	grupo de presión *m*
Interessent (D)	—	person interested	intéressé *m*	interessato *m*	interesado *m*
Interessenvertretung (D)	—	representation of interests	représentation des intérêts *f*	rappresentanza degli interessi *f*	representación de intereses *f*
interessi (I)	Zins *m*	interest	intérêt *m*	—	interés *m*
interessi composti (I)	Zinseszins *m*	compound interest	intérêt composé *m*	—	interés compuesto *m*
interessi creditori (I)	Habenzinsen *pl*	credit interest	intérêts créditeur *m*	—	intereses acreedores *m pl*
interessi debitori (I)	Sollzinsen *pl*	debtor interest rates	intérêt débiteur *m*	—	intereses deudores *m pl*
interessi di mora (I)	Verzugszinsen *pl*	default interest	intérêts moratoires *m pl*	—	intereses de demora *m pl*
interessi effettivi (I)	Effektivverzinsung *f*	effective interest yield	taux effectif (de l'intérêt) *m*	—	interés efectivo *m*
interessi maturati (I)	Stückzinsen *f*	broken period interest	intérêts courus *m pl*	—	intereses por fracción de período *m pl*
interessi per lo stanziamento (I)	Bereitstellungszinsen *pl*	commitment interests	intérêts de disponibilité *m pl*	—	interés de disponibilidad *m*
interest¹ (E)	Zins *m*	—	intérêt *m*	interessi *m pl*	interés *m*
interest² (E)	Interesse *n*	—	intérêt *m*	interesse *m*	interés *m*
interest account (E)	Zinsrechnung *f*	—	calcul des intérêts *m*	conteggio degli interessi *m*	cómputo de intereses *m*
interest group (E)	Interessengruppe *f*	—	groupe d'intérêts *m*	gruppo d'interesse *m*	grupo de presión *m*
interest margin (E)	Zinsmarge *f*	—	marge entre les taux d'intérêt créditeur et débiteur *f*	margine degli interessi *m*	margen de interés *m*
interest on capital (E)	Kapitalzins *m*	—	intérêt du capital *m*	interesse del capitale *m*	renta del capital *f*
interest rate (E)	Zinsfuß *m*	—	taux d'intérêt *m*	tasso d'interesse *m*	tipo de interés *m*
interest rate level (E)	Zinsniveau *n*	—	niveau du taux d'intérêt *m*	livello degli interessi *m*	nivel de interés *m*
interest rate policy (E)	Zinspolitik *f*	—	politique en matière d'intérêts *f*	politica dei tassi d'interesse *f*	política en materia de intereses *f*
interest service (E)	Zinsendienst *m*	—	service de l'intérêt *m*	servizio degli interessi *m*	servicio de intereses *m*
interés variable (Es)	variabler Zins *m*	variable rate of interest	intérêt variable *m*	tasso d'interesse variabile *m*	—
intérêt¹ (F)	Interesse *n*	interest	—	interesse *m*	interés *m*
intérêt² (F)	Zins *m*	interest	—	interessi *m pl*	interés *m*
intérêt composé (F)	Zinseszins *m*	compound interest	—	interessi composti *m pl*	interés compuesto *m*
intérêt débiteur (F)	Sollzinsen *pl*	debtor interest rates	—	interessi debitori *m pl*	intereses deudores *m pl*
intérêt du capital (F)	Kapitalzins *m*	interest on capital	—	interesse del capitale *m*	renta del capital *f*
intérêt effectif (F)	Effektivzins *m*	effective interest	—	tasso d'interesse effettivo *m*	intereses reales *m pl*
intérêt fixe (F)	fester Zins *m*	fixed interest rate	—	tasso d'interesse fisso *m*	interés fijo *m*
intérêts courus (F)	Stückzinsen *f*	broken period interest	—	interessi maturati *m pl*	intereses por fracción de período *m pl*
intérêts créditeur (F)	Habenzinsen *pl*	credit interest	—	interessi creditori *m pl*	intereses acreedores *m pl*
intérêts de disponibilité (F)	Bereitstellungszinsen *pl*	commitment interests	—	interessi per lo stanziamento *m pl*	interés de disponibilidad *m*
intérêts moratoires (F)	Verzugszinsen *pl*	default interest	—	interessi di mora *m pl*	intereses de demora *m pl*
intérêt variable (F)	variabler Zins *m*	variable rate of interest	—	tasso d'interesse variabile *m*	interés variable *m*
interim account (E)	Zwischenkonto *n*	—	compte provisoire *m*	conto transitorio *m*	cuenta provisional *f*
interim balance sheet (E)	Zwischenbilanz *f*	—	bilan intermédiaire *m*	bilancio provvisorio *m*	balance intermedio *m*
interim report (E)	Zwischenzeugnis *n*	—	certificat provisoire *m*	certificato provvisorio *m*	certificado provisional *m*
Interimslösung (D)	—	interim solution	solution intérimaire *f*	soluzione ad interim *f*	solución interina *f*

	D	E	F	I	Es
interim solution (E)	Interimslösung f	—	solution intérimaire f	soluzione ad interim f	solución interina f
intermédiaire (F)	Zwischenhändler m	middleman	—	intermediario m	intermediario m
intermediario (Es)	Zwischenhändler m	middleman	intermédiaire m	intermediario m	—
intermediario (I)	Zwischenhändler m	middleman	intermédiaire m		intermediario m
intermediate purchase (E)	Zwischenabnahme f	—	achat intermédiaire m	acquisto intermediario m	compra intermediaria f
intermediazione di crediti (I)	Kreditvermittlung f	arranging for a credit	médiation du crédit f	—	mediación de créditos f
intern (D)	—	internal	interne	interno	interno
internal (E)	intern	—	interne	interno	interno
Internal Market of the European Community (E)	EG-Binnenmarkt m	—	Marché Intérieur de la Communauté Européenne m	mercato unico m	Mercado Unico m
International Commodity Agreements (E)	Rohstoff-abkommen n	—	accord sur les matières premières m	accordo sulle materie prime m	acuerdo de materias primas m
international economic order (E)	Weltwirtschafts-ordnung f	—	ordre économique mondial m	sistema economico mondiale m	orden económico mundial m
international monetary system (E)	Weltwährungs-system n	—	système monétaire international m	sistema monetario internazionale m	sistema monetario internacional m
(international) price system (E)	Preiszusammen-hang m	—	système des prix m	contesto dei prezzi m	sistema de precios m
interne (F)	intern	internal	—	interno	interno
interno (Es)	intern	internal	interne	interno	—
interno (I)	intern	internal	interne	—	interno
inter-office sale (E)	Telefonverkauf m	—	vente par téléphone f	vendita per telefono f	venta por teléfono f
intérprete (Es)	Dolmetscher m	interpreter	interprète m	interprete m	—
interprète (F)	Dolmetscher m	interpreter	—	interprete m	intérprete m
interprete (I)	Dolmetscher m	interpreter	interprète m	—	intérprete m
interpreter (E)	Dolmetscher m	—	interprète m	interprete m	intérprete m
interrogazione (I)	Befragung f	poll	enquête f	—	encuesta f
intervención (Es)	Intervention f	intervention	intervention f	intervento m	—
Intervention (D)	—	intervention	intervention f	intervento m	intervención f
intervention (E)	Intervention f	—	intervention f	intervento m	intervención f
intervention (F)	Intervention f	intervention	—	intervento m	intervención f
intervention buying (E)	Interventionskäufe pl	—	achats d'intervention m pl	acquisti d'intervento m pl	compras de intervención f pl
intervention point (E)	Interventionspunkt m	—	point d'intervention m	punto d'intervento m	punto de intervención m
Interventionskäufe (D)	—	intervention buying	achats d'intervention m pl	acquisti d'intervento m pl	compras de intervención f pl
Interventionspflicht (D)	—	obligation to intervene	obligation d'intervention f	obbligo d'intervento m	obligación de intervención f
Interventionspunkt (D)	—	intervention point	point d'intervention m	punto d'intervento m	punto de intervención m
intervento (I)	Intervention f	intervention	intervention f	—	intervención f
Interview (D)	—	interview	enquête f	intervista f	entrevista f
interview (E)	Interview n	—	enquête f	intervista f	entrevista f
intervista (I)	Interview n	interview	enquête f	—	entrevista f
intervista ai clienti (I)	Kundenbefragung f	customer survey	enquête parmi les clients f	—	encuesta entre los clientes f
intestazione (I)	Briefkopf m	letterhead	en-tête m	—	encabezamiento m
(in) the red (E)	rote Zahlen pl	—	chiffres en déficit m pl	conti in rosso m pl	cifras rojas f pl
intransmisible (Es)	nicht übertragbar	non-assignable	ne pas transférable	non trasferibile	—
introductory discount (E)	Einführungsrabatt m	—	rabais d'introduction m	sconto di lancio m	rebaja de lanzamiento f
introiti base (I)	Basiseinkommen n	basic income	revenu de base m	—	salario base m
introito disponibile (I)	verfügbares Einkommen n	disposable income	revenu disponible m	—	ingresos disponibles m pl
inutilizzato (I)	ungenutzt	unused	pas utilisé	—	no utilizado
inventaire¹ (F)	Inventur f	taking of the inventory	—	redazione d'inventario f	inventario m

	D	E	F	I	Es
inventaire² (F)	Inventar *n*	inventory	—	inventario *m*	inventario *m*
Inventar (D)	—	inventory	inventaire *m*	inventario *m*	inventario *m*
inventario¹ (Es)	Inventur *f*	taking of the inventory	inventaire *m*	redazione d'inventario *f*	—
inventario² (Es)	Inventar *n*	inventory	inventaire *m*	inventario *m*	—
inventario (I)	Inventar *n*	inventory	inventaire *m*	—	inventario *m*
inventory (E)	Inventar *n*	—	inventaire *m*	inventario *m*	inventario *m*
Inventur (D)	—	taking of the inventory	inventaire *m*	redazione d'inventario *f*	inventario *m*
inversión (Es)	Investition *f*	investment	investissement *m*	investimento *m*	—
inversión de capital (Es)	Kapitalanlage *f*	capital investment	investissement de capitaux *m*	investimento di capitale *m*	—
inversión de reposición (Es)	Ersatzinvestition *f*	replacement of capital assets	investissement pour remplacement des moyens de production *m*	investimento di ampliamento e di sostituzione *m*	—
inversión equivocada (Es)	Fehlinvestition *f*	misconceived capital projects	mauvais investissement *m*	investimento sbagliato *m*	—
inversiones directas (Es)	Direktinvestitionen *pl*	direct investments	investissements directs *m pl*	investimenti diretti *m pl*	—
inversión fija (Es)	Anlageinvestition *f*	investment in fixed assets	investissement productif *m*	investimento fisso *m*	—
inversión inmobiliaria (Es)	Bauinvestitionen *pl*	structural investments	investissements à la construction *m pl*	investimenti edili *m pl*	—
inversión neta (Es)	Nettoinvestition *f*	net investment	investissement net *m*	investimento netto *m*	—
investigación (Es)	Forschung *f*	research	recherche *f*	ricerca *f*	—
investigación espacial (Es)	Raumforschung *f*	space research	recherches spatiales *f pl*	ricerche spaziali *f pl*	—
investigación tributaria (Es)	Steuerfahndung *f*	investigation into su-spected tax offences	recherche de la fraude fiscale *f*	inchiesta tributaria *f*	—
investigation (E)	Nachforschung *f*	—	recherche *f*	indagine *f*	pesquisas *f pl*
investigation by the tax authorities (E)	Betriebsprüfung *f*	—	vérification des livres de l'entreprise *f*	revisione aziendale *f*	inspección de la explotación *f*
investigation into suspected tax offences (E)	Steuerfahndung *f*	—	recherche de la fraude fiscale *f*	inchiesta tributaria *f*	investigación tributaria *f*
investimenti diretti (I)	Direktinvestitionen *pl*	direct investments	investissements directs *m pl*	—	inversiones directas *f pl*
investimenti edili (I)	Bauinvestitionen *pl*	structural investments	investissements à la construction *m pl*	—	inversión inmobiliaria *f*
investimento (I)	Investition *f*	investment	investissement *m*	—	inversión *f*
investimento di ampliamento e di sostituzione (I)	Ersatzinvestition *f*	replacement of capital assets	investissement pour remplacement des moyens de production *m*	—	inversión de reposición *f*
investimento di capitale (I)	Kapitalanlage *f*	capital investment	investissement de capitaux *m*	—	inversión de capital *f*
investimento fisso (I)	Anlageinvestition *f*	investment in fixed assets	investissement productif *m*	—	inversión fija *f*
investimento netto (I)	Nettoinvestition *f*	net investment	investissement net *m*	—	inversión neta *f*
investimento sbagliato (I)	Fehlinvestition *f*	misconceived capital projects	mauvais placement *m*	—	inversión equivocada *f*
investissement (F)	Investition *f*	investment	—	investimento *m*	inversión *f*
investissement de capitaux (F)	Kapitalanlage *f*	capital investment	—	investimento di capitale *m*	inversión de capital *f*
investissement net (F)	Nettoinvestition *f*	net investment	—	investimento netto *m*	inversión neta *f*
investissement productif (F)	Anlageinvestition *f*	investment in fixed assets	—	investimento fisso *m*	inversión fija *f*
investissements à la construction (F)	Bauinvestitionen *pl*	structural investments	—	investimenti edili *m pl*	inversión inmobiliaria *f*
investissements directs (F)	Direktinvestitionen *pl*	direct investments	—	investimenti diretti *m pl*	inversiones directas *f pl*
Investition (D)	—	investment	investissement *m*	investimento *m*	inversión *f*
Investitionsboom (D)	—	investment boom	boom d'investissement *m*	boom d'investimento *m*	boom de inversión *m*

	D	E	F	I	Es
Investitions-förderung (D)	—	investment promotion	promotion de l'investissement f	promozione degli investimenti f	estímulo a la inversión m
Investitionsgüter (D)	—	capital goods	biens d'investisse-ment m pl	beni di investimento m pl	bienes de inversión m pl
Investitions-kontrolle (D)	—	investment control	contrôle d'investissement m	controllo degli investimenti m	control de las inversiones m
Investitionskredit (D)	—	investment credit	crédit d'investissement m	credito d'investimento m	crédito de inversión m
Investitionslenkung (D)	—	investment control	politique d'investissement f	politica d'investimento f	dirección de inversiones f
Investitionsplan (D)	—	investment scheme	plan des investissements m	piano d'investimento m	plan de inversión m
Investitionssteuer (D)	—	investment tax	impôt sur les investissements m	imposta sugli investimenti f	impuesto sobre las inversiones m
Investitionszulage (D)	—	investment grant	prime d'investissement f	premio d'investimento m	prima a la inversión f
investment (E)	Investition f	—	investissement m	investimento m	inversión f
Investmentbank (D)	—	investment bank	banque d'investissement f	banca d'investimento f	banco de inversiones m
investment bank (E)	Investmentbank f	—	banque d'investissement f	banca d'investimento f	banco de inversiones m
investment boom (E)	Investitionsboom m	—	boom d'investissement m	boom d'investimento m	boom de inversión m
investment business (E)	Emissionsgeschäft n	—	opération succédant à une émission f	operazione d'emissione f	operación de emisión f
investment certificate (E)	Investmentzertifikat n	—	certificat émis par un fonds commun de placement m	certificato d'investimento m	certificado de participación m
investment company (E)	Investment-gesellschaft f	—	société d'investissement f	società d'investimento f	sociedad de inversiones f
investment control¹ (E)	Investitionskontrolle f	—	contrôle d'investissement m	controllo degli investimenti m	control de las inversiones m
investment control² (E)	Investitionslenkung f	—	politique d'investissement f	politica d'investimento f	dirección de inversiones f
investment credit (E)	Investitionskredit m	—	crédit d'investissement m	credito d'investimento m	crédito de inversión m
Investmentfonds (D)	—	unit trust	fonds commun de placement m	fondo d'investimento m	fondo de inversiones m
Investment-gesellschaft (D)	—	investment company	société d'investissement f	società d'investimento f	sociedad de inversiones f
investment grant (E)	Investitionszulage f	—	prime d'investissement f	premio d'investimento m	prima a la inversión f
investment in fixed assets (E)	Anlageinvestition f	—	investissement productif m	investimento fisso m	inversión fija f
investment promotion (E)	Investitions-förderung f	—	promotion de l'investisse-ment f	promozione degli investimenti f	estímulo a la inversión m
investment scheme (E)	Investitionsplan m	—	plan des investissements m	piano d'investimento m	plan de inversión m
investment securities (E)	Anlagepapiere pl	—	valeurs de placement f	titoli d'investimento m pl	valores de inversión m pl
investment tax (E)	Investitionssteuer f	—	impôt sur les investissements m	imposta sugli investimenti f	impuesto sobre las inversiones m
Investmentzertifikat (D)	—	investment certificate	certificat émis par un fonds commun de placement m	certificato d'investimento m	certificado de participación m
invitar (Es)	einladen	invite	inviter	invitare	—
invitare (I)	einladen	invite	inviter	—	invitar
invite (E)	einladen	—	inviter	invitare	invitar
inviter (F)	einladen	invite	—	invitare	invitar
invoice¹ (E)	Faktura f	—	facture f	fattura f	factura f
invoice² (E)	Rechnung f	—	facture f	fattura f	factura f
invoice amount (E)	Rechnungssumme f	—	montant de la facture m	importo della fattura m	suma de la factura f
invoice number (E)	Rechnungsnummer f	—	numéro de la facture m	numero della fattura m	número de la factura m

	D	E	F	I	Es
invoicing (E)	Rechnungsstellung f	—	établissement d'une facture m	fatturazione f	facturación f
in vigore (I)	in Kraft	effective/in force	en vigueur	—	en vigor
in visione (I)	zur Ansicht	on approval	à vue	—	para examen
in zweifacher Ausfertigung (D)	—	in duplicate	en deux exemplaires	in due copie	por duplicado
iperinflazione (I)	Hyperinflation f	hyperinflation	hyperinflation f	—	hiperinflación f
ipermercato (I)	Verbrauchermarkt m	consumer market	marché des consommateurs m	—	mercado favorable al consumidor m
ipoteca (I)	Hypothek f	mortgage	hypothéque f	—	hipoteca f
ipotesi (I)	Hypothese f	hypothesis	hypothèse f	—	hipótesis f
irregolarità (I)	Unregelmäßigkeit f	irregularity	irrégularité f	—	irregularidad f
irregularidad (Es)	Unregelmäßigkeit f	irregularity	irrégularité f	irregolarità f	—
irrégularité (F)	Unregelmäßigkeit f	irregularity	—	irregolarità f	irregularidad f
irrégularité en matière de chèque (F)	Scheckbetrug m	cheque fraud	—	emissione di assegno a vuoto f	falsificación de cheques f
irregularity (E)	Unregelmäßigkeit f	—	irrégularité f	irregolarità f	irregularidad f
irrevocable letter of credit (E)	unwiderrufliches Akkreditiv n	—	accréditif irrévocable m	apertura di credito documentario irrevocabile f	crédito documentario irrevocable m
Irrtum vorbehalten (D)	—	errors excepted	sauf erreur	salvo errore	salvo error
issue (E)	Emission f	—	émission f	emissione f	emisión f
issuing restriction (E)	Emissions- begrenzung f	—	limitation d'émission f	limitazione d'emissione f	limitación de emisiones f
istanza (I)	Instanz f	instance	instance f	—	instancia f
istituto della ricerca di mercato (I)	Marktforschungs- institut n	market research institute	institut d'études de marché m	—	instituto de investiga- ción del mercado m
istituto di credito (I)	Kreditinstitut n	credit institution	établissement de crédit m	—	instituto de crédito m
istituto previdenziale (I)	Versorgungs- einrichtung f	pension scheme	institution de retraite f	—	institución de prevision f
istituzione a finalità mutualistiche (I)	Selbsthilfe- einrichtung f	mutual assistance institution	organisation d'assistance mutuelle f	—	organización de asistencia mutua f
Istkosten (D)	—	actual costs	coûts réels m pl	costi effettivi m pl	gastos efectivos m pl
istruttore (I)	Ausbilder m	trainer	instructeur m	—	instructor m
istruzione (I)	Anleitung f	instructions	instruction f	—	instrucción f
istruzione per la riparazione (I)	Reparaturanleitung f	repair instructions	instruction de réparation f	—	instrucción de reparación m
Istzahlen (D)	—	actual figures	résultats effectifs m pl	dati effettivi m pl	cifras efectivas f pl
item of real estate (E)	Immobilie f	—	bien immobilier m	immobile m	inmueble m
itinéraire¹ (F)	Reiseroute f	route	—	itinerario m	itinerario m
itinéraire² (F)	Tourenplan m	tour schedule	—	programma dell'itinerario m	itinerario m
itinerant trade (E)	ambulantes Gewerbe n	—	commerce ambulant m	commercio ambulante m	comercio ambulante m
itinerario¹ (Es)	Reiseroute f	route	itinéraire m	itinerario m	—
itinerario² (Es)	Tourenplan m	tour schedule	itinéraire m	programma dell'itinerario m	—
itinerario (I)	Reiseroute f	route	itinéraire m	—	itinerario m
Jahresabschluß (D)	—	annual accounts	clôture annuelle des comptes f	chiusura d'esercizio f	cierre de cuentas m
Jahresarbeitszeit (D)	—	annual hours of work	temps de travail annuel m	orario di lavoro annuale m	jornada anual f
Jahresbedarf (D)	—	annual need	besoin annuel m	bisogno annuale m	necesidad anual f
Jahreseinkommen (D)	—	annual income	revenu annuel m	reddito annuale m	renta anual f
Jahresfixum (D)	—	fixed annual salary	fixe annuel m	fisso annuale m	fijo anual m
Jahresgewinn (D)	—	annual profit	bénéfice annuel m	utile dell'anno m	beneficio del ejercicio m
Jahreshaupt- versammlung (D)	—	annual meeting of shareholders	assemblée générale annuelle f	assemblea generale annuale f	junta general anual f

	D	E	F	I	Es
Jahresüberschuß (D)	—	annual surplus	excédent annuel *m*	surplus dell'anno *m*	superávit del ejercicio *m*
Jahreswirtschafts-bericht (D)	—	Annual Economic Report	compte rendu d'activité économique annuel *m*	relazione generale sulla situazione economica *f*	informe económico anual *m*
jährlich (D)	—	annual	annuel	annuale	anual
jauger (F)	eichen	gauge	—	tarare	contrastar
jefe (Es)	Chef *m*	head	chef *m*	capo *m*	—
jefe del departamento de expedición (Es)	Versandleiter *m*	manager of shipping department	chef du service des expéditions *m*	capo reparto spedizioni *m*	—
jefe de personal (Es)	Personalleiter *m*	staff manager	chef du personnel *m*	capo reparto personale *m*	—
jefe de sección (Es)	Abteilungsleiter *m*	head of department	chef de service *m*	capo reparto *m*	—
jefe de sucursal (Es)	Filialleiter *m*	branch manager	directeur d'agence *m*	direttore della filiale *m*	—
jefe de venta regional (Es)	Gebietsverkaufs-leiter *m*	area sales manager	chef de vente régionale *m*	direttore di vendita regionale *m*	—
jerarquía (Es)	Hierarchie *f*	hierarchy	hiérarchie *f*	gerarchia *f*	—
jeu d'écritures (F)	Umbuchung *f*	transfer of an entry	—	giro di partite *m*	asiento en otra cuenta *m*
jeu d'entreprise (F)	Planspiel *n*	management games	—	gioco di strategia imprenditoriale *m*	juego de ensayo *m*
job demand (E)	Arbeitsnachfrage *f*	—	demande d'emploi *f*	domanda di lavoro *f*	demanda de trabajo *f*
job description (E)	Stellenbeschreibung *f*	—	description de l'emploi *f*	descrizione d'impiego *f*	descripción del puesto de trabajo *f*
job evaluation (E)	Arbeitsbewertung *f*	—	qualification du travail *f*	valutazione del lavoro *f*	evaluación del trabajo *f*
job preparation (E)	Arbeitsvorbereitung *f*	—	préparation du travail *f*	preparazione del lavoro *f*	preparación laboral *f*
job satisfaction (E)	Arbeitszufriedenheit *f*	—	satisfaction de travail *f*	soddisfazione del lavoro *f*	satisfacción en el trabajo *f*
joint publicity (E)	Gemeinschafts-werbung *f*	—	publicité collective *f*	pubblicità collettiva *f*	publicidad colectiva *f*
joint stock company (E)	Aktiengesellschaft *f*	—	société anonyme *f*	società per azioni *f*	sociedad anónima *f*
jornada anual (Es)	Jahresarbeitszeit *f*	annual hours of work	temps de travail annuel *m*	orario di lavoro annuale *m*	—
jornada laboral (Es)	Arbeitszeit *f*	working hours	heures de travail *f pl*	orario di lavoro *m*	—
jour de bourse (F)	Börsentag *m*	market day	—	giorno di borsa *m*	sesión bursátil *f*
jour de la liquidation (F)	Abrechnungstag *m*	settling day	—	giorno di liquidazione *m*	fecha de liquidación *f*
jour de l'échéance (F)	Verfalltag *m*	day of expiry	—	giorno di scadenza *m*	día de vencimiento *m*
jour de paye (F)	Zahltag *m*	payday	—	giorno di paga *m*	día de pago *m*
jour de travail (F)	Arbeitstag *m*	working day	—	giorno lavorativo *m*	día laboral *m*
journal destiné à la clientèle (F)	Kundenzeitschrift *f*	customer magazine	—	periodico per i clienti *m*	revista para los clientes *f*
journeyman (E)	Geselle *m*	—	ouvrier artisan *m*	garzone *m*	oficial *m*
joven empresario (Es)	Jungunternehmer *m*	young businessman	entrepreneur débutant *m*	imprenditore giovane *m*	—
jubilee (E)	Geschäftsjubiläum *n*	—	anniversaire de l'entreprise *m*	anniversario aziendale *m*	aniversario de la empresa *m*
judge (E)	Richter *m*	—	juge *m*	giudice *m*	juez *m*
judiciaire (F)	gerichtlich	judicial	—	giudiziario	judicial
judicial (E)	gerichtlich	—	judiciaire	giudiziario	judicial
judicial (Es)	gerichtlich	judicial	judiciaire	giudiziario	—
judicial execution (E)	Zwangs-vollstreckung *f*	—	exécution forcée *f*	esecuzione forzata *f*	ejecución forzosa *f*
juego de ensayo (Es)	Planspiel *n*	management games	jeu d'entreprise *m*	gioco di strategia imprenditoriale *m*	—
juez (Es)	Richter *m*	judge	juge *m*	giudice *m*	—
juge (F)	Richter *m*	judge	—	giudice *m*	juez *m*
Jungunternehmer (D)	—	young businessman	entrepreneur débutant *m*	imprenditore giovane *m*	joven empresario *m*
junior partner (E)	Junior-Partner *m*	—	fils du partenaire *m*	junior partner *m*	socio menor *m*

	D	E	F	I	Es
junior partner (I)	Junior-Partner *m*	junior partner	fils du partenaire *m*	—	socio menor *m*
Junior-Partner (D)	—	junior partner	fils du partenaire *m*	junior partner *m*	socio menor *m*
junta de acreedores (Es)	Gläubigerversammlung *f*	creditors' meeting	assemblée des créanciers *f*	riunione dei creditori *f*	—
junta directiva (Es)	Direktion *f*	board of directors	direction *f*	direzione *f*	—
junta general anual (Es)	Jahreshauptversammlung *f*	annual meeting of shareholders	assemblée générale annuelle *f*	assemblea generale annuale *f*	—
junta social (Es)	Gesellschafterversammlung *f*	meeting of shareholders	réunion des associés *f*	assemblea dei soci *f*	—
jurídicamente capaz (Es)	rechtsfähig	capable of acting in law	capable de jouir des droits	avendo capacità giuridica *f*	—
juridiction compétente (F)	Gerichtsstand *m*	jurisdiction	—	foro competente *m*	tribunal competente *m*
jurisdiction (E)	Gerichtsstand *m*	—	juridiction compétente *f*	foro competente *m*	tribunal competente *m*
jurisprudence (F)	Rechtsprechung *f*	administration of justice	—	giurisprudenza *f*	jurisprudencia *f*
jurisprudencia (Es)	Rechtsprechung *f*	administration of justice	jurisprudence *f*	giurisprudenza *f*	—
juristische Person (D)	—	legal person	personne juridique *f*	persona giuridica *f*	persona jurídica *f*
justificado (Es)	gerechtfertigt	justified	justifié	giustificato	—
justificatif (F)	Beleg *m*	voucher	—	quietanza *f*	justificativo *m*
justificativo (Es)	Beleg *m*	voucher	justificatif *m*	quietanza *f*	—
justifié (F)	gerechtfertigt	justified	—	giustificato	justificado
justified (E)	gerechtfertigt	—	justifié	giustificato	justificado
Kabelfernsehen (D)	—	cable television	télévision par câble *f*	televisione via cavo *f*	televisión por cable *f*
Kabeltelegramm (D)	—	cablegram	câblogramme *m*	cablogramma *m*	cablegrama *f*
Kabelüberweisung (D)	—	cable transfer	virement par câble *m*	bonifico telegrafico *m*	giro telegráfico *m*
Kalenderjahr (D)	—	calendar year	année civile *f*	anno solare *m*	año civil *m*
Kalkulation (D)	—	calculation	calcul *m*	calcolazione *f*	calculación *f*
Kampagne (D)	—	campaign	campagne *f*	campagna *f*	campaña *f*
Kapazität (D)	—	capacity	capacité *f*	capacità *f*	capacidad *f*
Kapazitätsauslastung (D)	—	utilization of capacity	utilisation de la capacité *f*	sfruttamento delle capacità *m*	utilización de las capacidades *f*
Kapazitätsausweitung (D)	—	increase in capacity	extension de la capacité *f*	ampliamento delle capacità *m*	ampliación de la capacidad *f*
Kapazitätsengpaß (D)	—	bottleneck in capacity	goulot d'étranglement de capacité *m*	strettoia di capacità *f*	escasez de capacidad *f*
Kapital (D)	—	capital	capital *m*	capitale *m*	capital *m*
Kapitalabfindung (D)	—	lump sum settlemnt	indemnité en capital *f*	indennità in capitale *f*	indemnización en capital *f*
Kapitalanlage (D)	—	capital investment	investissement de capitaux *m*	investimento di capitale *m*	inversión de capital *f*
Kapitalanteil (D)	—	share in capital	part de capital *f*	quota di capitale *f*	participación en el capital *f*
Kapitalausstattung (D)	—	capital resources	dotation en capital *f*	dotazione di capitale *f*	dotación de capital *f*
Kapitalbasis (D)	—	capital base	base de capital *f*	base di capitale *f*	base de capital *f*
Kapitalbedarf (D)	—	capital requirements	besoin en capital *m*	domanda di capitale *m*	necesidad de capital *f*
Kapitalbilanz (D)	—	balance of capital transactions	balance des opérations en capital *f*	bilancia dei capitali *f*	balanza de capitales *f*
Kapitaleinkommen (D)	—	unearned income	revenu du capital *m*	reddito del capitale *m*	ganancias de capital *f pl*
Kapitalerhöhung (D)	—	increase of the share capital	augmentation de capital *f*	aumento del capitale *m*	aumento de capital *m*
Kapitalertrag (D)	—	income from capital	produit du capital *m*	rendita del capitale *f*	rendimiento del capital *m*
Kapitalertragsteuer (D)	—	tax on investment income	impôt sur le revenu du capital *m*	imposta sulla rendita del capitale *f*	impuesto sobre la renta del capital *m*
Kapitalexport (D)	—	capital export	exportation de capitaux *f*	esportazione di capitale *f*	exportación de capital *f*
Kapitalflucht (D)	—	flight of capital	évasion des capitaux *f*	fuga dei capitali *f*	fuga de capital *f*

	D	E	F	I	Es
Kapitalgesellschaft (D)	—	company limited by shares	société de capitaux *f*	società di capitale *f*	sociedad capitalista *f*
Kapitalherabsetzung (D)	—	reduction of capital	diminution du capital *f*	riduzione del capitale *f*	reducción de capital *f*
Kapitalhilfe (D)	—	capital aid	aide financière *f*	aiuto finanziario *m*	ayuda financiera *f*
Kapitalimport (D)	—	capital import	importation de capitaux *f*	importazione di capitali *f*	importación de capital *f*
kapitalintensiv (D)	—	capital-intensive	avec grande intensité de capital	ad alta incidenza di capitale	con gran intensidad de capital
Kapitalisierung (D)	—	capitalization	capitalisation *f*	capitalizzazione *f*	capitalización *f*
Kapitalismus (D)	—	capitalism	capitalisme *m*	capitalismo *m*	capitalismo *m*
Kapitalmarkt (D)	—	capital market	marché des capitaux *m*	mercato finanziario *m*	mercado financiero *m*
Kapitalproduktivität (D)	—	productivity of capital	productivité du capital *f*	produttività del capital *f*	productividad del capital *f*
Kapitalrentabilität (D)	—	return on investment	rentabilité du capital *f*	redditività del capitale *f*	rentabilidad del capital *f*
Kapitalstock (D)	—	capital stock	réserve de capital *f*	riserva di capitale *f*	fondo de capital *m*
Kapitaltheorie (D)	—	capital theory	théorie du capital *f*	teoria del capitale *f*	teoría financiera *f*
Kapitalumschlag (D)	—	capital turnover	roulement des capitaux *m*	rotazione del capitale *f*	rotación del capital *f*
Kapitalverkehr (D)	—	capital transactions	mouvement des capitaux *m*	movimento dei capitali *m*	circulación de capitales *f*
Kapitalwert (D)	—	capital value	valeur en capital *f*	valore del capitale *m*	valor capitalizado *m*
Kapitalzins (D)	—	interest on capital	intérêt du capital *m*	interesse del capitale *m*	renta del capital *f*
Karat (D)	—	carat	carat *m*	carato *m*	quilate *m*
Karenzzeit (D)	—	qualifying period	délai de carence *m*	periodo d'attesa *m*	período carencial *m*
Kartei (D)	—	card-index	cartothèque	schedario *m*	fichero *m*
Karteikarte (D)	—	index card	fiche *f*	scheda *f*	ficha *f*
Kartell (D)	—	cartel	cartel *m*	cartello *m*	cártel *m*
Kartellbehörde (D)	—	cartel authority	office de surveillance des cartels et ententes *m*	autorità antimonopoli *f pl*	oficina de cártels *f*
Kartellbildung (D)	—	cartel formation	cartellisation *f*	costituzione di cartelli *f*	formación de carteles *f*
Kartellgesetz (D)	—	Cartel Law	loi sur les cartels *f*	legge sui cartelli *f*	ley relativa a los cártels *f*
Kaskoversicherung (D)	—	comprehensive insurance	assurance tous risques *f*	assicurazione corpi del ramo trasporto *f*	seguro de casco *m*
Kassakurs (D)	—	spot price	cours au comptant *m*	corso a pronti *m*	cotización al contado *f*
Kassenbuch (D)	—	cash book	compte de caisse *m*	libro di cassa *m*	libro de caja *m*
Kassierer (D)	—	cashier	caissier *m*	cassiere *m*	cajero *m*
Katalog (D)	—	catalogue	catalogue *m*	catalogo *m*	catálogo *m*
Katalysator (D)	—	catalytic converter	catalyseur *m*	catalizzatore *m*	catalizador *m*
Kataster (D)	—	cadaster	cadastre *m*	catasto *m*	catastro *m*
Kauf (D)	—	purchase	achat *m*	acquisto *m*	compra *f*
Kaufabschluß (D)	—	conclusion of a sales contract	conclusion du marché *f*	conclusione d'acquisto *f*	convenio de compra *m*
Kaufanlaß (D)	—	buying motive	motif d'achat *m*	motivo d'acquisto *m*	motivo de compra *m*
Kauf auf Probe (D)	—	sale on approval	achat à l'éssai *m*	acquisto a titolo di prova *m*	compra a prueba *f*
Kaufbereitschaft (D)	—	buying intention	propension à l'achat *f*	propensione all'acquisto *f*	disposición a comprar *f*
kaufen (D)	—	buy	acheter	acquistare	comprar
Kaufentscheidung (D)	—	decision to purchase	décision d'acheter *f*	decisione d'acquisto *f*	decisión de compra *f*
Käufer (D)	—	purchaser	acheteur *m*	acquirente *m*	adquirente *m*
Käufermarkt (D)	—	buyer's market	marché d'acheteurs *m*	mercato favorevole all'acquirente *m*	mercado favorable al comprador *m*
Käuferprovision (D)	—	buyer's commission	commission d'acheteur *f*	provvigione dell'acquirente *f*	comisión al comprador *f*
Käuferstil (D)	—	style of the purchaser	style des acheteurs *m*	stile dell'acquirente *m*	estilo de compra *m*

	D	E	F	I	Es
Kaufhaus (D)	—	department store	grand magasin m	grande magazzino m	gran almacén m
Kaufkraft (D)	—	purchasing power	pouvoir d'achat m	potere d'acquisto m	poder adquisitivo m
Kaufkraftanalyse (D)	—	spending capacity analysis	analyse du pouvoir d'achat f	analisi del potere d'acquisto f	análisis del poder adquisitivo m
Kaufkraftänderung (D)	—	changes in the purchasing power	modification du pouvoir d'achat f	mutamento del potere d'acquisto m	cambio en el poder adquisitivo m
Kaufleute (D)	—	businessmen	commerçants m pl	commercianti m pl	comerciantes m pl
Kaufmann (D)	—	businessman	négociant m	commerciante m	comerciante m
kaufmännische Lehre (D)	—	commercial apprenticeship	apprentissage commercial m	apprendistato di commercio m	aprendizaje comercial m
Kaufpreis (D)	—	purchase price	prix d'achat m	prezzo d'acquisto m	precio de compra m
Kaufverhalten (D)	—	purchase pattern	comportement d'achat m	filosofia d'acquisto f	comportamiento de compra m
Kaufvertrag (D)	—	contract of sale	contrat de vente m	contratto di compravendita m	contrato de compraventa m
Kaution (D)	—	security/bond	caution f	cauzione f	caución f garantía f
keeping of an account (E)	Kontoführung f	—	tenue de compte f	tenuta di un conto f	administración de una cuenta f
Kennzahlen (D)	—	code numbers	numéros de référence m pl	numeri d'identificazione m pl	números índice m pl
Kennziffern (D)	—	code numbers	indice m	cifre d'identificazione f pl	cifras índice f pl
Kernenergie (D)	—	nuclear energy	énergie nucléaire f	energia nucleare f	energía nuclear f
keyboard (E)	Tastatur f	—	clavier m	tastiera f	teclado m
key currency (E)	Leitwährung f	—	monnaie-clé f	valuta guida f	moneda de referencia f
key rate (E)	Leitzins m	—	taux-clé d'intérêt bancaire	tasso d'interesse guida m	tipos de referencia m pl
key word (E)	Schlüsselwort n	—	mot-clé m	parola chiave f	palabra clave f
Kilometergeld (D)	—	allowance per kilometre	indemnité par kilomètre f	indennità per chilometro f	kilometraje m
kilometraje (Es)	Kilometergeld n	allowance per kilometre	indemnité par kilomètre f	indennità per chilometro f	—
Kiste (D)	—	box	caisse f	cassa f	caja f
kiteflying (E)	Wechselreiterei f	—	tirage d'une traite de cavalerie m	emissione di tratte incrociate f	libramiento de letras cruzadas m
Klage (D)	—	legal action	action en justice f	citazione in giudizio f	demanda f
Klausel (D)	—	clause	clause f	clausola f	cláusula f
Kleincontainer (D)	—	small container	petit conteneur m	mini container m	pequeño contenedor m
Kleinpalette (D)	—	small pallet	petite palette f	mini paletta f	pequeña paleta f
Klein- und Mittelbetriebe (D)	—	small and medium-sized enterprises	petites et moyennes entreprises f pl	piccole e medie imprese f pl	pequeñas y medianas empresas f pl
Klientel (D)	—	clientele	clients m pl	clientela f	clientela f
knapp (D)	—	scarce	rare	scarso	escaso
Knappheit (D)	—	shortage	rareté f	scarsità f	escasez f
know-how (E)	Sachkenntnis f	—	compétence f	competenza f	conocimiento de causa m
Koalitionsfreiheit (D)	—	freedom of association	liberté d'association f	libertà di coalizione f	libertad de coalición f
Kollektiv (D)	—	collective	collectif m	collettivo m	colectivo m
Kollektivgüter (D)	—	collective goods	biens collectifs m pl	beni collettivi m pl	bienes sociales m pl
Kollektivismus (D)	—	collectivism	collectivisme m	collettivismo m	colectivismo m
Kommanditgesellschaft (D)	—	limited partnership	société en commandite f	società in accomandita semplice f	sociedad comanditaria f
Kommanditgesellschaft auf Aktien (D)	—	partnership limited by shares	société en commandite par action f	società in accomandita per azioni f	sociedad comanditaria por acciones f
Kommanditist (D)	—	limited partner	commanditaire m	socio accomandante m	comanditario m
Kommerz (D)	—	commerce	commerce m	commercio m	comercio m
Kommission (D)	—	commission	commission f	commissione f	comisión f
Kommissionär (D)	—	commission agent	commissionnaire m	commissionario m	comisionista m

	D	E	F	I	Es
Kommissions-geschäft (D)	—	commission business	affaire en commission	operazione di commissione f	operación de comisión f
Kommissionsgüter (D)	—	goods for sale on commission	marchandises en commssion f pl	beni in conto deposito m pl	mercancías en comisión f pl
Kommissions-handel (D)	—	commission trade	commissionnage m	commercio di commissione m	comercio de comisión m
Kommunal-anleihen (D)	—	local authorities loan	emprunt communal m	prestiti comunali m pl	empréstito municipal m
Kommunal-obligation (D)	—	corporation stock	obligation communale f	obbligazioni comunali f pl	obligación comunal f
Kommune (D)	—	municipality	commune f	comune m	municipalidad f
Kompensation (D)	—	compensation	compensation f	compensazione f	compensación f
Kompensations-geschäft (D)	—	barter transaction	affaire de compensation f	operazione di compensazione f	operacion de compensación f
Kompetenz (D)	—	competence	compétence f	competenza f	competencia f
Komplementär (D)	—	general partner	commandité m	socio accomandatario m	socio colectivo m
komplementäre Güter (D)	—	complementary goods	produits de complément m pl	beni complementari m pl	bienes comple-mentarios m pl
Kondition (D)	—	condition	condition f	condizione f	condición f
Konferenz (D)	—	conference	conférence f	conferenza f	conferencia f
Konferenzraum (D)	—	conference room	salle de conférences f	sala conferenze f	sala de conferencia f
Konjunktur (D)	—	business cycle	conjoncture f	congiuntura f	conyuntura f
Konjunkturanalyse (D)	—	economic analysis	analyse de la conjoncture f	analisi congiunturale f	análisis de la si-tuación económica m
konjunkturanfällig (D)	—	depending on the cyclical trend	sensible aux oscilla-tions de la conjoncture	soggetto ad influssi congiunturali	sensible a las fluctua-ciones coyunturales
Konjunkturbelebung (D)	—	economic upturn	relance économique f	ripresa congiunturale f	recuperación coyuntural f
Konjunktur-entwicklung (D)	—	economic trend	évolution de la conjoncture f	sviluppo congiunturale m	evolución de la coyuntura f
Konjunkturpolitik (D)	—	economic policy	politique de conjoncture f	politica congiunturale f	política de coyuntura f
Konjunkturzyklus (D)	—	business cycle	cycle conjoncturel m	ciclo congiunturale m	ciclo económico m
Konkurrent (D)	—	competitor	concurrent m	concorrente m	competidor m
Konkurrenz (D)	—	competition	concurrence f	concorrenza f	competencia f
Konkurrenz-beobachtung (D)	—	observation of the competitors	observation de la concurrence f	studio della concorrenza m	observación de la competencia f
Konkurrenzfirma (D)	—	competing firm	maison concurrente f	ditta concorrente f	empresa competidora f
konkurrenzlos (D)	—	without competition	défiant toute concurrence	senza concorrenza	sin competencia
Konkurrenzsituation (D)	—	competitive situation	situation de concurrence f	situazione concorrenziale f	situación de competencia f
Konkurrenz-unternehmen (D)	—	competing undertaking	entreprise concurrente f	impresa concorrente f	empresa competitoria f
Konkurs (D)	—	bankruptcy	faillite f	fallimento m	quiebra f
Konkursantrag (D)	—	bankruptcy petition	demande en déclara-tion de faillite f	domanda di dichiara-zione del fallimento f	petición de quiebra f
Konkursgericht (D)	—	bankruptcy court	tribunal de la faillite m	tribunale fallimentare m	tribunal de quiebras m
Konkursgläubiger (D)	—	bankrupt's creditor	créancier de la faillite m	creditore della massa fallimentare m	acreedor de la quiebra m
Konkursmasse (D)	—	bankrupt's estate	masse de la faillite f	massa fallimentare f	masa de la quiebra f
Konkursordnung (D)	—	Bankruptcy Act	régime juridique de la faillite m	legge fallimentare f	ley de las quiebras f
Konkursverfahren (D)	—	proceedings in bankruptcy	procédure de faillite f	procedura fallimentare f	procedimiento de quiebra m
Konkursverwalter (D)	—	administrator in bank-ruptcy proceedings	liquidateur de la faillite m	curatore fallimentare m	síndico de quiebra m
Konnossement (D)	—	bill of lading	connaissement m	polizza di carico f	conocimiento m
konsolidierte Bilanz (D)	—	consolidated balance sheet	bilan consolidé m	bilancio consolidato m	balance consolidado m
Konsolidierung (D)	—	consolidation	consolidation f	consolidamento m	consolidación f

	D	E	F	I	Es
Konsortium (D)	—	consortium	consortium *m*	consorzio *m*	consorcio *m*
Konsul (D)	—	consul	consul *m*	console *m*	cónsul *m*
Konsulat (D)	—	consulate	consulat *m*	consolato *m*	consulado *m*
Konsum (D)	—	consumption	consommation *f*	consumo *m*	consumo *m*
Konsument (D)	—	consumer	consommateur *m*	consumatore *m*	consumidor *m*
Konsumenten-information (D)	—	consumer information	information des consommateurs *f*	informazione per i consumatori *f*	información a los comsumidores *f*
Konsum-finanzierung (D)	—	financing consumption	financement de la vente à crédit *m*	finanziamento del consumo *m*	financiación del consumo *f*
Konsumfreiheit (D)	—	freedom of consumption	liberté de consommation *f*	libertà di consumo *f*	libertad de consumo *f*
Konsumgüter (D)	—	consumer goods	biens de consommation *m pl*	beni di consumo *m pl*	bienes de consumo *m pl*
Konsumgüter-industrie (D)	—	consumer goods industry	industrie des biens de consommation *f*	industria dei beni di consumo *f*	industria de bienes de consumo *f*
konsumieren (D)	—	consume	consommer	consumare	consumir
Konsumkredit (D)	—	consumer credit	crédit à la consommation *m*	credito al consumatore *m*	crédito de consumo *m*
Konsumstruktur (D)	—	consumption structure	structure de la consommation	struttura del consumo *f*	estructura del consumo *f*
Konsumverzicht (D)	—	voluntary constraint in consumption	renonciation à la consommation *f*	rinuncia al consumo *f*	renuncia al consumo *f*
Kontaktfähigkeit (D)		capability to establish public relations	capacité d'entrer en contact *f*	comunicativa *f*	capacidad de anudar contactos *f*
Kontamination (D)	—	contamination	contamination *f*	contaminazione *f*	contaminación *f*
Kontingent (D)	—	quota	contingent *m*	contingente *m*	contingente *m*
Kontingentierung (D)	—	fixing of a quota	contingentement *m*	contingentamento *m*	contingentación *f*
Konto (D)	—	account	compte *m*	conto *m*	cuenta *f*
Kontoausgleich (D)	—	settlement of an account	solde de compte *m*	liquidazione del conto *f*	saldo de cuenta *m*
Kontoauszug (D)	—	statement of account	extrait de compte *m*	estratto conto *m*	extracto de cuenta *m*
Kontobuch (D)	—	account book	livre de compte *m*	libro dei conti *m*	libro de cuentas *m*
Kontoeröffnung (D)	—	opening of an account	ouverture de compte *f*	apertura di un conto *f*	apertura de una cuenta *f*
Kontoführung (D)	—	keeping of an account	tenue de compte *f*	tenuta di un conto *f*	administración de una cuenta *f*
Kontogebühren (D)	—	bank charges	frais de tenue de compte *m pl*	diritti di conto *m pl*	gastos de administración de una cuenta *m pl*
Kontoinhaber (D)	—	account holder	titulaire d'un compte *m*	titolare del conto *m*	titular de una cuenta *f*
Kontokorrent (D)	—	account current	compte courant *m*	conto corrente *m*	cuenta corriente *f*
Kontokorrentkonto (D)	—	current account	compte tenu en compte courant *m*	conto corrente *m*	cuenta corriente *f*
Kontokorrentkredit (D)	—	current account credit	crédit en compte courant *m*	credito in conto corrente *m*	crédito en cuenta corriente *m*
Kontonummer (D)	—	account number	numéro de compte *m*	numero di conto *m*	número de cuenta *m*
Kontoüberziehung (D)	—	overdraft of an account	découvert d'un compte *m*	scoperto di conto *m*	descubierto *m*
Kontrakt (D)	—	contract	contrat *m*	contratto *m*	contrato *m*
Kontrolle (D)	—	control	contrôle *m*	controllo *m*	control *m*
Konventionalstrafe (D)	—	contractual penalty	pénalité *f*	penalità convenzionale *f*	pena convencional *f*
konvertibel (D)	—	convertible	convertible	convertibile	convertible
Konvertibilität (D)	—	convertibility	convertibilité *f*	convertibilità *f*	convertibilidad *f*
Konzentration (D)	—	concentration	concentration *f*	concentrazione *f*	concentración *f*
Konzept (D)	—	concept	brouillon *m*	piano *m*	bosquejo *m*
Konzeption (D)	—	conception	conception *f*	concezione *f*	concepción *f*
konzeptionelles Denken (D)	—	conceptional thinking	penser conceptionnel *m*	mentalità concezionale *f*	pensar concepcional *m*
Konzern (D)	—	group/combine	groupe industriel *m*	gruppo *m*	consorcio *m*

	D	E	F	I	Es
Konzernbilanz (D)	—	balance sheet of a group	bilan consolidé d'un groupement de sociétés *m*	bilancio del gruppo *m*	balance del consorcio *m*
Konzession (D)	—	licence	concession *f*	concessione *f*	concesión *f*
Kooperation (D)	—	cooperation	coopération *f*	cooperazione *f*	cooperación *f*
kooperativ (D)	—	cooperative	coopératif	cooperativo	cooperativo
Koordination (D)	—	coordination	coordination *f*	coordinazione *f*	coordinación *f*
Kopie (D)	—	copy	copie *f*	copia *f*	copia *f*
Koppelproduktion (D)	—	tied production	production couplée *f*	produzione abbinata *f*	coproducción *f*
Kopplungsgeschäft (D)	—	tie-in transaction	affaire couplée *f*	operazione abbinata *f*	negocio acoplado *m*
Körperschaft (D)	—	corporation	collectivité *f*	ente *m*	corporación *f*
Körperschaftsteuer (D)	—	corporation tax	taxe sur les sociétés *f*	imposta sul reddito delle società *f*	impuesto de corporaciones *m*
Korrelation (D)	—	correlation	corrélation *f*	correlazione *f*	correlación *f*
korrigieren (D)	—	correct	corriger	correggere	corrigir
Kosten (D)	—	costs	coût *m*	costi *m pl*	gastos *m pl*
Kostenarten (D)	—	cost types	coûts par nature *m pl*	tipi di costi *m pl*	clases de costes *f pl*
Kostendämpfung (D)	—	combatting rising costs	réduction des coûts *f*	contenimento dei costi *m*	disminución de costes *f*
Kostendegression (D)	—	cost degression	dégressivité des coûts *f*	riduzione dei costi *f*	reducción de costes *f*
Kostenexplosion (D)	—	cost escalation	explosion des coûts *f*	esplosione dei costi *f*	incremento desmesurado de los costes *m*
kostenlos (D)	—	free of charge	gratuit	gratuito	libre de gastos
Kostenminimierung (D)	—	minimization of costs	minimalisation des coûts *f*	diminuzione dei costi *f*	minimación de gastos *f*
Kosten-Nutzen-Analyse (D)	—	cost-benefit analysis	analyse du ratio coût à profit *f*	analisi costi-benefici *f*	análisis de coste-beneficio *m*
Kostenplan (D)	—	cost schedule	planning des coûts *m*	piano dei costi *m*	planilla de costas *f*
Kostenrechnungs-system (D)	—	cost accounting system	méthode de calcul des coûts *f*	sistema dei costi *m*	sistema de costes *m*
Kostensenkung (D)	—	cost reduction	diminution des coûts *f*	ribasso dei costi *m*	reducción de coste
Kostenstelle (D)	—	departmental expense account	compte de frais par secteurs *m*	posizione costi *f*	posición de costes *f*
Kostenträger (D)	—	unit assuming costs	poste de production absorbant des coûts *m*	chi si assume i costi	que sufraga los costes
Kostenverrechnung (D)	—	cost allocation	répartition des frais *f*	repartizione dei costi *f*	repartición de costes *f*
Kostenvoranschlag (D)	—	estimate of cost	devis estimatif des frais *m*	preventivo dei costi *m*	presupuesto de coste *m*
Kostenvorteil (D)	—	cost advantage	avantage de coût *m*	vantaggio di costo *m*	ventaja de costes *f*
Kraftfahrzeug (D)	—	motor vehicle	véhicule à moteur *m*	automobile *f*	automóvil *m*
Kraftfahrzeugsteuer (D)	—	motor vehicle tax	taxe sur les véhicules à moteur *f*	imposta sulla circolazione degli autoveicoli *f*	impuesto sobre vehículos *m*
Kraftfahrzeug-versicherung (D)	—	motor insurance	assurance responsa-bilité civile automobile *f*	assicurazione autoveicoli *f*	seguro de automóviles *m*
Kranken-versicherung (D)	—	health insurance	assurance maladie *f*	assicurazione contro le malattie *f*	seguro de enfermedad *m*
kreativ (D)	—	creative	créatif	creativo	creativo
kreatives Denken (D)	—	creative thinking	créativité conceptionnelle *f*	mentalità creativa *f*	creatividad concepcional *f*
Kredit (D)	—	credit	crédit *m*	credito *m*	crédito *m*
Kreditbank (D)	—	commercial bank	banque de crédit *f*	banca di credito *f*	banco de crédito *m*
Kreditbeschaffungs-kosten (D)	—	cost of borrowing	coûts d'obtention de crédits *m pl*	spese d'approvvi-gionamento di credito *f pl*	costes de apelación al crédito *m pl*
Kreditbrief (D)	—	letter of credit	lettre de crédit *f*	lettera di credito *f*	carta de crédito *f*
Kreditfähigkeit (D)	—	financial standing	solvabilité *f*	capacità di credito *f*	crédito *m*
Kreditgeschäft (D)	—	credit business	achat à crédit *m*	operazione di credito *f*	operaciones de crédito *f pl*

	D	E	F	I	Es
Kreditinstitut (D)	—	credit institution	établissement de crédit *m*	istituto di credito *m*	instituto de crédito *m*
Kreditkarte (D)	—	credit card	carte accréditive *f*	carta di credito *f*	tarjeta de crédito *f*
Kreditkauf (D)	—	credit purchase	achat à crédit *m*	acquisto a credito *m*	compra de crédito *f*
Kreditlaufzeit (D)	—	duration of credit	durée de l'allocation de crédit *f*	scadenza del credito *f*	período concesional de un crédito *m*
Kreditlimit (D)	—	borrowing limit	plafond du crédit alloué *m*	limite di credito *m*	límite de crédito *m*
Kreditlinie (D)	—	credit line	plafond du crédit accordé *m*	linea creditizia *f*	línea de crédito *f*
Kreditnehmer (D)	—	borrower	bénéficiaire d'un crédit *m*	beneficiario del credito *m*	prestatario *m*
Kreditor (D)	—	creditor	créditeur *m*	creditore *m*	acreedor *m*
Kreditpolitik (D)	—	credit policy	politique favorisant le crédit *f*	politica creditizia *f*	política de crédito *f*
Kreditprovision (D)	—	credit commission	frais de commissions d'ouverture de crédit *m pl*	provvigione di credito *f*	comisión de apertura de crédito *f*
Kreditrahmen (D)	—	credit margin	marge de crédit accordé *f*	plafond di credito *m*	margen de crédito *m*
Kreditrestriktion (D)	—	credit restriction	restriction du crédit *f*	restrizione creditizia *f*	restricción de créditos *f*
Kreditvermittlung (D)	—	arranging for a credit	médiation du crédit *f*	intermediazione di crediti *f*	mediación de créditos *f*
Kreditversicherung (D)	—	credit insurance	assurance crédit *f*	assicurazione dei crediti *f*	seguro crediticio *m*
kreditwürdig (D)	—	creditworthy	solvable	degno di credito	solvente
Kreditwürdigkeit (D)	—	creditworthiness	solvabilité *f*	essere degno di credito	crédito *m*
Kreditzusage (D)	—	promise of credit	promesse de crédit *f*	consenso di credito *m*	promesa de créditos *f*
Krise (D)	—	crisis	crise *f*	crisi *f*	crisis *f*
krisenfest (D)	—	slump-proof	insensible aux influences de la crise économique	resistente alle crisi	a prueba de crisis
Kühlwagen (D)	—	cold storage lorry	wagon frigorifique *m*	vagone frigorifero *m*	vagón frigorífico *m*
kulant (D)	—	accommodating	arrangeant	corrente	de fácil avenencia
Kulanz (D)	—	accommodation	souplesse en affaires *f*	correntezza *f*	facilidad en los negocios *f*
kündbar (D)	—	redeemable/callable	résiliable/ remboursable	risolubile/redimibile	revocable/rescindible
Kunde (D)	—	customer	client *m*	cliente *m*	cliente *m*
Kundenbefragung (D)	—	customer survey	enquête parmi les clients *f*	intervista ai clienti *f*	encuesta entre los clientes *f*
Kundendienst (D)	—	after-sales service	service après vente *m*	servizio d'assistenza *m*	servicio posventa *m*
Kundendienst-organisation (D)	—	service organization	organisation du service après vente *f*	organizzazione del servizio d'assistenza *f*	organización de servicio posventa *f*
Kundenkreis (D)	—	clientele	clientèle *f*	clientela *f*	clientela *f*
Kundennummer (D)	—	customer's reference number	numéro de référence du client *m*	numero di cliente *m*	número del cliente *m*
Kundenstamm (D)	—	regular customers	clients en portefeuille *m pl*	clientela fissa *f*	clientela fija *f*
Kundenzeitschrift (D)	—	customer magazine	journal destiné à la clientèle *m*	periodico per i clienti *m*	revista para los clientes *f*
kündigen (D)	—	terminate	résilier	disdire	denunciar/dar aviso de despido
Kündigung (D)	—	notice of termination	résiliation *f*	disdetta *f*	rescisión *f*
Kündigungsfrist (D)	—	period of notice	délai de préavis *m*	termine di preavviso la disdetta *m*	plazo de preaviso *m*
Kündigungsschutz (D)	—	protection against dismissal	protection en matière de licenciement *f*	protezione contro il licenziamento *f*	protección contra el despido *f*
Kündigungsschutz-gesetz (D)	—	Termination of Employment Act	loi sur le délai-congé en matière de licenciement *f*	legge sulla tutela contro il licenziamento *f*	ley de protección contra el despido *f*

	D	E	F	I	Es
Kundschaft (D)	—	clientele	clientèle *f*	clientela *f*	clientela *f*
Kurs (D)	—	exchange rate	cours (du change) *m*	corso *m*/cambio *m*	cotización *f*/tipo de cambio *m*
Kursfestsetzung (D)	—	fixing of prices	détermination des cours *f*	fissazione dei corsi *f*	fijación de los cambios *f*
Kurs-Gewinn-Verhältnis (D)	—	price-earnings ratio	relation cours-bénéfice *f*	rapporto corso-profitto *m*	relación cotización-ganancia *f*
Kursmakler (D)	—	stock broker/ exchange broker	courtier en bourse *m*	agente di borsa *m*	agente cambio y bolsa *m*/corredor de cambios *m*
Kursnotierung (D)	—	quotation of prices	cotation *f*	quotazione dei corsi *f*	cotización *m*
Kurspflege (D)	—	price nursing	soutien des cours *m*	sostegno dei corsi *m*	compras de sostén *f pl*
Kursrisiko (D)	—	price risk	risque de change *m*	rischio di cambio *m*	riesgo de cambio *m*
Kurssteigerung (D)	—	price advance	hausse *f*	aumento dei corsi *m*	alza de las cotizaciones *f*
Kursstützung (D)	—	price support	soutiens des cours *m*	difesa dei corsi *f*	sostén de las cotizaciones *m*
Kursvergleich (D)	—	comparison of prices	comparaison des cours *f*	confronto dei corsi *m*	comparación de las cotizaciones *f*
Kursverlust (D)	—	loss in exchange	perte sur les cours *f*	perdita sul cambio *f*	pérdida en bolsa *f*
Kurszettel (D)	—	stock exchange list	bulletin des cours *m*	listino di borsa *m*	boletín de bolsa *m*
Kurszusammen-bruch (D)	—	collapse of prices	chute des cours *f*	crollo delle quotazioni *m*	caída de los cambios *f*
Kurzarbeit (D)	—	short-time work	travail à temps réduit *m*	lavoro ad orario ridotto *m*	trabajo reducido *m*
kurzfristig (D)	—	short-term	à court terme	a breve scadenza	a corto plazo
kurzfristiger Kredit (D)	—	short-term credit	crédit à court terme *m*	credito a breve scadenza *m*	crédito a corto plazo *m*
Küstengewässer (D)	—	coastal waters	eaux côtières *f pl*	acque territoriali *f pl*	zona costera *f*
Kuvert (D)	—	envelope	enveloppe *f*	busta *f*	sobre *m*
Kybernetik (D)	—	cybernetics	cybernétique *f*	cibernetica *f*	cibernética *f*
label (E)	Etikett *n*	—	étiquette *f*	etichetta *f*	etiqueta *f*
labour-intensive (E)	arbeitsintensiv	—	déterminé par le facteur main-d'œuvre	ad alta incidenza di lavoro	con gran intensidad de mano de obra
labour law (E)	Arbeitsrecht *n*	—	législation industrielle *f*	diritto di lavoro *m*	derecho laboral *m*
labour market (E)	Arbeitsmarkt *m*	—	marché du travail *m*	mercato del lavoro *m*	mercado laboral *m*
lacuna di mercato (I)	Marktlücke *f*	market gap	créneau du marché *m*	—	sector del mercado no abarcado por la oferta *m*
Ladegebühren (D)	—	loading charges	taxe de chargement *f*	spese di carico *f pl*	derechos de carga *m pl*
Ladenpreis (D)	—	retail price	prix de vente *m*	prezzo di vendita *m*	precio de venta *m*
Ladeschein (D)	—	bill of lading	avis de chargement *m*	bolletta di carico *f*	póliza de carga *f*
Ladung (D)	—	freight	charge *f*	carico *m*	carga *f*
Lager (D)	—	warehouse	magasin *m*	magazzino *m*	almacén *m*
Lagerhaltung (D)	—	stockkeeping	entreposage *m*	magazzinaggio *m*	almacenaje *m*
Lagerkapazität (D)	—	storage capacity	capacité de stockage *f*	capacità di magazzino *f*	capacidad de almacenaje *f*
Lagermiete (D)	—	warehouse rent	location d'une surface pour magasinage *f*	spese di magazzinaggio *f pl*	alquiler de almacén *m*
Lagerraum (D)	—	storage space	halle de dépôt *f*	magazzino *m*	almacén *m*
Lagerschein (D)	—	warehouse warrant	certificat de dépot *m*	ricevuta di deposito *f*	resguardo de almacén *m*
Lagerung (D)	—	storage	stockage *m*	magazzinaggio *m*	almacenaje *m*
Lagerverwaltung (D)	—	stockkeeping	entreposage *m*	amministrazione del magazzino *f*	administración de almacén *f*
Lagerzyklus (D)	—	stock cycle	cycle de stockage *m*	ciclo di magazzinaggio *m*	período de almacenaje *m*
lag salariale (I)	Lohnlag *m*	wage lag	décalage entre les prix et les salaires *m*	—	diferencial entre precios y salarios *m*
lanciare sul mercato (I)	vermarkten	market	commercialiser	—	comercializar
land policy (E)	Bodenpolitik *f*	—	politique de la terre *f*	politica del suolo *f*	política de suelo *f*

	D	E	F	I	Es
land price (E)	Bodenpreis *m*	—	prix du terrain *m*	prezzo del suolo *m*	precio de suelo *m*
land reform (E)	Bodenreform *f*	—	réforme agraire *f*	riforma agraria *f*	reforma agraria *f*
Landweg (D)	—	overland transportation	voie de terre *f*	via terra *f*	vía terrestre *m*
Landwirtschafts-ministerium (D)	—	Ministry of Agriculture	ministère de l'agriculture *m*	ministero dell'agricoltura *m*	minsterio de Agricultura, Pesca y Alimentación *m*
langage de programmation (F)	Programmier-sprache *f*	common business-oriented language	—	linguaggio di programmazione *m*	lenguaje de programación *m*
langfristig (D)	—	long-term	à long terme	a lunga scadenza	a largo plazo
langfristiger Kredit (D)	—	long-term credit	crédit à long terme *m*	credito a lunga scadenza *m*	crédito a largo plazo *m*
langfristiges Kapital (D)	—	long-term capital	capital à long terme *m*	capitale a lungo termine *m*	capital a largo plazo *m*
large container (E)	Großcontainer *m*	—	conteneur à grand volume *m*	container di grande dimensione *m*	gran contenedor *m*
large-scale operation (E)	Großbetrieb *m*	—	grande exploitation *f*	azienda di grande dimensione *f*	gran explotación *f*
large-scale order (E)	Großauftrag *m*	—	grosse commande *f*	ordine di grandi quantità *m*	importante pedido *m*
Lärmbekämpfung (D)	—	noise abatement	lutte contre le bruit *f*	lotta contro i rumori *f*	lucha contra el ruido *f*
Laserdrucker (D)	—	laser printer	imprimante au laser *f*	stampante laser *f*	impresora laser *m*
laser printer (E)	Laserdrucker *m*	—	imprimante au laser *f*	stampante laser *f*	impresora laser *m*
Lastschrift (D)	—	debit note	note de débit *f*	addebito *m*	cargo en cuenta *m*
last will (E)	Testament *n*	—	testament *m*	testamento *m*	testamento *m*
latent funds (E)	stille Rücklage *f*	—	réserve cachée *f*	riserva latente *m*	reserva tácita *f*
laufende Rechnung (D)	—	current account	compte courant *m*	conto corrente *m*	cuenta corriente *f*
Laufzeit (D)	—	term	durée *f*	scadenza *f*/durata *f*	plazo de vencimiento *m*
lavabo (Es)	Toilette *f*	toilet	toilettes *f pl*	toilette *f*	—
lavora a cottimo (I)	Akkordarbeit *f*	piecework	travail à la tâche *m*	—	trabajo a destajo *m*
lavorazione (I)	Verarbeitung *f*	processing	transformation *f*	—	transformación *f*
lavoro (I)	Arbeit *f*	work	travail *m*	—	trabajo *m*
lavoro abusivo (I)	Schwarzarbeit *f*	illicit work	travail noir *m*	—	trabajo clandestino *m*
lavoro a domicilio (I)	Heimarbeit *f*	homework	travail à domicile *m*	—	trabajo a domicilio *m*
lavoro ad orario ridotto (I)	Kurzarbeit *f*	short-time work	travail à temps réduit *m*	—	trabajo reducido *m*
lavoro d'équipe (I)	Teamarbeit *f*	team work	travail d'équipe *m*	—	trabajo en equipo *m*
lavoro domenicale (I)	Sonntagsarbeit *f*	Sunday work	travail du dimanche *m*	—	trabajo dominical *m*
lavoro manuale (I)	Handarbeit *f*	handwork	travail manuel *m*	—	trabajo a mano *m*
lavoro part-time (I)	Teilzeitarbeit *f*	part-time work	travail à temps partiel *m*	—	trabajo a tiempo parcial *m*
lavoro supplementare (I)	Mehrarbeit *f*	additional work	travail supplémentaire *m*	extraordinario *m*	trabajo
lavoro video (I)	Bildschirmarbeit *f*	screen work	travail à l'écran *m*	—	trabajo de pantalla *m*
law¹ (E)	Recht *n*	—	droit *m*	diritto *m*	derecho *m*
law² (E)	Gesetz *n*	—	loi *f*	legge *f*	ley *f*
Law on Collective Agreements (E)	Tarifvertragsgesetz *n*	—	loi réglant les conventions collectives *f*	legge sui contratti salariali *f pl*	ley de convenios colectivos *f*
law on competition (E)	Wettbewerbsrecht *n*	—	législation en matière de concurrence commerciale *f*	diritto della concorrenza *m*	derecho de la competencia *m*
lawyer¹ (E)	Anwalt *m*	—	avocat *m*	avvocato *m*	abogado *m*
lawyer² (E)	Rechtsanwalt *m*	—	avocat *m*	avvocato *m*	abogado *m*
lawyer's office (E)	Anwaltskanzlei *f*	—	cabinet d'avocat *m*	studio d'avvocato *m*	bufete de abogado *m*
lay days (E)	Liegetage *pl*	—	staries *f pl*	stallie *f pl*	estadías *f pl*
Layout (D)	—	layout	maquette *f*	layout *m*	layout *m*
layout (E)	Layout *n*	—	maquette *f*	layout *m*	layout *m*
layout (Es)	Layout *n*	layout	maquette *f*	layout *m*	—
layout (I)	Layout *n*	layout	maquette *f*	—	layout *m*

	D	E	F	I	Es
lay-out of an advertisement (E)	Anzeigengestaltung f	—	arrangement de l'annonce m	tipo d'inserzione m	estructuración del anuncio f
leader (E)	Anführer m	—	chef m	leader m	líder m
leader (I)	Anführer m	leader	chef m	—	líder m
leader en matière de prix (F)	Preisführerschaft f	price leadership	—	leader in materia di prezzi m	precio hegemónico m
leader in materia di prezzi (I)	Preisführerschaft f	price leadership	leader en matière de prix m	—	precio hegemónico m
leaflet (E)	Prospekt m	—	feuille publicitaire f/ prospectus m	prospetto m/ dépliant m	prospecto m/ folleto m
Leasing (D)	—	leasing	crédit-bail m	leasing m	leasing m
leasing (E)	Leasing n	—	crédit-bail m	leasing m	leasing m
leasing (Es)	Leasing n	leasing	crédit-bail m	leasing m	—
leasing (I)	Leasing n	leasing	crédit-bail m	—	leasing m
leasing company (E)	Leasing-Gesellschaft f	—	société de leasing f	società di leasing f	sociedad de leasing f
leasing contract (E)	Leasing-Vertrag m	—	contrat de leasing m	contratto leasing m	contrato de arrendamiento financiero m
leasing de biens immobiliers (F)	Immobilien-Leasing n	leasing of real estate	—	leasing immobiliare m	leasing de inmuebles m
leasing de inmuebles (Es)	Immobilien-Leasing n	leasing of real estate	leasing de biens immobiliers m	leasing immobiliare m	leasing de inmuebles m
leasing de personal (Es)	Personal-Leasing n	personnel leasing	leasing de personnel m	leasing di personale m	—
leasing de personnel (F)	Personal-Leasing n	personnel leasing	—	leasing di personale m	leasing de personal m
leasing di personale (I)	Personal-Leasing n	personnel leasing	leasing de personnel m	—	leasing de personal m
Leasing-Geber (D)	—	lessor	donneur de leasing m	concedente del leasing m	arrendatario financiero m
Leasing-Gesellschaft (D)	—	leasing company	société de leasing f	società di leasing f	sociedad de leasing f
leasing immobiliare (I)	Immobilien-Leasing n	leasing of real estate	leasing de biens immobiliers m	—	leasing de inmuebles m
Leasing-Nehmer (D)	—	lessee	preneur de leasing m	utente del leasing m	arrendatante financiero m
leasing object (E)	Leasing-Objekt n	—	objet de leasing m	oggetto del leasing m	objeto de leasing m
Leasing-Objekt (D)	—	leasing object	objet de leasing m	oggetto del leasing m	objeto de leasing m
leasing of real estate (E)	Immobilien-Leasing n	—	leasing de biens immobiliers m	leasing immobiliare m	leasing de inmuebles m
leasing payment (E)	Leasing-Rate f	—	taux de leasing m	rata leasing f	plazo de arrendamiento financiero m
Leasing-Rate (D)	—	leasing payment	taux de leasing m	rata leasing f	plazo de arrendamiento financiero m
Leasing-Vertrag (D)	—	leasing contract	contrat de leasing m	contratto leasing m	contrato de arrendamiento financiero m
Lebenserwartung (D)	—	expectation of life	espérance de vie f	durata probabile della vita f	expectativa de vida f
Lebenslauf (D)	—	curriculum vitae	curriculum vitae m	curriculum vitae m	curriculum vitae m
Lebensqualität (D)	—	quality of life	qualité de la vie f	qualità di vita f	calidad de vida m
Lebensstandard (D)	—	standard of living	niveau de vie m	tenore di vita m	nivel de vida m
Lebens- versicherung (D)	—	life insurance	assurance vie f	assicurazione sulla vita f	seguro de vida m
Lebenszyklus (D)	—	life cycle	cycle de vie m	ciclo di vita m	ciclo de vida m
Leerverkauf (D)	—	bear sale	vente à découvert f	vendita allo scoperto f	venta al descubierto f
legal action[1] (E)	Rechtsstreit m	—	litige m	causa f	conflicto jurídico m
legal action[2] (E)	Klage f	—	action en justice f	citazione in giudizio f	demanda f
legal adviser (E)	Syndikus	—	syndic m	consulente legale m	síndico m
legal capacity (E)	Rechtsfähigkeit f	—	capacité de jouissance des droits f	capacità giuridica f	capacidad jurídica f
legal claim (E)	Rechtsanspruch m	—	titre m	pretesa giuridica f	pretensión legal f
legal costs (E)	Gerichtskosten pl	—	frais judiciaires taxables exposés m pl	spese giudiziarie f pl	gastos judiciales m pl
legal department (E)	Rechtsabteilung f	—	bureau juridique m	ufficio legale m	sección jurídica f

	D	E	F	I	Es
legal form (E)	Rechtsform f	—	forme juridique f	forma giuridica f	forma jurídica f
legalización (Es)	Beglaubigung f	authentication	certification f	autenticazione f	—
legal norm (E)	Rechtsnorm f	—	règle de droit f	norma giuridica f	norma jurídica f
legal person (E)	juristische Person f	—	personne juridique f	persona giuridica f	persona jurídica f
legal relationship (E)	Rechtsverhältnis n	—	rapport juridique m	rapporto giuridico m	relación jurídica f
legal responsibility (E)	Rechtshaftung f	—	responsabilité légale f	responsabilità giuridica f	responsabilidad jurídica f
legal situation (E)	Rechtslage f	—	situation juridique f	situazione giuridica f	situación jurídica f
legal tender (E)	gesetzliches Zahlungsmittel n	—	monnaie légale f	mezzo di pagamento legale m	medio legal de pago m
legal transaction (E)	Rechtsgeschäft n	—	acte juridique m	negozio giuridico m	negocio jurídico m
legge (I)	Gesetz n	law	loi f	—	ley f
legge fallimentare (I)	Konkursordnung f	Bankruptcy Act	régime juridique de la faillite m	—	ley de las quiebras f
legge sui cartelli (I)	Kartellgesetz n	Cartel Law	loi sur les cartels f	—	ley relativa a los cártels f
legge sulla tutela contro il licenziamento (I)	Kündigungs-schutzgesetz n	Termination of Employment Act	loi sur le délai-congé en matière de licenciement f	—	ley de protección contra el despido f
legge sulla tutela dei dati (I)	Datenschutzgesetz n	Data Protection Act	loi sur l'informatique f	—	ley de protección de datos f
legge sulle società per azioni (I)	Aktiengesetz n	Companies Act	loi sur les sociétés par actions f	—	ley sobre sociedades anónimas f
législation économique (F)	Wirtschaftsrecht n	economic law	—	diritto economico m	derecho económico m
législation en matière de concurrence commerciale (F)	Wettbewerbsrecht n	law on competition	—	diritto della concorrenza m	derecho de la competencia m
législation industrielle (F)	Arbeitsrecht n	labour law	—	diritto di lavoro m	derecho laboral m
legislative sovereignty (E)	Gesetzgebungs-hoheit f	—	compétence législative f	sovranità legislativa f	soberanía legislativa f
Leihwagen (D)	—	hired car	voiture de location f	vettura da noleggio f	coche de alquiler m
Leistung (D)	—	performance	rendement m	rendimento m	rendimiento m
Leistungsbilanz (D)	—	balance of goods and services	balance des opéra-tions courantes f	bilancia delle partite correnti f	balanza por cuenta corriente f
Leistungsfähigkeit (D)	—	efficiency	efficience f	efficienza f	capacidad productiva f
Leistungslohn (D)	—	payment by result	salaire au rendement m	salario a rendimento m	salario por rendimiento m
leistungsorientiert (D)	—	performance-oriented	orienté vers le rendement	orientato al rendimento	orientado hacia el rendimiento
Leistungssteigerung (D)	—	increase in efficiency	amélioration du rendement f	aumento della produttività m	incremento del rendimiento m
Leitkurs (D)	—	central rate	taux central m	parità centrale f	tipo pivote m
Leitung (D)	—	management	direction f	direzione f	dirección f
Leitwährung (D)	—	key currency	monnaie-clé f	valuta guida f	moneda de referencia f
Leitzins (D)	—	key rate	taux-clé d'intérêt bancaire	tasso d'interesse guida m	tipos de referencia m pl
lending on securities (E)	Lombardgeschäft n	—	prêt sur gage m	anticipazioni f pl	operaciones de pignoración f pl
lenguaje de programación (Es)	Programmier-sprache f	common business-oriented language	langage de programmation m	linguaggio di programmazione m	—
le plus vite possible (F)	schnellstmöglich	as quickly as possible	—	al più presto possibile	tan rápido como sea posible
lessee (E)	Leasing-Nehmer m	—	preneur de leasing m	utente del leasing m	arrendatante financiero m
lessor (E)	Leasing-Geber m	—	donneur de leasing m	concedente del leasing m	arrendatario financiero m
letra comercial (Es)	Warenwechsel m	commercial bill	traite commerciale f	cambiale commerciale f	—
letra con valor declarado (Es)	Wertbrief m	insured letter	lettre avec valeur déclarée f	lettera con valore dichiarato m	—
letra de cambio (Es)	Wechsel m	bill of exchange	lettre de change f	cambiale f	

	D	E	F	I	Es
letra domiciliada (Es)	Domizilwechsel *m*	domiciliary bill	effet domicilier *m*	cambiale domiciliata *f*	—
letra sobre el exterior (Es)	Auslandswechsel *n*	foreign bill of exchange	traite tirée sur l'étranger *f*	cambiale estera *f*	—
letrero de establecimiento (Es)	Firmenschild *n*	company's name plate	enseigne commerciale *f*	insegna dell'impresa *f*	—
letter (E)	Brief *m*	—	lettre *f*	lettera *f*	carta *f*
lettera (I)	Brief *m*	letter	lettre *f*	—	carta *f*
lettera con valore dichiarato (I)	Wertbrief *m*	insured letter	lettre avec valeur déclarée *f*	—	letra con valor declarado *f*
lettera di conferma (I)	Schlußbrief *m*	fixing letter	lettre de confirmation des conditions *f*	—	carta de confirmación *f*
lettera di credito commerciale (I)	Handelskreditbrief *m*	commercial letter of credit	lettre de crédit commercial *f*	—	carta de crédito comercial *f*
lettera di credito¹ (I)	Bankakkreditiv *n*	bank letter of credit	accréditif bancaire *m*	—	carta de crédito bancaria *f*
lettera di credito² (I)	Kreditbrief *m*	letter of credit	lettre de crédit *f*	—	carta de crédito *f*
lettera di raccomandazione (I)	Empfehlungs-schreiben *n*	letter of recommendation	lettre de recommandation *f*	—	carta de recomendación *f*
lettera di ringraziamento (I)	Dankschreiben *n*	letter of thanks	lettre de remerciement *f*	—	carta de agradecimiento *f*
lettera di sollecito (I)	Mahnbrief *m*	reminder	lettre d'avertissement *f*	—	carta (ad)monitoria *f*
lettera di trasporto aereo (I)	Luftfrachtbrief *m*	air waybill	lettre de transport aérien *f*	—	transporte aéreo *m*
lettera di vettura (I)	Frachtbrief *m*	consignment note	lettre de voiture *f*	—	carta de porte *f*
lettera espresso (I)	Eilbrief *m*	express letter	lettre par exprès *f*	—	carta urgente *f*
lettera pubblicitaria (I)	Werbebrief *m*	advertising letter	lettre publicitaire *f*	—	circular de publicidad *m*
lettera raccomandata (I)	Einschreibebrief *m*	registered letter	lettre recommandée *f*	—	carta certificada *f*
lettera raccomandata con ricevuta di ritorno (I)	Einschreiben-Rückschein *m*	recorded delivery letter with advice	lettre recommandée avec avis de réception *f*	—	carta certificada con talón de recibo *f*
letterhead (E)	Briefkopf *m*	—	en-tête *m*	intestazione *f*	encabezamiento *m*
letter of application (E)	Bewerbungs-schreiben *n*	—	lettre de demande d'emploi *f*	domanda d'impiego *f*	carta de solicitud *f*
letter of confirmation (E)	Schlußbrief *m*	—	lettre de confirmation des conditions *f*	lettera di conferma *f*	carta de confirmación *f*
letter of credit¹ (E)	Kreditbrief *m*	—	lettre de crédit *f*	lettera di credito *f*	carta de crédito *f*
letter of credit² (E)	Akkreditiv *n*	—	accréditif *m*	credito documentario *m*	crédito documentario *m*
letter of credit clause (E)	Akkreditivklausel *f*	—	clause de payement par accréditif *f*	clausola del credito documentario *f*	cláusula de crédito documentario *f*
letter of recommendation (E)	Empfehlungs-schreiben *n*	—	lettre de recommandation *f*	lettera di raccomandazione *f*	carta de recomendación *f*
letter of thanks (E)	Dankschreiben *n*	—	lettre de remerciement *f*	lettera di ringraziamento *f*	carta de agradecimiento *f*
letter scales (E)	Briefwaage *f*	—	pèse-lettres *m*	bilancia per corrispondenza *f*	pesacartas *m*
lettre (F)	Brief *m*	letter	—	lettera *f*	carta *f*
lettre avec valeur déclarée (F)	Wertbrief *m*	insured letter	—	lettera con valore dichiarato *f*	letra con valor declarado *f*
lettre circulaire (F)	Rundschreiben *n*	circular (letter)	—	circolare *f*	circular *m*
lettre d'avertissement (F)	Mahnbrief *m*	reminder	—	lettera di sollecito *f*	carta (ad)monitoria *f*
lettre de change (F)	Wechsel *m*	bill of exchange	—	cambiale *f*	letra de cambio *f*
lettre de confirmation des conditions (F)	Schlußbrief *m*	letter of confirmation	—	lettera di conferma *f*	carta de confirmación *f*
lettre de crédit (F)	Kreditbrief *m*	letter of credit	—	lettera di credito *f*	carta de crédito *f*
lettre de crédit commercial (F)	Handelskreditbrief *m*	commercial letter of credit	—	lettera di credito commerciale *f*	carta de crédito comercial *f*
lettre de demande d'emploi (F)	Bewerbungs-schreiben *n*	letter of application	—	domanda d'impiego *f*	carta de solicitud *f*
lettre de recommandation (F)	Empfehlungs-schreiben *n*	letter of recommendation	—	lettera di raccomandazione *f*	carta de recomendación *f*

	D	E	F	I	Es
lettre de remerciement (F)	Dankschreiben *n*	letter of thanks	—	lettera di ringraziamento *f*	carta de agradecimiento *f*
lettre de transport aérien (F)	Luftfrachtbrief *m*	air waybill	—	lettera di trasporto aereo *f*	transporte aéreo *m*
lettre de voiture (F)	Frachtbrief *m*	consignment note	—	lettera di vettura *f*	carta de porte *f*
lettre par exprès (F)	Eilbrief *m*	express letter	—	lettera espresso *f*	carta urgente *f*
lettre publicitaire (F)	Werbebrief *m*	advertising letter	—	lettera pubblicitaria *f*	circular de publicidad *m*
lettre recommandée (F)	Einschreibebrief *m*	registered letter	—	lettera raccomandata *f*	carta certificada *f*
lettre recommandée avec avis de réception (F)	Einschreiben-Rückschein *m*	recorded delivery letter with advice	—	lettera raccomandata con ricevuta di ritorno *f*	carta certificada con talón de recibo *f*
Leumund (D)	—	reputation	réputation *f*	reputazione *f*	reputación *f*
level of employment (E)	Beschäftigungsgrad *m*	—	taux d'emploi *m*	tasso d'occupazione *m*	grado de empleo *m*
ley[1] (Es)	Feingehalt *m*	fine gold content	titre *m*	titolo *m*	—
ley[2] (Es)	Gesetz *n*	law	loi *f*	legge *f*	—
ley de las quiebras (Es)	Konkursordnung *f*	Bankruptcy Act	régime juridique de la faillite *m*	legge fallimentare *f*	—
ley de protección contra el despido (Es)	Kündigungsschutzgesetz *n*	Termination of Employment Act	loi sur le délai-congé en matière de licenciement *f*	legge sulla tutela contro il licenziamento *f*	—
ley de protección de datos (Es)	Datenschutzgesetz *n*	Data Protection Act	loi sur l'informatique	legge sulla tutela dei dati *f*	—
ley relativa a los cártels (Es)	Kartellgesetz *n*	Cartel Law	loi sur les cartels *f*	legge sui cartelli *f*	—
ley sobre sociedades anónimas (Es)	Aktiengesetz *n*	Companies Act	loi sur les sociétés par actions *f*	legge sulle società per azioni *f*	—
liabilities (E)	Passiva *n*	—	passif *m*	passivo *m*	pasivo *m*
liability[1] (E)	Obligo *n*	—	engagement *m*	obbligo *m*	obligación *f*
liability[2] (E)	Verbindlichkeiten *pl*	—	obligation *f*/ dettes *f pl*	obblighi *m pl*/ debiti *m pl*	obligaciones *f pl*/ deudas *f pl*/créditos pasivos *m pl*
liability[3] (E)	Haftung *f*	—	responsabilité *f*	responsabilità *f*	responsabilidad *f*
liability for breach of warranty (E)	Gewährleistungshaftung *f*	—	responsabilité en matière de garantie *f*	responsabilità di garanzia *f*	responsabilidad de garantía *f*
liability for damages (E)	Schadensersatzpflicht *f*	—	obligation de dédommager *f*	obbligo di risarcimento danni *m*	obligación indemnizatoria *f*
liability to insure (E)	Versicherungspflicht *f*	—	assujettissement obligatoire à l'assurance *m*	obbligo d'assicurazione *m*	obligatoriedad del seguro *f*
liable to prosecution (E)	straffällig	—	encourir une peine	passibile di pena	criminal
liable to tax (E)	abgabenpflichtig	—	soumis à l'impôt	soggetto a contributi	sujeto a impuestos
libbra (I)	Pfund *n*	pound	livre *f*	—	libra *f*
libera circolazione dei capitali (I)	freier Kapitalverkehr *m*	free movement of capital	libre circulation des capitaux *f*	—	libre circulación de capitales
liberalism (E)	Liberalismus *m*	—	libéralisme *m*	liberalismo *m*	liberalismo *m*
libéralisme (F)	Liberalismus *m*	liberalism	—	liberalismo *m*	liberalismo *m*
liberalismo (Es)	Liberalismus *m*	liberalism	libéralisme *m*	liberalismo *m*	—
liberalismo (I)	Liberalismus *m*	liberalism	libéralisme *m*	—	liberalismo *m*
Liberalismus (D)	—	liberalism	libéralisme *m*	liberalismo *m*	liberalismo *m*
libero professionista (I)	Freiberufler *m*	self-employed person	personne exerçant une profession libérale *f*	—	profesional *m*
libertà contrattuale (I)	Vertragsfreiheit *f*	freedom of contract	liberté de contracter *f*	—	libertad contractual *f*
libertad contractual (Es)	Vertragsfreiheit *f*	freedom of contract	liberté de contracter *f*	libertà contrattuale *f*	—
libertad de coalición (Es)	Koalitionsfreiheit *f*	freedom of association	liberté d'association *f*	libertà di coalizione *f*	—
libertad de consumo (Es)	Konsumfreiheit *f*	freedom of consumption	liberté de consommation *f*	libertà di consumo *f*	—
libertad de industria (Es)	Gewerbefreiheit *f*	freedom of trade	liberté des professions industrielles et commerciales *f*	libertà d'industria *f*	—

licensee

	D	E	F	I	Es
libertà di coalizione (I)	Koalitionsfreiheit *f*	freedom of association	liberté d'association *f*	—	libertad de coalición *f*
libertà di commercio estero (I)	Außenhandels-freiheit *f*	free trade	libre-échange *m*	—	librecambio *m*
libertà di consumo (I)	Konsumfreiheit *f*	freedom of consumption	liberté de consommation *f*	—	libertad de consumo *f*
libertà d'industria (I)	Gewerbefreiheit *f*	freedom of trade	liberté des professions industrielles et commerciales *f*	—	libertad de industria *f*
liberté d'association (F)	Koalitionsfreiheit *f*	freedom of association	—	libertà di coalizione *f*	libertad de coalición *f*
liberté de consommation (F)	Konsumfreiheit *f*	freedom of consumption	—	libertà di consumo *f*	libertad de consumo *f*
liberté de contracter (F)	Vertragsfreiheit *f*	freedom of contract	—	libertà contrattuale *f*	libertad contractual *f*
liberté des professions industrielles et commerciales (F)	Gewerbefreiheit *f*	freedom of trade	—	libertà d'industria *f*	libertad de industria *f*
libra (Es)	Pfund *n*	pound	livre *f*	libbra *f*	—
librado (Es)	Bezogener *m*	drawee	tiré *m*	trattario *m*	—
libramiento de letras cruzadas (Es)	Wechselreiterei *f*	kiteflying	tirage d'une traite de cavalerie *m*	emissione di tratte incrociate *f*	—
librecambio¹ (Es)	Außenhandels-freiheit *f*	free trade	libre-échange *m*	libertà di commercio estero *f*	—
librecambio² (Es)	Freihandel *m*	free trade	commerce libre *m*	scambio libero *m*	—
libre circulación de capitales (Es)	freier Kapitalverkehr *m*	free movement of capital	libre circulation des capitaux *f*	libera circolazione dei capitali *f*	—
libre circulation des capitaux (F)	freier Kapitalverkehr *m*	free movement of capital	—	libera circolazione dei capitali *f*	libre circulación de capitales *f*
libre de gastos (Es)	kostenlos	free of charge	gratuit	gratuito	—
libre de impuesto (Es)	steuerfrei	tax-free	dispensé de l'impôt	esente da imposte	—
libre-échange (F)	Außenhandels-freiheit *f*	free trade	—	libertà di commercio estero *f*	librecambio *m*
libreta de cheques (Es)	Scheckheft *n*	cheque book	carnet de chèques *m*	carnet degli assegni *m*	—
libretto degli assegni (I)	Scheckbuch *n*	cheque book	livre d'enregistre-ment des chéques *m*	—	libro de cheques *m*
libri contabili (I)	Geschäftsbücher *pl*	account books	livres de commerce *m pl*	—	libros de contabilidad *m pl*
libro de caja (Es)	Kassenbuch *n*	cash book	compte de caisse *m*	libro di cassa *m*	—
libro de cheques (Es)	Scheckbuch *n*	cheque book	livre d'enregistre-ment des chéques *m*	libretto degli assegni *m*	—
libro de cuentas (Es)	Kontobuch *n*	account book	livre de compte *m*	libro dei conti *m*	—
libro dei conti (I)	Kontobuch *n*	account book	livre de compte *m*	—	libro de cuentas *m*
libro di cassa (I)	Kassenbuch *n*	cash book	compte de caisse *m*	—	libro de caja *m*
libros de contabilidad (Es)	Geschäftsbücher *pl*	account books	livres de commerce *m pl*	libri contabili *m pl*	—
libro specializzato (I)	Fachbuch *n*	technical book	livre technique *m*	—	libro técnico *m*
libro técnico (Es)	Fachbuch *n*	technical book	livre technique *m*	libro specializzato *m*	—
licence¹ (E)	Konzession *f*	—	concession *f*	concessione *f*	concesión *f*
licence² (E)	Lizenzen *pl*	—	licence *f*	licenze *f pl*	licencias *f pl*
licence agreement (E)	Lizenzvertrag *m*	—	contrat de concession de licence *m*	contratto di licenza *m*	contrato de licencia *m*
licence de brevet (F)	Patentlizenz *f*	patent licence	—	licenza di brevetto *f*	licencia de patente *f*
licences (F)	Lizenzen *pl*	licence	—	licenze *f pl*	licencias *f pl*
licencia de exportación (Es)	Ausfuhr-genehmigung *f*	export licence	autorisation d'exportation *f*	autorizzazione per le esportazioni *f*	—
licencia de patente (Es)	Patentlizenz *f*	patent licence	licence de brevet *f*	licenza di brevetto *f*	—
licenciado (Es)	Lizenznehmer *m*	licensee	preneur d'une licence *m*	concessionario di licenza *m*	—
licencias (Es)	Lizenzen *pl*	licence	licences *f*	licenze *f pl*	—
licenciement (F)	Entlassung *f*	dismissal	—	licenziamento *m*	despido *m*
licensee (E)	Lizenznehmer *m*	—	preneur d'une licence *m*	concessionario di licenza *m*	licenciado *m*

licenser

	D	E	F	I	Es
licenser (E)	Lizenzgeber *m*	—	concédant de licence *m*	concedente di licenza *m*	licitador *m*
licenza di brevetto (I)	Patentlizenz *f*	patent licence	licence de brevet *f*	—	licencia de patente *f*
licenze (I)	Lizenzen *pl*	licence	licences *f*	—	licencias *f pl*
licenziamento (I)	Entlassung *f*	dismissal	licenciement *m*	—	despido *m*
licitador (Es)	Lizenzgeber *m*	licenser	concédant de licence *m*	concedente di licenza *m*	—
líder (Es)	Anführer *m*	leader	chef *m*	leader *m*	—
Liebhaberpreis (D)	—	connoisseur's price	prix d'amateur *m*	prezzo d'affezione *m*	precio afectivo *m*
Lieferant (D)	—	supplier	fournisseur *m*	fornitore *m*	suministrador *m*
Lieferantenkredit (D)	—	supplier's credit	crédit de fournisseurs *m*	credito al fornitore *m*	crédito comercial *m*
lieferbar (D)	—	deliverable	livrable	disponibile	suministrable
Lieferbedingungen (D)	—	terms of delivery	conditions de livraison *f pl*	condizioni di consegna *f pl*	condiciones de suminstro *f pl*
Lieferfrist (D)	—	time for delivery	délai de livraison *m*	termine di consegna *m*	plazo de entrega *m*
Lieferkapazität (D)	—	delivery capacity	capacité de livraison *f*	capacità di fornitura *f*	capacidad de entrega *f*
Lieferklausel (D)	—	delivery clause	clause de livraison *f*	clausola di fornitura *f*	cláusulas comerciales *f pl*
Lieferprogramm (D)	—	delivery programme	programme de livraison *m*	programma di fornitura *m*	programa de entrega *m*
Lieferschein (D)	—	delivery note	bulletin de livraison *m*	bolletta di consegna *f*	recibo de entrega *m*
Liefersperre (D)	—	delivery ban	blocage de livraisons *m*	blocco delle forniture *m*	embargo *m*
Liefertermin (D)	—	date of delivery	délai de livraison *m*	termine di consegna *m*	plazo de entrega *m*
Lieferung (D)	—	delivery	livraison *f*	fornitura *f*/consegna *f*	suministro *m*
Lieferung gegen Nachnahme (D)	—	cash on delivery	livraison contre remboursement *f*	consegna contro assegno *f*	entrega contra reembolso *f*
Lieferungs-verzögerung (D)	—	delay in delivery	retard dans la livraison *m*	ritardo della consegna *m*	demora en la entrega *f*
Liefervertrag (D)	—	supply contract	contrat de fourniture *m*	contratto di consegna *m*	contrata *f*
Lieferverzug (D)	—	delay in delivery	demeure du fournisseur *f*	mora nella consegna *f*	demora en la entrega *f*
Liegetage (D)	—	lay days	staries *f pl*	stallie *f pl*	estadías *f pl*
lieu de destination (F)	Bestimmungsort *m*	place of destination	—	luogo di destinazione *m*	lugar de de destino *m*
lieu de naissance (F)	Geburtsort *m*	place of birth	—	luogo di nascita *m*	lugar de nacimiento *m*
lieu de travail (F)	Arbeitsraum *m*	workroom	—	locale di lavoro *m*	sala de trabajo *f*
lieu d'implantation (F)	Standort *m*	location	—	ubicazione *f*	ubicación *f*
life cycle (E)	Lebenszyklus *m*	—	cycle de vie *m*	ciclo di vita *m*	ciclo de vida *m*
life insurance (E)	Lebensversicherung *f*	—	assurance vie *f*	assicurazione sulla vita *f*	seguro de vida *m*
ligne des produits (F)	Produktlinie *f*	production scheduling	—	linea dei prodotti *f*	línea de productos *f*
lignite (F)	Braunkohle *f*	brown coal	—	lignite *f*	lignito *m*
lignite (I)	Braunkohle *f*	brown coal	lignite *m*	—	lignito *m*
lignito (Es)	Braunkohle *f*	brown coal	lignite *m*	lignite *f*	—
Limit (D)	—	limit	limite *f*	limite *m*	límite *m*
limit (E)	Limit *n*	—	limite *f*	limite *m*	límite *m*
limitación de cultivos (Es)	Anbau-beschränkung *f*	restriction on cultivation	limitation des cultures *f*	restrizione di coltivazione *f*	—
limitación de emisiones (Es)	Emissions-begrenzung *f*	issuing restriction	limitation d'émission *f*	limitazione d'emissione *f*	—
limitación de precios[1] (Es)	Preisbindung *f*	obligation to main-tain fixed prices	obligation de respecter les prix *f*	obbligo di mantenere il prezzo fissato *m*	—
limitación de precios[2] (Es)	Preisstopp *m*	price stop	blocage des prix *m*	blocco dei prezzi *m*	—
limitation d'émission (F)	Emissions-begrenzung *f*	issuing restriction	—	limitazione d'emissione *f*	limitación de emisiones *f*

	D	E	F	I	Es
limitation des cultures (F)	Anbaubeschränkung f	restriction on cultivation	—	restrizione di coltivazione f	limitación de cultivos f
limitation des importations (F)	Einfuhrbeschränkung f	import restriction	—	restrizione d'importazione f	restricción a la importación f
limitation of actions (E)	Verjährung f	—	prescription f	prescrizione f	prescripción f
limitazione d'emissione (I)	Emissionsbegrenzung f	issuing restriction	limitation d'émission f	—	limitación de emisiones f
límite (Es)	Limit n	limit	limite f	limite m	—
limite (F)	Limit n	limit	—	limite m	límite m
limite (I)	Limit n	limit	limite f	—	límite m
limite d'âge (F)	Altersgrenze f	age limit	—	limite d'età m	limite de edad m
límite de crédito (Es)	Kreditlimit n	borrowing limit	plafond du crédit alloué m	limite di credito m	—
limite de edad (Es)	Altersgrenze f	age limit	limite d'âge f	limite d'età m	—
limite de producción (Es)	Förderlimit n	production limit	limite de production f	limite d'estrazione m	—
limite de production (F)	Förderlimit n	production limit	—	limite d'estrazione m	limite de producción m
limite d'estrazione (I)	Förderlimit n	production limit	limite de production f	—	limite de producción m
limite d'età (I)	Altersgrenze f	age limit	limite d'âge f	—	limite de edad m
limite di credito (I)	Kreditlimit n	borrowing limit	plafond du crédit alloué m	—	límite de crédito m
limited liability company (E)	Gesellschaft mit beschränkter Haftung f	—	société à responsabilité limitée f	società a responsabilità limitata f	sociedad de responsabilidad limitada f
limited partner (E)	Kommanditist m	—	commandmaire m	socio accommandante m	comanditario m
limited partnership (E)	Kommanditgesellschaft f	—	société en commandite f	società in accomandita semplice f	sociedad comanditaria f
límite inferior de los precios (Es)	Preisuntergrenze f	price floor	plancher des prix m	limite inferiore di prezzo m	—
límite inferior de rentabilidad (Es)	Rentabilitätsschwelle f	break-even point	seuil de rentabilité f	soglia di redditività f	—
limite inferiore di prezzo (I)	Preisuntergrenze f	price floor	plancher des prix m	—	límite inferior de los precios m
limite massimo di prezzo (I)	Preisobergrenze f	price ceiling	limite supérieur des prix f	—	límite superior de los precios m
límite máximo (Es)	Plafond m	ceiling	plafond m	plafond m	—
limite supérieur des prix (F)	Preisobergrenze f	price ceiling	—	limite massimo di prezzo m	límite superior de los precios m
límite superior de los precios (Es)	Preisobergrenze f	price ceiling	limite supérieur des prix f	limite massimo di prezzo m	—
limiting value (E)	Grenzwert m	—	valeur marginale f	valore limite m	valor límite m
linea creditizia (I)	Kreditlinie f	credit line	plafond du crédit accordé m	—	línea de crédito f
línea de crédito (Es)	Kreditlinie f	credit line	plafond du crédit accordé m	linea creditizia f	—
linea dei prodotti (I)	Produktlinie f	production scheduling	ligne des produits f	—	línea de productos f
línea de productos (Es)	Produktlinie f	production scheduling	ligne des produits f	linea dei prodotti f	—
linear depreciation (E)	lineare Abschreibung f	—	amortissement constant m	ammortamento lineare m	amortización constante f
lineare Abschreibung (D)	—	linear depreciation	amortissement constant m	ammortamento lineare m	amortización constante f
lineare Programmierung (D)	—	linear programming	programmation linéaire f	programmazione lineare f	programación lineal f
lineares Wachstum (D)	—	linear growth	accroissement constant m	crescita lineare f	crecimiento lineal m
linear growth (E)	lineares Wachstum n	—	accroissement constant m	crescita lineare f	crecimiento lineal m
linear programmation (E)	lineare Programmierung f	—	programmation linéaire f	programmazione lineare f	programación lineal f
line of business (E)	Branche f	—	branche f	categoria f	ramo m
lingot d'ór (F)	Goldbarren m	gold bar	—	lingotto d'oro m	lingote de oro m

	D	E	F	I	Es
lingote de oro (Es)	Goldbarren *m*	gold bar	lingot d'ór *m*	lingotto d'oro *m*	—
lingotto d'oro (I)	Goldbarren *m*	gold bar	lingot d'ór *m*	—	lingote de oro *m*
linguaggio di programmazione (I)	Programmiersprache *f*	common business-oriented language	langage de programmation *m*	—	lenguaje de programación *m*
liquid (E)	liquide		solvable	liquido	líquido
liquidación[1] (Es)	Ausverkauf *m*	clearance sale	soldes *m pl*	svendita *f*	—
liquidación[2] (Es)	Abrechnung *f*	settlement of accounts	règlement *m*	liquidazione *f*	—
liquidación[3] (Es)	Liquidation *f*	liquidation	liquidation *f*	liquidazione *f*	—
liquidación de gastos (Es)	Spesenabrechnung *f*	statement of expenses	décompte des frais *m*	conteggio delle spese *m*	—
liquidación de impuestas (Es)	Steuerbescheid *m*	notice of assessment	avis d'imposition *m*	cartella delle imposte *f*	—
liquidación de la comisión (Es)	Provisionsabrechnung *f*	statement of a commission	compte des commissions *m*	conteggio delle provvigioni *m*	—
liquidación de los gastos de viaje (Es)	Reisekostenabrechnung *f*	travel expense accounting	règlement des frais de voyage *m*	conteggio dei costi di viaggio *m*	—
liquidador[1] (Es)	Liquidator *m*	liquidator	liquidateur *m*	liquidatore *m*	—
liquidador[2] (Es)	Abwickler *m*	liquidator	liquidateur *m*	liquidatore *m*	—
liquidar (Es)	liquidieren	liquidate	liquider	liquidare	—
liquidare (I)	liquidieren	liquidate	liquider	—	liquidar
liquidate (E)	liquidieren	—	liquider	liquidare	liquidar
liquidateur[1] (F)	Liquidator *m*	liquidator	—	liquidatore *m*	liquidador *m*
liquidateur[2] (F)	Abwickler *m*	liquidator	—	liquidatore *m*	liquidador *m*
liquidateur de la faillite (F)	Konkursverwalter *m*	administrator in bankruptcy proceedings	—	curatore fallimentare *m*	síndico de quiebra *m*
Liquidation (D)	—	liquidation	liquidation *f*	liquidazione *f*	liquidación *f*
liquidation (E)	Liquidation *f*	—	liquidation *f*	liquidazione *f*	liquidación *f*
liquidation[1] (F)	Auflösung *f*	dissolution	—	scioglimento *m*	disolución *f*
liquidation[2] (F)	Liquidation *f*	liquidation	—	liquidazione *f*	liquidación *f*
liquidation des commissions (F)	Provisionsabrechnung *f*	statement of a commission	—	conteggio delle provvigioni *m*	liquidación de la comisión *f*
liquidation des stocks (F)	Räumungsverkauf *m*	clearance sale	—	liquidazione totale *f*	venta total *f*
Liquidationserlös (D)	—	remaining assets after liquidation	produit de la liquidation *m*	ricavo della liquidazione *m*	haber social repartible *m*
Liquidator (D)	—	liquidator	liquidateur *m*	liquidatore *m*	liquidador *m*
liquidator[1] (E)	Liquidator *m*	—	liquidateur *m*	liquidatore *m*	liquidador *m*
liquidator[2] (E)	Abwickler *m*	—	liquidateur *m*	liquidatore *m*	liquidador *m*
liquidatore[1] (I)	Liquidator *m*	liquidator	liquidateur *m*	—	liquidador *m*
liquidatore[2] (I)	Abwickler *m*	liquidator	liquidateur *m*	—	liquidador *m*
liquidazione[1] (I)	Abrechnung *f*	settlement of accounts	règlement *m*	—	liquidación *f*
liquidazione[2] (I)	Liquidation *f*	liquidation	liquidation *f*	—	liquidación *f*
liquidazione del conto (I)	Kontoausgleich *m*	settlement of an account	solde de compte *m*	—	saldo de cuenta *m*
liquidazione totale (I)	Räumungsverkauf *m*	clearance sale	liquidation des stocks *f*	—	venta total *f*
liquide (D)	—	liquid	solvable	liquido	líquido
liquider (F)	liquidieren	liquidate	—	liquidare	liquidar
liquidez (Es)	Liquidität *f*	liquidity	liquidité *f*	liquidità *f*	—
liquidieren (D)	—	liquidate	liquider	liquidare	liquidar
liquidità (I)	Liquidität *f*	liquidity	liquidité *f*	—	liquidez *f*
Liquidität (D)	—	liquidity	liquidité *f*	liquidità *f*	liquidez *f*
Liquiditätsengpaß (D)	—	liquidity squeeze	goulot d'étranglement dans la trésorerie	strettoia di liquidità *f*	restricción de la liquidez *f*
Liquiditätsplan (D)	—	cash forecasting plan	plan de liquidité *m*	piano della liquidità *m*	plan de liquidez *m*
Liquiditätsrechnung (D)	—	liquidity calculation	compte de liquidité *m*	calcolo della liquidità *m*	cálculo de liquidez *m*

	D	E	F	I	Es
Liquiditätsreserve (D)	—	liquidity reserves	réserves de liquidité f pl	riserva di liquidità f	reserva de liquidez f
Liquiditäts-überschuß (D)	—	excess liquidity	excédent de liquidité m	eccedenza di liquidità f	exceso de liquidez m
liquidité (F)	Liquidität f	liquidity	—	liquidità f	liquidez f
liquidity (E)	Liquidität f	—	liquidité f	liquidità f	liquidez f
liquidity calculation (E)	Liquiditätsrechnung f	—	compte de liquidité m	calcolo della liquidità m	cálculo de liquidez m
liquidity reserves (E)	Liquiditätsreserve f	—	réserves de liquidité f pl	riserva di liquidità f	reserva de liquidez f
liquidity squeeze (E)	Liquiditätsengpaß m	—	goulot d'étranglement dans la trésorerie	strettoia di liquidità f	restricción de la liquidez f
líquido (Es)	liquide	liquid	solvable	liquido	—
liquido (I)	liquide	liquid	solvable	—	líquido
lista de control (Es)	Checkliste f	checklist	liste de contrôle f	lista di controllo f	—
lista de correos (Es)	postlagernd	poste restante	poste restante	fermo posta m	—
lista dei partecipanti (I)	Teilnehmerliste f	list of participants	liste des participants f	—	lista de participantes f
lista de participantes (Es)	Teilnehmerliste f	list of participants	liste des participants f	lista dei partecipanti f	—
lista de precios (Es)	Preisliste f	price list	liste des prix f	listino prezzi m	—
lista de precios de exportación (Es)	Exportpreisliste f	export price list	liste des prix à l'exportation f	listino prezzi delle esportazioni m	—
lista di controllo (I)	Checkliste f	checklist	liste de contrôle f	—	lista de control f
liste de contrôle (F)	Checkliste f	checklist	—	lista di controllo f	lista de control f
liste des participants (F)	Teilnehmerliste f	list of participants	—	lista dei partecipanti f	lista de participantes f
liste des prix (F)	Preisliste f	price list '	—	listino prezzi m	lista de precios f
liste des prix à l'exportation (F)	Exportpreisliste f	export price list	—	listino prezzi delle esportazioni m	lista de precios de exportación f
Listenpreis (D)	—	list price	prix du tarif m	prezzo di listino m	precio-lista m
listino di borsa (I)	Kurszettel m	stock exchange list	bulletin des cours m	—	boletín de bolsa m
listino prezzi (I)	Preisliste f	price list	liste des prix f	—	lista de precios f
listino prezzi delle esportazioni (I)	Exportpreisliste f	export price list	liste des prix à l'exportation f	—	lista de precios de exportación f
list of participants (E)	Teilnehmerliste f	—	liste des participants f	lista dei partecipanti f	lista de participantes f
listo para la recogida (Es)	abholbereit	ready for collection	disponible	pronto per il ritiro	—
listo para ser expedido (Es)	versandbereit	ready for dispatch	prêt à être expédié	pronto per la spedizione	—
list price (E)	Listenpreis m	—	prix du tarif m	prezzo di listino m	precio-lista m
litige (F)	Rechtsstreit m	legal action	—	causa f	conflicto jurídico m
litigio hereditario (Es)	Erbstreit m	dispute concerning an inheritance	action successorale f	causa ereditaria f	—
livello degli interessi (I)	Zinsniveau n	interest rate level	niveau du taux d'intérêt m	—	nivel de interés m
livello dei prezzi (I)	Preisniveau n	price level	niveau des prix m	—	nivel de precios m
livestock breeding (E)	Tierzucht f	—	élevage m	zootecnia f	cría de animales f
livrable (F)	lieferbar	deliverable	—	disponibile	suministrable
livraison (F)	Lieferung f	delivery	—	fornitura f/consegna f	suministro m
livraison à titre d'essai (F)	Probelieferung f	trial shipment	—	fornitura a titolo di prova f	envío de prueba m
livraison contre remboursement (F)	Lieferung gegen Nachnahme f	cash on delivery	—	consegna contro assegno f	entrega contra reembolso f
livraison de remplacement (F)	Ersatzlieferung f	substitute delivery	—	fornitura di compensazione f	entrega de reposición f
livraison en quantité inférieure (F)	Minderlieferung f	short delivery	—	fornitura ridotta f	envío incompleto m
livraison immédiate (F)	sofortige Lieferung f	immediate delivery	—	consegna immediata f	entrega inmediata f
livraison partielle (F)	Teillieferung f	partial delivery	—	fornitura parziale	entrega parcial f
livraison supplémentaire (F)	Mehrlieferung f	additional delivery	—	fornitura supplementare f	exceso m

	D	E	F	I	Es
livraison totale (F)	Gesamtlieferung *f*	total delivery	—	fornitura completa *f*	suministro total *m*
livre (F)	Pfund *n*	pound	—	libbra *f*	libra *f*
livre de compte (F)	Kontobuch *n*	account book	—	libro dei conti *m*	libro de cuentas *m*
livre d'enregistrement des chèques (F)	Scheckbuch *n*	cheque book	—	libretto degli assegni *m*	libro de cheques *m*
livrer (F)	abliefern	hand over	—	consegnare	entregar
livres de commerce (F)	Geschäftsbücher *pl*	account books	—	libri contabili *m pl*	libros de contabilidad *m pl*
livre technique (F)	Fachbuch *n*	technical book	—	libro specializzato *m*	libro técnico *m*
Lizenzen (D)	—	licence	licences *f pl*	licenze *f pl*	licencias *f pl*
Lizenzgeber (D)	—	licenser	concédant de licence *m*	concedente di licenza *m*	licitador *m*
Lizenzgebühr (D)	—	royalty	taxe d'expoitation de licence *f*	tassa di licenza *f*	derecho de licencia *m*
Lizenznehmer (D)	—	licensee	preneur d'une licence *m*	concessionario di licenza *m*	licenciado *m*
Lizenzvertrag (D)	—	licence agreement	contrat de concession de licence *m*	contratto di licenza *m*	contrato de licencia *m*
llamada en causa (Es)	Beiladung *f*	summons to interested parties/ additional load	assignation en intervention *f*/complément de fret *m*	intervento per ordine del giudice *m*/spedizione in collettanze *f*	—
lluvia ácida (Es)	saurer Regen *m*	acid rain	pluie acide *f*	pioggia acida *f*	—
load¹ (E)	verladen	—	charger	caricare	expedir
load² (E)	Belastung *f*	—	charge *f*	addebito *m*	gravamen *m*
load³ (E)	belasten	—	débiter	addebitare	cargar/adeudar
loading charges¹ (E)	Ladegebühren *pl*	—	taxe de chargement *f*	spese di carico *f pl*	derechos de carga *m pl*
loading charges² (E)	Verladekosten *pl*	—	coût du chargement *m*	costi di caricamento *m pl*	gastos de carga *m pl*
loan¹ (E)	Anleihe *f*	—	emprunt *m*	prestito *m*	empréstito *m*
loan² (E)	Darlehen *n*	—	prêt *m*	mutuo *m*	préstamo *m*
Lobby (D)	—	lobbying group	lobby *m*	lobby *m*	grupo de presión *m*
lobby (F)	Lobby *f*	lobbying group	—	lobby *m*	grupo de presión *m*
lobby (I)	Lobby *f*	lobbying group	lobby *m*	—	grupo de presión *m*
local agent (E)	Bezirksvertreter *m*	—	agent local *m*	rappresentante di zona *m*	agente regional *m*
local à usage commercial (F)	Geschäftsräume *pl*	business premises	—	locali commerciali *m pl*	local comercial *m*
local authorities loan (E)	Kommunalanleihen *pl*	—	emprunt communal *m*	prestiti comunali *m pl*	empréstito municipal *m*
local comercial (Es)	Geschäftsräume *pl*	business premises	local à usage commercial *m*	locali commerciali *m pl*	—
locale di lavoro (I)	Arbeitsraum *m*	workroom	lieu de travail *m*	—	sala de trabajo *f*
locali commerciali (I)	Geschäftsräume *pl*	business premises	local à usage commercial *m*	—	local comercial *m*
locataire (F)	Mieter *m*	tenant	—	locatario *m*	inquilino *m*/arrendatario *m*
locatario (I)	Mieter *m*	tenant	locataire *m*	—	inquilino *m*/arrendatario *m*
location (E)	Standort *m*	—	lieu d'implantation *m*	ubicazione *f*	ubicación *f*
location (F)	Miete *f*	rent	—	canone di locazione *m*	alquiler *m*
location decision (E)	Standortentscheidung *f*	—	décision de l'implantation *f*	determinazione dell'ubicazione *f*	decisión de ubicación *f*
location d'une surface pour magasinage (F)	Lagermiete *f*	warehouse rent	—	spese di magazzinaggio *f pl*	alquiler de almacenaje *m*
location factors (E)	Standortfaktoren *pl*	—	facteurs dépendant du lieu d'implantation *m pl*	fattori d'ubicazione *m pl*	factores de ubicación *m pl*
lock-down period for interest rates (E)	Zinsbindungsfrist *f*	—	délai d'engagement sur le taux d'intérêt accordé *m*	scadenza degli interessi vincolati *f*	plazo de vinculación al tipo de interés pactado *m*
lockout (E)	Aussperrung *f*	—	lock-out *m*	serrata *f*	cierre patronal *m*
lock-out (F)	Aussperrung *f*	lockout	—	serrata *f*	cierre patronal *m*

	D	E	F	I	Es
logement en propriété (F)	Eigentumswohnung f	freehold flat	—	appartamento in condominio m	piso en propiedad m
logística (Es)	Logistik f	logistics	logistique f	logistica f	—
logistica (I)	Logistik f	logistics	logistique f	—	logística f
logistics (E)	Logistik f	—	logistique f	logistica f	logística f
Logistik (D)	—	logistics	logistique f	logistica f	logística f
logistique (F)	Logistik f	logistics	—	logistica f	logística f
Logo (D)	—	logo	logotype m	logo m	logo m
logo (E)	Logo n	—	logotype m	logo m	logo m
logo (Es)	Logo n	logo	logotype m	logo m	—
logo (I)	Logo n	logo	logotype m	—	logo m
logotype (F)	Logo n	logo	—	logo m	logo m
Lohn (D)	—	wage	salaire m	salario m	salario m
Lohnbüro (D)	—	pay office	bureau de la paye m	ufficio paga m	departamento de nóminas m
Lohnerhöhung (D)	—	increase in wages	augmentation du salaire f	aumento salariale m	aumento de salario m
Lohnforderung (D)	—	wage claim	revendication de salaire f	rivendicazione salariale f	reivindicación salarial f
lohnintensiv (D)	—	wage-intensive	déterminé par le facteur salaire	ad alta incidenza salariale	con gran intensidad de costos salariales
Lohnkosten (D)	—	cost of wages	coût du travail m	costo del lavoro m	coste de salarios m
Lohnlag (D)	—	wage lag	décalage entre les prix et les salaires m	lag salariale m	diferencial entre precios y salarios m
Lohnnebenkosten (D)	—	ancillary wage costs	charges salariales annexes f pl	costi complementari del lavoro m pl	cargas salariales accesorias f pl
Lohnpfändung (D)	—	attachment of earnings	saisie-arrêt sur le salaire f	pignoramento del salario m	embargo de salario m
Lohnpolitik (D)	—	wage policy	politique des salaires f	politica salariale f	política salarial f
Lohn-Preis-Spirale (D)	—	wage-price spiral	course des prix et des salaires f	spirale prezzi-salari f	espiral salarios-precios m
Lohnsteuer (D)	—	wage tax	impôt sur les traitements et salaires m	imposta sui salari f	impuesto sobre los rendimientos del trabajo personal m
Lohnstopp (D)	—	wage freeze	blocage des salaires m	blocco dei salari m	congelación salarial f
Lohnvereinbarung (D)	—	wage agreement	accord de salaires m	accordo salariale m	pacto salarial m
loi (F)	Gesetz n	law	—	legge f	ley f
loi sur le délai-congé en matière de licenciement (F)	Kündigungsschutzgesetz n	Termination of Employment Act	—	legge sulla tutela contro il licenziamento f	ley de protección contra el despido f
loi sur les cartels (F)	Kartellgesetz n	Cartel Law	—	legge sui cartelli f	ley relativa a los cártels f
loi sur les sociétés anonymes (F)	Aktienrecht n	company law	—	diritto azionario m	derecho de sociedades anónimas m
loi sur les sociétés par actions (F)	Aktiengesetz n	Companies Act	—	legge sulle società per azioni f	ley sobre sociedades anónimas f
loi sur l'informatique (F)	Datenschutzgesetz n	Data Protection Act	—	legge sulla tutela dei dati f	ley de protección de datos f
Lombardgeschäft (D)	—	lending on securities	prêt sur gage m	anticipazioni f pl	operaciones de pignoración f pl
Lombardkredit (D)	—	credit against securities	crédit garanti par nantissement m	credito su pegno m	crédito pignoraticio m
Lombardpolitik (D)	—	policy of advances on securities	politique des prêts sur gages f	politica delle anticipazioni f	política de pignoración f
Lombardsatz (D)	—	rate for advances on securities	taux d'intérêt de l'argent prêté sur gage m	tasso sulle anticipazioni m	tipo de pignoración m
long distance traffic (E)	Fernverkehr m	—	trafic sur longues distances m	traffico a grande distanza m	transporte a distancia m
long-term (E)	langfristig	—	à long terme	a lunga scadenza	a largo plazo
long-term capital (E)	langfristiges Kapital n	—	capital à long terme m	capitale a lungo termine m	capital a largo plazo m

	D	E	F	I	Es
long-term credit (E)	langfristiger Kredit m	—	crédit à long terme m	credito a lunga scadenza m	crédito a largo plazo m
lorryload (E)	Wagenladung f	—	charge de voiture f	carico di autocarro m	carga de un vagón f
Löschgebühren (D)	—	discharging expenses	droit de déchargement m	spese di scarico f pl	gastos de descarga m pl
losing business (E)	Verlustgeschäft n	—	affaire déficitaire f	affare in perdita m	venta con pérdida f
loss (E)	Verlust m	—	perte f	perdita f	pérdida f
loss in exchange (E)	Kursverlust m	—	perte sur les cours f	perdita sul cambio f	pérdida en bolsa f
loss of production (E)	Produktionsausfall m	—	perte dans la production f	perdita di produzione f	pérdida de producción f
loss of value (E)	Wertverfall m	—	dévalorisation f	deprezzamento m	depreciación f
loss prevention (E)	Schadenverhütung f	—	mesure préventive contre les sinistres f	prevenzione danni f	prevención de siniestros f
lost shipment (E)	verlorengegangene Sendung f	—	envoi perdu m	spedizione andata persa f	envío perdido m
lot (E)	Posten m	—	lot de merchandises m	partita f	partida f
lot restant (F)	Restposten m	remnants	—	rimanenze f pl	partida restante f
lotería (Es)	Lotterie f	lottery	loterie f	lotteria f	—
loterie (F)	Lotterie f	lottery	—	lotteria f	lotería f
lotta contro i rumori (I)	Lärmbekämpfung f	noise abatement	lutte contre le bruit f	—	lucha contra el ruido f
lotteria (I)	Lotterie f	lottery	loterie f	—	lotería f
Lotterie (D)	—	lottery	loterie f	lotteria f	lotería f
lottery (E)	Lotterie f	—	loterie f	lotteria f	lotería f
lubricants (E)	Schmierstoffe pl	—	lubrifiants m pl	lubrificanti m pl	lubricantes m pl
lubrifiants (F)	Schmierstoffe pl	lubricants	—	lubrificanti m pl	lubricantes m pl
lubrificantes (Es)	Schmierstoffe pl	lubricants	lubrifiants m pl	lubrificanti m pl	—
lubrificanti (I)	Schmierstoffe pl	lubricants	lubrifiants m pl	—	lubricantes m pl
lucha contra el ruido (Es)	Lärmbekämpfung f	noise abatement	lutte contre le bruit f	lotta contro i rumori f	—
Luftfracht (D)	—	air freight	fret aérien m	nolo aereo m	flete aéreo m
Luftfrachtbrief (D)	—	air waybill	lettre de transport aérien f	lettera di trasporto aereo f	transporte aéreo m
Luftfrachtführer (D)	—	air carrier	voiturier aérien m	vettore aereo m	transportista m
Luftfrachtverkehr (D)	—	air freight traffic	transport aérien des marchandises m	traffico aereo commerciale m	tráfico de flete aéreo m
Luftpost (D)	—	air mail	par avion	posta aerea f	correo aéreo m
Luftweg (D)	—	air route	voie aérienne f	via aerea f	vía aérea f
lugar de destino (Es)	Bestimmungsort m	place of destination	lieu de destination m	luogo di destinazione m	—
lugar de la cita (Es)	Treffpunkt m	meeting place	rendez-vous m	punto d'incontro m	—
lugar de nacimiento (Es)	Geburtsort m	place of birth	lieu de naissance m	luogo di nascita m	—
lujo (Es)	Luxus m	luxury	luxe m	lusso m	—
lump sum settlement (E)	Kapitalabfindung f	—	indemnité en capital f	indennità in capitale f	indemnización en capital f
luogo di destinazione (I)	Bestimmungsort m	place of destination	lieu de destination m	—	lugar de de destino m
luogo di nascita (I)	Geburtsort m	place of birth	lieu de naissance m	—	lugar de nacimiento m
lusso (I)	Luxus m	luxury	luxe m	—	lujo m
lutte contre le bruit (F)	Lärmbekämpfung f	noise abatement	—	lotta contro i rumori f	lucha contra el ruido f
luxe (F)	Luxus m	luxury	—	lusso m	lujo m
luxury (E)	Luxus m	—	luxe m	lusso m	lujo m
luxury goods (E)	Luxusgüter pl	—	produits de luxe m pl	beni di lusso m pl	bienes de lujo m pl
luxury tax (E)	Luxussteuer f	—	taxe de luxe f	imposta sui consumi di lusso f	impuesto de lujo m
Luxus (D)	—	luxury	luxe m	lusso m	lujo m
Luxusgüter (D)	—	luxury goods	produits de luxe m pl	beni di lusso m pl	bienes de lujo m pl
Luxussteuer (D)	—	luxury tax	taxe de luxe f	imposta sui consumi di lusso f	impuesto de lujo m

	D	E	F	I	Es
macchina (I)	Maschine f	machine	machine f	—	máquina f
machine (E)	Maschine f	—	machine f	macchina f	máquina f
machine (F)	Maschine f	machine	—	macchina f	máquina f
machine insurance (E)	Maschinen-versicherung f	—	assurance des machines f	assicurazione delle macchine f	seguro de maquinaria m
macroeconomía (Es)	Makroökonomie f	macroeconomics	macroéconomie f	macroeconomia m	—
macroeconomia (I)	Makroökonomie f	macroeconomics	macroéconomie f	—	macroeconomía f
macroeconomics (E)	Makroökonomie f	—	macroéconomie f	macroeconomia m	macroeconomía f
macroéconomie (F)	Makroökonomie f	macroeconomics	—	macroeconomia m	macroeconomía f
maestranza (I)	Belegschaft f	staff	personnel m	—	plantilla f
magasin (F)	Lager n	warehouse	—	magazzino m	almacén m
magasins de test (F)	Testläden pl	test shops	—	negozi pilota m pl	tiendas piloto f pl
magazzinaggio¹ (I)	Lagerhaltung f	stockkeeping	entreposage m	—	almacenaje m
magazzinaggio² (I)	Lagerung f	storage	stockage m	—	almacenaje m
magazzino¹ (I)	Lagerraum m	storage space	halle de dépôt f	—	almacén m
magazzino² (I)	Lager n	warehouse	magasin m	—	almacén m
magazzino³ (I)	Warenlager n	stock room	stock de marchandises m	—	depósito de mercancías m
maggioranza (I)	Majorität f	majority	majorité f	—	mayoría f
maggioranza dei voti (I)	Stimmenmehrheit f	majority of votes	majorité des voix f	—	mayoría de votos f
maggioranza delle azioni (I)	Aktienmehrheit f	majority of shares	majorité d'actions f	—	mayoría de acciones f
maggiorazione dell'utile (I)	Gewinnaufschlag m	profit mark-up	majoration de bénéfice f	—	margen de benificio f
magnitud (Es)	Bestandsgröße f	stock variable	stock variable m	entità dell'inventario f	—
Mahnbrief (D)	—	reminder	lettre d'avertissement f	lettera di sollecito f	carta (ad)monitoria f
Mahnung (D)	—	demand for payment	mise en demeure f	sollecito m	(ad)monición f
mail box (E)	Briefkasten m	—	boîte aux lettres f	cassetta postale f	buzón m
mail order business (E)	Versandhandel m	—	commerce de vente au détail par correspondance m	vendita per corrispondenza f	venta por correspondencia f
main memory (E)	Hauptspeicher m	—	mémoire principale f	memoria principale f	memoria principal f
maintained (E)	behauptet	—	affirmé	affermato	sostenido
maintaining the real value (E)	Substanzerhaltung f	—	maintien de la substance m	mantenimento della sostanza m	conservación de la sustancia f
maintenance of secrecy (E)	Geheimhaltung f	—	conservation du secret f	segretezza f	mantenimiento del secreto m
maintien de la substance (F)	Substanzerhaltung f	maintaining the real value	—	mantenimento della sostanza m	conservación de la sustancia f
maison concurrente (F)	Konkurrenzfirma f	competing firm	—	ditta concorrente f	empresa competidora f
maison d'édition (F)	Verlag m	publishing house	—	casa editrice f	editorial f
maison mère¹ (F)	Mutterhaus n	mother house	—	casa madre f	casa matriz f
maison mère² (F)	Stammhaus n	parent company	—	casa madre f	casa matriz f
majoration de bénéfice (F)	Gewinnaufschlag m	profit mark-up	—	maggiorazione dell'utile f	margen de benificio f
Majorität (D)	—	majority	majorité f	maggioranza f	mayoría f
majorité (F)	Majorität f	majority	—	maggioranza f	mayoría f
majorité d'actions (F)	Aktienmehrheit f	majority of shares	—	maggioranza delle azioni f	mayoría de acciones f
majorité des voix (F)	Stimmenmehrheit f	majority of votes	—	maggioranza dei voti f	mayoría de votos f
majority (E)	Majorität f	—	majorité f	maggioranza f	mayoría f
majority of shares (E)	Aktienmehrheit f	—	majorité d'actions f	maggioranza delle azioni f	mayoría de acciones f
majority of votes (E)	Stimmenmehrheit f	—	majorité des voix f	maggioranza dei voti f	mayoría de votos f
majority-ownership (E)	Mehrheitsbesitz m	—	possession majoritaire f	possesso maggioritario m	mayoría f
making out an invoice (E)	Fakturierung f	—	facturation f	fatturazione f	facturación f

	D	E	F	I	Es
Makler (D)	—	broker	courtier *m*	mediatore *m*	corredor *m*
Makroökonomie (D)	—	macroeconomics	macroéconomie *f*	macroeconomia *m*	macroeconomía *f*
mala calidad (Es)	schlechte Qualität *f*	poor quality	mauvaise qualité *f*	qualità scadente *f*	—
malnutrition (E)	Unterernährung *f*	—	sous-alimentation *f*	denutrizione *f*	subalimentación *f*
malversación (Es)	Veruntreuung *f*	misappropriation	détournement *m*	abuso di fiducia *m*	—
Management (D)	—	management	management *m*	management *m*	alta dirección *f*
management[1] (E)	Leitung *f*	—	direction *f*	direzione *f*	dirección *f*
management[2] (E)	Führung *f*	—	direction *f*	gestione *f*	gestión *f*
management[3] (E)	Geschäftsleitung *f*	—	direction commerciale *f*	direzione *f*	dirección *f*
management[4] (E)	Management *n*	—	management *m*	management *m*	alta dirección *f*
management[5] (E)	Geschäftsführung *f*	—	gestion *f*	amministrazione *f*	gestión *f*
management (F)	Management *n*	management	—	management *m*	alta dirección *f*
management (I)	Management *n*	management	management *m*	—	alta dirección *f*
management di progetto (I)	Projekt-Management *n*	project management	gestion d'un projet *f*	—	administración del proyecto *f*
management games (E)	Planspiel *n*	—	jeu d'entreprise *m*	gioco di strategia imprenditoriale *m*	juego de ensayo *m*
Manager (D)	—	manager	manager *m*	manager *m*	alto directivo *m*
manager[1] (E)	Geschäftsführer *m*	—	gérant d'une affaire *m*	amministratore *m*	gerente *m*
manager[2] (E)	Manager *m*	—	manager *m*	manager *m*	alto directivo *m*
manager (F)	Manager *m*	manager	—	manager *m*	alto directivo *m*
manager (I)	Manager *m*	manager	manager *m*	—	alto directivo *m*
manager of shipping department (E)	Versandleiter *m*	—	chef du service des expéditions *m*	capo reparto spedizioni *m*	jefe del departamento de expedición *m*
mancanza di personale (I)	Personalmangel *m*	shortage of staff	manque de personnel *m*	—	falta der personal *f*
mandamiento de pago (Es)	Zahlungsbefehl *m*	order for payment	ordre de payement *m*	ingiunzione di pagamento *f*	—
mandante (Es)	Auftraggeber *m*	client	commettant *m*	committente *m*	—
mandante (I)	Vollmachtgeber *m*	grantor of a power of attorney	auteur de la procuration *m*	—	poderdante *m*
mandare allo scoperto (I)	überziehen	overdraw	faire un prélèvement à découvert	—	sobrepasar
mandat (F)	Anweisung *f*	transfer	—	ordine di pagamento *m*	transferencia *f*
mandatario commerciale (I)	Handlungsbevoll-mächtigter *m*	commercial agent	personne ayant le pouvoir commercial *f*	—	apoderado especial *m*
mandat-carte (F)	Zahlkarte *f*	money order	—	modulo di versamento *m*	carta de pago *f*
mandat de payement (F)	Zahlungsanweisung *f*	order to pay	—	ordine di pagamento *m*	orden de pago *f*
mandat-poste (F)	Postanweisung *f*	postal money order	—	vaglia postale *m*	vale postal *m*
mandat télégraphique (F)	telegrafische Anweisung *f*	telegraphic payment order	—	vaglia telegrafico *m*	orden telegráfica *f*
Mangel (D)	—	defect	défaut *m*	vizio *m*	defecto *m*/vicio *m*
Mängelanzeige (D)	—	notice of defect	notification d'un vice *f*	denuncia dei vizi	aviso de vicios *m*
mangelfrei (D)	—	free of defects	sans défaut	esente da vizi	sin vicios
manifattura (I)	Manufaktur *f*	manufactory	manufacture *f*	—	manufactura *f*
manifesto (I)	Plakat *n*	poster	affiche *f*	—	cartel *m*
manifesto promozionale (I)	Aktionsplakat *n*	advertising bill	affiche d'action *f*	—	cartel de acción *m*
manner of delivery (E)	Versandform *f*	—	forme d'expédition *f*	tipo di spedizione *m*	forma de envío *f*
Mannschaft (D)	—	team/crew	équipe *f*/équipage *m*	équipe *f*/equipaggio *m*	equipo *m*/tripulación *f*
man of straw (E)	Strohmann *m*	—	prête-nom *m*	prestanome *m*	testaferro *m*
mano pubblica (I)	öffentliche Hand *f*	public authorities	secteur public *m*	—	sector público *m*
manque de personnel (F)	Personalmangel *m*	shortage of staff	—	mancanza di personale *f*	falta de personal *f*
manque de trésorerie (F)	Illiquidität *f*	illiquidity	—	illiquidità *f*	falta de liquidez *f*

	D	E	F	I	Es
mantenimento della sostanza (I)	Substanzerhaltung f	maintaining the real value	maintien de la substance m	—	conservación de la sustancia f
mantenimiento del secreto (Es)	Geheimhaltung f	maintenance of secrecy	conservation du secret f	segretezza f	—
manual (E)	Handbuch n	—	manuel m	manuale m	manual m
manual (Es)	Handbuch n	manual	manuel m	manuale m	—
manuale (I)	Handbuch n	manual	manuel m	—	manual m
manuel (F)	Handbuch n	manual	—	manuale m	manual m
manufactory (E)	Manufaktur f	—	manufacture f	manifattura f	manufactura f
manufactura (Es)	Manufaktur f	manufactory	manufacture f	manifattura f	—
manufacture (F)	Manufaktur f	manufactory	—	manifattura f	manufactura f
manufactured quantity (E)	Fertigungsmenge f	—	quantité fabriquée f	quantitativo di produzione m	cantidad producida f
manufactured to measure (E)	maßgefertigt	—	travaillé sur mesure	prodotto su misura	hecho a medida
manufacturer (E)	Erzeuger m	—	producteur m	produttore m	productor m
manufacture to customer's specifications (E)	Sonderanfertigung f	—	fabrication spéciale f	produzione fuori serie f	fabricación especial f
manufacturing industry (E)	verarbeitende Industrie f	—	industrie transformatrice f	industria di trasformazione f	industria transformadora f
Manufaktur (D)	—	manufactory	manufacture f	manifattura f	manufactura f
maquette (F)	Layout n	layout	—	layout m	layout m
máquina (Es)	Maschine f	machine	machine f	macchina f	—
máquina de dictar (Es)	Diktiergerät n	dictaphone	appareil à dicter m	dittafono m	—
marca (Es)	Warenzeichen n	trade mark	marque f	marchio m	—
marca (I)	Marke f	mark	marque f	—	característica f
marchandise (F)	Ware f	goods	—	merce f	mercancía f
marchandise à transporter (F)	Frachtgut n	cargo	—	merce di trasporto f	mercancías en pequeña velocidad f pl
marchandise en grande vitesse (F)	Eilgut n	goods sent by express	—	merce a grande velocità f	mercancía en gran velocidad f
marchandises en commission (F)	Kommissionsgüter pl	goods for sale on commission	—	beni in conto deposito m pl	mercancías en comisión f pl
marchandises en vrac (F)	Massengüter pl	bulk goods	—	beni di massa m pl	productos a granel m pl
marché (F)	Markt m	market	—	mercato m	mercado m
marché agricole (F)	Agrarmarkt m	agricultural market	—	mercato agrario m	mercado agrícola m
marché avant le marché officiel (F)	Vorbörse f	before hours dealing	—	mercato preborsistico m	operaciones antes de la apertura de la bolsa f pl
marché commun (F)	gemeinsamer Markt m	common market	—	mercato comune m	mercado común m
marché d'acheteurs (F)	Käufermarkt m	buyer's market	—	mercato favorevole all'acquirente m	mercado favorable al comprador m
marché de l'ór (F)	Goldmarkt m	gold market	—	mercato dell'oro m	mercado del oro m
marché des capitaux (F)	Kapitalmarkt m	capital market	—	mercato finanziario m	mercado financiero m
marché des changes[1] (F)	Devisenhandel m	foreign exchange dealings	—	commercio delle divise m	operaciones de divisas f pl
marché des changes[2] (F)	Devisenmarkt m	foreign exchange market	—	mercato valutario m	mercado de divisas m
marché des consommateurs (F)	Verbrauchermarkt m	consumer market	—	ipermercato m	mercado favorable al consumidor m
marché des effets publics (F)	Rentenmarkt m	bond market	—	mercato dei titoli a reddito fisso m	mercado de títulos de renta fija m
marché de test (F)	Testmarkt m	test market	—	mercato pilota m	mercado piloto m
marché de vendeurs (F)	Verkäufermarkt m	seller's market	—	mercato favorevole ai venditori m	mercado favorable al vendedor m
marché d'exportation (F)	Exportmarkt m	export market	—	mercato delle esportazioni m	mercado de exportación m
marché du travail (F)	Arbeitsmarkt m	labour market	—	mercato del lavoro m	mercado laboral m
marché en disponible (F)	Spotmarkt m	spot market	—	mercato spot m	mercado de operaciones al contado y de entrega inmediata m

	D	E	F	I	Es
marché gris (F)	Grauer Markt m	grey market	—	mercato grigio m	mercado gris m
Marché Intérieur de la Communauté Européenne (F)	EG-Binnenmarkt m	Internal Market of the European Community	—	mercato unico m	Mercado Unico m
marché monétaire (F)	Geldmarkt m	money market	—	mercato monetario m	mercado monetario m
marché national (F)	Binnenmarkt m	home market	—	mercato nazionale m	mercado interior m
marché noir (F)	Schwarzmarkt m	black market	—	mercato nero m	mercado negro m
marchés des matières premières (F)	Rohstoffmarkt m	commodity market	—	mercato delle materie prime m	mercado de materias primas m
marchés extérieurs (F)	Auslandsmärkte pl	foreign markets	—	mercati esteri m pl	mercado exterior m
marchio[1] (I)	Markenzeichen n	trademark	marque déposée f	—	emblema comercial m/marca registrada f
marchio[2] (I)	Warenzeichen n	trade mark	marque f	—	marca f
Marge (D)	—	margin	marge f	margine m	margen m
marge[1] (F)	Marge f	margín	—	margine m	margen m
marge[2] (F)	Bandbreite f	margin	—	margine m	margen de fluctuación f
marge[3] (F)	Spanne f	margin	—	margine m	margen f
marge[4] (F)	Spielraum m	margin	—	tolleranza f	margen f
marge bénéficiaire (F)	Gewinnmarge f	profit margin	—	margine dell'utile m	margen de beneficios f
marge de bénéfice (F)	Gewinnspanne f	margin of profit	—	margine dell'utile m	margen de beneficios f
marge de crédit accordé (F)	Kreditrahmen m	credit margin	—	plafond di credito m	margen de crédito m
marge de détail (F)	Einzelhandels-spanne f	retail price margin	—	margine del commercio al dettaglio m	margen del comercio al por menor m
marge de la fluctuation (F)	Schwankungsbreite f	margin of fluctuation	—	margine d'oscillazione m	margen de fluctuación f
marge de sécurité (F)	Sicherheitsmarge f	margin	—	margine di sicurezza m	margen de seguridad f
marge entre les taux d'intérêt créditeur et débiteur (F)	Zinsmarge f	interest margin	—	margine degli interessi m	margen de interés m
margen[1] (Es)	Spielraum m	margin	marge f	tolleranza f	—
margen[2] (Es)	Marge f	margin	marge f	margine m	—
margen[3] (Es)	Spanne f	margin	marge f	margine m	—
margen comercial (Es)	Handelsspanne f	trading margin	bénéfice brut m	margine commerciale m	—
margen de beneficios[1] (Es)	Gewinnmarge f	profit margin	marge bénéficiaire f	margine dell'utile m	—
margen de beneficios[2] (Es)	Gewinnspanne f	margin of profit	marge de bénéfice f	margine dell'utile m	—
margen de benificio (Es)	Gewinnaufschlag m	profit mark-up	majoration de bénéfice f	maggiorazione dell'utile f	—
margen de crédito (Es)	Kreditrahmen m	credit margin	marge de crédit accordé f	plafond di credito m	—
margen de fluctuación[1] (Es)	Bandbreite f	margin	marge f	margine m	—
margen de fluctuación[2] (Es)	Schwankungsbreite f	margin of fluctuation	marge de la fluctuation f	margine d'oscillazione m	—
margen de interés (Es)	Zinsmarge f	interest margin	marge entre les taux d'intérêt créditeur et débiteur f	margine degli interessi m	—
margen del comercio al por menor (Es)	Einzelhandels-spanne f	retail price margin	marge de détail f	margine del commercio al dettaglio m	—
margen de seguridad (Es)	Sicherheitsmarge f	margin	marge de sécurité f	margine di sicurezza m	—
margin[1] (E)	Marge f	—	marge f	margine m	margen m
margin[2] (E)	Spielraum m	—	marge f	tolleranza f	margen m
margin[3] (E)	Spanne f	—	marge f	margine m	margen m
margin[4] (E)	Sicherheitsmarge f	—	marge de sécurité f	margine di sicurezza m	margen de seguridad f

	D	E	F	I	Es
margin⁵ (E)	Bandbreite f	—	marge f	margine m	margen de fluctuación f
marginal costing (E)	Grenzkosten-rechnung f	—	détermination du coût marginal f	conto dei costi limite m	cálculo de los costes marginales m
marginal value (E)	Marginalwert m	—	valeur marginale f	valore marginale m	valor marginal m
Marginalwert (D)	—	marginal value	valeur marginale f	valore marginale m	valor marginal m
margin between interest rates (E)	Zinsgefälle n	—	disparité des niveaux d'intérêts f	differenza dei tassi d'interesse f	diferencia entre los tipos de interés f
margine¹ (I)	Spanne f	margin	marge f	—	margen f
margine² (I)	Bandbreite f	within a limit of	marge f	—	margen de fluctuación f
margine³ (I)	Marge f	margin	marge f	—	margen f m
margine commerciale (I)	Handelsspanne f	trading margin	bénéfice brut m	—	margen comercial f
margine degli interessi (I)	Zinsmarge f	interest margin	marge entre les taux d'intérêt créditeur et débiteur f	—	margen de interés m
margine del commercio al dettaglio (I)	Einzelhandels-spanne f	retail price margin	marge de détail f	—	margen del comercio al por menor m
margine dell'utile¹ (I)	Gewinnmarge f	profit margin	marge bénéficiaire f	—	margen de beneficios f
margine dell'utile² (I)	Gewinnspanne f	margin of profit	marge de bénéfice f	—	margen de beneficios f
margine di sicurezza (I)	Sicherheitsmarge f	margin	marge de sécurité f	—	margen de seguridad f
margine d'oscillazione (I)	Schwankungsbreite f	margin of fluctuation	marge de la fluctuation f	—	margen de fluctuación f
margin of fluctuation (E)	Schwankungsbreite f	—	marge de la fluctuation f	margine d'oscillazione m	margen de fluctuación f
margin of profit (E)	Gewinnspanne f	—	marge de bénéfice f	margine dell'utile m	margen de beneficios f
mark (E)	Marke f	—	marque f	marca f	característica f
Marke (D)	—	mark	marque f	marca f	característica f
Markenartikel (D)	—	brandname article	produit de marque m	articolo di marca m	artículo de marca m
Markenzeichen (D)	—	trademark	marque deposée f	marchio m	emblema comercial m/ marca registrada f
market¹ (E)	vermarkten	—	commercialiser	lanciare sul mercato	comercializar
market² (E)	Markt m	—	marché m	mercato m	mercado m
marketable (E)	marktfähig	—	vendable	smerciabile	comerciable
market analysis (E)	Marktanalyse f	—	analyse du marché f	analisi di mercato f	anállsis de mercado m
market day (E)	Börsentag m	—	jour de bourse m	giorno di borsa m	sesión bursátil f
market details (E)	Marktdaten pl	—	données sur le marché f pl	dati di mercato m pl	datos del mercado m pl
market economy (E)	Marktwirtschaft f	—	économie de marché f	economia di mercato f	economía de mercado f
market forces (E)	Marktkräfte pl	—	forces du marché	forze di mercato f pl	fuerzas del mercado f pl
market gap (E)	Marktlücke f	—	créneau du marché m	lacuna di mercato f	sector del mercado no abarcado por la oferta m
Marketing (D)	—	marketing	marketing	marketing m	organización de ventas f
marketing¹ (E)	Marketing n	—	marketing m	marketing m	organización de ventas f
marketing² (E)	Absatzwirtschaft f	—	commercialisation f	marketing m	economía de distribución f
marketing (F)	Marketing n	marketing	—	marketing m	organización de ventas f
marketing¹ (I)	Marketing n	marketing	marketing m	—	organización de ventas f
marketing² (I)	Absatzwirtschaft f	marketing	commercialisation f	—	economía de distribución f
Marketingabteilung (D)	—	marketing department	bureau de marketing m	reparto marketing m	departamento de mercadeo m

	D	E	F	I	Es
Marketingberater (D)	—	marketing consultant	conseiller de marketing *m*	consulente di marketing *m*	asesor de marketing *m*
marketing consultant (E)	Marketingberater *m*	—	conseiller de marketing *m*	consulente di marketing *m*	asesor de marketing *m*
marketing department (E)	Marketingabteilung *f*	—	bureau de marketing *m*	reparto marketing *m*	departamento de mercadeo *m*
marketing in prima persona (I)	Direct-Marketing *n*	direct marketing	stratégie des ventes directes *f*	—	comercialización directa *f*
Marketing-Mix (D)	—	mixture of marketing strategies	mélange de marketing *f*	marketing-mix *m*	mezcla de marketing *f*
marketing-mix (I)	Marketing-Mix *m*	mixture of marketing strategies	mélange de marketing *f*	—	mezcla de marketing *f*
marketing-oriented (E)	Marketing-orientiert	—	orienté vers le marketing	orientato al marketing	orientado hacia el marketing
Marketing-orientiert (D)	—	marketing-oriented	orienté vers le marketing	orientato al marketing	orientado hacia el marketing
marketing planning (E)	Marketingplanung *f*	—	planning du marketing *m*	programmazione del marketing *f*	planificación de mercadeo *m*
Marketingplanung (D)	—	marketing planning	planning du marketing *m*	programmazione del marketing *f*	planificación de mercadeo *m*
marketing policy (E)	Absatzpolitik *f*	—	politique de vente *f*	politica di vendita *f*	política de ventas *f*
market organization (E)	Marktordnung *f*	—	organisation du marché *f*	ordinamento del mercato *m*	organización del mercado *f*
market position (E)	Marktposition *f*	—	position sur le marché *f*	posizione di mercato *f*	posición en el mercado *f*
market research (E)	Marktforschung *f*	—	recherche du marché *f*	ricerca di mercato *f*	estudio del mercado *m*
market research institute (E)	Marktforschungs-institut *n*	—	institut d'études de marché *m*	istituto della ricerca di mercato *m*	instituto de investigación del mercado *m*
market share (E)	Marktanteil *m*	—	participation au marché *f*	quota di mercato *f*	cuota del mercado *f*
market situation (E)	Marktsituation *f*	—	situation du marché *f*	situazione di mercato *f*	estado del mercado *m*
market survey (E)	Marktuntersuchung *f*	—	étude du marché *f*	analisi di mercato *f*	estudio del mercado *m*
market test (E)	Markttest *m*	—	test du marché *m*	test di mercato *m*	examinación del mercado *m*
market transparency (E)	Markttransparenz *f*	—	transparence du marché *f*	trasparenza di mercato *f*	transparencia del mercado *f*
Markt (D)	—	market	marché *m*	mercato *m*	mercado *m*
Marktanalyse (D)	—	market analysis	analyse du marché *f*	analisi di mercato *f*	análisis de mercado *m*
Marktanteil (D)	—	market share	participation au marché *f*	quota di mercato *f*	cuota del mercado *f*
Marktbeobachtung (D)	—	observation of markets	étude de marché *f*	sondaggio del mercato *m*	observación del mercado *f*
Marktdaten (D)	—	market details	données sur le marché *f pl*	dati di mercato *m pl*	datos del mercado *m pl*
Markteintritt (D)	—	entry into the market	entrée dans le marché *f*	apertura di mercato *f*	entrada en el mercado *f*
marktfähig (D)	—	marketable	vendable	smerciabile	comerciable
Marktformen (D)	—	types of markets	formes du marché *f pl*	tipi di mercato *m pl*	formas del mercado *f*
Marktforschung (D)	—	market research	recherche du marché *f*	ricerca di mercato *f*	estudio del mercado *m*
Marktforschungs-institut (D)	—	market research institute	institut d'études de marché *m*	istituto della ricerca di mercato *m*	instituto de investigación del mercado *m*
marktkonform (D)	—	in conformity with market conditions	conforme au marché	conforme al mercato	conforme al mercado
Marktkräfte (D)	—	market forces	forces du marché	forze di mercato *f pl*	fuerzas del mercado *f pl*
Marktlage (D)	—	state of the market	situation du marché *f*	situazione di mercato *f*	condiciones del mercado *f pl*
Marktlücke (D)	—	market gap	créneau du marché *m*	lacuna di mercato *f*	sector del mercado no abarcado por la oferta *m*

	D	E	F	I	Es
Marktordnung (D)	—	market organization	organisation du marché f	ordinamento del mercato m	organización del mercado f
Marktposition (D)	—	market position	position sur le marché f	posizione di mercato f	posición en el mercado f
Marktsituation (D)	—	market situation	situation du marché f	situazione di mercato f	estado del mercado m
Markttest (D)	—	market test	test du marché m	test di mercato m	examinación del mercado f
Markttransparenz (D)	—	market transparency	transparence du marché f	trasparenza di mercato f	transparencia del mercado f
Marktübersicht (D)	—	overall view of the market	vue d'ensemble du marché f	quadro del mercato m	panorama de mercado m
Marktuntersuchung (D)	—	market survey	étude du marché f	analisi di mercato f	estudio del mercado m
Marktwirtschaft (D)	—	market economy	économie de marché f	economia di mercato f	economía de mercado f
marque[1] (F)	Warenzeichen n	trademark	—	marchio m	marca f
marque[2] (F)	Marke f	mark	—	marca f	característica f
marque déposée (F)	Markenzeichen n	trademark	—	marchio m	emblema comercial m/ marca registrada f
masa de la quiebra (Es)	Konkursmasse f	bankrupt's estate	masse de la faillite f	massa fallimentare f	—
masa pasiva (Es)	Schuldenmasse f	total of indebtedness	passif m	massa passiva f	—
Maschine (D)	—	machine	machine f	macchina f	máquina f
maschinell (D)	—	by machine	mécanique	a macchina	a máquina
Maschinen- versicherung (D)	—	machine insurance	assurance des machines f	assicurazione delle macchine f	seguro de maquinaria m
Maß (D)	—	measure	mesure f	misura f	medida f
massa fallimentare (I)	Konkursmasse f	bankrupt's estate	masse de la faillite f	—	masa de la quiebra f
massa monetaria (I)	Geldmenge f	money supply	quantité de monnaie en circulation f	—	volumen monetario m
massa passiva (I)	Schuldenmasse f	total of indebtedness	passif m	—	masa pasiva f
masse active (F)	Aktiva pl	assets	—	attivo m	activo m
masse de la faillite (F)	Konkursmasse f	bankrupt's estate	—	massa fallimentare f	masa de la quiebra f
masse héréditaire (F)	Erbengemeinschaft f	community of heirs	—	comunità degli eredi f	comunidad sucesoria f
masse monétaire (F)	Geldvolumen n	volume of money	—	volume monetario m	volumen monetario m
Massenfertigung (D)	—	mass production	production en série f	fabbricazione di massa f	fabricación en masa f
Massengüter (D)	—	bulk goods	marchandises en vrac f pl	beni di massa m pl	productos a granel m pl
Massenproduktion (D)	—	mass production	production en grandes séries f	produzione di massa f	producción en masa f
maßgefertigt (D)	—	manufactured to measure	travaillé sur mesure	prodotto su misura	hecho a medida
massimizzazione dell'utile (I)	Gewinn- maximierung f	maximization of profits	maximisation du gain f	—	maximación de los beneficios f
massimo (I)	Maximum n	maximum	maximum m	—	máximo m
mass production[1] (E)	Massenfertigung f	—	production en série f	fabbricazione di massa f	fabricación en masa f
mass production[2] (E)	Massenproduktion f	—	production en grandes séries f	produzione di massa f	producción en masa f
Material (D)	—	material	matériel m	materiale m	material m
material (E)	Material n	—	matériel m	materiale m	material m
material (Es)	Material n	material	matériel m	materiale m	—
material assets (E)	Sachvermögen n	—	biens corporels m pl	capitale reale m	patrimonio real m
Materialaufwand (D)	—	material expenditure	dépenses en matières f pl	spese materiale f pl	coste de material m
material costs (E)	Materialaufwand m	—	dépenses en matériels f pl	spese materiale f pl	coste de material m
materiale (I)	Material n	material	matériel m	—	material m
materiale d'imballaggio (I)	Verpackungs- material n	packing material	matériel d'emballage m	—	empaque m
material expenditures (E)	Materialkosten pl	—	frais de matériel m pl	costi del materiale m pl	gastos de ma- terial m pl/coste de material m

	D	E	F	I	Es
Materialkosten (D)	—	material costs	frais de matériel *m pl*	costi del materiale *m pl*	gastos de material *m pl*/coste de material *m*
Materialkosten-anteil (D)	—	share in the material costs	proportion des frais de matériel *f*	quota dei costi del materiale *f*	parte de los gastos de material *m*
materia prima (Es)	Rohstoff *m*	raw materials	matière première *f*	materia prima *f*	—
materia prima (I)	Rohstoff *m*	raw materials	matière première *f*	—	materia prima *f*
matériel (F)	Material *n*	material	—	materiale *m*	material *m*
matériel d'emballage (F)	Verpackungsmittel *n*	means of packing	—	mezzi d'imballaggio *m pl*	medios de embalaje *m pl*
matière première (F)	Rohstoff *m*	raw materials	—	materia prima *f*	materia prima *f*
mauvaise qualité (F)	schlechte Qualität *f*	poor quality	—	qualità scadente *f*	mala calidad *f*
mauvais investissement (F)	Fehlinvestition *f*	misconceived capital projects	—	investimento sbagliato *m*	inversión equivocada *f*
maximación de los beneficios (Es)	Gewinn-maximierung *f*	maximization of profits	maximisation du gain *f*	massimizzazione dell'utile *f*	—
maximisation du gain (F)	Gewinn-maximierung *f*	maximization of profits	—	massimizzazione dell'utile *f*	maximación de los beneficios *f*
maximization of profits (E)	Gewinn-maximierung *f*	—	maximisation du gain *f*	massimizzazione dell'utile *f*	maximación de los beneficios *f*
máximo (Es)	Maximum *n*	maximum	maximum *m*	massimo *m*	—
Maximum (D)	—	maximum	maximum *m*	massimo *m*	máximo *m*
maximum (E)	Maximum *n*	—	maximum *m*	massimo *m*	máximo *m*
maximum (F)	Maximum *n*	maximum	—	massimo *m*	máximo *m*
mayoría (Es)	Majorität *f*	majority	majorité *f*	maggioranza *f*	—
mayoría de acciones (Es)	Aktienmehrheit *f*	majority of shares	majorité d'actions *f*	maggioranza delle azioni *f*	—
mayoría de votos (Es)	Stimmenmehrheit *f*	majority of votes	majorité des voix *f*	maggioranza dei voti *f*	—
mayorista (Es)	Grossist *m*	wholesaler	grossiste *m*	grossista *m*	—
means (E)	Mittel *n*	—	moyen *m*	mezzo *m*	medio *m*/recurso *m*
means of payment (E)	Zahlungsmittel *n*	—	moyen de payement *m*	mezzo di pagamento *m*	medio de pago *m*
means of transport (E)	Transportmittel *n*	—	moyen de transport *m*	mezzo di trasporto *m*	medio de transporte *m*
measure (E)	Maß *n*	—	mesure *f*	misura *f*	medida *f*
measurements (E)	Meßwerte *pl*	—	valeurs mesurées *f pl*	valori misurati *m pl*	valor de medida *m*
measures to encourage exports (E)	Ausfuhrförderung *f*	—	encouragement à l'exportation *m*	promozione delle esportazioni *f*	fomento de la exportación *m*
measuring (E)	Messung *f*	—	mesurage *m*	misurazione *f*	medición *f*
mécanicien (F)	Mechaniker *m*	mechanic	—	meccanico *m*	mecánico *m*
mecánico (Es)	Mechaniker *m*	mechanic	mécanicien *m*	meccanico *m*	—
mécanique (F)	maschinell	by machine	—	a macchina	a máquina
mécanisme des prix (F)	Preismechanismus *m*	price mechanism	—	meccanismo dei prezzi *m*	mecanismo de precios *m*
mecanismo de precios (Es)	Preismechanismus *m*	price mechanism	mécanisme des prix *m*	meccanismo dei prezzi *m*	—
meccanico (I)	Mechaniker *m*	mechanic	mécanicien *m*	—	mecánico *m*
meccanismo dei prezzi (I)	Preismechanismus *m*	price mechanism	mécanisme des prix *m*	—	mecanismo de precios *m*
mechanic (E)	Mechaniker *m*	—	mécanicien *m*	meccanico *m*	mecánico *m*
Mechaniker (D)	—	mechanic	mécanicien *m*	meccanico *m*	mecánico *m*
media (I)	Durchschnitt *m*	average	moyenne *f*	—	promedio *m*
mediación (Es)	Vermittlung *f*	mediation	médiation *f*	mediazione *f*	—
mediación de créditos (Es)	Kreditvermittlung *f*	arranging for a credit	médiation du crédit *f*	intermediazione di crediti *f*	—
mediante assegno (I)	bargeldlos	non-cash	par virement	—	por transferencia
média publicitaires (F)	Werbemedien *pl*	advertising media	—	mezzi pubblicitari *m pl*	medios de publicidad *m pl*
mediation (E)	Vermittlung *f*	—	médiation *f*	mediazione *f*	mediación *f*/conciliación *f*
médiation (F)	Vermittlung *f*	mediation	—	mediazione *f*	mediación *f*/conciliación *f*

	D	E	F	I	Es
médiation du crédit (F)	Kreditvermittlung *f*	arranging for a credit	—	intermediazione di crediti *f*	mediación de créditos *f*
mediatore (I)	Makler *m*	broker	courtier *m*	—	corredor *m*
mediatore d'assicurazione (I)	Versicherungsmakler *m*	insurance broker	courtier en assurance *m*	—	corredor de seguros *m*
mediazione (I)	Vermittlung *f*	mediation	médiation *f*	—	mediación *f*/ conciliación *f*
medición (Es)	Messung *f*	measuring	mesurage *m*	misurazione *f*	—
medida (Es)	Maß *n*	measure	mesure *f*	misura *f*	—
medidas de infraestructura (Es)	Infrastrukturmaßnahmen *f*	infrastructural measures	mesures pour l'amélioration de l'infrastructure *f pl*	misure per l'infrastruttura *f pl*	—
medio (Es)	Mittel *n*	means	moyen *m*	mezzo *m*	—
medio de datos (Es)	Datenträger *m*	data medium	porteur des données *m*	supporto dati *m*	—
medio de pago (Es)	Zahlungsmittel *n*	means of payment	moyen de payement *m*	mezzo di pagamento *m*	—
medio de publicidad (Es)	Werbeträger *m*	advertising medium	support publicitaire *m*	veicolo pubblicitario *m*	—
medio de transporte (Es)	Transportmittel *n*	means of transport	moyen de transport *m*	mezzo di trasporto *m*	—
medio de venta (Es)	Absatzweg *m*	channel of distribution	canal de distribution *m*	via della distribuzione *f*	—
medio legal de pago (Es)	gesetzliches Zahlungsmittel *n*	legal tender	monnaie légale *f*	mezzo di pagamento legale *m*	—
medio publicitario (Es)	Werbemittel *n*	advertising aids	moyen publicitaire *m*	mezzo pubblicitario *m*	—
medios de publicidad (Es)	Werbemedien *pl*	advertising media	média publicitaires *m pl*	mezzi pubblicitari *m pl*	—
medios publicitarios directos (Es)	Direktwerbemittel *n*	direct means of advertising	moyens publicitaires directs *m pl*	mezzo pubblicitario diretto *m*	—
medium-term (E)	mittelfristig	—	à moyen terme	a media scadenza	a medio plazo
medium-term credit (E)	mittelfristiger Kredit *m*	—	crédit à moyen terme *m*	credito a media scadenza *m*	crédito a medio plazo *m*
meeting (E)	Tagung *f*	—	congrès *m*	convegno *m*	reunión *f*
meeting date (E)	Besprechungstermin *m*	—	date de la conférence *f*	termine del colloquio *m*	fecha de conferencia *f*
meeting of shareholders (E)	Gesellschafterversammlung *f*	—	réunion des associés *f*	assemblea dei soci *f*	junta social *f*
meeting place (E)	Treffpunkt *m*	—	rendez-vous *m*	punto d'incontro *m*	lugar de la cita *m*
Mehrarbeit (D)	—	additional work	travail supplémentaire *m*	lavoro supplementare *m*	trabajo extraordinario *m*
Mehrbelastung (D)	—	additional burden	surcharge *f*	onere supplementare *m*	carga suplementaria *f*
Mehrlieferung (D)	—	additional delivery	livraison supplémentaire *f*	fornitura supplementare *f*	exceso *m*
Mehrwert (D)	—	value added	valeur ajoutée *f*	valore aggiunto *m*	plusvalía *f*
Mehrwertsteuer (D)	—	value-added tax	taxe à la valeur ajoutée *f*	imposta sul valore aggiunto *f*	impuesto sobre el valor añadido *m*
Meile (D)	—	mile	mille *m*	miglio *m*	milla *f*
Meinung (D)	—	opinion	opinion *f*	opinione *f*	opinión *f*
Meinungskäufe (D)	—	speculative buying	achats spéculatifs *m pl*	acquisti speculativi *m pl*	compras especulativas *f pl*
Meistbegünstigungsklausel (D)	—	most-favoured nation clause	clause de la nation la plus favorisée *f*	clausola della nazione più favorita *f*	cláusula de nación más favorecida *f*
mélange de marketing (F)	Marketing-Mix *m*	mixture of marketing strategies	—	marketing-mix *m*	mezcla de marketing *f*
member (E)	Mitglied *n*	—	membre *m*	membro *m*	miembro *m*
member of the European Commission (E)	EG-Kommissar *m*	—	commissaire européen *m*	commissario CEE *m*	comisario de la Comunidad Europea *m*
member of the managing board (E)	Vorstandsmitglied *n*	—	membre du comité de direction *m*	membro del consiglio di amministrazione *m*	consejero directivo *m*
membre (F)	Mitglied *n*	member	—	membro *m*	miembro *m*
membre du comité de direction (F)	Vorstandsmitglied *n*	member of the managing board	—	membro del consiglio di amministrazione *m*	consejero directivo *m*

	D	E	F	I	Es
membro (I)	Mitglied *n*	member	membre *m*	—	miembro *m*
membro del consiglio di amministrazione (I)	Vorstandsmitglied *n*	member of the managing board	membre du comité de direction *m*	—	consejero directivo *m*
mémoire principale (F)	Hauptspeicher *m*	main memory	—	memoria principale *f*	memoria principal *f*
memorandum (E)	Aktennotiz *f*	—	note *f*	annotazione *f*	nota *f*
memoria principal (Es)	Hauptspeicher *m*	main memory	mémoire principale *f*	memoria principale *f*	—
memoria principale (I)	Hauptspeicher *m*	main memory	mémoire principale *f*	—	memoria principal *f*
ménage privé (F)	privater Haushalt *m*	private household	—	famiglia *f*	economía doméstica *f*
Menge (D)	—	quantity	quantité *f*	quantità *f*	cantidad *f*
Mengenangabe (D)	—	indication of quantity	indication de la quantité *f*	indicazione della quantità *f*	indicación de cantidades *f*
Mengeneinheit (D)	—	quantity unit	unité de quantité *f*	unità quantitativa *f*	unidad cuantitativa *f*
Mengenkonjunktur (D)	—	quantitative boom	conjoncture de quantité *f*	congiuntura quantitativa *f*	coyuntura cuantitativa *f*
Mengenkontingent (D)	—	quantity quota	contingent de marchandises *m*	contingente di quantità *m*	contingente cuantitativo *m*
Mengennotierung (D)	—	fixed exchange	cotation de quantité *f*	cambio reale *m*	cotización real *f*
Mengenrabatt (D)	—	quantity discount	remise de quantité *f*	sconto di quantità *m*	rebaja de cantidad *f*
Mengenzoll (D)	—	specific duty	droit de douane par quantité *m*	dazio di quantità *m*	arancel aduanero cuantitativo *m*
menor de edad (Es)	minderjährig	under age	mineur	minorenne	—
mensaje publicitario (Es)	Werbebotschaft *f*	sales message	message publicitaire *m*	messaggio pubblicitario *m*	—
mensaje radiado (Es)	Funkspruch *m*	radio message	message par radio *m*	radiotelefonata *f*	—
mensile (I)	monatlich	monthly	par mois	—	mensual
mensual (Es)	monatlich	monthly	par mois	mensile	—
mensualité d'un achat à tempérament (F)	Teilzahlungsrate *f*	monthly instalment	—	rata *f*	plazo *m*
mentalità concezionale (I)	konzeptionelles Denken *n*	conceptional thinking	penser conceptionnel *m*	—	pensar concepcional *m*
mentalità creativa (I)	kreatives Denken *n*	creative thinking	créativité conceptionnelle *f*	—	creatividad concepcional *f*
mention des responsables de l'édition (F)	Impressum *n*	imprint	—	impressum *m*	pie de imprenta *m*
mercado (Es)	Markt *m*	market	marché *m*	mercato *m*	—
mercado agrícola (Es)	Agrarmarkt *m*	agricultural market	marché agricole *m*	mercato agrario *m*	—
mercado central (Es)	Großmarkt *m*	wholesale market	grand marché *m*	mercato all'ingrosso *m*	—
mercado común (Es)	gemeinsamer Markt *m*	common market	marché commun *m*	mercato comune *m*	—
mercado de divisas (Es)	Devisenmarkt *m*	foreign exchange market	marché des changes *m*	mercato valutario *m*	—
mercado de exportación (Es)	Exportmarkt *m*	export market	marché d'exportation *m*	mercato delle esportazioni *m*	—
mercado del oro (Es)	Goldmarkt *m*	gold market	marché de l'ór *m*	mercato dell'oro *m*	—
mercado de materias primas (Es)	Rohstoffmarkt *m*	commodity market	marchés des matières premières *m*	mercato delle materie prime *m*	—
mercado de operaciones al contado y de entrega inmediata (Es)	Spotmarkt *m*	spot market	marché en disponible *m*	mercato spot *m*	—
mercado de títulos de renta fija (Es)	Rentenmarkt *m*	bond market	marché des effets publics *m*	mercato dei titoli a reddito fisso *m*	—
mercado de valores (Es)	Wertpapierbörse *f*	securities market	bourse des titres et valeurs *f*	borsa valori *f*	—
mercado exterior (Es)	Auslandsmärkte *pl*	foreign markets	marchés extérieurs *m pl*	mercati esteri *m pl*	—
mercado favorable al comprador (Es)	Käufermarkt *m*	buyer's market	marché d'acheteurs *m*	mercato favorevole all'acquirente *m*	—
mercado favorable al consumidor (Es)	Verbrauchermarkt *m*	consumer market	marché des consommateurs *m*	ipermercato *m*	—
mercado favorable al vendedor (Es)	Verkäufermarkt *m*	seller's market	marché de vendeurs *m*	mercato favorevole ai venditori *m*	—
mercado financiero (Es)	Kapitalmarkt *m*	capital market	marché des capitaux *m*	mercato finanziario *m*	—
mercado gris (Es)	Grauer Markt *m*	grey market	marché gris *m*	mercato grigio *m*	—

	D	E	F	I	Es
mercado interior (Es)	Binnenmarkt *m*	home market	marché national *m*	mercato nazionale *m*	—
mercado laboral (Es)	Arbeitsmarkt *m*	labour market	marché du travail *m*	mercato del lavoro *m*	—
mercado monetario (Es)	Geldmarkt *m*	money market	marché monétaire *m*	mercato monetario *m*	—
mercado negro (Es)	Schwarzmarkt *m*	black market	marché noir *m*	mercato nero *m*	—
mercado piloto (Es)	Testmarkt *m*	test market	marché de test *m*	mercato pilota *m*	—
Mercado Unico (Es)	EG-Binnenmarkt *m*	Internal Market of the European Community	Marché Intérieur de la Communauté Européenne *m*	mercato unico *m*	—
mercancía (Es)	Ware *f*	goods	marchandise *f*	merce *f*	—
mercancía almacenada (Es)	Markenartikel *m*	branded article	produit de marque *m*	articolo di marca *m*	—
mercancía en gran velocidad (Es)	Eilgut *n*	goods sent by express	marchandise en grande vitesse *f*	merce a grande velocità *f*	—
mercancía pesada (Es)	Schwergut *n*	heavy freight	produit pondéreux *m*	carico pesante *m*	—
mercancías en comisión (Es)	Kommissionsgüter *pl*	goods for sale on commission	marchandises en commission *f pl*	beni in conto deposito *m pl*	—
mercancías en pequeña velocidad (Es)	Frachtgut *n*	cargo	marchandise à transporter *f*	merce di trasporto *f*	—
mercancía transportada (Es)	Speditionsgut *n*	forwarding merchandise	bien transporté *m*	merce spedita *f*	—
mercantile system (E)	Merkantilismus *m*	—	mercantilisme *m*	mercantilismo *m*	mercantilismo *m*
mercantilisme (F)	Merkantilismus *m*	mercantile system	—	mercantilismo *m*	mercantilismo *m*
mercantilismo (Es)	Merkantilismus *m*	mercantile system	mercantilisme *m*	mercantilismo *m*	—
mercantilismo (I)	Merkantilismus *m*	mercantile system	mercantilisme *m*	—	mercantilismo *m*
mercati esteri (I)	Auslandsmärkte *pl*	foreign markets	marchés extérieurs *m pl*	—	mercado exterior *m*
mercato (I)	Markt *m*	market	marché *m*	—	mercado *m*
mercato agrario (I)	Agrarmarkt *m*	agricultural market	marché agricole *m*	—	mercado agrícola *m*
mercato all'ingrosso (I)	Großmarkt *m*	wholesale market	grand marché *m*	—	mercado central *m*
mercato a termine (I)	Terminbörse *f*	futures market	bourse à terme *f*	—	bolsa de valores a término *f*
mercato comune (I)	gemeinsamer Markt *m*	common market	marché commun *m*	—	mercado común *m*
mercato dei titoli a reddito fisso (I)	Rentenmarkt *m*	bond market	marché des effets publics *m*	—	mercado de títulos de renta fija *m*
mercato del lavoro (I)	Arbeitsmarkt *m*	labour market	marché du travail *m*	—	mercado laboral *m*
mercato delle esportazioni (I)	Exportmarkt *m*	export market	marché d'exportation *m*	—	mercado de exportación *m*
mercato delle materie prime (I)	Rohstoffmarkt *m*	commodity market	marchés des matières premières *m*	—	mercado de materias primas *m*
mercato dell'oro (I)	Goldmarkt *m*	gold market	marché de l'ór *m*	—	mercado del oro *m*
mercato favorevole ai venditori (I)	Verkäufermarkt *m*	seller's market	marché de vendeurs *m*	—	mercado favorable al vendedor *m*
mercato favorevole all'acquirente (I)	Käufermarkt *m*	buyer's market	marché d'acheteurs *m*	—	mercado favorable al comprador *m*
mercato finanziario (I)	Kapitalmarkt *m*	capital market	marché des capitaux *m*	—	mercado financiero *m*
mercato grigio (I)	Grauer Markt *m*	grey market	marché gris *m*	—	mercado gris *m*
mercato monetario (I)	Geldmarkt *m*	money market	marché monétaire *m*	—	mercado monetario *m*
mercato nazionale (I)	Binnenmarkt *m*	home market	marché national *m*	—	mercado interior *m*
mercato nero (I)	Schwarzmarkt *m*	black market	marché noir *m*	—	mercado negro *m*
mercato pilota (I)	Testmarkt *m*	test market	marché de test *m*	—	mercado piloto *m*
mercato preborsistico (I)	Vorbörse *f*	before hours dealing	marché avant le marché officiel *m*	—	operaciones antes de la apertura de la bolsa *f pl*
mercato spot (I)	Spotmarkt *m*	spot market	marché en disponible *m*	—	mercado de operaciones al contado y de entrega inmediata *m*
mercato unico CEE (I)	EG-Binnenmarkt *m*	Internal Market of the European Community	Marché Intérieur de la Communauté Européenne *m*	—	Mercado Unico *m*
mercato valutario (I)	Devisenmarkt *m*	foreign exchange market	marché des changes *m*	—	mercado de divisas *m*

	D	E	F	I	Es
merce (I)	Ware *f*	goods	marchandise *f*	—	mercancía *f*
merce a grande velocità (I)	Eilgut *n*	goods sent by express	marchandise en grande vitesse *f*	—	mercancía en gran velocidad *f*
merce di trasporto (I)	Frachtgut *n*	cargo	marchandise a'transporter *f*	—	mercancías en pequeña velocidad *f pl*
merce immagazzinata (I)	Stapelware *f*	staple commodities	produit de stockage *m*	—	mercancía almacenada *f*
merce spedita (I)	Speditionsgut *n*	forwarding merchandise	bien transporté *m*	—	mercancía transportada *f*
merce spedita per espresso (I)	Expressgut *n*	express goods	colis express *m*	—	carga por expreso *f*
merchant bank (E)	Handelsbank *f*	—	banque de commerce *f*	banca commerciale *f*	banco comercial *m*
merger (E)	Verschmelzung *f*	—	fusion *f*	fusione *f*	fusión *f*
merger control (E)	Fusionskontrolle *f*	—	contrôle de fusion *m*	controllo delle fusioni *m*	control de fusiones *m*
merger of companies (E)	Unternehmensfusion *f*	—	fusion de sociétés *f*	fusione d'imprese *f*	fusión de empresas *f*
Merkantilismus (D)	—	mercantile system	mercantilisme *m*	mercantilismo *m*	mercantilismo *m*
message par radio (F)	Funkspruch *m*	radio message	—	radiotelefonata *f*	mensaje radiado *m*
message publicitaire (F)	Werbebotschaft *f*	sales message	—	messaggio pubblicitario *m*	mensaje publicitario *m*
messaggio pubblicitario (I)	Werbebotschaft *f*	sales message	message publicitaire *m*	—	mensaje publicitario *m*
Messe (D)	—	fair	foire *f*	fiera *f*	feria *f*
Messung (D)	—	measuring	mesurage *m*	misurazione *f*	medición *f*
Meßwerte (D)	—	measurements	valeurs mesurées *f pl*	valori misurati *m pl*	valor de medida *m*
mesure¹ (F)	Messung *f*	measuring	—	misurazione *f*	medición *f*
mesure² (F)	Maß *n*	measure	—	misura *f*	medida *f*
mesure préventive contre les sinistres (F)	Schadenverhütung *f*	loss prevention	—	prevenzione danni *f*	prevención de siniestros *f*
mesures pour l'amélioration de l'infrastructure (F)	Infrastrukturmaßnahmen *f*	infrastructural measures	—	misure per l'infrastruttura *f pl*	medidas de infraestructura *f pl*
metallo pesante (I)	Schwermetall *n*	heavy metal	métal lourd *m*	—	metal pesado *m*
métal lourd (F)	Schwermetall *n*	heavy metal	—	metallo pesante *m*	metal pesado *m*
metal pesado (Es)	Schwermetall *n*	heavy metal	métal lourd *m*	metallo pesante *m*	—
method (E)	Methode *f*	—	méthode *f*	metodo *m*	método *m*
Methode (D)	—	method	méthode *f*	metodo *m*	método *m*
méthode¹ (F)	Methode *f*	method	—	metodo *m*	método *m*
méthode² (F)	Verfahren *n*	procedure/process	—	procedimento *m*/procedura *f*	proceso *m*/procedimiento *m*
méthode de calcul des coûts (F)	Kostenrechnungssystem *n*	cost accounting system	—	sistema dei costi *m*	sistema de costes *m*
méthode de l'apurement des comptes (F)	Abrechnungsverfahren *n*	settling procedure	—	metodo di liquidazione *m*	operaciones de descuento *f pl*
méthode d'enquête par sondage (F)	Stichprobeverfahren *n*	sampling procedure	—	metodo del campionamento *m*	muestreo *m*
méthode de production (F)	Fertigungsverfahren *n*	production process	—	procedimento produttivo *m*	procedimiento de fabricación *m*
méthodes de vente (F)	Verkaufsmethoden *pl*	sales strategy	—	metodi di vendita *m pl*	métodos de venta *m pl*
metodi di vendita (I)	Verkaufsmethoden *pl*	sales strategy	méthodes de vente *f pl*	—	métodos de venta *m pl*
método (Es)	Methode *f*	method	méthode *f*	metodo *m*	—
metodo (I)	Methode *f*	method	méthode *f*	—	método *m*
metodo del campionamento (I)	Stichprobeverfahren *n*	sampling procedure	méthode d'enquête par sondage *f*	—	muestreo *m*
metodo di chiusura (I)	Abschlußtechnik *f*	finishing technique	technique de conclusion *f*	—	técnica de conclusión *f*
metodo di liquidazione (I)	Abrechnungsverfahren *n*	settling procedure	méthode de l'apurement des comptes	—	operaciones de descuento *f pl*
métodos de venta (Es)	Verkaufsmethoden *pl*	sales strategy	méthodes de vente *f pl*	metodi di vendita *m pl*	—

	D	E	F	I	Es
mettre à la ferraille (F)	verschrotten	scrap	—	ridurre a rottame	hacer quincalla/ desguazar
mezcla de marketing (Es)	Marketing-Mix *m*	mixture of marketing strategies	mélange de marketing *f*	marketing-mix *m*	—
mezzi pubblicitari (I)	Werbemedien *pl*	advertising media	média publicitaires *m pl*	—	medios de publicidad *m pl*
mezzo (I)	Mittel *n*	means	moyen *m*	—	medio *m*/recurso *m*
mezzo di pagamento (I)	Zahlungsmittel *n*	means of payment	moyen de payement *m*	—	medio de pago *m*
mezzo di pagamento legale (I)	gesetzliches Zahlungsmittel *n*	legal tender	monnaie légale *f*	—	medio legal de pago *m*
mezzo di trasporto (I)	Transportmittel *n*	means of transport	moyen de transport *m*	—	medio de transporte *m*
mezzo pubblicitario (I)	Werbemittel *n*	advertising aids	moyen publicitaire *m*	—	medio publicitario *m*
mezzo pubblicitario diretto (I)	Direktwerbemittel *n*	direct means of advertising	moyens publicitaires directs *m pl*	—	medios publicitarios directos *m pl*
microchip (E)	Mikrochip *m*	—	microplaquette *f*	microchip *m*	microchip *m*
microchip (Es)	Mikrochip *m*	microchip	microplaquette *f*	microchip *m*	—
microchip (I)	Mikrochip *m*	microchip	microplaquette *f*	—	microchip *m*
microeconomía (Es)	Mikroökonomie *f*	microeconomics	microéconomie *f*	microeconomia *f*	—
microeconomia (I)	Mikroökonomie *f*	microeconomics	microéconomie *f*	—	microeconomía *f*
microeconomics (E)	Mikroökonomie *f*	—	microéconomie *f*	microeconomia *f*	microeconomía *f*
microéconomie (F)	Mikroökonomie *f*	microeconomics	—	microeconomia *f*	microeconomía *f*
microplaquette (F)	Mikrochip *m*	microchip	—	microchip *m*	microchip *m*
microprocesor (Es)	Mikroprozessor *m*	microprocessor	microprocesseur *m*	microprocessore *m*	—
microprocesseur (F)	Mikroprozessor *m*	microprocessor	—	microprocessore *m*	microprocesor *m*
microprocessor (E)	Mikroprozessor *m*	—	microprocesseur *m*	microprocessore *m*	microprocesor *m*
microprocessore (I)	Mikroprozessor *m*	microprocessor	microprocesseur *m*	—	microprocesor *m*
middle class(es) (E)	Mittelstand *m*	—	classe moyenne *f*	ceto medio *m*	clase media *f*
middleman (E)	Zwischenhändler *m*	—	intermédiaire *m*	intermediario *m*	intermediario *m*
miembro (Es)	Mitglied *n*	member	membre *m*	membro *m*	—
Miete (D)	—	rent	location *f*	canone di locazione *m*	alquiler *m*
Mieter (D)	—	tenant	locataire *m*	locatario *m*	inquilino *m*/ arrendatario *m*
Mieterschutz (D)	—	protection of tenants	protection en matière de location *f*	tutela del locatario *f*	protección al arrendatario *f*
Mietwucher (D)	—	exorbitant rent	hausse illicite des loyers *f*	strozzinaggio sui canoni di locazione *m*	usura arrendaticia *f*
Mietzins (D)	—	rent	prix de location *m*	canone di locazione *m*	arrendamiento *m*
miglio (I)	Meile *f*	mile	mille *m*	—	milla *f*
miglio marino (I)	Seemeile *f*	nautical mile	mille nautique *m*	—	milla marina *f*
Mikrochip (D)	—	microchip	microplaquette *f*	microchip *m*	microchip *m*
Mikroökonomie (D)	—	microeconomics	microéconomie *f*	microeconomia *f*	microeconomía *f*
Mikroprozessor (D)	—	microprocessor	microprocesseur *m*	microprocessore *m*	microprocesor *m*
mile (E)	Meile *f*	—	mille *m*	miglio *m*	milla *f*
milla (Es)	Meile *f*	mile	mille *m*	miglio *m*	—
milla marina (Es)	Seemeile *f*	nautical mile	mille nautique *m*	miglio marino *m*	—
mille (F)	Meile *f*	mile	—	miglio *m*	milla *f*
mille nautique (F)	Seemeile *f*	nautical mile	—	miglio marino *m*	milla marina *f*
mina de oro (Es)	Goldmine *f*	goldmine	mine d'or *f*	miniera d'oro *f*	—
minderjährig (D)	—	under age	mineur	minorenne	menor de edad
Minderlieferung (D)	—	short delivery	livraison en quantité inférieure *f*	fornitura ridotta *f*	envío incompleto *m*
Minderung (D)	—	reduction	diminution *f*	riduzione *f*	reducción *f*
Mindestabnahme (D)	—	minimum purchase	achat d'une quantité minimum *m*	quantitativo minimo di fornitura *m*	recogida mínima *f*
Mindestbestellmenge (D)	—	minimum quantity order	quantité commandée minimum *f*	quantitativo minimo di ordine *m*	cantidad mínima de pedido *f*
Mindestdauer (D)	—	minimum length/ minimum duration	durée minimum *f*	durata minima *f*	duración mínima *m*/ plazo mínimo *m*

	D	E	F	I	Es
Mindest-einfuhrpreise (D)	—	minimum import price	prix minimum d'importation *m pl*	prezzi minimi all'import *m pl*	precio mínimo a la importación *m*
Mindesthöhe (D)	—	minimum amount	montant minimum *m*	importo minimo *m*	cantidad mínima *f*
Mindestkapital (D)	—	minimum capital	capital minimum *m*	capitale minimo *m*	capital mínimo *m*
Mindestlohn (D)	—	minimum wage	salaire minimum *m*	salario minimo *m*	salario mínimo *m*
Mindestmenge (D)	—	minimum quantity	quantité minimum *f*	quantitativo minimo *m*	cantidad mínima *f*
Mindestpreis (D)	—	minimum price	prix minimum *m*	prezzo minimo *m*	precio mínimo *m*
Mindestreserve (D)	—	minimum reserves	réserve minimum *f*	riserva minima obbligatoria *f*	reserva mínima *f*
mine d'or (F)	Goldmine *f*	goldmine	—	miniera d'oro *f*	mina de oro *f*
Mineral (D)	—	mineral	minéral *m*	minerale *m*	mineral *m*
mineral (E)	Mineral *n*	—	minéral *m*	minerale *m*	mineral *m*
mineral (Es)	Mineral *n*	mineral	minéral *m*	minerale *m*	—
minéral (F)	Mineral *n*	mineral	—	minerale *m*	mineral *m*
minerale (I)	Mineral *n*	mineral	minéral *m*	—	mineral *m*
mineral oil (E)	Erdöl *n*	—	pétrole *m*	petrolio *m*	crudo *m*
mineral oil tax (E)	Mineralölsteuer *f*	—	taxe sur les carburants *f*	imposta sugli olii minerali *f*	impuesto sobre la gasolina *m*
Mineralölsteuer (D)	—	mineral oil tax	taxe sur les carburants *f*	imposta sugli olii minerali *f*	impuesto sobre la gasolina *m*
minería (Es)	Bergbau *m*	mining	industrie extractive *f*	industria mineraria *f*	—
mineur (F)	minderjährig	under age	—	minorenne	menor de edad
mini container (I)	Kleincontainer *m*	small container	petit conteneur *m*	—	pequeño contenedor *m*
miniera d'oro (I)	Goldmine *f*	goldmine	mine d'or *f*	—	mina de oro *f*
minimación de gastos[1] (Es)	Kostenminimierung *f*	minimization of costs	minimalisation des coûts *f*	diminuzione dei costi *f*	—
minimación de gastos[2] (Es)	Aufwands-minimierung *f*	expenditure minimization	minimiser les frais	riduzione delle spese *f*	—
minimal damage (E)	Bagatellschaden *m*	—	dommage mineur *m*	danno piccolo *m*	siniestro leve *m*
minimalisation des coûts (F)	Kostenminimierung *f*	minimization of costs	—	diminuzione dei costi *f*	minimación de gastos *f*
minimiser les frais (F)	Aufwands-minimierung *f*	expenditure minimization	—	riduzione delle spese *f*	minimación de gastos *f*
minimization of costs (E)	Kostenminimierung *f*	—	minimalisation des coûts *f*	diminuzione dei costi *f*	minimación de gastos *f*
minimo di esistenza (I)	Existenzminimum *n*	subsistence minimum	minimum vital *m*	—	minimo vital *m*
minimo vital (Es)	Existenzminimum *n*	subsistence minimum	minimum vital *m*	minimo di esistenza *m*	—
minimum amount (E)	Mindesthöhe *f*	—	montant minimum *m*	importo minimo *m*	cantidad mínima *f*
minimum capital (E)	Mindestkapital *n*	—	capital minimum *m*	capitale minimo *m*	capital mínimo *m*
minimum import price (E)	Mindest-einfuhrpreise *pl*	—	prix minimum d'importation *m pl*	prezzi minimi all'import *m pl*	precio mínimo a la importación *m*
minimum length (E)	Mindestdauer *f*	—	durée minimum *f*	durata minima *f*	duración mínima *m*/ plazo mínimo *m*
minimum nominal amount (E)	Mindestnennbetrag *m*	—	montant nominal minimum *m*	importo nominale minimo *m*	valor nominal mínimo *m*
minimum price (E)	Mindestpreis *m*	—	prix minimum *m*	prezzo minimo *m*	precio mínimo *m*
minimum purchase (E)	Mindestabnahme *f*	—	achat d'une quantité minimum *m*	quantitativo minimo di fornitura *m*	recogida mínima *f*
minimum quantity (E)	Mindestmenge *f*	—	quantité minimum *f*	quantitativo minimo *m*	cantidad mínima *f*
minimum quantity order (E)	Mindest-bestellmenge *f*	—	quantité commandée minimum *f*	quantitativo minimo di ordine *m*	cantidad mínima de pedido *f*
minimum reserves (E)	Mindestreserve *f*	—	réserve minimum *f*	riserva minima obbligatoria *f*	reserva mínima *f*
minimum turnover (E)	Mindestumsatz *m*	—	chiffre d'affaires minimum *m*	fatturato minimo *m*	cifra de venta mínima *f*
minimum vital (F)	Existenzminimum *n*	subsistence minimum	—	minimo di esistenza *m*	minimo vital *m*
minimum wage (E)	Mindestlohn *m*	—	salaire minimum *m*	salario minimo *m*	salario mínimo *m*
mining (E)	Bergbau *m*	—	industrie extractive *f*	industria mineraria *f*	minería *f*

	D	E	F	I	Es
mining industry (E)	Montanindustrie *f*	—	industrie minière *f*	industria mineraria e siderurgica *f*	industria minera *f*
mini paletta (I)	Kleinpalette *f*	small pallet	petite palette *f*	—	pequña paleta *f*
ministère de l'agriculture (F)	Landwirtschafts-ministerium *n*	Ministry of Agriculture	—	ministero dell'agricoltura *m*	minsterio de Agricultura, Pesca y Alimentación *m*
ministère des finances (F)	Finanzministerium *n*	Ministry of Finance	—	ministero delle Finanze *m*	Hacienda *f*
ministerio de Agricultura, Pesca y Alimentación (Es)	Landwirtschafts-ministerium *n*	Ministry of Agriculture	ministère de l'agriculture *m*	ministero dell'agricoltura	
ministero dell'agricoltura (I)	Landwirtschafts-ministerium *n*	Ministry of Agriculture	ministère de l'agriculture *m*	—	minsterio de Agricultura, Pesca y Alimentación *m*
ministero delle Finanze (I)	Finanzministerium *n*	Ministry of Finance	ministère des finances *m*	—	Hacienda *f*
Ministry of Agriculture (E)	Landwirtschafts-ministerium *n*	—	ministère de l'agriculture *m*	ministero dell'agricoltura	minsterio de Agricultura, Pesca y Alimentación *m*
Ministry of Finance (E)	Finanzministerium *n*	—	ministère des finances *m*	ministero delle Finanze *m*	Hacienda *f*
minoration de l'intérêt (F)	Zinserleichterung *f*	reduction of interest	—	agevolazione sugli interessi *f*	reducción de intereses *f*
minorenne (I)	minderjährig	under age	mineur	—	menor de edad
minoría de bloqueo (Es)	Sperrminorität *f*	blocking minority	minorité suffisante pour bloquer qch. *f*	sindacato di blocco *m*	—
minorista (Es)	Einzelhändler *m*	retailer	commerçant détaillant *m*	dettagliante *m*	—
minorité suffisante pour bloquer qch. (F)	Sperrminorität *f*	blocking minority	—	sindacato di blocco *m*	minoría de bloqueo *f*
misappropriation (E)	Veruntreuung *f*	—	détournement *m*	abuso di fiducia *m*	malversación *f*
miscalculation (E)	Rechenfehler *m*	—	erreur de calcul *f*	errore di calcolo *m*	error de cálculo *m*
misconceived capital projects (E)	Fehlinvestition *f*	—	mauvais investissement *m*	investimento sbagliato *m*	inversión equivocada *f*
mise à profit (F)	Nutzung *f*	use/utilization	—	utilizzazione *f*	utilización *f*
mise au concours d'une place (F)	Stellen-ausschreibung *f*	advertisement of a vacancy	—	bando di concorso per impiegati *m*	convocatoria de oposiciones *f*
mise en demeure (F)	Mahnung *f*	demand for payment	—	sollecito *m*	(ad)monición *f*
mise en gage (F)	Verpfändung *f*	pledge	—	pignoramento *m*	pignoración *f*
misión comercial (Es)	Handelsmission *f*	trade mission	mission commerciale *f*	missione commerciale *f*	—
mission commerciale (F)	Handelsmission *f*	trade mission	—	missione commerciale *f*	misión comercial *f*
missione commerciale (I)	Handelsmission *f*	trade mission	mission commerciale *f*	—	misión comercial *f*
mistake (E)	Fehler *m*	—	faute *f*	errore *m*	error *m*
mistake of law (E)	Rechtsirrtum *m*	—	erreur de droit *m*	errore di diritto *m*	error de derecho *m*
misura (I)	Maß *n*	measure	mesure *f*	—	medida *f*
misurazione (I)	Messung *f*	measuring	mesurage *m*	—	medición *f*
misure per l'infrastruttura (I)	Infrastruktur-maßnahmen *f*	infrastructural measures	mesures pour l'amélioration de l'infrastructure *f pl*	—	medidas de infraestructura *f pl*
Mitarbeit (D)	—	collaboration	collaboration *f*	collaborazione *f*	colaboración *f*
Mitbestimmung (D)	—	codetermination of labour	cogestion *f*	cogestione *f*	cogestión *f*
Mitbewerber (D)	—	competitor	concurrent *m*	competitore *m*	contendiente *m*
Miteigentum (D)	—	co-ownership	copropriété *f*	comproprietà *f*	copropiedad *f*
mit getrennter Post (D)	—	under separate cover	sous pli séparé	in plico a parte	por correo aparte
Mitglied (D)	—	member	membre *m*	membro *m*	miembro *m*
Mitteilung (D)	—	information	notification *f*	comunicazione *f*	aviso *m*
Mittel (D)	—	means	moyen *m*	mezzo *m*	medio *m*/recurso *m*
mittelfristig (D)	—	medium-term	à moyen terme	a media scadenza	a medio plazo
mittelfristiger Kredit (D)	—	medium-term credit	crédit à moyen terme *m*	credito a media scadenza *m*	crédito a medio plazo *m*

	D	E	F	I	Es
Mittelstand (D)	—	middle class(es)	classe moyenne *f*	ceto medio *m*	clase media *f*
mittente (I)	Absender *m*	sender	envoyeur *m*	—	remitente *m*
mixed cargo (E)	Stückgut *n*	—	colis de détail *m*	collettame *m*	fardos *m pl*
mixture of marketing strategies (E)	Marketing-Mix *m*	—	mélange de marketing *f*	marketing-mix *m*	mezcla de marketing *f*
mobilidad (Es)	Mobilität *f*	mobility	mobilité *f*	mobilità *f*	—
mobilità (I)	Mobilität *f*	mobility	mobilité *f*	—	mobilidad *f*
Mobilität (D)	—	mobility	mobilité *f*	mobilità *f*	mobilidad *f*
mobilité (F)	Mobilität *f*	mobility	—	mobilità *f*	mobilidad *f*
mobility (E)	Mobilität *f*	—	mobilité *f*	mobilità *f*	mobilidad *f*
Modeartikel (D)	—	fashion article	article de mode *m*	articolo di moda *m*	artículos de moda *m pl*
Modemesse (D)	—	fashion fair	foire de la mode *f*	fiera della moda *f*	feria de moda *f*
modificación de contrato (Es)	Vertragsänderung *f*	modification of a contract	modification du contrat *f*	modificazione del contratto *f*	—
modificación de los estatutos (Es)	Satzungsänderung *f*	amendment of the statutes	modification des statuts *f*	modificazione dello statuto *f*	—
modification des statuts (F)	Satzungsänderung *f*	amendment of the statutes	—	modificazione dello statuto *f*	modificación de los estatutos *f*
modification du contrat (F)	Vertragsänderung *f*	modification of a contract	—	modificazione del contratto *f*	modificación de contrato *f*
modification du pouvoir d'achat (F)	Kaufkraftänderung *f*	changes in the purchasing power	—	mutamento del potere d'acquisto *m*	cambio en el poder adquisitivo *m*
modification of a contract (E)	Vertragsänderung *f*	—	modification du contrat *f*	modificazione del contratto *f*	modificación de contrato *f*
modificazione del contratto (I)	Vertragsänderung *f*	modification of a contract	modification du contrat *f*	—	modificación de contrato *f*
modificazione dello statuto (I)	Satzungsänderung *f*	amendment of the statutes	modification des statuts *f*	—	modificación de los estatutos *f*
modulo¹ (I)	Formular *n*	form	formulaire *m*	—	formulario *m*
modulo² (I)	Vordruck *m*	printed form	imprimé *m*	—	impreso *m*
modulo di domanda (I)	Antragsformular *n*	application form	formulaire de demande *m*	—	formulario de solicitud *m*
modulo di versamento (I)	Zahlkarte *f*	money order	mandat-carte *m*	—	carta de pago *f*
modulo d'ordinazione (I)	Bestellformular *n*	order form	bon de commande *m*	—	formulario de pedido *m*
modulo in bianco (I)	Blankoformular *n*	blank form	imprimé en blanc *m*	—	formulario en blanco *m*
monatlich (D)	—	monthly	par mois	mensile	mensual
moneda¹ (Es)	Münze *f*	coin	monnaie *f*	moneta *f*	—
moneda² (Es)	Währung *f*	currency	monnaie *f*	valuta *f*/moneta *f*	—
moneda blanda (Es)	weiche Währung *f*	soft currency	monnaie faible *f*	moneta debole *f*	—
moneda de referencia (Es)	Leitwährung *f*	key currency	monnaie-clé *f*	valuta guida *f*	—
moneda de reserva (Es)	Reservewährung *f*	reserve currency	monnaie de réserve *f*	valuta di riserva *f*	—
moneda dura (Es)	harte Währung *f*	hard currency	monnaie solide *f*	moneta forte *f*	—
moneda extranjera (Es)	Valuta *f*	foreign exchange/value	monnaie étrangère *f*	valuta *f*/divise *f pl*	—
moneda oro (Es)	Goldwährung *f*	gold currency	monnaie à couverture or *f*	valuta aurea *f*	—
moneda única (Es)	Einheitswährung *f*	uniform currency	monométallisme *m*	moneta unitaria *f*	—
moneta (I)	Münze *f*	coin	monnaie *f*	—	moneda *f*
moneta bancaria (I)	Buchgeld *n*	money in account	monnaie de crédit *f*	—	dinero bancario *m*
moneta debole (I)	weiche Währung *f*	soft currency	monnaie faible *f*	—	moneda blanda *f*
moneta forte (I)	harte Währung *f*	hard currency	monnaie solide *f*	—	moneda dura *f*
moneta metallica (I)	Hartgeld *n*	specie	pièce de monnaie *f*	—	dinero metálico *m*
moneta unitaria (I)	Einheitswährung *f*	uniform currency	monométallisme *m*	—	moneda única *f*
monétaire (F)	monetär	monetary		monetario	monetario
monetär (D)	—	monetary	monétaire	monetario	monetario
monetario (Es)	monetär	monetary	monétaire	monetario	—

	D	E	F	I	Es
monetario (I)	monetär	monetary	monétaire	—	monetario
monetarism (E)	Monetarismus *m*	—	monétarisme *m*	monetarismo *m*	monetarismo *m*
monétarisme (F)	Monetarismus *m*	monetarism	—	monetarismo *m*	monetarismo *m*
monetarismo (Es)	Monetarismus *m*	monetarism	monétarisme *m*	monetarismo *m*	—
monetarismo (I)	Monetarismus *m*	monetarism	monétarisme *m*	—	monetarismo *m*
Monetarismus (D)	—	monetarism	monétarisme *m*	monetarismo *m*	monetarismo *m*
monetary (E)	monetär	—	monétaire	monetario	monetario
monetary authority (E)	Währungsbehörde *f*	—	autorité monétaire *f*	autorità monetaria *f*	autoridad monetaria *f*
monetary expert (E)	Währungsexperte *m*	—	expert monétaire *m*	esperto in materia monetaria *m*	experto en materia monetaria *m*
monetary policy[1] (E)	Währungspolitik *f*	—	politique monétaire *f*	politica monetaria *f*	política monetaria *f*
monetary policy[2] (E)	Geldpolitik *f*	—	politique monétaire *f*	politica monetaria *f*	política monetaria *f*
monetary restriction (E)	Geldverknappung *f*	—	pénurie d'argent *f*	riduzione del denaro *f*	restricción monetaria *f*
monetary theory (E)	Geldtheorie *f*	—	théorie monétaire *f*	teoria del denaro *f*	teoría monetaria *f*
monetary union (E)	Währungsunion *f*	—	union monétaire *f*	unione monetaria *f*	uníon monetaria *f*
money (E)	Geld *n*	—	argent *m*	denaro *m*	dinero *m*/efectivo *m*
money creation (E)	Geldschöpfung *f*	—	création de trésorerie *f*	creazione di denaro *f*	creación de dinero *f*
money in account (E)	Buchgeld *n*	—	monnaie de crédit *f*	moneta bancaria *f*	dinero bancario *m*
money market (E)	Geldmarkt *m*	—	marché monétaire *m*	mercato monetario *m*	mercado monetario *m*
money order (E)	Zahlkarte *f*	—	mandat-carte *m*	modulo di versamento *m*	carta de pago *f*
money owed (E)	Guthaben *n*	—	avoir *m*	saldo attivo *m*	haber *m*
money supply (E)	Geldmenge *f*	—	quantité de monnaie en circulation *f*	massa monetaria *f*	volumen monetario *m*
monnaie[1] (F)	Währung *f*	currency	—	valuta *f*/moneta *f*	moneda *f*
monnaie[2] (F)	Münze *f*	coin	—	moneta *f*	moneda *f*
monnaie à couverture or (F)	Goldwährung *f*	gold currency	—	valuta aurea *f*	moneda oro *f*
monnaie-clé (F)	Leitwährung *f*	key currency	—	valuta guida *f*	moneda de referencia *f*
monnaie de crédit (F)	Buchgeld *n*	money in account	—	moneta bancaria *f*	dinero bancario *m*
monnaie de papier (F)	Papiergeld *n*	paper money	—	banconote *f pl*	papel-moneda *m*
monnaie de réserve (F)	Reservewährung *f*	reserve currency	—	valuta di riserva *f*	moneda de reserva *f*
monnaie étrangère (F)	Valuta *f*	foreign exchange	—	divise *f pl*	moneda extranjera *f*/ divisas *f pl*
monnaie faible (F)	weiche Währung *f*	soft currency	—	moneta debole *f*	moneda blanda *f*
monnaie légale (F)	gesetzliches Zahlungsmittel *n*	legal tender	—	mezzo di pagamento legale *m*	medio legal de pago *m*
monnaie solide (F)	harte Währung *f*	hard currency	—	moneta forte *f*	moneda dura *f*
monocoltura (I)	Monokultur *f*	monoculture	monoculture *f*	—	monocultivo *m*
monocultivo (Es)	Monokultur *f*	monoculture	monoculture *f*	monocoltura *f*	—
monoculture (E)	Monokultur *f*	—	monoculture *f*	monocoltura *f*	monocultivo *m*
monoculture (F)	Monokultur *f*	monoculture	—	monocoltura *f*	monocultivo *m*
Monokultur (D)	—	monoculture	monoculture *f*	monocoltura *f*	monocultivo *m*
monométallisme (F)	Einheitswährung *f*	uniform currency	—	moneta unitaria *f*	moneda única *f*
Monopol (D)	—	monopoly	monopole *m*	monopolio *m*	monopolio *m*
monopole (F)	Monopol *n*	monopoly	—	monopolio *m*	monopolio *m*
monopole du commerce extérieur (F)	Außenhandelsmonopol *n*	foreign trade monopoly	—	monopolio del commercio estero *m*	monopolio del commercio exterior *m*
monopole fiscal (F)	Finanzmonopol *n*	fiscal monopoly	—	monopolio fiscale *m*	monopolio financiero *m*
monopolio (Es)	Monopol *n*	monopoly	monopole *m*	monopolio *m*	—
monopolio (I)	Monopol *n*	monopoly	monopole *m*	—	monopolio *m*
monopolio del comercio exterior (Es)	Außenhandelsmonopol *n*	foreign trade monopoly	monopole du commerce extérieur *m*	monopolio del commercio estero *m*	—
monopolio del commercio estero (I)	Außenhandelsmonopol *n*	foreign trade monopoly	monopole du commerce extérieur *m*	—	monopolio del commercio exterior *m*

	D	E	F	I	Es
monopolio financiero (Es)	Finanzmonopol n	fiscal monopoly	monopole fiscal m	monopolio fiscale m	—
monopolio fiscale (I)	Finanzmonopol n	fiscal monopoly	monopole fiscal m	—	monopolio financiero m
monopoly (E)	Monopol n	—	monopole m	monopolio m	monopolio m
Montage (D)	—	installation	montage m	montaggio m	montaje m
montage (F)	Montage f	installation	—	montaggio m	montaje m
montaggio (I)	Montage f	installation	montage m	—	montaje m
montaje (Es)	Montage f	installation	montage m	montaggio m	—
Montanindustrie (D)	—	mining industry	industrie minière f	industria mineraria e siderurgica f	industria minera f
montant (F)	Betrag m	amount	—	importo m	suma f
montant de l'accréditif (F)	Akkreditivsumme f	amount of the letter of credit	—	importo del credito documentario m	suma del crédito documentario f
montant de la facture[1] (F)	Rechnungssumme f	invoice amount	—	importo della fattura m	suma de la factura f
montant de la facture[2] (F)	Rechnungsbetrag m	amount of invoice	—	ammontare della fattura m	importe de la factura m
montant de la garantie (F)	Beleihungswert m	value as security for a loan	—	valore finanziabile m	valor para préstamos m
montant de l'assurance (F)	Versicherungssumme f	insurance sum	—	somma assicurata f	suma asegurada f
montant de rachat (F)	Ablösesumme f	redemption sum	—	importo di rimborso m	suma de amortización f
montante nominal (Es)	Nominalbetrag m	nominal amount	montant nominal m	importo nominale m	—
montant minimum (F)	Mindesthöhe f	minimum amount	—	importo minimo m	cantidad mínima f
montant nominal (F)	Nominalbetrag m	nominal amount	—	importo nominale m	montante nominal m
montant nominal minimum (F)	Mindestnennbetrag m	minimum nominal amount	—	importo nominale minimo m	valor nominal mínimo m
montant total (F)	Gesamtsumme f	total amout	—	importo totale m	suma total f
monthly (E)	monatlich	—	par mois	mensile	mensual
monthly instalment (E)	Teilzahlungsrate f	—	mensualité d'un achat à tempérament f	rata f	plazo m
mora (I)	Verzug m	delay	demeure f	—	retraso m/demora f
mora nella consegna (I)	Lieferverzug m	delay in delivery	demeure du fournisseur f	—	demora en la entrega f
moratoria (Es)	Stundung f	respite	prorogation f	dilazione f/proroga f	—
morosità di pagamento[1] (I)	Zahlungsverzug m	failure to pay on due date	demeure du débiteur f	—	retraso en el pago m
morosità di pagamento[2] (I)	Zahlungsrückstand m	payment in arrears	arriéré de payement m	—	pago atrasado m
moroso (Es)	säumig	dilatory	retardataire	moroso	—
moroso (I)	säumig	dilatory	retardataire	—	moroso
mortgage[1] (E)	Hypothek f	—	hypothéque f	ipoteca f	hipoteca f
mortgage[2] (E)	Grundschuld f	—	dette foncière f	debito fondiario m	hipoteca f
mortgage bank (E)	Hypothekenbank f	—	banque hypothécaire f	banca ipotecaria f	banco hipotecario m
mortgage bond (E)	Pfandbrief m	—	obligation hypothécaire f	titolo ipotecario m	cédula hipotecaria f
most favourable offer (E)	günstigstes Angebot n	—	offre favorable f	offerta vantaggiosa f	oferta favorable f
most-favoured nation clause (E)	Meistbegünstigungsklausel f	—	clause de la nation la plus favorisée f	clausola della nazione più favorita f	cláusula de la nación más favorecida f
mot-clé (F)	Schlüsselwort n	key word	—	parola chiave f	palabra clave f
mot de code (F)	Codewort n	code	—	parola di codice f	palabra de clave f
mother house (E)	Mutterhaus n	—	maison mère f	casa madre f	casa matriz f
motif (F)	Motiv n	motive	—	motivo m	motivo m
motif d'achat (F)	Kaufanlaß m	buying motive	—	motivo d'acquisto m	motivo de compra m
Motiv (D)	—	motive	motif m	motivo m	motivo m
motivación (Es)	Motivation f	motivation	motivation f	motivazione f	—
Motivation (D)	—	motivation	motivation f	motivazione f	motivación f

	D	E	F	I	Es
motivation (E)	Motivation f	—	motivation f	motivazione f	motivación f
motivation (F)	Motivation f	motivation	—	motivazione f	motivación f
motivazione (I)	Motivation f	motivation	motivation f	—	motivación f
motive (E)	Motiv n	—	motif m	motivo m	motivo m
motivo (Es)	Motiv n	motive	motif m	motivo m	—
motivo (I)	Motiv n	motive	motif m	—	motivo m
motivo d'acquisto (I)	Kaufanlaß m	buying motive	motif d'achat m	—	motivo de compra m
motivo de compra (Es)	Kaufanlaß m	buying motive	motif d'achat m	motivo d'acquisto m	—
motor insurance (E)	Kraftfahrzeug-versicherung f	—	assurance responsabilité civile automobile f	assicurazione autoveicoli f	seguro de automóviles m
motor vehicle (E)	Kraftfahrzeug n	—	véhicule à moteur m	automobile f	automóvil m
motor vehicle tax (E)	Kraftfahrzeugsteuer f	—	taxe sur les véhicules à moteur f	imposta sulla circolazione degli autoveicoli f	impuesto sobre vehículos m
mousse synthétique (F)	Schaumstoff m	foam material	—	espanso m	plástico espumoso m
mouvement ascendant (F)	Aufwärtstrend m	upward trend	—	tendenza al rialzo f	tendencia alcista f
mouvement des capitaux (F)	Kapitalverkehr m	capital transactions	—	movimento dei capitali m	circulación de capitales f
mouvement des devises (F)	Devisenverkehr m	foreign exchange dealings	—	commercio dei cambi m	tráfico de divisas m
mouvements dans le personnel (F)	Personalwechsel m	staff changes	—	cambio del personale m	cambio de personal m
mouvements saisonniers (F)	Saison-schwankungen pl	seasonal fluctuations	—	oscillazioni stagionali f pl	oscilaciones estacionales f pl
movable goods (E)	bewegliche Güter pl	—	biens meubles m pl	beni mobili m pl	bienes muebles m pl
movimento dei capitali (I)	Kapitalverkehr m	capital transactions	mouvement des capitaux m	—	circulación de capitales f
moyen (F)	Mittel n	means	—	mezzo m	medio m/recurso m
moyen de payement (F)	Zahlungsmittel n	means of payment	—	mezzo di pagamento m	medio de pago m
moyen de transport (F)	Transportmittel n	means of transport	—	mezzo di trasporto m	medio de transporte m
moyenne (F)	Durchschnitt m	average	—	media f	promedio m
moyen publicitaire (F)	Werbemittel n	advertising aids	—	mezzo pubblicitario m	medio publicitario m
moyens financiers (F)	Geldvermögen n	financial assets	—	patrimonio monetario m	activo monetario m
moyens publicitaires directs (F)	Direktwerbemittel n	direct means of advertising	—	mezzo pubblicitario diretto m	medios publicitarios directos m pl
mudanza (Es)	Umzug m	change of residence	déménagement m	trasferimento m	—
muestra[1] (Es)	Probepackung f	trial package	échantillon m	confezione campione f	—
muestra[2] (Es)	Warenprobe f	sample	échantillon m	campione m	—
muestrario (Es)	Mustermappe f	sample bag	dossier à échantillons m	cartella campioni f	—
muestra sin valor (Es)	Muster ohne Wert n	sample, no commercial value	échantillon sans valeur m	campione senza valore m	—
muestreo (Es)	Stichprobe-verfahren n	sampling procedure	méthode d'enquête par sondage f	metodo del campionamento m	—
multa[1] (Es)	Geldbuße f	fine	amende f	pena pecuniaria f	—
multa[2] (Es)	Bußgeld n	administration fee	amende f	pena pecuniaria f	—
multa[3] (Es)	Geldstrafe f	fine	peine pécuniaire f	multa f	—
multa (I)	Geldstrafe f	fine	peine pécuniaire f	—	multa f
multilateral (D)	—	multilateral	multilatéral	multilaterale	multilateral
multilateral (E)	multilateral	—	multilatéral	multilaterale	multilateral
multilateral (Es)	multilateral	multilateral	multilatéral	multilaterale	—
multilatéral (F)	multilateral	multilateral	—	multilaterale	multilateral
multilaterale (I)	multilateral	multilateral	multilatéral	—	multilateral
multinational enterprise (E)	multinationale Unternehmen n	—	entreprises multinationales f pl	imprese multinazionali f pl	empresa multinacional f

	D	E	F	I	Es
multinationaler Konzern (D)	—	multinational group	groupe multinational *m*	gruppo multinazionale *m*	grupo multinacional *m*
multinationale Unternehmen (D)	—	multinational enterprise	entreprises multinationales *f pl*	imprese multinazionali *f pl*	empresa multinacional *f*
multinational group (E)	multinationaler Konzern *m*	—	groupe multinational *m*	gruppo multinazionale *m*	grupo multinacional *m*
mündlich (D)	—	verbal	verbal	verbale	oral
municipalidad (Es)	Kommune *f*	municipality	commune *f*	comune *m*	—
municipality (E)	Kommune *f*	—	commune *f*	comune *m*	municipalidad *f*
Münze (D)	—	coin	monnaie *f*	moneta *f*	moneda *f*
Muster (D)	—	sample	échantillon *m*	campione *m*	muestra *f*/dibujo *m*
Mustermappe (D)	—	sample bag	dossier à échantillons *m*	cartella campioni *f*	muestrario *m*
Mustermesse (D)	—	trade fair	foire d'échantillons *f*	fiera campionaria *f*	feria de muestras *f*
Muster ohne Wert (D)	—	sample, no commercial value	échantillon sans valeur *m*	campione senza valore *m*	muestra sin valor *f*
Mustersendung (D)	—	sample consignment	envoi d'échantillons *m*	spedizione di campioni *f*	envío de muestras *m*
mutamento del potere d'acquisto (I)	Kaufkraftänderung *f*	changes in the purchasing power	modification du pouvoir d'achat *f*	—	cambio en el poder adquisitivo *m*
Mutmaßung (D)	—	conjecture	présomption *f*	presunzione *f*	suposición *f*
Muttergesellschaft (D)	—	parent company	société mère *f*	società madre *f*	sociedad matriz *f*
Mutterhaus (D)	—	mother house	maison mère *f*	casa madre *f*	casa matriz *f*
Mutterschutz (D)	—	protection for motherhood	protection maternelle et infantile *f*	tutela della maternità *f*	protección de la madre *f*
mutua assicurazione (I)	Versicherung auf Gegenseitigkeit *f*	mutual insurance	assurance mutuelle *f*	—	caja de socorros mutuos *f*
mutual insurance (E)	Versicherung auf Gegenseitigkeit *f*	—	assurance mutuelle *f*	mutua assicurazione *f*	caja de socorros mutuos *f*
mutuo (I)	Darlehen *n*	loan	prêt *m*	—	préstamo *m*
mutuo residuo (I)	Restdarlehen *n*	purchase-money loan	prêt restant *m*	—	restante de un préstamo *m*
nach Erhalt der Rechnung (D)	—	on receipt of the invoice	après avoir réçu la facture	a ricevimento della fattura	después de haber recibo la factura
Nachbereitung (D)	—	aftertreatment	remise en ordre *f*	rielaborazione *f*	tratamiento ulterior *m*
Nachbestellung (D)	—	repeat order	nouvel ordre *m*	ordinazione supplementare *f*	pedido suplementario *m*
nachdatiert (D)	—	postdated	postdaté	postdatato	pos(t)datado
Nachforschung (D)	—	investigation	recherche *f*	indagine *f*	pesquisas *f pl*
Nachfrage (D)	—	demand	demande *f*	domanda *f*	demanda *f*
Nachfragerückgang (D)	—	decrease in demand	recul de la demande *m*	flessione della domanda *f*	disminución en la demanda *f*
Nachfrist (D)	—	additional period	prolongation *f*	termine supplementare *m*	plazo de gracia *m*
Nachkalkulation (D)	—	historical costing	calcul des coûts a posteriori *m*	computisteria *f*	cálculo de costes a posteriori *m*
Nachlaß (D)	—	inheritance	héritage *m*	eredità *f*	herencia *f*
Nachlaßverwalter (D)	—	administrator of the deceased's estate	administrateur de la succession *m*	amministratore dell'eredità *m*	administrador de la herencia *m*
Nachlieferungsanspruch (D)	—	claim to subsequent delivery	droit à livraison complémentaire *m*	diritto alla fornitura supplementare *m*	derecho de suministro adicional *m*
Nachnahme (D)	—	cash on delivery	remboursement *m*	contrassegno *m*	reembolso *m*
Nachprüfung (D)	—	reexamination	vérification *f*	revisione *f*	revisión *f*
Nachricht (D)	—	news	avis *m*/nouvelle *f*	notizia *f*	noticia *f*
Nachteil (D)	—	disadvantage	désavantage *m*	svantaggio *m*	desventaja *f*
Nachtschicht (D)	—	night shift	équipe de nuit *f*	turno notturno *m*	turno de noche *m*
Nachttresor (D)	—	night safe	dépôt de nuit *m*	cassa continua *f*	depósito de noche *m*
Nachzahlung (D)	—	supplementary payment	versement complémentaire *m*	pagamento supplementare *m*	pago suplementario *m*
nacionalización (Es)	Verstaatlichung *f*	nationalization	nationalisaiton *f*	nazionalizzazione *f*	—
Namensaktie (D)	—	registered shares	action nominative *f*	azione nominativa *f*	acción nominal *f*

	D	E	F	I	Es
Natale (I)	Weihnachten *n*	Christmas	Noël *m*	—	Navidad *f*
national (F)	Inländer *m*	national resident	—	persona residente *f*	residente *m*
national accounting (E)	Volkswirtschaftliche Gesamtrechnung *f*	—	comptabilité nationale *f*	contabilità nazionale *f*	contabilidad nacional *f*
national economy (E)	Volkswirtschaft *f*	—	économie nationale *f*	economia politica *f*	economía nacional *f*
nationale Souveräni-tätsrechte (D)	—	national sovereignty rights	droits de souveraineté nationale *m pl*	diritti di sovranità nazionale *m pl*	derechos de sobera-nía nacional *m pl*
national income (E)	Volkseinkommen *n*	—	revenu national *m*	reddito nazionale *m*	renta nacional *f*
nationalisation (F)	Verstaatlichung *f*	nationalization	—	nazionalizzazione *f*	nacionalización *f*
nationalization (E)	Verstaatlichung *f*	—	nationalisation *f*	nazionalizzazione *f*	nacionalización *f*
Nationalökonomie (D)	—	economics	économie nationale *f*	economia nazionale *f*	economía nacional *f*
national product (E)	Sozialprodukt *n*	—	produit national *m*	prodotto nazionale *m*	producto nacional *m*
national resident (E)	Inländer *m*	—	habitant du pays *m*	persona residente *f*	residente *m*
national sovereignty rights (E)	nationale Souveräni-tätsrechte *pl*	—	droits de souveraineté nationale *m pl*	diritti di sovranità nazionale *m pl*	derechos de sobera-nía nacional *m pl*
Naturalabgabe (D)	—	duty in kind	taxe acquittée en nature *f*	imposta in natura *f*	impuesto en especie *m*
natural gas (E)	Erdgas *n*	—	gaz naturel *m*	gas naturale *m*	gas natural *m*
Naturallohn (D)	—	wages (paid) in kind	rémunérarion du travail en nature *f*	remunerazione in natura *f*	salario en especie *m*
natural person (E)	natürliche Person *f*	—	personne physique *f*	persona fisica *f*	persona natural *f*
natürliche Person (D)	—	natural person	personne physique *f*	persona fisica *f*	persona natural *f*
nautical mile (E)	Seemeile *f*	—	mille nautique *m*	miglio marino *m*	milla marina *f*
naval blockade (E)	Seeblockade *f*	—	blocus maritime *m*	blocco marittimo *m*	bloqueo marítimo *m*
navegable (Es)	schiffbar	navigable	navigable	navigabile	—
navegación fluvial (Es)	Binnenschiffahrt *f*	inland navigation	navigation fluviale *f*	navigazione interna *f*	—
Navidad (Es)	Weihnachten *n*	Christmas	Noël *m*	Natale *m*	
navigabile (I)	schiffbar	navigable	navigable	—	navegable
navigable (E)	schiffbar	—	navigable	navigabile	navegable
navigable (F)	schiffbar	navigable	—	navigabile	navegable
navigation fluviale (F)	Binnenschiffahrt *f*	inland navigation	—	navigazione interna *f*	navegación fluvial *f*
navigazione interna (I)	Binnenschiffahrt *f*	inland navigation	navigation fluviale *f*	—	navegación fluvial *f*
nazionalizzazione (I)	Verstaatlichung *f*	nationalization	nationalisation *f*	—	nacionalización *f*
Nebenkosten (D)	—	ancillary costs	coûts accessoires *m pl*	costi accessori *m pl*	gastos adicionales *m pl*
Nebenprodukt (D)	—	by-product	produit dérivé *m*	prodotto secondario *m*	producto accesorio *m*
necesidad (Es)	Bedürfnis *n*	need	besoin *m*	bisogno *m*	—
necesidad anual (Es)	Jahresbedarf *m*	annual need	besoin annuel *m*	bisogno annuale *m*	—
necesidad de capital (Es)	Kapitalbedarf *m*	capital requirements	besoin en capital *m*	domanda di capitale *m*	—
necesidad de información (Es)	Informationsbedarf *m*	requirement of information	besoin d'information *m*	bisogno d'informazioni *m*	—
necesidades (Es)	Bedarf *m*	need/demand	besoin *m*/demande *f*	fabbisogno *m*/domanda *f*	—
necesidades individuales (Es)	Individualbedürfnis *n*	individual need	besoin individuel *m*	fabbisogno individuale *m*	—
need[1] (E)	Bedürfnis *n*	—	besoin *m*	bisogno *m*	necesidad *f*
need[2] (E)	Bedarf *m*	—	besoin *m*/demande *f*	fabbisogno *m*/domanda *f*	necesidades *f*/demanda *f*
negativa (Es)	Absage *f*	refusal	refus *m*	risposta negativa *f*	—
negligence (E)	Fahrlässigkeit *f*	—	négligence *f*	negligenza *f*	descuido *m*
negligenza (I)	Fahrlässigkeit *f*	negligence	négligence *f*	—	descuido *m*
negociación (Es)	Verhandlung *f*	negotiation	négociation *f*	trattativa *f*	—
negociación bursátil (Es)	Börsenhandel *m*	stock exchange transactions	transactions boursiaires *f pl*	commercio in borsa *m*	—
négociant (F)	Kaufmann *m*	businessman	—	commerciante *m*	comerciante *m*
négociation (F)	Verhandlung *f*	negotiation	—	trattativa *f*	negociación *f*
négociation des actions (F)	Aktienhandel *m*	dealing in shares	—	commercio azionario *m*	constratación de acciones *f pl*

	D	E	F	I	Es
negocio (Es)	Geschäft n	business	affaire f	negozio m	—
negocio acoplado (Es)	Kopplungsgeschäft n	tie-in transaction	affaire couplée f	operazione abbinata f	—
negocio de exportación o importación (Es)	Auslandsgeschäft n	foreign business	opération avec l'étranger f	affare con l'estero m	—
negocio de inmuebles (Es)	Immobilien-geschäft n	property transactions	affaire immobilière f	operazione immobiliare f	—
negocio jurídico (Es)	Rechtsgeschäft n	legal transaction	acte juridique m	negozio giuridico m	—
negocios de transporte (Es)	Beförderungs-geschäfte pl	transport services	transports m pl	operazioni di trasporto f pl	—
negotiation (E)	Verhandlung f	—	négociation f	trattativa f	negociación f
negotiation skills (E)	Verhandlungs-geschick n	—	habileté en matière de négociations f	abilità nel trattare f	tino de negociar m
negozi pilota (I)	Testläden pl	test shops	magasins de test m pl	—	tiendas piloto f pl
negozio (I)	Geschäft n	business	affaire f	—	negocio m
negozio giuridico (I)	Rechtsgeschäft n	legal transaction	acte juridique m	—	negocio jurídico m
negozio simulato (I)	Scheingeschäft n	fictitious transaction	opération simulée f	—	operación ficticia f
Nennwert (D)	—	nominal value	valeur nominale f	valore nominale m	valor nominal m
ne pas transférable (F)	nicht übertragbar	non-assignable	—	non trasferibile	intransmisible
net (E)	netto	—	net	netto	neto
net (F)	netto	net	—	netto	neto
net assets[1] (E)	Reinvermögen n	—	avoir net m	patrimonio netto m	patrimonio neto m
net assets[2] (E)	Nettovermögen n	—	patrimoine net m	patrimonio netto m	patrimonio neto m
net earnings (E)	Nettoertrag m	—	produit net m	ricavo netto m	producto neto m
net income (E)	Nettoeinkommen n	—	revenu net m	reddito netto m	ingreso neto m
net income percentage of turnover (E)	Umsatzrendite f	—	rendement du chiffre d'affaires m	rendita del fatturato f	rédito de la cifra de ventas m
net indebtedness (E)	Nettoverschuldung f	—	endettement net m	indebitamento netto m	deuda neta m
net investment (E)	Nettoinvestition f	—	investissement net m	investimento netto m	inversión neta f
net national product (E)	Nettosozialprodukt n	—	produit national net m	prodotto nazionale netto m	producto nacional neto m
neto (Es)	netto	net	net	netto	—
net price (E)	Nettopreis m	—	prix net m	prezzo netto m	precio neto m
net production (E)	Nettoproduktion f	—	production nette f	produzione netta f	producción neta f
net profit (E)	Reingewinn m	—	bénéfice net m	utile netto m	ganancia neta f
netto (D)	—	net	net	netto	neto
netto (I)	netto	net	net	—	neto
Nettoeinkommen (D)	—	net income	revenu net m	reddito netto m	ingreso neto m
Nettoertrag (D)	—	net earnings	produit net m	ricavo netto m	producto neto m
Nettoinvestition (D)	—	net investment	investissement net m	investimento netto m	inversión neta f
Nettolohn (D)	—	take-home pay	salaire net m	salario netto m	salario neto m
Nettopreis (D)	—	net price	prix net m	prezzo netto m	precio neto m
Nettoproduktion (D)	—	net production	production nette f	produzione netta f	producción neta f
Nettosozialprodukt (D)	—	net national product	produit national net m	prodotto nazionale netto m	producto nacional neto m
Nettoumsatz (D)	—	net turnover	chiffre d'affaires net m	fatturato netto m	ventas netas f pl
Nettovermögen (D)	—	net assets	patrimoine net m	patrimonio netto m	patrimonio neto m
Nettoverschuldung (D)	—	net indebtedness	endettement net m	indebitamento netto m	deuda neta m
net turnover (E)	Nettoumsatz m	—	chiffre d'affaires net m	fatturato netto m	ventas netas f pl
network (E)	Netzwerk n	—	réseau m	rete f	red f
network planning (E)	Netzplan m	—	réseau linéaire pour planification m	pianificazione reticolare f	planificación reticular f
Netzplan (D)	—	network planning	réseau linéaire pour planification m	pianificazione reticolare f	planificación reticular f
Netzwerk (D)	—	network	réseau m	rete f	red f
Neugründung (D)	—	new foundation	création d'une nouvelle société f	costituzione nuova f	fundación nueva f

	D	E	F	I	Es
Neujahr (D)	—	New Year	Nouvel An *m*	Capodanno *m*	(día de) Año Nuevo *m*
new foundation (E)	Neugründung *f*	—	création d'une nouvelle société *f*	costituzione nuova *f*	fundación nueva *f*
newly industrialized countries (E)	Schwellenland *n*	—	pays dans le seuil à l'industrialisation *m*	paese emergente *m*	país en el umbral hacia la industrializa- ción *m*
news (E)	Nachricht *f*	—	nouvelle *f*	notizia *f*	noticia *f*
newspaper and maga- zine advertising (E)	Anzeigenwerbung *f*	—	publicité par la presse *f*	pubblicità per inserzione *f*	publicidad por anuncios *f*
New Year (E)	Neujahr *n*	—	Nouvel An *m*	Capodanno *m*	(día de) Año Nuevo *m*
Nichterfüllung (D)	—	non-performance	inexécution *f*	inadempienza *f*	incumplimiento *m*
nichtig (D)	—	void	non valable	nullo	nulo
nicht übertragbar (D)	—	non-assignable	ne pas transférable	non trasferibile	intransmisible
Niederlassung (D)	—	establishment	succursale *f*	succursale *f*	sucursal *f*
Niedrigstkurs (D)	—	floor price	cours le plus bas *m*	corso minimo *m*	cotización mínima *f*
Nießbrauch (D)	—	usufruct	usufruit *m*	usufrutto *m*	usufructo *m*
night safe (E)	Nachttresor *m*	—	dépôt de nuit *m*	cassa continua *f*	depósito de noche *m*
night shift (E)	Nachtschicht *f*	—	équipe de nuit *f*	turno notturno *m*	turno de noche *m*
nil tariff (E)	Nulltarif *m*	—	tarif gratuit *m*	tariffa zero *f*	tarifa gratuita *f*
nitric oxide (E)	Stickoxid *n*	—	oxyde azotique *m*	ossido di azoto *m*	óxido nítrico *m*
niveau de gestion (F)	Führungsebene *f*	executive level	—	quadri dirigenti *m*	nivel de dirección *m*
niveau de l'endettement (F)	Verschuldungsgrad *m*	debt ratio	—	tasso d'indebitamento *m*	grado de endeudamiento *m*
niveau des prix (F)	Preisniveau *n*	price level	—	livello dei prezzi *m*	nivel de precios *m*
niveau de vie (F)	Lebensstandard *m*	standard of living	—	tenore di vita *m*	nivel de vida *m*
niveau du rendement (F)	Ertragslage *f*	earning situation	—	situazione economica *f*	situación del beneficio *f*
niveau du taux d'intérêt (F)	Zinsniveau *n*	interest rate level	—	livello degli interessi *m*	nivel de interés *m*
nivel de dirección (Es)	Führungsebene *f*	executive level	niveau de gestion *m*	quadri dirigenti *m*	—
nivel de interés (Es)	Zinsniveau *n*	interest rate level	niveau du taux d'intérêt *m*	livello degli interessi *m*	—
nivel de precios (Es)	Preisniveau *n*	price level	niveau des prix *m*	livello dei prezzi *m*	—
nivel de vida (Es)	Lebensstandard *m*	standard of living	niveau de vie *m*	tenore di vita *m*	—
no asegurado (Es)	ungesichert	unsecured	non garanti	non assicurato	—
no contaminante (Es)	umweltfreundlich	beneficial to the environment	favorable à l'environnement	ecologico	—
Noël (F)	Weihnachten *n*	Christmas	—	Natale *m*	Navidad *f*
no en efectivo (Es)	unbar	non cash	non comptant	non in contanti	—
noise abatement (E)	Lärmbekämpfung *f*	—	lutte contre le bruit *f*	lotta contro i rumori *f*	lucha contra el ruido *f*
nolo (I)	Fracht *f*	freight	fret *m*	—	carga *f*
nolo aereo (I)	Luftfracht *f*	air freight	fret aérien *m*	—	flete aéreo *m*
nolo ferroviario (I)	Bahnfracht *f*	rail freight	fret par rail *m*	—	transporte ferroviario *m*
nolo pagato (I)	Fracht bezahlt	freight paid	fret payé	—	flete pagado
nombramiento (Es)	Ernennung *f*	apointment	nomination *f*	nomina *f*	—
nombre (F)	Zahl *f*	number/figure	—	numero *m*/cifra *f*	número *m*/cifra *f*
nom de la maison (F)	Firmenname *m*	company name	—	denominazione *f*/ ragione sociale *f*	razón social *f*
nomina (I)	Ernennung *f*	apointment	nomination *f*	—	nombramiento *m*
nominal amount (E)	Nominalbetrag *m*	—	montant nominal *m*	importo nominale *m*	montante nominal *m*
Nominalbetrag (D)	—	nominal amount	montant nominal *m*	importo nominale *m*	montante nominal *m*
Nominaleinkommen (D)	—	nominal income	revenu nominal *m*	reddito nominale *m*	ingresos nominales *m*
nominal income (E)	Nominaleinkommen *n*	—	revenu nominal *m*	reddito nominale *m*	ingresos nominales *m*
Nominallohn (D)	—	nominal wage	salaire nominal *m*	salario nominale *m*	salario nominal *m*
nominal value (E)	Nennwert *m*	—	valeur nominale *f*	valore nominale *m*	valor nominal *m*
nominal wage (E)	Nominallohn *m*	—	salaire nominal *m*	salario nominale *m*	salario nominal *m*
nomination[1] (F)	Beförderung *f*	promotion	—	promozione *f*	ascenso *m*

	D	E	F	I	Es
nomination² (F)	Ernennung f	apointment	—	nomina f	nombramiento m
non adéquat (F)	unsachgemäß	improper	—	non idoneo	con falta de objetividad
No-name-Produkt (D)	—	generic product	produit sans nom m	prodotto senza nome m	producto genérico m
non assicurato (I)	ungesichert	unsecured	non garanti	—	no asegurado
non-assignable (E)	nicht übertragbar	—	ne pas transférable	non trasferibile	intransmisible
non cash (E)	unbar	—	non comptant	non in contanti	no en efectivo
non-cash (E)	bargeldlos	—	par virement	mediante assegno	por transferencia
non comptant (F)	unbar	non cash	—	non in contanti	no en efectivo
non dédouané (F)	unverzollt	duty unpaid	—	non sdoganato	aduana aparte
non garanti (F)	ungesichert	unsecured	—	non assicurato	no asegurado
non idoneo (I)	unsachgemäß	improper	non adéquat	—	con falta de objetividad
non imballato (I)	unverpackt	unpacked	sans emballage	—	sin embalar
non in contanti (I)	unbar	non cash	non comptant	—	no en efectivo
non-material damage (E)	immaterieller Schaden m	—	dommage immatériel m	danno immateriale m	daño inmaterial m
non-performance (E)	Nichterfüllung f	—	inexécution f	inadempienza f	incumplimiento m
non-recourse financing (E)	Forfaitierung f	—	financement sans recours m	forfetizzazione f	financiación sin recurso f
non sdoganato (I)	unverzollt	duty unpaid	non dédouané	—	aduana aparte
non trasferibile (I)	nicht übertragbar	non-assignable	ne pas transférable	—	intransmisible
non valable (F)	nichtig	void	—	nullo	nulo
Norm (D)	—	standard	standard m	norma f	norma f
norma (Es)	Norm f	standard	standard m	norma f	—
norma (I)	Norm f	standard	standard m	—	norma f
norma de producción (Es)	Arbeitsnorm f	fair labour standards	norme de travail f	norma di lavoro f	—
norma di lavoro (I)	Arbeitsnorm f	fair labour standards	norme de travail f	—	norma de producción f
norma giuridica (I)	Rechtsnorm f	legal norm	règle de droit f	—	norma jurídica f
norma industrial alemana (Es)	Deutsche Industrie-Norm f	German Industrial Standards	norme industrielle allemande f	norma tedesca di normalizzazione f	—
norma jurídica (Es)	Rechtsnorm f	legal norm	règle de droit f	norma giuridica f	—
normalisé (F)	genormt	standardized	—	standardizzato	normalizado
normalización (Es)	Normung f	standardization	standardisation f	standardizzazione f	—
normalizado (Es)	genormt	standardized	normalisé	standardizzato	—
normas técnicas (Es)	technische Normen pl	technical standards	normes techniques f pl	norme tecniche f pl	—
norma tedesca di normalizzazione (I)	Deutsche Industrie-Norm f	German Industrial Standards	norme industrielle allemande f	—	norma industrial alemana f
norme de travail (F)	Arbeitsnorm f	fair labour standards	—	norma di lavoro f	norma de producción f
norme industrielle allemande (F)	Deutsche Industrie-Norm f	German Industrial Standards	—	norma tedesca di normalizzazione f	norma industrial alemana f
normes techniques (F)	technische Normen pl	technical standards	—	norme tecniche f pl	normas técnicas f pl
norme tecniche (I)	technische Normen pl	technical standards	normes techniques f pl	—	normas técnicas f pl
Normung (D)	—	standardization	standardisation f	standardizzazione f	normalización f
nota¹ (Es)	Aktennotiz f	memorandum	note f	annotazione f	—
nota² (Es)	Vermerk m	note	remarque f	annotazione f	—
nota de cobertura (Es)	Deckungszusage f	confirmation of cover	acceptation de prendre le risque en charge f	impegno di copertura m	—
nota de prensa (Es)	Pressenotiz f	press report	note de presse f	notizia stampa f	—
nota di accredito (I)	Gutschriftsanzeige f	credit advice	avis de crédit m	—	aviso de abono m
notaio (I)	Notar m	(public) notary	notaire m	—	notario m
notaire (F)	Notar m	(public) notary	—	notaio m	notario m
Notar (D)	—	(public) notary	notaire m	notaio m	notario m
notario (Es)	Notar m	(public) notary	notaire m	notaio m	—
not binding (E)	unverbindlich	—	sans obligation	senza impegno	sin compromiso

	D	E	F	I	Es
note¹ (E)	Vermerk *m*	—	remarque *f*	annotazione *f*	nota *f*
note² (E)	Notiz *f*	—	note *f*	annotazione *f*	noticia *f*
note¹ (F)	Notiz *f*	note	—	annotazione *f*	noticia *f*
note² (F)	Aktennotiz *f*	memorandum	—	annotazione *f*	nota *f*
note de débit (F)	Lastschrift *f*	debit entry	—	addebito *m*	cargo en cuenta *m*
note de presse (F)	Pressenotiz *f*	press report	—	notizia stampa *f*	nota de prensa *f*
Notenbank (D)	—	central bank	banque d'émission *f*	banca d'emissione *f*	banco emisor *m*
Notenumlauf (D)	—	notes in circulation	circulation fiduciaire *f*	circolazione delle banconote *f*	circulación fiduciaria *f*
notes in circulation (E)	Notenumlauf *m*	—	circulation fiduciaire *f*	circolazione delle banconote *f*	circulación fiduciaria *f*
notice of assessment (E)	Steuerbescheid *m*	—	avis d'imposition *m*	cartella delle imposte *f*	liquidación de impuestos *f*
notice of defect (E)	Mängelanzeige *f*	—	notification d'un vice *f*	denuncia dei vizi *f*	aviso de vicios *m*
notice of termination (E)	Kündigung *f*	—	résiliation *f*	disdetta *f*	rescisión *f*
noticia¹ (Es)	Notiz *f*	note	note *f*	annotazione *f*	—
noticia² (Es)	Nachricht *f*	news	nouvelle *f*	notizia *f*	—
Notierung (D)	—	quotation	cotation *f*	quotazione *f*	cotización *f*
notifica (I)	Zustellung *f*	delivery	remise *f*	—	envío *m*
notification (F)	Mitteilung *f*	information	—	comunicazione *f*	aviso *m*
notification d'un vice (F)	Mängelanzeige *f*	notice of defect	—	denuncia dei vizi *f*	aviso de vicios *m*
notification of damage (E)	Schadensmeldung *f*	—	déclaration du sinistre *f*	avviso di danni *m*	aviso de siniestro *m*
Notiz (D)	—	note	note *f*	annotazione *f*	noticia *f*
notizia (I)	Nachricht *f*	news	nouvelle *f*	—	noticia *f*
notizia stampa (I)	Pressenotiz *f*	press report	note de presse *f*	—	nota de prensa *f*
no utilizado (Es)	ungenutzt	unused	pas utilisé	inutilizzato	—
Nouvel An (F)	Neujahr *n*	New Year	—	Capodanno *m*	(día de) Año Nuevo *m*
nouvel ordre (F)	Nachbestellung *f*	repeat order	—	ordinazione supplementare *f*	pedido suplementario *m*
no vinculante (Es)	freibleibend	subject to confirmation	sans engagement	senza impegno	—
nuclear energy (E)	Kernenergie *f*	—	énergie nucléaire *f*	energia nucleare *f*	energía nuclear *f*
nuclear power plant (E)	Atomkraftwerk *n*	—	centrale nucléaire *f*	centrale nucleare *f*	central nuclear *f*
nuisible à l'environnement (F)	umweltschädlich	causing environmental damages	—	inquinante	contaminante
nullo (I)	nichtig	void	non valable	—	nulo
Nulltarif (D)	—	nil tariff	tarif gratuit *m*	tariffa zero *f*	tarifa gratuita *f*
Nullwachstum (D)	—	zero growth	croissance zéro *f*	crescita zero *f*	crecimiento cero *m*
nulo (Es)	nichtig	void	non valable	nullo	—
number (E)	Zahl *f*	—	nombre *m*/chiffre *m*	numero *m*/cifra *f*	número *m*/cifra *f*
numbered account (E)	Nummernkonto *n*	—	compte anonyme *m*	conto cifrato *m*	cuenta cifrada *f*
numeri d'identificazione (I)	Kennzahlen *pl*	code numbers	numéros de référence *m pl*	—	números índice *m pl*
número (Es)	Zahl *f*	number/figure	nombre *m*/chiffre *m*	numero *m*/cifra *f*	—
numero (I)	Zahl *f*	number/figure	nombre *m*/chiffre *m*	—	número *m*/cifra *f*
numéro de commande (F)	Auftragsnummer *f*	order number	—	numero d'ordine *m*	número de pedido *m*
numéro de compte (F)	Kontonummer *f*	account number	—	numero di conto *m*	número de cuenta *m*
número de cuenta (Es)	Kontonummer *f*	account number	numéro de compte *m*	numero di conto *m*	—
número de la factura (Es)	Rechnungsnummer *f*	invoice number	numéro de la facture *m*	numero della fattura *m*	—
numéro de la facture (F)	Rechnungsnummer *f*	invoice number	—	numero della fattura *m*	número de la factura *m*
número del cliente (Es)	Kundennummer *f*	customer's reference number	numéro de référence du client *m*	numero di cliente *m*	—
numero della fattura (I)	Rechnungsnummer *f*	invoice number	numéro de la facture *m*	—	número de la factura *m*

	D	E	F	I	Es
número de pedido (Es)	Auftragsnummer f	order number	numéro de commande m	numero d'ordine m	—
numéro de référence du client (F)	Kundennummer f	customer's reference number	—	numero di cliente m	número del cliente m
número de telefax (Es)	Telefaxnummer f	telefax number	numéro de téléfax m	numero telefax m	—
numéro de téléfax (F)	Telefaxnummer f	telefax number	—	numero telefax m	número de telefax m
número de teléfono (Es)	Telefonnummer f	telephone number	numéro de téléphone m	numero di telefono m	—
numéro de téléphone (F)	Telefonnummer f	telephone number	—	numero di telefono m	número de teléfono m
número de téletex (Es)	Teletexnummer f	teletex number	numéro de télétex m	numero teletex m	—
numéro de télétex (F)	Teletexnummer f	teletex number	—	numero teletex m	número de téletex m
número de télex (Es)	Telexnummer f	telex number	numéro de télex m	numero telex m	—
numéro de télex (F)	Telexnummer f	telex number	—	numero telex m	número de télex m
numero di cliente (I)	Kundennummer f	customer's reference number	numéro de référence du client m	—	número del cliente m
numero di conto (I)	Kontonummer f	account number	numéro de compte m	—	número de cuenta m
numero di telefono (I)	Telefonnummer f	telephone number	numéro de téléphone m	—	número de teléfono m
numero d'ordine (I)	Auftragsnummer f	order number	numéro de commande m	—	número de pedido m
numéros de référence (F)	Kennzahlen pl	code numbers	—	numeri d'identificazione m pl	números índice m pl
números índice (Es)	Kennzahlen pl	code numbers	numéros de référence m pl	numeri d'identificazione m pl	—
numero telefax (I)	Telefaxnummer f	telefax number	numéro de téléfax m	—	número de telefax m
numero teletex (I)	Teletexnummer f	teletex number	numéro de télétex m	—	número de téletex m
numero telex (I)	Telexnummer f	telex number	numéro de télex m	—	número de télex m
Nummernkonto (D)	—	numbered account	compte anonyme m	conto cifrato m	cuenta cifrada f
Nutzen (D)	—	utility	utilité f	utilità f	utilidad f
Nutzkosten (D)	—	utility costs	coûts fixes utiles m pl	costi fissi di utilizzo m pl	gastos fijos de utilización m pl
Nutzung (D)	—	use/utilization	mise à profit f	utilizzazione f	utilización f
oasi fiscale (I)	Steueroase f	tax haven	oasis fiscale f	—	oasis fiscal m
oasis fiscal (Es)	Steueroase f	tax haven	oasis fiscale f	oasi fiscale f	—
oasis fiscale (F)	Steueroase f	tax haven	—	oasi fiscale f	oasis fiscal m
obbligazione (I)	Schuld-verschreibung f	debenture stock	obligation f	—	obligación f
obbligazione convertibile (I)	Wandelschuld-verschreibung f	convertible bonds	obligation convertible f	—	obligaciones convertibles f pl
obbligazione perpetua (I)	Dauerschuld-verschreibung f	unredeemable bond	obligation perpétuelle f	—	obligación perpetua f
obbligazioni comunali (I)	Kommunal-obligation f	corporation stock	obligation communale f	—	obligación comunal f
obbligazioni industriali (I)	Industrie-obligationen pl	industrial bonds	obligations de l'industrie f pl	—	obligaciones industriales f pl
obblighi (I)	Verbindlichkeiten pl	liability/debts	obligation f/dettes f pl	—	obligaciónes f pl/ deudas f pl/créditos pasivos m pl
obbligo (I)	Obligo n	liability	engagement m	—	obligación f
obbligo d'assicurazione (I)	Versicherungs-pflicht f	liability to insure	assujettissement obligatoire à l'assurance m	—	obligatoriedad del seguro f
obbligo del segreto professionale (I)	Schweigepflicht f	professional discretion	discretion professionnelle f	—	secreto profesional m
obbligo di accettare la consegna (I)	Abnahmepflicht f	obligation to accept delivery	obligation d'acceptation de la marchandise f	—	obligación de recepción f
obbligo di conservazione (I)	Aufbewahrungs-pflicht f	obligation to preserve records	obligation de conservation f	—	deber de conservación m
obbligo di fornitura (I)	Belieferungspflicht f	duty to supply	obligation de livraison f	—	obligación de suministro f
obbligo di garanzia (I)	Garantie-verpflichtung f	guarantee obligation	engagement de garantie m	—	obligación de garantía f

	D	E	F	I	Es
obbligo di mantenere il prezzo fissato (I)	Preisbindung *f*	obligation to maintain fixed prices	obligation de respecter les prix *f*	—	limitación de precios *f*
obbligo d'intervento (I)	Interventionspflicht *f*	obligation to intervene	obligation d'intervention *f*	—	obligación de intervención *f*
obbligo di relazione (I)	Berichtspflicht *f*	obligation to report	obligation d'information *f*	—	obligación de información *f*
obbligo di risarcimento danni (I)	Schadensersatz-pflicht *f*	liability for damages	obligation de dédommager *f*	—	obligación indemnizatoria *f*
obbligo di sorveglianza (I)	Aufsichtspflicht *f*	duty of supervision	obligation de surveillance *f*	—	obligación de vigilancia *f*
obiettivi pubblicitari (I)	Werbeziele *pl*	advertising objective	objectifs publicitaires *m pl*	—	objetivos de la publicidad *m pl*
obiettivo (I)	Ziel *n*	objective	but *m*	—	objetivo *m*
obiettivo della politica economica (I)	wirtschaftspolitische Zielsetzung *f*	economy policy objectives	objectifs commandés par une politique économique *m pl*	—	objetivos de la política económica *m pl*
obiettivo di vendita (I)	Absatzziel *n*	sales target	objectif de vente *m*	—	fin de venta *m*
obiettivo imprenditoriale (I)	Unternehmensziel *n*	company objective	objectif de l'entreprise *m*	—	objetivo empresarial *m*
objectif de l'entreprise (F)	Unternehmensziel *n*	company objective	—	obiettivo imprenditoriale *m*	objetivo empresarial *m*
objectif de vente (F)	Absatzziel *n*	sales target	—	obbiettivo di vendita *m*	fin de venta *m*
objectifs commandés par une politique économique (F)	wirtschaftspolitische Zielsetzung *f*	economy policy objectives	—	obiettivo della politica economica *m*	objetivos de la política económica *m pl*
objectifs publicitaires (F)	Werbeziele *pl*	advertising objective	—	obiettivi pubblicitari *m pl*	objetivos de la publicidad *m pl*
objection (F)	Beanstandung *f*	objection	—	reclamo *m*	queja *f*
objection¹ (E)	Beanstandung *f*	—	objection *f*	reclamo *m*	queja *f*
objection² (E)	Protest *m*	—	protestation *f*/protêt *m*	opposizione *f*/protesta *f*	oposición *f*/protesta *f*
objective (E)	Ziel *n*	—	but *m*	obiettivo *m*	objetivo *m*
objectivo de facturación (Es)	Umsatzplan *m*	turnover plan	plan du chiffre d'affaires *m*	programma del fatturato *m*	—
object of depreciation (E)	Abschreibungs-objekt *n*	—	objet d'amortissement *m*	oggetto da ammortizzare *m*	objeto de amortización *m*
object of speculation (E)	Spekulationsobjekt *n*	—	objet de spéculation *m*	oggetto di speculazioni *m*	objeto de especulación *m*
objet d'amortissement (F)	Abschreibungs-objekt *n*	object of depreciation	—	oggetto da ammortizzare *m*	objeto de amortización *m*
objet de leasing (F)	Leasing-Objekt *n*	leasing object	—	oggetto del leasing *m*	objeto de leasing *m*
objet de spéculation (F)	Spekulationsobjekt *n*	object of speculation	—	oggetto di speculazioni *m*	objeto de especulación *m*
objetivo (Es)	Ziel *n*	objective	but *m*	obiettivo *m*	—
objetivo empresarial (Es)	Unternehmensziel *n*	company objective	objectif de l'entreprise *m*	obiettivo imprenditoriale *m*	—
objetivos de la política económica (Es)	wirtschaftspolitische Zielsetzung *f*	economy policy objectives	objectifs commandés par une politique économique *m pl*	obiettivo della politica economica *m*	—
objetivos de la publicidad (Es)	Werbeziele *pl*	advertising objective	objectifs publicitaires *m pl*	obiettivi pubblicitari *m pl*	—
objeto de amortización (Es)	Abschreibungs-objekt *n*	object of depreciation	objet d'amortissement *m*	oggetto da ammortizzare *m*	—
objeto de especulación (Es)	Spekulationsobjekt *n*	object of speculation	objet de spéculation *m*	oggetto di speculazioni *m*	—
objeto de leasing (Es)	Leasing-Objekt *n*	leasing object	objet de leasing *m*	oggetto del leasing *m*	—
obligación¹ (Es)	Obligo *n*	liability	engagement *m*	obbligo *m*	—
obligación² (Es)	Schuldverschreibung *f*	debenture stock	obligation *f*	obbligazione *f*	—
obligación comunal (Es)	Kommunalobligation *f*	corporation stock	obligation communale *f*	obbligazioni comunali *f pl*	—
obligación de garantía (Es)	Garantie-verpflichtung *f*	guarantee obligation	engagement de garantie *m*	obbligo di garanzia *m*	—
obligación de información (Es)	Berichtspflicht *f*	obligation to report	obligation d'information *f*	obbligo di relazione *m*	—

	D	E	F	I	Es
obligación de intervención (Es)	Interventionspflicht f	obligation to intervene	obligation d'intervention f	obbligo d'intervento m	—
obligación de recepción (Es)	Abnahmepflicht f	obligation to accept delivery	obligation d'acceptation de la marchandise f	obbligo di accettare la consegna m	—
obligación de suministro (Es)	Belieferungspflicht f	duty to supply	obligation de livraison f	obbligo di fornitura m	—
obligación de vigilancia (Es)	Aufsichtspflicht f	duty of supervision	obligation de surveillance f	obbligo di sorveglianza m	—
obligaciones (Es)	Verbindlichkeiten pl	liability/debts	obligation f/ dettes f pl	obblighi m pl/ debiti m pl	—
obligaciones convertibles (Es)	Wandelschuld-verschreibung f	convertible bonds	obligation convertible f	obbligazione convertibile f	—
obligaciones industriales (Es)	Industrie-obligationen pl	industrial bonds	obligations de l'industrie f pl	obbligazioni industriali f pl	—
obligación indemnizatoria (Es)	Schadens-ersatzpflicht f	liability for damages	obligation de dédommager f	obbligo di risarcimento danni m	—
obligación perpetua (Es)	Dauerschuld-verschreibung f	unredeemable bond	obligation perpétuelle f	obbligazione perpetua f	—
obligation¹ (F)	Schuld-verschreibung f	debenture stock	—	obbligazione f	obligación f
obligation² (F)	Verbindlichkeiten pl	liability/debts	—	obblighi m pl/ debiti m pl	obligaciónes f pl/ deudas f pl/créditos pasivos m pl
obligation communale (F)	Kommunal-obligation f	corporation stock	—	obbligazioni comunali f pl	obligación comunal f
obligation convertible (F)	Wandelschuld-verschreibung f	convertible bonds	—	obbligazione convertibile f	obligaciones convertibles f pl
obligation d'acceptation de la marchandise (F)	Abnahmepflicht f	obligation to accept delivery	—	obbligo di accettare la consegna m	obligación de recepción f
obligation de conservation (F)	Aufbewahrungs-pflicht f	obligation to preserve records	—	obbligo di conservazione m	deber de conservación m
obligation de dédommager (F)	Schadensersatz-pflicht f	liability for damages	—	obbligo di risarcimento danni m	obligación indemnizatoria f
obligation de livraison (F)	Belieferungspflicht f	duty to supply	—	obbligo di fornitura m	obligación de suministro f
obligation de respecter les prix (F)	Preisbindung f	obligation to maintain fixed prices	—	obbligo di mantenere il prezzo fissato m	limitación de precios f
obligation de surveillance (F)	Aufsichtspflicht f	duty of supervision	—	obbligo di sorveglianza m	obligación de vigilancia f
obligation d'information (F)	Berichtspflicht f	obligation to report	—	obbligo di relazione m	obligación de información f
obligation d'intervention (F)	Interventionspflicht f	obligation to intervene	—	obbligo d'intervento m	obligación de intervención f
obligation hypothécaire (F)	Pfandbrief m	mortgage bond	—	titolo ipotecario m	cédula hipotecaria f
obligation perpétuelle (F)	Dauerschuld-verschreibung f	unredeemable bond	—	obbligazione perpetua f	obligación perpetua f
Obligationsanleihe (D)	—	debenture loan	emprunt obligataire m	prestito obbligazionario m	empréstito sobre obligaciones m
obligations de l'industrie (F)	Industrie-obligationen pl	industrial bonds	—	obbligazioni industriali f pl	obligaciones industriales f pl
obligation to accept delivery (E)	Abnahmepflicht f	—	obligation d'acceptation de la marchandise f	obbligo di accettare la consegna m	obligación de recepción f
obligation to intervene (E)	Interventionspflicht f	—	obligation d'intervention f	obbligo d'intervento m	obligación de intervención f
obligation to maintain fixed prices (E)	Preisbindung f	—	obligation de respecter les prix f	obbligo di mantenere il prezzo fissato m	limitación de precios f
obligation to preserve records (E)	Aufbewahrungs-pflicht f	—	obligation de conservation f	obbligo di conservazione m	deber de conservación m
obligation to report (E)	Berichtspflicht f	—	obligation d'information f	obbligo di relazione m	obligación de información f
obligatoriedad del seguro (Es)	Versicherungs-pflicht f	liability to insure	assujettissement obligatoire à l'assurance m	obbligo d'assicurazione m	—
Obligo (D)	—	liability	engagement m	obbligo m	obligación f

	D	E	F	I	Es
observación de la competencia (Es)	Konkurrenzbeobachtung f	observation of the competitors	observation de la concurrence f	studio della concorrenza m	—
observación del mercado (Es)	Marktbeobachtung f	observation of markets	recherche du marché f	sondaggio del mercato m	—
observation de la concurrence (F)	Konkurrenzbeobachtung f	observation of the competitors	—	studio della concorrenza m	observación de la competencia f
observation of markets (E)	Marktbeobachtung f	—	étude de marché f	sondaggio del mercato m	observación del mercado f
observation of the competitors (E)	Konkurrenzbeobachtung f	—	observation de la concurrence f	studio della concorrenza m	observación de la competencia f
occupation (F)	Beschäftigung f	employment	—	occupazione f	ocupación f
occupational hazard (E)	Berufsrisiko n	—	risque professionnel m	rischio professionale m	riesgo profesional m
occupazione (I)	Beschäftigung f	employment	occupation f	—	ocupación f
occupazione eccedente (I)	Überbeschäftigung f	overcharge	surchargement m	—	exceso de empleo m/ superempleo m
occupazione part-time (I)	Teilzeitbeschäftigung f	part-time employment	emploi à temps partiel m	—	empleo parcial m
octroi d'un délai (F)	Fristgewährung f	granting a respite	—	concessione di un termine f	concesión de un plazo f
ocupación (Es)	Beschäftigung f	employment	occupation f	occupazione f	—
oferta (Es)	Offerte f	offer	offre f	offerta f	—
oferta de empleo (Es)	Stellenangebot n	offer of employment	offre d'emploi f	offerta d'impiego f	—
oferta de indemnización (Es)	Abfindungsangebot n	compensation offer	offre d'indemnité f	offerta d'indennità f	—
oferta especial (Es)	Sonderangebot n	special offer	offre spéciale f	offerta speciale f	—
oferta favorable[1] (Es)	preisgünstiges Angebot n	well-priced offer	offre à un prix avantageux f	offerta a buon prezzo f	—
oferta favorable[2] (Es)	günstigstes Angebot n	most favourable offer	offre favorable f	offerta vantaggiosa f	—
offene Rechnung (D)	—	unsettled account	facture pas encore payée f	conto aperto m	factura pendiente f
Offenlegung (D)	—	disclosure	révélation des derniers bilans du postulant d'un prêt f	pubblicità del bilancio f	publicidad para fines de inspección f
öffentliche Ausgaben (D)	—	public spending	dépenses publiques f pl	spesa pubblica f	gastos públicos m pl
öffentliche Betriebe (D)	—	public sector industrial enterprises	entreprises publiques f pl	aziende pubbliche f pl	empresa pública f
öffentliche Einnahmen (D)	—	public revenues	recettes publiques f pl	entrate pubbliche f pl	ingresos públicos m pl
öffentliche Güter (D)	—	public goods	biens publics m pl	beni pubblici m pl	bienes públicos m pl
öffentliche Hand (D)	—	public authorities	secteur public m	mano pubblica f	sector público m
öffentliche Unternehmen (D)	—	public enterprise	entreprises publiques f pl	imprese pubbliche f pl	empresa pública f
öffentliche Wirtschaft (D)	—	public sector of the economy	économie publique f	economia pubblica f	economía pública f
Öffentlichkeitsarbeit (D)	—	public relations (work)	relations publiques f pl	relazioni pubbliche f pl	relaciones públicas f pl
öffentlich-rechtlich (D)	—	under public law	de droit public	di diritto pubblico	de derecho público
offer[1] (E)	Angebot n	—	proposition f	offerta f	oferta f
offer[2] (E)	Offerte f	—	offre f	offerta f	oferta f
offer[3] (E)	anbieten	—	offrir	offrire	ofrecer
offer of employment (E)	Stellenangebot n	—	offre d'emploi f	offerta d'impiego f	oferta de empleo f
offerta[1] (I)	Offerte f	offer	offre f	—	oferta f
offerta[2] (I)	Angebot n	offer	proposition f	—	oferta f
offerta a buon prezzo (I)	preisgünstiges Angebot n	well-priced offer	offre à un prix avantageux f	—	oferta favorable f
offerta d'impiego (I)	Stellenangebot n	offer of employment	offre d'emploi f	—	oferta de empleo f
offerta d'indennità (I)	Abfindungsangebot n	compensation offer	offre d'indemnité f	—	oferta de indemnización f
offerta pubblica d'acquisto (I)	Tenderverfahren n	tender procedure	offre d'emprunts pour la régulation monétaire f	—	subasta de prestamos de regulación monetaria f

	D	E	F	I	Es
offerta speciale (I)	Sonderangebot n	special offer	offre spéciale f	—	oferta especial f
offerta vantaggiosa (I)	günstigstes	most favourable offer Angebot n	offre favorable f	—	oferta favorable f
Offerte (D)	—	offer	offre f	offerta f	oferta f
office de surveillance des cartels et ententes (F)	Kartellbehörde f	cartel authority	—	autorità antimonopoli f pl	oficina de cártels f
office des brevets (F)	Patentamt n	Patent Office	—	ufficio brevetti m	oficina del registro de patentes f
Office Européen de Brevets (F)	Europäisches Patentamt n	European Patent Office	—	Ufficio Europeo Brevetti m	Oficina Europea de Patentes f
office¹ (E)	Amt n	—	bureau m	ufficio m	cargo m
office² (E)	Geschäftsstelle f	—	agence f	ufficio m	oficina f
official (E)	Beamter m	—	fonctionnaire m	funzionario m	funcionario m
official car (E)	Dienstwagen m	—	voiture de service f	vettura di servizio f	coche de servicio m
official secret (E)	Dienstgeheimnis n	—	secret de service m	segreto d'ufficio m	secreto profesional m
offre (F)	Offerte f	offer	—	offerta f	oferta f
offre à un prix avantageux (F)	preisgünstiges Angebot n	well-priced offer	—	offerta a buon prezzo f	oferta favorable f
offre d'emploi (F)	Stellenangebot n	offer of employment	—	offerta d'impiego f	oferta de empleo f
offre d'emprunts pour la régulation monétaire (F)	Tenderverfahren n	tender procedure	—	offerta pubblica d'acquisto f	subasta de prestamos de regulación monetaria f
offre d'indemnité (F)	Abfindungsangebot n	compensation offer	—	offerta d'indennità f	oferta de indemnización f
offre favorable (F)	günstigstes Angebot n	most favourable offer	—	offerta vantaggiosa f	oferta favorable f
offre spéciale (F)	Sonderangebot n	special offer	—	offerta speciale f	oferta especial f
offrir (F)	anbieten	offer	—	offrire	ofrecer
offrire (I)	anbieten	offer	offrir	—	ofrecer
offset (F)	Offsetdruck m	offset (printing)	—	stampa offset f	impresión offset f
Offsetdruck (D)	—	offset (printing)	offset m	stampa offset f	impresión offset f
offset (printing) (E)	Offsetdruck m	—	offset m	stampa offset f	impresión offset f
oficial (Es)	Geselle m	journeyman	ouvrier artisan m	garzone m	—
oficina (Es)	Geschäftsstelle f	office	agence f	ufficio m	—
oficina de aduanas (Es)	Zollstelle f	customs office	bureau de douane m	posto di dogana m	—
oficina de cártels (Es)	Kartellbehörde f	cartel authority	office de surveillance des cartels et ententes f	autorità antimonopoli f pl	—
oficina de cheques postales (Es)	Postscheckamt n	postal giro centre	bureau de chèques postaux m	ufficio dei conti correnti postali m	—
oficina de información (Es)	Auskunftei f	information bureau	agence de renseignements f	agenzia d'informazioni f	—
oficina del censo (Es)	Einwohnermelde-amt n	residents' registration office	bureau de déclaration de résidence m	ufficio anagrafe m	—
oficina del registro de patentes (Es)	Patentamt n	Patent Office	office des brevets m	ufficio brevetti m	—
oficina de personal (Es)	Personalbüro n	personnel office	bureau du personnel m	ufficio del personale m	—
Oficina Europea de Patentes (Es)	Europäisches Patentamt n	European Patent Office	Office Européen de Brevets f	Ufficio Europeo Brevetti m	—
ofrecer (Es)	anbieten	offer	offrir	offrire	—
oggetto da ammortizzare (I)	Abschreibungs-objekt n	object of depreciation	objet d'amortissement m	—	objeto de amortización m
oggetto del leasing (I)	Leasing-Objekt n	leasing object	objet de leasing m	—	objeto de leasing m
oggetto di speculazioni (I)	Spekulationsobjekt n	object of speculation	objet de spéculation m	—	objeto de especulación m
ohne Dividende (D)	—	with non-distributed dividend	sans dividende m	senza dividendo	sin dividendo
ohne Gewähr (D)	—	without garanty	sous toute réserve	senza garanzia	sin garantía
ohne Obligo (D)	—	without obligation	sans engagement	senza obbligo	sin obligación
Ökologie (D)	—	ecology	écologie f	ecologia f	ecología f

	D	E	F	I	Es
Ökonomie (D)	—	economy	économie f	economia f	economía f
old age insurance (E)	Altersversicherung f	—	assurance-vieillesse f	assicurazione per la vecchiaia f	seguro de vejez m
old-age pension insurance (E)	Rentenversicherung f	—	assurance sociale invalidité-vieillesse f	assicurazione invalidità e vecchiaia f	seguro de pensiones m
Oligopol (D)	—	oligopoly	oligopole m	oligopolio m	oligopolio m
oligopole (F)	Oligopol m	oligopoly	—	oligopolio m	oligopolio m
oligopolio (Es)	Oligopol m	oligopoly	oligopole m	oligopolio m	—
oligopolio (I)	Oligopol m	oligopoly	oligopole m	—	oligopolio m
oligopoly (E)	Oligopol m	—	oligopole m	oligopolio m	oligopolio m
olio usato (I)	Altöl n	waste oil	huile usée f	—	aceite usado m
oltremare (I)	Übersee	oversea(s)	outre-mer	—	ultramar m
omaggio pubblicitario (I)	Werbegeschenk n	advertising gift	cadeau publicitaire m	—	regalo publicitario m
omogeneità (I)	Homogenität f	homogeneity	homogénéité f	—	homogeneidad f
on account of payment (E)	zahlungshalber	—	pour raison de payement	a titolo di pagamento	a título de pago
on a commission basis[1] (E)	auf Provisionsbasis	—	à la commission	a provvigione	a comisión
on a commission basis[2] (E)	auf Kommissionsbasis	—	en commission	in base commissionaria	en comisión
on approval (E)	zur Ansicht	—	à vue	in visione	para examen
on call (E)	auf Abruf	—	à convenance	su richiesta	a requerimiento
onere di prova (I)	Beweislast f	burden of proof	charge de la preuve f	—	carga de la prueba f
onere supplementare (I)	Mehrbelastung f	additional burden	surcharge f	—	carga suplementaria f
oneri straordinari (I)	außergewöhnliche Belastung f	extraordinary expenses	charges exceptionnelles f pl	—	carga extraordinaria f
onorario[1] (I)	Gage f	salary	cachet m	—	remuneración
onorario[2] (I)	Honorar n	professional fee	honoraires m pl	—	honorario m
on receipt of the invoice (E)	nach Erhalt der Rechnung	—	après avoir réçu la facture	a ricevimento della fattura	después de haber recibo la factura
on schedule (E)	termingerecht	—	dans les délais	puntuale	en la fecha fijada
on trial (E)	auf Probe	—	à l'essai	in prova	a prueba
opción (Es)	Option f	option	option f	opzione f	—
opción de venta (Es)	Verkaufsoption f	option to sell	option de vente f	opzione di vendita f	—
open cheque (E)	Barscheck m	—	chèque non barré m	assegno circolare m	cheque de caja m
open credit (E)	Blankokredit m	—	crédit en compte courant m	credito scoperto m	crédito en blanco m
opening balance sheet (E)	Eröffnungsbilanz f	—	bilan d'ouverture m	bilancio d'apertura m	balance inicial m
opening capital (E)	Anfangskapital n	—	capital initial m	capitale iniziale m	capital inicial m
opening inventory (E)	Anfangsbestand m	—	stock initial m	scorte iniziali f pl	existencias iniciales f pl
opening of a business (E)	Geschäftseröffnung f	—	ouverture d'une affaire f	apertura di un negozio f	apertura de los establecimientos f
opening of a letter of credit (E)	Akkreditiveröffnung f	—	ouverture d'un accréditif f	apertura del credito documentario f	apertura de un crédito documentario f
opening of an account (E)	Kontoeröffnung f	—	ouverture de compte f	apertura di un conto f	apertura de una cuenta f
opening of the will (E)	Testaments-eröffnung f	—	ouverture du testament f	apertura del testamento f	apertura de testamento f
open price (E)	Preis freibleibend	—	prix sans engagement m	prezzo non vincolante m	precio sin compromiso m
operación al contado (Es)	Tagesgeschäft n	day-to-day operations	affaire au comptant f	contratto a contanti m	—
operación a plazo[1] (Es)	Termingeschäft n	time bargain	opération à terme f	operazione a termine f	—
operación a plazo[2] (Es)	Teilzahlungs-geschäft n	partial payment transaction	achat à tempérament m	vendita a rate f	—
operación a plazo de mercancías (Es)	Warentermin-geschäft n	commodity forward transaction	opération de livraison à terme f	operazione a termine su merci f	—

	D	E	F	I	Es
operación bursátil (Es)	Börsengeschäfte pl	stock market transactions	opérations de bourse f pl	operazioni di borsa f pl	—
operación con valores (Es)	Wertpapiergeschäft n	securities business	opérations sur titres f pl	operazioni su titoli f pl	—
operación de comisión (Es)	Kommissions-geschäft n	commission business	affaire en commission f	operazione di commissione f	—
operacion de compensación (Es)	Kompensations-geschäft n	barter transaction	affaire de compensation f	operazione di compensazione f	—
operación de emisión (Es)	Emissionsgeschäft n	investment business	opération succédant à une émission f	operazione d'emissione f	—
operación de especulación (Es)	Spekulations-geschäft n	speculative operations	affaire spéculative f	operazione speculativa f	—
operación de exportación (Es)	Exportgeschäft n	export business	affaire d'exportation f	operazione d'esportazione f	—
operación de moneda extranjera (Es)	Sortenhandel m	dealing in foreign notes and coins	commerce de change m	cambio valuta m	—
operacion de valores (Es)	Effektengeschäft n	securities business	commerce des valeurs mobilières m	operazione su titoli f	—
operaciones activas (Es)	Aktivgeschäft n	credit transaction	opération active f	operazione attiva f	—
operaciones antes de la apertura de la bolsa (Es)	Vorbörse f	before hours dealing	marché avant le marché officiel m	mercato preborsistico m	
operaciones de crédito (Es)	Kreditgeschäft n	credit business	achat à crédit m	operazione di credito f	—
operaciones de descuento (Es)	Abrechnungs-verfahren n	settling procedure	méthode de l'apure-ment des comptes	metodo di liquidazione m	—
operaciones de divisas (Es)	Devisenhandel m	foreign exchange dealings	marché des changes m	commercio delle divise m	—
operaciones de pignoración (Es)	Lombardgeschäft n	lending on securities	prêt sur gage m	anticipazioni f pl	—
operación ficticia (Es)	Scheingeschäft n	fictitious transaction	opération simulée f	negozio simulato m	—
operación pasiva (Es)	Passivgeschäft n	passive deposit transactions	opération passive f	operazione passiva f	—
operación swap (Es)	Swapgeschäft n	swap transaction	opération swap f	operazione swap f	—
operación triangular (Es)	Dreiecksgeschäft n	triangular transaction	opération commer-ciale triangulaire f	operazione triangolare f	—
operaio (I)	Arbeiter m	worker	travailleur m	—	trabajador m
operating company (E)	Betriebsgesellschaft f	—	entreprise d'exploitation f	società d'esercizio f	empresa de explotación f
operating costs (E)	Betriebskosten pl	—	charges d'exploitation f pl	spese d'esercizio f pl	gastos de explotación m pl
operating permit (E)	Betriebserlaubnis f	—	droit d'exploitation m	autorizzazione per l'esercizio f	autorización de funcionamiento f
opération active (F)	Aktivgeschäft n	credit transaction	—	operazione attiva f	operaciones activas f pl
operational statistics (E)	Betriebsstatistik f	—	statistique commer-ciale et industrielle f	statistica aziendale f	estadística de la empresa f
operation analysis (E)	Betriebsanalyse f	—	situation analytique de l'expoitation f	analisi aziendale f	análisis de la empresa m
opération à terme (F)	Termingeschäft n	time bargain	—	operazione a termine f	operación a plazo f
opération avec l'étranger (F)	Auslandsgeschäft n	foreign business	—	affare con l'estero m	negocio de exporta-ción o importación m
opération commer-ciale triangulaire (F)	Dreiecksgeschäft n	triangular transaction	—	operazione triangolare f	operación triangular f
opération de livraison à terme (F)	Warentermin-geschäft n	commodity forward transaction	—	operazione a termine su merci f	operación a plazo de mercancías f
opération passive (F)	Passivgeschäft n	passive deposit transactions	—	operazione passiva f	operación pasiva m
opérations à terme sur les changes (F)	Devisentermin-geschäft n	forward exchange dealings	—	operazione valutaria a termine f	transacciones a tér-mino en divisas f pl
opérations de bourse (F)	Börsengeschäfte pl	stock market transactions	—	operazioni di borsa f pl	operación bursátil f
opérations de payement (F)	Zahlungsverkehr m	payment transactions	—	operazioni di pagamento f pl	servicio de pagos m pl
opération simulée (F)	Scheingeschäft n	fictitious transaction	—	negozio simulato m	operación ficticia f

optimization

	D	E	F	I	Es
opérations sur titres (F)	Wertpapiergeschäft *n*	securities business	—	operazioni su titoli *f pl*	operación con valores *f*
opération succédant à une émission (F)	Emissionsgeschäft *n*	investment business	—	operazione d'emissione *f*	operación de emisión *f*
opération swap (F)	Swapgeschäft *n*	swap transaction	—	operazione swap *f*	operación swap *f*
operazione abbinata (I)	Kopplungsgeschäft *n*	tie-in transaction	affaire couplée *f*	—	negocio acoplado *m*
operazione a termine (I)	Termingeschäft *n*	time bargain	opération à terme *f*	—	operación a plazo *f*
operazione a termine su merci (I)	Warentermingeschäft *n*	commodity forward transaction	opération de livraison à terme *f*	—	operación a plazo de mercancías *f*
operazione attiva (I)	Aktivgeschäft *n*	credit transaction	opération active *f*	—	operaciones activas *f pl*
operazione con pagamento a rate (I)	Abzahlungsgeschäft *n*	hire purchase transaction	achat à tempérament *m*	—	venta a plazos *f*
operazione d'emissione (I)	Emissionsgeschäft *n*	investment business	opération succédant à une émission *f*	—	operación de emisión *f*
operazione d'esportazione (I)	Exportgeschäft *n*	export business	affaire d'exportation *f*	—	operación de exportación *f*
operazione di commissione (I)	Kommissionsgeschäft *n*	commission business	affaire en commission *f*	—	operación de comisión *f*
operazione di compensazione (I)	Kompensationsgeschäft *n*	barter transaction	affaire de compensation *f*	—	operacion de compensación *f*
operazione di credito (I)	Kreditgeschäft *n*	credit business	achat à crédit *m*	—	operaciones de crédito *f pl*
operazione di deposito (I)	Depotgeschäft *n*	deposit banking	garde des titres *f*	—	custodia de valores *f*
operazione immobiliare (I)	Immobiliengeschäft *n*	property transactions	affaire immobiliée *f*	—	negocio de inmuebles *m*
operazione passiva (I)	Passivgeschäft *n*	passive deposit transactions	opération passive *f*	—	operación pasiva *m*
operazione speculativa (I)	Spekulationsgeschäft *n*	speculative operations	affaire spéculative *f*	—	operación de especulación *f*
operazione su titoli (I)	Effektengeschäft *n*	securities business	commerce des valeurs mobilières *m*	—	operacion de valores *f*
operazione swap (I)	Swapgeschäft *n*	swap transaction	opération swap *f*	—	operación swap *f*
operazione triangolare (I)	Dreiecksgeschäft *n*	triangular transaction	opération commerciale triangulaire *f*	—	operación triangular *f*
operazione valutaria a termine (I)	Devisentermingeschäft *n*	forward exchange dealings	opérations à terme sur les changes *f pl*	—	transacciones a término en divisas *f pl*
operazioni a termine su merci (I)	Warenterminhandel *m*	commodity forward dealing	commerce d'opérations à terme *m*	—	tráfico de futuro *m*
operazioni di borsa (I)	Börsengeschäfte *pl*	stock market transactions	opérations de bourse *f pl*	—	operación bursátil *f*
operazioni di pagamento (I)	Zahlungsverkehr *m*	payment transactions	opérations de payement *f pl*	—	servicio de pagos *m pl*
operazioni di trasporto (I)	Beförderungsgeschäfte *pl*	transport services	transports *m pl*	—	negocios de transporte *m pl*
operazioni su titoli (I)	Wertpapiergeschäft *n*	securities business	opérations sur titres *f pl*	—	operación con valores *f*
opinion (E)	Meinung *f*	—	opinion *f*	opinione *f*	opinión *f*
opinión (Es)	Meinung *f*	opinion	opinion *f*	opinione *f*	—
opinion (F)	Meinung *f*	opinion	—	opinione *f*	opinión *f*
opinione (I)	Meinung *f*	opinion	opinion *f*	—	opinión *f*
oposición (Es)	Protest *m*	objection/protest	protestation *f/* protêt *m*	opposizione *f/* protesta *f*	—
opportunity costs (E)	Alternativkosten *pl*	—	coûts alternatifs *m pl*	costi alternativi *m pl*	coste alternativo *m*
opposition au payement d'un chèque (F)	Schecksperrung *f*	stopping payment of cheque	—	blocco d'assegno *m*	bloqueo de un cheque *m*
opposizione (I)	Protest *m*	objection/protest	protestation *f*/protêt *m*	—	oposición *f*/protesta *f*
optima (E)	Optimum *n*	—	optimum *m*	optimum *m*	óptimo *m*
Optimierung (D)	—	optimization	optimisation *f*	ottimizzazione *f*	optimización *f*
optimisation (F)	Optimierung *f*	optimization	—	ottimizzazione *f*	optimización *f*
optimización (Es)	Optimierung *f*	optimization	optimisation *f*	ottimizzazione *f*	—
optimization (E)	Optimierung *f*	—	optimisation *f*	ottimizzazione *f*	optimización *f*

	D	E	F	I	Es
óptimo (Es)	Optimum *n*	optima	optimum *m*	optimum *m*	—
Optimum (D)	—	optima	optimum *m*	optimum *m*	óptimo *m*
optimum (F)	Optimum *n*	optima	—	optimum *m*	óptimo *m*
optimum (I)	Optimum *n*	optima	optimum *m*	—	óptimo *m*
Option (D)	—	option	option *f*	opzione *f*	opción *f*
option (E)	Option *f*	—	option *f*	opzione *f*	opción *f*
option (F)	Option *f*	option	—	opzione *f*	opción *f*
option de vente (F)	Verkaufsoption *f*	option to sell	—	opzione di vendita *f*	opción de venta *f*
option to sell (E)	Verkaufsoption *f*	—	option de vente *f*	opzione di vendita *f*	opción de venta *f*
opzione (I)	Option *f*	option	option *f*	—	opción *f*
opzione di vendita (I)	Verkaufsoption *f*	option to sell	option de vente *f*	—	opción de venta *f*
or (F)	Gold *n*	gold	—	oro *m*	oro *m*
oral (Es)	mündlich	verbal	verbal	verbale	—
orario d'apertura (I)	Geschäftszeit *f*	business hours	heures d'ouverture *f pl*	—	hora de despacho *f pl*
orario di lavoro (I)	Arbeitszeit *f*	working hours	heures de travail *f pl*	—	jornada laboral *f*
orario di lavoro annuale (I)	Jahresarbeitszeit *f*	annual hours of work	temps de travail annuel *m*	—	jornada anual *f*
ora straordinaria (I)	Überstunde *f*	overtime	heure supplémentaire *f*	—	hora extraordinaria *f*
orden¹ (Es)	Anordnung *f*	order/arrangement	ordre *m*/disposition *f*	ordine *m*/disposizione *f*	—
orden² (Es)	Ordnung *f*	order	ordre *m*	ordinamento *m*	—
ordenación del territorio (Es)	Raumordnung *f*	regional policy	aménagement des espaces *m*	ordinamento territoriale *m*	—
ordenador¹ (Es)	Computer *m*	computer	ordinateur *m*	computer *m*	—
ordenador² (Es)	Datenverarbeitungsanlage *f*	data processing system	installation de traitement électronique des informations *f*	elaboratore elettronico di dati *m*	—
ordenador³ (Es)	Rechner *m*	computer/calculator	ordinateur *m*/calculateur de poche *m*	calcolatore *m*	—
ordenador personal (Es)	Personalcomputer *m*	personal computer	ordinateur individuel *m*	personal computer *m*	—
orden al mejor cambio posible (Es)	Bestensorder	order at best	ordre non limité *m*	ordine al miglior corso *m*	—
ordenanza (Es)	Verordnung *f*	decree	décret *m*	regolamento *m*	—
orden de pago (Es)	Zahlungsanweisung *f*	order to pay	mandat de payement *m*	ordine di pagamento *m*	—
orden económico (Es)	Wirtschaftsordnung *f*	economic order	ordre économique *m*	ordinamento economico *m*	—
orden económico mundial (Es)	Weltwirtschaftsordnung *f*	international economic order	ordre économique mondial *m*	sistema economico mondiale *m*	—
órden permanente (Es)	Dauerauftrag *m*	standing order	ordre régulier *m*	ordine permanente *m*	—
orden sucesivo (Es)	Folgeauftrag *m*	follow-up order	commande consécutive *f*	ordine successivo *m*	—
orden telegráfica (Es)	telegrafische Anweisung *f*	telegraphic payment order	mandat télégraphique *m*	vaglia telegrafico *m*	—
Order (D)	—	order	ordre *m*	ordine *m*	pedido *m*
order¹ (E)	Anordnung *f*	—	ordre *m*/disposition *f*	ordine *m*/disposizione *f*	orden *f*/disposición *f*
order² (E)	Ordnung *f*	—	ordre *m*	ordinamento *m*	orden *m*/leyes *f pl*
order³ (E)	Order *f*	—	ordre *m*	ordine *m*	pedido *m*
order⁴ (E)	Bestellung *f*	—	commande *f*	ordinazione *f*	pedido *m*
order⁵ (E)	Auftrag *m*	—	commande *f*	ordine *m*	pedido *m*
order at best (E)	Bestensorder	—	ordre non limité *m*	ordine al miglior corso *m*	orden al mejor cambio posible *f*
order cheque (E)	Orderscheck *m*	—	chèque à ordre *m*	assegno all'ordine *m*	cheque a la orden *m*
order form¹ (E)	Bestellschein *m*	—	bulletin de commande *m*	bolletta d'ordinazione *f*	hoja de pedido *f*
order form² (E)	Bestellformular *n*	—	bon de commande *m*	modulo d'ordinazione *m*	formulario de pedido *m*

	D	E	F	I	Es
order for payment (E)	Zahlungsbefehl *m*	—	ordre de payement *m*	ingiunzione di pagamento *f*	mandamiento de pago *m*
ordering quantity (E)	Bestellmenge *f*	—	quantité commandée *f*	quantità d'ordinazione *f*	cantidad pedida *f*
orderly (E)	ordnungsgemäß	—	correct(e)	regolare	debidamente
order number (E)	Auftragsnummer *f*	—	numéro de commande *m*	numero d'ordine *m*	número de pedido *m*
order opening a trial (E)	Eröffnungs-beschluß *m*	—	arrêt de mise en accusation *m*	decreto di citazione in giudizio *m*	acuerdo de apertura *m*
Orderpapier (D)	—	instruments (made out) to order	papier à ordre *m*	titolo all'ordine *m*	título a la orden *m*
order processing (E)	Auftragsbearbeitung *f*	—	réalisation d'une commande *f*	esecuzione ordini *f*	tramitación de pedidos *f*
Orderscheck (D)	—	order cheque	chèque à ordre *m*	assegno all'ordine *m*	cheque a la orden *m*
order scheduling (E)	Auftragsplanung *f*	—	planification des commandes *f*	pianificazione degli ordini *f*	planificación de la ejecución de pedidos *f*
order to pay (E)	Zahlungsanweisung *f*	—	mandat de payement *m*	ordine di pagamento *m*	orden de pago *f*
ordinamento (I)	Ordnung *f*	order	ordre *m*	—	orden *m*/leyes *f pl*
ordinamento del mercato (I)	Marktordnung *f*	market organization	organisation du marché *f*	—	organización del mercado *f*
ordinamento economico (I)	Wirtschaftsordnung *f*	economic order	ordre économique *m*	—	orden económico *m*
ordinamento territoriale (I)	Raumordnung *f*	regional policy	aménagement des espaces *m*	—	ordenación del territorio *f*
ordinary shares (E)	Stammaktie *f*	—	action ordinaire *f*	azione ordinaria *f*	acción ordinaria *f*
ordinateur[1] (F)	Computer *m*	computer	—	computer *m*	ordenador *m*
ordinateur[2] (F)	Rechner *m*	computer/calculator	—	calcolatore *m*	ordenador *m*/calculadora de bolsillo *f*
ordinateur individuel (F)	Personalcomputer *m*	personal computer	—	personal computer *m*	ordenador personal *m*
ordinazione[1] (I)	Auftragserteilung *f*	placing of an order	passation d'une commande *f*	—	otorgamiento de un pedido *m*
ordinazione[2] (I)	Bestellung *f*	order	commande *f*	—	pedido *m*
ordinazione anticipata (I)	Vorbestellung *f*	reservation	commande préalable *f*	—	pedidio anticipado *m*
ordinazione diretta (I)	Direktbestellung *f*	direct ordering	commande directe *f*	—	pedido directo *m*
ordinazione supplementare (I)	Nachbestellung *f*	repeat order	nouvel ordre *m*	—	pedido suplementario *m*
ordine[1] (I)	Auftrag *m*	order	commande *f*	—	pedido *m*
ordine[2] (I)	Order *f*	order	ordre *m*	—	pedido *m*
ordine[3] (I)	Anordnung *f*	order/arrangement	ordre *m*/disposition *f*	—	orden *f*/disposición *f*
ordine al miglior corso (I)	Bestensorder	order at best	ordre non limité *m*	—	orden al mejor cambio posible *f*
ordine a titolo di prova (I)	Probeauftrag *m*	trial order	ordre d'essai *m*	—	pedido de prueba *m*
ordine d'esportazione (I)	Exportauftrag *m*	export order	commande d'exportation *f*	—	pedido destinado a la exportación *m*
ordine di grandi quantità (I)	Großauftrag *m*	large-scale order	grosse commande *f*	—	importante pedido *m*
ordine di pagamento (I)	Zahlungsanweisung *f*	order to pay	mandat de payement *m*	—	orden de pago *f*
ordine permanente (I)	Dauerauftrag *m*	standing order	ordre régulier *m*	—	órden permanente *f*
ordine successivo (I)	Folgeauftrag *m*	follow-up order	commande consécutive *f*	—	orden sucesivo *f*
Ordnung (D)	—	order	ordre *m*	ordinamento *m*	orden *m*/leyes *f pl*
ordnungsgemäß (D)	—	orderly	correct(e)	regolare	debidamente
ordonnance sur référé civil (F)	einstweilige Verfügung *f*	temporary injunction	—	provvedimento temporaneo *m*	interdicto provisorio *m*
ordre[1] (F)	Anordnung *f*	order/arrangement	—	ordine *m*/disposizione *f*	orden *f*/disposición *f*
ordre[2] (F)	Order *f*	order	—	ordine *m*	pedido *m*
ordre[3] (F)	Ordnung *f*	order	—	ordinamento *m*	orden *m*/leyes *f pl*

	D	E	F	I	Es
ordre de payement (F)	Zahlungsbefehl *m*	order for payment	—	ingiunzione di pagamento *f*	mandamiento de pago *m*
ordre d'essai (F)	Probeauftrag *m*	trial order	—	ordine a titolo di prova *m*	pedido de prueba *m*
ordre économique (F)	Wirtschaftsordnung *f*	economic order	—	ordinamento economico *m*	orden económico *m*
ordre économique mondial (F)	Weltwirtschafts-ordnung *f*	international economic order	—	sistema economico mondiale *m*	orden económico mundial *m*
ordre non limité (F)	Bestensorder	order at best	—	ordine al miglior corso *m*	orden al mejor cambio posible *f*
ordre régulier (F)	Dauerauftrag *m*	standing order	—	ordine permanente *m*	órden permanente *f*
or en lingot (F)	Barrengold *n*	gold in bars	—	oro in lingotti *m*	oro en barras *m*
organigrama de flujo de datos (Es)	Datenflußplan *m*	data flow chart	organigramme de flux des données *m*	diagramma flusso dati *m*	—
organigramme de flux des données (F)	Datenflußplan *m*	data flow chart	—	diagramma flusso dati *m*	organigrama de flujo de datos *m*
Organisation (D)	—	organization	organisation *f*	organizzazione *f*	organización *f*
organisation (F)	Organisation *f*	organization	—	organizzazione *f*	organización *f*
organisation de service après vente (F)	Kundendienst-organisation *f*	service organization	—	organizzazione del servizio d'assistenza *f*	organización de servicio posventa *f*
organisation des consommateurs (F)	Verbraucher-organisation *f*	consumer protection organization	—	organizzazione dei consumatori *f*	orgnización de defensa del consumidor *f*
organisation de vente (F)	Absatzorganisation *f*	sales organization	—	organizzazione di vendita *f*	organización de ventas *f*
organisation des marchés agricoles (F)	Agrarmarktordnung *f*	agricultural market organization	—	regolamento del mercato agrario *m*	reglamentación del mercado agrícola *f*
organisation du marché (F)	Marktordnung *f*	market organization	—	ordinamento del mercato *m*	organización del mercado *f*
organisation du service (F)	Abteilungs-organisation *f*	department organization	—	organizzazione reparto *f*	organización de sección *f*
organisation fonction-nelle de l'entreprise (F)	Ablauforganisation *f*	scheduling organization	—	organizzazione del lavoro *f*	organización funcional *f*
Organisationsform (D)	—	pattern of organization	forme de l'organisation *f*	forma di organizzazione *f*	forma de organización *f*
organización (Es)	Organisation *f*	organization	organisation *f*	organizzazione *f*	—
organización de defen-sa del consumidor (Es)	Verbraucher-organisation *f*	consumer protection organization	organisation des consommateurs *f*	organizzazione dei consumatori *f*	—
organización del mercado (Es)	Marktordnung *f*	market organization	organisation du marché *f*	ordinamento del mercato *m*	—
organización de sección (Es)	Abteilungs-organisation *f*	department organization	organisation du service *f*	organizzazione reparto *f*	—
organización de servicio posventa (Es)	Kundendienst-organisation *f*	service organization	organisation de service après-vente *f*	organizzazione del servizio d'assistenza *f*	—
organización de ventas[1] (Es)	Absatzorganisation *f*	sales organization	organisation de vente *f*	organizzazione di vendita *f*	—
organización de ventas[2] (Es)	Marketing *n*	marketing	marketing *m*	marketing *m*	—
organización funcional (Es)	Ablauforganisation *f*	scheduling organization	organisation fonction-nelle de l'entreprise *f*	organizzazione del lavoro *f*	—
organization (E)	Organisation *f*	—	organisation *f*	organizzazione *f*	organización *f*
organization costs (E)	Gründungskosten *pl*	—	frais de fondation *m pl*	costi della costituzione *m pl*	gastos de fundación *m pl*
organizzazione (I)	Organisation *f*	organization	organisation *f*	—	organización *f*
organizzazione dei consumatori (I)	Verbraucher-organisation *f*	consumer protection organization	organisation des consommateurs *f*	—	orgnización de defen-sa del consumidor *f*
organizzazione del lavoro (I)	Ablauforganisation *f*	scheduling organization	organisation fonction-nelle de l'entreprise *f*	—	organización funcional *f*
organizzazione del servizio d'assistenza (I)	Kundendienst-organisation *f*	service organization	organisation de service après vente *f*	—	organización de servicio posventa *f*
organizzazione di vendita (I)	Absatzorganisation *f*	sales organization	organisation de vente *f*	—	organización de ventas *f*
organizzazione reparto (I)	Abteilungs-organisation *f*	department organization	organisation du service *f*	—	organización de sección *f*
orientado hacia el éxito (Es)	erfolgsorientiert	success-oriented	orienté vers le succès	orientato al successo	—

	D	E	F	I	Es
orientado hacia el marketing (Es)	Marketing-orientiert	marketing-oriented	orienté vers le marketing	orientato al marketing	—
orientado hacia el rendimiento (Es)	leistungsorientiert	performance-oriented	orienté vers le rendement	orientato al rendimento	—
orientato al marketing (I)	Marketing-orientiert	marketing-oriented	orienté vers le marketing	—	orientado hacia el marketing
orientato al rendimento (I)	leistungsorientiert	-performance-oriented	orienté vers le rendement	—	orientado hacia el rendimiento
orientato al successo (I)	erfolgsorientiert	success-oriented	orienté vers le succès	—	orientado hacia el éxito
orienté vers le marketing (F)	Marketing-orientiert	marketing-oriented	—	orientato al marketing	orientado hacia el marketing
orienté vers le rendement (F)	leistungsorientiert	performance-oriented	—	orientato al rendimento	orientado hacia el rendimiento
orienté vers le succès (F)	erfolgsorientiert	success-oriented	—	orientato al successo	orientado hacia el éxito
Orientierungspreis (D)	—	guide price	prix d'orientation *m*	prezzo d'orientamento *m*	precio de orientación *m*
oro (Es)	Gold *n*	gold	or *m*	oro *m*	—
oro (I)	Gold *n*	gold	or *m*	—	oro *m*
oro en barras (Es)	Barrengold *n*	gold in bars	or en lingot *m*	oro in lingotti *m*	—
oro in lingotti (I)	Barrengold *n*	gold in bars	or en lingot *m*	—	oro en barras *m*
oscilación de precios (Es)	Preisschwankung *f*	price fluctuation	fluctuation des prix *f*	fluttuazione dei prezzi *f*	—
oscilaciones estacionales (Es)	Saison-schwankungen *pl*	seasonal fluctuations	mouvements saisonniers *m pl*	oscillazioni stagionali *f pl*	—
oscillations de la demande (F)	Bedarfsschwankung *f*	fluctuations in requirements	—	oscillazioni del fabbisogno *f pl*	fluctuación de las necesidades *f*
oscillazione della produzione (I)	Produktions-schwankung *f*	fluctuations in production	fluctuation de la production *f pl*	—	fluctuaciones en la producción *f pl*
oscillazioni del fabbisogno (I)	Bedarfsschwankung *f*	fluctuations in requirements	oscillations de la demande *f pl*	—	fluctuación de las necesidades *f*
oscillazioni stagionali (I)	Saison-schwankungen *pl*	seasonal fluctuations	mouvements saisonniers *m pl*	—	oscilaciones estacionales *f pl*
ospitalità (I)	Bewirtung *f*	hospitality/catering	hospitalité *f*/accueil *m*	—	hospedaje *m*/ atenciones *f pl*
ossido di azoto (I)	Stickoxid *n*	nitric oxide	oxyde azotique *m*	—	óxido nítrico *m*
Ost-West-Handel (D)	—	East-West trade	commerce Est-Ouest *m*	scambio est-ovest *m*	comercio este-oeste *m*
otorgamiento de un pedido (Es)	Auftragserteilung *f*	placing of an order	passation d'une commande *f*	ordinazione *f*	—
ottimizzazione (I)	Optimierung *f*	optimization	optimisation *f*	—	optimización *f*
ottimo (I)	bestens	at best	au mieux	—	al mejor cambio
outdoor publicity (E)	Außenwerbung *f*	—	publicité extérieure *f*	pubblicità all'aperto *f*	publicidad al aire libre *f*
outgoing goods (E)	Warenausgang *m*	—	sortie de marchandieses *f*	uscita merci *f*	salida de mercancías *f*
Output (D)	—	output/production	output *m*/ production totale *f*	output *m*/ produzione totale *f*	output *m*/ producción total *f*
output (Es)	Output *n*	output/production	output *m*/ production totale *f*	output *m*/ produzione totale *f*	—
output (F)	Output *n*	output/production	—	output *m*/ produzione totale *f*	output *m*/ producción total *f*
output (I)	Output *n*	output/production	output *m*/ production totale *f*	—	output *m*/ producción total *f*
output¹ (E)	Fördermenge *f*	—	quantité extraite *f*	quantitativo d'estrazione *m*	cantidad producida *f*
output² (E)	Output *n*	—	output *m*/ production totale *f*	output *m*/ produzione totale *f*	output *m*/ producción total *f*
outre-mer (F)	Übersee	oversea(s)	—	oltremare *m*	ultramar *m*
outstanding debts (E)	Außenstände *pl*	—	dettes actives *f pl*	crediti *m pl*	cobros pendientes *m pl*
ouverture de compte (F)	Kontoeröffnung *f*	opening of an account	—	apertura di un conto *f*	apertura de una cuenta *f*
ouverture d'un accréditif (F)	Akkreditiveröffnung *f*	opening of a letter of credit	—	apertura del credito documentario *f*	apertura de un crédito documentario *f*

	D	E	F	I	Es
ouverture d'une affaire (F)	Geschäftseröffnung f	opening of a business	—	apertura di un negozio f	apertura de los establecimientos f
ouverture du testament (F)	Testaments-eröffnung f	opening of the will	—	apertura del testamento f	apertura de testamento f
ouvrier artisan (F)	Geselle m	journeyman	—	garzone m	oficial m
overall conception (E)	Gesamtkonzeption f	—	conception générale f	concezione universale f	concepción general f
overall view of the market (E)	Marktübersicht f	—	vue d'ensemble du marché f	quadro del mercato m	panorama de mercado m
overcapacity (E)	Überkapazität f	—	surcapacité f	capacità eccessiva f	supercapacidad f
overcapitalization (E)	Überkapitalisierung f	—	surcapitalisation f	sovracapitalizzazione f	sobrecapitalización f
overcharge (E)	Überbeschäftigung f	—	surchargement m	occupazione eccedente f	exceso de empleo m/ superempleo m
overdraft of an account (E)	Kontoüberziehung f	—	découvert de compte m	scoperto di conto m	descubierto m
overdraw (E)	überziehen	—	faire un prélèvement à découvert	mandare allo scoperto	sobrepasar
overhead expenses (E)	Gemeinkosten pl	—	coûts indirects m pl	costi comuni m pl	gastos generales m pl
overinsurance (E)	Überversicherung f	—	surassurance f	soprassicurazione f	sobreseguro m
overland transportation (E)	Landweg m	—	voie de terre f	via terra f	vía terrestre m
overnight expenses (E)	Übernachtungs-kosten pl	—	coûts de nuitée m pl	spese di pernottamento f pl	gastos de alojamiento m pl
overpopulation (E)	Überbevölkerung f	—	surpopulation f	sovrappopolazione f	superpoblación f
overproduction (E)	Überproduktion f	—	surproduction f	produzione eccessiva f	sobreproducción f
oversea(s) (E)	Übersee	—	outre-mer	oltremare m	ultramar m
oversea(s) trade (E)	Überseehandel m	—	commerce d'outre-mer m	commercio d'oltremare m	comercio de ultramar m
overtime (E)	Überstunde f	—	heure supplémentaire f	ora straordinaria f	hora extraordinaria f
overvaluation (E)	Überbewertung f	—	surestimation f	sopravvalutazione f	sobrevaloración f
owner of a house (E)	Hauseigentümer m	—	propriétaire de maison m	proprietario di casa m	propietario de una casa m
ownership of a flat (E)	Wohnungs-eigentum n	—	propriété du logement m	proprietà edilizia f	propiedad de vivienda f
óxido nítrico (Es)	Stickoxid n	nitric oxide	oxyde azotique m	ossido di azoto m	—
oxyde azotique (F)	Stickoxid n	nitric oxide	—	ossido di azoto m	óxido nítrico m
ozone layer (E)	Ozonschicht f	—	ozonosphère f	strato d'ozono m	capa del ozono f
ozonosphère (F)	Ozonschicht f	ozone layer	—	strato d'ozono m	capa del ozono f
Ozonschicht (D)	—	ozone layer	ozonosphère f	strato d'ozono m	capa del ozono f
pacchetto (I)	Päckchen n	small package	petit paquet m	—	pequeño paquete m
pacchetto delle azioni (I)	Aktienpaket n	block of shares	paquet d'actions m	—	paquete de acciones m
pacco (I)	Paket n	parcel	colis m	—	bulto m
pacco espresso (I)	Eilpaket n	express parcel	colis exprès m	—	paquete urgente m
packages (E)	Frachtstücke pl	—	colis m	colli m pl	fardo m
Päckchen (D)	—	small package	petit paquet m	pacchetto m	pequeño paquete m
packing (E)	Verpackung	—	emballage m	imballaggio m	embalaje m
packing instructions (E)	Verpackungs-vorschriften pl	—	prescriptions concernant l'emballage f pl	prescrizioni per l'imballaggio f pl	prescripciones de embalaje f pl
packing material (E)	Verpackungs-material n	—	matériel d'emballage m	materiale d'imballaggio m	empaque m
packing unit (E)	Verpackungseinheit f	—	unité d'emballage f	unità d'imballaggio f	unidad de embalaje f
pacto salarial (Es)	Lohnvereinbarung f	wage agreement	accord de salaires m	accordo salariale m	—
paese acquirente[1] (I)	Einkaufsland n	country of purchase	pays où l'on achète m	—	país de compra m
paese acquirente[2] (I)	Abnehmerland n	buyer country	pays acheteur m	—	país comprador m
paese agrario (I)	Agrarstaat m	agricultural state	état agricole m	—	estado agrario m
paese d'origine[1] (I)	Ursprungsland n	country of origin	pays d'origine m	—	país de origen m
paese d'origine[2] (I)	Herkunftsland n	country of origin	pays de provenance m	—	país de origen m

	D	E	F	I	Es
paese emergente (I)	Schwellenland *n*	newly industrialized countries	pays dans le seuil à l'industrialisation *m*	—	país en el umbral hacia la industrialización *m*
paesi debitori (I)	Schuldnerländer *pl*	debtor countries	pays débiteurs *m pl*	—	países deudores *m pl*
paesi sottosviluppati (I)	unterentwickelte Länder *pl*	less-developed countries	pays sous-développé *m pl*	—	países subdesarrollados *m pl*
paesi terzi (I)	Drittländer *pl*	third countries	pays tiers *m pl*	—	terceros países *m pl*
pagabile (I)	zahlbar	payable	payable	—	pagable
pagable (Es)	zahlbar	payable	payable	pagabile	—
pagado (Es)	verzollt	duty paid	dédouané	sdoganato	—
pagamento[1] (I)	Auszahlung *f*	paying out	payement *m*	—	pago *m*
pagamento[2] (I)	Einlösung *f*	payment	payement *m*	—	pago *m*
pagamento[3] (I)	Zahlung *f*	payment	payement *m*	—	pago *m*
pagamento a conto (I)	a-conto-Zahlung *f*	payment on account	payement acompte *m*	—	pago a cuenta *m*
pagamento anticipato (I)	Vorauszahlung *f*	payment in advance	payement anticipé *m*	—	adelanto *m*
pagamento anticipato delle imposte (I)	Steuervorauszahlung *f*	advanced payment of taxes	acompte provisionnel sur l'imposition *m*	—	impuestos adelantados *m pl*
pagamento a rate[1] (I)	Teilzahlung *f*	partial payment	payement partiel *m*	—	pago parcial *m*
pagamento a rate[2] (I)	Abschlagszahlung *f*	partial payment/ payment on account	premier versement *m*/ acompte *m*	—	pago parcial *m*/ pago a cuenta *m*
pagamento arretrato delle imposte (I)	Steuernachzahlung *f*	additional payment of taxes	payement d'un rappel d'impôt *m*	—	pago de impuestos atrasados *m*
pagamento contro assegno (I)	Zahlung per Nachnahme *f*	cash on delivery	payement contre remboursement *m*	—	pago contra reembolso *m*
pagamento contro credito documentario (I)	Akkreditivzahlung *f*	payment by letter of credit	payement par accréditif *m*	—	pago por crédito documentario *m*
pagamento contro documenti (I)	Dokumente gegen Zahlung *pl*	documents against payments	documents contre payement *m pl*	—	al contado contra documentos
pagamento delle imposte (I)	Steuerzahlung *f*	payment of taxes	payement de l'impôt *m*	—	tributación *f*
pagamento di provvigione (I)	Provisionszahlung *f*	commission payment	payement de commission *m*	—	pago de comisión *m*
pagamento di un effetto (I)	Akzepteinlösung *f*	honouring of an acceptance	honorer la traite acceptée	—	descuento de una letra aceptada *m*
pagamento immediato (I)	sofortige Zahlung *f*	immediate payment	payement immédiat *m*	—	pago inmediato *m*
pagamento in acconto (I)	Anzahlung *f*	deposit	acompte *m*	—	pago a cuenta *m*
pagamento in contanti (I)	Barzahlung *f*	cash payment	payement comptant *m*	—	pago al contado *m*
pagamento rateale (I)	Ratenzahlung *f*	payment by instalments	payement par versements fractionnés *m*	—	pago a plazos *m*
pagamento sotto protesta (I)	Zahlung unter Protest *f*	payment supra protest	payement sous protêt *m*	—	pago bajo protesta *m*
pagamento supplementare (I)	Nachzahlung *f*	supplementary payment	versement complémentaire *m*	—	pago suplementario *m*
pagamento totale (I)	vollständige Bezahlung *f*	payment in full	payement complet *m*	—	pago íntegro *m*
pagaré[1] (Es)	Schuldschein *m*	certificate of indebtedness	billet de créance *m*	certificato di debito *m*	—
pagaré[2] (Es)	Solawechsel *m*	promissory note	seule lettre de change *f*	pagherò *m*	—
pagare a rate (I)	abzahlen	pay off	régler par acompte	—	pagar por cuotas
pagare interessi (I)	verzinsen	pay interest on	compter des intérêts	—	pagar interés
pagar interés (Es)	verzinsen	pay interest on	compter des intérêts	pagare interessi	—
pagar por cuotas (Es)	abzahlen	pay off	régler par acompte	pagare a rate	—
pagella (I)	Zeugnis *n*	school report	certificat scolaire *m*	—	certificado de escuela *m*
pagherò (I)	Solawechsel *m*	promissory note	seule lettre de change *f*	—	pagaré *m*
pago[1] (Es)	Auszahlung *f*	paying out	payement *m*	pagamento *m*	—
pago[2] (Es)	Einlösung *f*	payment	payement *m*	pagamento *m*	—

	D	E	F	I	Es
pago³ (Es)	Zahlung f	payment	payement m	pagamento m	—
pago a cuenta¹ (Es)	a-conto-Zahlung f	payment on account	payement acompte m	pagamento a conto m	—
pago a cuenta² (Es)	Anzahlung f	deposit	acompte m	pagamento in acconto m	—
pago al contado (Es)	Barzahlung f	cash payment	payement comptant m	pagamento in contanti m	—
pago aplazado (Es)	Zahlungsaufschub m	extension of time for payment	sursis de payement m	dilazione del pagamento f	—
pago a plazos (Es)	Ratenzahlung f	payment by instalments	payement par versements fractionnés m	pagamento rateale m	—
pago atrasado¹ (Es)	Rückstand m	arrear	arriéré m	arretrato m	—
pago atrasado² (Es)	Zahlungsrückstand m	payment in arrearse	arriéré de payement m	morosità di pagamento f	—
pago bajo protesta (Es)	Zahlung unter Protest f	payment supra protest	payement sous protêt m	pagamento sotto protesta m	—
pago contra reembolso (Es)	Zahlung per Nachnahme f	cash on delivery	payement contre remboursement m	pagamento contro assegno m	—
pago de comisión (Es)	Provisionszahlung f	commission payment	payement de commission m	pagamento di provvigione m	—
pago de compensación (Es)	Ausgleichszahlung f	compensation payment	payement pour solde de compte m	conguaglio m	—
pago de impuestos atrasados (Es)	Steuernachzahlung f	additional payment of taxes	payement d'un rappel d'impôt m	pagamento arretrato delle imposte m	—
pago inmediato (Es)	sofortige Zahlung f	immediate payment	payement immédiat m	pagamento immediato m	—
pago íntegro (Es)	vollständige Bezahlung f	payment in full	payement complet m	pagamento totale m	—
pago parcial¹ (Es)	Teilzahlung f	partial payment	payement partiel m	pagamento a rate m	—
pago parcial² (Es)	Abschlagszahlung f	partial payment/ payment on account	premier versement m/ acompte m	pagamento a rate m/ pagamento in acconto m	—
pago por crédito documentario (Es)	Akkreditivzahlung f	payment by letter of credit	payement par accréditif m	pagamento contro credito documentario m	—
pago suplementario (Es)	Nachzahlung f	supplementary payment	versement complémentaire m	pagamento supplementare m	—
paid-up capital (E)	eingezahltes Kapital n	—	capital versé m	capitale versato m	capital desembolsado m
paid vacation (E)	bezahlter Urlaub m	—	congé payé m	ferie pagate f pl	vacaciones con goce de sueldo f pl
país comprador (Es)	Abnehmerland n	buyer country	pays acheteur m	paese acquirente m	—
país de compra (Es)	Einkaufsland n	country of purchase	pays où l'on achète m	paese acquirente m	—
país de origen¹ (Es)	Ursprungsland n	country of origin	pays d'origine m	paese d'origine m	—
país de origen² (Es)	Herkunftsland n	country of origin	pays de provenance m	paese d'origine m	—
país en el umbral hacia la industrialización (Es)	Schwellenland n countries	newly industrialized l'industrialisation m	pays dans le seuil à	paese emergente m	—
países deudores (Es)	Schuldnerländer pl	debtor countries	pays débiteurs m pl	paesi debitori m pl	—
países subdesarrollados (Es)	unterentwickelte Länder pl	less developed countries	pays sous-développés m pl	paesi sottosviluppati m pl	—
Paket (D)	—	parcel	colis m	pacco m	bulto m
palabra clave (Es)	Schlüsselwort n	key word	mot-clé m	parola chiave f	—
palabra de clave (Es)	Codewort n	code	mot de code m	parola di codice f	—
paleta (Es)	Palette f	pallet	palette f	paletta f	—
paletta (I)	Palette f	pallet	palette f	—	paleta m
Palette (D)	—	pallet	palette f	paletta f	paleta m
palette (F)	Palette f	pallet	—	paletta f	paleta m
pallet (E)	Palette f	—	palette f	paletta f	paleta m
panorama de mercado (Es)	Marktübersicht f	overall view of the market	vue d'ensemble du marché f	quadro del mercato m	—
pantalla (Es)	Bildschirm m	screen	écran m	video m	—
papel-moneda (Es)	Papiergeld n	paper money	monnaie de papier f	banconote f pl	—

	D	E	F	I	Es
paper money (E)	Papiergeld n	—	monnaie de papier f	banconote f pl	papel-moneda m
papier à ordre (F)	Orderpapier n	instruments (made out) to order	—	titolo all'ordine m	título a la orden m
Papiergeld (D)	—	paper money	monnaie de papier f	banconote f pl	papel-moneda m
papiers d'affaires (F)	Geschäftspapiere pl	business papers	—	documenti commerciali m pl	documentos comerciales m pl
paquet d'actions (F)	Aktienpaket n	block of shares	—	pacchetto delle azioni m	paquete de acciones m
paquete de acciones (Es)	Aktienpaket n	block of shares	paquet d'actions m	pacchetto delle azioni m	—
paquete urgente (Es)	Eilpaket n	express parcel	colis exprès m	pacco espresso m	—
para examen (Es)	zur Ansicht	on approval	à vue	in visione	—
Parameter (D)	—	parameter	paramètre m	parametro m	parámetro m
parameter (E)	Parameter m	—	paramètre m	parametro m	parámetro m
paramètre (F)	Parameter m	parameter	—	parametro m	parámetro m
paramètre d'action (F)	Aktionsparameter m	action parameter	—	parametro d'azione m	parámetro de acción m
parámetro (Es)	Parameter m	parameter	paramètre m	parametro m	—
parametro (I)	Parameter m	parameter	paramètre m	—	parámetro m
parametro d'azione (I)	Aktionsparameter m	action parameter	paramètre d'action m	—	parámetro de acción m
parámetro de acción (Es)	Aktionsparameter m	action parameter	paramètre d'action m	parametro d'azione m	—
par avion (F)	Luftpost f	air mail	—	posta aerea f	correo aéreo m
par camion (F)	per Lastkraftwagen	by lorry	—	per autocarro	por camión
parcel (E)	Paket n	—	colis m	pacco m	bulto m
par écrit (F)	schriftlich	written	—	per iscritto	por escrito
pareggio di bilancio (I)	Budgetausgleich m	balancing of the budget	équilibrage du budget m	—	balance del presupuesto m
parent company[1] (E)	Muttergesellschaft f	—	société mère f	società madre f	sociedad matriz f
parent company[2] (E)	Stammhaus n	—	maison mère f	casa madre f	casa matriz f
par exprès (F)	per Express	by express (mail)	—	per espresso	por expreso
paridad (Es)	Parität f	parity	parité f	parità f	—
paridad adquisitiva (Es)	Kaufkraftparität f	purchasing power parity	parité du pouvoir d'achat f	parità del potere d'acquisto f	—
paridad-oro (Es)	Goldparität f	gold parity	parité de l'or f	parità aurea f	—
parità (I)	Parität f	parity	parité f	—	paridad f
parità aurea (I)	Goldparität f	gold parity	parité de l'or f	—	paridad-oro f
parità centrale (I)	Leitkurs m	central rate	taux central m	—	tipo pivote m
parità del potere d'acquisto (I)	Kaufkraftparität f	purchasing power parity	parité du pouvoir d'achat f	—	paridad adquisitiva f
Parität (D)	—	parity	parité f	parità f	paridad f
parité (F)	Parität f	parity	—	parità f	paridad f
parité de l'or (F)	Goldparität f	gold parity	—	parità aurea f	paridad-oro f
parité du pouvoir d'achat (F)	Kaufkraftparität f	purchasing power parity	—	parità del potere d'acquisto f	paridad adquisitiva f
parity (E)	Parität f	—	parité f	parità f	paridad f
Parlamento Europeo (Es)	Europäisches Parlament n	European Parliament	Parlement européen m	Parlamento Europeo m	—
Parlamento Europeo (I)	Europäisches Parlament n	European Parliament	Parlement européen m	—	Parlamento Europeo m
Parlement européen (F)	Europäisches Parlament n	European Parliament	—	Parlamento Europeo m	Parlamento Europeo m
par mois (F)	monatlich	monthly	—	mensile	mensual
paro estacional (Es)	saisonale Arbeitslosigkeit f	seasonal unemployment	chômage saisonnier m	disoccupazione stagionale f	—
paro estructural (Es)	strukturelle Arbeitslosigkeit f	structural unemployment	chômage structurel m	disoccupazione strutturale f	—
parola chiave (I)	Schlüsselwort n	key word	mot-clé m	—	palabra clave f
parola di codice (I)	Codewort n	code	mot de code m	—	palabra de clave f
par ordre (F)	im Auftrag	by order	—	per ordine	por poder

	D	E	F	I	Es
par procuration (F)	per procura	by procuration	—	per procura	por poder
par retour du courrier (F)	postwendend	by return of post	—	a giro di posta	a vuelta de correo
part de capital (F)	Kapitalanteil *m*	share in capital	—	quota di capitale *f*	participación en el capital *f*
partecipante (I)	Teilnehmer *m*	participant	participant *m*	—	participante *m*
partecipazione (I)	Beteiligung *f*	participation	participation *f*	—	participación *f*
partecipazione all'utile (I)	Gewinnbeteiligung *f*	participation in profits	participation aux bénéfices *f*	—	participación en los beneficios *f*
partecipazione al reddito (I)	Ertragsbeteiligung *f*	participation in profits	participation aux bénéfices *f*	—	participación en los resultados *f*
partecipazione dei prestatori d'opera (I)	Arbeitnehmer-beteiligung *f*	worker participation	participation du personnel *f*	—	participación de los empleados *f*
parte contratante en un convenio colectivo (Es)	Tarifpartner *m*	parties to a collective agreement	signataire d'une convention collective *m*	parti sociali *f pl*	—
parte de los gastos de material (Es)	Materialkosten-anteil *m*	share in the material costs	proportion des frais de matériel *f*	quota dei costi del materiale *f*	—
parte fraccionaria (Es)	Bruchteil *m*	fraction	fraction *f*	frazione *f*	—
partenaire (F)	Partner *m*	partner	—	partner *m*	socio *m*
partenaire commercial (F)	Handelspartner *m*	trading partner	—	partner commerciale *m*	socio comercial *m*
partes integrantes esencial (Es)	wesentliche Bestandteile *pl*	integral part	parties constitutives essentielles *f pl*	componenti essenziali *f pl*	—
par tête d'habitant (F)	pro Kopf	per capita	—	pro capite	per cápita
partial analysis (E)	Teil-Analyse *f*	—	analyse partielle *f*	analisi parziale *f*	análisis parcial *m*
partial balance sheet (E)	Teilbilanz *f*	—	bilan partiel *m*	bilancio parziale *m*	balance parcial *m*
partial delivery (E)	Teillieferung *f*	—	livraison partielle *f*	fornitura parziale	entrega parcial *f*
partial denationalization (E)	Teilprivatisierung *f*	—	privatisation partielle *f*	privatizzazione parziale *f*	privatización parcial *f*
partial edition (E)	Teilauflage *f*	—	édition partielle *f*	emissione parziale *f*	emisión parcial *f*
partial loss (E)	Teilverlust *m*	—	perte partielle *f*	perdita parziale *f*	pérdida parcial *f*
partial payment¹ (E)	Teilzahlung *f*	—	payement partiel *m*	pagamento a rate *m*	pago parcial *m*
partial payment² (E)	Abschlagszahlung *f*	—	premier versement *m*/ acompte *m*	pagamento a rate *m*/ pagamento in acconto *m*	pago parcial *m*/ pago a cuenta *m*
partial payment price (E)	Teilzahlungspreis *m*	—	prix d'un achat à tempérament *m*	prezzo rateale *m*	precio de compras a plazo *m*
partial payment transaction (E)	Teilzahlungs-geschäft *n*	—	achat à tempérament *m*	vendita a rate *f*	operación a plazo *f*
partial value (E)	Teilwert *m*	—	valeur partielle *f*	valore parziale *m*	valor parcial *m*
participación¹ (Es)	Anteilnahme *f*	sympathy	participation *f*	interesse *m*	—
participación² (Es)	Geschäftsanteil *m*	share	part sociale *f*	quota sociale *f*	—
participación³ (Es)	Beteiligung *f*	participation	participation *f*	partecipazione *f*	—
participación de los empleados (Es)	Arbeitnehmer-beteiligung *f*	worker participation	participation du personnel *f*	partecipazione dei prestatori d'opera *f*	—
participación en el capital (Es)	Kapitalanteil *m*	share in capital	part de capital *f*	quota di capitale *f*	—
participación en los beneficios (Es)	Gewinnbeteiligung *f*	participation in profits	participation aux bénéfices *f*	partecipazione all'utile *f*	—
participación en los resultados (Es)	Ertragsbeteiligung *f*	participation in profits	participation aux bénéfices *f*	partecipazione al reddito *f*	—
participant (E)	Teilnehmer *m*	—	participant *m*	partecipante *m*	participante *m*
participant (F)	Teilnehmer *m*	participant	—	partecipante *m*	participante *m*
participante (Es)	Teilnehmer *m*	participant	participant *m*	partecipante *m*	—
participation (E)	Beteiligung *f*	—	participation *f*	partecipazione *f*	participación *f*
participation¹ (F)	Anteilnahme *f*	sympathy	—	interesse *m*	participación *f*
participation² (F)	Beteiligung *f*	participation	—	partecipazione *f*	participación *f*
participation au marché (F)	Marktanteil *m*	market share	—	quota di mercato *f*	cuota del mercado *f*
participation aux bénéfices¹ (F)	Ertragsbeteiligung *f*	participation in profits	—	partecipazione al reddito *f*	participación en los resultados *f*

	D	E	F	I	Es
participation aux bénéfices² (F)	Gewinnbeteiligung f	participation in profits	—	partecipazione all'utile f	participación en los beneficios f
participation du personnel (F)	Arbeitnehmer-beteiligung f	worker participation	—	partecipazione dei prestatori d'opera f	participación de los empleados f
participation in profits¹ (E)	Gewinnbeteiligung f	—	participation aux bénéfices f	partecipazione all'utile f	participación en los beneficios f
participation in profits² (E)	Ertragsbeteiligung f	—	participation aux bénéfices f	partecipazione al reddito f	participación en los resultados f
participations (F)	Beiträge pl	contributions	—	contributi m pl	contribuciones f pl
partida restante (Es)	Restposten m	remnants	lot restant m	rimanenze f pl	—
parties constitutives essentielles (F)	wesentliche Bestandteile pl	integral part	—	componenti essenziali f pl	partes integrantes esencial f pl
parties to a collective agreement (E)	Tarifpartner m	—	signataire d'une convention collective m	parti sociali f pl	parte contratante en un convenio colectivo f
parti sociali (I)	Tarifpartner m	parties to a collective agreement	signataire d'une convention collective m	—	parte contratante en un convenio colectivo f
Partner (D)	—	partner	partenaire m	partner m	socio m
partner¹ (E)	Teilhaber m	—	associé m	socio m	socio m
partner² (E)	Partner m	—	partenaire m	partner m	socio m
partner³ (E)	Gesellschafter m	—	associé m	socio m	socio m
partner (I)	Partner m	partner	partenaire m	—	socio m
partner commerciale¹ (I)	Handelspartner m	trading partner	partenaire commercial m	—	socio comercial m
partner commerciale² (I)	Geschäftspartner m	business partner	associé m	—	socio m
partner d'affari (I)	Geschäftsfreund m	business friend	correspondant m	—	corresponsal m
partnership¹ (E)	Sozietät f	—	groupe de sociétaires m	associazione f	sociedad f
partnership² (E)	Personen-gesellschaft n	—	société de personnes f	società di persone f	sociedad personalista f
partnership assets (E)	Gesellschafts-vermögen n	—	patrimoine social m	patrimonio sociale m	patrimonio social m
partnership limited by shares (E)	Kommanditgesell-schaft auf Aktien f	—	société en commandite par action f	società in accomandita per azioni f	sociedad comandita-ria por acciones f
part sociale (F)	Geschäftsanteil m	share	—	quota sociale f	participación f
part-time employment (E)	Teilzeit-beschäftigung f	—	emploi à temps partiel m	occupazione part-time f	empleo parcial m
part-time job (E)	Teilzeitstelle f	—	poste à temps partiel m	posto di lavoro part-time m	puesto de trabajo a tiempo parcial m
part-time work (E)	Teilzeitarbeit f	—	travail à temps partiel m	lavoro part-time m	trabajo a tiempo parcial m
par virement (F)	bargeldlos	non-cash	—	mediante assegno	por transferencia
pasavante (Es)	Durchgangs-schein m	transit certificate	acquit de transit m	bolletta di transito f	—
pasivo (Es)	Passiva n	liabilities	passif m	passivo m	—
passation d'une commande (F)	Auftragserteilung f	placing of an order	—	ordinazione f	otorgamiento de un pedido m
passibile di pena (I)	straffällig	liable to prosecution	encourir une peine	—	criminal
passif¹ (F)	Schuldenmasse f	total of indebtedness	—	massa passiva f	masa pasiva f
passif² (F)	Passiva n	liabilities	—	passivo m	pasivo m
passing on (E)	Überwälzung f	—	répercussion f	accollamento m	traslación f
Passiva (D)	—	liabilities	passif m	passivo m	pasivo m
Passivgeschäft (D)	—	passive deposit transactions	opération passive f	operazione passiva f	operación pasiva m
passivo¹ (I)	Soll m	debit	doit m	—	debe m
passivo² (I)	Passiva pl	liabilities	passif m	—	pasivo m
pas utilisé (F)	ungenutzt	unused	—	inutilizzato	no utilizado
Patent (D)	—	patent	brevet d'invention m	brevetto m	patente f
patent (E)	Patent n	—	brevet d'invention m	brevetto m	patente f
Patentamt (D)	—	Patent Office	office des brevets m	ufficio brevetti m	oficina del registro de patentes f

	D	E	F	I	Es
patent document (E)	Patenturkunde f	—	certificat d'attestation du brevet d'invention m	brevetto m	patente f
patente[1] (Es)	Patent n	patent	brevet d'invention m	brevetto m	—
patente[2] (Es)	Patenturkunde f	patent document	certificat d'attestation du brevet d'invention m	brevetto m	—
patente (F)	Gewerbesteuer f	trade tax	—	imposta industriale f	impuesto industrial m
patente europea (Es)	Europapatent n	European patent	brevet européen m	brevetto europeo m	—
patent licence (E)	Patentlizenz f	—	licence de brevet f	licenza di brevetto f	licencia de patente f
Patentlizenz (D)	—	patent licence	licence de brevet f	licenza di brevetto f	licencia de patente f
Patent Office (E)	Patentamt n	—	office des brevets m	ufficio brevetti m	oficina del registro de patentes f
patent pool (E)	Patentpool m	—	pool de brevet m	pool dei brevetti m	pool de patentes m
Patentpool (D)	—	patent pool	pool de brevet m	pool dei brevetti m	pool de patentes m
Patenturkunde (D)	—	patent document	certificat d'attestation du brevet d'invention m	brevetto m	patente f
patriarcal (Es)	patriarchalisch	patriarchal	patriarcal	patriarcale	—
patriarcal (F)	patriarchalisch	patriarchal	—	patriarcale	patriarcal
patriarcale (I)	patriarchalisch	patriarchal	patriarcal	—	patriarcal
patriarchal (E)	patriarchalisch	—	patriarcal	patriarcale	patriarcal
patriarchalisch (D)	—	patriarchal	patriarcal	patriarcale	patriarcal
patrimoine (F)	Vermögen n	property	—	patrimonio m	patrimonio m
patrimoine net (F)	Nettovermögen n	net assets	—	patrimonio netto m	patrimonio neto m
patrimoine réel (F)	Realvermögen n	real wealth	—	patrimonio reale m	activo inmobiliario m
patrimoine social (F)	Gesellschafts- vermögen n	partnership assets	—	patrimonio sociale m	patrimonio social m
patrimonio (Es)	Vermögen n	property	patrimoine m	patrimonio m	—
patrimonio (I)	Vermögen n	property	patrimoine m	—	patrimonio m
patrimonio circolante (I)	Umlaufvermögen n	current assets/ floating assets	capital de roulement m	—	capital circulante m
patrimonio estero (I)	Auslandsvermögen n	foreign assets	avoirs à l'étranger m pl	—	activo exterior m
patrimonio in contanti (I)	Barvermögen n	cash assets	valeurs réalisables à court terme ou disponibles f pl	—	activo efectivo m
patrimonio monetario (I)	Geldvermögen n	financial assets	moyens financiers m	—	activo monetario m
patrimonio neto[1] (Es)	Nettovermögen n	net assets	patrimoine net m	patrimonio netto m	—
patrimonio neto[2] (Es)	Reinvermögen n	net assets	avoir net m	patrimonio netto m	—
patrimonio netto[1] (I)	Reinvermögen n	net assets	avoir net m	—	patrimonio neto m
patrimonio netto[2] (I)	Nettovermögen n	net assets	patrimoine net m	—	patrimonio neto m
patrimonio productivo (Es)	Produktivvermögen n	productive property	capital productif m	patrimonio produttivo m	—
patrimonio produttivo (I)	Produktivvermögen n	productive property	capital productif m	—	patrimonio produttivo m
patrimonio público (Es)	Staatseigentum n	public ownership	propriété d'Etat f	proprietà demaniale f	—
patrimonio real (Es)	Sachvermögen n	material assets	biens corporels m pl	capitale reale m	—
patrimonio reale (I)	Realvermögen n	real wealth	patrimoine réel m	—	activo inmobiliario m
patrimonio social (Es)	Gesellschafts- vermögen n	partnership assets	patrimoine social m	patrimonio sociale m	—
patrimonio sociale (I)	Gesellschafts- vermögen n	partnership assets	patrimoine social m	—	patrimonio social m
patrón (Es)	Arbeitgeber m	employer	employeur m	datore di lavoro m	—
patrón-oro (Es)	Goldstandard m	gold standard	étalon or m	gold standard m	—
pattern of organization (E)	Organisationsform f	—	forme de l'organisation f	forma di organizzazione f	forma de organización f
paupérisme (F)	Massenarmut f	pauperism	—	pauperismo m	pauperismo m
pauperismo (Es)	Massenarmut f	pauperism	paupérisme m	pauperismo m	—
pauperismo (I)	Massenarmut f	pauperism	paupérisme m	—	pauperismo m

	D	E	F	I	Es
Pauschalbetrag (D)	—	flat rate amount	somme forfaitaire *f*	somma forfettaria *f*	suma global *f*
pay (E)	Besoldung *f*	—	rétribution *f*	retribuzione *f*	sueldo *m*
payable (E)	zahlbar	—	payable	pagabile	pagable
payable (F)	zahlbar	payable	—	pagabile	pagable
payday (E)	Zahltag *m*	—	jour de paye *m*	giorno di paga *m*	día de pago *m*
payee (E)	Remittent *m*	—	remettant *m*	beneficiario *m*	remitente *m*
payement¹ (F)	Einlösung *f*	payment	—	pagamento *m*	pago *m*
payement² (F)	Zahlung *f*	payment	—	pagamento *m*	pago *m*
payement³ (F)	Auszahlung *f*	paying out	—	pagamento *m*	pago *m*
payement acompte (F)	a-conto-Zahlung *f*	payment on account	—	pagamento a conto *m*	pago a cuenta *m*
payement anticipé (F)	Vorauszahlung *f*	payment in advance	—	pagamento anticipato *m*	adelanto *m*
payement complet (F)	vollständige Bezahlung *f*	payment in full	—	pagamento totale *m*	pago íntegro *m*
payement comptant (F)	Barzahlung *f*	cash payment	—	pagamento in contanti *m*	pago al contado *m*
payement contre remboursement (F)	Zahlung per Nachnahme *f*	cash on delivery	—	pagamento contro assegno *m*	pago contra reembolso *m*
payement de commission (F)	Provisionszahlung *f*	commission payment	—	pagamento di provvigione *m*	pago de comisión *m*
payement de l'impôt (F)	Steuerzahlung *f*	payment of taxes	—	pagamento delle imposte *m*	tributación *f*
payement d'un rappel d'impôt (F)	Steuernachzahlung *f*	additional payment of taxes	—	pagamento arretrato delle imposte *m*	pago de impuestos atrasados *m*
payement immédiat (F)	sofortige Zahlung *f*	immediate payment	—	pagamento immediato *m*	pago inmediato *m*
payement par accréditif (F)	Akkreditivzahlung *f*	payment by letter of credit	—	pagamento contro credito documentario *m*	pago por crédito documentario *m*
payement partiel (F)	Teilzahlung *f*	partial payment	—	pagamento a rate *m*	pago parcial *m*
payement par versements fractionnés (F)	Ratenzahlung *f*	payment by instalments	—	pagamento rateale *m*	pago a plazos *m*
payement pour solde de compte (F)	Ausgleichszahlung *f*	compensation payment	—	conguaglio *m*	pago de compensación *m*
payement sous protêt (F)	Zahlung unter Protest *f*	payment supra protest	—	pagamento sotto protesta *m*	pago bajo protesta *m*
paying out (E)	Auszahlung *f*	—	payement *m*	pagamento *m*	pago *m*
pay interest on (E)	verzinsen	—	compter des intérêts	pagare interessi	pagar interés
payment¹ (E)	Einlösung *f*	—	payement *m*	pagamento *m*	pago *m*
payment² (E)	Zahlung *f*	—	payement *m*	pagamento *m*	pago *m*
payment by instalments (E)	Ratenzahlung *f*	—	payement par versements fractionnés *m*	pagamento rateale *m*	pago a plazos *m*
payment by letter of credit (E)	Akkreditivzahlung *f*	—	payement par accréditif *m*	pagamento contro credito documentario *m*	pago por crédito documentario *m*
payment by result (E)	Leistungslohn *m*	—	salaire au rendement *m*	salario a rendimento *m*	salario por rendimiento *m*
payment in advance (E)	Vorauszahlung *f*	—	payement anticipé *m*	pagamento anticipato *m*	adelanto *m*
payment in arrears (E)	Zahlungsrückstand *m*	—	arriéré de payement *m*	morosità di pagamento *f*	pago atrasado *m*
payment in full (E)	vollständige Bezahlung *f*	—	payement complet *m*	pagamento totale *m*	pago íntegro *m*
payment of taxes (E)	Steuerzahlung *f*	—	payement de l'impôt *m*	pagamento delle imposte *m*	tributación *f*
payment on account (E)	a-conto-Zahlung *f*	—	payement acompte *m*	pagamento in acconto *m*	pago a cuenta *m*
payments arrangement (E)	Zahlungsabkommen *n*	—	accord de payement *m*	accordo di pagamento *m*	acuerdo de pagos *m*
payment supra protest (E)	Zahlung unter Protest *f*	—	payement sous protêt *m*	pagamento sotto protesta *m*	pago bajo protesta *m*
payment system (E)	Zahlungsform *f*	—	forme de payement *f*	tipo di pagamento *m*	forma de pago *f*
payment transactions (E)	Zahlungsverkehr *m*	—	opérations de payement *f pl*	operazioni di pagamento *f pl*	servicio de pagos *m pl*

	D	E	F	I	Es
pay off (E)	abzahlen	—	régler par acompte	pagare a rate	pagar por cuotas
pay office (E)	Lohnbüro n	—	bureau de la paye m	ufficio paga m	departamento de nóminas m
pays acheteur (F)	Abnehmerland n	buyer country	—	paese acquirente m	país comprador m
pays dans le seuil à l'industrialisation (F)	Schwellenland n	newly industrialized countries	—	paese emergente m	país en el umbral hacia la industrialización m
pays débiteurs (F)	Schuldnerländer pl	debtor countries	—	paesi debitori m pl	países deudores m pl
pays de provenance (F)	Herkunftsland n	country of origin	—	paese d'origine m	país de origen m
pays d'origine (F)	Ursprungsland n	country of origin	—	paese d'origine m	país de origen m
pays où l'on achète (F)	Einkaufsland n	country of purchase	—	paese acquirente m	país de compra m
pays sous-développé (F)	unterentwickelte Länder pl	less developed countries	—	paesi sottosviluppati m pl	países subdesarrollados m pl
pays tiers (F)	Drittländer pl	third countries	—	paesi terzi m pl	terceros países m pl
pêcherie (F)	Fischerei f	fishing	—	pesca f	pesca f
pedido[1] (Es)	Auftrag m	order	commande f	ordine m	—
pedido[2] (Es)	Order f	order	ordre m	ordine m	—
pedido[3] (Es)	Bestellung f	order	commande f	ordinazione f	—
pedido anticipado (Es)	Vorbestellung f	reservation	commande préalable f	ordinazione anticipata f	—
pedido de prueba (Es)	Probeauftrag m	trial order	ordre d'essai m	ordine a titolo di prova m	—
pedido destinado a la exportación (Es)	Exportauftrag m	export order	commande d'exportation f	ordine d'esportazione m	—
pedido directo (Es)	Direktbestellung f	direct ordering	commande directe f	ordinazione diretta f	—
pedido suplementario (Es)	Nachbestellung f	repeat order	nouvel ordre m	ordinazione supplementare f	—
pegatina (Es)	Aufkleber m	sticker	étiquette f	etichetta adesiva f	—
peine pécuniaire (F)	Geldstrafe f	fine	—	multa f	multa f
película promocional (Es)	Werbefilm m	advertising film	film publicitaire m	film pubblicitario m	—
peligro (Es)	Gefahr f	danger	danger m	pericolo m	—
pena convencional (Es)	Konventionalstrafe f	contractual penalty	pénalité f	penalità convenzionale f	—
penalità convenzionale (I)	Konventionalstrafe f	contractual penalty	pénalité f	—	pena convencional f
pénalité (F)	Konventionalstrafe f	contractual penalty	—	penalità convenzionale f	pena convencional f
pena pecuniaria[1] (I)	Geldbuße f	fine	amende f	—	multa f
pena pecuniaria[2] (I)	Bußgeld n	administration fee	amende f	—	multa f
Pendelverkehr (D)	—	shuttle service	trafic de va-et-vient m	traffico pendolare m	vaivén m
pensar concepcional (Es)	konzeptionelles Denken n	conceptional thinking	penser conceptionnel m	mentalità concezionale f	—
penser conceptionnel (F)	konzeptionelles Denken n	conceptional thinking	—	mentalità concezionale f	pensar concepcional m
pensión básica (Es)	Grundrente f	basic pension	pension de base f	pensione base f	—
pension de base (F)	Grundrente f	basic pension	—	pensione base f	pensión básica f
pensione base (I)	Grundrente f	basic pension	pension de base f	—	pensión básica f
pension fund (E)	Rentenfonds m	—	fonds d'Etat m/ effets publics m pl	fondo obbligazionario m	fondo de bonos m
pension scheme (E)	Versorgungs-einrichtung f	—	institution de retraite f	istituto previdenziale m	institución de previsión f
pénurie d'argent (F)	Geldverknappung f	monetary restriction	—	riduzione del denaro f	restricción monetaria f
pénurie de marchandises (F)	Warenknappheit f	shortage of goods	—	scarsità di merci f	escasez de mercancías f
pénurie de matières premières (F)	Rohstoffknappheit f	raw materials shortage	—	scarsità di materie prime f	escasez de materias primas f
pequeña paleta (Es)	Kleinpalette f	small pallet	petite palette f	mini paletta f	—
pequeñas y medianas empresas (Es)	Klein- und Mittelbetriebe pl	small and medium-sized enterprises	petites et moyennes entreprises f pl	piccole e medie imprese f pl	—

	D	E	F	I	Es
pequeño contenedor (Es)	Kleincontainer m	small container	petit conteneur m	mini container m	—
pequeño paquete (Es)	Päckchen n	small package	petit paquet m	pacchetto m	—
per autocarro (I)	per Lastkraftwagen	by lorry	par camion	—	por camión
per capita (E)	pro Kopf	—	par tête d'habitant	pro capite	per cápita
per cápita (Es)	pro Kopf	per capita	par tête d'habitant	pro capite	—
per cent (E)	Prozent n	—	pour-cent m	percento m	por ciento m
percentage¹ (E)	Prozentsatz m	—	pourcentage m	percentuale f	porcentaje m
percentage² (E)	Tantieme f	—	tantième m	percentuale f	tanto por ciento m
percento (I)	Prozent n	per cent	pour-cent m	—	por ciento m
percentuale¹ (I)	Tantieme f	percentage	tantième m	—	tanto por ciento m
percentuale² (I)	Prozentsatz m	percentage	pourcentage m	—	porcentaje m
percepciónes en especie (Es)	Sachbezüge pl	remuneration in kind	prestations en nature f pl	retribuzioni in natura f pl	—
per conto proprio (I)	für eigene Rechnung	for one's own account	pour son propre compte	—	por cuenta propia
per conto terzi (I)	für fremde Rechnung	for account of a third party	pour compte de tiers	—	por cuenta ajena
pérdida¹ (Es)	Verlust m	loss	perte f	perdita f	—
pérdida² (Es)	Damnum n	damnum	perte f	perdita f	—
pérdida de valor (Es)	Werteinbuße f	loss of value	perte de valeur f	perdita di valore f	—
pérdida en bolsa (Es)	Kursverlust m	loss in exchange	baisse sur les cours f	perdita sul cambio f	—
perdita¹ (I)	Verlust m	loss	perte f	—	pérdida f
perdita² (I)	Damnum n	damnum	perte f	—	pérdida f
perdita di valore (I)	Werteinbuße f	loss of value	perte de valeur f	—	pérdida de valor f
perdita sul cambio (I)	Kursverlust m	loss in exchange	baisse sur les cours f	—	pérdida en bolsa f
perecedero (Es)	verderblich	perishable	périssable	deperibile	—
per Einschreiben (D)	—	by registered post	sous pli recommandé	per raccomandata	certificado
péréquation fiscale des revenus des deux époux (F)	Splitting n	splitting	—	splittaggio m	imposición separada e igual de los conyúges f
per espresso (I)	per Express	by express (mail)	par exprès	—	por expreso
per Express (D)	—	by express (mail)	par exprès	per espresso	por expreso
perfeccionamiento (Es)	Veredelung f	processing	perfectionnement m	perfezionamento m	—
perfectionnement (F)	Veredelung f	processing	—	perfezionamento m	perfeccionamiento m
perfezionamento (I)	Veredelung f	processing	perfectionnement m	—	perfeccionamiento m
perforadora (Es)	Datentypistin f	terminal operator	perforatrice f	dattilografa f	—
perforatrice (F)	Datentypistin f	terminal operator	—	dattilografa f	perforadora f
performance (E)	Leistung f	—	rendement m	rendimento m	rendimiento m
performance-oriented (E)	leistungsorientiert	—	orienté vers le rendement	orientato al rendimento	orientado hacia el rendimiento
pericolo (I)	Gefahr f	danger	danger m	—	peligro m
period¹ (E)	Periode f	—	période f	periodo m	período m
period² (E)	Frist f	—	délai m	termine m	plazo m
Periode (D)	—	period	période f	periodo m	período m
période (F)	Periode f	period	—	periodo m	período m
période comptable (F)	Abrechnungs-zeitraum m	accounting period	—	periodo di liquidazione m	período contable m
période de base (F)	Basisperiode f	base period	—	periodo di base m	período básico m
période de mise en marche (F)	Anlaufperiode f	initial period	—	periodo iniziale m	período de puesta en marcha m
période d'essai (F)	Probezeit f	trial period	—	periodo di prova m	período de prueba m
period for payment (E)	Zahlungsziel n	—	délai de payement m	termine di pagamento m	plazo de pago m
periodico per i clienti (I)	Kundenzeitschrift f	customer magazine	journal destiné à la clientèle m	—	revista para los clientes f
período (Es)	Periode f	period	période f	periodo m	—
periodo (I)	Periode f	period	période f	—	período m

	D	E	F	I	Es
período básico (Es)	Basisperiode f	base period	période de base f	periodo di base m	—
período carencial (Es)	Karenzzeit f	qualifying period	délai de carence m	periodo d'attesa m	—
período concesional de un crédito (Es)	Kreditlaufzeit f	duration of credit	durée de l'allocation de crédit f	scadenza del credito f	—
período contable (Es)	Abrechnungs- zeitraum m	accounting period	période comptable f	periodo di liquidazione m	—
periodo d'adattamento (I)	Einarbeitung f	vocational adjustment	entraînement m	—	entrenamiento m
periodo d'attesa (I)	Karenzzeit f	qualifying period	délai de carence m	—	período carencial m
periodo de almacenaje (Es)	Lagerzyklus m	stock cycle	cycle de stockage m	ciclo di magazzinaggio m	—
período de financiación (Es)	Finanzierungsdauer f	period of financing	durée du financement f	durata del finanziamento f	—
período de prueba (Es)	Probezeit f	trial period	période d'essai f	periodo di prova m	—
período de puesta en marcha (Es)	Anlaufperiode f	initial period	période de mise en marche f	periodo iniziale m	—
periodo di base (I)	Basisperiode f	base period	période de base f	—	período básico m
periodo di liquidazione (I)	Abrechnungs- zeitraum m	accounting period	période comptable f	—	período contable m
periodo di prova (I)	Probezeit f	trial period	période d'essai f	—	período de prueba m
period of financing (E)	Finanzierungsdauer f	—	durée du financement f	durata del finanziamento f	período de financiación m
period of notice (E)	Kündigungsfrist f	—	délai de préavis m	termine di preavviso per la disdetta m	plazo de preaviso m
periodo iniziale (I)	Anlaufperiode f	initial period	période de mise en marche f	—	período de puesta en marcha m
per iscritto (I)	schriftlich	written	par écrit	—	por escrito
perishable (E)	verderblich	—	périssable	deperibile	perecedero
périssable (F)	verderblich	perishable	—	deperibile	perecedero
perito publicitario (Es)	Werbefachmann m	advertising expert	technicien publicitaire m	esperto di pubblicità m	—
perizia (I)	Expertise f	expert opinion	expertise f	—	dictamen pericial m
per Lastkraftwagen (D)	—	by lorry	par camion	per autocarro	por camión
permesso (I)	Erlaubnis f	permission	permission f	—	permiso m
permesso di lavoro (I)	Arbeitserlaubnis f	work permit	permis de travail m	—	permiso de trabajo m
permesso d'importazione (I)	Einfuhr- genehmigung f	import licence	autorisation d'importation f	—	permiso de importación m
permesso di soggiorno (I)	Aufenthalts- erlaubnis f	residence permit	autorisation de séjour f	—	permiso de residencia m
permis de travail (F)	Arbeitserlaubnis f	work permit	—	permesso di lavoro m	permiso de trabajo m
permiso (Es)	Erlaubnis f	permission	permission f	permesso m	—
permiso de importación (Es)	Einfuhr- genehmigung f	import licence	autorisation d'importation f	permesso d'importazione m	—
permiso de residencia (Es)	Aufenthalts- erlaubnis f	residence permit	autorisation de séjour f	permesso di soggiorno m	—
permiso de trabajo (Es)	Arbeitserlaubnis f	work permit	permis de travail m	permesso di lavoro m	—
permission (F)	Erlaubnis f	permission	—	permesso m	permiso m
permission¹ (E)	Genehmigung f	—	autorisation f	autorizzazione f	autorización f
permission² (E)	Erlaubnis f	—	permission f	permesso m	permiso m
per nome proprio (I)	im eigenen Namen	in one's own name	en nom propre	—	en nombre propio
per ordine (I)	im Auftrag	by order	par ordre	—	por poder
per procura (D)	—	by procuration	par procuration	per procura	por poder
per procura (I)	per procura	by procuration	par procuration	—	por poder
per raccomandata (I)	per Einschreiben	by registered post	sous pli recommandé	—	certificado
persona activa (Es)	Erwerbstätiger m	gainfully employed person	personne ayant un emploi m	persona attiva f	—
persona attiva¹ (I)	Erwerbstätiger m	gainfully employed person	personne ayant un emploi m	—	persona activa f
persona attiva² (I)	Erwerbsperson f	gainfully employed person	personne active f	—	persona en activo f

	D	E	F	I	Es
persona avente capacità giuridica (I)	rechtsfähig	capable to act in law	capable de jouir des droits	—	jurídicamente capaz
persona en activo (Es)	Erwerbsperson f	gainfully employed person	personne active f	persona attiva f	—
persona fisica (I)	natürliche Person f	natural person	personne physique f	—	persona natural f
persona giuridica (I)	juristische Person f	legal person	personne juridique f	—	persona jurídica f
persona jurídica (Es)	juristische Person f	legal person	personne juridique f	persona giuridica f	—
Personal (D)	—	staff	personnel m	personale m	personal m
personal (Es)	Personal n	staff	personnel m	personale m	—
Personalabbau (D)	—	reduction of staff	réduction de personnel f	riduzione del personale f	reducción de personal f
personal accident insurance (E)	Unfallversicherung f	—	assurance accidents corporels f	assicurazione contro infortuni f	seguro de accidentes m
Personalausweis (D)	—	identity card	pièce d'identité f	carta d'identità f	carné de identidad m
Personalbüro (D)	—	personnel office	bureau du personnel m	ufficio del personale m	oficina de personal f
Personalcomputer (D)	—	personal computer	ordinateur individuel m	personal computer m	ordenador personal m
personal computer (E)	Personalcomputer m	—	ordinateur individuel m	personal computer m	ordenador personal m
personal computer (I)	Personalcomputer m	personal computer	ordinateur individuel m	—	ordenador personal m
personal consumption (E)	Eigenverbrauch m	—	consommation personnelle f	consumo proprio m	consumo propio m
personal conversation (E)	persönliches Gespräch n	—	conversation personnelle f	colloquio personale m	conversación personal f
personal data (E)	Personalien pl	—	identité f	generalità f pl	datos personales m pl
personal de formación (Es)	Schulungspersonal n	training staff	personnel d'instruction m	personale d'addestramento m	—
personal drawings (E)	Privatentnahmen pl	—	prélèvement personnel m	prelevamento a titolo personale m	detracción privada f
personale (I)	Personal n	staff	personnel m	—	personal m
personale d'addestramento (I)	Schulungspersonal n	training staff	personnel d'instruction m	—	personal de formación m
Personalführung (D)	—	personnel management	direction du personnel f	gestione del personale f	dirección de personal m
Personalien (D)	—	personal data	identité f	generalità f pl	datos personales m pl
Personalkredit (D)	—	personal loan	crédit personnel m	credito al personale m	crédito personal m
Personal-Leasing (D)	—	personnel leasing	leasing de personnel m	leasing di personale m	leasing de personal m
Personalleiter (D)	—	staff manager	chef du personnel m	capo reparto personale m	jefe de personal m
personal loan (E)	Personalkredit m	—	crédit personnel m	credito al personale m	crédito personal m
Personalmangel (D)	—	shortage of staff	manque de personnel m	mancanza di personale f	falta der personal f
Personalsituation (D)	—	personnel situation	effectif du personnel m	situazione occupazionale f	situación de personal f
Personalstrategie (D)	—	personnel strategy	stratégie en matière de personnel f	strategia occupazionale f	estrategia de personal f
Personalwechsel (D)	—	staff changes	mouvements dans le personnel m pl	cambio del personale m	cambio de personal m
Personalwerbung (D)	—	hiring of personnel	recrutement de personnel m	reclutazione di personale f	reclutamiento de personal m
persona natural (Es)	natürliche Person f	natural person	personne physique f	persona fisica f	—
persona residente[1] (I)	Deviseninländer m	resident	résident m	—	residente m
persona residente[2] (I)	Inländer m	national resident	national m	—	residente m
Personenbeförderung (D)	—	carriage of passengers	transport de personnes m	trasporto di persone m	transporte de personas m
Personengesellschaft (D)	—	partnership	société de personnes f	società di persone f	sociedad personalista f
Personenversicherung (D)	—	insurance of persons	assurance des personnes f	assicurazione di persone f	seguro personal m
person interested (E)	Interessent m	—	intéressé m	interessato m	interesado m
persönliches Gespräch (D)	—	personal conversation	conversation personelle f	colloquio personale m	conversación personal f

	D	E	F	I	Es
personne ayant le pouvoir commercial (F)	Handlungsbevoll-mächtigter *m*	commercial agent	—	mandatario commerciale *m*	apoderado especial *m*
personne ayant un emploi (F)	Erwerbsperson *f*	gainfully employed person	—	persona attiva *f*	persona en activo *f*
personne exerçant une profession libérale (F)	Freiberufler *m*	selfemployed person	—	libero professionista *m*	profesional *m*
personne juridique (F)	juristische Person *f*	legal person	—	persona giuridica *f*	persona jurídica *f*
personnel¹ (F)	Personal *n*	staff	—	personale *m*	personal *m*
personnel² (F)	Belegschaft *f*	staff	—	maestranza *f*	plantilla *f*
personnel d'instruction (F)	Schulungspersonal *n*	training staff	—	personale d'addestramento *m*	personal de formación *m*
personnel du service extérieur (F)	Außendienst-mitarbeiter *m*	field staff	—	collaboratore del servizio esterno *m*	colaborador en el servicio exterior *m*
personnel leasing (E)	Personal-Leasing *n*	—	leasing de personnel *m*	leasing di personale *m*	leasing de personal *m*
personnel management (E)	Personalführung *f*	—	direction du personnel *f*	gestione del personale *f*	dirección de personal *m*
personnel office (E)	Personalbüro *n*	—	bureau du personnel *m*	ufficio del personale *m*	oficina de personal *f*
personnel situation (E)	Personalsituation *f*	—	effectif du personnel *m*	situazione occupazionale *f*	situación de personal *f*
personnel strategy (E)	Personalstrategie *f*	—	stratégie en matière de personnel *f*	strategia occupazionale *f*	estrategia de personal *f*
personne physique (F)	natürliche Person *f*	natural person	—	persona fisica *f*	persona natural *f*
perspective (F)	Prognose *f*	forecast(ing)	—	prognosi *f*	pronóstico *m*
perspectives d'avenir (F)	Zukunftschance *f*	future prospects	—	prospettiva *f*	posibilidades futuras *f pl*
perspectives de promotion (F)	Aufstiegs-möglichkeit *f*	promotion possibility	—	possibilità di carriera *f*	posibilidades de ascenso *f pl*
perte¹ (F)	Verlust *m*	loss	—	perdita *f*	pérdida *f*
perte² (F)	Damnum *n*	damnum	—	perdita *f*	pérdida *f*
perte dans la production (F)	Produktionsausfall *m*	loss of production	—	perdita di produzione *f*	pérdida de producción *f*
pesacartas (Es)	Briefwaage *f*	letter scales	pèse-lettres *m*	bilancia per corrispondenza *f*	—
pesca (Es)	Fischerei *f*	fishing	pêcherie *f*	pesca *f*	—
pesca (I)	Fischerei *f*	fishing	pêcherie *f*	—	pesca *f*
pèse-lettres (F)	Briefwaage *f*	letter scales	—	bilancia per corrispondenza *f*	pesacartas *m*
peso (Es)	Gewicht *n*	weight	poids *m*	peso *m*	—
peso (I)	Gewicht *n*	weight	poids *m*	—	peso *m*
peso de descarga (Es)	Abladegewicht *n*	shipping (delivered) weight	poids au déchargement *m*	peso di scarico *m*	—
peso di scarico (I)	Abladegewicht *n*	shipping (delivered) weight	poids au déchargement *m*	—	peso de descarga *m*
peso fino (Es)	Feingewicht *n*	weight of fine gold	poids de métal fin *m*	peso fino *m*	—
peso fino (I)	Feingewicht *n*	weight of fine gold	poids de métal fin *m*	—	peso fino *m*
pesquisas (Es)	Nachforschung *f*	investigation	recherche *f*	indagine *f*	—
petición de quiebra (Es)	Konkursantrag *m*	bankruptcy petition	demande en déclara-tion de faillite *f*	domanda di dichiarazione del fallimento *f*	—
petit conteneur (F)	Kleincontainer *m*	small container	—	mini container *m*	pequeño contenedor *m*
petite palette (F)	Kleinpalette *f*	small pallet	—	mini paletta *f*	pequña paleta *f*
petites et moyennes entreprises (F)	Klein- und Mittelbetriebe *pl*	small and medium-sized enterprises	—	piccole e medie imprese *f pl*	pequeñas y medianas empresas *f pl*
petit paquet (F)	Päckchen *n*	small package	—	pacchetto *m*	pequeño paquete *m*
petrol (E)	Benzin *n*	—	essence *f*	benzina *f*	gasolina *f*
pétrole (F)	Erdöl *n*	mineral oil	—	petrolio *m*	crudo *m*
pétrole brut (F)	Rohöl *n*	crude oil	—	petrolio greggio *m*	crudo *m*
petrolio (I)	Erdöl *n*	mineral oil	pétrole *m*	—	crudo *m*
petrolio greggio (I)	Rohöl *n*	crude oil	pétrole brut *m*	—	crudo *m*
petrol voucher (E)	Benzingutscheine *pl*	—	bon d'essence *m*	coupons *m pl*	bono de gasolina *m*

	D	E	F	I	Es
pezzo di ricambio (I)	Ersatzteil *n*	spare part	pièce de rechange *f*	—	pieza de recambio *f*
Pfandbrief (D)	—	mortgage bond	obligation hypothécaire *f*	titolo ipotecario *m*	cédula hipotecaria *f*
Pfandrecht (D)	—	pledge	droit de gage *m*	diritto di pegno *m*	derecho de garantía real *m*
Pfändung (D)	—	seizure	saisie *f*	pignoramento *m*	pignoración *f*
Pfund (D)	—	pound	livre *f*	libbra *f*	libra *f*
phase d'organisation (F)	Aufbauphase *f*	development phase	—	fase di costruzione *f*	fase de desarrollo *f*
Phosphat (D)	—	phosphate	phosphate *m*	fosfato *m*	fosfato *m*
phosphate (E)	Phosphat *n*	—	phosphate *m*	fosfato *m*	fosfato *m*
phosphate (F)	Phosphat *n*	phosphate	—	fosfato *m*	fosfato *m*
phosphatfrei (D)	—	free of phosphate	sans phosphate	privo di fosfato	sin fosfato
photocopie (F)	Fotokopie *f*	photocopy	—	fotocopia *f*	fotocopia *f*
photocopier (E)	Fotokopierer *m*	—	photocopieur *m*	copialettere *m*	fotocopiadora *f*
photocopieur (F)	Fotokopierer *m*	photocopier	—	copialettere *m*	fotocopiadora *f*
photocopy (E)	Fotokopie *f*	—	photocopie *f*	fotocopia *f*	fotocopia *f*
pianificazione (I)	Planifikation *f*	planning	planification *f*	—	planificación *f*
pianificazione alternativa (I)	Alternativplanung *f*	alternative planning	planification alternative *f*	—	planificación alternativa *f*
pianificazione degli ordini (I)	Auftragsplanung *f*	order scheduling	planification des commandes *f*	—	planificación de la ejecución de pedidos *f*
pianificazione delle vendite (I)	Absatzplanung *f*	sales planning	planning de la distribution *m*	—	planificación de ventas *f*
pianificazione finanziaria a media scadenza (I)	mittelfristige Finanzplanung *f*	medium-term fiscal planning	gestion financière à moyen terme *f*	—	planificación financiera a medio plazo
pianificazione regionale (I)	Regionalplanung *f*	regional planning	aménagement régional *m*	—	planificación regional *f*
pianificazione reticolare (I)	Netzplan *m*	network planning	réseau linéaire pour planification *m*	—	planificación reticular *f*
pianificazione territoriale (I)	Raumplanung *f*	regional planning	plan d'aménagement des espaces *m*	—	planificación del espacio *m*
piano (I)	Konzept *n*	concept	brouillon *m*	—	bosquejo *m*
piano dei costi (I)	Kostenplan *m*	cost schedule	planning des coûts *m*	—	planilla de costas *f*
piano della liquidità (I)	Liquiditätsplan *m*	cash forecasting plan	plan de liquidité *m*	—	plan de liquidez *m*
piano d'investimento (I)	Investitionsplan *m*	investment scheme	plan des investissements *m*	—	plan de inversión *m*
piano di produzione (I)	Produktionsplan *m*	production plan	plan de production *m*	—	plan de producción *m*
piano economico (I)	Wirtschaftsplan *m*	economic plan	plan économique *m*	—	plan económico *m*
piano finanziario (I)	Finanzplan *m*	financial plan	plan financier *m*	—	presupuesto *m*
piano imprenditoriale (I)	Unternehmenskonzept *n*	business concept	stratégie de l'entreprise *f*	—	concepto comercial *m*
piazza (I)	Börsenplatz *m*	stock exchange centre	place boursière *f*	—	plaza bursátil *f*
piazza commerciale (I)	Handelsplatz *m*	trade centre	place marchande *f*	—	plaza comercial *f*
piccole e medie imprese (I)	Klein- und Mittelbetriebe *pl*	small and medium-sized enterprises	petites et moyennes entreprises *f pl*	—	pequeñas y medianas empresas *f pl*
pièce de monnaie (F)	Hartgeld *n*	specie	—	moneta metallica *f*	dinero metálico *m*
pièce de rechange (F)	Ersatzteil *n*	spare part	—	pezzo di ricambio *m*	pieza de recambio *f*
pièce d'identité (F)	Personalausweis *m*	identity card	—	carta d'identità *f*	carné de identidad *m*
pièce d'identité de l'entreprise (F)	Betriebsausweis *m*	staff identification card	—	tessera aziendale *f*	carné de empresa *f*
pièce jointe (F)	Anlage *f*	enclosure	—	allegato *m*	anexo *m*
pièces accompagnant l'envoi (F)	Begleitpapiere *pl*	accompanying documents	—	bolle di accompagnamento *f pl*	documentos adjuntos *m pl*
piece time (E)	Stückzeit *f*	—	temps par pièce *m*	tempo pezzo *m*	tiempo por unidad *m*
piecework (E)	Akkordarbeit *f*	—	travail à la tâche *m*	lavora a cottimo *m*	trabajo a destajo *m*
piece work (E)	Akkord *m*	—	convention de salaire à la tâche *f*	cottimo *m*	destajo *m*
piece work pay (E)	Stücklohn *m*	—	salaire à la tâche *m*	salario a cottimo *m*	salario a destajo *m*

	D	E	F	I	Es
piece work system (E)	Akkordsystem *n*	—	système du travail aux pièces *m*	sistema del lavoro a cottimo *m*	régimen de trabajo a destajo *m*
piece work wages (E)	Akkordlohn *m*	—	salaire à la pièce *m*	retribuzione per il lavoro a cottimo *f*	salario a destajo *m*
pie de imprenta (Es)	Impressum *n*	imprint	mention des responsables de l'édition *f*	impressum *m*	—
piena occupazione (I)	Vollbeschäftigung *f*	full employment	plein emploi *m*	—	empleo total *m*
pieza de recambio (Es)	Ersatzteil *n*	spare part	pièce de rechange *f*	pezzo di ricambio *m*	—
pig cycle (E)	Schweinezyklus *m*	—	cycle de porc *m*	teorema cobweb sul ciclo produttivo *m*	ciclo de puerco *m*
piggyback advertisement (E)	Huckepackwerbung *f*	—	publicité pick-a-back *f*	pubblicità per il trasporto strada-rotaia *f*	publicidad combinada ferrocarril-carretera *f*
piggyback service (E)	Huckepackverkehr *m*	—	transport pick-a-back *m*	trasporto strada-rotaia *m*	transporte combinado ferrocarril-carretera *m*
pignoración[1] (Es)	Verpfändung *f*	pledge	mise en gage *f*	pignoramento *m*	—
pignoración[2] (Es)	Pfändung *f*	seizure	saisie *f*	pignoramento *m*	—
pignoramento[1] (I)	Verpfändung *f*	pledge	mise en gage *f*	—	pignoración *f*
pignoramento[2] (I)	Pfändung *f*	seizure	saisie *f*	—	pignoración *f*
pignoramento del salario (I)	Lohnpfändung *f*	attachment of earnings	saisie-arrêt sur le salaire *f*	—	embargo de salario *m*
pioggia acida (I)	saurer Regen *m*	acid rain	pluie acide *f*	—	lluvia ácida *f*
pirating (E)	Abwerbung *f*	—	débauchage *m*	accaparramento *m*	sonsacamiento *m*
piso en propiedad (Es)	Eigentumswohnung *f*	freehold flat	logement en propriété *m*	appartamento in condominio *m*	—
place (E)	plazieren	—	placer	collocare	colocar
place boursière (F)	Börsenplatz *m*	stock exchange centre	—	piazza *f*	plaza bursátil *f*
place marchande (F)	Handelsplatz *m*	trade centre	—	piazza commerciale *f*	plaza comercial *f*
placement (E)	Plazierung *f*	—	placement *m*	collocamento *m*	colocación
placement (F)	Plazierung *f*	placing	—	collocamento *m*	colocación *f*
placement de l'annonce (F)	Anzeigenschaltung *f*	insertion of an advertisement	—	posizionamento dell'inserzione *m*	inserción del anuncio *m*
placement of an advertisement (E)	Anzeigenplazierung *f*	—	disposition de l'annonce *f*	collocamento dell'inserzione *m*	colocación del anuncio *f*
place of birth (E)	Geburtsort *m*	—	lieu de naissance *m*	luogo di nascita *m*	lugar de nacimiento *m*
place of destination (E)	Bestimmungsort *m*	—	lieu de destination *m*	luogo di destinazione *m*	lugar de de destino *m*
place of employment (E)	Arbeitsplatz *m*	—	poste de travail *m*	posto di lavoro *m*	puesto de trabajo *m*
placer (F)	plazieren	place	—	collocare	colocar
placing (E)	Plazierung *f*	—	placement *m*	collocamento *m*	colocación *f*
placing of an order (E)	Auftragserteilung *f*	—	passation d'une commande *f*	ordinazione *f*	otorgamiento de un pedido *m*
Plafond (D)	—	ceiling	plafond *m*	plafond *m*	límite máximo *m*
plafond (F)	Plafond *m*	ceiling	—	plafond *m*	límite máximo *m*
plafond (I)	Plafond *m*	ceiling	plafond *m*	—	límite máximo *m*
plafond di credito (I)	Kreditrahmen *m*	credit margin	marge de crédit accordé *f*	—	margen de crédito *m*
plafond du crédit accordé (F)	Kreditlinie *f*	credit line	—	linea creditizia *f*	línea de crédito *f*
plafond du crédit alloué (F)	Kreditlimit *n*	borrowing limit	—	limite di credito *m*	límite de crédito *m*
Plakat (D)	—	poster	affiche *f*	manifesto *m*	cartel *m*
plancher des prix (F)	Preisuntergrenze *f*	price floor	—	limite inferiore di prezzo *m*	límite inferior de los precios *m*
plan d'aménagement des espaces (F)	Raumplanung *f*	regional planning	—	pianificazione territoriale *f*	planificación del espacio *m*
plan de inversión (Es)	Investitionsplan *m*	investment scheme	plan des investissements *m*	piano d'investimento *m*	—
plan de liquidez (Es)	Liquiditätsplan *m*	cash forecasting plan	plan de liquidité *m*	piano della liquidità *m*	—
plan de liquidité (F)	Liquiditätsplan *m*	cash forecasting plan	—	piano della liquidità *m*	plan de liquidez *m*
plan de producción (Es)	Produktionsplan *m*	production plan	plan de production *m*	piano di produzione *m*	—

	D	E	F	I	Es
plan de production (F)	Produktionsplan *m*	production plan	—	piano di produzione *m*	plan de producción *m*
plan des investissements (F)	Investitionsplan *m*	investment scheme	—	piano d'investimento *m*	plan de inversión *m*
plan du chiffre d'affaires (F)	Umsatzplan *m*	turnover plan	—	programma del fatturato *m*	objectivo de facturación *m*
plan económico (Es)	Wirtschaftsplan *m*	economic plan	plan économique *m*	piano economico *m*	—
plan économique (F)	Wirtschaftsplan *m*	economic plan	—	piano economico *m*	plan económico *m*
plan financier (F)	Finanzplan *m*	financial plan	—	piano finanziario *m*	presupuesto *m*
planificación¹ (Es)	Planifikation *f*	planning	planification *f*	pianificazione *f*	—
planificación² (Es)	Planung *f*	planning	planning *m*	programmazione *f*	—
planificación alternativa (Es)	Alternativplanung *f*	alternative planning	planification alternative *f*	pianificazione alternativa *f*	—
planificación de la ejecución de pedidos (Es)	Auftragsplanung *f*	order scheduling	planification des commandes *f*	pianificazione degli ordini *f*	—
planificación de la fundación (Es)	Gründungsplanung *f*	formation plan	planification de fondation *f*	progettazione della costituzione *f*	—
planificación de las vacaciones (Es)	Urlaubsplanung *f*	vacation scheduling	planification des vacances *f*	programmazione delle ferie *f*	—
planificación del espacio (Es)	Raumplanung *f*	regional planning	plan d'aménagement des espaces *m*	pianificazione territoriale *f*	—
planificación del presupuesto (Es)	Budgetplanung *f*	budgetary planning	planification du budget *f*	pianificazione del bilancio *f*	—
planificación de mercadeo (Es)	Marketingplanung *f*	marketing planning	planning du marketing *m*	programmazione del marketing *f*	—
planificación de plazos (Es)	Terminplanung *f*	scheduling	planning de rendez-vous *m*	programmazione dei termini *f*	—
planificación de ventas (Es)	Absatzplanung *f*	sales planning	planning de la distribution *m*	pianificazione delle vendite *f*	—
planificación regional (Es)	Regionalplanung *f*	regional planning	aménagement régional *m*	pianificazione regionale *f*	—
planificación reticular (Es)	Netzplan *m*	network planning	réseau linéaire pour planification *m*	pianificazione reticolare *f*	—
planification (F)	Planifikation *f*	planning	—	pianificazione *f*	planificación *f*
planification alternative (F)	Alternativplanung *f*	alternative planning	—	pianificazione alternativa *f*	planificación alternativa *f*
planification de fondation (F)	Gründungsplanung *f*	formation plan	—	progettazione della costituzione *f*	planificación de la fundación *f*
planification des commandes (F)	Auftragsplanung *f*	order scheduling	—	pianificazione degli ordini *f*	planificación de la ejecución de pedidos *f*
planification des vacances (F)	Urlaubsplanung *f*	vacation scheduling	—	programmazione delle ferie *f*	planificación de las vacaciones *f*
planification du budget (F)	Budgetplanung *f*	budgetary planning	—	programmazione del bilancio *f*	planificación del presupuesto *m*
Planifikation (D)	—	planning	planification *f*	pianificazione *f*	planificación *f*
planilla de costas (Es)	Kostenplan *m*	cost schedule	planning des coûts *m*	piano dei costi *m*	—
Plankalkulation (D)	—	target calculation	calcul des coûts prévisionnels *m*	calcolo pianificato *m*	cálculo de los objetivos *m*
Plankosten-rechnung (D)	—	calculation of the budget costs	calcul de l'écart sur cadence de fabrication *m*	calcolo dei costi pianificati *m*	cálculo de costes normalizados *m*
planned economy (E)	Planwirtschaft *f*	—	économie planifiée *f*	economia pianificata *f*	economía planificada *f*
planning¹ (E)	Planifikation *f*	—	planification *f*	pianificazione *f*	planificación *f*
planning² (E)	Planung *f*	—	planning *m*	programmazione *f*	planificación *f*
planning (F)	Planung *f*	planning	—	programmazione *f*	planificación *f*
planning control (E)	Planungskontrolle *f*	—	contrôle de la planification *f*	controllo della programmazione *m*	contol de planificación *m*
planning de la distribution (F)	Absatzplanung *f*	sales planning	—	pianificazione delle vendite *f*	planificación de ventas *f*
planning de rendez-vous (F)	Terminplanung *f*	scheduling	—	programmazione dei termini *f*	planificación de plazos *f*
planning des coûts (F)	Kostenplan *m*	cost schedule	—	piano dei costi *m*	planilla de costas *f*
planning du marketing (F)	Marketingplanung *f*	marketing planning	—	programmazione del marketing *f*	planificación de mercadeo *m*

	D	E	F	I	Es
planning figures (E)	Planwerte *pl*	—	valeurs prévisionnelles *f pl*	valori pianificati *m pl*	valores previstos *m pl*
Planrevision (D)	—	budget adjustment	révision des coûts marginaux *f*	revisione del piano *f*	ajuste presupuestario *m*
Planspiel (D)	—	management games	jeu d'entreprise *m*	gioco di strategia imprenditoriale *m*	juego de ensayo *m*
plant (E)	Werk *n*	—	usine *f*	stabilimento *m*	planta *f*
planta (Es)	Werk *n*	plant	usine *f*	stabilimento *m*	—
planta industrial (Es)	Industrieanlage *f*	industrial plant	installation industrielle *f*	impianto industriale *m*	—
plantilla (Es)	Belegschaft *f*	staff	personnel *m*	maestranza *f*	—
Planung (D)	—	planning	planning *m*	programmazione *f*	planificación *f*
Planungskontrolle (D)	—	planning control	contrôle de la planification *f*	controllo della programmazione *m*	contol de planificación *m*
Planwerte (D)	—	planning figures	valeurs prévisionnelles *f pl*	valori pianificati *m pl*	valores previstos *m pl*
Planwirtschaft (D)	—	planned economy	économie planifiée *f*	economia pianificata *f*	economía planificada *f*
plata (Es)	Silber *n*	silver	argent *m*	argento *m*	—
plaza bursátil (Es)	Börsenplatz *m*	stock exchange centre	place boursière *f*	piazza *f*	—
plaza comercial (Es)	Handelsplatz *m*	trade centre	place marchande *f*	piazza commerciale *f*	—
plazieren (D)	—	place	placer	collocare	colocar
Plazierung (D)	—	placing	placement *m*	collocamento *m*	colocación *f*
plazo[1] (Es)	Teilzahlungsrate *f*	monthly instalment	mensualité d'un achat à tempérament *f*	rata *f*	—
plazo[2] (Es)	Rate *f*	instalment	acompte *m*	rata *f*	—
plazo[3] (Es)	Frist *f*	period	délai *m*	termine *m*	—
plazo de arrendamiento financiero (Es)	Leasing-Rate *f*	leasing payment	taux de leasing *m*	rata leasing *f*	—
plazo de entrega[1] (Es)	Lieferfrist *f*	time for delivery	délai de livraison *m*	termine di consegna *m*	—
plazo de entrega[2] (Es)	Liefertermin *m*	date of delivery	délai de livraison *m*	termine di consegna *m*	—
plazo de gracia (Es)	Nachfrist *f*	additional period	prolongation *f*	termine supplementare *m*	—
plazo de pago[1] (Es)	Zahlungsziel *n*	period for payment	délai de payement *m*	termine di pagamento *m*	—
plazo de pago[2] (Es)	Zahlungstermin *m*	date of payment	terme du payement *m*	termine di pagamento *m*	—
plazo de pago[3] (Es)	Zahlungsfrist *f*	terms of payment	délai de payement *m*	scadenza di pagamento *f*	—
plazo de preaviso (Es)	Kündigungsfrist *f*	period of notice	délai de préavis *m*	termine di preavviso per la disdetta *m*	—
plazo de protección (Es)	Schutzfrist *f*	term of protection	délai de protection *m*	durata della protezione *f*	—
plazo de solicitud (Es)	Anmeldefrist *f*	time for application	délai de déclaration *m*	termine di denuncia *m*	—
plazo de vencimiento (Es)	Laufzeit *f*	term	durée *f*	scadenza *f*/durata *f*	—
plazo de vencimiento restante (Es)	Restlaufzeit *f*	residual time to maturity	durée restante *f*	scadenza residua *f*	—
plazo de vinculación al tipo de interés pactado (Es)	Zinsbindungsfrist *f*	lock-down period for interest rates	délai d'engagement sur le taux d'intérêt accordé *m*	scadenza degli interessi vincolati *f*	—
pledge[1] (E)	Verpfändung *f*	—	mise en gage *f*	pignoramento *m*	pignoración *f*
pledge[2] (E)	Pfandrecht *n* ·	—	droit de gage *m*	diritto di pegno *m*	derecho de garantía real *m*
plein emploi (F)	Vollbeschäftigung *f*	full employment	—	piena occupazione *f*	empleo total *m*
plein pouvoir (F)	Vollmacht *f*	full power/ power of attorney	—	autorizzazione *f*/ procura *f*	poder *m*/ autorización *f* /escritura de poder *f*
pluie acide (F)	saurer Regen *m*	acid rain	—	pioggia acida *f*	lluvia ácida *f*
plusvalía[1] (Es)	Mehrwert *m*	value added	valeur ajoutée *f*	valore aggiunto *m*	—

politica dei prezzi

	D	E	F	I	Es
plusvalía² (Es)	Wertzuwachs m	appreciation	accroissement de valeur m	incremento di valore m	—
población (Es)	Bevölkerung f	population	population f	popolazione f	—
poder (Es)	Vollmacht f	full power/power of attorney	plein pouvoir m/ mandat m	autorizzazione f/ procura f	—
poder adquisitivo (Es)	Kaufkraft f	purchasing power	pouvoir d'achat m	potere d'acquisto m	—
poderdante (Es)	Vollmachtgeber m	grantor of a power of attorney	auteur de la procuration m	mandante m	—
poder general¹ (Es)	Prokura f	Prokura (procuration)	procuration commerciale générale f	procura f	—
poder general² (Es)	Generalvollmacht f	general power	pouvoir général m	procura generale f	—
poids (F)	Gewicht n	weight	—	peso m	peso m
poids au déchargement (F)	Abladegewicht n	shipping (delivered) weight	—	peso di scarico m	peso de descarga m
poids de métal fin (F)	Feingewicht n	weight of fine gold	—	peso fino m	peso fino m
point d'intervention (F)	Interventionspunkt m	intervention point	—	punto d'intervento m	punto de intervención m
Police (D)	—	policy	police f	polizza f	póliza f
police (F)	Police f	policy	—	polizza f	póliza f
police certificate of good conduct (E)	polizeiliches Führungszeugnis n	—	certificat de bonnes vie et moeurs m	certificato di buona condotta m	certificado policial m
police d'assurance (F)	Versicherungspolice f	insurance policy	—	polizza d'assicurazione f	seguro m
policía de la empresa (Es)	Werkschutz m	works protection force	corps de sécurité d'entreprise m	servizio di sorveglianza aziendale m	—
policy (E)	Police f	—	police f	polizza f	póliza f
policy of advances on securities (E)	Lombardpolitik f	—	politique des prêts sur gages f	politica delle anticipazioni f	política de pignoración f
policy relating to capital formation (E)	Vermögenspolitik f	—	politique financière f	politica patrimoniale f	política de los patrimonios f
política (Es)	Politik f	politics	politique f	politica f	—
politica (I)	Politik f	politics	politique f	—	política f
politica agraria (I)	Agrarpolitik f	agricultural policy	politique agricole f	—	política agrícola f
política agrícola (Es)	Agrarpolitik f	agricultural policy	politique agricole f	politica agraria f	—
política comercial (Es)	Handelspolitik f	commercial policy	politique commerciale f	politica commerciale f	—
política comercial exterior (Es)	Außenhandelspolitik f	foreign trade policy	politique de commerce extérieur f	politica del commercio estero f	—
politica commerciale (I)	Handelspolitik f	commercial policy	politique commerciale f	—	política comercial f
politica concorrenziale (I)	Wettbewerbspolitik f	competition policy	politique de concurrence f	—	política de competencia f
politica congiunturale (I)	Konjunkturpolitik f	economic policy	politique de conjoncture f	—	política de coyuntura f
politica creditizia (I)	Kreditpolitik f	credit policy	politique favorisant le crédit f	—	política de crédito f
política de competencia (Es)	Wettbewerbspolitik f	competition policy	politique de concurrence f	politica concorrenziale f	—
política de coyuntura (Es)	Konjunkturpolitik f	economic policy	politique de conjoncture f	politica congiunturale f	—
política de crecimiento económico (Es)	Wachstumspolitik f	growth policy	politique d'accroissement f	politica di crescita f	—
política de crédito (Es)	Kreditpolitik f	credit policy	politique favorisant le crédit f	politica creditizia f	—
política de descuento (Es)	Diskontpolitik f	discount policy	politique d'escompte f	politica di sconto f	—
política de distribución (Es)	Verteilungspolitik f	distribution policy	politique de répartition f	politica della distribuzione f	—
política de empleo (Es)	Beschäftigungspolitik f	employment policy	politique d'emploi f	politica d'occupazione f	—
política de estabilidad económica (Es)	Stabilitätspolitik f	stability policy	politique de stabilité f	politica di consolidamento f	—
politica dei prezzi (I)	Preispolitik f	price policy	politiques des prix f		política de precios f

	D	E	F	I	Es
politica dei tassi d'interesse (I)	Zinspolitik f	interest rate policy	politique en matière d'intérêts f	—	política en materia de intereses f
politica del commercio estero (I)	Außenhandelspolitik f	foreign trade policy	politique de commerce extérieur f	—	política comercial exterior f
politica della bilancia dei pagamenti (I)	Zahlungsbilanz-politik f	balance of payments policy	politique en matière de la balance des payements f	—	política en materia de balanza de pagos f
politica della distribuzione (I)	Verteilungspolitik f	distribution policy	politique de répartition f	—	política de distribución f
politica dell'assortimento (I)	Sortimentspolitik f	assortment policy	politique de sortiment f	—	política de surtido f
politica delle anticipazioni (I)	Lombardpolitik f	policy of advances on securities	politique des prêts sur gages f	—	política de pignoración f
política de los patrimonios (Es)	Vermögenspolitik f	policy relating to capital formation	politique financière f	politica patrimoniale f	—
politica del suolo (I)	Bodenpolitik f	land policy	politique de la terre f	—	política de suelo f
politica del traffico (I)	Verkehrspolitik f	transport policy	politique des transports f	—	política de transportes f
política demográfica (Es)	Bevölkerungspolitik f	population policy	politique démographi-que populationniste f	politica demografica f	—
politica demografica (I)	Bevölkerungspolitik f	population policy	politique démographi-que populationniste f	—	política demográfica f
política de pignoración (Es)	Lombardpolitik f	policy of advances on securities	politique des prêts sur gages f	politica delle anticipazioni f	—
política de precios (Es)	Preispolitik f	price policy	politiques des prix f	politica dei prezzi f	—
política de suelo (Es)	Bodenpolitik f	land policy	politique de la terre f	politica del suolo f	—
política de surtido (Es)	Sortimentspolitik f	assortment policy	politique de sortiment f	politica dell'assortimento f	—
política de transportes (Es)	Verkehrspolitik f	transport policy	politique des transports f	politica del traffico f	—
política de ventas (Es)	Absatzpolitik f	marketing policy	politique de vente f	politica di vendita f	—
politica di bilancio (I)	Bilanzpolitik f	balance policy	politique du bilan f	—	política en materia de balanzas f
politica di consolidamento (I)	Stabilitätspolitik f	stability policy	politique de stabilité f	—	política de estabilidad económica f
politica di crescita (I)	Wachstumspolitik f	growth policy	politique d'accroissement f	—	política de crecimien-to económico f
politica d'investimento (I)	Investitionslenkung f	investment control	politique d'investissement f	—	dirección de inversiones f
politica di sconto (I)	Diskontpolitik f	discount policy	politique d'escompte f	—	política de descuento f
politica di vendita (I)	Absatzpolitik f	marketing policy	politique de vente f	—	política de ventas f
politica d'occupazione (I)	Beschäftigungs-politik f	employment policy	politique d'emploi f	—	política de empleo f
política económica (Es)	Wirtschaftspolitik f	economic policy	politique économique f	politica economica f	—
politica economica (I)	Wirtschaftspolitik f	economic policy	politique économique f	—	política económica f
política en materia de balanza de pagos (Es)	Zahlungsbilanz-politik f	balance of payments policy	politique en matière de la balance des payements f	politica della bilancia dei pagamenti f	—
política en materia de balanzas (Es)	Bilanzpolitik f	balance policy	politique du bilan f	politica di bilancio f	—
política en materia de intereses (Es)	Zinspolitik f	interest rate policy	politique en matière d'intérêts f	politica dei tassi d'interesse f	—
política estructural (Es)	Strukturpolitik f	structural policy	politique structurelle f	politica strutturale f	—
política financiera (Es)	Finanzpolitik f	fiscal policy	politique financière f	politica finanziaria f	—
politica finanziaria (I)	Finanzpolitik f	fiscal policy	politique financière f	—	política financiera f
política fiscal (Es)	Steuerpolitik f	fiscal policy	politique fiscale f	politica fiscale f	—
politica fiscale (I)	Steuerpolitik f	fiscal policy	politique fiscale f	—	política fiscal f
política monetaria¹ (Es)	Geldpolitik f	monetary policy	politique monétaire f	politica monetaria f	—
política monetaria² (Es)	Währungspolitik f	monetary policy	politique monétaire f	politica monetaria f	—
politica monetaria¹ (I)	Geldpolitik f	monetary policy	politique monétaire f	—	política monetaria f
politica monetaria² (I)	Währungspolitik f	monetary policy	politique monétaire f	—	política monetaria f

	D	E	F	I	Es
politica patrimoniale (I)	Vermögenspolitik *f*	policy relating to capital formation	politique financière *f*	—	política de los patrimonios *f*
política regional (Es)	Regionalpolitik *f*	regional policy	politique régionale *f*	politica regionale *f*	—
politica regionale (I)	Regionalpolitik *f*	regional policy	politique régionale *f*	—	política regional *f*
política salarial (Es)	Lohnpolitik *f*	wage policy	politique des salaires *f*	politica salariale *f*	—
politica salariale (I)	Lohnpolitik *f*	wage policy	politique des salaires *f*	—	política salarial *f*
política social (Es)	Sozialpolitik *f*	social policy	politique sociale *f*	politica sociale *f*	—
politica sociale (I)	Sozialpolitik *f*	social policy	politique sociale *f*	—	política social *f*
politica strutturale (I)	Strukturpolitik *f*	structural policy	politique structurelle *f*	—	política estructural *f*
politics (E)	Politik *f*	—	politique *f*	politica *f*	política *f*
Politik (D)	—	politics	politique *f*	politica *f*	política *f*
politique (F)	Politik *f*	politics	—	politica *f*	política *f*
politique agricole (F)	Agrarpolitik *f*	agricultural policy	—	politica agraria *f*	política agrícola *f*
politique commerciale (F)	Handelspolitik *f*	commercial policy	—	politica commerciale *f*	política comercial *f*
politique d'accroissement (F)	Wachstumspolitik *f*	growth policy	—	politica di crescita *f*	política de crecimiento económico *f*
politique de commerce extérieur (F)	Außenhandelspolitik *f*	foreign trade policy	—	politica del commercio estero *f*	política comercial exterior *f*
politique de concurrence (F)	Wettbewerbspolitik *f*	competition policy	—	politica concorrenziale *f*	política de competencia *f*
politique de conjoncture (F)	Konjunkturpolitik *f*	economic policy	—	politica congiunturale *f*	política de coyuntura *f*
politique de l'assortiment (F)	Sortimentspolitik *f*	assortment policy	—	politica dell'assortimento *f*	política de surtido *f*
politique de la terre (F)	Bodenpolitik *f*	land policy	—	politica del suolo *f*	política de suelo *f*
politique démographique populationniste (F)	Bevölkerungspolitik *f*	population policy	—	politica demografica *f*	política demográfica *f*
politique d'emploi (F)	Beschäftigungspolitik *f*	employment policy	—	politica d'occupazione *f*	política de empleo *f*
politique de répartition (F)	Verteilungspolitik *f*	distribution policy	—	politica della distribuzione *f*	política de distribución *f*
politique d'escompte (F)	Diskontpolitik *f*	discount policy	—	politica di sconto *f*	política de descuento *f*
politique des prêts sur gages (F)	Lombardpolitik *f*	policy of advances on securities	—	politica delle anticipazioni *f*	política de pignoración *f*
politique des salaires (F)	Lohnpolitik *f*	wage policy	—	politica salariale *f*	política salarial *f*
politique de stabilité (F)	Stabilitätspolitik *f*	stability policy	—	politica di consolidamento *f*	política de estabilidad económica *f*
politique des transports (F)	Verkehrspolitik *f*	transport policy	—	politica del traffico *f*	política de transportes *f*
politique de vente (F)	Absatzpolitik *f*	marketing policy	—	politica di vendita *f*	política de ventas *f*
politique d'investissement (F)	Investitionslenkung *f*	investment control	—	politica d'investimento *f*	dirección de inversiones *f*
politique du bilan (F)	Bilanzpolitik *f*	balance policy	—	politica di bilancio *f*	política en materia de balanzas *f*
politique économique (F)	Wirtschaftspolitik *f*	economic policy	—	politica economica *f*	política económica *f*
politique en matière de la balance des payements (F)	Zahlungsbilanzpolitik *f*	balance of payments policy	—	politica della bilancia dei pagamenti *f*	política en materia de balanza de pagos *f*
politique en matière d'intérêts (F)	Zinspolitik *f*	interest rate policy	—	politica dei tassi d'interesse *f*	política en materia de intereses *f*
politique favorisant le crédit (F)	Kreditpolitik *f*	credit policy	—	politica creditizia *f*	política de crédito *f*
politique financière[1] (F)	Finanzpolitik *f*	fiscal policy	—	politica finanziaria *f*	política financiera *f*
politique financière[2] (F)	Vermögenspolitik *f*	policy relating to capital formation	—	politica patrimoniale *f*	política de los patrimonios *f*
politique fiscale (F)	Steuerpolitik *f*	fiscal policy	—	politica fiscale *f*	política fiscal *f*
politique monétaire[1] (F)	Geldpolitik *f*	monetary policy	—	politica monetaria *f*	política monetaria *f*
politique monétaire[2] (F)	Währungspolitik *f*	monetary policy	—	politica monetaria *f*	política monetaria *f*

	D	E	F	I	Es
politique régionale (F)	Regionalpolitik f	regional policy	—	politica regionale f	política regional f
politiques des prix (F)	Preispolitik f	price policy	—	politica dei prezzi f	política de precios f
politique sociale (F)	Sozialpolitik f	social policy	—	politica sociale f	política social f
politique structurelle (F)	Strukturpolitik f	structural policy	—	politica strutturale f	política estructural f
póliza¹ (Es)	Seefrachtbrief m	bill of lading	connaissement maritime m	polizza di carico f	—
póliza² (Es)	Police f	policy	police f	polizza f	—
póliza de carga (Es)	Ladeschein m	bill of lading	avis de chargement m	bolletta di carico f	—
polizeiliches Führungszeugnis (D)	—	police certificate of good conduct	certificat de bonnes vie et moeurs m	certificato di buona condotta m	certificado policial m
polizza (I)	Police f	policy	police f	—	póliza f
polizza d'assicurazione (I)	Versicherungspolice f	insurance policy	police d'assurance f	—	seguro m
polizza di carico¹ (I)	Konnossement n	bill of lading	connaissement m	—	conocimiento m
polizza di carico² (I)	Seefrachtbrief m	bill of lading	connaissement maritime m	—	póliza f
poll (E)	Befragung f	—	enquête f	interrogazione f	encuesta f
pollutants (E)	Schadstoff m	—	élément polluant m	sostanza nociva f	substancia nociva f
polluter pays principle (E)	Verursacherprinzip n	—	principe du pol. pollueur payeur m	principio della colpa oggettiva m	principio contamina-dor-pagador m
pollution de l'environnement (F)	Umwelt-verschmutzung f	environmental pollution	—	inquinamento dell'ambiente m	contaminación del medio ambiente f
polvere secondaria (I)	Sekundärstaub m	secondary dust	poussière secondaire f	—	polvo secundario m
polvo secundario (Es)	Sekundärstaub m	secondary dust	poussière secondaire f	polvere secondaria f	—
Pool (D)	—	pool	pool m	pool m	pool m
pool (E)	Pool m	—	pool m	pool m	pool m
pool (Es)	Pool m	pool	pool m	pool m	—
pool (F)	Pool m	pool	—	pool m	pool m
pool (I)	Pool m	pool	pool m	—	pool m
pool de brevet (F)	Patentpool m	patent pool	—	pool dei brevetti m	pool de patentes m
pool dei brevetti (I)	Patentpool m	patent pool	pool de brevet m	—	pool de patentes m
pool de patentes (Es)	Patentpool m	patent pool	pool de brevet m	pool dei brevetti m	—
pool d'imprese (I)	Unternehmens-konzentration f	business concentration	concentration d'entreprises f	—	concentración de empresas f
poor quality (E)	schlechte Qualität f	—	mauvaise qualité f	qualità scadente f	mala calidad f
popolazione (I)	Bevölkerung f	population	population f	—	población f
population (E)	Bevölkerung f	—	population f	popolazione f	población f
population (F)	Bevölkerung f	population	—	popolazione f	población f
population policy (E)	Bevölkerungspolitik f	—	politique démo-graphique populationniste f	politica demografica f	política demográfica f
population statistics (E)	Bevölkerungs-statistik f	—	statistique démographique f	statistica demografica f	estadística de población f
population structure (E)	Bevölkerungs-struktur f	—	structure démographique f	struttura demografica f	estructura demográfica f
por camión (Es)	per Lastkraftwagen	by lorry	par camion	per autocarro	—
porcentaje (Es)	Prozentsatz m	percentage	pourcentage m	percentuale f	—
por ciento (Es)	Prozent n	per cent	pour-cent m	percento m	—
por correo aparte (Es)	mit getrennter Post	under separate cover	sous pli séparé	in plico a parte	—
por cuenta ajena (Es)	für fremde Rechnung	for account of a third party	pour compte de tiers	per conto terzi	—
por cuenta propia (Es)	für eigene Rechnung	for one's own account	pour son propre compte	per conto proprio	—
por duplicado (Es)	in zweifacher Ausfertigung	in duplicate	en deux exemplaires	in due copie	—
por escrito (Es)	schriftlich	written	par écrit	per iscritto	—
por expreso (Es)	per Express	by express (mail)	par exprès	per espresso	—
por poder¹ (Es)	per procura	by procuration	par procuration	per procura	—

possessore di casa

	D	E	F	I	Es
por poder² (Es)	im Auftrag	by order	par ordre p.o.	per ordine	—
port (E)	Hafen *m*	—	port *m*	porto *m*	puerto *m*
port¹ (F)	Hafen *m*	port	—	porto *m*	puerto *m*
port² (F)	Porto *n*	postage	—	porto *m*	porte *m*
portador (Es)	Überbringer *m*	bearer	porteur *m*	portatore *m*	—
portafoglio (I)	Portfolio *n*	portfolio	portefeuille *m*	—	cartera *f*
portafoglio di azioni (I)	Aktienbestand *m*	shareholding	portefeuille d'actions *m*	—	cartera de acciones *f*
portalettere (I)	Postbote *m*	postman	facteur *m*	—	cartero *m*
portatore (I)	Überbringer *m*	bearer	porteur *m*	—	portador *m*
porte (Es)	Porto *m*	postage	port *m*	porto *m*	—
portefeuille (F)	Portfolio *n*	portfolio	—	portafoglio *m*	cartera *f*
portefeuille d'actions (F)	Aktienbestand *m*	shareholding	—	portafoglio di azioni *m*	cartera de acciones *f*
porte pagado (Es)	portofrei	post-free	franco de port	franco di porto	—
porteur (F)	Überbringer *m*	bearer	—	portatore *m*	portador *m*
porteur des données (F)	Datenträger *m*	data medium	—	supporto dati *m*	medio de datos *m*
Portfolio (D)	—	portfolio	portefeuille *m*	portafoglio *m*	cartera *f*
portfolio (E)	Portfolio *n*	—	portefeuille *m*	portafoglio *m*	cartera *f*
port franc (F)	Freihafen *m*	free port	—	porto franco *m*	puerto franco *m*
Porto (D)	—	postage	port *m*	porto *m*	porte *m*
porto¹ (I)	Porto *n*	postage	port *m*	—	porte *m*
porto² (I)	Hafen *m*	port	port *m*	—	puerto *m*
Portoabzug (D)	—	postage deduction	déduction de port *f*	detrazione porto *f*	deducción de porte *f*
porto franco (I)	Freihafen *m*	free port	port franc *m*	—	puerto franco *m*
portofrei (D)	—	post-free	franco de port	franco di porto	porte pagado
por transferencia (Es)	bargeldlos	non-cash	par virement	mediante assegno	—
poscritto (I)	Postskriptum *n*	postscript	post-scriptum *m*	—	pos(t)data *m*
posesión (Es)	Besitz *m*	possession	possession *f*	possesso *m*	—
posibilidades de ascenso (Es)	Aufstiegsmöglichkeit *f*	promotion possibility	perspectives de promotion *f pl*	possibilità di carriera *f*	—
posibilidades de venta¹ (Es)	Verkaufschance *f*	sales possibilities	possibilité de vente *f*	prospettiva dello smercio *f*	—
posibilidades de venta² (Es)	Absatzchance *f*	sales prospects	possibilités de réussite des ventes *f pl*	prospettive di smercio *f pl*	—
posibilidades futuras (Es)	Zukunftschance *f*	future prospects	perspectives d'avenir *f pl*	prospettiva *f*	—
posición de costes (Es)	Kostenstelle *f*	departmental expense account	compte de frais par secteurs *m*	posizione costi *f*	—
posición en el mercado (Es)	Marktposition *f*	market position	position sur le marché *f*	posizione di mercato *f*	—
position (E)	Stellung *f*	—	position *f*	posizione *f*	empleo *m*
position (F)	Stellung *f*	position	—	posizione *f*	empleo *m*
position offered (E)	Stellenanzeige *f*	—	annonce d'emploi *f*	inserzione d'impiego *f*	anuncio de empleo *m*
position sur le marché (F)	Marktposition *f*	market position	—	posizione di mercato *f*	posición en el mercado *f*
posizionamento dell'inserzione (I)	Anzeigenschaltung *f*	insertion of an advertisement	placement de l'annonce *m*	—	inserción del anuncio *f*
posizione (I)	Stellung *f*	position	position *f*	—	empleo *m*
posizione costi (I)	Kostenstelle *f*	departmental expense account	compte des frais por secteurs *m*	—	posición de costes *f*
posizione di mercato (I)	Marktposition *f*	market position	position sur le marché *f*	—	posición en el mercado *f*
possession (E)	Besitz *m*	—	possession *f*	possesso *m*	posesión *f*
possession (F)	Besitz *m*	possession	—	possesso *m*	posesión *f*
possesso (I)	Besitz *m*	possession	possession *f*	—	posesión *f*
possessore di casa (I)	Hausbesitzer *m*	home property owner	propriétaire d'immeuble *m*	—	propietario de una casa *m*

	D	E	F	I	Es
possibilità di carriera (I)	Aufstiegsmöglichkeit *f*	promotion possibility	perspectives de promotion *f pl*	—	posibilidades de ascenso *f pl*
possibilité de vente (F)	Verkaufschance *f*	sales possibilities	—	prospettiva dello smercio *f*	posibilidades de venta *f pl*
possibilités de réussite des ventes (F)	Absatzchance *f*	sales prospects	—	prospettive di smercio *f pl*	posibilidades de venta *f pl*
posta aerea (I)	Luftpost *f*	air mail	par avion	—	correo aéreo *m*
postage (E)	Porto *n*	—	port *m*	porto *m*	porte *m*
postage deduction (E)	Portoabzug *m*	—	déduction de port *f*	detrazione porto *f*	deducción de porte *f*
postagiro (I)	Postgiro *n*	postal giro	virement postal *m*	—	giro postal *m*
postal code (E)	Postleitzahl *f*	—	chiffre de code postal *m*	codice d'avviamento postale *m*	código postal *m*
postal giro¹ (E)	Postscheck *m*	—	chèque postal *m*	assegno postale *m*	cheque postal *m*
postal giro² (E)	Postgiro *n*	—	virement postal *m*	postagiro *m*	giro postal *m*
(postal) giro account (E)	Postscheckkonto *n*	—	compte chèque postal *m*/compte courant postal *m*	conto corrente postale *m*	cuenta corriente postal *f*
postal giro centre (E)	Postscheckamt *n*	—	bureau de chèques postaux *m*	ufficio dei conti correnti postali *m*	oficina de cheques postales *f*
postal money order (E)	Postanweisung *f*	—	mandat-poste *m*	vaglia postale *m*	vale postal *m*
postal remittance (E)	Postüberweisung *f*	—	virement postal *m*	bonifico postale *m*	giro postal *m*
postal wrapper (E)	Streifband *f*	—	bande étiquette *f*	fascia *f*	precinto *m*
Postamt (D)	—	post office	bureau de poste *m*	ufficio postale *m*	correos *m pl*
Postanweisung (D)	—	postal money order	mandat-poste *m*	vaglia postale *m*	vale postal *m*
Postbote (D)	—	postman	facteur *m*	portalettere *m*	cartero *m*
postcard (E)	Postkarte *f*	—	carte postale *f*	cartolina postale *f*	tarjeta postal *f*
pos(t)data (Es)	Postskriptum *n*	postscript	post-scriptum *m*	poscritto *m*	—
pos(t)datado (Es)	nachdatiert	postdated	postdaté	postdatato	—
postdatato (I)	nachdatiert	postdated	postdaté	—	pos(t)datado
postdaté (F)	nachdatiert	antedated	—	postdatato	pos(t)datado
postdated (E)	nachdatiert	—	postdaté	postdatato	pos(t)datado
poste (F)	Posten *m*	item/lot	—	voce *f*/partita *f*	puesto *m*/partida *f*
poste à temps partiel (F)	Teilzeitstelle *f*	part-time job	—	posto di lavoro part-time *m*	puesto de trabajo a tiempo parcial *m*
poste de production absorbant des coûts (F)	Kostenträger *m*	unit assuming costs	—	chi si assume i costi	que sufraga los costes
poste de travail (F)	Arbeitsplatz *m*	place of employment	—	posto di lavoro *m*	puesto de trabajo *m*
poste de travail à l'écran (F)	Bildschirmarbeitsplatz *m*	screen job	—	posto di lavoro video *m*	puesto de trabajo de pantalla *m*
Posten (D)	—	item/lot	poste *m*/lot de marchandieses *m*	voce *f*/partita *f*	puesto *m*/partida *f*
poster (E)	Plakat *n*	—	affiche *f*	manifesto *m*	cartel *m*
poste restante¹ (E)	postlagernd	—	poste restante	fermo posta	lista de correos *m*
poste restante² (F)	postlagernd	poste restante	—	fermo posta	lista de correos *m*
Postfach (D)	—	post office box	boîte postale *f*	casella postale *f*	apartado postal *m*
post-free (E)	portofrei	—	franco de port	franco di porto	porte pagado
Postgeheimnis (D)	—	secrecy of the post	secret postal *m*	segreto postale *m*	secreto postal *m*
Postgiro (D)	—	postal giro	virement postal *m*	postagiro *m*	giro postal *m*
Postkarte (D)	—	postcard	carte postale *f*	cartolina postale *f*	tarjeta postal *f*
postlagernd (D)	—	poste restante	poste restante	fermo posta	lista de correos *m*
Postleitzahl (D)	—	postal code	chiffre de code postal *m*	codice d'avviamento postale *m*	código postal *m*
postman (E)	Postbote *m*	—	facteur *m*	portalettere *m*	cartero *m*
postmark (E)	Poststempel *m*	—	cachet de la poste *m*	timbro postale *m*	sello postal *m*
posto di dogana (I)	Zollstelle *f*	customs office	bureau de douane *m*	—	oficina de aduanas *f*
posto di lavoro (I)	Arbeitsplatz *m*	place of employment	poste de travail *m*	—	puesto de trabajo *m*
posto di lavoro part-time (I)	Teilzeitstelle *f*	part-time job	poste à temps partiel *m*	—	puesto de trabajo a tiempo parcial *m*

	D	E	F	I	Es
posto di lavoro video (I)	Bildschirm-arbeitsplatz *m*	screen job	poste de travail à l'écran *f*	—	puesto de trabajo de pantalla *m*
post office (E)	Postamt *n*	—	bureau de poste principal *m*	ufficio postale *m*	correos *m pl*
post office box (E)	Postfach *n*	—	boîte postale *f*	casella postale *f*	apartado postal *m*
postpone (E)	Vertagung *f*	—	ajournement *m*	rinvio *m*	aplazamiento *m/* suspensión *f*
postponement (E)	Aufschiebung *f*	—	remise *f*	rinvio *m*	aplazamiento *m*
Postscheck (D)	—	postal giro	chèque postal *m*	assegno postale *m*	cheque postal *m*
Postscheckamt (D)	—	postal giro centre	bureau de chèques postaux *m*	ufficio dei conti correnti postali *m*	oficina de cheques postales *f*
Postscheckkonto (D)	—	(postal) giro account	compte chèque postal *m*	conto corrente postale *m*	cuenta corriente postal *f*
postscript (E)	Postskriptum *n*	—	post-scriptum *m*	poscritto *m*	pos(t)data *m*
post-scriptum (F)	Postskriptum *n*	postscript	—	poscritto *m*	pos(t)data *m*
Postskriptum (D)	—	postscript	post-scriptum *m*	poscritto *m*	pos(t)data *m*
Poststempel (D)	—	postmark	cachet de la poste *m*	timbro postale *m*	sello postal *m*
Postüberweisung (D)	—	postal remittance	virement postal *m*	bonifico postale *m*	giro postal *m*
postwendend (D)	—	by return of post	par retour du courrier	a giro di posta	a vuelta de correo
Postwurfsendung (D)	—	printed papers or samples of merchandise posted in bulk	envoi publicitaire collectif *m*	spedizione postale cumulativa di stampati *f*	envío postal colectivo *m*
potencial productivo (Es)	Produktions-potential *n*	production potential	potentiel de production *m*	potenziale produttivo *m*	—
potentiel de production (F)	Produktions-potential *n*	production potential	—	potenziale produttivo *m*	potencial productivo *m*
potenziale produttivo (I)	Produktions-potential *n*	production potential	potentiel de production *m*	—	potencial productivo *m*
potere d'acquisto (I)	Kaufkraft *f*	purchasing power	pouvoir d'achat *m*	—	poder adquisitivo *m*
pound (E)	Pfund *n*	—	livre *f*	libbra *f*	libra *f*
pouperism (E)	Massenarmut *f*	—	paupérisme *m*	paupersimo *m*	pauperismo *m*
pourboire (F)	Bedienungsgeld *n*	tip	—	diritto di servizio *m*	propina *f*
pour-cent (F)	Prozent *n*	per cent	—	percento *m*	por ciento *m*
pourcentage (F)	Prozentsatz *m*	percentage	—	percentuale *f*	porcentaje *m*
pour compte de tiers (F)	für fremde Rechnung	for account of a third party	—	per conto terzi	por cuenta ajena
pour raison de payement (F)	zahlungshalber	on account of payment	—	a titolo di pagamento	título de pago
pour son propre compte (F)	für eigene Rechnung	for one's own account	—	per conto proprio	por cuenta propia
poussière secondaire (F)	Sekundärstaub *m*	secondary dust	—	polvere secondaria *f*	polvo secundario *m*
pouvoir¹ (F)	Bevollmächtigung *f*	authorization	—	autorizzazione *f*	apoderamiento *m*
pouvoir² (F)	Befugnis *f*	authorization	—	prerogativa *f*	autorización *f*
pouvoir d'achat (F)	Kaufkraft *f*	purchasing power	—	potere d'acquisto *m*	poder adquisitivo *m*
pouvoir général (F)	Generalvollmacht *f*	general power	—	procura generale *f*	poder general *m*
power of administration (E)	Verwaltungshoheit *f*	—	autonomie d'administration *f*	sovranità amministrativa *f*	soberanía administrativa *f*
power station (E)	Kraftwerk *n*	—	centrale électrique *f*	centrale elettrica *f*	circulación de automóviles *f*
práctica de pago (Es)	Zahlungs-gewohnheit *f*	practice of payment	habitude de payement *f*	consuetudine di pagamento *f*	—
practice of payment (E)	Zahlungs-gewohnheit *f*	—	habitude de payement *f*	consuetudine di pagamento *f*	práctica de pago *f*
Präferenz (D)	—	preference	préférence *f*	preferenza *f*	preferencia *f*
Präferenzzoll (D)	—	preferential duty	taxe préférentielle de douane *f*	dazio preferenziale *m*	aduanas preferenciales *f pl*
Prämie (D)	—	bonus/premium	prime *f*	premio *m*	gratificación *f*/prima *f*
Prämiensystem (D)	—	bonus system	système de primes *m*	sistema dei premi *m*	sistema de primas *m*
Prämisse (D)	—	premise	prémisse *f*	premessa *f*	premisa *f*
pranzo di lavoro (I)	Arbeitsessen *n*	working lunch	déjeuner de travail *m*	—	comida de trabajo *f*
Präsentation (D)	—	presentation	présentation *f*	presentazione *f*	presentación *f*

	D	E	F	I	Es
Präsident (D)	—	president	président *m*	presidente *m*	presidente *m*
pratica (I)	Akte *f*	file	dossier *m*	—	documento *m*
précieux (F)	wertvoll	valuable	—	prezioso	precioso
precinto (Es)	Streifband *f*	postal wrapper	bande étiquette *f*	fascia *f*	—
precinto aduanero (Es)	Zollverschluß *m*	customs seal	fermeture douanière *f*	sigillo doganale *m*	—
precio (Es)	Preis *m*	price	prix *m*	prezzo *m*	—
precio afectivo (Es)	Liebhaberpreis *m*	connoisseur's price	prix d'amateur *m*	prezzo d'affezione *m*	—
precio agrícola (Es)	Agrarpreis *m*	prices of farm products	prix agricole *m*	prezzo agrario *m*	—
precio-base (Es)	Schwellenpreis *m*	threshold price	prix de seuil *m*	prezzo soglia *m*	—
precio bruto (Es)	Bruttopreis *m*	gross price	prix brut *m*	prezzo lordo *m*	—
precio de compra (Es)	Einkaufspreis *m*	purchase price	prix d'achat *m*	prezzo d'acquisto *m*	—
precio de compras a plazo (Es)	Teilzahlungspreis *m*	partial payment price	prix d'un achat à tempérament *m*	prezzo rateale *m*	—
precio de coste[1] (Es)	Selbstkostenpreis *m*	cost price	prix coûtant *m*	prezzo di costo *m*	—
precio de coste[2] (Es)	Einstandspreis *m*	cost price	prix coûtant *m*	prezzo di costo *m*	—
precio de equilibrio (Es)	Gleichgewichts-preis *m*	equilibrium price	prix équilibré *m*	prezzo d'equilibrio *m*	—
precio de la travesía (Es)	Fahrgeld *n*	fare	coût du voyage *m*	spese di trasferta *f pl*	—
precio del crudo (Es)	Rohölpreis *m*	crude oil price	prix du pétrole brut *m*	prezzo del petrolio greggio *m*	—
precio del mercado mundial (Es)	Weltmarktpreis *m*	world market price	prix du marché mondial *m*	prezzo di mercato mondiale *m*	—
precio del oro (Es)	Goldpreis *m*	gold price	prix de l'ór *m*	prezzo dell'oro *m*	—
precio de orientación (Es)	Orientierungspreis *m*	guide price	prix d'orientation *m*	prezzo d'orientamento *m*	—
precio de producción (Es)	Erzeugerpreis *m*	producer price	prix à la production *m*	prezzo di fabbrica *m*	—
precio de reventa (Es)	Wiederverkaufs-preis *m*	resale price	prix de revente *m*	prezzo di rivendita *m*	—
precio de suelo (Es)	Bodenpreis *m*	land price	prix du terrain *m*	prezzo del terreno *m*	—
precio de venta (Es)	Ladenpreis *m*	retail price	prix de vente *m*	prezzo di vendita *m*	—
precio fijo (Es)	Festpreis *m*	fixed price	prix fixe *m*	prezzo fisso *m*	—
precio hegemónico (Es)	Preisführerschaft *f*	price leadership	leader en matière de prix *m*	leader in materia di prezzi *m*	—
precio indicativo (Es)	Richtpreis *m*	recommended retail price	prix indicatif *m*	prezzo indicativo *m*	—
precio-lista (Es)	Listenpreis *m*	list price	prix au tarif *m*	prezzo di listino *m*	—
precio máximo (Es)	Höchstpreis *m*	top price	prix plafond *m*	prezzo massimo *m*	—
precio mayorista (Es)	Großhandelspreise *pl*	wholesale prices	prix de gros *m*	prezzo all'ingrosso *m*	—
precio mínimo (Es)	Mindestpreis *m*	minimum price	prix minimum *m*	prezzo minimo *m*	—
precio mínimo a la importación (Es)	Mindesteinfuhr-preise *pl*	minimum import price	prix minimum d'importation *m pl*	prezzi minimi all'importazione *m pl*	—
precio neto (Es)	Nettopreis *m*	net price	prix net *m*	prezzo netto *m*	—
precio recomendado (Es)	Preisempfehlung *f*	price recommendation	recommendation de prix *f*	suggerimento di prezzo *m*	—
precios administrados (Es)	administrierte Preise *pl*	administered prices	prix administrés *m pl*	prezzi amministrati *m pl*	—
precios escalonados (Es)	Staffelpreis *m*	graduated price	prix échelonné *m*	prezzo differenziato *m*	—
precios ficticios (Es)	Mondpreise *pl*	ficticious prices	prix fictifs *m pl*	prezzi alle stelle *m pl*	—
precio sin compromiso (Es)	Preis freibleibend	open price	prix sans engagement	prezzo non vincolante *m*	—
precioso (Es)	wertvoll	valuable	précieux	prezioso	—
precio único (Es)	Einheitspreis *m*	uniform price	prix unique *m*	prezzo unitario *m*	—
precondition (E)	Voraussetzung *f*	—	condition préalable *f*	presupposto *m*	condición previa *f*
preemption right (E)	Vorkaufsrecht *n*	—	droit de préemption *m*	diritto di prelazione *m*	derecho de preferencia *m*
preference (E)	Präferenz *f*	—	préférence *f*	preferenza *f*	preferencia *f*
préférence (F)	Präferenz *f*	preference	—	preferenza *f*	preferencia *f*

	D	E	F	I	Es
preference share (E)	Vorzugsaktie f	—	action privilégiée f	azione privilegiata f	acción preferente f
preferencia (Es)	Präferenz f	preference	préférence f	preferenza f	—
preferential discount (E)	Vorzugsrabatt m	—	remise de faveur f	ribasso preferenziale m	rebaja preferencial f
preferential duty (E)	Präferenzzoll m	—	taxe préférentielle de douane f	dazio preferenziale m	aduanas preferenciales f pl
preferenza (I)	Präferenz f	preference	préférence f	—	preferencia f
Preis (D)	—	price	prix m	prezzo m	precio m
Preisabsprache (D)	—	price fixing	accord sur les prix m	accordo sui prezzi m	acuerdo de precios m
Preisabzug (D)	—	price deduction	réduction de prix f	riduzione del prezzo f	descuento m
Preisanstieg (D)	—	price rise	hausse des prix f	aumento del prezzo m	aumento de precios m
Preisauszeichnung (D)	—	pricemarking	affichage des prix f	indicazione del prezzo f	indicación de precios f
Preisbildung (D)	—	formation of prices	formation des prix f	formazione dei prezzi f	formación de precios f
Preisbindung (D)	—	obligation to maintain fixed prices	obligation de respecter les prix f	obbligo di mantenere il prezzo fissato m	limitación de precios f
Preisdifferenzierung (D)	—	price differentiation	différenciation de prix f	differenziazione dei prezzi f	diferenciación de los precios f
Preisempfehlung (D)	—	price recommendation	recommendation de prix f	suggerimento di prezzo m	precio recomendado m
Preiserhöhung (D)	—	price increase	augmentation des prix f	rialzo dei prezzi m	aumento de precios m
Preis freibleibend (D)	—	open price	prix sans engagement	prezzo non vincolante m	precio sin compromiso m
Preisführerschaft (D)	—	price leadership	leader en matière de prix m	leader in materia di prezzi m	precio hegemónico m
preisgünstiges Angebot (D)	—	well-priced offer	offre à un prix avantageux f	offerta a buon prezzo f	oferta favorable f
Preisindex (D)	—	price index	indice des prix m	indice dei prezzi m	ínidce de precios m
Preiskontrolle (D)	—	price control	contrôle des prix m	controllo dei prezzi m	control de precios m
Preislenkung (D)	—	administration of prices	réglementation des prix f	gestione dei prezzi f	reglamentación de precios f
Preisliste (D)	—	price list	liste des prix f	listino prezzi m	lista de precios f
Preismechanismus (D)	—	price mechanism	mécanisme des prix m	meccanismo dei prezzi m	mecanismo de precios m
Preisnachlaß (D)	—	price reduction	remise sur le prix f	ribasso del prezzo m	rebaja f
Preisniveau (D)	—	price level	niveau des prix m	livello dei prezzi m	nivel de precios m
Preisnotierung (D)	—	prices quoted	cotation des prix f	quotazione dei prezzi f	cotización de precios f
Preisobergrenze (D)	—	price ceiling	limite supérieure des prix f	limite massimo di prezzo m	límite superior de los precios m
Preispolitik (D)	—	price policy	politiques des prix f	politica dei prezzi f	política de precios f
Preisschwankung (D)	—	price fluctuation	fluctuation des prix f	fluttuazione dei prezzi f	oscilación de precios f
Preisschwelle (D)	—	threshold price	seuil du prix m	soglia dei prezzi f	umbral de precios m
Preissenkung (D)	—	price reduction	réduction des prix f	riduzione dei prezzi f	reducción de precios f
Preisstabilität (D)	—	stability of prices	stabilité des prix f	stabilità dei prezzi f	estabilidad de precios f
Preissteigerung (D)	—	price increase	hausse des prix f	aumento dei prezzi m	aumento de precios m
Preisstopp (D)	—	price stop	blocage des prix m	blocco dei prezzi m	limitación de precios f
Preistheorie (D)	—	theory of prices	théorie des prix f	teoria del prezzo f	teoría de los precios f
Preisuntergrenze (D)	—	price floor	plancher des prix m	limite inferiore di prezzo m	límite inferior de los precios m
Preisunterschied (D)	—	price difference	écart de prix m	differenza dei prezzi f	diferencia de precios f
Preisverfall (D)	—	decline in prices	chute des prix f	caduta dei prezzi f	caída de precios f
Preiswettbewerb (D)	—	competition in prices	concurrence des prix f	competizione dei prezzi f	competencia de precios f
prelevamento a titolo personale (I)	Privatentnahmen pl	personal drawings	prélèvement personnel m	—	detracción privada f
prélèvement personnel (F)	Privatentnahmen pl	personal drawings	—	prelevamento a titolo personale m	detracción privada f

	D	E	F	I	Es
prelievo di campioni (I)	Stichprobener-hebung *f*	sample survey	enquête par sondage *f*	—	encuesta por muestreo *f*
premessa (I)	Prämisse *f*	premise	prémisse *f*	—	premisa *f*
première qualité (F)	beste Qualität	first class quality	—	qualità ottima *f*	primera calidad *f*
premier versement (F)	Abschlagszahlung *f*	partial payment/ payment on account	—	pagamento a rate *m*/ pagamento in acconto *m*	pago parcial *m*/ pago a cuenta *m*
premio[1] (I)	Bonus *m*	bonus	bonification *f*	—	gratificación *f*
premio[2] (I)	Prämie *f*	bonus/premium	prime *f*	—	gratificación *f*/prima *f*
premio[3] (I)	Zulage *f*	increase/ additional pay	prime *f*/complément de salaire *m*	—	suplemento *m*/plus *m*
premio d'assicurazione (I)	Versicherungs-prämie *f*	insurance premium	prime d'assurance *f*	—	prima de seguro *f*
premio d'investimento (I)	Investitionszulage *f*	investment grant	prime d'investissement *f*	—	prima a la inversión *f*
premio di rischio[1] (I)	Risikoprämie *f*	risk premium	prime de risque *f*	—	prima de riesgo *f*
premio di rischio[2] (I)	Gefahrenzulage *f*	danger money	prime de danger *f*	—	incremento por peligrosidad *m*
premisa (Es)	Prämisse *f*	premise	prémisse *f*	premessa *f*	—
premise (E)	Prämisse *f*	—	prémisse *f*	premessa *f*	premisa *f*
prémisse (F)	Prämisse *f*	premise	—	premessa *f*	premisa *f*
preneur de leasing (F)	Leasing-Nehmer *m*	lessee	—	utente del leasing *m*	arrendatante financiero *m*
preneur d'une licence (F)	Lizenznehmer *m*	licensee	—	concessionario di licenza *m*	licenciado *m*
preneur final (F)	Endabnehmer *m*	ultimate buyer	—	acquirente finale *m*	comprador final *m*
prenotazione (I)	Reservierung *f*	reservation	réservation *f*	—	reservación *f*
prensa (Es)	Presse *f*	press	presse *f*	stampa *f*	—
preparación (Es)	Vorbereitung *f*	preparation	préparation *f*	preparazione *f*	—
preparación laboral (Es)	Arbeitsvorbereitung *f*	job preparation	préparation du travail *f*	preparazione del lavoro *f*	—
preparation (E)	Vorbereitung *f*	—	préparation *f*	preparazione *f*	preparación *f*
préparation (F)	Vorbereitung *f*	preparation	—	preparazione *f*	preparación *f*
préparation du travail (F)	Arbeitsvorbereitung *f*	job preparation	—	preparazione del lavoro *f*	preparación laboral *f*
preparazione (I)	Vorbereitung *f*	preparation	préparation *f*	—	preparación *f*
preparazione del lavoro (I)	Arbeitsvorbereitung *f*	job preparation	préparation du travail *f*	—	preparación laboral *f*
prepay the postage (E)	frankieren	—	affranchir	affrancare	franquear
prerogativa (I)	Befugnis *f*	authorization	pouvoir *m*	—	autorización *f*
prérogative (F)	Vorrecht *n*	privilege	—	privilegio *m*	derecho preferente *m*
presa di posizione (I)	Stellungnahme *f*	comment	prise de position *f*	—	dictamen *m*
presa visione (I)	Einsichtnahme *f*	inspection	contrôle des livres comptables *m*	—	inspección *f*
prescripción (Es)	Verjährung *f*	limitation of actions	prescription *f*	prescrizione *f*	—
prescripciones de embalaje (Es)	Verpackungs-vorschriften *pl*	packing instructions	prescriptions concernant l'emballage *f pl*	prescrizioni per l'imballaggio *f pl*	—
prescription (F)	Verjährung *f*	limitation of actions	—	prescrizione *f*	prescripción *f*
prescriptions concernant l'emballage (F)	Verpackungs-vorschriften *pl*	packing instructions	—	prescrizioni per l'imballaggio *f pl*	prescripciones de embalaje *f pl*
prescriptions concernant l'expédition (F)	Versandvorschrift *f*	forwarding instructions	—	prescrizione per la spedizione *f*	instrucción para el envío *f*
prescrizione (I)	Verjährung *f*	limitation of actions	prescription *f*	—	prescripción *f*
prescrizione per la spedizione (I)	Versandvorschrift *f*	forwarding instructions	prescriptions concernant l'expédition *f pl*	—	instrucción para el envío *f*
prescrizioni per l'imballaggio (I)	Verpackungs-vorschriften *pl*	packing instructions	prescriptions concernant l'emballage *f pl*	—	prescripciones de embalaje *f pl*
presentación (Es)	Präsentation *f*	presentation	présentation *f*	presentazione *f*	—
presentation (E)	Präsentation *f*	—	présentation *f*	presentazione *f*	presentación *f*
présentation (F)	Präsentation *f*	presentation	—	presentazione *f*	presentación *f*

	D	E	F	I	Es
présentation d'un produit (F)	Produktgestaltung *f*	product design	—	creazione del prodotto *f*	diseño del producto *m*
presentazione (I)	Präsentation *f*	presentation	présentation *f*	—	presentación *f*
présidence (F)	Vorsitz *m*	chairmanship	—	presidenza *f*	presidencia *f*
presidencia (Es)	Vorsitz *m*	chairmanship	présidence *f*	presidenza *f*	—
president (E)	Präsident *m*	—	président *m*	presidente *m*	presidente *m*
président (F)	Präsident *m*	president	—	presidente *m*	presidente *m*
président du comité de direction (F)	Vorstands-vorsitzender *m*	chairman of the board	—	presidente del consiglio di amministrazione *m*	presidente del consejo *m*
président du conseil de surveillance (F)	Aufsichtsrats-vorsitzender *m*	chairman of the supervisory board	—	presidente del consiglio di sorveglianza *m*	presidente del consejo devigilancia *m*
presidente (Es)	Präsident *m*	president	président *m*	presidente *m*	—
presidente (I)	Präsident *m*	president	président *m*	—	presidente *m*
presidente del consejo (Es)	Vorstands-vorsitzender *m*	chairman of the board	président du comité de direction *m*	presidente del consiglio di amministrazione *m*	—
presidente del consejo devigilancia (Es)	Aufsichtsrats-vorsitzender *m*	chairman of the supervisory board	président du conseil de surveillance *m*	presidente del consiglio di sorveglianza *m*	—
presidente del consiglio di amministrazione (I)	Vorstands-vorsitzender *m*	chairman of the board	président du comité de direction *m*	—	presidente del consejo *m*
presidente del consiglio di sorveglianza (I)	Aufsichtsrats-vorsitzender *m*	chairman of the supervisory board	président du conseil de surveillance *m*	—	presidente del consejo devigilancia *m*
presidenza (I)	Vorsitz *m*	chairmanship	présidence *f*	—	presidencia *f*
présomption (F)	Mutmaßung *f*	conjecture	—	presunzione *f*	suposición *f*
press (E)	Presse *f*	—	presse *f*	stampa *f*	prensa *f*
press campaign (E)	Presseaktion *f*	—	action de presse *f*	azione stampa *f*	campaña de prensa *f*
press conference (E)	Pressekonferenz *f*	—	conférence de presse *f*	conferenza stampa *f*	rueda de prensa *f*
Presse (D)	—	press	presse *f*	stampa *f*	prensa *f*
presse (F)	Presse *f*	press	—	stampa *f*	prensa *f*
Presseaktion (D)	—	press campaign	action de presse *f*	azione stampa *f*	campaña de prensa *f*
Pressekonferenz (D)	—	press conference	conférence de presse *f*	conferenza stampa *f*	rueda de prensa *f*
Pressemitteilung (D)	—	press release	commentaire de presse *m*	comunicazione stampa *f*	remitido a la prensa *m*
Pressenotiz (D)	—	press report	note de presse *f*	notizia stampa *f*	nota de prensa *f*
press release (E)	Pressemitteilung *f*	—	commentaire de presse *m*	comunicazione stampa *f*	remitido a la prensa *m*
press report (E)	Pressenotiz *f*	—	note de presse *f*	notizia stampa *f*	nota de prensa *f*
pressure group (E)	Lobby *f*	—	lobby *m*	lobby *m*	grupo de presión *m*
prestación de servicio (Es)	Dienstleistung *f*	service	prestation de service *f*	servizio *m*	—
prestaciones por desempleo (Es)	Arbeitslosen-unterstützung *f*	unemployment benefits	indemnité de chômage *f*	sussidio di disoccupazione *m*	—
prestación social (Es)	Sozialleistung *f*	social services	prestations des caisses d'assurance sociale *f pl*/ prestation sociale *f*	prestazione sociale *f*	—
prestamista (Es)	Geldgeber *m*	financial backer	bailleur de fonds *m*	finanziatore *m*	—
préstamo (Es)	Darlehen *n*	loan	prêt *m*	mutuo *m*	—
prestanome (I)	Strohmann *m*	man of straw/ dummy	prête-nom *m*	—	testaferro *m*
prestatario (Es)	Kreditnehmer *m*	borrower	bénéficiaire d'un crédit *m*	beneficiario del credito *m*	—
prestation de garantie (F)	Gewährleistung *f*	warranty	—	garanzia *f*	garantía *f*
prestation de service (F)	Dienstleistung *f*	service	—	servizio *m*	prestación de servicio *m*
prestations des caisses d'assurance sociale (F)	Sozialleistung *f*	social services	—	prestazione sociale *f*	prestacion social *f*/ seguridad social *f*

	D	E	F	I	Es
prestations en nature (F)	Sachbezüge *pl*	remuneration in kind	—	retribuzioni in natura *f pl*	percepciónes en especie *f pl*
prestatore d'opera (I)	Arbeitnehmer *m*	employee	salarié *m*	—	empleado *m*
prestatori d'opera stranieri (I)	ausländische Arbeitnehmer *m*	foreign worker	travailleur étranger *m*	—	trabajadores extranjeros *m*
prestazione di garanzia (I)	Garantieleistung *f*	guarantee	fourniture sous garantie *f*	—	aplicación de la garantía *f*
prestazione sociale (I)	Sozialleistung *f*	social services	prestations des caisses d'assurance sociale *f pl*/ prestation sociale *f*	—	prestacion social *f*/ seguridad social *f*
prestiti comunali (I)	Kommunalanleihen *pl*	local authorities loan	emprunt communal *m*	—	empréstito municipal *m*
prestito (I)	Anleihe *f*	loan	emprunt *m*	—	empréstito *m*
prestito a reddito fisso (I)	Rentenanleihe *f*	annuity bonds	effet public *m*	—	empréstito por anualidades *m*
prestito estero (I)	Auslandsanleihe *f*	foreign bond	emprunt extérieur *m*	—	empréstito exterior *m*
prestito giornaliero (I)	Tagesgeld *n*	day-to-day money	argent au jour le jour *m*	—	dinero de día a día *m*
prestito obbligazionario (I)	Obligationsanleihe *f*	debenture loan	emprunt obligataire *m*	—	empréstito sobre obligaciones *m*
prestito rimborsabile in annualità (I)	Annuitätendarlehen *n*	annuity loan	prêt amortissable par annuités *m*	—	empréstito por anualidades *m*
presunzione (I)	Mutmaßung *f*	conjecture	présomption *f*	—	suposición *f*
presupposto (I)	Voraussetzung *f*	precondition	condition préalable *f*	—	condición previa *f*
presupuesto¹ (Es)	Haushaltsplan *m*	budget	budget *m*	bilancio preventivo *m*	—
presupuesto² (Es)	Budget *n*/Etat *m*	budget	budget *m*	bilancio *m*	—
presupuesto³ (Es)	Finanzplan *m*	financial plan	plan financier *m*	piano finanziario *m*	—
presupuesto⁴ (Es)	Voranschlag *m*	estimate	devis *m*	preventivo *m*	—
presupuesto de coste (Es)	Kostenvoranschlag *m*	estimate of cost	devis estimatif des frais *m*	preventivo dei costi *m*	—
presupuesto publicitario (Es)	Werbebudget *n*	advertising budget	budget de publicité *m*	budget pubblicitario *m*	—
prêt (F)	Darlehen *n*	loan	—	mutuo *m*	préstamo *m*
prêt à être expédié (F)	versandbereit	ready for dispatch	—	pronto per la spedizione	listo para ser expedido
prêt amortissable par annuités (F)	Annuitätendarlehen *n*	annuity loan	—	prestito rimborsabile in annualità *m*	empréstito por anualidades *m*
prête-nom (F)	Strohmann *m*	man of straw/ dummy	—	prestanome *m*	testaferro *m*
pretensión de indemnización (Es)	Schadensforderung *f*	claim for damages	prétention à dommages-intérêts *f*	credito da danni *m*	—
pretensión legal (Es)	Rechtsanspruch *m*	legal claim	titre *m*	pretesa giuridica *f*	—
prétention (F)	Anspruch *m*	claim	—	pretesa *f*	reivindicación *f*
prétention à dommages-intérêts (F)	Schadensforderung *f*	claim for damages	—	credito da danni *m*	pretensión de indemnización *f*
pretesa (I)	Anspruch *m*	claim	prétention *f*	—	reivindicación *f*
pretesa giuridica (I)	Rechtsanspruch *m*	legal claim	titre *m*	—	pretensión legal *f*
prêt restant (F)	Restdarlehen *n*	purchase-money loan	—	mutuo residuo *m*	restante de un préstamo *m*
prêt sur gage (F)	Lombardgeschäft *n*	lending on securities	—	anticipazioni *f pl*	operaciones de pignoración *f pl*
preuve (F)	Beweis *m*	proof	—	prova *f*	prueba *f*
prevención de siniestros (Es)	Schadenverhütung *f*	loss prevention	mesure préventive contre les sinistres *f*	prevenzione danni *f*	—
preventivo (I)	Voranschlag *m*	estimate	devis *m*	—	presupuesto *m*
preventivo dei costi (I)	Kostenvoranschlag *m*	estimate of cost	devis estimatif des frais *m*	—	presupuesto de coste *m*
prevenzione danni (I)	Schadenverhütung *f*	loss prevention	mesure préventive contre les sinistres *f*	—	prevención de siniestros *f*
previdenza per la vecchiaia (I)	Altersversorgung *f*	provision for old age	prévoyance vieillesse *f*	—	previsión para la vejez *f*
previdenza sociale (I)	Sozialversicherung *f*	social insurance	assurance sociale *m*	—	seguro social *m*

	D	E	F	I	Es
previsión de la evolución del volumen de ventas (Es)	Umsatzprognose *f*	turnover forecast	prévision de l'évolution du chiffre d'affaires *f*	prognosi del fatturato *f*	—
prévision de l'évolution du chiffre d'affaires (F)	Umsatzprognose *f*	turnover forecast	—	prognosi del fatturato *f*	previsión de la evolución del volumen de ventas *f*
previsión para la vejez (Es)	Altersversorgung *f*	provision for old age	prévoyance vieillesse *f*	previdenza per la vecchiaia *f*	—
prévoyance vieillesse (F)	Altersversorgung *f*	provision for old age	—	previdenza per la vecchiaia *f*	previsión para la vejez *f*
prezioso (I)	wertvoll	valuable	précieux	—	precioso
prezzi alle stelle (I)	Mondpreise *pl*	ficticious prices	prix fictifs *m pl*	—	precios ficticios *m pl*
prezzi amministrati (I)	administrierte Preise *pl*	administered prices	prix administrés *m pl*	—	precios administrados *m pl*
prezzi minimi all'importaz (I)	Mindesteinfuhrpreise *pl*	minimum import price	prix minimum d'importation *m pl*	—	precio mínimo a la importación *m*
prezzo (I)	Preis *m*	price	prix *m*	—	precio *m*
prezzo agrario (I)	Agrarpreis *m*	prices of farm products	prix agricole *m*	—	precio agrícola *m*
prezzo all'ingrosso (I)	Großhandelspreise *pl*	wholesale prices	prix de gros *m*	—	precio mayorista *m*
prezzo d'acquisto¹ (I)	Einkaufspreis *m*	purchase price	prix d'achat *m*	—	precio de compra *m*
prezzo d'acquisto² (I)	Bezugskosten *f pl*	purchasing costs	coûts d'acquisition *m pl*	—	gastos de adquisición *m pl*
prezzo d'affezione (I)	Liebhaberpreis *m*	connoisseur's price	prix d'amateur *m*	—	precio afectivo *m*
prezzo dell'oro (I)	Goldpreis *m*	gold price	prix de l'ór *m*	—	precio del oro *m*
prezzo del petrolio greggio (I)	Rohölpreis *m*	crude oil price	prix du pétrole brut *m*	—	precio del crudo *m*
prezzo del suolo (I)	Bodenpreis *m*	land price	prix du terrain *m*	—	precio de suelo *m*
prezzo d'emissione (I)	Emissionskurs *m*	price of issue	cours d'émission *m*	—	tipo de emisión *m*
prezzo d'equilibrio (I)	Gleichgewichtspreis *m*	equilibrium price	prix équilibré *m*	—	precio de equilibrio *m*
prezzo di costo¹ (I)	Selbstkostenpreis *m*	cost price	prix coûtant *m*	—	precio de coste *m*
prezzo di costo² (I)	Einstandspreis *m*	cost price	prix coûtant *m*	—	precio de coste *m*
prezzo di domanda (I)	Geldkurs *m*	demand price	cours de la demande *m*	—	cotización demandada *f*/precio ofrecido *m*
prezzo di fabbrica (I)	Erzeugerpreis *m*	producer price	prix à la production *m*	—	precio de producción *m*
prezzo differenziato (I)	Staffelpreis *m*	graduated price	prix échelonné *m*	—	precios escalonados *m pl*
prezzo di listino (I)	Listenpreis *m*	list price	prix au tarif *m*	—	precio-lista *m*
prezzo di mercato mondiale (I)	Weltmarktpreis *m*	world market price	prix du marché mondial *m*	—	precio del mercado mundial *m*
prezzo di rivendita (I)	Wiederverkaufspreis *m*	resale price	prix de revente *m*	—	precio de reventa *m*
prezzo di vendita (I)	Ladenpreis *m*	retail price	prix de vente *m*	—	precio de venta *m*
prezzo d'offerta (I)	Briefkurs *m*	ask price	cours de vente *m*	—	cotización ofrecida *f*
prezzo d'orientamento (I)	Orientierungspreis *m*	guide price	prix d'orientation *m*	—	precio de orientación *m*
prezzo fisso (I)	Festpreis *m*	fixed price	prix fixe *m*	—	precio fijo *m*
prezzo indicativo (I)	Richtpreis *m*	recommended retail price	prix indicatif *m*	—	precio indicativo *m*
prezzo lordo (I)	Bruttopreis *m*	gross price	prix brut *m*	—	precio bruto *m*
prezzo massimo (I)	Höchstpreis *m*	top price	prix plafond *m*	—	precio máximo *m*
prezzo minimo (I)	Mindestpreis *m*	minimum price	prix minimum *m*	—	precio mínimo *m*
prezzo netto (I)	Nettopreis *m*	net price	prix net *m*	—	precio neto *m*
prezzo non vincolante (I)	Preis freibleibend	open price	prix sans engagement	—	precio sin compromiso *m*
prezzo rateale (I)	Teilzahlungspreis *m*	partial payment price	prix d'un achat à tempérament *m*	—	precio de compras a plazo *m*
prezzo soglia (I)	Schwellenpreis *m*	threshold price	prix de seuil *m*	—	precio-base *m*
prezzo unitario (I)	Einheitspreis *m*	uniform price	prix unique *m*	—	precio único *m*
price (E)	Preis *m*	—	prix *m*	prezzo *m*	precio *m*

	D	E	F	I	Es
price advance (E)	Kurssteigerung f	—	hausse f	aumento dei corsi m	alza de las cotizaciones f
price calculation (E)	Preiskalkulation f	—	calcul des prix m	calcolo dei prezzi m	cálculo de precios m
price ceiling (E)	Preisobergrenze f	—	limite supérieure des prix f	limite massimo di prezzo m	límite superior de los precios m
price control (E)	Preiskontrolle f	—	contrôle des prix m	controllo dei prezzi m	control de precios m
price deduction (E)	Preisabzug m	—	réduction de prix f	riduzione del prezzo f	descuento m
price difference (E)	Preisunterschied m	—	écart de prix m	differenza dei prezzi f	diferencia de precios f
price differentiation (E)	Preisdifferenzierung f	—	différenciation de prix f	differenziazione dei prezzi f	diferenciación de los precios f
price-earnings ratio (E)	Kurs-Gewinn-Verhältnis n	—	relation cours-bénéfice f	rapporto corso-profitto m	relación cotización-ganancia f
price fixing (E)	Preisabsprache f	—	accord sur les prix m	accordo sui prezzi m	acuerdo de precios m
price floor (E)	Preisuntergrenze f	—	plancher des prix m	limite inferiore di prezzo m	límite inferior de los precios m
price fluctuation (E)	Preisschwankung f	—	fluctuation des prix f	fluttuazione dei prezzi f	oscilación de precios f
price increase[1] (E)	Preissteigerung f	—	hausse des prix f	aumento dei prezzi m	aumento de precios m
price increase[2] (E)	Preiserhöhung f	—	augmentation des prix f	rialzo dei prezzi m	aumento de precios m
price index (E)	Preisindex m	—	indice des prix m	indice dei prezzi m	índice de precios m
price leadership (E)	Preisführerschaft f	—	leader en matière de prix m	leader in materia di prezzi m	precio hegemónico m
price level (E)	Preisniveau n	—	niveau des prix m	livello dei prezzi m	nivel de precios m
price list (E)	Preisliste f	—	liste des prix f	listino prezzi m	lista de precios f
pricemarking (E)	Preisauszeichnung f	—	affichage des prix f	indicazione del prezzo f	indicación de precios f
price mechanism (E)	Preismechanismus m	—	mécanisme des prix m	meccanismo dei prezzi m	mecanismo de precios m
price nursing (E)	Kurspflege f	—	soutien des cours m	sostegno dei corsi m	compras de sostén f pl
price of issue (E)	Emissionskurs m	—	cours d'émission m	prezzo d'emissione m	tipo de emisión m
price policy (E)	Preispolitik f	—	politiques des prix f	politica dei prezzi f	política de precios f
price recommendation (E)	Preisempfehlung f	—	recommendation de prix f	suggerimento di prezzo m	precio recomendado m
price reduction[1] (E)	Preisnachlaß m	—	remise sur le prix f	ribasso del prezzo m	rebaja f
price reduction[2] (E)	Preissenkung f	—	réduction des prix f	riduzione dei prezzi f	reducción de precios f
price rise (E)	Preisanstieg m	—	hausse des prix f	aumento del prezzo m	aumento de precios m
price risk (E)	Kursrisiko n	—	risque de change m	rischio di cambio m	riesgo de cambio m
prices of farm products (E)	Agrarpreis m	—	prix agricole m	prezzo agrario m	precio agrícola m
prices quoted (E)	Preisnotierung f	—	cotation des prix f	quotazione dei prezzi f	cotización de precios f
price stop (E)	Preisstopp m	—	blocage des prix m	blocco dei prezzi m	limitación de precios f
price support (E)	Kursstützung f	—	soutiens des cours m	difesa dei corsi m	sostén de las cotizaciones m
prima a la inversión (Es)	Investitionszulage f	investment grant	prime d'investissement f	premio d'investimento m	—
prima de riesgo (Es)	Risikoprämie f	risk premium	prime de risque f	premio di rischio m	—
prima de seguro (Es)	Versicherungsprämie f	insurance premium	prime d'assurance f	premio d'assicurazione m	—
Primäraufwand (D)	—	primary expenses	charge primaire f	spese primarie f pl	gastos directos m pl
Primärenergie (D)	—	primary energy	énergie primaire f	energia primaria f	energía primaria f
Primärhaftung (D)	—	primary responsibility	responsabilité primaire f	responsabilità primaria f	responsabilidad primaria f
primary energy (E)	Primärenergie f	—	énergie primaire f	energia primaria f	energía primaria f
primary expenses (E)	Primäraufwand m	—	charge primaire f	spese primarie f pl	gastos directos m pl
primary responsibility (E)	Primärhaftung f	—	responsabilité primaire f	responsabilità primaria f	responsabilidad primaria f
prime[1] (F)	Aufgeld n	agio	—	aggio m	agio m
prime[2] (F)	Prämie f	bonus/premium	—	premio m	gratificación f/prima f

	D	E	F	I	Es
prime³ (F)	Zugabe f	extra	—	aggiunta f	suplemento m
prime⁴ (F)	Zulage f	increase/additional pay	—	premio m/indennità f	suplemento m/plus m
prime d'assurance (F)	Versicherungsprämie f	insurance premium	—	premio d'assicurazione m	prima de seguro f
prime de danger (F)	Gefahrenzulage f	danger money		premio di rischio m	incremento por peligrosidad m
prime de risque (F)	Risikoprämie f	risk premium	—.	premio di rischio m	prima de riesgo f
prime de vacances (F)	Urlaubsgeld n	holiday allowance		indennità di ferie f	retribución por vacaciones f
prime d'investissement (F)	Investitionszulage f	investment grant		premio d'investimento m	prima a la inversión f
primera calidad (Es)	beste Qualität	first class quality	première qualité f	qualità ottima f	—
primer asegurador (Es)	Erstversicherer m	direct insurer	assureur direct m	assicuratore diretto m	—
principe d'accélération (F)	Akzelerationsprinzip n	acceleration principle		principio di accelerazione m	principio de aceleracaión m
principe du pollueur payeur (F)	Verursacherprinzip n	polluter pays principle		principio della colpa oggettiva m	principio contaminador-pagador m
principes budgétaires (F)	Budgetgrundsätze f	budget principles		principi di bilancio m pl	principios presupuestarios m pl
principi di bilancio (I)	Budgetgrundsätze f	budget principles	principes budgétaires m pl	—	principios presupuestarios m pl
principio contaminador-pagador (Es)	Verursacherprinzip n	polluter pays principle	principe du pollueur payeur m	principio della colpa oggettiva m	—
principio de aceleración (Es)	Akzelerationsprinzip n	acceleration principle	principe d'accélération m	principio di accelerazione m	—
principio della colpa oggettiva (I)	Verursacherprinzip n	polluter pays principle	principe du pollueur payeur m	—	principio contaminador-pagador m
principio di accelerazione (I)	Akzelerationsprinzip n	acceleration principle	principe d'accélération m	—	principio de aceleración m
principios presupuestarios (Es)	Budgetgrundsätze f	budget principles	principes budgétaires m pl	principi di bilancio m pl	—
printed form (E)	Vordruck m	—	imprimé m	modulo m	impreso m
printed matter (E)	Drucksache f	—	imprimé m	stampa f	impreso m
printed papers or samples of merchandise posted in bulk (E)	Postwurfsendung f	—	envoi publicitaire collectif m	spedizione postale cumulativa di stampati f	envío postal colectivo m
printer (E)	Drucker m	—	imprimante f	stampante f	impresora f
prise de position (F)	Stellungnahme f	comment	—	presa di posizione f	dictamen m
private account (E)	Privatkonto n	—	compte privé m	conto privato m	cuenta particular f
private contribution (E)	Privateinlagen pl	—	apport personnel m	depositi privati m pl	depósitos privados m pl
private household (E)	privater Haushalt m	—	ménage privé m	famiglia f	economía doméstica f
Privateigentum (D)	—	private property	propriété privée f	proprietà privata f	propiedad privada f
Privateinlagen (D)	—	private contribution	apport personnel m	depositi privati m pl	depósitos privados m pl
private insurance (E)	Privatversicherung f	—	assurance privée f	assicurazione privata f	seguro privado m
Privatentnahmen (D)	—	personal drawings	prélèvement personnel m	prelevamento a titolo personale m	detracción privada f
private property (E)	Privateigentum n	—	propriété privée f	proprietà privata f	propiedad privada f
privater Haushalt (D)	—	private household	ménage privé m	famiglia f	economía doméstica f
private sector of the economy (E)	Privatwirtschaft f	—	économie privée f	economia privata f	economía privada f
privatisation (F)	Privatisierung f	denationalization	—	privatizzazione f	privatización f
privatisation partielle (F)	Teilprivatisierung f	partial denationalization	—	privatizzazione parziale f	privatización parcial f
Privatisierung (D)	—	denationalization	privatisation f	privatizzazione f	privatización f
privatización (Es)	Privatisierung f	denationalization	privatisation f	privatizzazione f	—
privatización parcial (Es)	Teilprivatisierung f	partial denationalization	privatisation partielle f	privatizzazione parziale f	—
privatizzazione (I)	Privatisierung f	denationalization	privatisation f	—	privatización f

	D	E	F	I	Es
privatizzazione parziale (I)	Teilprivatisierung f	partial denationalization	privatisation partielle f	—	privatización parcial f
Privatkonto (D)	—	private account	compte privé m	conto privato m	cuenta particular f
Privatversicherung (D)	—	private insurance	assurance privée f	assicurazione privata f	seguro privado m
Privatwirtschaft (D)	—	private sector of the economy	économie privée f	economia privata f	economía privada f
privilege (E)	Vorrecht n	—	prérogative f	privilegio m	derecho preferente m
privilegio (I)	Vorrecht n	privilege	prérogative f	—	derecho preferente m
privo di fosfato (I)	phosphatfrei	free of phosphate	sans phosphate	—	sin fosfato
prix (F)	Preis m	price	—	prezzo m	precio m
prix administrés (F)	administrierte Preise pl	administered prices	—	prezzi amministrati m pl	precios administrados m pl
prix agricole (F)	Agrarpreis m	prices of farm products	—	prezzo agrario m	precio agrícola m
prix à la production (F)	Erzeugerpreis m	producer price	—	prezzo di fabbrica m	precio de producción m
prix au tarif (F)	Listenpreis m	list price	—	prezzo di listino m	precio-lista m
prix brut (F)	Bruttopreis m	gross price	—	prezzo lordo m	precio bruto m
prix coûtant¹ (F)	Einstandspreis m	cost price	—	prezzo di costo m	precio de coste m
prix coûtant² (F)	Selbstkostenpreis m	cost price	—	prezzo di costo m	precio de coste m
prix d'achat (F)	Einkaufspreis m	purchase price	—	prezzo d'acquisto m	precio de compra m
prix d'amateur (F)	Liebhaberpreis m	connoisseur's price	—	prezzo d'affezione m	precio afectivo m
prix de gros (F)	Großhandelspreise pl	wholesale prices	—	prezzo all'ingrosso m	precio mayorista m
prix de location (F)	Mietzins m	rent	—	canone di locazione m	arrendamiento m
prix de l'ór (F)	Goldpreis m	gold price	—	prezzo dell'oro m	precio del oro m
prix de revente (F)	Wiederverkaufspreis m	resale price	—	prezzo di rivendita m	precio de reventa m
prix de revient (F)	Herstellungswert m	production value	—	valore di produzione m	valor de fabricación m
prix de seuil (F)	Schwellenpreis m	threshold price	—	prezzo soglia m	precio-base m
prix de vente (F)	Ladenpreis m	retail price	—	prezzo di vendita m	precio de venta m
prix d'orientation (F)	Orientierungspreis m	guide price	—	prezzo d'orientamento m	precio de orientación m
prix du marché mondial (F)	Weltmarktpreis m	world market price	—	prezzo di mercato mondiale m	precio del mercado mundial m
prix d'un achat à tempérament (F)	Teilzahlungspreis m	partial payment price	—	prezzo rateale m	precio de compras a plazo m
prix du pétrole brut (F)	Rohölpreis m	crude oil price	—	prezzo del petrolio greggio m	precio del crudo m
prix du terrain (F)	Bodenpreis m	land price	—	prezzo del suolo m	precio de suelo m
prix échelonné (F)	Staffelpreis m	graduated price	—	prezzo differenziato m	precios escalonados m pl
prix équilibré (F)	Gleichgewichtspreis m	equilibrium price	—	prezzo d'equilibrio m	precio de equilibrio m
prix fictifs (F)	Mondpreise pl	ficticious prices	—	prezzi alle stelle m pl	precios ficticios m pl
prix fixe (F)	Festpreis m	fixed price	—	prezzo fisso m	precio fijo m
prix indicatif (F)	Richtpreis m	recommended retail price	—	prezzo indicativo m	precio indicativo m
prix minimum (F)	Mindestpreis m	minimum price	—	prezzo minimo m	precio mínimo m
prix minimum d'importation (F)	Mindesteinfuhrpreise pl	minimum import price	—	prezzi minimi all'importazione m pl	precio mínimo a la importación m
prix net (F)	Nettopreis m	net price	—	prezzo netto m	precio neto m
prix plafond (F)	Höchstpreis m	top price	—	prezzo massimo m	precio máximo m
prix sans engagement (F)	Preis freibleibend	open price	—	prezzo non vincolante m	precio sin compromiso m
prix unique (F)	Einheitspreis m	uniform price	—	prezzo unitario m	precio único m
probar (Es)	probieren	try	essayer	provare	—
Probeauftrag (D)	—	trial order	ordre d'essai m	ordine a titolo di prova m	pedido de prueba m
Probelieferung (D)	—	trial shipment	livraison à titre d'essai f	fornitura a titolo di prova f	envío de prueba m

procura generale

	D	E	F	I	Es
Probepackung (D)	—	trial package	échantillon m	confezione campione f	muestra f
Probezeit (D)	—	trial period	période d'essai f	periodo di prova m	período de prueba m
probieren (D)	—	try	essayer	provare	probar
pro capite (I)	pro Kopf	per capita	par tête d'habitant	—	per cápita
procedimento¹ (I)	Verfahren n	procedure/process	méthode f/ procédure f	—	proceso m/ procedimiento m
procedimento² (I)	Prozeß m	process	processus m	—	proceso m
procedimento produttivo (I)	Fertigungs- verfahren n	production process	méthode de production f	—	procedimiento de fabricación m
procedimiento conciliatorio (Es)	Vergleichs- verfahren n	composition proceedings	procédure de conciliation f	procedura di concordato f	—
procedimiento de fabricación (Es)	Fertigungs- verfahren n	production process	méthode de production f	procedimento produttivo m	—
procedimiento de quiebra (Es)	Konkursverfahren n	proceedings in bankruptcy	procédure de faillite f	procedura fallimentare f	—
procedura d'ammis- sione in franchigia (I)	Zollfreischreibungs- verfahren n	procedure of duty free admission	régime de l'admission en franchise m	—	régimen de admisión en franquicia m
procedura del credito documentario (I)	Akkreditiv- abwicklung f	settlement by letter of credit	exécution par crédit documentaire f	—	ejecución por crédito documentario f
procedura di concordato (I)	Vergleichsverfahren n	composition proceedings	procédure de conciliation f	—	procedimiento conciliatorio m
procedura fallimentare (I)	Konkursverfahren n	proceedings in bankruptcy	procédure de faillite f	—	procedimiento de quiebra m
procédure de conciliation (F)	Vergleichsverfahren n	composition proceedings	—	procedura di concordato f	procedimiento conciliatorio m
procédure de faillite (F)	Konkursverfahren n	proceedings in bankruptcy	—	procedura fallimentare f	procedimiento de quiebra m
procedure doganali (I)	Zollverkehr m	customs procedure	régime douanier m	—	régimen aduanero de mercancías m
procedure of duty free admission (E)	Zollfreischreibungs- verfahren n	—	régime de l'admission en franchise m	procedura d'ammis- sione in franchigia f	régimen de admisión en franquicia m
proceedings in bankruptcy (E)	Konkursverfahren n	—	procédure de faillite f	procedura fallimentare f	procedimiento de quiebra m
proceeds (E)	Erlös m	—	produit des ventes m	ricavo m	beneficio m
procesamiento de datos (Es)	Datenverarbeitung f	data processing	traitement des information m	elaborazione dati f	—
proceso¹ (Es)	Prozeß m	process	processus m	procedimento m	—
proceso² (Es)	Verfahren n	procedure/process	méthode f/ procédure f	procedimento m/ procedura f	—
proceso de producción¹ (Es)	Fertigungsprozeß m	production procedure	déroulement de la fabrication m	processo produttivo m	—
proceso de producción² (Es)	Produktionsprozeß m	process of production	processus de production m	processo produttivo m	—
process¹ (E)	Prozeß m	—	processus m	procedimento m	proceso m
process² (E)	aufbereiten	—	élaborer/traiter	elaborare/lavorare	elaborar/tratar
processing¹ (E)	Veredelung f	—	perfectionnement m	perfezionamento m	perfeccionamiento m
processing² (E)	Verarbeitung f	—	transformation f	lavorazione f	transformación f
process of production (E)	Produktionsprozeß m	—	processus de production m	processo produttivo m	proceso de producción m
processo produttivo¹ (I)	Fertigungsprozeß m	production procedure	déroulement de la fabrication m	—	proceso de producción m
processo produttivo² (I)	Produktionsprozeß m	process of production	processus de production m	—	proceso de producción m
processus (F)	Prozeß m	process	—	procedimento m	proceso m
processus de production (F)	Produktionsprozeß m	process of production	—	processo produttivo m	proceso de producción m
procès-verbal (F)	Protokoll n	record/minutes	—	protocollo m/ verbale m	protocolo m/acta f
procès-verbal de fondation (F)	Gründungsbericht m	formation report	—	relazione di costituzione f	informe de los fundadores m
procura (I)	Prokura f	Prokura (procuration)	procuration commer- ciale générale f	—	poder general m
procura generale (I)	Generalvollmacht f	general power	pouvoir général m	—	poder general m

	D	E	F	I	Es
procuration commer-ciale générale (F)	Prokura *f*	Prokura (procuration)	—	procura *f*	poder general *m*
procuratore (I)	Prokurist *m*	Prokurist (authorized clerk)	fondé de procuration *m*	—	apoderado general *m*
prodotto (I)	Produkt *n*	product	produit *m*	—	producto *m*
prodotto agricolo[1] (I)	Agrarprodukt *n*	farm produce	produit agricole *m*	—	producto agrario *m*
prodotto agricolo[2] (I)	Agrarerzeugnis *n*	agricultural produce	produit agricole *m*	—	producto agrícola *m*
prodotto finito[1] (I)	Endprodukt *n*	finished product	produit final *m*	—	producto final *m*
prodotto finito[2] (I)	Fertigprodukt *n*	finished product	produit fini *m*	—	producto acabado *m*
prodotto interno lordo (I)	Bruttoinlands-produkt *n*	gross domestic product	produit intérieur brut *m*	—	producto interior bruto *m*
prodotto nazionale (I)	Sozialprodukt *n*	national product	produit national *m*	—	producto nacional *m*
prodotto nazionale lordo (I)	Bruttosozialprodukt *n*	gross national product	produit national brut *m*	—	producto nacional bruto *m*
prodotto nazionale netto (I)	Nettosozialprodukt *n*	net national product	produit national net *m*	—	producto nacional neto *m*
prodotto secondario (I)	Nebenprodukt *n*	by-product	produit dérivé *m*	—	producto accesorio *m*
prodotto semifinito (I)	Halberzeugnis *n*	semi-finished product	produit demi-fini *m*	—	producto semielaborado *m*
prodotto senza nome (I)	No-name-Produkt *n*	generic product	produit sans nom *m*	—	producto genérico *m*
prodotto su misura (I)	maßgefertigt	manufactured to measure	travaillé sur mesure	—	hecho a medida
producción (Es)	Produktion *f*	production	production *f*	produzione *f*	—
producción bruta (Es)	Bruttoproduktion *f*	gross production	production brutte *f*	produzione lorda *f*	—
producción de materias primas (Es)	Rohstoffgewinnung *f*	raw material production	extraction de matières premières *f*	produzione delle materie prime *f*	—
producción en masa (Es)	Massenproduktion *f*	mass production	production en grandes séries *f*	produzione di massa *f*	—
producción en serie (Es)	Serienfertigung *f*	series production	fabrication de série *f*	produzione in serie *f*	—
producción neta (Es)	Nettoproduktion *f*	net production	production nette *f*	produzione netta *f*	—
produce or to buy in addition (E)	Herstellen-oder-Zukaufen	—	produire ou acheter additionnellement	produrre o comprare in aggiunta	producir o comprar adicionalmente
producer[1] (E)	Hersteller *m*	—	fabricant *m*	produttore *m*	fabricante *m*
producer[2] (E)	Produzent *m*	—	producteur *m*	produttore *m*	productor *m*
producer goods industry (E)	Produktionsgüter-Industrie *f*	—	industrie des biens de production *f*	industria dei beni strumentali *f*	industria de bienes de producción *f*
producer price (E)	Erzeugerpreis *m*	—	prix à la production *m*	prezzo di fabbrica *m*	precio de producción *m*
producer price index (E)	Erzeugerpreisindex *m*	—	indice des prix à la production *m*	indice dei prezzi di fabbrica *m*	índice de precios de producción *m*
producer's cooperative (E)	Produktions-genossenschaft *f*	—	société coopérative de production *f*	cooperativa di produzione *f*	cooperativa de producción *f*
producer's surplus (E)	Produzentenrente *f*	—	rente du vendeur *f*	rendita del produttore *f*	superávit del productor *m*
producir o comprar adicionalmente (Es)	Herstellen-oder-Zukaufen	produce or to buy in addition	produire ou acheter additionnellement	produrre o comprare in aggiunta	—
product (E)	Produkt *n*	—	produit *m*	prodotto *m*	producto *m*
product design (E)	Produktgestaltung *f*	—	présentation d'un produit *f*	creazione del prodotto *f*	diseño del producto *m*
producteur[1] (F)	Erzeuger *m*	manufacturer	—	produttore *m*	productor *m*
producteur[2] (F)	Produzent *m*	producer	—	produttore *m*	productor *m*
production (E)	Produktion *f*	—	production *f*	produzione *f*	producción *f*
production (F)	Produktion *f*	production	—	produzione *f*	producción *f*
production agricole (F)	Ackerbau *m*	agriculture	—	agricoltura *f*	agricultura *f*
production brutte (F)	Bruttoproduktion *f*	gross production	—	produzione lorda *f*	producción bruta *m*
production capacity (E)	Produktions-kapazität *f*	—	capacité de production *f*	capacità produttiva *f*	capacidad de producción *f*
production control (E)	Produktions-kontrolle *f*	—	contrôle de la production *m*	controllo della produzione *m*	control de producción *m*
production costs (E)	Herstellungskosten *pl*	—	frais de fabrication *m pl*	costi di produzione *m pl*	costo de la producción *m*

	D	E	F	I	Es
production couplée (F)	Koppelproduktion f	tied production	—	produzione abbinata f	coproducción f
production en grandes séries (F)	Massenproduktion f	mass production	—	produzione di massa f	producción en masa f
production en série (F)	Massenfertigung f	mass production	—	fabbricazione di massa f	fabricación en masa f
production facilities (E)	Produktions-anlagen pl	—	installations industrielles f pl	impianti di produzione m pl	instalaciones de producción f pl
production limit (E)	Förderlimit n	—	limite de production f	limite d'estrazione m	límite de producción m
production nette (F)	Nettoproduktion f	net production	—	produzione netta f	producción neta f
production plan (E)	Produktionsplan m	—	plan de production m	piano di produzione m	plan de producción m
production potential (E)	Produktions-potential n	—	potentiel de production m	potenziale produttivo m	potencial productivo m
production procedure (E)	Fertigungs-prozeß m	—	déroulement de la fabrication m	processo produttivo m	proceso de producción m
production process (E)	Fertigungsverfahren n	—	méthode de production f	procedimento produttivo m	procedimiento de fabricación m
production programme[1] (E)	Produktions-programm n	—	gamme f	programma di produzione m	programa de producción m
production programme[2] (E)	Fertigungs-programm n	—	programme de fabrication m	programma di produzione m	programa de producción m
production quota (E)	Förderquote f	—	quote-part de production f	quota d'estrazione f	cuota de producción f
production scheduling (E)	Produktlinie f	—	ligne des produits f	linea dei prodotti f	línea de productos f
production theory (E)	Produktionstheorie f	—	théorie de la production f	teoria della produzione f	teoría de producción f
production value[1] (E)	Produktionswert m	—	valeur de production f	valore produttivo m	valor de la producción m
production value[2] (E)	Herstellungswert m	—	prix de revient m	valore di produzione m	valor de fabricación m
productive property (E)	Produktivvermögen n	—	capital productif m	patrimonio produttivo m	patrimonio productivo m
productividad[1] (Es)	Produktivität f	productivity	productivité f	produttività f	—
productividad[2] (Es)	Arbeitsleistung f	productivity	rendement m	produttività f	—
productividad del capital (Es)	Kapitalproduktivität f	productivity of capital	productivité du capital f	produttività del capitale f	—
productivité (F)	Produktivität f	productivity	—	produttività f	productividad f
productivité du capital (F)	Kapitalproduktivität f	productivity of capital	—	produttività del capitale f	prodicutividad del capital f
productivity[1] (E)	Produktivität f	—	productivité f	produttività f	productividad f
productivity[2] (E)	Arbeitsleistung f	—	rendement m	produttività f	productividad f
productivity of capital (E)	Kapitalproduktivität f	—	productivité du capital f	produttività del capitale f	prodicutividad del capital f
product liability[1] (E)	Produkthaftung f	—	responsabilité du fabricant f	responsabilità prodotto f	responsabilidad del productor f
product liability[2] (E)	Produzentenhaftung f	—	responsabilité du producteur f	responsabilità di produttore f	responsabilidad civil del fabricante f
product line (E)	Warengruppe f	—	groupe de marchandises m	gruppo merci m	grupo de mercancías m
producto (Es)	Produkt n	product	produit m	prodotto m	—
producto acabado (Es)	Fertigprodukt n	finished product	produit fini m	prodotto finito m	—
producto accesorio (Es)	Nebenprodukt n	by-product	produit dérivé m	prodotto secondario m	—
producto agrario (Es)	Agrarprodukt n	farm produce	produit agricole m	prodotto agricolo m	—
producto agrícola (Es)	Agrarerzeugnis n	agricultural produce	produit agricole m	prodotto agricolo m	—
producto bruto (Es)	Rohertrag m	gross proceeds	produit brut m	reddito lordo m	—
producto de la venta (Es)	Verkaufserlös m	sale proceeds	produit des ventes m	ricavo delle vendite m	—
producto final (Es)	Endprodukt n	finished product	produit final m	prodotto finito m	—
producto genérico (Es)	No-name-Produkt n	generic product	produit sans nom m	prodotto senza nome m	—

	D	E	F	I	Es
producto interior bruto (Es)	Bruttoinlands-produkt *n*	gross domestic product	produit intérieur brut *m*	prodotto interno lordo *m*	—
producto nacional (Es)	Sozialprodukt *n*	national product	produit national *m*	prodotto nazionale *m*	—
producto nacional bruto (Es)	Bruttosozialprodukt *n*	gross national product	produit national brut *m*	prodotto nazionale lordo *m*	—
producto nacional neto (Es)	Nettosozialprodukt *n*	net national product	produit national net *m*	prodotto nazionale netto *m*	—
producto neto (Es)	Nettoertrag *m*	net earnings	produit net *m*	ricavo netto *m*	—
productor¹ (Es)	Erzeuger *m*	manufacturer	producteur *m*	produttore *m*	—
productor² (Es)	Produzent *m*	producer	producteur *m*	produttore *m*	—
productos a granel (Es)	Massengüter *pl*	bulk goods	marchandises en vrac *f pl*	beni di massa *m pl*	—
producto semielaborado (Es)	Halberzeugnis *n*	semi-finished good	produit demi-fini *m*	prodotto semifinito *m*	—
produire ou acheter additionnellement (F)	Herstellen-oder-Zukaufen	produce or to buy in addition	—	produrre o comprare in aggiunta	producir o comprar adicionalmente
produit (F)	Produkt *n*	product	—	prodotto *m*	producto *m*
produit agricole¹ (F)	Agrarprodukt *n*	farm produce	—	prodotto agricolo *m*	producto agrario *m*
produit agricole² (F)	Agrarerzeugnis *n*	agricultural produce	—	prodotto agricolo *m*	producto agrícola *m*
produit brut (F)	Rohertrag *m*	gross proceeds	—	reddito lordo *m*	producto bruto *m*
produit de la liquidation (F)	Liquidationserlös *m*	remaining assets after liquidation	—	ricavo della liquidazione *m*	haber social repartible *m*
produit de marque (F)	Markenartikel *m*	brandname article	—	articolo di marca *m*	artículo de marca *m*
produit demi-fini (F)	Halberzeugnis *n*	semi-finished product	—	prodotto semifinito *m*	producto semielaborado *m*
produit dérivé (F)	Nebenprodukt *n*	by-product	—	prodotto secondario *m*	producto accesorio *m*
produit de stockage (F)	Stapelware *f*	staple commodities	—	merce immagazzinata *f*	mercancía almacenada *f*
produit des ventes¹ (F)	Verkaufserlös *m*	sale proceeds	—	ricavo delle vendite *m*	producto de la venta *m*
produit des ventes² (F)	Erlös *m*	proceeds	—	ricavo *m*	beneficio *m*
produit du capital (F)	Kapitalertrag *m*	income from capital	—	rendita del capitale *f*	rendimiento del capital *m*
produit final (F)	Endprodukt *n*	finished product	—	prodotto finito *m*	producto final *m*
produit fini (F)	Fertigprodukt *n*	finished product	—	prodotto finito *m*	producto acabado *m*
produit intérieur brut (F)	Bruttoinlands-produkt *n*	gross domestic product	—	prodotto interno lordo *m*	producto interior brutom
produit national (F)	Sozialprodukt *n*	national product	—	prodotto nazionale *m*	producto nacional *m*
produit national brut (F)	Bruttosozialprodukt *n*	gross national product	—	prodotto nazionale lordo *m*	producto nacional bruto *m*
produit national net (F)	Nettosozialprodukt *n*	net national product	—	prodotto nazionale netto *m*	producto nacional neto *m*
produit net (F)	Nettoertrag *m*	net earnings	—	ricavo netto *m*	producto neto *m*
produit pondéreux (F)	Schwergut *n*	heavy freight	—	carico pesante *m*	mercancía pesada *f*
produits agricoles (F)	Agrargüter *pl*	agricultural goods	—	beni agricoli *m pl*	bienes agrícolas *m pl*
produit sans nom (F)	No-name-Produkt *n*	generic product	—	prodotto senza nome *m*	producto genérico *m*
produits de complément (F)	komplementäre Güter *pl*	complementary goods	—	beni complementari *m pl*	bienes comple-mentarios *m pl*
produits de luxe (F)	Luxusgüter *pl*	luxury goods	—	beni di lusso *m pl*	bienes de lujo *m pl*
Produkt (D)	—	product	produit *m*	prodotto *m*	producto *m*
Produktgestaltung (D)	—	product design	présentation d'un produit *f*	creazione del prodotto *f*	diseño del producto *m*
Produkthaftung (D)	—	product liability	responsabilité du fabricant *f*	responsabilità prodotto *f*	responsabilidad del productor *f*
Produktion (D)	—	production	production *f*	produzione *f*	producción *f*
Produktionsanlagen (D)	—	production facilities	installations industrielles *f pl*	impianti di produzione *m pl*	instalaciones de producción *f pl*
Produktionsausfall (D)	—	loss of production	perte dans la production *f*	perdita di produzione *f*	pérdida de producción *f*
Produktionsfaktoren (D)	—	factors of production	facteurs de production *m pl*	fattori di produzione *m pl*	factores de producción *m pl*

	D	E	F	I	Es
Produktions-genossenschaft (D)	—	producer's cooperative	société coopérative de production *f*	cooperativa di produzione *f*	cooperativa de producción *f*
Produktionsgüter-Industrie (D)	—	producer goods industry	industrie des biens de production *f*	industria dei beni strumentali *f*	industria de bienes de producción *f*
Produktions-kapazität (D)	—	production capacity	capacité de production *f*	capacità produttiva *f*	capacidad de producción *f*
Produktions-kontrolle (D)	—	production control	contrôle de la production *m*	controllo della produzione *m*	control de producción *m*
Produktionskosten (D)	—	cost of production	coût de production *m*	costi produttivi *m pl*	gastos de producción *m pl*
Produktionsplan (D)	—	production plan	plan de production *m*	piano di produzione *m*	plan de producción *m*
Produktions-potential (D)	—	production potential	potentiel de production *m*	potenziale produttivo *m*	potencial productivo *m*
Produktions-programm (D)	—	production programme	gamme *f*	programma di produzione *m*	programa de producción *m*
Produktionsprozeß (D)	—	process of production	processus de production *m*	processo produttivo *m*	proceso de producción *m*
Produktions-schwankung (D)	—	fluctuations in production	fluctuation de la production *f pl*	oscillazione della produzione *f*	fluctuaciones en la producción *f pl*
Produktionstheorie (D)	—	production theory	théorie de la production *f*	teoria della produzione *f*	teoría de producción *f*
Produktionswert (D)	—	production value	valeur de production *f*	valore produttivo *m*	valor de la producción *m*
Produktivität (D)	—	productivity	productivité *f*	produttività *f*	productividad *f*
Produktivvermögen (D)	—	productive property	capital productif *m*	patrimonio produttivo *m*	patrimonio productivo *m*
Produktlinie (D)	—	production scheduling	ligne des produits *f*	linea dei prodotti *f*	línea de productos *f*
Produktpalette (D)	—	range of products	gamme des produits *f*	gamma dei prodotti *f*	gama de productos *f*
produrre o comprare in aggiunta (I)	Herstellen-oder-Zukaufen	produce or buy in addition	produire ou acheter additionnellement	—	producir o comprar adicionalmente
produttività[1] (I)	Produktivität *f*	productivity	productivité *f*	—	productividad *f*
produttività[2] (I)	Arbeitsleistung *f*	productivity	rendement *m*	—	productividad *f*
produttività del capitale (I)	Kapitalproduktivität *f*	productivity of capital	productivité du capital *f*	—	producituvidad del capital *f*
produttore[1] (I)	Erzeuger *m*	manufacturer	producteur *m*	—	productor *m*
produttore[2] (I)	Hersteller *m*	producer	fabricant *m*	—	fabricante *m*
produttore[3] (I)	Produzent *m*	producer	producteur *m*	—	productor *m*
Produzent (D)	—	producer	producteur *m*	produttore *m*	productor *m*
Produzentenhaftung (D)	—	product liability	responsabilité du producteur *f*	responsabilità di produttore *f*	responsabilidad civil del fabricante *f*
Produzentenrente (D)	—	producer's surplus	rente du vendeur *f*	rendita del produttore *f*	superávit del productor *m*
produzione (I)	Produktion *f*	production	production *f*	—	producción *f*
produzione abbinata (I)	Koppelproduktion *f*	tied production	production couplée *f*	—	coproducción *f*
produzione delle materie prime (I)	Rohstoffgewinnung *f*	raw material production	extraction de matières premières *f*	—	producción de materias primas *f*
produzione di massa (I)	Massenproduktion *f*	mass production	production en grandes séries *f*	—	producción en masa *f*
produzione eccessiva (I)	Überproduktion *f*	overproduction	surproduction *f*	—	sobreproducción *f*
produzione fuori serie (I)	Sonderanfertigung *f*	manufacture to customer's specifications	fabrication spéciale *f*	—	fabricación especial *f*
produzione in serie (I)	Serienfertigung *f*	series production	fabrication de série *f*	—	producción en serie *f*
produzione lorda (I)	Bruttoproduktion *f*	gross production	production brutte *f*	—	producción bruta *m*
produzione netta (I)	Nettoproduktion *f*	net production	production nette *f*	—	producción neta *f*
profesión (Es)	Beruf *m*	profession	profession *f*	professione *f*	—
profesional (Es)	Freiberufler *m*	self-employed person	personne exerçant une profession libérale *f*	libero professionista *m*	—
profession (E)	Beruf *m*	—	profession *f*	professione *f*	profesión *f*
profession (F)	Beruf *m*	profession	—	professione *f*	profesión *f*

	D	E	F	I	Es
professional discretion (E)	Schweigepflicht f	—	discretion professionnelle f	obbligo del segreto professionale m	secreto profesional m
professional fee (E)	Honorar n	—	honoraires m pl	onorario m	honorario m
professional knowledge (E)	Fachwissen n	—	connaissances professionnelles f pl	cognizioni professionali f pl	conocimientos especializados m pl
professional secret (E)	Berufsgeheimnis n	—	secret professionnel m	segreto professionale m	secreto profesional m
professional training (E)	Berufsausbildung f	—	formation professionnelle f	formazione professionale f	formación profesional f
professione (I)	Beruf m	profession	profession f	—	profesión f
Profit (D)	—	profit	profit m	profitto m	beneficio m
profit¹ (E)	Gewinn m	—	bénéfice m	utile m	beneficio m/ superávit m
profit² (E)	Profit m	—	profit m	profitto m	beneficio m
profit (F)	Profit m	profit	—	profitto m	beneficio m
profitability (E)	Rentabilität f	—	rentabilité f	redditività f	rentabilidad f
profit account (E)	Erfolgskonto n	—	compte de résultats m	conto profitti m	cuenta de beneficios y pérdidas f
profit and loss account¹ (E)	Ertragsrechnung f	—	solde net de l'exploitation m	conto economico m	cuenta de ganancias f pl
profit and loss account² (E)	Gewinn- und Verlustrechnung f	—	compte de pertes et profits m	conto profitti e perdite m	cuenta de pérdidas y ganancias f
profit de rationalisation (F)	Rationalisierungs- gewinn m	rationalization profit	—	profitto di razionalizzazione m	beneficio de racionalización m
profit margin (E)	Gewinnmarge f	—	marge bénéficiaire f	margine dell'utile m	margen de beneficios f
profit mark-up (E)	Gewinnaufschlag m	—	majoration de bénéfice f	maggiorazione dell'utile f	margen de benificio f
profit of the enterprise (E)	Unternehmens- gewinn m	—	bénéfice d'exploitation m	utile d'impresa m	beneficio empresarial m
Profitrate (D)	—	profit rate	taux de profit m	tasso di profitto m	tasa de beneficio f
profit rate (E)	Profitrate f	—	taux de profit m	tasso di profitto m	tasa de beneficio f
profitto (I)	Profit m	profit	profit m	—	beneficio m
profitto di razionalizzazione (I)	Rationalisierungs- gewinn m	rationalization profit	profit de rationalisation m	—	beneficio de racionalización m
pro forma invoice (E)	Proforma-Rechnung f	—	facture pro forma f	fattura pro forma f	factura proforma f
Proforma-Rechnung (D)	—	pro forma invoice	facture pro forma f	fattura pro forma f	factura proforma f
progettazione della costituzione (I)	Gründungsplanung f	formation plan	planification de fondation f	—	planificación de la fundación f
progetto (I)	Entwurf m	draft	projet m	—	proyecto m
Prognose (D)	—	forecast(ing)	perspective f	prognosi f	pronóstico m
Prognosetechnik (D)	—	forecasting techniques	technique de pronostic f	tecnica della prognosi f	técnica de pronóstico f
prognosi (I)	Prognose f	forecast(ing)	perspective f	—	pronóstico m
prognosi del fatturato (I)	Umsatzprognose f	turnover forecast	prévision de l'évolution du chiffre d'affaires f	—	previsión de la evolución del volumen de ventas f
programa (Es)	Programm n	programme	programme m	programma m	—
programación (Es)	Programmierung f	programming	programmation f	programmazione f	—
programación lineal (Es)	lineare Programmierung f	linear programmation	programmation linéaire f	programmazione lineare f	—
programa de entrega (Es)	Lieferprogramm n	delivery programme	programme de livraison m	programma di fornitura m	—
programa de producción¹ (Es)	Fertigungs- programm n	production programme	programme de fabrication m	programma di produzione m	—
programa de producción² (Es)	Produktions- programm n	production programme	gamme f	programma di produzione m	—
programa de venta (Es)	Verkaufsprogramm n	sales programme	programme de vente m	programma di vendita m	—
programador (Es)	Programmierer m	programmer	programmeur m	programmatore m	—
Programa Europeo de Recuperación (Es)	Europäisches Wieder- aufbauprogramm n	European Recovery Programme	Programme Européen de Récupération m	Programma di Rico- struzione Europea m	—
Programm (D)	—	programme	programme m	programma m	programa m

	D	E	F	I	Es
programma (I)	Programm *n*	programme	programme *m*	—	programa *m*
programma del fatturato (I)	Umsatzplan *m*	turnover plan	plan du chiffre d'affaires *m*	—	objectivo de facturación *m*
programma dell'itinerario (I)	Tourenplan *m*	tour schedule	itinéraire *m*	—	itinerario *m*
programma di fornitura (I)	Lieferprogramm *n*	delivery programme	programme de livraison *m*	—	programa de entrega *m*
programma di produzione[1] (I)	Produktionsprogramm *n*	production programme	gamme *f*	—	programa de producción *m*
programma di produzione[2] (I)	Fertigungsprogramm *n*	production programme	programme de fabrication *m*	—	programa de producción *m*
programma di vendita (I)	Verkaufsprogramm *n*	sales programme	programme de vente *m*	—	programa de venta *m*
programmation (F)	Programmierung *f*	programming	—	programmazione *f*	programación *f*
programmation linéaire (F)	lineare Programmierung *f*	linear programmation	—	programmazione lineare *f*	programación lineal *f*
programmatore (I)	Programmierer *m*	programmer	programmeur *m*	—	programador *m*
programmazione[1] (I)	Planung *f*	planning	planning *m*	—	planificación *f*
programmazione[2] (I)	Programmierung *f*	programming	programmation *f*	—	programación *f*
programmazione dei termini (I)	Terminplanung *f*	scheduling	planning de rendez-vous *m*	—	planificación de plazos *f*
programmazione del bilancio (I)	Budgetplanung *f*	budgetary planning	planification du budget *f*	—	planificación del presupuesto *m*
programmazione delle ferie (I)	Urlaubsplanung *f*	vacation scheduling	planification des vacances *f*	—	planificación de las vacaciones *f*
programmazione del marketing (I)	Marketingplanung *f*	marketing planning	planning du marketing *m*	—	planificación de mercadeo *m*
programmazione lineare (I)	lineare Programmierung *f*	linear programmation	programmation linéaire *f*	—	programación lineal *f*
programme (E)	Programm *n*	—	programme *m*	programma *m*	programa *m*
programme (F)	Programm *n*	programme	—	programma *m*	programa *m*
programme de fabrication (F)	Fertigungsprogramm *n*	production programme	—	programma di produzione *m*	programa de producción *m*
programme de livraison (F)	Lieferprogramm *n*	delivery programme	—	programma di fornitura *m*	programa de entrega *m*
programme de vente (F)	Verkaufsprogramm *n*	sales programme	—	programma di vendita *m*	programa de venta *m*
programmer (E)	Programmierer *m*	—	programmeur *m*	programmatore *m*	programador *m*
programmeur (F)	Programmierer *m*	programmer	—	programmatore *m*	programador *m*
Programmierer (D)	—	programmer	programmeur *m*	programmatore *m*	programador *m*
Programmiersprache (D)	—	common business-oriented language	langage de programmation *m*	linguaggio di programmazione *m*	lenguaje de programación *m*
Programmierung (D)	—	programming	programmation *f*	programmazione *f*	programación *f*
programming (E)	Programmierung *f*	—	programmation *f*	programmazione *f*	programación *f*
progresión (Es)	Progression *f*	progression	progression *f*	progressione *f*	—
progressif (F)	gestaffelt	graduated	—	differenziato	escalonado
Progression (D)	—	progression	progression *f*	progressione *f*	progresión *f*
progression (E)	Progression *f*	—	progression *f*	progressione *f*	progresión *f*
progression (F)	Progression *f*	progression	—	progressione *f*	progresión *f*
progressione (I)	Progression *f*	progression	progression *f*	—	progresión *f*
progressive Abschreibung (D)	—	progressive depreciation	amortissement progressif *m*	ammortamento progressivo *m*	amortización progresiva *f*
progressive depreciation (E)	progressive Abschreibung *f*	—	amortissement progressif *m*	ammortamento progressivo *m*	amortización progresiva *f*
prohibición de competencia (Es)	Wettbewerbsverbot *n*	prohibition of competition	interdiction en matière de concurrence *f*	divieto di concorrenza *m*	—
prohibición de publicidad (Es)	Werbeverbot *n*	ban on advertising	défense de publicité *f*	divieto di pubblicità *m*	—
prohibition of competition (E)	Wettbewerbsverbot *n*	—	interdiction en matière de concurrence *f*	divieto di concorrenza *m*	prohibición de competencia *f*
prohibitive duty (E)	Prohibitivzoll *m*	—	droit prohibitif *m*	dazio proibitivo *m*	derechos prohibitivos *m pl*

	D	E	F	I	Es
Prohibitivzoll (D)	—	prohibitive duty	droit prohibitif *m*	dazio proibitivo *m*	derechos prohibitivos *m pl*
proiettore per diapositive (I)	Diaprojektor *m*	slide projector	projecteur pour diapositives *m*	—	projector de diapositivas *m*
proiezione (I)	Projektion *f*	projection	projection *f*	—	proyección *f*
proiezione degli obiettivi (I)	Zielprojektion *f*	target projection	projection d'objectifs *f*	—	proyección de objetivos *f*
projecteur pour diapositives (F)	Diaprojektor *m*	slide projector	—	proiettore per diapositive *m*	projector de diapositivas *m*
projection (E)	Projektion *f*	—	projection *f*	proiezione *f*	proyección *f*
projection (F)	Projektion *f*	projection	—	proiezione *f*	proyección *f*
projection d'objectifs (F)	Zielprojektion *f*	target projection	—	proiezione degli obiettivi *f*	proyección de objetivos *f*
project management (E)	Projekt-Management *n*	—	gestion d'un projet *f*	management di progetto *m*	administración del proyecto *f*
projector de diapositivas (Es)	Diaprojektor *m*	slide projector	projecteur pour diapositives *m*	proiettore per diapositive *m*	—
project write-off company (E)	Abschreibungsgesellschaft *f*	—	société d'amortissement *f*	società di ammortamento *f*	sociedad de amortización *f*
Projektion (D)	—	projection	projection *f*	proiezione *f*	proyección *f*
Projekt-Management (D)	—	project management	gestion d'un projet *f*	management di progetto *m*	administración del proyecto *f*
projet (F)	Entwurf *m*	draft	—	progetto *m*	proyecto *m*
pro Kopf (D)	—	per capita	par tête d'habitant	pro capite	per cápita
Prokura (D)	—	Prokura (procuration)	procuration commerciale générale *f*	procura *f*	poder general *m*
Prokura (E)	Prokura *f*	—	procuration commerciale générale *f*	procura *f*	poder general *m*
Prokurist (D)	—	Prokurist (authorized clerk)	fondé de procuration *m*	procuratore *m*	apoderado general *m*
Prokurist (E)	Prokurist *m*	—	fondé de procuration *m*	procuratore *m*	apoderado general *m*
prolongación (Es)	Prolongation *f*	extension/prolongation	prolongation *f*/report *m*	proroga *f*/riporto *m*	—
Prolongation (D)	—	extension/prolongation	prolongation *f*/report *m*	proroga *f*/riporto *m*	prolongación *f*/renovación *f*/prórroga *f*
prolongation¹ (F)	Nachfrist *f*	additional period	—	termine supplementare *m*	plazo de gracia *m*
prolongation² (F)	Prolongation *f*	extension/prolongation	—	proroga *f*/riporto *m*	prolongación *f*/renovación *f*/prórroga *f*
prolongation³ (F)	Verlängerung *f*	extension	—	prolungamento *m*	prórroga *f*
prolungamento (I)	Verlängerung *f*	extension	prolongation *f*	—	prórroga *f*
promedio (Es)	Durchschnitt *m*	average	moyenne *f*	media *f*	—
promesa (Es)	Zusage *f*	promise	promesse *f*	conferma *f*	—
promesa de créditos (Es)	Kreditzusage *f*	promise of credit	promesse de crédit *f*	consenso di credito *m*	—
promesse (F)	Zusage *f*	promise	—	conferma *f*	promesa *f*
promesse de crédit (F)	Kreditzusage *f*	promise of credit	—	consenso di credito *m*	promesa de créditos *f*
promise (E)	Zusage *f*	—	promesse *f*	conferma *f*	promesa *f*
promise of credit (E)	Kreditzusage *f*	—	promesse de crédit *f*	consenso di credito *m*	promesa de créditos *f*
promissory note (E)	Solawechsel *m*	—	seule lettre de change *f*	pagherò *m*	pagaré *m*
promoción comercial (Es)	Absatzförderung *f*	sales promotion	promotion des ventes *f*	promozione dello smercio *f*	—
promoción de las ventas (Es)	Verkaufsförderung *f*	sales promotion	encouragement à la vente *m*	promozione di vendita *f*	—
promotion (E)	Beförderung *f*	—	nomination *f*	promozione *f*	ascenso *m*
promotion de l'investissement (F)	Investitionsförderung *f*	investment promotion	—	promozione degli investimenti *f*	estímulo a la inversión *m*
promotion des ventes (F)	Absatzförderung *f*	sales promotion	—	promozione dello smercio *f*	promoción comercial *f*
promotion possibility (E)	Aufstiegsmöglichkeit *f*	—	perspectives de promotion *f pl*	possibilità di carriera *f*	posibilidades de ascenso *f pl*

	D	E	F	I	Es
promozione (I)	Beförderung f	promotion	nomination f	—	ascenso m
promozione degli investimenti (I)	Investitionsförderung f	investment promotion	promotion de l'investissement f	—	estímulo a la inversión m
promozione delle esportazioni (I)	Ausfuhrförderung f	measures to encourage exports	encouragement à l'exportation m	—	fomento de la exportació m
promozione dello smercio (I)	Absatzförderung f	sales promotion	promotion des ventes f	—	promoción comercial f
promozione di vendita (I)	Verkaufsförderung f	sales promotion	encouragement à la vente m	—	promoción de las ventas f
pronóstico (Es)	Prognose f	forecast(ing)	perspective f	prognosi f	—
pronto per il ritiro (I)	abholbereit	ready for collection	disponible		listo para la recogida
pronto per la spedizione (I)	versandbereit	ready for dispatch	prêt à être expédié	—	listo para ser expedido
proof (E)	Beweis m	—	preuve f	prova f	prueba f
propension à l'achat (F)	Kaufbereitschaft f	buying intention	—	propensione all'acquisto f	disposición a comprar f
propensione all'acquisto (I)	Kaufbereitschaft f	buying intention	propension à l'achat f	—	disposición a comprar f
property¹ (E)	Eigentum n	—	propriété f	proprietà f	propiedad f
property² (E)	Vermögen n	—	patrimoine m	patrimonio m	patrimonio m
property insurance (E)	Sachversicherung f	—	assurance de choses f	assicurazione di cose f	seguro de cosas m
property relations (E)	Eigentumsverhältnisse pl	—	régime de la propriété m	rapporti di proprietà m pl	régimen de tenencia m
property transactions (E)	Immobiliengeschäft n	—	affaire immobilière f	operazione immobiliare f	negocio de inmuebles m
propiedad (Es)	Eigentum n	property	propriété f	proprietà f	—
propiedad colectiva (Es)	Gemeinschaftseigentum n	collective property	propriété collective f	proprietà collettiva f	—
propiedad común (Es)	Gemeineigentum n	public property	propriété publique f	proprietà collettiva f	—
propiedad del Estado (Es)	Staatsbesitz m	government property	propriété de l'Etat f	demanio m	—
propiedad de vivienda (Es)	Wohnungseigentum n	ownership of a flat	propriété du logement f	proprietà edilizia f	—
propiedad privada (Es)	Privateigentum n	private property	propriété privée f	proprietà privata f	—
propietario (Es)	Inhaber m	proprietor	propriétaire m	proprietario m	—
propietario de una casa¹ (Es)	Hausbesitzer m	home property owner	propriétaire d'immeuble m	possessore di casa m	—
propietario de una casa² (Es)	Hauseigentümer m	owner of a house	propriétaire d'une maison m	proprietario di casa m	—
propietario exclusivo (Es)	Alleininhaber m	sole owner	seul propriétaire m	titolare unico m	—
propina (Es)	Bedienungsgeld n	tip	pourboire m	diritto di servizio m	—
proporción de la población activa (Es)	Erwerbsquote f	activity rate	proportion de la population active f	quota della popolazione attiva f	—
proportion (E)	Verhältnis n	—	relation f	rapporto m	relación f
proportion de garantie (F)	Deckungsbeitrag m	contribution margin	—	contributo per copertura m	aportación de cobertura f
proportion de la population active (F)	Erwerbsquote f	activity rate	—	quota della popolazione attiva f	proporción de la población activa f
proportion des frais afférents aux matières (F)	Materialkostenanteil m	share in the material costs	—	quota della popolazione attiva f	parte de los gastos de material m
proposal (E)	Vorschlag m	—	proposition f	proposta f	proposición f
proposición (Es)	Vorschlag m	proposal	proposition f	proposta f	—
proposition¹ (F)	Angebot n	offer	—	offerta f	oferta f
proposition² (F)	Vorschlag m	proposal	—	proposta f	proposición f
proposition d'amélioration (F)	Verbesserungsvorschlag m	suggestion for improvement	—	proposta di miglioramento f	propuesta de mejora f
proposta (I)	Vorschlag m	proposal	proposition f	—	proposición f
proposta di miglioramento (I)	Verbesserungsvorschlag m	suggestion for improvement	proposition d'amélioration f	—	propuesta de mejora f
proprietà (I)	Eigentum n	property	propriété f	—	propiedad f

	D	E	F	I	Es
proprietà collettiva¹ (I)	Gemeineigentum n	public property	proprietà publique f	—	propiedad común m
proprietà collettiva² (I)	Gemeinschafts-eigentum n	collective property	proprietà collective f	—	propiedad colectiva f
proprietà demaniale (I)	Staatseigentum n	public ownership	propriété d'Etat f	—	patrimonio público m
proprietà edilizia (I)	Wohnungs-eigentum n	ownership of a flat	propriété du logement f	—	propiedad de vivienda f
proprietaire (F)	Inhaber m	proprietor	—	proprietario m	propietario m
propriétaire d'immeuble (F)	Hausbesitzer m	home property owner	—	possessore di casa m	propietario de una casa m
propriétaire d'une maison (F)	Hauseigentümer m	owner of a house	—	proprietario di casa m	propietario de una casa m
proprietà privata (I)	Privateigentum n	private property	propriété privée f	—	propiedad privada f
proprietario (I)	Inhaber m	proprietor	propriétaire m	—	propietario m
proprietario di casa (I)	Hauseigentümer m	owner of a house	propriétaire d'une maison m	—	propietario de una casa m
propriété (F)	Eigentum n	property	—	proprietà f	propiedad f
propriété collective (F)	Gemeinschafts-eigentum n	collective property	—	proprietà collettiva f	propiedad colectiva f
propriété d'Etat (F)	Staatseigentum n	public ownership	—	proprietà demaniale f	patrimonio público m
propriété du logement (F)	Wohnungseigentum n	ownership of a flat	—	proprietà edilizia f	propiedad de vivienda f
propriété privée (F)	Privateigentum n	private property	—	proprietà privata f	propiedad privada f
propriété publique (F)	Gemeineigentum n	public property	—	proprietà collettiva f	propiedad común m
proprietor (E)	Inhaber m	—	propriétaire m	proprietario m	propietario m
propuesta de mejora (Es)	Verbesserungs-vorschlag m	suggestion for improvement	proposition d'amélioration f	proposta di miglioramento f	—
proroga (I)	Prolongation f	extension/prolongation	prolongation f/report m	—	prolongación f/renovación f/prórroga f
prorogation (F)	Stundung f	respite	—	dilazione f/proroga f	moratoria f
prórroga (Es)	Verlängerung f	extension	prolongation f	prolungamento m	—
prospecto (Es)	Prospekt m	leaflet/prospectus	feuille publicitaire f/prospectus m	prospetto m/dépliant m	—
prospectus (F)	Broschüre f	brochure	—	dépliant m	folleto m
Prospekt (D)	—	leaflet/prospectus	feuille publicitaire f/prospectus m	prospetto m/dépliant m	prospecto m/folleto m
prospérité (F)	Wohlstand m	prosperity	—	benessere m	bienestar m
prosperity (E)	Wohlstand m	—	prospérité f	benessere m	bienestar m
prospettiva (I)	Zukunftschance f	future prospects	perspectives d'avenir f pl	—	posibilidades futuras f pl
prospettiva dello smercio (I)	Verkaufschance f	sales possibilities	possibilité de vente f	—	posibilidades de venta f pl
prospettive di smercio (I)	Absatzchance f	sales prospects	possibilités de réussite des ventes f pl	—	posibilidades de venta f pl
prospetto (I)	Prospekt m	leaflet/prospectus	feuille publicitaire f/prospectus m	—	prospecto m/folleto m
protección (Es)	Protektion f	protection	protection f	protezione f	—
protección al arrendatario (Es)	Mieterschutz m	protection of tenants	protection en matière de location f	tutela del locatario f	—
protección contra el despido (Es)	Kündigungsschutz m	protection against dismissal	protection en matière de licenciement f	protezione contro il licenziamento f	—
protección contra incendios (Es)	Brandschutz m	protection against fire	protection contre l'incendie f	protezione antincendio f	—
protección de datos (Es)	Datensicherung f	data protection	protection de données f	protezione dei dati f	—
protección de la madre (Es)	Mutterschutz m	protection of motherhood	protection maternelle et infantile f	tutela della maternità f	—
protección del medio ambiente (Es)	Umweltschutz m	protection of the environment	protection de l'environnement f	tutela dell'ambiente f	—
protección de los acreedores (Es)	Gläubigerschutz m	protection of creditors	garantie des créanciers f	tutela del creditore f	—
protección de los consumidores¹ (Es)	Konsumenten-schutz m	consumer protection	protection des consommateurs f	tutela del consumatore f	—

	D	E	F	I	Es
protección de los consumidores² (Es)	Verbraucherschutz m	consumer protection	protection des consommateurs f	tutela dei consumatori f	—
protección de los datos (Es)	Datenschutz m	data securing	sauvegarde des données f	tutela dei dati f	—
protección del trabajo (Es)	Arbeitsschutz m	employment protection	protection sociale du travail f	tutela del lavoro f	—
proteccionismo (Es)	Protektionismus m	protectionism	protectionnisme m	protezionismo m	—
protección territorial (Es)	Gebietsschutz m	territory protection	exclusivité territoriale f	tutela territoriale f	—
protection (E)	Protektion f	—	protection f	protezione f	protección f
protection (F)	Protektion f	protection	—	protezione f	protección f
protection against dismissal (E)	Kündigungsschutz m	—	protection en matière de licenciement f	protezione contro il licenziamento f	protección contra el despido f
protection against fire (E)	Brandschutz m	—	protection contre l'incendie f	protezione antincendio f	protección contra incendios f
protection contre l'incendie (F)	Brandschutz m	protection against fire	—	protezione antincendio f	protección contra incendios f
protection de données (F)	Datensicherung f	data protection	—	protezione dei dati f	protección de datos f
protection de l'environnement (F)	Umweltschutz m	protection of the environment	—	tutela dell'ambiente f	protección del medio ambiente f
protection des consommateurs (F)	Verbraucherschutz m	consumer protection	—	tutela dei consumatori f	protección de los consumidores f
protection en matière de licenciement (F)	Kündigungsschutz m	protection against dismissal	—	protezione contro il licenziamento f	protección contra el despido f
protection en matière de location (F)	Mieterschutz m	protection of tenants	—	tutela del locatario f	protección al arrendatario f
protectionism (E)	Protektionismus m	—	protectionnisme m	protezionismo m	proteccionismo m
protection maternelle et infantile (F)	Mutterschutz m	protection of motherhood	—	tutela della maternità f	protección de la madre f
protectionnisme (F)	Protektionismus m	protectionism	—	protezionismo m	proteccionismo m
protection of creditors (E)	Gläubigerschutz m	—	garantie des créanciers f	tutela del creditore f	protección de los acreedores f
protection of endangered species (E)	Artenschutz m	—	protection d'espèces f	protezione delle speci f	protección de la especie f
protection of motherhood (E)	Mutterschutz m	—	protection maternelle et infantile f	tutela della maternità f	protección de la madre f
protection of tenants (E)	Mieterschutz m	—	protection en matière de location f	tutela del locatario f	protección al arrendatario f
protection of the environment (E)	Umweltschutz m	—	protection de l'environnement f	tutela dell'ambiente f	protección del medio ambiente f
protection sociale du travail (F)	Arbeitsschutz m	employment protection	—	tutela del lavoro f	protección del trabajo f
protective duty (E)	Schutzzoll m	—	droit de protection m	dazio protettivo m	aduana proteccionista f
Protektion (D)	—	protection	protection f	protezione f	protección f
Protektionismus (D)	—	protectionism	protectionnisme m	protezionismo m	proteccionismo m
Protest (D)	—	objection/protest	protestation f/ protêt m	opposizione f/ protesta f	oposición f/protesta f
protest (E)	Wechselprotest m	—	protêt de traite m	protesto cambiario m	protesto de letra m
protesta (I)	Beschwerde f	complaint	réclamation f	—	recurso m
protestation (F)	Protest m	objection/protest	—	opposizione f/ protesta f	oposición f/protesta f
protesto cambiario (I)	Wechselprotest m	protest	protêt de traite m	—	protesto de letra m
protesto de letra (Es)	Wechselprotest m	protest	protêt de traite m	protesto cambiario m	—
protêt de traite (F)	Wechselprotest m	protest	—	protesto cambiario m	protesto de letra m
protezione (I)	Protektion f	protection	protection f	—	protección f
protezione antincendio (I)	Brandschutz m	protection against fire	protection contre l'incendie f	—	protección contra incendios f
protezione contro il licenziamento (I)	Kündigungsschutz m	protection against dismissal	protection en matière de licenciement f	—	protección contra el despido f
protezione dei dati (I)	Datensicherung f	data protection	protection de données f	—	protección de datos f
protezionismo (I)	Protektionismus m	protectionism	protectionnisme m	—	proteccionismo m

	D	E	F	I	Es
protocole d'erreurs (F)	Fehlerprotokoll *n*	record of errors	—	protocollo errori *m*	protocolo de errores *m*
protocollo (I)	Protokoll *n*	record/minutes	procès-verbal *m*/ compte-rendu *m*	—	protocolo *m*/acta *f*
protocollo errori (I)	Fehlerprotokoll *n*	record of errors	protocole d'erreurs *m*	—	protocolo de errores *m*
protocolo (Es)	Protokoll *n*	record/minutes	procès-verbal *m*/ compte-rendu *m*	protocollo *m*/ verbale *m*	—
protocolo de errores (Es)	Fehlerprotokoll *n*	record of errors	protocole d'erreurs *m*	protocollo errori *m*	—
Protokoll (D)	—	record/minutes	procès-verbal *m*/ compte-rendu *m*	protcollo *m*/verbale *m*	protocolo *m*/acta *f*
prototipo (Es)	Prototyp *m*	prototype	prototype *m*	prototipo *m*	—
prototipo (I)	Prototyp *m*	prototype	prototype *m*	—	prototipo *m*
Prototyp (D)	—	prototype	prototype *m*	prototipo *m*	prototipo *m*
prototype (E)	Prototyp *m*	—	prototype *m*	prototipo *m*	prototipo *m*
prototype (F)	Prototyp *m*	prototype	—	prototipo *m*	prototipo *m*
prova (I)	Beweis *m*	proof	preuve *f*	—	prueba *f*
provare (I)	probieren	try	essayer	—	probar
Provision (D)	—	commission	commission *f*	provvigione *f*	comisión *f*/ corretaje *m*
provisional (Es)	einstweilig	temporary	provisoire	temporaneo	—
provision for old age (E)	Altersversorgung *f*	—	prévoyance vieillesse *f*	previdenza per la vecchiaia *f*	previsión para la vejez *f*
provisioning with raw materials (E)	Rohstoffversorgung *f*	—	approvisionnement de matières premières *m*	approvvigionamento di materie prime *m*	aprovisionamiento de materias primas *m*
provision pour pertes et charges (F)	Rückstellung *f*	reserves	—	accantonamento *m*	reserva *f*
Provisions-abrechnung (D)	—	statement of a commission	liquidation des commissions *f*	conteggio delle provvigioni *m*	liquidación de la comisión *f*
Provisionsgarantie (D)	—	commission guarantee	garantie de commission *f*	garanzia di provvigione *f*	garantía de comisión *f*
Provisionszahlung (D)	—	commission payment	payement de commission *m*	pagamento di provvigione *m*	pago de comisión *m*
provisiore (F)	einstweilig	temporary	—	temporaneo	provisional
provvedimento temporaneo (I)	einstweilige Verfügung *f*	temporary injunction	ordonnance sur référé civil *f*	—	interdicto provisorio *m*
provvigione (I)	Provision *f*	commission	commission *f*	—	comisión *f*/corretaje *m*
provvigione dell'acquirente (I)	Käuferprovision *f*	buyer's commission	commission d'acheteur *f*	—	comisión al comprador *f*
provvigione dello star del credere (I)	Delkredereprovision *f*	del credere commission	commission ducroire *f*	—	comisión de garantía *f*
provvigione di credito (I)	Kreditprovision *f*	credit commission	frais de commissions d'ouverture de crédit *m pl*	—	comisión de apertura de crédito *f*
provvigione del venditore (I)	Verkäuferprovision *f*	sales commission	commission sur les ventes *f*	—	comisión sobre la venta *f*
provvigione sul fatturato (I)	Umsatzprovision *f*	commission on turnover	commission sur le chiffre d'affaires *f*	—	comisión sobre la cifra de ventas *f*
proyección (Es)	Projektion *f*	projection	projection *f*	proiezione *f*	—
proyección de objetivos (Es)	Zielprojektion *f*	target projection	projection d'objectifs *f*	proiezione degli obiettivi *f*	—
proyecto (Es)	Entwurf *m*	draft	projet *m*	progetto *m*	—
Prozent (D)	—	per cent	pour-cent *m*	percento *m*	por ciento *m*
Prozentsatz (D)	—	percentage	pourcentage *m*	percentuale *f*	porcentaje *m*
Prozeß (D)	—	process	processus *m*	procedimento *m*	proceso *m*
prueba (Es)	Beweis *m*	proof	preuve *f*	prova *f*	—
prueba por sondeo (Es)	Stichproben *pl*	random test	sondage *m*	campioni *m pl*	—
Prüfung (D)	—	inspection/ examination	vérification *f*/ examen *m*	controllo *m*/ esame *m*	verificación *f*/ examen *m*
pseudoditta (I)	Scheinfirma *f*	bogus firm	raison sociale imaginaire *f*	—	casa ficticia *f*
psicologia del lavoro (I)	Arbeitspsychologie *f*	industrial psychology	psychologie de travail *f*	—	psicología laboral *f*

	D	E	F	I	Es
psicología industrial (Es)	Industriepsychologie f	psychology of industry	psychologie industrielle f	psicologia industriale f	—
psicologia industriale (I)	Industriepsychologie f	psychology of industry	psychologie industrielle f	—	psicología industrial
psicología laboral (Es)	Arbeitspsychologie f	industrial psychology	psychologie de travail f	psicologia del lavoro f	—
psychologie de travail (F)	Arbeitspsychologie f	industrial psychology	—	psicologia del lavoro f	psicología laboral f
psychologie industrielle (F)	Industriepsychologie f	psychology of industry	—	psicologia industriale f	psicología industrial
psychology of industry (E)	Industriepsychologie f	—	psychologie industrielle f	psicologia industriale f	psicología industrial
pubblicazione (I)	Veröffentlichung f	publication	publication f	—	publicación f
pubblicità (I)	Werbung f	publicity	publicité f	—	publicidad f
pubblicità all'aperto (I)	Außenwerbung f	outdoor publicity	publicité extérieure f	—	publicidad al aire libre f
pubblicità collettiva[1] (I)	Gemeinschaftswerbung f	joint publicity	publicité collective f	—	publicidad colectiva f
pubblicità collettiva[2] (I)	Sammelwerbung f	collective advertisement	publicité groupée f	—	publicidad colectiva f
pubblicità comparativa (I)	vergleichende Werbung f	comparative advertising	publicité comparative f	—	publicidad comparativa f
pubblicità del bilancio (I)	Offenlegung f	disclosure	révélation des derniers bilans du postulant d'un prêt f	—	publicidad para fines de inspección f
pubblicità per il trasporto strada-rotaia (I)	Huckepackwerbung f	piggyback advertisement	publicité pick-a-back f	—	publicidad combinada ferrocarril-carretera f
pubblicità per inserzione (I)	Anzeigenwerbung f	newspaper and magazine advertising	publicité par la presse f	—	publicidad por anuncios f
pubblicità radiofonica (I)	Rundfunkwerbung f	radio advertising	publicité à la radio f	—	publicidad radiada f
pubblicità televisiva (I)	Fernsehwerbung f	television advertising	émission publicitaire télévisée f	—	publicidad televisiva f
publicación (Es)	Veröffentlichung f	publication	publication f	pubblicazione f	—
public assistance (E)	Sozialhilfe f	—	aide sociale f	assistenza sociale f	ayuda social f
publication (E)	Veröffentlichung f	—	publication f	pubblicazione f	publicación f
publication (F)	Veröffentlichung f	publication	—	pubblicazione f	publicación f
public authorities (E)	öffentliche Hand f	—	secteur public m	mano pubblica f	sector público m
public enterprise (E)	öffentliche Unternehmen n	—	entreprises publiques f pl	imprese pubbliche f pl	empresa pública f
public goods (E)	öffentliche Güter n pl	—	biens publics m pl	beni pubblici m pl	bienes públicos m pl
public health (E)	Gesundheitswesen n	—	santé publique f	sanità f	sanidad f
publicidad[1] (Es)	Werbung f	publicity	publicité f	pubblicità f	—
publicidad[2] (Es)	Reklame f	advertising	publicité f	réclame f	—
publicidad al aire libre (Es)	Außenwerbung f	outdoor publicity	publicité extérieure f	pubblicità all'aperto f	—
publicidad colectiva[1] (Es)	Sammelwerbung f	collective advertisement	publicité groupée f	pubblicità collettiva f	—
publicidad colectiva[2] (Es)	Gemeinschaftswerbung f	joint publicity	publicité collective f	pubblicità collettiva f	—
publicidad combinada ferrocarril-carretera (Es)	Huckepackwerbung f	piggyback advertisement	publicité pick-a-back f	pubblicità per il trasporto strada-rotaia f	—
publicidad comparativa (Es)	vergleichende Werbung f	comparative advertising	publicité comparative f	pubblicità comparativa f	—
publicidad para fines de inspección (Es)	Offenlegung f	disclosure	révélation des derniers bilans du postulant d'un prêt f	pubblicità del bilancio f	—
publicidad por anuncios (Es)	Anzeigenwerbung f	newspaper and magazine advertising	publicité par la presse f	pubblicità per inserzione f	—
publicidad radiada (Es)	Rundfunkwerbung f	radio advertising	publicité à la radio f	pubblicità radiofonica f	—
publicidad televisiva (Es)	Fernsehwerbung f	television advertising	émission publicitaire télévisée f	pubblicità televisiva f	—
public institution (E)	gemeinnütziges Unternehmen n	—	entreprise d'utilité publique f	impresa di utilità pubblica f	empresa de beneficio común f

	D	E	F	I	Es
publicité¹ (F)	Reklame f	advertising	—	réclame f	publicidad f
publicité² (F)	Werbung f	publicity	—	pubblicità f	publicidad f
publicité à la radio (F)	Rundfunkwerbung f	radio advertising	—	pubblicità radiofonica f	publicidad radiada f
publicité collective (F)	Gemeinschafts-werbung f	joint publicity	—	pubblicità collettiva f	publicidad colectiva f
publicité comparative (F)	vergleichende Werbung f	comparative advertising	—	pubblicità comparativa f	publicidad comparativa f
publicité extérieure (F)	Außenwerbung f	outdoor publicity	—	pubblicità all'aperto f	publicitad al aire libre f
publicité groupée (F)	Sammelwerbung f	collective advertisement	—	pubblicità collettiva f	publicidad colectiva f
publicité par la presse (F)	Anzeigenwerbung f	newspaper and magazine advertising	—	pubblicità per inserzione f	publicidad por anuncios f
publicité pick-a-back (F)	Huckepackwerbung f	piggyback advertisement	—	pubblicità per il trasporto strada-rotaia f	publicidad combinada ferrocarril-carretera f
publicity¹ (E)	Publizität f	—	publicité f	pubblicità f	publicidad f
publicity² (E)	Werbung f	—	publicité f	pubblicità f	publicidad f
publicity department (E)	Werbeabteilung f	—	service de publicité m	reparto pubblicità m	sección de publicidad f
publicly owned enterprise (E)	Regiebetrieb m	—	établissement en régie m	gestione in economia f	empresa estatal f
(public) notary (E)	Notar m	—	notaire m	notaio m	notario m
public opinion research (E)	Demoskopie f	—	sondage de l'opinion publique m	demoscopia f	demoscopia f
public ownership (E)	Staatseigentum n	—	propriété d'Etat f	proprietà demaniale f	patrimonio público m
public property (E)	Gemeineigentum n	—	propriété publique f	proprietà collettiva f	propiedad común m
Public Relations (D)	—	public relations	relations publiques f pl	public relations f pl	relaciones públicas f pl
public relations (E)	Public Relations	—	relations publiques f pl	public relations f pl	relaciones públicas f pl
public relations (I)	Public Relations	public relations	relations publiques f pl	—	relaciones públicas f pl
public relations (work) (E)	Öffentlichkeitsarbeit f	—	relations publiques f pl	relazioni pubbliche f pl	relaciones públicas f pl
public revenue (E)	Staatseinnahmen pl	—	recettes de l'Etat f pl	entrate pubbliche f pl	ingresos del Estado m pl
public revenues (E)	öffentliche Einnahmen pl	—	recettes publiques f pl	entrate pubbliche f pl	ingresos públicos m pl
public sector industrial enterprise (E)	öffentliche Betriebe pl	—	entreprises publiques f pl	aziende pubbliche f pl	empresa pública f
public sector of the economy (E)	öffentliche Wirtschaft f	—	économie publique f	economia pubblica f	economía pública f
public spending¹ (E)	Staatsausgaben pl	—	dépenses publiques f pl	spese pubbliche f pl	gastos públicos m pl
public spending² (E)	öffentliche Ausgaben pl	—	dépenses publiques f pl	spesa pubblica f	gastos públicos m pl
public supervision of banking (E)	Bankenaufsicht f	—	contrôle des banques m	commissione bancaria f	supervisión bancaria f
(public) utility (E)	Versorgungs-betrieb m	—	services publics de distribution urbaine m pl	impresa di pubblici servizi f	empresa de suministros f
public welfare (E)	Allgemeinwohl n	—	bien général m	benestare pubblico m	bienestar público m
publisher (E)	Verleger m	—	éditeur m	editore m	editor m
publishing house (E)	Verlag m	—	maison d'édition f	casa editrice f	editorial f
puerto (Es)	Hafen m	port	port m	porto m	—
puerto franco (Es)	Freihafen m	free port	port franc m	porto franco m	—
puesto (Es)	Posten m	item	poste m	voce f	—
puesto de trabajo (Es)	Arbeitsplatz m	place of employment	poste de travail m	posto di lavoro m	—
puesto de trabajo a tiempo parcial (Es)	Teilzeitstelle f	part-time job	poste à temps partiel m	posto di lavoro part-time m	—
puesto de trabajo de pantalla (Es)	Bildschirm-arbeitsplatz m	screen job	poste de travail à l'écran f	posto di lavoro video m	—

qualitativo

	D	E	F	I	Es
puesto en estación (Es)	ab Bahnhof	ex rail	départ gare	franco stazione	—
punibile (I)	strafbar	punishable	punissable	—	punible
punible (Es)	strafbar	punishable	punissable	punibile	—
punishable (E)	strafbar	—	punissable	punibile	punible
punissable (F)	strafbar	punishable	—	punibile	punible
punto de intervención (Es)	Interventionspunkt *m*	intervention point	point d'intervention *m*	punto d'intervento *m*	—
punto d'incontro (I)	Treffpunkt *m*	meeting place	rendez-vous *m*	—	lugar de la cita *m*
punto d'intervento (I)	Interventionspunkt *m*	intervention point	point d'intervention *m*	—	punto de intervención *m*
punto por punto (Es)	Zug um Zug	concurrent	de point en point	contestualmente	—
puntuale (I)	termingerecht	on schedule	dans les délais	—	en la fecha fijada
purchase¹ (E)	Einkauf *m*	—	achat *m*	acquisto *m*	compra *f*
purchase² (E)	Kauf *m*	—	achat *m*	acquisto *m*	compra *f*
purchase costs (E)	Anschaffungs-kosten *pl*	—	frais d'acquisition *m pl*	costi d'acquisto *m pl*	coste de adquisición *m*
purchased quantity (E)	Abnahmemenge *f*	—	quantité commercialisée *f*	quantità d'acquisto *f*	cantidad de compra *f*
purchase guarantee (E)	Ankaufgarantie *f*	—	garantie d'achat *f*	garanzia d'acquisto *f*	garantía de compra *f*
purchase-money loan (E)	Restdarlehen *n*	—	prêt restant *m*	mutuo residuo *m*	restante de un préstamo *m*
purchase on credit (E)	Zielkauf *m*	—	achat à terme *m*	acquisto a termine *m*	compra a plazos *m*
purchase pattern (E)	Kaufverhalten *n*	—	comportement d'achat *m*	filosofia d'acquisto *f*	comportamiento de compra *m*
purchase price¹ (E)	Kaufpreis *m*	—	prix d'achat *m*	prezzo d'acquisto *m*	precio de compra *m*
purchase price² (E)	Einkaufspreis *m*	—	prix d'achat *m*	prezzo d'acquisto *m*	precio de compra *m*
purchaser (E)	Käufer *m*	—	acheteur *m*	acquirente *m*	adquirente *m*
purchasing costs (E)	Bezugskosten *pl*	—	coûts d'acquisition *m pl*	prezzo d'acquisto *m*	gastos de adquisición *m pl*
purchasing power (E)	Kaufkraft *f*	—	pouvoir d'achat *m*	potere d'acquisto *m*	poder adquisitivo *m*
purchasing power parity (E)	Kaufkraftparität *f*	—	parité du pouvoir d'achat *f*	parità del potere d'acquisto *f*	paridad adquisitiva *f*
purchasing terms (E)	Einkaufs-bedingungen *pl*	—	conditions d'achat *f pl*	condizioni d'acquisto *f pl*	condiciones de compra *f pl*
purification of sewage (E)	Abwasserreinigung *f*	—	clarification des eaux usées *f*	depurazione delle acque di scarico *f*	depuración de las aguas residuales *f*
putting on the index (E)	Indizierung *f*	—	indexation *f*	indicizzazione *f*	indiciación *f*
quadri dirigenti (I)	Führungsebene *f*	executive level	niveau de gestion *m*	—	nivel de dirección *m*
quadro del mercato (I)	Marktübersicht *f*	overall view of the market	vue d'ensemble du marché *f*	—	panorama de mercado *m*
qualification (E)	Qualifikation *f*	—	qualification *f*	qualificazione *f*	cualificación *f*
qualification (F)	Qualifikation *f*	qualification	—	qualificazione *f*	cualificación *f*
qualification du travail (F)	Arbeitsbewertung *f*	job evaluation	—	valutazione del lavoro *f*	evaluación del trabajo *f*
qualificazione (I)	Qualifikation *f*	qualification	qualification *f*	—	cualificación *f*
Qualifikation (D)	—	qualification	qualification *f*	qualificazione *f*	cualificación *f*
qualifying period (E)	Karenzzeit *f*	—	délai de carence *m*	periodo d'attesa *m*	período carencial *m*
qualità¹ (I)	Güteklasse *f*	grade	catégorie de qualité *f*	—	categoría de calidad *f*
qualità² (I)	Qualität *f*	quality	qualité *f*	—	calidad *f*
qualità dell'acqua potabile (I)	Trinkwasserqualität *f*	drinking water quality	qualité de l'eau potable *f*	—	calidad del agua potable *f*
qualità di vita (I)	Lebensqualität *f*	quality of life	qualité de la vie *f*	—	calidad de vida *m*
qualità ottima (I)	beste Qualität	first class quality	première qualité *f*	—	primera calidad *f*
qualità scadente (I)	schlechte Qualität *f*	poor quality	mauvaise qualité *f*	—	mala calidad *f*
Qualität (D)	—	quality	qualité *f*	qualità *f*	calidad *f*
qualitatif (F)	qualitativ	qualitative	—	qualitativo	cualitativo
qualitativ (D)	—	qualitative	qualitatif	qualitativo	cualitativo
qualitative (E)	qualitativ	—	qualitatif	qualitativo	cualitativo
qualitativo (I)	qualitativ	qualitative	qualitatif	—	cualitativo

	D	E	F	I	Es
Qualitäts-abweichung (D)	—	deviation from quality	écart qualitatif *m*	differenza di qualità *f*	diferencia de calidad *f*
Qualitätskontrolle (D)	—	quality control	contrôle de la qualité *m*	controllo di qualità *m*	verificación de la calidad *f*
Qualitätssicherung (D)	—	quality assurance	garantie de la qualité *f*	garanzia di qualità *f*	garantía de la calidad *f*
qualité (F)	Qualität *f*	quality	—	qualità *f*	calidad *f*
qualité de la vie (F)	Lebensqualität *f*	quality of life	—	qualità di vita *f*	calidad de vida *m*
qualité de l'eau potable (F)	Trinkwasserqualität *f*	drinking water quality	—	qualità dell'acqua potabile *f*	calidad del agua potable *f*
qualité fongible d'un bien (F)	Fungibilität *f*	fungibility	—	fungibilità *f*	fungibilidad *f*
qualité promise (F)	zugesicherte Eigenschaften *pl*	warranted characteristics	—	caratteristiche promesse *f pl*	calidades aseguradas *f pl*
quality (E)	Qualität *f*	—	qualité *f*	qualità *f*	calidad *f*
quality assurance (E)	Qualitätssicherung *f*	—	garantie de la qualité *f*	garanzia di qualità *f*	garantía de la calidad *f*
quality control (E)	Qualitätskontrolle *f*	—	contrôle de la qualité *m*	controllo di qualità *m*	verificación de la calidad *f*
quality of life (E)	Lebensqualität *f*	—	qualité de la vie *f*	qualità di vita *f*	calidad de vida *m*
quantità (I)	Menge *f*	quantity	quantité *f*	—	cantidad *f*
quantità d'acquisto (I)	Abnahmemenge *f*	purchased quantity	quantité commercialisée *f*	—	cantidad de compra *f*
quantità d'ordinazione (I)	Bestellmenge *f*	ordering quantity	quantité commandée *f*	—	cantidad pedida *f*
quantitatif (F)	quantitativ	quantitative	—	quantitativo	cuantitativo
quantitativ (D)	—	quantitative	quantitatif	quantitativo	cuantitativo
quantitative (E)	quantitativ	—	quantitatif	quantitativo	cuantitativo
quantitative boom (E)	Mengenkonjunktur *f*	—	conjoncture de quantité *f*	congiuntura quantitativa *f*	coyuntura cuantitativa *f*
quantitativo (I)	quantitativ	quantitative	quantitatif	—	cuantitativo
quantitativo d'estrazione (I)	Fördermenge *f*	output	quantité extraite *f*	—	cantidad producida *f*
quantitativo di produzione (I)	Fertigungsmenge *f*	manufactured quantity	quantité fabriquée *f*	—	cantidad producida *f*
quantitativo minimo (I)	Mindestmenge *f*	minimum quantity	quantité minimum *f*	—	cantidad mínima *f*
quantitativo minimo di fornitura (I)	Mindestabnahme *f*	minimum purchase	achat d'une quantité minimum *m*	—	recogida mínima *f*
quantitativo minimo di ordine (I)	Mindest-bestellmenge *f*	minimum quantity order	quantité commandée minimum *f*	—	cantidad mínima de pedido *f*
quantité (F)	Menge *f*	quantity	—	quantità *f*	cantidad *f*
quantité commandée (F)	Bestellmenge *f*	ordering quantity	—	quantità d'ordinazione *f*	cantidad pedida *f*
quantité commandée minimum (F)	Mindest-bestellmenge *f*	minimum quantity order	—	quantitativo minimo di ordine *m*	cantidad mínima de pedido *f*
quantité commercialisée (F)	Abnahmemenge *f*	purchased quantity	—	quantità d'acquisto *f*	cantidad de compra *f*
quantité de monnaie en circulation (F)	Geldmenge *f*	money supply	—	massa monetaria *f*	volumen monetario *m*
quantité extraite (F)	Fördermenge *f*	output	—	quantitativo d'estrazione *m*	cantidad producida *f*
quantité fabriquée (F)	Fertigungsmenge *f*	manufactured quantity	—	quantitativo di produzione *m*	cantidad producida *f*
quantité minimum (F)	Mindestmenge *f*	minimum quantity	—	quantitativo minimo *m*	cantidad mínima *f*
quantity (E)	Menge *f*	—	quantité *f*	quantità *f*	cantidad *f*
quantity discount (E)	Mengenrabatt *m*	—	remise de quantité *f*	sconto di quantità *m*	rebaja de cantidad *f*
quantity quota (E)	Mengenkontingent *n*	—	contingent de marchandises *m*	contingente di quantità *m*	contingente cuantitativo *m*
quantity unit (E)	Mengeneinheit *f*	—	unité de quantité *f*	unità quantitativa *f*	unidad cuantitativa *f*
Quartal (D)	—	quarter	trimestre *m*	trimestre *m*	trimestre *m*
Quartalsende (D)	—	end of a quarter	fin de trimestre *f*	fine trimestre *f*	final del trimestre *m*
Quartalsrechnung (D)	—	quarterly invoice	compte trimestriel *m*	conto trimestrale *m*	cuenta trimestral *f*

	D	E	F	I	Es
quarter (E)	Quartal *n*	—	trimestre *m*	trimestre *m*	trimestre *m*
quarterly (E)	vierteljährlich	—	trimestriel	trimestrale	trimestral
quarterly invoice (E)	Quartalsrechnung *f*	—	compte trimestriel *m*	conto trimestrale *m*	cuenta trimestral *f*
queja (Es)	Beanstandung *f*	objection	objection *f*	reclamo *m*	—
que sofrage los costes (Es)	Kostenträger *m*	assuming unit costs	poste de production absorbant des coûts *m*	chi si assume i costi	—
questionario (I)	Fragebogen *m*	questionnaire	questionnaire *m*	—	cuestionario *m*
questionnaire (E)	Fragebogen *m*	—	questionnaire *m*	questionario *m*	cuestionario *m*
questionnaire (F)	Fragebogen *m*	questionnaire	—	questionario *m*	cuestionario *m*
queue up (E)	Schlange stehen	—	faire la queue	fare la coda	hacer la cola
quiebra[1] (Es)	Konkurs *m*	bankruptcy	faillite *f*	fallimento *m*	—
quiebra[2] (Es)	Bankrott *m*	bankruptcy	banqueroute *f*	bancarotta	—
quietanza[1] (I)	Quittung *f*	receipt	quittance *f*	—	recibo *m*
quietanza[2] (I)	Beleg *m*	voucher	justificatif *m*	—	justificativo *m*
quilate (Es)	Karat *n*	carat	carat *m*	carato *m*	—
química (Es)	Chemie *f*	chemistry	chimie *f*	chimica *f*	—
quince días (Es)	vierzehn Tage	fortnight	quinze jours	quindici giorni	—
quindici giorni (I)	vierzehn Tage	fortnight	quinze jours	—	quince días *m pl*
quinze jours (F)	vierzehn Tage	fortnight	—	quindici giorni	quince días *m pl*
quittance (F)	Quittung *f*	receipt	—	quietanza *f*	recibo *m*
Quittung (D)	—	receipt	quittance *f*	quietanza *f*	recibo *m*
quota[1] (E)	Quote *f*	—	quota *m*	quota *f*	cuota *f*
quota[2] (E)	Kontingent *n*	—	contingent *m*	contingente *m*	contingente *m*
quota (F)	Quote *f*	quota	—	quota *f*	cuota *f*
quota (I)	Quote *f*	quota	quota *m*	—	cuota *f*
quota dei costi del materiale (I)	Materialkostenanteil *m*	share in the material costs	proportion des frais de matériel *f*	—	parte de los gastos de material *m*
quota della popolazione attiva (I)	Erwerbsquote *f*	activity rate	proportion de la population active *f*	—	proporción de la población activa *f*
quota d'estrazione (I)	Förderquote *f*	production quota	quote-part de production *f*	—	cuota de producción *f*
quota d'exportation (F)	Exportquote *f*	export quota	—	contingente d'esportazione *m*	cupo de exportación *m*
quota di capitale (I)	Kapitalanteil *m*	share in capital	part de capital *f*	—	participación en el capital *f*
quota di mercato (I)	Marktanteil *m*	market share	participation au marché *f*	—	cuota del mercado *f*
quota d'importazione (I)	Importquote *f*	import quota	contingent d'importation *m*	—	cuota de importación *f*
quota di risparmio (I)	Sparquote *f*	savings ratio	quote-part de revenu réservée à des fins d'épargne *f*	—	cuota de ahorro *f*
quota sociale[1] (I)	Stammeinlage *f*	initial contribution	apport social *m*	—	capital suscrito *m*
quota sociale[2] (I)	Geschäftsanteil *m*	share	part sociale *f*	—	participación *f*
quota system (E)	Quotensystem *n*	—	système de quote-parts *m*	sistema di contingentamento *m*	sistema de cuotas *m*
quotation (E)	Notierung *f*	—	cotation *f*	quotazione *f*	cotización *f*
quotation of prices (E)	Kursnotierung *f*	—	cotation *f*	quotazione dei corsi *f*	cotización *m*
quotation on the stock exchange[1] (E)	Börsennotierung *f*	—	cotation des cours en bourse *f*	quotazione di borsa *f*	cotización de bolsa *f*
quotation on the stock exchange[2] (E)	Börsenkurs *m*	—	cours de bourse *m pl*	corso di borsa *m*	cotización en bolsa *f*
quotazione (I)	Notierung *f*	quotation	cotation *f*	—	cotización *f*
quotazione dei corsi (I)	Kursnotierung *f*	quotation of prices	cotation *f*	—	cotización *m*
quotazione dei prezzi (I)	Preisnotierung *f*	prices quoted	cotation des prix *f*	—	cotización de precios *f*
quotazione delle azioni (I)	Aktiennotierung *f*	share quotation	cotation des actions *f*	—	cotización de acciones *f*
quotazione di borsa (I)	Börsennotierung *f*	quotation on the stock exchange	cotation des cours en bourse *f*	—	cotización de bolsa *f*

	D	E	F	I	Es
quotazione di chiusura (I)	Schlußkurs *m*	closing price	dernier cours *m*	—	cotización final *f*
Quote (D)	—	quota	quota *m*	quota *f*	cuota *f*
Quotensystem (D)	—	quota system	système de quote-parts *m*	sistema di contingentamento *m*	sistema de cuotas *m*
quote-part de production (F)	Förderquote *f*	production quota	—	quota d'estrazione *f*	cuota de producción *f*
quote-part de revenu réservée à des fins d'épargne (F)	Sparquote *f*	savings ratio	—	quota di risparmio *f*	cuota de ahorro *f*
quotidien (F)	täglich	daily	—	giornaliero	diario
Quotient (D)	—	quotient	quotient *m*	quoziente *m*	cociente *m*
quotient (E)	Quotient *m*	—	quotient *m*	quoziente *m*	cociente *m*
quotient (F)	Quotient *m*	quotient	—	quoziente *m*	cociente *m*
quoziente (I)	Quotient *m*	quotient	quotient *m*	—	cociente *m*
rabais d'introduction (F)	Einführungsrabatt *m*	introductory discount	—	sconto di lancio *m*	rebaja de lanzamiento *f*
Rabatt (D)	—	discount	remise *f*	ribasso *m*	rebaja *f*
raccolta dati (I)	Datenerfassung *f*	data collection	saisie des données informatiques *f*	—	recogida de datos *f*
raccomandata (I)	Einschreiben *n*	Registered	en recommandé	—	certificado *m*
raccomandazione (I)	Empfehlung *f*	recommendation	recommandation *f*	—	recomendación *f*
racionalización (Es)	Rationalisierung *f*	rationalization	rationalisation *f*	razionalizzazione *f*	—
racionamiento (Es)	Rationierung *f*	rationing	rationnement *m*	razionamento *m*	—
radio advertising (E)	Rundfunkwerbung *f*	—	publicité à la radio *f*	pubblicità radiofonica *f*	publicidad radiada *f*
radio message (E)	Funkspruch *m*	—	message par radio *m*	radiotelefonata	mensaje radiado *m*
radiotelefonata (I)	Funkspruch *m*	radio message	message par radio *m*	—	mensaje radiado *m*
raggio d'azione della pubblicità (I)	Werbereichweite *f*	scope of advertising effect	zone de rayonnement de la publicité *f*	—	alcance publicitario *m*
ragioneria (I)	Rechnungswesen *n*	accounting system	comptabilité *f*	—	contabilidad *f*
ragioniere (I)	Buchhalter *m*	bookkeeper	comptable *m*	—	tenedor de libros *m*
rail freight (E)	Bahnfracht *f*	—	fret par rail *m*	nolo ferroviario *m*	transporte ferroviario *m*
railway tariff (E)	Eisenbahntarif *m*	—	tarif ferroviaire *m*	tariffa ferroviaria *f*	tarifa ferroviaria *f*
raising of money (E)	Geldaufnahme *f*	—	emprunt *m*	accensione di un mutuo *f*	dinero tomado a préstamo *m*
raison sociale imaginaire (F)	Scheinfirma *f*	bogus firm	—	pseudoditta *f*	casa ficticia *f*
ramo (Es)	Branche *f*	line of business	branche *f*	categoria *f*	—
ramo de la construcción (Es)	Bauwirtschaft *f*	building and construction industry	(industrie du) bâtiment *f*	edilizia *f*	—
ramo económico (Es)	Wirtschaftszweig *m*	field of the economy	secteur économique *m*	settore economico *m*	—
random test (E)	Stichproben *pl*	—	sondage *m*	campioni *m pl*	prueba por sondeo *f*
range of production (E)	Produktionspalette *f*	—	gamme de production *f*	gamma di produzione *f*	gama de producción *f*
rapport (F)	Report *m*	report	—	rapporto *m*	informe *m*
rapport de confiance (F)	Vertrauensverhältnis *n*	confidential relationship	—	rapporto di fiducia *m*	relación de confianza *f*
rapport de gestion (F)	Geschäftsbericht *m*	business report	—	relazione sull'esercizio commerciale *f*	informe *m*
rapport de travail (F)	Arbeitsverhältnis *n*	employee-employer relationship	—	rapporto di lavoro *m*	relación laboral *f*
rapport de vente (F)	Verkaufsbericht *m*	sales report	—	rapporto sulle vendite *m*	informe de venta *m*
rapport financier (F)	Finanzbericht *m*	financial report	—	relazione finanziaria *f*	informe financiero *m*
rapporti commerciali (I)	Handelsbeziehungen *pl*	trade relations	relations commerciales *f pl*	—	relaciones comerciales *f pl*
rapporti d'affari (I)	Geschäftsbeziehung *f*	business relation	relations d'affaires *f pl*	—	relaciones comerciales *f pl*
rapporti di proprietà (I)	Eigentumsverhältnisse *pl*	property relations	régime de la propriété *m*	—	régimen de tenencia *m*

	D	E	F	I	Es
rapport juridique (F)	Rechtsverhältnis *n*	legal relationship	—	rapporto giuridico *m*	relación jurídica *f*
rapporto¹ (I)	Verhältnis *n*	proportion	relation *f*	—	relación *f*
rapporto² (I)	Report *m*	report	rapport *m*	—	informe *m*
rapporto corso-profitto (I)	Kurs-Gewinn-Verhältnis *n*	price-earnings ratio	relation cours-bénéfice *f*	—	relación cotización-ganancia *f*
rapporto di fiducia (I)	Vertrauens-verhältnis *n*	confidential relationship	rapport de confiance *m*	—	relación de confianza *f*
rapporto di lavoro (I)	Arbeitsverhältnis *n*	employee-employer relationship	rapport de travail *m*	—	relación laboral *f*
rapporto di lavoro in prova (I)	Arbeitsverhältnis auf Probe *n*	employee-employer relationship on a trial basis	contrat de travail convenu à l'essai *m*		relación laboral a prueba *f*
rapporto giuridico (I)	Rechtsverhältnis *n*	legal relationship	rapport juridique *m*	—	relación jurídica *f*
rapporto sulle vendite (I)	Verkaufsbericht *m*	sales report	rapport de vente *m*	—	informe de venta *m*
rappresaglia (I)	Repressalie *f*	reprisals	représaille *f*	—	represalia *f*
rappresentante (I)	Vertreter *m*	representative	représentant *m*	—	representante *m*
rappresentante commerciale (I)	Handelsvertreter *m*	commercial agent	représentant de commerce *m*	—	representante comercial *m*
rappresentante di zona (I)	Bezirksvertreter *m*	local agent	agent local *m*	—	agente regional *m*
rappresentante esclusivo (I)	Alleinvertreter *m*	sole agent	agent exclusive *m*	—	representante exclusivo *m*
rappresentante generale (I)	Generalvertreter *m*	general agent	agent général *m*	—	representante general *m*
rappresentanza (I)	Vertretung *f*	representation	représentation *f*	—	representación *f*
rappresentanza commerciale (I)	Handelsvertretung *f*	commercial agency	représentation commerciale *f*	—	representación comercial *f*
rappresentanza degli interessi (I)	Interessen-vertretung *f*	representation of interests	représentation des intérêts *f*	—	representación de intereses *f*
rappresentanza esclusiva (I)	Alleinvertretung *f*	sole agency	agence exclusive *f*	—	representación exclusiva *f*
rappresentanza estera (I)	Auslandsvertretung *f*	agency abroad	agence à l'étranger *f*	—	representación en el exterior *f*
rare (F)	knapp	scarce	—	scarso	escaso
rareté (F)	Knappheit *f*	shortage	—	scarsità *f*	escasez *f*
rata¹ (I)	Rate *f*	instalment	acompte *m*	—	plazo *m*
rata² (I)	Teilzahlungsrate *f*	monthly instalment	mensualité d'un achat à tempérament *f*	—	plazo *m*
rata leasing (I)	Leasing-Rate *f*	leasing payment	taux de leasing *m*	—	plazo de arrenda-miento financiero *m*
Rate (D)	—	instalment	acompte *m*	rata *f*/tasso *m*	plazo *m*
rate for advances on securities (E)	Lombardsatz *m*	—	taux d'intérêt de l'argent prêté sur gage *m*	tasso sulle anticipazioni *m*	tipo de pignoración *m*
rate for foreign notes and coin (E)	Sortenkurs *m*	—	cours des monnaies étrangères *m*	corso dei cambi *m*	tipo de cambio de billetes y monedas extranjeras *m*
ratei e risconti (I)	Rechnungs-abgrenzung *f*	apportionment of payments between accounting periods	délimitation des comptes non encore soldés *f*	—	ajuste de cuentas *m*
Ratengeschäft (D)	—	instalment sale transaction	vente à tempérament *f*	vendita a rate *f*	venta a plazo *f*
Ratenkauf (D)	—	hire-purchase transaction	achat à tempérament *m*	acquisto a rate *m*	compra a plazo *f*
Ratenzahlung (D)	—	payment by instalments	payement par verse-ments fractionnés *m*	pagamento rateale *m*	pago a plazos *m*
rate of conversion (E)	Umrechnungskurs *m*	—	cours de conversion *m*	corso di cambio *m*	tasa de cambio *f*
rate of growth (E)	Wachstumsrate *f*	—	taux d'accroissement *m*	tasso di crescita *m*	tasa de crecimiento *f*
rate of inflation (E)	Inflationsrate *f*	—	taux d'inflation *m*	tasso d'inflazione *m*	tasa de inflación *f*
ratificación (Es)	Ratifikation *f*	ratification	ratification *f*	ratificazione *f*	—
ratification (E)	Ratifikation *f*	—	ratification *f*	ratificazione *f*	ratificación *f*
ratification (F)	Ratifikation *f*	ratification	—	ratificazione *f*	ratificación *f*

	D	E	F	I	Es
ratificazione (I)	Ratifikation f	ratification	ratification f	—	ratificación f
Ratifikation (D)	—	ratification	ratification f	ratificazione f	ratificación f
ratio de perte (F)	Ausfallquote f	default rate	—	tasso di perdita m	cuota de pérdida f
rational behaviour (E)	Rationalverhalten n	—	comportement rationnel m	atteggiamento razionale m	comportamiento racional m
rationalisation (F)	Rationalisierung f	rationalization	—	razionalizzazione f	racionalización f
Rationalisierung (D)	—	rationalization	rationalisation f	razionalizzazione f	racionalización f
Rationalisierungs-gewinn (D)	—	rationalization profit	profit de rationalisation m	profitto di razionalizzazione m	beneficio de racionalización m
rationalization (E)	Rationalisierung f	—	rationalisation f	razionalizzazione f	racionalización f
rationalization profit (E)	Rationalisierungs-gewinn m	—	profit de rationalisation m	profitto di razionalizzazione m	beneficio de racionalización m
Rationalverhalten (D)	—	rational behaviour	comportement rationnel m	atteggiamento razionale m	comportamiento racional m
Rationierung (D)	—	rationing	rationnement m	razionamento m	racionamiento m
rationing (E)	Rationierung f	—	rationnement m	razionamento m	racionamiento m
rationnement (F)	Rationierung f	rationing	—	razionamento m	racionamiento m
Raubbau (D)	—	ruinous exploitation	exploitation abusive f	sfruttamento abusivo m	explotación abusiva f
Raumforschung (D)	—	space research	recherches spatiales f pl	ricerche spaziali f pl	investigación espacial f
Raumordnung (D)	—	regional policy	aménagement des espaces m	ordinamento territoriale m	ordenación del territorio f
Raumplanung (D)	—	regional planning	plan d'aménagement des espaces m	pianificazione territoriale f	planificación del espacio m
Raumstruktur (D)	—	spatial structure	structure des espaces f	struttura territoriale f	estructura territorial f
Räumung (D)	—	evacuation	évacuation f	evacuazione f	desalojamiento m
Räumungsverkauf (D)	—	clearance sale	liquidation des stocks f	liquidazione totale f	venta total f
raw material production (E)	Rohstoff-gewinnung f	—	extraction de matières premières f	produzione delle materie prime f	producción de materias primas f
raw materials (E)	Rohstoff m	—	matière première f	materia prima f	materia prima f
raw materials marketing (E)	Rohstoff-vermarktung f	—	commercialisation des matières premières f	smercio delle materie prime m	comercialización de las materias primas f
raw materials shortage (E)	Rohstoffknappheit f	—	pénurie de matières premières f	scarsità di materie prime f	escasez de materias primas f
razionalizzazione (I)	Rationalisierung f	rationalization	rationalisation f	—	racionalización f
razionamento (I)	Rationierung f	rationing	rationnement m	—	racionamiento m
razón social (Es)	Firmenname m	company name	nom de la maison m	denominazione f/ ragione sociale f	—
reacción (Es)	Reaktion f	reaction	réaction f	reazione f	—
reacoplamiento (Es)	Rückkopplung f	feedback	accouplement réactif m	accoppiamento a reazione m	—
reaction (E)	Reaktion f	—	réaction f	reazione f	reacción f
réaction (F)	Reaktion f	reaction	—	reazione f	reacción f
readaptación profesional (Es)	Umschulung f	retraining	rééducation professionnelle f	riqualificazione professionale f	—
ready for collection (E)	abholbereit	—	disponible	pronto per il ritiro	listo para la recogida
ready for dispatch (E)	versandbereit	—	prêt à être expédié	pronto per la spedizione	listo para ser expedido
Reaktion (D)	—	reaction	réaction f	reazione f	reacción f
real account (E)	Bestandskonto n	—	compte d'existences m	conto merci m	cuenta de existencias f
real capital (E)	Realkapital n	—	biens corporels immobilisés m pl	capitale reale m	capital real m
Realeinkommen (D)	—	real income	revenu réel m	reddito reale m	ingreso real m
real estate (E)	Grundstück n	—	terrain m	terreno m	terreno m
real estate fund (E)	Immobilienfonds m	—	fonds immobilier m	fondo immobiliare m	fondo inmobiliario f
real income (E)	Realeinkommen n	—	revenu réel m	reddito reale m	ingreso real m
real indebtedness (E)	effektive Verschuldung f	—	endettement effectif m	indebitamento effettivo m	endeudamiento efectivo m

	D	E	F	I	Es
real (rate of) interest (E)	Realzins *m*	—	rendement réel *m*	tasso d'interesse reale *m*	interés real *m*
réalisation (F)	Durchführung *f*	realization	—	esecuzione *f*	ejecución *f*
réalisation d'une commande (F)	Auftragsbearbeitung *f*	order processing	—	esecuzione ordini *f*	tramitación de pedidos *f*
realization (E)	Durchführung *f*	—	réalisation *f*	esecuzione *f*	ejecución *f*
Realkapital (D)	—	real capital	biens corporels immobilisés *m pl*	capitale reale *m*	capital real *m*
Realkredit (D)	—	credit secured by real property	crédit sur gage mobilier *m*	credito reale *m*	crédito real *m*
Reallohn (D)	—	real wage	salaire réel *m*	salario reale *m*	salario real *m*
real right (E)	dingliches Recht *n*	—	droit réel *m*	diritto reale *m*	derecho real *m*
real security (E)	dingliche Sicherung *f*	—	sécurité réelle *f*	garanzia reale *f*	garantía real *f*
Realsteuern (D)	—	impersonal taxes	impôt réel *m*	imposte reali *f pl*	impuestos reales *m pl*
real value (E)	Sachwert *m*	—	valeur matérielle *f*	valore reale *m*	valor real *m*
Realvermögen (D)	—	real wealth	patrimoine réel *m*	patrimonio reale *m*	activo inmobiliario *m*
real wage (E)	Reallohn *m*	—	salaire réel *m*	salario reale *m*	salario real *m*
real wealth (E)	Realvermögen *n*	—	patrimoine réel *m*	patrimonio reale *m*	activo inmobiliario *m*
Realzins (D)	—	real (rate of) interest	rendement réel *m*	tasso d'interesse reale *m*	interés real *m*
réapprovisionnement (F)	Wiederbeschaffung *f*	replacement	—	riapprovvigionamento *m*	reposición *f*
reaseguro (Es)	Rückversicherung *f*	reinsurance	réassurance *f*	riassicurazione *f*	—
réassurance (F)	Rückversicherung *f*	reinsurance	—	riassicurazione *f*	reaseguro *m*
reazione (I)	Reaktion *f*	reaction	réaction *f*	—	reacción *f*
rebaja[1] (Es)	Rabatt *m*	discount	remise *f*	ribasso *m*	—
rebaja[2] (Es)	Preisnachlaß *m*	price reduction	remise sur le prix *f*	ribasso del prezzo *m*	—
rebaja de cantidad (Es)	Mengenrabatt *m*	quantity discount	remise de quantité *f*	sconto di quantità *m*	—
rebaja de lanzamiento (Es)	Einführungsrabatt *m*	introductory discount	rabais d'introduction *m*	sconto di lancio *m*	—
rebaja preferencial (Es)	Vorzugsrabatt *m*	preferential discount	remise de faveur *f*	ribasso preferenziale *m*	—
rebajas de invierno (Es)	Winterschlußverkauf *m*	winter clearance sale	solde d'hiver *m*	svendita di fine inverno *f*	—
recargo (Es)	Aufschlag *m*	surcharge	hausse *f*	aggiunta *f*	—
receipt (E)	Quittung *f*	—	quittance *f*	quietanza *f*	recibo *m*
receipt for payment (E)	Zahlungsbestätigung *f*	—	confirmation de payement *f*	conferma di pagamento *f*	confirmación de pago *f*
receipts (E)	Einnahmen *pl*	—	revenu *m*	entrate *f pl*	ingresos *m pl*
receiver (E)	Empfänger *m*	—	destinataire *m*	destinatario *m*	destinatario *m*
receivership (E)	Zwangsverwaltung *f*	—	séquestre judiciare *m*	amministrazione giudiziaria *f*	administración forzosa *f*
recensement démographique (F)	Volkszählung *f*	census of population	—	censimento *m*	censo *m*
réception (F)	Abnahme *f*	acceptance/decrease	—	accettazione *f*/riduzione *f*	aceptación *f*/disminución *f*
recesión (Es)	Rezession *f*	recession	récession *f*	recessione *f*	—
recession (E)	Rezession *f*	—	récession *f*	recessione *f*	recesión *f*
récession (F)	Rezession *f*	recession	—	recessione *f*	recesión *f*
recessione (I)	Rezession *f*	recession	récessinn *f*	—	recesión *f*
recettes de l'Etat (F)	Staatseinnahmen *pl*	public revenue	—	entrate pubbliche *f pl*	ingresos del Estado *m pl*
recettes publiques (F)	öffentliche Einnahmen *pl*	public revenues	—	entrate pubbliche *f pl*	ingresos públicos *m pl*
Recheneinheit (D)	—	calculation unit	unité de calcul *f*	unità di conteggio *f*	unidad de cuenta *f*
Rechenfehler (D)	—	miscalculation	erreur de calcul *f*	errore di calcolo *m*	error de cálculo *m*
Rechenzentrum (D)	—	computer centre	centre de calcul *m*	centro da computer *m*	centro de computación *m*
recherche[1] (F)	Forschung *f*	research	—	ricerca *f*	investigación *f*
recherche[2] (F)	Nachforschung *f*	investigation	—	indagine *f*	pesquisas *f pl*

	D	E	F	I	Es
recherche de la fraude fiscale (F)	Steuerfahndung f	investigation into suspected tax offences	—	inchiesta tributaria f	investigación tributaria f
recherches spatiales (F)	Raumforschung f	space research	—	ricerche spaziali f pl	investigación espacial f
Rechner (D)	—	computer/calculator	ordinateur m/calculateur de poche m	computer m/calcolatore m	ordenador m/calculadora de bolsillo m
Rechnung (D)	—	invoice/calculation	facture f/calcul m	fattura f/calcolo m	factura f/cálculo m
Rechnungsbetrag (D)	—	amount of invoice	montant de la facture m	ammontare della fattura m	importe de la factura m
Rechnungseinheit (D)	—	unit of account	unité de compte f	unità di conto f	unidad de cuenta f
Rechnungsjahr (D)	—	financial year	exercice comptable m	anno d'esercizio m	ejercicio m
Rechnungsnummer (D)	—	invoice number	numéro de la facture m	numero della fattura m	número de la factura m
Rechnungsprüfer (D)	—	auditor	commissaire aux comptes m	revisore dei conti m	revisor contable m
Rechnungsstellung (D)	—	invoicing	établissement d'une facture m	fatturazione f	facturación f
Rechnungssumme (D)	—	invoice amount	montant de la facture m	importo della fattura m	suma de la factura f
Rechnungswesen (D)	—	accounting system	comptabilité f	ragioneria f	contabilidad f
Recht (D)	—	law	droit m	diritto m	derecho m
Rechtsabteilung (D)	—	legal department	bureau juridique m	ufficio legale m	sección jurídica f
Rechtsanspruch (D)	—	legal claim	titre m	pretesa giuridica f	pretensión legal f
Rechtsanwalt (D)	—	lawyer	avocat m	avvocato m	abogado m
rechtsfähig (D)	—	capable to act in law	capable de jouir des droits	persona avente capacità giuridica f	jurídicamente capaz
Rechtsfähigkeit (D)	—	legal capacity	capacité de jouissance des droits f	capacità giuridica f	capacidad jurídica f
Rechtsform (D)	—	legal form	forme juridique f	forma giuridica f	forma jurídica f
Rechtsgeschäft (D)	—	legal transaction	acte juridique m	negozio giuridico m	negocio jurídico m
Rechtshaftung (D)	—	legal responsibility	responsabilité légale f	responsabilità giuridica f	responsabilidad jurídica f
Rechtsirrtum (D)	—	mistake of law	erreur de droit m	errore di diritto m	error de derecho m
Rechtslage (D)	—	legal situation	situation juridique f	situazione giuridica f	situación jurídica f
Rechtsnorm (D)	—	legal norm	règle de droit f	norma giuridica f	norma jurídica f
Rechtsprechung (D)	—	administration of justice	jurisprudence f	giurisprudenza f	jurisprudencia f
Rechtsstreit (D)	—	legal action	litige m	causa f	conflicto jurídico m
Rechtsverhältnis (D)	—	legal relationship	rapport juridique m	rapporto giuridico m	relación jurídica f
recibo[1] (Es)	Quittung f	receipt	quittance f	quietanza f	—
recibo[2] (Es)	Empfangsbestätigung f	acknowledgement of receipt	accusé de réception m	ricevuta f	—
recibo de entrega (Es)	Lieferschein m	delivery note	bulletin de livraison m	bolletta di consegna f	—
reciclaje (Es)	Recycling n	recycling	recyclage m	riciclaggio m	—
reciprocidad (Es)	Reziprozität f	reciprocity	réciprocité f	reciprocità f	—
reciprocità (I)	Reziprozität f	reciprocity	réciprocité f	—	reciprocidad f
réciprocité (F)	Reziprozität f	reciprocity	—	reciprocità f	reciprocidad f
reciprocity (E)	Reziprozität f	—	réciprocité f	reciprocità f	reciprocidad f
reclamación (Es)	Reklamation f	complaint	réclamation f	reclamo m	—
reclamación de la entrega de un pedido (Es)	Abruf m	call	appel m	richiesta f	—
réclamation[1] (F)	Reklamation f	complaint	—	reclamo m	reclamación f
réclamation[2] (F)	Beschwerde f	complaint	—	protesta f	recurso m
réclame (I)	Reklame f	advertising	publicité f	—	publicidad f
reclamo[1] (I)	Reklamation f	complaint	réclamation f	—	reclamación f
reclamo[2] (I)	Beanstandung f	objection	objection f	—	queja f
reclutamento (I)	Anwerbung f	recruitment	recrutement m	—	contratación f
reclutamiento de personal (Es)	Personalwerbung f	hiring of personnel	recrutement de personnel m	reclutazione di personale f	—

	D	E	F	I	Es
reclutazione di personale (I)	Personalwerbung f	hiring of personnel	recrutement de personnel m	—	reclutamiento de personal m
recogida de datos (Es)	Datenerfassung f	data collection	saisie des données informatiques f	raccolta dati f	—
recogida mínima (Es)	Mindestabnahme f	minimum purchase	achat d'une quantité minimum m	quantitativo minimo di fornitura m	—
recognize (E)	erkennen	—	reconnaître	riconoscere	reconocer
recomendación (Es)	Empfehlung f	recommendation	recommandation f	raccomandazione f	—
recommandation (F)	Empfehlung f	recommendation	—	raccomandazione f	recomendación f
recommendation (E)	Empfehlung f	—	recommandation f	raccomandazione f	recomendación f
recommendation de prix (F)	Preisempfehlung f	price recommendation	—	suggerimento di prezzo m	precio recomendado m
recommended retail price (E)	Richtpreis m	—	prix indicatif m	prezzo indicativo m	precio indicativo m
reconnaissance de dette (F)	Schuldanerkennung f	acknowledgement of a debt	—	riconoscimento del debito m	reconocimiento de la deuda m
reconnaître (F)	erkennen	recognize	—	riconoscere	reconocer
reconocer (Es)	erkennen	recognize	reconnaître	riconoscere	—
reconocimiento de la deuda (Es)	Schuldanerkennung f	acknowledgement of a debt	reconnaissance de dette f	riconoscimento del debito m	—
reconstrucción (Es)	Wiederaufbau m	reconstruction	reconstruction f	ricostruzione f	—
reconstruction (E)	Wiederaufbau m	—	reconstruction f	ricostruzione f	reconstrucción f
reconstruction (F)	Wiederaufbau m	reconstruction	—	ricostruzione f	reconstrucción f
record (E)	Protokoll n	—	procès-verbal m/ compte-rendu m	protocollo m/ verbale m	protocolo m/acta f
recorded delivery letter (with advice) (E)	Einschreiben-Rückschein m	—	lettre recommandée avec avis de réception f	lettera raccomandata con ricevuta di ritorno f	carta certificada con talón de recibo f
record of errors (E)	Fehlerprotokoll n	—	protocole d'erreurs m	protocollo errori m	protocolo de errores m
recours¹ (F)	Regreß m	recourse	—	regresso m	regreso m
recours² (F)	Rückgriff m	recourse	—	regresso m	recurso m
recourse¹ (E)	Rückgriff m	—	recours m	regresso m	recurso m
recourse² (E)	Regreß m	—	recours m	regresso m	regreso m
recouvrement (F)	Inkasso n	collection	—	incasso m	encobro m
recruitment (E)	Anwerbung f	—	recrutement m	reclutamento m	contratación f
recrutement (F)	Anwerbung f	recruitment	—	reclutamento m	contratación f
recrutement de personnel (F)	Personalwerbung f	hiring of personnel	—	reclutazione di personale f	reclutamiento de personal m
rectificación (Es)	Berichtigung f	correction	rectification f	correzione f	—
rectificación de valor (Es)	Wertberichtigung f	value adjustment	réévaluation f	rettifica del valore f	—
rectification (F)	Berichtigung f	correction	—	correzione f	rectificación f
recul de la demande (F)	Nachfrage-rückgang m	decrease in demand	—	flessione della domanda f	disminución en la demanda f
recul du chiffre d'affaires (F)	Umsatzrückgang m	decrease of turnover	—	calo del fatturato m	disminución de la cifra de facturación f
recuperable (Es)	wiederverwertbar	recyclable	réutilisable	riutilizzabile	—
recuperación coyuntural (Es)	Konjunkturbelebung f	economic upturn	relance économique f	ripresa congiunturale f	—
recurso¹ (Es)	Beschwerde f	complaint	réclamation f	protesta f	—
recurso² (Es)	Ressource f	resources	ressource f	risorsa f	—
recurso³ (Es)	Rückgriff m	recourse	recours m	regresso m	—
recusación (Es)	Ablehnung f	refusal/rejection	refus m/rejet m	rifiuto m/rigetto m	—
recyclable (E)	wiederverwertbar	—	réutilisable	riutilizzabile	recuperable
recyclage (F)	Recycling n	recycling	—	riciclaggio m	reciclaje m
Recycling (D)	—	recycling	recyclage m	riciclaggio m	reciclaje m
recycling (E)	Recycling n	—	recyclage m	riciclaggio m	reciclaje m
recycling exchange (E)	Abfallbörse f	—	bourse de recyclage f	borsa dei rifiuti f	bolsa de reciclaje f
red (Es)	Netzwerk n	network	réseau m	rete f	—

	D	E	F	I	Es
redazione del testo (I)	Textgestaltung f	text configuration	structure du texte f	—	estructuración del texto f
redazione d'inventario (I)	Inventur f	taking of the inventory	inventaire m	—	inventario m
red de carreteras (Es)	Straßennetz n	road network	réseau routier m	rete stradale f	—
red de sucursales (Es)	Filialnetz n	branch network	réseau de succursales m	rete delle filiali f	—
redditività¹ (I)	Ertragskraft f	earning capacity	force productive f	—	rentabilidad f
redditività² (I)	Rentabilität f	profitability	rentabilité f	—	rentabilidad f
redditività del capitale (I)	Kapitalrentabilität f	return on investment	rentabilité du capital f	—	rentabilidad del capital f
reddito¹ (I)	Einkommen n	income	revenu m	—	ingresos m pl/ renta f
reddito² (I)	Ertrag m	income/earnings	rendement m/ revenu m	—	producto m/ rendimiento m/ renta f
reddito annuale (I)	Jahreseinkommen n	annual income	revenu annuel m	—	renta anual f
reddito da possesso (I)	Besitzeinkommen n	unearned income	revenu du patrimoine m	—	renta de la propiedad f
reddito del capitale (I)	Kapitaleinkommen n	unearned income	revenu du capital m	—	ganancias de capital f pl
reddito fisso (I)	Festeinkommen n	fixed income	revenu fixe m	—	salario fijo m
reddito lordo¹ (I)	Rohertrag m	gross proceeds	produit brut m	—	producto bruto m
reddito lordo² (I)	Bruttoeinkommen n	gross income	revenu brut m	—	ingreso bruto m
reddito nazionale (I)	Volkseinkommen n	national income	revenu national m	—	renta nacional f
reddito netto (I)	Nettoeinkommen n	net income	revenu net m	—	ingreso neto m
reddito nominale (I)	Nominal-einkommen n	nominal income	revenu nominal m	—	ingresos nominales m
reddito reale (I)	Realeinkommen n	real income	revenu réel m	—	ingreso real m
redeem (E)	ablösen	—	amortir	rimborsare	amortizar
Redegewandtheit (D)	—	eloquence	élocution aisée f	eloquenza f	elocuencia f
redemption (E)	Tilgung f	—	amortissement m	ammortamento m	amortización f
redemption financing (E)	Ablösungs-finanzierung f	—	financement du rachat m	finanziamento del rimborso m	financiamiento de amortización m
redemption sum (E)	Ablösesumme f	—	montant de rachat m	importo di rimborso m	suma de amortización f
redescontar (Es)	rediskontieren	rediscount	réescompter	riscontare	—
rediscount (E)	rediskontieren	—	réescompter	riscontare	redescontar
rediskontieren (D)	—	rediscount	réescompter	riscontare	redescontar
redistribución (Es)	Redistribution f	redistribution	redistribution f	ridistribuzione f	—
redistribución de la renta (Es)	Einkommens-umverteilung f	redistribution of income	redistribution des revenus f pl	ridistribuzione dei redditi f	—
Redistribution (D)	—	redistribution	redistribution f	ridistribuzione f	redistribución f
redistribution (E)	Redistribution f	—	redistribution f	ridistribuzione f	redistribución f
redistribution (F)	Redistribution f	redistribution	—	ridistribuzione f	redistribución f
redistribution des revenues (F)	Einkommens-umverteilung f	redistribution of income	—	ridistribuzione dei redditi f	redistribución de la renta f
redistribution of income (E)	Einkommens-umverteilung f	—	redistribution des revenus f pl	ridistribuzione dei redditi f	redistribución de la renta f
rédito de la cifra de ventas (Es)	Umsatzrendite f	net income percent-age of turnover	rendement du chiffre d'affaires m	rendita del fatturato f	—
redondance (F)	Redundanz f	redundancy	—	ridondanza f	redundancia f
reducción¹ (Es)	Abbau m	reduction/lay off	réduction f/ diminution f	riduzione f/ diminuzione f	—
reducción² (Es)	Ermäßigung f	reduction	réduction f	riduzione f	—
reducción³ (Es)	Minderung f	reduction	diminution f	riduzione f	—
reducción de capital (Es)	Kapitalherabsetzung f	reduction of capital	diminution du capital f	riduzione del capitale f	—
reducción de coste (Es)	Kostensenkung f	cost reduction	diminution des coûts f	ribasso dei costi m	—
reducción de costes (Es)	Kostendegression f	cost degression	dégressivité des coûts f	riduzione dei costi f	—

	D	E	F	I	Es
reducción de gastos (Es)	Ausgabensenkung f	drop in expenditure	diminution des dépenses f	riduzione delle spese f	—
reducción de intereses (Es)	Zinserleichterung f	reduction of interest	minoration de l'intérêt m	agevolazione sugli interessi f	—
reducción de las subvenciones (Es)	Subventionsabbau m	reduction of subsidy	réduction des subventions f	riduzione delle sovvenzioni f	—
reducción del tipo de interés (Es)	Zinssenkung f	reduction of interest	diminution du taux de l'intérêt f	riduzione degli interessi f	—
reducción de personal (Es)	Personalabbau m	reduction of staff	réduction de personnel f	riduzione del personale f	—
reducción de precios (Es)	Preissenkung f	price reduction	réduction des prix f	riduzione dei prezzi f	—
reduced tariffs (E)	ermäßigte Tarife pl	—	tarifs reduits m pl	tariffe ridotte f pl	tarifas reducidas f pl
reduction¹ (E)	Abschlag m	—	déduction f	detrazione f	descuento m
reduction² (E)	Abbau m	—	réduction f/ diminution f	riduzione f/ diminuzione f	reducción f/ disminución f
reduction³ (E)	Minderung f	—	diminution f	riduzione f	reducción f
réduction¹ (F)	Abbau m	reduction/lay off	—	riduzione f/ diminuzione f	reducción f/ disminución f
réduction² (F)	Ermäßigung f	reduction	—	riduzione f	reducción f
réduction de prix (F)	Preisabzug m	price deduction	—	riduzione del prezzo f	descuento m
réduction des coûts (F)	Kostendämpfung f	combatting rising costs	—	contenimento dei costi m	disminución de costes f
réduction des prix (F)	Preissenkung f	price reduction	—	riduzione dei prezzi f	reducción de precios f
réduction des subventions (F)	Subventionsabbau m	reduction of subsidy	—	riduzione delle sovvenzioni f	reducción de las subvenciones f
réduction du prix (F)	Verbilligung f	cheapening	—	ribasso m	abaratamiento m
reduction of capital (E)	Kapitalherabsetzung f	—	diminution du capital f	riduzione del capitale f	reducción de capital f
reduction of interest¹ (E)	Zinssenkung f	—	diminution du taux de l'intérêt f	riduzione degli interessi f	reducción del tipo de interés f
reduction of interest² (E)	Zinserleichterung f	—	minoration de l'intérêt m	agevolazione sugli interessi f	reducción de intereses f
reduction of staff (E)	Personalabbau m	—	réduction de personnel f	riduzione del personale f	reducción de personal f
reduction of subsidy (E)	Subventionsabbau m	—	réduction des subventions f	riduzione delle sovvenzioni f	reducción de las subvenciones f
redundancia (Es)	Redundanz f	redundancy	redondance f	ridondanza f	—
redundancy (E)	Redundanz f	—	redondance f	ridondanza f	redundancia f
Redundanz (D)	—	redundancy	redondance f	ridondanza f	redundancia f
Reeder (D)	—	shipowner	armateur m	armatore m	armador m
Reederei (D)	—	shipping company	société d'armateurs f pl	compagnia armatoriale f	compañía naviera f
rééducation professionnelle (F)	Umschulung f	retraining	—	riqualificazione professionale f	readaptación profesional f
reembolso (Es)	Nachnahme f	cash on delivery	remboursement m	contrassegno m	—
reempaquetar (Es)	umpacken	repack	remballer	rifare l'imballaggio	—
réescompter (F)	rediskontieren	rediscount	—	riscontare	redescontar
reestructuración (Es)	Umstrukturierung f	restructuring	restructuration f	ristrutturazione f	—
réévaluation (F)	Wertberichtigung f	value adjustment	—	rettifica del valore f	rectificación de valor f
reexamination (E)	Nachprüfung f	—	vérification f	revisione f	revisión f
reexportación (Es)	Wiederausfuhr f	reexportation	réexportation f	riesportazione f	—
reexportation (E)	Wiederausfuhr f	—	réexportation f	riesportazione f	reexportación f
réexportation (F)	Wiederausfuhr f	reexportation	—	riesportazione f	reexportación f
reference¹ (E)	Referenz f	—	référence f	referenza f	referencia f
reference² (E)	Diktatzeichen n	—	références f pl	sigla f	referencias f pl
reference³ (E)	Bezug m	—	référence f	riferimento m	referencia f
référence¹ (F)	Referenz f	reference	—	referenza f	referencia f
référence² (F)	Bezug m	reference	—	riferimento m	referencia f
références (F)	Diktatzeichen n	reference	—	sigla f	referencias f pl

	D	E	F	I	Es
références de commande (F)	Bestelldaten *pl*	details of order	—	dati delle ordinazioni *m pl*	datos de pedido *m pl*
referencia[1] (Es)	Bezug *m*	reference	référence *f*	riferimento *m*	—
referencia[2] (Es)	Referenz *f*	reference	référence *f*	referenza *f*	—
referencias (Es)	Diktatzeichen *n*	reference	références *f pl*	sigla *f*	—
Referenz (D)	—	reference	référence *f*	referenza *f*	referencia *f*
referenza (I)	Referenz *f*	reference	référence *f*		referencia *f*
referring to (E)	bezugnehmend	—	se référant (à)	con riferimento	con referencia a
refinancement (F)	Refinanzierung *f*	refinancing	—	rifinanziamento *m*	refinanciación *f*
refinanciación (Es)	Refinanzierung *f*	refinancing	refinancement *m*	rifinanziamento *m*	—
refinancing (E)	Refinanzierung *f*	—	refinancement *m*	rifinanziamento *m*	refinanciación *f*
Refinanzierung (D)	—	refinancing	refinancement *m*	rifinanziamento *m*	refinanciación *f*
reforma agraria (Es)	Bodenreform *f*	land reform	réforme agraire *f*	riforma agraria *f*	—
réforme agraire (F)	Bodenreform *f*	land reform	—	riforma agraria *f*	reforma agraria *f*
refus[1] (F)	Absage *f*	refusal	—	risposta negativa *f*	negativa *f*
refus[2] (F)	Ablehnung *f*	refusal/rejection	—	rifiuto *m*/rigetto *m*	recusación *f*/repulsa *f*
refus d'acceptation (F)	Annahme-verweigerung *f*	refusal of delivery	—	rifiuto d'accettazione *m*	rehuso de aceptación *m*
refusal[1] (E)	Absage *f*	—	refus *m*	risposta negativa *f*	negativa *f*
refusal[2] (E)	Ablehnung *f*	—	refus *m*/rejet *m*	rifiuto *m*/rigetto *m*	recusación *f*/repulsa *f*
refusal of delivery (E)	Annahme-verweigerung *f*	—	refus d'acceptation *m*	rifiuto d'accettazione *m*	rehuso de aceptación *m*
regalo publicitario (Es)	Werbegeschenk *n*	advertising gift	cadeau publicitaire *m*	omaggio pubblicitario *m*	—
Regiebetrieb (D)	—	publicly owned enterprise	établissement en régie *m*	gestione in economia *f*	empresa estatal *m*
Regierung (D)	—	government/Ministry	gouvernement *m*	governo *m*	gobierno *m*
régime de l'admission en franchise (F)	Zollfreischreibungs-verfahren *n*	procedure of duty free admission	—	procedura d'ammis-sione in franchigia *f*	régimen de admisión en franquicia *m*
régime de la propriété (F)	Eigentums-verhältnisse *pl*	property relations	—	rapporti di proprietà *m pl*	régimen de tenencia *m*
regime di prelievo (I)	Abschöpfungs-system *n*	absorption system	système d'absorption *m*	—	sistema de gravámenes *m*
régime douanier (F)	Zollverkehr *m*	customs procedure	—	procedure doganali *f pl*	régimen aduanero de mercancías *m*
régime juridique de la faillite (F)	Konkursordnung *f*	Bankruptcy Act	—	legge fallimentare *f*	ley de las quiebras *f*
régime monétaire international (F)	internationale Währungsordnung *f*	international monetary system	—	regolamento valutario internazionale *m*	régimen monetario internacional *m*
régimen aduanero de mercancías (Es)	Zollverkehr *m*	customs procedure	régime douanier *m*	procedure doganali *f pl*	—
régimen de admisión en franquicia (Es)	Zollfreischreibungs-verfahren *n*	procedure of duty-free admission	régime de l'admission en franchise *m*	procedura d'ammis-sione in franchigia *f*	—
régimen de tenencia (Es)	Eigentums-verhältnisse *pl*	property relations	régime de la propriété *m*	rapporti di proprietà *m pl*	—
régimen de trabajo a destajo (Es)	Akkordsystem *n*	piece work system	système du travail aux pièces *m*	sistema del lavoro a cottimo *m*	—
régimen monetario internacional (Es)	internationale Währungsordnung *f*	international monetary system	régime monétaire international *m*	regolamento valutario internazionale *m*	—
Regionalbank (D)	—	regional bank	banque régionale *f*	banca regionale *f*	banco regional *m*
regional bank (E)	Regionalbank *f*	—	banque régionale *f*	banca regionale *f*	banco regional *m*
regional planning[1] (E)	Raumplanung *f*	—	plan d'aménagement des espaces *m*	pianificazione territoriale *f*	planificación del espacio *m*
regional planning[2] (E)	Regionalplanung *f*	—	aménagement régional *m*	pianificazione regionale *f*	planificación regional *f*
Regionalplanung (D)	—	regional planning	aménagement régional *m*	pianificazione regionale *f*	planificación regional *f*
regional policy[1] (E)	Raumordnung *f*	—	aménagement des espaces *m*	ordinamento territoriale *m*	ordenación del territorio *f*
regional policy[2] (E)	Regionalpolitik *f*	—	politique régionale *f*	politica regionale *f*	política regional *f*
Regionalpolitik (D)	—	regional policy	politique régionale *f*	politica regionale *f*	política regional *f*
región industrial (Es)	Industriegebiet *n*	industrial area	région industrielle *f*	zona industriale *f*	—

	D	E	F	I	Es
région industrielle (F)	Industriegebiet *n*	industrial area	—	zona industriale *f*	región industrial *f*
Register (D)	—	register	registre *m*	registro *m*	registro *m*
register (E)	Register *n*	—	registre *m*	registro *m*	registro *m*
Registered (E)	Einschreiben *n*	—	en recommandé	raccomandata *f*	certificado *m*
Registered-Advice of Delivery (E)	Einschreiben-Rückschein *m*	—	lettre recommandée avec avis de réception *f*	lettera racommandata con ricevuta di ritorno *f*	carta certificada con talón de recibo *f*
registered letter (E)	Einschreibebrief *m*	—	lettre recommandée *f*	lettera raccomandata *f*	carta certificada *f*
registered shares (E)	Namensaktie *f*	—	action nominative *f*	azione nominativa *f*	acción nominal *f*
register of ships (E)	Schiffsregister *n*	—	répertoire des navires *m*	registro navale *m*	registro marítimo *m*
register ton (E)	Registertonne *f*	—	tonneau de jauge *m*	tonnellata di registro *f*	tonelada de registro *f*
Registertonne (D)	—	register ton	tonneau de jauge *m*	tonnellata di registro *f*	tonelada de registro *f*
registration (E)	Anmeldung *f*	—	inscription *f*/ déclaration *f*	avviso *m*/ dichiarazione *f*	solicitud *f*/ declaración *f*
registre (F)	Register *n*	register	—	registro *m*	registro *m*
registre du commerce (F)	Handelsregister *n*	commercial register	—	registro commerciale *m*	registro mercantil *m*
registro (Es)	Register *n*	register	registre *m*	registro *m*	—
registro (I)	Register *n*	register	registre *m*	—	registro *m*
registro commerciale (I)	Handelsregister *n*	commercial register	registre du commerce *m*	—	registro mercantil *m*
registro marítimo (Es)	Schiffsregister *n*	register of ships	répertoire des navires *m*	registro navale *m*	—
registro mercantil (Es)	Handelsregister *n*	commercial register	registre du commerce *m*	registro commerciale *m*	—
registro navale (I)	Schiffsregister *n*	register of ships	répertoire des navires *m*	—	registro marítimo *m*
reglamentación del mercado agrícola (Es)	Agrarmarktordnung *f*	agricultural market organization	organisation des marchés agricoles *f*	regolamento del mercato agrario *m*	—
reglamentación de precios (Es)	Preislenkung *f*	administration of prices	réglementation des prix *f*	gestione dei prezzi *f*	—
reglamento de exportación (Es)	Ausfuhr-bestimmungen *pl*	export regulations	dispositions d'exportation *f pl*	disposizioni per le esportazioni *f pl*	—
reglamento del artesanado (Es)	Handwerksordnung *f*	Handicrafts Regulation Act	code de l'artisanat *m*	codice dell'artigianato *m*	—
règle de droit (F)	Rechtsnorm *f*	legal norm	—	norma giuridica *f*	norma jurídica *f*
règlement (F)	Abrechnung *f*	settlement of accounts	—	liquidazione *f*	liquidación *f*
réglementation des prix (F)	Preislenkung *f*	administration of prices	—	gestione dei prezzi *f*	reglamentación de precios *f*
règlement des frais de voyage (F)	Reisekosten-abrechnung *f*	travel expense accounting	—	conteggio dei costi di viaggio *m*	liquidación de los gastos de viaje *f*
règlement immédiat (F)	sofortige Regulierung *f*	settlement with immediate effect	—	regolazione immediata *f*	regulación inmediata *f*
règlement transitoire (F)	Übergangsregelung *f*	transitional arrangement	—	regolamento transitorio *m*	regulación transitoria *f*
régler par compte (F)	abzahlen	pay off	—	pagare a rate	pagar por cuotas
regolamento (I)	Verordnung *f*	decree	décret *m*	—	ordenanza *f*
regolamento del mercato agrario (I)	Agrarmarktordnung *f*	agricultural market organization	organisation des marchés agricoles *f*	—	reglamentación del mercado agrícola *f*
regolamento transitorio (I)	Übergangsregelung *f*	transitional arrangement	règlement transitoire *m*	—	regulación transitoria *f*
regolamento valutario internazionale (I)	internationale Währungsordnung *f*	international monetary system	régime monétaire international *m*	—	régimen monetario internacional *m*
regolare (I)	ordnungsgemäß	orderly	correct(e)	—	debidamente
regolazione immediata (I)	sofortige Regulierung *f*	settlement with immediate effect	règlement immédiat *m*	—	regulación inmediata *f*
regreso (Es)	Regreß *m*	recourse	recours *m*	regresso *m*	—
Regreß (D)	—	recourse	recours *m*	regresso *m*	regreso *m*
regresso[1] (I)	Rückgriff *m*	recourse	recours *m*	—	recurso *m*
regresso[2] (I)	Abschwung *m*	down-swing	dépression *f*	—	baja *f*

	D	E	F	I	Es
regresso³ (I)	Regreß *m*	recourse	recours *m*	—	regreso *m*
regulación global (Es)	Globalsteuerung *f*	global control	régulation globale *f*	controllo globale *m*	—
regulación inmediata (Es)	sofortige Regulierung *f*	settlement with immediate effect	règlement immédiat *m*	regolazione immediata *f*	—
regulación transitoria (Es)	Übergangsregelung *f*	transitional arrangement	règlement transitoire *m*	regolamento transitorio *m*	—
regular customer (E)	Stammkunde *f*	—	client habituel *m*	cliente fisso *m*	cliente habitual *m*
regular customers (E)	Kundenstamm *m*	—	clients en portefeuille *m pl*	clientela fissa *f*	clientela fija *f*
regular meeting (E)	ordentliche Versammlung *f*	—	assemblée ordinaire *f*	assemblea ordinaria *f*	asamblea ordinaria *f*
régulation globale (F)	Globalsteuerung *f*	global control	—	controllo globale *m*	regulación golbal *f*
rehuso de aceptación (Es)	Annahmeverweigerung *f*	refusal of delivery	refus d'acceptation *m*	rifiuto d'accettazione *m*	—
Re-Import (D)	—	reimportation	réimportation *f*	reimportazione *f*	reimportación *f*
reimportación (Es)	Re-Import *m*	reimportation	réimportation *f*	reimportazione *f*	—
reimportation (E)	Re-Import *m*	—	réimportation *f*	reimportazione *f*	reimportación *f*
réimportation (F)	Re-Import *m*	reimportation	—	reimportazione *f*	reimportación *f*
reimportazione (I)	Re-Import *m*	reimportation	réimportation *f*	—	reimportación *f*
Reingewinn (D)	—	net profit	bénéfice net *m*	utile netto *m*	ganancia neta *f*
reinsurance (E)	Rückversicherung *f*	—	réassurance *f*	riassicurazione *f*	reaseguro *m*
reintegro (Es)	Abzahlung *f*	hire purchase	payement par acomptes *m*	pagamento a rate *m*	—
Reinvermögen (D)	—	net assets	avoir net *m*	patrimonio netto *m*	patrimonio neto *m*
reinversión (Es)	Reinvestition *f*	reinvestment	réinvestissement *m*	reinvestimento *m*	—
reinvestimento (I)	Reinvestition *f*	reinvestment	réinvestissement *m*	—	reinversión *f*
réinvestissement (F)	Reinvestition *f*	reinvestment	—	reinvestimento *m*	reinversión *f*
Reinvestition (D)	—	reinvestment	réinvestissement *m*	reinvestimento *m*	reinversión *f*
reinvestment (E)	Reinvestition *f*	—	réinvestissement *m*	reinvestimento *m*	reinversión *f*
Reisebüro (D)	—	travel agency	agence de voyages *f*	ufficio viaggi *m*	agencia de viajes *f*
Reisegepäckversicherung (D)	—	baggage insurance	assurance des bagages *f*	assicurazione del bagaglio *f*	seguro de equipajes *m*
Reisekostenabrechnung (D)	—	travel expense accounting	règlement des frais de voyage *m*	conteggio dei costi di viaggio *m*	liquidación de los gastos de viaje *f*
Reiseroute (D)	—	route	itinéraire *m*	itinerario *m*	itinerario *m*
Reiserücktrittsversicherung (D)	—	travel cancellation insurance	assurance de résiliation du voyage *f*	assicurazione recessione viaggio *f*	seguro de rescisión del viaje *m*
Reisescheck (D)	—	traveller's cheque	chèque de voyage *m*	assegno turistico *m*	cheque de viaje *m*
Reisespesen (D)	—	travel(l)ing expenses	frais de voyage *m pl*	spese di viaggio *f pl*	gastos de viaje *m pl*
reivindicación (Es)	Anspruch *m*	claim	prétention *f*	pretesa *f*	—
reivindicación salarial (Es)	Lohnforderung *f*	wage claim	revendication de salaire *f*	rivendicazione salariale *f*	—
Reklamation (D)	—	complaint	réclamation *f*	reclamo *m*	reclamación *f*
Reklame (D)	—	advertising	publicité *f*	réclame *f*	publicidad *f*
relación¹ (Es)	Relation *f*	relation	relation *f*	relazione *f*	—
relación² (Es)	Verhältnis *n*	proportion	relation *f*	rapporto *m*	—
relación comercial (Es)	Geschäftsverbindung *f*	business relation	relation d'affaires *f*	relazione d'affari *f*	—
relación cotización-ganancia (Es)	Kurs-Gewinn-Verhältnis *n*	price-earnings ratio	relation cours-bénéfice *f*	rapporto corso-profitto *m*	—
relación de confianza (Es)	Vertrauensverhältnis *n*	confidential relationship	rapport de confiance *f*	rapporto di fiducia *m*	—
relaciones comerciales¹ (Es)	Handelsbeziehungen *pl*	trade relations	relations commerciales *f pl*	rapporti commerciali *m pl*	—
relaciones comerciales² (Es)	Geschäftsbeziehung *f*	business relation	relations d'affaires *f pl*	rapporti d'affari *m pl*	—
relaciones públicas¹ (Es)	Öffentlichkeitsarbeit *f*	public relations (work)	relations publiques *f pl*	relazioni pubbliche *f pl*	—
relaciones públicas² (Es)	Public Relations	public relations	relations publiques *f pl*	public relations *f pl*	—
relación jurídica (Es)	Rechtsverhältnis *n*	legal relationship	rapport juridique *m*	rapporto giuridico *m*	—

	D	E	F	I	Es
relación laboral (Es)	Arbeitsverhältnis *n*	employee-employer relationship	rapport de travail *m*	rapporto di lavoro *m*	—
relación laboral a prueba (Es)	Arbeitsverhältnis auf Probe *n*	employee-employer relationship on a trial basis	contrat de travail convenu à l'essai *m*	rapporto di lavoro in prova *m*	—
relance économique (F)	Konjunkturbelebung *f*	economic upturn	—	ripresa coyunturale *f*	recuperación coyuntural *f*
Relation (D)	—	relation	relation *f*	relazione *f*	relación *f*
relation (E)	Relation *f*	—	relation *f*	relazione *f*	relación *f*
relation¹ (F)	Verhältnis *n*	proportion	—	rapporto *m*	relación *f*
relation² (F)	Relation *f*	relation	—	relazione *f*	relación *f*
relation cours-bénéfice (F)	Kurs-Gewinn-Verhältnis *n*	price-earnings ratio	—	rapporto corso-profitto *m*	relación cotización-ganancia *f*
relation d'affaires (F)	Geschäfts-verbindung *f*	business relation	—	relazione d'affari *f*	relación comercial *f*
relations commerciales (F)	Handels-beziehungen *pl*	trade relations	—	rapporti commerciali *m pl*	relaciones comerciales *f pl*
relations d'affaires (F)	Geschäfts-beziehung *f*	business relation	—	rapporti d'affari *m pl*	relaciones comerciales *f pl*
relations publiques (F)	Öffentlichkeitsarbeit *f*	public relations (work)	—	relazioni pubbliche *f pl*	relaciones públicas *f pl*
relazione¹ (I)	Berichterstattung *f*	reporting	compte rendu *m*	—	reportaje *m*
relazione² (I)	Relation *f*	relation	relation *f*	—	relación *f*
relazione d'affari (I)	Geschäfts-verbindung *f*	business relation	relation d'affaires *f*	—	relación comercial *f*
relazione di costituzione (I)	Gründungsbericht *m*	formation report	procès-verbal de fondation *m*	—	informe de los fundadores *m*
relazione finanziaria (I)	Finanzbericht *m*	financial report	rapport financier *m*	—	informe financiero *m*
relazione generale sulla situazione economica (I)	Jahreswirtschafts-bericht *m*	Annual Economic Report	compte rendu d'activité économique annuel *m*	—	informe económico anual *m*
relazione sull'eserci-zio commerciale (I)	Geschäftsbericht *m*	business report	rapport de gestion *m*	—	informe *m*
relazioni pubbliche (I)	Öffentlichkeitsarbeit *f*	public relations (work)	relations publiques *f pl*	—	relaciones públicas *f pl*
relevant (D)	—	relevant	significatif	rilevante	importante
relevant (E)	relevant	—	significatif	rilevante	importante
relève d'équipe (F)	Schichtwechsel *m*	change of shift	—	cambio di turno *m*	cambio del equipo de obreros *m*
relèvement des impôts (F)	Steuererhöhung *f*	increase of taxes	—	aumento delle imposte *m*	aumento de los impuestos *m*
reliable (E)	zuverlässig	—	de confiance	affidabile	de confianza
remaining assets after liquidation (E)	Liquidationserlös *m*	—	produit de la liquidation *m*	ricavo della liquidazione *f*	haber social repartible *m*
remarque (F)	Vermerk *m*	note	—	annotazione *f*	nota *f*
remballer (F)	umpacken	repack	—	rifare l'imballaggio	reempaquetar
remboursement¹ (F)	Abzahlung *f*	repayment/hire purchase	—	rimborso *m*/pagamento a rate *m*	reintegro *m*/pago a plazos *m*
remboursement² (F)	Rückerstattung *f*	repayment	—	rimborso *m*	restitución *f*
remboursement³ (F)	Nachnahme *f*	cash on delivery	—	contrassegno *m*	reembolso *m*
Rembourskredit (D)	—	documentary acceptance credit	crédit documentaire confirmé *m*	credito di rimborso *m*	crédito de reembolso *m*
remembrement parcellaire (F)	Flurbereinigung *f*	compulsory consoli-dation of farmland	—	ricomposizione fondiaria *f*	concentración parcelaria *f*
remesa (Es)	Rimesse *f*	remittance	remise *f*	rimessa *f*	—
remettant (F)	Remittent *m*	payee	—	beneficiario *m*	remitente *m*
remettre en mains sûres (F)	zu treuen Händen	for safekeeping	—	alla particolare attenzione	a la atención
reminder (E)	Mahnbrief *m*	—	lettre d'avertissement *f*	lettera di sollecito *f*	carta (ad)monitoria *f*
remise¹ (F)	Übergabe *f*	delivery	—	consegna *f*	entrega *f*
remise² (F)	Rimesse *f*	remittance	—	rimessa *f*	remesa *f*
remise³ (F)	Zustellung *f*	delivery	—	notifica *f*/recapito *m*	envío *m*

	D	E	F	I	Es
remise⁴ (F)	Rabatt m	discount	—	ribasso m	rebaja f
remise⁵ (F)	Aufschiebung f	postponement	—	rinvio m	aplazamiento m
remise de faveur (F)	Vorzugsrabatt m	preferential discount	—	ribasso preferenziale m	rebaja preferencial f
remise de quantité (F)	Mengenrabatt m	quantity discount	—	sconto di quantità m	rebaja de cantidad f
remise en ordre (F)	Nachbereitung f	aftertreatment	—	rielaborazione f	tratamiento ulterior m
remise par exprès (F)	Eilzustellung f	express delivery	—	consegna per espresso f	entrega urgente f
remise pour payement au comptant (F)	Barzahlungs-nachlaß m	discount for cash payment	—	sconto per pagamento in contanti m	descuento por pago al contado m
remise pour payement comptant (F)	Barzahlungsrabatt m	cash discount	—	ribasso per paga-mento in contanti m	descuento por pago al contado m
remise sur le prix (F)	Preisnachlaß m	price reduction	—	ribasso del prezzo m	rebaja f
remitente¹ (Es)	Remittent m	payee	remettant m	beneficiario m	—
remitente² (Es)	Absender m	sender	envoyeur m	mittente m	—
remitido a la prensa (Es)	Pressemitteilung f	press release	commentaire de presse m	comunicazione stampa f	—
remittance¹ (E)	Überweisung f	—	virement m	rimessa f	transferencia f
remittance² (E)	Rimesse f	—	remise f	rimessa f	remesa f
Remittent (D)	—	payee	remettant m	beneficiario m	remitente m
remnants (E)	Restposten m	—	lot restant m	rimanenze f pl	partida restante f
remote data transmission (E)	Datenfern-übertragung f	—	télétransmission des données informatiques f	teletrasmissione dati f	transmisión de datos f
remuneración¹ (Es)	Gage f	salary	cachet m	onorario m	—
remuneración² (Es)	Vergütung f	remuneration	rémunération f	ricompensa f	—
remuneración del empresario (Es)	Unternehmerlohn m	entrepreneurial income	rémunération de l'entrepreneur f	retribuzione dell'imprenditore f	—
remuneration (E)	Vergütung f	—	rémunération f	ricompensa f	remuneración f
rémunération (F)	Vergütung f	remuneration	—	ricompensa f	remuneración f
rémunération de l'entrepreneur (F)	Unternehmerlohn m	entrepreneurial income	—	retribuzione dell'imprenditore f	remuneración del empresario f
rémunération du tra-vail en nature (F)	Naturallohn m	wages (paid) in kind	—	remunerazione in natura f	salario en especie m
remuneration in kind (E)	Sachbezüge pl	—	prestations en nature f pl	retribuzioni in natura f pl	percepciónes en especie f pl
rémunération spéciale (F)	Sondervergütung f	special remuneration	—	compenso straordinario m	gratificación f
remunerazione in natura (I)	Naturallohn m	wages (paid) in kind	rémunérarion du tra-vail en nature f	—	salario en especie m
rendement¹ (F)	Leistung f	performance	—	rendimento m	rendimiento m
rendement² (F)	Arbeitsleistung f	productivity	—	produttività f	productividad f
rendement³ (F)	Rendite f	yield	—	rendita f	rentabilidad f
rendement du chiffre d'affaires (F)	Umsatzrendite f	net income per-centage of turnover	—	rendita del fatturato f	rédito de la cifra de ventas m
rendement du travail (F)	Arbeitsertrag m	work performed	—	rendimento del lavoro m	rendimiento del trabajo m
rendement réel (F)	Realzins m	real (rate of) interest	—	tasso d'interesse reale m	interés real m
rendez-vous (F)	Treffpunkt m	meeting place	—	punto d'incontro m	lugar de la cita m
rendez-vous de présentation (F)	Vorstellungstermin m	date of interview	—	appuntamento di presentazione m	fecha de entrevista personal f
rendimento (I)	Leistung f	performance	rendement m	—	rendimiento m
rendimento del lavoro (I)	Arbeitsertrag m	work performed	rendement du travail m	—	rendimiento del trabajo m
rendimiento del capital (Es)	Kapitalertrag m	income from capital	produit du capital m	rendita del capitale f	—
rendimiento del trabajo (Es)	Arbeitsertrag m	work performed	rendement du travail m	rendimento del lavoro m	—
rendita (I)	Rendite f	yield	rendement m	—	rentabilidad f
rendita del capitale (I)	Kapitalertrag m	income from capital	produit du capital m	—	rendimiento del capital m

	D	E	F	I	Es
rendita del fatturato (I)	Umsatzrendite f	net income percentage of turnover	rendement du chiffre d'affaires m	—	rédito de la cifra de ventas m
rendita del produttore (I)	Produzentenrente f	producer's surplus	rente du vendeur f	—	superávit del productor m
Rendite (D)	—	yield	rendement m	rendita f	rentabilidad f
renewal costs (E)	Sanierungskosten pl	—	coûts d'assainissement m pl	costi di risanamento m pl	gastos de saneamiento m pl/ gastos de rehabilitación m pl
renonciation à la consommation (F)	Konsumverzicht m	voluntary constraint in consumption	—	rinuncia al consumo f	renuncia al consumo f
renseignement (F)	Auskunft f	information	—	informazione f	información f
renseignement fourni par l'intéressé lui-même (F)	Selbstauskunft f	voluntary disclosure	—	informazione volontaria f	información de sí mismo f
rent¹ (E)	Mietzins m	—	prix de location m	canone di locazione m	arrendamiento m
rent² (E)	Miete f	—	location f	canone di locazione m	alquiler m
renta (Es)	Rente f	annuity	rente f	rendita f	—
rentabilidad¹ (Es)	Ertragskraft f	earning capacity	force productive f	redditività f	—
rentabilidad² (Es)	Wirtschaftlichkeit f	economic efficiency	rentabilité f	economicità f	—
rentabilidad³ (Es)	Rendite f	yield	rendement m	rendita f	—
rentabilidad⁴ (Es)	Rentabilität f	profitability	rentabilité f	redditività f	—
rentabilidad del capital (Es)	Kapitalrentabilität f	return on investment	rentabilité du capital f	redditività del capitale f	—
Rentabilität (D)	—	profitability	rentabilité f	redditività f	rentabilidad f
Rentabilitätschwelle (D)	—	break-even point	seuil de rentabilité m	soglia di redditività f	límite inferior de rentabilidad m
rentabilité¹ (F)	Rentabilität f	profitability	—	redditività f	rentabilidad f
rentabilité² (F)	Wirtschaftlichkeit f	economic efficiency	—	economicità f	rentabilidad f
rentabilité du capital (F)	Kapitalrentabilität f	return on investment	—	redditività del capitale f	rentabilidad del capital f
renta del capital (Es)	Kapitalzins m	interest on capital	intérêt du capital m	interesse del capitale m	—
renta de la propiedad (Es)	Besitzeinkommen n	unearned income	revenu du patrimoine m	reddito da possesso m	—
Rente (D)	—	annuity	rente f	rendita f	renta f
rente (F)	Rente f	annuity	—	rendita f	renta f
rente du vendeur (F)	Produzentenrente f	producer's surplus	—	rendita del produttore f	superávit del productor m
Rentenanleihe (D)	—	annuity bonds	effet public m	prestito a reddito fisso m	empréstito por anualidades m
Rentenfonds (D)	—	pension fund	fonds d'Etat m/ effets publics m pl	fondo obbligazionario m	fondo de bonos m
Rentenmarkt (D)	—	bond market	marché des effets publics m	mercato dei titoli a reddito fisso m	mercado de títulos de renta fija m
Rentenpapiere (D)	—	bonds	titres de rente m pl	titoli a reddito fisso m pl	títulos de renta fija m pl
Rentenversicherung (D)	—	old-age pension insurance	assurance sociale invalidité-vieillesse f	assicurazione invalidità e vecchiaia f	seguro de pensiones m
renuncia al consumo (Es)	Konsumverzicht m	voluntary constraint in consumption	renonciation à la consommation f	rinuncia al consumo f	—
renvoi (F)	Rücksendung f	return	—	rispedizione f	devolución f
repack (E)	umpacken	—	remballer	rifare l'imballaggio	reempaquetar
repair¹ (E)	reparieren	—	réparer	riparare	reparar
repair² (E)	Reparatur f	—	réparation f	riparazione f	reparación f
repair instructions (E)	Reparaturanleitung f	—	instruction de réparation f	istruzione per la riparazione f	instrucción de reparación f
reparación (Es)	Reparatur f	repair	réparation f	riparazione f	—
reparar (Es)	reparieren	repair	réparer	riparare	—
réparation (F)	Reparatur f	repair	—	riparazione f	reparación f
Reparatur (D)	—	repair	réparation f	riparazione f	reparación f
Reparaturanleitung (D)	—	repair instructions	instruction de réparation f	istruzione per la riparazione f	instrucción de reparación f

	D	E	F	I	Es
réparer (F)	reparieren	repair	—	riparare	reparar
reparieren (D)	—	repair	réparer	riparare	reparar
répartition¹ (F)	Umlage f	charge levied	—	ripartizione f	reparto m
répartition² (F)	Zuteilung f	allocation	—	attribuzione f/ ripartizione f	asignación f
répartition des bénéfices (F)	Gewinnverteilung f	distribution of profits	—	ripartizione dell'utile f	reparto de beneficios m
répartition du patrimoine (F)	Vermögens-verteilung f	distribution of wealth	—	ripartizione del patrimonio f	reparto de la riqueza m
reparto (I)	Abteilung f	division/department	service m	—	sección f
reparto de beneficios (Es)	Gewinnverteilung f	distribution of profits	répartition des bénéfices f	ripartizione dell'utile f	—
reparto de la riqueza (Es)	Vermögens-verteilung f	distribution of wealth	repartition du patrimoine f	ripartizione del patrimonio f	—
reparto esportazioni (I)	Exportabteilung f	export department	service d'exportation m	—	departamento de exportación m
reparto marketing (I)	Marketingabteilung f	marketing department	bureau de marketing m	—	departamento de mercadeo m
reparto pubblicità (I)	Werbeabteilung f	publicity department	service de publicité m	—	sección de publicidad f
reparto spedizioni (I)	Versandabteilung f	dispatch department	service des expéditions m	—	departamento de expedición m
reparto tecnico (I)	technische Abteilung f	engineering department	service technique m	—	departamento técnico m
repayment¹ (E)	Abzahlung f	—	remboursement m/ payement par acomptes m	rimborso m/ pagamento a rate m	reintegro m/ pago a plazos m
repayment² (E)	Rückerstattung f	—	rembourse-ment m	rimborso m	restitución f
repeat (E)	Reprise f	—	tendance à la hausse f	ripresa f	segunda lectura en el corro f
repeat order (E)	Nachbestellung f	—	nouvel ordre m	ordinazione supplementare f	pedido suplementario m
repercusión (Es)	Feedback n	feedback	feed-back m	feedback m	—
répercussion (F)	Überwälzung f	passing on	—	accollamento m	traslación f
répertoire des navires (F)	Schiffsregister n	register of ships	—	registro navale m	registro marítimo m
replaceable (E)	substituierbar	—	interchangeable	sostituibile	sustituible
replacement (E)	Wiederbeschaffung f	—	réapprovisionne-ment m	riapprovvigiona-mento m	reposición f
reply (E)	Antwort f	—	réponse f	risposta f	respuesta f
répondeur automatique (F)	Anrufbeantworter m	answering machine	—	segreteria telefonica f	contestador de llamadas m
réponse (F)	Antwort f	reply	—	risposta f	respuesta f
Report (D)	—	report	rapport m	rapporto m	informe m
report (E)	Report m	—	rapport m	rapporto m	informe m
reportaje (Es)	Berichterstattung f	reporting	compte rendu m	relazione f	—
reporting (E)	Berichterstattung f	—	compte rendu m	relazione f	reportaje m
reposición (Es)	Wiederbeschaffung f	replacement	réapprovisionne-ment m	riapprovvigiona-mento m	—
Repräsentant (D)	—	representative	représentant m	rappresentante m	representante m
représaille (F)	Repressalie f	reprisals	—	rappresaglia f	represalia f
represalia (Es)	Repressalie f	reprisals	représaille f	rappresaglia f	—
representación (Es)	Vertretung f	representation	représentation f	rappresentanza f	—
representación comercial (Es)	Handelsvertretung f	commercial agency	représentation commerciale f	rappresentanza commerciale f	—
representación de intereses (Es)	Interessen-vertretung f	representation of interests	représentation des intérêts f	rappresentanza degli interessi f	—
representación en el exterior (Es)	Auslandsvertretung f	agency abroad	agence à l'étranger f	rappresentanza estera f	—
representación exclusiva (Es)	Alleinvertretung f	sole agency	agence exclusive f	rappresentanza esclusiva f	—
représentant (F)	Vertreter m	representative	—	rappresentante m	representante m

	D	E	F	I	Es
représentant de commerce (F)	Handelsvertreter *m*	commercial agent	—	rappresentante commerciale *m*	representante comercial *m*
representante (Es)	Vertreter *m*	representative	représentant *m*	rappresentante *m*	—
representante comercial (Es)	Handelsvertreter *m*	commercial agent	représentant de commerce *m*	rappresentante commerciale *m*	—
representante general (Es)	Generalvertreter *m*	general agent	agent général *m*	rappresentante generale *m*	—
representante regional (Es)	Gebietsvertreter *m*	area representative	représentant régional *m*	agente di zona *m*	—
représentant régional (F)	Gebietsvertreter *m*	area representative	—	agente di zona *m*	representante regional *m*
representation (E)	Vertretung *f*	—	représentation *f*	rappresentanza *f*	representación *f*
représentation (F)	Vertretung *f*	representation	—	rappresentanza *f*	representación *f*
représentation commerciale (F)	Handelsvertretung *f*	commercial agency	—	rappresentanza commerciale *f*	representación comercial *f*
représentation des intérêts (F)	Interessen-vertretung *f*	representation of interests	—	rappresentanza degli interessi *f*	representación de intereses *f*
representation of interests (E)	Interessen-vertretung *f*	—	représentation des intérêts *f*	rappresentanza degli interessi *f*	representación de intereses *f*
representative (E)	Vertreter *m*	—	représentant *m*	rappresentante *m*	representante *m*
Repressalie (D)	—	reprisals	représaille *f*	rappresaglia *f*	represalia *f*
reprisals (E)	Repressalie *f*	—	représaille *f*	rappresaglia *f*	represalia *f*
Reprise (D)	—	repeat	tendance à la hausse *f*	ripresa *f*	segunda lectura en el corro *f*
reprise d'une affaire (F)	Geschäfts-übernahme *f*	business acquisition	—	acquisto di un'azienda *m*	adquisición de una empresa *f*
Reprivatisierung (D)	—	reversion to private ownership	dénationalisation *f*	riprivatizzazione *f*	desnacionalización *f*
reproducción (Es)	Vervielfältigung *f*	reproduction	reproduction *f*	riproduzione *f*	—
reproduction (E)	Vervielfältigung *f*	—	reproduction *f*	riproduzione *f*	reproducción *f*/multiplicación *f*
reproduction (F)	Vervielfältigung *f*	reproduction	—	riproduzione *f*	reproducción *f*/multiplicación *f*
reproduction cost (E)	Reproduktions-kosten *pl*	—	coût de reproduction *m*	costi di riproduzione *m pl*	gastos de reprducción *m pl*
reproduction value (E)	Reproduktionswert *m*	—	valeur de remplacement *f*	valore di riproduzione *m*	valor de reproducción *m*
Reproduktion (D)	—	reproduction	reproduction *f*	riproduzione *f*	reproducción *f*
Reproduktions-kosten (D)	—	reproduction cost	coût de reproduction *m*	costi di riproduzione *m pl*	gastos de reprducción *m pl*
Reproduktionswert (D)	—	reproduction value	valeur de remplacement *f*	valore di riproduzione *m*	valor de reproducción *m*
reputación (Es)	Leumund *m*	reputation	réputation *f*	reputazione *f*	—
reputation (E)	Leumund *m*	—	réputation *f*	reputazione *f*	reputación *f*
réputation (F)	Leumund *m*	reputation	—	reputazione *f*	reputación *f*
reputazione (I)	Leumund *m*	reputation	réputation *f*	—	reputación *f*
requirement characteristics (E)	Anforderungs-merkmal *n*	—	caractéristique d'exigences *f*	caratteristica richiesta *f*	característica de requisitos *f*
requirement factors (E)	Bedarfsfaktoren *pl*	—	éléments pouvant influencer la demande *m pl*	fattori del fabbisogno *m pl*	factores determinantes de las necesidades *m pl*
requirement of information (E)	Informationsbedarf *m*	—	besoin d'information *m*	bisogno d'informazioni *m*	necesidad de información *f*
resale price (E)	Wieder-verkaufspreis *m*	—	prix de revente *m*	prezzo di rivendita *m*	precio de reventa *m*
rescisión (Es)	Kündigung *f*	notice of termination (of employment)	licenciement *m*	licenziamento *m*	—
rescission (E)	Rücktritt *m*	—	démission *f*/résolution du contrat *f*	recesso *m*	rescisión *f*
research (E)	Forschung *f*	—	recherche *f*	ricerca *f*	investigación *f*
réseau (F)	Netzwerk *n*	network	—	rete *f*	red *f*
réseau de succursales (F)	Filialnetz *n*	branch network	—	rete delle filiali *f*	red de sucursales *f*

	D	E	F	I	Es
réseau linéaire pour planification (F)	Netzplan *m*	network planning	—	pianificazione reticolare *f*	planificación reticular *f*
réseau routier (F)	Straßennetz *n*	road network	—	rete stradale *f*	red de carreteras *f*
reseller (E)	Wiederverkäufer *m*	—	revendeur *m*	rivenditore *m*	revendedor *m*
reserva (Es)	Rückstellung *f*	reserves	provision pour pertes et charges *f*	accantonamento *m*	—
reservación (Es)	Reservierung *f*	reservation	réservation *f*	prenotazione *f*	—
reserva de liquidez (Es)	Liquiditätsreserve *f*	liquidity reserves	réserves de liquidité *f pl*	riserva di liquidità *f*	—
reserva mínima (Es)	Mindestreserve *f*	minimum reserves	réserve minimum *f*	riserva minima obbligatoria *f*	—
reservas (Es)	Rücklagen *pl*	reserves	réserve *f*	riserve *f pl*	—
reserva tácita[1] (Es)	stille Rücklage *f*	latent funds	réserve cachée *f*	riserva latente *m*	—
reserva tácita[2] (Es)	stille Reserve *f*	hidden reserves	réserve cachée *f*	riserva occulta *f*	—
reservation[1] (E)	Vorbestellung *f*	—	commande préalable *f*	ordinazione anticipata *f*	pedidio anticipado *m*
reservation[2] (E)	Reservierung *f*	—	réservation *f*	prenotazione *f*	reservación *f*
réservation (F)	Reservierung *f*	reservation	—	prenotazione *f*	reservación *f*
reservation confirmation (E)	Reservierungs-bestätigung *f*	—	confirmation de réservation *f*	conferma della prenotazione *f*	confirmación de la reservación *f*
Reserve (D)	—	reserve stock/ reserves	stocks de ré-serve *m pl*/réserve *f*	scorte *f pl*/ riserva *f*	existencias *f pl*/ reserva *f*
réserve (F)	Rücklagen *pl*	reserves	—	riserve *f pl*	reservas *f pl*
réserve cachée[1] (F)	stille Rücklage *f*	latent funds	—	riserva latente *m*	reserva tácita *f*
réserve cachée[2] (F)	stille Reserve *f*	hidden reserves	—	riserva occulta *f*	reserva tácita *f*
reserve currency (E)	Reservewährung *f*	—	monnaie de réserve *f*	valuta di riserva *f*	moneda de reserva *f*
réserve de capital (F)	Kapitalstock *m*	capital stock	—	riserva di capitale *f*	fondo de capital *m*
Reservefonds (D)	—	reserve fund	fonds de réserve *m*	fondo di riserva *m*	fondo de reserva *m*
reserve fund (E)	Reservefonds *m*	—	fonds de réserve *m*	fondo di riserva *m*	fondo de reserva *m*
réserve minimum (F)	Mindestreserve *f*	minimum reserves	—	riserva minima obbligatoria *f*	reserva mínima *f*
reserves[1] (E)	Rücklagen *pl*	—	réserve *f*	riserve *f*	reservas *f pl*
reserves[2] (E)	Rückstellung *f*	—	provision pour pertes et charges *f*	accantonamento *m*	reserva *f*
réserves de liquidité (F)	Liquiditätsreserve *f*	liquidity reserves	—	riserva di liquidità *f*	reserva de liquidez *f*
reserve stock (E)	Reserve *f*	—	stocks de ré-serve *m pl*/réserve *f*	scorte *f pl*/ riserva *f*	existencias *f pl*/ reserva *f*
Reservewährung (D)	—	reserve currency	monnaie de réserve *f*	valuta di riserva *f*	moneda de reserva *f*
Reservierung (D)	—	reservation	réservation *f*	prenotazione *f*	reservación *f*
Reservierungs-bestätigung (D)	—	reservation confirmation	confirmation de réservation *f*	conferma della prenotazione *f*	confirmación de la reservación *f*
resguardo de almacén (Es)	Lagerschein *m*	warehouse warrant	certificat de dépôt *m*	ricevuta di deposito *f*	—
residence permit (E)	Aufenthaltserlaubnis *f*	—	autorisation de séjour *f*	permesso di soggiorno *m*	permiso de residencia *m*
resident (E)	Deviseninländer *m*	—	résident *m*	persona residente *f*	residente *m*
résident (F)	Deviseninländer *m*	resident	—	persona residente *f*	residente *m*
residente (Es)	Deviseninländer *m*	resident	résident *m*	persona residente *f*	—
residents' registration office (E)	Einwohnermelde-amt *n*	—	bureau de déclaration de résidence *m*	ufficio anagrafe *m*	oficina del censo *f*
residual time to maturity (E)	Restlaufzeit *f*	—	durée restante *f*	scadenza residua *f*	plazo de vencimiento restante *m*
residual value (E)	Restwert *m*	—	valeur résiduelle *f*	valore rimanente *f*	valor residual *m*/ valor contable residual *m*
residues (E)	Rückstände *pl*	—	déchet *m*	residui *m pl*	residuos *m pl*
residui (I)	Rückstände *pl*	residues	déchet *m*	—	residuos *m pl*
residuos (Es)	Rückstände *pl*	residues	déchet *m*	residui *m pl*	—
résiliation (F)	Kündigung *f*	notice of termination	—	disdetta *f*	rescisión *f*

	D	E	F	I	Es
resistente alle crisi (I)	krisenfest	slump-proof	insensible aux influences de la crise économique	—	a prueba de crisis
resolución (Es)	Resolution f	resolution	résolution f	risoluzione f	—
Resolution (D)	—	resolution	résolution f	risoluzione f	resolución f
resolution (E)	Resolution f	—	résolution f	risoluzione f	resolución f
résolution (F)	Resolution f	resolution	—	risoluzione f	resolución f
resources (E)	Ressource f	—	ressource f	risorsa f	recurso m
respite (E)	Stundung f	—	prorogation f	dilazione f/proroga f	moratoria f
responsabilidad (Es)	Haftung f	liability	responsabilité f	responsabilità f	—
responsabilidad civil del fabricante (Es)	Produzentenhaftung f	product liability	responsabilité du producteur f	responsabilità di produttore f	—
responsabilidad de garantía (Es)	Gewährleistungs-haftung f	liability for breach of warranty	responsabilité en matière de garantie f	responsabilità di garanzia f	—
responsabilidad del productor (Es)	Produkthaftung f	product liability	responsabilité du fabricant f	responsabilità prodotto f	—
responsabilidad jurídica (Es)	Rechtshaftung f	legal responsibility	responsabilité légale f	responsabilità giuridica f	—
responsabilidad primaria (Es)	Primärhaftung f	primary responsibility	responsabilité primaire f	responsabilità primaria f	—
responsabilità (I)	Haftung f	liability	responsabilité f	—	responsabilidad f
responsabilità di garanzia (I)	Gewährleistungs-haftung f	liability for breach of warranty	responsabilité en matière de garantie f	—	responsabilidad de garantía f
responsabilità di produttore (I)	Produzentenhaftung f	product liability	responsabilité du producteur f	—	responsabilidad civil del fabricante f
responsabilità giuridica (I)	Rechtshaftung f	legal responsibility	responsabilité légale f	—	responsabilidad jurídica f
responsabilità primaria (I)	Primärhaftung f	primary responsibility	responsabilité primaire f	—	responsabilidad primaria f
responsabilità prodotto (I)	Produkthaftung f	product liability	responsabilité du fabricant f	—	responsabilidad del productor f
responsabilité (F)	Haftung f	liability	—	responsabilità f	responsabilidad f
responsabilité du fabricant (F)	Produkthaftung f	product liability	—	responsabilità prodotto f	responsabilidad del productor f
responsabilité du producteur (F)	Produzentenhaftung f	product liability	—	responsabilità di produttore f	responsabilidad civil del fabricante f
responsabilité en matière de garantie (F)	Gewährleistungs-haftung f	liability for breach of warranty	—	responsabilità di garanzia f	responsabilidad de garantía f
responsabilité légale (F)	Rechtshaftung f	legal responsibility	—	responsabilità giuridica f	responsabilidad jurídica f
responsabilité primaire (F)	Primärhaftung f	primary responsibility	—	responsabilità primaria f	responsabilidad primaria f
respuesta (Es)	Antwort f	reply	réponse f	risposta f	—
Ressource (D)	—	resources	ressource f	risorsa f	recurso m
ressource (F)	Ressource f	resources	—	risorsa f	recurso m
Restdarlehen (D)	—	purchase-money loan	prêt restant m	mutuo residuo m	restante de un préstamo m
restitución[1] (Es)	Rückgabe f	return	restitution f	restituzione f	—
restitución[2] (Es)	Rückerstattung f	repayment	remboursement m	rimborso m	—
restitution (F)	Rückgabe f	return	—	restituzione f	restitución f
restituzione (I)	Rückgabe f	return	restitution f	—	restitución f
Restlaufzeit (D)	—	residual time to maturity	durée restante f	scadenza residua f	plazo de vencimiento restante m
Restposten (D)	—	remnants	lot restant m	rimanenze f pl	partida restante f
restraint of competition (E)	Wettbewerbs-beschränkung f	—	restriction apportée à la concurrence f	restrizione della concorrenza f	restricciones a la competencia f pl
restricción (Es)	Restriktion f	restriction	restriction f	restrizione f	—
restricción a la exportación (Es)	Ausfuhr-beschränkung f	export restriction	contingentement de l'exportation m	restrizione delle esportazioni f	—
restricción a la importación (Es)	Einfuhr-beschränkung f	import restriction	limitation des importations f	restrizione d'importazione f	—
restricción de créditos (Es)	Kreditrestriktion f	credit restriction	restriction du crédit f	restrizione creditizia f	—

	D	E	F	I	Es
restricción de la liquidez (Es)	Liquiditätsengpaß *m*	liquidity squeeze	goulot d'étranglement dans la trésorerie	strettoia di liquidità *f*	—
restricciones a la competencia (Es)	Wettbewerbs-beschränkung *f*	restraint of competition	restriction apportée à la concurrence *f*	restrizione della concorrenza *f*	—
restricciones commerciales (Es)	Handels-beschränkungen *pl*	trade restrictions	restrictions au commerce *f pl*	restrizioni commerciali *f pl*	—
restricción monetaria (Es)	Geldverknappung *f*	monetary restriction	pénurie d'argent *f*	riduzione del denaro *f*	—
restriction (E)	Restriktion *f*	—	restriction *f*	restrizione *f*	restricción *f*
restriction (F)	Restriktion *f*	restriction	—	restrizione *f*	restricción *f*
restriction apportée à la concurrence (F)	Wettbewerbs-beschränkung *f*	restraint of competition	—	restrizione della concorrenza *f*	restricciones a la competencia *f pl*
restriction du crédit (F)	Kreditrestriktion *f*	credit restriction	—	restrizione creditizia *f*	restricción de créditos *f*
restriction on cultivation (E)	Anbau-beschränkung *f*	—	limitation des cultures *f*	restrizione di coltivazione *f*	limitación de cultivos *f*
restrictions au commerce (F)	Handels-beschränkungen *pl*	trade restrictions	—	restrizioni commerciali *f pl*	restricciones commerciales *f pl*
Restriktion (D)	—	restriction	restriction *f*	restrizione *f*	restricción *f*
Restrisiko (D)	—	acceptable risk	risque acceptable *m*	rischio rimanente *m*	riesgo aceptable *m*
restrizione (I)	Restriktion *f*	restriction	restriction *f*	—	restricción *f*
restrizione creditizia (I)	Kreditrestriktion *f*	credit restriction	restriction du crédit *f*	—	restricción de créditos *f*
restrizione della concorrenza (I)	Wettbewerbs-beschränkung *f*	restraint of competition	restriction apportée à la concurrence *f*	—	restricciones a la competencia *f pl*
restrizione delle esportazioni (I)	Ausfuhr-beschränkung *f*	export restriction	contingentement de l'exportation *m*	—	restricción a la exportación *f*
restrizione di coltivazione (I)	Anbau-beschränkung *f*	restriction on cultivation	limitation des cultures *f*	—	limitación de cultivos *f*
restrizione d'importazione (I)	Einfuhr-beschränkung *f*	import restriction	limitation des importations *f*	—	restricción a la importación *f*
restrizioni commerciali (I)	Handels-beschränkungen *pl*	trade restrictions	restrictions au commerce *f pl*	—	restricciones commerciales *f pl*
restructuration (F)	Umstrukturierung *f*	restructuring	—	ristrutturazione *f*	reestructuración *f*
restructuring (E)	Umstrukturierung *f*	—	restructuration *f*	ristrutturazione *f*	reestructuración *f*
Restwert (D)	—	residual value/ net book value	valeur résiduelle *f*	valore rimanente *m*	valor residual *m*/valor contable residual *m*
result (E)	Ergebnis *n*	—	résultat *m*	risultato *m*	resultado *m*
resultado (Es)	Ergebnis *n*	result	résultat *m*	risultato *m*	—
résultat (F)	Ergebnis *n*	result	—	risultato *m*	resultado *m*
résultats effectifs (F)	Istzahlen *pl*	actual figures	—	dati effettivi *m pl*	cifras efectivas *f pl*
retailer (E)	Einzelhändler *m*	—	commerçant détaillant *m*	dettagliante *m*	minorista *m*
retail merchant (E)	Einzelhandels-kaufmann *m*	—	détaillant *m*	commerciante al dettaglio *m*	comerciante particular *m*
retail price (E)	Ladenpreis *m*	—	prix de vente *m*	prezzo di vendita *m*	precio de venta *m*
retail price margin (E)	Einzelhandels-spanne *f*	—	marge de détail *f*	margine del com-mercio al dettaglio *m*	margen del comercio al por menor *m*
retail trade (E)	Einzelhandel *m*	—	commerce de détail *m*	commercio al dettaglio *m*	comercio al por menor *m*
retard (F)	Verspätung *f*	delay	—	ritardo *m*	retraso *m*
retardataire (F)	säumig	dilatory	—	moroso	moroso
retard d'adaptation (F)	Anpassungs-verzögerung *f*	adjustment lag	—	ritardo d'adattamento *m*	retraso de adaptación *m*
retard dans la livraison (F)	Lieferungs-verzögerung *f*	delay in delivery	—	ritardo della consegna *m*	demora en la entrega *f*
rete (I)	Netzwerk *n*	network	réseau *m*	—	red *f*
rete delle filiali (I)	Filialnetz *n*	branch network	réseau de succursales *m*	—	red de sucursales *f*
rete di distribuzione (I)	Vertriebsweg *m*	distribution channel	canal de distribution *m*	—	circuito de distribución *f*
rete stradale[1] (I)	Straßennetz *n*	road network	réseau routier *m*	—	red de carreteras *f*
rete stradale[2] (I)	Wegenetz *n*	road network	voirie *f*	—	comunicaciones *f pl*

	D	E	F	I	Es
retórica (Es)	Rhetorik *f*	rhetoric	rhétorique *f*	retorica *f*	—
retorica (I)	Rhetorik *f*	rhetoric	rhétorique *f*	—	retórica *f*
retraining (E)	Umschulung *f*	—	rééducation professionnelle *f*	riqualificazione professionale *f*	readaptación profesional *f*
retraso¹ (Es)	Verspätung *f*	delay	retard *m*	ritardo *m*	—
retraso² (Es)	Verzug *m*	delay	demeure *f*	mora *f*	—
retraso de adaptación (Es)	Anpassungs-verzögerung *f*	adjustment lag	retard d'adaptation *m*	ritardo d'adattamento *m*	
retraso en el pago (Es)	Zahlungsverzug *m*	failure to pay on due date	demeure du débiteur *f*	morosità di pagamento *f*	—
retribuciones (Es)	Bezüge *pl*	earnings	émoluments *m pl*	entrate *f pl*	—
retribución por vacaciones (Es)	Urlaubsgeld *n*	holiday allowance	prime de vacances *f*	indennità di ferie *f*	—
retribuzione (I)	Besoldung *f*	pay	rétribution *f*	—	sueldo *m*
retribuzione dell'imprenditore (I)	Unternehmerlohn *m*	entrepreneurial income	salaire de l'entrepreneur *m*	—	remuneración del empresario *f*
retribuzione per il lavoro a cottimo (I)	Akkordlohn *m*	piece work wages	salaire à la pièce *m*	—	salario a destajo *m*
retribuzioni in natura (I)	Sachbezüge *pl*	remuneration in kind	prestations en nature *f pl*	—	percepciónes en especie *f pl*
rétroactif (F)	rückwirkend	retrospective	—	con effetto retroattivo	retroactivo
retroactivo (Es)	rückwirkend	retrospective	rétroactif	con effetto retroattivo	—
retrospective (E)	rückwirkend	—	rétroactif	con effetto retroattivo	retroactivo
rettifica del valore (I)	Wertberichtigung *f*	value adjustment	réévaluation *f*	—	rectificación de valor *f*
return¹ (E)	Rücksendung *f*	—	renvoi *m*	rispedizione *f*	devolución *f*
return² (E)	Rückgabe *f*	—	restitution *f*	restituzione *f*	restitución *f*
return on investment (E)	Kapitalrentabilität *f*	—	rentabilité du capital *f*	redditività del capitale *f*	rentabilidad del capital *f*
return ticket (E)	Rückfahrkarte *f*	—	billet d'aller et retour *m*	biglietto di andata e ritorno *m*	billete de ida y vuelta *m*
reunión (Es)	Tagung *f*	meeting	congrès *m*	convegno *m*	—
réunion des associés (F)	Gesellschafter-versammlung *f*	meeting of shareholders	—	assemblea dei soci *f*	junta social *f*
réutilisable (F)	wiederverwertbar	recyclable	—	riutilizzabile	recuperable
revalorisation (F)	Aufwertung *f*	revaluation	—	rivalutazione *f*	revalorización *f*
revalorización (Es)	Aufwertung *f*	revaluation	revalorisation *f*	rivalutazione *f*	—
revaluation (E)	Aufwertung *f*	—	revalorisation *f*	rivalutazione *f*	revalorización *f*
revendedor (Es)	Wiederverkäufer *m*	reseller	revendeur *m*	rivenditore *m*	—
revendeur (F)	Wiederverkäufer *m*	reseller	—	rivenditore *m*	revendedor *m*
revendication de salaire (F)	Lohnforderung *f*	wage claim	—	rivendicazione salariale *f*	reivindicación salarial *f*
revenu¹ (F)	Einkommen *n*	income	—	reddito *m*	ingresos *m pl*/renta *f*
revenu² (F)	Einnahmen *pl*	receipts	—	entrate *f pl*	ingresos *m pl*
revenu annuel (F)	Jahreseinkommen *n*	annual income	—	reddito annuale *m*	renta anual *f*
revenu brut (F)	Bruttoeinkommen *n*	gross income	—	reddito lordo *m*	ingreso bruto *m*
revenu de base (F)	Basiseinkommen *n*	basic income	—	introiti base *m pl*	salario base *m*
revenu disponible (F)	verfügbares Einkommen *n*	disposable income	—	introito disponibile *m*	ingresos disponibles *m pl*
revenu du capital (F)	Kapitaleinkommen *n*	unearned income	—	reddito del capitale *m*	ganancias de capital *f pl*
revenu du patrimoine (F)	Besitzeinkommen *n*	unearned income	—	reddito da possesso *m*	renta de la propiedad *f*
revenu fixe (F)	Festeinkommen *n*	fixed income	—	reddito fisso *m*	salario fijo *m*
revenu national (F)	Volkseinkommen *n*	national income	—	reddito nazionale *m*	renta nacional *f*
revenu net (F)	Nettoeinkommen *n*	net income	—	reddito netto *m*	ingreso neto *m*
revenu nominal (F)	Nominal-einkommen *n*	nominal income	—	reddito nominale *m*	ingresos nominales *m pl*
revenu réel (F)	Realeinkommen *n*	real income	—	reddito reale *m*	ingreso real *m*
reversion to private ownership (E)	Reprivatisierung *f*	—	dénationalisation *f*	riprivatizzazione *f*	desnacionalización *f*

	D	E	F	I	Es
Revision (D)	—	audit/examination	vérification f/ contrôle m	revisione f/verifica f	revisión f/ examinación f
revisión¹ (Es)	Nachprüfung f	reexamination	vérification f	revisione f	—
revisión² (Es)	Revision f	audit/examination	vérification f/ contrôle m	revisione f/verifica f	—
revisión contable (Es)	Abschlußprüfung f	audit	vérification des comptes f	revisione f	—
revisione¹ (I)	Revision f	audit/examination	vérification f/ contrôle m	—	revisión f/ examinación f
revisione² (I)	Nachprüfung f	reexamination	vérification f	—	revisión f
revisione³ (I)	Wirtschaftsprüfung f	auditing	contrôle de la gestion et des comptes m	—	revisoría f
revisione⁴ (I)	Abschlußprüfung f	audit	vérification des comptes f	—	revisión contable f
revisione aziendale (I)	Betriebsprüfung f	investigation by the tax authorities	vérification des livres de l'entreprise f	—	inspección de la explotación f
revisione del piano (I)	Planrevision f	budget adjustment	révision des coûts marginaux f	—	ajuste presupuestario m
revisor contable¹ (Es)	Rechnungsprüfer m	auditor	commissaire aux comptes m	revisore dei conti m	—
revisor contable² (Es)	Abschlußprüfer m	auditor	vérificateur des comptes m	revisore m	—
revisor de cuentas (Es)	Wirtschaftsprüfer m	auditor	expert comptable économique et financier m/commissaire aux comptes m	revisore dei conti m	—
revisore (I)	Abschlußprüfer m	auditor	vérificateur des comptes m	—	revisor contable m
revisore aziendale (I)	Betriebsprüfer m	auditor	expert-comptable m	—	contador público m
revisore dei conti¹ (I)	Rechnungsprüfer m	auditor	commissaire aux comptes m	—	revisor contable m
revisore dei conti² (I)	Wirtschaftsprüfer m	auditor	expert comptable économique et financier m	—	revisor de cuentas m/ experto contable m
revisoría (Es)	Wirtschaftsprüfung f	auditing	contrôle de la gestion et des comptes m	revisione f	—
revista para los clientes (Es)	Kundenzeitschrift f	customer magazine	journal destiné à la clientèle m	periodico per i clienti m	—
revocable (Es)	kündbar	redeemable/callable	résiliable/ remboursable	risolubile/redimibile	—
revocar (Es)	widerrufen	revoke	révoquer	revocare	—
revocare (I)	widerrufen	revoke	révoquer	—	revocar
revocation clause (E)	Widerrufsklausel f	—	clause de révocation f	clausola di revoca f	cláusula revocatoria f
revoke (E)	widerrufen	—	révoquer	revocare	revocar
revolving credit (E)	Revolving-Kredit m	—	crédit rotatif m	credito rotativo m	crédito rotativo m
Revolving-Kredit (D)	—	revolving credit	crédit rotatif m	credito rotativo m	crédito rotativo m
révoquer (F)	widerrufen	revoke	—	revocare	revocar
Rezession (D)	—	recession	récession f	recessione f	recesión f
Reziprozität (D)	—	reciprocity	réciprocité f	reciprocità f	reciprocidad f
rhetoric (E)	Rhetorik f	—	rhétorique f	retorica f	retórica f
Rhetorik (D)	—	rhetoric	rhétorique f	retorica f	retórica f
rhétorique (F)	Rhetorik f	rhetoric	—	retorica f	retórica f
rialzo dei prezzi (I)	Preiserhöhung f	price increase	augmentation des prix f	—	aumento de precios m
riapprovigiona-mento (I)	Wiederbeschaffung f	replacement	réapprovisionne-ment m	—	reposición f
riassicurazione (I)	Rückversicherung f	reinsurance	réassurance f	—	reaseguro m
ribasso¹ (I)	Rabatt m	discount	remise f	—	rebaja f
ribasso² (I)	Verbilligung f	cheapening	réduction du prix f	—	abaratamiento m
ribasso dei costi (I)	Kostensenkung f	cost reduction	diminution des coûts f	—	reducción de coste f
ribasso del prezzo (I)	Preisnachlaß m	price reduction	remise sur le prix f	—	rebaja f

riduzione delle spese

	D	E	F	I	Es
ribasso per ordinazioni anticipate (I)	Vorbestellrabatt *m*	discount on advance orders	escompte de suscription *m*	—	descuento de suscripción *m*
ribasso per pagamento in contanti (I)	Barzahlungsrabatt *m*	cash discount	remise pour payement comptant *f*	—	descento por pago al contado *m*
ribasso preferenziale (I)	Vorzugsrabatt *m*	preferential discount	remise de faveur *f*	—	rebaja preferencial *f*
ribasso speciale (I)	Sonderrabatt *m*	special discount	ristourne exceptionnelle *f*	—	descuento suplementario *m*
ricavo della liquidazione (I)	Liquidationserlös *m*	remaining assets after liquidation	produit de la liquidation *m*	—	haber social repartible *m*
ricavo delle vendite (I)	Verkaufserlös *m*	sale proceeds	produit des ventes *m*	—	producto de la venta *m*
ricavo netto (I)	Nettoertrag *m*	net earnings	produit net *m*	—	producto neto *m*
ricerca (I)	Forschung *f*	research	recherche *f*	—	investigación *f*
ricerca di mercato (I)	Marktforschung *f*	market research	recherche du marché *f*	—	estudio del mercado *m*
ricerca di mercato empirica (I)	empirische Marktforschung *f*	empirical market research	étude de marché empirique *f*	—	estudio del mercado empírico *m*
ricerche spaziali (I)	Raumforschung *f*	space research	recherches spatiales *f pl*	—	investigación espacial *f*
ricevuta (I)	Empfangsbestätigung *f*	acknowledgement of receipt	accusé de réception *m*	—	recibo *m*
ricevuta di deposito (I)	Lagerschein *m*	warehouse warrant	certificat de dépôt *m*	—	resguardo de almacén *m*
ricevuta di ritorno (I)	Rückschein *m*	advice of delivery	avis de réception *m*	—	acuse de recibo *m*
richiesta[1] (I)	Anfrage *f*	inquiry	demande *f*	—	demanda *f*
richiesta[2] (I)	Abruf *m*	call	appel *m*	—	reclamación de la entrega de un pedido *f*
Richter (D)	—	judge	juge *m*	giudice *m*	juez *m*
Richtpreis (D)	—	recommended retail price	prix indicatif *m*	prezzo indicativo *m*	precio indicativo *m*
riciclaggio (I)	Recycling *n*	recycling	recyclage *m*	—	reciclaje *m*
ricompensa (I)	Vergütung *f*	remuneration	rémunération *f*	—	remuneración *f*
ricomposizione fondiaria (I)	Flurbereinigung *f*	compulsory consolidation of farmland	remembrement parcellaire *m*	—	concentración parcelaria *f*
riconoscere (I)	erkennen	recognize	reconnaître	—	reconocer
riconoscimento del debito (I)	Schuldanerkennung *f*	acknowledgement of a debt	reconnaissance de dette *f*	—	reconocimiento de la deuda *m*
ricostruzione (I)	Wiederaufbau *m*	reconstruction	reconstruction *f*	—	reconstrucción *f*
ricupero (I)	Bergung *f*	salvage	sauvetage *m*	—	salvamento *m*
ridistribuzione (I)	Redistribution *f*	redistribution	redistribution *f*	—	redistribución *f*
ridistribuzione dei redditi (I)	Einkommensumverteilung *f*	redistribution of income	redistribution des revenus *f pl*	—	redistribución de la renta *f*
ridondanza (I)	Redundanz *f*	redundancy	redondance *f*	—	redundancia *f*
ridurre a rottame (I)	verschrotten	scrap	mettre à la ferraille	—	hacer quincalla desguazar
riduzione[1] (I)	Abbau *m*	reduction/lay off	réduction *f*/ diminution *f*	—	reducción *f*/ disminución *f*
riduzione[2] (I)	Ermäßigung *f*	reduction	réduction *f*	—	reducción *f*
riduzione[3] (I)	Minderung *f*	reduction	diminution *f*	—	reducción *f*
riduzione degli interessi (I)	Zinssenkung *f*	reduction of interest	diminution du taux de l'intérêt *f*	—	reducción del tipo de interés *f*
riduzione dei costi (I)	Kostendegression *f*	cost degression	dégressivité des coûts *f*	—	reducción de costes *f*
riduzione dei prezzi (I)	Preissenkung *f*	price reduction	baisse des prix *f*	—	reducción de precios *f*
riduzione del capitale (I)	Kapitalherabsetzung *f*	reduction of capital	diminution du capital *f*	—	reducción de capital *f*
riduzione del denaro (I)	Geldverknappung *f*	monetary restriction	pénurie d'argent *f*	—	restricción monetaria *f*
riduzione delle sovvenzioni (I)	Subventionsabbau *m*	reduction of subsidy	réduction des subventions *f*	—	reducción de las subvenciones *f*
riduzione delle spese[1] (I)	Aufwandsminimierung *f*	expenditure minimization	minimiser les frais	—	minimación de gastos *f*

	D	E	F	I	Es
riduzione delle spese[2] (I)	Ausgabensenkung f	drop in expenditure	diminution des dépenses f	—	reducción de gastos f
riduzione del personale (I)	Personalabbau m	reduction of staff	réduction de personnel f	—	reducción de personal f
riduzione del prezzo (I)	Preisabzug m	price deduction	réduction de prix f	—	descuento m
riduzione di valore (I)	Wertminderung f	decrease in value	diminution de la valeur f	—	depreciación f
rielaborazione (I)	Nachbereitung f	aftertreatment	remise en ordre f	—	tratamiento ulterior m
riesgo[1] (Es)	Wagnis n	venture	risque m	rischio m	—
riesgo[2] (Es)	Risiko n	risk	risque m	rischio m	—
riesgo aceptable (Es)	Restrisiko n	acceptable risk	risque acceptable m	rischio rimanente m	—
riesgo de cambio (Es)	Kursrisiko n	price risk	risque de change m	rischio di cambio m	—
riesgo de pago (Es)	Zahlungsrisiko n	risk of payment	risque de payement m	rischio di pagamento m	—
riesgo de pérdida (Es)	Ausfallrisiko n	default risk	risque de perte m	rischio di perdita m	—
riesgo de transferencia (Es)	Transferrisiko n	risk of transfer	risque de transfert m	rischio di trasferimento m	—
riesgo monetario (Es)	Währungsrisiko n	currency risk	risque de change m	rischio monetario m	—
riesgo profesional (Es)	Berufsrisiko n	occupational hazard	risque professionnel m	rischio professionale m	—
riesportazione (I)	Wiederausfuhr f	reexportation	réexportation f	—	reexportación f
rifare l'imballaggio (I)	umpacken	repack	remballer	—	reempaquetar
riferimento (I)	Referenz	reference	référence f	—	referencia f
rifinanziamento (I)	Refinanzierung f	refinancing	refinancement m	—	refinanciación f
rifiuti (I)	Abfall m	waste	déchet m	—	desechos m pl
rifiuti da imballaggi (I)	Verpackungsmüll m	packing waste	déchets d'emballage m pl	—	basura de embalaje f
rifiuti speciali (I)	Sondermüll m	special refuse	détritus spéciaux m pl	—	basura especial f
rifiuto (I)	Ablehnung f	refusal/rejection	refus m/rejet m	—	recusación f/repulsa f
rifiuto d'accettazione (I)	Annahmeverweigerung f	refusal of delivery	refus d'acceptation m	—	rehuso de aceptación m
riforma agraria (I)	Bodenreform f	land reform	réforme agraire f	—	reforma agraria f
right of redemption (E)	Rückgaberecht n	—	droit à restitution m	diritto alla restituzione m	derecho de devolución m
right of revocation (E)	Widerrufsrecht n	—	droit de révocation m	diritto di revoca m	derecho de revocación m
right to vote (E)	Stimmrecht n	—	droit de vote m	diritto al voto m	derecho a voto m
rilevante (I)	relevant	relevant	significatif	—	importante
rimanenze (I)	Restposten m	remnants	lot restant m	—	partida restante f
rimborsare (I)	ablösen	redeem	amortir	—	amortizar
rimborso[1] (I)	Rückerstattung f	repayment	remboursement m	—	restitución f
rimborso[2] (I)	Abzahlung f	repayment/ hire purchase	remboursement m/ payement par acomptes m	—	reintegro m/ pago a plazos m
rimessa[1] (I)	Rimesse f	remittance	remise f	—	remesa f
rimessa[2] (I)	Überweisung f	remittance	virement m	—	transferencia f
rimessa bancaria (I)	Banküberweisung f	bank transfer	virement bancaire m	—	transferencia bancaria f
Rimesse (D)	—	remittance	remise f	rimessa f	remesa f
rincaro (I)	Verteuerung f	rise in price	enchérissement m	—	encarecimiento m
rinuncia al consumo (I)	Konsumverzicht m	voluntary constraint in consumption	renonciation à la consommation f	—	renuncia al consumo f
rinvio[1] (I)	Vertagung f	postponement	ajournement m	—	aplazamiento m/ suspensión f
rinvio[2] (I)	Aufschiebung f	postponement	remise f	—	aplazamiento m
riparare (I)	reparieren	repair	réparer	—	reparar
riparazione (I)	Reparatur f	repair	réparation f	—	reparación f
ripartizione (I)	Umlage f	charge levied	répartition f	—	reparto m
ripartizione dell'utile[1] (I)	Gewinnverteilung f	distribution of profits	répartition des bénéfices f	—	reparto de beneficios m

	D	E	F	I	Es
ripartizione dell'utile² (I)	Gewinn-ausschüttung f	distribution of profits	distribution de bénéfices f	—	distribución de beneficios f
ripartizione del patrimonio (I)	Vermögens-verteilung f	distribution of wealth	répartition du patrimoine f	—	reparto de la riqueza m
ripresa (I)	Reprise f	repeat	tendance à la hausse f	—	segunda lectura en el corro f
ripresa congiunturale (I)	Konjunkturbelebung f	economic upturn	relance économique f	—	recuperación coyuntural f
riprivatizzazione (I)	Reprivatisierung f	reversion to private ownership	dénationalisation f	—	desnacionalización f
riproduzione (I)	Vervielfältigung f	reproduction	reproduction f	—	reproducción f/ multiplicación f
riqualificazione professionale (I)	Umschulung f	retraining	rééducation professionnelle f	—	readaptación profesional f
risanamento (I)	Sanierung f	urban renewal/ reconstruction	assainissement m	—	saneamiento m/ rehabilitación f
risarcimento danni (I)	Schadensersatz m	compensation for loss suffered	dommages-intérêts m pl	—	indemnización f
rischio¹ (I)	Wagnis n	venture	risque m	—	riesgo m
rischio² (I)	Risiko n	risk	risque m	—	riesgo m
rischio di cambio (I)	Kursrisiko n	price risk	risque de change m	—	riesgo de cambio m
rischio di pagamento (I)	Zahlungsrisiko n	risk of payment	risque de payement m	—	riesgo de pago m
rischio di perdita (I)	Ausfallrisiko n	default risk	risque de perte m	—	riesgo de pérdida m
rischio di trasferimento (I)	Transferrisiko n	risk of transfer	risque de transfert m	—	riesgo de transferencia m
rischio monetario (I)	Währungsrisiko n	currency risk	risque de change m	—	riesgo monetario m
rischio professionale (I)	Berufsrisiko n	occupational hazard	risque professionnel m	—	riesgo profesional m
rischio rimanente (I)	Restrisiko n	acceptable risk	risque acceptable m	—	riesgo aceptable m
rischioso (I)	riskant	risky	risqué	—	arriesgado
riscontare (I)	rediskontieren	rediscount	réescompter	—	redescontar
rise in income (E)	Einkommens-erhöhung f	—	augmentation du revenu f	aumento del reddito m	aumento de salario m
rise in price (E)	Verteuerung f	—	enchérissement m	rincaro m	encarecimiento m
riserva di capitale (I)	Kapitalstock m	capital stock	réserve de capital f	—	fondo de capital m
riserva di liquidità (I)	Liquiditätsreserve f	liquidity reserves	réserves de liquidité f pl	—	reserva de liquidez f
riserva latente (I)	stille Rücklage f	latent funds	réserve cachée f	—	reserva tácita f
riserva minima obbligatoria (I)	Mindestreserve f	minimum reserves	réserve minimum f	—	reserva mínima f
riserva occulta (I)	stille Reserve f	hidden reserves	réserve cachée f	—	reserva tácita f
riserve (I)	Rücklagen pl	reserves	réserve f	—	reservas f pl
Risiko (D)	—	risk	risque m	rischio m	riesgo m
Risiko-Lebens-versicherung (D)	—	term life insurance	assurance-vie temporaire f	assicurazione rischio-vita f	seguro de vida temporal m
Risikoprämie (D)	—	risk premium	prime de risque f	premio di rischio m	prima de riesgo f
rising (E)	steigend	—	croissant(e)	in aumento	ascendente
risk (E)	Risiko n	—	risque m	rischio m	riesgo m
riskant (D)	—	risky	risqué	rischioso	arriesgado
risk of payment (E)	Zahlungsrisiko n	—	risque de payement m	rischio di pagamento m	riesgo de pago m
risk of transfer (E)	Transferrisiko n	—	risque de transfert m	rischio di trasferimento m	riesgo de transferencia m
risk premium (E)	Risikoprämie f	—	prime de risque f	premio di rischio m	prima de riesgo f
risky (E)	riskant	—	risqué	rischioso	arriesgado
risolubile (I)	kündbar	redeemable/callable	résiliable/ remboursable	—	revocable/rescindible
risoluzione (I)	Resolution f	resolution	résolution f	—	resolución f
risorsa (I)	Ressource f	resources	ressource f	—	recurso m
risparmio¹ (I)	Ersparnis f	savings	épargne f	—	ahorro m

	D	E	F	I	Es
risparmio² (I)	Sparen n	saving	épargne f	—	ahorro m
risparmio coatto (I)	Zwangssparen n	compulsory saving	épargne forcée f	—	ahorro forzoso m
rispedizione (I)	Rücksendung f	return	renvoi m	—	devolución f
risposta (I)	Antwort f	reply	réponse f	—	respuesta f
risposta negativa (I)	Absage f	refusal	refus m	—	negativa f
risque¹ (F)	Wagnis n	venture	—	rischio m	riesgo m
risque² (F)	Risiko n	risk	—	rischio m	riesgo m
risqué³ (F)	riskant	risky	—	rischioso	arriesgado
risque acceptable (F)	Restrisiko n	acceptable risk	—	rischio rimanente m	riesgo aceptable m
risque de change¹ (F)	Kursrisiko n	price risk	—	rischio di cambio m	riesgo de cambio m
risque de change² (F)	Währungsrisiko n	currency risk	—	rischio monetario m	riesgo monetario m
risque de payement (F)	Zahlungsrisiko n	risk of payment	—	rischio di pagamento m	riesgo de pago m
risque de perte (F)	Ausfallrisiko n	default risk	—	rischio di perdita m	riesgo de pérdida m
risque de transfert (F)	Transferrisiko n	risk of transfer	—	rischio di trasferimento m	riesgo de transferencia m
risque professionnel (F)	Berufsrisiko n	occupational hazard	—	rischio professionale m	riesgo profesional m
ristourne des droits de douane (F)	Rückzoll m	customs drawback	—	restituzione di dazi f	drawback m
ristourne exceptionnelle (F)	Sonderrabatt m	special discount	—	ribasso speciale m	descuento suplementario m
ristrutturazione (I)	Umstrukturierung f	restructuring	restructuration f	—	reestructuración f
risultato (I)	Ergebnis n	result	résultat m	—	resultado m
ritardo (I)	Verspätung f	delay	retard m	—	retraso m
ritardo d'adattamento (I)	Anpassungs-verzögerung f	adjustment lag	retard d'adaptation m	—	retraso de adaptación m
ritardo della consegna (I)	Lieferungs-verzögerung f	delay in delivery	retard dans la livraison m	—	demora en la entrega f
ritmo de trabajo (Es)	Arbeitsrhythmus m	work rhythm	rythme de travail m	ritmo di lavoro m	—
ritmo di lavoro (I)	Arbeitsrhythmus m	work rhythm	rythme de travail m	—	ritmo de trabajo m
riunione dei creditori (I)	Gläubiger-versammlung f	creditors' meeting	assemblée des créanciers f	—	junta de acreedores f
riutilizzabile (I)	wiederverwertbar	recyclable	réutilisable	—	recuperable
rival (E)	Rivale m	—	rival m	rivale m	rival m
rival (Es)	Rivale m	rival	rival m	rivale m	—
rival (F)	Rivale m	rival	—	rivale m	rival m
Rivale (D)	—	rival	rival m	rivale m	rival m
rivale (I)	Rivale m	rival	rival m	—	rival m
rivalutazione (I)	Aufwertung f	revaluation	revalorisation f	—	revalorización f
rivendicazione salariale (I)	Lohnforderung f	wage claim	revendication de salaire f	—	reivindicación salarial f
rivenditore (I)	Wiederverkäufer m	reseller	revendeur m	—	revendedor m
road network¹ (E)	Wegenetz n	—	voirie f	rete stradale f	comunicaciones f pl
road network² (E)	Straßennetz n	—	réseau routier m	rete stradale f	red de carreteras f
road traffic (E)	Straßenverkehr m	—	trafic routier m	traffico stradale m	circulación f
robo (Es)	Diebstahl m	theft	vol m	furto m	—
Rohgewinn (D)	—	gross profit on sales	bénéfice brut m	utile lordo m	ganancia bruta f
Rohöl (D)	—	crude oil	pétrole brut m	petrolio greggio m	crudo m
Rohölpreis (D)	—	crude oil price	prix du pétrole brut m	prezzo del petrolio greggio m	precio del crudo m
Rohstoff (D)	—	raw materials	matière première f	materia prima f	materia prima f
Rohstoffgewinnung (D)	—	raw material production	extraction de matières premières f	produzione delle materie prime f	producción de materias primas f
Rohstoffknappheit (D)	—	raw materials shortage	pénurie de matières premières f	scarsità di materie prime f	escasez de materias primas f
Rohstoffmarkt (D)	—	commodity market	marchés des matières premières m	mercato delle materie prime m	mercado de materias primas m

	D	E	F	I	Es
Rohstoff-vermarktung (D)	—	raw materials marketing	commercialisation des matières premières f	smercio delle materie prime m	comercialización de las materias primas f
Rohstoffversorgung (D)	—	provisioning with raw materials	approvisionnement de matières premières m	approvvigionamento di materie prime m	aprovisionamiento de materias primas m
Rollgeld (D)	—	haulage	camionnage m	spese di trasporto f pl	derechos de acarreo m pl
roll-over credit (E)	Roll-over-Kredit m	—	crédit roll-over m	credito roll-over m	crédito roll over m
Roll-over-Kredit (D)	—	roll-over credit	crédit roll-over m	credito roll-over m	crédito roll over m
room reservation (E)	Zimmerbestellung f	—	réservation de chambre f	prenotazione di una camera f	reservación f
rotación del capital (Es)	Kapitalumschlag m	capital turnover	roulement des capitaux m	rotazione del capitale f	—
rotazione del capitale (I)	Kapitalumschlag m	capital turnover	roulement des capitaux m	—	rotación del capital f
rote Zahlen (D)	—	(in) the red	chiffres en déficit f pl	conti in rosso m pl	cifras rojas f pl
roulement des capitaux (F)	Kapitalumschlag m	capital turnover	—	rotazione del capitale f	rotación del capital f
route (E)	Reiseroute f	—	itinéraire m	itinerario m	itinerario m
route of transportation (E)	Transportweg m	—	voie de transport f	via di trasporto f	vía de transporte f
royalty (E)	Lizenzgebühr f	—	taxe d'exploitation de licence f	tassa di licenza f	derecho de licencia m
Rückerstattung (D)	—	repayment	remboursement m	rimborso m	restitución f
Rückfahrkarte (D)	—	return ticket	billet d'aller et retour m	biglietto di andata e ritorno m	billete de ida y vuelta m
Rückgabe (D)	—	return	restitution f	restituzione f	restitución f
Rückgaberecht (D)	—	right of redemption	droit à restitution m	diritto alla restituzione m	derecho de devolución m
Rückgriff (D)	—	recourse	recours m	regresso m	recurso m
Rückkopplung (D)	—	feedback	accouplement réactif m	accoppiamento a reazione m	reacoplamiento m
Rücklagen (D)	—	reserves	réserve f	riserve f pl	reservas f pl
Rückschein (D)	—	advice of delivery	avis de réception m	ricevuta di ritorno f	acuse de recibo m
Rücksendung (D)	—	return	renvoi m	rispedizione f	devolución f
Rückstand (D)	—	arrear	arriéré m	arretrato m	pago atrasado m/ atraso m
Rückstände (D)	—	residues	déchet m	residui m pl	residuos m pl
Rückstellung (D)	—	reserves	provision pour pertes et charges f	accantonamento m	reserva f
Rücktritt (D)	—	rescission	résolution du contrat f	recesso m	rescisión f
Rücktrittsklausel (D)	—	escape clause	clause de résolution du contrat f	clausola di recesso f	cláusula de arrepentimiento f
Rückversicherung (D)	—	reinsurance	réassurance f	riassicurazione f	reaseguro m
rückwirkend (D)	—	retrospective	rétroactif	con effetto retroattivo	retroactivo
Rückzoll (D)	—	customs drawback	ristourne des droits de douane f	restituzione di dazi f	drawback m
rue (F)	Straße f	street/road	—	via f/strada f	calle f/carretera f
rueda de prensa (Es)	Pressekonferenz f	press conference	conférence de presse f	conferenza stampa f	—
ruinous exploitation (E)	Raubbau m	—	exploitation abusive f	sfruttamento abusivo m	explotación abusiva f
Rundfunkwerbung (D)	—	radio advertising	publicité à la radio f	pubblicità radiofonica f	publicidad radiada f
Rundschreiben (D)	—	circular (letter)	lettre circulaire f	circolare f	circular m
rythme de travail (F)	Arbeitsrhythmus m	work rhythm	—	ritmo di lavoro m	ritmo de trabajo m
Sabotage (D)	—	sabotage	sabotage m	sabotaggio m	sabotaje m
sabotage (E)	Sabotage f	—	sabotage m	sabotaggio m	sabotaje m
sabotage (F)	Sabotage f	sabotage	—	sabotaggio m	sabotaje m
sabotaggio (I)	Sabotage f	sabotage	sabotage m	—	sabotaje m
sabotaje (Es)	Sabotage f	sabotage	sabotage m	sabotaggio m	—
sac (F)	Sack m	sack	—	sacco m	saco m

	D	E	F	I	Es
sacco (I)	Sack *m*	sack	sac *m*	—	saco *m*
Sachanlagen (D)	—	fixed assets	immobilisations corporelles *f pl*	immobilizzazioni *f pl*	inmuebles y utillaje *m pl*
Sachbezüge (D)	—	remuneration in kind	prestations en nature *f pl*	retribuzioni in natura *f pl*	percepciónes en especie *f pl*
Sachkenntnis (D)	—	know-how	compétence *f*	competenza *f*	conocimiento de causa *m*
Sachvermögen (D)	—	material assets	biens corporels *m pl*	capitale reale *m*	patrimonio real *m*
Sachversicherung (D)	—	property insurance	assurance de choses *f*	assicurazione di cose *f*	seguro de cosas *m*
Sachwert (D)	—	real value	valeur matérielle *f*	valore reale *m*	valor real *m*
Sack (D)	—	sack	sac *m*	sacco *m*	saco *m*
sack (E)	Sack *m*	—	sac *m*	sacco *m*	saco *m*
saco (Es)	Sack *m*	sack	sac *m*	sacco *m*	—
Safe (D)	—	safe	coffre-fort *m*	cassetta di sicurezza *f*	caja de seguridad *f*
safe¹ (E)	Tresor *m*	—	coffre-fort *m*	cassaforte *f*	caja fuerte *f*
safe² (E)	Safe *m*	—	coffre-fort *m*	cassetta di sicurezza *f*	caja de seguridad *f*
safety at work (E)	Arbeitssicherheit *f*	—	sécurité du travail *f*	sicurezza del lavoro *f*	seguridad del trabajo *f*
saggio di sconto (I)	Diskontsatz *m*	discount rate	taux d'escompte *m*	—	tasa de descuento *f*
saisie¹ (F)	Beschlagnahme *f*	confiscation	—	sequestro *m*	confiscación *f*
saisie² (F)	Pfändung *f*	seizure	—	pignoramento *m*	pignoración *f*
saisie des données informatiques (F)	Datenerfassung *f*	data collection	—	raccolta dati *f*	recogida de datos *f*
saisie-arrêt sur le salaire (F)	Lohnpfändung *f*	attachment of earnings	—	pignoramento del salario *m*	embargo de salario *m*
Saison (D)	—	season	saison *f*	stagione *f*	temporada *f*
saison (F)	Saison *f*	season		stagione *f*	temporada *f*
saisonale Arbeitslosigkeit (D)	—	seasonal unemployment	chômage saisonnier *m*	disoccupazione stagionale *f*	paro estacional *m*
Saison-schwankungen (D)	—	seasonal fluctuations	mouvements saisonniers *m pl*	oscillazioni stagionali *f pl*	oscilaciones estacionales *f pl*
sala conferenze (I)	Konferenzraum *m*	conference room	salle de conférences *f*	—	sala de conferencia *f*
sala de conferencia¹ (Es)	Konferenzraum *m*	conference room	salle de conférences *f*	sala conferenze *f*	—
sala de conferencia² (Es)	Sitzungszimmer *n*	conference room	salle de réunion *f*	sala riunioni *f*	—
salaire (F)	Lohn *m*	wage	—	salario *m*	salario *m*
salaire à la pièce (F)	Akkordlohn *m*	piece work wages	—	retribuzione per il lavoro a cottimo *f*	salario a destajo *m*
salaire à la tâche (F)	Stücklohn *m*	piece work pay	—	salario a cottimo *m*	salario a destajo *m*
salaire au rendement (F)	Leistungslohn *m*	payment by result	—	salario a rendimento *m*	salario por rendimiento *m*
salaire au temps (F)	Zeitlohn *m*	time wage	—	salario a tempo *m*	salario por unidad de tiempo *m*
salaire brut (F)	Bruttolohn *m*	gross pay	—	salario lordo *m*	salario bruto *m*
salaire de référence (F)	Basislohn *m*	basic wage	—	salario base *m*	sueldo base *m*
salaire effectif (F)	Effektivlohn *m*	actual wage	—	salario effettivo *m*	salario efectivo *m*
salaire horaire (F)	Stundenlohn *m*	hourly wage	—	salario ad ora *m*	salario-hora *m*
salaire indexé (F)	Indexlohn *m*	index-linked wages	—	salario indicizzato *m*	salario-índice *m*
salaire initial (F)	Anfangsgehalt *n*	starting salary	—	stipendio iniziale *m*	salario inicial *m*
salaire maximum (F)	Spitzenlohn *m*	top wage	—	salario massimo *m*	salario máximo *m*
salaire minimum (F)	Mindestlohn *m*	minimum wage	—	salario minimo *m*	salario mínimo *m*
salaire net (F)	Nettolohn *m*	take-home pay	—	salario netto *m*	salario neto *m*
salaire nominal (F)	Nominallohn *m*	nominal wage	—	salario nominale *m*	salario nominal *m*
salaire réel (F)	Reallohn *m*	real wage	—	salario reale *m*	salario real *m*
salaire tarifaire (F)	Tariflohn *m*	standard wage	—	salario contrattuale *m*	salario tarifado *m*
salarié (F)	Arbeitnehmer *m*	employee	—	prestatore d'opera *m*	empleado *m*
Salaried Employees' Pension Insurance (E)	Angestellten-versicherung *f*	—	assurance invalidité-vieillesse des employés *f*	assicurazione degli impiegati *f*	seguro de empleados *m*

sale

	D	E	F	I	Es
salario (Es)	Lohn *m*	wage	salaire *m*	salario *m*	—
salario (I)	Lohn *m*	wage	salaire *m*	—	salario *m*
salario a cottimo (I)	Stücklohn *m*	piece work pay	salaire à la tâche *m*	—	salario a destajo *m*
salario a destajo¹ (Es)	Akkordlohn *m*	piece work wages	salaire à la pièce *m*	retribuzione per il lavoro a cottimo *f*	—
salario a destajo² (Es)	Stücklohn *m*	piece work pay	salaire à la tâche *m*	salario a cottimo *m*	—
salario ad ora (I)	Stundenlohn *m*	hourly wage	salaire horaire *m*	—	salario-hora *m*
salario a rendimento (I)	Leistungslohn *m*	payment by result	salaire au rendement *m*	—	salario por rendimiento *m*
salario a tempo (I)	Zeitlohn *m*	time wage	salaire au temps *m*	—	salario por unidad de tiempo *m*
salario base (I)	Basislohn *m*	basic wage	salaire de référence *m*	—	sueldo base *m*
salario base¹ (Es)	Grundgehalt *n*	basic salary	traitement de base *m*	stipendio base *m*	—
salario base² (Es)	Basiseinkommen *n*	basic income	revenu de base *m*	introiti base *m pl*	—
salario bruto (Es)	Bruttolohn *m*	gross pay	salaire brut *m*	salario lordo *m*	—
salario contrattuale (I)	Tariflohn *m*	standard wage	salaire tarifaire *m*	—	salario tarifado *m*
salario efectivo (Es)	Effektivlohn *m*	actual wage	salaire effectif *m*	salario effettivo *m*	—
salario effettivo (I)	Effektivlohn *m*	actual wage	salaire effectif *m*	—	salario efectivo *m*
salario en especie (Es)	Naturallohn *m*	wages (paid) in kind	rémunérarion du travail en nature *f*	remunerazione in natura *f*	—
salario fijo (Es)	Festeinkommen *n*	fixed income	revenu fixe *m*	reddito fisso *m*	—
salario-hora (Es)	Stundenlohn *m*	hourly wage	salaire horaire *m*	salario ad ora *m*	—
salario-índice (Es)	Indexlohn *m*	index-linked wages	salaire indexé *m*	salario indicizzato *m*	—
salario indicizzato (I)	Indexlohn *m*	index-linked wages	salaire indexé *m*	—	salario-índice *m*
salario inicial (Es)	Anfangsgehalt *n*	starting salary	salaire initial *m*	stipendio iniziale *m*	—
salario lordo (I)	Bruttolohn *m*	gross pay	salaire brut *m*	—	salario bruto *m*
salario massimo (I)	Spitzenlohn *m*	top wage	salaire maximum *m*	—	salario máximo *m*
salario máximo (Es)	Spitzenlohn *m*	top wage	salaire maximum *m*	salario massimo *m*	—
salario mínimo (Es)	Mindestlohn *m*	minimum wage	salaire minimum *m*	salario minimo *m*	—
salario minimo (I)	Mindestlohn *m*	minimum wage	salaire minimum *m*	—	salario mínimo *m*
salario neto (Es)	Nettolohn *m*	take-home pay	salaire net *m*	salario netto *m*	—
salario netto (I)	Nettolohn *m*	take-home pay	salaire net *m*	—	salario neto *m*
salario nominal (Es)	Nominallohn *m*	nominal wage	salaire nominal *m*	salario nominale *m*	—
salario nominale (I)	Nominallohn *m*	nominal wage	salaire nominal *m*	—	salario nominal *m*
salario por rendimiento (Es)	Leistungslohn *m*	payment by result	salaire au rendement *m*	salario a rendimento *m*	—
salario por unidad de tiempo (Es)	Zeitlohn *m*	time wage	salaire au temps *m*	salario a tempo *m*	—
salario real (Es)	Reallohn *m*	real wage	salaire réel *m*	salario reale *m*	—
salario reale (I)	Reallohn *m*	real wage	salaire réel *m*	—	salario real *m*
salario tarifado (Es)	Tariflohn *m*	standard wage	salaire tarifaire *m*	salario contrattuale *m*	—
sala riunioni (I)	Sitzungszimmer *n*	conference room	salle de réunion *f*	—	sala de conferencia *f*
salary¹ (E)	Gage *f*	—	cachet *m*	onorario *m*	remuneración *f*
salary² (E)	Gehalt *n*	—	traitement *m*	stipendio *m*	sueldo *m*
salary account (E)	Gehaltskonto *n*	—	compte de domiciliation du salaire *m*	conto stipendi *m*	cuenta de salario *f*
Saldo (D)	—	balance	solde *m*	saldo *m*	saldo *m*
saldo (Es)	Saldo *m*	balance	solde *m*	saldo *m*	—
saldo (I)	Saldo *m*	balance	solde *m*	—	saldo *m*
saldo activo (Es)	Aktivsaldo *m*	active balance	solde créditeur *m*	saldo attivo *m*	—
saldo attivo¹ (I)	Aktivsaldo *m*	active balance	solde créditeur *m*	—	saldo activo *m*
saldo attivo² (I)	Guthaben *n*	money owed	avoir *m*	—	haber *m*
saldo de cuenta (Es)	Kontoausgleich *m*	settlement of an account	solde de compte *m*	liquidazione del conto *f*	—
saldo en efectivo (Es)	Bargeldbestand *m*	cash in hand	espèces en caisse *f pl*	denaro contante in cassa *m*	—
sale¹ (E)	Verkauf *m*	—	vente *f*	vendita *f*	venta *f*

	D	E	F	I	Es
sale² (E)	Veräußerung f	—	aliénation f	alienazione f	enajenación f
sale³ (E)	Absatz m	—	volume des ventes m	vendita f	cifra de ventas f
sale by court order (E)	Zwangs-versteigerung f	—	vente de biens par justice f	asta giudiziaria f	subasta forzosa f
sale on approval (E)	Kauf auf Probe m	—	achat à l'éssai m	acquisto a titolo di prova m	compra a prueba f
sale proceeds (E)	Verkaufserlös m	—	produit des ventes m	ricavo delle vendite m	producto de la venta m
sales analysis¹ (E)	Absatzanalyse f	—	analyse de la distribution f	analisi di mercato f	análisis de venta m
sales analysis² (E)	Verkaufsanalyse f	—	analyse des ventes f	analisi delle vendite f	análisis de las ventas m
sales campaign (E)	Verkaufskampagne f	—	campagne de vente f	campagna di vendita f	campaña de venta f
sales commission (E)	Verkäuferprovision f	—	commission sur les ventes f	provvigione del venditore f	comisión sobre la venta f
sales conception (E)	Verkaufskonzeption f	—	conception de vente f	concezione di vendita f	concepción de venta f
sales contract (E)	Verkaufsabschluß m	—	contrat de vente m	conclusione di vendita f	conclusión de la venta f
sales crisis (E)	Absatzkrise f	—	crise de vente f	crisi di mercato f	crisis en la venta f
sales financing (E)	Absatzfinanzierung f	—	financement des ventes m	finanziamento delle vendite m	financiación de las ventas f
sales meeting (E)	Vertretertagung f	—	réunion de représentants f	convegno dei rappresentanti m	conferencia de representantes f
sales message (E)	Werbebotschaft f	—	message publicitaire m	messaggio pubblicitario m	mensaje publicitario m
sales organization (E)	Absatzorganisation f	—	organisation de vente f	organizzazione di vendita f	organización de ventas f
sales planning (E)	Absatzplanung f	—	planning de la distribution m	pianificazione delle vendite f	planificación de ventas f
sales possibilities (E)	Verkaufschance f	—	possibilité de vente f	prospettiva dello smercio	posibilidades de venta f pl
sales programme (E)	Verkaufsprogramm n	—	programme de vente m	programma di vendita f	programa de venta m
sales promotion¹ (E)	Verkaufsförderung f	—	encouragement à la vente f	promozione di vendita f	promoción de las ventas f
sales promotion² (E)	Absatzförderung f	—	promotion des ventes f	promozione dello smercio f	promoción comercial f
sales prospects (E)	Absatzchance f	—	possibilités de réus-site des ventes f pl	prospettive di smercio f pl	posibilidades de venta f pl
sales report (E)	Verkaufsbericht m	—	rapport de vente m	rapporto sulle vendite m	informe de venta m
sales representative (E)	festangestellter Reisender m	—	voyageur de commerce m	commesso viaggiatore m	viajante m
sales segment (E)	Absatzsegment n	—	segment de vente m	segmento di vendita m	segmento de venta m
sales staff (E)	Verkaufsstab m	—	équipe de vente f	staff di venditori m	equipo de venta m
sales statistics (E)	Absatzstatistik f	—	statistique de la vente f	statistica delle vendite f	estadística de ventas f
sales strategy¹ (E)	Verkaufsmethoden pl	—	méthodes de vente f pl	metodi di vendita m pl	métodos de venta m pl
sales strategy² (E)	Absatzstrategie f	—	stratégie de vente f	strategia di vendita f	estrategia de ventas f
sales target (E)	Absatzziel n	—	objectif de vente m	obbiettivo di vendita m	fin de venta m
sales technique (E)	Verkaufstechnik f	—	art de vendre m	tecnica di vendita f	técnica de venta f
sales territory (E)	Verkaufsgebiet n	—	territoire de vente m	zona di vendita f	territorio de venta m
sales training (E)	Verkäuferschulung f	—	formation des vendeurs f	addestramento dei venditori f	formación de los vendedores f
sale talk (E)	Verkaufsgespräch n	—	conversation de vente f	colloquio di vendita m	conversación de venta f
salida de mercancías (Es)	Warenausgang m	outgoing goods	sortie de marchandises f	uscita merci f	—
salle de conférences (F)	Konferenzraum m	conference room	—	sala conferenze f	sala de conferencia f

	D	E	F	I	Es
salle de réunion (F)	Sitzungszimmer n	conference room	—	sala riunioni f	sala de conferencia f
saludo (Es)	Begrüßung f	salutation	salutations f pl	saluto m	—
salutation (E)	Begrüßung f	—	salutations f pl	saluto m	saludo m
salutations (F)	Begrüßung f	salutation	—	saluto m	saludo m
saluto (I)	Begrüßung f	salutation	salutations f pl	—	saludo m
salvage (E)	Bergung f	—	sauvetage m	ricupero m	salvamento m
salvamento (Es)	Bergung f	salvage	sauvetage m	ricupero m	—
salvo buen cobro (Es)	Eingang vorbehalten	due payment reserved	sauf bonne fin	salvo buon fine	—
salvo buon fine (I)	Eingang vorbehalten	due payment reserved	sauf bonne fin	—	salvo buen cobro m
salvo error (Es)	Irrtum vorbehalten	errors excepted	sauf erreur	salvo errore	—
salvo errore (I)	Irrtum vorbehalten	errors excepted	sauf erreur	—	salvo error
Sammelladung (D)	—	collective consignment	envoi par groupage m	carico a collettame m	carga colectiva f
Sammeltransport (D)	—	collective transport	transport de groupage m	trasporto a collettame m	transporte colectivo m
Sammelwerbung (D)	—	collective advertisement	publicité groupée f	pubblicità collettiva f	publicidad colectiva f
sample[1] (E)	Muster n	—	échantillon m	campione m	muestra f
sample[2] (E)	Warenprobe f	—	échantillon m	campione m	muestra f
sample bag (E)	Mustermappe f	—	dossier à échantillons m	cartella campioni f	muestrario m
sample consignment (E)	Mustersendung f	—	envoi d'échantillons m	spedizione di campioni f	envío de muestras m
sample, no commercial value (E)	Muster ohne Wert n	—	échantillon sans valeur m	campione senza valore m	muestra sin valor f
sample survey (E)	Stichproben- erhebung f	—	enquête par sondage f	prelievo di campioni m	encuesta por muestreo f
sampling procedure (E)	Stichprobe- verfahren n	—	méthode d'enquête par sondage f	metodo del campionamento m	muestreo m
sanción (Es)	Sanktion f	sanction	sanction f	sanzione f	—
sanction (E)	Sanktion f	—	sanction f	sanzione f	sanción f
sanction (F)	Sanktion f	sanction	—	sanzione f	sanción f
saneamiento (Es)	Sanierung f	urban renewal/ reconstruction	assainissement m	risanamento m	—
sanidad (Es)	Gesundheitswesen n	public health	santé publique f	sanità f	—
Sanierung (D)	—	urban renewal/ reconstruction	assainissement m	risanamento m	saneamiento m
sanità (I)	Gesundheitswesen n	public health	santé publique f	—	sanidad f
Sanktion (D)	—	sanction	sanction f	sanzione f	sanción f
sans défaut (F)	mangelfrei	free of defects	—	esente da vizi	sin vicios
sans délai (F)	fristlos	without prior notice	—	senza preavviso	sin plazo
sans dividende (F)	ohne Dividende	with non-distributed dividend	—	senza dividendo	sin dividendo
sans emballage (F)	unverpackt	unpacked	—	non imballato/ alla rinfusa	sin embalar
sans engagement[1] (F)	freibleibend	subject to confirmation	—	senza impegno	no vinculante
sans engagement[2] (F)	ohne Obligo	without obligation	—	senza obbligo	sin obligación
sans obligation (F)	unverbindlich	not binding	—	senza impegno	sin compromiso
sans phosphate (F)	phosphatfrei	free of phosphate	—	privo di fosfato	sin fosfato
santé publique (F)	Gesundheitswesen n	public health	—	sanità f	sanidad f
sanzione (I)	Sanktion f	sanction	sanction f	—	sanción f
satélite (Es)	Satellit m	satellite	satellite f	satellite m	—
Satellit (D)	—	satellite	satellite f	satellite m	satélite m
satellite (E)	Satellit m	—	satellite f	satellite m	satélite m
satellite (F)	Satellit m	satellite	—	satellite m	satélite m
satellite (I)	Satellit m	satellite	satellite f	—	satélite m
Satellitenstation (D)	—	space station	station de satellite f	stazione satellite f	estación satélite f

	D	E	F	I	Es
satisfacción de las necesidades (Es)	Bedürfnisbefriedigung f	satisfaction of needs	satisfaction des besoins f	soddisfazione dei bisogni f	—
satisfacción en el trabajo (Es)	Arbeitszufriedenheit f	job satisfaction	satisfaction de travail f	soddisfazione del lavoro f	—
satisfaction des besoins (F)	Bedürfnisbefriedigung f	satisfaction of needs	—	soddisfazione dei bisogni f	satisfacción de las necesidades f
satisfaction de travail (F)	Arbeitszufriedenheit f	job satisfaction	—	soddisfazione del lavoro f	satisfacción en el trabajo f
satisfaction of needs (E)	Bedürfnisbefriedigung f	—	satisfaction des besoins f	soddisfazione dei bisogni f	satisfacción de las necesidades f
Sättigung (D)	—	saturation	saturation f	saturazione f	saturación f
saturazione (I)	Sättigung f	saturation	saturation f	—	saturación f
saturación (Es)	Sättigung f	saturation	saturation f	saturazione f	—
saturation (E)	Sättigung f	—	saturation f	saturazione f	saturación f
saturation (F)	Sättigung f	saturation	—	saturazione f	saturación f
Satzung (D)	—	statutes	statut m	statuto m	estatuto m
Satzungsänderung (D)	—	amendment of the statutes	modification des statuts f	modificazione dello statuto f	modificación de los estatutos f
sauf bonne fin (F)	Eingang vorbehalten	due payment reserved	—	salvo buon fine	salvo buen cobro m
sauf erreur (F)	Irrtum vorbehalten	errors excepted	—	salvo errore	salvo error
säumig (D)	—	dilatory	retardataire	moroso	moroso
sauvegarde des données (F)	Datenschutz m	data securing	—	tutela dei dati f	protección de los datos f
sauvetage (F)	Bergung f	salvage	—	ricupero m	salvamento m
saving (E)	Sparen n	—	épargne f	risparmio m	ahorro m
savings (E)	Ersparnis f	—	épargne f	risparmio m	ahorro m
savings bank (E)	Sparkasse f	—	institut bancaire d'épargne m	cassa di risparmio f	caja de ahorros f
savings deposits (E)	Spareinlagen pl	—	dépôt d'épargne m	depositi di risparmio m pl	imposiciones de ahorro f pl
savings ratio (E)	Sparquote f	—	quote-part de revenu réservée à des fins d'épargne f	quota di risparmio f	cuota de ahorro f
scadenza (I)	Laufzeit f	term	durée f	—	plazo de vencimiento m
scadenza degli interessi vincolati (I)	Zinsbindungsfrist f	lock-down period for interest rates	délai d'engagement sur le taux d'intérêt accordé m	—	plazo de vinculación al tipo de interés pactado m
scadenza del credito (I)	Kreditlaufzeit f	duration of credit	durée de l'allocation de crédit f	—	período concesional de un crédito m
scadenza di pagamento (I)	Zahlungsfrist f	terms of payment	délai de payement f	—	plazo de pago m
scadenza residua (I)	Restlaufzeit f	residual time to maturity	durée restante f	—	plazo de vencimiento restante m
scaduto (I)	anstehen	be due	échu	—	estar pendiente
scambio (I)	Tausch m	exchange/barter	échange m/troc m	—	cambio m/trueque m
scambio est-ovest (I)	Ost-West-Handel m	East-West trade	commerce Est-Ouest m	—	comercio este-oeste m
scambio libero (I)	Freihandel m	free trade	commerce libre m	—	librecambio m
scambio merci (I)	Warenaustausch m	exchange of goods	échanges commerciaux m pl	—	intercambio de mercancías m
scarce (E)	knapp	—	rare	scarso	escaso
scarsità (I)	Knappheit f	shortage	rareté f	—	escasez f
scarsità di materie prime (I)	Rohstoffknappheit f	raw materials shortage	pénurie de matières premières f	—	escasez de materias primas f
scarsità di merci (I)	Warenknappheit f	shortage of goods	pénurie de marchandises f	—	escasez de mercancías f
scarso (I)	knapp	scarce	rare	—	escaso
scarto tipo (I)	Standardabweichung f	standard deviation	déviation standard f	—	desviación standard f
sceau (F)	Siegel n	seal	—	sigillo m	sello m
scelta dell'ubicazione (I)	Standortwahl f	choice of location	choix du lieu d'implantation m	—	elección de la ubicación f

	D	E	F	I	Es
Schaden (D)	—	damage	dommage *m*	danno *m*	daño *m*
Schadenersatz-ansprüche (D)	—	claim for damages	droit à l'indemnité *m*	diritti al risarcimento danni *m pl*	derecho a indemnización por daños y perjuicios *m*
Schadensersatz (D)	—	compensation for loss suffered	dommages-intérêts *m pl*	risarcimento danni *m*	indemnización *f*
Schadensersatz-klage (D)	—	action for damages	action en dommages-intérêts *f*	azione di risarcimento danni *f*	demanda de daños y perjuicios *f*
Schadensersatz-pflicht (D)	—	liability for damages	obligation de dédommager *f*	obbligo di risarcimento danni *m*	obligación indemnizatoria *f*
Schadensforderung (D)	—	claim for damages	prétention à dommages-intérêts *f*	credito da danni *m*	pretensión de indemnización *f*
Schadensmeldung (D)	—	notification of damage	déclaration du sinistre *f*	avviso di danni *m*	aviso de siniestro *m*
Schadenverhütung (D)	—	loss prevention	mesure préventive contre les sinistres *f*	prevenzione danni *f*	prevención de siniestros *f*
Schadstoff (D)	—	pollutants	élément polluant *m*	sostanza nociva *f*	substancia nociva *f*
Schatzamt (D)	—	Treasury	trésor *m*	tesoreria *f*	tesorería *f*
Schätzwert (D)	—	estimated value	valeur d'estimation *f*	valore stimato *m*	estimación *f*
Schaubild (D)	—	graph	graphique *m*	diagramma *m*	cuadro *m*
Schaufenster (D)	—	shop-window	vitrine *f*	vetrina *f*	escaparate *m*
Schaufenster-dekoration (D)	—	window dressing	décoration de vitrine *f*	allestimento di vetrina *m*	adorno del escaparate *m*
Schaumstoff (D)	—	foam material	mousse synthétique *f*	espanso *m*	plástico espumoso *m*
Scheck (D)	—	cheque	chèque *m*	assegno *m*	cheque *m*
Scheckbetrug (D)	—	cheque fraud	irrégularité en matière de chèque *f*	emissione di assegno a vuoto *f*	falsificación de cheques *f*
Scheckbuch (D)	—	cheque book	livre d'enregistre-ment des chèques *m*	libretto degli assegni *m*	libro de cheques *m*
Scheckheft (D)	—	cheque book	carnet de chèques *m*	carnet degli assegni *m*	libreta de cheques *f*
Scheckkarte (D)	—	cheque card	carte d'identité eurochèque *f*	carta assegni *f*	tarjeta de cheques *f*
Schecksperrung (D)	—	stopping payment of cheque	opposition au paye-ment d'un chèque *f*	blocco d'assegno *m*	bloqueo de un cheque *m*
scheda (I)	Karteikarte *f*	index card	fiche *f*	—	ficha *f*
schedario (I)	Kartei *f*	card-index	cartothèque	—	fichero *m*
scheduling (E)	Terminplanung *f*	—	planning de rendez-vous *m*	programmazione dei termini *f*	planificación de plazos *f*
scheduling organization (E)	Ablauforganisation *f*	—	organisation fonction-nelle de l'entreprise *f*	organizzazione del lavoro *f*	organización funcional *f*
Scheinfirma (D)	—	bogus firm	raison sociale imaginaire *f*	pseudoditta *f*	casa ficticia *f*
Scheingeschäft (D)	—	fictitious transaction	opération simulée *f*	negozio simulato *m*	operación ficticia *f*
Scheingewinn (D)	—	fictitious profit	gain fictif *m*	utile fittizio *m*	beneficio simulado *m*
Schenkung (D)	—	donation	donation *f*	donazione *f*	donación *f*
Schenkungssteuer (D)	—	gift tax	impôt sur les donations *m*	imposta sulle donazioni *f*	impuesto sobre donaciones *m*
Schichtwechsel (D)	—	change of shift	relève d'équipe *f*	cambio di turno *m*	cambio del equipo de obreros *m*
Schiedsgericht (D)	—	court of arbitration	tribunal d'arbitrage *m*	tribunale arbitrale *m*	tirbunal arbitral *m*
schiffbar (D)	—	navigable	navigable	navigabile	navegable
Schiffsmakler (D)	—	shipbroker	courtier maritime *m*	agente marittimo *m*	corredor marítimo *m*
Schiffsregister (D)	—	register of ships	répertoire des navires *m*	registro navale *m*	registro marítimo *m*
Schlange stehen (D)	—	queue up	faire la queue	fare la coda	hacer la cola
schlechte Qualität (D)	—	poor quality	mauvaise qualité *f*	qualità scadente *f*	mala calidad *f*
schleichende Inflation (D)	—	creeping inflation	inflation rampante *f*	inflazione strisciante *f*	inflación latente *f*
Schlußbilanz (D)	—	closing balance	bilan de clôture *m*	bilancio consuntivo *m*	balance final *m*/ba-lanza de saldos definitivos *f*

	D	E	F	I	Es
Schlußbrief (D)	—	letter of confirmation	lettre de confirmation des conditions *f*	lettera di conferma *f*	carta de confirmación *f*
Schlußkurs (D)	—	closing price	dernier cours *m*	quotazione di chiusura *f*	cotización final *f*
Schlußverkauf (D)	—	seasonal sale	vente de fin de saison *f*	svendita di fine stagione *f*	venta de liquidación *f*
Schlüsselwort (D)	—	key word	mot-clé *m*	parola chiave *f*	palabra clave *f*
Schmierstoffe (D)	—	lubricants	lubrifiants *m pl*	lubrificanti *m pl*	lubrificantes *m pl*
Schmuggel (D)	—	smuggling	contrebande *f*	contrabbando *m*	contrabando *m*
Schneeballsystem (D)	—	snowball system	système de la boule de neige *m*	sistema di vendite a catena aperta *m*	venta en cadena *f*
schnellstmöglich (D)	—	as quickly as possible	le plus vite possible	al più presto possibile	tan rápido como sea posible
school (E)	Schule *f*	—	école *f*	scuola *f*	escuela *f*
school report (E)	Zeugnis *n*	—	certificat scolaire *m*	pagella *f*	certificado de escuela *m*
Schreibtisch (D)	—	desk	bureau *m*	scrivania *f*	escritorio *m*
Schriftform (D)	—	written form	forme par écrit *f*	forma scritta *f*	forma escrita *f*
schriftlich (D)	—	written	par écrit	per iscritto	por escrito
Schuld (D)	—	debt	dette *f*	debito *m*	deuda *f*
Schuldanerkennung (D)	—	acknowledgement of a debt	reconnaissance de dette *f*	riconoscimento del debito *m*	reconocimiento de la deuda *f*
Schulden (D)	—	debts	dettes *f pl*	debiti *m pl*	deudas *f pl*
Schuldendienst (D)	—	debt service	service de la dette *m*	servizio dei debiti *m*	servicio de la deuda *m*
Schuldenmasse (D)	—	total of indebtedness	passif *m*	massa passiva *f*	masa pasiva *f*
schuldhaft (D)	—	culpable	coupable	colposo	culpable
Schuldner (D)	—	debtor	débiteur *m*	debitore *m*	deudor *m*
Schuldnerländer (D)	—	debtor countries	pays débiteurs *m pl*	paesi debitori *m pl*	países deudores *m pl*
Schuldschein (D)	—	certificate of indebtedness	billet de créance *m*	certificato di debito *m*	pagaré *m*
Schuldverschreibung (D)	—	debenture stock	obligation *f*	obbligazione *f*	obligación *f*
Schule (D)	—	school	école *f*	scuola *f*	escuela *f*
Schulungspersonal (D)	—	training staff	personnel d'instruction *m*	personale d'addestramento *m*	personal de formación *m*
Schutzfrist (D)	—	term of protection	délai de protection *m*	durata della protezione *f*	plazo de protección *m*
Schutzzoll (D)	—	protective duty	droit de protection *m*	dazio protettivo *m*	aduana proteccionista *f*
Schwankungsbreite (D)	—	margin of fluctuation	marge de la fluctuation *f*	margine d'oscillazione *m*	margen de fluctuación *f*
Schwarzarbeit (D)	—	illicit work	travail noir *m*	lavoro abusivo *m*	trabajo clandestino *m*
schwarze Zahlen (D)	—	surplus	excédent *m*	conti in nero *m pl*	superávit *m*
Schwarzmarkt (D)	—	black market	marché noir *m*	mercato nero *m*	mercado negro *m*
Schweigepflicht (D)	—	professional discretion	discrétion professionnelle *f*	obbligo del segreto professionale *m*	secreto profesional *m*
Schwellenland (D)	—	newly industrialized countries	pays dans le seuil à l'industrialisation *m*	paese emergente *m*	país en el umbral hacia la industrialización *m*
Schwellenpreis (D)	—	threshold price	prix de seuil *m*	prezzo soglia *m*	precio-base *m*
Schwergut (D)	—	heavy freight	produit pondéreux *m*	carico pesante *m*	mercancía pesada *f*
Schwermetall (D)	—	heavy metal	métal lourd *m*	metallo pesante *m*	metal pesado *m*
Schwestergesellschaft (D)	—	affiliated company	société affiliée *f*	consorella *f*	compañía asociada *f*
Schwindel (D)	—	swindle	tromperie *f*	truffa *f*	engaño *m*
(science de la) gestion industrielle et commerciale (F)	Betriebswirtschaftslehre *f*	business administration	—	economia aziendale *f*	teoría de la empresa *f*
sciences économiques (F)	Wirtschaftswissenschaften *pl*	economics	—	scienze economiche *f pl*	ciencias económicas *f pl*
scienze economiche (I)	Wirtschaftswissenschaften *pl*	economics	sciences économiques *f pl*	—	ciencias económicas *f pl*

	D	E	F	I	Es
scioglimento (I)	Auflösung f	dissolution	liquidation f	—	disolución f
sciopero (I)	Streik m	strike	grève f	—	huelga f
sciopero generale (I)	Generalstreik m	general strike	grève générale f	—	huelga general f
sconto¹ (I)	Diskont m	discount	escompte m	—	descuento m
sconto² (I)	Skonto n	discount	escompte m	—	descuento m
sconto di lancio (I)	Einführungsrabatt m	introductory discount	rabais d'introduction m	—	rebaja de lanzamineto f
sconto di quantità (I)	Mengenrabatt m	quantity discount	remise de quantité f	—	rebaja de cantidad f
sconto per pagamento in contanti¹ (I)	Barzahlungs-nachlaß m	discount for cash payment	remise pour paye-ment au comptant f	—	descuento por pago al contado m
sconto per pagamento in contanti² (I)	Barzahlungskonto n	cash discount	escompte de caisse m	—	descuento de pago al contado f
scope of advertising effect (E)	Werbereichweite f	—	zone de rayonnement de la publicité f	raggio d'azione della pubblicità m	alcance publicitario m
scoperto di conto (I)	Kontoüberziehung f	overdraft of an account	découvert de compte m	—	descubierto m
scorte¹ (I)	Reserve f	reserve stock/ reserves	stocks de ré-serve m pl/réserve f	—	existencias f pl/ reserva f
scorte² (I)	Vorrat m	stock	stock m	—	existencias f pl
scorte iniziali (I)	Anfangsbestand m	opening inventory	stock initial m	—	existencias iniciales f pl
scorte merci (I)	Warenbestand m	stock	stock de marchandises m	—	existencias de mercancías f pl
scrap (E)	verschrotten	—	mettre à la ferraille	ridurre a rottame	hacer quincalla desguazar
screen (E)	Bildschirm m	—	écran m	video m	pantalla f
screen job (E)	Bildschirm-arbeitsplatz m	—	poste de travail à l'écran f	posto di lavoro video m	puesto de trabajo de pantalla m
screen work (E)	Bildschirmarbeit f	—	travail à l'écran	lavoro video m	trabajo de pantalla m
scrivania (I)	Schreibtisch m	desk	bureau m	—	escritorio m
scuola (I)	Schule f	school	école f	—	escuela f
sdoganamento delle esportazioni (I)	Ausfuhrabfertigung f	customs clearance of exports	formalités en douane à l'exportation f pl	—	despacho de exportación m
sdoganato (I)	verzollt	duty paid	dédouané	—	pagado
seal (E)	Siegel n	—	sceau m	sigillo m	sello m
séance extraordinaire (F)	Sondersitzung f	special meeting	—	seduta straordinaria f	sesión especial f
seaproof packing (E)	seemäßige Verpackung f	—	emballage maritime m	imballaggio marittimo m	embalaje marítimo m
season (E)	Saison f	—	saison f	stagione f	temporada f
sea route (E)	Seeweg m	—	voie maritime f	via marittima f	vía marítima f
seasonal fluctuations (E)	Saison-schwankungen pl	—	mouvements saisonniers m pl	oscillazioni stagionali f pl	oscilaciones estacionales f pl
seasonally adjusted (E)	saisonbereinigt	—	corrigé du mouve-ment saisonnier	al netto degli influssi stagionali	desestacionalizado
seasonal sale (E)	Schlußverkauf m	—	vente de fin de saison f	svendita di fine stagione f	venta de liquidación f
seasonal unemployment (E)	saisonale Arbeitslosigkeit f	—	chômage saisonnier m	disoccupazione stagionale f	paro estacional m
sección (Es)	Abteilung f	division/department	service m	reparto m	—
sección de publicidad (Es)	Werbeabteilung f	publicity department	service de publicité m	reparto pubblicità m	—
sección jurídica (Es)	Rechtsabteilung f	legal department	bureau juridique m	ufficio legale m	—
secondary dust (E)	Sekundärstaub m	—	poussière secondaire f	polvere secondaria f	polvo secundario m
secondary energy (E)	Sekundärenergie f	—	énergie secondaire f	energia secondaria f	energía secundaria f
secrecy of the post (E)	Postgeheimnis n	—	secret postal m	segreto postale m	secreto postal m
secret¹ (E)	geheim	—	secret	segreto	secreto
secret² (E)	Geheimnis n	—	secret m	segreto m	secreto m
secret¹ (F)	geheim	secret	—	segreto	secreto
secret² (F)	Geheimnis n	secret	—	segreto m	secreto m

	D	E	F	I	Es
secrétaire¹ (F)	Sekretärin *f*	secretary	—	segretaria *f*	secretaria *f*
secrétaire² (F)	Sekretär *m*	secretary	—	segretario *m*	secretario *m*
secretaria (Es)	Sekretärin *f*	secretary	secrétaire *f*	segretaria *f*	—
secretario (Es)	Sekretär *m*	secretary	secrétaire *m*	segretario *m*	—
secretary¹ (E)	Sekretär *m*	—	secrétaire *m*	segretario *m*	secretario *m*
secretary² (E)	Sekretärin *f*	—	secrétaire *f*	segretaria *f*	secretaria *f*
secret bancaire (F)	Bankgeheimnis *n*	banker's duty of secrecy	—	segreto bancario *m*	secreto bancario *m*
secret d'affaires (F)	Geschäftsgeheimnis *n*	business secret	—	segreto commerciale *m*	secreto comercial *m*
secret de service (F)	Dienstgeheimnis *n*	official secret	—	segreto d'ufficio *m*	secreto profesional *m*
secret d'exploitation (F)	Betriebsgeheimnis *n*	trade secret	—	segreto aziendale *m*	secreto empresarial *m*
secreto¹ (Es)	geheim	secret	secret	segreto	—
secreto² (Es)	Geheimnis *n*	secret	secret *m*	segreto *m*	—
secreto bancario (Es)	Bankgeheimnis *n*	banker's duty of secrecy	secret bancaire *m*	segreto bancario *m*	—
secreto comercial (Es)	Geschäftsgeheimnis *n*	business secret	secret d'affaires *m*	segreto commerciale *m*	—
secreto empresarial (Es)	Betriebsgeheimnis *n*	trade secret	secret d'exploitation *m*	segreto aziendale *m*	—
secreto postal (Es)	Postgeheimnis *n*	secrecy of the post	secret postal *m*	segreto postale *m*	—
secreto profesional¹ (Es)	Berufsgeheimnis *n*	professional secret	secret professionnel *m*	segreto professionale *m*	—
secreto profesional² (Es)	Schweigepflicht *f*	professional discretion	discrétion professionnelle *f*	obbligo del segreto professionale *m*	—
secreto profesional³ (Es)	Dienstgeheimnis *n*	official secret	secret de service *m*	segreto d'ufficio *m*	—
secret postal (F)	Postgeheimnis *n*	secrecy of the post	—	segreto postale *m*	secreto postal *m*
secret professionnel (F)	Berufsgeheimnis *n*	professional secret	—	segreto professionale *m*	secreto profesional *m*
secteur (F)	Sektor *m*	sector	—	settore *m*	sector *m*
secteur économique (F)	Wirtschaftszweig *m*	field of the economy	—	settore economico *m*	ramo económico *m*
secteur public (F)	öffentliche Hand *f*	public authorities	—	mano pubblica *f*	sector público *m*
sector (E)	Sektor *m*	—	secteur *m*	settore *m*	sector *m*
sector (Es)	Sektor *m*	sector	secteur *m*	settore *m*	—
sector del mercado no abarcado por la oferta (Es)	Marktlücke *f*	market gap	créneau du marché *m*	lacuna di mercato *f*	—
sector público (Es)	öffentliche Hand *f*	public authorities	secteur public *m*	mano pubblica *f*	—
sécurité (F)	Sicherheit *f*	security	—	sicurezza *f*	seguridad *f*
sécurité du travail (F)	Arbeitssicherheit *f*	safety at work	—	sicurezza del lavoro *f*	seguridad del trabajo *f*
sécurité réelle (F)	dingliche Sicherung *f*	real security	—	garanzia reale *f*	garantía real *f*
sécurité sociale (F)	soziale Sicherheit *f*	social security	—	sicurezza sociale *f*	seguridad social *f*
securities (E)	Effekten *f*	—	valeurs mobilières *f pl*	titoli *m pl*	efectos *m pl*
securities business¹ (E)	Effektengeschäft *n*	—	commerce des valeurs mobilières *m*	operazione su titoli *f*	operacion de valores *f*
securities business² (E)	Wertpapiergeschäft *n*	—	opérations sur titres *f pl*	operazioni su titoli *f pl*	operación con valores *f*
securities fund (E)	Wertpapierfonds *m*	—	fonds de valeurs mobilières *m*	fondo titoli *m*	fondo de inversión mobiliaria *m*
securities market (E)	Wertpapierbörse *f*	—	bourse des titres et valeurs *f*	borsa valori *f*	mercado de valores *m*
security¹ (E)	Kaution *f*	—	caution *f*	cauzione *f*	caución *f*/garantía *f*
security² (E)	Wertpapier *n*	—	titre *m*/valeur *f*	titolo *m*	título *m*/valor *m*
security³ (E)	Sicherheit *f*	—	sécurité *f*	sicurezza *f*	seguridad *f*
sede (I)	Firmensitz *m*	domicile of the company	siège social *m*	—	sede social *f*
sede social (Es)	Firmensitz *m*	domicile of the company	siège social *m*	sede *f*	—

seguro de empleados

	D	E	F	I	Es
seduta straordinaria (I)	Sondersitzung f	special meeting	séance extraordinaire f	—	sesión especial f
Seeblockade (D)	—	naval blockade	blocus maritime m	blocco marittimo m	bloqueo marítimo m
Seefrachtbrief (D)	—	bill of lading	connaissement maritime m	polizza di carico f	póliza f
seemäßige Verpackung (D)	—	seaproof packing	emballage maritime m	imballaggio marittimo m	embalaje marítimo m
Seemeile (D)	—	nautical mile	mille nautique m	miglio marino m	milla marina f
Seeweg (D)	—	sea route	voie maritime f	via marittima f	vía marítima f
segment de vente (F)	Absatzsegment n	sales segment	—	segmento di vendita m	segmento de venta m
segmento de venta (Es)	Absatzsegment n	sales segment	segment de vente m	segmento di vendita m	—
segmento di vendita (I)	Absatzsegment n	sales segment	segment de vente m	—	segmento de venta m
segretaria (I)	Sekretärin f	secretary	secrétaire f	—	secretaria f
segretario (I)	Sekretär m	secretary	secrétaire m	—	secretario m
segreteria telefonica (I)	Anrufbeantworter m	answering machine	répondeur automatique m	—	contestador de llamadas m
segretezza (I)	Geheimhaltung f	maintenance of secrecy	conservation du secret f	—	mantenimiento del secreto m
segreto¹ (I)	Geheimnis n	secret	secret m	—	secreto m
segreto² (I)	geheim	secret	secret	—	secreto
segreto aziendale (I)	Betriebsgeheimnis n	trade secret	secret d'exploitation m	—	secreto empresarial m
segreto bancario (I)	Bankgeheimnis n	banker's duty of secrecy	secret bancaire m	—	secreto bancario m
segreto commerciale (I)	Geschäftsgeheimnis n	business secret	secret d'affaires m	—	secreto comercial m
segreto d'ufficio (I)	Dienstgeheimnis n	official secret	secret de service m	—	secreto profesional m
segreto postale (I)	Postgeheimnis n	secrecy of the post	secret postal m	—	secreto postal m
segreto professionale (I)	Berufsgeheimnis n	professional secret	secret professionnel m	—	secreto profesional m
segunda lectura en el corro (Es)	Reprise f	repeat	tendance à la hausse f	ripresa f	—
según lo acordado (Es)	vereinbarungsgemäß	as agreed	comme convenu	come convenuto	—
seguridad (Es)	Sicherheit f	security	sécurité f	sicurezza f	—
seguridad del trabajo (Es)	Arbeitssicherheit f	safety at work	sécurité du travail f	sicurezza del lavoro f	—
seguridad social (Es)	soziale Sicherheit f	social security	sécurité sociale f	sicurezza sociale f	—
seguro¹ (Es)	Assekuranz f	assurance	assurance f	assicurazione f	—
seguro² (Es)	Versicherungspolice f	insurance policy	police d'assurance f	polizza d'assicurazione f	—
seguro³ (Es)	Versicherung f	insurance	assurance f	assicurazione f	—
seguro contra el robo (Es)	Diebstahlversicherung f	theft insurance	assurance contre le vol f	assicurazione contro il furto f	—
seguro contra incendios (Es)	Feuerversicherung f	fire insurance	assurance contre l'incendie f	assicurazione contro incendi f	—
seguro contra robo con fractura (Es)	Einbruchversicherung f	housebreaking insurance	assurance contre le vol avec effraction f	assicurazione contro il furto con scasso f	—
seguro crediticio (Es)	Kreditversicherung f	credit insurance	assurance crédit f	assicurazione dei crediti f	—
seguro de accidentes (Es)	Unfallversicherung f	personal accident insurance	assurance accidents corporels f	assicurazione contro infortuni f	—
seguro de automóviles (Es)	Kraftfahrzeugversicherung f	motor insurance	assurance responsabilité civile automobile f	assicurazione autoveicoli f	—
seguro de casco (Es)	Kaskoversicherung f	comprehensive insurance	assurance tous risques f	assicurazione corpi del ramo trasporto f	—
seguro de cosas (Es)	Sachversicherung f	property insurance	assurance de choses f	assicurazione di cose f	—
seguro de empleados (Es)	Angestelltenversicherung f	Salaried Employees' Pension Insurance	assurance invalidité-vieillesse des employés f	assicurazione degli impiegati f	—

	D	E	F	I	Es
seguro de enfermedad (Es)	Krankenversicherung *f*	health insurance	assurance maladie *f*	assicurazione contro le malattie	—
seguro de equipajes (Es)	Reisegepäckversicherung *f*	baggage insurance	assurance des bagages *f*	assicurazione del bagaglio *f*	—
seguro de maquinaria (Es)	Maschinenversicherung *f*	machine insurance	assurance des machines *f*	assicurazione delle macchine *f*	—
seguro de pensiones (Es)	Rentenversicherung *f*	old-age pension insurance	assurance sociale invalidité-vieillesse *f*	assicurazione invalidità e vecchiaia *f*	—
seguro de rescisión del viaje (Es)	Reiserücktrittsversicherung *f*	travel cancellation insurance	assurance de résiliation du voyage *f*	assicurazione recessione viaggio *f*	—
seguro de responsabilidad civil (Es)	Haftpflichtversicherung *f*	third party liability insurance	assurance responsabilité civile *f*	assicurazione della responsabilità civile *f*	—
seguro de transporte (Es)	Transportversicherung *f*	transportation insurance	assurance transports *f*	assicurazione dei trasporti *f*	—
seguro de vejez (Es)	Altersversicherung *f*	old age insurance	assurance-vieillesse *f*	assicurazione per la vecchiaia *f*	—
seguro de vida (Es)	Lebensversicherung *f*	life insurance	assurance vie *f*	assicurazione sulla vita *f*	—
seguro de vida temporal (Es)	Risiko-Lebensversicherung *f*	term life insurance	assurance-vie temporaire *f*	assicurazione rischio-vita *f*	—
seguro inmobiliario (Es)	Gebäudeversicherung *f*	insurance on buildings	assurance des bâtiments *f*	assicurazione dei fabbricati *f*	—
seguro personal (Es)	Personenversicherung *f*	insurance of persons	assurance des personnes *f*	assicurazione di persone *f*	—
seguro privado (Es)	Privatversicherung *f*	private security	assurance privée *f*	assicurazione privata *f*	—
seguro social (Es)	Sozialversicherung *f*	social insurance	assurance sociale *m*	previdenza sociale *f*	—
Sekretär (D)	—	secretary	secrétaire *m*	segretario *m*	secretario *m*
Sekretärin (D)	—	secretary	secrétaire *f*	segretaria *f*	secretaria *f*
Sektor (D)	—	sector	secteur *m*	settore *m*	sector *m*
Sekundärenergie (D)	—	secondary energy	énergie secondaire *f*	energia secondaria *f*	energía secundaria *f*
Sekundärstaub (D)	—	secondary dust	poussière secondaire *f*	polvere secondaria *f*	polvo secundario *m*
selbständig (D)	—	independent	indépendant	indipendente	independiente/no asalariado/autónomo
Selbstauskunft (D)	—	voluntary disclosure	renseignement fourni par l'intéressé lui-même *m*	informazione volontaria *f*	información de sí mismo *f*
Selbstbedienung (D)	—	self-service	self-service *m*	self service *m*	autoservicio *m*
Selbstfinanzierung (D)	—	self-financing	autofinancement *m*	autofinanziamento *m*	autofinanciación *f*
Selbstkosten (D)	—	cost	coût de revient *m*	spese vive *f pl*	costes propios *m pl*
Selbstkostenpreis (D)	—	cost price	prix coûtant *m*	prezzo di costo *m*	precio de coste *m*
selección (Es)	Selektion *f*	selection	sélection *f*	selezione *f*	—
sélectif (F)	selektiv	selective	—	selettivo	selectivo
selection (E)	Selektion *f*	—	sélection *f*	selezione *f*	selección *f*
sélection (F)	Selektion *f*	selection	—	selezione *f*	selección *f*
selective (E)	selektiv	—	sélectif	selettivo	selectivo
selectivo (Es)	selektiv	selective	sélectif	selettivo	—
Selektion (D)	—	selection	sélection *f*	selezione *f*	selección *f*
selektiv (D)	—	selective	sélectif	selettivo	selectivo
selettivo (I)	selektiv	selective	sélectif	—	selectivo
selezione (I)	Selektion *f*	selection	sélection *f*	—	selección *f*
selfemployed person (E)	Freiberufler *m*	—	personne exerçant une profession libérale *f*	libero professionista *m*	profesional *m*
self-financing (E)	Eigenfinanzierung *f*	—	autofinancement *m*	autofinanziamento *m*	financiación propia *f*
self-service (E)	Selbstbedienung *f*	—	self-service *m*	self service *m*	autoservicio *m*
self-service (F)	Selbstbedienung *f*	self-service	—	self service *m*	autoservicio *m*
self service (I)	Selbstbedienung *f*	self-service	self-service *m*	—	autoservicio *m*
sell (E)	verkaufen	—	vendre	vendere	vender
sellers competition (E)	Verkäuferwettbewerb *m*	—	compétition des vendeurs *f*	concorrenza dei venditori *f*	competición de vendedores *f*

	D	E	F	I	Es
seller's market (E)	Verkäufermarkt *m*	—	marché de vendeurs *m*	mercato favorevole ai venditori *m*	mercado favorable al vendedor *m*
sello¹ (Es)	Briefmarke *f*	stamp	timbre-poste *m*	francobollo *m*	—
sello² (Es)	Siegel *n*	seal	sceau *m*	sigillo *m*	—
sello postal (Es)	Poststempel *m*	postmark	cachet de la poste *m*	timbro postale *m*	—
semaine de travail (F)	Arbeitswoche *f*	working week	—	settimana lavorativa *f*	semana laboral *f*
semana laboral (Es)	Arbeitswoche *f*	working week	semaine de travail *f*	settimana lavorativa *f*	—
semestral (Es)	halbjährlich	half-yearly	semestriel	semestrale	—
semestrale (I)	halbjährlich	half-yearly	semestriel	—	semestral
semestriel (F)	halbjährlich	half-yearly	—	semestrale	semestral
semi-finished good (E)	Halberzeugnis *n*	—	produit demi-fini *m*	prodotto semifinito *m*	producto semielaborado *m*
semi-qualificato (I)	angelernt	semi-skilled	semi-qualifié	—	semicualificado
semi-qualifié (F)	angelernt	semi-skilled	—	semi-qualificato	semicualificado
semi-skilled (E)	angelernt	—	semi-qualifié	semi-qualificato	semicualificado
send a telegram (E)	telegrafieren	—	télégraphier	telegrafare	telegrafiar
sender (E)	Absender *m*	—	envoyeur *m*	mittente *m*	remitente *m*
Sendung (D)	—	consignment	envoi *m*	spedizione *f*	envío *m*
sensible a las fluctuaciones coyunturales (Es)	konjunkturanfällig	depending on the cyclical trend	sensible aux oscillations de la conjoncture	soggetto ad influssi congiunturali	—
sensible aux oscillations de la conjoncture (F)	konjunkturanfällig	depending on the cyclical trend	—	soggetto ad influssi congiunturali	sensible a las fluctuaciones coyunturales
senza concorrenza (I)	konkurrenzlos	without competition	défiant toute concurrence	—	sin competencia
senza dividendo (I)	ohne Dividende	with non-distributed dividend	sans dividende *m*	—	sin dividendo
senza garanzia (I)	ohne Gewähr	without garanty	sous toute réserve	—	sin garantía
senza impegno¹ (I)	unverbindlich	not binding	sans obligation	—	sin compromiso
senza impegno² (I)	freibleibend	subject to confirmation	sans engagement	—	no vinculante
senza obbligo (I)	ohne Obligo	without obligation	sans engagement	—	sin obligación
senza preavviso (I)	fristlos	without prior notice	sans délai	—	sin plazo
séquestre judiciare (F)	Zwangsverwaltung *f*	receivership	—	amministrazione giudiziaria *f*	administración forzosa *f*
sequestro (I)	Beschlagnahme *f*	confiscation	saisie *f*	—	confiscación *f*
se référant (F)	bezugnehmend	referring to	—	con riferimento	con referencia a
Serienfertigung (D)	—	series production	fabrication de série *f*	produzione in serie *f*	producción en serie *f*
series production (E)	Serienfertigung *f*	—	fabrication de série *f*	produzione in serie *f*	producción en serie *f*
serietà (I)	Seriosität *f*	seriousness	caractère sérieux *m*	—	buena reputación *f*
Seriosität (D)	—	seriousness	caractère sérieux *m*	serietà *f*	buena reputación *f*
seriousness (E)	Seriosität *f*	—	caractère sérieux *m*	serietà *f*	buena reputación *f*
serpente monetario (I)	Währungsschlange *f*	currency snake	serpent monétaire *m*	—	serpiente monetaria *f*
serpent monétaire (F)	Währungsschlange *f*	currency snake	—	serpente monetario *m*	serpiente monetaria *f*
serpiente monetaria (Es)	Währungsschlange *f*	currency snake	serpent monétaire *m*	serpente monetario *m*	—
serrata (I)	Aussperrung *f*	lock out	lock-out *m*	—	cierre patronal *m*
Service (D)	—	service	service *m*	servizio *m*	servicio *m*
service¹ (E)	Service *m*	—	service *m*	servizio *m*	servicio *m*
service² (E)	Dienst *m*	—	service *m*	servizio *m*	servicio *m*
service³ (E)	Dienstleistung *f*	—	prestation de service *f*	servizio *m*	prestación de servicio *m*
service¹ (F)	Service *m*	service	—	servizio *m*	servicio *m*
service² (F)	Abteilung *f*	division/department	—	reparto *m*	sección *f*
service³ (F)	Dienst *m*	service	—	servizio *m*	servicio *m*
service après vente (F)	Kundendienst *m*	after-sales service	—	servizio d'assistenza *m*	servicio posventa *m*

	D	E	F	I	Es
service de contributions (F)	Finanzamt n	inland revenue office	—	ufficio delle imposte m	Hacienda f
service de la dette (F)	Schuldendienst m	debt service	—	servizio dei debiti m	servicio de la deuda m
service de l'intérêt (F)	Zinsendienst m	interest service	—	servizio degli interessi m	servicio de intereses m
service de publicité (F)	Werbeabteilung f	publicity department	—	reparto pubblicità m	sección de publicidad f
service des expéditions (F)	Versandabteilung f	dispatch department	—	reparto spedizioni m	departamento de expedición m
service de télécommunication (F)	Fernmeldeamt n	telephone exchange	—	ufficio telecomunicazioni m	central interurbana f
service d'exportation (F)	Exportabteilung f	export department	—	reparto esportazioni m	departamento de exportación m
service du téléphone (F)	Telefondienst m	telephone service	—	servizio telefonico m	servicio telefónico m
service extérieur (F)	Außendienst m	field work	—	servizio esterno m	servicio exterior m
service organization (E)	Kundendienstorganisation f	—	organisation de service après-vente f	organizzazione del servizio d'assistenza f	organización de servicio posventa f
service technique (F)	technische Abteilung f	engineering department	—	reparto tecnico m	departamento técnico m
servicio¹ (Es)	Dienst m	service	service m	servizio m	—
servicio² (Es)	Service m	service	service m	servizio m	—
servicio de colocación (Es)	Arbeitsnachweis m	vacancies employment	emploi vacant m	informazioni sui posti vacanti f pl	—
servicio de intereses (Es)	Zinsendienst m	interest service	service de l'intérêt m	servizio degli interessi m	—
servicio de la deuda (Es)	Schuldendienst m	debt service	service de la dette m	servizio dei debiti m	—
servicio de pagos (Es)	Zahlungsverkehr m	payment transactions	opérations de payement f pl	operazioni di pagamento f pl	—
servicio exterior (Es)	Außendienst m	field work	service extérieur m	servizio esterno m	—
servicio posventa (Es)	Kundendienst m	after-sales service	service après vente m	servizio d'assistenza m	—
servicio telefónico (Es)	Telefondienst m	telephone service	service du téléphone m	servizio telefonico m	—
servizio¹ (I)	Service m	service	service m	—	servicio m
servizio² (I)	Dienst m	service	service m	—	servicio m
servizio³ (I)	Dienstleistung f	service	prestation de service f	—	prestación de servicio m
servizio d'assistenza (I)	Kundendienst m	after-sales service	service après vente m	—	servicio posventa m
servizio degli interessi (I)	Zinsendienst m	interest service	service de l'intérêt m	—	servicio de intereses m
servizio dei debiti (I)	Schuldendienst m	debt service	service de la dette m	—	servicio de la deuda m
servizio di sorveglianza aziendale (I)	Werkschutz m	works protection force	corps de sécurité d'entreprise m	—	policía de la empresa f
servizio esterno (I)	Außendienst m	field work	service extérieur m	—	servicio exterior m
servizio telefonico (I)	Telefondienst m	telephone service	service du téléphone m	—	servicio telefónico m
sesión bursátil (Es)	Börsentag m	market day	jour de bourse m	giorno di borsa m	—
sesión especial (Es)	Sondersitzung f	special meeting	séance extraordinaire f	seduta straordinaria f	—
set-off (E)	Aufrechnung f	—	compensation f	compensazione f	compensación f
settimana lavorativa (I)	Arbeitswoche f	working week	semaine de travail f	—	semana laboral f
settimanale (I)	wöchentlich	weekly	hebdomadaire	—	semanal
setting up of new business (E)	Existenzgründung f	—	fondation d'existence f	costituzione di un lavoro indipendente f	fundación de existencia f
settlement (E)	Abwicklung f	—	exécution f/ liquidation f	esecuzione f	ejecución f
settlement account (E)	Abwicklungskonto n	—	compte de liquidation m	conto di liquidazione f	cuenta de liquidación f
settlement by letter of credit (E)	Akkreditivabwicklung f	—	exécution par crédit documentaire f	procedura del credito documentario f	ejecución por crédito documentario f

	D	E	F	I	Es
settlement of accounts (E)	Abrechnung f	—	règlement m	liquidazione f	liquidación f
settlement of an account (E)	Kontoausgleich m	—	solde de compte m	liquidazione del conto f	saldo de cuenta m
settlement with immediate effect (E)	sofortige Regulierung f	—	règlement immédiat m	regolazione immediata f	regulación inmediata f
settling day (E)	Abrechnungstag m	—	jour de la liquidation m	giorno di liquidazione m	fecha de liquidación f
settling procedure (E)	Abrechnungs-verfahren n	—	méthode de l'apure-ment des comptes	metodo di liquidazione m	operaciones de descuento f pl
settore (I)	Sektor m	sector	secteur m	—	sector m
settore economico (I)	Wirtschaftszweig m	field of the economy	secteur économique m	—	ramo económico m
seuil de rentabilité[1] (F)	Gewinnschwelle f	break even point	—	soglia dell'utile f	umbral de la rentabilidad m
seuil de rentabilité[2] (F)	Rentabilitätschwelle f	break-even point	—	soglia di redditività f	límite inferior de rentabilidad m
seuil du prix (F)	Preisschwelle f	threshold price	—	soglia dei prezzi f	umbral de precios m
seule de change (F)	Solawechsel m	promissory note	—	pagherò m	pagaré m
seul propriétaire (F)	Alleininhaber m	sole owner	—	titolare unico m	propietario exclusivo m
sewage disposal costs (E)	Abwasserkosten pl	—	coûts de traitement des eaux usées m pl	costi per le acque di scarico m pl	gastos para aguas residuales m pl
sfruttamento abusivo (I)	Raubbau m	ruinous exploitation	exploitation abusive f	—	explotación abusiva f
sfruttamento delle capacità (I)	Kapazitäts-auslastung f	utilization of capacity	utilisation de la capacité f	—	utilización de las capacidades f
sgravio (I)	Entlastung f	discharge	décharge f	—	desgravamen m
share[1] (E)	Geschäftsanteil m	—	part sociale f	quota sociale f	participación f
share[2] (E)	Aktie f	—	action f	azione f	acción f
share capital[1] (E)	Grundkapital n	—	capital initial m	capitale sociale m	capital social m
share capital[2] (E)	Stammkapital n	—	capital social m	capitale sociale m	capital social m
share capital[3] (E)	Aktienkapital n	—	fonds social m	capitale azionario m	capital en acciones m
share deposit (E)	Aktiendepot n	—	dépôt d'actions m	deposito di azioni m	depósitio de acciones m
shareholder (E)	Aktionär m	—	actionnaire m	azionista m	accionista m
shareholder's agreement (E)	Gesellschafts-vertrag m	—	acte de société m	contratto di società m	contrato social m
shareholding (E)	Aktienbestand m	—	portefeuille d'actions m	portafoglio di azioni m	cartera de acciones f
share in capital (E)	Kapitalanteil m	—	part de capital f	quota di capitale f	participación en el capital f
share index (E)	Aktienindex m	—	indice du cours des actions m	indice azionario m	índice de cotización de acciones m
share in the material costs (E)	Materialkosten-anteil m	—	proportion des frais de matériel f	quota dei costi del materiale f	parte de los gastos de material m
share issue[1] (E)	Aktienemision f	—	émission d'actions f	emissione di azioni f	emisión de acciones f
share issue[2] (E)	Aktienausgabe f	—	émission d'actions f	emissione di azioni f	emisión de acciones f
share price (E)	Aktienkurs m	—	cours des actions m	corso delle azioni m	cotización de las acciones f
share quotation (E)	Aktiennotierung f	—	cotation des actions f	quotazione delle azioni f	cotización de acciones f
shares (E)	Aktien pl	—	actions f pl	azioni f	acciones f pl
shipbroker (E)	Schiffsmakler m	—	courtier maritime m	agente marittimo m	corredor marítimo m
shipment (E)	Verschiffung f	—	embarquement m	imbarco m	embarque m
shipowner (E)	Reeder m	—	armateur m	armatore m	armador m
shipping company (E)	Reederei f	—	société d'armateurs f	compagnia armatoriale f	compañía naviera f
shipping (delivered) weight (E)	Abladegewicht n	—	poids au déchargement m	peso di scarico m	peso de descarga m
shipping document (E)	Versanddokument n	—	documents d'expédition m pl	documento di spedizione m	documentos de expedición m pl
Shopping Center (D)	—	shopping centre	centre commercial m	centro commerciale m	centro comercial m
shopping centre (E)	Shopping Center n	—	centre commercial m	centro commerciale m	centro comercial m

	D	E	F	I	Es
shop-window (E)	Schaufenster n	—	vitrine f	vetrina f	escaparate m
shortage (E)	Knappheit f	—	rareté f	scarsità f	escasez f
shortage of goods (E)	Warenknappheit f	—	pénurie de marchandises f	scarsità di merci f	escasez de mercancías f
shortage of staff (E)	Personalmangel m	—	manque de personnel m	mancanza di personale f	falta der personal f
short delivery (E)	Minderlieferung f	—	livraison en quantité inférieure f	fornitura ridotta f	envío incompleto m
short distance traffic (E)	Nahverkehr m	—	transport à courte distance m	traffico a breve distanza m	tráfico a corta distancia m
short sale (E)	Blankoverkauf m	—	vente à découvert f	vendita allo scoperto f	venta al descubierto f
short-term (E)	kurzfristig	—	à court terme	a breve scadenza	a corto plazo
short-term credit (E)	kurzfristiger Kredit m	—	crédit à court terme m	credito a breve scadenza m	crédito a corto plazo m
short-time work (E)	Kurzarbeit f	—	travail à temps réduit m	lavoro ad orario ridotto m	trabajo reducido m
shuttle service (E)	Pendelverkehr m	—	trafic de va-et-vient m	traffico pendolare m	vaivén m
Sicherheit (D)	—	security	sécurité f	sicurezza f	seguridad f
Sicherheitsmarge (D)	—	margin	marge de sécurité f	margine di sicurezza m	margen de seguridad f
sicurezza (I)	Sicherheit f	security	sécurité f	—	seguridad f
sicurezza del lavoro (I)	Arbeitssicherheit f	safety at work	sécurité du travail f	—	seguridad del trabajo f
sicurezza sociale (I)	soziale Sicherheit f	social security	sécurité sociale f	—	seguridad social f
Siegel (D)	—	seal	sceau m	sigillo m	sello m
siège social (F)	Firmensitz m	domicile of the company	—	sede f	sede social f
sigillo (I)	Siegel n	seal	sceau m	—	sello m
sigillo doganale (I)	Zollverschluß m	customs seal	fermeture douanière f	—	precinto aduanero m
sigla (I)	Diktatzeichen n	reference	références f pl	—	referencias f pl
sign (E)	unterschreiben	—	signer	firmare	signar
signar (Es)	unterschreiben	sign	signer	firmare	—
signataire d'une convention collective (F)	Tarifpartner m	parties to a collective agreement	—	parti sociali f pl	parte contratante en un convenio colectivo f
signature (E)	Unterschrift f	—	signature f	firma f	firma f
signature (F)	Unterschrift f	signature	—	firma f	firma f
signature en blanc (F)	Blankounterschrift f	blank signature	—	firma in bianco f	firma en blanco f
signer (F)	unterschreiben	sign	—	firmare	signar
significatif (F)	relevant	relevant	—	rilevante	importante
Silber (D)	—	silver	argent m	argento m	plata f
silver (E)	Silber n	—	argent m	argento m	plata f
silvicultura (Es)	Forstwirtschaft f	forestry	économie forestière f	economia forestale f	—
simulación (Es)	Simulation f	simulation	simulation f	simulazione f	—
Simulation (D)	—	simulation	simulation f	simulazione f	simulación f
simulation (E)	Simulation f	—	simulation f	simulazione f	simulación f
simulation (F)	Simulation f	simulation	—	simulazione f	simulación f
simulazione (I)	Simulation f	simulation	simulation f	—	simulación f
sinceridad del balance (Es)	Bilanzwahrheit f	truth in the balance sheet	sincérité du bilan f	chiarezza di bilancio f	—
sincérité du bilan (F)	Bilanzwahrheit f	truth in the balance sheet	—	chiarezza di bilancio f	sinceridad del balance f
sin competencia (Es)	konkurrenzlos	without competition	défiant toute concurrence	senza concorrenza	—
sin compromiso (Es)	unverbindlich	not binding	sans obligation	senza impegno	—
sindacati (I)	Gewerkschaften pl	trade union	syndicat m	—	sindicato m
sindacato (I)	Syndikat n	syndicate	syndicat m	—	sindicato m
sindacato di blocco (I)	Sperrminorität f	blocking minority	minorité suffisante pour bloquer qch. f	—	minoría de bloqueo f
sindicación (Es)	Syndizierung f	syndication	syndication f	costituzione di un sindacato f	—

	D	E	F	I	Es
sindicato¹ (Es)	Gewerkschaften pl	trade union	syndicat m	sindacati m pl	—
sindicato² (Es)	Syndikat n	syndicate	syndicat m	sindacato m	—
síndico (Es)	Syndikus	legal adviser	syndic m	consulente legale m	—
síndico de quiebra (Es)	Konkursverwalter m	administrator in bankruptcy proceedings	liquidateur de la faillite m	curatore fallimentare m	—
sin dividendo (Es)	ohne Dividende	with non-distributed dividend	sans dividende m	senza dividendo	—
sin embalar (Es)	unverpackt	unpacked	sans emballage	non imballato/ alla rinfusa	—
sin fosfato (Es)	phosphatfrei	free of phosphate	sans phosphate	privo di fosfato	—
sin garantía (Es)	ohne Gewähr	without garanty	sous toute réserve	senza garanzia	—
sin obligación (Es)	ohne Obligo	without obligation	sans engagement	senza obbligo	—
siniestro leve (Es)	Bagatellschaden m	minimal damage	dommage mineur m	danno piccolo m	—
sinistre (F)	Versicherungsfall m	event insured against	—	caso di sinistro m	situación de siniestro f
sin plazo (Es)	fristlos	without prior notice	sans délai	senza preavviso	—
sin vicios (Es)	mangelfrei	free of defects	sans défaut	esente da vizi	—
sistema (Es)	System n	system	système m	sistema m	—
sistema (I)	System n	system	système m	—	sistema m
sistema de costes (Es)	Kostenrechnungs- system n	cost accounting system	méthode de calcul des coûts f	sistema dei costi m	—
sistema de cuotas (Es)	Quotensystem n	quota system	système de quote-parts m	sistema di contingentamento m	—
sistema de gravámenes (Es)	Abschöpfungs- system n	absorption system	système d'absorption m	regime di prelievo m	—
sistema dei costi (I)	Kostenrechnungs- system n	cost accounting system	méthode de calcul des coûts f	—	sistema de costes m
sistema de incentivos (Es)	Anreizsystem n	incentive system	système d'incitation m	sistema d'incentivo m	—
sistema de información (Es)	Informations- system n	information system	système d'information m	sistema d'informazione m	—
sistema de información asistido por ordenador (Es)	computergestütztes Informations- system n	computer-aided information system	système d'informa- tion assisté par ordinateur m	sistema di informazione computerizzato m	—
sistema dei premi (I)	Prämiensystem n	bonus system	système de primes m	—	sistema de primas m
sistema del lavoro a cottimo (I)	Akkordsystem n	piece work system	système du travail aux pièces m	—	régimen de trabajo a destajo m
sistema de primas (Es)	Prämiensystem n	bonus system	système de primes m	sistema dei premi m	—
sistema di contingentamento (I)	Quotensystem n	quota system	système de quote-parts m	—	sistema de cuotas m
sistema di informazione computerizzato (I)	computergestütztes Informations- system n	computer-aided information system	système d'informa- tion assisté par ordinateur m	—	sistema de informa- ción asistido por ordenador m
sistema d'incentivo (I)	Anreizsystem n	incentive system	système d'incitation m	—	sistema de incentivos m
sistema d'informazione (I)	Informations- system n	information system	système d'information m	—	sistema de información m
sistema di vendite a catena aperta (I)	Schneeballsystem n	snowball system	système de la boule de neige m	—	venta en cadena f
sistema economico mondiale (I)	Weltwirtschafts- ordnung f	international economic order	ordre économique mondial m	—	orden económico mundial m
sistema fiscal (Es)	Steuersystem n	system of taxation	système fiscal m	sistema fiscale m	—
sistema fiscale (I)	Steuersystem n	system of taxation	système fiscal m	—	sistema fiscal m
Sistema Monetario Europeo (Es)	Europäisches Währungssystem n	European Monetary System	Système Monétaire Européen m	Sistema Monetario Europeo m	—
Sistema Monetario Europeo (I)	Europäisches Währungssystem n	European Monetary System	Système Monétaire Européen m	—	Sistema Monetario Europeo m
sistema monetario internacional (Es)	Weltwährungs- system n	international monetary system	système monétaire international m	sistema monetario internazionale m	—
sistema monetario internazionale (I)	Weltwährungs- system n	international monetary system	système monétaire international m	—	sistema monetario internacional m
situación de competencia (Es)	Konkurrenzsituation f	competitive situation	situation de concurrence f	situazione concorrenziale f	—

	D	E	F	I	Es
situación del beneficio (Es)	Ertragslage *f*	earning situation	niveau du rendement *m*	situazione economica *f*	—
situación de personal (Es)	Personalsituation *f*	personnel situation	effectif du personnel *m*	situazione occupazionale *f*	—
situación de siniestro (Es)	Versicherungsfall *m*	event insured against	sinistre *m*	caso di sinistro *m*	—
situación económica (Es)	Vermögensverhältnisse *pl*	financial situation	situation financière *f*	situazione patrimoniale *f*	—
situación jurídica (Es)	Rechtslage *f*	legal situation	situation juridique *f*	situazione giuridica *f*	—
situation analytique de l'expoitation (F)	Betriebsanalyse *f*	operation analysis	—	analisi aziendale *f*	análisis de la empresa *m*
situation de concurrence (F)	Konkurrenzsituation *f*	competitive situation	—	situazione concorrenziale *f*	situación de competencia *f*
situation du marché[1] (F)	Marktsituation *f*	market situation	—	situazione di mercato *f*	estado del mercado *m*
situation du marché[2] (F)	Marktlage *f*	state of the market	—	situazione di mercato *f*	condiciones del mercado *f pl*
situation financière (F)	Vermögensverhältnisse *pl*	financial situation	—	situazione patrimoniale *f*	situación económica *f*
situation juridique (F)	Rechtslage *f*	legal situation	—	situazione giuridica *f*	situación jurídica *f*
situation wanted (E)	Stellengesuch *n*	—	demande d'emploi *f*	domanda d'impiego *f*	solicitud de colocación *f*
situazione concorrenziale (I)	Konkurrenzsituation *f*	competitive situation	situation de concurrence *f*	—	situación de competencia *f*
situazione di mercato[1] (I)	Marktsituation *f*	market situation	situation du marché *f*	—	estado del mercado *m*
situazione di mercato[2] (I)	Marktlage *f*	state of the market	situation du marché *f*	—	condiciones del mercado *f pl*
situazione economica (I)	Ertragslage *f*	earning situation	niveau du rendement *m*	—	situación del beneficio *f*
situazione giuridica (I)	Rechtslage *f*	legal situation	situation juridique *f*	—	situación jurídica *f*
situazione occupazionale (I)	Personalsituation *f*	personnel situation	effectif du personnel *m*	—	situación de personal *f*
situazione patrimoniale (I)	Vermögensverhältnisse *pl*	financial situation	situation financière *f*	—	situación económica *f*
Sitzungszimmer (D)	—	conference room	salle de réunion *f*	sala riunioni *f*	sala de conferencia *f*
size of an advertisement (E)	Anzeigenformat *n*	—	format de l'annonce *m*	formato dell'inserzione *m*	tamaño del anuncio *m*
size of the company[1] (E)	Betriebsgröße *f*	—	dimension de l'entreprise *f*	dimensione dell'azienda *f*	tamaño de la explotación *m*
size of the company[2] (E)	Unternehmensgröße *f*	—	dimension de l'entreprise *f*	dimensione dell'impresa *f*	dimensión de la empresa *f*
Skonto (D)	—	discount	escompte *m*	sconto *m*	descuento *m*
Skontoabzug (D)	—	discount deduction	déduction de l'escompte *f*	detrazione di sconto *f*	deducción del descuento *f*
slide projector (E)	Diaprojektor *m*		projecteur pour diapositives *m*	proiettore per diapositive *m*	projector de diapositivas *m*
slump-proof (E)	krisenfest	—	insensible aux influences de la crise économique	resistente alle crisi	a prueba de crisis
small and medium-sized enterprises (E)	Klein- und Mittelbetriebe *pl*	—	petites et moyennes entreprises *f pl*	piccole e medie imprese *f pl*	pequeñas y medianas empresas *f pl*
small container (E)	Kleincontainer *m*	—	petit conteneur *m*	mini container *m*	pequeño contenedor *m*
small package (E)	Päckchen *n*	—	petit paquet *m*	pacchetto *m*	pequeño paquete *m*
small pallet (E)	Kleinpalette *f*	—	petite palette *f*	mini paletta *f*	pequña paleta *f*
smaltimento (I)	Entsorgung *f*	waste disposal	dépollution *f*	—	eliminación *f*
smaltimento dei rifiuti (I)	Abfallbeseitigung *f*	waste disposal	élimination de déchets *f*	—	evacuación de residuos *f*
smaltimento dell'olio usato (I)	Altölbeseitigung *f*	disposal of waste oil	élimination d'huile usée *f*	—	eliminación de petróleo usado *f*
smerciabile (I)	marktfähig	marketable	vendable	—	comerciable
smercio delle materie prime (I)	Rohstoffvermarktung *f*	raw materials marketing	commercialisation des matières premières *f*	—	comercialización de las materias primas *f*
Smog (D)	—	smog	smog *m*	smog *m*	smog *m*
smog (E)	Smog *m*	—	smog *m*	smog *m*	smog *m*

	D	E	F	I	Es
smog (Es)	Smog *m*	smog	smog *m*	smog *m*	—
smog (F)	Smog *m*	smog	—	smog *m*	smog *m*
smog (I)	Smog *m*	smog	smog *m*	—	smog *m*
Smogalarm (D)	—	smog warning	alerte au smog *f*	allarme smog *m*	alarma de smog *f*
smog warning (E)	Smogalarm *m*	—	alerte au smog *f*	allarme smog *m*	alarma de smog *f*
smuggling (E)	Schmuggel *m*	—	contrebande *f*	contrabbando *m*	contrabando *m*
snob effect (E)	Snob-Effekt *m*	—	effet snob *m*	effetto snob *m*	efecto snob *m*
Snob-Effekt (D)	—	snob effect	effet snob *m*	effetto snob *m*	efecto snob *m*
snowball system (E)	Schneeballsystem *n*	—	système de la boule de neige *m*	sistema di vendite a catena aperta *m*	venta en cadena *f*
soberanía (Es)	Hoheitsrecht *n*	sovereign right	droit de souveraineté *m*	diritto di sovranità *m*	—
soberanía administrativa (Es)	Verwaltungshoheit *f*	power of administration	autonomie d'administration *f*	sovranità amministrativa *f*	—
soberanía financiera (Es)	Finanzhoheit *f*	financial sovereignty	souveraineté en matière budgétaire *f*	sovranità finanziaria *f*	—
soberanía legislativa (Es)	Gesetzgebungshoheit *f*	legislative sovereignty	compétence législative *f*	sovranità legislativa *f*	—
soberanía territorial (Es)	Gebietshoheit *f*	territorial jurisdiction	souveraineté territoriale *f*	sovranità territoriale *f*	—
soborno (Es)	Bestechung *f*	bribe	corruption *f*	corruzione *f*	—
sobre¹ (Es)	Kuvert *n*	envelope	enveloppe *f*	busta *f*	—
sobre² (Es)	Briefumschlag *m*	envelope	enveloppe de lettre *f*	busta *f*	—
sobrecapitalización (Es)	Überkapitalisierung *f*	overcapitalization	surcapitalisation *f*	sovracapitalizzazione *f*	—
sobrepasar (Es)	überziehen	overdraw	faire un prélèvement à découvert	mandare allo scoperto	—
sobreporte (Es)	Frachtzuschlag *m*	additional freight charges	supplément de fret *m*	supplemento di nolo *m*	—
sobrepreso (Es)	Übergewicht *n*	excess weight	surcharge *f*	sovrappeso *m*	—
sobreproducción (Es)	Überproduktion *f*	overproduction	surproduction *f*	produzione eccessiva *f*	—
sobreseguro (Es)	Überversicherung *f*	overinsurance	surassurance *f*	soprassicurazione *f*	—
sobreseimiento del proceso (Es)	Verfahrenseinstellung *f*	abatement of an action	arrêt d'une procédure *m*	sospensione del procedimento *f*	—
sobrevaloración (Es)	Überbewertung *f*	overvaluation	surestimation *f*	sopravvalutazione *f*	—
social insurance (E)	Sozialversicherung *f*	—	assurance sociale *m*	previdenza sociale *f*	seguro social *m*
socialisation (F)	Sozialisierung *f*	socialization	—	socializzazione *f*	socialización *f*
socialización (Es)	Sozialisierung *f*	socialization	socialisation *f*	socializzazione *f*	—
socialization (E)	Sozialisierung *f*	—	socialisation *f*	socializzazione *f*	socialización *f*
socializzazione (I)	Sozialisierung *f*	socialization	socialisation *f*	—	socialización *f*
social market economy (E)	soziale Marktwirtschaft *f*	—	économie sociale du marché *f*	economia sociale di mercato *f*	economía de mercado social *f*
social policy (E)	Sozialpolitik *f*	—	politique sociale *f*	politica sociale *f*	política social *f*
social security (E)	soziale Sicherheit *f*	—	sécurité sociale *f*	sicurezza sociale *f*	seguridad social *f*
social services (E)	Sozialleistung *f*	—	prestation sociale *f*	prestazione sociale *f*	prestacion social *f*/ seguridad social *f*
social state based on the rule of law (E)	Sozialstaat *m*	—	Etat social *m*	stato sociale *m*	Estado social *m*
sociedad (Es)	Sozietät *f*	partnership	groupe de sociétaires *m*	associazione *f*	—
sociedad anónima (Es)	Aktiengesellschaft *f*	joint stock company	société anonyme *f*	società per azioni *f*	—
sociedad capitalista (Es)	Kapitalgesellschaft *f*	company limited by shares	société de capitaux *f*	società di capitale *f*	—
sociedad comanditaria (Es)	Kommanditgesellschaft *f*	limited partnership	société en commandite *f*	società in accomandita semplice *f*	—
sociedad comanditaria por acciones (Es)	Kommanditgesellschaft auf Aktien *f*	partnership limited by shares	société en commandite par action *f*	società in accomandita per azioni *f*	—
sociedad comercial (Es)	Handelsgesellschaft *f*	trading company	société commerciale *f*	società commerciale *f*	—
sociedad controladora (Es)	Besitzgesellschaft *f*	controlling company	société contrôleuse *f*	società finanziaria *f*	—

	D	E	F	I	Es
sociedad cooperativa (Es)	Genossenschaft f	co-operative	société coopérative f	cooperativa f	—
sociedad de amortización (Es)	Abschreibungs-gesellschaft f	project write-off company	société d'amortissement f	società di ammortamento f	—
sociedad de bienestar (Es)	Wohlstands-gesellschaft f	affluent society	société de bien-être f	società del benessere f	—
sociedad de inversiones (Es)	Investment-gesellschaft f	investment company	société d'investissement f	società d'investimento f	—
sociedad de leasing (Es)	Leasing-Gesellschaft f	leasing company	société de leasing f	società di leasing f	—
sociedad de responsa-bilidad limitada (Es)	Gesellschaft mit beschränkter Haftung f	limited liability company	société à responsabilité limitée f	società a responsabilità limitata f	—
sociedad de seguros (Es)	Versicherungs-gesellschaft f	insurance company	société d'assurance f	compagnia di assicurazione f	—
sociedad en participación (Es)	stille Gesellschaft f	dorment partnership	association commer-ciale en participation f	associazione in partecipazione f	—
sociedad holding (Es)	Dachgesellschaft f	holding company	société holding f	società finanziaria f	—
sociedad matriz (Es)	Muttergesellschaft f	parent company	société mère f	società madre f	—
sociedad personalista (Es)	Personen-gesellschaft n	partnership	société de personnes f	società di persone f	—
società affiliata (I)	Tochtergesellschaft f	subsidiary	société filiale f	—	filial f
società a responsa-bilità limitata (I)	Gesellschaft mit beschränkter Haftung f	limited liability company	société à responsabilité limitée f	—	sociedad de responsabilidad limitada f
società bucalettere (I)	Briefkastenfirma f	bubble company	entreprise fantôme f	—	empresa ficticia f
società commerciale (I)	Handelsgesellschaft f	trading company	société commerciale f	—	sociedad comercial f
società del benessere (I)	Wohlstands-gesellschaft f	affluent society	société de bien-être f	—	sociedad de bienestar f
società d'esercizio (I)	Betriebsgesellschaft f	operating company	entreprise d'exploitation f	—	empresa de explotación f
società di ammortamento (I)	Abschreibungs-gesellschaft f	project write-off company	société d'amortissement f	—	sociedad de amortización f
società di capitale (I)	Kapitalgesellschaft f	company limited	société de capitaux f by shares	—	sociedad capitalista f
società di leasing (I)	Leasing-Gesellschaft f	leasing company	société de leasing f	—	sociedad de leasing f
società d'investimento (I)	Investment-gesellschaft f	investment company	société d'investissement f	—	sociedad de inversiones f
società di persone (I)	Personen-gesellschaft n	partnership	société de personnes f	—	sociedad personalista f
società finanziaria¹ (I)	Besitzgesellschaft f	controlling company	société contrôleuse f	—	sociedad controladora f
società finanziaria² (I)	Dachgesellschaft f	holding company	société holding f	—	sociedad holding f
società in accoman-dita per azioni (I)	Kommanditgesell-schaft auf Aktien f	partnership limited by shares	société en comman-dite par action f	—	sociedad comandita-ria por acciones f
società in accoman-dita semplice (I)	Kommandit-gesellschaft f	limited partnership	société en commandite f	—	sociedad comandítaria f
società madre (I)	Muttergesellschaft f	parent company	société mère f	—	sociedad matriz f
società per azioni (I)	Aktiengesellschaft f	joint stock company	société anonyme f	—	sociedad anónima f
société affiliée (F)	Schwester-gesellschaft f	affiliated company	—	consorella f	compañía asociada f
société anonyme (F)	Aktiengesellschaft f	joint stock company	—	società per azioni f	sociedad anónima f
société à responsa-bilité limitée (F)	Gesellschaft mit beschränkter Haftung f	limited liability company	—	società a responsabilità limitata f	sociedad de responsabilidad limitada f
société commerciale (F)	Handelsgesellschaft f	trading company	—	società commerciale f	sociedad comercial f
société contrôleuse (F)	Besitzgesellschaft f	controlling company	—	società finanziaria	sociedad controladora f
société coopérative (F)	Genossenschaft f	co-operative	—	cooperativa f	sociedad cooperativa f
société coopérative de production (F)	Produktions-genossenschaft f	producer's cooperative	—	cooperativa di produzione f	cooperativa de producción f
société d'amortissement (F)	Abschreibungs-gesellschaft f	project write-off company	—	società di ammortamento f	sociedad de amortización f

	D	E	F	I	Es
société d'assurance (F)	Versicherungs-gesellschaft f	insurance company	—	compagnia di assicurazione f	sociedad de seguros f
société de bien-être (F)	Wohlstands-gesellschaft f	affluent society	—	società del benessere f	sociedad de bienestar f
société de capitaux (F)	Kapitalgesellschaft f	company limited by shares	—	società di capitale f	sociedad capitalista f
société de leasing (F)	Leasing-Gesellschaft f	leasing company	—	società di leasing f	sociedad de leasing f
société de personnes (F)	Personen-gesellschaft n	partnership	—	società di persone f	sociedad personalista f
société d'investissement (F)	Investment-gesellschaft f	investment company	—	società d'investimento f	sociedad de inversiones f
société en commandite (F)	Kommandit-gesellschaft f	limited partnership	—	società in accoman-dita semplice f	sociedad comanditaria f
société en comman-dite par action (F)	Kommanditgesell-schaft auf Aktien f	partnership limited by shares	—	società in accoman-dita per azioni f	sociedad comandita-ria por acciones f
société filiale (F)	Tochtergesellschaft f	subsidiary	—	società affiliata f	filial f
société holding (F)	Dachgesellschaft f	holding company	—	società finanziaria f	sociedad holding f
société mère (F)	Muttergesellschaft f	parent company	—	società madre f	sociedad matriz f
socio[1] (Es)	Teilhaber m	partner	associé m	socio m	—
socio[2] (Es)	Partner m	partner	partenaire m	partner m	—
socio[3] (Es)	Geschäftspartner m	business partner	associé m	partner commerciale m	—
socio[4] (Es)	Gesellschafter m	partner	associé m	socio m	—
socio[1] (I)	Teilhaber m	partner	associé m	—	socio m
socio[2] (I)	Gesellschafter m	partner	associé m	—	socio m
socio accomandante (I)	Kommanditist m	limited partner	associé m	—	comanditario m
socio accomandatario (I)	Komplementär m	general partner	commandité m	—	socio colectivo m
socio activo (Es)	aktiver Teilhaber m	active partner	associé prenant part à la gestion m	socio attivo m	—
socio attivo (I)	aktiver Teilhaber m	active partner	associé prenant part à la gestion m	—	socio activo m
socio colectivo (Es)	Komplementär m	general partner	commandité m	socio accomandatario m	—
socio comercial (Es)	Handelspartner m	trading partner	partenaire commercial m	partner commerciale m	—
socio menor (Es)	Junior-Partner m	junior partner	fils du partenaire m	junior partner m	—
soddisfazione dei bisogni (I)	Bedürfnis-befriedigung f	satisfaction of needs	satisfaction des besoins f	—	satisfacción de las necesidades f
soddisfazione del lavoro (I)	Arbeitszufriedenheit f	job satisfaction	satisfaction de travail f	—	satisfacción en el trabajo f
sofortige Lieferung (D)	—	immediate delivery	livraison immédiate f	consegna immediata f	entrega inmediata f
sofortige Regulierung (D)	—	settlement with immediate effect	règlement immédiat m	regolazione immediata f	regulación inmediata f
sofortige Zahlung (D)	—	immediate payment	payement immédiat m	pagamento immediato m	pago inmediato m
soft currency (E)	weiche Währung f	—	monnaie faible f	moneta debole f	moneda blanda f
soggetto a contributi (I)	abgabenpflichtig	liable to tax	soumis à l'impôt	—	sujeto a impuestos
soggetto ad influssi congiunturali (I)	konjunkturanfällig	depending on the cyclical trend	sensible aux oscillations de la conjoncture	—	sensible a las fluctuaciones coyunturales
soglia dei prezzi (I)	Preisschwelle f	threshold price	seuil du prix m	—	umbral de la rentabilidad m
soglia dell'utile (I)	Gewinnschwelle f	break-even point	seuil de rentabilité m	—	umbral de la rentabilidad m
soglia di redditività (I)	Rentabilitätsschwelle f	break-even point	seuil de rentabilité m	—	límite inferior de rentabilidad m
sol (F)	Boden m	ground/soil	—	terra f/suolo m	suelo m/terreno m
Solawechsel (D)	—	promissory note	seule lettre de change f	pagherò m	pagaré m
solde (F)	Saldo m	balance	—	saldo m	saldo m
solde créditeur (F)	Aktivsaldo m	active balance	—	saldo attivo m	saldo activo m

	D	E	F	I	Es
solde de compte (F)	Kontoausgleich m	settlement of an account	—	liquidazione del conto f	saldo de cuenta m
solde d'hiver (F)	Winterschlußverkauf m	winter clearance sale	—	svendita di fine inverno f	rebajas de invierno f pl
solde net de l'exploitation (F)	Ertragsrechnung f	profit and loss account	—	conto economico m	cuenta de ganancias f pl
soldes (F)	Ausverkauf m	clearance sale	—	svendita f	liquidación f
sole agency (E)	Alleinvertretung f	—	agence exclusive f	rappresentanza esclusiva f	representación exclusiva f
sole agent (E)	Alleinvertreter m	—	agent exclusif m	rappresentante esclusivo m	representante exclusivo m
sole and exclusive agency right (E)	Alleinvertretungsrecht n	—	droit exclusif de représentation m	diritto di rappresentanza esclusiva m	derecho de representación exclusiva m
sole owner (E)	Alleininhaber m	—	seul propriétaire m	titolare unico m	propietario exclusivo m
solicitud[1] (Es)	Anmeldung f	registration/ declaration	inscription f/ déclaration f	avviso m/ dichiarazione f	—
solicitud[2] (Es)	Antrag m	application	demande f	domanda f	—
solicitud de aduana (Es)	Zollantrag m	customs application	demande de dédouanement f	domanda di sdoganamento f	—
solicitud de colocación (Es)	Stellengesuch n	situation wanted/ application for a job	demande d'emploi f	domanda d'impiego f	—
Soll (D)	—	debit	doit m	passivo m	debe m
sollecito (I)	Mahnung f	demand for payment	mise en demeure f	—	(ad)monición f
Soll/Ist-Vergleich (D)	—	comparison of estimates with results	comparaison entre les résultats effectifs et les prévisions f	confronto costi calcolati/costi reali m	comparación entre los resultados efectivos y las previsiones f
Sollkosten (D)	—	budgeted costs	coûts ex ante m pl	costi calcolati m pl	gastos precalculados m pl
Sollzahlen (D)	—	target figures	chiffres prévisionnels m pl	cifre calcolate f pl	cifras e estimadas f pl
Sollzinsen (D)	—	debtor interest rates	intérêt débiteur m	interessi debitori m pl	intereses deudores m pl
solución interina (Es)	Interimslösung f	interim solution	solution intérimaire f	soluzione ad interim f	—
solution intérimaire (F)	Interimslösung f	interim solution	—	soluzione ad interim f	solución interina f
soluzione ad interim (I)	Interimslösung f	interim solution	solution intérimaire f	—	solución interina f
solvabilité[1] (F)	Kreditfähigkeit f	financial standing	—	capacità di credito f	crédito m
solvabilité[2] (F)	Bonität f	solvency	—	solvibilità f	solvencia f
solvabilité[3] (F)	Kreditwürdigkeit f	creditworthiness	—	essere degno di credito	crédito m
solvabilité[4] (F)	Zahlungsfähigkeit f	solvency	—	solvibilità f	solvencia f
solvable[1] (F)	liquide	liquid	—	liquido	líquido
solvable[2] (F)	zahlungsfähig	solvent	—	solvibile	solvente
solvable[3] (F)	kreditwürdig	creditworthy	—	degno di credito	solvente
solvencia (Es)	Bonität f	solvency	solvabilité f	solvibilità f	—
solvency (E)	Zahlungsfähigkeit f	—	solvabilité f	solvibilità f	solvencia f
solvent (E)	zahlungsfähig	—	solvable	solvibile	solvente
solvente (Es)	kreditwürdig	creditworthy	solvable	degno di credito	—
solvibile (I)	zahlungsfähig	solvent	solvable	—	solvente
solvibilità[1] (I)	Zahlungsfähigkeit f	solvency	solvabilité f	—	solvencia f
solvibilità[2] (I)	Bonität f	solvency	solvabilité f	—	solvencia f
somma assicurata (I)	Versicherungssumme f	insurance sum	montant de l'assurance m	—	suma asegurada f
somma di denaro (I)	Geldbetrag m	amount of money	somme d'argent f	—	suma de dinero f
somma fissa (I)	Fixum n	fixed sum	somme fixe f	—	fijo m
somma forfettaria (I)	Pauschalbetrag m	flat rate amount	somme forfaitaire f	—	suma global f
somme d'argent (F)	Geldbetrag m	amount of money	—	somma di denaro f	suma de dinero f
somme fixe (F)	Fixum n	fixed sum	—	somma fissa f	fijo m
somme forfaitaire (F)	Pauschalbetrag m	flat rate amount	—	somma forfettaria f	suma global f
sondage (F)	Stichproben pl	random test	—	campioni m pl	prueba por sondeo f
sondage de l'opinion publique (F)	Demoskopie f	public opinion research	—	demoscopia f	demoscopia f

	D	E	F	I	Es
sondaggio del mercato (I)	Marktbeobachtung f	observation of markets	étude de marché f	—	observación del mercado f
Sonder-abschreibungen (D)	—	special depreciatipn	amortissement extraordinaire m	ammortamenti straordinari m pl	amortización extraordinaria f
Sonderaktion (D)	—	special action	action spéciale f	azione speciale f	acción especial f
Sonderanfertigung (D)	—	manufacture to customer's specifications	fabrication spéciale f	produzione fuori serie f	fabricación especial f
Sonderangebot (D)	—	special offer	offre spéciale f	offerta speciale f	oferta especial f
Sonderausgaben (D)	—	special expenses	dépense spéciale f	spese straordinarie f pl	gastos extraordinarios m pl
Sondermüll (D)	—	special refuse	détritus spéciaux m pl	rifiuti speciali m pl	basura especial f
Sonderrabatt (D)	—	special discount	ristourne exceptionnelle f	ribasso speciale m	descuento suplementario m
Sondersitzung (D)	—	special meeting	séance extraordinaire f	seduta straordinaria f	sesión especial f
Sondervereinbarung (D)	—	special agreement	accord particulier m	accordo speciale m	acuerdo especial m
Sondervergütung (D)	—	special remuneration	rémunération spéciale f	compenso straordinario m	gratificación f
Sonderziehungs-rechte (D)	—	special drawing rights	droits de tirage spécial m pl	diritti speciali di prelievo m pl	derechos de giro especial m pl
Sonntagsarbeit (D)	—	Sunday work	travail du dimanche m	lavoro domenicale m	trabajo dominical m
sonsacamiento (Es)	Abwerbung f	pirating	débauchage m	accaparramento m	—
soprassicurazione (I)	Überversicherung f	overinsurance	surassurance f	—	sobreseguro m
sopravvalutazione (I)	Überbewertung f	overvaluation	surestimation f	—	sobrevaloración f
Sorte (D)	—	variety/foreign notes and coins	genre m/ devises f pl	categoria f/ valuta estera f	especie f/calidad f/ marca f/ moneda extranjera f
Sortenhandel (D)	—	dealing in foreign notes and coins	commerce de change m	cambio valuta m	operación de moneda extranjera f
Sortenkurs (D)	—	rate for foreign notes and coins	cours des monnaies étrangères m	corso dei cambi m	tipo de cambio de billetes y monedas extranjeras m
sortie de devises (F)	Devisenabfluß m	foreign exchange outflow	—	deflusso di divise m	drenaje de divisas m
sortie de marchandieses (F)	Warenausgang m	outgoing goods	—	uscita merci f	salida de mercancías f
Sortiment (D)	—	assortment	assortiment m	assortimento m	surtido m
Sortimentsanalyse (D)	—	analysis of assortment	analyse d'assortiment f	analisi dell'assortimento f	análisis del surtido m
Sortiments-gestaltung (D)	—	assortment structuring	structure d'ssortiment f	composizione dell'assortimento f	configuración del surtido f
Sortimentspolitik (D)	—	assortment policy	politique d'assortiment f	politica dell'assortimento f	política de surtido f
sorveglianza (I)	Aufsicht f	supervision	surveillance f	—	inspección f
sorvegliare (I)	überwachen	supervise	surveiller	—	vigilar
sospensione del procedimento (I)	Verfahrens-einstellung f	abatement of an action	arrêt d'une procédure m	—	sobreseimiento del proceso m
sostanza (I)	Substanz f	substance	substance f	—	sustancia f
sostanza nociva (I)	Schadstoff m	pollutants	élément polluant m	—	substancia nociva f
sostegno dei corsi (I)	Kurspflege f	price nursing	soutien des cours m	—	compras de sostén f pl
sostén de las cotizaciones (Es)	Kursstützung f	price support	soutiens des cours m	difesa dei corsi f	—
sostenido (Es)	behauptet	maintained	affirmé	affermato	—
sostituibile (I)	substituierbar	replaceable	interchangeable	—	sustituible
sostituto (I)	Stellvertreter m	deputy	adjoint m	—	sustituto m
sottassicurazione (I)	Unterversicherung f	underinsurance	insuffisance d'assurance f	—	infraseguro m
sottoccupazione (I)	Unterbeschäftigung f	underemployment	sous-emploi m	—	subempleo m
sottoscrizione (I)	Suskription f	subscription	souscription f	—	suscripción f
sottovalutazione (I)	Unterbewertung f	undervaluation	sous-estimation f	—	subvaloración f
soumis à l'impôt (F)	abgabenpflichtig	liable to tax	—	soggetto a contributi	sujeto a impuestos
soumission (F)	Ausschreibung f	tender	—	appalto m	concurso-subasta m

	D	E	F	I	Es
source d'approvisionnement (F)	Bezugsquelle *f*	source of supply	—	fonte d'acquisto *f*	fuente de suministro *f*
source of supply (E)	Bezugsquelle *f*	—	source d'approvisionnement *f*	fonte d'acquisto *f*	fuente de suministro *f*
sous-agent (F)	Untervertreter *m*	subagent	—	subagente *m*	subagente *m*
sous-alimentation (F)	Unterernährung *f*	malnutrition	—	denutrizione *f*	subalimentación *f*
souscripteur d'une assurance (F)	Versicherungsnehmer *m*	insured person	—	assicurato *m*	asegurado *m*
souscription (F)	Suskription *f*	subscription	—	sottoscrizione *f*	suscripción *f*
sous-emploi (F)	Unterbeschäftigung *f*	underemployment	—	sottoccupazione *f*	subempleo *m*
sous-entrepreneur (F)	Subunternehmer *m*	subcontractor	—	subimprenditore *m*	subcontratista *m*
sous-estimation (F)	Unterbewertung *f*	undervaluation	—	sottovalutazione *f*	subvaloración *f*
sous-location (F)	Untervermietung *f*	subletting	—	subaffitto *m*	subalquiler *m*
sous pli recommandé (F)	per Einschreiben	by registered post	—	per raccomandata	certificado
sous pli séparé (F)	mit getrennter Post	under separate cover	—	in plico a parte	por correo aparte
sous toute réserve (F)	ohne Gewähr	without garanty	—	senza garanzia	sin garantía
sous-traitant (F)	Zulieferer *m*	supplier	—	fornitore *m*	abastecedor *m*
soutien des cours¹ (F)	Kurspflege *f*	price nursing	—	sostegno dei corsi *m*	compras de sostén *f pl*
soutien des cours² (F)	Kursstützung *f*	price support	—	difesa dei corsi *f*	sostén de las cotizaciones *m*
souveraineté en matière budgétaire (F)	Finanzhoheit *f*	financial sovereignty	—	sovranità finanziaria *f*	soberanía financiera *f*
souveraineté territoriale (F)	Gebietshoheit *f*	territorial jurisdiction	—	sovranità territoriale *f*	soberanía territorial *f*
sovereign right (E)	Hoheitsrecht *n*	—	droit de souveraineté *m*	diritto di sovranità *m*	soberanía *f*
sovracapitalizzazione (I)	Überkapitalisierung *f*	overcapitalization	surcapitalisation *f*	—	sobrecapitalización *f*
sovranità amministrativa (I)	Verwaltungshoheit *f*	power of administration	autonomie d'administration *f*	—	soberanía administrativa *f*
sovranità finanziaria (I)	Finanzhoheit *f*	financial sovereignty	souveraineté en matière budgétaire *f*	—	soberanía financiera *f*
sovranità legislativa (I)	Gesetzgebungshoheit *f*	legislative sovereignty	compétence législative *f*	—	soberanía legislativa *f*
sovranità territoriale (I)	Gebietshoheit *f*	territorial jurisdiction	souveraineté territoriale *f*	—	soberanía territorial *f*
sovrappeso (I)	Übergewicht *n*	excess weight	surcharge *f*	—	sobrepreso *m*
sovvenzione¹ (I)	Subvention *f*	subsidy	subvention *f*	—	subvención *f*
sovvenzione² (I)	Zuschuß *m*	allowance	allocation *f*	—	subvención *f*
sovvenzione pubblica (I)	Staatszuschuß *m*	government grant	subvention de l'Etat *f*	—	subvenciones del Estado *f pl*
sovvenzioni agrarie (I)	Agrarsubventionen *pl*	agricultural subsidies	subventions de l'agriculture *f pl*	—	subvención a la agricultura *f*
soziale Marktwirtschaft (D)	—	social market economy	économie sociale du marché *f*	economia sociale di mercato *f*	economía de mercado social *f*
soziale Sicherheit (D)	—	social security	sécurité sociale *f*	sicurezza sociale *f*	seguridad social *f*
Sozialhilfe (D)	—	public assistance	aide sociale *f*	assistenza sociale *f*	ayuda social *f*
Sozialisierung (D)	—	socialization	socialisation *f*	socializzazione *f*	socialización *f*
Sozialkosten (D)	—	social insurance costs	coûts sociaux *m pl*	costi sociali *m pl*	costo social *m*/ cargas sociales *f pl*
Sozialleistung (D)	—	social services	prestation sociale *f*	prestazione sociale *f*	prestacion social *f*/ seguridad social *f*
Sozialpolitik (D)	—	social policy	politique sociale *f*	politica sociale *f*	política social *f*
Sozialprodukt (D)	—	national product	produit national *m*	prodotto nazionale *m*	producto nacional *m*
Sozialversicherung (D)	—	social insurance	assurance sociale *m*	previdenza sociale *f*	seguro social *m*
Sozietät (D)	—	partnership	groupe de sociétaires *m*	associazione *f*	sociedad *f*
space research (E)	Raumforschung *f*	—	recherches spatiales *f pl*	ricerche spaziali *f pl*	investigación espacial *f*
space station (E)	Satellitenstation *f*	—	station de satellite *f*	stazione satellite *f*	estación satélite *f*
Spanne (D)	—	margin	marge *f*	margine *m*	margen *f*

	D	E	F	I	Es
Spareinlagen (D)	—	savings deposits	dépôt d'épargne *m*	depositi di risparmio *m pl*	imposiciones de ahorro *f pl*
Sparen (D)	—	saving	épargne *f*	risparmio *m*	ahorro *m*
spare part (E)	Ersatzteil *n*	—	pièce de rechange *f*	pezzo di ricambio *m*	pieza de recambio *f*
Sparkasse (D)	—	savings bank	institut bancaire d'épargne *m*	cassa di risparmio *f*	caja de ahorros *f*
Sparquote (D)	—	savings ratio	quote-part de revenu réservée à des fins d'épargne *f*	quota di risparmio *f*	cuota de ahorro *f*
spatial structure (E)	Raumstruktur *f*	—	structure des espaces *f*	struttura territoriale *f*	estructura territorial *f*
special action (E)	Sonderaktion *f*	—	action spéciale *f*	azione speciale *f*	acción especial *f*
special agreements (E)	Sondervereinbarung *f*	—	accord particulier *m*	accordo speciale *m*	acuerdo especial *m*
special depreciation (E)	Sonderabschreibungen *f*	—	amortissement extraordinaire *m*	ammortamenti straordinari *m pl*	amortización extraordinaria *f*
special discount (E)	Sonderrabatt *m*	—	ristourne exceptionnelle *f*	ribasso speciale *m*	descuento suplementario *m*
special drawing rights (E)	Sonderziehungsrechte *pl*	—	droits de tirage spécial *m pl*	diritti speciali di prelievo, DSP *m pl*	derechos de giro especial *m pl*
special expenses (E)	Sonderausgaben *pl*	—	dépense spéciale *f*	spese straordinarie *f pl*	gastos extraordinarios *m pl*
spécialisation (F)	Spezialisierung *f*	specialization	—	specializzazione *f*	especialización *f*
specialization (E)	Spezialisierung *f*	—	spécialisation *f*	specializzazione *f*	especialización *f*
specializzazione (I)	Spezialisierung *f*	specialization	spécialisation *f*	—	especialización *f*
special meeting (E)	Sondersitzung *f*	—	séance extraordinaire *f*	seduta straordinaria *f*	sesión especial *f*
special offer (E)	Sonderangebot *n*	—	offre spéciale *f*	offerta speciale *f*	oferta especial *f*
special purpose association (E)	Zweckverband *m*	—	association à but déterminé *f*	consorzio intercomunale *m*	asociación con un fin determinado *f*
special refuse (E)	Sondermüll *m*	—	détritus spéciaux *m pl*	rifiuti speciali *m pl*	basura especial *f*
special remuneration (E)	Sondervergütung *f*	—	rémunération spéciale *f*	compenso straordinario *m*	gratificación *f*
specie (E)	Hartgeld *n*	—	pièce de monnaie *f*	moneta metallica *f*	dinero metálico *m*
specification (E)	Spezifikation *f*	—	spécification *f*	specificazione *f*	especificación *f*
spécification (F)	Spezifikation *f*	specification	—	specificazione *f*	especificación *f*
specificazione (I)	Spezifikation *f*	specification	spécification *f*	—	especificación *f*
specific duty (E)	Mengenzoll *m*	—	droit de douane par quantité *m*	dazio di quantità *m*	arancel aduanero cuantitativo *m*
speculation (E)	Spekulation *f*	—	spéculation *f*	speculazione *f*	especulación *f*
spéculation (F)	Spekulation *f*	speculation	—	speculazione *f*	especulación *f*
speculative buying (E)	Meinungskäufe *pl*	—	achats spéculatifs *m pl*	acquisti speculativi *m pl*	compras especulativas *f pl*
speculative operations (E)	Spekulationsgeschäft *n*	—	affaire spéculative *f*	operazione speculativa *f*	operación de especulación *f*
speculazione (I)	Spekulation *f*	speculation	spéculation *f*	—	especulación *f*
Spediteur (D)	—	forwarder	commissionnaire de transport *m*	spedizioniere *m*	expeditor *m*
Speditionsgut (D)	—	forwarding merchandise	bien transporté *m*	merce spedita *f*	mercancía transportada *f*
spedizione[1] (I)	Absendung *f*	dispatch	expédition *f*	—	expedición *f*
spedizione[2] (I)	Abfertigung *f*	dispatch/clearance	expédition *f*/expédition en douane *f*	—	despacho *m*/despacho de aduana *m*
spedizione[3] (I)	Sendung *f*	consignment	envoi *m*	—	envío *m*
spedizione[4] (I)	Versand *m*	dispatch	expédition *f*	—	envío *m*
spedizione andata persa (I)	verlorengegangene Sendung *f*	lost shipment	envoi perdu *m*	—	envío perdido *m*
spedizione con valore dichiarato (I)	Wertsendung *f*	consignment with value declared	envoi avec valeur déclarée *m*	—	envío con valor declarado *m*
spedizione di campioni (I)	Mustersendung *f*	sample consignment	envoi d'échantillons *m*	—	envío de muestras *m*
spedizione di merci (I)	Warensendung *f*	consignment of goods	expédition de marchandises *f*	—	envío de mercancías *m*

	D	E	F	I	Es
spedizione postale cumulativa di stampati (I)	Postwurfsendung f	printed papers or samples of merchandise posted in bulk	envoi publicitaire collectif m	—	envío postal colectivo m
spedizioniere (I)	Spediteur m	forwarder	commissionnaire de transport m	—	expeditor m
speedy (E)	beschleunigt	—	accéléré	accelerato	acelerado
Spekulation (D)	—	speculation	spéculation f	speculazione f	especulación f
Spekulationsgeschäft (D)	—	speculative operations	affaire spéculative f	operazione speculativa f	operación de especulación f
Spekulationsobjekt (D)	—	object of speculation	objet de spéculation m	oggetto di speculazioni m	objeto de especulación m
spending capacity analysis (E)	Kaufkraftanalyse f	—	analyse du pouvoir d'achat f	analisi del potere d'acquisto f	análisis del poder adquisitivo m
Sperrkonto (D)	—	blocked account	compte bloqué m	conto vincolato m	fondos bloqueados m pl
Sperrminorität (D)	—	blocking minority	minorité suffisante pour bloquer qch. f	sindacato di blocco m	minoría de bloqueo f
spesa pubblica (I)	öffentliche Ausgaben pl	public spending	dépenses publiques f pl	—	gastos públicos m pl
spese¹ (I)	Ausgaben pl	expenses	dépenses f pl	—	gastos m pl
spese² (I)	Aufwendung f	expenditure	dépenses f pl	—	gasot m
spese³ (I)	Aufwand m	expenditure	charge f	—	gastos m pl
spese⁴ (I)	Spesen pl	expenses	frais m pl	—	gastos m pl
spese aziendali (I)	Betriebsausgaben f	(current) operational expenses	charges d'exploitation f pl	—	gastos de explotación m pl
spese d'approvvigionamento di credito (I)	Kreditbeschaffungskosten pl	cost of borrowing	coûts d'obtention de crédits m pl	—	costes de apelación al crédito m pl
spese d'esercizio (I)	Betriebskosten pl	operating costs	charges d'exploitation f pl	—	gastos de explotación m pl
spese del procedimento (I)	Verfahrenskosten pl	costs of the proceedings	frais de procédure m pl	—	costas f pl
spese di carico (I)	Ladegebühren pl	loading charges	taxe de chargement f	—	derechos de carga m pl
spese di magazzinaggio (I)	Lagermiete f	warehouse rent	location d'une surface pour magasinage f	—	alquiler de almacenaje m
spese di pernottamento (I)	Übernachtungskosten pl	overnight expenses	coûts de nuitée m pl	—	gastos de alojamiento m pl
spese di scaricamento (I)	Entladungskosten pl	discharging expenses	coûts de déchargement m pl	—	gastos de descargo m pl
spese di scarico (I)	Löschgebühren pl	discharging expenses	droit de déchargement m	—	gastos de descarga m pl
spese di stanziamento (I)	Bereitstellungskosten pl	commitment fee	coûts administratifs m pl	—	gastos fijos m pl
spese di trasferta (I)	Fahrgeld n	fare	coût du voyage m	—	precio de la travesía m
spese di trasporto¹ (I)	Frachtkosten pl	freight charges	frais de transport m pl	—	gastos de transporte m pl
spese di trasporto² (I)	Rollgeld n	haulage	camionnage m	—	derechos de acarreo m pl
spese di viaggio (I)	Reisespesen pl	travelling expenses	frais de voyage m pl	—	gastos de viaje m pl
spese giudiziarie (I)	Gerichtskosten pl	legal costs	frais judiciaires taxables exposés m pl	—	gastos judiciales m pl
spese materiale (I)	Materialaufwand m	material expenditure	dépenses en matières f	—	coste de material m
Spesen (D)	—	expenses	frais m pl	spese f pl	gastos m pl
Spesenabrechung (D)	—	statement of expenses	décompte des frais m	conteggio delle spese m	liquidación de gastos f
Spesenpauschale (D)	—	allowance for expenses	forfait de frais m	forfait di spese m	suma global de gastos f
spese primarie (I)	Primäraufwand m	primary expenses	charge primaire f	—	gastos directos m pl
spese pubbliche (I)	Staatsausgaben pl	public spending	dépenses publiques f pl	—	gastos públicos m pl
spese straordinarie (I)	Sonderausgaben pl	special expenses	dépense spéciale f	—	gastos extraordinarios m pl
spese vive (I)	Selbstkosten pl	cost	coût de revient m	—	costes propios m pl
Spezialisierung (D)	—	specialization	spécialisation f	specializzazione f	especialización f

	D	E	F	I	Es
Spezifikation (D)	—	specification	spécification f	specificazione f	especificación f
sphère d'influence (F)	Einflußbereich m	sphere of influence	—	sfera d'influenza f	esfera de influencia f
sphere of influence (E)	Einflußbereich m	—	sphère d'influence f	sfera d'influenza f	esfera de influencia f
Spielraum (D)	—	margin	marge f	tolleranza f	margen m
spinta innovativa (I)	Innovationsschub m	technology push	animation d'innovation f	—	empuje innovador m
Spionage (D)	—	espionage	espionnage m	spionaggio m	espionaje m
spionaggio (I)	Spionage f	espionage	espionnage m	—	espionaje m
spionaggio aziendale[1] (I)	Betriebsspionage f	industrial espionage	espionnage dans l'entreprise	—	espionaje industrial m
spionaggio aziendale[2] (I)	Werkspionage f	industrial espionage	espionnage industriel m	—	espionaje industrial m
spionaggio industriale (I)	Industriespionage f	industrial espionage	espionnage industriel m	—	espionaje industrial m
spirale inflationniste (F)	Inflationsspirale f	inflationary spiral	—	spirale inflazionistica f	espiral inflacionista m
spirale inflazionistica (I)	Inflationsspirale f	inflationary spiral	spirale inflationniste f	—	espiral inflacionista m
spirale prezzi-salari (I)	Lohn-Preis-Spirale f	wage-price spiral	course des prix et des salaires f	—	espiral salarios-precios m
Spitzenlohn (D)	—	top wage	salaire maximum m	salario massimo m	salario máximo m
splittaggio (I)	Splitting n	splitting	péréquation fiscale des revenus des deux époux f	—	imposición separada e igual de los cónyuges f
Splitting (D)	—	splitting	péréquation fiscale des revenus des deux époux f	splittaggio m	imposición separada e igual de los cónyuges f
splitting (E)	Splitting n	—	péréquation fiscale des revenus des deux époux f	splittaggio m	imposición separada e igual de los cónyuges f
spot market (E)	Spotmarkt m	—	marché en disponible m	mercato spot m	mercado de operaciones al contado y de entrega inmediata m
Spotmarkt (D)	—	spot market	marché en disponible m	mercato spot m	mercado de operaciones al contado y de entrega inmediata m
spot price[1] (E)	Einheitskurs m	—	cours unique m	cambio unitario m	cotización única f
spot price[2] (E)	Kassakurs m	—	cours au comptant m	corso a pronti m	cotización al contado f
spot pubblicitario (I)	Werbespot m	commercial	spot publicitaire m	—	spot publicitario m
spot publicitaire (F)	Werbespot m	commercial	—	spot pubblicitario m	spot publicitario m
spot publicitario (Es)	Werbespot m	commercial	spot publicitaire m	spot pubblicitario m	—
Staat (D)	—	state	Etat m	stato m	Estado m
staatlich (D)	—	state	de l'Etat	statale	estatal
staatliche Betriebe (D)	—	state-owned enterprise	entreprise publique f	aziende statali f pl	empresas públicas f pl
Staatsanleihen (D)	—	government loan	emprunt d'Etat m	titoli pubblici m pl	empréstito estatal m
Staatsausgaben (D)	—	public spending	dépenses publiques f pl	spese pubbliche f pl	gastos públicos m pl
Staatsbank (D)	—	state bank	banque nationale f	Banca Centrale f	banco del Estado m
Staatseigentum (D)	—	public ownership	propriété d'Etat f	proprietà demaniale f	patrimonio público m
Staatseinnahmen (D)	—	public revenue	recettes de l'Etat f pl	entrate pubbliche f pl	ingresos del Estado m pl
Staatstätigkeit (D)	—	state activity	activité de l'Etat f	attività pubblica f	actividad del Estado f
Staatsverschuldung (D)	—	state indebtedness	endettement de l'Etat m	debito pubblico m	endeudamiento público m
Staatszuschuß (D)	—	government grant	subvention de l'Etat f	sovvenzione pubblica f	subvenciones del Estado f pl
stabilimento (I)	Werk n	plant	usine f	—	planta f
stabilimento di lavorazione del rame (I)	Kupferhütte f	copper smelting work	cuivrerie f	—	fábrica metalúrgica de cobre f
Stabilisierung (D)	—	stabilization	stabilisation f	stabilizzazione f	estabilización f
stabilità (I)	Stabilität f	stability	stabilité f	—	estabilidad f
stabilità dei prezzi (I)	Preisstabilität f	stability of prices	stabilité des prix f	—	estabilidad de precios f

	D	E	F	I	Es
stabilità monetaria (I)	Geldwertstabilität f	stability of the value of money	stabilité monétaire f	—	estabilidad monetaria f
Stabilität (D)	—	stability	stabilité f	stabilità f	estabilidad f
Stabilitätspolitik (D)	—	stability policy	politique de stabilité f	politica di consolidamento f	política de estabilidad económica f
stabilité (F)	Stabilität f	stability	—	stabilità f	estabilidad f
stabilité des prix (F)	Preisstabilität f	stability of prices	—	stabilità dei prezzi f	estabilidad de precios f
stabilité monétaire (F)	Geldwertstabilität f	stability of the value of money	—	stabilità monetaria f	estabilidad monetaria f
stability (E)	Stabilität f	—	stabilité f	stabilità f	estabilidad f
stability of prices (E)	Preisstabilität f	—	stabilité des prix f	stabilità dei prezzi f	estabilidad de precios f
stability of the value of money (E)	Geldwertstabilität f	—	stabilité monétaire f	stabilità monetaria f	estabilidad monetaria f
stability policy (E)	Stabilitätspolitik f	—	politique de stabilité f	politica di consolidamento f	política de estabilidad económica f
stabilization (E)	Stabilisierung f	—	stabilisation f	stabilizzazione f	estabilización f
stabilizzazione (I)	Stabilisierung f	stabilization	stabilisation f	—	estabilización f
stable value clause (E)	Wertsicherungsklausel f	—	clause de stabilité f	clausola di garanzia monetaria f	cláusula de índice variable f
Städtebau (D)	—	town planning	urbanisme m	urbanistica f	urbanización f
staff¹ (E)	Personal n	—	personnel m	personale m	personal m
staff² (E)	Belegschaft f	—	personnel m	maestranza f	plantilla f
staff changes (E)	Personalwechsel m	—	mouvements dans le personnel m pl	cambio del personale m	cambio de personal m
staff di venditori (I)	Verkaufsstab m	sales staff	équipe de vente f	—	equipo de venta m
Staffelpreis (D)	—	graduated price	prix échelonné m	prezzo differenziato m	precios escalonados m pl
Staffeltarif (D)	—	graduated tariff	tarif échelonné m	tariffa differenziata f	tarifa diferencial f
staff identification card (E)	Betriebsausweis m	—	pièce d'identité de l'entreprise f	tessera aziendale f	carné de empresa f
staff manager (E)	Personalleiter m	—	chef du personnel m	capo reparto personale m	jefe de personal m
Stagflation (D)	—	stagflation	stagflation f	stagflazione f	estanflación f
stagflation (E)	Stagflation f	—	stagflation f	stagflazione f	estanflación f
stagflation (F)	Stagflation f	stagflation	—	stagflazione f	estanflación f
stagflazione (I)	Stagflation f	stagflation	stagflation f	—	estanflación f
stagione (I)	Saison f	season	saison f	—	temporada f
Stagnation (D)	—	stagnation	stagnation f	stagnazione f	estancamiento m
stagnation (E)	Stagnation f	—	stagnation f	stagnazione f	estancamiento m
stagnation (F)	Stagnation f	stagnation	—	stagnazione f	estancamiento m
stagnazione (I)	Stagnation f	stagnation	stagnation f	—	estancamiento m
stallie (I)	Liegetage pl	lay days	staries f pl	—	estadías f pl
Stammaktie (D)	—	ordinary shares	action ordinaire f	azione ordinaria f	acción ordinaria f
Stammeinlage (D)	—	initial contribution	apport social m	quota sociale f	capital suscrito m
Stammhaus (D)	—	parent company	maison mère f	casa madre f	casa matriz f
Stammkapital (D)	—	share capital/nominal capital	capital social m	capitale sociale m	capital social m
Stammkunde (D)	—	regular customer	client habituel m	cliente fisso m	cliente habitual m
stamp (E)	Briefmarke f	—	timbre-poste m	francobollo m	sello m
stampa¹ (I)	Presse f	press	presse f	—	prensa f
stampa² (I)	Drucksache f	printed matter	imprimé m	—	impreso m
stampante (I)	Drucker m	printer	imprimante f	—	impresora f
stampante laser (I)	Laserdrucker m	laser printer	imprimante au laser f	—	impresora laser m
stampa offset (I)	Offsetdruck m	offset (printing)	offset m	—	impresión offset f
stamp duty (E)	Stempelgebühr f	—	droit de timbre m	tassa di bollo f	derechos de timbre m pl
Standard (D)	—	standard	standard m	standard m	estándar m

	D	E	F	I	Es
standard¹ (E)	Norm f	—	standard m	norma f	norma f
standard² (E)	Standard m	—	standard m	standard m	estándar m
standard¹ (F)	Standard m	standard	—	standard m	estándar m
standard² (F)	Norm f	standard	—	norma f	norma f
standard (I)	Standard m	standard	standard m	—	estándar m
Standard-abweichung (D)	—	standard deviation	déviation standard f	scarto tipo m	desviación standard f
standard deviation (E)	Standard-abweichung f	—	déviation standard f	scarto tipo m	desviación standard f
standardisation (F)	Normung f	standardization	—	standardizzazione f	normalización f
standardisé (F)	standardisiert	standardized	—	standardizzato	estandardizado
standardisiert (D)	—	standardized	standardisé	standardizzato	estandardizado
standardization (E)	Normung f	—	standardisation f	standardizzazione f	normalización f
standardized¹ (E)	genormt	—	normalisé	standardizzato	normalizado
standardized² (E)	standardisiert	—	standardisé	standardizzato	estandardizado
standardized within the European Community (E)	EG-einheitlich	—	uniforme au niveau communautaire	uniforme all'interno della CEE	armonizado a nivel comunitario
standardizzato¹ (I)	standardisiert	standardized	standardisé	—	estandardizado
standardizzato² (I)	genormt	standardized	normalisé	—	normalizado
standardizzazione (I)	Normung f	standardization	standardisation f	—	normalización f
standard of living (E)	Lebensstandard m	—	niveau de vie m	tenore di vita m	nivel de vida m
standard technique (F)	technischer Standard m	technical standard	—	standard tecnico m	standard técnico m
standard técnico (Es)	technischer Standard m	technical standard	standard technique m	standard tecnico m	—
standard tecnico (I)	technischer Standard m	technical standard	standard technique m	—	standard técnico m
standard wage (E)	Tariflohn m	—	salaire tarifaire m	salario contrattuale m	salario tarifado m
Standardwerte (D)	—	standard values	valeur standard f	valori standard m pl	valores representativos m pl
stand-by credits (E)	Stand-by-Kredite pl	—	crédit stand-by m	crediti stand-by m pl	créditos stand-by m pl
Stand-by-Kredite (D)	—	stand-by credits	crédit stand-by m	crediti stand-by m pl	créditos stand-by m pl
standing order (E)	Dauerauftrag m	—	ordre régulier m	ordine permanente m	órden permanente f
Standort (D)	—	location	lieu d'implantation m	ubicazione f	ubicación f
Standort-entscheidung (D)	—	location decision	décision de l'implantation f	determinazione dell'ubicazione f	decisión de ubicación f
Standortfaktoren (D)	—	location factors	facteurs dépendant du lieu d'implantation m pl	fattori d'ubicazione m pl	factores de ubicación m pl
Standortwahl (D)	—	choice of location	choix du lieu d'implantation m	scelta dell'ubicazione f	elección de la ubicación f
stanza centrale di compensazione (I)	Girozentrale f	central giro institution	banque centrale de virement f	—	central de giros f
Stapelware (D)	—	staple commodities	produit de stockage m	merce immagazzinata f	mercancía almacenada f
staple commodities (E)	Stapelware f	—	produit de stockage m	merce immagazzinata f	mercancía almacenada f
star del credere (I)	Delkredere n	del credere	ducroire m	—	delcrédere m
staries (F)	Liegetage pl	lay days	—	stallie f pl	estadías f pl
starting salary (E)	Anfangsgehalt n	—	salaire initial m	stipendio iniziale m	salario inicial m
statale (I)	staatlich	state	de l'Etat	—	estatal
state¹ (E)	Staat m	—	Etat m	stato m	Estado m
state² (E)	staatlich	—	de l'Etat	statale	estatal
state activity (E)	Staatstätigkeit f	—	activité de l'Etat f	attività pubblica f	actividad del Estado f
state bank (E)	Staatsbank f	—	banque nationale f	Banca Centrale f	banco del Estado m
state indebtedness (E)	Staatsverschuldung f	—	endettement de l'Etat m	debito pubblico m	endeudamiento público m
statement of account (E)	Kontoauszug m	—	extrait de compte m	estratto conto m	extracto de cuenta m

	D	E	F	I	Es
statement of a commission (E)	Provisions-abrechnung f	—	liquidation des commissions f	conteggio delle provvigioni m	liquidación de la comisión f
statement of expenses (E)	Spesenabrechung f	—	décompte des frais m	conteggio delle spese m	liquidación de gastos f
state of the market (E)	Marktlage f	—	situation du marché f	situazione di mercato f	condiciones del mercado f pl
state-owned enterprise (E)	staatliche Betriebe pl	—	entreprise publique f	aziende statali f pl	empresas públicas f pl
station de satellite (F)	Satellitenstation f	space station	—	stazione satellite f	estación satélite f
station of destination (E)	Bestimmungs-bahnhof m	—	gare destinataire f	stazione di destinazione f	estación de destino f
statistica (I)	Statistik f	statistics	statistique f	—	estadística f
statistica agraria (I)	Agrarstatistik f	agricultural statistics	statistique agricole f	—	estadística agrícola f
statistica aziendale (I)	Betriebsstatistik f	operational statistics	statistique commerciale et industrielle f	—	estadística de la empresa f
statistica delle vendite (I)	Absatzstatistik f	sales statistics	statistique de la vente f	—	estadística de ventas f
statistica demografica (I)	Bevölkerungs-statistik f	population statistics	statistique démographique f	—	estadística de población f
statistica di categoria (I)	Branchenstatistik f	trade statistics	statistique sur les différentes branches économiques f	—	estadística del ramo f
statistica economica (I)	Wirtschaftsstatistik f	housekeeping account	statistique économique f	—	estadística económica f
statistics (E)	Statistik f	—	statistique f	statistica f	estadística f
Statistik (D)	—	statistics	statistique f	statistica f	estadística f
statistique (F)	Statistik f	statistics	—	statistica f	estadística f
statistique agricole (F)	Agrarstatistik f	agricultural statistics	—	statistica agraria f	estadística agrícola f
statistique commerciale et industrielle (F)	Betriebsstatistik f	operational statistics	—	statistica aziendale f	estadística de la empresa f
statistique de la vente (F)	Absatzstatistik f	sales statistics	—	statistica delle vendite f	estadística de ventas f
statistique démographique (F)	Bevölkerungs-statistik f	population statistics	—	statistica demografica f	estadística de población f
statistique économique (F)	Wirtschaftsstatistik f	housekeeping account	—	statistica economica f	estadística económica f
statistique sur les différentes branches économiques (F)	Branchenstatistik f	trade statistics	—	statistica di categoria f	estadística del ramo f
stato[1] (I)	Status m	status	état m	—	status m
stato[2] (I)	Staat m	state	Etat m	—	Estado m
stato assistenziale (I)	Wohlfahrtsstaat m	welfare state	Etat social m	—	estado de bienestar m
stato sociale (I)	Sozialstaat m	social state based on the rule of law	Etat social m	—	Estado social m
Status (D)	—	status	état m	stato m	status m
status (E)	Status m	—	état m	stato m	status m
status (Es)	Status m	status	état m	stato m	—
statut (F)	Satzung f	statutes	—	statuto m	constitución f/ estatuto m
statutes (E)	Satzung f	—	statut m	statuto m	estatuto m
statuto (I)	Satzung f	statutes	statut m	—	estatuto m
stazione di destinazione (I)	Bestimmungs-bahnhof m	station of destination	gare destinataire f	—	estación de destino f
stazione satellite (I)	Satellitenstation f	space station	station de satellite f	—	estación satélite f
steigend (D)	—	rising	croissant(e)	in aumento	ascendente
Steinkohle (D)	—	hard coal	houille f	carbone fossile m	hulla f
Stellenangebot (D)	—	offer of employment	offre d'emploi f	offerta d'impiego f	oferta de empleo f
Stellenanzeige (D)	—	position offered	annonce d'emploi f	inserzione d'impiego f	anuncio de empleo m
Stellen-ausschreibung (D)	—	advertisement of a vacancy	mise au concours d'une place f	bando di concorso per impiegati m	convocatoria de oposiciones f
Stellen-beschreibung (D)	—	job description	description de l'emploi f	descrizione d'impiego f	descripción del puesto de trabajo f

	D	E	F	I	Es
Stellengesuch (D)	—	situation wanted/ application for a job	demande d'emploi f	domanda d'impiego f	solicitud de colocación f
Stellung (D)	—	position	position f	posizione f	empleo m
Stellungnahme (D)	—	comment	prise de position f	presa di posizione f	dictamen m
Stellungswechsel (D)	—	change of employment	changement d'emploi m	cambiamento del posto di lavoro m	cambio de empleo m
Stellvertreter (D)	—	deputy	adjoint m	sostituto m	sustituto m
Stempelgebühr (D)	—	stamp duty	droit de timbre m	tassa di bollo f	derechos de timbre m pl
Steuer (D)	—	tax	impôt m	imposta f	impuesto m
Steuerbehörden (D)	—	tax authority	administration des contributions f	autorità fiscali f pl	administración de hacienda f
Steuerberater (D)	—	tax adviser	conseiller fiscal m	consulente fiscale m	asesor fiscal m
Steuerbescheid (D)	—	notice of assessment	avis d'imposition m	cartella delle imposte f	liquidación de impuestos f
Steuerbetrug (D)	—	fiscal fraud	fraude fiscale f	frode fiscale f	fraude fiscal m
Steuerbilanz (D)	—	tax balance-sheet	bilan fiscal m	bilancio fiscale m	balance impositivo m
Steuererhöhung (D)	—	increase of taxes	relèvement des impôts m	aumento delle imposte m	aumento de los impuestos m
Steuererklärung (D)	—	tax return	déclaration d'impôts f	dichiarazione dei redditi f	declaración a efectos fiscales f
Steuerfahndung (D)	—	investigation into suspected tax offences	recherche de la fraude fiscale f	inchiesta tributaria f	investigación tributaria f
steuerfrei (D)	—	tax-free	dispensé de l'impôt	esente da imposte	libre de impuesto
Steuer- hinterziehung (D)	—	tax evasion	dissimulation en matière fiscale f	evasione fiscale f	defraudación fiscal f
Steuernachzahlung (D)	—	additional payment of taxes	payement d'un rappel d'impôt m	pagamento arretrato delle imposte m	pago de impuestos atrasados m
Steueroase (D)	—	tax haven	oasis fiscale f	oasi fiscale f	oasis fiscal m
Steuerpolitik (D)	—	fiscal policy	politique fiscale f	politica fiscale f	política fiscal f
Steuersystem (D)	—	system of taxation	système fiscal m	sistema fiscale m	sistema fiscal m
Steuerung (D)	—	control	contrôle m	controllo m	control m
Steuerveranlagung (D)	—	tax assessment	taxation fiscale f	accertamento tributario m	tasación de los impuestos f
Steuervoraus- zahlung (D)	—	advanced payment of taxes	acompte provisionnel sur l'imposition m	pagamento anticipato delle imposte m	impuestos adelantados m pl
Steuerzahler (D)	—	taxpayer	contribuable m	contribuente m	contribuyente m
Steuerzahlung (D)	—	payment of taxes	payement de l'impôt m	pagamento delle imposte m	tributación f
Stichprobe (D)	—	random test	sondage m	campioni pl	prueba for sondeo f
Stichprobe- verfahren (D)	—	sampling procedure	méthode d'enquête par sondage f	metodo del campionamento m	muestreo m
sticker (E)	Aufkleber m	—	étiquette f	etichetta adesiva f	pegatina f
Stickoxid (D)	—	nitric oxide	oxyde azotique m	ossido di azoto m	óxido nítrico m
Stiftung (D)	—	foundation	fondation f	fondazione f	fundación f
stile dell'acquirente (I)	Käuferstil m	style of the purchaser	style des acheteurs m	—	estilo de compra m
stille Gesellschaft (D)	—	dormant partnership	association commer- ciale en participation f	associazione in partecipazione f	sociedad en participación f
stille Reserve (D)	—	hidden reserves	réserve cachée f	riserva occulta f	reserva tácita f
stille Rücklage (D)	—	latent funds	réserve cachée f	riserva latente f	reserva tácita f
Stimmabgabe (D)	—	vote	vote m	votazione f	voto m
Stimme (D)	—	voting	voix f	voto m	voz f
Stimmenmehrheit (D)	—	majority of votes	majorité des voix f	maggioranza dei voti f	mayoría de votos f
Stimmrecht (D)	—	right to vote	droit de vote m	diritto al voto m	derecho a voto m
Stimmungs- barometer (D)	—	barometer of public opinion	baromètre de la tendance m	barometro economico m	barómetro de la opinión pública m
stimulation de l'accroissement (F)	Wachstumsimpuls m	growth impulse	—	impulso di crescita m	impulso de crecimiento m
stipendio (I)	Gehalt n	salary	traitement m	—	sueldo m
stipendio base (I)	Grundgehalt n	basic salary	traitement de base m	—	salario base m

	D	E	F	I	Es
stipendio iniziale (I)	Anfangsgehalt *n*	starting salary	salaire initial *m*	—	salario inicial *m*
stipulazione (I)	Abschluß *m*	conclusion/business deal/balancing	conclusion *f*/ règlement *m*/clôture *f*	—	contratación *f*/ conclusión *f*/cierre *m*
stipulazione del contratto (I)	Vertragsabschluß *m*	conclusion of a contract	conclusion du contrat *f*	—	conclusión de un contrato *f*
stock¹ (E)	Warenbestand *m*	—	stock de marchandises *m*	scorte merci *f pl*	existencias de mercancías *f pl*
stock² (E)	Vorrat *m*	—	stock *m*	scorte *f pl*	existencias *f pl*
stock (F)	Vorrat *m*	stock	—	scorte *f pl*	existencias *f pl*
stockage¹ (F)	Lagerung *f*	storage	—	magazzinaggio *m*	almacenaje *m*
stockage² (F)	Vorratshaltung *f*	stock piling	—	gestione delle scorte *f*	formación de stocks *f*
stockbroker (E)	Börsenmakler *m*	—	courtier en bourse *m*	agente di cambio *m*	corredor de bolsa *m*
stock broker (E)	Kursmakler *m*	—	courtier en bourse *m*	agente di borsa *m*	agente cambio y bolsa *m*/corredor de cambios *m*
stock cycle (E)	Lagerzyklus *m*	—	cycle de stockage *m*	ciclo di magazzinaggio *m*	período de almacenaje *m*
stock de marchandises¹ (F)	Warenbestand *m*	stock	—	scorte merci *f pl*	existencias de mercancías *f pl*
stock de marchandises² (F)	Warenlager *n*	stock room	—	magazzino *m*	depósito de mercancías *m*
(stock) exchange (E)	Börse *f*	—	bourse *f*	borsa *f*	bolsa *f*
stock exchange (E)	Effektenbörse *f*	—	bourse des titres et valeurs mobilières *f*	borsa valori *f*	Bolsa de valores *f*
stock exchange centre (E)	Börsenplatz *m*	—	place boursière *f*	piazza *f*	plaza bursátil *f*
stock exchange index (E)	Börsenindex *m*	—	indice des cours des actions *m*	indice delle quotazioni *m*	índice bursátil *m*
stock exchange list (E)	Kurszettel *m*	—	bulletin des cours *m*	listino di borsa *m*	boletín de bolsa *m*
stockkeeping¹ (E)	Lagerhaltung *f*	—	entreposage *m*	magazzinaggio *m*	almacenaje *m*
stockkeeping² (E)	Lagerverwaltung *f*	—	entreposage *m*	amministrazione del magazzino *f*	administración de almacén *f*
stockmarket crash (E)	Börsenkrach *m*	—	débâcle boursière *f*	crollo di borsa *m*	caída en picado de la bolsa *f*
stock exchange transactions (E)	Börsenhandel *m*	—	transactions boursiaires *f pl*	commercio in borsa *m*	negociación bursátil *f*
stock exchange turnover tax (E)	Börsenumsatz- steuer *f*	—	droit de transaction sur les opérations boursières *m*	imposta sulle operazioni di borsa *f*	impuesto de negociación bursátil *m*
stock initial (F)	Anfangsbestand *m*	opening inventory	—	scorte iniziali *f pl*	existencias iniciales *f pl*
stock market transactions (E)	Börsengeschäfte *pl*	—	opérations de bourse *f pl*	operazioni di borsa *f pl*	operación bursátil *f*
stock piling (E)	Vorratshaltung *f*	—	stockage *m*	gestione delle scorte *f*	formación de stocks *f*
stock room (E)	Warenlager *n*	—	stock de marchandises *m*	magazzino *m*	depósito de mercancías *m*
stock variable (F)	Bestandsgröße *f*	stock variable	—	entità dell'inventario *f*	magnitud *f*
stopping payment of cheque (E)	Scheckssperrung *f*	—	opposition au paye- ment d'un chèque *f*	blocco d'assegno *m*	bloqueo de un cheque *m*
storage¹ (E)	Einlagerung *f*	—	entreposage *m*	immagazzinamento *m*	almacenamiento *m*
storage² (E)	Lagerung *f*	—	stockage *m*	magazzinaggio *m*	almacenaje *m*
storage capacity (E)	Lagerkapazität *f*	—	capacité de stockage *f*	capacità di magazzino *f*	capacidad de almacenaje *f*
storage space (E)	Lagerraum *m*	—	halle de dépôt *f*	magazzino *m*	almacén *m*
storia economica (I)	Wirtschafts- geschichte *f*	economic history	histoire économique *f*	—	historia económica *f*
Stornierung (D)	—	cancellation	annulation *f*	storno *m*	cancelación *f*/anula- ción *f*/contrapartida *f*
Storno (D)	—	counter entry	écriture de contre-passation *f*	storno *m*	extorno *m*
storno¹ (I)	Storno *n*	counter entry	écriture de contre-passation *f*	—	extorno *m*
storno² (I)	Stornierung *f*	cancellation	annulation *f*	—	cancelación *f*/anula- ción *f*/contrapartida *f*
strafbar (D)	—	punishable	punissable	punibile	punible

structure

	D	E	F	I	Es
straffällig (D)	—	liable to prosecution	encourir une peine	passibile di pena	criminal
straniero (I)	Ausländer *m*	foreigner	étranger *m*	—	extranjero *m*
Straße (D)	—	street/road	rue *f*/route *f*	via *f*/strada *f*	calle *f*/carretera *f*
Straßenbahn (D)	—	tramway	tramway *m*	tram *m*	tranvía *m*
Straßennetz (D)	—	road network	réseau routier *m*	rete stradale *f*	red de carreteras *f*
Straßenverkehr (D)	—	road traffic	trafic routier *m*	traffico stradale *m*	circulación *f*
strategia (I)	Strategie *f*	strategy	stratégie *f*	—	estrategia *f*
strategia di vendita (I)	Absatzstrategie *f*	sales strategy	stratégie de vente *f*	—	estrategia de ventas *f*
strategia imprenditoriale (I)	Unternehmens-strategie *f*	corporate strategy	stratégie de l'entreprise *f*	—	estrategia empresarial *f*
strategia occupazionale (I)	Personalstrategie *f*	personnel strategy	stratégie en matière de personnel *f*	—	estrategia de personal *f*
strategic (E)	strategisch	—	stratégique	strategico	estratégico
strategico (I)	strategisch	strategic	stratégique	—	estratégico
Strategie (D)	—	strategy	stratégie *f*	strategia *f*	estrategia *f*
stratégie (F)	Strategie *f*	strategy	—	strategia *f*	estrategia *f*
stratégie de l'entreprise[1] (F)	Unternehmens-konzept *n*	business concept	—	piano imprenditoriale *m*	concepto comercial *m*
stratégie de l'entreprise[2] (F)	Unternehmens-strategie *f*	corporate strategy	—	strategia imprenditoriale *f*	estrategia empresarial *f*
stratégie des ventes directes (F)	Direct-Marketing *n*	direct marketing	—	marketing in prima persona *m*	comercialización directa *f*
stratégie de vente (F)	Absatzstrategie *f*	sales strategy	—	strategia di vendita *f*	estrategia de ventas *f*
stratégie en matière de personnel (F)	Personalstrategie *f*	personnel strategy	—	strategia occupazionale *f*	estrategia de personal *f*
stratégique (F)	strategisch	strategic	—	strategico	estratégico
strategisch (D)	—	strategic	stratégique	strategico	estratégico
strategy (E)	Strategie *f*	—	stratégie *f*	strategia *f*	estrategia *f*
strato d'ozono (I)	Ozonschicht *f*	ozone layer	ozonosphère *f*	—	capa del ozono *f*
street (E)	Straße *f*	—	rue *f*/route *f*	via *f*/strada *f*	calle *f*/carretera *f*
Streifband (D)	—	postal wrapper	bande étiquette *f*	fascia *f*	precinto *m*
Streik (D)	—	strike	grève *f*	sciopero *m*	huelga *f*
streng vertraulich (D)	—	strictly confidential	strictement confidentiel	strettamente confidenziale	absolutamente confidencial
Stress (D)	—	stress	stress *m*	stress *m*	estrés *m*
stress (E)	Stress *m*	—	stress *m*	stress *m*	estrés *m*
stress (I)	Stress *m*	stress	stress *m*	—	estrés *m*
strettamente confidenziale (I)	streng vertraulich	strictly confidential	strictement confidentiel	—	absolutamente confidencial
strettoia di capacità (I)	Kapazitätsengpaß *m*	bottleneck in capacity	goulot d'étrangle-ment de capacité *m*	—	escasez de capacidad *f*
strettoia di liquidità (I)	Liquiditätsengpaß *m*	liquidity squeeze	goulot d'étranglement dans la trésorerie	—	restricción de la liquidez *f*
strictement confidentiel (F)	streng vertraulich	strictly confidential	—	strettamente confidenziale	absolutamente confidencial
strictly confidential (E)	streng vertraulich	—	strictement confidentiel	strettamente confidenziale	absolutamente confidencial
strike (E)	Streik *m*	—	grève *f*	sciopero *m*	huelga *f*
Strohmann (D)	—	man of straw/dummy	prête-nom *m*	prestanome *m*	testaferro *m*
Strom (D)	—	current	courant *m*	corrente *f*	corriente *f*
strozzinaggio sui canoni di locazione (I)	Mietwucher *m*	exorbitant rent	hausse illicite des loyers *f*	—	usura arrendaticia *f*
structural change (E)	Strukturwandel *m*	—	changement dans les structures *m*	cambiamenti strutturali *m pl*	cambio de estructuras *m*
structural investments (E)	Bauinvestitionen *pl*	—	investissements à la construction *m pl*	investimenti edili *m pl*	inversión inmobiliaria *f*
structural policy (E)	Strukturpolitik *f*	—	politique structurelle *f*	politica strutturale *f*	política estructural *f*
structural unemployment (E)	strukturelle Arbeitslosigkeit *f*	—	chômage structurel *m*	disoccupazione strutturale *f*	paro estructural *m*
structure (E)	Struktur *f*	—	structure *f*	struttura *f*	estructura *f*

	D	E	F	I	Es
structure (F)	Struktur f	structure	—	struttura f	estructura f
structure agraire (F)	Agrarstruktur f	agricultural structure	—	struttura agraria f	estructura agraria f
structure d'assortiment (F)	Sortiments-gestaltung f	assortment structuring	—	composizione dell'assortimento f	configuración del surtido f
structure de la consommation (F)	Konsumstruktur f	consumption structure	—	struttura del consumo f	estructura del consumo f
structure de distribution (F)	Vertriebsstruktur f	structure of distribution	—	struttura della distribuzione f	estructura de distribución f
structure de la branche (F)	Branchenstruktur f	trade structure	—	struttura di categoria f	estructura del ramo f
structure démographique (F)	Bevölkerungs-struktur f	population structure	—	struttura demografica f	estructura demográfica f
structure des espaces (F)	Raumstruktur f	spatial structure	—	struttura territoriale f	estructura territorial f
structure du texte (F)	Textgestaltung f	text configuration	—	redazione del testo f	estructuración del texto f
structure économique (F)	Wirtschaftsstruktur f	economic structure	—	struttura economica f	estructura económica f
structure of distribution (E)	Vertriebsstruktur f	—	structure de distribution f	struttura della distribuzione f	estructura de distribución f
Struktur (D)	—	structure	structure f	struttura f	estructura f
strukturelle Arbeitslosigkeit (D)	—	structural unemployment	chômage structurel m	disoccupazione strutturale f	paro estructural m
Strukturpolitik (D)	—	structural policy	politique structurelle f	politica strutturale f	política estructural f
Strukturwandel (D)	—	structural change	changement dans les structures m	cambiamenti strutturali m pl	cambio de estructuras m
strumento (I)	Instrument n	instrument	instrument m	—	instrumento m
struttura (I)	Struktur f	structure	structure f	—	estructura f
struttura agraria (I)	Agrarstruktur f	agricultural structure	structure agraire f	—	estructura agraria f
struttura del consumo (I)	Konsumstruktur f	consumption structure	structure de la consommation	—	estructura del consumo f
struttura della distribuzione (I)	Vertriebsstruktur f	structure of distribution	structure de distribution f	—	estructura de distribución f
struttura demografica (I)	Bevölkerungs-struktur f	population structure	structure démographique f	—	estructura demográfica f
struttura di categoria (I)	Branchenstruktur f	trade structure	structure de la branche f	—	estructura del ramo f
struttura economica (I)	Wirtschaftsstruktur f	economic structure	structure économique f	—	estructura económica f
struttura territoriale (I)	Raumstruktur f	spatial structure	structure des espaces f	—	estructura territorial f
Stückgut (D)	—	mixed cargo	colis de détail m	collettame m	fardos m pl
Stückgutverkehr (D)	—	general cargo trade	expéditions de détail f	trasporto di collettame m	tráfico de mercanías en bultos sueltos m
Stückkosten (D)	—	costs per unit	coût unitaire de production m	costi unitari m pl	coste por unidad m
Stücklohn (D)	—	piece work pay	salaire à la tâche m	salario a cottimo m	salario a destajo m
Stückzeit (D)	—	piece time	temps par pièce m	tempo pezzo m	tiempo por unidad m
Stückzinsen (D)	—	broken period interest	intérêts courus m pl	interessi maturati m pl	intereses por fracción de período m pl
studio d'avvocato (I)	Anwaltskanzlei f	lawyer's office	cabinet d'avocat m	—	bufete de abogado m
studio della concorrenza (I)	Konkurrenz-beobachtung f	observation of the competitors	observation de la concurrence f	—	observación de la competencia f
Stundenlohn (D)	—	hourly wage	salaire horaire m	salario ad ora m	salario-hora m
Stundung (D)	—	respite	prorogation f	dilazione f/proroga f	moratoria f
Stützungskauf (D)	—	support buying	achat de soutien m	acquisto di sostegno m	compra para sostener precios f
style des acheteurs (F)	Käuferstil m	style of the purchaser	—	stile dell'acquirente m	estilo de compra m
style of the purchaser (E)	Käuferstil m	—	style des acheteurs m	stile dell'acquirente m	estilo de compra m
subaffitto (I)	Untervermietung f	subletting	sous-location f	—	subalquiler m
subagent (E)	Untervertreter m	—	sous-agent m	subagente m	subagente m
subagente (Es)	Untervertreter m	subagent	sous-agent m	subagente m	—

	D	E	F	I	Es
subagente (I)	Untervertreter *m*	subagent	sous-agent *m*	—	subagente *m*
subalimentación (Es)	Unterernährung *f*	malnutrition	sous-alimentation *f*	denutrizione *f*	—
subalquiler (Es)	Untervermietung *f*	subletting	sous-location *f*	subaffitto *m*	—
subalterne (F)	Untergebener *m*	subordinate	—	dipendente *m*	subordinado *m*
subasta¹ (Es)	Versteigerung *f*	auction	vente à l'enchère *f*	vendita all'asta *f*	—
subasta² (Es)	Auktion *f*	auction	vente à l'enchère *f*	asta *f*	—
subasta de préstamos de regulación monetaria (Es)	Tenderverfahren *n*	tender procedure	offre d'emprunts pour la régulation monétaire *f*	offerta pubblica d'acquisto *f*	—
subasta forzosa (Es)	Zwangsversteigerung *f*	sale by court order	vente de biens par justice *f*	asta giudiziaria *f*	—
subcontractor (E)	Subunternehmer *m*	—	sous-entrepreneur *m*	subimprenditore *m*	subcontratista *m*
subcontratista (Es)	Subunternehmer *m*	subcontractor	sous-entrepreneur *m*	subimprenditore *m*	—
subempleo (Es)	Unterbeschäftigung *f*	underemployment	sous-emploi *m*	sottoccupazione *f*	—
subimprenditore (I)	Subunternehmer *m*	subcontractor	sous-entrepreneur *m*	—	subcontratista *m*
subject to confirmation (E)	freibleibend	—	sans engagement	senza impegno	no vinculante
subletting (E)	Untervermietung *f*	—	sous-location *f*	subaffitto *m*	subalquiler *m*
subordinado (Es)	Untergebener *m*	subordinate	subalterne *m*	dipendente *m*	—
subordinate (E)	Untergebener *m*	—	subalterne *m*	dipendente *m*	subordinado *m*
subscriber (E)	Abonnent *m*	—	abonné *m*	abbonato *m*	suscriptor *m*
subscription¹ (E)	Abonnement *n*	—	abonnement *m*	abbonamento *m*	suscripción *f*
subscription² (E)	Suskription *f*	—	souscription *f*	sottoscrizione *f*	suscripción *f*
subsidiary (E)	Tochtergesellschaft *f*	—	société filiale *f*	società affiliata *f*	filial *f*
subsidy (E)	Subvention *f*	—	subvention *f*	sovvenzione *f*	subvención *f*
subsistence minimum (E)	Existenzminimum *n*	—	minimum vital *m*	minimo di esistenza *m*	minimo vital *m*
Subkription (D)	—	subscription	souscription *f*	sottoscrizione *f*	suscripción *f*
substance (E)	Substanz *f*	—	substance *f*	sostanza *f*	sustancia *f*
substance (F)	Substanz *f*	substance	—	sostanza *f*	sustancia *f*
substancia nociva (Es)	Schadstoff *m*	pollutants	élément polluant *m*	sostanza nociva *f*	—
Substanz (D)	—	substance	substance *f*	sostanza *f*	sustancia *f*
Substanzerhaltung (D)		maintaining the real value	maintien de la substance *m*	mantenimento della sostanza *m*	conservación de la sustancia *f*
Substanzwert (D)	—	assets value	valeur de remplacement *f*	valore sostanziale *m*	valor sustancial *m*
substituierbar (D)	—	replaceable	interchangeable	sostituibile	sustituible
substitute delivery (E)	Ersatzlieferung *f*	—	livraison de remplacement *f*	fornitura di compensazione *f*	entrega de reposición *f*
substitute purchase (E)	Ersatzkauf *m*	—	achat de remplacement *m*	acquisto di compensazione *m*	compra de sustitución *f*
Subunternehmer (D)	—	subcontractor	sous-entrepreneur *m*	subimprenditore *m*	subcontratista *m*
subvaloración (Es)	Unterbewertung *f*	undervaluation	sous-estimation *f*	sottovalutazione *f*	—
subvención¹ (Es)	Subvention *f*	subsidy	subvention *f*	sovvenzione *f*	—
subvención² (Es)	Zuschuß *m*	allowance	allocation *f*	sovvenzione *f*	—
subvención a la agricultura (Es)	Agrarsubventionen *pl*	agricultural subsidies	subventions de l'agriculture *f pl*	sovvenzioni agrarie *f pl*	—
subvenciones del Estado (Es)	Staatszuschuß *m*	government grant	subvention de l'Etat *f*	sovvenzione pubblica *f*	—
Subvention (D)	—	subsidy	subvention *f*	sovvenzione *f*	subvención *f*
subvention (F)	Subvention *f*	subsidy	—	sovvenzione *f*	subvención *f*
subvention à l'exportatoin (F)	Exporthilfe *f*	export subsidy	—	aiuto all'esportazione *m*	ayuda a la exportación *f*
subvention de l'Etat (F)	Staatszuschuß *m*	government grant	—	sovvenzione pubblica *f*	subvenciones del Estado *f pl*
Subventionsabbau (D)	—	reduction of subsidy	réduction des subventions *f*	riduzione delle sovvenzioni *f*	reducción de las subvenciones *f*
subventions de l'agriculture (F)	Agrarsubventionen *pl*	agricultural subsidies	—	sovvenzioni agrarie *f pl*	subvención a la agricultura *f*

	D	E	F	I	Es
success-oriented (E)	erfolgsorientiert	—	orienté vers le succès	orientato al successo	orientado hacia el éxito
succursale[1] (F)	Niederlassung f	establishment	—	succursale f	sucursal f
succursale[2] (F)	Zweigniederlassung f	branch office	—	succursale f	filial f
succursale[1] (I)	Niederlassung f	establishment	succursale f	—	sucursal f
succursale[2] (I)	Zweigniederlassung f	branch office	succursale f	—	filial f
succursale à l'étranger (F)	Auslands-niederlassung f	branch abroad	—	succursale estera f	filial en el exterior m
succursale à l'intérieur (F)	Inlands-niederlassung f	domestic establishment	—	succursale nazionale f	sucursal en el interior f
succursale estera (I)	Auslands-niederlassung f	branch abroad	succursale à l'étranger f	—	filial en el exterior m
succursale nazionale (I)	Inlands-niederlassung f	domestic establishment	succursale à l'intérieur f	—	sucursal en el interior f
sucursal (Es)	Zweigbetrieb m	branch business	établissement secondaire m	filiale f	—
sucursal en el interior (Es)	Inlands-niederlassung f	domestic establishment	succursale à l'intérieur f	succursale nazionale f	—
sueldo[1] (Es)	Besoldung f	pay	rétribution f	retribuzione f	—
sueldo[2] (Es)	Gehalt n	salary	traitement m	stipendio m	—
sueldo base (Es)	Basislohn m	basic wage	salaire de référence m	salario base m	—
suelo (Es)	Boden m	ground/soil	sol m/terrain m	terra f/suolo m	—
sugestionable (Es)	beeinflußbar	be influenced	influençable	influenzabile	—
suggerimento di prezzo (I)	Preisempfehlung f	price recommendation	recommendation de prix f	—	precio recomendado m
suggestion for improvement (E)	Verbesserungs-vorschlag m	—	proposition d'amélioration f	proposta di miglioramento f	propuesta de mejora f
sujeto a impustos (Es)	abgabenpflichtig	liable to tax	soumis à l'impôt	soggetto a contributi	—
suma (Es)	Betrag m	amount	montant m	importo m	—
suma asegurada (Es)	Versicherungs-summe f	insurance sum	montant de l'assurance m	somma assicurata f	—
suma de amortización (Es)	Ablösesumme f	redemption sum	montant de rachat m	importo di rimborso m	—
suma de dinero (Es)	Geldbetrag m	amount of money	somme d'argent f	somma di denaro f	—
suma de la factura (Es)	Rechnungssumme f	invoice amount	montant de la facture m	importo della fattura m	—
suma del crédito documentario (Es)	Akkreditivsumme f	amount of the letter of credit	montant de l'accréditif m	importo del credito documentario m	—
suma global (Es)	Pauschalbetrag m	flat rate amount	somme forfaitaire f	somma forfettaria f	—
suma global de gastos (Es)	Spesenpauschale f	allowance for expenses	forfait de frais m	forfait di spese m	—
sumar (Es)	addieren	add	additionner	addizionare	—
suma total (Es)	Gesamtsumme f	total amount	montant total m	importo totale m	—
suministrable (Es)	lieferbar	deliverable	livrable	disponibile	—
suministrador (Es)	Lieferant m	supplier	fournisseur m	fornitore m	—
suministro (Es)	Lieferung f	delivery	livraison f	fornitura f/consegna f	—
suministro total (Es)	Gesamtlieferung f	total delivery	livraison totale f	fornitura completa f	—
Sunday work (E)	Sonntagsarbeit f	—	travail du dimanche m	lavoro domenicale m	trabajo dominical m
superávit (Es)	schwarze Zahlen pl	surplus	excédent m	conti in nero m pl	—
superávit del ejercicio (Es)	Jahresüberschuß m	annual surplus	excédent annuel m	surplus dell'anno m	—
superávit del productor (Es)	Produzentenrente f	producer's surplus	rente du vendeur f	rendita del produttore f	—
superávit en la balanza de pagos (Es)	Zahlungsbilanz-überschuß m	surplus in the balance of payments	balance des paye-ments excédentaire f	eccedenza della bilan-cia dei pagamenti f	—
supercapacidad (Es)	Überkapazität f	overcapacity	surcapacité f	capacità eccessiva f	—
superficie agrícola utilizada (Es)	Anbaufläche f	area under cultivation	surface plantée f	area coltivata f	—
supermarché (F)	Supermarkt m	supermarket	—	supermercato m	supermercado m
supermarket (E)	Supermarkt m	—	supermarché m	supermercato m	supermercado m
Supermarkt (D)	—	supermarket	supermarché m	supermercato m	supermercado m

	D	E	F	I	Es
supermercado (Es)	Supermarkt *m*	supermarket	supermarché *m*	supermercato *m*	—
supermercato (I)	Supermarkt *m*	supermarket	supermarché *m*	—	supermercado *m*
superpoblación (Es)	Überbevölkerung *f*	overpopulation	surpopulation *f*	sovrappopolazione *f*	—
supervision (E)	Aufsicht *f*	—	surveillance *f*	sorveglianza *f*	inspección *f*
supervisión bancaria (Es)	Bankenaufsicht *f*	public supervision of banking	contrôle des banques *m*	commissione bancaria *f*	—
supervisory board (E)	Aufsichtsrat *m*	—	conseil de surveillance *m*	consiglio di sorveglianza *m*	consejo de vigilancia *m*
suplemento[1] (Es)	Beilage *f*	supplement	encart non broché à la revue *m*	inserto *m*	—
suplemento[2] (Es)	Zugabe *f*	extra	prime *f*	aggiunta *f*	—
suplemento[3] (Es)	Zuschlag *m*	extra charge	supplément *m*	supplemento *m*/ premio *m*	—
suplemento[4] (Es)	Zulage *f*	increase/ additional pay	prime *f*/complément de salaire *m*	premio *m*/indennità *f*	—
suposición (Es)	Mutmaßung *f*	conjecture	présomption *f*	presunzione *f*	—
supplement (E)	Beilage *f*	—	encart non broché à la revue *m*	inserto *m*	suplemento *m*
supplément (F)	Zuschlag *m*	extra charge	—	supplemento *m*/ premio *m*	suplemento *m*/ prima *f*
supplementary payment (E)	Nachzahlung *f*	—	versement complémentaire *m*	pagamento supplementare *m*	pago suplementario *m*
supplément de fret (F)	Frachtzuschlag *m*	additional freight charges	—	supplemento di nolo *m*	sobreporte *m*
supplemento (I)	Zuschlag *m*	extra charge	supplément *m*	—	supplemento *m*/ prima *f*
supplemento di nolo (I)	Frachtzuschlag *m*	additional freight charges	supplément de fret *m*	—	sobreporte *m*
supplier[1] (E)	Zulieferer *m*	—	sous-traitant *m*	fornitore *m*	abastecedor *m*
supplier[2] (E)	Lieferant *m*	—	fournisseur *m*	fornitore *m*	suministrador *m*
supplier's credit (E)	Lieferantenkredit *m*	—	crédit de fournisseurs *m*	credito al fornitore *m*	crédito comercial *m*
supply (E)	Versorgung *f*	—	approvisionnement *m*	approvvigiona- mento *m*	abastecimiento *m*
supply contract (E)	Liefervertrag *m*	—	contrat de fourniture *m*	contratto di consegna *m*	contrata *f*
support buying (E)	Stützungskauf *m*	—	achat de soutien *m*	acquisto di sostegno *m*	compra para sostener precios *f*
supporto dati (I)	Datenträger *m*	data medium	porteur des données *m*	—	medio de datos *m*
support publicitaire (F)	Werbeträger *m*	advertising medium	—	veicolo pubblicitario *m*	medio de publicidad *m*
surassurance (F)	Überversicherung *f*	overinsurance	—	soprassicurazione *f*	sobreseguro *m*
surcapacité (F)	Überkapazität *f*	overcapacity	—	capacità eccessiva *f*	supercapacidad *f*
surcapitalisation (F)	Überkapitali- sierung *f*	overcapitalization	—	sovracapitalizzazione *f*	sobrecapitalización *f*
surcharge (E)	Aufschlag *m*	—	hausse *f*	aggiunta *f*	recargo *m*
surcharge[1] (F)	Übergewicht *n*	excess weight	—	sovrappeso *m*	sobrepreso *m*
surcharge[2] (F)	Mehrbelastung *f*	additional burden	—	onere supplementare *m*	carga suplementaria *f*
surchargement (F)	Überbeschäftigung *f*	overcharge	—	occupazione eccedente *f*	exceso de empleo *m*/ superempleo *m*
surendettement (F)	Überschuldung *f*	excessive indebtedness	—	indebitamento eccessivo *m*	exceso de deudas *m*
surestimation (F)	Überbewertung *f*	overvaluation	—	sopravvalutazione *f*	sobrevaloración *f*
surface plantée (F)	Anbaufläche *f*	area under cultivation	—	area coltivata *f*	superficie agrícola utilizada *f*
su richiesta (I)	auf Abruf	on call	à convenance	—	a requerimiento
surplus (E)	schwarze Zahlen *pl*	—	excédent *m*	conti in nero *m pl*	superávit *m*
surplus dell'anno (I)	Jahresüberschuß *m*	annual surplus	excédent annuel *m*	—	superávit del ejercicio *m*
surplus d'offres (F)	Angebotsüberhang *m*	excess of supply over demand	—	eccedenza d'offerta *f*	exceso de oferta *m*

	D	E	F	I	Es
surplus in the balance of payments (E)	Zahlungsbilanz-überschuß *m*	—	balance des paye-ments excédentaires *f*	eccedenza della bilan-cia dei pagamenti *f*	superávit en la ba-lanza de pagos *m*
surpopulation (F)	Überbevölkerung *f*	overpopulation	—	sovrappopolazione *f*	superpoblación *f*
surproduction (F)	Überproduktion *f*	overproduction	—	produzione eccessiva *f*	sobreproducción *f*
sursis de payement (F)	Zahlungsaufschub *m*	extension of time for payment	—	dilazione del pagamento *f*	pago aplazado *m*
surtido (Es)	Sortiment *n*	assortment	assortiment *m*	assortimento *m*	—
surveillance (F)	Aufsicht *f*	supervision	—	sorveglianza *f*	inspección *f*
surveiller (F)	überwachen	supervise	—	sorvegliare	vigilar
survey report (E)	Havariezertifikat *n*	—	certificat d'avarie *m*	certificato d'avaria *m*	certificado de avería *m*
suscripción¹ (Es)	Abonnement *n*	subscription	abonnement *m*	abbonamento *m*	—
suscripción² (Es)	Suskription *f*	subscription	souscription *f*	sottoscrizione *f*	—
suscriptor (Es)	Abonnent *m*	subscriber	abonné *m*	abbonato *m*	—
suspensión de pagos (Es)	Zahlungseinstellung *f*	cessation of payments	suspension de payement *f*	cessazione dei pagamenti *f*	—
suspension de payement (F)	Zahlungseinstellung *f*	cessation of payments	—	cessazione dei pagamenti *f*	suspensión de pagos *f*
sussidio di disoccupazione (I)	Arbeitslosen-unterstützung *f*	unemployment benefits	indemnité de chômage *f*	—	prestaciones por desempleo *f pl*
sustancia (Es)	Substanz *f*	substance	substance *f*	sostanza *f*	—
sustituible (Es)	substituierbar	replaceable	interchangeable	sostituibile	—
sustituto (Es)	Stellvertreter *m*	deputy	adjoint *m*	sostituto *m*	—
svalutazione (I)	Abwertung *f*	devaluation	dévaluation *f*	—	devaluación *f*
svantaggio (I)	Nachteil *m*	disadvantage	désavantage *m*	—	desventaja *f*
svendita (I)	Ausverkauf *m*	clearance sale	soldes *m pl*	—	liquidación *f*
svendita di fine inverno (I)	Winterschluß-verkauf *m*	winter clearance sale	solde d'hiver *m*	—	rebajas de invierno *f pl*
svendita di fine stagione (I)	Schlußverkauf *m*	seasonal sale	vente de fin de saison *f*	—	venta de liquidación *f*
sviluppo (I)	Entwicklung *f*	development	développement *m*	—	desarrollo *m*
sviluppo congiunturale (I)	Konjunktur-entwicklung *f*	economic trend	évolution de la conjoncture *f*	—	evolución de la coyuntura *f*
sviluppo del fatturato (I)	Umsatzentwicklung *f*	turnover trend	évolution du chiffre d'affaires *f*	—	evolución del volu-men de facturación *f*
Swapgeschäft (D)	—	swap transaction	opération swap *f*	operazione swap *f*	operación swap *f*
swap rate (E)	Swapsatz *m*	—	taux de swap *m*	tasso swap *m*	tasa swap *f*
Swapsatz (D)	—	swap rate	taux de swap *m*	tasso swap *m*	tasa swap *f*
swap transaction (E)	Swapgeschäft *n*	—	opération swap *f*	operazione swap *f*	operación swap *f*
swindle (E)	Schwindel *m*	—	tromperie *f*	truffa *f*	engaño *m*
Swing (D)	—	swing	swing *m*	swing *m*	swing *m*
swing (E)	Swing *m*	—	swing *m*	swing *m*	swing *m*
swing (Es)	Swing *m*	swing	swing *m*	swing *m*	—
swing (F)	Swing *m*	swing	—	swing *m*	swing *m*
swing (I)	Swing *m*	swing	swing *m*	—	swing *m*
sworn statement (E)	beeidigte Erklärung *f*	—	déclaration sous serment *f*	dichiarazione giurata *f*	declaración jurada *f*
sympathy (E)	Anteilnahme *f*	—	participation *f*	interesse *m*	participación *f*
syndic (F)	Syndikus	legal adviser	—	consulente legale *m*	síndico *m*
syndicat¹ (F)	Syndikat *n*	syndicate	—	sindacato *m*	sindicato *m*
syndicat² (F)	Gewerkschaften *pl*	trade union	—	sindacati *m pl*	sindicato *m*
syndicate (E)	Syndikat *n*	—	syndicat *m*	sindacato *m*	sindicato *m*
syndication (E)	Syndizierung *f*	—	syndication *f*	costituzione di un sindacato *f*	sindicación *f*
syndication (F)	Syndizierung *f*	syndication	—	costituzione di un sindacato *f*	sindicación *f*
Syndikat (D)	—	syndicate	syndicat *m*	sindacato *m*	sindicato *m*
Syndikus (D)	—	legal adviser	syndic *m*	consulente legale *m*	síndico *m*
Syndizierung (D)	—	syndication	syndication *f*	costituzione di un sindacato *f*	sindicación *f*

	D	E	F	I	Es
System (D)	—	system	système m	sistema m	sistema m
system (E)	System n	—	système m	sistema m	sistema m
Systemanalyse (D)	—	systems analysis	analyse du système f	analisi di sistema f	análisis de los sistemas m
system control (E)	Systemsteuerung f	—	contrôle du système m	controllo del sistema m	control del sistema m
système (F)	System n	system	—	sistema m	sistema m
système d'absorption (F)	Abschöpfungssystem n	absorption system	—	regime di prelievo m	sistema de gravámenes m
système de la boule de neige (F)	Schneeballsystem n	snowball system	—	sistema di vendite a catena aperta m	venta en cadena f
système de primes (F)	Prämiensystem n	bonus system	—	sistema dei premi m	sistema de primas m
système de quote-parts (F)	Quotensystem n	quota system	—	sistema di contingentamento m	sistema de cuotas m
système des changes flottants (F)	Floating n	floating	—	floating m	flotación f
système d'incitation (F)	Anreizsystem n	incentive system	—	sistema d'incentivo m	sistema de incentivos m
système d'information (F)	Informationssystem n	information system	—	sistema d'informazione m	sistema de información m
système d'information assisté par ordinateur (F)	computergestützes Informationssystem n	computer-aided information system	—	sistema di informazione computerizzato m	sistema de información asistido por ordenador m
système du travail aux pièces (F)	Akkordsystem n	piece work system	—	sistema del lavoro a cottimo m	régimen de trabajo a destajo m
système fiscal (F)	Steuersystem n	system of taxation	—	sistema fiscale m	sistema fiscal m
Système Monétaire Européen (F)	Europäisches Währungssystem n	European Monetary System	—	Sistema Monetario Europeo m	Sistema Monetario Europeo m
système monétaire international (F)	Weltwährungssystem n	international monetary system	—	sistema monetario internazionale m	sistema monetario internacional m
systems analysis (E)	Systemanalyse f	—	analyse du système f	analisi di sistema f	análisis de los sistemas m
system of taxation (E)	Steuersystem n	—	système fiscal m	sistema fiscale m	sistema fiscal m
Systemsteuerung (D)	—	system control	contrôle du système m	controllo del sistema m	control del sistema m
tabella (I)	Tabelle f	table	tableau m	—	tabla f
Tabelle (D)	—	table	tableau m	tabella f	tabla f
tabla (Es)	Tabelle f	table	tableau m	tabella f	—
table (E)	Tabelle f	—	tableau m	tabella f	tabla f
tableau (F)	Tabelle f	table	—	tabella f	tabla f
tableau économique input-output (F)	Input-Output-Analyse f	input-output analysis	—	analisi input-output f	análisis de input-output m
Tagesgeld (D)	—	day-to-day money	argent au jour le jour m	prestito giornaliero m	dinero de día a día m
Tagesgeschäft (D)	—	day-to-day operations	affaire au comptant f	contratto a contanti m	operación al contado f
Tageswert (D)	—	current value	valeur du jour f	valore del giorno m	valor del día m
täglich (D)	—	daily	quotidien	giornaliero	diario
Tagung (D)	—	meeting	congrès m	convegno m	reunión f
taking of the inventory (E)	Inventur f	—	inventaire m	redazione d'inventario f	inventario m
talent for argumentation (E)	Argumentationsstärke f	—	capacité d'argumentation f	forza d'argomentazione f	fuerza de argumentación f
tamaño de la explotación (Es)	Betriebsgröße f	size of the company	dimension de l'entreprise f	dimensione dell'azienda f	—
tamaño del anuncio (Es)	Anzeigenformat n	size of an advertisement	format de l'annonce f	formato dell'inserzione m	—
tan rápido como sea posible (Es)	schnellstmöglich	as quickly as possible	le plus vite possible	al più presto possibile	—
Tantieme (D)	—	percentage	tantième m	percentuale f	tanto por ciento m
tantième (F)	Tantieme f	percentage	—	percentuale f	tanto por ciento m

	D	E	F	I	Es
tanto por ciento (Es)	Tantieme *f*	percentage	tantième *m*	percentuale *f*	—
Tara (D)	—	tare	tare *f*	tara *f*	tara *f*
tara (Es)	Tara *f*	tare	tare *f*	tara *f*	—
tara (I)	Tara *f*	tare	tare *f*	—	tara *f*
tarare (I)	eichen	gauge	jauger	—	contrastar
tare (E)	Tara *f*	—	tare *f*	tara *f*	tara *f*
tare (F)	Tara *f*	tare	—	tara *f*	tara *f*
target calculation (E)	Plankalkulation *f*	—	calcul des coûts prévisionnels *m*	calcolo pianificato *m*	cálculo de los objetivos *m*
target figures (E)	Sollzahlen *pl*	—	chiffres prévisionnels *m pl*	cifre calcolate *f pl*	cifras estimadas *f pl*
target group (E)	Zielgruppe *f*	—	groupe destinataire *m*	gruppo di riferimento *m*	grupo destinatario *m*
target projection (E)	Zielprojektion *f*	—	projection d'objectifs *f*	proiezione degli obiettivi *f*	proyección de objetivos *f*
Tarif (D)	—	tariff	tarif *m*	tariffa *f*	tarifa *f*
tarif (F)	Tarif *m*	tariff	—	tariffa *f*	tarifa *f*
tarifa (Es)	Tarif *m*	tariff	tarif *m*	tariffa *f*	—
tarifa arancelaria (Es)	Zolltarif *m*	customs tariff	tarif des douanes *m*	tariffa doganale *f*	—
tarifa de transporte (Es)	Gütertarif *m*	trade tariff	tarif marchandises *m*	tariffa merci *f*	—
tarifa diferencial (Es)	Staffeltarif *m*	graduated tariff	tarif échelonné *m*	tariffa differenziata *f*	—
tarifa ferroviaria (Es)	Eisenbahntarif *m*	railway tariff	tarif ferroviaire *m*	tariffa ferroviaria *f*	—
tarifas reducidas (Es)	ermäßigte Tarife *pl*	reduced tariffs	tarifs reduits *m pl*	tariffe ridotte *f pl*	—
tarifa única (Es)	Einheitstarif *m*	uniform tariff	tarif standard *m*	tariffa unitaria *f*	—
tarif des douanes (F)	Zolltarif *m*	customs tariff	—	tariffa doganale *f*	tarifa arancelaria *f*
tarif échelonné (F)	Staffeltarif *m*	graduated tariff	—	tariffa differenziata *f*	tarifa diferencial *f*
tariff (E)	Tarif *m*	—	tarif *m*	tariffa *f*	tarifa *f*
tariffa (I)	Tarif *m*	tariff	tarif *m*	—	tarifa *f*
tariffa differenziata (I)	Staffeltarif *m*	graduated tariff	tarif échelonné *m*	—	tarifa diferencial *f*
tariffa di nolo (I)	Frachtrate *f*	(freight) rate	taux de fret *m*	—	tipo de flete *m*
tariffa doganale (I)	Zolltarif *m*	customs tariff	tarif des douanes *m*	—	tarifa arancelaria *f*
tariffa ferroviaria (I)	Eisenbahntarif *m*	railway tariff	tarif ferroviaire *m*	—	tarifa ferroviaria *f*
tariffa merci (I)	Gütertarif *m*	trade tariff	tarif marchandises *m*	—	tarifa de transporte *f*
tariffa unitaria (I)	Einheitstarif *m*	uniform tariff	tarif standard *m*	—	tarifa única *f*
tariffa zero (I)	Nulltarif *m*	nil tariff	tarif gratuit *m*	—	tarifa gratuita *f*
tariffe ridotte (I)	ermäßigte Tarife *pl*	reduced tariffs	tarifs réduits *m pl*	—	tarifas reducidas *f pl*
tarif ferroviaire (F)	Eisenbahntarif *m*	railway tariff	—	tariffa ferroviaria *f*	tarifa ferroviaria *f*
tarif gratuit (F)	Nulltarif *m*	nil tariff	—	tariffa zero *f*	tarifa gratuita *f*
Tariflohn (D)	—	standard wage	salaire tarifaire *m*	salario contrattuale *m*	salario tarifado *m*
tarif marchandises (F)	Gütertarif *m*	trade tariff	—	tariffa merci *f*	tarifa de transporte *f*
Tarifpartner (D)	—	parties to a collective agreement	signataire d'une convention collective *m*	parti sociali *f pl*	parte contratante en un convenio colectivo *f*
tarifs reduits (F)	ermäßigte Tarife *pl*	reduced tariffs	—	tariffe ridotte *f pl*	tarifas reducidas *f pl*
tarif standard (F)	Einheitstarif *m*	uniform tariff	—	tariffa unitaria *f*	tarifa única *f*
Tarifvertrag (D)	—	collective agreement	convention collective *f*	contratto salariale *m*	contrato colectivo *m*
tarjeta de cheques (Es)	Scheckkarte *f*	cheque card	carte d'identité eurochèque *f*	carta assegni *f*	—
tarjeta de crédito (Es)	Kreditkarte *f*	credit card	carte accréditive *f*	carta di credito *f*	—
tarjeta de garantía (Es)	Garantiekarte *f*	certificate of warranty	carte de garantie *f*	certificato di garanzia *m*	—
tarjeta postal (Es)	Postkarte *f*	postcard	carte postale *f*	cartolina postale *f*	—
tasa a la importación (Es)	Einfuhrabgabe *f*	import duties	taxe à l'importation *f*	tassa d'importazione *f*	—

	D	E	F	I	Es
tasación de los impuestos (Es)	Steuerveranlagung f	tax assessment	taxation fiscale f	accertamento tributario m	—
tasa de beneficio (Es)	Profitrate f	profit rate	taux de profit m	tasso di profitto m	—
tasa de cambio (Es)	Umrechnungskurs m	rate of conversion	cours de conversion m	corso di cambio m	—
tasa de descuento (Es)	Diskontsatz m	discount rate	taux d'escompte m	saggio di sconto m	—
tasa de inflación (Es)	Inflationsrate f	rate of inflation	taux d'inflation m	tasso d'inflazione m	—
tasa de natalidad (Es)	Geburtenrate f	birth rate	taux de natalité m	tasso di natalità m	—
tasa de utilización (Es)	Auslastungsgrad m	capacity utilisation rate	dégré de saturation m	grado di sfruttamento m	—
tasa swap (Es)	Swapsatz m	swap rate	taux de swap m	tasso swap m	—
tassa (I)	Gebühr f	fee	taxe f	—	derecho m
tassa di bollo (I)	Stempelgebühr f	stamp duty	droit de timbre m	—	derechos de timbre m pl
tassa di licenza (I)	Lizenzgebühr f	royalty	taxe d'exploitation de licence f	—	derecho de licencia m
tassa d'importazione (I)	Einfuhrabgabe f	import duties	taxe à l'importation f	—	tasa a la importación f
tasso di crescita (I)	Wachstumsrate f	rate of growth	taux d'accroissement m	—	tasa de crecimiento f
tasso di natalità (I)	Geburtenrate f	birth rate	taux de natalité m	—	tasa de natalidad f
tasso d'indebitamento (I)	Verschuldungsgrad m	debt ratio	niveau de l'endettement m	—	grado de endeudamiento m
tasso d'inflazione (I)	Inflationsrate f	rate of inflation	taux d'inflation m	—	tasa de inflación f
tasso d'interesse (I)	Zinsfuß m	interest rate	taux d'intérêt m	—	tipo de interés m
tasso d'interesse effettivo (I)	Effektivzins m	effective interest	intérêt effectif m	—	intereses reales m pl
tasso d'interesse fisso (I)	fester Zins m	fixed interest rate	intérêt fixe m	—	interés fijo m
tasso d'interesse guida (I)	Leitzins m	key rate	taux-clé d'intérêt bancaire m	—	tipos de referencia m pl
tasso d'interesse reale (I)	Realzins m	real (rate of) interest	rendement réel m	—	interés real m
tasso d'interesse variabile (I)	variabler Zins m	variable rate of interest	intérêt variable m	—	interés variable m
tasso di perdita (I)	Ausfallquote f	default rate	ratio de perte m	—	cuota de pérdida f
tasso di profitto (I)	Profitrate f	profit rate	taux de profit m	—	tasa de beneficio f
tasso d'occupazione (I)	Beschäftigungs-grad m	level of employment	taux d'emploi m	—	grado de empleo m
tasso interbancario (I)	Interbankrate f	interbank rate	taux interbancaire m	—	tipo interbancario m
tasso sulle anticipazioni (I)	Lombardsatz m	rate for advances on securities	taux d'intérêt de l'argent prêté sur gage m	—	tipo de pignoración m
tasso swap (I)	Swapsatz m	swap rate	taux de swap m	—	tasa swap f
Tastatur (D)	—	keyboard	clavier m	tastiera f	teclado m
tastiera (I)	Tastatur f	keyboard	clavier m	—	teclado m
Tätigkeitsfeld (D)	—	field of activity	champ d'acivité m	campo d'azione m	campo de actividad m
Tausch (D)	—	exchange/barter	échange m/troc m	scambio m/baratto m	cambio m/trueque m
Täuschung (D)	—	deceit	tromperie f	inganno m	engaño m
taux central (F)	Leitkurs m	central rate	—	parità centrale f	tipo pivote m
taux-clé d'intérêt bancaire (F)	Leitzins m	key rate	—	tasso d'interesse guida m	tipos de referencia m pl
taux d'accroissement (F)	Wachstumsrate f	rate of growth	—	tasso di crescita m	tasa de crecimiento f
taux de change (F)	Devisenkurs m	foreign exchange rate	—	cambio delle divise m	cambio m
taux de change fixe (F)	feste Wechselkurse pl	fixed exchange rates	—	cambi fissi m pl	tipos de cambio fijos m pl
taux de change flottant (F)	flexibler Wechselkurs m	flexible exchange rate	—	cambio flessibile m	tipo flotante de cambio m
taux de fret (F)	Frachtrate f	(freight) rate	—	tariffa di nolo f	tipo de flete m

	D	E	F	I	Es
taux de leasing (F)	Leasing-Rate *f*	leasing payment	—	rata leasing *f*	plazo de arrendamiento financiero *m*
taux d'emploi (F)	Beschäftigungsgrad *m*	level of employment	—	tasso d'occupazione *m*	grado de empleo *m*
taux de natalité (F)	Geburtenrate *f*	birth rate	—	tasso di natalità *m*	tasa de natalidad *f*
taux de profit (F)	Profitrate *f*	profit rate	—	tasso di profitto *m*	tasa de beneficio *f*
taux d'escompte (F)	Diskontsatz *m*	discount rate	—	saggio di sconto *m*	tasa de descuento *f*
taux de swap (F)	Swapsatz *m*	swap rate	—	tasso swap *m*	tasa swap *f*
taux d'inflation (F)	Inflationsrate *f*	rate of inflation	—	tasso d'inflazione *m*	tasa de inflación *f*
taux d'intérêt (F)	Zinsfuß *m*	interest rate	—	tasso d'interesse *m*	tipo de interés *m*
taux d'intérêt de l'argent prêté sur gage (F)	Lombardsatz *m*	rate for advances on securities	—	tasso sulle anticipazioni *m*	tipo de pignoración *m*
taux d'utilisation (F)	Ausnutzungsgrad *m*	utilization rate	—	grado di utilizzazione *m*	grado de utilización *m*
taux effectif (de l'intérêt) (F)	Effektivverzinsung *f*	effective interest yield	—	interessi effettivi *m pl*	interés efectivo *m*
taux interbancaire (F)	Interbankrate *f*	interbank rate	—	tasso interbancario *m*	tipo interbancario *m*
tax[1] (E)	Steuer *f*	—	impôt *m*	imposta *f*	impuesto *m*
tax[2] (E)	Abgabe *f*	—	taxe *f*	imposta *f*/dazio *m*	impuesto *m*/arancel *m*
tax adviser (E)	Steuerberater *m*	—	conseiller fiscal *m*	consulente fiscale *m*	asesor fiscal *m*
tax assessment (E)	Steuerveranlagung *f*	—	taxation fiscale *f*	accertamento tributario *m*	tasación de los impuestos *f*
taxation fiscale (F)	Steuerveranlagung *f*	tax assessment	—	accertamento tributario *m*	tasación de los impuestos *f*
tax authority (E)	Steuerbehörden *pl*	—	administration des contributions *f*	autorità fiscali *f pl*	administración de hacienda *f*
tax balance-sheet (E)	Steuerbilanz *f*	—	bilan fiscal *m*	bilancio fiscale *m*	balance impositivo *m*
taxe[1] (F)	Gebühr *f*	fee	—	tassa *f*	derecho *m*
taxe[2] (F)	Abgabe *f*	tax/duty	—	imposta *f*/dazio *m*	impuesto *m*/arancel *m*
taxe acquittée en nature (F)	Naturalabgabe *f*	duty in kind	—	imposta in natura *f*	impuesto en especie *m*
taxe à la valeur ajoutée (F)	Mehrwertsteuer *f*	value-added tax	—	imposta sul valore aggiunto *f*	impuesto sobre el valor añadido *m*
taxe à l'importation (F)	Einfuhrabgabe *f*	import duties	—	tassa d'importazione *f*	tasa a la importación *f*
taxe de chargement (F)	Ladegebühren *pl*	loading charges	—	spese di carico *f pl*	derechos de carga *m pl*
taxe de douane ad valorem (F)	Wertzoll *m*	ad valorem duty	—	dazio ad valorem *m*	aduanas ad valorem *f pl*
taxe de luxe (F)	Luxussteuer *f*	luxury tax	—	imposta sui consumi di lusso *f*	impuesto de lujo *m*
taxe de sortie (F)	Ausfuhrzoll *m*	export duty	—	dazio sull'esportazione *m*	derechos de exportación *m pl*
taxe d'expoitation de licence (F)	Lizenzgebühr *f*	royalty	—	tassa di licenza *f*	derecho de licencia *m*
taxe préférentielle de douane (F)	Präferenzzoll *m*	preferential duty	—	dazio preferenziale *m*	aduanas preferenciales *f pl*
taxe sur les sociétés (F)	Körperschaftsteuer *f*	corporation tax	—	imposta sul reddito delle società *f*	impuesto de corporaciones *m*
taxe sur les véhicules à moteur (F)	Kraftfahrzeugsteuer *f*	motor vehicle tax	—	imposta sulla circolazione degli autoveicoli *f*	impuesto sobre vehículos *m*
tax evasion (E)	Steuerhinterziehung *f*	—	dissimulation en matière fiscale *f*	evasione fiscale *f*	defraudación fiscal *f*
tax-free[1] (E)	abgabenfrei	—	exempt de taxes	esente da contributi	exento de derechos
tax-free[2] (E)	steuerfrei	—	dispensé de l'impôt	esente da imposte	libre de impuesto
tax haven (E)	Steueroase *f*	—	oasis fiscale *f*	oasi fiscale *f*	oasis fiscal *m*
tax on alcohol (E)	Alkoholsteuer *f*	—	impôt sur l'alcool *m*	imposta sugli alcolici *f*	impuesto sobre el alcohol *m*

	D	E	F	I	Es
tax on income (E)	Ertragsteuer f	—	impôt assis sur le produit m	imposta cedolare f/ imposta sul reddito f	impuesto sobre beneficios m
tax on investment income (E)	Kapitalertragsteuer f	—	impôt sur le revenu du capital m	imposta sulla rendita del capitale f	impuesto sobre la renta del capital m
taxpayer (E)	Steuerzahler m	—	contribuable m	contribuente m	contribuyente m
tax return (E)	Steuererklärung f	—	déclaration d'impôts f	dichiarazione dei redditi f	declaración a efectos fiscales f
Taxwert (D)	—	estimated value	valeur de taxation f	valore stimato m	valor de tasación m
Team (D)	—	team	équipe f	équipe f	equipo m
team¹ (E)	Mannschaft f	—	équipe f/équipage m	équipe f/ equipaggio m	equipo m/ tripulación f
team² (E)	Team n	—	équipe f	équipe f	equipo m
Teamarbeit (D)	—	team work	travail d'équipe m	lavoro d'équipe m	trabajo en equipo m
team work (E)	Teamarbeit f	—	travail d'équipe m	lavoro d'équipe m	trabajo en equipo m
technical (E)	technisch	—	technique	tecnico	técnico
technical book (E)	Fachbuch n	—	livre technique m	libro specializzato m	libro técnico m
technical standard (E)	technischer Standard m	—	standard technique m	standard tecnico m	standard técnico m
technical standards (E)	technische Normen pl	—	normes norme techniques f pl	tecniche f pl	normas técnicas f pl
technicien publicitaire (F)	Werbefachmann m	advertising expert	—	esperto di pubblicità m	perito publicitario m
Technik (D)	—	technique	technique f	tecnica f	técnica f/método m
technique (E)	Technik f	—	technique f	tecnica f	técnica f/método m
technique¹ (F)	Technik f	technique	—	tecnica f	técnica f/método m
technique² (F)	technisch	technical	—	tecnico	técnico
technique de conclusion (F)	Abschlußtechnik f	finishing technique	—	metodo di chiusura m	técnica de conclusión f
technique de pronostic (F)	Prognosetechnik f	forecasting techniques	—	tecnica della prognosi f	técnica de pronóstico f
technique de travail (F)	Arbeitstechnik f	working technique	—	tecnica lavorativa f	técnica del trabajo f
technique informatique (F)	Computertechnik f	computer technology	—	tecnica dei computer f	técnica informática f
technisch (D)	—	technical	technique	tecnico	técnico
technische Abteilung (D)	—	engineering department	service technique m	reparto tecnico m	departamento técnico m
technische Normen (D)	—	technical standards	normes techniques f pl	norme tecniche f pl	normas técnicas f pl
technischer Standard (D)	—	technical standard	standard technique m	standard tecnico m	standard técnico m
Technologie (D)	—	technology	technologie f	tecnologia f	tecnología f
technologie (F)	Technologie f	technology	—	tecnologia f	tecnología f
technologie d'information (F)	Informationstechnologie f	information technology	—	tecnologia d'informazione f	tecnología de información f
technology (E)	Technologie f	—	technologie f	tecnologia f	tecnología f
technology push (E)	Innovationsschub m	—	animation d'innovation f	spinta innovativa f	empuje innovador m
teclado (Es)	Tastatur f	keyboard	clavier m	tastiera f	—
técnica (Es)	Technik f	technique	technique f	tecnica f	—
tecnica (I)	Technik f	technique	technique f	—	técnica f/ método m
técnica de conclusión (Es)	Abschlußtechnik f	finishing technique	technique de conclusion f	metodo di chiusura m	—
tecnica dei computer (I)	Computertechnik f	computer technology	technique informatique f	—	técnica informática f
tecnica del trabajo (Es)	Arbeitstechnik f	working technique	technique de travail f	tecnica lavorativa f	—
tecnica della prognosi (I)	Prognosetechnik f	forecasting techniques	technique de pronostic f	—	técnica de pronóstico f
técnica de pronóstico (Es)	Prognosetechnik f	forecasting techniques	technique de pronostic f	tecnica della prognosi f	—

	D	E	F	I	Es
técnica de venta (Es)	Verkaufstechnik f	sales technique	art de vendre m	tecnica di vendita f	—
tecnica di vendita (I)	Verkaufstechnik f	sales technique	art de vendre m	—	técnica de venta f
técnica informática (Es)	Computertechnik f	computer technology	technique informatique f	tecnica dei computer f	—
tecnica lavorativa (I)	Arbeitstechnik f	working technique	technique de travail f	—	técnica del trabajo f
técnico (Es)	technisch	technical	technique	tecnico	—
tecnico (I)	technisch	technical	technique	—	técnico
tecnología (Es)	Technologie f	technology	technologie f	tecnologia f	—
tecnologia (I)	Technologie f	technology	technologie f	—	tecnología f
tecnología de información (Es)	Informations technologie f	information technology	technologie d'information f	tecnologia d'informazione f	—
tecnologia d'informazione (I)	Informations-technologie f	information technology	technologie d'information f	—	tecnología de información f
Teilhaber (D)	—	partner	associé m	socio m	socio m
Teillieferung (D)	—	partial delivery	livraison partielle f	fornitura parziale f	entrega parcial f
Teilnehmer (D)	—	participant	participant m	partecipante m	participante m
Teilnehmerliste (D)	—	list of participants	liste des participants f	lista dei partecipanti f	lista de participantes f
Teilprivatisierung (D)	—	partial denationalization	privatisation partielle f	privatizzazione parziale f	privatización parcial f
Teilwert (D)	—	partial value	valeur partielle f	valore parziale m	valor parcial m
Teilzahlung (D)	—	partial payment	payement partiel m	pagamento a rate m	pago parcial m
Teilzahlungs-geschäft (D)	—	partial payment transaction	achat à tempérament m	vendita a rate f	operación a plazo f
Teilzahlungspreis (D)	—	partial payment price	prix d'un achat à tempérament m	prezzo rateale m	precio de compras a plazo m
Teilzahlungsrate (D)	—	monthly instalment	mensualité d'un achat à tempérament f	rata f	plazo m
Teilzeitarbeit (D)	—	part-time work	travail à temps partiel m	lavoro part-time m	trabajo a tiempo parcial m
Teilzeitstelle (D)	—	part-time job	poste à temps partiel m	posto di lavoro part-time m	puesto de trabajo a tiempo parcial m
telefax number (E)	Telefaxnummer f	—	numéro de téléfax m	numero telefax m	número de telefax m
Telefaxnummer (D)	—	telefax number	numéro de téléfax m	numero telefax m	número de telefax m
Telefon (D)	—	telephone	téléphone m	telefono m	teléfono m
telefonata (I)	Telefongespräch n	telephone conversation	conversation téléphonique f	—	conferencia telefónica f
Telefondienst (D)	—	telephone service	service du téléphone m	servizio telefonico m	servicio telefónico m
Telefongespräch (D)	—	telephone conversation	conversation téléphonique f	telefonata f	conferencia telefónica f
Telefonnummer (D)	—	telephone number	numéro de téléphone m	numero di telefono m	número de teléfono m
teléfono¹ (Es)	Fernsprecher m	telephone	appareil téléphonique m	telefono m	—
teléfono² (Es)	Telefon n	telephone	téléphone m	telefono m	—
telefono¹ (I)	Fernsprecher m	telephone	appareil téléphonique m	—	teléfono m
telefono² (I)	Telefon n	telephone	téléphone m	—	teléfono m
Telefonverkauf (D)	—	inter-office sale	vente par téléphone f	vendita per telefono f	venta por teléfono f
Telegraf (D)	—	telegraph	télégraphe m	telegrafo m	telégrafo m
telegrafare (I)	telegrafieren	send a telegram	télégraphier	—	telegrafiar
telegrafiar (Es)	telegrafieren	send a telegram	télégraphier	telegrafare	—
telegrafieren (D)	—	send a telegram	télégraphier	telegrafare	telegrafiar
telegrafische Anweisung (D)	—	telegraphic payment order	mandat télégraphique m	vaglia telegrafico m	orden telegráfica f
telégrafo (Es)	Telegraf m	telegraph	télégraphe m	telegrafo m	—
telegrafo (I)	Telegraf m	telegraph	télégraphe m	—	telégrafo m
telegram (E)	Telegramm n	—	télégramme m	telegramma m	telegrama m

	D	E	F	I	Es
telegrama (Es)	Telegramm n	telegram	télégramme m	telegramma m	—
Telegramm (D)	—	telegram	télégramme m	telegramma m	telegrama m
telegramma (I)	Telegramm n	telegram	télégramme m	—	telegrama m
télégramme (F)	Telegramm n	telegram	—	telegramma m	telegrama m
telegraph (E)	Telegraf m	—	télégraphe m	telegrafo m	telégrafo m
télégraphe (F)	Telegraf m	telegraph	—	telegrafo m	telégrafo m
telegraphic payment order (E)	telegrafische Anweisung f	—	mandat télégraphique m	vaglia telegrafico m	orden telegráfica f
télégraphier (F)	telegrafieren	send a telegram	—	telegrafare	telegrafiar
téléimprimeur (F)	Fernschreiber m	teleprinter	—	telescrivente m	télex m
telephone¹ (E)	Telefon n	—	téléphone m	telefono m	teléfono m
telephone² (E)	Fernsprecher m	—	appareil téléphonique m	telefono m	teléfono m
téléphone (F)	Telefon n	telephone	—	telefono m	teléfono m
telephone conversation (E)	Telefongespräch n	—	conversation téléphonique f	telefonata f	conferencia telefónica f
telephone exchange (E)	Fernmeldeamt n	—	service de télécommunication m	ufficio telecomunicazioni m	central interurbana f
telephone number (E)	Telefonnummer f	—	numéro de téléphone m	numero di telefono m	número de teléfono m
telephone service (E)	Telefondienst m	—	service du téléphone m	servizio telefonico m	servicio telefónico m
teleprinter (E)	Fernschreiber m	—	téléimprimeur m	telescrivente m	télex m
telescrivente (I)	Fernschreiber m	teleprinter	téléimprimeur m	—	télex m
teletex number (E)	Teletexnummer f	—	numéro de télétex m	numero teletex m	número de téletex m
Teletexnummer (D)	—	teletex number	numéro de télétex m	numero teletex m	número de téletex m
teletexto (Es)	Bildschirmtext m	videotext	videotex international m	videotex m	—
télétransmission des données informatiques (F)	Datenfern-übertragung f	remote data transmission	—	teletrasmissione dati f	transmisión de datos f
teletrasmissione dati (I)	Datenfern-übertragung f	remote data transmission	télétransmission des données informatiques f	—	transmisión de datos f
television advertising (E)	Fernsehwerbung f	—	émission publicitaire télévisée f	pubblicità televisiva f	publicidad televisiva f
televisione via cavo (I)	Kabelfernsehen n	cable television	télévision par câble f	—	televisión por cable f
télévision par câble (F)	Kabelfernsehen n	cable television	—	televisione via cavo f	televisión por cable f
televisión por cable (Es)	Kabelfernsehen n	cable television	télévision par câble f	televisione via cavo f	—
télex (Es)	Fernschreiber m	teleprinter	téléimprimeur m	telescrivente m	—
Telexanschluß (D)	—	telex connection	communication de télex f	collegamento telex m	comunicación de télex f
telex connection (E)	Telexanschluß m	—	communication de télex f	collegamento telex m	comunicación de télex f
telex number (E)	Telexnummer f	—	numéro de télex m	numero telex m	número de télex m
Telexnummer (D)	—	telex number	numéro de télex m	numero telex m	número de télex m
tempo d'attesa (I)	Wartezeit f	waiting time	temps d'attente m	—	tiempo de espera m
tempo impiegato (I)	Zeitaufwand m	expenditure of time	temps passé m	—	tiempo consagrado m
tempo pezzo (I)	Stückzeit f	piece time	temps par pièce m	—	tiempo por unidad m
temporada (Es)	Saison f	season	saison f	stagione f	—
temporaneo (I)	einstweilig	temporary	provisoire	—	provisional
temporary (E)	einstweilig	—	provisoire	temporaneo	provisional
temporary injunction (E)	einstweilige Verfügung f	—	ordonnance sur référé civil f	provvedimento temporaneo m	interdicto provisorio m
temps d'attente (F)	Wartezeit f	waiting time	—	tempo d'attesa m	tiempo de espera m
temps de travail annuel (F)	Jahresarbeitszeit f	annual hours of work	—	orario di lavoro annuale m	jornada anual f

	D	E	F	I	Es
temps par pièce (F)	Stückzeit f	piece time	—	tempo pezzo m	tiempo por unidad m
temps passé (F)	Zeitaufwand m	expenditure of time	—	tempo impiegato m	tiempo consagrado m
tenant (E)	Mieter m	—	locataire m	locatario m	inquilino m/ arrendatario m
tendance (F)	Tendenz f	tendency	—	tendenza f	tendencia f
tendance à la hausse (F)	Reprise f	repeat	—	ripresa f	segunda lectura en el corro f
tendance générale (F)	Trend m	trend	—	tendenza f	tendencia f
tendant à l'expansion (F)	expansiv	expansive	—	espansivo	expansivo
tendencia[1] (Es)	Tendenz f	tendency	tendance f	tendenza f	—
tendencia[2] (Es)	Trend m	trend	tendance générale f	tendenza f	—
tendencia alcista (Es)	Aufwärtstrend m	upward trend	mouvement ascendant m	tendenza al rialzo f	—
tendencia bajista (Es)	Abwärtstrend m	downward trend	baisse f	tendenza al ribasso f	—
tendency (E)	Tendenz f	—	tendance f	tendenza f	tendencia f
Tendenz (D)	—	tendency	tendance f	tendenza f	tendencia f
tendenza[1] (I)	Tendenz f	tendency	tendance f	—	tendencia f
tendenza[2] (I)	Trend m	trend	tendance générale f	—	tendencia f
tendenza al rialzo (I)	Aufwärtstrend m	upward trend	mouvement ascendant m	—	tendencia alcista f
tendenza al ribasso (I)	Abwärtstrend m	downward trend	baisse f	—	tendencia bajista f
tender (E)	Ausschreibung f	—	soumission f	appalto m	concurso-subasta m
tender guarantee (E)	Bietungsgarantie f	—	cautionnement provisoire m	garanzia d'offerta f	caución de licitación f
tender procedure (E)	Tenderverfahren n	—	offre d'emprunts pour la régulation monétaire f	offerta pubblica d'acquisto f	subasta de prestamos de regulación monetaria f
Tenderverfahren (D)	—	tender procedure	offre d'emprunts pour la régulation monétaire f	offerta pubblica d'acquisto f	subasta de prestamos de regulación monetaria f
tenedor de libros (Es)	Buchhalter m	bookkeeper	comptable m	ragioniere m	—
tener en almacén (Es)	auf Lager haben	have in stock	avoir en stock	avere in magazzino	—
tenore di vita (I)	Lebensstandard m	standard of living	niveau de vie m		nivel de vida m
tenue de compte (F)	Kontoführung f	keeping of an account	—	tenuta di un conto f	administración de una cuenta f
tenuta di un conto (I)	Kontoführung f	keeping of an account	tenue de compte f	—	administración de una cuenta f
teoría (Es)	Theorie f	theory	théorie f	teoria f	
teoria (I)	Theorie f	theory	théorie f	—	teoría f
teoría de la empresa (Es)	Betriebswirtschafts-lehre f	business administration	(science de la) gestion industrielle et commerciale f	economia aziendale f	—
teoría de la información (Es)	Informationstheorie f	information theory	théorie d'information f	teoria dell'informazione f	—
teoria del capitale (I)	Kapitaltheorie f	capital theory	théorie du capital f	—	teoría financiera f
teoria del denaro (I)	Geldtheorie f	monetary theory	théorie monétaire f	—	teoría monetaria f
teoría del empleo (Es)	Beschäftigungs-theorie f	employment theory	théorie d'emploi f	teoria dell'occupazione f	—
teoria della produzione (I)	Produktionstheorie f	production theory	théorie de la production f	—	teoría de producción f
teoria dell'economia (I)	Wirtschaftstheorie f	economic theory	théorie économique f	—	teoría económica f
teoria dell'inflazione (I)	Inflationstheorie f	inflationary theory	théorie d'inflation f	—	teoria inflacionista f
teoria dell'informazione (I)	Informationstheorie f	information theory	théorie d'information f	—	teoría de la información f
teoria dell'occupazione (I)	Beschäftigungs-theorie f	employment theory	théorie d'emploi f	—	teoría del empleo f
teoría de los precios (Es)	Preistheorie f	theory of prices	théorie des prix f	teoria del prezzo f	—

	D	E	F	I	Es
teoría del prezzo (I)	Preistheorie *f*	theory of prices	théorie des prix *f*	—	teoría de los precios *f*
teoría de producción (Es)	Produktionstheorie *f*	production theory	théorie de la production *f*	teoria della produzione *f*	—
teoría económica (Es)	Wirtschaftstheorie *f*	economic theory	théorie économique *f*	teoria dell'economia *f*	—
teoría financiera (Es)	Kapitaltheorie *f*	capital theory	théorie du capital *f*	teoria del capitale *f*	—
teoría inflacionista (Es)	Inflationstheorie *f*	inflationary theory	théorie d'inflation *f*	teoria dell'inflazione *f*	—
teoría monetaria (Es)	Geldtheorie *f*	monetary theory	théorie monétaire *f*	teoria del denaro *f*	—
terceros países (Es)	Drittländer *pl*	third countries	pays tiers *m pl*	paesi terzi *m pl*	—
term (E)	Laufzeit *f*	—	durée *f*	scadenza *f*/durata *f*	plazo de vencimiento *m*
terme du payement (F)	Zahlungstermin *m*	date of payment	—	termine di pagamento *m*	plazo de pago *m*
Termin (D)	—	deadline	date limite *f*	termine *m*	fecha *f*/cita *f*/ plazo *m*
terminación total (Es)	Fertigstellung *f*	completion	achèvement *m*	completamento *m*	—
Terminal (D)	—	terminal	terminal *m*	terminale *m*	terminal *m*
terminal (E)	Terminal *m*	—	terminal *m*	terminale *m*	terminal *m*
terminal (Es)	Terminal *m*	terminal	terminal *m*	terminale *m*	—
terminal (F)	Terminal *m*	terminal	—	terminale *m*	terminal *m*
terminale (I)	Terminal *m*	terminal	terminal *m*	—	terminal *m*
terminal operator (E)	Datentypistin *f*	—	perforatrice *f*	dattilografa *f*	perforadora *f*
terminate (E)	kündigen	—	résilier	disdire	denunciar/dar aviso de despido
Termination of Employment Act (E)	Kündigungsschutz-gesetz *n*	—	loi sur le délai-congé en matière de licenciement *f*	legge sulla tutela contro il licenziamento *f*	ley de protección contra el despido *f*
Terminbörse (D)	—	futures market	bourse à terme *f*	mercato a termine *m*	bolsa de valores a término *f*
termine[1] (I)	Termin *m*	deadline	date limite *f*	—	fecha *f*/cita *f*/ plazo *m*
termine[2] (I)	Frist *f*	period	délai *m*	—	plazo *m*
termine del colloquio (I)	Besprechungs-termin *m*	meeting date	date de la conférence *f*	—	fecha de conferencia *f*
termine di consegna[1] (I)	Liefertermin *m*	date of delivery	délai de livraison *m*	—	plazo de entrega *m*
termine di consegna[2] (I)	Lieferfrist *f*	time for delivery	délai de livraison *m*	—	plazo de entrega *m*
termine di denuncia (I)	Anmeldefrist *f*	time for application	délai de déclaration *m*	—	plazo de solicitud *m*
termine di pagamento[1] (I)	Zahlungsziel *n*	period for payment	délai de payement *m*	—	plazo de pago *m*
termine di pagamento[2] (I)	Zahlungstermin *m*	date of payment	terme du payement *m*	—	plazo de pago *m*
termine di preavviso per la disdetta (I)	Kündigungsfrist *f*	period of notice	délai de préavis *m*	—	plazo de preaviso *m*
termine di scadenza (I)	Ablauffrist *f*	time limit	délai *m*	—	vencimiento *m*
termine supplementare (I)	Nachfrist *f*	additional period	prolongation *f*	—	plazo de gracia *m*
termingerecht (D)	—	on schedule	dans les délais	puntuale	en la fecha fijada
Termingeschäft (D)	—	time bargain	opération à terme *f*	operazione a termine *f*	operación a plazo *f*
Terminkontrakt (D)	—	forward contract	contrat à terme *m*	contratto a termine *m*	contrato de entrega futura *m*
Terminkurs (D)	—	forward price	cours de bourse à terme *m*	corso a termine *m*	cambio a término *m*
Terminplanung (D)	—	scheduling	planning de rendez-vous *m*	programmazione dei termini *f*	planificación de plazos *f*
term life insurance (E)	Risiko-Lebens-versicherung *f*	—	assurance-vie temporaire *f*	assicurazione rischio-vita *f*	seguro de vida temporal *m*
term of contract (E)	Vertragsbedingung *f*	—	condition du contrat *f*	condizione del contratto *f*	condiciones contractuales *f pl*

	D	E	F	I	Es
term of protection (E)	Schutzfrist f	—	délai de protection m	durata della protezione f	plazo de protección m
terms of conveyance (E)	Beförderungsbedingungen f	—	conditions de transport f pl	condizioni di trasporto f pl	condiciones de transporte f pl
terms of delivery (E)	Lieferbedingungen pl	—	conditions de livraison f pl	condizioni di consegna f pl	condiciones de suminstro f pl
terms of payment¹ (E)	Zahlungsbedingung f	—	conditions de payement f pl	condizione di pagamento f	condiciones de pago f pl
terms of payment² (E)	Zahlungsfrist f	—	délai de payement f	scadenza di pagamento f	plazo de pago m
terra (I)	Boden m	ground/soil	sol m/terrain m	—	suelo m/ terreno m
terrain (F)	Grundstück n	real estate	—	terreno m	terreno m
terreno (Es)	Grundstück n	real estate	terrain m	terreno m	—
terreno (I)	Grundstück n	real estate	terrain m	—	terreno m
terreno edificable (Es)	Bauland n	building land	espace à bâtir m	area edificabile f	—
territoire considéré hors frontière douanière nationale (F)	Zollausschluß m	territory inside political but outside customs frontier	—	zona franca f	exclave aduanero m
territoire de surveillance douanière (F)	Zollgrenzgebiet n	customs frontier district	—	area doganale di confine f	territorio aduanero fronterizo m
territoire de vente (F)	Verkaufsgebiet n	sales territory	—	zona di vendita f	territorio de venta m
territoire douanier¹ (F)	Zollgebiet n	customs territory	—	territorio doganale m	distrito aduanero m
territoire douanier² (F)	Zollinland n	domestic customs territory	—	territorio doganale nazionale m	territorio aduanero interior m
territoire hors du contrôle de la douane (F)	Zollausland n	foreign customs territory	—	territorio doganale estero m	territorio aduanero exterior m
territorial jurisdiction (E)	Gebietshoheit f	—	souveraineté territoriale f	sovranità territoriale f	soberanía territorial f
territorio aduanero exterior (Es)	Zollausland n	foreign customs territory	territoire hors du contrôle de la douane m	territorio doganale estero m	—
territorio aduanero fronterizo (Es)	Zollgrenzgebiet n	customs frontier district	territoire de surveillance douanière m	area doganale di confine f	—
territorio aduanero interior (Es)	Zollinland n	domestic customs territory	territoire douanier national m	territorio doganale nazionale m	—
territorio de venta (Es)	Verkaufsgebiet n	sales territory	territoire de vente m	zona di vendita f	—
territorio doganale (I)	Zollgebiet n	customs territory	territoire douanier m	—	distrito aduanero m
territorio doganale estero (I)	Zollausland n	foreign customs territory	territoire hors du contrôle de la douane m	—	territorio aduanero exterior m
territorio doganale nazionale (I)	Zollinland n	domestic customs territory	territoire douanier national m	—	territorio aduanero interior m
territory inside political but outside customs frontier (E)	Zollausschluß m	—	territoire considéré hors frontière douanière nationale m	zona franca f	exclave aduanero m
territory protection (E)	Gebietsschutz m	—	exclusivité territoriale f	tutela territoriale f	protección territorial f
tesorería (Es)	Schatzamt n	Treasury	trésor m	tesoreria f	—
tesoreria (I)	Schatzamt n	Treasury	trésor m	—	tesorería f
tessera aziendale (I)	Betriebsausweis m	staff identification card	pièce d'identité de l'entreprise f	—	carné de empresa f
Test (D)	—	test	test m	test m	test m
test (E)	Test m	—	test m	test m	test m
test (Es)	Test m	test	test m	test m	—
test (F)	Test m	test	—	test m	test m
test (I)	Test m	test	test m	—	test m
testaferro (Es)	Strohmann m	man of straw/ dummy	prête-nom m	prestanome m	—
Testament (D)	—	last will	testament m	testamento m	testamento m
testament (F)	Testament n	last will	—	testamento m	testamento m
testamento (Es)	Testament n	last will	testament m	testamento m	—
testamento (I)	Testament n	last will	testament m	—	testamento m

	D	E	F	I	Es
Testaments-eröffnung (D)	—	opening of the will	ouverture du testament *f*	apertura del testamento *f*	apertura de testamento *f*
test di mercato (I)	Markttest *m*	market test	test du marché *m*	—	examinación del mercado *f*
test du marché (F)	Markttest *m*	market test	—	test di mercato *m*	examinación del mercado *f*
Testläden (D)	—	test shops	magasins de test *m pl*	negozi pilota *m pl*	tiendas piloto *f pl*
test market (E)	Testmarkt *m*	—	marché de test *m*	mercato pilota *m*	mercado piloto *m*
Testmarkt (D)	—	test market	marché de test *m*	mercato pilota *m*	mercado piloto *m*
testo pubblicitario (I)	Werbetext *m*	advertising copy	texte publicitaire *m*	—	texto publicitario *m*
test shops (E)	Testläden *pl*	—	magasins de test *m pl*	negozi pilota *m pl*	tiendas piloto *f pl*
text configuration (E)	Textgestaltung *f*	—	structure du texte *f*	redazione del testo *f*	estructuración del texto *f*
texte publicitaire (F)	Werbetext *m*	advertising copy	—	testo pubblicitario *m*	texto publicitario *m*
Textgestaltung (D)	—	text configuration	structure du texte *f*	redazione del testo *f*	estructuración del texto *f*
texto publicitario (Es)	Werbetext *m*	advertising copy	texte publicitaire *m*	testo pubblicitario *m*	—
Textverarbeitung (D)	—	word processing	élaboration de texte *f*	elaborazione testi *f*	tratamiento de textos *m*
theft (E)	Diebstahl *m*	—	vol *m*	furto *m*	robo *m*
Theorie (D)	—	theory	théorie *f*	teoria *f*	teoría *f*
théorie (F)	Theorie *f*	theory	—	teoria *f*	teoría *f*
théorie de la production (F)	Produktionstheorie *f*	production theory	—	teoria della produzione *f*	teoría de producción *f*
théorie d'emploi (F)	Beschäftigungs-theorie *f*	employment theory	—	teoria dell'occupazione *f*	teoría del empleo *f*
théorie des prix (F)	Preistheorie *f*	theory of prices	—	teoria del prezzo *f*	teoría de los precios *f*
théorie d'inflation (F)	Inflationstheorie *f*	inflationary theory	—	teoria dell'inflazione *f*	teoría inflacionista *f*
théorie d'information (F)	Informationstheorie *f*	information theory	—	teoria dell'informazione *f*	teoría de la información *f*
théorie du capital (F)	Kapitaltheorie *f*	capital theory	—	teoria del capitale *f*	teoría financiera *f*
théorie économique (F)	Wirtschaftstheorie *f*	economic theory	—	teoria dell'economia *f*	teoría económica *f*
théorie monétaire (F)	Geldtheorie *f*	monetary theory	—	teoria del denaro *f*	teoría monetaria *f*
theory (E)	Theorie *f*	—	théorie *f*	teoria *f*	teoría *f*
theory of prices (E)	Preistheorie *f*	—	théorie des prix *f*	teoria del prezzo *f*	teoría de los precios *f*
third countries (E)	Drittländer *pl*	—	pays tiers *m pl*	paesi terzi *m pl*	terceros países *m pl*
third party liability insurance (E)	Haftpflicht-versicherung *f*	—	assurance responsabilité civile *f*	assicurazione della responsabilità civile *f*	seguro de responsabilidad civil *m*
three months papers (E)	Dreimonatspapier *n*	—	titre à trois mois *m*	titolo trimestrale *m*	títulos a tres meses *m*
threshold price[1] (E)	Schwellenpreis *m*	—	prix de seuil *m*	prezzo soglia *m*	precio-base *m*
threshold price[2] (E)	Preisschwelle *f*	—	seuil du prix *m*	soglia dei prezzi *f*	umbral de precios *m*
tied production (E)	Koppelproduktion *f*	—	production couplée *f*	produzione abbinata *f*	coproducción *f*
tie-in transaction (E)	Kopplungsgeschäft *n*	—	affaire couplée *f*	operazione abbinata *f*	negocio acoplado *m*
tiempo consagrado (Es)	Zeitaufwand *m*	expenditure of time	temps passé *m*	tempo impiegato *m*	—
tiempo de espera (Es)	Wartezeit *f*	waiting time	temps d'attente *m*	tempo d'attesa *m*	—
tiendas piloto (Es)	Testläden *pl*	test shops	magasins de test *m pl*	negozi pilota *m pl*	—
Tierzucht (D)	—	livestock breeding	élevage *m*	zootecnia *f*	cría de animales *f*
Tilgung (D)	—	redemption	amortissement *m*	ammortamento *m*	amortización *f*
timbre-poste (F)	Briefmarke *f*	stamp	—	francobollo *m*	sello *m*

	D	E	F	I	Es
timbro postale (I)	Poststempel m	postmark	cachet de la poste m	—	sello postal m
time bargain (E)	Termingeschäft n	—	opération à terme f	operazione a termine f	operación a plazo f
time deposit account (E)	Festgeldkonto n	—	compte de dépôt à terme m	deposito vincolato m	cuenta a plazo f
time for application (E)	Anmeldefrist f	—	délai de déclaration m	termine di denuncia m	plazo de solicitud m
time for delivery (E)	Lieferfrist f	—	délai de livraison m	termine di consegna m	plazo de entrega m
time limit (E)	Ablauffrist f	—	délai m	termine di scadenza m	vencimiento m
timely (E)	fristgerecht	—	dans les délais	entro il termine convenuto	dentro del plazo fijado
time study (E)	Zeitstudie f	—	étude des temps f	analisi sul tempo impiegato f	estudio de tiempo m
time wage (E)	Zeitlohn m	—	salaire au temps m	salario a tempo m	salario por unidad de tiempo m
tino de negociar (Es)	Verhandlungs-geschick n	negotiation skills	habileté en matière de négociations f	abilità nel trattare f	—
tip (E)	Bedienungsgeld n	—	pourboire m	diritto di servizio m	propina f
tipi di costi (I)	Kostenarten pl	cost types	coûts par nature m pl	—	clases de costes f pl
tipi di mercato (I)	Marktformen pl	types of markets	formes du marché f pl	—	formas del mercado f
tipo de cambio (Es)	Wechselkurs m	exchange rate	cours du change m	cambio m	—
tipo de cambio de billetes y monedas extranjeras (Es)	Sortenkurs m	rate for foreign notes and coin	cours des monnaies étrangères m	corso dei cambi m	—
tipo de cambio múltiple (Es)	gespaltene Wechselkurse pl	two-tier exchange rate	cours du change multiple m	cambi multipli m pl	—
tipo de emisión (Es)	Emissionskurs m	price of issue	cours d'émission m	prezzo d'emissione m	—
tipo de flete (Es)	Frachtrate f	(freight) rate	taux de fret m	tariffa di nolo f	—
tipo de interés (Es)	Zinsfuß m	interest rate	taux d'intérêt m	tasso d'interesse m	—
tipo de pignoración (Es)	Lombardsatz m	rate for advances on securities	taux d'intérêt de l'argent prêté sur gage m	tasso sulle anticipazioni m	—
tipo di merce (I)	Warenart f	class of goods	catégorie de marchandise f	—	categoría de mercancías f
tipo d'inserzione (I)	Anzeigengestaltung f	lay out of an advertisement	arrangement de l'annonce m	—	estructuración del anuncio f
tipo di pagamento (I)	Zahlungsform f	payment system	forme de payement f	—	forma de pago f
tipo di spedizione (I)	Versandform f	manner of delivery	forme d'expéditoin f	—	forma de envío f
tipo flotante de cambio (Es)	flexibler Wechselkurs m	flexible exchange rate	taux de change flottant m	cambio flessibile m	—
tipo interbancario (Es)	Interbankrate f	interbank rate	taux interbancaire m	tasso interbancario m	—
tipo pivote (Es)	Leitkurs m	central rate	taux central m	parità centrale f	—
tipos de cambio fijos (Es)	feste Wechselkurse pl	fixed exchange rates	taux de change fixe m	cambi fissi m pl	—
tipos de referencia (Es)	Leitzins m	key rate	taux-clé d'intérêt bancaire	tasso d'interesse guida m	—
tirage d'une traite de cavalerie (F)	Wechselreiterei f	kiteflying	—	emissione di tratte incrociate f	libramiento de letras cruzadas m
tiré (F)	Bezogener m	drawee	—	trattario m	librado m
Titel (D)	—	title	titre m	titolo m	título m
title (E)	Titel m	—	titre m	titolo m	título m
titolare del conto (I)	Kontoinhaber m	account holder	titulaire d'un compte m	—	titular de una cuenta m
titolare unico (I)	Alleininhaber m	sole owner	seul propriétaire m	—	propietario exclusivo m
titoli (I)	Effekten f	securities	valeurs mobilières f pl	—	efectos m pl
titoli a reddito fisso (I)	Rentenpapiere pl	bonds	titres de rente m pl	—	títulos de renta fija m pl

	D	E	F	I	Es
titoli a reddito variabile (I)	Dividendenpapiere *pl*	dividend-bearing shares	titre donnant droit à des dividendes *m*	—	títulos de renta variable *m pl*
titoli d'investimento (I)	Anlagepapiere *pl*	investment securities	valeurs de placement *f*	—	valores de inversión *m pl*
titoli pubblici (I)	Staatsanleihen *pl*	government loan	emprunt d'Etat *m*	—	empréstito estatal *m*
titolo¹ (I)	Titel *m*	title	titre *m*	—	título *m*
titolo² (I)	Feingehalt *m*	fine gold content	titre *m*	—	ley *f*
titolo³ (I)	Anrede *f*	form of address	début de lettre *m*	—	tratamiento *m*
titolo⁴ (I)	Wertpapier *n*	security	titre *m*/valeur *f*	—	título *m*/valor *m*
titolo all'ordine (I)	Orderpapier *n*	instruments (made out) to order	papier à ordre *m*	—	título a la orden *m*
titolo al portatore (I)	Inhaberpapier *n*	bearer instrument	titre souscrit au porteur *m*	—	título al portador *m*
titolo ipotecario (I)	Pfandbrief *m*	mortgage bond	obligation hypothécaire *f*	—	cédula hipotecaria *f*
titolo trimestrale (I)	Dreimonatspapier *n*	three months papers	titre à trois mois *m*	—	títulos a tres meses *m*
titre¹ (F)	Titel *m*	title	—	titolo *m*	título *m*
titre² (F)	Rechtsanspruch *m*	legal claim	—	pretesa giuridica *f*	pretensión legal *f*
titre³ (F)	Wertpapier *n*	security	—	titolo *m*	título *m*/valor *m*
titre à trois mois (F)	Dreimonatspapier *n*	three months papers	—	titolo trimestrale *m*	títulos a tres meses *m*
titre donnant droit à des dividendes (F)	Dividendenpapiere *pl*	dividend-bearing shares	—	titoli a reddito variabile *m pl*	títulos de renta variable *m pl*
titre souscrit au porteur (F)	Inhaberpapier *n*	bearer instrument	—	titolo al portatore *m*	título al portador *m*
titulaire d'un compte (F)	Kontoinhaber *m*	account holder	—	titolare del conto *m*	titular de una cuenta *m*
titular de una cuenta (Es)	Kontoinhaber *m*	account holder	titulaire d'un compte *m*	titolare del conto *m*	—
título¹ (Es)	Wertpapier *n*	security	titre *m*/valeur *f*	titolo *m*	—
título² (Es)	Titel *m*	title	titre *m*	titolo *m*	—
título al portador (Es)	Inhaberpapier *n*	bearer instrument	titre souscrit au porteur *m*	titolo al portatore *m*	—
títulos a tres meses (Es)	Dreimonatspapier *n*	three months papers	titre à trois mois *m*	titolo trimestrale *m*	—
títulos de renta fija (Es)	Rentenpapiere *pl*	bonds	titres de rente *m pl*	titoli a reddito fisso *m pl*	—
títulos de renta variable (Es)	Dividendenpapiere *pl*	dividend-bearing shares	titre donnant droit à des dividendes *m*	titoli a reddito variabile *m pl*	—
Tochter-gesellschaft (D)	—	subsidiary	société filiale *f*	società affiliata *f*	filial *f*
toilet (E)	Toilette *f*	—	toilettes *f pl*	toilette *f*	lavabo *m*
Toilette (D)	—	toilet	toilettes *f pl*	toilette *f*	lavabo *m*
toilette (I)	Toilette *f*	toilet	toilettes *f pl*	—	lavabo *m*
toilettes (F)	Toilette *f*	toilet	—	toilette *f*	lavabo *m*
tolleranza (I)	Spielraum *m*	margin	marge *f*	—	margen *f*
tomador (Es)	Abnehmer *m*	buyer/purchaser/customer	acheteur *m*	acquirente *m*/cliente *m*	—
tonelada de registro (Es)	Registertonne *f*	register ton	tonneau de jauge *m*	tonnellata di registro *f*	—
tonelada de registro bruto (Es)	Bruttoregistertonne *f*	gross register(ed) ton	tonneau de jauge brute *m*	tonnellata di stazza lorda *f*	—
tonneau de jauge (F)	Registertonne *f*	register ton	—	tonnellata di registro *f*	tonelada de registro *f*
tonneau de jauge brute (F)	Bruttoregistertonne *f*	gross register(ed) ton	—	tonnellata di stazza lorda *f*	tonelada de registro bruto *f*
tonnellata di registro (I)	Registertonne *f*	register ton	tonneau de jauge *m*	—	tonelada de registro *f*
tonnellata di stazza lorda (I)	Bruttoregistertonne *f*	gross register(ed) ton	tonneau de jauge brute *m*	—	tonelada de registro bruto *f*
top price (E)	Höchstpreis *m*	—	prix plafond *m*	prezzo massimo *m*	precio máximo *m*

	D	E	F	I	Es
top wage (E)	Spitzenlohn *m*	—	salaire maximum *m*	salario massimo *m*	salario máximo *m*
total amout (E)	Gesamtsumme *f*	—	montant total *m*	importo totale *m*	suma total *f*
total costs (E)	Gesamtkosten *pl*	—	coût total *m*	costi totali *m pl*	gastos generales *m pl*
total delivery (E)	Gesamtlieferung *f*	—	livraison totale *f*	fornitura completa *f*	suministro total *f*
total loss (E)	Totalschaden *m*	—	dommage total *m*	danno totale *m*	daño total *m*
total of indebtedness (E)	Schuldenmasse *f*	—	passif *m*	massa passiva *f*	masa pasiva *f*
Totalschaden (D)	—	total loss	dommage total *m*	danno totale *m*	daño total *m*
totes Kapital (D)	—	unproductive capital	capital improductif *m*	capitale infruttifero *m*	capital improductivo *m*
tour schedule (E)	Tourenplan *m*	—	itinéraire *m*	programma dell'itinerario *m*	itinerario *m*
Tourenplan (D)	—	tour schedule	itinéraire *m*	programma dell'itinerario *m*	itinerario *m*
town planning (E)	Städtebau *m*	—	urbanisme *m*	urbanistica *f*	urbanización *f*
trabajador (Es)	Arbeiter *m*	worker	travailleur *m*	operaio *m*	—
trabajadores extranjeros (Es)	ausländische Arbeitnehmer *m*	foreign workers	travailleurs étrangers *m*	prestatori d'opera stranieri *m pl*	—
trabajo (Es)	Arbeit *f*	work	travail *m*	lavoro *m*	—
trabajo a destajo (Es)	Akkordarbeit *f*	piecework	travail à la tâche *m*	lavora a cottimo *m*	—
trabajo a domicilio (Es)	Heimarbeit *f*	homework	travail à domicile *m*	lavoro a domicilio *m*	—
trabajo a mano (Es)	Handarbeit *f*	handwork	travail manuel *m*	lavoro manuale *m*	—
trabajo a tiempo parcial (Es)	Teilzeitarbeit *f*	part-time work	travail à temps partiel *m*	lavoro part-time *m*	—
trabajo clandestino (Es)	Schwarzarbeit *f*	illicit work	travail noir *m*	lavoro abusivo *m*	—
trabajo de pantalla (Es)	Bildschirmarbeit *f*	screen work	travail à l'écran	lavoro video *m*	—
trabajo dominical (Es)	Sonntagsarbeit *f*	Sunday work	travail du dimanche *m*	lavoro domenicale *m*	—
trabajo en equipo (Es)	Teamarbeit *f*	team work	travail d'équipe *m*	lavoro d'équipe *m*	—
trabajo extraordinario (Es)	Mehrarbeit *f*	additional work	travail supplémentaire *m*	lavoro supplementare *m*	—
trabajo reducido (Es)	Kurzarbeit *f*	short-time work	travail à temps réduit *m*	lavoro ad orario ridotto *m*	—
trade¹ (E)	Gewerbe *n*	—	activité professionnelle *f*/industrie *f*/ arsanat *f*	commercio *m*/ industria *f*/ artigianato *m*	industria *f*/ comercio *m*/ artesanía *f*
trade² (E)	Handel *m*	—	commerce *m*	commercio *m*	comercio *m*
trade analysis (E)	Branchenanalyse *f*	—	analyse des branches *f*	analisi di categoria *f*	análisis del ramo *m*
trade association (E)	Wirtschaftsverband *m*	—	association économique *f*	associazione economica *f*	asociación económica *f*
trade centre (E)	Handelsplatz *m*	—	place marchande *f* commerciale *f*	piazza	plaza comercial *f*
trade comparison (E)	Branchenvergleich *m*	—	comparaison des différentes branches *f*	comparazione delle categorie *f*	comparación de ramos *f*
trade credit (E)	Warenkredit *m*	—	avance sur marchandises *f*	credito su merci *m*	crédito comercial *m*
trade deficit (E)	Außenhandelsdefizit *n*	—	déficit de la balance du commerce extérieur *m*	deficit del commercio estero *m*	déficit del comercio exterior *m*
trade embargo (E)	Handelsembargo *n*	—	embargo commercial *m*	embargo commerciale *m*	embargo comercial *m*
trade fair¹ (E)	Handelsmesse *f*	—	foire commerciale *f*	fiera commerciale *f*	feria comercial *f*
trade fair² (E)	Fachausstellung *f*	—	exposition spécialisée *f*	esposizione specializzata *f*	exposición especializada *f*
trade fair³ (E)	Mustermesse *f*	—	foire d'échantillons *f*	fiera campionaria *f*	feria de muestras *f*
trade mark (E)	Warenzeichen *n*	—	marque *f*	marchio *m*	marca *f*
trade mission (E)	Handelsmission *f*	—	mission commerciale *f*	missione commerciale *f*	misión comercial *f*
trade practice (E)	Handelsusancen *pl*	—	usages commerciaux *m pl*	usanze commerciali *f pl*	usos comerciales *m pl*

	D	E	F	I	Es
trader (E)	Händler *m*	—	commerçant *m*	commerciante *m*	comerciante *m*
trade relations (E)	Handels-beziehungen *pl*	—	relations commerciales *f pl*	rapporti commerciali *m pl*	relaciones comerciales *f pl*
trade restrictions (E)	Handels-beschränkungen *pl*	—	restrictions au commerce *f pl*	restrizioni commerciali *f pl*	restricciones comerciales *f pl*
trade secret (E)	Betriebsgeheimnis *n*	—	secret d'exploitation *m*	segreto aziendale *m*	secreto empresarial *m*
trade statistics (E)	Branchenstatistik *f*	—	statistique sur les différentes branches économiques *f*	statistica di categoria *f*	estadística del ramo *f*
trade structure (E)	Branchenstruktur *f*	—	structure de la branche *f*	struttura di categoria *f*	estructura del ramo *f*
trade surplus (E)	Handelsüberschuß *m*	—	excédent commercial *m*	eccedenza commerciale *f*	excedente comercial *m*
trade tariff (E)	Gütertarif *m*	—	tarif marchandises *m*	tariffa merci *f*	tarifa de transporte *f*
trade tax (E)	Gewerbesteuer *f*	—	patente *f*	imposta industriale *f*	impuesto industrial *m*
trade terms (E)	Handelsklausel *f*	—	clause commerciale *f*	clausola commerciale *f*	cláusula comercial *f*
trade union (E)	Gewerkschaften *pl*	—	syndicat *m*	sindacati *m pl*	sindicato *m*
trade war (E)	Handelskrieg *m*	—	guerre commerciale *f*	guerra commerciale *f*	guerra comercial *f*
trading company (E)	Handelsgesellschaft *f*	—	société commerciale *f*	società commerciale *f*	sociedad comercial *f*
trading conditions (E)	Handels-bedingungen *pl*	—	conditions commerciales *f pl*	condizioni commerciali *f pl*	condiciones comerciales *f pl*
trading margin (E)	Handelsspanne *f*	—	bénéfice brut *m*	margine commerciale *m*	margen comercial *f*
trading partner (E)	Handelspartner *m*	—	partenaire commercial *m*	partner commerciale *m*	socio comercial *m*
traffic (E)	Verkehr *m*	—	circulation *f*	traffico *m*	circulación *f*
traffico (I)	Verkehr *m*	traffic	circulation *f*	—	circulación *f*
traffico a breve distanza (I)	Nahverkehr *m*	short distance traffic	transport à courte distance *m*	—	tráfico a corta distancia *m*
traffico aereo commerciale (I)	Luftfrachtverkehr *m*	air freight traffic	transport aérien des marchandises *m*	—	tráfico de flete aéreo *m*
traffico a grande distanza (I)	Fernverkehr *m*	long distance traffic	trafic sur longues distances *m*	—	transporte a distancia *m*
traffico pendolare (I)	Pendelverkehr *m*	shuttle service	trafic de va-et-vient *m*	—	vaivén *m*
traffico stradale (I)	Straßenverkehr *m*	road traffic	trafic routier *m*	—	circulación *f*
tráfico a corta distancia (Es)	Nahverkehr *m*	short distance traffic	transport à courte distance *m*	traffico a breve distanza *m*	—
tráfico de divisas (Es)	Devisenverkehr *m*	foreign exchange dealings	mouvement des devises *m*	commercio dei cambi *m*	—
tráfico de flete aéreo (Es)	Luftfrachtverkehr *m*	air freight traffic	transport aérien des marchandises *m*	traffico aereo commerciale *m*	—
tráfico de futuro (Es)	Warentermin-handel *m*	commodity forward dealing	commerce d'opéra-tions à terme *m*	operazioni a termine su merci *f pl*	—
tráfico de mercancías en bultos sueltos (Es)	Stückgutverkehr *m*	general cargo trade	expéditions de détail *f*	trasporto di collettame *m*	—
trafic routier (F)	Straßenverkehr *m*	road traffic	—	traffico stradale *m*	circulación *f*
trafic sur longues distances (F)	Fernverkehr *m*	long distance traffic	—	traffico a grande distanza *m*	transporte a distancia *m*
Trainee (D)	—	trainee	apprenti *m*	trainee *m*	entrenamiento *m*
trainee (E)	Trainee *m*	—	apprenti *m*	trainee *m*	entrenamiento *m*
trainee (I)	Trainee *m*	trainee	apprenti *m*	—	entrenamiento *m*
trainer (E)	Ausbilder *m*	—	instructeur *m*	istruttore *m*	instructor *m*
training staff (E)	Schulungspersonal *n*	—	personnel d'instruction *m*	personale d'addestramento *m*	personal de formación *m*
traite acceptée (F)	Akzept *n*	accepted bill	—	accettazione *f*	aceptación *f*
traite commerciale (F)	Warenwechsel *m*	commercial bill	—	cambiale commerciale *f*	letra comercial *f*

	D	E	F	I	Es
traitement (F)	Gehalt *n*	salary	—	stipendio *m*	sueldo *m*
traitement de base (F)	Grundgehalt *n*	basic salary	—	stipendio base *m*	salario base *m*
traitement des informations (F)	Datenverarbeitung *f*	data processing	—	elaborazione dati *f*	procesamiento de datos *m*
traite tirée sur l'étranger (F)	Auslandswechsel *n*	foreign bill of exchange	—	cambiale estera *f*	letra sobre el exterior *f*
tram (I)	Straßenbahn *f*	tramway	tramway *m*	—	tranvía *m*
tramitación de pedidos (Es)	Auftragsbearbeitung *f*	order processing	réalisation d'une commande *f*	esecuzione ordini *f*	—
tramway (E)	Straßenbahn *f*	—	tramway *m*	tram *m*	tranvía *m*
tramway (F)	Straßenbahn *f*	tramway	—	tram *m*	tranvía *m*
Tranche (D)	—	tranche	tranche *f*	tranche *f*	emisión parcial *f*
tranche (E)	Tranche *f*	—	tranche *f*	tranche *f*	emisión parcial *f*
tranche (F)	Tranche *f*	tranche	—	tranche *f*	emisión parcial *f*
tranche (I)	Tranche *f*	tranche	tranche *f*	—	emisión parcial *f*
transacción (Es)	Transaktion *f*	transaction	transaction *f*	transazione *f*	—
transacciones a término en divisas (Es)	Devisentermin- geschäft *n*	forward exchange dealings	opérations à terme sur les changes *f pl*	operazione valutaria a termine *f*	—
transaction (E)	Transaktion *f*	—	transaction *f*	transazione *f*	transacción *f*
transaction (F)	Transaktion *f*	transaction	—	transazione *f*	transacción *f*
transactions boursiaires (F)	Börsenhandel *m*	stock exchange transactions	—	commercio in borsa *m*	negociación bursátil *f*
Transaktion (D)	—	transaction	transaction *f*	transazione *f*	transacción *f*
transazione (I)	Transaktion *f*	transaction	transaction *f*	—	transacción *f*
transbordement (F)	Umschlag *m*	transshipment	—	trasbordo *m*	transbordo de carga *m*
transbordo de carga (Es)	Umschlag *m*	transshipment	transbordement *m*	trasbordo *m*	—
transcription error (E)	Übertragungsfehler *m*	—	erreur de transcription *f*	errore di trascrizione *m*	error de transcripción *m*
Transfer (D)	—	transfer	transfert *m*	trasferimento *m*	transferencia *f*
transfer¹ (E)	Anweisung *f*	—	mandat *m*	ordine di pagamento *m*	transferencia *f*
transfer² (E)	Transfer *m*	—	transfert *m*	trasferimento *m*	transferencia *f*
transferencia¹ (Es)	Transfer *m*	transfer	transfert *m*	trasferimento *m*	—
transferencia² (Es)	Anweisung *f*	transfer	mandat *m* pagamento *m*	ordine di	—
transferencia³ (Es)	Überweisung *f*	remittance	virement *m*	rimessa *f*	—
transferencia bancaria (Es)	Banküberweisung *f*	bank transfer	virement bancaire *m*	rimessa bancaria *f*	—
transfer of an entry (E)	Umbuchung *f*	—	jeu d'écritures *m*	giro di partite *m*	asiento en otra
transfer of profit (E)	Gewinnabführung *f*	—	transfert du bénéfice *m*	trasferimento dell'utile *m*	tranferencia de beneficios *f*
transferencia de beneficios (Es)	Gewinnabführung *f*	transfer of profit	transfert du bénéfice *m*	trasferimento dell'utile *m*	—
Transferrisiko (D)	—	risk of transfer	risque de transfert *m*	rischio di trasferimento *m*	riesgo de transferencia *m*
transfert¹ (F)	Transfer *m*	transfer/transmission	—	trasferimento *m*/ trasmissione *f*	transferencia *f*
transfert² (F)	Übertragung *f*	transfer/transmission	—	trasferimento *m*/ trasmissione *f*	transmisión *f*
transfert de résidence (F)	Wohnungswechsel *m*	change of residence	—	cambiamento dell'abitazione *m*	cambio de vivienda *m*
transfert du bénéfice (F)	Gewinnabführung *f*	transfer of profit	—	trasferimento dell'utile *m*	tranferencia de beneficios *f*
transformación (Es)	Verarbeitung *f*	processing	transformation *f*	lavorazione *f*	—
transformation (F)	Verarbeitung *f*	processing	—	lavorazione *f*	transformación *f*
transformation complémentaire (F)	Weiterverarbeitung *f*	further processing	—	trasformazione *f*	elaboración ulterior *f*
Transit (D)	—	transit	transit *m*	transito *m*	tránsito *m*
transit (E)	Transit *m*	—	transit *m*	transito *m*	tránsito *m*

	D	E	F	I	Es
transit (F)	Transit *m*	transit	—	transito *m*	tránsito *m*
transit certificate (E)	Durchgangsschein *m*	—	acquit de transit *m*	bolletta di transito *f*	pasavante *m*
transit clause (E)	Transitklausel *f*	—	clause de transit *f*	clausola di transito *f*	cláusula de tránsito *f*
transit duty (E)	Transitzoll *m*	—	droit de transit *m*	diritti di transito *m pl*	derecho de tránsito *m*
Transithandel (D)	—	transit trade	commerce de transit *m*	commercio di transito *m*	comercio de tránsito *m*
transitional arrangement (E)	Übergangsregelung *f*	—	règlement transitoire *m*	regolamento transitorio *m*	regulación transitoria *f*
Transitklausel (D)	—	transit clause	clause de transit *f*	clausola di transito *f*	cláusula de tránsito *f*
tránsito (Es)	Transit *m*	transit	transit *m*	transito *m*	—
transito (I)	Transit *m*	transit	transit *m*	—	tránsito *m*
transit trade (E)	Transithandel *m*	—	commerce de transit *m*	commercio di transito *m*	comercio de tránsito *m*
Transitzoll (D)	—	transit duty	droit de transit *m*	diritti di transito *m pl*	derecho de tránsito *m*
transmisión (Es)	Übertragung *f*	transfer/transmission	transfert *m*/ transmission *f*	trasferimento *m*/ trasmissione *f*	—
transmisión de datos[1] (Es)	Datenübertragung *f*	data transmission	transmission de dates *f*	trasmissione dati *f*	—
transmisión de datos[2] (Es)	Datenfern- übertragung *f*	remote data transmission	télétransmission des données informatiques *f*	teletrasmissione dati *f*	—
transmission de dates (F)	Datenübertragung *f*	data transmission	—	trasmissione dati *f*	transmisión de datos *f*
transparence (F)	Transparenz *f*	transparency	—	trasparenza *f*	transparencia *f*
transparence du marché (F)	Markttransparenz *f*	market transparency	—	trasparenza di mercato *f*	transparencia del mercado *f*
transparencia (Es)	Transparenz *f*	transparency	transparence *f*	trasparenza *f*	—
transparencia del mercado (Es)	Markttransparenz *f*	market transparency	transparence du marché *f*	trasparenza di mercato *f*	—
transparency (E)	Transparenz *f*	—	transparence *f*	trasparenza *f*	transparencia *f*
Transparenz (D)	—	transparency	transparence *f*	trasparenza *f*	transparencia *f*
Transport (D)	—	transport	transport *m*	trasporto *m*	transporte *m*
transport (E)	Transport *m*	—	transport *m*	trasporto *m*	transporte *m*
transport (F)	Transport *m*	transport	—	trasporto *m*	transporte *m*
transport à courte distance (F)	Nahverkehr *m*	short distance traffic	—	traffico a breve distanza *m*	tráfico a corta distancia *m*
transport aérien des marchandises (F)	Luftfrachtverkehr *m*	air freight traffic	—	traffico aereo commerciale *m*	tráfico de flete aéreo *m*
transportación en contenedores (Es)	Behälterverkehr *m*	container transport	transport utilisant des containers *m*	trasporto container *m*	—
transport(ation) (E)	Transport- wesen *n*	—	transports *m pl*	trasporti *m pl*	transportes *m pl*
transportation insurance (E)	Transport- versicherung *f*	—	assurance transports *f*	assicurazione dei trasporti *f*	seguro de transporte *m*
transport de groupage (F)	Sammeltransport *m*	collective transport	—	trasporto a collettame *m*	transporte colectivo *m*
transport de marchandises (F)	Güterbeförderung *f*	carriage of goods	—	trasporto di merci *m*	transporte de mercancías *m*
transport de personnes (F)	Personen- beförderung *f*	carriage of passengers	—	trasporto di persone *m*	transporte de personas *m*
transporte (Es)	Transport *m*	transport	transport *m*	trasporto *m*	—
transporte a distancia (Es)	Fernverkehr *m*	long distance traffic	trafic sur longues distances *m*	traffico a grande distanza *m*	—
transporte aéreo (Es)	Luftfrachtbrief *m*	air waybill	lettre de transport aérien *f*	lettera di trasporto aereo *f*	—
transporte colectivo (Es)	Sammeltransport *m*	collective transport	transport de groupage *m*	trasporto a collettame *m*	—
transporte combinado ferrocarril- carretera (Es)	Huckepackverkehr *m*	piggyback service	transport pick-a-back *m*	trasporto strada-rotaia *m*	—

	D	E	F	I	Es
transporte de mercancías (Es)	Güterbeförderung f	carriage of goods	transport de marchandises m	trasporto di merci m	—
transporte de personas (Es)	Personen-beförderung f	carriage of passengers	transport de personnes m	trasporto di persone m	—
transporte ferroviario (Es)	Bahnfracht f	rail freight	fret par rail m	nolo ferroviario m	—
transporteur (F)	Frachtführer m	carrier	—	vettore m	transportista m
transportista¹ (Es)	Luftfrachtführer m	air carrier	voiturier aérien m	vettore aereo m	—
transportista² (Es)	Frachtführer m	carrier	transporteur m	vettore m	—
Transportmittel (D)	—	means of transport	moyen de transport m	mezzo di trasporto m	medio de transporte m
Transportpapiere (D)	—	documents covering transportation	documents de transport m pl	documenti di trasporto m pl	documentos de transporte m pl
transport pick-a-back (F)	Huckepackverkehr m	piggyback service	—	trasporto strada-rotaia m	transporte combinado ferrocarril-carretera m
transport policy (E)	Verkehrspolitik f	—	politique des transports f	politica del traffico f	política de transportes f
transports (F)	Beförderungs-geschäfte pl	transport services	—	operazioni di trasporto f pl	negocios de transporte m pl
Transportschaden (D)	—	damage to goods in transit	dommage au cours d'un transport m	danno di trasporto m	daño de transporte m
transport services (E)	Beförderungs-geschäfte pl	—	transports m pl	operazioni di trasporto f pl	negocios de transporte m pl
transport utilisant des containers (F)	Behälterverkehr m	container transport	—	trasporto container m	transportación en contenedores f
Transport-versicherung (D)	—	transportation insurance	assurance transports f	assicurazione dei trasporti f	seguro de transporte m
Transportweg (D)	—	route of transportation	voie de transport f	via di trasporto f	vía de transporte f
transshipment (E)	Umschlag m	—	transbordement m	trasbordo m	transbordo de carga m
transshipment frequencies (E)	Umschlags-häufigkeit f	—	fréquence de transboredement f	velocità di rotazione f	frecuencia de transbordo f
tranvía (Es)	Straßenbahn f	tramway	tramway m	tram m	—
trasbordo (I)	Umschlag m	transshipment	transbordement m	—	transbordo de carga m
trasferimento¹ (I)	Umzug m	change of residence	déménagement m	—	mudanza f
trasferimento² (I)	Übertragung f	transfer/transmission	transfert m/transmission f	—	transmisión f
trasferimento³ (I)	Transfer m	transfer	transfert m	—	transferencia f
trasferimento dell'utile (I)	Gewinnabführung f	transfer of profit	transfert du bénéfice m	—	tranferencia de beneficios f
trasformazione (I)	Weiterverarbeitung f	further processing	transformation complémentaire f	—	elaboración ulterior f
traslación (Es)	Überwälzung f	passing on	répercussion f	accollamento m	—
trasmissione dati (I)	Datenübertragung f	data transmission	transmission de dates f	—	transmisión de datos f
trasparenza (I)	Transparenz f	transparency	transparence f	—	transparencia f
trasparenza di bilancio (I)	Bilanzklarheit f	balance transparency	clarté du bilan f	—	claridad del balance f
trasparenza di mercato (I)	Markttransparenz f	market transparency	transparence du marché f	—	transparencia del mercado f
trasporto (I)	Transport m	transport	transport m	—	transporte m
trasporto a collettame (I)	Sammeltransport m	collective transport	transport de groupage m	—	transporte colectivo m
trasporto container (I)	Behälterverkehr m	container transport	transport utilisant des containers m	—	transportación en contenedores f
trasporto di collettame (I)	Stückgutverkehr m	general cargo trade	expéditions de détail f	—	tráfico de mercanías en bultos sueltos m
trasporto di merci (I)	Güterbeförderung f	carriage of goods	transport de marchandises m	—	transporte de mercancías m
trasporto di persone (I)	Personen-beförderung f	carriage of passengers	transport de personnes m	—	transporte de personas m
trasporto marittimo (I)	Verfrachtung f	carriage of goods by sea	affrètement m	—	expedición f

	D	E	F	I	Es
trasporto strada-rotaia (I)	Huckepackverkehr *m*	piggyback service	transport pick-a-back *m*	—	transporte combinado ferrocarril-carretera *m*
tratamiento (Es)	Anrede *f*	form of address	début de lettre *m*	titolo *m*	—
tratamiento de textos (Es)	Textverarbeitung *f*	word processing	élaboration de texte *f*	elaborazione testi *f*	—
tratamiento ulterior (Es)	Nachbereitung *f*	aftertreatment	remise en ordre *f*	rielaborazione *f*	—
trattario (I)	Bezogener *m*	drawee	tiré *m*	—	librado *m*
trattativa (I)	Verhandlung *f*	negotiation	négociation *f*	—	negociación *f*
travail (F)	Arbeit *f*	work	—	lavoro *m*	trabajo *m*
travail à domicile (F)	Heimarbeit *f*	homework	—	lavoro a domicilio *m*	trabajo a domicilio *m*
travail à exécuter (F)	Arbeitsanfall *m*	volume of work	—	volume di lavoro *m*	volumen de trabajo *m*
travail à la tâche (F)	Akkordarbeit *f*	piecework	—	lavora a cottimo *m*	trabajo a destajo *m*
travail à l'écran (F)	Bildschirmarbeit *f*	screen work	—	lavoro video *m*	trabajo de pantalla *m*
travail à temps partiel (F)	Teilzeitarbeit *f*	part-time work	—	lavoro part-time *m*	trabajo a tiempo parcial *m*
travail à temps réduit (F)	Kurzarbeit *f*	short-time work	—	lavoro ad orario ridotto *m*	trabajo reducido *m*
travail d'équipe (F)	Teamarbeit *f*	team work	—	lavoro d'équipe *m*	trabajo en equipo *m*
travail du dimanche (F)	Sonntagsarbeit *f*	Sunday work	—	lavoro domenicale *m*	trabajo dominical *m*
travaillé sur mesure (F)	maßgefertigt	manufactured to measure	—	prodotto su misura	hecho a medida
travailleur (F)	Arbeiter *m*	worker	—	operaio *m*	trabajador *m*
travailleur ayant un emploi (F)	Erwerbstätiger *m*	gainfully employed person	—	persona attiva *f*	persona activa *f*
travailleurs étrangers (F)	ausländische Arbeitnehmer *m*	foreign workers	—	prestatori d'opera stranieri *m pl*	trabajadores extranjeros *m*
travail manuel (F)	Handarbeit *f*	handwork	—	lavoro manuale *m*	trabajo a mano *m*
travail noir (F)	Schwarzarbeit *f*	illicit work	—	lavoro abusivo *m*	trabajo clandestino *m*
travail supplémentaire (F)	Mehrarbeit *f*	additional work	—	lavoro supplementare *m*	trabajo extraordinario *m*
travel agency (E)	Reisebüro *n*	—	agence de voyages *f*	ufficio viaggi *m*	agencia de viajes *f*
travel cancellation insurance (E)	Reiserücktrittsversicherung *f*	—	assurance de résiliation du voyage *f*	assicurazione recessione viaggio *f*	seguro de rescisión del viaje *m*
traveller's cheque (E)	Reisescheck *m*	—	chèque de voyage *m*	assegno turistico *m*	cheque de viaje *m*
travel(l)ing expenses (E)	Reisespesen *pl*	—	frais de voyage *m pl*	spese di viaggio *f pl*	gastos de viaje *m pl*
Treasury (E)	Schatzamt *n*	—	trésor *m*	tesoreria *f*	tesorería *f*
Treffpunkt (D)	—	meeting place	rendez-vous *m*	punto d'incontro *m*	lugar de la cita *m*
Treibhauseffekt (D)	—	global warming	effet de serre *m*	effetto serra *m*	efecto invernadero *m*
Treibstoff (D)	—	fuel	carburant *m*	carburante *m*	combustible *m*
Trend (D)	—	trend	tendance générale *f*	tendenza *f*	tendencia *f*
trend (E)	Trend *m*	—	tendance générale *f*	tendenza *f*	tendencia *f*
Trendanalyse (D)	—	trend analysis	analyse de la tendance générale *f*	analisi delle tendenze *f*	análisis de tendencia *m*
trend analysis (E)	Trendanalyse *f*	—	analyse de la tendance générale *f*	analisi delle tendenze *f*	análisis de tendencia *m*
Tresor (D)	—	safe	coffre-fort *m*	cassaforte *f*	caja fuerte *f*
trésor (F)	Schatzamt *n*	Treasury	—	tesoreria *f*	tesorería *f*
trial order (E)	Probeauftrag *m*	—	ordre d'essai *m*	ordine a titolo di prova *m*	pedido de prueba *m*
trial package (E)	Probepackung *f*	—	échantillon *m*	confezione campione *f*	muestra *f*
trial period (E)	Probezeit *f*	—	période d'essai *f*	periodo di prova *m*	período de prueba *m*

	D	E	F	I	Es
trial shipment (E)	Probelieferung f	—	livraison à titre d'essai f	fornitura a titolo di prova f	envío de prueba m
triangular transaction (E)	Dreiecksgeschäft n	—	opération commerciale triangulaire f	operazione triangolare f	operación triangular f
tribunal arbitral (Es)	Schiedsgericht n	court of arbitration	tribunal d'arbitrage m	tribunale arbitrale m	—
tribunal competente (Es)	Gerichtsstand m	jurisdiction	juridiction compétente f	foro competente m	—
tribunal d'appel (F)	Berufungsgericht n	appeal court	—	corte d'appello f	tribunal de apelación m
tribunal d'arbitrage (F)	Schiedsgericht n	court of arbitration	—	tribunale arbitrale m	tirbunal arbitral m
tribunal de apelación (Es)	Berufungsgericht n	appeal court	tribunal d'appel m	corte d'appello f	—
Tribunal de Justicia de las Comunidades Europeas (Es)	Europäischer Gerichtshof m	European Court	Cour de Justice Européenne f	Corte di Giustizia Europea f	—
tribunal de la faillite (F)	Konkursgericht n	bankruptcy court	—	tribunale fallimentare m	tribunal de quiebras m
tribunal de quiebras (Es)	Konkursgericht n	bankruptcy court	tribunal de la faillite m	tribunale fallimentare m	—
tribunale arbitrale (I)	Schiedsgericht n	court of arbitration	tribunal d'arbitrage m	—	tirbunal arbitral m
tribunale fallimentare (I)	Konkursgericht n	bankruptcy court	tribunal de la faillite m	—	tribunal de quiebras m
tributación (Es)	Steuerzahlung f	payment of taxes	payement de l'impôt m	pagamento delle imposte m	—
trimestral (Es)	vierteljährlich	quarterly	trimestriel	trimestrale	—
trimestrale (I)	vierteljährlich	quarterly	trimestriel	—	trimestral
trimestre (Es)	Quartal n	quarter	trimestre m	trimestre m	—
trimestre (F)	Quartal n	quarter	—	trimestre m	trimestre m
trimestre (I)	Quartal n	quarter	trimestre m	—	trimestre m
trimestriel (F)	vierteljährlich	quarterly	—	trimestrale	trimestral
tromperie[1] (F)	Täuschung f	deceit	—	inganno m	engaño m
tromperie[2] (F)	Schwindel m	swindle	—	truffa f	engaño m
truffa (I)	Schwindel m	swindle	tromperie f	—	engaño m
Trust (D)	—	trust	trust m	trust m	trust m
trust (E)	Trust m	—	trust m	trust m	trust m
trust (Es)	Trust m	trust	trust m	trust m	—
trust (F)	Trust m	trust	—	trust m	trust m
trust (I)	Trust m	trust	trust m	—	trust m
truth in the balance sheet (E)	Bilanzwahrheit f	—	sincérité du bilan f	chiarezza di bilancio f	sinceridad del balance f
try (E)	probieren	—	essayer	provare	probar
turno de noche (Es)	Nachtschicht f	night shift	équipe de nuit f	turno notturno m	—
turno notturno (I)	Nachtschicht f	night shift	équipe de nuit f	—	turno de noche m
turnover (E)	Umsatz m	—	chiffre d'affaires m	fatturato m	volumen de ventas m
turnover forecast (E)	Umsatzprognose f	—	prévision de l'évolution du chiffre d'affaires f	prognosi del fatturato f	previsión de la evolución del volumen de ventas f
turnover increase (E)	Umsatzanstieg m	—	augmentation du chiffre d'affaires f	aumento del fatturato m	aumento del volumen de facturación m
turnover plan (E)	Umsatzplan m	—	plan du chiffre d'affaires m	programma del fatturato m	objectivo de facturación m
turnover tax (E)	Umsatzsteuer f	—	impôt sur le chiffre d'affaires m	imposta generale sulle entrate f	impuesto sobre el volumen de ventas m
turnover trend (E)	Umsatzentwicklung f	—	évolution du chiffre d'affaires f	sviluppo del fatturato m	evolución del volumen de facturación f
tutela dei consumatori (I)	Verbraucherschutz m	consumer protection	protection des consommateurs f	—	protección de los consumidores f
tutela dei dati (I)	Datenschutz m	data securing	sauvegarde des données f	—	protección de los datos f

	D	E	F	I	Es
tutela del creditore (I)	Gläubigerschutz *m*	protection of creditors	garantie des créanciers *f*	—	protección de los acreedores *f*
tutela dell'ambiente (I)	Umweltschutz *m*	protection of the environment	protection de l'environment *f*	—	protección del medio ambiente *f*
tutela della maternità (I)	Mutterschutz *m*	protection of motherhood	protection maternelle et infantile *f*	—	protección de la madre *f*
tutela del lavoro (I)	Arbeitsschutz *m*	employment protection	protection sociale du travail *f*	—	protección del trabajo *f*
tutela del locatario (I)	Mieterschutz *m*	protection of tenants	protection en matière de location *f*	—	protección al arrendatario *f*
tutela territoriale (I)	Gebietsschutz *m*	territory protection	exclusivité territoriale *f*	—	protección territorial *f*
two-tier exchange rate (E)	gespaltene Wechselkurse *pl*	—	cours du change multiple *m*	cambi multipli *m pl*	tipo de cambio múltiple *m*
types of markets (E)	Marktformen *pl*	—	formes du marché *f pl*	tipi di mercato *m pl*	formas del mercado *f*
Überbeschäftigung (D)	—	overcharge	surchargement *m*	occupazione eccedente *f*	exceso de empleo *m*/ superempleo *m*
Überbevölkerung (D)	—	overpopulation	surpopulation *f*	sovrappopolazione *f*	superpoblación *f*
Überbewertung (D)	—	overvaluation	surestimation *f*	sopravvalutazione *f*	sobrevaloración *f*
Überbringer (D)	—	bearer	porteur *m*	portatore *m*	portador *m*
Überbringerscheck (D)	—	bearer cheque	chèque au porteur *m*	assegno al portatore *m*	cheque al portador *m*
Überbrückungskredit (D)	—	bridging loan	crédit transitoire *m*	credito ponte *m*	crédito transitorio *m*
Überfremdung (D)	—	control by foreign capital	majorité d'étrangers *f*	inforestierimento *m*	extranjerización *f*
Übergabe (D)	—	delivery	remise *f*	consegna *f*	entrega *f*
Übergangsregelung (D)	—	transitional arrangement	règlement transitoire *m*	regolamento transitorio *m*	regulación transitoria *f*
Übergewicht (D)	—	excess weight	surcharge *f*	sovrappeso *m*	sobrepreso *m*
Überkapazität (D)	—	overcapacity	surcapacité *f*	capacità eccessiva *f*	supercapacidad *f*
Überkapitalisierung (D)	—	overcapitalization	surcapitalisation *f*	sovracapitalizzazione *f*	sobrecapitalización *f*
übermäßig (D)	—	excessive	excessif	eccessivo	excesivo
Übernachtungskosten (D)	—	overnight expenses	coûts de nuitée *m pl*	spese di pernottamento *f pl*	gastos de alojamiento *m pl*
Überproduktion (D)	—	overproduction	surproduction *f*	produzione eccessiva *f*	sobreproducción *f*
Überschuldung (D)	—	excessive indebtedness	surendettement *m*	indebitamento eccessivo *m*	exceso de deudas *m*
Überschuß (D)	—	excess	excédent *m*	eccedenza *f*	excedente *m*
Übersee (D)	—	oversea	outre-mer	oltremare *m*	ultramar *m*
Überseehandel (D)	—	oversea trade	commerce d'outre-mer *m*	commercio d'oltremare *m*	comercio de ultramar *m*
Überstunde (D)	—	overtime	heure supplémentaire *f*	ora straordinaria *f*	hora extraordinaria *f*
Übertragung (D)	—	transfer/transmission	transfert *m*/ transmission *f*	trasferimento *m*/ trasmissione *f*	transmisión *f*
Übertragungsfehler (D)	—	transcription error	erreur de transcription *f*	errore di trascrizione *m*	error de transcripción *m*
Überversicherung (D)	—	overinsurance	surassurance *f*	soprassicurazione *f*	sobreseguro *m*
überwachen (D)	—	supervise	surveiller	sorvegliare	vigilar
Überwälzung (D)	—	passing on	répercussion *f*	accollamento *m*	traslación *f*
Überweisung (D)	—	remittance	virement *m*	rimessa *f*	transferencia *f*
überziehen (D)	—	overdraw	faire un prélèvement à découvert	mandare allo scoperto	sobrepasar
ubicación (Es)	Standort *m*	location	lieu d'implantation *m*	ubicazione *f*	—
ubicazione (I)	Standort *m*	location	lieu d'implantation *m*	—	ubicación *f*
Überziehungskredit (D)	—	credit by way of overdraft	avance sur compte courant *f*	credito allo scoperto *m*	crédito en descubierto *m*

	D	E	F	I	Es
ufficiale giudiziario (I)	Gerichtsvollzieher *m*	bailiff	huissier de justice *m*	—	ejecutor judicial *m*
ufficio¹ (I)	Amt *n*	office	bureau *m*	—	cargo *m*
ufficio² (I)	Geschäftsstelle *f*	office	agence *f*	—	oficina *f*
ufficio anagrafe (I)	Einwohnermelde-amt *n*	residents' registration office	bureau de déclaration de résidence *m*	—	oficina del censo *f*
ufficio brevetti (I)	Patentamt *n*	Patent Office	office des brevets *m*	—	oficina del registro de patentes *f*
ufficio dei conti correnti postali (I)	Postscheckamt *n*	postal giro centre	bureau de chèques postaux *m*	—	oficina de cheques postales *f*
ufficio delle imposte (I)	Finanzamt *n*	inland revenue office	service de contributions *m*	—	Hacienda *f*
ufficio del personale (I)	Personalbüro *n*	personnel office	bureau du personnel *m*	—	oficina de personal *f*
ufficio di collocamento (I)	Arbeitsvermittlung *f*	employment agency	bureau de placement *m*	—	agencia laboral *f*
Ufficio Europeo Brevetti (I)	Europäisches Patentamt *n*	European Patent Office	Office Européen de Brevets *m*	—	Oficina Europea de Patentes *f*
ufficio legale (I)	Rechtsabteilung *f*	legal department	bureau juridique *m*	—	sección jurídica *f*
ufficio paga (I)	Lohnbüro *n*	pay office	bureau de la paye *m*	—	departamento de nóminas *m*
ufficio postale (I)	Postamt *n*	post office	bureau de poste *m*	—	correos *m pl*
ufficio tele-comunicazioni (I)	Fernmeldeamt *n*	telephone exchange	service de télécommunication *m*	—	central interurbana *f*
ufficio viaggi (I)	Reisebüro *n*	travel agency	agence de voyages *f*	—	agencia de viajes *f*
ultimate buyer (E)	Endabnehmer *m*	—	preneur final *m*	acquirente finale *m*	comprador final *m*
ultimate consumer (E)	Endverbraucher *m*	—	consommateur final *m*	consumatore finale *m*	consumidor final *m*
Ultimo (D)	—	end of the month	fin de mois *f*	fine mese *m*	fin de mes *m*
ultramar (Es)	Übersee	oversea(s)	outre-mer	oltremare *m*	—
umbral de precios (Es)	Preisschwelle *f*	threshold price	seuil du prix *m*	soglia dei prezzi *f*	—
Umbuchung (D)	—	transfer of an entry	jeu d'écritures *m*	giro di partite *m*	asiento en otra cuenta *m*
Umfang (D)	—	volume	volume *m*	volume *m*	volumen *m*/ dimensión *f*
umgehend (D)	—	immediate(ly)	immédiatement	immediato	inmediatamente
Umlage (D)	—	charge levied	répartition *f*	ripartizione *f*	reparto *m*
Umlaufvermögen (D)	—	current assets/ floating assets	capital de roulement *m*	patrimonio circolante *m*	capital circulante *m*
umpacken (D)	—	repack	remballer	rifare l'imballaggio	reempaquetar
Umrechnungskurs (D)	—	rate of conversion	cours de conversion *m*	corso di cambio *m*	tasa de cambio *f*
Umsatz (D)	—	turnover	chiffre d'affaires *m*	fatturato *m*	volumen de ventas *m*
Umsatzanstieg (D)	—	turnover increase	augmentation du chiffre d'affaires *f*	aumento del fatturato *m*	aumento del volumen de facturación *m*
Umsatzentwicklung (D)	—	turnover trend	évolution du chiffre d'affaires *f*	sviluppo del fatturato *m*	evolución del volu-men de facturación *f*
Umsatzplan (D)	—	turnover plan	plan du chiffre d'affaires *m*	programma del fatturato *m*	objectivo de facturación *m*
Umsatzprognose (D)	—	turnover forecast	prévision de l'évolution du chiffre d'affaires *f*	prognosi del fatturato *f*	previsión de la evo-lución del volumen de ventas *f*
Umsatzprovision (D)	—	commission on turnover	commission sur le chiffre d'affaires *f*	provvigione sul fatturato *f*	comisión sobre la cifra de ventas *f*
Umsatzrendite (D)	—	net income percentage of turnover	rendement du chiffre d'affaires *m*	rendita del fatturato *f*	rédito de la cifra de ventas *m*
Umsatzrückgang (D)	—	decrease of turnover	recul du chiffre d'affaires *m*	calo del fatturato *m*	disminución de la cifra de facturación *f*
Umsatzsteuer (D)	—	turnover tax	impôt sur le chiffre d'affaires *m*	imposta generale sulle entrate *f*	impuesto sobre el volumen de ventas *m*

	D	E	F	I	Es
Umschlag (D)	—	transshipment	transbordement *m*	trasbordo *m*	transbordo de carga *m*
Umschlags-häufigkeit (D)	—	transshipment frequencies	fréquence de transbordement *f*	frequenza di trasbordo *f*	frecuencia de transbordo *f*
Umschulung (D)	—	retraining	rééducation professionnelle *f*	riqualificazione professionale *f*	readaptación profesional *f*
Umstrukturierung (D)	—	restructuring	restructuration *f*	ristrutturazione *f*	reestructuración *f*
Umtausch (D)	—	exchange	échange *m*	cambio *m*	cambio *m*/ conversión *f*
umweltbewußt (D)	—	environmental-conscious	conscient de la réalité écologique	con rispetto dell'ambiente	consciente del medio ambiente
umweltfreundlich (D)	—	beneficial to the environment	favorable à l'environnement	ecologico	no contaminante
umweltschädlich (D)	—	causing environmental damages	nuisible à l'environnement	inquinante	contaminante
Umweltschutz (D)	—	protection of the environment	protection de l'environnement *f*	tutela dell'ambiente *f*	protección del medio ambiente *f*
Umwelt-verschmutzung (D)	—	environmental pollution	pollution de l'environnement *f*	inquinamento dell'ambiente *m*	contaminación del medio ambiente *f*
Umzug (D)	—	change of residence	déménagement *m*	trasferimento *m*	mudanza *f*
Unabhängigkeit (D)	—	independence	indépendance *f*	indipendenza *f*	independencia *f*
unbar (D)	—	non cash	non comptant	non in contanti	no en efectivo
unbezahlter Urlaub (D)	—	unpaid vacation	congé non payé *m*	ferie non pagate *f pl*	vacaciones no pagadas *f pl*
uncertainty (E)	Unsicherheit *f*	—	insécurité *f*	insicurezza *f*	inseguridad *f*
under age (E)	minderjährig	—	mineur	minorenne	menor de edad
underemployment (E)	Unter-beschäftigung *f*	—	sous-emploi *m*	sottoccupazione *f*	subempleo *m*
underinsurance (E)	Unterversicherung *f*	—	insuffisance d'assurance *f*	sottassicurazione *f*	infraseguro *m*
under public law (E)	öffentlich-rechtlich	—	de droit public	di diritto pubblico	de derecho público
under separate cover (E)	mit getrennter Post	—	sous pli séparé	in plico a parte	por correo aparte
undervaluation (E)	Unterbewertung *f*	—	sous-estimation *f*	sottovalutazione *f*	subvaloración *f*
unearned income[1] (E)	Kapitaleinkommen *n*	—	revenu du capital *m*	reddito del capitale *m*	ganancias de capital *f pl*
unearned income[2] (E)	Besitzeinkommen *n*	—	revenu du patrimoine *m*	reddito da possesso *m*	renta de la propiedad *f*
unemployment (E)	Arbeitslosigkeit *f*	—	chômage *m*	disoccupazione *f*	desempleo *m*
unemployment benefits (E)	Arbeitslosen-unterstützung *f*	—	indemnité de chômage *f*	sussidio di disoccupazione *m*	prestaciones por desempleo *m*
unentgeltlich (D)	—	free of charge	à titre gracieux	gratuito	gratuito
unfair competition (E)	unlauterer Wettbewerb *m*	—	concurrence déloyale *f*	concorrenza sleale *f*	competencia desleal *f*
Unfallversicherung (D)	—	personal accident insurance	assurance accidents corporels *f*	assicurazione contro infortuni *f*	seguro de accidentes *m*
ungenutzt (D)	—	unused	pas utilisé	inutilizzato	no utilizado
ungesetzlich (D)	—	illegal	contraire à la loi	illegale	ilegal
ungesichert (D)	—	unsecured	non garanti	non assicurato	no asegurado
unidad central (Es)	Zentraleinheit *f*	central unit	unité centrale *f*	unità centrale *f*	—
unidad cuantitativa (Es)	Mengeneinheit *f*	quantity unit	unité de quantité *f*	unità quantitativa *f*	—
unidad de compensación (Es)	Verrechnungs-einheit *f*	clearing unit	unité de compte *f*	unità di compensazione *f*	—
unidad de cuenta[1] (Es)	Recheneinheit *f*	calculation unit	unité de calcul *f*	unità di conteggio *f*	—
unidad de cuenta[2] (Es)	Rechnungseinheit *f*	unit of account	unité de compte *f*	unità di conto *f*	—
unidad de embalaje (Es)	Verpackungseinheit *f*	packing unit	unité d'emballage *f*	unità d'imballaggio *f*	—
unidad monetaria europea (Es)	Europäische Währungseinheit *f*	European Currency Unit	unité de compte européenne *f*	unità monetaria europea *f*	—
uniform currency (E)	Einheitswährung *f*	—	monométallisme *m*	moneta unitaria *f*	moneda única *f*

	D	E	F	I	Es
uniform duty (E)	Einheitszoll *m*	—	droit unique *m*	dazio unitario *m*	aduanas uniformes *f pl*
uniforme all'interno della CEE (I)	EG-einheitlich	standardized within the European Community	uniforme au niveau communautaire	—	armonizado a nivel comunitario
uniforme au niveau communautaire (F)	EG-einheitlich	standardized within the European Community	—	uniforme all'interno della CEE	armonizado a nivel comunitario
uniform price (E)	Einheitspreis *m*	—	prix unique *m*	prezzo unitario *m*	precio único *m*
uniform tariff (E)	Einheitstarif *m*	—	tarif standard *m*	tariffa unitaria *f*	tarifa única *f*
unión aduanera (Es)	Zollunion *f*	customs union	union douanière *f*	unione doganale *f*	—
unión agrícola (Es)	Agrarunion *f*	agricultural union	union agricole *f*	unione agraria *f*	—
union agricole (F)	Agrarunion *f*	agricultural union	—	unione agraria *f*	unión agrícola *f*
union douanière (F)	Zollunion *f*	customs union	—	unione doganale *f*	unión aduanera *f*
unione agraria (I)	Agrarunion *f*	agricultural union	union agricole *f*	—	unión agrícola *f*
unión económica (Es)	Wirtschaftsunion *f*	economic union	union économique *f*	unione economica *f*	—
union économique (F)	Wirtschaftsunion *f*	economic union	—	unione economica *f*	unión económica *f*
unione degli imprenditori (I)	Unternehmer-verband *m*	employers' association	association des chefs d'entreprise *f*	—	asociación empresarial *f*
unione doganale (I)	Zollunion *f*	customs union	union douanière *f*	—	unión aduanera *f*
unione economica (I)	Wirtschaftsunion *f*	economic union	union économique *f*	—	unión económica *f*
Unione Europea dei Pagamenti (I)	Europäische Zahlungsunion *f*	European Payments Union	union européenne des payements *f*	—	Unión Europea de Pagos *f*
unione monetaria (I)	Währungsunion *f*	monetary union	union monétaire *f*	—	unión monetaria *f*
Unión Europea de Pagos (Es)	Europäische Zahlungsunion *f*	European Payments Union	union européenne des payements *f*	Unione Europea dei Pagamenti *f*	—
union européenne des payements (F)	Europäische Zahlungsunion *f*	European Payments Union	—	Unione Europea dei Pagamenti *f*	Unión Europea de Pagos *f*
union monétaire (F)	Währungsunion *f*	monetary union	—	unione monetaria *f*	unión monetaria *f*
unión monetaria (Es)	Währungsunion *f*	monetary union	union monétaire *f*	unione monetaria *f*	—
unità centrale (I)	Zentraleinheit *f*	central unit	unité centrale *f*	—	unidad central *f*
unità di compensazione (I)	Verrechnungs-einheit *f*	clearing unit	unité de compte *f*	—	unidad de compensación *f*
unità di conteggio (I)	Recheneinheit *f*	calculation unit	unité de calcul *f*	—	unidad de cuenta *f*
unità di conto (I)	Rechnungseinheit *f*	unit of account	unité de compte *f*	—	unidad de cuenta *f*
unità d'imballaggio (I)	Verpackungseinheit *f*	packing unit	unité d'emballage *f*	—	unidad de embalaje *f*
unità monetaria europea (I)	Europäische Währungseinheit *f*	European Currency Unit	unité de compte européenne *f*	—	unidad monetaria europea *f*
unità quantitativa (I)	Mengeneinheit *f*	quantity unit	unité de quantité *f*	—	unidad cuantitativa *f*
unité centrale (F)	Zentraleinheit *f*	central unit	—	unità centrale *f*	unidad central *f*
unité de calcul (F)	Recheneinheit *f*	calculation unit	—	unità di conteggio *f*	unidad de cuenta *f*
unité de compte[1] (F)	Rechnungseinheit *f*	unit of account	—	unità di conto *f*	unidad de cuenta *f*
unité de compte[2] (F)	Verrechnungs-einheit *f*	clearing unit	—	unità di compensazione *f*	unidad de compensación *f*
unité de compte européenne (F)	Europäische Währungseinheit *f*	European Currency Unit	—	unità monetaria europea *f*	unidad monetaria europea *f*
unité d'emballage (F)	Verpackungs-einheit *f*	packing unit	—	unità d'imballaggio *f*	unidad de embalaje *f*
unité de quantité (F)	Mengeneinheit *f*	quantity unit	—	unità quantitativa *f*	unidad cuantitativa *f*
unit of account (E)	Rechnungseinheit *f*	—	unité de compte *f*	unità di conto *f*	unidad de cuenta *f*
unit trust (E)	Investmentfonds *m*	—	fonds commun de placement *m*	fondo d'investimento *m*	fondo de inversiones *m*
universidad (Es)	Universität *f*	university	université *f*	università *f*	—

	D	E	F	I	Es
università (I)	Universität *f*	university	université *f*	—	universidad *f*
Universität (D)	—	university	université *f*	università *f*	universidad *f*
université (F)	Universität *f*	university	—	università *f*	universidad *f*
university (E)	Universität *f*	—	université *f*	università *f*	universidad *f*
unlauterer Wettbewerb (D)	—	unfair competition	concurrence déloyale *f*	concorrenza sleale *f*	competencia desleal *f*
unpacked (E)	unverpackt	—	sans emballage	non imballato/ alla rinfusa	sin embalar
unpaid vacation (E)	unbezahlter Urlaub *m*	—	congé non payé *m*	ferie non pagate *f pl*	vacaciones no pagadas *f pl*
unproductive capital (E)	totes Kapital *n*	—	capital improductif *m*	capitale infruttifero *m*	capital improductivo *m*
unredeemable bond (E)	Dauerschuld- verschreibung *f*	—	obligation perpétuelle *f*	obbligazione perpetua *f*	obligación perpetua *f*
Unregelmäßigkeit (D)	—	irregularity	irrégularité *f*	irregolarità *f*	irregularidad *f*
unsachgemäß (D)	—	improper	non adéquat	non idoneo	con falta de objetividad
unsecured (E)	ungesichert	—	non garanti	non assicurato	no asegurado
unsettled account (E)	offene Rechnung *f*	—	facture pas encore payée *f*	conto aperto *m*	factura pendiente *f*
Unsicherheit (D)	—	uncertainty	insécurité *f*	insicurezza *f*	inseguridad *f*
Unterbeschäftigung (D)	—	underemployment	insuffisance de charge *f*	sottoccupazione *f*	subempleo *m*
Unterbewertung (D)	—	undervaluation	sous-estimation *f*	sottovalutazione *f*	subvaloración *f*
unterentwickelte Länder (D)	—	underdeveloped countries	pays sous- développé *m pl*	paesi sottosviluppati *m pl*	países subdesa- rrollados *m pl*
Unterernährung (D)	—	malnutrition	sous-alimentation *f*	denutrizione *f*	subalimentación *f*
Untergebener (D)	—	subordinate	subalterne *m*	dipendente *m*	subordinado *m*
Unternehmen (D)	—	enterprise	entreprise *f*	impresa *f*	empresario *m*
Unternehmensform (D)	—	form of business	forme de l'entreprise *f*	forma d'impresa *f*	forma de organización empresarial *f*
Unternehmens- fusion (D)	—	merger of companies	fusion de sociétés *f*	fusione d'imprese *f*	fusión de empresas *f*
Unternehmens- gewinn (D)	—	profit of the enterprise	bénéfice d'exploitation *m*	utile d'impresa *m*	beneficio empresarial *m*
Unternehmens- größe (D)	—	size of the company	dimension de l'entreprise *f*	dimensione dell'impresa *f*	dimensión de la empresa *f*
Unternehmens- konzentration (D)	—	business concentration	concentration d'entreprises *f*	pool d'imprese *m*	concentración de empresas *f*
Unternehmens- konzept (D)	—	business concept	stratégie de l'entreprise *f*	piano imprenditoriale *m*	concepto comercial *m*
Unternehmens- kultur (D)	—	entrepreneurial culture	culture de l'entreprise *f*	cultura imprenditoriale *f*	cultura empresarial *f*
Unternehmens- leitung (D)	—	executive management	direction de l'entreprise *f*	direzione dell'impresa *f*	dirección de la empresa *f*
Unternehmens- strategie (D)	—	corporate strategy	stratégie de l'entreprise *f*	strategia imprenditoriale *f*	estrategia empresarial *f*
Unternehmensziel (D)	—	company objective	objectif de l'entreprise *m*	obiettivo i mprenditoriale *m*	objetivo empresarial *m*
Unternehmer (D)	—	entrepreneur	entrepreneur *m*	imprenditore *m*	empresario *m*
Unternehmerlohn (D)	—	entrepreneurial income	rémunération de l'entrepreneur *f*	retribuzione dell'imprenditore *f*	remuneración del empresario *f*
Unternehmer- verband (D)	—	employers' association	association des chefs d'entreprise *f*	unione degli imprenditori *f*	asociación empresarial *f*
Unterredung (D)	—	discussion	entretien *m*	colloquio *m*	conversación *f*
Unterschlagung (D)	—	embezzlement	détournement *m*	appropriazione indebita *f*	defraudación *f*
unterschreiben (D)	—	sign	signer	firmare	signar
Unterschrift (D)	—	signature	signature *f*	firma *f*	firma *f*
Untersuchung (D)	—	examination	étude *f*	indagine *f*	inspección *f*
Untervermietung (D)	—	subletting	sous-location *f*	subaffitto *m*	subalquiler *m*
Unterversicherung (D)	—	underinsurance	insuffisance d'assurance *f*	sottassicurazione *f*	infraseguro *m*

	D	E	F	I	Es
Untervertreter (D)	—	subagent	sous-agent m	subagente m	subagente m
unused (E)	ungenutzt	—	pas utilisé	inutilizzato	no utilizado
unverbindlich (D)	—	not binding	sans obligation	senza impegno	sin compromiso
unverpackt (D)	—	unpacked	sans emballage	non imballato/ alla rinfusa	sin embalar
unverzollt (D)	—	duty unpaid	non dédouané	non sdoganato	aduana aparte
unvollständig (D)	—	incomplete	incomplet	incompleto	incompleto
unwiderrufliches Akkreditiv (D)	—	irrevocable letter of credit	accréditif irrévocable m	apertura di credito documentario irrevocabile f	crédito documentario irrevocable m
upward trend (E)	Aufwärtstrend m	—	mouvement ascendant m	tendenza al rialzo f	tendencia alcista f
urban renewal (E)	Sanierung f	—	assainissement m	risanamento m	saneamiento m/ rehabilitación f
urbanisme (F)	Städtebau m	town planning	—	urbanistica f	urbanización f
urbanistica (I)	Städtebau m	town planning	urbanisme m	—	urbanización f
urbanización (Es)	Städtebau m	town planning	urbanisme m	urbanistica f	—
Urheberrecht (D)	—	copyright	droit d'auteur m	diritto d'autore m	derecho del autor m
Urkunde (D)	—	document	document m	documento m	documento m
Urlaub (D)	—	annual holidays/ vacation	congé m/ vacances f pl	ferie f pl/ vacanze f pl	vacaciones f pl
Urlaubsgeld (D)	—	holiday allowance	prime de vacances f	indennità di ferie f	retribución por vacaciones f
Urlaubsplanung (D)	—	vacation scheduling	planification des vacances f	programmazione delle ferie f	planificación de las vacaciones f
Ursprungsland (D)	—	country of origin	pays d'origine m	paese d'origine m	país de origen m
Ursprungszeugnis (D)	—	certificate of origin	certificat d'origine m	certificato d'origine m	certificado de origen m
usage (E)	Usancen pl	—	usages m pl	usanze f pl	usanza f
usage commercial (F)	Handelsbrauch m	business practice	—	usanza commerciale f	uso comercial m
usages (F)	Usancen pl	usage	—	usanze f pl	usanza f
usages commerciaux (F)	Handelsusancen pl	trade practice	—	usanze commerciali f pl	usos comerciales m pl
Usancen (D)	—	usage	usages m pl	usanze f pl	usanza f
usanza (Es)	Usancen pl	usage	usages m pl	usanze f pl	—
usanza commerciale (I)	Handelsbrauch m	business practice	usage commercial m	—	uso comercial m
usanze (I)	Usancen pl	usage	usages m pl	—	usanza f
usanze commerciali (I)	Handelsusancen pl	trade practice	usages commerciaux m pl	—	usos comerciales m pl
uscita merci (I)	Warenausgang m	outgoing goods	sortie de marchandises f	—	salida de mercancías f
use of a computer (E)	Computereinsatz m	—	emploi d'ordinateurs m	impiego di computer m	utilización de ordenadores f
use¹ (E)	Gebrauch m	—	utilisation f	uso m	uso m
use² (E)	Nutzung f	—	mise à profit f	utilizzazione f	utilización f
used car (E)	Gebrauchtwagen m	—	voiture d'occasion f	automobile usata f	coche de segunda mano m
usine¹ (F)	Betrieb m	factory	—	azienda f	fábrica f
usine² (F)	Werk n	plant	—	stabilimento m	planta f
uso (Es)	Gebrauch m	use	utilisation f	uso m	—
uso (I)	Gebrauch m	use	utilisation f	—	uso m
uso comercial (Es)	Handelsbrauch m	business practice	usage commercial m	usanza commerciale f	—
usos comerciales (Es)	Handelsusancen pl	trade practice	usages commerciaux m pl	usanze commerciali f pl	—
usuary (E)	Wucher m	—	usure f	usura f	usura f
usufruct (E)	Nießbrauch m	—	usufruit m	usufrutto m	usufructo m

vaglia postale

	D	E	F	I	Es
usufructo (Es)	Nießbrauch *m*	usufruct	usufruit *m*	usufrutto *m*	—
usufruit (F)	Nießbrauch *m*	usufruct	—	usufrutto *m*	usufructo *m*
usufrutto (I)	Nießbrauch *m*	usufruct	usufruit *m*	—	usufructo *m*
usura (Es)	Wucher *m*	usuary	usure *f*	usura *f*	—
usura¹ (I)	Wucher *m*	usuary	usure *f*	—	usura *f*
usura² (I)	Abnutzung *f*	wear and tear	dépréciation *f*	—	desgaste *m*
usura arrendaticia (Es)	Mietwucher *m*	exorbitant rent	hausse illicite des loyers *f*	strozzinaggio sui canoni di locazione *m*	—
usure (F)	Wucher *m*	usuary	—	usura *f*	usura *f*
utente del leasing (I)	Leasing-Nehmer *m*	lessee	preneur de leasing *m*	—	arrendatante financiero *m*
utile (I)	Gewinn *m*	profit/surplus	bénéfice *m*	—	beneficio *m*/ superávit *m*
utile contabile (I)	Buchgewinn *m*	book profit	bénéfice comptable *m*	—	beneficio contable *m*
utile dell'anno (I)	Jahresgewinn *m*	annual profit	bénéfice annuel *m*	—	beneficio del ejercicio *m*
utile d'impresa (I)	Unternehmens- gewinn *m*	profit of the enterprise	bénéfice d'exploitation *m*	—	beneficio empresarial *m*
utile fittizio (I)	Scheingewinn *m*	ficticious profit	gain fictif *m*	—	beneficio simulado *m*
utile lordo (I)	Rohgewinn *m*	gross profit on sales	bénéfice brut *m*	—	ganancia bruta *f*
utile netto (I)	Reingewinn *m*	net profit	bénéfice net *m*	—	ganancia neta *f*
utilidad (Es)	Nutzen *m*	utility	utilité *f*	utilità *f*	—
utilisation (F)	Gebrauch *m*	use	—	uso *m*	uso *m*
utilisation de la capacité (F)	Kapazitäts- auslastung *f*	utilization of capacity	—	sfruttamento delle capacità *m*	utilización de las capacidades *f*
utilisation des bénéfices (F)	Gewinnverwendung *f*	appropriation of net income	—	impiego dell'utile *m*	aplicación de los resultados *f*
utilisation du revenu (F)	Einkommens- verwendung *f*	appropriation of income	—	impiego dei redditi *m*	distribución de la renta *f*
utilisation économique (F)	wirtschaftliche Nutzung *f*	economic use	—	utilizzo economico *m*	utilización económica *f*
utilité (F)	Nutzen *m*	utility	—	utilità *f*	utilidad *f*
utility (E)	Nutzen *m*	—	utilité *f*	utilità *f*	utilidad *f*
utility costs (E)	Nutzkosten *pl*	—	coûts fixes utiles *m pl*	costi fissi di utilizzo *m pl*	gastos fijos de utilización *m pl*
utilización (Es)	Nutzung *f*	use/utilization	mise à profit *f*	utilizzazione *f*	—
utilización de las capacidades (Es)	Kapazitäts- auslastung *f*	utilization of capacity	utilisation de la capacité *f*	sfruttamento delle capacità *m*	utilización de las capacidades *f*
utilización de ordenadores (Es)	Computereinsatz *m*	use of a computer	emploi d'ordinateurs *m*	impiego di computer *m*	—
utilización económica (Es)	wirtschaftliche Nutzung *m*	economic use	utilisation économique *f*	utilizzo economico *m*	—
utilization of capacity (E)	Kapazitäts- auslastung *f*	—	utilisation de la capacité *f*	sfruttamento delle capacità *m*	utilización de las capacidades *f*
utilization rate (E)	Ausnutzungsgrad *m*	—	taux d'utilisation *m*	grado di utilizzazione *m*	grado de utilización *m*
utilizzazione (I)	Nutzung *f*	use/utilization	mise à profit *f*	—	utilización *f*
utilizzo economico (I)	wirtschaftliche Nutzung *m*	economic use	utilisation économique *f*	—	utilización económica *f*
vacaciones (Es)	Urlaub *m*	annual holidays/ vacation	congé *m*/ vacances *f pl*	ferie *f pl*/ vacanze *f pl*	—
vacaciones con goce de sueldo (Es)	bezahlter Urlaub *m*	paid vacation	congé payé *m*	ferie pagate *f pl*	—
vacaciones de la empresa (Es)	Betriebsferien *pl*	annual holiday	clôture annuelle de l'établissement *f*	ferie aziendali *f pl*	—
vacaciones no pagadas (Es)	unbezahlter Urlaub *m*	unpaid vacation	congé non payé *m*	ferie non pagate *f pl*	—
vacation scheduling (E)	Urlaubsplanung *f*	—	planification des vacances *f*	programmazione delle ferie *f*	planificación de las vacaciones *f*
vaglia postale (I)	Postanweisung *f*	postal money order	mandat-poste *m*	—	vale postal *m*

	D	E	F	I	Es
vaglia telegrafico (I)	telegrafische Anweisung *f*	telegraphic payment order	mandat télégraphique *m*	—	orden telegráfica *f*
vagone frigorifero (I)	Kühlwagen *m*	cold storage lorry	wagon frigorifique *m*	—	vagón frigorífico *m*
vagón frigorífico (Es)	Kühlwagen *m*	cold storage lorry	wagon frigorifique *m*	vagone frigorifero *m*	—
vale postal (Es)	Postanweisung *f*	postal money order	mandat-poste *m*	vaglia postale *m*	—
valeur (F)	Wert *m*	value	—	valore *m*	valor *m*
valeur ajoutée (F)	Mehrwert *m*	value added	—	valore aggiunto *m*	plusvalía *f*
valeur à une certaine date (F)	Zeitwert *m*	current market value	—	valore corrente *m*	valor actual *m*
valeur commerciale[1] (F)	Firmenwert *m*	goodwill	—	goodwill *m*	fondo de comercio *m*
valeur commerciale[2] (F)	Geschäftswert *m*	goodwill	—	valore d'avviamento *m*	valor comercial *m*
valeur comptable (F)	Buchwert *m*	book value	—	valore contabile *m*	valor contable *m*
valeur d'acquisition (F)	Anschaffungswert *m*	acquisition value	—	valore d'acquisto *m*	valor de adquisición *m*
valeur de l'argent (F)	Geldwert *m*	value of money	—	valore monetario *m*	valor monetario *m*
valeur de production (F)	Produktionswert *m*	production value	—	valore produttivo *m*	valor de la producción *m*
valeur de remplacement (F)	Substanzwert *m*	assets value	—	valore sostanziale *m*	valor sustancial *m*
valeur de remplacement (F)	Reproduktionswert *m*	reproduction value	—	valore di riproduzione *m*	valor de reproducción *m*
valeur d'estimation (F)	Schätzwert *m*	estimated value	—	valore stimato *m*	estimación *f*
valeur de taxation (F)	Taxwert *m*	estimated value	—	valore stimato *m*	valor de tasación *m*
valeur du jour (F)	Tageswert *m*	current value	—	valore del giorno *m*	valor del día *m*
valeur d'une chose mesurée à son rendement (F)	Ertragswert *m*	capitalized value	—	valore del reddito *m*	valor de rendimiento *m*
valeur en capital (F)	Kapitalwert *m*	capital value	—	valore del capitale *m*	valor capitalizado *m*
valeur immobilisée (F)	Anlagegüter *pl*	capital goods	—	beni d'investimento *m pl*	bienes de inversión *m pl*
valeur marginale[1] (F)	Grenzwert *m*	limiting value	—	valore limite *m*	valor límite *m*
valeur marginale[2] (F)	Marginalwert *m*	marginal value	—	valore marginale *m*	valor marginal *m*
valeur matérielle (F)	Sachwert *m*	real value	—	valore reale *m*	valor real *m*
valeur nominale (F)	Nennwert *m*	nominal value	—	valore nominale *m*	valor nominal *m*
valeur partielle (F)	Teilwert *m*	partial value	—	valore parziale *m*	valor parcial *m*
valeur résiduelle (F)	Restwert *m*	residual value/ net book value	—	valore rimanente *m*	valor residual *m*/ valor contable residual *m*
valeurs de placement (F)	Anlagepapiere *pl*	investment securities	—	titoli d'investimento *m pl*	valores de inversión *m pl*
valeurs immobilisées (F)	Anlagevermögen *n*	fixed assets	—	attivo fisso *m*	activo fijo *m*
valeurs mesurées (F)	Meßwerte *pl*	measurements	—	valori misurati *m pl*	valor de medida *m*
valeurs mobilières (F)	Effekten *f*	securities	—	titoli *m pl*	efectos *m pl*
valeurs prévisionnelles (F)	Planwerte *pl*	planning figures	—	valori pianificati *m pl*	valores previstos *m pl*
valeurs réalisables à court terme ou disponibles (F)	Barvermögen *n*	cash assets	—	patrimonio in contanti *m*	activo efectivo *m*
valeur standard (F)	Standardwerte *pl*	standard values	—	valori standard *m pl*	valores representativos *m pl*
valor (Es)	Wert *m*	value	valeur *f*	valore *m*	—
valoración (Es)	Bewertung *f*	valuation	valorisation *f*	valutazione *f*	—

	D	E	F	I	Es
valor actual (Es)	Zeitwert *m*	current market value	valeur à une certaine date *f*	valore corrente *m*	—
valor capitalizado (Es)	Kapitalwert *m*	capital value	valeur en capital *f*	valore del capitale *m*	—
valor comercial (Es)	Geschäftswert *m*	goodwill	valeur commerciale *f*	valore d'avviamento *m*	—
valor contable (Es)	Buchwert *m*	book value	valeur comptable *f*	valore contabile *m*	—
valor de adquisisción (Es)	Anschaffungswert *m*	acquisition value	valeur d'acquisition *f*	valore d'acquisto *m*	—
valor de fabricación (Es)	Herstellungswert *m*	production value	prix de revient *m*	valore di produzione *m*	—
valor de la producción (Es)	Produktionswert *m*	production value	valeur de production *f*	valore produttivo *m*	—
valor del día (Es)	Tageswert *m*	current value	valeur du jour *f*	valore del giorno *m*	—
valor de medida (Es)	Meßwerte *pl*	measurements	valeurs mesurées *f pl*	valori misurati *m pl*	—
valor de rendimiento (Es)	Ertragswert *m*	capitalized value	valeur d'une chose mesurée à son rendement *f*	valore del reddito *m*	—
valor de reproducción (Es)	Reproduktionswert *m*	reproduction value	valeur de remplacement *f*	valore di riproduzione *m*	—
valor de tasación (Es)	Taxwert *m*	estimated value	valeur de taxation *f*	valore stimato *m*	—
valore (I)	Wert *m*	value	valeur *f*	—	valor *m*
valore aggiunto[1] (I)	Mehrwert *m*	value added	valeur ajoutée *f*	—	plusvalía *f*
valore aggiunto[2] (I)	Wertschöpfung *f*	value added	création de valeurs *f*	—	creación de riqueza *f*
valore contabile (I)	Buchwert *m*	book value	valeur comptable *f*	—	valor contable *m*
valore corrente (I)	Zeitwert *m*	current market value	valeur à une certaine date *f*	—	valor actual *m*
valore d'acquisto (I)	Anschaffungswert *m*	acquisition value	valeur d'acquisition *f*	—	valor de adquisisción *m*
valore d'avviamento (I)	Geschäftswert *m*	goodwill	valeur commerciale *f*	—	valor comercial *m*
valore del capitale (I)	Kapitalwert *m*	capital value	valeur en capital *f*	—	valor capitalizado *m*
valore del giorno (I)	Tageswert *m*	current value	valeur du jour *f*	—	valor del día *m*
valore del reddito (I)	Ertragswert *m*	capitalized value	valeur d'une chose mesurée à son rendement *f*	—	valor de rendimiento *m*
valore di produzione (I)	Herstellungswert *m*	production value	prix de revient *m*	—	valor de fabricación *m*
valore di riproduzione (I)	Reproduktionswert *m*	reproduction value	valeur de remplacement *f*	—	valor de reproducción *m*
valore finanziabile (I)	Beleihungswert *m*	value as security for a loan	montant de la garantie *m*	—	valor para préstamos *m*
valore limite (I)	Grenzwert *m*	limiting value	valeur marginale *f*	—	valor límite *m*
valore marginale (I)	Marginalwert *m*	marginal value	valeur marginale *f*	—	valor marginal *m*
valore monetario (I)	Geldwert *m*	value of money	valeur de l'argent *f*	—	valor monetario *m*
valore nominale (I)	Nennwert *m*	nominal value	valeur nominale *f*	—	valor nominal *m*
valore parziale (I)	Teilwert *m*	partial value	valeur partielle *f*	—	valor parcial *m*
valore produttivo (I)	Produktionswert *m*	production value	valeur de production *f*	—	valor de la producción *m*
valore reale (I)	Sachwert *m*	real value	valeur matérielle *f*	—	valor real *m*
valore rimanente (I)	Restwert *m*	residual value/ net book value	valeur résiduelle *f*	—	valor residual *m*/valor contable residual *m*
valores de inversión (Es)	Anlagepapiere *pl*	investment securities	valeurs de placement *f*	titoli d'investimento *m pl*	—
valore sostanziale (I)	Substanzwert *m*	assets value	valeur de remplacement *f*	—	valor sustancial *m*
valores previstos (Es)	Planwerte *pl*	planning figures	valeurs prévisionnelles *f pl*	valori pianificati *m pl*	—
valore stimato[1] (I)	Taxwert *m*	estimated value	valeur de taxation *f*	—	valor de tasación *m*
valore stimato[2] (I)	Schätzwert *m*	estimated value	valeur d'estimation *f*	—	estimación *f*

	D	E	F	I	Es
valori misurati (I)	Meßwerte *pl*	measurements	valeurs mesurées *f pl*	—	valor de medida *m*
valori pianificati (I)	Planwerte *pl*	planning figures	valeurs prévisionnelles *f pl*	—	valores previstos *m pl*
valorisation (F)	Bewertung *f*	valuation	—	valutazione *f*	valoración *f*
valori standard (I)	Standardwerte *pl*	standard values	valeur standard *f*	—	valores representativos *m pl*
valor límite (Es)	Grenzwert *m*	limiting value	valeur marginale *f*	valore limite *m*	—
valor marginal (Es)	Marginalwert *m*	marginal value	valeur marginale *f*	valore marginale *m*	—
valor monetario (Es)	Geldwert *m*	value of money	valeur de l'argent *f*	valore monetario *m*	—
valor nominal (Es)	Nennwert *m*	nominal value	valeur nominale *f*	valore nominale *m*	—
valor nominal mínimo (Es)	Mindest-nennbetrag *m*	minimum nominal amount	montant nominal minimum *m*	importo nominale minimo *m*	—
valor para préstamos (Es)	Beleihungswert *m*	value as security for a loan	montant de la garantie *m*	valore finanziabile *m*	—
valor parcial (Es)	Teilwert *m*	partial value	valeur partielle *f*	valore parziale *m*	—
valor real (Es)	Sachwert *m*	real value	valeur matérielle *f*	valore reale *m*	—
valor residual (Es)	Restwert *m*	residual value/ net book value	valeur résiduelle *f*	valore rimanente *m*	—
valor sustancial (Es)	Substanzwert *m*	assets value	valeur de remplacement *f*	valore sostanziale *m*	—
valuable (E)	wertvoll	—	précieux	prezioso	precioso
value (E)	Wert *m*	—	valeur *f*	valore *m*	valor *m*
value added[1] (E)	Mehrwert *m*	—	valeur ajoutée *f*	valore aggiunto *m*	plusvalía *f*
value added[2] (E)	Wertschöpfung *f*	—	création de valeurs *f*	valore aggiunto *m*	creación de riqueza *f*
value-added tax (E)	Mehrwertsteuer *f*	—	taxe à la valeur ajoutée *f*	imposta sul valore aggiunto *m*	impuesto sobre el valor añadido *m*
value adjustment (E)	Wertberichtigung *f*	—	réévaluation *f*	rettifica del valore *f*	rectificación de valor *f*
value as security for a loan (E)	Beleihungswert *m*	—	montant de la garantie *m*	valore finanziabile *m*	valor para préstamos *m*
value of money (E)	Geldwert *m*	—	valeur de l'argent *f*	valore monetario *m*	valor monetario *m*
Valuta (D)	—	foreign exchange/ value	monnaie étrangère *f*	valuta *f*/divise *f pl*	moneda extranjera *f*/ divisas *f pl*/valuta *f*
valuta[1] (I)	Valuta *f*	foreign exchange/ value	monnaie étrangère *f*	—	moneda extranjera *f*/ divisas *f pl*/valuta *f*
valuta[2] (I)	Währung *f*	currency	monnaie *f*	—	moneda *f*
valuta aurea (I)	Goldwährung *f*	gold currency	monnaie à couverture or *f*	—	moneda oro *f*
valuta di riserva (I)	Reservewährung *f*	reserve currency	monnaie de réserve *f*	—	moneda de reserva *f*
valuta guida (I)	Leitwährung *f*	key currency	monnaie-clé *f*	—	moneda de referencia *f*
valutazione (I)	Bewertung *f*	valuation	valorisation *f*	—	valoración *f*
valutazione approssimativa (I)	vorsichtige Schätzung *f*	conservative estimate	évaluation approximative *f*	—	evaluación aproximativa *f*
valutazione del lavoro (I)	Arbeitsbewertung *f*	job evaluation	qualification du travail *f*	—	evaluación del trabajo *f*
vantaggio (I)	Vorteil *m*	advantage	avantage *m*	—	ventaja *f*
vantaggio concorrenziale (I)	Wettbewerbs-vorteil *m*	competitive advantage	avantage de concurrence *m*	—	ventaja de competencia *f*
vantaggio di costo (I)	Kostenvorteil *m*	cost advantage	avantage de coût *m*	—	ventaja de costes *f*
variabel (D)	—	variable	variable	variabile	variable
variabile (I)	variabel	variable	variable	—	variable
variable (E)	variabel	—	variable	variabile	variable
variable (Es)	variabel	variable	variable	variabile	—
variable (F)	variabel	variable	—	variabile	variable

	D	E	F	I	Es
variable costs (E)	variable Kosten pl	—	coûts variables m pl	costi variabili m pl	gastos variables m pl
variable Kosten (D)	—	variable costs	coûts variables m pl	costi variabili m pl	gastos variables m pl
variable rate of interest (E)	variabler Zins m	—	intérêt variable m	tasso d'interesse variabile m	interés variable m
variabler Zins (D)	—	variable rate of interest	intérêt variable m	tasso d'interesse variabile m	interés variable m
variety (E)	Sorte f	—	genre m	categoria f	especie f
véhicule à moteur (F)	Kraftfahrzeug n	motor vehicle	—	automobile f	automóvil m
veicolo pubblicitario (I)	Werbeträger m	advertising medium	support publicitaire m	—	medio de publicidad m
vencimiento (Es)	Ablauffrist f	time limit	délai m	termine di scadenza m	—
vendable (F)	marktfähig	marketable	—	smerciabile	comerciable
vender (Es)	verkaufen	sell	vendre	vendere	—
vendere (I)	verkaufen	sell	vendre	—	vender
vending machine[1] (E)	Verkaufsautomat m	—	distributeur automatique m	distributore automatico m	distribuidor automático m
vending machine[2] (E)	Automat m	—	appareil automatique m	distributore automatico m	distribuidor automático m
vendita[1] (I)	Absatz m	sale/distribution	volume des ventes m	—	cifra de ventas f
vendita[2] (I)	Verkauf m	sale	vente f	—	venta f
vendita all'asta (I)	Versteigerung f	auction	vente à l'enchère f	—	subasta f
vendita allo scoperto[1] (I)	Leerverkauf m	bear sale	vente à découvert f	—	venta al descubierto f
vendita allo scoperto[2] (I)	Blankoverkauf m	short sale	vente à découvert f	—	venta al descubierto f
vendita a rate[1] (I)	Teilzahlungs-geschäft n	partial payment transaction	achat à tempérament m	—	operación a plazo f
vendita a rate[2] (I)	Ratengeschäft n	instalment sale transaction	vente à tempérament f	—	venta a plazo f
vendita complementare (I)	Zusatzverkauf m	additional sale	vente additionnelle f	—	venta adicional f
vendita diretta (I)	Direktverkauf m	direct selling	vente directe f	—	venta directa f
vendita esclusiva (I)	Alleinvertrieb m	exclusive distribution	vente exclusive f	—	distribución exclusiva f
vendita giudiziaria (I)	Zwangsverkauf m	forced sale	vente forcée f	—	venta forzada f
vendita per corrispondenza (I)	Versandhandel m	mail order business	commerce de vente au détail par correspondance m	—	venta por correspondencia f
vendita per distributori automatici (I)	Automatenverkauf m	automatic vending	vente par distributeur automatique f	—	venta por distribuido-res automáticos f
vendita per telefono (I)	Telefonverkauf m	inter-office sale	vente par téléphone f	—	venta por teléfono f
vendre (F)	verkaufen	sell	—	vendere	vender
venta (Es)	Verkauf m	sale	vente f	vendita f	—
venta adicional (Es)	Zusatzverkauf m	additional sale	vente additionnelle f	vendita complementare f	—
venta al descubierto[1] (Es)	Blankoverkauf m	short sale	vente à découvert f	vendita allo scoperto f	—
venta al descubierto[2] (Es)	Leerverkauf m	bear sale	vente à découvert f	vendita allo scoperto f	—
venta a plazo (Es)	Ratengeschäft n	instalment sale transaction	vente à tempérament f	vendita a rate f	—
venta a plazos (Es)	Abzahlungs-geschäft n	hire purchase transaction	achat à tempérament m	operazione con pagamento a rate f	—
venta con pérdida (Es)	Verlustgeschäft n	losing business	affaire déficitaire f	affare in perdita m	—
venta de liquidación (Es)	Schlußverkauf m	seasonal sale	vente de fin de saison f	svendita di fine stagione f	—
venta directa (Es)	Direktverkauf m	direct selling	vente directe f	vendita diretta f	—

	D	E	F	I	Es
venta en cadena (Es)	Schneeballsystem n	snowball system	système de la boule de neige m	sistema di vendite a catena aperta m	—
venta forzada (Es)	Zwangsverkauf m	forced sale	vente forcée f	vendita giudiziaria f	—
ventaja (Es)	Vorteil m	advantage	avantage m	vantaggio m	—
ventaja de competencia (Es)	Wettbewerbsvorteil m	competitive advantage	avantage de concurrence m	vantaggio concorrenziale m	—
ventaja de costes (Es)	Kostenvorteil m	cost advantage	avantage de coût m	vantaggio di costo m	—
venta por correspondencia (Es)	Versandhandel m	mail order business	commerce de vente au détail par correspondance m	vendita per corrispondenza f	—
venta por distribuidores automáticos (Es)	Automatenverkauf m	automatic vending	vente par distributeur automatique f	vendita per distributori automatici f	—
venta por teléfono (Es)	Telefonverkauf m	inter-office sale	vente par téléphone f	vendita per telefono f	—
ventas netas (Es)	Nettoumsatz m	net turnover	chiffre d'affaires net m	fatturato netto m	—
venta total (Es)	Räumungsverkauf m	clearance sale	liquidation des stocks f	liquidazione totale f	—
vente (F)	Verkauf m	sale	—	vendita f	venta f
vente additionnelle (F)	Zusatzverkauf m	additional sale	—	vendita complementare f	venta adicional f
vente à découvert[1] (F)	Blankoverkauf m	short sale	—	vendita allo scoperto f	venta al descubierto f
vente à découvert[2] (F)	Leerverkauf m	bear sale	—	vendita allo scoperto f	venta al descubierto f
vente à l'enchère[1] (F)	Versteigerung f	auction	—	vendita all'asta f	subasta f
vente à l'enchère[2] (F)	Auktion f	auction	—	asta f	subasta f
vente à tempérament (F)	Ratengeschäft n	instalment sale transaction	—	vendita a rate f	venta a plazo f
vente de biens par justice (F)	Zwangsversteigerung f	sale by court order	—	asta giudiziaria f	subasta forzosa f
vente de fin de saison (F)	Schlußverkauf m	seasonal sale	—	svendita di fine stagione f	venta de liquidación f
vente directe (F)	Direktverkauf m	direct selling	—	vendita diretta f	venta directa f
vente exclusive (F)	Alleinvertrieb m	exclusive distribution	—	vendita esclusiva f	distribución exclusiva f
vente forcée (F)	Zwangsverkauf m	forced sale	—	vendita giudiziaria f	venta forzada f
vente par distributeur automatique (F)	Automatenverkauf m	automatic vending	—	vendita per distributori automatici f	venta por distribuidores automáticos f
vente par téléphone (F)	Telefonverkauf m	inter-office sale	—	vendita per telefono f	venta por teléfono f
venture (E)	Wagnis n	—	risque m	rischio m	riesgo m
verarbeitende Industrie (D)	—	manufacturing industry	industrie transformatrice f	industria di trasformazione f	industria transformadora f
Verarbeitung (D)	—	processing	transformation f	lavorazione f	transformación f
Veräußerung (D)	—	sale/alienation	aliénation f	alienazione f	enajenación f
verbale (I)	mündlich	verbal	verbal	—	oral
Verband (D)	—	association	association f	associazione f	asociación f
Verbesserungsvorschlag (D)	—	suggestion for improvement	proposition d'amélioration f	proposta di miglioramento f	propuesta de mejora f
Verbilligung (D)	—	cheapening	réduction du prix f	ribasso m	abaratamiento m
Verbindlichkeiten (D)	—	liability/debts	obligation f/ dettes f pl	obblighi m pl/ debiti m pl	obligaciones f pl/ deudas f pl/créditos pasivos m pl
Verbrauch (D)	—	consumption	consommation f	consumo m	consumo m
verbrauchen (D)	—	consume	consommer	consumare	consumir
Verbraucher (D)	—	consumer	consommateur m	consumatore m	consumidor m
Verbraucherinformation (D)	—	consumer information	information des consommateurs f	informazione per i consumatori f	información de consumidores f
Verbrauchermarkt (D)	—	consumer market	marché des consommateurs m	ipermercato m	mercado favorable al consumidor m

	D	E	F	I	Es
Verbraucher-organisation (D)	—	consumer protection organization	organisation des consommateurs f	organizzazione dei consumatori f	orgnización de defensa del consumidor f
Verbraucherschutz (D)	—	consumer protection	protection des consommateurs f	tutela dei consumatori f	protección de los consumidores f
Verbrauchsgüter (D)	—	consumer goods	biens de consommation m pl	beni non durevoli m pl	bienes de consumo m pl
Verbrennung (D)	—	incineration	combustion f	combustione f	combustión f
verderblich (D)	—	perishable	périssable	deperibile	perecedero
Veredelung (D)	—	processing	perfectionnement m	perfezionamento m	perfeccionamiento m
Verein (D)	—	association	association f	associazione f	asociación f
vereinbarungs-gemäß (D)	—	as agreed	comme convenu	come convenuto	según lo acordado
Verfahren (D)	—	procedure/process	méthode f/ procédure f	procedimento m/ procedura f	proceso m/ procedimiento m
Verfahrens-einstellung (D)	—	abatement of an action	arrêt d'une procédure	sospensione del procedimento f	sobreseimiento del proceso m
Verfahrenskosten (D)	—	costs of the proceedings	frais de procédure m pl	spese del procedimento f pl	costas f pl
Verfallsdatum (D)	—	expiry date	date d'échéance f	data di scadenza f	fecha de vencimiento f
Verfalltag (D)	—	day of expiry	jour de l'échéance m	giorno di scadenza m	día de vencimiento m
verfrachten (D)	—	freight/ship	fréter/embarquer	imbarcare	expedir/fletar
Verfrachtung (D)	—	carriage of goods by sea	affrètement m	trasporto marittimo m	expedición f
verfügbares Einkommen (D)	—	disposable income	revenu disponible m	introito disponibile m	ingresos disponibles m pl
Verfügung (D)	—	disposal/order disposition m	disposition f/acte de	disposizione f/ ordinanza f	disposición f/ decreto m
Vergleich (D)	—	comparison	comparaison f	confronto m	comparación f
vergleichende Werbung (D)	—	comparative advertising	publicité comparative f	pubblicità comparativa f	publicidad comparativa f
Vergleichs-verfahren (D)	—	composition proceedings	procédure de conciliation f	procedura di concordato f	procedimiento conciliatorio m
Vergütung (D)	—	remuneration	rémunération f	ricompensa f	remuneración f
Verhältnis (D)	—	proportion	relation f	rapporto m	relación f
Verhandlung (D)	—	negotiation	négociation f	trattativa f	negociación f/ juicio m/ vista oral f
Verhandlungs-geschick (D)	—	negotiation skills	habileté de négociation f	abilità nel trattare f	tino de negociar m
verificación (Es)	Prüfung f	inspection/ examination	vérification f/ examen m	controllo m/ esame m	—
verificación de la calidad (Es)	Qualitätskontrolle f	quality control	contrôle de la qualité m	controllo di qualità m	—
vérificateur des comptes (F)	Abschlußprüfer m	auditor	—	revisore m	revisor contable m
vérification¹ (F)	Prüfung f	inspection/ examination	—	controllo m/ esame m	verificación f/ examen m
vérification² (F)	Nachprüfung f	reexamination	—	revisione f	revisión f
vérification des comptes (F)	Abschlußprüfung f	audit	—	revisione f	revisión contable f
vérification des livres de l'entreprise (F)	Betriebsprüfung f	investigation by the tax authorities	—	revisione aziendale f	inspección de la explotación f
Verjährung (D)	—	limitation of actions	prescription f	prescrizione f	prescripción f
Verkauf (D)	—	sale	vente f	vendita f	venta f
verkaufen (D)	—	sell	vendre	vendere	vender
Verkäufermarkt (D)	—	seller's market	marché de vendeurs m	mercato favorevole ai venditori m	mercado favorable al vendedor m
Verkäuferprovision (D)	—	sales commission	commission sur les ventes f	provvigione del venditore f	comisión sobre la venta f
Verkäuferschulung (D)	—	sales training	formation des vendeurs f	addestramento dei venditori f	formación de los vendedores f
Verkäufer-wettbewerb (D)	—	sellers competition	compétition des vendeurs f	concorrenza dei venditori f	competición de vendedores f

	D	E	F	I	Es
Verkaufsabschluß (D)	—	sales contract	contrat de vente *m*	conclusione di vendita *f*	conclusión de la venta *f*
Verkaufsanalyse (D)	—	sales analysis	analyse des ventes *f*	analisi delle vendite *f*	análisis de las ventas *m*
Verkaufsautomat (D)	—	vending machine	distributeur automatique *m*	distributore automatico *m*	distribuidor automático *m*
Verkaufsbericht (D)	—	sales report	rapport de vente *m*	rapporto sulle vendite *m*	informe de venta *m*
Verkaufschance (D)	—	sales possibilities	possibilité de vente *f*	prospettiva dello smercio *f*	posibilidades de venta *f pl*
Verkaufserlös (D)	—	sale proceeds	produit des ventes *m*	ricavo delle vendite *m*	producto de la venta *m*
Verkaufsförderung (D)	—	sales promotion	encouragement à la vente *m*	promozione di vendita *f*	promoción de las ventas *f*
Verkaufsgebiet (D)	—	sales territory	territoire de vente *m*	zona di vendita *f*	territorio de venta *m*
Verkaufsgespräch (D)	—	sale talk	conversation de vente *f*	colloquio di vendita *m*	conversación de venta *f*
Verkaufskampagne (D)	—	sales campaign	campagne de vente *f*	campagna di vendita *f*	campaña de venta *f*
Verkaufskonzeption (D)	—	sales conception	conception de vente *f*	concezione di vendita *f*	concepción de venta *f*
Verkaufsmethoden (D)	—	sales strategy	méthodes de vente *f pl*	metodi di vendita *m pl*	métodos de venta *m pl*
Verkaufsoption (D)	—	option to sell	option de vente *f*	opzione di vendita *f*	opción de venta *f*
Verkaufsprogramm (D)	—	sales programme	programme de vente *m*	programma di vendita *m*	programa de venta *m*
Verkaufsstab (D)	—	sales staff	équipe de vente *f*	staff di venditori *m*	equipo de venta *m*
Verkaufstechnik (D)	—	sales technique	art de vendre *m*	tecnica di vendita *f*	técnica de venta *f*
Verkehr (D)	—	traffic	circulation *f*	traffico *m*	circulación *f*
Verkehrspolitik (D)	—	transport policy	politique des transports *f*	politica del traffico *f*	política de transportes *f*
Verladekosten (D)	—	loading charges	coût du chargement *m*	costi di caricamento *m pl*	gastos de carga *m pl*
verladen (D)	—	load	charger	caricare	expedir
Verlag (D)	—	publishing house	maison d'édition *f*	casa editrice *f*	editorial *f*
Verlängerung (D)	—	extension	prolongation *f*	prolungamento *m*	prórroga *f*
Verleger (D)	—	publisher	éditeur *m*	editore *m*	editor *m*
verlorengegangene Sendung (D)	—	lost shipment	envoi perdu *m*	spedizione andata persa *f*	envío perdido *m*
Verlust (D)	—	loss	perte *f*	perdita *f*	pérdida *f*
Verlustgeschäft (D)	—	losing business	affaire déficitaire *f*	affare in perdita *m*	venta con pérdida *f*
vermarkten (D)	—	market	commercialiser	lanciare sul mercato	comercializar
Vermerk (D)	—	note	remarque *f*	annotazione *f*	nota *f*
Vermittlung (D)	—	mediation	médiation *f*	mediazione *f*	mediación *f*
Vermögen (D)	—	property	patrimoine *m*	patrimonio *m*	patrimonio *m*
Vermögensbildung (D)	—	capital formation	formation de capital *f*	formazione del patrimonio *f*	formación de capital *f*
Vermögenspolitik (D)	—	policy relating to capital formation	politique financière *f*	politica patrimoniale *f*	política de los patrimonios *f*
Vermögens-rechnung (D)	—	capital account	calcul du patrimoine *m*	calcolo del patrimonio *m*	cálculo del valor neto *m*
Vermögens-verhältnisse (D)	—	financial situation	situation financière *f*	situazione patrimoniale *f*	situación económica *f*
Vermögens-verteilung (D)	—	distribution of wealth	répartition du patrimoine *f*	ripartizione del patrimonio *f*	reparto de la riqueza *m*
Veröffentlichung (D)	—	publication	publication *f*	pubblicazione *f*	publicación *f*
Verordnung (D)	—	decree	décret *m*	regolamento *m*	ordenanza *f*
Verpackung (D)	—	packing	emballage *m*	imballaggio *m*	embalaje *m*
Verpackungseinheit (D)	—	packing unit	unité d'emballage *f*	unità d'imballaggio *f*	unidad de embalaje *f*

	D	E	F	I	Es
Verpackungs-material (D)	—	packing material	matériel d'emballage m	materiale d'imballaggio m	empaque m
Verpackungsmüll (D)	—	packing waste	déchets d'emballage m pl	rifiuti da imballaggi m pl	basura de embalaje f
Verpackungs-vorschriften (D)		packing instructions	prescriptions concernant l'emballage f pl	prescrizioni per l'imballaggio f pl	prescripciones de embalaje f pl
Verpfändung (D)	—	pledge	mise en gage f	pignoramento m	pignoración f
Verrechnung (D)	—	compensation	compensation f	compensazione f	compensación f
Verrechnungs-einheit (D)	—	clearing unit	unité de compte f	unità di compensazione f	unidad de compensación f
Verrechnungs-scheck (D)	—	crossed cheque	chèque à porter en compte m	assegno sbarrato m	cheque cruzado m
Versand (D)	—	dispatch	expédition f	spedizione f	envío m
Versandabteilung (D)	—	dispatch department	service des expéditions m	reparto spedizioni m	departamento de expedición m
Versandavis (D)	—	advice of dispatch	avis d'expédition m	avviso di spedizione m	aviso de envío m
versandbereit (D)	—	ready for dispatch	prêt à être expédié	pronto per la spedizione	listo para ser expedido
Versanddokument (D)	—	shipping document	documents d'expédition m pl	documento di spedizione m	documentos de expedición m pl
Versandform (D)	—	manner of delivery	forme d'expédition f	tipo di spedizione m	forma de envío f
Versandhandel (D)	—	mail order business	commerce de vente au détail par correspondance m	vendita per corrispondenza f	venta por correspondencia f
Versandleiter (D)	—	manager of shipping department	chef du service des expéditions m	capo reparto spedizioni m	jefe del departamento de expedición m
Versandvorschrift (D)	—	forwarding instruction	prescriptions concernant l'expédition f pl	prescrizione per la spedizione f	instrucción para el envío f
Verschiffung (D)	—	shipment	embarquement m	imbarco m	embarque m
Verschmelzung (D)	—	merger	fusion f	fusione f	fusión f
verschrotten (D)	—	scrap	mettre à la ferraille	ridurre a rottame	hacer quincalla u/c/ desguazar
Verschuldung (D)	—	indebtedness	endettement m	indebitamento m	endeudamiento m
Verschuldungsgrad (D)	—	debt ratio	niveau de l'endettement m	tasso d'indebitamento m	grado de endeudamiento m
versement complémentaire (F)	Nachzahlung f	supplementary payment	—	pagamento supplementare m	pago suplementario m
Versicherung (D)	—	insurance	assurance f	assicurazione f	seguro m
Versicherung auf Gegenseitigkeit (D)	—	mutual insurance	assurance mutuelle f	mutua assicurazione f	caja de socorros mutuos f
Versicherungsagent (D)	—	insurance agent	agent d'assurance m	agente d'assicurazione m	agente de seguros m
Versicherungsfall (D)	—	event insured against	sinistre m	caso di sinistro m	situación de siniestro f
Versicherungs-gesellschaft (D)	—	insurance company	société d'assurance f	compagnia di assicurazione f	sociedad de seguros f
Versicherungs-makler (D)	—	insurance broker	courtier en assurance m	mediatore d'assicurazione m	corredor de seguros m
Versicherungs-nehmer (D)	—	insured person	souscripteur d'une assurance m	assicurato m	asegurado m
Versicherungs-pflicht (D)	—	liability to insure	assujettissement obligatoire à l'assurance m	obbligo d'assicurazione m	obligatoriedad del seguro f
Versicherungs-police (D)	—	insurance policy	police d'assurance f	polizza d'assicurazione f	seguro m
Versicherungs-prämie (D)	—	insurance premium	prime d'assurance f	premio d'assicurazione m	prima de seguro f
Versicherungs-schutz (D)	—	insurance cover	couverture de l'assurance f	copertura assicurativa f	cobertura de seguro f
Versicherungs-summe (D)	—	insurance sum	montant de l'assurance m	somma assicurata f	suma asegurada f
Versicherungs-vertrag (D)	—	insurance contract	contrat d'assurance m	contratto d'assicurazione m	contrato de seguro m

	D	E	F	I	Es
Versorgung (D)	—	supply	approvisionne-ment *m*	approvvigiona-mento *m*	abastecimiento *m*
Versorgungs-einrichtung (D)	—	pension scheme	institution de retraite *f*	istituto previdenziale *m*	insitución de previsón *f*
Verspätung (D)	—	delay	retard *m*	ritardo *m*	retraso *m*
Verstaatlichung (D)	—	nationalization	nationalisaiton *f*	nazionalizzazione *f*	nacionalización *f*
Versteigerung (D)	—	auction	vente à l'enchère *f*	vendita all'asta *f*	subasta *f*
Vertagung (D)	—	postponement	ajournement *m*	rinvio *m*	aplazamiento *m*/suspensión *f*
Verteilung (D)	—	distribution	distribution *f*	distribuzione *f*	distribución *f*
Verteilungspolitik (D)	—	distribution policy	politique de répartition *f*	politica della distribuzione *f*	política de distribución *f*
Verteuerung (D)	—	rise in price	enchérissement *m*	rincaro *m*	encarecimiento *m*
Vertrag (D)	—	contract/treaty/agreement	contrat *m*/traité *m*/accord *m*	contratto *m*	contrato *m*/tratado *m*/acuerdo *m*
Vertragsabschluß (D)	—	conclusion of a contract	conclusion du contrat *f*	stipulazione del contratto *f*	conclusión de un contrato *f*
Vertragsänderung (D)	—	modification of a contract	modification du contrat *f*	modificazione del contratto *f*	modificación de contrato *f*
Vertragsbedingung (D)	—	term of contract	condition du contrat *f*	condizione del contratto *f*	condiciones contractuales *f pl*
Vertragsdauer (D)	—	contract period	durée du contrat *f*	durata del contratto *f*	duración del contrato *f*
Vertragsfreiheit (D)	—	freedom of contract	liberté de contracter *f*	libertà contrattuale *f*	libertad contractual *f*
Vertragsstrafe (D)	—	contractual penalty	pénalité *f*	penalità convenzionale *f*	pena convencional *f*
Vertrauens-verhältnis (D)	—	confidential relationship	rapport de confiance *m*	rapporto di fiducia *m*	relación de confianza *f*
vertraulich (D)	—	confidential	confidentiel	confidenziale	confidencial
Vertreter (D)	—	representative	représentant *m*	rappresentante *m*	representante *m*
Vertretertagung (D)	—	sales meeting	réunion de représentants *f*	convegno dei rappresentanti *m*	conferencia de representantes *f*
Vertretung (D)	—	representation	représentation *f*	rappresentanza *f*	representación *f*
Vertretungs-berechtigung (D)	—	authorized to represent	autorisation de représentation *f*	autorizzazione alla rappresentanza *f*	derecho de representación *m*
Vertrieb (D)	—	distribution	distribution *f*	distribuzione *f*	distribución *f*
Vertriebsfirma (D)	—	distributor	distributeur *m*	ditta di distribuzione *f*	compañia distribuidora *f*
Vertriebsstruktur (D)	—	structure of distribution	structure de distribution *f*	struttura della distribuzione *f*	estructura de distribución *f*
Vertriebsweg (D)	—	distribution channel	canal de distribution *m*	rete di distribuzione *f*	circuito de distribución *f*
Veruntreuung (D)	—	misappropriation	détournement *m*	abuso di fiducia *m*	malversación *f*
Verursacherprinzip (D)	—	polluter pays principle	principe du pollueur payeur *m*	principio della colpa oggettiva *m*	principio contamina-dor-pagador *m*
Vervielfältigung (D)	—	reproduction	reproduction *f*	riproduzione *f*	reproducción *f*/multiplicación *f*
Verwahrung (D)	—	custody	dépôt *m*	custodia *f*	custodia *f*/incautación *f*
Verwalter (D)	—	administrator	administrateur *m*	amministratore *m*	administrador *m*
Verwaltung (D)	—	administration	administration *f*	amministrazione *f*	administración *f*
Verwaltungsakt (D)	—	administrative act	acte administratif *m*	atto amministrativo *m*	acto administrativo *m*
Verwaltungshoheit (D)	—	power of administration	autonomie d'administration *f*	sovranità amministrativa *f*	soberanía administrativa *f*
verzinsen (D)	—	pay interest on	compter des intérêts	pagare interessi	pagar interés
verzollt (D)	—	duty paid	dédouané	sdoganato	aranceles pagados
Verzug (D)	—	delay	demeure *f*	mora *f*	retraso *m*/demora *f*
Verzugszinsen (D)	—	default interest	intérêts moratoires *m pl*	interessi di mora *m pl*	intereses de demora *m pl*
vetrina[1] (I)	Schaufenster *n*	shop-window	vitrine *f*	—	escaparate *m*

	D	E	F	I	Es
vetrina² (I)	Auslage f	display/ expenditure	étalage f/ débours m	—	vitrina f/ gastos m pl
vettore (I)	Frachtführer m	carrier	transporteur m	—	transportista m
vettore aereo (I)	Luftfrachtführer m	air carrier	voiturier aérien m	—	transportista m
vettura aziendale (I)	Firmenwagen m	company car	voiture appartenant à l'entreprise f	—	coche de empresa m
vettura da noleggio (I)	Leihwagen m	hired car	voiture de location f	—	coche de alquiler m
vettura di servizio (I)	Dienstwagen m	official car	voiture de service f	—	coche de servicio m
via (I)	Straße f	street/road	rue f/route f	—	calle f/carretera f
vía aérea (Es)	Luftweg m	air route	voie aérienne f	via aerea f	—
via aerea (I)	Luftweg m	air route	voie aérienne f	—	vía aérea f
via d'acqua (I)	Wasserstraße f	waterway	voie d'eau f	—	vía navegable f
vía de transporte (Es)	Transportweg m	route of transportation	voie de transport f	via di trasporto f	—
via della distribuzione (I)	Absatzweg m	channel of distribution	canal de distribution m	—	medio de venta f
via di trasporto (I)	Transportweg m	route of transportation	voie de transport f	—	vía de transporte f
viajante (Es)	festangestellter Reisender m	sales representative	voyageur de commerce m	commesso viaggiatore m	—
vía marítima (Es)	Seeweg m	sea route	voie maritime f	via marittima f	—
via marittima (I)	Seeweg m	sea route	voie maritime f	—	vía marítima f
vía navegable (Es)	Wasserstraße f	waterway	voie d'eau f	via d'acqua f	—
via terra (I)	Landweg m	overland transportation	voie de terre f	—	vía terrestre m
vía terrestre (Es)	Landweg m	overland transportation	voie de terre f	via terra f	—
video (I)	Bildschirm m	screen	écran m	—	pantalla f
videotex (I)	Bildschirmtext m	videotext	videotex international m	—	teletexto m
videotex international (F)	Bildschirmtext m	videotext	—	videotex m	teletexto m
videotext (E)	Bildschirmtext m	—	videotex international m	videotex m	teletexto m
vierteljährlich (D)	—	quarterly	trimestriel	trimestrale	trimestral
vierzehn Tage (D)	—	fortnight	quinze jours	quindici giorni	quince días m pl
vigilar (Es)	überwachen	supervise	surveiller	sorvegliare	—
violación de las reglas de competencia (Es)	Wettbewerbs- verstoß m	violation of competition rules	violation de concurrence f	violazione delle re- gole di concorrenza f	—
violation de concurrence (F)	Wettbewerbs- verstoß m	violation of competition rules	—	violazione delle regole di concorrenza f	violación de las reglas de competencia f
violation of competition rules (E)	Wettbewerbs- verstoß m	—	violation de concurrence f	violazione delle regole di concorrenza f	violación de las reglas de competencia f
violazione delle re- gole di concorrenza (I)	Wettbewerbs- verstoß m	violation of competition rules	violation de concurrence f	—	violación de las reglas de competencia f
virement¹ (F)	Giro n	credit transfer	—	giro m	giro m
virement² (F)	Überweisung f	remittance	—	rimessa f	transferencia f
virement bancaire (F)	Banküberweisung f	bank transfer	—	rimessa bancaria f	transferencia bancaria f
virement par câble (F)	Kabelüberweisung f	cable transfer	—	bonifico telegrafico m	giro telegráfico m
virement postal¹ (F)	Postüberweisung f	postal remittance	—	bonifico postale m	giro postal m
virement postal² (F)	Postgiro n	postal giro	—	postagiro m	giro postal m
visa (E)	Visum n	—	visa m	visto m	visado m
visa (F)	Visum n	visa	—	visto m	visado m
visado (Es)	Visum n	visa	visa m	visto m	—
visto (I)	Visum n	visa	visa m	—	visado m
Visum (D)	—	visa	visa m	visto m	visado m
vitrine (F)	Schaufenster n	shop-window	—	vetrina f	escaparate m

	D	E	F	I	Es
vivienda (Es)	Wohnung f	apartment	appartement m	abitazione f	—
vizio (I)	Mangel m	defect	défaut m	—	defecto m/ vicio m
vocational adjustment (E)	Einarbeitung f	—	entraînement m	periodo d'adattamento m	entrenamiento m
voce (I)	Posten m	item	poste m	—	puesto m
void (E)	nichtig	—	non valable	nullo	nulo
voie aérienne (F)	Luftweg m	air route	—	via aerea f	vía aérea f
voie d'eau (F)	Wasserstraße f	waterway	—	via d'acqua f	vía navegable f
voie de terre (F)	Landweg m	overland transportation	—	via terra f	vía terrestre m
voie de transport (F)	Transportweg m	route of transportation	—	via di trasporto f	vía de transporte f
voie maritime (F)	Seeweg m	sea route	—	via marittima f	vía marítima f
voirie (F)	Wegenetz n	road network	—	rete stradale f	comunicaciones f pl
voiture appartenant à l'entreprise (F)	Firmenwagen m	company car	—	vettura aziendale f	coche de empresa m
voiture de location (F)	Leihwagen m	hired car	—	vettura da noleggio f	coche de alquiler m
voiture de service (F)	Dienstwagen m	official car	—	vettura di servizio f	coche de servicio m
voiture d'occasion (F)	Gebrauchtwagen m	used car	—	automobile usata f	coche de segunda mano m
voiturier aérien (F)	Luftfracht-führer m	air carrier	—	vettore aereo m	transportista m
voix (F)	Stimme f	voting	—	voto m	voz f
vol (F)	Diebstahl m	theft	—	furto m	robo m
vol charter (F)	Charterflug m	charter flight	—	volo charter m	vuelo fletado m
Volkseinkommen (D)	—	national income	revenu national m	reddito nazionale m	renta nacional f
Volkswirtschaft (D)	—	national economy	économie nationale f	economia politica f	economía nacional f
Volkswirtschaftliche Gesamtrechnung (D)	—	national accounting	comptabilité nationale f	contabilità nazionale f	contabilidad nacional f
Volkswirtschafts-lehre (D)	—	economics	économie politique f	economia politica f	ciencias económicas f pl
Volkszählung (D)	—	census of population	recensement démographique m	censimento m	censo m
Vollbeschäftigung (D)	—	full employment	plein emploi m	piena occupazione f	empleo total m
Vollmacht (D)	—	full power/power of attorney	plein pouvoir m/ mandat m	mandato m	poder m/ autorización f/ escritura de poder f
Vollmachtgeber (D)	—	grantor of a power of attorney	auteur de la procuration m	mandante m	poderdante m
vollständige Bezahlung (D)	—	payment in full	payement complet m	pagamento totale m	pago íntegro m
Vollstreckung (D)	—	enforcement	exécution f	esecuzione f	ejecución f
volo charter (I)	Charterflug m	charter flight	vol charter m	—	vuelo fletado m
volume¹ (E)	Umfang m	—	volume m	entità f	volumen m/ dimensión f
volume² (E)	Volumen n	—	volume m	volume m	volumen m
volume (F)	Volumen n	volume	—	volume m	volumen m
volume (I)	Volumen n	volume	volume m	—	volumen m
volume des ventes (F)	Absatz m	sale/distribution	—	vendita f	cifra de ventas f
volume di lavoro (I)	Arbeitsanfall m	volume of work	travail à exécuter m	—	volumen de trabajo m
volume monetario (I)	Geldvolumen n	volume of money	masse monétaire f	—	volumen monetario m
Volumen (D)	—	volume	volume m	volume m	volumen m
volumen (Es)	Volumen n	volume	volume m	volume m	—
volumen de trabajo (Es)	Arbeitsanfall m	volume of work	travail à exécuter m	volume di lavoro m	—
volumen de ventas (Es)	Umsatz m	turnover	chiffre d'affaires m	fatturato m	—

	D	E	F	I	Es
volumen monetario¹ (Es)	Geldvolumen *n*	volume of money	masse monétaire *f*	volume monetario *m*	—
volumen monetario² (Es)	Geldmenge *f*	money supply	quantité de monnaie en circulation *f*	massa monetaria *f*	—
volume of money (E)	Geldvolumen *n*	—	masse monétaire *f*	volume monetario *m*	volumen monetario *m*
volume of work (E)	Arbeitsanfall *m*	—	travail à exécuter *m*	volume di lavoro *m*	volumen de trabajo *m*
voluntary constraint in consumption (E)	Konsumverzicht *m*	—	renonciation à la consommation *f*	rinuncia al consumo *f*	renuncia al consumo *f*
voluntary disclosure (E)	Selbstauskunft *f*	—	renseignement fourni lui-même *m*	informazione volontaria *f*	información de sí mismo *f*
Voranschlag (D)	—	estimate	devis *m*	preventivo *m*	presupuesto *m*
Voraussetzung (D)	—	precondition	condition préalable *f*	presupposto *m*	condición previa *f*
Vorauszahlung (D)	—	payment in advance	payement anticipé *m*	pagamento anticipato *m*	adelanto *m*
Vorbereitung (D)	—	preparation	préparation *f*	preparazione *f*	preparación *f*
Vorbestellrabatt (D)	—	discount on advance orders	escompte de suscription *m*	ribasso per ordinazioni anticipate *m*	descuento de suscripción *m*
Vorbestellung (D)	—	reservation	commande préalable *f*	ordinazione anticipata *f*	pedidio anticipado *m*
Vorbörse (D)	—	before hours dealing	marché avant le marché officiel *m*	mercato preborsistico *m*	operaciones antes de la apertura de la bolsa *f pl*
vordatierter Scheck (D)	—	antidated cheque	chèque antidaté *m*	assegno antidatato *m*	cheque de fecha adelantada *m*
Vordruck (D)	—	printed form	imprimé *m*	modulo *m*	impreso *m*
Vorkalkulation (D)	—	estimation of cost	calcul des coûts a priori *m*	calcolo preventivo *m*	cálculo provisional *m*
Vorkaufsrecht (D)	—	preemption right	droit de préemption *m*	diritto di prelazione *m*	derecho de preferencia *m*
Vorrat (D)	—	stock	stock *m*	scorte *f pl*	existencias *f pl*
Vorratshaltung (D)	—	stockpiling	stockage *m*	gestione delle scorte *f*	formación de stocks *f*
Vorrecht (D)	—	privilege	prérogative *f*	privilegio *m*	derecho preferente *m*
Vorschlag (D)	—	proposal	proposition *f*	proposta *f*	proposición *f*
Vorschuß (D)	—	advance	avance *f*	anticipo *m*	anticipo *m*
vorsichtige Schätzung (D)	—	conservative estimate	évaluation approximative *f*	valutazione approssimativa *f*	evaluación aproximativa *f*
Vorsitz (D)	—	chairmanship	présidence *f*	presidenza *f*	presidencia *f*
Vorstand (D)	—	board	comité directeur *m*	consiglio di amministrazione *m*	consejo de dirección *m*
Vorstandsmitglied (D)	—	member of the managing board	membre du comité de direction *m*	membro del consiglio di amministrazione *m*	consejero directivo *m*
Vorstandsvorsitzender (D)	—	chairman of the board	président du comité de direction *m*	presidente del consiglio di amministrazione *m*	presidente del consejo *m*
Vorstellungstermin (D)	—	date of interview	rendez-vous de présentation *m*	appuntamento di presentazione *m*	fecha de entrevista personal *f*
Vorsteuer (D)	—	input tax	impôt perçu en amont *m*	imposta sul fatturato d'acquisto *f*	impuesto sobre el valor añadido deducible *m*
Vorteil (D)	—	advantage	avantage *m*	vantaggio *m*	ventaja *f*
Vorzugsaktie (D)	—	preference share	action privilégiée *f*	azione privilegiata *f*	acción preferente *f*
Vorzugsrabatt (D)	—	preferential discount	remise de faveur *f*	ribasso preferenziale *m*	rebaja preferencial *f*
votazione (I)	Stimmabgabe *f*	vote	vote *m*	—	voto *m*
vote (E)	Stimmabgabe *f*	—	vote *m*	votazione *f*	voto *m*
vote (F)	Stimmabgabe *f*	vote	—	votazione *f*	voto *m*
voting (E)	Stimme *f*	—	voix *f*	voto *m*	voz *f*
voto (Es)	Stimmabgabe *f*	vote	vote *m*	votazione *f*	—
voto (I)	Stimme *f*	voting	voix *f*	—	voz *f*
voucher¹ (E)	Beleg *m*	—	justificatif *m*	quietanza *f*	justificativo *m*

	D	E	F	I	Es
voucher² (E)	Bon m	—	bon m	buono m	bono m
voyageur de commerce (F)	festangestellter Reisender m	sales representative	—	commesso viaggiatore m	viajante m
voz (Es)	Stimme f	voting	voix f	voto m	—
vue d'ensemble du marché (F)	Marktübersicht f	overall view of the market	—	quadro del mercato m	panorama de mercado m
vuelo fletado (Es)	Charterflug m	charter flight	vol charter m	volo charter m	—
Wachstum (D)	—	growth	croissance f	crescita f	crecimiento m
Wachstumsimpuls (D)	—	growth impulse	stimulation de l'accroissement f	impulso di crescita m	impulso de crecimiento m
Wachstumspolitik (D)	—	growth policy	politique d'accroissement f	politica di crescita f	política de crecimiento económico f
Wachstumsrate (D)	—	rate of growth	taux d'accroissement m	tasso di crescita m	tasa de crecimiento f
wage (E)	Lohn m	—	salaire m	salario m	salario m
wage agreement (E)	Lohnvereinbarung f	—	accord de salaires m	accordo salariale m	pacto salarial m
wage claim (E)	Lohnforderung f	—	revendication de salaire f	rivendicazione salariale f	reivindicación salarial f
wage freeze (E)	Lohnstopp m	—	blocage des salaires m	blocco dei salari m	congelación salarial f
wage-intensive (E)	lohnintensiv	—	déterminé par le facteur salaire	ad alta incidenza salariale	con gran intensidad de costos salariales
wage lag (E)	Lohnlag m	—	décalage entre les prix et les salaires m	lag salariale m	diferencial entre precios y salarios m
Wagenladung (D)	—	cartload	charge de voiture f	carico di autocarro m	carga de un vagón f
wage policy (E)	Lohnpolitik f	—	politique des salaires f	politica salariale f	política salarial f
wage-price spiral (E)	Lohn-Preis-Spirale f	—	course des prix et des salaires f	spirale prezzi-salari f	espiral salarios-precios m
wages (paid) in kind (E)	Naturallohn m	—	rémunérarion du travail en nature f	remunerazione in natura f	salario en especie m
wage tax (E)	Lohnsteuer f	—	impôt sur les traitements et salaires m	imposta sui salari f	impuesto sobre los rendimientos del trabajo personal f
Wagnis (D)	—	venture	risque m	rischio m	riesgo m
wagon frigorifique (F)	Kühlwagen m	cold storage lorry	—	vagone frigorifero m	vagón frigorífico m
Wahlkonsul (D)	—	honorary consul	consul honoraire m	console onorario m	cónsul honorario m
Wahrscheinlichkeitsrechnung (D)	—	calculation of probabilities	calcul des probabilités m	calcolo della probabilità m	cálculo de probabilidades m
Währung (D)	—	currency	monnaie f	valuta f/moneta f	moneda f
Währungsabkommen (D)	—	currency agreement	accord monétaire m	accordo monetario m	acuerdo monetario m
Währungsbehörde (D)	—	monetary authority	autorité monétaire f	autorità monetaria f	autoridad monetaria f
Währungsexperte (D)	—	monetary expert	expert monétaire m	esperto in materia monetaria m	experto en materia monetaria m
Währungsgebiet (D)	—	currency area	zone monétaire f	area monetaria f	área monetaria f
Währungsklausel (D)	—	currency clause	clause monétaire f	clausola monetaria f	cláusula monetaria f
Währungskonto (D)	—	currency account	compte en monnaies étrangères m	conto in valuta m	cuenta de moneda extranjera f
Währungspolitik (D)	—	monetary policy	politique monétaire f	politica monetaria f	política monetaria f
Währungsrisiko (D)	—	currency risk	risque de change m	rischio monetario m	riesgo monetario m
Währungsschlange (D)	—	currency snake	serpent monétaire m	serpente monetario m	serpiente monetaria f
Währungsunion (D)	—	monetary union	union monétaire f	unione monetaria f	unión monetaria f
Währungszone (D)	—	currency zone	zone monétaire f	zona monetaria f	zona monetaria f
waiting time (E)	Wartezeit f	—	temps d'attente m	tempo d'attesa m	tiempo de espera m
Wandelschuldverschreibung (D)	—	convertible bonds	obligation convertible f	obbligazione convertibile f	obligaciones convertibles f pl

	D	E	F	I	Es
Ware (D)	—	goods	marchandise f	merce f	mercancía f
warehouse (E)	Lager n	—	magasin m	magazzino m	almacén m
warehouse rent (E)	Lagermiete f	—	location d'une surface pour magasinage f	spese di magazzinaggio f pl	alquiler de almacenaje m
warehouse warrant (E)	Lagerschein m	—	certificat de dépot m	ricevuta di deposito f	resguardo de almacén m
Warenart (D)	—	class of goods	catégorie de marchandise f	tipo di merce m	categoría de mercancías f
Warenausgang (D)	—	outgoing goods	sortie de marchandises f	uscita merci f	salida de mercancías f
Warenaustausch (D)	—	exchange of goods	échanges commerciaux m pl	scambio merci m	intercambio de mercancías m
Warenbestand (D)	—	stock	stock de marchandises m	scorte merci f pl	existencias de mercancías f pl
Warenbörse (D)	—	commodity exchange	bourse de marchandises f	borsa merci f	bolsa de mercancías f
Wareneingang (D)	—	arrival of goods	entrée de marchandises f	entrata merci f	entrada de mercancías f
Warengruppe (D)	—	product line	groupe de marchandises m	gruppo merci m	grupo de mercancías m
Warenhaus (D)	—	department store	grand magasin m	grande magazzino m	gran almacén m
Warenknappheit (D)	—	shortage of goods	pénurie de marchandises f	scarsità di merci f	escasez de mercancías f
Warenkredit (D)	—	trade credit	avance sur marchandises f	credito su merci m	crédito comercial m
Warenlager (D)	—	stock room	stock de marchandises m	magazzino m	depósito de mercancías m
Warenprobe (D)	—	sample	échantillon m	campione m	muestra f
Warensendung (D)	—	consignment of goods	expédition de marchandises f	spedizione di merci f	envío de mercancías m
Warenterminbörse (D)	—	commodity forward exchange	bourse d'opérations à livrer f	borsa merci a termine f	bolsa de mercancías a plazo m
Warentermin-geschäft (D)	—	commodity forward transaction	opération de livraison à terme f	operazione a termine su merci f	operación a plazo de mercancías f
Warenterminhandel (D)	—	commodity forward dealing	commerce d'opéra-tions à terme m	operazioni a termine su merci f pl	tráfico de futuro m
Warenwechsel (D)	—	commercial bill	traite commerciale f	cambiale commerciale f	letra comercial f
Warenzeichen (D)	—	trade mark	marque f	marchio m	marca f
warranted characteristics (E)	zugesicherte Eigenschaften pl	—	qualité promise f	caratteristiche promesse f pl	calidades aseguradas f pl
warranty¹ (E)	Garantie f	—	garantie f	garanzia f	garantía f
warranty² (E)	Gewährleistung f	—	prestation de garantie f	garanzia f	garantía f
Wartezeit (D)	—	waiting time	temps d'attente m	tempo d'attesa m	tiempo de espera m
Wasserschaden (D)	—	damage caused by water	dommage causé par l'eau m	danno dovuto all'acqua m	daño causado por el agua m
Wasserstraße (D)	—	waterway	voie d'eau f	via d'acqua f	vía navegable f
Wasser-verschmutzung (D)	—	water pollution	contamination des eaux f	inquinamento delle acque m	contaminación del agua f
waste (E)	Abfall m	—	déchet m	rifiuti m pl	desechos m pl
waste disposal¹ (E)	Abfallbeseitigung f	—	élimination de déchets f	smaltimento dei rifiuti m	evacuación de residuos f
waste disposal² (E)	Entsorgung f	—	dépollution f	smaltimento m	eliminación f
waste management (E)	Abfallwirtschaft f	—	industrie de déchets f	industria dei rifiuti f	industria de desperdicios f
waste oil (E)	Altöl n	—	huile usée f	olio usato m	aceite usado m
waste water (E)	Abwasser n	—	eaux résiduelles f pl	acque di scarico f pl	aguas residuales f pl
water pollution (E)	Wasser-verschmutzung f	—	contamination des eaux f	inquinamento delle acque m	contaminación del agua f
waterway (E)	Wasserstraße f	—	voie d'eau f	via d'acqua f	vía navegable f
wear and tear (E)	Abnutzung f	—	dépréciation f	usura f	desgaste m

	D	E	F	I	Es
Wechsel (D)	—	bill of exchange	lettre de change f	cambiale f	letra de cambio f
Wechselkredit (D)	—	acceptance credit	crédit d'escompte m	credito cambiario m	crédito cambiario m
Wechselkurs (D)	—	exchange rate	cours du change m	cambio m	tipo de cambio m
Wechselprotest (D)	—	protest	protêt de traite m	protesto cambiario m	protesto de letra m
Wechselreiterei (D)	—	kiteflying	tirage d'une traite de cavalerie m	emissione di tratte incrociate f	libramiento de letras cruzadas m
weekly (E)	wöchentlich	—	hebdomadaire	settimanale	semanal
Wegenetz (D)	—	road network	voirie f	rete stradale f	comunicaciones f pl
weiche Währung (D)	—	soft currency	monnaie faible f	moneta debole f	moneda blanda f
weight (E)	Gewicht n	—	poids m	peso m	peso m
weight of fine gold (E)	Feingewicht n	—	poids de métal fin m	peso fino m	peso fino m
Weihnachten (D)	—	Christmas	Noël m	Natale m	Navidad f
Weiterverarbeitung (D)	—	further processing	transformation complémentaire f	trasformazione f	elaboración ulterior f
welfare state (E)	Wohlfahrtsstaat m	—	Etat social m	stato assistenziale m	estado de bienestar m
well-price offer (E)	preisgünstiges Angebot n	—	offre à un avantageux f	offerta a buon prezzo f	oferta favorable f
Weltbank (D)	—	World Bank	banque mondiale f	Banca Mondiale f	Banco Mundial m
Welthandel (D)	—	world trade	commerce mondial m	commercio mondiale m	comercio internacional m
Weltmarktpreis (D)	—	world market price	prix du marché mondial m	prezzo di mercato mondiale m	precio del mercado mundial m
Weltwährungs-system (D)	—	international monetary system	système monétaire international m	sistema monetario internazionale m	sistema monetario internacional m
Weltwirtschaft (D)	—	world economy	économie mondiale f	economia mondiale f	economía internacional f
Weltwirtschafts-krise (D)	—	worldwide economic crisis	crise économique mondiale f	crisi dell'economia mondiale f	crisis económica internacional f
Weltwirtschafts-ordnung (D)	—	international economic order	ordre économique mondial m	sistema economico mondiale m	orden económico mundial m
Werbeabteilung (D)	—	publicity department	service de publicité m	reparto pubblicità m	sección de publicidad f
Werbeagentur (D)	—	advertising agency	agence de publicité f	agenzia pubblicitaria f	agencia publicitaria f
Werbeaktion (D)	—	advertising activity	campagne publicitaire f	azione pubblicitaria f	campaña publicitaria f
Werbebotschaft (D)	—	sales message	message publicitaire m	messaggio pubblicitario m	mensaje publicitario m
Werbebrief (D)	—	advertising letter	lettre publicitaire f	lettera pubblicitaria f	circular de publicidad m
Werbebudget (D)	—	advertising budget	budget de publicité m	budget pubblicitario m	presupuesto publicitario m
Werbeerfolgs-kontrolle (D)	—	advertising control	contrôle du résultat de la publicité f	controllo del successo pubblicitario m	análisis del resultado publicitario m
Werbefachmann (D)	—	advertising expert	technicien publicitaire m	esperto di pubblicità m	perito publicitario m
Werbefilm (D)	—	advertising film	film publicitaire m	film pubblicitario m	película promocional f
Werbefrequenz (D)	—	advertising frequency	fréquence publicitaire f	frequenza della pubblicità f	frecuencia publicitaria f
Werbegeschenk (D)	—	advertising gift	cadeau publicitaire m	omaggio pubblicitario m	regalo publicitario m
Werbekampagne (D)	—	advertising campaign	campagne publicitaire f	campagna pubblicitaria f	campaña publicitaria f
Werbemedien (D)	—	advertising media	médias publicitaires m pl	mezzi pubblicitari m pl	medios de publicidad m pl
Werbemittel (D)	—	advertising aids	moyen publicitaire m	mezzo pubblicitario m	medio publicitario m
Werbereichweite (D)	—	scope of advertising effect	zone de rayonne-ment de la publicité f	raggio d'azione della pubblicità m	alcance publicitario m
Werbespot (D)	—	commercial	spot publicitaire m	spot pubblicitario m	spot publicitario m
Werbetext (D)	—	advertising copy	texte publicitaire m	testo pubblicitario m	texto publicitario m

	D	E	F	I	Es
Werbeträger (D)	—	advertising medium	support publicitaire *m*	veicolo pubblicitario *m*	medio de publicidad *m*
Werbeverbot (D)	—	ban on advertising	défense de publicité *f*	divieto di pubblicità *m*	prohibición de publicidad *f*
Werbeziele (D)	—	advertising objective	objectifs publicitaires *m pl*	obiettivi pubblicitari *m pl*	objetivos de la publicidad *m pl*
Werbung (D)	—	publicity	publicité *f*	pubblicità *f*	publicidad *f*
Werft (D)	—	shipyard	chantier naval *m*	cantiere navale *m*	astillero *m*
Werk (D)	—	plant	usine *f*	stabilimento *m*	planta *f*
Werkschutz (D)	—	works protection force	corps de sécurité d'entreprise *m*	servizio di sorveglianza aziendale *m*	policía de la empresa *f*
Werkspionage (D)	—	industrial espionage	espionnage industriel *m*	spionaggio aziendale *m*	espionaje industrial *m*
Werkvertrag (D)	—	contract for work and services	contrat de louage d'ouvrage et d'industrie *m*	contratto d'appalto *m*	contrato de obra *m*
Wert (D)	—	value	valeur *f*	valore *m*	valor *m*
Wertberichtigung (D)	—	value adjustment	réévaluation *f*	rettifica del valore *f*	rectificación de valor *f*
Wertbrief (D)	—	insured letter	lettre avec valeur déclarée *f*	lettera con valore dichiarato *f*	letra con valor declarado *f*
Wertminderung (D)	—	decrease in value	diminution de la valeur *f*	riduzione di valore *f*	depreciación *f*
Wertpapier (D)	—	security	titre *m*/valeur *f*	titolo *m*	título *m*/valor *m*
Wertpapierbörse (D)	—	securities market	bourse des titres et valeurs *f*	borsa valori *f*	mercado de valores *m*
Wertpapierfonds (D)	—	securities fund	fonds de valeurs mobilières *m*	fondo titoli *m*	fondo de inversión mobiliaria *f*
Wertpapiergeschäft (D)	—	securities business	opérations sur titres *f pl*	operazioni su titoli *f pl*	operación con valores *f*
Wertschöpfung (D)	—	value added	création de valeurs *f*	valore aggiunto *m*	creación de riqueza *f*
Wertsendung (D)	—	consignment with value declared	envoi avec valeur déclarée *m*	spedizione con valore dichiarato *f*	envío con valor declarado *m*
Wertsicherungsklausel (D)	—	stable value clause	clause de stabilité *f*	clausola di garanzia monetaria *f*	cláusula de índice variable *f*
Wertverfall (D)	—	loss of value	dévalorisation *f*	deprezzamento *m*	depreciación *f*
wertvoll (D)	—	valuable	précieux	prezioso	precioso
Wertzoll (D)	—	ad valorem duty	taxe de douane ad valorem *f*	dazio ad valorem *m*	aduanas ad valorem *f pl*
Wertzuwachs (D)	—	appreciation	accroissement de valeur *m*	incremento di valore *m*	plusvalía *f*
wesentliche Bestandteile (D)	—	integral part	parties constitutives essentielles *f pl*	componenti essenziali *f pl*	partes integrantes esencial *f pl*
Wettbewerb (D)	—	competition	compétition *f*	concorrenza *f*	competencia *f*
Wettbewerbsbeschränkung (D)	—	restraint of competition	restriction apportée à la concurrence *f*	restrizione della concorrenza *f*	restricciones a la competencia *f pl*
Wettbewerbsfähigkeit (D)	—	competitiveness	compétitivité *f*	competitività *f*	competitividad *f*
Wettbewerbspolitik (D)	—	competition policy	politique de concurrence *f*	politica concorrenziale *f*	política de competencia *f*
Wettbewerbsrecht (D)	—	law on competition	législation en matière de concurrence commerciale *f*	diritto della concorrenza *m*	derecho de la competencia *m*
Wettbewerbsverbot (D)	—	prohibition of competition	interdiction en matière de concurrence *f*	divieto di concorrenza *m*	prohibición de competencia *f*
Wettbewerbsverstoß (D)	—	violation of competition rules	violation de concurrence *f*	violazione delle regole di concorrenza *f*	violación de las reglas de competencia *f*
Wettbewerbsvorteil (D)	—	competitive advantage	avantage de concurrence *m*	vantaggio concorrenziale	ventaja de competencia *f*
white-collar crime (E)	Wirtschaftskriminalität *f*	—	délinquance économique *f*	criminalità economica *f*	criminalidad económica *f*
white-collar delinquency (E)	White-collar-Kriminalität *f*	—	délinquance économique *f*	criminalità dei colletti bianchi *f*	criminalidad económica *f*

	D	E	F	I	Es
White-collar Kriminalität (D)	—	white-collar delinquency	délinquance économique f	criminalità dei colletti bianchi f	criminalidad económica f
wholesale prices (E)	Großhandelspreise pl	—	prix de gros m	prezzo all'ingrosso m	precio mayorista m
wholesaler (E)	Grossist m	—	grossiste m	grossista m	mayorista m
wholesale trade (E)	Großhandel m	—	commerce de gros m	commercio all'ingrosso m	comercio mayorista m
widerrufen (D)	—	revoke	révoquer	revocare	revocar
Widerrufsklausel (D)	—	revocation clause	clause de révocation f	clausola di revoca f	cláusula revocatoria f
Widerrufsrecht (D)	—	right of revocation	droit de révocation m	diritto di revoca m	derecho de revocación m
Wiederaufbau (D)	—	reconstruction	reconstruction f	ricostruzione f	reconstrucción f
Wiederausfuhr (D)	—	reexportation	réexportation f	riesportazione f	reexportación f
Wiederbeschaffung (D)	—	replacement	réapprovisionnement m	riapprovvigionamento m	reposición f
Wiederverkäufer (D)	—	reseller	revendeur m	rivenditore m	revendedor m
Wiederverkaufspreis (D)	—	resale price	prix de revente m	prezzo di rivendita m	precio de reventa m
wiederverwertbar (D)	—	recyclable	réutilisable	riutilizzabile	recuperable
Willenserklärung (D)	—	declaration of intent	déclaration de volonté f	dichiarazione di volontà f	declaración de la voluntad f
Windenergie (D)	—	eolian energy	énergie éolienne f	energia eolica f	energía eólica f
window dressing (E)	Schaufensterdekoration f	—	décoration de vitrine f	allestimento di vetrina m	adorno del escaparate m
Wirtschaft (D)	—	economy	économie f	economia f	economía f
wirtschaftliche Integration (D)	—	economic integration	intégration économique f	integrazione economica f	integración económica f
wirtschaftliche Nutzung (D)	—	economic use	utilisation économique f	utilizzo economico m	utilización económica f
wirtschaftliches Prinzip (D)	—	economic principle	principe économique m	principio economico m	principio económico m
Wirtschaftlichkeit (D)	—	economic efficiency	rentabilité f	economicità f	rentabilidad f
Wirtschaftsanalyse (D)	—	economic analysis	analyse de l'économie f	analisi economica f	análisis económico m
Wirtschaftsboykott (D)	—	economic boycott	boycottage économique m	boicottaggio economico m	boicot económico m
Wirtschaftsexperte (D)	—	economic expert	expert économique m	esperto in materia economica	economista m
Wirtschaftsgemeinschaft (D)	—	economic community	communauté économique f	comunità economica f	comunidad económica f
Wirtschaftsgeographie (D)	—	economic geography	géographie économique f	geografia economica f	geografía económica f
Wirtschaftsgeschichte (D)	—	economic history	histoire économique f	storia economica f	historia económica f
Wirtschaftsgut (D)	—	economic good	bien économique m	bene economico m	bien económico m
Wirtschaftsjahr (D)	—	business year	exercice comptable m	esercizio m	ejercicio m
Wirtschaftskonzentration (D)	—	economic concentration	concentration économique f	concentrazione economica f	concentración económica f
Wirtschaftskreislauf (D)	—	economic cycle	circuit économique m	circuito economico m	circuito económico m
Wirtschaftskrieg (D)	—	economic war	guerre économique f	guerra economica f	guerra económica f
Wirtschaftskriminalität (D)	—	white-collar crime	délinquance économique f	criminalità economica f	criminalidad económica f
Wirtschaftskrise (D)	—	economic crisis	crise économique f	crisi economica f	crisis económica f
Wirtschaftsordnung (D)	—	economic order	ordre économique m	ordinamento economico m	orden económico m
Wirtschaftsplan (D)	—	economic plan	plan économique m	piano economico m	plan económico m
Wirtschaftspolitik (D)	—	economic policy	politique économique f	politica economica f	política económica f

	D	E	F	I	Es
wirtschaftspolitische Zielsetzung (D)	—	economy policy objectives	objectifs commandés par une politique économique *m pl*	obiettivo della politica economica *m*	objetivos de la política económica *m pl*
Wirtschaftsprüfer (D)	—	auditor	expert comptable économique et financier *m*	revisore dei conti *m*	revisor de cuentas *m/* experto contable *m*
Wirtschaftsprüfung (D)	—	auditing	contrôle de la gestion et des comptes *m*	revisione *f*	revisoría *f*
Wirtschafts-rechnung (D)	—	economic account	comptabilisation économique *f*	conto economico *m*	contabilización económica *f*
Wirtschaftsrecht (D)	—	economic law	législation économique *f*	diritto economico *m*	derecho económico *m*
Wirtschaftsstatistik (D)	—	housekeeping account	statistique économique *f*	statistica economica *f*	estadística económica *f*
Wirtschaftsstruktur (D)	—	economic structure	structure économique *f*	struttura economica *f*	estructura económica *f*
Wirtschafts-theorie (D)	—	economic theory	théorie économique *f*	teoria dell'economia *f*	teoría económica *f*
Wirtschaftsunion (D)	—	economic union	union économique *f*	unione economica *f*	unión económica *f*
Wirtschaftsverband (D)	—	trade association	association économique *f*	associazione economica *f*	asociación económica *f*
Wirtschaftsverlauf (D)	—	course of the economic evolution	évolution économique *f*	andamento dell'economia *m*	evolución económica *f*
Wirtschafts-wachstum (D)	—	economic growth	croissance économique *f*	crescita economica *f*	crecimiento económico *m*
Wirtschafts-wissenschaften (D)	—	economics	sciences économiques *f pl*	scienze economiche *f pl*	ciencias económicas *f pl*
Wirtschaftszweig (D)	—	field of the economy	secteur économique *m*	settore economico *m*	ramo económico *m*
within (E)	binnen	—	dans le délai de	entro	en el término de
with non-distributed dividend (E)	ohne Dividende	—	sans dividende *m*	senza dividendo	sin dividendo
without competition (E)	konkurrenzlos	—	défiant toute concurrence	senza concorrenza	sin competencia
without obligation (E)	ohne Obligo	—	sans engagement	senza obbligo	sin obligación
without garanty (E)	ohne Gewähr	—	sous toute réserve	senza garanzia	sin garantía
without prior notice (E)	fristlos	—	sans délai	senza preavviso	sin plazo
wöchentlich (D)	—	weekly	hebdomadaire	settimanale	semanal
Wohlfahrtsstaat (D)	—	welfare state	Etat social *m*	stato assistenziale *m*	estado de bienestar *m*
Wohlstand (D)	—	prosperity	prospérité *f*	benessere *m*	bienestar *m*
Wohlstands-gesellschaft (D)	—	affluent society	société de bien-être *f*	società del benessere *f*	sociedad de bienestar *f*
Wohnung (D)	—	flab	appartement *m*	abitazione *f*	vivienda *f*
Wohnungsbau (D)	—	housing construction	construction de logements *f*	edilizia abitativa *f*	construcción de viviends *f*
Wohnungs-eigentum (D)	—	ownership of a flat	propriété du logement *f*	proprietà edilizia *f*	propiedad de vivienda *f*
Wohnungswechsel (D)	—	change of residence	transfert de résidence *m*	cambiamento dell'abitazione *m*	cambio de vivienda *m*
word processing (E)	Textverarbeitung *f*	—	élaboration de texte *f*	elaborazione testi *f*	tratamiento de textos *m*
work (E)	Arbeit *f*	—	travail *m*	lavoro *m*	trabajo *m*
worker (E)	Arbeiter *m*	—	travailleur *m*	operaio *m*	trabajador *m*
worker participation (E)	Arbeitnehmer-beteiligung *f*	—	participation du personnel *f*	partecipazione dei prestatori d'opera *f*	participación de los empleados *f*
working capital (E)	Betriebskapital *n*	—	capital de roulement *m*	capitale d'esercizio *m*	capital de explotación *m*
working class (E)	Arbeiterklasse *f*	—	classe ouvrière *f*	classe degli operai *f*	clase obrera *f*
working conditions and human relations (E)	Betriebsklima *n*	—	climat social *m*	atmosfera di lavoro *f*	ambiente de trabajo *m*
working day (E)	Arbeitstag *m*	—	jour de travail *m*	giorno lavorativo *m*	día laboral *m*

	D	E	F	I	Es
working hours (E)	Arbeitszeit f	—	heures de travail f pl	orario di lavoro m	jornada laboral f
working lunch (E)	Arbeitsessen n	—	déjeuner de travail m	pranzo di lavoro m	comida de trabajo f
working technique (E)	Arbeitstechnik f	—	technique de travail f	tecnica lavorativa f	técnica del trabajo f
working week (E)	Arbeitswoche f	—	semaine de travail f	settimana lavorativa f	semana laboral f
work performed (E)	Arbeitsertrag m	—	rendement du travail m	rendimento del lavoro m	rendimiento del trabajo m
work permit (E)	Arbeitserlaubnis f	—	permis de travail m	permesso di lavoro m	permiso de trabajo m
work rhythm (E)	Arbeitsrhythmus m	—	rythme de travail m	ritmo di lavoro m	ritmo de trabajo m
workroom (E)	Arbeitsraum m	—	lieu de travail m	locale di lavoro m	sala de trabajo f
works protection force (E)	Werkschutz m	—	corps de sécurité d'entreprise m	servizio di sorveglianza aziendale m	policía de la empresa f
World Bank (E)	Weltbank f	—	banque mondiale f	Banca Mondiale f	Banco Mundial m
world economy (E)	Weltwirtschaft f	—	économie mondiale f	economia mondiale f	economía internacional f
world market price (E)	Weltmarktpreis m	—	prix du marché mondial m	prezzo di mercato mondiale m	precio del mercado mundial m
world trade (E)	Welthandel m	—	commerce mondial m	commercio mondiale m	comercio internacional m
worldwide economic crisis (E)	Weltwirtschaftskrise f	—	crise économique mondiale f	crisi dell'economia mondiale f	crisis económica internacional f
written (E)	schriftlich	—	par écrit	per iscritto	por escrito
written form (E)	Schriftform f	—	forme par écrit f	forma scritta f	forma escrita f
Wucher (D)	—	usuary	usure f	usura f	usura f
yield (E)	Rendite f	—	rendement m	rendita f	rentabilidad f
young businessman (E)	Jungunternehmer m	—	entrepreneur débutant m	imprenditore giovane m	joven empresario m
Zahl (D)	—	number/ figure	nombre m/ chiffre m	numero m/ cifra f	número m/ cifra f
zahlbar (D)	—	payable	payable	pagabile	pagable
Zahlkarte (D)	—	money order	mandat-carte m	modulo di versamento m	carta de pago f
Zahltag (D)	—	payday	jour de paye m	giorno di paga m	día de pago m
Zahlung (D)	—	payment	payement m	pagamento m	pago m
Zahlung per Nachnahme (D)	—	cash on delivery	payement contre remboursement m	pagamento contro assegno m	pago contra reembolso m
Zahlungsabkommen (D)	—	payments arrangement	accord de payement m	accordo di pagamento m	acuerdo de pagos m
Zahlungsanweisung (D)	—	order to pay	mandat de payement m	ordine di pagamento m	orden de pago f
Zahlungsaufschub (D)	—	extension of time for payment	sursis de payement m	dilazione del pagamento f	pago aplazado m
Zahlungsbedingung (D)	—	terms of payment	conditions de payement f pl	condizione di pagamento f	condiciones de pago f pl
Zahlungsbefehl (D)	—	order for payment	ordre de payement m	ingiunzione di pagamento f	mandamiento de pago m
Zahlungsberechtigter (D)	—	beneficiary of payment	bénéficiaire du payement m	beneficiario del pagamento m	beneficiario del pago m
Zahlungsbestätigung (D)	—	receipt for payment	confirmation de payement f	conferma di pagamento f	confirmación de pago f
Zahlungsbilanz (D)	—	balance of payments	balance des payements f	bilancia dei pagamenti f	balanza de pagos f
Zahlungsbilanzdefizit (D)	—	deficit in the balance of payments	balance des payements déficitaire f	disavanzo della bilancia dei pagamenti m	déficit en la balanza de pagos m
Zahlungsbilanzgleichgewicht (D)	—	equilibrium of the balance of payments	balance des payements équilibrée f	equilibrio della bilancia dei pagamenti m	balanza de pagos equilibrada f
Zahlungsbilanzpolitik (D)	—	balance of payments policy	politique en matière de la balance des payements f	politica della bilancia dei pagamenti f	política en materia de balanza de pagos f
Zahlungsbilanzüberschuß (D)	—	surplus in the balance of payments	balance des payements excédentaire f	eccedenza della bilancia dei pagamenti f	superávit en la balanza de pagos m

	D	E	F	I	Es
Zahlungs-einstellung (D)	—	cessation of payments	suspension de payement f	cessazione dei pagamenti f	suspensión de pagos f
zahlungsfähig (D)	—	solvent	solvable	solvibile	solvente
Zahlungs-fähigkeit (D)	—	solvency	solvabilité f	solvibilità f	solvencia f
Zahlungsform (D)	—	payment system	forme de payement f	tipo di pagamento m	forma de pago f
Zahlungsfrist (D)	—	terms of payment	délai de payement f	scadenza di pagamento f	plazo de pago m
Zahlungs-gewohnheit (D)	—	practice of payment	habitude de payement f	consuetudine di pagamento f	práctica de pago f
zahlungshalber (D)	—	on account of payment	pour raison de payement	a titolo di pagamento	a título de pago
Zahlungsmittel (D)	—	means of payment	moyen de payement m	mezzo di pagamento m	medio de pago m
Zahlungsrisiko (D)	—	risk of payment	risque de payement m	rischio di pagamento m	riesgo de pago m
Zahlungsrückstand (D)	—	payment in arrears	arriéré de payement m	morosità di pagamento f	pago atrasado m
Zahlungs-schwierigkeit (D)	—	financial difficulties	difficultés financières f pl	difficoltà di pagamento f	dificultades de pago f pl
zahlungsstatt (D)	—	in lieu of payment	à titre de payement	a titolo di pagamento	a título de pago
Zahlungstermin (D)	—	date of payment	terme du payement m	termine di pagamento m	plazo de pago m
Zahlungs-unfähigkeit (D)	—	insolvency	insolvabilité f	insolvenza f	insolvencia f
Zahlungsverkehr (D)	—	payment transaction	opérations de payement f pl	operazioni di pagamento f pl	servicio de pagos m pl
Zahlungsverzug (D)	—	failure to pay on due date	demeure du débiteur f	morosità di pagamento f	retraso en el pago m
Zahlungsziel (D)	—	period for payment	délai de payement m	termine di pagamento m	plazo de pago m
Zahlung unter Protest (D)	—	payment supra protest	payement sous protêt m	pagamento sotto protesta f	pago bajo protesta m
Zedent (D)	—	assignor	cédant m	cedente m	cedente m
Zeichnungs-berechtigung (D)	—	authority to sign	autorisation de signer f	diritto di firma m	facultad de firma f
Zeitaufwand (D)	—	expenditure of time	temps passé m	tempo impiegato m	tiempo consagrado m
Zeitlohn (D)	—	time wage	salaire au temps m	salario a tempo m	salario por unidad de tiempo m
Zeitstudie (D)	—	time study	étude des temps f	analisi sul tempo impiegato f	estudio de tiempo m
Zeitungsanzeige (D)	—	advertisement	annonce de journal f	inserzione sul giornale f	anuncio de prensa m
Zeitwert (D)	—	current market value	valeur à une certaine date f	valore corrente m	valor actual m
Zentralbank (D)	—	central bank	banque centrale f	Banca Centrale f	banco emisor m
Zentralbankrat (D)	—	Central Bank Council	Conseil de la Banque Centrale m	consiglio superiore della Banca Centrale m	Consejo del Banco Central m
Zentraleinheit (D)	—	central unit	unité centrale f	unità centrale f	unidad central f
zentrale Planwirtschaft (D)	—	centrally controlled economy	économie planifiée centrale f	economia pianificata f	economía planificada central f
Zentralisierung (D)	—	centralization	centralisation f	centralizzazione f	centralización f
zero growth (E)	Nullwachstum n	—	croissance zéro f	crescita zero f	crecimiento cero m
Zertifikat (D)	—	certificate	certificat m	certificato m	certificado m
Zession (D)	—	assignment	cession f	cessione f	cesión f
Zessionar (D)	—	assignee	cessionnaire m	cessionario m	cesionario m
Zeugnis (D)	—	school report/ certificate/evidence	certificat scolaire m/ certificat m/ témoignage m	pagella f/ certificato m/ testimonianza f	certificado de escuela m/ certificado m/ testimonio m
Ziehungsrechte (D)	—	drawing rights	droits de tirage m pl	diritti di prelievo m pl	derechos de giro m pl

	D	E	F	I	Es
Ziel (D)	—	objective	but *m*	obiettivo *m*	objetivo *m*
Zielgruppe (D)	—	target group	groupe destinataire *m*	gruppo di riferimento *m*	grupo destinatario *m*
Zielkauf (D)	—	purchase on credit	achat à terme *m*	acquisto a termine *m*	compra a plazos *m*
Zielkonflikt (D)	—	conflicting goals	conflit d'objectifs *m*	incompatibilità degli obiettivi *f*	conflicto de objectivos *m*
Zielprojektion (D)	—	target projection	projection d'objectifs *f*	proiezione degli obiettivi *f*	proyección de objetivos *f*
Zins (D)	—	interest	intérêt *m*	interessi *m pl*	interés *m*
Zinsberechnung (D)	—	calculating the interest	calcul des intérêts *m*	calcolo degli interessi *m*	cálculo de intereses *m*
Zinsbindungsfrist (D)	—	lock-down period for interest rates	délai d'engagement sur le taux d'intérêt accordé *m*	scadenza degli interessi vincolati *f*	plazo de vinculación al tipo de interés pactado *f*
Zinsendienst (D)	—	interest service	service de l'intérêt *m*	servizio degli interessi *m*	servicio de intereses *m*
Zinserleichterung (D)	—	reduction of interest	minoration de l'intérêt *m*	agevolazione sugli interessi *f*	reducción de intereses *f*
Zinseszins (D)	—	compound interest	intérêt composé *m*	interessi composti *m pl*	interés compuesto *m*
Zinsfuß (D)	—	interest rate	taux d'intérêt *m*	tasso d'interesse *m*	tipo de interés *m*
Zinsgefälle (D)	—	margin between interest rates	disparité des niveaux d'intérêts *f*	differenza dei tassi d'interesse *f*	diferencia entre los tipos de interés *f*
Zinsmarge (D)	—	interest margin	marge entre les taux d'intérêt créditeur et débiteur *f*	margine degli interessi *m*	margen de interés *m*
Zinsniveau (D)	—	interest rate level	niveau du taux d'intérêt *m*	livello degli interessi *m*	nivel de interés *m*
Zinspolitik (D)	—	interest rate policy	politique en matière d'intérêts *f*	politica dei tassi d'interesse *f*	política en materia de intereses *f*
Zinsrechnung (D)	—	interest account	calcul des intérêts *m*	conteggio degli interessi *m*	cómputo de intereses *m*
Zinssatz (D)	—	interest rate	taux de l'intérêt *m*	tasso d'interesse *m*	tipo de interés *m*
Zinssenkung (D)	—	reduction of interest	diminution du taux de l'intérêt *f*	riduzione degli interessi *f*	reducción del tipo de interés *f*
Zoll (D)	—	customs/ customs duty	douane *f*/ droit de douane *m*	dogana *f*/dazio *m*	aduana *f*/arancel *m*
Zollabkommen (D)	—	customs convention	accord douanier *m* doganali *m*	accordo sulle tariffe	convenio aduanero *m*
Zollagerung (D)	—	customs warehouse procedure	dépôt en entrepôt sous douane *m*	immagazzinamento doganale *m*	depósito de aduana *m*
Zollanmeldung (D)	—	customs declaration	déclaration en douane *f*	dichiarazione doganale *f*	declaración arancelaria *f*
Zollantrag (D)	—	customs application	demande de dédouanement *f*	domanda di sdoganamento *f*	solicitud de aduana *f*
Zollausland (D)	—	foreign customs territory	territoire hors du contrôle de la douane *m*	territorio doganale estero *m*	territorio aduanero exterior *m*
Zollausschluß (D)	—	territory inside political but outside customs frontier	territoire considéré hors frontière douanière nationale *m*	zona franca *f*	exclave aduanero *m*
Zolleinfuhrschein (D)	—	bill of entry	acquit d'entrée *m*	bolletta d'entrata *m*	certificado de aduana *m*
Zollerklärung (D)	—	customs declaration	déclaration en douane *f*	dichiarazione doganale *f*	declaración arancelaria *f*
Zollfaktura (D)	—	customs invoice	facture douanière *f*	fattura doganale *f*	factura arancelaria *f*
Zollformalität (D)	—	customs formalities	formalité douanières *f*	formalità doganale *f*	formalidades aduaneras *f pl*
Zollfreischreibungs-verfahren (D)	—	procedure of duty free admission	régime de l'admission en franchise *m*	procedura d'ammissione in franchigia *f*	régimen de admisión en franquicia *m*
Zollgebiet (D)	—	customs territory	territoire douanier *m*	territorio doganale *m*	distrito aduanero *m*
Zollgebühren (D)	—	customs duties	droit de douane *m*	diritti doganali *m pl*	derechos arancelarios *m pl*
Zollgrenze (D)	—	customs frontier	frontière douanière *f*	confine doganale *f*	frontera aduanera *f*

	D	E	F	I	Es
Zollgrenzgebiet (D)	—	customs frontier district	territoire de surveillance douanière *m*	area doganale di confine *f*	territorio aduanero fronterizo *m*
Zollinland (D)	—	domestic customs territory	territoire douanier national *m*	territorio doganale nazionale *m*	territorio aduanero interior *m*
Zollpapiere (D)	—	customs documents	documents douaniers *m pl*	documenti doganali *m pl*	documentos aduaneros *m pl*
Zollstelle (D)	—	customs office	bureau de douane *m*	posto di dogana *m*	oficina de aduanas *f*
Zolltarif (D)	—	customs tariff	tarif des douanes *m*	tariffa doganale *f*	tarifa arancelaria *f*
Zollunion (D)	—	customs union	union douanière *f*	unione doganale *f*	unión aduanera *f*
Zollverkehr (D)	—	customs procedure	régime douanier *m*	procedure doganali *f pl*	régimen aduanero de mercancías *m*
Zollverschluß (D)	—	customs seal	fermeture douanière *f*	sigillo doganale *m*	precinto aduanero *m*
zona (Es)	Zone *f*	zone	zone *f*	zona *f*	—
zona (I)	Zone *f*	zone	zone *f*	—	zona *f*
zona costera (Es)	Küstengewässer *n*	coastal waters	eaux côtières *f pl*	acque territoriali *f pl*	—
zona de librecambio (Es)	Freihandelszone *f*	free trade area	zone de libre-échange *f*	zona di libero scambio *f*	—
zona di libero scambio (I)	Freihandelszone *f*	free trade area	zone de libre-échange *f*	—	zona de librecambio *f*
zona di vendita (I)	Verkaufsgebiet *n*	sales territory	territoire de vente *m*	—	territorio de venta *m*
zona franca (I)	Zollausschluß *m*	territory inside political but outside customs frontier	territoire considéré hors frontière douanière nationale *m*	—	exclave aduanero *m*
zona industriale (I)	Industriegebiet *n*	industrial area	région industrielle *f*	—	región industrial *f*
zona monetaria (Es)	Währungszone *f*	currency zone	zone monétaire *f*	zona monetaria *f*	—
zona monetaria (I)	Währungszone *f*	currency zone	zone monétaire *f*	—	zona monetaria *f*
Zone (D)	—	zone	zone *f*	zona *f*	zona *f*
zone (E)	Zone *f*	—	zone *f*	zona *f*	zona *f*
zone (F)	Zone *f*	zone	—	zona *f*	zona *f*
zone de libre-échange (F)	Freihandelszone *f*	free trade area	—	zona di libero scambio *f*	zona de librecambio *f*
zone de rayonnement de la publicité (F)	Werbereichweite *f*	scope of advertising effect	—	raggio d'azione della pubblicità *m*	alcance publicitario *m*
zone monétaire¹ (F)	Währungszone *f*	currency zone	—	zona monetaria *f*	zona monetaria *f*
zone monétaire² (F)	Währungsgebiet *n*	currency area	—	area monetaria *f*	área monetaria *f*
zootecnia (I)	Tierzucht *f*	livestock breeding	élevage *m*	—	cría de animales *f*
Zugabe (D)	—	extra	prime *f*	aggiunta *f*	suplemento *m*
Zugang (D)	—	access	entrée *f*	accesso *m*	acceso *m*
zugesicherte Eigenschaften (D)	—	warranted characteristics	qualité promise *f*	caratteristiche promesse *f pl*	calidades aseguradas *f pl*
Zug um Zug (D)	—	concurrent	de point en point	contestualmente	punto por punto
Zukunftschance (D)	—	future prospects	perspectives d'avenir *f pl*	prospettiva *f*	posibilidades futuras *f pl*
Zulage (D)	—	increase/ additional pay	prime *f*/complément de salaire *m*	premio *m*/indennità *f*	suplemento *m*/plus *m*
Zulassung (D)	—	admission	admission *f*	ammissione *f*	admisión *f*
zu Lasten (D)	—	chargeable to	à la charge de qn	a carico di	a cargo de
Zulieferer (D)	—	supplier	sous-traitant *m*	fornitore *m*	abastecedor *m*
zur Ansicht (D)	—	on approval	à vue	in visione	para examen
Zusage (D)	—	promise	promesse *f*	conferma *f*	promesa *f*
Zusammenarbeit (D)	—	cooperation	collaboration *f*	collaborazione *f*	cooperación *f*
Zusatzverkauf (D)	—	additional sale	vente additionnelle *f*	vendita complementare *f*	venta adicional *f*
Zuschlag (D)	—	extra charge	supplément *m*	supplemento *m*/ premio *m*	suplemento *m*/ prima *f*
Zuschuß (D)	—	allowance	allocation *f*	sovvenzione *f*	subvención *f*
Zustellung (D)	—	delivery	remise *f*	notifica *f*/ recapito *m*	envío *m*

	D	E	F	I	Es
Zustimmung (D)	—	consent	accord *m*	consenso *m*	consentimiento *m*
Zuteilung (D)	—	allocation	répartition *f*	attribuzione *f*/ ripartizione *f*	asignación *f*
zu treuen Händen (D)	—	for safekeeping	remettre en mains sûres	alla particolare attenzione	a la atención
zuverlässig (D)	—	reliable	de confiance	affidabile	de confianza
Zuwendung (D)	—	bestowal	affectation *f*	assegnazione *f*	gratificación *f*
Zwangssparen (D)	—	compulsory saving	épargne forcée *f*	risparmio coatto *m*	ahorro forzoso *m*
Zwangsvergleich (D)	—	compulsory settlement	arrangement forcé *m*	concordato fallimentare *m*	convenio forzoso *m*
Zwangsverkauf (D)	—	forced sale	vente forcée *f*	vendita giudiziaria *f*	venta forzada *f*
Zwangs-versteigerung (D)	—	sale by court order	vente de biens par justice *f*	asta giudiziaria *f*	subasta forzosa *f*
Zwangsverwaltung (D)	—	receivership	séquestre judiciare *m*	amministrazione giudiziaria *f*	administración forzosa *f*
Zwangs-vollstreckung (D)	—	judicial execution	exécution forcée *f*	esecuzione forzata *f*	ejecución forzosa *f*
Zweckverband (D)	—	special purpose association	association à but déterminé *f*	consorzio intercomunale *m*	asociación con un fin determinado *f*
zweifelhafte Forderung (D)	—	doubtful account	créance douteuse *f*	credito dubbio *m*	créditos dudosos *m pl*
Zweigbetrieb (D)	—	branch business	établissement secondaire *m*	filiale *f*	sucursal *f*
Zweig-niederlassung (D)	—	branch office	succursale *f*	succursale *f*	filial *f*
Zweigstelle (D)	—	branch	agence *f*	agenzia *f*	filial *f*
Zwischenabnahme (D)	—	intermediate purchase	achat intermédiaire *m*	acquisto intermediario *m*	compra intermediaria *f*
Zwischenbilanz (D)	—	interim balance sheet	bilan intermédiaire *m*	bilancio provvisorio *m*	balance intermedio *m*
Zwischenhändler (D)	—	middleman	intermédiaire *m*	intermediario *m*	intermediario *m*
Zwischenkonto (D)	—	interim account	compte provisoire *m*	conto transitorio *m*	cuenta provisional *f*
Zwischenzeugnis (D)	—	interim report	certificat provisoire *m*	certificato provvisorio *m*	certificado provisional *m*
Zyklus (D)	—	cycle	cycle *m*	ciclo *m*	ciclo *m*

	D	E	F	I	Es
	Grundzahlen	**cardinal numbers**	**nombres cardinaux**	**numeri cardinali**	**números cardinales**
1	eins	one	un, une	uno	uno
2	zwei	two	deux	due	dos
3	drei	three	trois	tre	tres
4	vier	four	quatre	quattro	cuatro
5	fünf	five	cinq	cinque	cinco
6	sechs	six	six	sei	seis
7	sieben	seven	sept	sette	siete
8	acht	eight	huit	otto	ocho
9	neun	nine	neuf	nove	nueve
10	zehn	ten	dix	diece	diez
11	elf	eleven	onze	undici	once
12	zwölf	twelf	douze	dodici	doce
13	dreizehn	thirteen	treize	tredici	trece
14	vierzehn	fourteen	quatorze	quattordici	catorce
15	fünfzehn	fifteen	quinze	quindici	quince
16	sechzehn	sixteen	seize	seidici	dieciséis
17	siebzehn	seventeen	dix-sept	diciasette	diecisiete
18	achtzehn	eighteen	dix-huit	dicio	dieciocho
19	neunzehn	nineteen	dix-neuf	dicinove	diecinueve
20	zwanzig	twenty	vingt	venti	veinte
21	einundzwanzig	twenty-one	vingt et un	ventuno	veintiuno
22	zweiundzwanzig	twenty-two	vingt-deux	ventidue	veintidos
30	dreißig	thirty	trente	trenta	treinta
40	vierzig	forty	quarante	quaranta	cuarenta
50	fünfzig	fifty	cinquante	cinquanta	cincuenta
60	sechzig	sixty	soixante	settanta	sesanta
70	siebzig	seventy	soixante-dix	settanta	setenta
80	achtzig	eighty	quatre-vingts	ottanta	ochenta
90	neunzig	ninety	quatre-vingt-dix	novanta	noventa
100	hundert	(one) hundred	cent	cento	cien(to)
200	zweihundert	two hundred	deux cents	duecento	descientos, -as
300	dreihundert	three hundred	trois cents	trecento	trescientos, -as
400	vierhundert	four hundred	quatre cents	quattrocento	cuatrocientos, -as
500	fünfhundert	five hundred	cinq cents	cinquacento	quinientos, -as
600	sechshundert	six hundred	six cents	seicento	seiscientos, -as
700	siebenhundert	seven hundred	sept cents	settecento	setecientos, -as
800	achthundert	eight hundred	huit cents	ottocento	ochocientos, -as
900	neunhundert	nine hundred	neuf cents	novecento	novecientos, -as
1000	tausend	(one) thousand	mille	mille	mil
5000	fünftausend	five thousand	cinq mille	cinquemilla	cinco mil
10.000	zehntausend	ten thousand	dix mille	diecemilla	diez mil
100.000	hunderttausend	hundred thousand	cent mille	centomilla	cien mil
200.000	zweihundert-tausend	two hundred thousand	deux cents mille	duecentamilla	descientos mil
500.000	fünfhundert-tausend	five hundred thousand	cinq cents mille	cinquacentamilla	quinientos mil
1.000.000	eine Million	(one) million	un million	un millione	un millón

D	E	F	I	Es
Wochentage	**weekdays**	**jours de la semaine**	**giorni della settimana**	**días de semana**
Montag	Monday	lundi	lunedì	lunes
Dienstag	Tuesday	mardi	martedì	martes
Mittwoch	Wednesday	mercredi	mercoledì	miércoles
Donnerstag	Thursday	jeudi	giovedì	jueves
Freitag	Friday	vendredi	venerdì	viernes
Samstag	Saturday	samedi	sabato	sábado
Sonntag	Sunday	dimanche	domenica	domingo

D	E	F	I	Es
Monate	**months**	**mois**	**mesi**	**meses**
Januar	January	janvier	gennoaio	enero
Februar	February	février	febbraio	febrero
März	March	mars	marzo	marzo
April	April	avril	aprile	abril
Mai	May	mai	maggio	mayo
Juni	June	juin	giugno	junio
Juli	July	juillet	luglio	julio
August	August	août	agosto	agosto
September	September	septembre	settembre	septiembre
Oktober	October	octobre	ottobre	octubre
November	November	novembre	novembre	noviembre
Dezember	December	décembre	dicembre	diciembre

DANGEROUS LADY

Mart...... y...) – ...order of publication.
All avail..... from Headline.

Dangerous Lady (1992)
The Ladykiller: DI Kate Burrows 1 (1993)
Goodnight Lady (1994)
The Jump (1995)
The Runaway (1997)
Two Women (1999)
Broken: DI Kate Burrows 2 (2000)
Faceless (2001)*
Maura's Game: Dangerous Lady 2 (2002)*
The Know (2003)*
The Graft (2004)*
The Take (2005)*
Close (2006)*
Faces (2007)*
The Business (2008)*
Hard Girls: DI Kate Burrows 3 (2009)*
The Family (2010)*
The Faithless (2011)*
The Life (2012)*
Revenge (2013)*
The Good Life (2014)*
Get Even (2015)
Betrayal (2016)*

On Screen:
Dangerous Lady (ITV 1995)
The Jump (ITV 1998)
Martina Cole's Lady Killers (ITV3 documentary 2003)
The Take (Sky 1 2009)
Martina Cole's Girl Gangs (Sky Factual documentary 2009)
The Runaway (Sky 1 2011)

*Martina Cole's No. 1 bestsellers – at time of press she has spent more weeks at No. 1 than any other author

MARTINA COLE
DANGEROUS LADY

25th Anniversary Edition

HEADLINE

Foreword © 2016 Denise Welch

First published in Great Britain in 1992 by
HEADLINE BOOK PUBLISHING

This 25th anniversary edition published in Great Britain in 2017 by
HEADLINE PUBLISHING GROUP

1

Cataloguing in Publication Data is available from the British Library

ISBN 978 1 4722 4477 2 (Hardback)
ISBN 978 1 4722 4728 5 (Trade paperback)

Typeset in Galliard by Letterpart Limited, Reigate, Surrey

Printed and bound in Great Britain by Clays Ltd, St Ives plc

Headline's policy is to use papers that are natural, renewable and recyclable
products and made from wood grown in sustainable forests. The logging
and manufacturing processes are expected to conform to the environmental
regulations of the country of origin.

HEADLINE PUBLISHING GROUP
An Hachette UK Company
Carmelite House
50 Victoria Embankment
London EC4Y 0DZ

www.headline.co.uk
www.hachette.co.uk

To my parents

Foreword

About ten years ago, back in my partying days, I struck up a late-night conversation with a bubbly blonde in Gerry's Club in Soho. She recognised me from the telly and asked me lots of questions about my career, my personal life and my family. I was very flattered by her attention and enjoyed our quite-drunken ramblings. Eventually, after I had regaled her with many a showbiz tale, I asked her what she did for a living.

'I'm a writer,' she replied. 'I've written a few novels.'

'Oh, how exciting!' I politely enthused. 'Have any been published?'

She smiled at me and in her wonderful, husky Cockney voice said, 'Have you ever heard of Martina Cole?'

'Yes, of course,' I said, 'I'm reading *Dangerous Lady* now!'

'Well, that's me!'

I was speechless for once – and as embarrassed as alcohol allowed me to be! And that was the start of our friendship as I remember it.

Martina is a wonderful storyteller. She transports her readers to the dark underbelly of a world most of us know very little about, and yet she knows intimately. It's the world of the London criminal – frightening, brutal, violent and often glamorous, for which she makes no apology.

Dangerous Lady, her first novel, is one of my favourites. It's a belter of a book, a real page-turner – and it's incredible to think that she wrote it, aged twenty, in a carpetless council flat, during snatched moments while her baby was sleeping.

The characters are so utterly convincing. Beautiful, ruthless Maura Ryan and her terrifying older brother, Michael – the underworld kingpin who rules Soho along with his seven gangster brothers – remain as fresh in my mind as when I was first introduced to them, a decade ago. Now, as then, part of me wanted these bad guys to get their comeuppance, but Martina cleverly evokes sympathy for each and every one of them, no matter how evil the crimes. She asks you to question how much choice people have over their destiny when they have endured the direst of upbringings. She highlights police corruption and asks whether bent coppers are any better than the criminals from whom they are taking hush money.

Martina's great skill is in showing how relationships are built and broken when siblings, friends, enemies and lovers come into conflict. As her plots twist and turn, her characters encompass the deepest and strongest of human emotions, from love, passion and loyalty to bitter rivalry and regret. Every sentence she writes is vivid, every paragraph compelling. It's no wonder that several of her novels have been adapted into acclaimed television dramas and stage plays – including, of course, *Dangerous Lady*.

I am honoured to have been asked to write the foreword for this anniversary edition of Martina's first novel, the book that set its author on the road to being the much-loved, bestselling novelist she is today.

I was, and remain, Martina Cole's greatest fan, both as an amazing crime writer and an exceptional human being.

Denise Welch, 2016

Book One

LONDON, NOTTING HILL

If possible honestly, if not,
somehow,
make money – Horace, 65–8 BC

Am I my brother's keeper? – *Genesis, iv, 9*

Chapter One

1950

'You took your bloody time!'

Dr Martin O'Reilly stared down into the child's face and sighed. 'I had to see another patient. Now where's your ma?'

'In bed, of course.'

The little boy went back to sit on the stairs with his seven brothers. They ranged in age from three to fourteen. The doctor lit a cigar. He stood in the hallway puffing on it for a few seconds to make sure it was fully alight. The smell of the Ryans en masse was enough to turn the strongest of stomachs, though the slum stench was in his blood now, he reckoned. It permeated his clothes and skin. He started to pick his way up the stairs, careful not to tread on any little fingers. The children shuffled left and right on their bottoms to let him pass. He was also careful not to touch the wall. The smell he could combat with his cigar, but the roaches – he would never get used to them. How the buggers ran up the walls he would never know. They defied gravity.

On the landing he pushed open the first bedroom door, and there in front of him was Sarah Ryan. She was lying on a large double bed, her belly huge and swollen. He smiled at her, his heart breaking. Sarah Ryan was thirty-four years old. Her faded blonde hair was scraped back from her face into a bun, her skin was pale and dry. If her eyes had not been so bright and alert, she could have been mistaken for a corpse. He could remember coming to this house fifteen years earlier to deliver her first child. A fine-looking woman she had been then. Now her body was fat and scarred from constant childbearing, and her face wrinkled prematurely from habitual frowning.

'It's well on then?' His voice was gentle.

Sarah tried to hitch herself up in the bed. The old newspapers that had been placed underneath her crackled at the movement. 'Yeah. It's good of you to come, Martin. I told the little sods to get their dad, but as usual he ain't nowhere to be seen.'

She gripped her belly as another pain shot through her. 'Oh, it's dying to be born this one.' She smiled faintly. Then her eyes stretched wide as she saw the doctor take a syringe out of his bag.

'You ain't sticking that thing in me! We had all this out the last time. I ain't having any bloody injections. This is me thirteenth child and I never had one with any of them. Not even the stillborns. I ain't starting now.'

'Come on, Sarah. This will ease you.'

She put up her hand to stem his protests. 'I'm sorry but them things hurt like hell, whereas giving birth . . . it's nothing. Nothing . . .'

Martin put the needle on the small bedside table and, sighing heavily, pulled back the blankets covering her legs. His expert hands felt around her sides and then he slipped two fingers inside her vagina. When he had finished he pulled the blankets back over her.

'I think this one's breech.'

Sarah shrugged.

'First one if it is. I ain't done so bad. Ben was saying the other day that soon they would drop out as I walked down to the shops!'

She laughed and the doctor laughed with her.

'That would do me out of a job. Now you relax for a minute, I won't be long. I want one of the boys to run an errand for me.' He left the room, shutting the door quietly behind him.

'She had it then?' This from eight-year-old Leslie who had let him in earlier.

'No, she hasn't had it yet. Be patient, you young bugger.'

The doctor turned to the eldest boy, Michael. At nearly fifteen he was already over six feet tall and towered over the little Irish doctor in front of him.

'Michael, go and get old Mother Jenkins. I'm going to need help with this one.'

The boy stared down at the doctor for a few seconds. 'Me muvver's gonna be all right, ain't she?' His voice was deep and concerned.

The doctor nodded. 'Of course.'

The boy still did not move.

'She's never had old Mother Jenkins before.'

The doctor stared up at the boy impatiently. 'Look, Michael, I can't stand around here all day talking to you. Your ma's bad, but if we can get this baby born she'll be all right. The sooner you get Mrs Jenkins the better. Time's short.'

Michael turned slowly away from the doctor and placing one hand on the banister and the other on the wall he slid down, jumping over the younger boys' heads. As he landed heavily on the linoleum, the doctor called to him: 'Tell her I'll be paying the ten shillings or she won't come.'

4

Michael waved to let the doctor know he had heard, then, opening the front door, he rushed out.

The doctor looked down on to the younger children's heads and his teeth clamped down even harder on his cigar. Michael's foray down the stairs had caused the cockroaches to fall from the walls. The youngest child, Benny, not only had them crawling in his clothes, but one adventurous roach was slowly making its way across his face. Martin watched the child flick it gently away and made a mental note to see the landlord about getting the house stoved. It would never get rid of the damned things permanently but at least it would give the Ryans a breathing space.

'Now then, I want a couple of you to go and find your father.' Geoffrey, Anthony and Leslie all stood up. The doctor pointed at them in turn. 'You, Geoffrey, try the Latimer Arms. You, Anthony, go up the Roundhouse. And you . . .'

Leslie nodded, his eyes fixed on the floor.

'. . . go to the Kensington Park Hotel. If you can't find him in any of those places then try the Bramley Arms. If by any chance you do find your da, tell him that he is needed at home. Can you all remember that?'

The three heads nodded and they went on their way. Martin went back into the bedroom with Sarah.

'Sure they're good boys you've got there.'

Her voice sounded sceptical. 'I don't know about that, Doctor. They're a bit wild at times. It's the old man. He takes the belt to them for nicking one minute, and then the next he's sending them out to do it. The poor little sods can't win.'

She doubled up as another pain hit her.

'Relax now, Sarah.' He pushed a few stray hairs from her face. It was getting dark so he pulled the curtains and put on the overhead light. He lit himself another cigar from the butt of the previous one. Then, with it firmly clamped between his teeth, he examined her again. When he had finished he had a worried look on his face. He visibly relaxed as he heard a voice in the hallway. A few seconds later Matilda Jenkins had pushed open the bedroom door. She stood at the end of Sarah's bed, all eighteen stone of her.

'All right, Doctor?' This was a form of address, not a question.

'All right, Sarah? The bloody stairs knacker me these days. But them boys!' She flapped her hand at Sarah. 'Talk about scatter them. One look at me coming up 'em and they run like mad!' Her deep booming laugh reverberated around the bedroom. The doctor was paying her the ten shillings, she could afford to be friendly.

'It's a big woman you are, Matilda, to be sure. Now get yourself back down the stairs and heat me up lots of water. I want to

5

sterilise me things. This little fellow's breech.'

Matilda nodded her head vigorously.

'Righto, Doc. I'll send around the neighbours, get them to put their kettles on. We might even get a cuppa out of them!'

As she stamped from the room, Sarah glared at the doctor.

'What's she doing here? I ain't got ten shillings, and if I did have I'd give it to the kids. They ain't eaten since yesterday, and until that man of mine comes home, they won't eat at all! Knowing him, he's shacked up with some old sort somewhere and won't be home till the morning!'

She was near to tears.

'Calm down now, Sarah. I'm paying her.' He grasped one of her hands. 'Now be quiet, woman. I can't cope with this on me own. So you whisht now, and save your strength.'

Sarah lay back against the pillows, her face drenched with sweat. Her lips were cracked and dry. Turning awkwardly towards the bedside table, she picked up a glass of water and sipped the warm liquid gratefully. A little later Matilda brought up a bucket of steaming water. The doctor set about sterilising his things, including a large pair of scissors.

By nine in the evening Sarah was in great distress, as was the child within her. Twice the doctor had tried to push his arm inside her to turn the child and each time he had failed. He wiped his hands on a towel he had brought with him.

This child had to be born, and soon, or he would lose the pair of them. Blast Benjamin Ryan! It was always the same. He gave her a child every year, but was never there when it came into the world.

The little boys kept their vigil on the stairs. All were tired and hungry. Michael, waiting at the top, was silently cursing his father as he looked at his younger brothers' little faces. Benny was sucking the arm of his jumper.

Suddenly there was a loud banging on the front door. Six-year-old Garry answered it, only to be knocked flying as two policemen came crashing in. Michael took one look at them and, swearing under his breath, ran into his mother's bedroom. Cries could be heard from the stairs as the policemen tried to make their way up to the landing, the remaining boys making it as difficult as possible for them in the hope that their brother would get away.

Michael had opened the bedroom window and was half in and half out as the policemen burst into the room.

Then the lights went out.

'Who turned off the lights, you little bastards?'

'No one turned off the bleeding lights. The electric's gone.' Sarah's voice was faint. The policemen turned on their torches.

'Bring those over here. This woman is in danger of her life.' The

6

urgency in the doctor's voice brought both men to the bed. The boy was long gone, they both knew that. Sarah was writhing in agony, tears on her cheeks.

'You lot want slaughtering. My boy ain't done nothing.'

Matilda Jenkins broke in, 'Look, has anyone got a shilling for the meter?'

'I have.' The smaller of the two policemen fished some change out of his pocket. Leaving his colleague to help the doctor, he walked from the room and carefully made his way down the stairs. Stepping through the children as gently as he could, he went to the cupboard under the stairs and, locating the meter, put a shilling in. He put in another, and turned off his torch as he stepped out of the cupboard. Seven pairs of eyes were looking at him with open hostility, even the youngest's who was not yet four. The man looked at the boys as if seeing them for the first time. At the heads close-cropped to combat the lice and the holey jumpers with elbows poking through. He stood for a while staring at them. He felt for the first time in his life what it must be like to be one of them and was overwhelmed with a feeling of sadness and futility. Taking out his wallet, he pulled out a ten-shilling note and offered it to Geoffrey, the second eldest.

'Get yourself over the Messer's and get some fish and chips.'

'We don't want old Bill's money!'

'Hark at the hard man! Well, clever clogs, your little brothers are starving, so go and do what I tell you.'

He pushed the money into Geoffrey's hands. All the boy's instincts told him to throw the money back at the policeman, their natural enemy, but his little brothers' faces changed his mind. They had not eaten for nearly two days. Sullenly, he pushed past the man, who held on to his arm.

'Tell that brother of yours that we'll catch him in the end so he might as well give himself up.'

Geoffrey pulled his arm roughly away. Then, looking at the man as if he was so much dirt, he let himself out of the front door. The constable walked back up the stairs, shaking his head.

In the bedroom, Sarah was fighting to get the child born. The other policeman was holding her down, while the doctor was cutting her down below. As he cut she gave an almighty push and ripped open to her behind. The child slipped into the world, still in its birth sac. The doctor punched this open and looked at the little blue face inside. He cleaned its nose and gently blew into its mouth while he pressed tenderly on its tiny ribcage. The baby coughed and gave a little cry. Then, taking a deep breath, began to bawl its head off. Quick as a flash the doctor had cut the cord, passed the child to Matilda

Jenkins, and was stitching away at Sarah as if his own life depended on it.

She lay against the pillows, her whole body numb. She swore to herself that this was going to be the last child.

'Your first girl, Sarah.' Matilda's voice was kind.

She sat up in the bed, dumbstruck, her face aglow as if lit from the inside. She grinned, showing all her large yellowing teeth.

'You're joking! I thought it was another boy! A girl! It is really a girl?'

Even the policemen smiled at her. She was genuinely amazed.

'Oh, let me have her. Let me hold her! A daughter at last, thank Gawd!'

Matilda placed the child in her arms. The baby was now cleaned up and Sarah looked down into the bluest eyes she had ever seen.

'She's a beauty, Sarah.'

She stared down at her daughter in wonderment. This was her thirteenth child, but her first girl. All tiredness was forgotten as she gazed at her daughter. Then she looked around her at the other smiling faces, and remembered why the policemen were there. The elder of the two had been coming to the house for nigh on fifteen years. Ben had even been at it all through the war.

'What's my Mickey supposed to have done now?' Her voice was flat.

'He's been running for a bookie again, Sarah. I've warned him twice now. This time I'm going to nick him. So you tell him to come and see me.'

She looked back at her daughter. The doctor had finished, and, after removing the old newspapers from under Sarah, covered her up. She looked back at the policeman.

'I'll tell him, Frank, but he's like the old man. He goes his own way.' Her voice was low.

Matilda Jenkins opened the bedroom door and called the rest of the boys in. They all trooped in, eating their fish and chips, and clustered around the bed. Benny could not see anything so pulled on the doctor's coat.

'What do you want, child?'

Benny looked up with his little monkey face. His mouth was full of food.

'Is it Hovis, then?'

'Hovis? The doctor's voice was puzzled. 'What are you on about, boy?'

'Hovis . . . you know, brown bread. Well, is it?'

The doctor looked around him for enlightenment.

'Brown bread? Are you delirious, child?'

'He means is it dead? Brown bread . . . dead. Get it?'

8

This was spoken by Anthony, and his tone indicated that if anyone was stupid it was not his little brother.

'Brown bread, bejasus! No, it's not. It's very much alive. Now eat your chips, you little heathen. Brown bread indeed!'

The policemen laughed.

'How long you been in London, Doc?' the elder asked. 'Twenty years? And you still don't know the lingo.' They thought this highly amusing. 'We'd better be off, Sar. Don't forget to tell Michael when he gets in.'

'I won't forget, Frank. I'll tell him, but he won't come. You know that.'

'Well, try and persuade him. Good luck with the new arrival. See you all.' The two men left.

Sarah looked at her sons' faces and smiled.

'It's a girl!'

All the boys grinned at her.

'A daughter for me old age.' She hugged the child to her. 'I'm going to call her Maura. Maura Ryan. I like that.'

'Shall I go and get Mickey, Mum? I saved him some chips.'

'Yeah, Geoff. Tell him the coast is clear.'

The doctor stopped packing away his instruments and looked at Sarah sternly.

'You knew where he was all along?'

She grinned at him. 'Course I did. He's in the Anderson shelter at number 119. He always hides there.'

Seeking the funny side of what Sarah said, Martin O'Reilly threw back his head and laughed out loud. Seven mouths stopped chewing as the boys stared at him.

'What a night! Your little girl certainly picked her time to arrive. She saved young Michael's bacon tonight, that's a fact.'

Sarah chuckled with him. 'She did that all right!'

Pat Johnstone, Sarah's best friend and next-door neighbour, came into the bedroom with a tray of tea. She ushered all the boys out and poured Sarah a strong cup.

'Here you are, girl. Get your laughing gear around that. What about you, Doc? Fancy a cuppa?'

'That would be grand. I'm parched.'

Pat poured the doctor out a cup of tea and placed it on the bedside table. Then she sat on the bed next to Sarah. She looked at the baby and gasped with surprise.

'Oh, my Gawd! She's a cracker, ain't she?' Her naturally loud voice seemed to bounce off the walls. 'Gis' a little hold, Sar.'

Sarah passed the child to her and took a deep drink of her tea. 'This is just what I needed, Pat.'

'Is that right the filth came in looking for your Mickey and the

9

electric went? I nearly wet meself laughing when Mrs Jenkins told me, I thought it was so funny.'

Sarah rolled her eyes to the ceiling. 'Oh, please, Pat. Don't remind me!'

The doctor finished putting his things away and drank his tea. 'That was lovely. It just hit the right spot. Now I'll be off, Sarah. Don't get out of bed until I tell you that it's safe. I've had to put in a lot of stitches. If you start to bleed, send one of the lads around for me, OK?'

'I will, Martin. And thanks for everything.'

'That's all right. I'll see you in the morning. 'Bye now.'

He went out of the bedroom and down the stairs to the hallway where Matilda Jenkins was waiting for him with her hand out. He slipped a ten-shilling note into her palm.

'Thanks, Matilda, 'Bye.'

''Bye, Doctor O'Reilly.'

She closed the front door behind him. He walked down the flight of stairs that led to the road and looked at his car, a Rover 90. It was his pride and joy. There was not a windscreen wiper to be seen. He should have known this would happen in Lancaster Road.

'Little buggers!'

He got into his car and drove off. On 2 May 1950 he had brought Maura Ryan into the world.

Chapter Two

1953

Sarah Ryan glanced around her kitchen. A feeling of satisfaction swept over her. It looked beautiful. Taking a deep breath she sighed with contentment. She had not felt this happy for years. The table was laden with food. Turkey, ham, a large joint of beef, all carefully prepared and waiting to go into the oven. The kitchen was filled with the aroma of mince pies and sausage rolls cooking to a golden crispness in the oven.

She was startled out of her reverie by a loud crash from above. Her mouth set in a grim line, she went to the kitchen door. Opening it wide, she shouted as loud as she could: 'I'm warning you lot, one more noise and I'll come up there and scalp the arses off yer!'

She stood listening for a few minutes, trying not to smile. Then, assured that the children were all in their beds, she went back to her preparations, humming a little tune. Her last task was to lay thick strips of bacon across the turkey. Finally she stepped back from the table to admire her handiwork. Then, picking up the poker from the hearth, she banged it three times against the back of the fireplace. A few seconds later the banging was answered by two sharp thuds. Going to the sink she filled the kettle with water and placed it on the gas. As the kettle came to the boil she heard the back door open and popped her head into the scullery to see her friend Pat Johnstone kicking snow off her shoes.

'Get yourself in, Pat, I've got the kettle on.'

'Oh, Sar, it's brass monkey weather out there tonight!'

Coming into the kitchen, Pat dropped into an easy chair by the fire. She looked around the kitchen, impressed.

'By Christ, you're well set up this year.'

Her voice held a hint of jealousy. Sarah poured the steaming water into the tea pot and smiled at her friend.

'Michael brought the lot in this morning. I couldn't believe it meself when I saw it! There's sweets and biscuits as well as nuts and fruit. He's a good boy.'

Pat nodded her head, reckoning up the cost of everything in her

11

mind. She realised that what was being said about Michael must be true. You couldn't buy all this working at Lyons bakery or the Black Cat factory. Crime certainly did pay by the looks of it.

'And there's presents for all the kids,' Sarah chatted on happily, unaware of the animosity she was creating. Pouring the tea into two thick white mugs, she gave one to her friend. With a tea cloth around her hand she opened up the oven and took out the mince pies and sausage rolls, placing them on the top of the stove to cool as she put the turkey in to cook. Her movements were quick and confident. She straightened up, wiping her forehead with the bottom of her apron, and then went to the dresser to open the drawer. Taking out a package, she passed it to Pat.

'I nearly forgot! Happy Christmas.'

Pat Johnstone took the package and placed it on her lap. She looked at Sarah's face with troubled eyes.

'I didn't get you nothing, Sar . . . I ain't got the money.'

Sarah dismissed this. 'Oh, shut your face and open it.'

Slowly Pat tore the brown paper apart. Then her hand went to her mouth. Her voice shook as she tried to speak.

'Oh Sar! Oh, it's lovely . . .'

Sarah patted her friend's shoulder gently.

'I knew you'd like it!'

Pat pulled the white blouse out of the wrapper and held it to her cheek, rubbing the soft material against her skin.

'It feels like silk!'

'It *is* silk. As soon as I saw it, I knew it was for you.'

All the terrible things she had thought earlier rose up in Pat's mind. Jealousy of her friend had been steadily mounting in the last few months. It had started the day three months previously when Michael paid to have the house stoved. Sulphur candles had been burning for days, leaving the house free of vermin, then the whole place had been painted from top to bottom. Like most of the women in the street, Pat Johnstone had been angered by it all. By Lancaster Road standards, the Ryans had gone too far up in the world, making them aliens. If it wasn't for the fact that Michael Ryan was now a force to be reckoned with, the other families would have tried to force them out.

All this flickered through her mind in a split second and she felt ashamed. She had gone to school with Sarah, and they had helped one another over the years. Now Sarah was remembering her friend and Pat felt she didn't deserve it.

'It's absolutely gorgeous, Sar.'

Satisfied that her friend was happy, Sarah sat opposite her and took a quarter bottle of Black and White whisky from the mantelpiece.

12

She poured two generous measures into their cups of tea.

'This'll keep the cold out, Pat. God himself knows we need it in this weather.'

Picking up her mug, Pat toasted her friend. 'Merry Christmas to you, Sarah . . . and many more.'

Settling themselves into their chairs, warmed by the whisky, the two women began the serious business of the day: gossiping.

Michael Ryan walked down the Bayswater Road. He walked, as always, as if he owned it – head held high, even in the driving snow. At eighteen, Michael was magnificent. Over six foot two, he was built like an athlete, his dark brown overcoat emphasising the spread of his shoulders. He still had thick black unruly hair, which he now wore cut in a DA. His eyes, deep-set and a striking blue, seemed to drink in everything around him. The only softness about his rugged face was in his lips. They were full and sensuous like a woman's, though at times they gave him a hint of cruelty. Women and men were drawn to Michael Ryan, and he knew it. He used it to his advantage as he used everything.

Now he watched the women lounging against the railings of Hyde Park. Even in the snow on Christmas Eve the streetwalkers were out.

A few of the younger girls, new to their beat, looked at him with interest. One opened her coat to reveal a scantily clad body. Michael looked her up and down, his lips curling with contempt. He wouldn't touch a tom with a barge pole. An older woman, seeing the exchange, laughed out loud.

'Cover yourself up, girl. Before you get frostbite of the fanny!'

The other women laughed, glad of some light relief. Michael carried on walking. He didn't really mind the prostitutes. In fact, he admired them. To his mind theirs was a business, like any other. Supply and demand. What he didn't like was the way some of them looked at him as a potential John. He liked to think that people put him above that kind of thing. He crossed the road, dodging the traffic skilfully. The snow was easing up and last-minute shoppers were everywhere. The Portobello Road had been packed.

He walked into the warmth of the Bramley Arms. Pushing his way among the men he went to the bar, nodding a greeting here and there. Over the last year he had worked hard to create an image for himself and it was paying off. People were deferential towards him. He snapped his fingers at the barmaid and ordered a brandy. He didn't particularly like brandy, but it was part of his image. It set him above other people. The men at the bar moved to give him room.

He sipped his drink. Ranging around the crowded bar, his eyes

13

settled on a group by the window. He picked up his drink and made his way over to them. One of the men glanced at him, giving a double take as he realised who it was.

Tommy Blue felt a knot of fear somewhere in his bowels. The four other men at the table with him sensed his panic and stopped talking to look at the newcomer. Seeing Michael Ryan smiling at them, they seemed to crowd together, hunching in their seats. Enjoying the terror he was creating, Michael drank his brandy in one gulp. Then, wiping his hand across his mouth, he placed his glass gently on the table.

'I've been looking for you, Tommy.'

His voice was quiet.

Tommy Blue felt his heart sinking. He tried to smile, his lips trembling.

'I think me and you had better have a little walk.'

Looking around the table at the other men, Michael pointed at Tommy.

'I'll be waiting outside for you.'

Turning, he pushed his way to the door. Outside he leant against the wall of the pub. He bit on his lip, the feeling of excitement in his breast causing his heart beat to pound in his ears.

A group of Salvation Army singers were making their way along the road. Pulling a pack of Strands from his pocket, Michael lit one. The strains of 'Onward Christian Soldiers' gradually grew closer. He pulled hard on the cigarette. He would give Tommy Blue five minutes before going in after him.

Inside the Bramley Arms, Tommy was rooted to his seat.

'How much do you owe, Tom?' This from Dustbin Daley, a totter from Shepherd's Bush.

'Forty-five quid.' Tommy's voice was low.

One of his companions whistled.

'I'd better get out there . . . otherwise he'll come in after me.' Getting up unsteadily, Tommy made his way to the door.

Dustbin Daley shook his head. 'He must be bloody mad.'

The others agreed with him. Their earlier high spirits were gone now, out of the door with Tommy Blue.

Tommy shivered as the cold hit him. He was wearing a thin jacket, torn in places, and a thick multi-coloured scarf.

Michael threw his cigarette on the slush-filled pavement and ground it out with his boot. Pushing himself from the wall he grabbed Tommy's jacket and pulled him along the road. The Salvationists were alongside them. A young girl pushed a tin in their direction. She smiled at Michael as she rattled it.

'Merry Christmas, sir.' Her eyes held open admiration.

Pulling his coat open, he pushed his hand into his trouser pocket, and taking out two half crowns dropped them into the tin. The girl flushed with pleasure.

'Thank you, sir. Merry Christmas.'

Nodding at her, Michael resumed piloting Tommy Blue along the pavement. The tambourines and the singing faded into the distance. The two men walked in silence for five minutes. Tommy Blue could not feel the cold now. He couldn't feel anything. Fear had completely taken over. Tommy Blue was on automatic pilot. All he could do was wait. The beer he had been drinking steadily all day was now weighing heavily on his stomach.

Michael slowed down in Treadgold Street. The laundry here was known affectionately as the bagwash. Michael himself had brought his mother's laundry here on many occasions. Now it was deserted, shut up for the Christmas holidays. Taking a key from inside his coat Michael opened the double doors of the building and pushed Tommy inside. Pulling the doors shut behind him, he turned on the lights. Tommy stood immobile.

Taking out his pack of Strands, Michael lit one slowly. He pulled deeply on the cigarette and blew the smoke into Tommy's face.

'You've made me very cross.' As usual Michael's voice was quiet.

Tommy's face seemed to come to life. He blinked his eyes rapidly.

'Look, Mickey, I . . .I tried to get the money. I swear it!'

'Shut up, Tommy. You're beginning to annoy me.'

Dropping the cigarette he grabbed Tommy's scarf, forcing him backwards until he was against one of the huge machines. Bringing his right fist back over his shoulder he punched Tommy in the face with considerable force. Tommy's nose seemed to collapse underneath the blow. Michael let him drop on the filthy floor. Groaning, Tommy curled himself up into a ball, his hands covering his head. Michael kicked him in the back, the force of the blow sending Tommy across the dirt-strewn floor. Picking up one of the large wooden podgers the women used to push down the bagwashes, Michael prodded Tommy on the shoulder.

'Hold out your arm.' Michael's voice held no emotion whatsoever. Tommy was blubbering.

'Please . . . please, Mickey, I'm begging you.' He looked up at Michael, his face bloody and awash with tears. 'Don't do this . . .I swear I'll ge-get the money somehow.'

Kicking him in the legs, Michael brought the podger down on Tommy's shoulders.

'If you don't put your arm out, I'll break your bastard back for you. Now put your arm out!'

15

Michael's voice echoed around the laundry. Slowly Tommy placed his arm on the floor, his whole body jerking with fear. Twice the 'podger' smashed down on his elbow, shattering the bone. Tommy screamed with pain. He was struggling to keep conscious as red-hot waves of nausea washed over him. He threw up on the floor, beer mixed with bile steaming in the cold.

'Get up, Tommy.' Michael's voice was quiet again.

Slowly he dragged himself to his feet, his arm hanging awkwardly against his side, the sleeve of his jacket gradually staining crimson. Droplets of blood ran over his fingers and dripped on to the floor. He leant against the machine, crying quietly.

'You've got seven days, Tommy, that's all, to find the money. Now piss off.'

Michael watched Tommy stagger from the laundry. He checked himself over to make sure there was no blood on his clothes. Then, whistling to himself, he washed the podger clean and put it back where he'd found it, against the far wall. Then, still whistling, he turned off the lights and locked up.

Joe the Fish listened avidly to everything Michael said to him, nodding his head now and again and every so often muttering, 'Good . . . good.' When Michael had finished, Joe smiled at him. 'The arm was good and broken?'

'Yeah. Smashed to smithereens!'

Joe the Fish sighed. He had a distaste for violence, but in his business it was a necessity. He looked at Michael Ryan sitting opposite him. He liked the boy, could see himself in Michael. The boy had the same urge to better himself. That had been Joe's ambition as a young man. Like Michael he had started out as a 'breaker' – a heavy – until he had built up his own business. Now he was a respected member of the community. He owned shops, clubs and market stalls, from Petticoat Lane to the Portobello Road. His most lucrative business, though, was the bets. Joe had been a bookie for over twenty years, gradually moving into loan sharking. He had realised as soon as he had employed Michael that he had found himself a kindred spirit. Michael was innately honest. If he said the punter had paid him fifty quid, Joe knew that was what had been paid. Most of the breakers kept a portion for themselves, knowing that the unlucky punter would eventually pay that portion once again. Michael Ryan, though, had his own set of principles. He might beat a man up so badly he needed hospital treatment, yet Joe knew that in Michael's mind, keeping any money back would be tantamount to stealing. Joe liked him. He liked the way Michael looked at his home. He liked the respect that Michael afforded him.

16

He coughed and spat some phlegm into the fire, hearing it sizzle as it hit the coals.

'From January I want you to take over the "breaking" side of the business. I'll inform all the men that they're to take their orders from you.'

Michael stared at Joe. Then a wide grin broke out across his face and he shook his head in amazement.

'Thanks, Joe! Bloody hell!'

Joe, like most people, felt happy to see Michael grin. It was as if a blinding sun had emerged from behind a black cloud. Michael had the gift of making people *want* to please him, as if by giving him pleasure they were somehow indebted to him. Joe felt a rush of warmth go through him. He would enjoy working with this boy, teaching him the ropes. He let his eyes travel over Michael's body. He certainly was a fine-looking boy.

Michael watched Joe's eyes and a thrill of anticipation went through him. Joe the Fish was fifty years old. He had never married or had an association with any woman as far as Michael knew. What he did know was that Joe liked to be surrounded by young men. In the last few months he had consciously ingratiated himself with Joe, flattered him, let Joe think that he was grateful to him for giving him the breaker's job. He stared into Joe's face and smiled at him, his deep blue eyes seemingly full of gratitude and admiration. He watched Joe heave his bulk out of the chair. A flicker of repugnance crossed Michael's features, to be quickly replaced by the dazzling smile he knew caused Joe so much happiness.

Opening one of the drawers in his desk, Joe took out a small box. He walked around the desk and gave it to Michael.

'Just a little token of my appreciation.' Joe's voice was low and husky. Leaning against the desk he watched Michael's face as he opened the box. When he heard the deep intake of breath, Joe relaxed. He would not rush the boy, he had to let him come to him.

Michael stared at the tie pin glinting up from the red velvet lining. It was gold, in the shape of a large M, encrusted with diamonds. Looking up into Joe's face, Michael felt a moment of terror at what he had to do. Then, seeing the softness in Joe's eyes, he swallowed heavily. It was now or never.

Placing his hand on the top of Joe's thigh, he gently brushed his knuckles against the man's groin. Joe stared down at the large, rough hand gently rubbing against him. Closing his eyes momentarily, he felt a rush of ecstasy pulsing through his body. He opened his eyes and stared down into Michael's face. In the firelight, he looked like a dark angel. His blue eyes held an amber glow that caused Joe's heart to somersault inside his breast.

Dropping heavily on to his knees, he placed his hands on Michael's thighs, rubbing and kneading them, his breath coming heavily. Watching him, Michael smiled to himself. He thought Joe looked ridiculous, and noticed that he had a film of sweat above his lips which he licked at nervously.

As he felt Joe begin fumbling with his trousers Michael stifled an urge to slam his fist into Joe's head. He couldn't go back now, not after all the planning and scheming of the last few months. Joe was his ticket out of Notting Hill, his passport into the world of real villainy. Gritting his teeth he lay back in the chair and forced himself to relax. Outside, in the muffled stillness of the snow, Michael heard a lone voice singing 'Silent Night'. Looking down at the top of Joe's balding pate, Michael listened to the haunting childish voice and could have cried.

Sarah was basting the turkey when she heard Benjamin come in. The front door was slammed as loudly as possible, causing Sarah to wince. Putting the turkey back into the oven, she sat back in her chair. Benjamin stumbled into the kitchen, his hair and clothes still laden with snow. He grinned his wide toothless grin at her and made his way unsteadily across the room to her side.

'Hello, Sarah, my darling!'

As usual when drunk, he spoke to her as if she was at the other end of the street.

'Will you keep your voice down! You'll have all the bloody kids up!'

Benjamin stared down at his wife, blinking his eyes as he swayed unsteadily before her. The more he tried to concentrate, the more blurred she seemed to become. Finally seeing two Sarahs, he staggered into the seat vacated by Pat Johnstone not an hour ago. Lifting up one of his legs he broke wind loudly, causing Sarah to purse her lips. He sat in the chair smiling amiably at her, his clothes beginning to steam with the heat of the fire.

Wordlessly she pulled herself from her chair and swiftly began making him some ham sandwiches. She looked at the clock and noticed it was twenty-past one – everyone was in now except Michael. Placing the sandwiches on a plate, she gave them to her husband. She was bone tired. She had been working since seven in the morning.

Going through the scullery she pulled on an old coat and went out into the tiny back garden. Squatting down, she took a plate from the top of a large glass bowl. The snow had drifted up the sides and on to the plate. Carefully she wiped it clean. Then, touching the green mass inside the bowl softly, she smiled. The younger children loved jelly. That was one good thing about the

18

snow, it kept everything nice and fresh. Replacing the plate, she stood up and went back inside the house, banging her slippers on the step to get rid of the snow.

Back inside the kitchen she heard her husband snoring loudly. He was sprawled in his chair, his long legs outstretched, his hand holding the plate of sandwiches away from his body. Taking the plate gently from him she placed it in the sink, then checked the turkey one last time, turned the gas down as low as it would go and made her way up to bed.

As she undressed in the bedroom she saw her daughter had climbed into their big double bed. This was Maura's first real Christmas. Slipping into the bed Sarah looked down on the white-blonde head and felt the familiar tightening in her guts. The child stirred and burrowed deeper into the bed. Placing her thumb in her mouth, she sucked on it furiously for a few seconds before settling down once more into a deep sleep. If Benjamin had given her nothing else in their life together he had given her this child, and for that Sarah would forgive him anything.

Michael woke up and glanced at his watch. It was three-fifteen. Shaking his head to clear the fustiness he noticed a fat arm around his waist. In the dying firelight he looked down on the sleeping face of Joe the Fish. Somewhere inside himself he felt disgust at the events of the previous few hours. He was acutely aware of everything that had gone on in front of the then roaring fire. Mixed with his revulsion was also a tiny feeling of excitement. He now had Joe the Fish in his grasp, as he had sworn to himself that he would. A cruel smile played at the corners of his mouth. He would play Joe like a musical instrument. He would slowly become the focal point of his life. Then, when Joe had served his purpose, he would dispose of him. Michael knew what he had to do. He had been planning it long enough.

Gently, he brought his face down on to Joe's and kissed him on his lips. Joe's watery eyes opened and he smiled, displaying discoloured teeth.

'I've got to get going, Joe.'

Yawning lazily, the older man stretched his plump arms above his head.

'All right, Michael love. Try and get around tomorrow. I'm always alone on Christmas Day.' His voice sounded sad.

'I will. Don't worry.'

Joe watched Michael dressing in the firelight, his heart bursting in his breast. In his mind's eye he relived their love-making of a few hours before and the picture of Michael lying underneath him as he penetrated him rose in his mind. He couldn't quite believe

19

he had found himself such a beautiful animal. As Michael slipped on his overcoat Joe felt a wave of loneliness wash over him.

'See you tomorrow then.' Michael's voice was gentle and caressing. He favoured Joe with one of his blinding grins. Pulling himself up from the floor he stood before the dying fire, his short fat legs and large stomach making Michael feel sick inside.

'Haven't you forgotten something?' Joe's voice sounded like a young girl's – high and breathless with anticipation. Michael frowned at him, bewildered. Then seeing Joe's lips pucker, he walked over to the fireplace and embraced him. Joe pushed his tongue into Michael's mouth, kissing him with an energy that startled him. Breaking away gently, Michael smiled at him and quietly left the room.

The picture of Joe's doughy white body seemed to be imprinted on his mind. As he walked out into the silent white world Michael was glad of the freezing cold that seemed to cut down into his lungs. A light snow was falling and he raised his face to allow the soft flakes to fall on his skin, willing it to wash away the disgust he felt inside.

The street lights gave the pavements a glittering glow as if thousands of diamonds were lining his path. Picking up speed, Michael began to smile. He shook his head and shrugged in the stillness of the night. The worst was over now. He knew what he had let himself in for and he was glad. Let the fat old queen use his body. It had put food on his mother's table. It had brought the kids clothes. It would eventually bring him untold riches. Never would he allow himself to feel bad about it again.

He looked up into the black sky and waved his fist at the stars. This was a new beginning for the Ryans. He was going to pick them up out of the gutter and establish them in the monied world where he knew they belonged. Shoving his hands into the pockets of his overcoat he felt the little box that contained the tie pin. He grinned. As soon as the shops opened after the holidays he was going to go out and buy himself a tie!

When Michael saw the happy faces on Christmas Day, the food that seemed inexhaustible and the merriment his gifts had brought, he finally came to terms with himself. Anything, however bad, was worth all this. After a large, noisy Christmas dinner, Michael sat with his sister Maura asleep on his lap. As he looked down at her sleeping face, sucking contentedly on her thumb, he swore that he would commit murder if it kept his family as happy as they were now.

It was a promise he was to keep many times.

Chapter Three

1955

Garry and Benny Ryan were playing on the bombsite that was once Testerton Street. The day before they had noticed while coming home from school that an enormous mound of sand had been left there. That meant one of two things – the remaining houses were either being patched up or demolished to make way for pre-fabs. Either way they knew that their playground was going to disappear. Both boys had been up and out by six-thirty. If they timed it just right they could scavenge for a few hours before going to the Royalty in Ladbroke Grove for the Saturday morning minors.

They had played in the mound of sand for over an hour. Benny, at nine, was already a true Ryan. Big for his age, he towered over Garry who was eleven. Garry had a long thin body, giving him a waif-like appearance. He was the only Ryan to wear glasses, which he was forever pushing higher on his nose, the thick lenses giving him an owlish appearance. Where Benny was dark-haired with the characteristic Ryan dark blue eyes and full-lipped mouth, Garry was the opposite. He had light brown hair and a feral quality about him that made people do what he wanted. Garry was the acknowledged genius of the family, forever reading. His room was strewn with books and papers. He also fancied himself as an inventor – a pastime that had his mother caught between maternal pride and an almost uncontrollable urge to murder him.

The June sunshine gave their play an added vigour. All around them the world had come to life. The hum of the traffic was getting louder and every so often the rattling of a train set the dirt trembling. To the right of the mound of sand stood what remained of the houses in Testerton Street. The bomb had been a direct hit and only the last few dwellings had still been standing afterwards. These had no fronts left. Their rooms were great gaping caverns that miraculously still had wallpaper and broken furniture inside.

The two boys knew every inch of these houses. From the roof rafter of the most stable hung their 'bundle' swing. Now summer

was here the swing would become a focal point for the children around and about. Boys would come from as far away as Shepherd's Bush and Bayswater to play on it between fighting rival gangs. Providing the work didn't start too soon, it would be a good summer.

Scrambling down from the mound of sand, Garry began walking towards the houses, his hands and knees stained orange. Seeing his brother walking away Benny followed hastily, rubbing off the damp sand from his hands on his shorts. He caught up with Garry, puffing for breath.

'What we gonna do then?' As always he waited for Garry to decide what games were to be played.

Garry looked up at his brother, his thin face already grimy. 'We's gonna look for bombs and things. Lee's hid some gunpowder he swiped from under the Arches and I'm gonna pinch it off him.'

Benny looked worried for a second. Lee at thirteen was already as big as Roy, who was seventeen, nearly six feet tall, and was also bad-tempered.

'Lee'll smash us up!'

Garry smiled and pushed his glasses higher up his nose. 'He's got to catch us first!'

Benny laughed nervously. Lee would catch them, he always did, but he kept his own counsel because when Garry got mad he sent him home. Then he'd have to play with his sister! He followed Garry into the end house. The stairs were still sound and both boys made their way up to the top floor. Standing dangerously close to the crumbling edge, the two looked out across London. Over the last few years the landscape had changed. From their vantage point they could see the whole of their world. In the distance Garry saw that the fairground had arrived at Wormwood Scrubs Park. He poked Benny in the ribs and pointed to it, a thrill of expectation going through them both.

'I'm gonna get Mickey to give us some money! We'll go there later and see what rides they've got!'

In his excitement Benny jumped backwards and tripped over a lump of wood. As he landed on the floor boards he gasped, 'Here, Gal, look at this lot!'

Garry was already staring at what lay beneath his brother's large feet.

'Where'd you reckon they come from?'

Garry shook his head. Kneeling down on the floor, he picked up an empty cartridge case. There were over a dozen in all.

'I reckon someone nicked them and then left them here!'

Pushing his glasses up on to the bridge of his nose, Garry snapped: 'Trust you to state the bloody obvious. These have been hidden here by a little firm, and I think I know whose it was!'

Benny pulled himself up from the floor with difficulty. Both his hands were stinging where he'd skinned them.

'Who d'you reckon hid them then?'

'I bet it was that gang from Elgin Avenue.' Garry's voice was triumphant.

'Come on, let's nick them quick. Before anyone comes.'

Both boys began stuffing the empty cases down their shirts. Then they ran down the stairs as fast as they could. As they ran out of the house into the sunshine they both skidded to a halt. Lee, Leslie and Roy were walking towards them. Garry looked at Benny, his face troubled.

'Whatever you do, don't tell them about this lot.' He patted his shirt. Benny's hands were smarting and he rubbed them gently on his shirt. Tears were already forming in his eyes.

Roy noticed the boys and called to them. 'What you two standing there for? What you done?'

Garry as usual did the talking. 'We ain't done nothing. We thought you was looking for us, that's all.'

'What would we want with you two?' Roy's voice sounded incredulous. 'We get enough of you at home. Now sod off, the pair of you.'

Neither boy needed to be told twice. They ran off as fast as their legs would carry them. When they reached the safety of the pile of sand they sat on top of it and watched their brothers. The three older boys stood by the opening of the houses. They were all smoking.

'Did you smell them? I reckons they've been to the baths in Silchester Road. They've all got that smelly stuff on their hair.' Benny's voice was disgusted. In his mind anyone who could have a bath without being told to needed treatment. He himself had a bath every fortnight, a sixpenny one with soap and towels supplied. He hated it. If his mother didn't stand outside waiting for him he'd spend the money on something important, like caps for his gun and comics.

A little while later three girls arrived on the scene, two blondes and redhead. Garry laughed.

'Dirty bleeders! That's why they've been to the baths. They're going snogging!'

They watched the three girls pair off with their brothers and go off in different directions. Even more disgusted, Benny stood up.

'Come on, let's go home. I'm hungry.'

Silently the two boys made their way home.

It was three in the afternoon when Roy brought Janine into his house. It was the first time he had brought a girl home and both he and Janine were nervous. Grasping her hand in the hallway, he smiled at her.

'Everything's gonna be all right.'

He looked down into her green eyes and as always had the urge to kiss her. She had milk-white skin and long thick red hair. To Roy's mind Janine was class. She was also very tall – five feet eight inches. In a way he was glad that she was 'in trouble'. It would give them the push they needed to come out into the open.

He led her by the hand into his mother's kitchen. As usual Sarah was cooking. Even on days like this with the sun cracking the pavements Sarah still cooked. With nine children to feed, preparing a meal was a major event. She looked at Roy and Janine, her surprise showing on her face. Roy stood awkwardly in the kitchen and, still grasping Janine's hand, smiled at his mother.

'Mum, I'd like you to meet Janine . . . Janine Grierson.'

The girl stretched out her free hand and nodded her head. 'Pleased to meet you, I'm sure.'

Her voice was very low and refined. Wiping her hand on her apron, Sarah took the girl's hand and shook it gently.

'And you, love. Well, sit yourselves down. I've made some ginger beer. Would you like a glass?'

Without waiting for an answer, she went to the scullery and took the large jug from the table out there. She needed time to think. Grierson? Grierson? Where did she know that name from? She carried the jug back into the kitchen. Roy had sat Janine at the kitchen table and was standing beside her. Then, like a bolt out of the blue, it came to Sarah. This was Janine Grierson. Her heart sank in her chest. Her father owned the butcher's in the Portobello Road. He had also owned the house next door to Christie's round in Rillington Place. What on earth was Janine doing with her Roy? Not that she didn't think her son was good enough for her, oh no! But Eliza Grierson had great plans for her only daughter, Sarah knew that much.

Forcing a smile on to her face she poured out two glasses of ginger beer. As she placed them on the table, Roy spoke up. 'Janine's pregnant, Mum. And I'm the father.'

Outside in the garden, Maura was watching Garry and Benny working. Benny was holding the cartridges steady while Garry filled them with the gunpowder. After watching a particularly thrilling Lone Ranger at the Saturday morning minors, Garry had experienced a renewed interest in the making of bombs. He pushed the wadding carefully into the cartridge before taking it from Benny and placing it on the garden wall. He stepped back to admire his handiwork. That was the last one.

Maura sat on the wooden crate. Her long blonde hair seemed to come alive in the sunlight which gave it golden highlights. Her aquamarine eyes carefully watched every movement her brothers made. At five, Maura knew that if she wanted to be a part of their games she had to sit and watch quietly, otherwise they would sneak out of the garden leaving her alone.

She saw Garry give Benny a large hammer. Then Garry carefully took one of the filled cartridges and placed it on the grass. He had to press it down a couple of times to stop it falling over. Then he nodded at Benny who took the hammer and brought it back over his head, ready to smash it down on to the cartridge at a sign from his brother. Garry pushed his glasses higher on his nose and raising his hand as if he was starting a race, brought it down heavily to his side . . .

Inside the house Janine was crying quietly as Sarah spoke. 'It's nothing against you, lass, but think of your father. He'll go stark staring mad when he hears. Baby or no baby, there's no way he'll allow you to marry Roy. I know it.' Her voice had a finality about it that made Roy's blood run cold in his veins. He opened his mouth to answer. Both women were looking at him expectantly. They saw his eyes open wide until they seemed about to start from his head.

'Benny! Benny . . . don't you bloody dare!' His voice was so loud both women jumped in their seats. A split second later an almighty bang erupted from the garden, followed by Maura's frenzied screaming. The three adults seemed to be catapulted from their seats as they ran out into the back yard.

Maura had seen the hammer descend on to the cartridge just as she heard Roy's voice from the house. The impact of the hammer hitting the brass casing of the cartridge had caused a flash of blue light followed by an enormous bang. As if in slow motion she had seen Benny travel backwards through the air, landing heavily on his back among the rubbish that littered the end of the garden. That's when she started to scream. Through her tears she saw Garry scaling the wall as he made a run for it.

Roy ran to where Benny was lying, his heart pounding in his ears. This time Garry had really done it. He had finally killed somebody. Picking Benny up gently he cradled his head in his lap, conscious of his mother standing in the garden, her hand over her mouth as if terrified of what she might find. Benny was soot-blackened all over. The smell of burnt powder seemed to hang around him in a cloud. Looking down into his brother's face, Roy felt the tears come into his eyes.

'Benny . . . Benny!' Roy's anguished voice carried up into the pale blue sky. Janine, stunned, had gone to the little girl sitting on the crate. Instinctively she pulled the child to her breast, stroking the long blonde hair.

Roy clutched Benny to him, cuddling the dirty head to his breast. Opening his eyes Benny looked up into his brother's tearstained face.

'What happened?' His childish voice broke into everyone's shocked thoughts. 'One minute I was hammerin'. The next I was blown up!'

Benny looked around him, a bewildered expression on his face. 'Where's Garry gone?'

Picking him up, Roy felt the terror slowly leave his own body. 'When that little bastard gets home, I'm gonna murder him. If it's the last thing I do in this life . . .'

Maura clung to Janine, enjoying the flowery smell of her. Her cries had subsided to little hiccups. Sarah let Roy carry Benny into the house, and as she looked at Janine comforting her only daughter, the ice in her heart melted. Going to the girl, she put her arm around her shoulders.

'That Garry will be the death of me. Well, if you think you could stand the strain of being part of this family, you're welcome.'

Janine's white face made Sarah's natural good nature come to the fore. Pushing the girl's heavy red hair back from her face, she said, 'I'm warning you, though . . . excitement like this is an everyday occurrence!'

'Oh, Mrs Ryan, my father is going to go mad.'

Sarah waved her hand at the girl, her voice sounding more confident than she actually felt.

'He'll get over it, love. He'll get over it.'

James Grierson was stalking around his house in a fit of temper so acute he could almost taste it. Unlike his wife, who had taken herself off to bed like one of the heroines in the penny dramas, he, James Grierson, was going to *do* something. What exactly he wasn't sure, but he would think of something. Stamping up the stairs he went into the bedroom he shared with Eliza.

'How could a daughter of mine take up with that bloody scum? A filthy, stinking Ryan!' He clenched his fists and raised them to the ceiling. 'I could throttle the bitch. My God, my mother used to say: "Show me the company you keep and I'll tell you what you are." Never was a truer word said!'

Eliza closed her eyes and groaned. Since Janine had told them that morning that she was pregnant, her whole world had fallen

26

apart. Only a week ago, she had stood in their butcher's shop and completely demolished the reputation of young Carrie Davidson for the same thing: having to get married. She could hear herself talking to anyone who would listen about the shameless hussy. Now it had happened to her daughter and she didn't like it, she didn't like it one bit. Eliza Grierson was known as a gossip of Olympian standards. She prided herself on her ability to sift through the most innocent conversations and turn them into major scandals. She knew that this trouble with her daughter would be all the more enjoyed because it was a reflection on herself. She groaned again and pushed a pillow over her head. If it had been anyone but a Ryan . . . She felt tears of frustration stinging her eyes. She could cheerfully throttle Janine herself!

A loud banging at the front door stopped both of them in their tracks. Pulling back the curtain, James Grierson looked down into his garden and groaned. It was not a very good day today, and he had a terrible feeling that it was going to get worse.

Michael and Geoffrey stood in the Griersons' front garden. Like everything of Eliza Grierson's, the garden was what she described as 'classy'. It was also immaculate, as were the curtains at the windows and the shiny brass knocker on the door. This was opened by a rather subdued James who said gruffly: 'You'd better come in.'

Michael and Geoffrey walked into the spacious hallway as if they owned the house. Opening the parlour door, James ushered them inside.

Michael sat himself down in an armchair and looked around the room slowly. Geoffrey sat on the rather hard horsehair settee.

Taking a packet of Strands from his pocket Michael gave one to Geoffrey and after offering the pack to James, who refused, laboriously set about lighting the cigarettes. He knew that his slowness was annoying James Grierson. It was a calculated move. Drawing the smoke into his lungs he put his head back against the chair and blew two large smoke rings. Then, looking at James, he smiled.

'I understand, Mr Grierson, that my brother Roy has been shunting your daughter.'

Geoffrey watched the red flush creep up James Grierson's neck and continue until it reached his receding hairline. Stamping across the room, the man made as if to grab Michael's shirt. Grabbing Grierson's hand in a vice-like grip, Michael laughed.

'Naughty, naughty.'

Then pushing the older man from him, he sat forward in the chair. James was sent sprawling across his own parlour carpet, a blinding anger building inside him.

27

Michael pointed at him, the cigarette smoke curling around his finger.

'In three weeks' time, Mr Grierson, my brother is gonna marry your daughter, with or without your permission. Personally I would advise you to give them your blessing, what with the baby and all. A new little Ryan . . . a Ryan that your daughter is carrying inside her.'

Slowly James Grierson pulled himself up from the floor. Geoffrey put out his hand to help but was ignored. Waving his hand away, the older man slumped down on the chair opposite Michael.

Staring at him, Michael underwent one of his lightning changes of mood. From anger and animosity he turned in a split second to a benevolent caring brother only here to see justice done. His rugged face softened. All irritation seemingly forgotten, he leant forward in his chair and smiled at James Grierson – one of his most stunning smiles that seemed to wipe the cruelty from his face at a stroke. He began to speak in a man to man voice.

'Listen, James . . . may I call you James?' The man nodded, not at all happy with this bewildering change in his antagonist.

'The way I see it is this. Your daughter has been made pregnant by my brother.' He opened his arms out wide in a gesture of helplessness. 'They love one another, they want to marry. It's not as if Roy's had it on his toes, is it? He's quite willing to do the right thing by the girl. I know you've had a shock. No man likes to think of his daughter . . . well, you know what I mean. But, the only thing left to do is to get them married. I hope you will change your attitude, soften towards them?' His voice was now redolent with an underlying threat that was not wasted on James Grierson. Michael Ryan was offering him a face saver and he knew it. He was being told in no uncertain terms that he could come out of all this as the loving, caring father who would do anything to keep his daughter's reputation; who welcomed her choice of husband with open arms; who would not bow down in the face of adversity, but would rise up and conquer it.

For the first time in his life James Grierson felt a grudging respect for a Ryan. He knew he was being manipulated but, he asked himself, what was the alternative? He had heard stories about Michael Ryan. That he was as queer as a nine-bob note. That he had taken over Joe the Fish's businesses and made a name for himself among the villains. At nineteen Michael Ryan was already becoming a neighbourhood legend. 'Cruel but fair' was the local opinion. Could he really let his only child become a part of this family? Even as the question formed in his mind he knew it was useless. If he went against this young man sitting opposite

28

him, he would in effect dig his own grave. The course was already set. Janine was marrying Roy Ryan whether he liked it or not. What he had to do now was stretch out and take the hand of friendship being offered to him. He sighed heavily and his voice came out in a nervous croak.

'You're right, of course. If they really care for one another . . .'

He swallowed deeply as Michael Ryan took his hand and shook it, the animal strength of the handshake reminding him acutely of exactly what he had done. His lovely Janine had brought him this low, had brought Michael Ryan into his home. He could have wept.

Three weeks later, on the first Saturday of July, James Grierson gave away his only daughter to Roy Ryan. It wasn't until after the reception, once home in his bed, that he finally gave way to the tears that had been building up inside him since Michael's visit. He felt he had taken his only child like a lamb to the slaughter.

It would be twenty years before he discovered how right he had been.

Chapter Four

1957

Michael was fuming, his blue eyes dark with anger. He rubbed one hand across his face and stared stonily at Joe.

'Look, Michael, you had no right to borrow any money behind my back. This is *my* business.' Joe the Fish pushed a pudgy finger into his chest.

Making a fist Michael smashed it down on the desk in front of him, causing their empty coffee cups to rattle in their saucers.

'So it's your business now, is it?' Michael's voice was bitter. 'I suppose this is *your* office as well? Don't let's worry about the money *I've* brought in . . .'

Joe sighed loudly. He interrupted Michael as if he was talking to a little child.

'Oh, for Christ's sake, Michael. No one's disputing that you've done well. What's annoyed me is the fact that you borrowed out five grand without even bothering to mention it to me.' Joe's voice was cajoling. In his heart he was frightened of Michael, frightened of his phenomenal temper. 'Come on, son . . . try and see it from my point of view.'

Michael picked up his pack of Strands from the desk and lit one. He sat at the desk, his head hanging forward on his chest, taking quick drags on his cigarette. Joe was conscious that Michael's hands were shaking. He knew he was trying to calm himself down.

Joe sat in the chair opposite and placed his elbows on the desk. Michael was such a difficult boy. He gravitated from extreme happiness to a difficult and dangerous depression in the space of seconds.

Normally Joe would have let Michael have his head, he was a good businessman, but this latest flouting of the rules had angered him. He had loaned five thousand pounds to Phillip Wreck, one of the most notorious villains in Paddington, and in Joe's mind Michael had more chance of getting the Pope's inside leg measurement than he had of getting that money back.

Michael stubbed out his cigarette, grinding it into the ashtray with such force Joe thought it would surely break. Snapping his

31

head up he looked at Joe, his mouth clamped closed. In the quiet room Joe could hear his laboured breathing.

'I'm warning you, Joe . . . I'm warning you now . . . don't fight me on this. I know exactly what I'm doing. I'll get that money back. I'll get it and the interest on it, you just wait and see.'

There were tears in Michael's eyes. He's just like a child, Joe thought, it's as if I've taken his toys away from him. The difference being that when Michael was like this he was liable to explode into a raging temper at any moment.

Joe felt the familiar fingers of fear touching him. It was Michael's very unpredictability that drew Joe to him. Twice Michael had lashed out at him and hurt him, only to be contrite and loving in the next breath. Although Joe had never tried to analyse their relationship, inside himself he knew that it was the boy's vicious streak that attracted him.

'All right, Michael, I'll let it go this time. But in future, you come to me.'

Michael's face broke into one of his winning smiles and Joe felt himself relax.

As Michael looked at the man sitting opposite, his fat ugly face grinning like a Cheshire cat's, he felt an impulse to smash his fist into his teeth. Instead he carried on smiling. Joe didn't know it but his days were numbered. Soon he would be out of the way and he, Michael, could get on with his life.

Joe got out of his chair and walked around the desk. Standing behind Michael he began rubbing his taut muscular shoulders. Feeling the solid flesh beneath his fingers he felt himself harden, completely unaware that Michael was planning his demise.

Roy was in the butcher's shop in the Portobello Road. His father-in-law had given up trying to explain to him the different cuts of meat. Roy had been working for him since three weeks after his wedding, and he hated it. He felt like a kept man. He couldn't do the job, he knew it and his father-in-law knew it, but it was all part of the grand master plan: How To Keep Your Daughter At Home. They lived with Mr and Mrs Grierson. They ate with Mr and Mrs Grierson. And they watched from the sidelines as Mr and Mrs Grierson between them brought up the baby, Carla. It had been a few months before Roy realised he had married what his mother would have called 'a lazy bitch'. Janine was quite content to let her mother take over the baby, the cooking, everything. That left her free to play at being married which consisted of getting herself done up to the nines and visiting her friends all day, now and again taking the baby, all nice and clean, out in her pram. Playing at being mother of the year.

Roy winced as he thought of her. What had happened to the girl he had fallen in love with? The spirited young woman who had been as eager for life as he was? Admittedly they were only nineteen, but surely, he reasoned, there must be more to married life than this? If he mentioned moving out of her parents' house, she dissolved into tears. Last night had been the last straw. He had told her there was a flat going in Westbourne Park and she had had hysterics.

'How am I gonna cope with a baby on me own?'

That's when he had lost his temper. 'Well, we won't find that out until you try, will we? God Almighty, Janine, you've never once looked after the bloody kid for a whole day since it was born!'

After that her mother, Eliza, had come into the bedroom and led Janine out, taking her into her own bedroom. Then this morning she had told him that Janine was 'delicate' and needed her mother to look after her. He was frankly bewildered by it all. He wanted them to have their own little place, where Janine looked after the baby all day and cooked his meal in the evening. What he had was a pampered, spoilt brat whose only interest in life was lipstick and what was on at the pictures. She never looked at the child unless she had to. Even his mother had noticed it. She had asked him a few Saturdays ago if everything was all right between them. He had felt like telling her everything but just couldn't. He wouldn't even know where to begin.

'Hello, Bruv.' Roy was brought out of his reverie by Michael's voice.

'Hello, Mickey!' He hadn't been so pleased to see someone in all his life.

'Fancy skiving off for a few hours? I've got a bit of business I want to talk to you about.'

Roy wiped his bloody hands on his apron. 'I'll be with you in a tick.' He walked through to the back of the shop and called out to his father-in-law. James Grierson came down the stairs that led to the flat above the shop.

'What's all this row about?' His voice was loud and agitated. 'Can't you even look after the bloody shop? Want me to hold your hand now, I suppose.' Roy was conscious that Michael could hear every word and groaned inside.

'I've got to shoot off for a couple of hours.'

'You what!' Grierson's voice was incredulous. 'This is a bloody business here, not a bloody knocking shop where you pick your own hours . . .'

His voice faltered as he saw Michael slip through the doorway. Grierson paled.

33

'Who do you think you're talking to?' Michael's voice was icy. He pointed at Grierson. 'I'm talking to you. You had enough bunny just now . . . so answer me. Who d'you think you're talking to?'

As Michael stepped towards him, Grierson stepped backwards, his hands coming up to defend himself if the visitor lashed out.

Michael snapped at Roy: 'Get your coat.' Then walking to where Grierson was cowering against the wall, he grabbed him around the throat. 'Now, I don't know what's going down here, but I know this much – if you *ever* talk to my brother like that again, I'll rip your nuts off and ram them down your throat. Do you understand what I'm saying?'

Grierson was nodding his head furiously when Roy came back with his coat. Pulling Mickey away gently, he led him through the front of the shop and out into the street. He was ashamed that Michael had heard his father-in-law speak to him like that. He was ashamed that he himself let him.

'Come on, Roy, we're going to the KPH. I think we'd better have a talk.'

They walked in silence. The bright October day belied the cold wind. Roy noticed that everywhere they walked people acknowledged Michael. It was as if he was their sovereign and they his subjects. Depending on how influential people were, Mickey either nodded at them or gave them a hearty greeting. Roy was impressed. Michael's name was becoming synonymous with those of the Krays and the Richardsons, two of the most influential young gangs of that time. Roy knew that Michael kept up a friendship with them. An uneasy alliance. It seemed that once people met him they decided they were better off having him as a friend than an enemy.

They walked into the red warmth of the Kensington Park Hotel. Michael ordered them both hot whiskies and they settled down in the lounge bar.

Michael took his cigarettes from his overcoat pocket, and then slipped the coat from his shoulders. Folding it up carefully, he laid it across a chair. All his movements were performed with a natural grace. Roy shrugged off his own coat while still sitting, letting it fall over the back of his chair. Adjusting his trouser crease fastidiously Michael sat down again, settling himself into the over-upholstered chair. Then, pulling a large white ashtray towards him so it would be within easy reach, he lit a cigarette. Throwing the packet across the table at Roy, he finally spoke.

'How long has he been talking to you like that?' His voice was quiet.

Roy hung his head. 'I know it sounds bad, Mickey, but he is my father-in-law . . .'

34

'I couldn't give a fuck if he was the Immaculate Conception! There's something wrong, ain't there? The Roy I knew would never take that from anyone, not in a million years.' He lowered his voice. 'Come on, Bruv. What's the SP?'

The barman brought over their hot toddies and Roy was glad of the few seconds' reprieve. He could feel Michael's eyes boring into him. When they were settled again, Roy spoke.

'I don't know, Mickey. Since Carla was born it's as if I don't exist any more. Janine and her mum and dad act like she never got married. I feel like a lodger in the house. I eat their food, I sleep in their bed, I shag their daughter now and again.' All the bitterness of the last two years seemed to boil over and come tumbling out. 'And I mean, now and again. Every three weeks when they go and visit her bloody granny in Bethnal Green. She says she can't do it while Mummy's in the house. Then old man Grierson treats me like the village idiot. I'm not a butcher, Mickey. I hate looking at the meat, I hate touching it . . .' His voice trailed off.

'So what are you gonna do?'

Roy shrugged and took a gulp of his drink. 'I dunno.'

'You don't know? So that's it then, is it?' Michael was getting annoyed. 'Why don't you give her a right-hander? Show her who's boss. Tell her old man to go and stuff his bloody butcher's shop up his Jacksey. I knew she spelt trouble . . . I bloody knew it!'

'All right . . . All right, Mickey. Keep your hair on.'

'Why don't you come and work for me? That's what I wanted to talk to you about.' He saw a gleam of hope appear in Roy's eyes.

'I'd jump at the chance, you know that.'

Michael laughed. Roy was like a bloody kid at times. He looked at his brother's open face, and made a mental note to tell his mother what was going down with him. He knew that she was worried.

'That's settled then.' He looked at his watch. 'From two-twenty-five today you are a working member of the Ryan dynasty.' They both laughed. Anthony and Geoffrey worked for Michael already. Now he had Roy.

'What's the pay, Mickey?' Roy sounded uncertain.

'Bloody good, that's what.'

'I wouldn't ask, but what with the baby and everything . . .'

'No worries, I'll start you on thirty quid a week. That's a bit more than the others, so keep stumm about it.' Michael tapped his nose with his forefinger.

Roy was amazed. He was going to go and get Janine and the baby and if necessary drag her to the flat in Westbourne Park. This was gonna be a new start. Mickey was right. Maybe she needed a right-hander. And if his father-in-law stuck his oar in, he would get one and all!

He drank his whisky down and felt the warm glow through his body. It was partly the alcohol and partly the knowledge that he was finally going to do something about his life. The worry he had been feeling about Janine was replaced by elation. He would take a leaf out of Mickey's book. Hit first, ask questions later.

Michael watched his brother's face and guessed immediately what was going through his mind. He motioned to the barman to refill their glasses, a feeling of satisfaction running through him. He had a soft spot for Roy, the same as he did for Benny. They were both too nice for their own good. He was going to toughen Roy up. Make him into someone. Then, when Joe the Fish was out of the way, the businesses would be run exclusively by Ryans. He raised up his steaming glass to his brother.

'To the Ryans!'

'The Ryans!'

Geoffrey and Anthony were sitting at the end of Penzance Gardens, where it met Princedale Road. It was nearly two-fifteen in the morning. They sat in a black Humber Snipe. Both were freezing and both were nervous, especially Geoffrey. At twenty-one he was two years older than Anthony. They were identical to look at. Both had the Ryan dark hair and firm chin. Anthony had more of Michael's ruggedness whereas Geoffrey had softer features, almost effeminate.

Anthony spoke. His voice in the darkness caused Geoffrey to jump. 'How much longer have we got to wait?'

'How the hell do I know? What do you think I am? The Oracle or something?'

'Very funny. You get on my wick, do you know that?' Anthony's usual animosity was coming to the fore. Anthony Ryan was known in his family as able to pick a fight with his own fingernails. The only person he was even remotely respectful to was Mickey. 'You think because you've read a few crappy books you know it all.'

Geoffrey rolled his eyes up towards the roof of the car. 'Do me a favour, Ant . . . Save all your hag for what we've got to do tonight. I ain't in the mood.'

They were silent again. Anthony was frustrated because he wasn't as quick-brained as Geoffrey so always came off worse in an argument. It didn't deter him though. He tried a different tack.

'I saw that sort you've been knocking about with last night. I'd give her one meself.' Knowing that it would annoy Geoffrey, Anthony braced himself for the ensuing argument. Instead, Geoffrey put his hand over his brother's mouth. They listened.

Footsteps were approaching the car. They sat tense and nervous. Anthony's hard features looked as if they had been carved from stone. His fists were clenched tight on the steering wheel.

The man who was walking towards them stepped into the light of a streetlamp. It was Joe the Fish. He was walking unsteadily along the road, obviously the worse for drink. Geoffrey nodded and Anthony started the car. He did not put on the headlights. Reversing back a little, they waited until Joe began crossing the intersection between Penzance Gardens and Princedale Road. Pushing his foot down on the accelerator, Anthony thrust the car forward.

Hearing a loud noise through his drunken haze, Joe turned in time to see the car coming at him. He raised his arm as if to protect himself as the car hit him full on. His body flew into the air and landed on the bonnet. His head crashed against the windscreen. Anthony slammed his foot on the brake. As the car screeched to a halt, Joe's body slid from the bonnet on to the road. Anthony ran the car over him one more time before speeding off. The whole operation had taken less than three minutes. A woman who had been up getting herself a glass of water heard the commotion and ran out into the street. She took one look at Joe's face and began to scream. Lights began to go on all over Princedale Road.

Anthony and Geoffrey drove the car from Holland Park to Moscow Road in Bayswater. The streets were deserted. Parking the car they left it there and walked around to Porchester Terrace, throwing the keys to the Humber Snipe down a drainhole. In Porchester Terrace they picked up a blue Mark 1 Zephyr and drove sedately home to Lancaster Road. It was just three o'clock.

Inside a private house in Beauchamp Place, Knightsbridge, Michael picked up his cards and studied them carefully. He was on a winning streak tonight. He had three aces and two kings. Joe had left an hour earlier. He had been given a lift to the Bayswater Road by a mutual friend, Derek O'Connor. If everything had gone according to plan then Joe was well and truly out of the picture, and he, Michael, had the perfect alibi. He smiled smugly to himself as he raised the bet by fifty pounds. If Geoffrey and Anthony had bungled the job tonight, he would personally batter their brains out.

Sarah heard a loud banging on her front door. She glanced at the clock on the bedside table. It was five o'clock in the morning. Sleepily she dragged herself out of bed. Benjamin was snoring his head off as usual, so it wasn't the police after him – that would make a change. She yawned, went down the stairs and opened the front door. Two men stood there and she recognised at once that they were CID.

'Is Michael at home, love?'

Blinking her eyes rapidly to try and clear her head, Sarah said, 'Come inside and I'll go and look.'

The two men walked into the hallway.

She went upstairs and looked into Michael's room. The bed hadn't been slept in. As she walked back on to the landing, Geoffrey came out of his room.

'Who's that downstairs, Mum?'

'The old Bill. They're looking for Michael. What's going on?'

She knew her sons and would bet her last pound that Geoffrey had been awake waiting for something like this.

'You go back to bed, Mum. I'll sort out the filth.'

Both turned as they heard a door opening. Maura Ryan came out of her room, clutching a raggy doll. Sarah went to her, picking her up in her arms. Geoffrey went down the stairs.

'Mickey ain't in.'

'Well, where is he then?' This from the older of the policemen.

'He's up West. At a house in Knightsbridge. What do you want him for?' Geoffrey yawned in their faces, scratching his belly lazily. The younger policeman noticed that his pyjamas were hardly creased. Geoffrey Ryan hadn't been in bed. The trouble would be proving it.

'Somebody tried to murder Joe the Fish earlier.'

Geoffrey felt as if someone had thrown a bucket of cold water over him. 'What do you mean, tried to murder him?'

'Exactly what I say. And knowing how close Mickey is to him, I thought we had better let him know.' The older officer was trying to goad him.

Unlike Anthony, Geoffrey could keep a lid on his temper. Deliberately misconstruing the policeman's words, he shook his head sadly and said, 'Mickey's like a son to that man. This will come as a great shock to him. What exactly happened?' He had to know what was going on. Half of his mind was saying silent prayers. He'd been sure Joe was dead when they left him.

'Someone tried to run him over a few hours ago. He's fighting for his life in St Charles's Hospital. The hospital said to try and get his next-of-kin. We assumed that was Michael Ryan. Two men couldn't get any closer than those two have been over the last couple of years, could they?' The policeman raised his eyebrows and his colleague laughed.

Geoffrey was saved from answering by his mother's voice. She had been carrying Maura down the stairs and had heard the policeman's remark.

'What are you trying to say? I know you lot with your dirty insinuendos.' She hitched her daughter up on to her shoulder, holding her steady with her free hand. The other was gripping the banister rail, her knuckles white and bony. 'My Michael is a decent clean-living individual. Now I'll thank you two to get out of my house.'

Hiding a grin, Geoffrey took the heavy child from her as she came to the bottom of the stairs. Maura sat in his arms, an alert expression on her face. At seven she was already wise to the likes of the police. Sarah pushed angrily at the two policemen. She looked so tiny beside the two men, yet so ferocious, that Geoffrey laughed out loud.

'That's it, Muvver. Tell the bastards to sling their hooks.'

Opening the front door, Sarah let the men out. She was fuming. How dare they say that of her Michael! Her temper was caused by the fact that she had a terrible suspicion that what they said was true. Slamming the door on them, she turned her anger on her son.

'Well, don't stand there like a gormless eejit! Go and get dressed and find Mickey!'

Placing Maura carefully on the floor, Geoffrey ran up the stairs. Maura followed her mother into the kitchen, curling up on one of the easy chairs by the fire.

'Can I have a standing up egg, Mum?'

Sarah nodded. 'Of course you can have a boiled egg if that's what you want.'

She filled the kettle, her mind racing. If Joe the Fish died then it would be a murder charge for somebody. But who? Michael? She pushed the thought from her head. Whatever she thought about her boys, there was one thing she knew: they were not murderers. They were just tearaways. High-spirited tearaways. Or, at least, she hoped that's all they were. Putting the kettle on the gas, she went to her daughter and hugged her tightly.

Joe was lying in the hospital bed. Nurse Walton looked down at his battered face. She shook her head and turned to see the policeman by the bed grimacing at her. She blinked and sighed.

'Who would do such a thing?' Her voice sounded very young.

PC Blenkinsop pushed out his narrow chest and tried to look like an all-knowing, sophisticated officer.

'You'd be surprised. It's a wicked life out on the street these days. He might look like an old man who's been run over a few times to you, but to me . . .' he puffed his chest out even further '. . . he's a vicious criminal.'

Nurse Walton looked suitably impressed. 'Just wait until I tell my mum!'

PC Blenkinsop looked as if he was readjusting his shoulders inside his tunic top. He thrust out his chin and smiled.

Joe groaned and immediately had the attention of both of them. 'Mickey . . . Mickey.'

PC Blenkinsop was writing down Joe's words with a flourish of his pencil. Licking it, he waited expectantly.

Michael stood in the entrance to the ward. He had known that a policeman would be in attendance. Squaring his shoulders, he walked down the ward towards Joe's bed. He could see the young PC and the nurse through the inadequate screens. Putting a sober expression on his face, he went to the bed.

PC Blenkinsop noted Nurse Walton's reaction to Michael Ryan and it annoyed him. He thrust out his lip like a petulant schoolboy.

'And who might you be?' He stood up and seemed to roll on the balls of his feet. Michael gave him a scathing glance. He picked up Joe's hand which was heavily bandaged. He turned to the nurse and smiled sadly at her.

'How bad is he?' His voice sounded wretched. Nurse Walton stared into his dark blue eyes and was immediately filled with pity for him.

'He's very bad. The doctor says he'll be surprised if he lasts out the day.' If she had known Michael, she would have noticed the glimmer of relief that came into his eyes.

'Has he said anything at all?'

The PC interrupted. 'He has been calling for a . . .' he glanced importantly at his notebook '. . . Mickey.'

Michael nodded. 'That's me.'

The young nurse brought Michael a chair and he sat beside Joe, holding the old man's hand and stroking it every now and again. The PC watched him. So this was Michael Ryan. He couldn't wait to get back to the station and brag about how he'd seen him.

The nurse brought Michael a cup of tea and he thanked her, giving her one of his radiant smiles. PC Blenkinsop could have cried. She didn't even know he was there now.

Shortly before seven in the evening Joe opened his eyes and immediately recognised Michael. He passed his tongue over his cracked lips and tried to speak. Michael could see by the look in his eyes that he knew who had ordered his accident. Agitated, Joe tried to lift his head off the pillow.

'Mickey . . . Mickey . . . you . . .' Then his head fell back and he died.

Michael closed his eyes, a feeling of euphoria surging through him. He had got away with it! Then, as could happen with him, he felt a deep despondency replace his feeling of elation. Tears welled up in his eyes, spilling over on to his cheeks. In his own funny way he would miss Joe who had been his passport into the real world. For that he would always be grateful to him. He would give Joe the Fish the best send-off anyone had ever seen.

PC Blenkinsop looked embarrassed. Later on in the station canteen he had everyone hanging on his words.

'Yeah, I'm telling you. It was quite touching. Michael Ryan cried like a baby. Well, it was to be expected really. After all, the old boy died calling out his name.'

At Joe's funeral a week later, the police noted that all the gang bosses stopped to pay their respects to Michael Ryan. He was well and truly established now. That, together with the fact that Joe had willed him everything he possessed, made Michael Ryan a very happy man.

Chapter Five

1960

Sister Rosario looked at the pinched face of Maura Ryan and her heart went out to the child. She had noticed her being teased mercilessly all through the dinner hour, no doubt due to the fact that her brother Benjamin had been expelled the day before. The nun realised that now the child had no one to protect her, some of the other children were making up for lost time. She watched Margaret Lacey lean forward across her desk and pull hard on one of Maura Ryan's long blonde plaits. Sister Rosario didn't like Margaret Lacey. She didn't like any of the Laceys, with their carroty red hair and green malicious eyes. And this Margaret Lacey was the most brazen strap of a child she had ever come across. The nun leapt from her seat, causing her chair to fly backwards. The noise brought thirty pairs of eyes to rest on her.

'Margaret Lacey, come out here at once!' Her voice reverberated around the classroom. Margaret, her face pale with fright, slowly edged her way from behind her desk and began to walk to the front of the class. Sister Rosario was without doubt the hardest nun in the school. No amount of tears could shake her. Margaret stood before her, trembling. Tapping a ruler across the palm of her hand, Sister Rosario stared at the child for a few seconds. She knew from thirty years' experience that bullies were a breed apart. Most were inherent cowards who picked only on people who they knew were frightened of them.

The nun's countenance and dark brown close-set eyes challenged the child before her.

'Did I see you pull Maura Ryan's plait?'

Margaret's big green eyes seemed to have taken possession of the whole of her face. Her tiny pink mouth was trembling. Already, tears were beginning to glisten in her eyes.

'N . . . N . . . No, Miss . . . I mean, Sister.'

In her fright she had begun to stutter. This caused some of the other children to titter, quickly putting their hands over their mouths to stifle the sound.

Margaret Lacey was the class bully and the children enjoyed

43

seeing her get, for once, what she doled out so often.

'Are you calling me a liar?' The nun's eyes had narrowed.

'No, Sister!' Margaret's voice was stronger now. Whoever heard of calling a nun a liar? It was unthinkable. Her own mother would kill her if she knew. Her eyes were now riveted on the ruler in the nun's hand. She knew that it was liable to come swishing down on her hands and legs at any moment.

Sister Rosario was enjoying Margaret's discomfiture. Running her tongue across her teeth she glared down at the object of her annoyance. Her white wimple covered nearly all her head, revealing only wrinkled yellowing skin that, combined with her dark eyes, had earned her the epithet 'Lizard Features'.

'So . . . you admit to pulling Maura Ryan's plait then?'

Maura watched Sister Rosario completely demoralise Margaret Lacey. She sat in her chair, her face scarlet. She did not thank this nun for making her the centre of attention. She knew that whatever Margaret got she would make sure Maura got it back one hundredfold.

'Yes, Sister . . . I pulled Maura's plait.' This was said so low as to be virtually inaudible.

'Speak up, child.'

'Yes, Sister. I pulled Maura Ryan's plait.' The high piping little voice was trembling with fear.

Smiling smugly at the class, Sister Rosario lifted the ruler. 'Hold out your hand then.'

The thin little hand come out. Margaret closed her eyes tightly as the ruler came down hard six times across her palm. Against her will, hot scalding tears burst from her eyes and down her cheeks. She held her injured hand to her breast as if frightened it might drop off, and at a nod from Sister Rosario made her way back to her desk, rubbing at her injured palm with the thumb of her good hand.

Sister Rosario's beady eyes scanned the classroom for about twenty seconds before she said, 'Let that be a warning to any would-be bullies in this class. Next time it will be twelve strokes of the ruler and your name read out at mass.'

Thirty faces looked scandalised at the thought of having their name read out by Father McCormack. Picking up her chair, the nun turned to her blackboard and began writing on it.

Seizing her opportunity. Margaret leant forward across her desk and whispered to Maura.

'You're dead, Ryan. Come hometime I'm gonna kill you.'

Maura closed her eyes, a knot of fear already forming in her stomach. Everyone was frightened of Margaret Lacey, even some of the boys. Which was surprising really because she was so small.

44

But small or not, she could fight and that was all that counted. Maura sat back in her chair and looked out of the window to the side of her. A group of younger children were playing rounders. The voice of Miss Norman, the games teacher, drifted in at the window now and again. Always encouraging, never reprimanding. As Maura watched the dust motes flying through the air in the rays of the June sun she wished that she was outside with the younger children. That she was anywhere away from Margaret Lacey and her cronies who would without doubt be waiting for her as she left the school. Why was it that time always flew when you didn't want it to? The minutes sped by until the bell that heralded hometime.

Slowly Maura went to get her coat, hoping against hope that if she took long enough Margaret would get fed up and go home. She walked slowly from the school, across the playground and out of the gates into Latimer Road. Sure enough, Margaret was waiting for her, about twenty yards past the school gates. She had three of her cronies with her: Jennifer Howard, Betty Leeds and Vanessa Rouse. Maura began walking towards them like a condemned man on his way to the gallows. Prickles of sweat had broken out along her backbone. She bit down hard on her lip as she watched the four girls.

She saw that Jennifer and Vanessa were laughing at her and something inside her stirred. In all her ten years she had always had one or other of her brothers watching out for her. Now here for the first time she was fighting her own battle. And fight it she would! She swallowed deeply. She could hear her heart crashing in her ears. She decided then and there that she was not going to stand for it. She had eight brothers and had had to fight or argue with every one of them at some time or another. Holding her head high, she walked faster, swinging her schoolbag menacingly.

The four girls looked at each other, puzzled. This wasn't supposed to happen! First they were going to make her squirm, then Margaret was going to hit her . . . Betty Leeds began to hop from one foot to another, a sure sign of agitation. Vanessa and Jennifer stepped back behind Margaret. Maura stopped in front of them, still swinging her school bag. She gave a loud sniff.

'Well?' The insolent way she said it made the other girls gasp with astonishment. Margaret Lacey soon found her tongue.

'I'll "well" you, you ugly bitch you! I'm gonna smash your face in!'

The other girls smiled. This was more like it.

'Well then, don't just stand there talking about it . . . do it!'

All eyes were glued to the swinging schoolbag. Margaret was silent for a few seconds. She could feel the others losing their nerve. If she didn't do something, and soon, they would desert

45

her. She spat on to the pavement casually.

'I will when I'm good and ready!'

Margaret Lacey was getting more worried by the second. She had thought she'd give Maura's long blonde hair a few good tugs, a scratch or two on her face, and then home to tea, basking in the other girls' admiration. Now she wasn't sure what to do. She might even get hit herself! She decided on a delaying tactic. Kneeling down on the dusty pavement, she made as if to tie her shoelaces.

The next thing she knew, she was lying sprawled across the pavement. Maura's schoolbag had hit her straight in the side of the head. Next, her long red hair was pulled so hard she felt as if it was going to come out by the roots. Finally, she felt a kick on the knee that brought a shocked cry to her throat. She lay on the pavement staring up at Maura Ryan, amazed. Her three friends had already run off. As soon as Maura's schoolbag had hit Margaret in the head, they had made their escape, frightened in case Maura decided on a repeat performance on one of them!

Maura just stood there stunned, staring at Margaret lying at her feet. She had done that! She had knocked Margaret Lacey down! She could feel her chest swelling with the joy of it. She had actually defended herself against Margaret Lacey, the school bully, and she had won. She had done it alone without one of her brothers to defend her!

Seeing Margaret begin to pull herself up, Maura's natural kindness came to the fore. This would be all over the school tomorrow. She tentatively held out her hand to help Margaret up. The smaller girl looked at her long and hard before accepting it. Maura pulled her to her feet and began to brush down Margaret's uniform, which was covered in grey dust. This was all done in silence, except for the occasional sniff. Maura saw the small swelling on Margaret's grubby knee and felt ashamed of herself. She had kicked her very hard and Margaret *was* smaller than her. In silent agreement they walked together down Latimer Road, into Bramley Road and then through to Lancaster Road, where both girls lived. They stopped outside Margaret's house first and stood looking at one another.

Margaret sniffed loudly and said, 'Come in if you want. Me mum's at work.'

It was the hand of friendship. Maura shrugged nonchalantly. 'All right then.'

They walked up the steps that led to the front door. Margaret's house was the same as Maura's except it had been made into flats. Margaret's family lived on the top floor. Being large town houses they were three storeys high with large basements. As many as five families lived in them. As they made their way up the stairs the smell of cooking and urine seemed to overpower them. Margaret's flat had no lock on the door. There was no need for one, there was nothing to steal.

'You take off your things and I'll make us some bread and marmite.'

'Ooh, lovely. I love marmite.'

As Margaret made the sandwiches and a pot of weak tea, Maura glanced around her. The room was filthy, clothes and newspapers strewn everywhere. Unlike her own home that was stoved regularly, cockroaches were on everything. A particularly adventurous one with large quivering antennae was being slowly buried in the rancid margarine. Maura shuddered inwardly. The last few years her mother had been waging a war on all vermin, including bed bugs. Money was now plentiful in her home, thanks to Michael's employing her brothers in his business, while the majority of the people in Lancaster Road were still no better off than they had been before the war. Margaret's mother worked at the new Black Cat cigarette factory out in Harlow and her father still worked in Lyons bakery. Maura watched with distaste as Margaret flicked the cockroach out of the margarine with the breadknife. It landed on the floor where it lay on its back, its numerous legs doing cycling motions as it tried to right itself. Wrinkling her nose Margaret stepped on it, the crunching noise sounding like a gunshot in the hot evening air.

'I hate them bloody things.'

'So do I.' Maura's voice sounded small.

Soon the girls were eating their sandwiches and drinking weak tea. Neither of them mentioned what had taken place outside the school and neither of them would. From outside, the sounds of a game of cricket floated into the hot airless room. Finishing her tea, Maura got up to go. Margaret offered Maura her little finger with a shy smile. Maura linked it with her own, vowing that the two girls would be best friends for always – through thick and thin. This was the female way of becoming blood brothers – unlike the boys they did not cut each other's thumbs.

Margaret walked Maura down the stairs to the street. 'I'll be here in the morning to walk to school. OK?'

Margaret nodded her head vigorously. 'See you then, Maura.'

''Bye.' Maura walked towards her own house. She felt light-hearted and gay. What had started out as a bad day had suddenly become brighter.

In the road a gang of boys with a makeshift cricket bat stopped their game to look at her. Already the news was travelling fast. Dinny O'Brien, one of Garry's friends, smiled at her.

'That right you podgered Margaret Lacey, Maws?'

She nodded, feeling herself blush.

'We're friends now, Dinny.'

He looked away, disgusted. Trust girls! In Dinny's code, if you beat someone in a fight you made their life misery for as long as possible. You did not become friends with them.

Maura hurried home. As she let herself in at the front door her mother's voice came booming out of the kitchen.

'Is that you, Maura!'

'Yes, Mum.'

She went into the kitchen where Sarah was standing, hands on hips, her face like thunder.

'Where have you been, you bloody little sod? I've been out of my mind with worry about you.'

Maura chewed on her lip, staring at her mother. She very rarely got told off and when she did it upset her.

'Well? Answer me, you little cow.' Sarah's face was haggard.

'I went to me friend's house and had a bit of tea.' Her enormous blue eyes had tears glistening on their lashes. Sarah saw her daughter's face crumple and her heart melted. Pulling the child into her arms, she hugged her close.

'I'm sorry, love, but you gave me such a fright. It's not like you to stay out like that. You're normally the first one home. I was worried.'

'I'm sorry, Mum, I won't do it again, I promise,' She tried to smile at her mother, genuinely sorry to have vexed her.

'I sent Benny, Garry and Lee out looking for you.' As if her words had conjured them up, all three burst into the kitchen.

'Mum . . . Mum!' They were all talking at once. 'Have a guess what!'

'One at a time . . . One at a time.' She held up her hands for silence then pointed at Garry, the most honest of the three.

'Right then, Garry, you tell me what happened.'

He pointed at Maura who was beginning to panic.

'It's her.'

'What about her?' Sarah looked at Maura, a frown on her face.

'She's been and gone and smashed Margaret Lacey's face in!'

Sarah's eyes widened. 'She's what!'

The tone of her voice frightened Maura. She pulled on her mother's flowery apron.

'I had to, Mum. She was gonna kill me 'cos Sister Rosario gave her the ruler for pulling me plaits.' She looked into her mother's face, pleading for understanding.

'Am I hearing right? You . . .' she pointed at Maura '. . . had a fight with Margaret Lacey.' She screwed up her eyes as if she was having difficulty seeing her child.

Maura was gabbling with fright. 'I hit her with me bag but we're friends now, Mum. That's where I was earlier when you were looking for me.'

Sarah shook her head slowly as if to clear it. So this one had gone too, another fighter in the family.

'Go on, all of you . . . out in the street to play. Your dad will be in soon and I haven't got a bit of food on.' She pushed the children towards the kitchen door. She wanted them all away from her.

The three boys ran out. Maura stood for a second looking at her mother. 'I'm sorry, Mum . . . honestly.'

Sarah's voice was tired. 'Get yourself outside, Maws. Go on now.'

When she had gone, Sarah poured herself out a large mug of thick black tea. She spooned four heaped spoonsful of sugar into it and some condensed milk and sat at the kitchen table. She sipped her tea and her body seemed to sag in the chair. Her mind was racing, though.

Leslie, aged twenty, was doing three years for robbery. Anthony, aged twenty-two, was with him, doing five years for robbery and malicious wounding. Michael was like the local Mafia, everyone was frightened of him. He now had all the older boys working for him. Over the years she had forced these thoughts from her mind, telling herself that her sons were the product of their father. And now this! Her only daughter, the apple of her eye, had been brawling in the street. It just wasn't fair. Her mother used to say that what was bred in the bone came out in the blood, and she had been right.

Oh, Sarah had plenty of money these days and the house was lovely. After the lean years, she had been only too happy to take the money her sons thrust on her. She had never questioned where it came from, though she knew deep inside. But if their lifestyles affected her daughter, she would murder the lot of them. Maura was going to have the chances that she herself had never had. One of her children would achieve something in this world. She was determined on that.

Outside in the summer evening, Maura was the centre of attention.

'Well done, Maws.' This from Garry, who was very fond of his sister.

'I hit her with me bag, that's what done it.'

They all looked across the road as they heard their father call. Maura's eyes lit up and she skipped across the road to meet him. Benjamin Ryan had had a skinful, that much was evident. He was

49

flushed around his ample face and neck. Under one arm he had a large box of crisps and a bottle of Tizer. He passed the box to Lee who had followed Maura over the street and picked his daughter up in his arms. The old man, as they called him, worshipped his daughter and they all knew this and accepted it. In their own way they all felt the same. Maura rubbed her face against his cheek and felt his stubble scratching against her smooth skin. She breathed in his familiar odour of best bitter and Woodbines and snuggled against him, safe and secure.

'How's me best girl then?'

'All right, Dad. Had a win?'

He laughed at her cheek.

'How do you know I've had a win?' He asked the question in a mock stern voice.

'The box of crisps and Tizer for a start, and your beery breath.'

Benjamin looked at his sons, a theoretical scowl on his face. 'Hear that, boys? Typical woman! She'll drink the Tizer and eat the crisps, and still complain where they come from!'

Benny laughed with Maura, but Garry and Lee just smiled wanly. The memory of empty bellies because their father had gambled away all the National Assistance was still fresh in their minds. They all walked up the steps and into the house.

Sarah had started the evening meal. She completely ignored her husband until he fell asleep in his chair, whereupon she woke him up and berated him all the way up the stairs, their shouting and swearing affecting the children not one iota. Half an hour later they sat down to their tea. Maura was once more in high spirits. As they sat chatting around the table there was a loud knock on the front door. Garry answered it and came back into the kitchen with two policemen.

'Go and wake your dad up.' Sarah's voice was heavy.

The elder of the two policemen smiled at Sarah but she dropped her eyes and tried to busy herself at the sink. Every nerve in her body was jangling. Every time the police visited her house she felt a heavy sickness inside her. Maura and Benny carried on eating.

Benjamin Ryan shuffled into the kitchen in his trousers and string vest, his braces hanging down the sides of his legs.

'What the fuck do you want?' His voice was menacing.

The older policeman looked at the children, a question in his eyes.

'Never you mind them, they'll hear what you got to say sooner or later. Now spit it out, man. I ain't got all day.'

'Very well. We've got some bad news for you, concerning your son Anthony.'

'What about my Antney? Escaped, has he?' Benjamin's voice sounded hopeful.

'No, not exactly. I'm sorry to tell you, Mr Ryan, that your son is dead.'

'He's *what*!' Sarah's hand went to her chest and she struggled to find breath. Lee went to her and folded her in his arms. The younger children were pale and silent.

'He was stabbed to death this morning in Pentonville prison. In the showers. We're doing everything possible to find the people responsible.'

Sarah's sobbing was building to a crescendo. The younger policeman was watching her, fascinated.

'Jesus H. Christ!' Benjamin was trying to clear his drink-fuddled brain. 'Who would want to kill my Antney? Everyone liked him . . .'

The younger policeman dragged his eyes from Sarah and looked at Benjamin.

'Well, someone didn't. You don't stab your mates.'

Benjamin went for him. 'Why, you dirty little bastard!'

The other officer intervened, all formality forgotten now.

'Calm down, Benny. And you, Brown, shut your bloody big gob!' He pushed Benjamin back against the kitchen wall. 'Look, Ben, we've been questioning Leslie all morning and he won't say a dicky bird, but we think he knows who done it.'

Benjamin pushed the man away. 'Of course he won't tell you. He ain't a grass.'

'Grass or no, Ben, this person has killed his brother.'

'And that person will pay. Thanks for coming, Bill, but you can go now. I need to speak to me wife.'

His tone held dismissal and the two officers left the house. Benjamin pointed at Lee.

'Go up West to Mickey's and tell him what's happened. Tell him, Geoffrey and Roy to get their arses home – now.' Lee nodded. Still holding his mother, he walked her to his father. As Benjamin tried to comfort her, Sarah pushed him violently away.

'Don't you dare touch me! You've brought us to this, you conniving old bastard.'

Getting up from her seat, Maura ran to her mother. The two held on to each other tightly. Benjamin looked frightened by his wife's attitude. The hatred in her voice had shocked him.

'Garry, nip round and get the quack for your mother.'

The boy ran from the room, frightened. His mother's wailing, following him down the front steps, seemed to spur him on. Maura, tears running down her face, was frightened out of her wits. Anthony was dead . . . her brother Anthony who had alter-

51

nately teased and comforted her was lying somewhere dead, never to come home again. Fighting Margaret Lacey seemed so futile now. Why was it that bad things always happened when you were feeling happy?

The voices had been going on all evening. Maura could not sleep. She slipped out of bed, where her mother was snoring softly. The doctor had been in and given her some sleeping pills. He had tried to give her an injection but it had only made her more hysterical. Pulling the cover up over her mother's shoulders, Maura crept from the room and down the stairs.

The front room door was slightly open and she pressed her face to the crack. Her eldest brother Mickey was walking up and down the room talking, his face set in a dark scowl. Maura loved Mickey. He was her favourite brother. She thought he was the handsomest of them all. All the boys were dark, with deep-set blue eyes, but Mickey was magnificent. He had something that attracted people to him – men as well as women. Maura adored him. He was like a god to her. Now, though, she was seeing a Mickey that she didn't know. His teeth were gritted together and he had dark circles under his eyes. He looked ferocious.

'I swear I'll kill the bastards! So help me God, I'll kill them.'

'Calm down, Mickey. Calm down.' This from Geoffrey.

'Calm down, you say? When them bastards have stabbed our brother to death?'

Geoffrey took a long drink of his whisky.

'Calm down and think clearly, that's what I'm saying. Think with your head and not your heart.'

Michael stopped abruptly in his pacing and punched the wall.

'I'd rather have given the bastards the cab ranks than see Antney dead.'

Geoffrey sighed.

'Well, it's done now, Bruv. What we've got to decide is how we retaliate.'

'We'll blow the fuckers off the face of the earth, that's what we'll do!'

'I was thinking along those lines.' Everyone in the room stared at Gerry Jackson, one of Mickey's closest friends, and he coloured slightly.

'What I thought was, right, they've got a rank in Ilford, ain't they? In the High Street.'

All heads nodded in agreement.

'Well, on Saturday night, Lee here and a few of his mates can go up the Ilford Palais, right? Later on in the evening they go into the Greek bastard's cab rank, as for a cab to say . . . Wanstead.

52

Anywhere, just so they can get a good look in. If he's there, one of them can trot off and let us know, then we can poodle round and petrol bomb the place. We can sit round Green Lanes waiting for word. It must be someone they won't recognise. That would teach the saucy gits a lesson.'

Mickey nodded his head.

'Yeah, that sounds dawdy, Gerry, I'll have some of that. Meantime, me and Geoff and Roy, who'll be the main suspects, can be causing a disturbance somewhere else.'

'Brilliant! That's it then.'

Maura, listening to all this, was frightened. Her brothers were planning to blow someone up! She had heard people talk about her brothers. Tearaways and out of control, had become the prevalent opinion in Lancaster Road. Yet she realised that people were always nice to their faces, especially Mickey's. A couple of Saturdays previously, she had walked with him along the Portobello Road. They had stopped to get some fruit for her, and the stall-holder had insisted that it was a gift, refusing Michael's money as if it was the norm to give his produce away for free. Now she knew why people acted like they did. It was because her brothers blew people up.

She started to hop from one foot to the other. She was scared. Anthony was dead and her brothers were going to blow someone up. Suddenly, the door opened and Roy was standing in front of her.

She saw his face go pale.

'What's this then? Can't you sleep, Princess?' His voice was very loud. He picked her up and carried her into the front room. It was heavy with cigarette smoke and she coughed. Michael held out his arms to her and she shrank away from him, clinging to Roy. This Mickey frightened her. This was not her brother who cuddled her and bought her things . . . this was a man who blew people up. She looked fearfully into his face. He was so hurt by her attitude he was nearly in tears. With all that had happened with Anthony, he was near the end of his tether. Suddenly sensing this, Maura slipped out of Roy's arms and ran to him, big dry sobs bursting from her throat and bouncing off the walls.

He scooped her up into his arms and holding her tightly, rubbed his face into her soft, sweet-smelling hair.

She cried hard, wracking sobs distorting her voice. 'I want Antney to come home . . . I want Antney to come home! Blow the bad man up, Mickey. Blow the bad man up!'

He looked at the other men in the room, his eyes resting on his father. Through her tears Maura heard someone mutter, 'Jesus Christ!'

Michael held her until her sobs subsided. Holding her away

from him so he could look into her face, he spoke to her. His voice sounded worried.

'Listen, Princess. You must never . . . ever . . . tell anyone what you heard here tonight. Do you understand what I'm saying? If you tell anyone, even a friend, then the police will come and take us all away. Even Dad. Do you understand me?'

She nodded at him solemnly. 'I won't tell anyone, Mickey . . . not even Mum.'

Instinctively she knew that this was what he wanted to hear. He blinked and the relief in his eyes was evident. 'Good girl. You're a good girl. Now, let Dad put you back to bed.' He kissed her on the forehead and lips tenderly, then placed her on the floor. 'Good night, Princess.'

She took her father's outstretched hand and began to walk from the room. At the door she looked back over her shoulder at Mickey, her face serene. In her white nightdress she looked like a golden angel. She opened her mouth and spoke.

''I meant what I said, Mickey . . . get them that done in Antney.' With that she carried on walking with her father. Benjamin looked at her sadly. His little girl was learning the realities of life. He just wished she could have been spared them a little longer.

On 20 July 1960 they buried Anthony Ryan. The funeral cortège went slowly past Wormwood Scrubs prison, up past the wagon works and on to Saint Mary's Roman Catholic Cemetery at the top of Scrubs Lane. There were five cars from the funeral parlour following the coffin. Behind these were two dozen other cars containing friends and relatives. A police car containing Leslie, handcuffed but in his best suit, was last in the line.

In the first car Sarah sat dry-eyed, staring out at the passing roads. As they had passed by Du Cane Road, where the entrance to Wormwood Scrubs prison was, she had been reminded of how many times she had been there, visiting either her husband or one of the older boys. Her husband had been proud of how he had lived his life. 'I'm a ducker and diver.' How many times had she heard him tell someone that? Well, the result of his way of living was upon them today. Her lovely boy dead. She felt the hot tears bunch in her throat.

Looking into her troubled face, Benjamin placed his hand gently on her arm. She smacked it away. She blamed him for all this. He had encouraged the boys to be villains. Even when they had been little more than babies he had started to corrupt them. If they had been beaten in a fight, he would give them a good hiding and send them back out to do the job properly.

'None of my boys are Nancys,' had been one of his favourite

54

expressions, coupled with, 'All my boys are hard.' He had dragged them to dog tracks, pubs, bare knuckle fights. He had taught them how to pick a lock, steal a car, to shoplift . . . The list was endless.

What had he done? She asked herself. She felt an urge to fell him to the floor of the car, strike his face and hurt him as she was hurting inside. Her big manly husband – at this moment she hated him. She crossed her arms across her breasts and hugged herself. Her gaze lighted on her only daughter and her face softened. This one he could not touch. A beauty was her Maura. Sarah's pride in her daughter knew no bounds. With her white-blonde hair and dark blue eyes, she was exquisite. Now Maura's hair was hanging in long waves, unaccustomed to being out of plaits, her eyes sad and shining with unshed tears. Sarah knew that the child was bewildered by all that had happened. She leant across the car and grasped Maura's hand, forcing herself to give her daughter a little wink. The cars stopped and everyone got out, standing around in little groups, talking in hushed voices.

Sarah's seven remaining sons carried Anthony's coffin to the graveside. The main mass and requiem mass had already been said in the RC Church in Notting Hill. Now all that was left was to bury her boy. The youngest, Benny, although only thirteen, walked with his brothers, carrying the coffin. Michael had placed Maura, dressed in white, at the front of the coffin. She led them slowly through the graveyard to the burial site.

Father McCormack was standing silently by the yawning hole. The sun was high in the sky and beating down on the mourners' heads. In the yew trees nearby, birds sang and the hum of traffic and smell of exhaust fumes carried on the air. Outside the cemetery walls were carts carrying totters from Shepherd's Bush. The rag and bone men were grim-faced and silent. Benjamin Ryan's eldest brother was leading them. Their horses had the old-fashioned black plumes rising up from their harnesses. The carts had been washed down and polished for the day's event. Paddy Ryan wiped a tear from his eye as he watched his brother's son being lowered into the ground.

Bees were quietly going about their business, bumbling from flower to flower, the hot summer day bringing them out in force. The priest's voice droned on. The police had once again hand-cuffed Leslie. Funeral or no funeral they were not taking any chances. Maura was holding Michael's hand tightly, her face pale and troubled.

The policeman to whom Leslie was handcuffed was impressed by the turn-out. The Krays, Richardsons, and many more villains had come to pay their last respects. It showed the respect accorded to Michael Ryan.

Mickey stared stonily into the grave. Anthony's oak coffin had a large brass crucifix on the lid. The INRI above Jesus's head was glinting in the sunlight. In his mind's eye Michael could see Anthony's face inside it, staring upwards at darkness for the rest of eternity. He clenched his teeth together before he lost control and cried out. He prayed for the first time in years to the Holy Spirit to come and take his brother's soul. To care for him and protect him. He prayed to the Immaculate Conception and Holy Saint Anthony, the patron saint of miracles. He prayed to every saint and martyr he could remember from his years of Catholic schooling. Somehow, today, there being a God was important.

Out of the corner of his eye, he saw a movement. He turned his head. Being so tall he was head and shoulders above most of the mourners. To the left of him, standing about ten yards from the small crowd around the graveside, was a man. Michael stiffened. Feeling the change in him, Maura looked up into his face. She noticed that he was staring across the graveyard. She followed his gaze, through a small gap in the mourners opposite her, and saw the object of Michael's scrutiny.

The man was dark – not dark like her brothers but swarthy. His thick black curly hair seemed to grow around his head like a crown, leaving his forehead exposed where it had receded. He reminded her of the mad professor in her comics. The sun was behind him and she could see the glare that shone on his bald pate. Instinctively she knew that this was Stavros, the Greek man that her brothers had been constantly talking about since Anthony's death. The man was smiling slightly.

She looked from him to Michael and realised that her brother was going to go over to the man. He was pulling back his shoulders in his arrogant way. Holding Michael's hand tightly, she pulled on it. He looked down at her. When they both looked back a split second later the man was gone, but his face was stamped on Maura's memory. Then she felt the hot, scalding tears come into her eyes, spilling down her face and entering her mouth, their saltiness exploding on her tongue. From far off she heard shrieking. It was a few seconds before she realised that it was coming from her.

Michael picked her up in his arms and held her tightly to him, murmuring endearments into her hair and stroking her back until she was spent. After what seemed an age all that could be heard were little hiccups. Even the hardest of the men there was sobered by her outburst. Reggie Kray, always a lover of children, had tears in his eyes as he watched Michael comfort the girl. Like most Londoners from working-class backgrounds, family was important to them all. You looked after your own, no matter what.

A little while later, still holding Maura in his arms, Michael threw his handful of dirt on to the coffin. When the service was finished, he put her down gently by their mother and, picking up a shovel, filled in Anthony's grave, helped by Geoffrey and Roy.

One of the rag and bone men's wives, Lilly McNamara, had been asked to sing while this was being done. She was noted throughout Kensington and the surrounding areas as a fine singer. In the hush, broken only by the scraping of the shovels in the dirt and the soft thuds as it landed on the coffin, she sang 'Amazing Grace'. To outsiders it would have looked incongruous: men in black zoot suits, all with fashionable elephant's trunk hair styles, filling in a grave, surrounded by more men and women dressed in black. The women's hats and bright make-up made them look like exotic birds. To the Ryans and their like, Anthony had been given a magnificent send-off.

Sarah stood dignified and erect as her sons buried their brother. She would not cry here; she would wait until after the wake, when she was alone. In the scorching heat she had felt as if she would pass out; now she wished she had. It would have saved her having to watch this grisly ritual, the burying of her son's remains. She closed her eyes, her hand on her daughter's soft and springy hair.

When the singing was over and Anthony buried, the mourners went to the family and paid their respects. Diana Dors, the secret object of the young policeman's desire, hugged Michael long and hard. She was a firm favourite of everybody there, a kind, loving, generous woman who never in all her life judged anyone. Freddie Mills and his boyfriend Michael Holiday each clasped Michael to them. Freddie Mills had been Michael's boyhood hero. It had been worship of him that had aroused Michael's interest in boxing. Nowadays he met him socially, as an equal. A few days before Anthony's death they had been together at the Lancaster Road Baths watching local semi-professional boxers.

It did not escape Sarah's notice that Michael was treated as the head of the family and her husband relegated to second position. That was how it should be. After all, Michael was the main provider. He made sure that she had ample money. More than enough in fact. She did not feel overawed by the company at her son's funeral. She had known Violet Kray for many years. The Richardson boys had been visitors to her house for a long time. Many of the mourners were young men who had grown up with her sons. Petty criminals most of them, but good boys all the same.

Roy's wife looked depressed as usual. Sarah knew that it was not the funeral that had put the sad look on her daughter-in-law's face, but something quite different. Janine and Roy had problems, she was sure of that. Neither of them looked happy these days. Their daughter, Carla, nearly five now, looked as if she hadn't been washed for days. Sarah made a mental note to go and see Janine. Even in her grief she could still look out for her remaining children.

Finally, they began to make their way back to the cars. Sarah noticed Roy trying to take Janine's hand and being shrugged off. She frowned. As if there wasn't enough unhappiness in the family, they had to bring their petty squabbles into the cemetery with them.

Benny was staring at the mound of dirt that covered his brother. Benjamin walked back to get him, his old face looking more haggard and careworn than usual. He had been drinking steadily since the early morning.

'Come on, son.' His voice was slurred but gentle.

Benny was staring intently at a large worm wriggling on the pile of damp earth. In his mind's eye he saw it boring its way into the earth, down, down, until it reached his brother's face. Covering his own face with his hands, he was overtaken by silent sobs that made his shoulders shake. He was as tall as his father, and as Benjamin took his namesake into his arms, he felt the strength of him.

Sarah was watching them. She realised for the first time how Benjamin must be feeling. After all, Anthony had been his son too. A feeling she had not known in over a decade slipped through her body. All animosity towards her husband dissolved and a spark of affection for him seemed to light up inside her, as it had in the old days. She couldn't blame him entirely for what had happened. Children would go their own way in the end. In the environment they lived in it was inevitable that kids would turn to crime. All she could really blame him for was not working hard enough to get them out of it. She sighed heavily. How could he? He had never had the chance.

All this flashed through her head in an instant. She looked around the cemetery. The brilliant sunshine seemed to be mocking her. It was too nice a day to be burying a young life. It should have been cold and raining as befitted a funeral. She saw the flowers gently swaying in the light breeze, the lichen-covered gravestones that hid their contents from the world, and was overcome with sadness. The birds were still singing as she made her way slowly to the cars. Her body seemed to have shrunk since Anthony's death, giving her the appearance of an old woman. She was only forty-four.

Back at the house everyone was drinking. Maura pushed her way through the adults and stationed herself in the front room next to the table piled high with food. Presently she was joined by Margaret Lacey. This had been arranged the day before. That morning Margaret had complained of a bad bout of sickness. Her mother, anxious to get to work, had given her the day off school. Now she was up and dressed and holding her new best friend's hand. She could not even imagine what it must be like to have a brother who had been murdered. Her mum and dad had talked of nothing else for days. According to them it was a wonder something like this had not happened before. Margaret, though, wisely kept this bit of information to herself.

Mickey came up, and, taking the two girls by the hand, led them out of the house and into the back garden. He could not bear to be away from Maura today. She was so innocent and trusting. With his guilt over Anthony, he felt that at least she loved him and didn't blame him for the death. No one would dare say that it was his fault outright, but he knew what was going on in everyone else's mind.

He sat in an old deck chair and the two girls sat on the ground, each leaning against one of his legs. He was already half drunk. The sun was so hot it was impossible to open his eyes without being blinded. Eventually he dozed. Maura and Margaret sat by him for hours. The friendship of a lifetime was bonded that day. Maura and Margaret became a pair, the friendship only to end with the death of one of them.

That night in bed Maura had her first nightmare. It was of the man in the cemetery coming after her with her mother's bread knife. She was to have the same dream intermittently for the rest of her life.

Chapter Six

Carla Ryan opened her eyes. The sun was streaming in at the windows of her room. She lay for a few moments watching the patterns it made on the ceiling. A cool breeze drifted over her thin little body. She rubbed her arm, where she had a large bruise above the elbow. Her mother had picked her up bodily the night before and dragged her into her room where she had then thrown her on to her bed. She had bumped her arm on the little bedside cabinet. The pain had made her lose her breath for a few seconds. Lifting up her pink nightdress her mother had then smacked her behind as hard as she could, afterwards putting her face next to Carla's and telling her that she had had enough. Her mother's breath had been sour as it always was when she had been drinking.

What exactly her mother had had enough of Carla was not sure. All she had done the night before was make herself a sugar sandwich. She had asked her mother for something to eat over and over again, until finally she had decided to get it herself. She supposed it was the sugar all over the table and floor that had made her mother cross.

She sat herself up in bed and swung her little legs over the side. She yawned and her long brown hair fell over her face as she stretched her arms out. She winced as her bad arm was stretched. This was going to be a sore one, she reflected. Like the one she'd had on her leg a few weeks previously. Slipping off the bed she crept across her room, opening the door as silently as possible.

She looked through the crack into the hallway. Opposite her bedroom was the kitchen. She waited a few seconds for any sounds that might tell her that her mother was in there but out of her range of sight. Nothing. She walked across the hall and into the kitchen. The sugar she had spilt everywhere the night before was sticking to her bare feet. She was hungry again. She was always hungry. Sneaking across the kitchen she made herself some bread and margarine.

She was kneeling on a kitchen chair, her long hair trailing in the margarine, when she heard the steps. The heavy thudding steps that meant her mother was getting up. She froze. Her heart was fluttering in her chest. Her breathing came rapidly. Remembering the night before she threw her knife from her hand as if it was red hot, then tried to push the sticky mass of bread and margarine underneath the bread wrapper. In her haste she was clumsy and only succeeded in pushing the loaf of Dinkum bread and the sandwich off the table and on to the floor, already sticky from the sugar.

Tears of frustration stung her eyes. She felt her mother's presence before she turned and faced her, her little grubby hands clenching and unclenching with nerves. Janine looked at her coldly. Her daughter's face was exquisite even when she was terrified. Her eyes were a startling violet colour that made her look incredibly strong-minded. Coupled with her dark brown hair and high cheekbones, she looked like a miniature woman. Janine watched her daughter sweep her hair away from her face with a gesture that was more fitting to a sexy movie star than a four-year-old girl. Her long neck and strong pointed chin were shown to advantage by the gesture.

Janine chewed her lip, staring spitefully at her child. She knew that if she didn't speak Carla would get more and more nervous, eventually breaking the heavy silence herself. She noticed the black bruise on her arm and a wicked light glowed in the back of her eyes. She would have to keep the child's arms covered, because Roy would go crazy if he thought his little angel had been whipped. She gritted her teeth and, aping the child's earlier movement, theatrically swept her own thick red hair off her face. She looked like a sleek, tawny cat about to pounce on its prey. Carla stared back at her, every nerve in her body tensed and waiting. As her mother swept back her hair in a parody of her own action she dropped her eyes. Everything she did annoyed her mother. How she sat, how she stood, how she ate, how she spoke. Every movement was ridiculed and parodied.

She wished her father was home but he was very rarely around much these days, and when he was her mother fought with him. Carla would curl up on his lap and hold her hands over her ears desperately trying to block out their arguing. She loved her father and missed him when he was away. She thought of him as a big tree, with strong branches that enabled her to climb him, which she did when he was home. With Roy holding her by the arms she walked up his body until, reaching his shoulders, she flipped over and landed on her feet, screeching with laughter. She wished he was here now. Her mother daren't touch her when her father was at home. The tension in the kitchen had reached its peak and, stuttering in fright, the child spoke.

'Where's me dad?' As soon as she spoke the words she flinched inside. Why had she mentioned him? She closed her eyes tightly.

Somewhere inside her was a weak hope that she had not spoken. She heard her mother's slippers crunching across the sugar-strewn floor. She squeezed her eyes shut as tightly as possible. As she felt her hair being yanked, she screamed. The pain was searing through her scalp. Shaking her like a rag doll, Janine began to shout.

'You want your dad, do you? You little slut! He's out whoring as usual. Shacked up with some woman somewhere. He don't care about you.'

Carla was trying to drag her mother's fingers from her hair. Crying now, and frightened, she screamed back at her mother, 'Please, Mum . . . Please . . . Let go of me hair . . . You're hurting me!'

Sarah heard the screams from the entrance hall of the flats. Grabbing Maura's hand she ran up the stairs and banged on the front door with her fists, demanding to be let in. Janine heard the banging and shouting and went cold with fright. She threw Carla from her and looked around her wild-eyed, like an animal seeking an escape route. The state of the kitchen registered inside her mind somewhere. Carla lay sobbing where she had landed, holding her poor injured head in both hands. Her granny's banging on the door was like music to hear ears.

She watched her mother walk out of the kitchen as if in a trance and a few seconds later Carla was nestled in her granny's arms. Little kisses were planted on her wet face, and murmured endearments and gentle strokes administered. Gradually the child calmed down. A handful of her hair was lying on the floor.

Maura watched the whole thing wide-eyed. Janine was now sitting at the kitchen table smoking a cigarette. Maura took in the dirty sugar floor and the loaf of bread now scattered everywhere, the filthy table and the stacks of dirty dishes. She dragged her eyes from it all, disgusted. She didn't like Janine. Taking the weeping Carla out of the kitchen Sarah motioned with her head for Maura to follow her, which she did gratefully. Going into Carla's room, Sarah laid the child on the bed. Maura watched as her mother checked the little girl from head to toe, shaking her head and tutting as she did it. Finally, Sarah turned to her own daughter.

'You stay here with Carla. Find some half-decent clothes and get her dressed. I'll call you if I need you . . . all right?' Her voice was thick with emotion. Maura nodded wordlessly. In the kitchen Janine sat at the table smoking yet another cigarette. Pulling herself up to her full height, Sarah glared at her.

'Now then, Janine. I think you'd better tell me exactly what's been going on here.' Her voice was determined.

Janine glanced at her and, all the hatred and animosity falling from her, began to cry. Groaning as if in physical pain, she rocked herself back and forth in her chair – her teeth bared as if she was grinning at some diabolical joke. Sarah stared at her. Where on earth was the beautiful, vital girl her son had married? How did this scruffy, dirty-looking individual come into being? The girl was only twenty-two years old. She looked at the filthy kitchen. The windows were so grimy it was difficult for the sun to penetrate them. The whole place stank. She had always understood that Janine's mother was never off the doorstep, that's why she never came herself. Say what you like about Eliza Grierson, she was a very particular housewife, so how come the flat was in this state? She shook her head in puzzlement. And just how long had Janine been beating the child? By the looks of Carla she had not had a decent meal for weeks.

Sarah blamed herself. She should have come over sooner, she should have spoken to Roy, but how did you ask a grown man about his home life? Once they left home it was up to them surely? That had been her own mother's philosophy. She was distressed, unsure how to go about sorting this situation out. Suddenly Janine spoke.

'No one ever said it would be like this!' Her voice was high. 'I hate it all . . . I hate the cooking and the cleaning and the dirt and the washing and the mending. I hate this flat – it's like a prison to me. Sometimes I don't see anyone for weeks on end. I'm so lonely.'

Sarah was nonplussed. Janine took a deep breath and all the fears and worries inside her came tumbling out like a great canker that had finally burst. 'Roy's never here. He leaves me for days on end. And Carla . . . that bloody Carla is like a permanent reminder of my bloody mistake! If it hadn't been for her I wouldn't be here . . . I wouldn't be here!'

She began crying again in earnest. Sarah went to her. She hesitated a few seconds before putting her arm around the girl's thin shoulders.

'What about your mother, Janine? I thought she came to see you.'

She gave a harsh bitter laugh.

'Well, you thought wrong, Mrs Ryan. My mother . . . my darling mother . . . has nothing to do with me anymore.'

'But why, Janine? Why?'

'Oh, it's a long story. She told me that if I left Roy and went home she would forgive me having Carla and everything . . . forgive me bringing shame on them by marrying a hoodlum. That's her choice of word not mine. And as much as I hate Roy at times . . .' she began to cry again '. . . I know that if I left him, I would never be happy again. I can't live without him, Mrs Ryan! I

64

love him so desperately yet I can't seem to make him happy. When he's here I start fights and drive him out of the house. I want him to want me and he doesn't. I know he doesn't . . .'

'Dear God, Janine. What on earth's the matter with you, girl? Look around you, for Christ's sake. Who'd want to come home to this? It's like a bloody pig sty.' Janine's declaration of love for her son had softened Sarah up. She reasoned that if she could help the girl, she could save their marriage as well as the child. 'Look at yourself. You look like the wreck of the Hesperus! No woman likes housework, but it's got to be done. At your age I already had five children living and not the hope of a decent wage coming. You've got it made if only you'd realise it.' She began rolling up the sleeves of her best dress. 'I'll tell you what we'll do. First we'll have a cup of tea. Get ourselves nice and calm. Then we'll go through this place like a dose of salts. Scrub it out from top to bottom. With the two of us working like blacks we'll have it done in no time. What do you say?' Janine nodded but Sarah could see her heart wasn't in it. She tried a different tack.

'Then you can go and get your lovely hair done while I get some food cooked. Can you imagine Roy's face when he comes home to everything nice and clean and homely? I'll take the little one home with me for a few days to give you a break. Now what do you say to that?'

Janine brightened up and Sarah smiled but deep inside she was worried. The only reason Janine had cheered up was because she was taking her child from her. She sighed. Even when your children grew up they still made demands. You were never free of them. Wearily she put on the kettle for the tea. Already she was tired, and by the looks of the flat by the time she was finished she would be exhausted. Well, soonest done soonest mended, as her mother used to say. She made the tea.

In the bedroom Maura had dressed Carla in a fairly clean pinafore dress. All the child's socks were dirty so she had turned a pair inside out and put them on her. They looked pretty clean. She was sitting on the bed cuddling Carla when her mother came in and told her to go to the shops and get some bits and pieces. She was instructed to take Carla with her and get her a big ice cream, and one for herself also.

She was amazed at how quickly Carla seemed to get over what had happened to her. At the mention of ice cream the little girl became excited and animated, bouncing up and down on the bed. Maura felt so sorry for her. Her arms were like sticks and the purple-black bruise looked swollen and painful. Yet jumping on the bed she could almost be a normal, happy little girl. She had seen the pity in her mother's eyes and a great rage against Janine had rushed through Maura. If she was older she would go into that kitchen and tear her apart.

Instead she took the money from her mother and walked sedately down to the shops with Carla, playing with her and making her laugh. She knew that Carla was coming home with her and decided that she would take the little girl into her bed with her. After all, she was her aunt. She had a responsibility towards her.

Three hours later the little flat was sparkling clean. Janine seemed to get up some enthusiasm as her mother-in-law chatted to her, telling her about her own difficult marriage, and how it was hard when one was young and unsure of oneself. For the first time Janine felt that she had an ally, and it made all the difference to her. Sarah was consciously getting her confidence, telling her what she knew she wanted to hear.

When Janine finally opened up to her she felt the loneliness and unhappiness emanating from her. Sarah reproached herself. She should have visited her more often, should have taken more of an interest in her – and just wait until she went around to Eliza Grierson's! She'd floor that bitch with what she had to say to her! The supercilious old cow! Sarah was looking forward to it. She'd 'hoodlum' her before she was much older! Next on her agenda was that galloping big son of hers. Letting the girl get into this state, and neglect that little child. She'd annihilate him as well! When she got her hands on the bugger, that was. From what she'd gleaned from Janine he came and went like a bloody ghost, flitting in and out as it suited him. Sarah's mouth set in a grim line. He wasn't too big for a clout round the ear hole, whatever he thought.

Janine came into the kitchen dressed up for her trip to the hairdresser's. Sarah smiled at her.

'You look a picture, love. Like one of them girls on the adverts! Now get yourself off and I'll fix you something for your dinner.'

Janine smiled shyly at Sarah. She felt better than she had for months. 'Thank you, Mrs Ryan. You've been so good to me.' Her voice was trembling with emotion.

Sarah waved her hand impatiently. 'Don't you think it's about time you called me Sarah? As for thanking me . . . for what? I should have been here for you a long time ago. I'm ashamed of meself.'

Janine went to her and kissed her on the cheek.

'Thanks . . . Sarah.' She said her name timidly, as if it felt strange to address her so. Sarah just grinned at her.

'Get yourself off and I'll have a lovely meal waiting for you, OK?'

Janine nodded and left the flat, feeling lighter hearted than she had for many days. Sarah watched her go and wiped her arm across her brow. She was sweating. It had been a hot and sultry summer. In a way she was grateful to Janine. Today had been the first time since he died she had not been tortured with thoughts of her Anthony. She looked out of the now sparkling window and heaved a deep sigh. She began to cook the meal, briefly wondering how her own household was coping without her. She pictured Benjamin waiting for the food to run out of the cupboard and into the frying pan, and smiled. It would never occur to him to cook himself anything. Well, he would just have to wait. She had more pressing things on her mind.

As she prepared the vegetables, she heard the front door open. Thinking it was Maura and Carla she called out: 'I'm in here, lovelies.'

'What you doing here, Mum?' Roy was standing in the doorway, staring at the kitchen as if he was in the wrong house.

Sarah smirked at him nastily. 'Well, well. The Wandering Jew's returned to his home at last!'

She looked at his crumpled clothing, and the dark shadow on his jaw. 'Obviously your new lady love isn't looking after you very well.'

She slammed the saucepan of potatoes on to the draining board. Roy stared at her warily. There was something funny going on here.

'So, now that you're home, are you thinking of staying at all? Or are you just going to get a change of gear and go off again on your merry way?' She gripped the handle of the saucepan.

Roy looked at her, bewildered. 'Are you being funny? Where's Janine and the kid?' Too late he realised his mother's intention. The saucepan and potatoes hit him full in the chest, the water drenching him.

Sarah ran to him, slipping on the wet floor. Righting herself she slapped him across his face, a white hand print appearing as if by magic. 'I'll give you where's the kid . . . she's your daughter, Roy Ryan, and you fought hammer and tongs to marry her mother. When I think of the trouble you caused because you couldn't keep your private parts to yourself! You've driven that poor girl to distraction.'

'I've what! Now you hold up a minute, Muvver.'

Sarah screamed at him: 'No, I bloody well won't, you gormless eejit! Before that girl took up with you the most she ever did in her life was get dressed up for church. She wasn't brought up to do all this.' She gestured around the flat. 'She's been slowly going out of her mind stuck here day in day out, and do you care? Not on your bloody nellie! I'm ashamed to admit that you're my son! That poor innocent little child has taken the brunt of everything.

She's got a bruise on her arm like she's been ten rounds with Dempsey . . . and it's all your fault.'

Roy's mouth was hanging open with disbelief.

'Shut your bloody gob up! You look like a mental deficient standing there gawking.'

Roy's mouth snapped shut. 'Janine won't do anything around the place.'

'Shut your trap, I said, or you'll be getting another smack off me otherwise. You're not too big for a good hiding, you know.'

Roy wanted to laugh. He towered over his mother. He had to admire her though. She stuck by her guns. Inside him there was a little nagging doubt. What his mother had said was true. He didn't try to understand Janine. Slowly bending down Sarah picked up the saucepan. It was dented on one side. She stifled an urge to brain her son with it, and instead placed it in the sink. In unspoken agreement mother and son began clearing up the debris. Potatoes had flown to all four corners of the kitchen. Water was everywhere. When it was all put right, Sarah pushed Roy into a chair. Outwardly, she looked her old formidable self. Inside, she was gloating. She was actually enjoying herself! She had not had so much fun for a long time, since before she buried Anthony.

She made a pot of tea. Putting a cup in front of Roy, she said, 'I came here this morning because I knew that something wasn't right. I sensed it at the funeral. The child looked like the orphan of the storm, and Janine looked terrible. I admit that I'm as much to blame, I should have come to visit her, but I understood her mother was never off the doorstep, so I left her to it. When I came here this morning she was pulling the child's hair out of her head.'

She watched Roy's mouth harden. 'And don't you come the old biddy with me! If *you* had done your job properly, been a decent husband, then all this could have been avoided.' She poked him in the chest. 'You are going to get yourself sorted out, my man, and you're going to start coming home at nights. I sat in many a night myself when you were all younger, waiting for that piss artist of a father of yours to come home, knowing in my heart that he was down the Bayswater Road, spending desperately needed money on old brasses. How I never got a dose of clap I'll never know! Well, I won't have any of my sons going the same way.'

Roy sat staring at her. He knew, as all the boys had always known, that she had not had the best of lives with his father, but she had never before spoken to him like this. He knew that she was trying to help him save his marriage, and in a tiny part of himself he knew that she was right. He had left Janine to fend for herself. He had chosen to ignore the fact that she took out her frustrations on Carla. But he just didn't know what to do. He was ashamed that his mother had so accurately put her finger on where he spent his nights. Since Michael had opened a hostess club in the West End, he had literally had his pick of women to spend the night with. It had been easier than coming home to fighting and arguing. To a dirty home and an unhappy wife.

But he still loved Janine. He had thought that taking her away from her mother's influence would have encouraged her to stand on her own two feet. Instead she had leant even more on him and he just couldn't take it, so had chosen the easy way out. Now he had to face not only Janine and little Carla, but his mother. He heard the front door open and braced himself, looking at his mother for support. As Janine walked into the room, Sarah stood up and smiled at her.

'You look an absolute angel, doesn't she, Roy?' She poked him in the shoulder, her bright smile belying the force she had used. Janine smiled uncertainly at him. The tension in the kitchen was like an electric current. Janine did look like angel. Her hair was swept up off her finely boned face, emphasising her long neck. Her deep green eyes were made up expertly and there was a wistfulness in them that pierced Roy's heart. She was a cracker, he thought. She really looked the business. His mum was right, Janine was like a high-spirited thoroughbred. She needed gentle guidance. He got up from his chair and held out his arms to her. Janine hesitated for a few seconds before she slipped into them.

Sarah watched, a satisfied expression on her face. Now all she had to do was go and see Father McCormack and get him to sort out her Michael and she would be happy. Half an hour later she left the two love birds, Maura and Carla in tow. Her next stop was the Church and Father McCormack. She looked at her watch. If she hurried she would catch him as he finished six o'clock mass.

Sitting in the refectory with a glass of wine in front of her, Sarah poured out her heart to the priest.

'I feel ashamed to tell you this, Father, but Michael has bought himself another club, this time a bordello.' She sipped her wine to steady her voice. 'Men go there to . . . Well, I don't have to paint a picture, now do I?'

Father McCormack looked at her through shrewd eyes. He was sixty years old and had been the parish priest for over thirty years. His hair was grey and cut in an American crew-cut. He had heavy grey-flecked eyebrows that gave him a wise demeanour and looked on religion the way some men looked on marriage: as a necessary part of life. You made the best of it. He put his large, soft hands together.

'I see, I see.' His Irish accent was still thick even though he had left Ireland over forty years previously. 'Sure that Michael was always a difficult one. I can see why you're worrying.'

'I think that if *you* had a word with him, Father . . .' Her voice trailed off.

'Well, Sarah, I'll do my best. But your Michael was always a strong-minded fellow. He might not like the interference.'

Sarah was determined that before she left this room she would have an appointment to save her son's eternal soul! She tried a different approach.

'Oh, Father, I know what people say about my Mickey, but as you know yourself, stories get stretched in the telling. All he needs is a little gentle guidance. If you were to talk to him, I'm sure he would listen to a fine man like yourself. Even when he was an altar boy, he always had a high regard for you.'

The priest raised his eyebrows. When Michael had been an altar boy he had also stolen the lead from the church roof! But he had the glimmer of a plan forming in his mind, and it would please this poor soul sitting before him. He decided to do as she asked.

'Hostess club, you say? Well, I think that a few words from me are called for, as you say.' Sarah jumped in before he could change his mind.

'If you come to my house at eleven o'clock tomorrow morning, I'll make sure that he's there.'

He smiled at her, showing tobacco-stained teeth. 'Eleven o'clock it is then. Now tell me, how are the other children? I hear that all the older boys are driving big expensive cars and living the life of Riley. They all work for Michael, I take it?'

'Yes, Father, that's true. But if you can help to sort out Mickey, the others will follow suit, I'm sure.'

'Well, Sarah, we can only put our trust in the Lord.' He looked up at the ceiling as if expecting to see him floating there. 'As it says in the Bible, "God is no respecter of persons", Romans 2-11. Michael Ryan may be a big man on earth but in heaven he's just another of God's children.'

Sarah smiled at him. There was nothing, she thought, like a chunk of the Bible when spouted by a true believer. She left a little while later, happier than she had been for a long time. Over the years her religion had been a great comfort to her. As she had suffered one setback after another – no money, another still birth, one or other of the boys in trouble with the police – she had turned more and more to the church. Benjamin was no good at all. If she relied on him for anything, it never happened. Whether it was her housekeeping or anything, he always let her down. Michael, God love him, had been a good son in many ways. He had looked after his younger brothers and sister, he had made sure

70

that she always had enough money, but she had been hearing things of late that had frightened her. Anthony's death had been the last straw. She knew that her eldest son was involved in all manner of criminal activities, that he was thought of as a kind of mobster. She shuddered. She was all for a bit of ducking and diving, that's how everyone lived in her estimation, but from what she had gleaned recently about her sons, it was a completely different lifestyle they were after. She had seen the effect that Michael had on the people around and about. She herself was now treated like visiting royalty when she went anywhere.

She could, to an extent, understand Michael's craving for recognition. She was shrewd enough to understand that the way he had been treated as a child would give him the added drive and determination to better himself. But she herself drew the line at prostitution. In her mind it was the ultimate degradation, and any man who could live off the proceeds of it was the lowest of the low. She fervently hoped that Father McCormack would be able to talk some sense into her son. The robbing was bad enough though the insurance companies could afford the losses and money had no soul. But the wilful destruction of young lives was a different kettle of fish altogether. She had been shocked to read in the *News of the World* about the drugs that were available now to youngsters. What on earth was the world coming to? Young girls selling their bodies for drugs.

In the war years and after, women had sold their bodies to feed their children. That fitted in with Sarah's creed. You could do anything to feed the children, to keep the family fed or clothed. Even sell your body. But that had been for women with no man to protect them, so they had to do whatever they could and were respected for it. Sarah herself knew many women who had moonlighted down the Bayswater Road to supplement meagre war pensions or National Assistance. What Michael was doing was disgusting. He was putting them on the game, women and young girls who would otherwise never have dreamt of doing it. He was offering easy money, a far cry from the days when it was a means to an end.

She watched Maura and Carla skipping in front of her. Maura looked huge beside the tiny Carla. Dear Maura, she had taken the poor little thing under her wing. Sarah only hoped now that Janine and Roy sorted themselves out. That it wasn't too late for her to take to her daughter. Oh, the worry of having children! A Jewish woman Sarah had been friends with, before the war, used to say to her, 'When your children are young they tread on your feet. When they get older they tread on your heart!' How right she had been! The poor woman had died when she had been bombed in the blitz. A direct hit. Sarah often thought of her. Too many good people had died in the war, had suffered in one way or another. She sighed. She was dead tired. Now she had to go home and start her own cooking and cleaning. Still, she consoled herself, Father McCormack was coming in the morning and hopefully everything would right itself.

Father McCormack sat opposite Michael and appraised him. There was no doubt about it, he was a fearsome-looking individual.

From his dark expertly cut hair to his hand-made shoes he was the epitome of the new young man. His single-breasted suit was made of mohair and he flicked a trace of ash off his trousers with a perfectly manicured hand. His closely shaven face was tense and his usually sensuous mouth set in a grim line. The priest had guessed that he was well aware of the object of this visit.

Sarah had made a pot of tea and left them together in the overcrowded room. It was as if, after years of having no furniture at all, Sarah had gone mad for it. The room was filled with tables, knick-knacks, chairs, and a large horse-hair three-piece suite. Religious paintings were all over the walls. The Sacred Heart, the Last Supper and the Crucifixion stared down at them. Our Lady of Lourdes looked at the doorway opposite her in a gesture of supplication. On the large sideboard that covered nearly the whole of one wall statues of the Virgin and Child, as well as the holy family, stood silently. One particularly macabre statue of Saint Sebastian, arrows poking out of every limb, was given centre stage. The priest found his eyes drawn towards it and made a conscious effort to stop staring at it. He picked up his cup of tea and turned his gaze back to Michael.

'I expect you know why I'm here?'

Michael sniffed and uncrossed his legs. 'Yeah.' His voice was wary.

The priest nodded as if in understanding. 'Well, Michael, if you know then it's pointless me droning on now, isn't it?'

'Yeah.' This was said insolently. Michael's fear of priests and nuns was long gone.

Father McCormack sat forward in his chair and replaced his cup on the table. His face hardened. He spoke in a low voice. 'What I am here for today is something completely different. When your mother, good woman that she is, came to see me yesterday I was not shocked to hear what she had to say. I guessed that you were breaking the law in some way. I'm not a fool, you know. Anyway, that's all neither here nor there . . . I want to speak to you as a man of the world.'

Michael looked at him. His blue eyes were sceptical.

72

'What I'm after is a little donation.'

Michael sat up in the chair, stunned. 'A what!'

The priest became agitated. 'Whisht now, whisht. You'll have your mother galloping in here else. As you know, I am rather sympathetic to my countrymen. There's poor Paddies in London even now, God love them, who have been driven out of their homes by the Proddies. It's every Irishman's duty to help these poor unfortunates.'

'Look, Father, just because my name's Ryan don't mean I'm Irish.'

The priest banged his fist on the little table, causing the cups to jump in their saucers.

'Listen here, you, since nineteen-twenty the Catholics have been discriminated against in Ulster, Belfast, all the North. They can't even get a council house out there! The bloody Protestants run the whole fecking sheebang! I collect money for the IRA so we can build up an army and fight the bastards at their own game. One day, my laddo, we'll be ready for the eejits. We forced them out of the South and we'll fight the buggers in the North. We want an Irish Free State that spans the whole of Ireland.'

The priest's eyes were alight. Michael stared at him as if he was mad. He had heard stories of Ireland from the cradle, as most Catholic children had. He could still hear his granny singing 'Kevin Barry' on Saint Patrick's Day, still remember the stories of the Easter Uprising and the Famine. How his ancestors had left the meat that Queen Victoria had sent over to them to rot in the streets rather than accept help from the English. But this was nineteen-sixty, for Christ's sake. Who gave a toss what was happening out there?

Father McCormack drank his tea. Wiping his mouth with the back of his hand he spoke again.

'I know an awful lot about you, Michael Ryan. There's nothing I can't find out if I want to. All I am asking is a little donation now and again. You'd be surprised at how many people give money to the cause. The Americans have regular collections in their bars and churches. Ireland is a poor country and needs all the help it can get.'

Michael laughed.

'Supposing I give you some money . . . now and again . . . what would you do in return?'

The priest took a handkerchief from the pocket of his black cassock and mopped his forehead.

'I would tell your mother exactly what she wanted to hear. If it came from me she would believe it. I can be a very persuasive man.'

Michael ran his tongue over his lips, and shook his head.

'What about the poor orphans and the starving blacks?' His voice was sarcastic.

'Sure, they would get a bit as well, God love them. Though I think most of the blacks are in Notting Hill.'

Michael burst out laughing.

'All right then, Father. You've sold me. But I'm warning you now, you've got to keep my muvver sweet.'

Father McCormack smiled.

'I will, Michael son.' He sighed heavily. 'Sure, it's a terrible world we're living in today. Money makes it so much easier. I remember this room when there was hardly a thing in it . . . except children, of course. Your mother always seemed to have plenty of those. Well, I must be off. It's been grand chatting to you, Michael. I'll expect you at the Presbytery in a few days with your donation.' He held out his hand. 'I won't give you a blessing . . . I don't think you need one!'

Michael shook his hand. 'I have a feeling I've just been conned, Father. An Irish Catholic Northern Ireland? Donations to the IRA . . .?' He smiled. 'If it was anyone else I'd kick their arse out of the door.'

The priest's face straightened and he looked meaningfully at Michael.

'Don't mock what you don't fully understand. Your religion is the mightiest in the world. Remember this? *Dominus illuminatio mea, et salus mea, quem timebo?*'

Michael translated it for him, smiling as he did so. 'The Lord is the source of my light and my safety, so whom shall I fear?'

'Would you listen to that! You remembered your Latin.'

'Yeah, I remember it all right. And I don't fear anyone, not even God. *You* remember that.'

Father McCormack digested the veiled threat gracefully. 'How could I forget? But I'll tell you one thing before I go. One day the troubles in Northern Ireland will be known all over the world, and the British will have to listen to us. When that day comes you remember my words, Michael, because we won't forget our friends, whoever they are.'

With that the priest picked up his hat and left the room.

Michael watched him leave. He felt like laughing out loud. The old boy had lost his marbles somewhere along the line. Still, if it kept his mother off his back, he didn't care. He picked up the tray of tea things and took them to the kitchen where he glanced at the clock. If he got his head down for a couple of hours he would be nice and fresh for the evening. His new club was raking the money in. After the lean war years, people wanted a bit of fun. And he would make sure they got it!

74

Chapter Seven

1966

'You look nice, Maws. Where you off to?' Sarah's voice was tight.

'I'm going up Tiffany's with me mates.'

'Tiffany's? Where's that?'

Sarah's voice had taken on the tone of an interrogation. Garry answered for Maura.

'It's in Ilford. The old Allie Pallie.'

'What's she going up there for? What's wrong with the Hammersmith Palais?'

Maura sighed and tossed back her hair. 'There's nothing wrong with round here, Mum. I'm just meeting some of the girls from work, that's all.' Her voice was beginning to rise and she tried in vain to control it.

Sarah wiped her hands on her apron and stared at Maura, her face wrinkled in concern. 'Well, it's a bloody long way to go if you ask me.'

'Well, I'm *not* asking you, Mum. I'm nearly seventeen and I can do what I like.'

Sarah walked towards her daughter. Garry tried to pull her back, holding her arm gently.

'Let me tell you something, Madam. You *can't* do what you sodding well like . . .'

Her diatribe was cut off by Michael who stormed into the kitchen. The constant bickering between Maura and his mother was beginning to get on everyone's nerves.

'For Christ's sake, Muvver, give it a rest. Let the girl go out if she wants to. Anyway . . .' he put his arm around his mother's shoulders '. . . Garry's going up there tonight. He can give her a lift on the back of his scooter.'

'I'm not getting on the back of his scooter with all my new gear on!' Maura's voice was horrified.

'Just as well, 'cos I ain't going up the Palais.'

'Tiffany's.'

'Tiffany's then. I'm going to the pictures with me mates.'

Maura smiled triumphantly. 'Well, that's settled then.' She

75

picked up her shoulder bag. 'Gawd Blimey, it's worse than living in Scotland Yard here. Where you bin? What you been doing? What did you talk about? Did he kiss you? I wouldn't mind, but I can't get a bloody boyfriend! As soon as they find out who I am they shy off.

' "You Mickey Ryan's sister?" they say. "Yes," says I, and watch them poodle off down the road. So stop worrying about me getting in the club, Muvver, I don't get the bloody chance!'

She snatched her coat off the kitchen table and stormed out of the kitchen, shouting, 'And if by any chance I do need an escort, it won't be my bloody brother. Ta rah!'

She walked out of the front door and gave it a satisfying slam behind her. In the kitchen Michael and Sarah stared at one another, shocked. Garry went to the sink and washed his hands. In the back of his mind he was cheering Maura on.

'Well, I never, Michael. Did you hear the way she carried on?'

He sighed heavily. 'I think the whole of Notting Hill heard it.'

Garry wiped his hands on a tea towel and faced his brother. 'She's got a point though, ain't she?'

Michael looked at him. It was like looking at a miniature version of himself.

'What do you mean by that?' His voice was cold.

Garry plucked up every bit of courage he had.

'Well, the way that everyone's at her. If I was her, it would drive me up the wall.'

'If you was her you'd be getting the same treatment. She's our sister, our responsibility. If we don't look after her, who will? You want to put your brain in gear before you open your trap, Garry. Our Geoff was right about you. He said an original thought in your head would die of loneliness. After hearing the crap you just come out with, I'm inclined to agree with him.'

Garry's face was scarlet with embarrassment.

'Come on, you two, get a move on or you'll be late.' Sarah was worried. She knew that Michael was capable of attacking Garry for what he had said. In Michael's mind it was tantamount to mutiny and he would not stand for anyone disagreeing with him.

He took a comb from the pocket of his suit and stood at the sink. Looking in the mirror that was perched precariously on the windowsill, he combed back the hair that hung over his eyes. Then, turning to Garry, he pointed the long steel comb at him.

'In future, Bruv, keep your nose out of what don't concern you.'

He kissed his mother lightly on the forehead and walked out of the room. Garry was fuming inside. Sensing this, Sarah went to him.

'He don't mean it, Gal. But he's right about Maura, you know.

You should all look out for your sister.'

Garry shrugged her arm off and picked up his crash helmet. 'We're not looking out for her, Mother. We're trying to own her, and that's a completely different thing.'

When he had gone Sarah carried on with her chores, but Garry's words stayed with her all evening.

Maura breathed a sigh of relief as she slammed the front door. It was getting more claustrophobic in that house by the day. If it wasn't for Margaret she would go mad. They were as close as two friends could be. They worked in the same office, they ate their lunch together, they went down the Lane on Sundays and the Roman Road on Fridays. The only cloud on the horizon was a boy called Dennis Dawson. Margaret had been seeing him for nearly a year and Maura had the feeling that they were going to get married. Still, she consoled herself, she would always have Margaret as a friend.

Tonight the two girls were meeting Dennis and one of his mates up Tiffany's. She had nearly had heart failure at the thought of Garry going up there. That was all she needed. The only reason they were going there was because they could be pretty sure that one or other of her brothers would *not* be up there and Maura would have a bit of privacy. How she hated the way her brothers protected her, and her mother was all for it. She was beginning to dislike her mother. The last few years Sarah had practically suffocated her only daughter. Maura wished that she could meet a nice bloke and get right out of it. If she married, at least she would have a life of her own, away from prying eyes. She daydreamed sometimes about finding a little flat but knew they were just that – daydreams. There was no way she would ever be allowed to go and live alone.

She saw Margaret waiting for her outside her house and she gave her a little wave. They made a funny pair. Maura was tall, nearly five ten, and big-boned. She was what her father jokingly called 'a good eyeful', with her large breasts and wide hips. Her long blonde hair was backcombed up into a beehive, kept firmly in place with sugar and water, making her look even taller – like an amazon. Her eyes, still a startling blue, were now heavily made up, with black liner and white eye shadow, the false eyelashes giving her a startled doe look. In her short shirtwaist dress and white winklepicker shoes she was the height of fashion.

Margaret on the other hand was still under five feet tall. Her orange-red hair was worn bouffant, and her orange lipstick made her look like a small circus clown. She was very flat-chested but had big legs and a large behind. When they were younger the boys in the streets whistled the Laurel and Hardy music as they passed. Nowadays they took no notice if people stared at them, they were used to it.

'You managed to escape then?'

'Oh, don't talk to me about it, Marge.'

Margaret laughed her billy goat laugh.

'You'd better check in your bag. It might be bugged.'

'Don't even joke about it, Marge, I wouldn't put it past them.'

They began to walk to the bus stop.

'What's Dennis's mate like?'

'Well, he's tall and very good-looking. He's twenty-four years old.'

'What job's he got?'

Margaret shook her head. 'Dunno. Dennis did tell me but we was too busy . . . well, you know.'

'No, I don't know. And you know that. Come on, Marge, tell me. What's it like?'

Margaret pursed her bright orange lips. 'What?' Her voice was innocent.

'You know very well, Marge. A bit of the other?'

·'Maura Ryan! I am not discussing my sex life at a bus stop!'

Maura burst out laughing. 'Why not? It's never stopped you before!'

Both girls laughed and pushed each other in the chest.

'Come on, tell me.' Maura's face straightened and she looked earnestly at her little friend.

'Well, I've only done it a couple of times as you know. But . . . I like it. It's nice, but a bit embarrassing. Dennis said that I'll get over that. In fact, he says I'm a natural!' The last piece of information was given with a toss of her head.

'Oh, hark at the Duchess of Duke Street.' They both laughed again. The bus pulled up and they jumped on it, going upstairs so they could smoke.

'Two to Holborn, please.' As they lit their cigarettes Maura felt the familiar annoyance wash over her. This was another bugbear. Her brothers all smoked yet when Mickey had seen his sister smoking he had snatched the cigarette from her hand, grinding it out with his heel, shouting at her that only slags smoked. He had done it in the street in front of everyone. She had thought that she was going to die of shame. Now she could only smoke when well away from them.

They got off the bus at Holborn and got a train to Mile End, from there taking another train to Ilford. They were in Tiffany's at nine forty-five. If they got in before ten it cost only a pound. They went straight to the toilets and repaired their makeup and hair. As

78

they came out of the toilet and into the bar Maura's heart stood still in her chest. Standing beside Dennis was the best-looking man she had ever seen in her life. She looked at Margaret with a question in her eyes and when she nodded felt a burst of happiness like she had never felt before.

'Hello, darling'.' Dennis kissed Margaret on her cheek. 'Maura, this is me mate Terry. Terry, this is Maura.'

She shook the stranger's hand timidly. Terry Petherick was well over six foot. It seemed strange to Maura to look up at someone. He had dark blond hair yet his eyes were a light brown. Maura was besotted after one smile.

'Would you like a drink?' His voice was deep and it sent her pulses racing.

'Please.' Her throat was dry with nerves. 'I'll have a scotch and dry.'

She was surprised at her answer. What on earth had made her say that? She drank half of bitter normally, but somehow she couldn't say that to him. He would think her terribly unsophisticated.

'Ice?'

She nodded at him. As he took Margaret and Dennis's orders she watched him. When he went to the bar she whispered into Margaret's ear, 'He's gorgeous!'

At the bar Terry Petherick was thinking about Maura. He had been surprised at how big she was, but she was absolutely fantastic. She was incredibly sexy and didn't even realise it! As she had walked towards him he had felt a physical pain in his guts. She was like one great big present, just waiting to be unwrapped. He paid for the drinks and took them back to the others.

Maura gulped at her drink. The music seemed very loud all of a sudden. They were playing a Beatles number. 'Love Me Do' seemed to be reverberating off the walls. Maura could see Terry's lips moving but could not make out a word. She smiled and gestured that she couldn't hear him. He laughed, showing perfect white teeth, and putting his mouth to her ear, he shouted: 'Another drink?'

She looked at her glass and was amazed to find it was empty! She smiled and nodded.

When he brought her back another drink he moved close to her trying to have a conversation. 'Do you come here often?'

'No. Only in the mating season.'

The record ended just as she spoke and her voice caused people to stare at them. Terry's eyebrows went up and she felt herself blushing furiously. Why had she said that? It was a silly saying of Margaret's. Now he would think she was a tart. She could have kicked herself. She concentrated on her drink to hide her embarrassment, deciding that whisky was all right. Just like drinking ginger beer really. She noticed that it was getting very hot all of a sudden.

Terry grinned at her ruefully. 'Another?'

She was aware of the disbelief in his voice even above the din. He bought her another drink and she sipped it. A slow dance came on. Putting her glass on the bar, she went on to the dance floor with him. As it was quieter now, he began to talk to her.

'I thought I'd better dance with you in case you wanted another drink.' His voice was jocular.

'I don't drink shorts very often.'

'I thought so. Are you nervous or something?'

'Yes . . . Yes, I am.'

He smiled a funny little lopsided grin and pulled her closer. She could feel his heartbeat against her breast and it gave her a feeling of longing she had never experienced before. She closed her eyes.

'What do you do for a living?' he asked.

'I work with Marge. We're typists for a firm of accountants in Charing Cross.'

'That's right. I remember Dennis telling me now. I'm a policeman.'

He felt the change in her.

'You're a what!' Her voice sounded shocked.

'I said, I'm a policeman. What's wrong with that?' He was puzzled. Maura could hear it in his tone.

'Nothing! It's just that I've never met a policeman before.' God forgive me for lying, she thought.

He relaxed. 'Well, don't worry. I'm not on duty so I won't arrest you. Not tonight anyway.'

She tried to smile at him. Bobby Darren was crooning 'Dream Lover' and Maura stepped back into Terry's arms. They finished the dance in silence. When they went back to Dennis and Margaret, Maura picked up her drink and slugged it straight back. She signalled to Margaret and both girls went into the toilets.

As soon as they were in there Maura said: 'He's only an old Bill.'

'He ain't!' Margaret was stunned.

'Oh yes he is, Marge. What am I gonna do?'

Margaret put her finger to her bottom lip. Her tiny heart-shaped face was screwed up as she thought the problem over. She looked up at Maura.

'Do you like him, Maws?'

'Oh, yes, Marge. But a filth . . . Jesus!' Maura was nearly in tears.

'Then it's simple. Just don't tell him about your brothers.'

'Do you honestly think I could get away with it?'

Margaret grinned. 'It's a doddle!' Her green eyes widened as she thought of a plan. 'Look, Dennis obviously ain't said nothing to him about your family and I'll put him wise. He don't see that much of Terry anyway. You just carry on as if nothing's happened. Let's face it, your brothers are more well known on their own turf than around this way. Anyway, you're not responsible for them, are you?'

'No, Marge . . . I know that. But I would feel a bit snidey pretending that I don't know them.'

Margaret rolled her eyes at the ceiling. 'Look, pea brain, you're not denying them . . . you're just not mentioning them. There's a difference. Like in confession when I tell Father McCormack that I have sinned in a personal manner – I don't tell him I'm having it off, do I? It's just a matter of not letting on, that's all.'

Maura still wasn't convinced.

Margaret sighed. 'Well, it's up to you, Maws. But I think he's lovely, and you can tell a mile off that he likes you. Now let's get back to them before they send a search party out looking for us.'

Later in the evening Maura was sitting in a small Chinese restaurant with Terry. What Margaret had said earlier had been going through her mind over and over again. She tried to reason with herself. Just because he was a policeman didn't mean she couldn't go out with him, surely? She shook her head to clear it. It was all the whisky she'd had. She was drunk.

'Do you come from a large family, Maura?'

'Oh, the usual, Terry. A few brothers, that's all. How about you?'

'There's only me now. I had a brother but he died.'

Maura's heart went out to him.

'Oh . . . I'm sorry. One of my brothers died. I know how you must feel.'

'We lost Joey to cancer when he was twelve. I was sixteen at the time. Funny, though, I still miss him. How did you . . .?'

Maura looked at the tablecloth.

'He got run over. I was only a kid. I don't really remember it.' Another lie, she thought. Not a day went by but she saw Anthony's face, and superimposed on it the face of Stavros, smirking slightly as he had been in the cemetery.

No one in her family had been the same since Anthony's funeral. Her mother and father had aged dramatically overnight. Michael and the boys had become harder, more violent somehow. As for herself, she just missed him. Sometimes in the middle of a celebration, Christmas or Easter, she would think of him and the knowledge of how he had been murdered would cast a shadow over everything.

81

The food arrived. As they served themselves from the many little dishes, Maura surveyed her companion. She could really get to like Terry and the thought frightened her. She was going to murder Margaret tomorrow, going off with Dennis and leaving them like that. Now he had to take her home whether he wanted to or not.

'Eat up, Maura.' She smiled at him and brightened up. He wouldn't have asked her out for a meal if he didn't like her, she reasoned.

'Sorry. I was miles away.'

'Maura?'

'Yes.'

'Can I see you again? I don't think I've enjoyed myself so much with a girl for ages.'

He smiled at her with that lopsided grin and she was undone. Her whole body seemed to tingle with expectation. He liked her!

'Of course you can. Whenever you want!' She popped a prawn ball into her mouth and bit on it, showering him with sweet and sour sauce.

'Oh, I'm sorry!' She leant across the table to wipe his face with her napkin and knocked his glass of wine into his lap. Mortified at what she had done she leapt out of her seat and collided with a waiter, sending the plate of egg fried rice he was carrying flying through the air. She stood in the restaurant with her hand over her mouth and tears in her eyes. Terry burst out laughing, causing all the people in the restaurant to take their eyes off Maura and begin staring at him. He laughed so hard that he had a fit of coughing which, in turn, caused big tears to roll down his face. He stood up and, throwing a handful of money on the table for the bill, led a scarlet-faced and humiliated Maura out of the restaurant and into the night air.

'Now can I trust you with my car? You won't knock my wheels off or pull my radio to pieces?' Although it was said in a jocular fashion it was too much for Maura. The whisky, the heat, the Chinese food, the humiliation, and finally the cold night air all took their toll. She threw up in the gutter.

Terry rubbed her back as she heaved. When she had finished she leant against his car, gulping in the cold air. Her forehead had small beads of sweat on it that glistened in the lamp light. Her mascara was smudged under her eyes. One of her eyelashes had come unstuck. Gently he pulled it from her eyelid. Giving her his hanky, he went back to the restaurant and came back with a glass of iced water.

She stood there dejectedly looking at him, convinced that he would never want to lay eyes on her again. She looked at the red wine stain on his trousers and felt tears prickling her eyes. She frantically blinked them away.

'Feeling better now?' His voice was gentle. He handed her the glass of water. 'Drink this down and you'll feel much better, I promise you.'

She shook her head.

'Come on, drink it.' The authority in his voice surprised her and she took the glass and drank the water. The coolness eased her throat which was burning. She handed the glass back to him and he returned it to the restaurant. She breathed deeply, trying to settle her nerves.

He came back and unlocked the car, helping her into the passenger seat. As he pulled away from the kerb, he said, 'I think you drank too much.'

'It was the whisky. I've never drunk it before. Normally I drink a half of bitter.'

She looked at his profile. He looked solid, not just physically but mentally, with an air about him that denoted an inner strength. He smiled.

'Well, if it's any consolation, it happens to us all! I can remember the first time I got drunk on Scotch. I threw up all over my mum's slippers! Never touched the bloody stuff since, so you're in good company.' He poked himself in the chest. 'I can't take my drink either.'

He felt in his jacket pocket and brought out a pack of Juicy Fruits. 'Have one of these. It will freshen your mouth up.'

She took one gratefully.

'Where do you want dropping off? I know you live in Notting Hill.'

'Do you know the Bramley Arms?' He nodded. 'Well, there will do. I live nearby.'

'I'll take you right to your door.'

'No . . . That's all right. It's my dad. You know.'

He glanced at her and grinned. 'I get it. You're supposed to be coming home with Margaret.'

'That's it. He's a bit old fashioned.'

They chatted on until they came to the Bramley Arms. The water and the Juicy Fruit seemed to have done the trick because she felt great. And better still, the big hunk of man beside her made her feel terrific. He stopped the car and turned to face her.

'When will I see you then?'

'Whenever you like.'

He smiled at her eagerness. 'Let's see.' He put his head to one side as if he was thinking, closing one eye and giving his little grin. 'Tomorrow's Sunday. How about Monday night? I'll pick you up here at about seven-thirty. Is that all right?'

She nodded and he pulled her into his arms and kissed her, then waved his finger in her face and said: 'And no drinking whisky!'

She grinned and got out of the car.

'See you, Maura.'

''Bye.' She watched the car pull away. He wanted to see her again! She felt as if she could float up into the starry night. It was two in the morning and she walked the short distance to her home as if on a cushion of air. He wanted to see her again! She couldn't believe her luck!

She had a little nagging worry in the back of her mind about Mickey, but pushed it impatiently away. As Margaret had said, what people didn't know couldn't hurt them. Anyway, Mickey and the boys weren't really bad. They were just tearaways.

As she pushed the key into the lock of the front door she heard a row going on. She walked into the kitchen just in time to see Benny punch Garry in the face. She ran and stood between them.

'What on earth's going on?'

'Get out me way, Maws. I'm gonna kill that little runt.'

'Calm down, Benny. What's he done?'

'Calm down? You dozy cow! He's poached my fucking bird, that's what he's done. The no good dirty ponce!'

Garry pushed Maura out of the way and faced his brother. 'She ain't your bird. She can't stand you, she told me that herself.'

With that Benny launched himself at Garry. As they fought, their mother and father came into the room, followed by Leslie and Lee who separated their brothers.

'What the hell's all this row abaht?' Benjamin's voice was slurred as usual. He was still half drunk.

'That wanker's poached me bird, that's what.'

'For the last time, Benny, she ain't your bird.'

Leslie threw Garry across the kitchen where he fell against the fireplace. He pulled himself up slowly. Leslie pointed at him.

'What's her name?'

'Mandy Watkins.'

Leslie and Lee looked at one another and burst out laughing. 'Not Mandy Watkins from Bletchedon Street?'

Benny and Garry nodded warily. There was something going on here.

'What's she doing, Les, making a career out of the Ryans?' Lee and Leslie began hooting with glee.

'What do you mean?' This from a sullen Benny.

'Me and Lee's had her, and Geoffrey. Me and Lee had her at the same time. She's a dog.'

'You're lying, you . . .' Garry went for Leslie who grabbed his

84

arms and held him tightly, pushing his arms up behind his back expertly.

'Ain't we had her, Lee?'

He nodded, still smiling, then picked up a pack of cigarettes from the table and lit one.

'I take oath that we've all had her. Christ almighty, she's had more pricks than a second-hand dart board!'

'That's enough!' Sarah's voice echoed off the kitchen walls. 'I won't have this kind of talk. If you have no respect for me, your mother, at least have some for your sister.'

All the boys looked shamefaced.

Leslie spoke. 'Sorry, Mum. We're out of order.'

'Who wants a cuppa?' Maura tried to defuse the situation. The boys all nodded but Benjamin and Sarah went back to bed. Maura put the kettle on.

'Have a good time, Sis?'

'All right, Garry, I suppose.'

As she made the tea she thought about the way her brothers had talked about Mandy Watkins. She had known Mandy all her life. The papers might talk about the swinging sixties but the nearest most girls of Maura's age got to it was in the clothes they wore. If her brothers even suspected that she had been with a boy, all hell would break loose. She put their tea on the table. Benny and Garry were bosom pals once again. Kissing all the boys, she made her way up to bed, taking her tea with her. Her last thought before she fell asleep was the reaction she would get if they knew that she had been out with a policeman. She didn't care, though. She couldn't wait until Monday!

Chapter Eight

Margaret and Maura were in Maura's bedroom, painting their nails. They had worked out a system. On the nights that Maura saw Terry, Margaret would come to the house and they would get ready there as if they were going out together. In reality, Maura was meeting Terry and Margaret, Dennis. Maura had been seeing Terry for nearly five months, and miraculously had managed to keep him a secret. Sometimes though a terrible feeling of dread came over her. She knew that she was playing with fire but couldn't help herself. She was absolutely besotted with him.

'How's you and Den these days, Marge?'

'Great! We're getting engaged.'

Maura's eyes rounded. 'You're joking?'

'Oh no I ain't! We get on so well. He's got a good job and mine ain't that bad. We're thinking of saving up a deposit for a little house.'

Maura was impressed.

'Good luck to you, Marge. Dennis is lovely, and you can see how much he thinks of you.'

'He's all right, I suppose.' Margaret was embarrassed. 'How about you and Terry? You doo-dahed yet?'

'No, we most certainly have not!' Maura's voice sounded shocked even to her own ears. 'No disrespect to you, Marge, but I want to save myself for when I get married.' Even as she spoke she knew she was being a hypocrite. She wanted to do it more than anything in life.

Margaret laughed. 'You can't fool me, Maws. You're more worried about your brothers. It's 1966, for Christ's sake. Saving yourself for marriage, my Aunt Nellie!'

Maura ignored the jibe and started to apply mascara. 'I have all me life to do that.'

'That's just it though, ain't it? You don't! Imagine still doing it at forty!' Both girls laughed. To them forty seemed positively ancient.

'I'll think about what you said, Marge. Now can we drop the subject?'

87

'Be a damn sight better if you dropped your drawers and got it over with!'

'Marge!' Maura's voice had lost its joviality now and she sounded annoyed.

'All right, all right, keep your hair on! I'm sorry!'

'I should bloody well think so and all! You're obsessed with it.'

Margaret glanced at her watch and jumped off the bed. 'Come on, Maws. Get a move on. It's nearly a quarter past seven.'

Both girls scrambled into their coats. It was October and the nights had turned very cold. They hurried down the stairs. Michael and Geoffrey were in the hallway. Geoffrey whistled at them.

'You two look nice. Who's the lucky lads then?' Maura thought she was going to faint with fright.

Mickey glanced at Margaret and chucked her under the chin. 'You might be little, Margie, but you poke out in all the right places.'

Sarah's voice stopped Margaret from having to answer. 'Will you leave the poor girl alone! I don't know what comes over you sometimes, Michael. You can see she's embarrassed.'

He picked Margaret up and hugged her. 'She knows I'm only joking, don't you, Margie?' Margaret smiled shyly and nodded her head. He placed her gently on the floor and turned to Maura.

'Now you, Princess, you look absolutely gorgeous!' He frowned. 'I wish you'd lay off the make-up, though.'

Maura rolled her eyes up to the ceiling. 'Everyone wears their make-up like this, Mickey. It's the fashion.' Her voice, as usual when talking to Michael, was strained.

'Well, I think it suits her.' This from Garry who had just come in the front door. 'You look a cracker, girl.'

'Thanks, Gal.' Maura smiled gratefully at him. He was the only brother who allowed her to live her own life. He worked for Michael but wasn't as subservient towards him as the other boys. And though Michael acted as if he was annoyed with Garry when he spoke out of turn, Maura also got the impression that he admired Garry for it. Geoffrey snatched the books Garry was carrying from under his arm.

Garry and Geoffrey were the only readers in the family. They shared a common bond, a love of literature. The other boys revelled in baiting them about it, but in a good-natured way.

Michael put on his best voice and said, 'And what is one reading this week?'

Garry grimaced at him.

'I've read this, Gal. It's quite good. Heavy going at first, but then you can get into it.'

'I've read it before, Geoff. I like Voltaire.'

'I like revoltaire.' Michael parodied Garry's voice.

Everyone laughed. Geoffrey looked at Michael.

'In *Candide* it says, "If we do not find anything pleasant, at least we shall find something new." A very astute man. It's for that reason people like us read, ain't it, Gal?'

'Oh, for Gawd's sake, don't start on all that crap!' Mickey's voice was full of fun. 'I've read a few books in my time, and there's one thing I've learned . . . there's a difference between education and being well read.'

'Come on, Marge, before Robin Day turns up to join in the debate!'

'You saucy cow! Where you off to and we'll give you a lift?'

'Oh . . . we're just off to get the train to Holborn.'

'We'll drop you off. Come on then, Geoff, let's make tracks.'

Maura and Margaret exchanged dismayed looks.

'That's all right, Mickey. We don't want to put you out.'

'You're not. See you all.' He kissed his mother on the cheek. As he passed Garry he pretended to punch him in the arm. 'See you later, book features.'

'Tah rah, Mickey.' Garry took his books back from Geoffrey.

Inside the Mercedes, Margaret and Maura sat quietly in the back. Maura felt panic building inside her. She was meeting Terry at Holborn, and prayed her brothers would not see him there. If he came over to them she would have to introduce him, and that thought was enough to bring on near hysteria.

Michael's 280 sports car pulled out of Lancaster Road and into Bramley Street. It was already dark. As he turned the corner a police car pulled out in front of them. Slamming on the brakes, the car skidded to a halt. It was obvious to Michael and Geoffrey that the car had been waiting for them. A policeman waved Michael over to the side of the road. His face dark with temper, he parked the car.

A plainclothes policeman got leisurely out of the Panda car and walked across the road to them. He looked at the tax disc on the windscreen and motioned Michael to wind down his window. 'Insurance certificate, please.' Michael already had it in his hand.

The policeman took it and studied it.

'Well, well, well. I never thought I would see a Ryan driving a new Merc with all the rent paid.'

'Well, officer, we live and learn, don't we. Now fuck off!'

'That's not very nice, Mickey. You should have a bit more respect for the boys in blue.' The voice dripped sarcasm. 'It looks like pimping in the West End is a lucrative business. Who's that in the back? A couple of new girls?'

The policeman was knocked off his feet as Michael jumped from the car.

Geoffrey was trying to drag him back by holding on to his overcoat. He could see what the police were trying to do. They wanted Mickey to lose that famous temper of his so they could legitimately nick him.

'That's my sister you're talking about, you ponce!'

Two uniformed policemen got out of the Panda car and joined their boss. Geoffrey got out of the car and stood in front of Michael, willing him to calm down. If Mickey went berserk here there were too many witnesses.

Michael pushed him out of the way. 'No one talks about my family like that and gets away with it. Do you hear me?'

The two uniforms stood in front of their boss to protect him. They were both terrified. It was true what they had heard: he was crazy all right. 'Mad Mickey' they called him. Since the Krays had been sent down, Mickey Ryan was the Number One. The only one left of all the big-time crooks. And unlike the Krays and the Richardsons, Michael Ryan was as cunning as a fox.

'So that's your sister in there, is it? I'm sorry, Michael. It was an easy mistake to make. I should have guessed because you don't have a lot of time for girls, do you?' He was goading again. He noticed that the veins were standing out on Michael's forehead and against his will felt a surge of apprehension. Geoffrey tried to save the situation. He grabbed Mickey's arm.

'They're trying to wind you up. Ignore them. If you blow your top, they'll nick you double quick.'

Michael's breathing was returning to normal. Geoffrey faced the plainclothes officer. 'Look, what do you want?'

The man ignored him and carried on talking to Michael. 'Can't your club run without you? I heard you had a very good doorman. Gerry Jackson, ain't it? Another brainless Mick . . .'

Michael shook his head in disbelief.

'If I'm not mistaken, you're Detective Inspector Murphy, ain't you? So you would know all about brainless Micks, wouldn't you?'

The two uniforms laughed and the Inspector was annoyed. 'I wasn't born in Ireland, Ryan.'

'Neither was I, nor any of my brothers. Neither was Gerry Jackson, by the way. Now why don't you take these two little boys home? It's way past their bedtime.' The two uniforms sobered up instantly. Michael was calm now. Maura got out of the car and went to him.

'Can my brothers and I go now, please?'

The uniforms were giving her the once-over. One of them smiled at her.

'Who are you smiling at?' Michael's voice was loud. The young uniform was in a quandary. He didn't want to answer Michael, but at the same time didn't want to look like a coward. He was saved from answering by the DI.

'Very attractive girl, Michael.' He smiled at Maura, feeling a little bit sorry for her. He looked at her feet. In her winkle picker shoes they looked enormous. 'Do your feet go right to the end of those?'

He tried to sound jocular. She was only a kid. He had a daughter about that age himself. Maura looked at him with the arrogance of youth.

'Do their heads go right to the top of their helmets?' She jerked her head in the uniforms' direction.

Everyone looked at her in amazement. Michael and Geoffrey burst out laughing, surprised at Maura's front, but proud of her all the same.

'Now, Mr Murphy, can we go? Or would you like to ask us some more questions? Only I don't know about you, but we're very busy people.' She was as surprised as everyone else at her outburst. But she was annoyed. What gave this man the right to speak to people like he did! She would bet her last pound that her Terry didn't carry on like that. She got back into the car with Margaret. Now the excitement had worn off she was shaking.

She heard the DI saying, 'I'm gonna have you, Ryan.'

Michael laughed softly. 'Yeah, Murphy. Of course you are.'

Without bothering to speak again Michael and Geoffrey got back in the Mercedes. The three police stood watching them. Murphy knew when he was beaten and decided to retreat on this occasion. He made a mental note to have Maura Ryan checked out. Young girl she might be, but she was as streetwise as her brothers. She had made a fool of him and he wouldn't let that go. Once the uniforms had told their version in the canteen, he would be a laughing stock.

In the car everyone was congratulating her.

'Oh, Maura, how could you?' Margaret's voice was filled with awe.

'She's a Ryan, Margie. And she showed that tonight! I thought I was going to piss myself. Murphy's face!' Michael was roaring with laughter. 'I'll tell you something though, Geoff. I'll do for that bastard one day. I take oath on that. He winds me up!'

'You get wound up too easily. They can't touch us, Bruv. They can't prove nothing!' Geoffrey stressed the last two words.

'I thought we was all gonna get nicked!' Margaret's voice was still quavery. Michael looked in the mirror and caught her eye.

'I can just see you in Holloway, Marge. Them big butch warders would all be after a little thing like you!'

'Aaow, don't!' She put her hand over her mouth.

'Don't be rotten, Mickey. Marge, he's winding you up. What on earth would they nick us for?'

'That Murphy's all talk. He couldn't nick himself shaving.'

They all laughed and joked until they got to Holborn. Maura was praying that Terry was not about. Her prayers were answered. When she and Margaret got out of the car, Michael and Geoff drove off immediately.

'Sod that, Maura, I thought we was gonners there!'

'I know Mickey's my brother, but he scares even me when he gets annoyed.'

'Don't you think he's a bit weird, Maws? I mean, one minute he's foaming at the mouth and the next . . . laughing and joking.' Michael's quicksilver temperament made Margaret nervous. Maura was annoyed.

'No, Marge, I don't actually!'

'I wasn't criticising him, Maws . . .'

'He likes you, Marge. He always makes you feel welcome when you're round our house. There's nothing wrong with Mickey. He's just . . . highly strung.'

In her heart Maura agreed with Margaret's opinion of Michael, but she would never admit it openly. Maura was more like her brothers than she cared to think about. There was a loyalty in her family that would not, and could not, be understood by outsiders.

Margaret was contrite. 'I'm sorry, Maws. Here, imagine the old Bill thinking we was old brasses!' She tried to lighten the atmosphere between them.

Maura giggled. 'Bloody cheek!'

They stood outside the station until Dennis came up.

When Margaret and he had gone, Maura thought about what had happened. Tonight she had discovered a new side to herself. She had not intended to say what she had. It just came out. She shrugged and pulled her coat tighter around her. It was getting cold. She saw Terry walking towards her and smiled at him. The familiar lurch in her breast that always heralded his approach left her breathless. She ran into his arms for a kiss.

'Hello, Princess!' Maura froze in his arms then pulled away from him.

'Do me a favour, Terry. Don't ever call me that again.' Her voice was frosty. Terry couldn't believe her attitude.

'I'm sorry, Maura. I . . .' He held out his arms in supplication. Maura could see that he was bewildered.

'Look, it's no big deal. It's just that I hate that expression, that's all.' Her voice was rising.

'All right. Keep your hair on!' He was annoyed and she knew it.

'Terry.' She drew his name out softly and slipped her arm through his.

'What?' His voice was flat and expressionless. He had really been looking forward to seeing her tonight. Then, within two minutes, she had started an argument with him. He couldn't believe it.

'I'm sorry, Terry.' Her voice was small.

He relaxed. 'Let's forget it. I've booked a table for us up West in a snazzy restaurant.' He saw her face fall again. Now what was the matter with her?

Maura was in a state of acute agitation. She couldn't go up West with him! Supposing Mickey saw her? Or one of her other brothers? Not to mention all the people who worked for them. They all knew her. Michael might come into the restaurant to say hello! She felt faint just thinking about it.

'Are you all right? You've gone very white.' His voice was all concern. Maura's mind was reeling.

'I feel a bit under the weather. I haven't eaten all day. Can't we eat around here?' She knew she was clutching at straws but nothing would get her up the West End.

'But I booked the table especially. We're celebrating.'

'Celebrating what?'

'Never you mind. I'll tell you when we get to the restaurant.'

Oh, God, please help her.

'Oh, let's stay around here . . . please. I don't fancy travelling back up West.' Her voice was wheedling. He couldn't help smiling. She was some girl! Not two minutes in his company and she was biting his head off. Now she didn't want to go to an expensive restaurant in the West End. He shook his head at her.

'All right. You win as usual. What's it to be? Indian? Greek? What?'

Maura felt the tension drain out of her. She kissed him hard on the mouth.

'Greek, please. I just love taramasalata!'

She tucked her arm into his. Twenty minutes later they were sitting in a little restaurant drinking retsina.

'So what are we celebrating then?'

'I've been given a transfer. I applied for it about six months ago. Anyway, today I was told that it had been passed. From next month I will be at Vine Street! That's why I wanted to go up West tonight. Get the feel of the place.' He grinned at her.

Maura felt herself smile in response. She felt the muscles in her face moving. 'What exactly will you be doing up there?'

'It's hard to explain really. There's a lot of illegal gambling up there, always has been, as well as prostitution and drugs.'

The waiter placed two moussakas in front of them.

'Anyway, some firms – that's gangs to you – are using the hostess clubs as a front for many other things. Guns, blackmail . . . the list is endless. Well, I'll be a very small cog in the wheel that's trying to stamp it all out.'

'I see.' Maura was finding it increasingly difficult to swallow.

'You don't see, but never mind, love. You'll never have to worry about it. Or are you a closet villain?' She laughed with him, amazed that she was still able to function normally while her insides were doing the Twist!

'How about a toast to your new job?'

'I'll drink to that, Maura.'

They clinked glasses and Terry chattered on.

'It's so exciting. Do you know that there's men running clubs up there who would murder somebody like you or me would have a cup of tea? It's unbelievable. I tell you.'

She stared into her glass of wine. What was she worried about anyway? Michael wasn't involved with anything like that. And drugs? Never!

But a little nagging voice at the back of her mind kept reminding her of the way he had blown up the taxi rank after Anthony died. A little voice was whispering: 'They all work for Michael now.'

She pushed the thoughts firmly from her mind, forcing herself to concentrate on what Terry was saying. All the while icy fingers were touching the back of her neck – ghostly reminders of the past. Later on, when they left the restaurant arm in arm, she shivered. Terry pulled her closer to him.

'I want you, Maura.'

'I want you too, Terry.' And she was surprised because she meant it. At this moment she wanted him more than she had ever wanted anything in her life.

'Really?' His voice was husky with longing.

'Yes . . . really.'

'Oh, Maura, you don't know how much I wanted to hear you say that.' He clasped her hand and pulled her to his car. 'Come on, before you change your mind.'

'Where are we going?'

'You'll find out.'

She felt the thrill of sexual anticipation sweep over her body, wiping everything from her mind except Terry, herself, and their need.

Inside the car he kissed her, long and hard. He fumbled in his pocket and took out a key.

'Do you see this?' Maura nodded. 'Well, it's a key to a flat in

Islington. I rented it today. Not for this, Maura, I swear. But to be nearer my job. All that's in it is a bed and a camping stove, but it's home for us . . . if that's what you really want.'

Maura loved him just for those words. He wasn't trying to force her into anything.

'I want to go to your flat in Islington, Terry.'

He kissed her again and then started up the car. Tonight was his lucky night.

On the way to the flat, Terry had stopped and bought a bottle of wine. Maura sat nervously on the edge of the big double bed while he opened the bottle and brought her a glass. She took it from him. The bedroom had large bay windows covered with grubby nets. Grantbridge Street was the centre of bedsitterland. Even now, record players and radios could be heard. Occasionally a shout or a loud laugh broke the gloom. There was no light in the bedroom, only the moonlight and the subdued glare of the streetlights outside the window. Maura was glad. She drank the wine and placed the empty glass on the floor by the bed. Terry walked out to the kitchen, talking as he moved.

'It doesn't look much now, I know, but you wait until I've finished it – decorated it, I mean. Hey, why don't you help me? We could go to Camden Market together and pick out some furniture.' He walked back into the bedroom with the bottle of wine. 'What do you say?' His voice was eager.

Maura caught some of his enthusiasm. 'I'd love it.'

He refilled her glass and gave it to her.

'Look, Maura, you don't have to sleep with me, you know.' His voice was caressing. 'I'll understand if you're not ready.'

She looked up. In the half-light he looked boyish. She traced the contours of his face with her finger.

'I am sure, Terry. In fact, I'm positive!'

He sat on the bed beside her and kissed her gently. 'Well, as long as you're sure.'

He stood up and removed his shirt. Maura watched him, fascinated. The muscles of his arms and chest were rippling as he moved and she felt a hot flush creeping over her body. She took a deep breath and slipped off her coat. The room was not very warm and she felt goosebumps on her arms. Her dress fastened up the front and she began to undo the buttons. She could sense his eyes on her and felt a sudden bashfulness. She had never in her life undressed in front of a man – not even a doctor. She came to the last button and, plucking up all her courage, slipped the dress off her shoulders and let it drop to the floor.

Terry watched her. His throat was dry and his breathing heavy.

Standing there in the moonlight in her underwear she looked magnificent. Her breasts were huge – like giant orbs in the confines of her bra, spilling over the top like overripe melons. He couldn't believe his luck. She was like a larger than life fantasy that had just come true. He dragged his eyes from her breasts to her long legs. He was surprised at how small her waist was. She was like some voluptuous painting by Titian. He could feel himself hardening.

He slipped off his trousers and went to her. Putting his arms around her back he unhooked her bra, letting her opulent breasts free. He pulled the brassiere from her body and dropped it on to the floor. Instinctively her arms crossed over her chest. He gently pulled them away, staring down at her body. He groaned.

'Oh, Maura. You're beautiful . . . You're so beautiful!' He pressed his lips against her nipples and she jumped. She could feel them hardening under his tongue and was caught between pure ecstasy and an urge to run from the room. Her heart was hammering in her breast and her breathing was irregular. She could feel herself panting. He squeezed both her breasts together and licked and chewed on her nipples, sending delicious waves of euphoria through her. He pulled her gently on to the bed. They fell together, their arms and legs entwined. He loomed over her.

'I love you, Maura. God, I love you.'

If he never said it again, the way he had just expressed himself to her would last for the rest of her life. She felt his fingers hook into either side of her panties, and as she felt him pull them down her body she closed her eyes. It was finally happening. The mystery of man and woman was about to be unfurled before her. She bit on her lip, an exquisite agony tearing her apart. Her natural shyness was trying to overcome a new, bigger, and more intense feeling.

Unaware that she had even done it, Maura opened her legs wide. As his tongue flicked over her thighs she groaned out loud. Slowly, he pushed his forefinger inside her. She was like a juicy peach.

Terry was in a fever of excitement. Who would have dreamed she would be so fiery the first time? She was like an experienced woman, the way she moved her body and opened herself up to him. He loved everything about her – the way she looked, the way she acted – everything. He especially loved the smell of her.

Maura felt him push himself up on his arms. She opened her eyes, and as he straddled her watched his swollen member trying to push into her. Her eyes opened wide. It was too big, surely? She pushed her elbows into the bed to pull herself up, but she was too late. She felt a tearing pain as if Terry pushed against some kind of obstacle. Then she felt a wave of dizziness as he slipped right up inside her. As he moved backwards and forwards she thrust her hips up to meet him at every stroke, a jumble of feelings and emotions raging through them both. Suddenly, she felt a shuddering somewhere in her bowels. It seemed to be slowly creeping into her groin and up . . . up into her stomach. She arched her back, and as she lost control in the final throes of orgasm felt Terry biting on her breasts. She called out . . . All self-consciousness seemed to dissolve in this all-encompassing feeling. She was aware that she was wailing and moaning, but she didn't care. This feeling was too good, too exciting to let go of. She felt her legs grab Terry's thighs and was trying desperately to push him further inside her.

Above her Terry was watching her, fascinated. As he felt his own orgasm beginning to pulsate he felt her legs gripping him and drove his penis into her as hard as he could, bursting inside her like a dam.

They lay together, their bodies bathed in sweat, their hearts beating a tattoo on each other's chests. Terry kissed her gently, little tiny kisses, all over her face and neck. He licked her throat and tasted the saltiness of her.

'That was fantastic, Maura.'

She lay beneath him, shy again, amazed at her own feelings.

'Thank you, Maura. For letting me be the first. And if it lies with me, I will be your last. You're my girl now. You'll always be my girl.'

He kissed her again and was surprised to find that she was crying gently. He was immediately concerned. 'I didn't hurt you too much, did I?'

'No, you didn't hurt me. I'm crying because I'm happy. That's all.'

He gathered her into his arms and held her tightly. He had promised himself that he would not get too involved with her, but at this moment he could no more have parted from her than he could have cut his own throat.

Maura felt the heightened awareness that comes with love-making. That feeling of infinite perception that envelops lovers in its embrace. She was acutely aware that she had burnt her boats. That she now belonged to the man lying with her. That her family had taken a back seat in her life. But she was also aware that no matter how she felt, her family would never allow her to relegate them to second place. The fact that Terry was a policeman would be enough for Michael. He would never countenance her having an association with one. He would take it as a personal affront.

She felt Terry's hand running over her body, kneading her breasts and shoulders, and was caught up in a feeling of presentiment. They were doomed and she knew it. She closed her eyes

97

tightly, praying to her God to take pity on them. To help them find a way out of the morass they had jumped into. She wished fervently that they might be allowed to be together, that nothing would happen to make them part. And even as she prayed and wished, she knew, deep inside, that it was all useless. But with the foolishness of youth, she convinced herself that somehow, somewhere, there was an answer to their problem.

Finally, she abandoned herself to him once again, the moonlight playing on their bodies as they loved each other with a strength that surprised them both. Their whispering and low moans echoed around the empty flat, like ghosts that danced on the ceiling with their shadows.

Maura had never dreamt that she could feel like she felt at this moment. She had indeed burnt her boats. But she smiled while she did it.

Chapter Nine

Benjamin Ryan pushed his wife out of his way. He was drunk as usual, but today, instead of his normal boisterous drunkenness, he was in a violent, vindictive frame of mind.

Sarah watched him warily. Ever since Anthony's death her husband had suffered these fits of depression. His face was bloated and red-veined. His large nose was reddened and bulbous. His dark blue eyes, inherited by all the children, were now listless, the whites a sepia colour, like an old photograph. He looked terrible. His once black hair was grey, hanging across his face in greasy tendrils. Sarah shook her head sadly. He was grey-skinned and the weight that had once given him an air of affability had dropped off him, leaving only a large beergut that hung offensively over his trousers. He stalked across the bedroom to her. Sarah put her hands up to her face through years of habit. The chances were that she was going to get a good hiding. She braced herself for the blows.

'I want some money, Sar . . . I'm warning you.'

His breath was sour and she tried to turn her face away from him. He grasped her chin with his hand and pulled her face towards him. He grinned at her, showing yellowing teeth. 'What's the matter then? Turning your face away from me these days?' He squeezed her chin in his large hand, causing her to flinch. 'That's right, my lovely . . . You be scared of me, because if you don't give me some of the money you've got stashed, I'm gonna beat you all around this room. Now where is it?'

Sarah was trying desperately to pull herself away from him. He pulled his right arm back and punched her in the stomach. He used such force she fell to her knees, winded.

He grabbed her hair, forcing her head up to look at him. 'That's just a taster, Sarah.'

She nursed her injured stomach with her arm, feeling sick. She stared at her husband, and gathering all her strength she spat at him. She saw his lips draw back over his teeth.

'You old trout! I'll bloody murder you for that.'

As his fist was raised to begin his beating she screamed, holding her arms over her head. His first punch hit her on her wrist, causing her to cry out in pain. Somewhere above the din she heard the bedroom door opening, then she felt Benjamin being pulled away from her bodily. It was Garry and Lee.

Lee felt a rush of emotion he had never known before. Seeing his mother kneeling there while his father beat her caused him to lose control. He was aware that he was punching and kicking his father. He could feel the surge of adrenaline as his arms and legs came into contact with Benjamin's body. He could easily kill this man who had fathered him. Eventually Garry pulled him away, forcing him to sit on the big double bed. His breathing was loud and noisy. The effort he had used on his father had exhausted him. He felt his mother's arm go around his shoulder. He grasped her rough workworn hand. His knuckles were bleeding.

Benjamin was too drunk to feel anything. He lay on the bedroom floor staring up at a picture of Our Lady's Ascension into Heaven. Her pale blue and gold gown was swimming before his eyes. He could taste blood in his mouth. Running his tongue around his gums, he found that one of his few remaining teeth was loose. Garry looked at his father with a feeling of disgust coupled with distress. The older man's woeful face was like an open book. All the setbacks, troubles, humiliations and causes for discontent were there for anyone who wanted to look. Only nobody ever wanted to. Even his own sons regarded him as an object of derision, tempered with a love that came more from duty than any feeling of filial affection. Garry sighed.

'Help him up, son. We'll put him to bed to sleep the worst of it off.' Sarah's voice was flat, resigned. Before the boys had grown up, she would have endured the beating; years of experience had taught her that it was preferable to giving him the money.

Garry and Lee, calmer now, put their father to bed. Benjamin was pliable. He allowed his sons to strip him and bundle him under the covers. Within minutes he was asleep. The three went down the stairs together. In the kitchen Lee examined his mother's arms and face. She shrugged him off.

'I'm all right, Lee. Give it a rest now, for Gawd's sake.' She made one of her endless cups of tea.

Garry took his and went back upstairs to his room. He placed the tea on his dressing table and went back to what he had been doing before his mother's scream. He was making a car bomb. The main work had already been done in one of Michael's lock-ups. Now he was perfecting the detonator. He took his glasses off the bed where he had left them earlier and slipped them on.

Garry's years of being the inventor of the family had paid off.

Michael had taken his expertise and channelled it to his own advantage. Garry made everything, from molotov cocktails to delayed-action devices for robberies or personal revenge attacks. His natural misanthropy and lack of interest in possessions gave him the perfect temperament for an explosives manufacturer. In Garry's mind there was no black or white, just fuzzy grey areas that he could interpret to his own advantage. Like Michael, he was a psychopath. He could champion causes with a fervour that amazed those around him. He could also see two sides to an argument, could balance the debate in his mind or that of whoever happened to be interested. But there was another side to him that even his own brothers did not realise. He would not stand for anyone or anything getting in *his* way. He had no real feelings about anyone, except his sister Maura. He was incapable of deep feelings or emotion. If Garry had a girl friend, she was his property. He would be jealous and moody. The girl always seemed to think this was because he felt deeply for her, but Garry felt the same way about his car or his record player. It was *his*. Until the time came when he tired of it.

The bedroom door opened and Lee came in. 'Mickey just phoned and said that we're all to meet him at the club tonight. Nine-thirty, OK?'

'All right, Lee. Thanks.' Garry carried on with what he was doing. Lee walked out of the room. The earlier trouble with their father was now forgotten. In the Ryan code, if you didn't mention it then it had never happened. When Benjamin had slept off his drink and emerged once again into their world he would be treated with the usual haphazard affection.

Garry had finished his detonator and smiled to himself happily. He began clearing away. His room was so tidy, Garry would know if anyone had been in while he was out. He had everything strategically placed.

Like all the rooms in the house, this also had a religious print on the wall and a small crucifix over the bedroom door. Garry's religious painting was of Jesus's entrance into Jerusalem on Palm Sunday. Jesus sat on a donkey, the marks of the stigmata on his outstretched hands, his face as always serene with a hint of sadness. Around him were crowds of people holding their palm leaves, expressions of ecstasy on their faces. The print was in beautiful pastel shades of blue and pink. Picking up the detonator, Garry went to the picture. Holding the device under the Donkey of Christ, he laughed softly.

'Bang fucking bang!'

Jesus still sat there, the yellows and golds of his halo shadowed by Garry's body, still serene and still sad.

Mickey, Geoffrey and Roy sat in the offices above their club, Le Buxom, in Dean Street. All three were wearing the usual dark suit, brilliant white shirt and thin black tie. It was their uniform. Michael's tie had a grey stripe going through it horizontally. It was his way of being just that little bit different. He lit a cigarette and blew the smoke out noisily.

'So what else have you found out then?' He stared at Geoffrey.

'Plenty. He's a bit of a rogue, is old Hanley. He likes the gee gees for a start, and he's not averse to a bit of skirt now and again either. Both expensive pastimes for old Bill. He usually goes round to the wives of convicted criminals offering them a bit of consolation.'

Mickey laughed. 'In return for a bit of the other, I suppose.'

'Exactly. He now owes us about three hundred quid. He was betting quite heavily in our South London shops. I tipped the lads the wink to give him as much tick as he wanted, which they did. Now we have him right where we want him. By the short and curlies.'

'Good work, Geoff. Arrange for him to come and see me next week. Another face would be to our advantage. Especially a prat like Hanley.'

'How about we give him a free night here, before you see him? Let him have his leg over with one of the girls for nix. That should soften him up before you give him the bad news.'

'Yeah, I think that's what we'll do, Roy. Bent filth are ten a penny these days. What we want are the ones who can do us the most good. Hanley's at Vine Street, from what I understand. He's the one who liaises with all the other nicks. We'll cultivate him, I think.'

Geoffrey and Roy nodded in agreement.

'Now about the loan sharking. I had a visitor today . . . do you remember old Moses Mabele?'

Roy nodded. 'The old West Indian bloke who lived in our street?'

'That's him. His wife Verbeena was mates with Muvver. Used to help her out now and again with money. Old Moses used to work in the Docks.'

'Yeah. What about them?' Geoffrey's voice was puzzled.

'Well, they moved Plaistow way. They got one of the old Dockers' Mansions – he was working in the East India Docks. Anyway, to cut a long story short, Moses popped off a bit sudden like . . .'

'What's this got to do with us?'

'Well, if you'd listen, you might learn something, Roy. Now where was I?'

'Moses had popped off.'

'Thanks, Geoffrey. Moses popped off a bit sharpish and Verbeena couldn't afford to bury him like. So she went to one of our "borrowers" – no prizes for guessing who that was.'

Geoffrey groaned. 'Not George Denellan!'

Mickey smirked. 'The one and only. Anyway, the rub is she couldn't pay it back quick enough and Georgie boy sent round some heavies . . .'

'You're joking!'

'I wish I was, Roy. I bunged her a couple of ton for her trouble and told her the debt was scrubbed. What I want you two to do is go and see Denellan. Put him straight about a few things. She's an old lady, for Christ's sake. I want at least an arm broken. He's got to learn that he works for me, not the government. You don't belt old dears. In fact, you don't lend money to old dears, period, not without querying it with one of us first. He takes too much on himself and he's beginning to aggravate me.'

'I'll go, Mickey. I don't like Denellan anyway, he's a ponce.'

'All right then, Roy, you can sort him out. What an advert for us, eh? Beating up old ladies!'

They all laughed.

Geoffrey got up and poured them all a drink. 'What's happening with that Smithson, Mickey?'

Michael took the glass off him and sipped the brandy. 'Our Garry's made him a little surprise present. He should be getting it some time over the weekend.'

'You're definitely trouncing him them?'

'Yep. I don't like doing it, Geoff, but that saucy bugger's asked for it.' He poked his finger in the air. 'Nobody tucks me up and gets away with it. It'll be a lesson to all the blokes who work for us.'

'How much exactly did he poach?'

'Nigh on two grand.'

Roy whistled softly. 'That much?'

'It's not so much the money as the principle of the thing. One bloke owed us a monkey. He paid three oners over, and then the last two hundred plus the fifty quid interest. Next thing he knows he's got three blokes waiting for him as he leaves for work. They'd trashed his motor.' Mickey laughed softly. 'The poor bastard is informed that he still owes three hundred smackers. Anyway, he paid it . . . but he came to see our Lee and he told me about it and that's how we uncovered the little bastard's game. Fuck me! It ain't as if we don't pay him enough. For a bloke who came out of the South London slums he's done bloody well. Do you know, his kids go to private school? Straight up.'

103

'That don't surprise me, Mickey, he always fancied himself. He still brags in pubs about how he worked for the Richardsons.'

Michael snorted. 'Don't talk to me about him. He's history now.'

The three men were quiet for a few moments. Geoffrey got up from his chair. 'Shall I bring the other lot up then? See what's happening with their teams?'

'Yeah. Hang on, what's the time?'

'Eleven-thirty-five.'

'I bet you a tenner Benny's sitting in the club watching the stripper. She comes on at half-past.'

They all laughed.

'He's sex mad. Most of the girls don't have to "go case" with the punters, they can go home with Benny!'

Still laughing, Geoffrey made his way down the stairs to the club's foyer.

Gerry Jackson, the doorman, nodded at him. 'We're pretty full tonight, mostly Americans. Must be a convention on somewhere.'

'Plenty of money then?'

Gerry nodded. 'The touts reckon that the streets are full of them. I bet a few get rolled, don't you?'

'Bound to, ain't they? Stupid bastards. They flash their money about like it's going out of fashion. Someone's got to stomp them, it stands to reason.'

Geoffrey walked into the club itself. The air was thick with cigarette smoke and cheap perfume. At the bar area seats lined each wall to either side. They were plush red velvet, were upholstered and fixed to the wall. On them sprawled women and girls of every shape and colour. On entering the club, punters were able to see the merchandise and if a particular girl took their fancy, she accompanied them to their table. The hostesses were only allowed to drink champagne – which they tipped on to the carpet when the punter wasn't looking. With a different stripper on every twenty minutes this was not difficult. At the moment a tall blonde of about thirty was dancing semi-naked to 'Pretty Flamingo'. She bent over almost double and her long bleached blonde hair touched the floor. She swayed her buttocks suggestively before hooking her fingers into her sequinned panties and slowly pulling them down her legs.

Geoffrey smiled. Sure enough there was Benny, sitting on the edge of his seat, his tongue poking out of his mouth as he watched the girl in a state of hypnotic fascination. Stepping out of her panties, the stripper stood up and turned to face the audience. Her pubic hair was black, in stark contrast to the whiteness of her hair.

104

She raised her arms above her head and once more set the tassels on her small breasts spinning.

The music ended and she nonchalantly picked up her discarded clothes and walked from the stage. She would strip in six or seven different clubs during the course of the evening. She passed by Benny and Geoffrey saw him squeeze her buttocks. The girl smacked his hand away and glared at him, shouting at the top of her voice, 'When you're old enough, Little Boy!'

Benny laughed good-naturedly. Geoffrey called him and he walked over, his moon face wreathed in smiles.

'You never give up, Ben, do you?'

Benny grinned. 'Old slag! She's got a face like a carpenter's nailbag. Let's face it, I don't want to *marry* her, just fuck her.'

'Well, she obviously don't want to fuck you.'

Benny tapped his nose with his finger and winked lewdly. 'She will. It's just a matter of wearing her down! She'll come round in the end.'

Geoffrey laughed. 'You'll wear your dick out if you're not careful. Where's the others?'

'In the back bar as usual. You know they don't like sitting with the peasants!'

'Get upstairs, you ponce. Mickey's waiting for you. I'll go and get the others.'

He walked across the dance floor. All round the walls were large photographs of women in various stages of undress. Geoffrey stopped at a table where a small bald-headed man was sitting with two girls. He smiled at the girls warmly and shook the man's hand.

'How is everything, sir?' His voice was solicitous.

The small man grinned, showing expensive-looking teeth. 'Just fine, son. These here two ladies is just about as fine as you could get.' His voice had a southern drawl. The two girls giggled. Geoffrey noticed that one of them was high.

'I'm glad to hear it, sir. We like all our guests to enjoy themselves.' He nodded at the man and moved away from the table, his eyes taking in everything that was going on around him. One of the hostesses, a young lady who called herself Shirelle, had her head buried in a man's lap. Geoffrey sighed with annoyance and, pulling back a curtain at the end of the dance floor, walked into the back bar.

'What on earth's going on here?' His voice was loud. Two hostesses were sitting at a table. Geoffrey recognised them as Liverpool twins who Denise, the head girl, had taken on a few days previously. They were tiny little things with wide brown eyes and mousy blonde hair. They were not particularly pretty but their attraction was that they only worked together. They had little half-formed breasts and were no more than fifteen. From what he had gleaned they had been toms for quite a while. Looking at them, it was obvious they had been roughed up.

Garry spoke. 'We caught these two "doing a dolly".'

Geoffrey was stunned. 'You're joking!'

'Oh no I ain't! Me and Lee were walking across the dance floor to come in here and I saw them, as plain as day. One of them slipped her arms around the bloke and kissed him on the mouth. While she was doing it she lifted his wallet and passed it to the other one. They've obviously done it before because it was all over in a split second. In fact, if I'd have blinked I'd have missed it. The slags!'

Both girls looked at Geoffrey with frightened eyes. In Soho you could be striped up for less. No clubs liked their punters rolled. It brought them to the attention of the police – the last thing a hostess club needed.

'Where's the wallet now?'

'I've got it, Geoff. It's got over three hundred quid in it.'

He gave a low whistle.

'Look, Lee, go back in there and tell the punter that the girls had to go somewhere. I noticed as I passed through that Monique and Cynthia are still up in the meat seats. Bring them to him. They're good girls. Pretend to find the wallet under the table. Make a big thing out of it. Oh, you know what to do.'

'What about these two?' Garry nodded at the girls.

'Sling them out. Give them a slap, Garry, but don't go too far. All right.'

Garry nodded at him.

'When you've finished, get your arses upstairs. Mickey's waiting for you.'

He stormed out of the back bar and went to where Denise was standing. She was nearly fifty years old and weighed in at seventeen stone. Her face was heavily made up and she wore too much rhinestone jewellery. She had been a prostitute for over thirty years. Her bright orange hair was piled up high on her head, and somehow she had squeezed her enormous bulk into a lurex two-piece. Her huge pendulous breasts spilled over the top. She smelt of gin and Parma violets.

'I want a word with you, Denise. Garry and Lee just caught those scouse birds "doing a dolly".'

'Look, sonny, I ain't got eyes up me arse, you know. There's over thirty brasses in here. I can't watch them all.'

'Well, my advice to you, Denise, is to get some eyes put up there then! And in the back of your head. That slag Shirelle was giving a punter a blow job earlier. Now either get your act together or you

106

get another job! This is my last warning.'

He stormed off before she could answer him. Shrugging her ample shoulders, she cursed him in her head.

One of the girls on the meat seats had heard the exchange. She shouted to Denise: 'What's the matter then? You been a naughty girl?' All the other girls laughed.

Denise curled her lips back from her broken teeth. 'Oh, go fry your shite!'

The girl made a face at her and called out, 'She's a silver-tongued bastard, ain't she, girls?'

Denise picked up her Sobranie cigarette from an ashtray and pulled on it, stifling an urge to put it out on the girl's face.

She'd murder that bloody Shirelle!

Detective Inspector Murphy was driving home to his house in Putney. Since his run-in with Maura Ryan he had been doing some snooping and what he had found out had given him food for thought. She was as clean as a whistle, never even been cautioned, but she had an Achilles heel and he had found out what it was. Tomorrow morning a certain young DC was going to get a shock. He smiled to himself. He quite liked young Petherick as well! He began to whistle a little tune. He would teach Maura Ryan a lesson she shouldn't forget. If there was one thing he hated, it was mouthy young women.

Maura got out of bed and began to get dressed. Terry lay for a while watching her. She was the sexiest girl he had ever known. The secret of her allure was the fact that she was completely unaware of it. She sat on the edge of the bed and smoothed her stockings up her legs. He pulled her backwards and kissed her, fondling her breasts.

'Is it my imagination or are your boobs getting bigger?'

Maura pulled away from him. 'Don't be so rude!' She pursed her lips. 'Come on, Tel, get dressed. You've got to run me home.'

He got off the bed and stretched himself lazily. 'I wish you didn't have to go.' His voice was childlike.

'Well, I have. And soon. So hurry up.' She picked up a pillow and threw it at him. He caught it and threw it back, knowing it would cause a pillow fight. Five minutes later they lay semi-naked on the bed, both trying to catch their breath.

'I love you, Terry.' Maura's voice was low.

'And I love you, Maura. More than you think.'

She smiled at him. She hoped that what he said was true, because tomorrow she was going to find out whether she was indeed pregnant. She bit her lip. There was going to be murder, she could feel it in her bones.

Michael arranged to see Lee on his own. His brother stood in front of him, his face pale. As far as he knew he had done nothing wrong.

'That right you give the old man a hammering today?'

Lee swallowed noisily. 'He was belting the old woman.'

Michael smiled one of his radiant smiles that seemed to light him up from inside. 'You did good, Lee. Remember this . . . you always look after the womenfolk. You never, ever let anyone hurt them, no matter who they are. I'm proud of you, Lee.'

Lee smiled with relief.

'I'll bung the old man a few bob tomorrow. He'll be as sweet as a nut. Now get yourself off home.'

Lee left the little office with his heart singing. He could hear the first few bars of 'Jailhouse Rock' and hurried down into the club. The girl who stripped to this particular record was a six foot amazon with olive skin, jet black hair, large brown eyes, and the biggest tits he had ever seen in his life! He settled down next to Benny, who being a thoughtful kind of boy had saved him a seat!

Chapter Ten

'Detective Constable Petherick, the big boss wants to see you.'

The WPC who gave Terry the message was grinning all over her face. He looked across his desk at Detective Sergeant Jones and made a little face. Far from being amused DS Jones just stared at him sadly and shook his head.

'You must have been barmy, lad if you thought you could get away with it.'

Terry looked at him nonplussed. 'What are you on about?' His voice was genuinely bewildered.

Jones picked up some papers from in front of him and pretended to sort through them. 'Get yourself into the office, son. The Chief Inspector doesn't like to be kept waiting.'

Terry stood up. The WPC who had spoken to him was standing with one of her cronies and laughing. He had a sneaking feeling that the object of their amusement was himself. He racked his brains trying to think what he had done wrong. As far as he knew all the reports he had typed up were fine. He'd had two 'collars' in the last few weeks, and neither of them had been in any way abnormal. There was nothing that he could think of that would merit being seen by the Chief Inspector. He made his way across the crowded office to the glass partition that served as the Chief's office when he was down 'below' with his men and tapped on the door.

The Chief Inspector was deep in conversation with DI Dobin when he motioned with his hand for Terry to enter. He walked into the office tentatively, shutting the door quietly behind him. The two men stopped talking as he entered and the Chief told him to sit down. Both the Chief and the DI regarded him stonily. Terry sat down opposite the Chief. He could feel sweat coming out of every pore in his body. He wiped the palms of his hands on the front of his trousers. As far as he knew he had not done anything wrong. He was trying frantically to think of any slip-up he could have made when the Chief Inspector spoke.

'Well, Petherick. This is a nice kettle of fish, I must say.' His voice was hard. Never had Terry been reprimanded before, not even when he had inadvertently written down a suspect's number-plate wrongly and it had led the inquiry team to go to the house of a respected judge.

He cleared his throat. 'I'm sorry, sir. I'm not with you.'

'I've been wondering the same thing myself, young man.'

Terry watched his superior. He was not loved by his men but he was respected, which in Terry's mind was a much better thing. Chief Inspector Harris was an ample man who ran his squad along the lines of an army platoon. Indeed, he had been a colonel in the Lancers. He still sported large handlebar moustaches that had earned him the nickname 'Flying Officer Kite'. He was a large, extremely corpulent individual, much given to brightly coloured clothes that made him look like a confidence trickster. But for all that he was shrewd. Very shrewd indeed.

'I am sorry, sir. I really don't have any idea what you're talking about.'

The Chief looked up at DI Dobin, a smirk on his chubby red face.

'Hear that, Dobin? The cheeky young bugger's begging me pardon.'

Dobin nodded. Personally he thought that the Chief was an arsehole. He would not have given Murphy houseroom, but the Chief *was* the Chief, and if he saw fit to listen to Murphy . . . Dobin mentally shrugged. What could he do? He felt sorry for the boy. He was getting caught up in one of Murphy's little vendettas. Dobin had heard the chat in the canteen about how Maura Ryan had wiped the floor with him verbally. He had laughed, along with most of the others. Now it seemed Murphy had done a bit of digging and had uncovered poor Petherick's association with the girl. He was to be Murphy's sacrificial lamb.

Most of the plainclothes police had had associations with villains' female relations. There was nothing like a twelve stretch to bring the Casanovas out of the woodwork, especially if the villain's wife was a nice-looking sort, and the majority of them were. He felt sorry for the boy in front of him.

'Seen much of your girlfriend, Petherick?' The Chief's voice dripped with sarcasm and innuendo.

'I saw her last night, sir.' Dobin closed his eyes. He couldn't look! The Chief linked his fingers together and leant on his desk.

'How long have you been seeing this Miss "Ryan"?' He stressed the 'Ryan' and suddenly Terry had a terrible sick feeling in the pit of his stomach. His mind was screaming 'No' but it was all becoming frighteningly clear.

Ryan . . . Ryan . . . Ryan . . . seemed to be swimming around in his head, like a rogue shark waiting to pounce on him.

He licked his lips.

'I have been seeing her for about nine months, sir.'

'Nine months. How thrilling for you. Taken you home to meet Mummy and Daddy and the boys, has she? Especially her brother Michael . . . I bet he just loved you, didn't he?'

'No, sir, she has not.' He stared at the men defiantly. He was in a kind of Limbo now. The officers in front of him had already tried and convicted him in their minds and he was quietly furious.

The Chief's voice rose a few octaves at the tone of Terry's voice.

'Well, young fellow me lad, you have a decision to make. I suppose you realise that her family between them have done more time than bloody, Big Ben?'

'NO! No, sir . . . I didn't.'

The Chief's voice seemed to thunder from him. Terry and Dobin were aware that everyone outside had gone quiet and were listening to all that was taking place.

'Don't you take the piss of me, sonny. I was doing this job when you were just a drunken twinkle in your father's eye!'

Suddenly it was all too much for Terry. The enormity of what he had found out, coupled with the humiliation of being bawled out in full earshot of his colleagues, took its toll. He lost his temper. He stood up and, putting his hands on the desk in front of him, palms flat, shouted in the Chief Inspector's face.

'I'm not taking the piss out of you . . . you can't take the piss out of shit! Surely *you* know that? You seem to know everything else. As for Maura Ryan, it never occurred to me to run her through Interpol. Let's face it, if every bit of skirt that got pulled around this place was checked out for credibility, there wouldn't be any time to catch criminals. And another thing: Maura Ryan is a decent law-abiding girl who never mentioned her family. Now, I might add, I bloody well know why!'

He stood staring at his boss, flecks of spittle at the corners of his mouth. Somewhere in the distance he heard the sound of clapping. He guessed, rightly, that it was his partner, Jones. Obviously the whole of their slanging match had been witnessed. He felt his heart sink. He had just thrown away his career, all that he had worked for. He felt an insane urge to bang his head repeatedly on the desk in front of him.

DI Dobin was having trouble keeping his face straight. He wished he had the nerve to clap the boy. It was about time someone gave the sanctimonious old bastard a taste of his own medicine. Then, to the amazement of everyone, the Chief Inspector actually smiled. His large moustaches seemed to crawl upwards towards his eyelids and he was showing small, even white teeth.

'Good lad! The fact that you lost your rag shows me that you're not guilty of anything. You must understand that the last thing we need here is a bent copper. I know they exist, but please God not in my division.'

He sat back in his chair, placing his fingers together and resting his elbows on the arms of his chair. He stared at Terry for a while before he continued speaking. Then his voice was low and adamant.

'It's either her or the force. You realise that, don't you? I can't have one of my men running around with the sister of the biggest villain London's ever known. It would cast doubt, not only on your integrity but on the integrity of your colleagues. You can understand that, surely?'

All the fight had left Terry and he dropped into his chair, defeated. He nodded. Dobin handed him a cigarette and he took it gratefully. Taking his matches from his pocket he lit up, aware that his hands were shaking.

Dobin spoke for the first time. His gravelly voice was quiet. 'Has she ever asked you about your work, Terry?'

'Never, sir. In fact, she hated me even mentioning it. Now I know why. It's all falling into place. Why I could never pick her up from her house . . . never phone her there . . . Oh, lots of things.'

The Chief was sorry for the boy.

'Well, lad, I'll give you twenty-four hours to make your choice. I hope you decide to stay with us.' He held out his hand to show that the meeting was over. Terry shook hands with both men and left the office. In the main office, the hubbub of conversation had begun again. A few of his friends smiled at him and patted his back. WPC Lomax, who had brought him his summons, winked at him saucily. Terry ignored everyone and went to his desk. He picked up his jacket.

'I'm going home, Jonesy. I don't feel very well.'

'Go home, lad, and come in tomorrow. He's given you an ultimatum then, has he?'

'Yeah.' Terry's voice was tired. He needed time to think. Away from this place.

'Well, if it's any consolation, son, I think you have the makings of a good copper. Don't throw away a perfectly good career for a piece of skirt. They're not worth it.' Jones's wife had been one of an army of long-suffering women who, faced with the loneliness of being a policeman's wife, had got herself an alternative wage packet. Jonesy still carried a torch for her though he would never admit it.

'Thanks for the vote of confidence. God knows I need it at the moment.'

'That slag Murphy had told everyone before he saw the old

112

man. Never could stomach the bastard. There was talk once . . . a few years ago now . . . that he was in on the Train Robbery. Nothing was ever proven against him, mind, but he's had a hard job living it down, I can tell you. What's this Maura Ryan like?'

'She is one of the sweetest girls you are ever likely to meet. I just can't believe that she is in any way related to that shower.'

'Well, you know what they say, son. You can pick your friends, but not your relatives. I reckon the bloke who said that had never been in the police force.'

Terry tried to smile. 'See you tomorrow.' He slipped on his jacket and left the building. He sat outside in his car for ten minutes before pulling away, his mind screaming one question: Why?

Margaret and Maura walked into the little chemist's. They had both had the day off work and had spent the morning walking aimlessly around the shops. It was twenty minutes before they plucked up the courage to enter the chemist's shop, standing outside waiting for it to empty of people. Now they were finally inside, Maura felt as if she wanted to scream. An Asian man stood behind the counter.

'I . . . I would like the result of my test, please.'

The little man smiled, showing decaying teeth. 'Surely you would, madam. And the name?' He spoke with the inbred politeness particular to the Pakistani race.

'Miss . . . I mean, Mrs Ryan.'

He grinned at her. Oh, they were all Mrs in this country, he thought. Even those who were not. He went into the back of the shop and looked through the test results that had arrived that morning. He walked back into the shop and looked at Maura pityingly before he said, 'I am pleased to tell you that the test was positive.'

It was the standard reply that was hardly ever what the woman wanted to hear. 'You are three months pregnant.'

Maura's face dropped. Under normal circumstances she and Margaret would have had a laugh at this man's expense. Mimicked his voice to each other and remarked on his rotten teeth, saying he had a mouth full of dogends, the standard expression for tooth decay. Now she very much doubted if she would ever laugh again. She had a terrible feeling, as if her head was filling up with hot air. She felt much too hot, and prickles of warmth crept up her back to her neck. She was having trouble breathing. She put her hand up to pull her blouse away from her throat . . . As she fainted away on to the floor the last thing she heard was Marge's voice, coming from somewhere in the distance, high and croaky.

'Oh my Gawd! The bleeding shock's killed her! She's dropped down dead!'

Maura woke up on a little couch in the back of the chemist's shop. As she opened her eyes and took a deep breath she vaguely wondered how on earth the two tiny people looking at her anxiously had managed to carry her in there. Margaret's face had tears and mascara running down it.

'Oh, Maws, you gave me such a fright . . . I thought you'd copped it.'

The little chemist pointed at a cup of hot sweet tea beside her. 'Come along, madam. Be drinking it up, it will make you feel much better. It's the best thing for shock. And it's a terrible shock you had, I am thinking.' He looked at the two girls closely.

Maura pushed herself upright on the little couch and picked up the cup of tea. Her dress had somehow risen up over her thighs and she noticed the chemist staring at her legs. Hastily she tried to pull her dress back down, spilling her tea as she did so.

'I am having a friend who can help ladies like yourself . . . young ladies who cannot tell their mummies and daddies what has befallen them. I will write his name and address down and give it to you. Tell the man that Mr Patel sent you. It will cost you only eighty-five pounds. That is very cheap price.'

He hurried back into the shop. The two girls stared at his retreating back. Maura felt as if she was trapped in some kind of nightmare that would never end. She glanced around the room. It was chock-a-block with boxes and packs of shampoo, disinfectant, bleach, and all manner of weird-looking instruments. The only nice thing about it was that it smelt lovely . . . of pine-scented bath cubes and perfume.

The little man rushed back in with a piece of paper. 'This man is very very good, madam. A very nice man indeed.'

Maura took the piece of paper, because she didn't know what else to do, and placed it in her shoulderbag.

The man kept chattering on until finally Maura put down the tea and stood up. She felt absolutely terrible and as if he read her mind he pointed to a small door in the corner of the room. Entering the tiny toilet, Maura retched for what seemed like ages, the dank and musty smell of the carpet tiles mingled with the overpowering smell of urine seeming to spur her on. Cold droplets of perspiration were standing out on her forehead and she wiped them away with the back of her hand. She staggered out to the smell of the pine bath cubes.

'Come on, Maws, we better make a move.' Margaret took her arm and, thanking the little man, they left the shop. They walked for a while in silence before Margaret said: 'You should have seen that skinny little sod trying to lift you on to that couch . . . If I hadn't have been so worried. I'd have pissed myself laughing!'

Maura, seeing in her mind's eye the incongruousness of the situation, started to laugh. Margaret laughed with her, and soon the two girls began to scream with laughter. Passersby paused to stare at them, smiling themselves and thinking it must be a great joke. Maura's laughter was tinged with hysteria. They held on to one another, screeching, until Maura's laughter turned to deep racking sobs.

'What am I gonna do, Marge?'

Margaret led her into a small coffee shop and sat her down. She ordered a pot of coffee from a fat bored waitress and went back to her friend. When she was seated Maura repeated her question.

'What the hell am I gonna do? There's gonna be murders committed over this.'

'There's not a lot you *can* do, Maws, except tell everyone. People are funny like that. Remember Gina Blenkinsop? She got in the club by some bloke who had it on his toes. Well, she had her baby and now her mum and dad absolutely dote on the poor little thing.'

Maura snapped at her friend, 'Oh, yeah? I can just see Mickey, can't you? Holding the baby at the christening . . . every villain in London on one side of the Church and the best part of Vine Street nick on the other. Use your bloody head, Marge. This baby will be as welcome as a pork chop in a synagogue.'

The waitress brought over their pot of coffee. She laid out the cups and saucers and the two girls sat quietly until she had finished. When she went Margaret tried again. 'I still can't understand why you never went on the pill.'

Maura sipped her coffee and banged the cup back in the saucer.

'Oh, don't be so bloody ridiculous! How could I go to O'Reilly? He would have been straight round my mother's!'

Margaret swallowed her temper. Maura was in one of her moods and in fairness, Marge admitted, she would be the same if the boot was on the other foot. She took a deep breath.

'I told you to go to that doctor in Hampstead where I go. He'll give you slimming pills . . . anything you want, as long as you can pay.'

Maura screwed up her eyes and stared at Margaret. Her weight was a touchy subject. 'Are you being bleeding funny?'

'Of course not! Anyway, slimming pills would be a bit of a waste of time now, don't you think?'

She looked meaningfully at Maura's waist. The look brought Maura back to reality and she wailed: 'Oh, Marge, what am I gonna do!' Her voice held a plaintive note. She put her hands on her belly. She had a little life in there, and somewhere inside her she was pleased. She loved children. Her brother's daughter Carla had always been like a little sister to her. She had never resented the amount of time she spent at the house. Maura was aware that Janine did not really like her only child, but it had never mattered because Carla was doted on by herself and her brothers. Now she had a child growing in her own body and knew that it would be hated, despised, because its father was a policeman. The biggest cloud on her horizon was not Terry's reaction but Mickey's. He would want to kill Terry stone dead just for sleeping with his sister, and when he found out that Terry was a policeman . . . she felt sick with fright. He would kill Terry, then herself – in that order. He would take it as a personal affront. She closed her eyes tightly to block out her brother's image.

'I tell you what I'm going to do, Marge. I'm going to go and see Terry and tell him everything. About the baby . . . the boys . . . everything. He loves me, I know he does. We could go away together somewhere. I know that he'll stand by me. He's got to!' Her voice was full of panic. Margaret wondered who she was trying to convince with her talk about going away.

'I hope he stands by you, Maws.' Her voice sounded sceptical.

Maura wailed, 'Oh, don't put the mockers on me, Marge! As if I haven't got enough troubles.'

Margaret stretched her hand across the table and held on to Maura's. Squeezing it tightly, she smiled at her best friend. They had come a long way together since the fight outside their school. She just wished that she had as much faith in Terry Petherick. She liked him well enough, but couldn't see him standing by Maura, somehow. She might not have any qualifications but she was cute enough to realise that Terry Petherick would not want relations like the Ryans in his job. She said a quick Hail Mary, as she used to when she was a child, and prayed that Maura would not come unstuck. Though another part of her mind said: She already has.

Terry was sitting in his flat in Islington. The chair he was sitting on had been a present from Maura. They had been strolling through Camden Market when they had seen it. It was large, high-backed, and upholstered in green leather. They had homed in on it together, both of the same mind. Instead of a settee they would have the chair, then they could cuddle up in it together. Something they had since done many times. They had bartered with the stall owner for it, laughing and joking until a compromise had been reached. For the grand total of six pounds they had got their 'loveseat'. Maura had then bought some material, a riot of green and blue brocade, and had made the curtains for the windows. He remembered thinking as he watched her sewing them: She's a natural homemaker.

Over the months they had been together he had fallen deeply in love with her. Her smile, her cheeky quips, her long legs and incredible breasts . . . Now he had to decide whether that love was strong enough. All day a little voice had been nagging at him, telling him that if he really loved her he would have thrown in his job there and then . . . Oh, he had defended her, but not vehemently enough to tell his boss where to stick his job, and logic told him that's what he would have done if he really, really loved her.

He stood up and went to the window. It was cold outside and a solitary little boy was kicking a football around the road. He turned abruptly from the window and walked into the bedroom. He stared at the bed. Maura had really abandoned herself there. She had shocked him at times with the intensity of her loving. She wasn't a girl who would give herself lightly, he knew that. Was that why he was feeling such a bastard? Because deep inside he knew that there was no competition really. Maura Ryan was an also-ran.

He went back into the small living room and opened the bottle of Teacher's he had bought on the way home from work. What he needed was a stiff drink. He poured himself a large Scotch. He needed something to numb his mind for what he was thinking of doing. He checked himself. What he was *going* to do. He had decided then, and not even realised it.

He took a large gulp of his Scotch, grateful for the burning sensation it created in his throat. All his life he had had one ambition: to be a policeman. He had studied long and hard with that one thought in mind. Now he had to choose between the job he loved and the woman he loved, and the woman had lost. He had to admit that to himself . . . Oh God!

If she had been anyone's sister but Michael Ryan's! The thought of Michael brought his heart leaping into his mouth. He took another long pull of his whisky and sat back in the armchair. Everyone knew about Michael Ryan and his brothers – they were notorious. There was talk of their being involved not just with drugs and whores, but arms too. Not just the odd sawn-off either, but high velocity rifles, rocket launchers, and anything else that the British Army wouldn't miss. Jesus Christ, how did he ever get personally involved with all this! He was starting to sweat. He had before him the awesome task of giving Michael Ryan's baby sister the Big E. He put the glass he was holding to his forehead. The enormity of it all was breaking into his consciousness.

All day he had been worried about Maura . . . Her reaction. How to let her down gently. In his worried state he had

117

concentrated wholly on Maura. Now the thought of her brother invaded his mind. He rolled the glass along his skin, savouring the coldness as he became unbearably hot.

He sat back in the chair. Everything in the room seemed to be mocking him. Even the TV set in the corner. Once again the dreadful feeling of foreboding pervaded his being. Michael Ryan would not like his sister being with a policeman, he would lay money on that.

He closed his eyes again. In his mind he could see Michael standing over him, threatening him with bodily harm. Suddenly he tensed. He could hear the scraping noise of a key going into a lock. His whole body was taut. In his mind's eye he could see Michael Ryan letting himself into his flat. He sat in the chair paralysed with fright, the knuckles of his hand white as he clutched the glass. He heard the door swing open with its familiar creaking groan. Every nerve in his body was jangling. For the first time he knew the smell of fear. It seemed to rise up into his nostrils, an overpowering aroma of hot sticky stale sweat. Supposing Ryan had taken the key off Maura? They could have been seen out together. A hundred different thoughts whirled around in his head, leaving him breathless and dizzy . . .

Instead of Michael's heavy footfall, he heard the familiar clatter of Maura's heels as she stepped into the hall on to the worn linoleum. He collapsed into the chair like a rag doll. A thin trickle of sweat slipped down his forehead, over his eyebrow and down on to his cheek. A feeling of euphoria swept over him. It was Maura . . . Maura . . . Her name bounced around inside his head like a crazy pattern in a child's kaleidoscope. She walked into the lounge and smiled at him.

'You all right? You look as if you've seen a ghost.'

He stood up awkwardly. Placing his glass on the small coffee table he went to her. Maura was in the process of putting her key back into her bag. Reaching out, he took it from her gently and slipped it into his trouser pocket. Maura looked at him.

'What did you do that for?' Her big luminous eyes held a hint of fear. He tried to smile and succeeded only in grimacing.

As he looked at her he didn't see her lovely trusting face. Terry saw only Michael Ryan. A very angry Michael Ryan.

'I think that we're getting a bit too serious, love.' It sounded lame even to his own ears. 'I think we should cool it for a while. We're both young . . .' His voice trailed off. He felt so bad he could not meet her eyes. Maura just stood there thunderstruck.

'I beg your pardon?' Her voice sounded small and hurt.

Terry still could not bring himself to look at her so he walked back over to the window.

'It's quite simple really, Maura . . . I don't want to get involved right now. I want to be free. Go out with other women. I don't want to get tied down just yet.'

'I see.' Her voice was flat. Pride had taken over. 'And just when did you come to this earth-shattering conclusion, may I ask? Only I was under the impression that you was my bloke . . . My chap, if you like that expression better. Now I find that I was just a screw.' She stormed across the room to him, pulling him around to face her with considerable strength. 'Let me tell you something, Terry bloody "I want to see other women" Petherick! I'm . . .'

She stopped herself there and then. How could she tell him about the baby? Her eyes darted around the room, looking for a chance of escape. It was all going wrong. All the words she had practised on her way over here dried up inside her head. The picture she had built up in her mind of Terry taking her in his arms and whispering that they would always be together, no matter what, faded in front of her eyes like chalk paintings in the rain. He was dumping her. He had had his bit of fun and now she was ancient history.

The fight left her as quickly as it had come. The urge to rip his face open with her nails dissolved along with all her dreams and hopes. She felt the hot salty tears come and forced them away. If she had to go, she would go with dignity. She glanced around the room. She had experienced so much pleasure in this little flat, the result of which was inside her at this very moment. Should she tell him? Should she scream it out into his face? Make him take the responsibility? Even as the words formed in her mind she knew that she would never say them to him. She would never tell him about the child. Having him on sufferance would be far worse than not having him at all. She bent down wearily and picked her bag up off the floor. She had not even realised that she had dropped it. She turned to leave and his voice stayed her.

'Believe me, Maws, I am really sorry about this.'

His voice sounded so sincere. She laughed bitterly. He had the knack of sounding sincere. Last night in bed he had told her that he loved her, and had sounded sincere. The lying, two-faced bastard!

Without facing him, she said: 'Terry.'

'Yes?' His heart was breaking.

Gathering up every ounce of strength and hatred she could muster she turned to face him, launching herself at him with arms flying. She felt his skin tear beneath her nails. Felt the pure rush of pleasure as she made him hurt, as she was hurting. As quickly as the attack began, it stopped. The sudden urge of energy left her drained.

'You can fuck off, Petherick!' She saw his hand go up to his face. Four deep grooves on his cheek were bleeding simultaneously. She smiled at him, a nasty evil smile, and pointed her finger at him. Her long scarlet-painted nails made him flinch.

'I never thought I would ever say this to you. You're a dirty rotten swine. You took me and you used me. I trusted you, Terry.' Her voice broke. 'But I tell you something now, boy. The day will come when you will want me . . . when you will need me. You'll live to regret this day, because if you live to one hundred years old you'll never find anyone to love you like I do.'

With that she turned away from him and left the flat, slamming the door behind her.

Terry watched her leave. In his heart he knew that what she said was true. She deserved much better than the treatment he had given her. She was his first love, the first woman to meet him on an equal plane, and he had destroyed her with a few simple words. He was not surprised to feel that he was crying. The tears were running into the scratches on his face, making them sting. He had a terrible feeling that although he had destroyed Maura, somewhere along the line he had also destroyed himself. He saw droplets of blood falling on to his shirt, their deep crimson colour spreading over the material.

Suddenly he couldn't let her go. He ran to the window. Pulling back the net curtain, he looked out on to the street. She was on the other side of the road, her head tucked into her coat. He knew that she too was crying. Fumbling with the ancient catch on the window he finally opened it and leant out, calling her at the top of his voice.

'Maura . . . Maura . . . come back!'

His voice carried to her on the wind.

He knew that she could hear him, saw her hesitate before walking away faster, her white-blonde head tucked even further into the collar of her coat. He watched her until she turned the corner, the hum of the traffic grating on his ears.

Pulling his head back inside, he closed the window. The once friendly little room looked alien now, and hostile. Everywhere he looked was Maura Ryan . . . He could see her flitting about, putting up the curtains, making sandwiches or curled up with him on their special armchair. He could breathe in her perfume and taste her musky body. She was everywhere around him. He sat in the chair.

He was still sitting there thinking about her when he passed out much later in the evening. He had drunk the whole bottle of Scotch.

★ ★ ★

120

Maura was devastated. If someone had told her that Terry would dump her like that she would have laughed at them. 'I want to see other women.' Those words kept echoing in her head. They would stay with her for the rest of her life. Anything he could have said, even that he hated her, would not have had the profound effect that those few words had. Well, let him see other women! She hoped to God that he caught a terrible disease from them.

She passed the Angel and made her way along the Pentonville Road. The fact remained that she was still pregnant. She had an urge to go and drown herself but dismissed it. It was getting dark and she wandered aimlessly, trying to figure out what on earth to do. All around her were couples, holding hands, laughing, kissing. She pushed her hands further into her pockets and carried on walking, letting her legs carry her wherever they wanted to go. Terry's face was fresh in her mind, his softness and his tenderness welcome memories to her in the cold evening wind.

She found herself at Kings Cross Station and was surprised at how far she had walked. A black cab came along the road and she hailed it, telling the driver to take her to Notting Hill. She sat in the back, huddled into a corner of the seat, staring listlessly out of the window at the rapidly moving landscape. A lone tear rolled down her face and she wiped it away impatiently. She was done with crying, she had more important things to think about.

The cab driver looked over his shoulder at her and asked cheerfully, 'Whereabouts in Notting Hill, love?'

'Lancaster Road, please.' She wouldn't go home just yet. She would go to Margaret's. Margaret would know what to do. She rested her head on the window, her breath coming in little gasps that barely managed to create steam on the glass surface. She felt so lonely, so frightened. Her bottom lip quivered as she tried to stop the tears of frustration and rage. She loved him so much!

'You all right, love?' The driver's voice was concerned.

She sat up in her seat and saw him watching her in the mirror above his windscreen.

She gave him a small childish smile. 'No, actually, I'm not.'

He had a broad good-natured face. 'You listen to me, girl. If it's boyfriend trouble that's put that frown on your boat, remember this. Us blokes ain't worth it!' He laughed at his own wit.

Maura looked back out of the window, then forced a large smile on to her face. 'Don't I bloody know it!'

Chapter Eleven

Michael Ryan was in the Valbonne nightclub in Kingly Street having a quick drink with his boyfriend, Jonny Fenwick. It was a well-known fact that Michael Ryan was a 'brown hatter'. Not that anyone would call him that to his face. Far from taking anything away from his street credibility it enhanced it, because queers were known to be nasty bastards. They had a cruel twist to their nature and the best thing to do was to keep on the good side of them. There was no queer bashing when Michael Ryan hit the streets. He also took a woman now and again which further puzzled his friends and adversaries alike. It was proof of his ever changing habits. He treated his friends like he treated his lovers. He could go one way or the other.

At the moment Michael was besotted by Jonny Fenwick's youth. He was a beautiful boy with thick blond curly hair and large, wide-spaced grey eyes. Mickey had put him up in a flat and paid him an allowance. He was Jonny Ryan now. Michael owned him, lock, stock and barrel. Jonny loved it, and loved being seen with Michael. Tonight, though, he was in a dilemma. He had heard a bit of gossip today concerning Michael's sister and was not sure whether to tell him or not. He certainly didn't want any comebacks off Michael if what he said turned out to be false. But Michael was in fine fettle tonight, full of laughter and jokes, and Jonny decided to risk it. Not only that, but that bitch Tommy was looking at him all gooey-eyed and Michael was loving it, so Jonny would use it as an excuse to get him away from the bar *and* Tommy! He tapped Michael's arm.

'What, mate?' Michael's voice was warm.

'It's a bit private, Mickey. I heard a bit of news today . . . I don't want to talk about it here.' He looked meaningfully at Tommy and pursed his lips. Michael nodded.

'Come and sit down then.'

He picked up their drinks and led Jonny over to an empty table away from listening ears. Jonny sat down and crossed his legs, placing his hands one on top of the other on his knee. He leant towards Michael theatrically.

'It's about a member of your family. But first I want your solemn promise that you won't go ape shit in here.'

Michael's eyes narrowed. 'I won't lose my temper. Now tell me what you heard.'

Jonny flicked his hair out of his eyes with a girlish gesture and said, 'I asked you to promise me, Michael.'

He gritted his teeth. 'For fuck's sake, Jonny, spit it out. I ain't got all night.'

Jonny licked his lips nervously. He wasn't at all sure that he was doing the right thing now. Michael spoke of his little sister as a mixture of the Virgin Mary and the Queen. Either way, she was completely beyond reproach.

'It's about your sister . . . She's got herself a boyfriend.'

Michael relaxed. 'Is that all? Who?'

Jonny took a sip of his gin and tonic before answering. 'It's a policeman from Vine Street.'

Michael looked as if he had been hit by a bus.

'A what!'

'Keep your voice down! Do you want the whole world to know? He's a young Detective Constable. Remember my friend little Mo, the fat queen from Kensington?' Michael nodded. 'Well, apparently he has a few friends at Vine Street, though myself I'd call them customers. Anyway, one of them told him. It seems a bigwig there . . . some bloke called Murphy . . . pulled the rug out from under him today. Told his Chief Inspector that he was seeing her . . . your sister. Apparently there was a big to-do about it. Anyway, little Mo rang me. And being a good boy, I thought you ought to know.'

Michael was staring at Jonny without seeing him. His face was dark with fury. The conniving little bitch! She'd been knocking about with a filth right under his nose. He felt a blinding compulsion to wring her neck.

'Phone this little Mo and find out who his customers are. Names, ranks, the works. Tell him from me that if he decides to become coy I'll break his fucking neck.'

Jonny nodded. 'All right, Mickey. First thing in the morning.'

Michael was in the throes of a violent rage. Maura had never even brought a fellow home. A small rational thought broke into his reverie. It said to him, Well, she wouldn't, would she? Of course not. She had a bit more sense than to bring an old Bill straight into her family of criminals. He could easily walk out of this club and smash her to a pulp. At least one good thing had come of it. He had the means to blackmail a few of the shirtlifters on the force. He consoled himself with that thought.

'Look, Jon, I have to get around to me own club now. I'll see you later on tonight.'

Jonny smiled his best smile. He had been the teller of very bad news and now he was scared. Michael was capable of taking the whole thing out on him.

'All right, Mickey love.' He fluttered his eyelashes as a woman might. Watching him, Michael experienced one of his lightning changes of mood. He laughed softly, guessing what was going through the boy's mind. Wagging his finger in Jonny's face, he said: 'Behave yourself, you!'

To which Jonny answered seriously, 'I don't have much choice do I?'

Michael squeezed his shoulder affectionately and left the club.

As he made his way to Dean Street he thought about what Jonny had told him. The doorman of the Pink Pussycat hailed him and he waved back halfheartedly. His arrogant, strutting walk and dark countenance were familiar features around Soho. Unlike most of his contemporaries Michael didn't feel the need to be surrounded by minders. His immense size, coupled with the fact that he was known to carry a piece, was warning enough for any would-be assassins. Since Michael had taken over as the Baron of the West End he had not had one serious threat. He was, to all intents and purposes, the business – the highest accolade that a villain could be awarded. As he walked to his club he was hailed by touts, prostitutes, bouncers and pimps. He crossed Shaftesbury Avenue into Dean Street itself and slowed his pace. If Maura was knocking about with a filth he would kill her. He hadn't fought tooth and nail since he was seventeen to have his little baby sister blow it all wide open for him. He gritted his teeth in temper. He had worshipped her, would have given her the earth if she had asked for it. But he wouldn't allow her to have this bloke. Never! He would find out everything he could about this copper and then he would nip it in the bud. He stormed into Le Buxom at ten-fifteen.

The club was just picking up. A few stray punters were having a drink. They were 'weekend warriors' – the nickname given to men who saved up their meagre earnings as civil servants or bank clerks and came up West once a month for a drink, sex and excitement. An experienced tom could tell them a mile off from their off-the-peg suits to their Freeman, Hardy and Willis shoes. The older women gravitated to them, secure in the knowledge that it would be an easy lay. These men were too scared of their wives and the police ever to cause any trouble. They were seldom rough, and because they had to make their money stretch were hardly choosy. The only bugbear for the club was the fact that they only ever

125

bought one bottle of champagne, making it last all night, until the final stripper had departed. A weekend warrior was the only sort of punter who provided the women with an opportunity actually to drink the stuff.

Michael looked around the club. It was half empty. He noticed Benny sitting at a table with one of the younger girls, a pretty little piece known affectionately as Pussy. Despite his anger Michael smiled. Benny had a permanent hard on. As soon as a new hostess arrived, Benny was there, cock standing to attention. There was a long-standing joke in all the rival clubs that without Benny, Le Buxom would have gone bankrupt years ago. Michael stood by the meat seats. For once the girls there were subdued. He had that effect on people. The girls rarely spoke to him unless he addressed them personally. The stench of cheap perfume was overpowering. Michael nodded to them and made his way out into the foyer and upstairs to the offices.

Geoffrey, Leslie and Garry were already in there having a drink. He greeted them and poured himself a large brandy. Sitting behind his desk, he looked directly at Garry. If anyone knew Maura's whereabouts it would be him.

'Do you know if our Maura's got a boyfriend?'

Garry looked at his brother in bewilderment. 'What if she has? It's none of our business.'

Michael was out of his seat and round the desk, knocking Leslie flying out of his chair as he pushed past him to get to Garry. He grabbed him by his shirt front, pulling him up out of the chair with considerable strength.

' "None of our business" you say . . . I heard a whisper on the street tonight that our sister is knocking about with a filth!' He threw Garry back into his seat. His temper was seething. If he didn't get some kind of answer soon he would explode.

Leslie stared at Garry, who was gasping for breath. There was no doubt about it . . . Mickey was an awesome bastard. There was no one to touch him. Mickey was the business. Well the business.

'Who told you all this then, Mick?' Geoffrey tried unsuccessfully to defuse the situation.

'Never you mind who bloody well told me! It's enough that I've heard. I want you two –' he pointed at Leslie and Garry – 'to find out how true it is.'

Geoffrey tried again. 'It's not definite then? What I mean is . . .'

Michael screwed up his face and bellowed at this brother, 'Oh, for fuck's sake, Geoffrey . . . I don't want a government White Paper on it all. I just want the facts! Now do what I fucking well told you to do!'

Leslie and Garry scrambled from the room. When Michael was

in one of his tempers, you did not argue with him.

Geoffrey poured himself a brandy. When Michael was like this, it was best not to rock the boat in any way.

Michael swallowed his own brandy in a gulp and grimaced. 'So what do you think, Geoffrey?' His voice was once again steady.

'Who told you?'

'Jonny actually.' He sounded wary.

'In that case . . . no way. Not our Maws.' His voice was dismissive. He did not like Jonny. He did not like the fact that Michael was homosexual, though he would never say it outright.

Michael guessed, rightly, exactly what had gone through Geoffrey's mind.

'I know you don't like Jonny. That's tough. But I'll tell you this much – for all his faults he ain't a liar. And there's one thing that seems to have escaped your notice . . . most people don't even know we have a sister.'

Geoffrey digested this bit of logic, watching Michael sitting at his desk chewing his thumbnail. Geoffrey knew from experience that Michael could sit like that for hours. Sighing, he poured himself another drink. He hoped for Maura's sake that what they had heard wasn't true.

Downstairs, Leslie and Garry had told Benny what had happened. He was still sitting with Pussy, except now the night had lost some of its enchantment. Sensing that she had lost his attention, the girl stroked his thigh, pouting at him prettily. He smiled at her with a crafty little grin guaranteed to melt the hardest of hearts.

'Pussy.' His voice was caressing.

'Yes?' She looked into his eyes. Their blue depths mirrored her features.

'Let's go, shall we?'

'All right then.' They stood up together. Benny wanted out of here before Michael decided to rope him in on everything. There were many things he would do for his eldest brother, but even he drew the line at a witch hunt on his only sister. Gathering up their things, they left the club. Hailing a cab outside, Benny jumped in, pulling Pussy in after him. There was a little hotel just off Leicester Square where he could hole up with her for the night. And that's what he intended to do. The thought of ringing home and warning his sister crossed his mind, but he soon dismissed it. He didn't want any part of this whatsoever.

The girl snuggled up to him in the back of the taxi, and for the first time in his life Benny wondered if he would be able to get it up.

The way he was feeling, he would need Charles Atlas to lift it for him.

★ ★ ★

Garry and Leslie got out of their car. They were going to see another policeman. This was their second visit in two hours. The first had been to a young PC who had been as bewildered as they were. They had left no wiser to their sister's antics than they had been before. It had cost them twenty quid to keep him quiet, but it was worth it. He was going to keep his ear to the ground. The man they were going to see now was a sergeant in Notting Dale police station. He had been on the Ryans' payroll for about five years. Well, now he could earn his money.

They knocked on his front door. It was nearly twelve-thirty. The small terraced house was in darkness. A light came on upstairs and Sergeant Potter's grizzled head appeared from a window.

'Who the bloody hell is it?'

He peered myopically down at them.

'It's Leslie Ryan. I wanna see you, Sarge.' Leslie's voice was a theatrical whisper.

Grunting and moaning, the old man retreated back inside the room. Leslie and Garry heard him clumping down his stairs. The hall light went on and the door was opened.

'What the hell are you playing at? Coming round here at this time of night?'

Garry and Leslie walked into the hallway.

'We've got a few questions, and we want you to give us the answers.'

The old man looked at them maliciously. He had a sneaking suspicion that he knew what they were going to ask. 'Would the questions be about your sister by any chance?'

'That's right, Sarge. What do you know about her then?' Garry sounded menacing and the man realised that he had forgotten for a moment just who he was dealing with. He licked his lips.

He started talking in a self-righteous tone of voice. 'Now you listen to me . . . I didn't know anything until today, I take oath on that. A friend of mine who's now at Vine Street gave me a ring at Notting Dale. He told me that there had been a bit of malarkey with one of the plainclothes there. He got hauled over the coals because he was knock – I mean, seeing your sister.'

He was fiddling with the cord of his plaid dressing gown, his short stubby fingers tobacco-stained. Leslie and Garry stood quietly staring at him.

The man began to babble. 'Honestly, boys, I didn't think you would be interested in it. I mean . . . I assumed you knew about it all.' He was getting desperate.

'What's the bloke's name?'

128

'The bloke who rang me or your sister's fancy man? Sorry, I mean boyfriend.'

Garry closed his eyes wearily. He spoke slowly and deliberately. 'Who was the man who rang you up?'

'Oh, it was an old friend.'

'Listen, you!' Garry pushed him across the hallway. 'I just want his name, not his fucking life story. Now who is he?'

The old man had fallen back on the stairs and sat there watching the two boys. Upstairs he could hear his wife getting out of bed. Her high-pitched, nasal voice floated down the stairs. 'Who's that down there, Albert? Sounds like an 'erd of bloody elephants from up here.'

He groaned. That was all he needed, his wife awake and sticking her oar in where it wasn't wanted.

'No one, dear. It's police business. You go back to sleep.'

'Well, just you tell them to keep their great big galloping feet off of my clean floor.'

'I will.'

Leslie had an urge to laugh and stifled it. 'The name of your informant?'

'It was a bloke called Jones . . . He's a DS at Vine Street.'

'Is he reliable? I mean, if he said something was true, would that be the case?'

'Oh, yeah. He's a rare one, old Jonesy. If he told me he had seen old Nick himself I'd believe him. He's not a spinner.'

Garry snorted. 'That makes a change in the police force. I thought you needed a degree in being a lying bastard before they would have you?'

Albert pursed his lips. Even though he was on the take, he still took a pride in being a policeman.

'What was the bloke's name who's been seeing my sister?'

'Petherick. Detective Constable Terence Petherick.'

'That's all we wanted to know. You can go back to bed with old vinegar tits now.'

As they left the house, Leslie slipped the old man a ten-pound note.

'Listen, Sarge, we want his address. If you can get it there'll be a pony in it for you, all right?'

'OK, son.' All his animosity was forgotten now. He could do a lot with twenty-five quid. Anyway, he reasoned, they'd get their information one way or the other so he might as well feather his nest while he had the chance. 'I'll keep me ear to the ground. Don't you worry.' He closed the door behind them.

His wife's voice came once more from above him. 'Al . . .bert!' She had the knack of singing his name out in such a way that her voice carried for about three miles.

'Oh, shut your row, you stupid old bitch!'

His wife sat in her bed, her face a mask of Pond's cold cream and abject disbelief. Her curlers were placed strategically around her head like a crash helmet. She hitched up her ample chest, her mouth settling to a grim line. A malevolent gleam in her eye, she pulled the covers off her. Swinging her legs out of bed, she placed her feet in her carpet slippers, stood up and picked up the heavy chamber pot from underneath the bed. She walked out of the bedroom on to the landing. As her husband reached the top of the stairs she flung the contents into his face . . . that would teach him to answer her back!

She clumped back into her bedroom leaving her husband clutching a soggy ten-pound note in his hand. He spat. Only his Gladys would have the nerve to empty an 'Edgar Allen' all over him. Sod them bloody Ryans! If they hadn't got him out of bed none of this would have happened.

Garry and Leslie drove back to Dean Street. It was just on one o'clock. They arrived at the club at one-thirty-five. The balloon went up at one-forty.

Maura was lying in bed wide awake. It was nearly two-thirty in the morning and she was no nearer sleep than she had been at nine o'clock when she had got into bed. Her mind was turning in circles, her thoughts drifting away on different tangents as she tried to see a way out of her predicament. There was none. She had talked everything over with Margaret, but neither girl could find a solution to her problem. A problem that was getting bigger in Maura's mind with every passing second.

She was in a quandary. If she told her family who the father was there would be murder. Especially if she told them he had dumped her. As much as Terry had hurt her, she wasn't going to be the cause of his getting beaten to death. And if she knew Mickey that would be the outcome. She placed her hands on her belly. There was a tiny little person in there, a completely new life waiting for her to bring it into the world. She turned over the bed again. The blankets and sheets were tangled around her.

How could he have dismissed her like that? She was still reeling from the shock. She had thought he would have been over the moon once the news had sunk in. She had seen him picking her up in his arms and kissing all her fears away. Telling her that he loved her. That they would go away and get married, away from her brothers, to Scotland or somewhere. Now, in bed, in the dark, she could see her plans for what they were: childish fantasies. Terry had no more need of her than he had of his car. When it was old

130

hat, you traded it in for a newer model.

She felt the familiar sting of tears. Well, he wouldn't hear about this child from her. She wouldn't lower herself. If he didn't want her then he didn't want his child either. But what was she going to do about the baby? She couldn't see herself as one of these unmarried mothers, brazenly having their babies and sod the neighbours. If it had been anyone else, her brothers would have been round the boy's house, given him a good hiding, and then the wedding would have been arranged, quick smart. But this was a situation that could not be resolved so easily. Even if Terry wanted to marry her, Michael would move heaven and earth to stop the marriage taking place.

She was hot again so she pushed off the blankets. In her short nylon nighty she looked far more seductive than she felt. Her long smooth legs were spreadeagled on the blankets, her arms were hugging her breasts. She had combed out her long hair before getting into bed and it fanned around her head giving her an ethereal appearance, like a saucy angel.

She rolled her head from side to side on her pillow. Oh, why was she being plagued like this! It was bad enough being pregnant without all this added worry. She turned herself over again in the bed. This time she was facing the window. She stared out into the darkness, only the light of the streetlights to illuminate her room. Earlier she had prayed – to the Immaculate Conception and Saint Jude, the patron saint of no hope! Above her bed was the Sacred Heart, a large golden vessel pulsing outside Christ's body. He had looked benevolently down on her for years. She began to pray to him again. In the half-light she could see his golden heart glinting. She began to murmur the Eucharistic prayer.

' "Father, you are holy indeed, and all creation rightly gives you praise." '

As she prayed she heard a car drive into Lancaster Road. She saw the car's headlights cast long shadows over her bedroom ceiling as the engine died down and guessed, rightly, that her brothers were home. She heard them coming into the house and carried on praying.

' "All life, all holiness comes from you . . ." '

They were coming up the stairs. She could hear the thud of their shoes.

' "Through our son, Jesus Christ our Lord." '

Her bedroom door was thrown open and the light turned on. She pulled herself up in the bed and put her hand over her eyes to shield them from the sudden glare. Michael and Geoffrey stood at the end of her bed like avenging angels.

She squinted at them. 'What's going on?'

131

'I was just gonna ask you the same thing.'

'I don't know what you're on about, Mickey. I ain't done nothing!' Her voice was full of fear.

With one bound he was across the room. He grabbed her hair, yanking her head back. 'You bloody tart! You've been knocking about with a filth, ain't ya?'

'No . . . Mickey, I swear!' She was screaming with fear.

'Don't lie to me, you slag.'

He pushed his face closer to hers. She could smell his breath as he shouted at her, 'Lover boy got an ultimatum today, Maura. Either his bit of skirt or his job. I understand the job won.'

Maura's head was reeling. That was why he had dumped her! That was why he had taken the key from her. He knew who she was!

'He was called into the Chief's office. Told what a naughty family you'd got. I'm the fucking laughing stock of the Metropolitan Police Force over you. Every villain from here to Liverpool will be laughing up their sleeves at me. I could bleeding well murder you!'

Maura was not listening to him. All she could think of was the fact that Terry had known about her when she had gone to him. It was the name Ryan that had created the rift between them. Somewhere deep down inside her a grain of contempt was forming. It was her family that he objected to, not her. Even though it proved that it was not anything she had done that had caused their rift, instead of pleasing her she felt a disdain for him that was so strong she could actually taste it. The gutless bastard! The dirty gutless bastard . . .

He didn't even have the nerve to tell her why he was dumping her. He'd said he wanted to see other women when in reality he meant: I am frightened of your brothers. He had destroyed her and didn't have the decency to tell her truthfully why. She was carrying his child inside her. The fruit of their so-called love. If he walked into her room now, Michael wouldn't be in it. She would rip him to shreds, Terry Gutless Petherick would be a dead man, and it wouldn't be her brothers who killed him.

Michael and Geoffrey were watching her, fascinated by the changing expressions on her face.

'Leave me alone, you!' she screamed at Michael at the top of her voice, all fear of him leaving her at the thought of what Terry had done to her. Michael brought back his fist. As he went to slam it into her body, Sarah's voice stayed him.

'Oi! What the bloody hell's going on in here? It's a wonder you ain't woken up the whole bleeding street.' She took in the picture before her and ran to her son. Raising herself up on her toes she grabbed hold of Michael's hair, shaking him like a dog with its prey.

'Don't you dare raise your hand to your sister, you great gormless bastard! Leave go of her hair before you pull it all out.' She pummelled Michael's chest with her fists. It said a lot for his feelings for her mother that he didn't strike her, but instead threw Maura back against the pillows.

'Go back to bed, Mum, and let me sort this out.'

'No, I bleeding well won't!' She looked at her husband who had followed her into the room. 'Tell him to leave her alone.'

She pulled her daughter into her arms.

Benjamin, as usual, was half drunk. He looked at everyone in the room with his drunken leer and, finding it difficult to concentrate, waved his hands at his wife. 'Leave Mickey alone. He knows what he's about.'

Sarah lost her temper.

'That's right, Ben, do what you always do. Pass the bloody buck. This time to your son. You drunken bastard! Get out of me sight.'

She turned her gaze on Mickey.

'Now you tell me what's going on here. Your father might be scared of you but I ain't. I'll never be frightened of something that came out of me own body, so just you remember that. Come on, I'm waiting. What's going on?'

Geoffrey answered for him. 'She's been seeing an old Bill.'

Maura's little sob was the only other sound. Sarah stroked her daughter's hair gently and sat herself on the bed.

'So what? Why should that worry you lot? Who the hell do you think you are . . . the Krays? You're nothing, do you hear me. Nothing!

'Out on the street you might be hard men, but in here . . .' she gestured around the room with her free hand. '. . . you're just my boys. That's all. And I never thought I would see the day when you raised your hand to your own sister.'

Sarah was aware that she was speaking for effect. She knew enough about her boys to know that they were greatly feared. She had found guns hidden in the coal house and had sat beside her sons in courtrooms. She had even read about them in the papers. The *News of the World* had had a big spread a few weeks earlier about the hostess clubs in Soho, and one of the clubs mentioned was owned by this great handsome son of hers. A son she was finding it increasingly difficult to love these days. And now on top of everything she had this – her only daughter, her pride and joy, being attacked in her own home. Just because she was seeing a policeman. A decent man more than likely. Yet she knew that her daughter's lovelife was doomed.

She looked down into Maura's tearstained face. 'Is it true, Maws?'

Maura couldn't lie to her mother so she nodded.

Benjamin, more alert now, said, 'Oh my God!'

Sarah turned on him like a mad dog.

'I'll give you "Oh my God", because your daughter's decent. By Christ, it's a wonder we haven't got a whore on our hands, being brought up with you lot. You're all whoremasters, the lot of you!' Her voice was thick with tears. 'I can't hold me head up in the street because everyone knows about you all ... everyone knows my sons are glorified pimps.' She turned on Michael. 'Well, my lad, I hope you get your just deserts in this life. That you pay for all that you've done. For the innocent lives you've ruined and for the death of my Anthony. I've always blamed you for that.' She wagged her head at him. 'If he hadn't been working for you he would be at home with me now.

'I also happen to know that you're a queer, Michael Ryan. And I hear that they're very good to their mothers. So perhaps you could make me a happy woman now by getting of this house and not coming back. It's high time you left anyway, at thirty-one. Go and live with your boyfriend, and take that little snipe with you!' She pointed at Geoffrey. 'Yes, you. You always walked in his footsteps, tried to emulate everything he did. Well, you can follow him out of this house tonight. Go on. Get out, the pair of you.'

Michael was staring at his mother as if she had grown another head right in front of his eyes. He worshipped her, lived for her. If she turned her back on him he had nothing. He stepped towards her, his voice wheedling.

'Mum? Don't be silly, Mum ... I don't want to leave you.'

Sarah cut him off. 'It's a fine thing we bred between us, Benjamin. A cruel, sadistic mummy's boy.' She put up her arm to push him away. 'Get out of my sight, Mickey. You're making me stomach turn. While you kept your violence outside this house I could ignore it, but to see you attacking your own sister ... and her no more than a child. That's finished you as far as I'm concerned. Now just get out.'

She turned her back to him and pulled Maura tightly to her breast. Michael stood there, dazed. Geoffrey went to him, taking him gently by the arm and leading him from the room. Neither looked at their father who stood staring at his wife as if she was a stranger. He had never heard her say so much in one go, in all their years of marriage. He heard the front

134

door slam. Turning slowly from his wife, he went back to their room.

Maura and Sarah cried together.

'Oh, Mum . . . poor Mickey!' Even after what had happened Maura could still find it in her heart to feel sorry for him. She knew that her mother was the most important thing in his life. For her to say all that to him, and for him to stand and take it, spoke volumes. Anyone else would have been dead.

'Don't waste any pity on him, Maws. He's no better than a wild animal. The thought of him with another man makes me sick to me guts.'

Sarah made herself comfortable on the bed and smoothed back her daughter's hair from her face. She loved Maura. She admitted to herself that she had been overprotective towards her, had allowed Michael and the other boys to run her life. But when she had walked in this room and seen Michael attacking her, something inside her had snapped. Garry had been right all along. What she had done was try and take over Maura's life, and this had been the outcome. Her daughter had found herself a man, a decent man more than likely, and the boys wanted to tear it apart.

She said softly, 'Who's the lucky man then?'

Maura sniffed and wiped her eyes with the back of her hand. 'That's the ironic part about it, Mum. As from today I'm not seeing him any more. He packed me in.'

Sarah smiled to herself. 'Listen, child, you will meet a lot of fellows and think that you love them. It's human nature, part of growing up. Don't make the same mistake as I did and marry the first man that comes along. I've regretted marrying your father all my life. You get yourself a decent man with a decent profession. Let me sort out Mickey and the rest of them.'

Maura cried harder. 'You don't understand, Mum. Terry . . . he was the one for me. I really loved him. When he finished with me today, I wanted to die.'

Sarah did smile now. Maura sounded so young and naïve. 'That'll pass. And in a few months someone else will be "the one". It's all part and parcel of growing up.'

Sarah's patronising tone made Maura angry. Rising up on her elbow she shouted, 'In a few months' time I'll be out here!' She gestured with her free hand.

Maura had a sneaking feeling of triumph when she saw the shock on her mother's face.

'Oh no, Maws! Never that. Is that why Michael . . .?'

Maura collapsed back on to the pillows. 'No, Mum. He doesn't know. I only found out myself today.' Her voice broke. 'I was gonna tell him . . . tell Terry everything. About the baby, Mickey . . . But before I got the chance he dumped me. Said he didn't want to get tied down. Wanted to see other women.' Her face screwed up into a mask of tragedy. 'Oh, Mum! What am I gonna do!'

Sarah was stunned. She sat on the bed staring at her daughter, the word 'pregnant' echoing inside her head. It made her squirm inside. She had become pregnant at eighteen. Her father had gone round to Benjamin's house and given him the 'hiding of his life', as he had boasted afterwards. Then the marriage had been arranged. Her life had been ruined because of a furtive, fumbling, sexual exploration up a dark alleyway. Well, that was not going to happen to her daughter. No, by Christ! Her only daughter would get a decent crack at life. She personally would see to that. She made a decision. 'You're going to get rid of it.'

'What!' Maura thought she was hearing things.

'I said, you're getting rid of it!'

'But, Mum!' Maura's voice was shocked. 'I can't do that. It's a sin!'

Sarah's thin-lipped mouth set in a grim line.

'It's a pity you didn't think of that when your knees were pointing at the ceiling. That was a sin as well! No, I've made up my mind. The child must go.' Seeing her daughter's sad face, her voice softened.

'Believe me, Maws, you will thank me for this some day. Could you imagine the trouble this would cause with Michael? His sister pregnant by a policeman – of all things – who'd dumped her? There'd be murder done.'

Maura felt numb inside. 'That's why he dumped me, Mum . . . because of who I am. A Ryan. He never told me that – Mickey did. That's how he found out about it all.'

Sarah kissed Maura's forehead lightly. Suddenly she felt weary, old. 'Get yourself off to sleep now. We'll make our plans in the morning.'

When her mother had settled her down and left the room Maura lay for a while in the darkness. Everything had gone wrong for her. Now she was not only pregnant, she was the cause of Michael and Geoffrey being thrown out of the house. She felt the useless tears run from her eyes and thought, I'll never sleep again. But she did. Only to be plagued by the old nightmare . . .

Downstairs Sarah had made herself a pot of tea and was on the second cup. There would be no sleep for her tonight, that much she was sure of. She finished her tea and settled herself into her chair. Closing her eyes, she began to pray to our Lady of Perpetual Succour.

' "Most holy Virgin Mary, who, to inspire me with boundless confidence, has been pleased to take that sweetest of name, Mother of Perpetual Succour . . ." ' Sarah's lips were barely moving in the dimness of the kitchen. ' ". . . I beseech thee to aid me at all times . . ." '

Chapter Twelve

It had finally been agreed between Maura and her mother to use the address given to her by the little chemist. Old Mother Jenkins would normally have been the one chosen to perform the operation but her encroaching senility, coupled with the fact she couldn't keep her mouth shut, had made Sarah chary of even approaching her. Though abortions were sometimes performed in the local hospital, the fact that the Ryans were a well-known family had put the damper on that idea as well. So it was that at three and a half months pregnant Maura finally went to the little flat in Peckham, accompanied by her mother. It was a high rise block, and Mr Patel lived on the tenth floor. Sarah had already visited the flat to arrange things. After the long journey up in the lift, she knocked on the front door.

Both women had been silent throughout their journey from Notting Hill. Maura felt sick with nerves. There was a part of her that was rebelling against all that was happening to her. Whenever these thoughts entered her head she reminded herself what Mickey would do if he knew, and the knowledge that he would commit a murder generally brought her back to her senses.

The door was opened by an Asian woman. She wore a canary yellow sari and smiled at them constantly, as if trying to make up for her lack of English with courteousness. Maura and Sarah found themselves nodding their heads at her like marionettes.

She showed them into the lounge. Maura had never seen so many colours in one room in all her life. There were greens and blues and reds of every shade imaginable; the walls had brightly coloured carpets hanging on them like paintings. Maura caught her mother's eye and felt an irresistible urge to laugh. She wasn't sure who was the more nervous.

A small untidy Asian man came into the room. 'How are you doing, madams?' He shook their hands and smiled at them so that the whole marionette game began again. 'If you plis follow me?' He led them through a small door into the kitchen.

The place stank of stale curry and there was a nasty undersmell that Maura couldn't pinpoint. It could have been blood. She wasn't sure. Whatever it was, it caught in her throat, burning it. The kitchen was small and in the middle was a large Formica-covered table. It was yellow with a small black pattern going through it. Maura stared at the table fearfully. To the right of her was a work surface and an array of stainless steel tools upon it. She was beginning to sweat. She felt her mother pull her coat and slipped it off her shoulders, letting it fall into her mother's arms.

'Please would you make sure your bladder is empty?'

'Er . . . I . . . it is.' Maura was stammering with fright.

'Good. Please be removing your undergarments and get on to the table.'

'What? You're going to do it in here?'

The man looked at her, puzzled. 'But of course.'

'Come on, Maws. Slip off your drawers.'

Burning with embarrassment, Maura slipped off her panties. With her mother's help she climbed on to the table. It wobbled under her weight and Maura had an awful vision of the whole lot collapsing underneath her. She closed her eyes for a second. On the ceiling above her she could see the naked light bulb. Years of cooking had left the flex with a coating of grease and fly droppings. She closed her eyes again. She must have been mad to come here.

'Mum . . . Mum! I've changed me mind.' Her voice was urgent.

'There now . . . there now. Quieten yourself. It will all be over soon.'

Maura pulled herself up with difficulty and Sarah forced her to lie down again.

'For goodness' sakes, Maura! Will you behave yourself?'

She was a child again, in the dentist's or the doctor's. Only this time it wasn't a filling she was having done, or a few stitches in a cut, it was to be the slaughter of her unborn child.

'Money, please.' The little Asian man had his hand outstretched.

Sarah took an envelope out of her bag and handed it to him. He ripped it open and took the money out. He counted it. Then putting the money back into the envelope, he pushed the lot into the pocket of his cardigan. He used such force he pushed the garment out of shape.

Sarah, watching him, was aware that his fingernails were filthy. She forced herself to look at her daughter. Maura was now gripping the sides of the table. Her long hair was hanging over the edge, nearly touching the floor.

Mr Patel smiled at his wife. He was happy now. He had the money, even if this silly girl changed her mind.

'Put your ankles together and let your legs drop open.'

Maura did as she was told, fear taking over. Mr Patel stood at the end of the stable staring at the opened body for a long while. He was sweating. The palms of his hands were damp and he wiped them on his grubby cardigan. He parted her pubic hair with his finger. Sarah saw him lick his lips and turned her head away in disgust, the bile rising up inside her. The man picked up one of his instruments and slipped it inside Maura. She felt the cold intrusion into her body and stiffened.

'Relax, madam, it will soon be over.'

Maura felt the stinging pain as the steel tip probed for the neck of the womb. When she felt the hard aching agony as he opened the cervix, she gasped. Picking up the curette, a long piece of metal with a strange-looking loop on the end, he began the scraping.

Sarah could hear the animal-like grunts coming from her daughter, could see large beads of sweat appearing on her forehead.

The man worked fast, scraping into the depths of her body. Sarah heard him mutter something in his native language as Maura tried desperately to sit up.

'Oh, Mum . . . please . . . the pain! I can't stand the pain!' Maura's voice was drenched with agony. Then she shrieked like a dog caught in a trap. The woman tried to clamp her hand over Maura's gaping mouth. Tears were rolling down her cheeks and into her ears. She could feel the wetness as she rolled her head from side to side on the hardness of the table. Pushing harder now, the man carried on his scraping. Sarah and the woman held Maura's shoulders to stop her rolling off the table. Sarah felt as if she was caught in some kind of nightmare.

'Just relax, Maws . . . relax.' Someone in the next flat turned their radio louder to drown out the screams. The strains of 'I wanna hold your hand' filled the little kitchen.

Maura tried to close her legs and Mr Patel forced them apart with his shoulders. 'Goodness gracious, woman. Will you keep still?'

'Mum . . . Stop him, Mum . . . I can't stand it. Please!'

Maura felt herself urinating. A bubble seemed to have burst inside her. Then she felt the hotness of the urine and blood. The man yanked out the instruments and shouted to his wife in their native tongue. Mrs Patel went to the sink and, tipping the dirty cups out of the washing up bowl, brought it over to the table. Somehow, between them, the couple managed to get Maura to squat over the bowl.

She felt a lump slowly leave her body, looked down through her sweatdamp hair and saw a baby, about four inches long, lying in mucus and blood at the bottom of the Dayglo orange washing up bowl. It was perfect. Her shoulders began to shake uncontrollably.

141

She felt the hysteria rising up inside her like a tidal wave. That was her baby. She began to cry, harder now, a high piercing crying that was tinged with mania.

Snot was hanging from her nose in long fat lines that dripped into the bowl and mixed with the blood and urine. She could see her white thighs smeared with blood on either side of her baby's orange coffin. She fainted, dropping forward on to the table, sending the washing up bowl and its grisly contents all over the kitchen floor. Sarah stared at the tiny foetus, her grandchild, and felt shame crawl over her body. It began in her legs and crept up her body to her heart. What had she done? Dear Lord, what on earth had she done?

Mrs Patel shook her arm and somehow Sarah was snapped back to life. She dragged her eyes from the tiny corpse and began to help the couple to clear up.

When Maura woke later her panties were back on and she could feel a sanitary towel between her legs. She felt dreadful. She noticed that she was lying on a strange bed in a strange room. She gazed around her, dazed. Then she remembered where she was, the scraping of the cold steel inside her, and felt the familiar panic return. The image of her baby rose up before her and she began to cry again.

Sarah, hearing that her daughter was awake, went into the room. She gathered her into her arms, her own heart breaking. Now she knew why her church outlawed abortion. Why it was considered a sin. She had been the instigator of a horrific deed. She had brought all this pain and suffering on to her daughter. She kissed Maura's head softly.

'It's all over, my love.' She helped her daughter to sit up.

'Oh, Mum, I do feel rough.'

Her stomach felt as if it had been ripped open. She had just had an abortion without any anaesthesia whatsoever. Although neither of them knew it, Maura would never be the same girl after what had happened that afternoon.

Half an hour later she and Sarah were in a taxi, on their way back to Notting Hill. Both sat in silence until, once again tucked up in her own bed, Maura said: 'I wish I'd had the guts to have kept it, Mum. Every time I think of it lying there . . .' Her voice broke. Sobbing, she turned her face into her pillows.

Sarah left the room. She could not face her daughter. She went down the stairs and into her front room where she poured herself a large whisky. She would not forget this day's work in a hurry.

Later in the evening, when she went to her daughter, Maura was asleep with the tears she had cried still glistening on her long lashes. Sarah pulled the blankets up around her daughter's shoulders, praying that her child would find some comfort in her rest, would wake up restored a little. She knew that it would be a long time before either of them felt their old selves again. If indeed they would ever feel anything again.

It was not until the next morning that Sarah found out why her daughter had slept so peacefully and for so long. Finding that she could not wake Maura, Sarah pulled the blankets from her, disturbed by her daughter's whiteness. A mass of deep red blood had seeped from her, till it covered nearly all her lower body and soaked the sheets and bedding. Maura Ryan was haemorrhaging her life's blood away.

Sarah's screams finally brought her friend Pat Johnstone running into the house. She took one look at the scene before her and phoned for an ambulance. The two women sat together as Maura was operated on, united in grief and worry.

Pat Johnstone had known immediately what had happened and she swore to her friend that the knowledge would go to her grave with her. After phoning the ambulance she had phoned Michael, not knowing what else to do. Now she held her friend's hand.

Sarah sat in limbo, waiting for the operation to be over. She would wish to her dying day that she had not taken her daughter to that little flat in Peckham, that she had let her have the baby in St Charles's hospital where they were fighting so valiantly to save her life. She closed her eyes tightly to blot out the troubling visions that kept disturbing her . . .

She heard the swish of the swing doors that led to the operating theatre and turned in the direction of the noise. It was the surgeon. His gown was covered in blood and his face strained. For one awful moment Sarah thought that her daughter had died. Then he spoke.

'Mrs Ryan, your daughter is over the worst now.'

Sarah heard her own voice. 'Thank God! Oh, thank God,'

'I wouldn't be so quick to thank him if I were you, Mrs Ryan. Your daughter was very badly smashed up inside. We've had to remove her ovaries. An infection had set in and I'm afraid she was in no fit state to fight it. Whoever the person was who operated on your daughter, they should be facing a life sentence.' He shook his head slowly. 'By rights she should be dead. As it is she will never have a child . . . another child. She still hasn't regained consciousness yet. But as I said before, the worst of it is over. Though how she will react mentally, I really couldn't say.'

'Thank you, Doctor. Thank you.' Sarah's voice was low and full of shame.

'Whoever it was who did this to your daughter should be put away. I have never, in all my years, seen anything like it. It was as if they had used a battering ram inside her. I'm afraid I must insist that you give me the address. I won't tell the police anything about your daughter. I feel she has been punished enough. But I cannot allow this ever to happen again.'

Sarah nodded. Opening her bag she gave the surgeon the piece of paper the chemist had given Maura. He took it. Patting Sarah's shoulder, he said, 'I know that sometimes the easy way out looks inviting. But it never works out, you know. In the end it pays to do things properly. Your daughter's being taken to Intensive Care if you would like to see her.' He walked off with the paper clutched in his hand.

When Sarah and Pat got to the Intensive Care Unit Michael was already there. He had just arrived in the hospital. Seeing him, Sarah forgot all the harsh words and ran into his outstretched arms. Michael held his mother to him, tears in his eyes. While all the staff looked at the big handsome man comforting his mother, Terry Petherick was being beaten mercilessly by two hired thugs. It would be three months before he came out of hospital and nearly a year before he went back to work.

Sitting his mother down, Michael asked one of the nurses to get her a cup of tea. He wiped her eyes with his handkerchief and then went into the little ward to see his sister. He stared down at her, shocked by what he saw. The years seemed to have been piled on her overnight. Her high cheekbones stood out starkly against her white skin; her cheeks had sunk into her face, leaving deep hollows. As he looked down at her he made a solemn vow to himself. No matter what she did, or what happened, he would always be there for her. He knew that if it had not been for him, she would not be lying there. That Petherick would not have dumped her. Now she was hurting and it was his fault. If it was left to him she would never know hurt again. Petherick was being paid out for his part in it, even as he stood there. Paid muscle was beating him to a pulp. And that was as it should be. As he had told Benny, you looked after your womenfolk.

He took her hand gently in his and Maura regained consciousness. She opened her eyes and looked up into Michael's face. She ran her tongue across cracked lips, trying to speak. He put his head nearer to her face and what she said caused him to sob into her shoulder.

'My poor baby, Mickey. My poor innocent baby.'

He gently enfolded her in his arms, their tears mingling together. If it cost him his life, she would never know sadness again.

A week later the surgeon, Mr Bernard Frobisher, was told by the police that the address he had given them had been firebombed three days previously. The tenants of the flat, Mr Ahman Patel, his wife Homina and eldest daughter Naimah, had been killed.

The police thought it was probably a racial attack; they had no idea who could have done it. Mr Frobisher wisely kept his opinion to himself. He had no intention of putting his own family in jeopardy. Especially not for a back-street abortionist.

Chapter Thirteen

Maura had been out of hospital six weeks and the whole family agreed that she was a changed girl. She had a brittleness that sat uneasily on her now slim shoulders. She had lost so much weight that Benny playfully nicknamed her 'Beanpole'. With her height and new svelteness she looked like a fashion model. Except for her breasts. Somehow, although they had shrunk with the rest of her body, they were still large enough to make her feel 'top heavy'. She had smiled at Benny's jokes about her body, but deep inside felt she had paid a high price for her newfound slimness.

She was sitting by her bedroom window looking out at the children playing in the street. She remembered when she had played the same games with Margaret. Tin Pan Alley, Hopscotch, Five Jacks. She longed for that safe world now, when the only worry she'd had was what time she had to be in by. Maura's profile, as she looked down on the children, showed the extent of the change in her. Her nose was more sharply defined, a Roman nose, her cheekbones looked as if they had been carved from ivory. Her dark blue eyes were deeper set. Earlier, she had creamed her face and hands, still unaware of how lovely she really was. Although she saw herself in the glass, she never really took any notice. It was as if the day she had left the hospital, Maura Ryan as was had ceased to exist. Now a beautiful outer shell, inside she felt nothing. Nothing at all. Until today. Today she had the beginnings of a plan forming in her mind, and she needed Michael's help to fulfil it.

She smiled as one of the children below her screamed and pointed to something on the pavement. She guessed, rightly, that it was some kind of insect. It brought back a memory from her subconscious. She could smell the dampness of the scullery, that cold dampness that seemed to seep into the bones. Anthony had locked her in there when she was a small child. Turning out the light, leaving her in the darkness. She had been far too small to reach the light switch. She had stood in the dank world he had created, knowing that the army of cockroaches was scrambling beneath her feet. She shuddered as she thought of it. The fear and panic it had created rose up inside her again, as it had on that day. She had imagined they were running up her legs, into her knickers. Until she had felt the hot wetness as the urine had run down her chubby legs, soaking her socks and shoes. That's when the screams had been forced from her throat, high piercing screams that had brought her mother and father and Michael . . . a very angry Michael who had taken off his belt and laid into Anthony until his screams had matched her own.

Again the image of her baby in the washing up bowl filled her head. She forced the picture away, shaking her head as if it would help to make it disappear. She did not blame anyone but herself for what had happened in that tiny flat. She told herself that at least twenty times a day. Not her mother or Michael. Not anyone but herself. And Terry.

She blamed him with all her heart and soul. From the moment she had seen the body of her child, their child, lying in that dirty bowl, hatred for him had entered her body. A seed had been planted that day, and Maura had nurtured it and cultivated it, until now it had grown tall, like a bedraggled beanstalk in a fairy tale. She had read about his beating in the *Daily Mirror* and felt nothing for him. No pity. No sorrow. Nothing. She was as empty where he was concerned as she was about herself. As the seed of contempt had grown inside her, it had strangled the memory of every nice thing he had ever said or done, until she had forgotten his goodness. Forgotten the fun they had had and the closeness they had shared. She knew that if he had not dumped her that day, she would have had the baby. Somehow she would have found a solution to her problems. She chose to forget her fear of Michael. Her fear of having a baby alone. In Terry Petherick she had found the perfect scapegoat. She knew that the police knew exactly who had ordered his beating but like so many things that happened thanks to the Ryan family, they could not prove it. She smiled to herself. Well, if everything went as she planned, she would soon be a real member of the Ryans. An active working member . . .

She hoped that Terry was in agony. That he was so badly hurt no one would ever look at his handsome face again. That was her prayer. The only good thing to come out of the whole sorry business was that Michael was back in her mother's good books. Although he had not come back home to live, he still visited frequently. It seemed that the day he had moved out had started the ball rolling for them all. Geoffrey, Leslie, Lee and Garry had all moved out. Only Benny and herself remained at home. Lee and Garry shared a flat off the Edgware Road; Geoffrey had bought himself a flat near Michael's, in Knightsbridge. The house was quiet now, unlike the old days when they were all young and it was noisy from early morning to late at night. In a funny way she missed the hustle and bustle of her younger days.

She was roused from her reverie by a tap on the bedroom door.

Michael walked in carrying a large box of chocolates. She gazed at him affectionately. There was no doubt about it, he was one hell of a good-looking man.

'You keep buying me chocolates, Mickey, and I don't eat them.'

'No . . . but I do!' He grinned at her mischievously, and then, throwing himself across the bed, rolled off on to the floor, rolled again sideways and was kneeling in front of her, offering the box of chocolates in a gesture of supplication. Arms outstretched, eyes raised to the ceiling, like a Japanese Geisha girl.

'And all because the lady loves Milk Tray!'

Maura burst out laughing. 'I wouldn't mind but they're Black Magic.'

'That's right, laugh at me after I risk life and limb for you.'

He sat back on his heels and looked at her. 'How are you feeling?' His voice was gentle.

Maura sighed. 'I feel OK. Though I would feel a damn' sight better if everyone stopped asking me that, I just want to forget it.' She slumped into her chair, her face closed again. She stared at him warily. 'Actually, Mickey, there is something I want to ask you.'

He shrugged. 'Ask away, Princess. Anything you want, you can have.'

'Honestly, Mickey? Anything?'

He put his hand on his heart. 'I give you my word, as they say on the telly.'

Maura leant forward in her chair and grinned at him. 'I want you to give me a job!'

Michael stared, his face a study in dismay. 'I don't know about that, Maws.'

'You promised me, Mickey.' Her voice was hard and shrewish. 'You promised me anything. Anything!'

'Yeah. But I never expected this.'

'Look, Mickey.' Her voice was wheedling now, cajoling. 'I have been thinking about this for a while now . . . I want to take over the ice cream and hot dogs.'

'You!' He sounded as if he had been poleaxed.

'Why not? I worked them often enough as a kid.'

He pushed her back into her seat. 'You don't understand, Princess.'

She pushed herself forward again, her voice desperate. 'Oh, but I do understand, Mickey. That's just where you're wrong. I know exactly how to run them. A bloody kid could do that. If you're worried that I ain't got the bottle then you can stop. I have got it,

Mickey. More than you would think. I've spent the best part of my life listening to you lot plan and scheme. I could piss it, Mickey, if you gave me the chance.'

'Look, Maws, it's a dangerous business for a bloke. Let alone a bird.'

'I know that, Michael, but I'm your sister. Not some nonsense bird out to make a few bob. I could do that on me back like your hostesses. I know that if you give me the chance, I could make a go of it. At first I would be respected because I'm your little sister, but I guarantee you that within a few months I'd be respected for myself.'

'But you don't understand, Maws . . .'

'I do! That's just what I'm trying to tell you if you'd listen to me. I know that if someone puts a van on one of our pitches, licence or no licence, they get warned off. Or you try to buy them out, depending. If they won't play your game, you petrol bomb them. They soon get the message. If you happen to know the person and like them, and the pitch isn't major, you arrange for a little percentage. Christ Almighty, Mickey, we're all from the same stable. If you can't trust me, who can you trust?'

Michael digested this bit of logic.

'I don't know, Maws.' She sensed that he was thawing towards her, and pressed home her advantage.

'I swear to you, Mickey, that I will make you proud of me. I'll run those pitches better than they have ever been run before!'

Seeing her face, so full of hope and anticipation, Michael couldn't deny her. After all she had been through, the pain and heartache, it seemed small compensation. He grinned. 'All right. You win.'

Maura threw herself into his arms, pulling them both to the floor. She kissed him full on the mouth.

'Oh, Mickey, thanks. Thanks! I'll work like a nigger for you, I promise. You won't regret it.'

I've got the ice cream and hot dogs, she thought, thrilled at the implications. If Terry Goody Two Shoes Petherick wanted to catch criminals . . . let him try to catch her!

'I promise you, Mickey, you will never regret this.'

And he didn't.

Maura walked across the Yard towards the small crowd of men. They were all staring at her. Some watched her with hostility, others with curiosity. She was their boss, and like most workforces they were waiting to see the outcome of a new regime. They were all aware that she was Michael Ryan's sister. Just seventeen years old. Most were amazed at the sheer size of her. She was taller than most of the men there. She smiled at them all, hiding her nervousness behind a façade of friendliness.

'Right, I expect you all know me, and over the next few weeks I hope to get to know you. I'm new at this business, I admit, and I will be open to any friendly advice you may wish to give me. But I must stress this one fact . . . at the end of the day it's my decision that counts. Now if any of you gentlemen find that hard to accept, I suggest you see me after I've finished the rotas. OK?'

She scanned the sea of faces before her, looking for any hint of trouble. Everyone looked neutral. Not bad for starters, she thought.

'Now if the runners would all stand aside, I would like to see the actual drivers and workers.'

Most of the younger men in the crowd broke away and made a smaller gang by themselves. The runners were the young men who kept a look out for the police. They stood at strategic points near the vans watching not only for beat policemen but also Panda cars. They also eyed up any competition that came on to their patch, reporting all back to the drivers – the mainstay of the business. It was not unusual to see an ice cream van wheelspin away, dragging a runner into the service hatch as it went, especially on the police patches: Westminster, the Houses of Parliament, Knightsbridge, outside Harrods, and Baker Street where Madame Tussaud's brought so many tourists.

The drivers and servers stood quietly. They employed and paid their own runners, the Ryans only paid these men. Eventually, if the runners proved any good, they were given new pitches as and when they came up. It was a close-knit community that these men lived in. If they were caught, and hauled into Bow Street court, they gave 'moody' names and Michael paid their fines. It was an arrangement that suited everyone. In the summer, especially, there was an awful lot of money to be made. And as with any lucrative business, many people who wanted a piece of the action.

Maura coughed to clear her throat. 'I think that for the time being, we stick to the usual rota. So you can all go to your usual pitch today. I will be looking over the takings and popping along to see you now and then.' She smiled again. 'I hope you will all bear with me on this.'

The men nodded at her, happier now they knew where they were to be stationed. Most knew their pitches like the back of their hands. They knew every road, alleyway, and escape route on their own particular manor.

'Off you go then. If you have any trouble, ring me. If I'm not here, someone will find me.'

She turned away and walked to the caravan that served as her office. Michael was watching her from the window. He had been listening to her address the men and was impressed. Against his better judgement, he began to think that she might just be able to do the job after all.

The men all gravitated to their vans. Most were subdued. None had ever worked for a woman before. All had lived on the fringes of crime, were petty burglars, car thieves or 'kiters' – people who bought stolen cheque books and then used them to buy goods that could be sold off to fences. Maura's advert into their masculine world was a shock. But she was Michael Ryan's sister and so they would afford her a trial period. If she didn't work out, and they were all sure she would not, Michael, being a business-man first and foremost, would 'out' her and they could all get back to normal!'

Maura walked into the caravan feeling sick with apprehension. It had gone much better than expected. Michael laughed and shook his head slowly. 'Sure you want all this hag, Princess?'

'Yes, Michael, I'm sure. Now, if you don't mind. I have some books to look over.'

'Oh, well. Pardon me for breathing.'

Maura laughed. 'Have a quick coffee before you go. There's still a few things I'm not sure of.'

'Okey doke. But I'll say this much to you now, Maws, you did well out there. They're the scum of the earth but they're good workers. But for Gawd's sake, watch them! If they kiss your hand, count your fingers. And if any get a bit too saucy, you let me know. Most of them would put their granny on the streets if they thought she could pull a few bob. Start as you mean to go on, love. Be fair but hard. That's the only law they know. Show that you're stronger than them and you've got friends for life. Show a chink of weakness and . . . well, to put it bluntly, you're fucked.'

'I'll remember that, Mickey. Now about these books?'

'You sort out the books, Maws. I know sod all about it. I told Benny to get his arse down here this morning and show you what he'd been doing. All I ever did was pick up the overall total. How Benny got to it, I don't know. So you'll have to sort that lot out yourself.'

'Well, Benny should be here soon. I'll ask him.'

'You do that. Now one last thing, Maws. In the drawer of your desk, on the right hand side, is a gun.'

'A gun?'

'Yes, a gun. I told you this was a dangerous business. But don't worry. I've left one of my best boys outside. No one will bother you while he's there. But just in case, that's where the gun is. If the filth come snooping about, tell them that they're paid up to next month. If they see you here they might try it on. On no account get rid of that firearm. Right?'

Maura nodded. She looked troubled and Michael laughed. 'Still think you can hack it?'

She straightened in her seat. 'Yes, I bloody well can. Now do you want a coffee or not?'

As she went to put the kettle on she had a fleeting feeling of being involved in something way over her head. She pushed the thought and the feeling firmly from her mind. This was her inauguration into the world of the Ryans. This was to be her career and she would make her name synonymous with villainy. Her brother Michael wouldn't be in it once she got started!

Danny Forster had been a runner for nearly two years. He worked for 'Big Bill' McEwan, a large extrovert Scotsman. He was standing at Baker Street tube station, watching for roving policemen and Panda cars. It was a bright spring day and the tourists were just arriving in force. He saw a strange van parking just down the road from him. It was a Milano Bros ice cream van. He frowned. Within minutes they were open for business. He walked quickly past the van. Inside were four men. He could not see any runners so he assumed that two of the men were breakers. He walked slowly back to Madame Tussaud's and told the Scotsman what he had seen.

Big Bill McEwan was not known for his quiet temperament. He was once described by a judge as 'a most obnoxious individual who should not be walking the streets with innocent people'. Big Bill had taken this as a compliment. He saw himself as different from the average person and was gratified that someone educated, as the judge so obviously was, should agree with him. Getting his considerable bulk out of the ice cream van he meandered down to the rival camp. When he arrived he realised that he had been expected.

'This is my patch. I want you lot to piss off – and sharpish!' His large stomach, hanging over his trousers, quivered as he spoke.

A very good-looking Italian smiled at him, displaying perfect teeth.

'We have a licence. Legally we are allowed to be here. I think it is yourself who is maybe . . . how you say? . . . in the wrong.'

Big Bill stared at the man through small piggy eyes. He decided that the Italian was probably a simpleton. Everyone in the 'creaming' business knew who he was. That's why he got to work 'The Sword', one of the best pitches in London.

'Are you going to fuck off or not?' His voice brooked no

153

argument. By now a crowd had gathered to watch the exchange. Tourists and Londoners alike sensed that a battle was taking place and stood waiting to see who would be the victor.

'No . . .'

Before the Italian could finish his sentence, Big Bill was already walking away and hauling himself back into his van, a bright pink and yellow affair with 'Dingle Dells Ice Cream' written in green letters along the sides. Without speaking to his server he started up the van and reversed out of his parking place. The server was still trying frantically to get a lid on the hotplate, which was covered in chopped onions and half-cooked hamburgers. He turned off the gas and the ice cream valves. He was not taking any chances.

Big Bill drove his ice cream van straight at the Milano Bros vehicle. The four men inside stood rooted to the spot as they realised his intention. He hit the back of their van so hard a box of flakes that had been standing on one of his own back shelves shot forward into the front seat, crumbling its contents all over Big Bill's trousers.

He reversed back again and once more rammed the Italians' van. They were hanging on to anything they could grab. Then, pulling his van up beside the driver's window. Big Bill shouted at the four men: 'I'll be back tomorrow with shooters and anything else it takes to shift you. This is your one and only warning.'

Then he drove away at a leisurely pace. The Hot Dog War of 1967 had started.

Maura listened to all that Big Bill had to say. In the few weeks she had been doing the job she had begged for, she had gained an insight into the world of the 'creamers'.

'So what are you going to do, Mrs?'

Maura sighed. If he called her 'Mrs' once more she would strangle him.

'Well, Bill, I'm not sure exactly what action I'll take yet, but I promise you that I'll have it sorted in the next twenty-four hours, OK?'

'You'd bloody well better have, Mrs. I've lost an awful lot of money today.'

Maura cut him off. 'I'm quite well aware of that, Bill. Now you shoot off home and leave this to me.' He turned to go and she called him back.

'One more thing. My name is either Maura or Miss Ryan. I don't care which you use. But, please, don't call me Mrs.' She smiled at him icily.

154

'Fair enough, Mrs. I'll let you know what I decide to call you.'

Maura mentally chalked one up to Big Bill.

Left alone she pondered what he had told her. This was the chance she had been waiting for. If she could successfully pull this off alone, without any help from her brothers, she would be set. She called in her minder, a large black man called Tony Dooley after his grandfather, an Irishman who had taken a West Indian woman as his wife. Tony stood in front of Maura as she outlined her plan. When she had finished, he smiled. Maura took the gun from the drawer and placed it in her shoulder bag. It was time to go and see the Milano Brothers.

George Milano surveyed the young girl before him. He let his gaze roam over her body. He decided she had good tits. He was disappointed that Michael Ryan could make such a bad decision. He had always understood that Michael was an astute business-man. He had respected him. Then this! It had hit the street that he had given his little sister the ice cream and hot dog business. Now she sat here, in his office, making veiled threats. It was laughable! He smiled at her.

'Listen, Miss Ryan, I appreciate you coming here today to speak to me, but I'm afraid that you are wasting your time. I have legitimate licences for all those vans of mine. My advice to you is to go and see your big brother . . . or has he given control of the rest of his businesses to your mother?' He spoke in a sarcastic manner, causing Maura to grit her teeth.

'So you won't listen to what I have to say?' Her voice was soft. He shook his head, still smiling that maddening smile. Maura stood up. She noticed him looking at her legs.

'Very well, Mr Milano. We shall have to come to some other arrangement.'

She left the office with Tony Dooley following her, her head held high. Milano might have won the first battle but she was determined to win the actual war. She went from the Milano Brothers' offices in Aldgate East to Brixton where she had a meet with one of Tony Dooley's brothers. Two hours later she left the meeting smiling.

Back in the caravan she had a telephone call from Michael. She assured him that it was all under control. All he had to do was wait. Tony made her a cup of coffee and they sat together companionably. News came in all day of different pitches that had been encroached on. Maura told each driver the same thing. To go home and come back the next day.

155

Geoffrey was annoyed and Michael knew it. 'She can't cope with all this on her own!'

'Let's just see how she gets on, Geoff. I think she might surprise us.'

'What if she gets hurt? Have you thought of that?'

Michael laughed. 'She won't. Why do you think I gave her Tony Dooley? Just leave her be, Geoff. If she cocks it up we can easily take over. If she gets a result, she's proved herself a worthy asset. Now let's forget it.'

Geoffrey was livid with Michael. How could a young girl like Maura be expected to cope with the likes of the Milano Brothers? 'Have you any idea how she's going to sort it all out?'

Michael lost his temper. Sometimes Geoffrey was like an old woman!

'No, I ain't! Now for fuck's sake give it a rest. She asked for twenty-four hours and she's gonna get it, all right?'

'All right . . . all right. Keep your hair on!'

They sat together in silence. Michael hoped that Maura did not let him down. He was well aware of the stir her appointment as head of the creamers had created on the street. He had been a laughing stock, not only among rival villains but among his own workforce. Not that anyone would ever say it to his face. In their world women were either wives or mistresses. They were not thought capable of running a 'moody' business, unless they were brasses; then they sold the only asset they had, their bodies, and nine times out of ten a man was behind that – either a pimp or a boyfriend. He crossed his fingers as he thought about what he had done. A lot lay on Maura's performance in the next twenty-four hours. He just hoped that he had not underestimated her.

George Milano was forty-five years old. His wife was twenty-two. She had flown over from Palermo two years earlier, a week before he married her. She had already given him two sons, and was lying beneath him passively as he puffed and panted on top of her when the telephone by the bed rang. George glanced at the clock. It was two o'clock in the morning. Not letting his stroke falter, he answered the phone, still pumping away at her. She watched his face, a detached expression in her eyes. She had been quick to learn that if she lay quietly he was soon finished. Even though she felt nothing for this fat old man on top of her, it annoyed her female pride that he answered the phone while he made love to her.

'Yeah?' His voice was breathy and stilted.

156

'Is that George Milano?' It was Maura Ryan's voice! He was so shocked he nearly missed his stroke.

'What do you want?'

'I just thought I'd let you know that your yard was blown up five minutes ago. I happened to be there when it went up.' The line went dead.

As did George's erection. He lay on top of his young wife with his mouth hanging open, the telephone receiver still in his hand.

Magdalena Milano brought up her long slender arms and, putting a finger under her husband's chin, pushed his mouth closed. She had to endure his nightly assaults, she accepted that, but she did not have to look at his false teeth and his yellow tongue.

The action spurred him back to life. He leapt from the bed, his flaccid penis lost in the roll of fat that was his stomach. Screaming abuse in Italian, he began to dress himself. Magdalena rolled over and closed her eyes, grateful to whoever was on the phone for cutting her husband's sexual appetite short. When he left the house five minutes later she was asleep.

By the time George got to his yard in Aldgate East the worst of the fires had been put out. He saw a police car and went straight to the officers standing by it.

'I know who did this thing! It was the Ryans! They rang me up to tell me . . .' His voice trailed off. Sitting in the police car was Maura Ryan.

She looked at him innocently. 'I beg your pardon?'

Suddenly George Milano realised exactly what he was up against. His vision of usurping the Ryans' position in London was replaced by one of his body floating in the Thames. He heard the two officers laughing. Turning from their grinning faces he went to what had once been his yard. Nearly all his vans were destroyed. As Maura watched the man's shoulders slump inside his suit she felt a moment of pity for him. She had just ruined his business. Then her heart hardened as she reminded herself that if he had had his way the boot would be on the other foot. She got out of the police car. Her brother owned most of the officers in this area. She went to George Milano and put her hand on his shoulder.

'I did try to warn you, Mr Milano.'

He nodded imperceptibly. 'I know that.'

'I'm not sorry for what happened here tonight, but I am sorry it had to come to this.'

He nodded again. She left him. Getting into her car with Tony Dooley, she went to her own yard. She would stay there for the rest of the night with Tony and a couple of his friends. If there were going to be any comebacks she would sort that out herself as well.

Tony bought the *Daily Mirror* at five-thirty. The explosion in the Milanos' yard had made the middle pages. It said that following the ramming of rival ice cream vans in Baker Street, a well-known Italian ice cream merchant's yard had been fire-bombed. The police believed it was the work of another Italian family. The Italians were known to be the main distributors of ice cream in London and the surrounding areas. The story went on to describe George Milano's father's rise to riches. From an ice cream barrow-boy in the late eighteen hundreds, he had built up the Milano Brothers business empire . . .

Maura, Tony and the other men laughed. They had done it!

Michael took the call from George Milano at nine-fifteen. 'Hello, Michael. It is George . . . George Milano. How are you?'

'I'm fine, Georgie. Which is more than I can say for you, ain't it?'

'I did not realise your sister had your protection . . .' His voice sounded desperate. Michael cut him off.

'My sister has my protection, Georgie, but only when she asks for it. Whoever done that bit of business last night works for *her*, Georgie, not me. It's her you've got to pacify.'

The line went quiet.

'I know what you was thinking, Georgie. Chatter always gets back to the person being chattered about. I know what the word was on the street. That I was a nutter for allowing my sister to take over the creamers. But it paid off, didn't it? She pissed all over your fireworks, didn't she? Well, I'll tell you again. If you wanna bargain, you do it with her.'

He replaced the telephone in its cradle, then laughed out loud. He looked at Geoffrey, and, pointing to the newspaper on his desk, said, 'She's a fucking girl ain't she?'

At six-thirty that morning Maura's workforce turned up for work. They greeted her warmly. She had not only their respect but their friendship. To Maura this was an added bonus. As she watched them sorting out their vans and stocking up, she felt a sudden pride in what she had done. They drove from the site with her watching. Then, as if all of one mind, they began to play their jingles. The noise was deafening. The Dingly Dell music was a clanging rendition of the old music hall favourite: 'How much is that doggy in the window?'

Maura laughed out loud as she placed her hands over her ears

158

to blot out the noise. All that day she found herself humming the tune. It was a turning point in her life. Within eighteen months she ran every site in London. Thanks to her own natural friendliness, coupled with a ruthless use of pickaxe handles and muscle men, Maura Ryan was well and truly on her way.

Book Two

Pecunia non olet
  (Money has no smell) – Emperor Vespasian, AD
  9–79

I fear the Greeks,
  even when they bring gifts – Virgil 70–19 BC

Chapter Fourteen

1975

Roy walked into the Lotus House Restaurant in Dagenham. It was three-thirty in the morning, 1 December 1975. He walked up to the tiny bar in the corner of the restaurant and banged on the counter. He frowned. Mr Wong was usually there to greet him, offer him a complimentary drink and pay him his money. Instinctively, Roy's hand went into his jacket, to the gun that he kept there. With his free hand he banged once more on the counter.

'Oi, anyone at home!'

He sensed rather than heard two men step from the shadows of the dimly lit room. He turned to face them.

'Mr Ryan? Mr Roy Ryan?' A short swarthy man stood there smiling at him – an oily smile that dripped from his face. Looking at him, Roy knew that if he got close enough the man would stink of garlic. His hand tightened on his gun. 'You have no need of your firearm tonight, Mr Ryan. I am intending to be very nice to you. Very friendly. I am a very generous man.'

He snapped his fingers at the large muscular young man beside him.

'Dimitri, get Mr Ryan and myself a drink.' As the younger man walked to the bar, the smaller one offered Roy a seat.

'Who are you?' His voice was careful and controlled.

'I am Mr Dopolis. You may laugh if you want.' He paused to allow Roy to chuckle. Roy ignored him. 'Normally you English hoot with laughter when you hear it.' He shrugged. 'Unfortunately, that was my father's name and his father's before him.' He smiled again. 'I could not have changed it.' His voice was conversational, as if they were old friends.

'Look, Mr Dopolpolis, or whatever your name is, what do you want and how do you know who I am?'

Mr Dopolis shook his head sadly.

'You young men! Always in a hurry!'

He snapped his fingers again and the boy brought over their drinks.

'Please, Mr Ryan. Sit down and have a drink with me.'

Roy sat down opposite the man. Up close he realised that his first thought had been correct. Dopolis *did* stink of garlic.

'Drink your whisky, Mr Ryan. We are going to have a little chat.'

Dimitri stood between the two of them and Roy noticed that he was carrying a gun. In his padded leather jacket it would have been virtually undetectable by anyone else. However, Roy was unnerved to observe that it was no ordinary handgun the youth was carrying. He would bet his last pound that the thigh-length leather the boy was wearing had a special 'long pocket' fitted inside it. That meant only one thing. Young Dimitri was carrying a sawn-off shotgun.

He glanced at the door, weighing up his chances of escape. Mr Dopolis laughed out loud, bringing Roy's head round to face him again.

'I know what you are thinking, young man.' Dopolis held his hand up as if to stop Roy leaving. 'You are free to go when you have heard what I have to say. You won't need *your* gun. Not tonight anyway.'

The man's voice was cold and calculating, as if he took great pains to pronounce his words properly.

Roy leant back in his chair nonchalantly and took a long sip of the Chivas Regal Dimitri had placed in front of him. He was well aware that he was not Brain of Britain. Roy had never overestimated himself. He could work the bookies, the hostess clubs, the minding. He was also first in line for any armed robberies that were in the offing. Roy was the eternal heavy. That's why he was in the Lotus House now. He was collecting the 'rents', the protection money. What he did not know was that Dopolis had picked him out for these very qualities. He wanted a message taken to Michael Ryan and Roy seemed to be the perfect messenger boy.

'I want you to tell your brother something for me, Roy. May I call you Roy?' He did not wait for an answer, but carried on as if taking everything he said for granted. 'I want you to tell Michael that although he has run the West End satisfactorily for many years, people are getting . . . how shall we say? . . . upset at the way he has gradually taken over East London and even parts of Essex!'

He laughed as if it was all a big misunderstanding. 'He collects the "rents" on the restaurants and bookies, not to mention the pubs and the clubs. He owns all the cab ranks. He even has the monopoly on the ice cream and hot dogs. Not forgetting that he gets a percentage of any blags that take place on the manor. Now I ask you, is that fair? My friends and I would like to know what is left for us? We want to earn a living as well. We have all joined forces, so to speak. We have only one avenue left for making money – drugs – and the blacks have always had the edge where they're concerned.'

His voice became low and conspiratorial, as if Roy was his dearest and oldest friend. 'You must tell your brother what we have been discussing. Tell him that myself and many others have joined forces. We will fight him if needs be. Tell him that we want the East End. The pubs, the clubs, the restaurants. Everything. He must make do with the West End, North London and South of the water. Surely that is enough for him? Tell him that he has my word we will not interfere with him.'

Roy burst out laughing. He sat and literally roared with laughter. Great bursting gales of merriment that rendered him incapable of talking. This man was some kind of nutter. He had to be. Everyone in the East End who was employed in a 'fringe' business, whether it was a jellied eel or a market stall, worked indirectly for Mickey. Even the blaggers, and they were getting more and more as the years went on, came and saw Mickey or one of his intermediaries before nipping into their local Tescos waving their sawn-offs at everyone. Now this little Greek twat wanted him to take a threatening message to Michael. He bubbled over with laughter again, forgetting the youth with his shotgun, forgetting everything except the crazy man before him.

Dopolis stared at him icily.

'You can laugh, Mr Ryan, but I am afraid that I and my friends are very serious. Very serious indeed. As you will soon find out.'

Roy wiped his eyes with his handkerchief. 'Listen, Cocker, Mickey has not, as you put it, muscled in on the East End. We fought for this shitheap and we won it fair and square.'

The little man sat straighter in his chair. 'Your brother –' he pointed at Roy – 'firebombed a taxi rank belonging to my cousin Stavros. Only two days after your brother's funeral my cousin was crippled for life. He was so badly hurt he could not control his armies.' Dopolis's face was red with temper and he had flecks of spittle at the corners of his lips.

Roy interrupted him rudely.

'Armies! What fucking armies? He couldn't control a bumper car. He had my brother murdered!' Roy was losing his own temper now. The last shred of fear dissolved in the face of Dopolis's argument. Anthony's death was still an open wound with all the Ryans.

Dopolis forced himself to remain calm. He smiled. 'That famous Irish temper of yours . . . it will be your downfall one of these days. Remember this – when you are in a temper you do not think straight. Michael should have worked out an agreement with my

165

cousin. Something that would have been satisfactory to both parties. If he had done that your brother would be alive today.'

'Bollocks!' Roy stood up. 'Let me tell you something, Mr Oppodopolis or whatever your fucking name is . . . Mickey will rip your ears off and shove them up your arse. And he'll smile while he's doing it. So do yourself a favour and piss off. I'm a very busy man.'

He pushed Dimitri out of the way. 'As for your Action Man, if you're gonna use your weapon, do it now. You've been standing there like the orphan of the storm . . . you big prat!'

The boy looked at Dopolis who shook his head slowly. Roy walked through the service door into the kitchen of the restaurant.

Mr Wong was sitting in there with his wife and daughter clutching him, frightened. His son was standing behind his father. He had recent bruises around his face. They all stared at him pathetically. Roy's blood was up now and taking his gun from its holster he stormed back into the restaurant. These people paid protection money. The least he could do was protect them. The restaurant was empty. He walked back to the kitchen.

'What happened?'

All four started talking at once, the mother and daughter in Cantonese. Roy put his hands over his ears and shouted: 'SHUT UP!' at the top of his voice. They all stopped speaking abruptly. Roy pointed to the son, Hap Ki, who spoke reasonable English, and said: 'You tell me what happened.'

'I tell you, Mr Ryan. The man took monry we had for you. In future, he say, you pay monry to us. Get bugger! I say we pay Mr Ryan. We always pay Mr Ryan. Nor anymore they say. If we no give monry, then place burned to ground by weekend. Still we not pay. My father tell them that Mr Ryan good friend and will protect us . . . So they start to bash me in face.' He pointed to his swollen eye. 'So my father gave them monry. We can't pay you now.'

Roy nodded. 'Never mind about that now. Look, I'll be back at the weekend as usual. If they come to see you before I get back here, phone me at this number.' He took a small card out of his jacket pocket. 'Now don't worry. This will all be sorted out in a few days.' He nodded to the women and walked out of the kitchen. He put his gun back in its holster. Then taking a serviette from the counter, carefully picked up the glass that Dopolis had used. Now, he thought, we'll see how good our friends at the Met are.

He left the restaurant and went to his car. Tessa, his Doberman, was lying on the back seat asleep. She shot into action as he unlocked his car, barking and growling. Roy spoke to her gently until she calmed down. She had been lying asleep on more than sixteen thousand pounds. As the dog settled back down Roy smiled to himself. He collected over sixty-four thousand a month. There was no way Michael was going to let that go, especially not to a relative of Stavros, the man who'd murdered Anthony. Roy started up the car. That Dopolis had to be some kind of head banger.

Michael Ryan was pacing up and down his office, a sure sign he was agitated. He pulled on his cigarette and blew the smoke out noisily from between his lips.

'Did he look familiar like? Have you ever seen him about?'

Roy shook his head.

'Nah, never seen him in my life before. He was a saucy fucker, though. The big bastard, Dimitri, was carrying a sawn-off, I'm certain of it. They'd collected old Wong's rent before I got there so they were definitely waiting for me.'

'What exactly did he say about Stavros?'

'Just that he was his cousin, that we had bombed him out and while he was hurt . . .' Roy laughed again '. . . he couldn't control his "armies". Armies, I ask you! Then he went on about you having the whole of London. Oh, Mickey, I tell you. He was a right prat.'

Geoffrey got up from his seat and glanced at his watch. 'How about we let Roy get home and get some shut-eye? It's nearly half-past four.' He looked at Roy. 'I expect you're dying to get home. The baby's due any day, isn't it?'

Roy nodded, a big grin on his face.

Michael rubbed his eyes with his fingers and leant against the wall of the office.

'I'm sorry, Roy. You get off home, mate. Tell Janine that she's got to phone the old woman as soon as she comes into labour. The old Dutch is like a cat on a hot tin roof over this baby.'

Roy laughed.

'If you could see the bloody stuff that they've got for it. Cots and cribs and bleeding layettes. It's enough to drive a man to drink, I tell ya!'

Michael smiled. 'You love it, mate. Is Carla going home when the baby's born?'

Roy's face dropped.

'I don't think so, Mickey. Maura's house is nearer her college and that.'

There was an embarrassed silence. It was a well-known fact that Janine could not stand her daughter around her. Carla gravitated between her grandmother's house and Maura's. Geoffrey coughed loudly.

167

'Anyway, mate, we'll see you later on. Give Janine our best.'

'I will, Geoff.' He got up to go. Michael took a package off his desk and passed it to Roy.

'One last thing, would you drop this off at Black Tony's house? Tell him it's a pound bag and I want the money for it by Saturday latest. Give it the big'un while you're there. He's been getting a bit lairy lately.'

Roy took the package.

'Okey doke. See you later then.'

When he had left, Geoffrey poured out two brandies. Giving one to Michael, he sat himself in the easy chair opposite the desk. Michael sat at the desk rolling the brandy in his glass.

'So, Mickey. What do you think? Trouble?'

Mickey sipped his drink. 'With a capital T, Bruv.'

He tossed back the rest of the brandy and stood up. 'Let's get off home, Geoffrey, I'm knackered. I can't think when I feel like this.'

Geoffrey gulped his own drink down. By the time he had pulled on his overcoat, Michael had already turned off the lights and made his way down the stairs. Outside the club they stood on the pavement, both gulping in the cool night air. Michael touched Geoffrey's shoulder before getting into his car and driving off.

As Geoffrey watched Michael's Mercedes pulling away he was aware of a feeling of annoyance. He walked slowly to where his own car was parked. He knew in his heart that Michael wanted Maura's opinion on the night's aggravation and he resented it. Over the last few years she had gradually moved up in the firm, until now, at only twenty-five, she practically ran the lot with Mickey. She was his right hand, as he never tired of telling anyone who would listen. She was the only person who could openly disagree with him and get away with it. This fact alone had earned her the respect not only of all her brothers but of the entire workforce, every man Jack of them. She had also master-minded a bank robbery that still had the police baffled eighteen months after the event. Geoffrey was beginning to hate her. Marvellous Fucking Maura . . . the Woman of the Century. He unlocked his car and sat in it for a few minutes, staring out into the night. His whole life had been built around Michael, and he was realising more and more each day that his brother did not really need him. It was a frightening thought. Without Michael, Geoffrey was nothing and he knew it. He started the car up. As he pulled away he turned on his radio. The soothing sound of the Carpenters filled the car. Geoffrey smiled to himself. Maura was like most women . . . give them enough rope and they generally hanged themselves. Eventually she would foul her nest and Michael would give her the bad news. All he had to do was wait.

He relaxed his grip on the steering wheel and allowed the strains of 'We've Only Just Begun' to wash over him.

Michael had driven from the club to Maura's house in Rainham, Essex. He had to see her about the events of the night. Maura had something that he would never have in a million years: she had a calculating nature. She never let her emotions interfere with her work. Michael respected this trait in her. Where he would lose his temper. Maura would calmly sort out a crisis. Her favourite expression was, 'Think with your head, not your heart.'

He looked at the house. It was in darkness. He got out of his car. When Maura had bought this house he had laughed at her. It was a large Georgian monstrosity that had seemed to be falling down. Now, a year later, it was beautiful. She had put in new windows, new doors, and the large overgrown frontage was now an in-and-out driveway. She had bought the place for pennies and if she sold it she would more than double her investment. In Michael's eyes this was another of Maura's clever schemes. Something that, until she had looked into and studied, he would never have dreamt of investing in.

He crunched across the pea-shingled drive up to the large double front door. He rang the bell. About five minutes later a bedraggled Carla opened the front door to him, her face lighting up as she smiled.

'Hello, Uncle Mickey. Auntie Maura's just getting dressed!' Michael playfully slapped her behind. 'Don't you let Maws catch you calling her "Auntie"! She'll skin you alive!' They walked into the lounge.

'Don't worry, I won't.' Her voice was full of fun.

In fact, Carla was one big bundle of fun and laughter. She was a natural mimic, and had the gift of making people laugh. It always amazed Michael that her own mother had so little time for her. Still, he reflected, she had Maura and his mother. They more than made up for Janine's indifference.

'Shall I make a pot of tea?'

'Yeah. There's a good girl.'

He watched her as she left the room. At twenty she was a lovely girl. She still had reddish-brown hair and freckles, but now had the grace that her mother had always had. She walked like a cat, with a long-legged stride. As she was now, in a shortie nightdress, her legs looked impossibly long. Michael sat himself on the Chesterfield and waited for Maura. When she walked into the lounge she looked as if she had never even been asleep. Her

169

blonde hair was now cut in a bob and it was immaculate. She wore a pink silk robe that barely covered her full breasts, and high-heeled mules. She grinned at her brother.

'So what brings you here at daybreak?'

'There's been some trouble, Maws.'

'I guessed as much. Ah, here's Carla with some tea!'

She took the tray and placed it on the Edwardian table to the left of the sofa. As she poured the tea Carla kept up a stream of chatter.

Michael smiled and answered Carla's seemingly endless supply of questions, relaxing back into his seat. Maura had good taste. The room was decorated in a mixture of peach tones and pinks. The carpets and heavy drapes were a deep burgundy. It was a cosy room. Even though it was full of expensive furniture it was a room that looked lived in, from the magazines on the coffee table to the Jacobean bookcase full of every title imaginable. Dickens and Trollope rubbed shoulders with Harold Robbins and Len Deighton. Maura's tastes in reading were as extreme as everything else in her life.

Carla did not think it at all strange that her uncle should get them out of bed at six in the morning. It was like everything else in her life with them. The unexpected was the norm around here and you had better get used to it or you were liable to go up the wall!

Michael and Maura allowed Carla to chatter to them. She was like the family mascot. Loved by them all, as if the rejection she had experienced when her mother had literally handed her over to Sarah, had made her their communal property. In their own ways, they tried to make up to her for what her mother had done. Though with Maura, Michael guessed, it went deeper. Carla was the child she had had aborted from her body. She was funding Carla through college. Maura made sure that Carla had every-thing, from decent clothes to a small car.

Carla finished telling them about her latest boyfriend and glanced at the ormolu clock on the mantelpiece of the Louis XVI fireplace.

She squealed: 'Oh, no it's nearly seven o'clock! I'd better get a move on. I've got to leave at eight!' She flitted from the room, all legs and hair. Michael laughed.

'She's a nice kid, Maws.' Even though Maura was only five years older than Carla, no one ever alluded to that fact. It was as if Maura had always been a woman. In Michael's eyes anyway she had never been any different. She had been a little sister for a long time, then she had become the mainstay of his life. There had never been an inbetween. Maura had never seemed to have that coltish look that Carla had. That magical illusion that was the turning point from adolescent to woman. Maura had become a woman overnight and had been one ever since. Maura Ryan had been a women from the age of seventeen.

'She's a good kid, Mickey, as well as a nice one. I miss her when she's at Mother's.'

'I bet you do. She's company in this great big rattling drum of yours.'

Maura laughed. 'You leave my house out of it. You're just gutted that you didn't buy it. Now what's all this about? What's happened?'

Michael explained to her. She sat curled up on the seat beside him, chain smoking as she listened. She did not interrupt him once. When he had finished, she smiled.

'So it's Stavros's cousin is it?

He smiled too.

'Well, we'll give the fat little bastard a run for his money!'

Michael grinned at her. Maura had said the words that he wanted to hear.

'That's exactly what I thought! Listen, Maws, I want you to think over what I've said. Get a few ideas together and then meet me later at the club. I'll get off home now or Jonny will think that I've been topped by someone. I'll see you later then.'

'All right, Mickey. What about the glass that Roy nicked? Shall I have it sent over to the Met? They might come up with a name . . . a legitimate name and address.'

Michael slapped his hand on his forehead. 'Bugger me, Maws. That went right out of me mind. I've left it in the club.'

'Never mind, Mick. Just you get home and get a bit of sleep. I'll sort that out.'

When Michael left, Maura went to her kitchen and made herself some tea and toast. The more she thought about what Michael had said, the more impossible it seemed. Who would wait over fifteen years to regain a territory? This bloke might be Stavros's cousin, but his story did not ring true.

Carla breezed into the kitchen and pinched a slice of toast from Maura's plate. 'I'll be late tonight, Maws. All right?'

'All right, love. Drive carefully.'

'I will.'

Then she was gone. As always when Carla left the house, it felt empty. She seemed to breathe life into it. Still pondering what Michael had said, Maura went up for a shower. She had a busy day ahead.

Chapter Fifteen

Maura walked into Le Buxom at ten-thirty-five. The hostesses were, as always, pleased to see her, unlike some of the men who worked for the Ryans who were wary of Maura. She was regarded as a hard-hearted bitch by the majority of them. Though if any one of them got hurt during the course of their work, it was Maura who saw to it that their wives were amply provided for. She half guessed what was said about her and made a conscious effort to keep the myth alive. Maura was happy enough with their respect, she did not want their love. She wanted to be known as a hard bitch. It suited her. The only people she could not con into disliking her were the hostesses.

They loved her. She always made sure that the girls with children got a good bonus around Christmas time, which was much appreciated. Also, most hostess clubs left the girl to sort out her hostess fee with the punter. Maura had a rule that the hostess fee, which was twenty-five pounds, went on the overall bill. Then, if there was a row over it, which was what frequently happened in the clubs, the bouncer would ensure that the hostess fee also was paid. A girl who had sat all night with a punter and talked him into buying champagne at two hundred pounds a bottle and cigarettes in packs of fifty that cost three times their retail price, could help run up a bill of over seven hundred pounds. If there was a fight over the payment she was hardly likely to be going on to a hotel with the punter. Therefore all she had for her efforts was the hostess fee. At least in Maura's club they could guarantee that. It was not unusual for a customer to be taken to the back bar where he was punched and threatened until the bill was paid.

Consequently, Le Buxom was known as the place to work. Maura offered them a degree of protection that had gradually wiped out pimping on their girls. For that they respected and loved her. They also kept their ears to the ground and let her in on anything that they heard. If they got any kind of venereal disease they were out, that was Maura's main stipulation, along with drugs and drinking. She had seen the effect that these things had on the prostitutes. It made them violent and aggressive. All prostitutes looked on one another as rivals. Hostess clubs were alive with gossip and back biting and trouble. Whores would rip one another apart, yet defend a sworn enemy to the police; would show a young 'greenie' the ropes, then try and muscle in on her punter. They lied, cheated and stole from one another.

All clubs had 'head girls', older, over the hill prostitutes who were as hard as nails. They were employed to keep order among the girls and liaise between them and the punters. In some clubs, if the head girl was offered a 'drink' – a percentage of the girls' 'case' fees – they would book these girls before their allotted time. (Hostesses generally lived by the rule that first into work was the first to be booked at a table.) So if a girl was offering a 'drink' she would be more likely to get a generous punter, either Arab or Chinese, both races known to be well heeled and unafraid of large fixed bills.

This form of hostessing had been gradually stamped out in Maura's club and the girls were grateful for it. Maura's club had waiting lists of girls who wanted to work for her. She ran her club like she ran her cab ranks and her hot dog stalls – fair and square. She was always on the right side of the police and had never had so much as a parking ticket herself. She was a very different person to the naïve young girl that Terry Petherick had known. She was frightened of no one. Even the large, hard-faced prostitutes, known lesbians and violent streetwalkers, held no terror for her. She walked the streets of Soho without a trace of fear. She had established her reputation long ago.

Tonight, an ex-hostess had brought in her baby and every woman in the club was clustered around the tiny bundle. Punters were left sitting alone while the child was duly praised and cuddled. The girl, Jenny Randle, had left the club a year earlier to marry one of her regular customers, a banker from Chiswick. She was radiantly happy. Maura took the baby into her arms and breathed in the smell of Johnson's baby powder and urine. The baby was wrapped in a white shawl and all that was visible was a tiny heart-shaped face, still red and wrinkled. The child opened its eyes and yawned, its tiny little rosebud mouth making a perfect 'O'. Maura felt the familiar longing rising inside her, and was embarrassed to find tears in her eyes. That was all she needed in front of the hostesses! Proof that she was soft.

'Oh, Jenny, she's beautiful . . . Gorgeous.'

'Thanks, Miss Ryan. I'm so happy.'

Michael walked down the stairs and into the club. All he saw was twenty-odd women huddled together at the entrance to the meat seats.

174

'What's going on here? A bloody union meeting?' His voice was annoyed. At his words the girls broke away from Maura. Michael was astonished to see her standing there, in a hundred-pound suit, holding a baby! As he looked into her face he saw the naked longing there, as did most of the hostesses, and suddenly he could not be cross with her. Maura treated the girls as if they were valued employees. Sometimes it drove him mad. She listened to their stupid quarrels, helped them when they were in trouble, financial or otherwise, arranged abortions for them, even paid for their baby-sitters if the woman was having a hard time getting 'case'. He admitted, grudgingly, that the club ran smoothly, but this was the ultimate piss take. It was like a secretary going into her office with new offspring. The bird was a brass, for Christ's sake. Next thing they'd be having Tupper-ware parties. Maura smiled at him.

'Jenny's new baby, Michael. Isn't she lovely?'

All the hostesses were on their guard, waiting for his reaction. Maura gave him a penetrating look that begged for his co-operation in front of the girls. He smiled to himself. She had so much front! Only Maura would expect him, Michael Ryan, the most feared man in London, to make a fuss of an old tom's baby. With all the aggravation they had at the moment with that nutty Greek, Maura expected him to act like the benevolent uncle! He took out his wallet, and pulling out a couple of ten-pound notes thrust them at Jenny. He smiled his most winning smile that secretly melted all the women's hearts.

'Get the baby something from us, Jenny.'

She took the proffered money and grinned at him.

'Thank you, Mr Ryan. I will.'

Feeling embarrassed, he left the women to carry on their inspection of the tiny scrap of humanity and went upstairs to his office.

Maura grinned at the hostesses who were all smiling at each other. It was at times like this that they were made aware of how lucky they were to have Maura Ryan's championship. She treated them as real people, not just whores. Even though they sold their bodies for a living, a fact that automatically made them second class citizens to the legitimate section of the female community, Maura made them feel like honest working girls. Like real people, doing a respectable job.

She handed the tiny baby back to Jenny and pulled down the jacket of her pale gold silk suit.

'She's a diamond, Jenny. You're very lucky. Now then, you lot!' She made her voice jocular. 'There's some lonely-looking punters sitting at the tables! Back to work!'

The girls who had left men sitting alone went meekly back to their tables, glad of the change in their nightly routine. Jenny's baby had been a little light relief.

Maura, leaving the other girls still cooing over the baby, followed Michael upstairs. In the office she put her finger to her lips and laughed.

'Not one word, Michael Ryan!'

He sat behind his desk, scowling at her.

'Well, Maws! What next? National Insurance stamps and baby showers?'

'Oh, shut up, you old bastard! What you seem to forget is that those women down there . . .' she pointed a perfectly manicured finger to the floor '. . . bring us in an awful lot of money. Jenny was one of the best hostesses in the West End. She brought thousands into this club.' Maura started to giggle. 'Not to mention a few highly respectable customers. If you remember rightly she worked the New Rockingham club before we poached her . . . *and* she brought her customers with her. So there!' She poked her tongue out at him saucily.

Michael ran his hands through his thick dark hair. There was a little glint of malevolence in his dark blue eyes. 'Have you by any chance thought over the problems of last night? Or was you out visiting the waifs and strays at Routen House?'

Maura walked behind her brother and slipped her arms around his neck. She kissed his cheek lightly, breathing in the smell of Old Spice aftershave.

'I love you when you're angry, Mickey. And Routen House was closed down years ago. They don't have workhouses no more. They have to go to the Salvation Army.'

Michael grabbed her hands and squeezed them. He laughed. 'You've got an answer for everything. And that Carla's getting just like you. Another trappy bird in the family is all I need!'

Maura pulled away from him and got herself a drink. She needed one. Holding Jenny's baby had unnerved her more than she liked to admit to herself. As she had clasped it to her breast she had felt a squeezing sensation in the pit of her stomach, similar to the feeling that preceded driving fast over a large hill. Her tummy had turned over. What she would not give to have a child of her own! She sipped her whisky.

'Well, down to business. What do you think about all that last night, Princess?'

Maura settled herself in the chair opposite her brother. She crossed her silk-clad legs and leant her right arm on the desk, staring at Michael.

'Well, it sounds to me like the bloke wants us to split territories.

176

Let's face it, we've got our fingers in a lot of pies, haven't we? I sent the glass over to the fingerprint boys this morning.' She shook her head. 'I don't know, Mickey. They make me laugh. They want their money for their little flutters and bits of skirt, then when you want them to return the favour, their arsehole goes. Well, I made a few go this morning, I can tell you! We should have a result late tonight. Realistically, Mickey, until this Dopolis makes his next move, or we find out something about him, we can't do much anyway.

'As for the protection money, he obviously knew that Wong's was Roy's last call, so taking the old boy's rent was just a token thing. A little bit of defiance. Roy had over sixteen grand in his motor. Even though he had Tessa in the car, if this Dopolis had wanted the money he could have got it. If what Roy said was right, and the young bloke had a sawn-off.' She shrugged. 'Well, they could have taken the lot, couldn't they? No, I think we had better wait until this Dopolis gets in touch. Then I bet if we offer him a little bit of action, he'll be as happy as Larry. The fact that he's Stavros's cousin does put the mockers on it a bit . . . it means we all hold grudges. But for Christ's sake, Bruv, who would be mug enough to take us lot on?' She waved her hand dismissively. 'We'll just wait and see, I ain't too trashed about it all.

'Now then, what about those houses out in Essex? Have you thought about them at all?'

Michael nodded. 'If you think they're worth it, it's up to you.'

He was digesting all that Maura had said. It made sense.

'Well, the thing is, Mickey, they're all knockdown rebuilds. And I've got a smashing little firm of NHBC housebuilders who would love the work. We'll make a fortune, Mickey. There's no doubt about it. Property is the business to be in these days.'

'Like all the old "tut" you've bought around the old docks?'

Maura smiled tolerantly.

'You crack me up, Maura. Imagine buying a load of old warehouses and Dockers' Mansions! . . .'

'Those old Dockers' Mansions will be worth a fortune one day, boy. You mark my words.'

'Oh, yeah, Maws! I can just see everyone dying to live in a two up two down, with a carzey in the garden and a tin bath in the front room. I bet you'll have queues of people just dying to buy them!'

Maura laughed. She sat back in her chair. She had never regained the weight she had lost after the abortion and was fashionably thin. In her gold silk suit and matching shoes and shirt she looked as if she had just stepped from the pages of a fashion magazine. Her white-blonde hair was freshly washed and framed her face like a platinum halo. Her bright blue eyes were expertly made up. She was, Michael reflected, a very beautiful and sophisticated woman. Yet she had never, to his knowledge, had a boyfriend. Not since the policeman. Michael guessed, rightly, that she still held a torch for him. Though they had never, ever discussed it. It was the only taboo subject between them. They discussed everything under the sun, except Terry Petherick.

'Do you remember Auntie Nellie's house, Mickey? I used to love staying there when I was a kid. I remember one New Year . . . the old man was in the 'ville, I think, and Mum dropped me off there for a couple of nights.' Maura closed her eyes as she remembered it all. 'I was only about six or seven, and as the clock chimed in the New Year Uncle Bertie opened the front door. It was foggy that night. I can see it so clearly. All of a sudden all the ships' hooters began to blast. It was as if all the boats were going to sail straight into their little front room. The noise was deafening. Uncle Bertie gave me a hot toddy to help me sleep . . . I loved that little house.'

Michael grimaced at her comically. 'Turn it up, Maws! You'll have me crying in a minute!'

'You rotten sod! You've got no soul, that's your trouble! For your information, Michael Ryan, those old places will be worth the National Debt in a few years. There's talk of them building a marina there, everything.'

'On the old docklands?' His voice was sceptical.

'On the old docklands.'

'Well, I still can't see it, Maws.'

She sobered as she looked at him. 'Property is the money making scheme of the future. I'm telling you, Mickey. Houses don't eat nothing and they make you a fortune. You buy them cheap and you sit on them until the prices rise.

'There's so much building going on in London at the moment, soon there'll not be any building land left except what can be reclaimed from the old dock areas: Wapping, Woolwich, all up the Thames.' She smiled. 'You just wait and see.'

'Do you know something, Maws?'

She looked at him, puzzled. 'No. What?'

'You are one clever bird. If you had been a bloke you could have taken over the world.' His voice held genuine admiration.

'Well, I've got you and the whole of London. That's all I want, Mickey.'

'You'll always have me, darling.' Michael's voice was soft. Maura smiled at him. As long as she had Mickey she didn't need a husband, a lover – anything. As she looked into his dark blue eyes she was aware of how much he had changed over the years. At forty years old he was still a handsome man but his body was more bulky now than it had been. He was beginning to run to fat. Yet he was still good-looking enough to gather glances wherever he went, from men as well as women. His dark hair was touched with grey. His face still had the high cheekbones and deepset eyes of his youth, except now he had the crow's feet and lines that denoted middle age. Like most handsome men, his age suited him. Unlike women who tried to keep young for as long as was physically possible, men like Michael wore their age with a panache that made it look like a desirable attribute. Maura poured them both out a whisky.

'Before I forget, Mickey. I had Mahoney on the blower today. He wants some more hardware, mainly M16 rifles. He said that Father McCormack would get them to Eire as usual. Don't ask me how. Probably by boat. He wants them by the end of the month and I said that was fine . . . provided he paid the money up front. I don't really like dealing with them, Mickey. But as you say – if we don't, someone else will.'

He nodded. Father McCormack's predictions in Sarah's front room all those years ago had proved startlingly accurate. Now they dealt with many aspects of the Irish Republican Army's operations. Not only arms, but also providing safe houses and, when possible, safe conduct for its soldiers.

'How much are they willing to spend?'

'A lot. The arms from Libya have dried up since the Arabs started fighting amongst themselves, but the money from America is astronomical now. They can't spend it quick enough. Shall I get in touch with Dixon then?'

Michael sighed. 'Yeah. Use Billy Bootnose as a go-between. I don't want you or me seen with them.'

'I will do. While you were sleeping the day away, Michael, I –' she poked herself in the chest '– have been sorting out the monthly accounts . . . as well as sorting out the fingerprint men!' She laughed. 'We've had a few big bets placed at the bookies, but no harm's been done. The club's doing all right. Considering it's nearly Christmas, the hot dogs are bringing in a small fortune. Especially on the new sites we took over.'

'You bought them out then?'

'Oh, yeah!' Her voice was indignant. 'It was all done legally and above board.'

'Except Roy had an axe in his hand when you went to negotiate!'

Maura made a little moue with her lips.

'Well, I think that did help. But I gave them a good price, Mickey. Well above the pitches' value. The cab ranks are booming, thanks to the cold weather and armfuls of Christmas presents. All in all, life is good. Once we sort the Greek prat out, we'll be laughing!'

'Thanks for sorting all that for me, Maws. What's the SP on the family front?'

She frowned. 'Not too good actually, Mickey. I had word today that Benny and Garry have been getting lairy in pubs and clubs all over town. Shouting their mouths off about you, me, and anything they can think of.'

'That don't sound like our Garry, Maws!'

'I know, but it's the truth. They haven't been working, Mickey. Sammy Goldbaum said he hadn't seen either of them for days. He's been running the ranks himself. I think we should give him a drink for that. I thought we could slip him a monkey as a Christmas box.'

Michael slammed his fist on to the desk.

'All right, do that. Fucking marvellous, ain't it! A pissing front wheel skid running me businesses, and me own brothers, who get paid a hefty portion, are doing fuck all! Well, I've just about had it this time. If they don't pull their socks up, they're out on their arses. I can't afford to have lazy bastards on my team.'

'I know what you're saying, Mickey, and I'll get Geoffrey to have a word with them. By the way, have you heard from any of the boys, today?'

He shook his head. 'No. Why?'

'Oh, nothing. It's just that I haven't seen hide nor hair of any of them, that's all.'

She yawned.

'You get yourself off home, Maws.'

'I might just do that, Mickey. I'm shattered. Not surprising considering I was woken out of my sleep this morning. Six o'clock this morning, to be precise.'

Michael laughed.

'I'll wait here for the bloke from the Met. As you say, we can't do anything until Dopolis makes a move or we find out more about him. We've got to find out exactly what we're dealing with.'

Maura walked around the desk and kissed his forehead. 'See you tomorrow, Mickey. Goodnight.'

'Goodnight, Princess.'

Maura left him and made her way to her car. As she drove home she hoped that Carla would be in when she arrived. She worried about her, especially with Janine having another baby. Though Carla seemed happy enough about the impending birth,

Maura was worried that the baby would further push her out of her parents' life. It was this overshadowing worry that made Maura shelve thoughts of the trouble with Dopolis. She wasn't to find out for a few days that he was a very dangerous man indeed.

Chapter Sixteen

Benny sat at the kitchen table eating an enormous breakfast. He insisted that his mother made him two eggs, five pieces of bacon, black pudding, mushrooms, and three giant sausages every morning. He ate this with five pieces of toast and washed it down with a whole pot of tea. He wiped the last of the toast around his plate and popped it into his mouth. He sat back in his chair replete, holding his stomach with both hands.

'That was handsome, Muvver.'

Sarah laughed. He was the last child to live at home and she was dreading the day when he, too, flew the nest.

'I don't know where you put it all, Benny.' She picked up his empty plate and placed it in the sink.

'I think I'll have a quick fag and then be on me way. It's about time I showed my boatrace at the betting office.' His voice sounded worried. Sarah turned to face him. Benny was her baby. She was aware of all his faults and still she loved him.

'Michael won't put up with you skiving off, you know. Or Maura.' Sarah's voice was tight when she spoke about her daughter. She could never get used to the fact that Maura ran the businesses with Michael. It bothered her more than she cared to admit. In Sarah's mind women married and had children. She admitted to herself, grudgingly, that Maura could not do that. But she still felt that no woman should live or work in what was to her a man's world. The shady life of Soho and hostess clubs was, to her, the lowest in the world, filled with the dregs of humanity.

Benny lit his Benson and Hedges cigarette and finished his cup of tea. He glanced at the old kitchen clock. It was nearly eight-thirty.

'I'm off then, Muvver. I'll see you tonight, about sixish.' He got up from the table and kissed his mother lightly on the cheek. Sarah smiled at him and said what she said to him every day.

'You be careful now, Benny. And do what our Michael tells you.'

'I will. See you.' He went from the house. Sarah carried on with her washing up. She'd had a bad feeling on her since she had got out of bed – like a dragging pain in her side. She wiped her hands and turned on her radio. Jimmy Young would be on soon and she liked him. She began her day's work. Janine would be around at about ten and they were going to plan the Christmas celebrations.

She now looked on Janine as her daughter and Maura as a distant relative. Sarah would never admit to herself or anyone that she actively disliked Maura these days, it seemed blasphemous somehow. She did not like Carla living with her either. She wished she could get Janine and Carla to become close, but she had resigned herself long ago to the fact that Janine would never like her child. That she could not stand being in the same room as her.

She sighed. Children were a bind really. You loved them but they never seemed to be out of your life. Wherever they were they demanded your time and energy. She consoled herself with the fact that at least there would be a new baby soon. If she waited on the other boys to make her a grandmother she would be disappointed. None of them seemed to want to settle down, Michael for obvious reasons. She knew he had a man living with him. She closed her eyes and shuddered. As for Geoffrey and the rest of the boys – they gravitated from woman to woman. Now here was Janine, in her thirties, having another baby – though she had a sneaking suspicion that if Janine had been able to get rid of this child she would have.

Sarah began to wipe the kitchen table with a damp cloth. She'd better get a move on. She wanted to get the house sorted before Benjamin decided to get out of bed. He was another one. At fifty-nine he was like a man of ninety, shuffling about the house waiting for the Bramley Arms to open. She carried on cleaning, unaware that before the day was out there would be trouble the like of which she had never even dreamed of.

It was eleven o'clock and Michael and Maura were in the small offices above Le Buxom. The glass had been sent back late the night before from West End Central police station. The prints on the glass were not known to them. Whoever it was had no criminal record. Michael and Maura were no nearer to finding out exactly who Dopolis was and what he dealt in than they'd been at the beginning.

'Well, we've had our people out on the street but this Dopolis is an unknown face. I don't know, Maura. The more I think about what went down in old Wong's, the more shirty I get.'

The phone rang and Maura answered it. While she took the call Michael lit himself a cigarette. There was something funny about all this and he could not put his finger on it. No one was an unknown quantity. There had to be someone who knew them, or

184

of them. Yet this Dopolis seemed to have appeared out of thin air.

Maura put down the phone and stared at Michael. 'That bloody Benny has gone on the missing list again. He ain't turned up for work.'

Michael groaned.

'What about Garry the boy wonder? 'as he turned up?'

'Funnily enough, he has. And according to Sammy Goldbaum, he was surprised that Benny hadn't turned in.'

'If I know Benny, Maws, he's got himself a new bird and he can't keep away. Well, I'm gonna dock the sod's pay this week. See how far he gets with the women then!' He laughed. 'As much as he annoys me, I have to laugh at him. He'd travel miles for a new conquest. He's like one of them wolves. He sniffs the air and can smell a bitch on heat from ten miles away.'

'Sex and food . . . that's our Benny. His two main occupations. Well, all joking aside, Mickey, he's got to be taught a lesson this time. He's twenty-nine, for Christ's sake, and he follows his dick like a teenager.' She pointed across the desk at Michael. 'You've got to put the hard word on him. He'll listen to you.'

'All right. When he finally turns up. Now, any more business before I shoot off home?'

Maura shook her head. 'I did the main work yesterday. There's just the usual today. Where's Geoffrey, by the way? I ain't seen him.'

Michael chewed his bottom lip and Maura, seeing this, sat back in her chair. She looked annoyed.

'Not again!'

'I'm afraid so, Maws. He thinks that I give you too much of my time. I had another row with him this morning.'

Maura lit herself a cigarette. She was fuming. 'What's it this time then?'

'He thinks you should be doing the cabs, not him.'

Maura pulled on her cigarette and stared at her brother. Geoffrey was beginning to get on her nerves. Although he was brought into everything that they did, was informed of every transaction that was made and was generally thought of as the main brother after Michael, he still kept up a petty coldness towards Maura. He acted as if she was just there to be humoured. At first Maura had accepted this. Now, nearly eight years later, he was getting on her nerves. Geoffrey could not be made to see that she was an asset to the businesses. That she was trying her hardest to make them more or less legal. Whatever she did he poured cold water on it. If she told him to do something, he nodded and smiled and then did exactly the opposite. What Geoffrey did not realise was that Michael was getting fed up with it all as well.

185

'Look, Mickey, can't you have a word with him?' Her voice was desperate. 'I understand that he feels put out, but if he would only try and work with me, instead of against me . . . I'll tell you something now that I was going to keep to myself. He goes through all the files.'

Michael's eyebrows rose and Maura laughed. 'Honestly, Mickey. He comes in here in the middle of the night and checks over all that I've done.'

Michael grinned. 'Sometimes I think he's a few sandwiches short of a picnic. Still, do me a favour and swallow. I've got enough on me plate at the moment, without you two going ten rounds.'

'You will have a word with him though?'

'Oh yeah, yeah, yeah.' He stood up, exasperated. 'Fucking real, ain't it? What with him and Benny, it's a wonder we ever get anything done!

'Well, I'm off, Princess. Unless there's anything else?'

'No, nothing, Mickey.'

'I'll be off then. See you.' He kissed her cheek. Maura watched him pull on his overcoat.

'See you later then, Mickey.'

She sat at the desk chewing on her pen. Outside the window she could hear the steady hum of traffic. It had been a bitter cold morning, but inside the office it was baking. She slipped off the suede shoes and wriggled her toes. In her plain green suit and white silk blouse, she looked very young and carefree. Like an office clerk. It always amazed people when they met her that she was Maura Ryan. Her name always preceded her, and though they were prepared for her height and magnificent bosom, they were always unprepared for her looks. They soon found, though, that behind her pretty face was an analytical brain that could pick up and dissect whatever was being said to her. She sat for a while thinking about Geoffrey. She had tried so hard to work with him and he would not play along. The jangling of the telephone broke into her thoughts.

'Hello.'

'Hello, Maws!' Margaret's nasal tones were instantly recognisable.

'Hello, Marge! I was going to ring you tonight. How's the kids?'

'Oh, they're all right, Maws. Looking forward to Christmas. The twins have got their Nativity play next week, that's why I was ringing you. They want you to come down and see them both in it. Can you make it?'

'Tell them it's a date. I wouldn't miss it for the world. I'll bring Carla. She should be on her holidays from college by then. How's baby Dennis?'

Marge groaned. 'He's in his playpen now, but about ten minutes ago he flushed the toilet roll down the loo. Honestly, Maws, he's worse than the girls ever were. You need eyes in the back of your head!'

Both women laughed.

'I must see them soon. I really miss them.'

'Well, don't come and spoil them. The girls are already too big for their boots.'

Maura's voice was cynical. 'Marge, girls can never be too big for their boots – or anyone else's come to that! Now, have you spotted any more houses?'

'Funnily enough, I have. Three. Two in Southend and one in Shoebury. They all have knockdown rebuilds on them.'

'Great. I'll have a look when I come over to see you.'

'How's your house coming along?'

'It's finished, Marge. You and Den must come to dinner one night. You'll love it.'

'Oh, I bet it's gorgeous. You're lucky, Maws.'

Maura went on the defensive. 'Luck don't enter into it, Marge. I work bloody hard for what I've got.'

Marge's placating voice came over the line. 'I know, I know. I didn't mean it like that and you know it. I meant lucky to have a good job, a nice home, and a lovely bank account! Especially the lovely bank account. Me and Den seem to spend the money before the poor bugger's even earned it!' Margaret was laughing.

'Listen, Marge, I'd swap everything I've got for a nice bloke and a couple of kids.'

'I know that, Maws. I wish you would meet someone.'

'Oh, Margie, get real, will you? Blokes my age want to settle down, have some babies. I can't give that to anyone so it's not worth the aggro. I mean, I can't see me being allowed to adopt, can you? No, Marge, I accepted that a long time ago. I'll have to make do with me wheeling and dealing!'

'Well, you certainly seem to have a flair for it.'

'Long may it last, Margie! Look, I've got to go. I'll give you a bell and let you know when I'll be over, all right?'

'Okey doke. See you.'

She hung up.

Maura lit herself another cigarette. What she wouldn't give to be Marge! She smiled to herself at the thought of little Dennis and his tricks. He was a case . . .

Geoffrey burst into the office.

'Where's Mickey?'

'He left a while ago. What's wrong?'

'We had a call at the cab rank in Manor Park. Some nutty

bastard reckons there's bombs in all the ranks we've got. I've phoned around and had the places cleared, sent all the drivers home.'

'You what!' Maura stubbed her cigarette out. 'On the strength of one bloody crank call!'

Geoffrey lost his temper.

'It was a crank all right . . . a crank called Dopolis. Can't you see this is the start? The prat wants war!'

Maura sat back in her chair, her face a study in disbelief. She stared at Geoffrey blankly for a moment then she shot into action. 'Get all the boys together at my warehouse in Wapping. Tell them me and Mickey will meet them there.'

Geoffrey stood looking at her. He curled his lip in contempt.

'I ain't your fucking messenger boy!'

Maura closed her eyes and said, through gritted teeth, 'It's bad enough we have this crisis with a nutty Greek. The last thing we want is to be arguing amongst ourselves. Now will you do as I ask . . . please?'

Geoffrey turned on his heel and stamped from the room. Maura turned her attention to the telephone and dialled Michael's number.

'Is that you, Jonny?'

'Oh, hello, Maura. Mickey's not . . .'

'Shut up and listen to me. Mickey will be home at any moment. You tell him that I am on my way over. Do not open the door to anyone except Michael or myself. Do you understand?'

The urgency in her voice communicated itself to him.

'What's going on!' His voice was high and frightened.

Maura slammed the phone down on him. She was in no mood to console that little faggot. She took a deep breath to control her heartbeat which was hammering in her ears, feeling a wave of apprehension wash over her. Slipping her shoes back on, she quickly left the office.

Michael and Maura walked into the club at eleven o'clock. It was a freezing night and a fine covering of snow was glistening in the light from the doorway. A surge of hot air hit them as they entered the club. Gerry Jackson took their damp coats from them.

'Brass monkey weather, ain't it?'

Michael nodded. 'Any news from Benny?' Everyone else had turned up at the warehouse meeting. Benny was the only exception. No one seemed to know where he was.

Gerry Jackson smiled.

'If I know your Benny, he's shacked up with some old bird somewhere!'

'Maybe, Gerry. Tell Geoff to come straight up when he gets here, OK? And get one of the hostesses out on reception.' Michael gave Gerry a small green address book. 'Tell them to try all these numbers. They'll get a ton if he's located. All right?'

Gerry took the battered address book. 'Will do. Shall I have some coffee sent up?'

Maura rubbed her hands together. 'That'll be just the thing, Gerry. How's Anne and the boys?'

He smiled sheepishly. 'She's pregnant again.'

'So I heard. I reckon she'll be like my mum. She won't get a girl for years!'

Gerry rolled his eyes at the ceiling.

'Oh, don't dare say that, Maura! We've got five boys already.'

Maura smiled at him. 'You shouldn't have married a good Catholic girl then.'

She followed Michael upstairs to the offices. As she entered behind him the telephone rang. Maura picked it up, hoping that it was Benny.

'May I speak to Michael Ryan, please?'

'Who's calling?'

'Tell him it's concerning his younger brother.'

Maura handed the phone to Michael and gently picked up the extension. She listened to a man's voice.

'Mr Ryan, I imagine you are missing one brother by now. Correct?'

Maura looked at Michael's set face and implored him with her eyes not to lose his temper.

'I have not missed my brother at all actually . . . Mr Dopolis. This is Mr Dopolis, I take it?'

The man laughed gently. 'How very astute of you, Mr Ryan.'

'Well, it wouldn't take a fucking contender for Mastermind to sus that much out, would it?'

'I hear from your voice that you are worried. I notice that you English always resort to bad language when you are in a tight corner . . . But I promise you that if it rests with me, no harm will come to your brother whatsoever.'

The words were spoken sincerely, but with a small underlying threat.

'Well, Mr Dopolis, what have you got my brother for? The rents and rates are fuck all to do with him.'

'I understand that, Mr Ryan. We want to use him to bargain with you. I know that you are a . . . how shall we say? . . . temperamental fellow. I want you to realise that we mean business. I knew that you would guess that the bomb threat was a hoax. I was just showing you my power, if you like. I know,

189

for example, that you had a meeting at the warehouse today. I know everything that you do.' His voice was smug. He was obviously enjoying himself. 'Perhaps we could meet at your warehouse tomorrow?'

Maura and Michael were astounded. How could he have got that kind of information?

'When do you want to meet?'

'Tomorrow at six-thirty. It will be nice and dark by then. Also, I want you to have plenty of time to think over my terms. I must stress to you here and now, Mr Ryan, that I am open to negotiation, providing it is in my favour . . .'

'And just what are your terms?' Michael was having trouble controlling his temper.

'Firstly, I want the East End of London for myself and my family. We have a few legitimate businesses there but it is not enough for us. We are not happy being such little fish. We are willing to make you a payment of half a million pounds for all your businesses there. A reasonable offer, I think.' He waited a few seconds before continuing.

'Secondly, I want your word that there will not be a gang war. Very sordid in this day and age, don't you think? We are both reasonable men. And, lastly, I will give you my word that we will never, ever, try and muscle in on the West End. That would remain wholly your domain.'

Michael chuckled, a grating phlegmy chuckle that should have warned Dopolis that he was not really amused.

'You don't want much, do you, cocker?'

The man's voice went cold.

'I want what I am entitled to, Mr Ryan. My cousin Stavros was willing to negotiate with you but you were young and hot-headed. You did not have the wisdom to talk things out. Sadly, you lost your brother and my cousin was crippled for life. I do not want a repeat of all that. But I am warning you now, I will fight if necessary. I have taken your young brother as a token, to show you that I know all that you do. I could have picked you all off one by one, your sister included, and have had the lot. The East and the West. But I am not a greedy man. No one can have everything. It just causes greed and envy, Mr Ryan.'

Michael listened to the man's voice as if fascinated by it. His eyes held the malevolent gleam that heralded one of his tempers.

'Yeah, well, the only thing you're causing right now, Mr Dopolis, is my blood pressure to rise! If anything should happen to my brother, either accidentally or deliberately, you will pay. Believe me, mate, that is a solemn promise.'

'Nothing will happen to your brother, Mr Ryan. Provided you

do what I ask of you. I will see you tomorrow at six-thirty.'

The line went dead.

As Michael and Maura replaced their receivers, Gerry Jackson came into the office with a tray of coffee.

'Any news, Mickey?'

'Tell the hostess who's ringing around not to bother. We've found him.'

'Where?'

Before Michael could answer, Maura spoke.

'We'll tell you later, Gerry, OK? Now if you don't mind I want to speak to Michael alone.'

Offended, Gerry placed the tray on the desk and walked out. Michael was annoyed.

'Here, hold up, Maws. Gerry is like family. You can't just dismiss him like that.'

Maura walked to the desk and began to pour the coffee. 'Mickey, that Dopolis just said that he knew where we all were today, right? He also said that he could have picked us off one by one, right? Now doesn't that tell you anything?' Her voice was peeved.

'Obviously someone in the firm is grassing.'

'Precisely.'

Michael banged his fist on the desk, causing the coffee to slop over the rim of the cups.

'Listen, you, Gerry would no more grass me than he would cut his own throat! You're out of order, Maura.'

She banged her own fist on the desk.

'Look, Mickey, I don't want to argue with you. All I'm thinking of is the fact that these people have got our Benny and I ain't taking any chances where his safety is concerned. We must play this one very close to our chests.'

Michael sighed and ran his hands through his hair. He looked old suddenly.

'Maybe you're right, Maws.'

She went to him and put her arms around his waist. 'We'll beat the buggers at their own game. With all the feelers we've got out in the street, something's bound to come up. It always does.'

'And what about his "terms", as he put it?'

'What about them?'

'Well, what are we going to do?'

'We play along with him, Mickey. To be honest, I wouldn't care if we let the East End go. It's pennies and halfpennies to what we can make once the building begins in London.'

Michael clenched his fists. 'Docklands . . . docklands, always the bloody docklands! Your brother is being held captive by a fucking nutter and that's all that you can think about. It's like a cancer with you!'

Maura was stunned. She looked up into Michael's face and what she saw there made her flinch. He was really worried about Dopolis.

She lost her temper again, this time deciding to tell him what she had been putting off for months.

'Can't you see further than that big hooter of yours? Sometimes you bloody well amaze me, Mickey. We are paper millionaires. We should take his money and get Benny back. Whoever controls the West End, controls the whole of London. It's always worked like that. Let the silly old bastard have it if he wants it so bad. He'll only be working for us anyway. Think about it, Mickey. We'll still get a pull off any blags that go down. We'll just be shifting the aggro, that's all. Then once the building starts, we'll be laughing all the way to the bank. Legally.'

'I ain't so sure about that . . .'

Maura clenched her fists. This was like a gift from the gods if he could only see it! She had wanted to lease out the East End anyway. Get rid of it. Now she had the perfect opportunity.

'Mickey, all that talk about luxury flats and the marina is true. I know for a fact that certain people have been buying up the place. They've been collecting money to fund the project for years. Oh, for God's sake, Michael. Do you want to be a hoodlum all your life? Well, do you? Answer me!' She pushed him in the chest.

Michael grabbed her hand and pushed her away from him. 'Why not? I ain't done too badly, and neither have you.'

Maura had tears in her eyes. If only he could be made to see. 'So you want to duck and dive all your life, is that it? This is a chance for us to be somebody in our own right. A legitimate way to spend our cash. I know that to the likes of you and me, living in the old dock areas would be anathema. We grew up in post-war slums, no better or worse than Tobacco Road or the Isle of Dogs. To us, you ain't made it unless your address has West One on it. But things are changing, Mickey . . . this country is going building mad at the moment. Everywhere you look, new housing estates are going up. People are even buying their council houses. We're cultivating a nation of home owners, and you can't see it! Soon all the sites will be played out, except for the old dock areas. And I want to be in on it. I want that *and* the West End.' Her voice trailed off. She could have cried her eyes out, but her pride stopped her.

Michael poured them both a large brandy. He passed Maura her glass and shook his head slowly. 'All right, Maws, you win. I'll take the half a mil. When Benny's back home I want to see all you've got on this docklands scam. I just hope that Dopolis hasn't roughed Benny up. For his sake . . . As you say, indirectly Dopolis would be working for us anyway.'

Maura put her glass on the filing cabinet beside her and ran into his arms.

'Oh, Mickey, Mickey . . . you little darling! I promise you won't regret it. I'll get on to our solicitor now and get him to draw up an agreement to take to the Greek bastard's meet. We'll show them! Just you wait and see. The name Ryan will be known the length and breadth of England. Just like Wimpey's!'

Michael laughed at her.

'What about Fitzpatrick's? Let's at least keep this thing Irish.'

Maura did a little dance of happiness. Michael smiled at her. She was right. They should let the East End go. Get Benny back safely. His dad had always said it was hard to own the two. That's what had happened to the Krays. He would let Dopolis have it, take his money, then pay him back one hundredfold for poaching his little brother. Dopolis would be made painfully aware of the fact that he worked for the Ryans.

He took a cigarette from his pocket and lit it. A thought had occurred to him. The only outsider to know about the meet today was Jonny. He made a mental note to have a word with his boyfriend. He was sick to death of him anyway. This had given him just the push he needed to out Jonny.

Michael drank his brandy and the two of them made their plans. When Geoffrey arrived the excitement was over. He realised that he had been too late. Again.

Downstairs, Roy, Leslie, Lee and Garry watched the strippers. When they were finally called upstairs into the office they were all glad to hear that their brother had been located, especially Garry. As Michael gave them their orders none of them realised that the real trouble was only just beginning. That events were being put into motion that would smash their world apart.

Chapter Seventeen

Benny watched as the man came into the room. It was the same man who had brought him some food earlier in the day. Benny smiled painfully, trying to get some response. In the fight that had occurred during Benny's kidnapping, he had lost two teeth and acquired a large black eye. The man was also sporting a black eye so Benny thought that evened things up. The man ignored Benny's smile and picked up the empty plate and cup. He checked that the handcuff which held Benny's right hand to the bed post was secure. Then he left the room, banging the door behind him.

Benny tried to get comfortable on the bed. The muscles in his right shoulder were screaming. He reckoned that he had been in the room twenty-four hours. He could smell the urine that was in a bucket by his bed. He had just enough space to kneel up and urinate into the bucket. As yet he had not been allowed to open his bowels. Not that he fancied going in front of an audience, and he had a sneaking suspicion that was what would happen. He rubbed his shoulder with his free hand.

The room he was in was some kind of office, he was sure of that. It had the hollow feel that was peculiar to Portakabins and the like. It was definitely not a house that he was being kept in. He felt the giant swelling above his eye and grinned – he had given them a run for their money. If they had not had the element of surprise he would have won the fight hands down. Now all he had to do was wait. He had been told briefly by his captors that he was being held until an agreement had been reached with Michael. He wasn't too worried about it. He knew that he was worth more to his captors alive than dead. He just hoped that someone had had the savvy to tell his mum that he was not coming home for a few days. She would be worried.

He tried to settle himself back against the bedpost. His round boyish face had a dark stubble around the jaw; he looked terrible. He ran his tongue over his teeth. He wished they would let him have a wash and brush up. He hated this dirty feeling. The bed was filthy and it stank. It was also damp. In the corner of the room was a paraffin heater which gave out a sickly smell as well as a sticky cloying heat.

He decided then and there that when he got home he would find out the names of the people who had held him here and would personally give each one a good hiding. This place was a dump. He wouldn't keep his dog, Driver, in conditions like this . . .

It never occurred to Benny that he was in any danger or that there was a good chance that he would never leave the room alive.

Maura and Michael walked into the warehouse at six-fifteen. Geoffrey, Roy and Leslie were already there. Garry and Lee arrived at six-twenty. Geoffrey had put up a set of spotlights. From outside the warehouse still looked empty. Dopolis arrived, accompanied by two big men, at six-thirty-five.

The two men with him were, Michael guessed, just brawn merchants. He also noted, as did his brothers, that they were both armed. Dopolis looked like a dark-skinned dwarf standing between them. The Greek nodded to them all, giving a half bow towards Maura.

It was freezing inside the warehouse. It seemed colder in there than it did outside. The snow was coming down harder and had decided to settle. In the bright glare from the spotlights they looked like characters rehearsing for a play. Dopolis was the first to speak. He cleared his throat theatrically. Dopolis had a taste for drama that spilled over into everything he did.

'I am so glad that we could have this little chat. I hope that you have thought over my proposition.'

'Where's Benny?' Michael's voice was flat.

Dopolis laughed and Maura saw the tendons stand out in Michael's neck. She touched his arm lightly to remind him that he was not to lose his temper.

'Surely, Mr Ryan, you do not think that I would be so foolish as to bring him here? I must first find out how the land lies.'

Garry was staring at the three men in front of him. He stifled an urge to open his coat and blow them away with his shotgun. He could feel the sweat slippery on his palms.

Maura could sense the mounting tension. Her voice seemed to echo around the building. 'We have decided that we like your offer, Mr Dopolis.'

The three Greeks stared at her in amazement. Surely Michael Ryan was not going to allow a woman to negotiate for him?

'Young lady,' Dopolis's voice was gentle, 'I have come here to do serious business.'

Maura's voice was brisk. 'I am well aware of that fact, Mr

Dopolis. My brother has every faith in me as I am sure you will soon realise.' She smiled. 'Now, shall we get down to business?'

Mr Dopolis was nonplussed. That much was clear to everyone watching. Never in his wildest imaginings had he envisaged discussing business with a woman. He had heard that Maura Ryan was a very astute business woman but nevertheless, he was a Greek and Greeks did not allow their women to interfere in men's business. It crossed his mind that this may be Michael Ryan's idea of an insult. Women were for pleasure or for childbearing as far as he was concerned. Maura could read the expressions on his face as if they were written on his forehead in indelible ink.

She began to talk in her best no-nonsense voice.

'You have offered to buy out our holdings in the East End for half a million pounds. We shall accept that offer with good grace. But only with the proviso that you work, indirectly of course, for us.

'We would only expect to be consulted on major issues. Everything else would be down to yourself. We shall keep our interests in the warehouses and the property . . .'

Dopolis seemed to have gathered his wits together.

'My dear girl, the half a million includes all this.' He gestured around the warehouse with his arms. 'I have a pressing need for these old warehouses myself. I want –' he paused for effect, 'everything you own from Dagenham to Tower Bridge. I want everything you have in Katherine Dock, East Dock. Around London Dock. I want all you possess on the Wapping Road, in Whitechapel and Shoreditch. I want Bethnal Green. In short, I want it all.'

Maura, Michael and Geoffrey were flabbergasted. Dopolis smiled coldly. 'Do not insult me by trying to negotiate with me. I have given you my terms. I would never work for you!' He spat out the words like bullets from a gun. 'I want it *all*, do you hear me? Every little bit, lock, stock and barrel. And if we can't settle this amicably then we will fight you. *I* will fight you to the death.'

He put a pudgy hand to his breast. 'I came here for an answer to my terms, that's all. Nothing else.'

'What about Benny?' This from Leslie, who was dying to start a fight.

'What about him?' Dopolis shrugged. 'He is my bargaining point. While I have him, I also have you.'

Michael stepped towards him, causing Dopolis to retreat; a fleeting expression of fear crossed his sallow face.

Michael pointed at him. 'You can't just demand, mate.'

'Oh, Mr Ryan, that's where you're wrong. While I have your brother I can demand all I want. And I will tell you something, Mr

197

Ryan . . . I have a man behind me who is so big that he would scare even you. Yes, even you! I am a trusted friend of this man and I can tell you now that he has much money and arms to fight you with. I know you are a force to be reckoned with but I have at my disposal a larger, more dangerous force. Do you understand what I am saying?'

Dopolis had a demonic look on his ugly face. In his temper he had spoken so forcefully that long strands of spit hung from his lower lip.

'Listen, mate.' Michael went to him. As he walked he clicked his fingers and Geoffrey, Roy, Leslie, Garry and Lee brought out their shotguns from beneath their coats. Maura stepped back from them. Despite herself she was getting frightened. She had never thought it would get this far.

Michael picked Dopolis up by his camel hair overcoat, lifting him off the ground as if he weighed nothing at all. 'You are beginning to get on my wick. Comprendez? Or whatever it is you bubbles say.' He threw Dopolis on to the filthy floor and turned to the minders. He could see they were frightened. 'Don't even think about getting your little pop-pops out. You'd never walk out of here. So just button your mutton while I tell your short-arse little mate here the score.' He went to where Dopolis was sprawling on the cold floor, his face like thunder. Grabbing him by the lapels of his coat, Michael dragged him upright and pushed his face down to his.

'You tell your Mr Big that if my brother ain't home by ten o'clock tonight, I am coming after him. If as much as one hair is harmed on Benny's pretty little head, I will kill you all. Slowly and painfully.'

He punched the Greek to the ground again. Dopolis watched as Michael took a length of lead piping from his pocket. He tried to scramble away. Michael brought the piping down on his legs.

'You want everything, do you? All that I've got? Don't want much do you, you wanker?' He brought the lead down on Dopolis's elbow and a powerful crack echoed around the warehouse. The two minders were staring, fascinated, at Michael Ryan in action. Leslie and Lee giggled as they heard Dopolis try to stifle a scream.

'Well, you'll get nothing, mate. Not a brass razoo, as the Aussies say. You've got more chance of getting a dose of clap off the fucking Pope than you've got of getting a job off me cleaning out toilets. You made a fatal mistake, Mr Dopolis. You were stupid enough to annoy me. I want me little brother and then I'm coming after you and your Mr Fucking Big. So you had better start saying your prayers, OK?'

He smashed the lead piping into the man's face, felt Dopolis's nose collapse and smiled. The Greek was a bloody mess.

He looked to where the two minders were standing and said calmly, 'Pick up him and take him home. He's annoying me.'

The two men stood paralysed with fear. They had never seen a look the like of which was on Michael Ryan's face now. He had enjoyed every second.

Mickey shouted at them: 'PICK HIM UP AND PISS OFF!'

They did as they were told, their movements jerky and awkward in their fright. Carrying Dopolis between them, his legs hanging uselessly, they began to drag him from the warehouse. Michael called to them, and then standing in front of them pushed his finger into Dopolis's broken nose. The bone and gristle were open to the freezing air.

'This is just for starters. You wait until I really lose me rag. I want me brother. And I want him tonight.' He jerked his head at the two men and they dragged Dopolis from the warehouse as fast as they possibly could. Michael pulled a handkerchief from his pocket and wiped the blood from his finger.

'Coo, Mickey . . . you scared me.'

'Listen, Princess, I might rant and rave but I would never hurt me own.'

'What about if they grassed you up?' This from Leslie, who always asked the wrong thing at the wrong time.

Michael stared at him nastily. 'Why? Are you thinking of trying it?'

Leslie blanched. He dropped his gun in fright and Michael laughed.

'No . . . No, Mickey. Not me. N-never!'

'I was only joking, you nonce.'

Michael was on a high. He was always the same after a bout of violence. 'Well, Maws, it seems your ideas about the docks are spot on.'

Geoffrey nodded. 'This Mr Big, whoever he is, must want all this. It's got to be something to do with all this chat about redevelopment. Why else would anyone want this heap of shit?'

Michael shrugged.

'Once our Benny's home we'll rip this town apart. No one can hide from us. Not for long anyway. This has taught me one thing, though. If we're going to keep any sort of order we must rent out the East End in little pieces. Geoffrey, I want you to keep your ear to the ground. See if any old wags are out and about looking for a bit of action. I'm getting sick of the lot of it. What's it the Yanks call it?' He laughed out loud. 'A conglomerate. That's what we'll become – a conglomerate! Take a leaf out of the big knobs' books.

Get loads of little firms to do the shitty work. Only there won't be any golden handshakes floating around!'

Maura was unnerved by how quickly Michael could forget what had just taken place. It was as if Dopolis had never existed. As if he had not been beaten to a pulp. She shuddered, and Lee put his arm around her.

'You cold, Maws?'

Michael carried on talking. 'I should have listened to you ages ago, Princess. We're going legal at last. Should please Mother anyway. Let's get back to the club. This place gives me the heebie jeebies.'

Ten minutes later they were all on their way to Dean Street. Maura and Michael travelled together and he talked to her all the time, not seeming to notice how quiet she was. They parked the Mercedes in Old Compton Street. For some reason Dean Street was cordoned off. There were people milling around everywhere. Maura and Michael saw that Geoffrey and the others had arrived before them. Maura walked up to Geoffrey. His skin looked grey in the twilight. She noticed police were everywhere. She heard the high screeching of an ambulance as it travelled along Shaftesbury Avenue. A large crowd had gathered, mainly bouncers and hostesses, a few punters and sightseers mixed in with them.

She felt Michael's breath on her neck as he spoke to Geoffrey. 'What's going on here?'

'It's the club, Michael. It was firebombed.' Geoffrey's voice was dead. As if he could not really comprehend what had happened.

'What!' Michael and Maura spoke in unison.

'I said it's been firebombed.'

'Is anyone hurt, Geoff?'

He shook his head. 'I don't know, Maura.'

She pushed her way through the crowd and stared at what had once been the entrance to Le Buxom. The wind was picking up and little flakes of snow were stinging her face. She could smell the burning.

Then her heart seemed to explode inside her chest. She felt her hands clench into fists and a breathlessness as if she had run for miles. Walking towards her, from the entrance of the club, was Terry Petherick. Even in the freezing cold she felt a wave of heat sweep through her body. He still had the same long-legged stride. The same dirty blond hair. The same lopsided grin. She was aware of her rapid heartbeat crashing through her body. For the first time in eight years she was seeing the man she hated. Only she did not hate him. She realised that she loved him . . . loved him with every ounce of her being.

200

The sights and sounds around her were blocked from her mind. All she was aware of was a feeling of being alive. Really alive. For the first time since she'd had the abortion she felt an overpowering urge to throw herself into his arms. Beg him to forgive her for what she had done to their child. He was getting closer to her. She could feel the heat creeping along her flesh . . .

'Hello, Maura. Long time no see.' His words were a vocal caress and she felt herself tremble. Her throat was dry and she knew that if she tried to speak to him she would begin to cry. The tears were already there, hot and aching behind her eyes. She bit down hard on her lip.

Terry Petherick was looking at her with his penetrating stare. He thought of the Maura he had known, the vulnerable young girl, and felt ashamed of what he had done to her. Through her sophisticated hair style and expensive clothes he could still see the girl she had been. The young woman he had made love to and whom he had nearly died for. She was still there, inside the new shell, looking at him through the blue stillness of her eyes. They would never change. When he had been beaten up he had lain in the hospital bed thinking about her. He had never held any grudge about what had happened to him. He had felt at the time that he deserved it. He deserved to feel the pain. He still felt that, especially now, looking at the face that had haunted him for eight long years.

Michael's voice broke into their private thoughts and snapped them both back to reality.

'Well, well, well. If it ain't the Casanova of Vine Street.'

Maura felt a flush come over her face and neck.

'Hello, Mr Ryan. I suppose you know that your club was firebombed?' Terry's voice was quiet and controlled. 'Your doorman, Gerry Jackson, was badly hurt, and a young lass, a young blonde girl called . . .' he looked at his notebook '. . . Sheree. No one seemed to know her surname.'

'Well, anything you want to ask you talk to my brother Geoffrey. He's over there.' Michael pointed to where Geoffrey was standing with Lee and Garry and Leslie. 'I want to get my sister home. This ain't no place for her. Especially now.'

'Quite.' Terry's voice was smooth. Maura noticed that he still had his baby soft skin. She wanted to reach up and touch his face. Feel his flesh beneath her fingers again. She closed her eyes and felt Michael's arm go around her.

'Come on, Maws. There's nothing we can do here.'

She wanted to throw Michael from her. She couldn't walk away from Terry now. Not when she had found him again. She felt Michael pulling her gently away and still she watched Terry, turning her head as Michael steered her through the crowd back to the car. And she knew in her heart that Terry felt the same as she did. It was written in his eyes and face. Suddenly all the noise and bustle around her became real once more. She came back to earth with a jolt that made her want to cry out in anguish.

'Come on, Princess. In the car, love.' Michael's voice was caressing, like a lover's. Only this time it was not enough for her.

In the space of a few minutes all the old longings had come back to haunt her. Long suppressed sights and sounds were rushing back. The little flat in Islington. Their favourite restaurant. The smell of his body as he slipped his maleness inside her. It was like a strong heady potion that had miraculously brought her back to life.

'Come on, Maws. Get in the car.'

She opened the door and sat in the car obediently. Leslie and Lee were already in the back, Garry squeezed in with them. For Maura the whole day's events had been wiped out by that one chance meeting.

Michael got into the driving seat and put the key in the ignition. He started up the car and pulled away. When they were driving along Shaftesbury Avenue, he spoke.

'I suppose you all realise what's happened, don't you?' Nobody answered him. 'The bombing of the club had already been arranged, well in advance. From five minutes after me belting Dopolis, the word had been sent out. It was a foregone conclusion. Whoever threw the petrol bomb was ready and waiting for word.'

Gradually, what Michael was saying penetrated Maura's brain.

'Benny ain't coming home, is he, Mickey?' Garry sounded as if he was going to cry.

'I doubt that very much, Gal. I doubt that very much indeed.'

'The dirty bastards! The filthy rotten dirty bastards . . .'

Leslie and Lee were both in shock.

'Well, I have an idea where some of Dopolis's information came from. And that's where we're all going now.'

They drove on in silence. Everyone was thinking about Benny. Michael gripped the steering wheel. Mr Big had better watch out. He was coming to get him.

The enormity of what had happened hit Maura like a bucket of icy water. Benny was probably dead already . . . She felt the shaking in her hands and legs that was caused by shock. As she looked out of the window of the car she saw that they were in Knightsbridge. Harrods had its Christmas decorations that brought people from miles around. Everywhere she looked were lights and Christmas messages, in the shops and the restaurants.

And Benny was dead. Or about to die. She closed her eyes and saw his face. Then Terry's face.

Garry was sitting hunched up in the back, racking his brains like Michael, trying to come up with a name. Someone who would have the guts to take on Michael Ryan. Someone who held a grudge . . .

Michael parked the car outside his flat. They all followed him inside. Maura realised that Roy was missing and asked Mickey where he was. He put his key into the lock of his front door.

'I sent him home, Maws. He's the only family man among us. After what happened at the club, I sent him home.'

She nodded as he opened the door. They all followed him into his lounge.

Jonny was sitting on the couch. He was wearing his straight gear: grey polo-necked sweater and black Staprest trousers. He was very white. His blond curly hair had been freshly washed. It was still damp. He stared up at Michael and smiled. Maura noticed that he was a bundle of nerves.

'Get us all a stiff drink, Jonny . . . now!' Michael sounded ferocious. Jonny leapt out of his seat to do his bidding. He was shaking so much he nearly dropped the decanter of whisky. Everyone sat down on Michael's deep green Habitat settee. Jonny brought them all a drink. Michael stood at the fireplace and, as Jonny handed him his drink, said: 'How much did they pay you?'

Jonny tried to bluff his way out of it. He knew that his life depended on it.

'I don't know what you're talking about, Mickey!'

Michael threw the contents of his glass into Jonny's face. Then, grabbing his blond curls, cried: 'Tell me, Jonny. Answer my question.'

'I swear to you, I don't know what you're talking about. Please!'

Michael brought his knee up into Jonny's groin, using such force that the boy's whole body was lifted from the ground. Michael let him drop on to the carpet in front of him. Then, taking out the lead piping he had used on Dopolis, he waved it in Jonny's face.

'You can make this hard for yourself or easy, Jonny. Either way you will answer my questions. Now, I ask you again, how much did they pay you?'

Jonny lay on the floor, heaving. His hands were holding his testicles, which felt as if they had been forced from their protective sac. He was in agony. Michael had dropped his glass and Jonny had a fleeting image of him smashing it into his face. Michael kicked the glass at him as if he had read the boy's mind.

Jonny hunched his shoulders up and held his testicles tighter. 'Five . . . five gr-grand.'

Michael laughed a bitter laugh.

'Five lousy grand? You let my brother die for five lousy grand? I'd have given you that if you'd asked me. You fucking scum queen!'

He brought the lead piping down on Jonny, busting his head open with the first blow.

Maura jumped from her seat and grabbed Michael's arm.

'Not here, Mickey. Don't kill him here. Find out who approached him. Then let them have him.' She poked her head in her brothers' direction. They were all sitting on Michael's giant settee watching him.

Maura stared down into Jonny's face.

'Who bought you off, Jonny? You may as well tell me. You're a dead man anyway. If you don't start talking, I'll let Michael and Garry torture you. I mean it, Jonny.'

He was crying, his tears mingling with the blood that was dripping down his face from his head.

'Maura . . . I . . . I swear I didn't mean any . . . harm. He made me do it! He said . . . you . . . was all finished. That I'd better get away . . .'

'Who was it, Jonny? Tell me who it was.'

'It . . . was . . . Sam. Sammy Goldbaum.'

Michael spat in Jonny's face.

'Not Sammy. Never! You poxy little shit stabber . . .'

'I swear to you, Mickey. Please believe me.' Jonny was crying hard now. 'I loved you, Mickey. I did. I'm so sorry . . .'

Michael kicked him in the legs. 'Yeah, you loved me all right. You ponce! You loved me so much you done a deal for money. Five shitty grand you sold me and my brother for. Wanker!'

He nodded his head and Garry and Leslie picked Jonny up from the floor between them. They did not need to be told that Jonny was not to come home. They would enjoy putting him away, for Benny's sake.

Jonny screamed out in fear. 'Please, Mickey! Please . . .' Tears were rolling down his face and mingling with blood and the mucus from his nose. 'I only told him things because I thought you wouldn't be there any more to protect me. I'm begging you, Mickey . . . please!'

Michael raised the lead piping above his head and smashed it down with all his might across Jonny's head. Jonny was suddenly quiet. He would never utter another word.

Garry, Leslie and Lee carried him from the flat.

Michael sat on his giant sofa and put his head in his hands.

'Benny's dead, Maws. Because that slag sold him for a lousy five grand. I want Goldbaum next. Sammy, my friend. Well, from now on, it's family always.' He wiped his streaming eyes.

'Come on, Mickey. Me and you will sort out Sammy together.'

They left the flat. As they got into the car, Maura heard the high piping voices of a group of carol singers. They were singing for charity outside the restaurants in Beauchamp Place. Maura could have wept herself. This had been one of the worst days of her life. Instead she lit them both a cigarette and braced herself for the night ahead. She knew that tonight she was going to commit a murder, and instead of being frightened felt a deadness in all her limbs. Thoughts of Terry Petherick were a luxury she could not afford. She had come too far with Mickey ever to be able to live a normal life again. Together they would pay back everyone responsible for Benny's death. The familiar hardness crept back into her deep blue eyes and she put away her childish dreams forever.

Terry was like the expensive present that all poor children wanted but could never hope to attain. She had felt for a few moments the agonising pleasure that he had always created in her, and she would have to make do with that for the rest of her life. She would think about it in her lonely bed when all this was over, but tonight they had a job to do.

As Michael's Mercedes sped through the streets of London Maura saw in her mind's eye the little baby in the washing up bowl and finally laid that ghost to rest.

She opened the window of the car and let the cold night air whip at her face. Benny was dead, love his heart. Big lovable Benny was dead. Her mother and father would be devastated.

As they drove past the Giorgiou used car lot in Bethnal Green, they were completely unaware that Benny was lying not twenty yards from where their car stopped at the junction with Roman Road. He had died at seven-ten precisely.

Chapter Eighteen

Sammy Goldbaum was sitting at his kitchen table, looking around the familiar room, breathing in the same old smells: gefilte fish and kanadelach soup. His wife Noola made the best Matzo balls he had ever tasted. On the wall to the right of his chair was a photograph of his three daughters. The eldest, Rebekka, had his large bulbous nose – the only one to inherit his Jewish legacy. The other two, Beatrice and Ruth, both had the blonde prettiness of his wife. He wiped his forehead again with a large handkerchief. He had been sweating profusely since he had heard the news. He was aware that Michael would be coming for him and so he waited, patiently but feeling very frightened.

His wife Noola sat opposite him. She was more than worried by the look of her husband. He looked terrible. You did not live with a man for over thirty years without knowing his every thought and action.

'Tell me, Sammy, what is ailing you? You sit there like a statue, staring into space. Is it the police you are frightened of? Have you got into trouble again?'

'Noola!' Sammy's deep voice was exasperated. 'Keep your nose out of my affairs. Always you must know everything. I tell you, Noola, it's not always healthy to know too much. Go to bed. God knows, you could do with the beauty sleep.'

He tried to smile at her but it did not quite work. She reached across the table and gripped his arm.

'Sammy, in all the years we've been married I've always stood by you. I've lied to the police. Even to the Rabbi, may God forgive me. But I did it for love. Now I see you scared out of your wits. You've sent the girls over to my mother's house for the night, and all you can say to me is: "Go to bed, Noola." Do you think I am a fool?'

He shook his head. Trust her to begin one of her arguments, tonight of all nights. She had been a good wife to him, an exemplary wife. Over the years he had grown to love her more than he had thought possible.

'No, Noola, my darling. I would never think that you were a

207

fool. But I tell you, you should have gone to your mother's with the girls. It could be very dangerous here tonight.'

'But why, Sammy? Tell me why?' Her voice was desperate. He looked into her faded eyes. Her grey hair was, as usual, rolled up in enormous curlers with a bright green chiffon scarf tied around them. Suddenly he saw her as she had been thirty-five years ago: a small thin young Jewish girl, with a trim figure and a bubbling, overpowering personality. She had made him laugh. Being a big man, he had wanted to protect the tiny scrap that was to become his wife; instead she had taken him over. But he had never once resented her for it. She would always be quicker than he to see the point of a debate or the way out of any trouble. He had begun to reply on her early in their marriage and it had never changed. Until tonight. No one could help him now. No one at all.

He took a deep breath. She deserved to know the truth.

'I sold out Michael Ryan, Noola.'

Noola's hand flew to her mouth. Her grey eyes screwed up into tiny slits until they finally closed, as if trying to blot out what her husband had said to her. She took her hand from her mouth and put it to her heart as if trying to stop its beat.

'Oh my God, Sammy! He will kill you.' Her voice cracked with emotion.

'I know that, Noola. I am waiting for him now. That's why I sent the girls away. I am sure he would not hurt them or you. But I think it would be better for all concerned if I was alone when he came.'

'But why, Sammy? Why?' Her voice was stronger now, truculent. 'He has always been a good friend to you, looked after you.'

Sammy wiped his forehead again.

'I know that. You think I don't know that?'

Noola sat back in her chair and stared at her husband. It all became as plain as day to her.

'Gold help you, Sammy Goldbaum. You've been gambling again. That's it, isn't it?'

He nodded his head.

'So, like Judas Iscariot, you betrayed your friend. Your very good friend.'

'I did not think that anyone would get hurt.' His voice was self-righteous. 'I swear, Noola. Then tonight I heard on the radio that his club, Le Buxom, had been firebombed. And I realised I had caused a lot of trouble. Now all I can do is sit and wait for my punishment. It is pointless trying to get away from him.'

Noola got up from her seat and went to her husband. She kissed his hot dry lips and sweaty forehead and she went to bed. She knew that she would never see her husband alive again. She took three Mogadon sleeping tablets, and when Maura and Michael arrived was out cold. As Sammy said, sometimes it was best not to know anything.

Janine looked at her husband Roy. He was eating his breakfast and it seemed to her that every mouthful was a trial to him. 'What's going on, Roy? I've already heard on the news about the bombing.'

He stopped chewing and glanced at his heavily pregnant wife. Then, putting down his knife and fork, he got up from the table and went to her, pulling her into his arms.

'Bombed!' He tried to make his voice light. 'It was a gas leak. You know what it's like if anything happens in Soho. The press always has a field day.'

'But a young girl died, and Gerry Jackson is seriously ill.'

'I know that, love. It was burns. Honestly, Jan, it was a gas leak from the building next door.' He caressed her swollen belly. 'You just worry about Junior here. I'll take care of everything else.'

'If it's trouble, Roy, I want to know.'

He turned her back towards the cooker and patted her behind. 'You just worry about making me a nice cup of Rosie Lee. Then I'd better be off.'

Janine filled the kettle and plugged it in. Then she turned the radio up. It was the eight-thirty news. The announcer's voice crackled around the kitchen as if unaccustomed to being listened to in this household.

'The bombing of the West End nightclub, Le Buxom, was this morning said to be a terrorist attack. The owner of the nightclub, Mr Michael Ryan, has been seen over the years with various IRA sympathisers. Mr Ryan is a known gangland figure, though attempts to bring charges against him have always failed. He was not available for comment this morning. Mr Heath . . .'

The voice droned on and Roy carried on eating his breakfast. Janine placed his cup of tea in front of him. She did not know what to do. She felt the baby kick and her hands went to her swollen belly protectively. She thought of ringing Carla and dismissed it. She would wait for him to leave then she would phone her mother-in-law.

Sarah Ryan looked terrible. She had not slept all night. Her straggly grey hair had escaped from its usual bun and her round open face looked more wrinkled than usual. Her body had grown fatter over the years and now everything about her seemed to sag – her breasts, her stomach, even the folds of skin under her neck. She had always looked older than her years, but in the last twenty-four hours had become positively decrepit-looking. She was just fifty-nine. Her eyes, though, were alert and filled with a bright intelligence that seemed to glow out of her wrinkled face. She was worried out of her mind about her youngest son. She had not seen him for over forty-eight hours, not since he had devoured one of his Olympian breakfasts. She knew that something had happened to him. She had tried unsuccessfully to contact Michael and Maura. Both were nowhere to be found. Carla had told her that she had not seen Maura for a couple of days. She had not seemed too bothered about it, but Sarah knew that her nervousness had communicated itself to the girl and now she too was worried.

Since the news about the bombing of the nightclub she had had a sick feeling in her guts. She had spoken to Roy late the night before but he was closemouthed about everything she had asked him. Protecting himself and the others, she guessed. She poured out a large mug of tea and took it up to her husband, who as usual had drunk himself into a stupor and gone to bed. She placed the tea on the bedside table and shook him roughly, the sour smell of his breath adding to her feeling of nausea.

'What? What do you want?'

She stared down at his sunken face. He had not shaved for nearly a week. He looked what he was . . . like dirty Irish scum. She had to stifle an overpowering urge to throw the mug of steaming hot tea into his face.

'Benjamin . . . he still hasn't come home.' She tried to get some response. Benjamin opened his eyes and stared around him blearily.

'Oh, piss off, Sar. Benny's a grown man. He's probably out shagging. You know what he's like.'

He sat up in bed and looked at the clock. It was just after nine.

'Jumping Jesus Christ! What you woke me up for?'

Sarah sat on the bed and gripped his arm. 'I think something terrible's happened. Michael's club was bombed last night.'

'What!'

'It was on the news. Roy said it was a gas leak but the man on the news said it was a terrorist attack.'

She watched the different expressions flicker over Benjamin's face and sighed. In his state he would have difficulty even working out what day it was, let alone following all this. It had always been the same. She could never rely on him to be of help in any way, shape or form. It was beyond him. For the first time in years she needed him and he was going to let her down. She heard the telephone ringing in the hallway and rushed off to answer it, hoping against hope that it was young Benny. It was Janine. Sarah felt the hope seep from her body as she heard her daughter-in-law's voice.

'Can you come over to me, Sarah? Please.'

'Yes, Janine, I'll come to you. Give me an hour.'

When she replaced the receiver she rang Carla. By ten-thirty the three women were closeted together in Janine's house. For once the atmosphere between mother and daughter was forged by a common bond. They were all frightened, but as yet did not really know what exactly they were frightened of.

Mr Desmond Buckingham Gooch walked his dog across Hampstead Heath every morning. He rose at five precisely and breakfasted on a soft boiled egg and one slice of toast. He then walked his dog Victory across the Heath. He was there by six o'clock every morning, come rain or shine. His neighbours called him 'Colonel Blimp', though never to his face. Victory was a cocker spaniel, a splendid animal, though scatty. She never came when he called her and completely disregarded his orders, and he loved her with all his heart. She was his sole companion.

This morning she had stopped by a litter bin attached to a lamp post. He called her in his most commanding voice. She ignored him as usual and stayed exactly where she was. She began to whine. She got up to her hind legs and tried to scratch the metal bin. The lamp post was giving out an eerie light. It was just becoming day in the cold twilight world of a winter's morning. A fine covering of snow had settled during the night and in the gloomy light of the breaking dawn the lamp post seemed to be radiating a burnt orange glow that barely illuminated itself. For a few seconds Desmond Buckingham Gooch felt a prickle of fear. Then, his natural common sense coming to the fore, he walked purposefully to the bin. Victory could probably smell one of those damned hamburgers that young people these days seemed to live on. If he had his way he would bring back the days of powdered egg and rationing. Youngsters today had it too easy, far too easy in his opinion. He looked into the bin.

A head stared up at him, covered with a layer of early morning frost. He staggered backwards, his hand going instinctively to his chest. He felt the vomit in his mouth, his boiled egg and toast mixed with bile burning his tongue and gums. He threw up on to the pavement. Taking deep breaths, he dragged Victory roughly away from the bin and put on her lead, then he half pulled and half kicked his beloved dog back to his flat. Inside his hallway he leant against the front door, trying to calm his heartbeat. He made his way into his bedroom and, sitting on his bed, opened his beside cabinet and took out the pills the doctor had given him for his heart. He placed one under his tongue with a trembling hand. Victory sat staring at him, her bright red coat glistening with snow. When he felt the life coming back to his limbs, he picked up the phone by his bed and called the police.

The news of the finding of the head did not hit the streets until twelve-thirty.

It was Benny Ryan's.

Mrs Carmen De'Sousa, a West Indian woman, was coming home from a nightshift at Ford's in Dagenham. She walked slowly up Lower Mardyke Avenue towards her block of maisonettes. She had had a bad night. Their union representative had wanted to call them all out. She shook her head in its large woolly hat. This country amazed her.

She heard the rubbery screech of car tyres as somebody attempted a wheelspin in the frosty morning. She ignored it. Cars came and went at all hours of the day and night. You became immune to the sound, as you became immune to the noise of radios, record players and ghetto blasters. If you were sensible on the Mardyke Estate, you kept your nose out of other people's business.

She started to walk up the steps that led to her landing, gripping the rail that ran parallel with the steps. It was very icy, the snow had settled, and all around her the world was blanketed in a white layer that made even the Mardyke Estate look pleasant. As she reached the top step she stopped. She could hear a faint mewling. She walked past the entrance to her landing and began to walk down the flight of steps that led to the garages that ran the whole length of the block of maisonettes. No one in their right mind kept their cars there these days. They were full of junk, old furniture, old bikes, mattresses and general rubbish.

She heard the soft mewling again and called out in the darkness, 'Marley? Id that you, boy?'

She reached the bottom of the steps and felt rather than saw that there was something lying sprawled out in front of her. She squinted and peered at the ground. The lights had been broken down here for over five years. She felt in the pocket of her heavy blanket coat and took out a box of Swan Vestas. She lit one and held it in front of her. It was to be an action she would regret all her life.

Lying on the floor in front of her was the body of a young man. A young blond man. She stared at the body for what seemed ages, a scream stuck in her throat. Then the match burnt her fingers and pain spurred her into action. She began to scream and wail at the top of her voice. Within five minutes nearly every resident from

212

her block of maisonettes was with her.

Jonny's body had been found.

Denise and Carol McBridge walked to the bus stop together. Both girls worked at Van Den Bergh and Jurgen's in West Thurrock. Their bus came at five minutes to seven. Two stops later they alighted and made their way from the London Road to the dirt track that had always been used as a short cut to their factory. As usual they were joking around, barely able to see in the winter half-light. Carol tripped over something and swore softly. It was a large rolled-up canvas. Nothing unusual about that. This was a known dumping ground. What was unusual was what was poking out of the bottom end of it. On closer inspection, the girls found that it was a pair of feet. Rather large feet. As if of one mind they scrambled over the bundle and ran as fast as they could to work, fear giving their feet wings.

Sammy Goldbaum's body had been found.

Denise's and Carol's manager was very good. He gave them the rest of the week off on full pay.

Maura sat in the interview room at Vine Street police station. She lit another cigarette and pulled on it hard. She was frightened, very frightened. But outwardly she looked as if she did not have a care in the world.

The WPC who had been assigned to stay with her looked her over critically. She approved of the pale grey suit Maura wore. It was plain but, with the single strand of pearls and the pearl earrings, it looked what it was: exclusive and expensive. WPC Cotter approved of everything about Maura Ryan, from her shiny white-blonde hair to her crocodile skin shoes and bag. It was common knowledge that this was the woman who had nearly ruined DS Petherick's career. It was an old story that had been embellished over the years until now it was part of Vine Street folklore.

DI Dobin came into the room. He smiled at Maura and she smiled back. She had been here for hours and they still had not charged her. She had called her brief and he was on his way from Cambridge. All she had to do was keep a clear head. They had nothing on her.

She forced the events of the night before from her mind. Sammy Goldbaum had deserved everything he got. Sammy was to become another blank spot in Maura's mind, along with everything else she had ever done that was decidedly wrong. DI Dobin and the WPC and everyone who touched Maura's life in some way, however trivial, were never in any way aware that she was like a time bomb: a dangerous time bomb that would eventually explode. Her outer veneer of calm and friendliness hid a mass of emotions and feelings that would one day spew out like a festering cancer.

'Am I going to be charged with anything?' Her voice was calm and controlled.

DI Dobin cleared his throat. Against his will he had taken a liking to this girl. Which was more than could be said of his feelings for her elder brother. The sad part was they both had perfect alibis and not even an outstanding parking ticket between them.

'I am afraid, Miss Ryan, that I have some bad news for you.'

Maura's face remained neutral. She took a long drag on her cigarette.

'Oh? And what's that?' She braced herself for what she knew was coming.

'A head was found earlier today in a litter bin in East Heath Road, just off Hampstead Heath. It was your brother Benjamin's.'

He watched her face blanch. The corner of her mouth began to twitch upwards. It was the only outward sign that she felt anything.

'Now, Miss Ryan, I ask you again – have you anything to tell me about the death of Jonny Fenwick or Samuel Goldbaum?'

Maura stared at him blankly. She put out her cigarette and immediately lit another. She shook her head. DI Dobin watched the tears begin to gather in her lovely eyes. He could see what had attracted young Petherick to her. Even with her height and her woman's body, she still had a naivete about her that made men want to protect her.

He knew as sure as eggs was eggs that if this lovely creature sitting in front of him had not actually committed the murders herself, she, along with her brother Michael, had ordered them. And he also knew that they would walk out of this police station because there was no evidence to go on. Michael had been with a 'friend', a young barrister who had already been in and given a sworn statement, and this young woman had been with Timothy Repton, a well-known actor who starred in a twice-weekly soap opera called 'Crossways'. Mr Repton had also been in and given a sworn statement. Both the witnesses to their whereabouts were beyond reproach and both were, in DI Dobin's opinion, lying bastards.

It was always the same with the Ryans. They were more slippery than a greased eel. Also, the Chief Super had been running around like a blue-arsed fly. He had received word from a big wig somewhere along the line, and now the Ryans were to be

214

'courteously' escorted off the premises. He sighed.

'Well, Miss Ryan, thank you very much for your time. You can go now.'

Maura stood up. She slipped her crocodile skin clutch bag underneath her arm and held out her free hand. Dobin shook it gently.

'Is my brother being released?'

'Yes, Miss Ryan, he's waiting for you at the reception desk.'

'Thank you. Thank you very much. Have you any idea who could have hurt . . . murdered my brother Benny?' Her voice was low.

'No, Miss. But rest assured we will do all that we can. As we will to investigate the bombing of your brother's club.'

Maura bowed her head and followed him from the room. Unlike her, Michael was making himself heard. Maura could hear him before she saw him.

As she turned the corner and walked to him, he pointed at her. 'Don't you worry, girl. These bastards will pay for this day's work. My little brother's dead and *you* arrest *me*!' His voice was indignant. 'And my little sister! My club's been bombed and you lot don't give a toss about it. I'm a taxpayer and I want me rights!'

The Chief Superintendent was nearly in tears. 'Please, Mr Ryan. We must follow every lead.'

'Why ain't you out looking for the real criminals, eh? The rapists and the child molesters. Why ain't you out looking for whoever murdered my little brother?'

Maura slipped her arm into his. 'Come on, Michael. Calm down, love. Let's just get out of here.' She led him out into the afternoon air. 'Please, Mickey, let's get home. I think I'm going to be sick.'

Michael put his arms around her and cuddled her to him. 'Don't worry, Dopolis will pay for what he's done, darlin', and he'll pay bloody dearly.'

At this moment Maura did not want anyone to pay for anything. She just wanted to run away from it all. Instead she smiled wanly. The worst was yet to come. They had to face their mother.

Sarah had been sitting in the darkness of her front room for hours. When the police brought her the news about Benny she had walked into the room, pulled the heavy curtains and sat in the chair by the fire. She felt nothing. Nothing at all. But she would. Oh, she knew that much. She would. It was like Anthony all over again. She had made Benjamin go with the policeman to identify young Benny's remains. Let him do some of the dirty work for a change.

In the flickering firelight her religious statues looked lifelike. Getting out of the seat, she went to the large sideboard that held them all. She opened one of the drawers and took out her wooden rosary. She went back to her seat. Kissing the Cross of Christ, she began to pray.

She could hear Carla's sobs coming from the bedroom above her, but did not really care. It would do the child good to find out just what her Auntie Maura and Uncle Michael had caused. It might take some of the shine off them for her. She had already refused to see Geoffrey. He had arrived just after the police and she had told him to bugger off out of it. She did not want to see any of her children except Maura and Michael. Oh, she wanted to see them all right! She wanted to throw them out of her house and her life. They were filthy . . . putrid.

She heard the click of the front room door opening and glanced towards it. In the light from the hall she could make out Maura and Michael's silhouettes. She said nothing. They walked into the room quietly, shutting the door behind them. Sarah carried on praying.

' "Hail Mary, full of grace, the Lord is with thee. Blessed art thou amongst sinners and blessed is the fruit of thy womb, Jesus . . ." '

Michael watched his mother. She was so short that her feet did not touch the floor properly as she sat on the large horsehair chair. The room had its own distinctive cloying stuffiness, a sickly sweet smell of lavender polish and dusty velvet.

'Mum? Shall I turn the light on?'

' "Holy Mary Mother of God, pray for us sinners, now and at the hour of our death, Amen." '

' "Hail Mary, full of grace . . ." '

'Come on, Michael. Let's leave her.'

Maura's voice sounded something in Sarah's head. It was as if her daughter's voice triggered an explosion. Sarah's voice came to them from the semi-darkness.

'So you want to leave, Maura Ryan, do you?' Her voice was low, conversational. As if they were having a friendly chat about the weather. 'Did you know that your brother's head was found this morning? In a litter bin, of all places.' She was amazed to hear herself laugh. 'Yes, a litter bin. Just the place to put rubbish, isn't it? In a dustbin. Where will they put you two, I wonder, when you're dead? Down in the sewers, I expect, with the rest of the shit and the effluent. Oh, yes. That will very likely be where you two will end up. In the filth and stink of the sewers!'

'Mum! For God's sake.' Michael's voice was shocked.

'Don't you "God" me, Michael Ryan. Because I'm finished

with you . . . I should never have forgiven you over my Anthony.'

Maura listened to their mother's voice. She knew that what Sarah was saying would break Michael's heart.

'And what about me, Mum? What about me?'

Maura's voice was hard. Sarah felt its iciness and shivered in her seat.

'You filthy whore! I know all about you, Maura Ryan. You and him.' She poked her head towards Michael. 'Do you know what people say? That you two sleep together. Did you know that? Only I know that's not true because he's as queer as a fish and you're a neuter. You're not capable of sleeping with any man, Maura Ryan.'

Maura felt a hot flush creep over her body. She went to the lightswitch and flipped it. The room was filled with the glaring brightness of a one hundred watt bulb.

Maura walked to her mother, her lovely face twisted into a mask of hatred.

'So I'm a neuter, am I? And whose bloody fault was that? Yours! Call yourself a mother? *You* took me to the abortionist. And *you* held me down on the bloody table while that Paki bastard ripped my baby from inside me. You turned us all into what we are, Mother. Even poor Benny. Another Mummy's boy, still at home at twenty-nine years old! You made it impossible for any of your children to lead a normal life. You drove your husband to drink and your kids into being neuters.

'I may end up in the gutter or the sewers. Who knows? But at least if I go there I'll have finally told you what I think of you. You're a nasty vindictive old bitch! You're even jealous of me and Carla, ain't you? Go on . . . admit it!'

Sarah stared at her daughter, mesmerised. Of all the things she had envisaged at this meeting with Maura and Michael, this was not one of them. She had expected silence as she read them the riot act. Not this.

'Sitting in the bloody dark saying the Rosary! You old hypocrite. Well, let me tell you something. Your old darling Father McCormack is an active IRA member. That's how we all got involved. When you sent him to talk some sense into Michael, the priest dragged him into it all. He was laughing at you, you stupid old cow!'

'No! I won't have you say that about the priest. You're a dirty liar!'

'SHUT YOUR BLOODY MOUTH UP!' Maura's voice bounced off the walls. 'Do you hear me? Shut up for once in your life. We may not be pillars of the church but we ain't got anything on our conscience where you're concerned, Mother. Everything you ever

217

had come from Mickey, later on from me and the other boys. You had nothing . . . NOTHING!'

Maura ran to where the religious statues stood bearing witness to their fight. Picking up the statue of Saint Sebastian, she threw it to the ground.

'Not even the money to buy this shower of shite!'

She stopped abruptly, gasping for breath. She saw her mother sitting in the chair. She looked like a very old woman. All the fight left Maura and she went to Michael.

'Come on, Mickey. Let's go.'

'Mum . . . You didn't mean what you said, did you, Maws? Mum, look at me.'

Sarah sighed heavily.

'Get him out of me sight, Maura, and take yourself with him. You both disgust me.'

Maura turned round to face the woman she had alternately loved and hated all her life.

'Not half as much as you disgust me, Mother.'

As Maura spoke, Michael seemed to snap out of his reverie. 'I worshipped you, Mother.' His voice was dangerously low. 'All my life it's been, "Michael, get me this, son." Or help with that. But you never really cared about me, did you? I was just a pair of hands as far as you were concerned.'

His eyes were moist and Maura felt her heart breaking as she watched him confront the most important person in his life. 'I helped you with the kids as they came along. I fetched and carried while you had your long . . . painfully long . . . pregnancies. Then as soon as you were delivered of yet another child, you allowed the old man back into your bed, didn't you? Even after the dead babies you were both back at it like a pair of dogs copulating.

'You wonder why I turned out like I did? Well, I'll tell you why. I never wanted a woman and all that it entailed. I never wanted an emotional leech sucking out my entrails like you did to all us. Anthony's dead, and our Benny – and I'd give anything to be with them! Away from this house and this family and *you* . . . especially you.

'Come on, Maws. Let's leave her to her prayers and her religious mania. It's all she's fit for.'

Sarah felt as if she had been stabbed to the heart. She'd never realised just how much she had come to rely on Michael's unquestioning support.

She sat still in her chair, trying to control her breathing. As Michael pulled Maura from the room they came face to face with Carla. She was standing in the hallway, her lovely face twisted in pain, arms hugging her slim body.

218

'Get your stuff together, Carla, we're leaving.'

She shook her head. Her long red-brown hair swirled about her face.

'I'm not going anywhere with you, Maura. I'm staying here with Nana.'

'I said, get your stuff together.' Maura's voice brooked no argument.

'No. I'm not going.'

Maura sighed. 'You do what you like, Carla. You know where I am when you want me.'

Carla curled her lips in contempt. 'I'll never want you. Never! You're nothing but murderers.'

Maura brought her hand back and slapped Carla a stinging blow across her face.

'You stay here with your precious Nana then . . . I don't give a toss any more. You can do what you like. Come on, Mickey. Let's go.'

As they left the house Benny's Alsatian, Driver, ran from the kitchen down the front steps. He leapt about in the snow, ecstatic to be out in the air.

Michael opened the door to his Mercedes and the dog jumped into the front seats then dived over into the back. He sat there with his tongue hanging out, his heavy tail thumping the seat as it wagged.

'I'll take him home with me, Mickey.'

They got into the car and Michael pulled away from the kerb with a heavy heart.

Inside the house Sarah and Carla held on to each other tightly.

Michael finally spoke as they drove along the Bayswater Road. 'When we get to your drum, Maws, we've got to round up the boys. The old Bill ain't got nothing on us but we have to plan our next moves cautiously.'

Maura did not answer him. He took one hand off the steering wheel and patted her leg.

'Listen, Maws, I ain't learnt much in this life but I have learnt this. When you hit a major setback you put it behind you as quick as possible. Benny's dead. Nothing will ever bring him back again. What we do now is decide when and how we retaliate.'

Maura nodded her head wearily. Her mum was right. Mickey was mad . . . and she had a sneaky feeling that she was as well.

Driver put his head on Maura's shoulder. She could feel his hot dog breath on her cheek and lifted her arm and caressed the dog's soft fur. Benny had loved his dog as he had loved his life – wholeheartedly. She realised with a curious insight that Benny had

219

probably not even realised he was in danger. That fact would never have occurred to him.

She closed her eyes tightly and instead of the tears she had been expecting, began to laugh. A slight giggle at first that gradually built up into a deep rollicking belly laugh. A laugh that made her shoulders shake and her tummy hurt. Somewhere in the distance, far off, she heard the dog begin to whine, and for some reason this just made her laugh harder.

Michael stopped the car and pulled her towards him. She could smell the dank dampness of the material of his coat. Then the tears came at last. She saw Terry Petherick, Anthony and Benny, as clear as a photograph in her mind. Then she saw her mother's face, old and wrinkled . . . a feeling of panic welled up in her and for a few minutes she thought she really had gone mad.

How had this happened to her? And, more importantly, how had she allowed it to happen? Both questions were to remain unanswered for many years, but as she sat in the car with Michael and Driver that night, she realised for the first time just how lonely and unhappy she really was.

'All right, Maws. All right, my love. I'll look after you. Don't you worry.' Michael's voice was soft and husky.

She did not want Michael to look after her. She wanted Terry Petherick to put his arms around her and whisper his words of love, as he had done before. Long ago. Before she had become bad. But, like many other bad things in her life, she forced the thoughts away. Where they waited patiently for the day they would all creep out into the open and torture her, like the long forgotten nightmares of her childhood.

Chapter Nineteen

'Merry Christmas, Auntie Maura!'

Margaret's twin daughters jumped on to the little bed where Maura was sleeping. She opened her eyes, not sure for a few seconds where she was. Then seeing the two bright faces, she tried to smile.

She was at Margaret's. She sat up in bed and hugged Patricia and Penelope. The sleeping tablets she had taken the night before made her feel groggy. She yawned. 'Merry Christmas, my lovelies.'

'Thank you for our Christmas presents, Auntie Maura. They were lovely.'

The two identical little faces beamed at her and she felt the familiar tightening in her guts. What she wouldn't give to be the mother of these two! She hugged them both to her tightly.

Margaret came into the bedroom carrying a tray. Maura could smell eggs and bacon.

'Oh, Marge. Don't be silly. I can get up.'

Margaret pursed her lips and shook her head. 'Oh no you won't, Maws. Oi, you two! Dad's got your breakfast waiting for you downstairs.'

The two girls got off the bed, their bright ginger hair telling anyone who looked at them who their mother was.

Patricia, the elder of the two by five minutes, grimaced. 'Oh, can't we stay up here, Mum?' Her voice had the whine that made Margaret feel like murdering her.

'N.O. spells no. Now hop it, the pair of you.'

The two girls ran from the room.

'Honest, Marge, I couldn't eat a thing.'

The greasy smell of the bacon and eggs was beginning to make her feel sick.

'You *will* bloody eat it. After all you've been through this last few weeks!' Margaret's voice was scandalised. 'You'll end up ill if you're not careful. Smoke, smoke, smoke! Drink, drink. And then sleeping pills to blot out the world.'

'Oh, give it a rest, Marge, for Christ's sake.'

Margaret put the tray across Maura's legs as if to trap her in the bed.

'No I won't give it a rest! You're my best friend and I feel that it's down to me to tell you a few home truths.'

'Such as?' Maura's voice was sarcastic.

'For a start, you look old and haggard. You're drinking too much. It's impossible to get a civil word out of you. You're moody, sarcastic, and to be honest, Maws, you're beginning to get on my tits!'

Maura closed her eyes and yawned again.

'Margie, just in case it's escaped your notice, I recently had a brother murdered. He was spread all over London like a paper chase. His left foot and various other parts of his anatomy are still unaccounted for. I had a big fight with my mother and Carla who are under the impression that me and Mickey were to blame for Benny's murder. I was arrested by the police and kept for over three hours on suspicion of *two* other murders. And you have the nerve to sit there and tell me that I am not my old self!' Maura's voice rose. 'It's enough to make the Queen feel depressed.'

Margaret sighed. She loved Maura wholeheartedly. 'Look, Maws, all I'm trying to say is, pull yourself together. If not for my sake then for the kids. I can't stand them seeing you like this. Last night you was so pissed Dennis had to carry you up to bed.'

'I know. Marge, I'm sorry. It's just that with all that's happened, I feel responsible . . .'

'That's crap and you know it! I can swallow a lot. Maws, but not self-pity. That's a luxury none of us can afford.'

Maura looked at Margaret as if for the first time. Since having the kids she had become huge. In her pink candlewick dressing gown she looked like a little pink Buddha. Her red hair was pinned up untidily and her face had the harassed look that seems to be worn only by mothers of young children. It was only her eyes, the deep sea-green eyes, that still held the image of the girl she had been. They were as sparkling and mischievous as ever.

Cutting off a small piece of bacon, Margaret held it to Maura's mouth. Reluctantly she ate it. Slowly Margaret fed her the whole breakfast. When the last piece of food had been eaten she placed a mug of tea in Maura's hands. Then, picking up the tray, she made her way out of the room. As she opened the bedroom door, holding the tray against her side with one hand, she looked back over her shoulder at Maura.

'You can't plan and scheme on an empty stomach, you know!'

'And just what do you mean by that?'

Marge smiled at her cheekily.

'I'm not as silly as I look, you know, Maura Ryan. So I'll thank you not to act as if I am.' She lowered her voice. 'What I know and what I've guessed will go to my grave with me. Now, you need your wits about you at this time, and I intend to see that you have them.'

She walked from the room and let the door slam shut behind her.

Maura leant back against the pillows and sighed. Good old Marge. The only real friend she had. She sat up in bed, and, putting the tea on the night table, picked up her packet of cigarettes. She lit one, drawing the smoke into her lungs. Margaret was right. She did need her wits about her. If only Carla would talk to her she would feel better. Every time she tried to get through to her, the phone was slammed down. She had even tried ringing Carla's friends. But nothing. She had not answered any of Maura's messages. Maura could imagine her mother, in her element, poisoning Carla against her. Oh, she had guessed her mother's game all right . . .

She took another pull on the cigarette and felt a wave of nausea sweep over her. The combination of fried food, cigarette smoke and acute hangover was suddenly too much for her stomach. With her hand pressed tightly to her mouth, she ran from the bedroom into the bathroom. Dropping her cigarette into the toilet pan she retched. She heaved until she thought her insides were going to come up. A cold sweat broke out all over her body. She leaned against the wall, trying to gather her wits about her. Turning on the shower, she slipped her nightie over her head and stood underneath the shower head. She shivered as ice cold water ran over her body, making her teeth chatter. Still she stood there, trying to bring some kind of life back into her limbs.

After a few minutes she felt the delicious sensation of warmth that only cold water can bring. She felt the tightening of her skin as the blood vessels beneath the surface tried desperately to pump warm blood around her aching body. Her nipples were rock hard and as she turned the water on to hot she savoured the exquisite sensation of the heat gradually invading her bones. She put her face up to let the water cleanse her from head to toe. Gradually she felt the life begin to come back to her. For the first time in days she actually felt something that was real and tangible.

Then the tears came. A torrent of salty rivulets that mixed with the heavy water from the shower and ran away, down her breasts, over her empty stomach, on to her feet and into the shower tray.

In her mind she saw the loathing on her mother's face. The handsome carefree face of Benny, the young boy who had always been in some kind of prank. She saw the face of Terry Petherick, as it had been the night of the club bombing. She had known then that he still cared for her, that if she had not been Maura Ryan they would have married. She would have been like Margie, juggling the bills, looking after the kids and just being loved. As Dennis loved Marge, even with her large mauve and silver stretch-marks and empty breasts. And she, Maura, would have loved it. Every second of it.

Instead she had more money than she knew what to do with. She ran a business that was more crooked than the Government of Cuba, and had a brother who was at this time almost totally dependent on her. As for the younger boys, they blamed *her* for Benny's death. Not Michael but her. They believed that if she had not wanted her dock properties so badly, and had given them to Dopolis, Benny would still be alive. And she had to be honest and admit to herself that they were right. She cried harder. Whoever said that money made you happy was a liar. A dirty rotten stinking liar! She would give every penny she had at this moment to be just plain ordinary Mrs Terry Petherick. He was the only man she would ever want, even if she lived to be a hundred. If only she had kept that little baby! If she had nothing else now she would have had that. She would never have taken over the ice cream and hot dogs. She would never have become the person she was now. The person who had watched her brother murder an old man, Sammy Goldbaum, who had been waiting patiently for them to arrive. He had walked so meekly to the car. And now she had his blood on her hands and could never escape from any of it.

She had always thought that if she ever came face to face with Terry Petherick she would spit in his eye. Instead she had felt an urge to tell him all that happened to her. About the baby and her life with Michael . . . everything. She had wanted to be like it had been once before. When she was young and free. She was still young, but too much had happened over the years ever to allow her to be the girl that she once had been.

She turned off the tap and stood in the confined space of the shower cubicle. The sudden silence was startling and broke her out of her reverie. Her tears were gone now and all they had left in their wake was a heavy tiredness. Stepping from the shower, she wrapped a large towel around her body. As she dried her hair she thought about what she was going to do next. Then she made a decision. All that she could do now was go forward into the future. No matter how exciting the past may have been you could never recapture it. What Margaret had said earlier was right. Self-pity was a destructive force. She would have to make herself stronger. Much stronger. What she really needed was to get laid!

She smiled to herself. That was what Marge had been telling her for years! She shrugged aggressively, as if throwing off all her

224

previous worries and cares. She wiped the steam from the mirror on the wall opposite the shower and stared at her face. Her hair hung in limp, damp strands around her face which was puffy from crying. She smiled to herself. She was going to pick herself up and slowly mend all the broken pieces. She and Michael could take on the world. She had absolutely no one else now. She had lost them all, one by one. But she knew that she would always have Michael and Margie. Good old Margie.

She remembered that it was Christmas Day. Back at her own house she had the mother-of-pearl jewellery box that she had bought for Carla . . . She forced the thought from her mind. Let the ungrateful little bitch stay with her mother! Maura did not need her. She did not need anyone.

She ran her hands through her hair, feeling the silky softness of it. Letting the towel fall from her body, she ran her hands down her neck and over her breasts, travelling down her tight stomach to her pubic hair, enjoying the sensation. Picking up her nightie from the floor she put it back on, then went back into the bedroom where her overnight bag was. She felt a lot better. Much better, in fact. As she plugged in her hair dryer she was actually humming a little tune. Margie was right. Self-pity was a bummer. All that she could do now was go forward.

When she finally went downstairs she had her make-up on and her hair done to perfection. She was wearing a dress that would have cost Marge two months' housekeeping and was gratified to hear the long low whistle that came from Dennis.

'If I wasn't so happy with my old Margie I'd be after you myself, Maws!'

Marge laughed. 'Listen here, Dennis Dawson. You couldn't pull a ligament these days, let alone a beauty like Maura. Especially not since you lost your hair.' She smiled at Maura. 'All he's got these days is six hairs and a nit!'

Maura laughed with her. Dennis had lost his hair early, and Maura knew that it was a sore point with him.

'Come out here and have a cuppa. You look much better.'

Maura followed her out into her little kitchen. 'I feel a lot better, Marge. Thanks for letting me come.'

Margaret plugged in the electric kettle. 'What you on about, you silly cow? This is your home for as long as you want to be here.' She opened her arms wide and Maura walked into them. Margaret's tiny plump body held on to Maura's tall thin frame. Maura got upset again at the show of emotion.

'If you knew what I'd done, Marge!'

'Shh.' Margaret stepped back from Maura and raised her finger to her lips. 'Look, Maws, I know that you and Michael ain't strictly kosher. I've always known and I don't care. You're me mate and that's all I'm interested in.'

Maura looked at her and frowned. 'Sometimes, Marge, I don't think that I'm all the ticket. I get so moody and I think really weird things.'

'Maws love, you've been through an awful lot, you know. Just let yourself heal naturally. Benny's death would make anyone feel rotten. It was horrific. You need time to get over it, that's all.'

'Maybe you're right, Marge.'

She wanted to tell Margaret what Mickey had done to Sammy Goldbaum and Jonny Fenwick. She wanted to tell her that she had helped him. She was experiencing that feeling again – as if she was on the outside of her body looking in. She had always known that Michael enjoyed inflicting pain on people. And until the night with Jonny Fenwick and Sammy Goldbaum it had not bothered her.

'Maura!' Margaret's voice broke into her thoughts. 'Mickey's on the phone for you.'

Maura stared around the kitchen blankly. Margaret looked at her curiously. 'You all right, girl?'

Maura nodded and walked out of the kitchen into the lounge. The twins were watching *Mary Poppins* on television and baby Dennis was now sitting on his dad's lap. Maura's mind registered the fact that the Christmas tree was falling to one side where the kids had been playing underneath it. She walked out into the hallway and picked up the receiver lying on the telephone table.

'Oh, darling. You'll never guess what?'

His voice was bubbling over with excitement.

'What?' Maura's voice was flat.

'I just had a visit from Sammy Goldbaum's daughter. You know her . . . the one with the big hooter?'

'Rebekka.'

'Yeah, that's it. Rebekka. Anyway, she said she had come to see me on Christmas Day to show that she bore me no ill will. Not that I give a toss anyway. Those front wheels are like the eye ties, full of crap. Anyway, the bottom line is she brought me some documents that belonged to Sammy. I've just been through them, and have a guess what I found along with a load of old betting slips?'

'What?'

'The name of the property developer we've been looking for. The mastermind behind Dopolis.'

'But Sammy said he had no idea who he was . . .'

'I don't think Sammy realised just what he had. You see, I found

226

an old cutting from a newspaper. The *Daily Mirror* in fact. It was from the racing section and it had a picture of Dopolis. And get this bit, Maws. He's in the Royal Enclosure at Ascot! Now what, I asked myself, was he doing in there? Then I realised that he was standing with none other than William Templeton! That's when it hit me. He's the Mr Big that Dopolis was talking about.'

Maura was stunned. 'But he's a peer of the Realm!'

Mickey laughed. 'I know. Saucy bastard! I bet he's even in You Know Who . . . or whatever that book's called.'

Maura laughed despite herself. 'It's *Who's Who*, you wally. Christ Almighty, Mickey, if you're right . . .'

'I know I'm right. I've got a gut feeling about it. Look, can you get over to me now?'

'I can't, Mickey. I promised Marge and Den I'd have Christmas dinner with them.'

'All right then, Princess. But get your arse over here as soon as you can. All right?'

'All right then, Mickey. Merry Christmas.' Her voice was sad.

Michael's voice lost its excitement. 'I know it's been a bad time, the last few weeks, but I promise you, Maws – I'll make it up to you somehow. Merry Christmas, my darling.'

Maura put the phone down gently. The implications of what Mickey had just said were phenomenal. She went back into the lounge and started to play with the children. She held them to the floor and tickled them till they screamed with laughter. Marge and Dennis watched her with amused expressions on their faces. This was more like it. This was the old Maura.

It wasn't until she was sitting at the dining table eating her enormous Christmas dinner that the excitement hit her. Lord William Templeton . . . Suddenly she could not wait to get started on him. Together Michael and she would eat him alive.

She picked up a bright blue cracker and pointed it at Patricia. 'Come on, Patty. Let's see who wins the paper hat!'

Lord Templeton was also sitting at his dinner table in his large rambling house in Kent. The house dated back to the fifteenth century and over the large inglenook fireplace was a painting of one of his ancestors. It had been executed by Holbein, one of Henry VIII's favourite painters. There was an old story in his family that it was this ancestor who had actually ordered the death of Sir Thomas More. William liked to think that the story was true.

At forty-five, he was a somewhat jaded man. Over the years he had used his vast wealth to engage in many pastimes, both sexual and otherwise. He had hunted big game in South Africa and had smoked hashish in Turkey. He had travelled to the Himalayas and had seen the Manta Rays leap from the sea in the Maldives. He had experimented with drugs, and did not think there was any country in the world that he had not visited. He had married once, when he was very young, a large voluptuous woman, years older than himself. She had left him after one year, taking with her a large amount of money and his good wishes. She had taught him much: that there was no pleasure without pain; that a man, especially a rich man, needs to use his wealth wisely. He had never, as far as he knew, fathered a child. Unlike most men. William Templeton did not have the urge to reproduce. He rather like his solitary life. If he wanted a woman they were easy enough to find.

He picked at his expertly cooked Christmas dinner. At this moment he was a very worried man. He was regretting getting involved with the Greek, Dopolis. For a start it had not achieved his objective – the warehouses that the Ryans owned in the old docklands. Dopolis had turned out to be a penny ante type villain. Not at all the hard man he had said he was. The Ryans had completely obliterated him. If only he had had the sense to keep his eye on the proceedings, then the young boy, Benjamin, would never have died. He shuddered. He had been impressed with Dopolis at first. Had admired his plan of action. How was he to know it was all going to backfire?

He pushed his plate away from him. He had no appetite. Dopolis should never have ordered the boy's killing, and such a horrible death . . . Now he would have to be very careful. The only avenue left to him was to get someone harder than Michael Ryan and from what he could gauge that would be a very tall order indeed.

His manservant, a rather pinched-faced man called Rankin, cleared the table in front of him. Templeton sat back in his large comfortable chair. His dining table could easily seat twenty-four people. Normally he would have accepted an invitation from a friend for the Christmas festivities, but this year, after all the trouble with Dopolis, he had a hankering for his own company and his own hearth. He conceded that he had made a fatal mistake with the Greek. He toyed with the idea of going to see Michael Ryan and offering him a good price for the warehouses, but pushed the idea away as quickly as it occurred to him.

Some of his best friends had done a stint in Ford Open Prison; in the circles he moved in it was inevitable that you would eventually meet someone who had either embezzled money from the bank that they had worked for or been involved with some kind of fraud. But that was a fact of life. This Ryan, though, was a rough type and his sister wasn't much better apparently. He lit up a Cuban cigar and poured himself a large Remy Martin into the glass that Rankin had left conveniently by his elbow. No, he had made a tragic mistake. What he had to do now was try to recoup his losses. But he was sure of one thing. He *would* get those warehouses. He would get all the Ryans' properties along the Thames.

He smiled to himself. As usual he was absolutely amazed by his own intelligence. He thought of himself as the epitome of the upper class male. God in heaven, he was a cousin to the Queen! Only by marriage, he admitted, but it was a close enough connection to get Nigel Dempster practically wetting himself with excitement every time he appeared in public. He relaxed. There was nothing whatsoever to tie him in with Dopolis.

He sat in his chair, smoking his cigar and drinking his brandy, planning his next move. When the building finally started in the old docklands, every foot would be worth a small fortune. He sat all evening scheming how he would get the Ryans' properties.

Luckily for him he was not aware that Maura and Michael Ryan were also planning and scheming along the same lines – how they were going to get *his* properties, and his co-operation.

Maura and Michael were now certain that William Templeton was their man. An old friend of Michael's who worked on one of the gutter papers had run his name through the newspaper's computer and supplied them with every piece of gossip ever written about him, as well as some facts that had never been published. And their friends in the IRA had been very helpful. Their final recourse had been to some paid 'informers' in the Foreign Office who had supplied information that had shocked even Michael. It seemed that Templeton was a major shareholder in an arms factory that had been supplying anyone with the readies for years. Templeton was certainly no angel, that much was apparent. And that he was protected by the old boy network was more than obvious. Though as Maura had pointed out, there had to be more people involved with him, and with all his businesses. His main buyers were North African countries; Iran, Iraq, Libya – the list was endless. He also supplied Romania and the Czechs. All in all, Templeton seemed like their kind of guy!

Michael was jubilant! The only cloud on their horizon was Dopolis. Although they now had just about everything they wanted to know about him, plans for his demise were put on hold for the time being. He was the bait with which they were going to lure William Templeton. As Michael had playfully remarked to Maura, 'Let him get over his injuries first. He can pay for Benny when he's better!'

Sarah Ryan had still not acknowledged either of them. This had cut Michael deeply. His mother had been his life. But the estrangement from her had brought brother and sister closer together. They spent every available minute in each other's company. Maura now needed Michael more than ever. When she was with him he could convince her that Sammy Goldbaum's and Jonny Fenwick's deaths were just the paying of a debt. While she was with him she could accept that. Away from him, she was frightened and lonely. Every day that passed was making her more bitter and confused. They had spent the days since Christmas following up their leads on Templeton, and decided they would pay him a visit on New Year's Day. Until then they would bide their time.

On the 29 December 1975 Roy's son was born. He rang the news through to Michael at seven in the evening. Maura and Michael arrived at St Mary's Hospital at eight-thirty. After looking at the new baby fleetingly, Michael and the rest of the boys took Roy out to celebrate, all feeling the loss of Benny more than ever.

Maura was left with Janine. She noticed that her mother was nowhere to be seen.

She held the baby, Benny Anthony, in her arms. 'He's beautiful, Janine. I hope you realise just how lucky you are?'

Janine smiled wearily. 'I'm a bit sore, Maws, but he was worth it.'

Maura nodded. She was staring at the baby so intently that Janine felt a prickle of fear.

'I nearly had a baby once, Janine. A long time ago.' Maura's voice was sad. For the first time ever Janine pitied her.

'I know, Maura. Roy told me.'

She held the baby tighter to her chest.

'It was a lovely gesture, naming the baby after Benny and Anthony. It brings them back somehow.' She kissed the baby's downy head. 'I think that if they'd at least let us bury Benny, half the battle would be over. I can't stand to think of him on ice.'

'Please, Maura. Don't talk about it.' Janine was nearly in tears.

Maura's sing-song voice as she spoke about her brother made Janine feel frightened. She had always been a little in awe of Maura. Now she was terrified.

Maura smiled radiantly at her.

'I'm sorry, Jan. I'm getting a bit morbid!' She kissed the baby's head again and squeezed him to her breast. It took all Janine's willpower not to snatch her baby away. Janine was sensitive and felt things very deeply. She did not want this woman anywhere near her child.

Roy had said recently that he did not think that Maura was right in the head. Looking at her now, Janine was sure that she was

230

capable of anything. She had a terrible feeling that Maura would even kill a baby if it would get her what she wanted. Janine shivered.

'You cold?'

'No, Maura, just tired. It takes a lot out of you, having a baby.'

'Like shitting a football, is how Marge described it!'

Janine pursed her lips. She had never understood the Ryans' use of bad language. They swore in much the same way as her mother said 'God bless you'.

Janine took all her courage into her hands and decided to approach Maura with an idea that had been floating around inside her head for months.

'Maura?'

'What?' She was rocking the baby in her arms, completely engrossed in his little face. He was looking up at her with the dark blue Ryan eyes.

Janine picked at her bedsheet, watching her sister-in-law warily.

'It's about Roy.'

Maura laughed gently. 'He's like a dog with three lamp posts! I've never seen him like this. All the boys are ribbing him terrible. You'd think this was the first baby ever born!'

'I know . . . I know.' Janine was finding it difficult to find the appropriate words.

Maura sensed that there was something going on and looked Janine in the face.

'What's on your mind? Come on, spit it out. I'm not really an ogre, whatever my Mum might say.' Her voice was bitter.

'I was wondering if you would help Roy set up a little business . . .'

Her voice trailed off as she saw the look of shock on Maura's face.

'You what! Roy work outside the family? You must be joking.'

Janine started to cry. 'Oh, Maura, I'm so frightened.' She put her face into her hands. 'I feel like a policeman's wife, wondering if he's going to come home. Then after what happened to Benny . . .'

Maura pulled her hands away from her face. 'You're just overwrought, that's all. Having a baby makes you go funny.'

'NO! It's not that!' Janine lost all caution. 'I don't want to be left a widow, bringing up the baby on my own. I want us to be a normal family. A real family. Roy's not meant to be a thug.'

Maura put the baby into the cot by the bed. Her face was set. She loomed over Janine and began to speak to her in a low and menacing voice.

'Shall I tell you something, Janine? In case it has escaped your notice. Roy, as much as I love him, is as thick as two short planks. He can barely count over fifty. He still reads *Marvel* comics, for Christ's sake! The best he could ever have expected out of life was a job on the council or with the Water Board. Either way, you'd not be spending the kind of hefty wedge you're used to now. Your father tried to turn him into a butcher and look where that got him. If Roy knew what you'd said here tonight he'd give you a well-deserved slap. Now about the other load of shit you was spouting . . .'

She pushed Janine back against the pillows hard and poked her in the chest. 'You want to be a real family, do you? You dumped your daughter on my mother if you remember rightly, love. If push ever comes to shove, you can dump your new arrival on her and all, can't you? Don't you ever try and bullshit me again. DO YOU HEAR ME?'

Maura's loud voice made the baby whimper in his cot. 'I'm going to forget what you've said in here tonight, Janine, because I know that having a baby can make you a bit distraught. I'm warning you, though, if I ever get wind that you've said this to anyone else, I'll come and sort you out myself. Get it?'

Janine nodded, her lips trembling. She realised that she had just made an enemy for life.

Maura watched her closely. Then she smiled a soft little smile that did not reach her eyes. Picking up her bag from the floor, she opened it, took out a blue velvet box and handed it to Janine.

'Well, open it then.' She snapped.

Janine was shaking so badly that Maura had to place her own hands on top of hers to help her open the box. Inside was a gold and platinum identity bracelet.

'I'll have his name put on it for you.'

Janine swallowed heavily. She did not want it. 'Tha . . . thanks. It's lovely. Beautiful.' A stray tear slid down her face. Maura wiped it away gently with her fingers.

'Cheer up, love. You just had a lovely little boy. You should be laughing, not crying.'

Janine forced a smile she did not think she had in her. 'As you say . . . it's my hormones or something.'

Maura laughed. 'That's the ticket. Now, I'm off to the Crown and Two Chairmen. If that lot are left on their own with Roy, he'll end up legless.' She put her bag under her arm and kissed Janine on the cheek.

'I heard a little saying the other day, Janine. It might give you something to think about. It was on a wall in some public toilets and Mickey read it. It said: "Life is like a shit sandwich. The more bread you've got, the less shit you have to eat." I'd think about that if I was you.'

With one last glance at the baby, Maura left the room. Janine was convinced that she was fuming inside and she was right. She sat in the bed staring at the identity bracelet. The tears came in a red hot rush. She felt like a trapped animal.

Her mother-in-law had been right. They would never let Roy go.

A while later a nurse came in and gave her a little talking to. And Janine sat in the bed silently as she was told all about 'the baby blues'. She was still crying when the nurse finally gave up and left her.

Maura drove to the Crown and Two Chairmen feeling better than she had for weeks. It had taken Janine's smugness and petty strivings for respectability to bring her out of her depression.

She was honest with herself, though. Holding the new baby had brought back all her maternal feelings and she had resented the fact that the baby was Janine's. Had she but known, Janine could not have picked a worse time to ask Maura for a favour.

Chapter Twenty

Maura walked into the Crown and Two Chairmen pub in Dean Street. As usual it was packed. She pushed her way through the throng of people and finally located the boys in the corner. Roy was already very drunk. The air was thick with cigarette smoke and camaraderie. Leslie saw Maura first and raised himself from his seat unsteadily. He was as drink as a lord. Maura smiled at him.

'Hello, Mawsh.' His voice was slurred.

'Sit down, Les, before you fall down.' She looked around the table. Her six remaining brothers were all sitting, looking like clones of one another, all in different states of inebriation. Only Michael was even remotely sober. He stood up and offered her his seat.

'Sit down, Maws, and I'll get you a drink. What'll it be? Scotch?'

Maura sat down and nodded at him. He went to the bar.

'Well, you lot seem to be enjoying yourselves.' She made her voice sound jovial. Five pairs of eyes stared at her blankly. Maura felt for the first time the impact of their combined wariness and it hurt her. Only Geoffrey looked different and she realised that he looked smug. Smug and very, very sure of himself. Maura mentally chalked one up to him.

'Well, Roy, you got a son at last.'

He nodded at her, a silly grin on his drunken face. Maura began to search in her bag for her cigarettes. It was obvious that she was not welcome. In her present state of mind she was not sure if it was over Benny or because it was a boys' night out. Michael came back with a tray of drinks and she took the double Scotch he gave her and drank it straight down.

'That bad, Maws?' Michael's voice was soft.

'No. Actually it's worse. If you boys will excuse me, I have got some work to do in the club. OK?'

She picked up her bag and left as quickly as possible. Outside in the freezing night she breathed a deep sigh. It was still snowy, though most of it had turned to slush and black ice. She walked carefully up Dean Street to Le Buxom. The main damage to the club had been in the foyer. The little reception desk where Sheree

235

Davidson had been sitting on the night of the bombing had taken most of the blast from the petrol bomb. The damage to the club had turned out to be minimal. Mainly cosmetic. But as Maura walked inside she was acutely aware of the fact that Sheree would never again walk in there with her tall stories and deep braying laugh. She had been popular with both punters and the other hostesses. She had left two children, who were now in the care of the courts. Their father, or fathers, no one was sure, were nowhere to be found. If indeed Sheree ever knew who they were.

As for Gerry Jackson, he had been taken to a Burns Unit in Billericay. His wife had already been made an interim payment of two thousand pounds to get her over Christmas and the New Year. She would receive a substantial weekly amount until it was decided by the doctors what would happen to Gerry. If he never worked again he would be more than amply provided for.

The club was once more up and running. It had been reopened less than a week after the 'trouble'. As Maura walked into the familiar blast of warm air she could hear 'My Eyes Adored You'. Her mind registered that Louise Barton was doing her act. Maura looked at her watch. It was nearly eleven and she was surprised that it was so late. She slipped off her fur coat and locked it in the little cloakroom just inside the entrance to the club.

Picking her bag up off the floor she went over to the meat seats and started her night's work. A new girl called Monique, for once a real Frenchwoman and not a phony, had started a few weeks previously. She was a very very beautiful girl, very intelligent, and not at all the usual class of tom. There was just one thing that had puzzled Maura: she would take literally any punter. And another of the girls had told Maura that she would 'go case' for as little as fifty pounds. The minimum that her girls usually worked for was one hundred pounds plus their hostess fee. That told Maura one thing: Monique either had a violent pimp who insisted on a night 'quota', or she had a drugs problem.

Maura guessed it was the latter, and if it was, then it would not be long before they were busted. The busts were well staged. They were told at least a week in advance when one was going to occur so they could put off any well-known citizens, such as judges or more rarely politicians. The police had no qualms about arresting any of the girls that were taking, or happened to possess, drugs. It gave the so-called raid credibility. But Maura did not work like that. She would not, like some club owners, employ 'stooges' to give their busts a veneer of realism.

Monique was sitting with two black girls. They were chatting together amicably, which was unusual in itself. There was a fierce rivalry between the black and white toms, but Monique seemed to be liked by everyone. Maura went to where they were sitting, and smiled.

'Hello.' She nodded at the three girls. 'I wonder, Monique, could I see you upstairs for a few minutes?' Maura's voice was friendly. The other girls would assume that Maura had a 'home-bird', a regular punter who had arranged to pay for the girl over the phone. That entailed stumping up for two bottles of champagne, fifty cigarettes, and a small administration fee. The girl would then be cabbed to the man's address.

Monique stood up and Maura noticed that she was very bright-eyed. Her pupils were dilated. She followed Maura upstairs to the office. Maura turned on the lights and, walking to the window, shut the venetian blinds. She turned back to face Monique and, smiling still, offered her a chair. The girl sat down. Instead of walking around the desk and sitting in her own chair, Maura stood in front of Monique, leaning on the edge of the desk.

'Monique, hold out your arms, please.'

'But why?'

Maura cleared her throat. She hated this. 'Would you please hold out your arms? You know why.'

Monique had long black hair and dark hazel eyes. In the bright light of the office Maura was surprised at how hard-faced she really was. In the muted light of the club she looked much younger. Maura had thought she was in her twenties. Looking at her now, though, she put her much nearer forty.

'Please, Monique. Don't make this any harder than it already is.'

Monique held out her arms. Maura checked them for track marks. There was nothing.

Monique looked at her triumphantly. 'You see, Miss Ryan. Nothing.'

Maura smiled apologetically. 'Take your stockings off, please.'

Monique's faced dropped. 'I beg your . . . how you say?'

Maura finished her sentence for her. 'Pardon. I beg your pardon. Now, if you don't mind, take your stockings off. I want a quick shufti at your calves and your shins, OK?'

Monique's eyes glittered with malevolence. She reminded Maura of a cornered rat.

'Take your stockings off, Monique. Either you do as I ask or I'll call one of the bouncers up here to have them forcibly removed. It's your choice.' She saw Monique's eyes go to the beaded bag on her lap. 'And don't even think about trying to shiv me, darling. It would only end in tears. And they wouldn't be mine.'

Maura's voice was as hard as concrete now. Monique surveyed her, weighing up the pros and cons. After a few seconds she dragged her tight black velour dress over her thighs. Slowly she

237

began to undo the suspender belt. Monique rolled the stocking down to below her knee and held her leg out for inspection. Maura grinned. She was used to every ploy in the book. She took off the black patent leather shoe that Monique was wearing and pulled the stocking off completely. The bottom of her leg was a mass of needle marks. Even between her toes. Maura threw the stocking back at her and sighed.

'You're a bloody mug to yourself. You know that, don't you, Monique?'

The woman shrugged. She began to put her stocking back on.

Maura carried on talking. 'I know for a fact that you can speak German, Arabic, and even a smattering of Japanese. You're not a fool. Why do you take drugs?'

Monique slipped her shoe back on and took the cigarette that Maura offered her. Maura offered her a light. Monique puffed on the cigarette.

'You people make me laugh. Oh, don't look so . . . how you say? . . . shocked. I come here night after night and I sleep with strange men. Some of them are very nice men. Very kind. Some, they are rough and they want to hurt you.'

She saw Maura's face change and laughed. 'You are a very funny girl. You do not want me in your club because I take drugs. Well, let me tell you, I have been a prostitute since I was seventeen. Over twenty years. I have to have something to give me a bit of happiness and I find it in drugs. I have slept with thousands of different men and while I work for people like you, I make you very much money. How many of my men have refused to pay their bills, eh? None. I can sweet talk any man I want. So please don't lecture me!

'I will leave your club. It's shit anyway since the bomb was thrown in here. All the girls are nervous.' She stood up and put her cigarette out in the ashtray on the desk. 'I will say one thing before I go. Who is worse, eh? Me because I sell my body, or you for earning good money off that fact?'

'I give all the girls a good deal here. I offer them a degree of protection that they would not get anywhere else in London.' Maura's voice was defensive.

Monique laughed. 'True. True. But you are still a pimp in my eyes *and* theirs.' She gave her Gallic shrug. 'Goodbye.'

Monique walked from the room and Maura suddenly felt flat. It seemed that she was not 'Miss Popular' these days. Even her own brothers were wary of her. Except for Michael, of course.

She laid her arms on the top of the desk and rested her head on them. What she would really like to do now was walk out of this office, out of this club, and in to her car. Then she would like to drive and drive and drive until she arrived somewhere where no one knew her and she could be exactly what she really was – a twenty-five-year-old girl. Not woman . . . girl.

She was startled to hear the door opening. It was another of the hostesses, a very young girl by the name of Candy. Whether or not that was her real name was debatable. She was carrying a cup of coffee. Maura sat up in her chair and tried to smile at her.

'I thought you looked as if you could do with this, Miss Ryan.' She placed the coffee on Maura's desk. Maura could smell the aroma of whisky. As if reading her mind, Candy smiled.

'It's an Irish coffee. A very strong Irish coffee.'

Maura smiled, her first real smile for days. 'Thanks, Candy.'

Candy sat in the chair vacated by Monique. She was a natural blonde, her hair lighter than Maura's which was unusual as Maura's was nearly white. Candy's was a silver blond and she had the most amazing brown eyes. It was a startling combination. A few weeks earlier, all the hostesses had put in five pounds each and Candy had shown every one of them her pubic hair. It was exactly the same colour as the hair on her head. She had stopped all the arguments about herself, and made herself nearly a hundred pounds richer.

The girl hitched up her strapless dress. The movement seemed to accentuate her childishness.

'You look right done in, Miss Ryan.'

'I feel it actually, Candy.'

The girl sniffed loudly. 'I wanted to see you about something personal.'

Maura sipped the steaming and fragrant coffee and lifted her eyebrows in an invitation for the girl to continue.

'A bloke was hanging around outside the club earlier.'

'What was he – a pimp?' Maura sounded bored. This was the last thing she wanted even to think about. Let alone *do* something about.

Candy shook her head. 'Oh, no. He was nothing like that. He was a policeman.'

'A what!'

'An old Bill. You know, lily law.' Candy laughed.

'What was he asking about? The night of the bombing? What?' Her voice was anxious.

Candy relaxed into her seat. 'No, nothing like that, Miss Ryan. He was asking about you.'

Maura's mouth dropped open. 'Me?'

'Yes, you. He gave me this to give to you.' Candy took a slip of paper from between her boobs. 'He asked me if you would be in tonight. I said I didn't know and then he offered me twenty quid

239

to deliver that to you. So I did. I hope I haven't done anything wrong?'

Maura's eyes were devouring the words on the piece of paper. 'No . . . No, Candy. You were right to take the message.'

She got up from her desk and, picking up her bag, slipped the note inside. Then she took out her purse and gave Candy three twenty-pound notes.

'Oh no, Miss Ryan, I couldn't. The bloke gave me a score.'

Maura pushed the notes into the girl's hands. 'You take it, Candy. You did very well tonight.'

Candy took the proffered money and smiled craftily. 'Well, if you're sure . . .'

Maura laughed out loud. She could feel the adrenaline pulsing through her body.

Candy stood up too and Maura did something that would make her a friend for life. She hugged the girl.

'Candy, can I trust you never to tell anyone about this?'

She put her hand gently on Maura's arm. 'Look, Miss Ryan, I don't know what was in that note. I didn't read it. And I'm not a grass. You've been good to me and if I can repay you somehow, I will.'

'Thanks, Candy. I appreciate it.'

Candy smiled and went back downstairs. She liked Maura Ryan. Whatever anyone said about her, she looked after the girls. And Candy, being honest in her own way, admitted that she would not get very far without her. It would be back to a pimp and either Park Lane or, when her looks went, King's Cross. At least at Le Buxom she had the chance to get herself a little stake. And for that she would be eternally grateful.

When Candy left the room Maura snatched the note from her bag. It was from Terry Petherick! She could not believe it! She read it again.

'IF EVER YOU NEED ME, CALL THIS NUMBER. LOVE, TERRY.'

Underneath was his phone number. Maura was ecstatic. He *did* still want her. Otherwise why would he bother to send her a note? She hugged the scrap of paper to her. Terry had put himself on the line to get this message to her. It crossed her mind that it was some kind of frame up but she had felt the attraction between them. And if nothing could ever come of it, at least she would always have the satisfaction of knowing that he had still wanted her, whatever she had done, because he must know everything that had transpired over the last few weeks. She sat back in her seat and drank the now stone cold coffee. The whisky bit into her taste buds and suddenly she realised that she was starving. She'd pack up here for the night and go home.

Home to her own house. Not Michael's flat.

She felt as if she was on a high. Monique, the reaction of her brothers to her in the Crown and Two Chairmen pub, Benny, Sammy, Jonny, Janine – all was wiped from her mind for a few precious moments as she thought about Terry. She wrote a note to Michael saying she would see him in the morning and, humming to herself, got her stuff ready to go home.

She sat on the edge of her desk and stared at the telephone. She glanced at her watch. It was twelve-fifteen. Was it too late to ring? She opened up the slip of paper and stared at the words. 'Love, Terry' seemed to leap off the paper. Love . . . She picked up the phone and dialled the number. Her mouth was dry and she felt lightheaded. Supposing he was asleep or had company? Her heart dropped a little at that thought. Then, before she knew it, she could hear his voice.

'Hello? Who is this? Is that you, Maura?'

His voice was soft and as he said her name she could hear the yearning that she was experiencing herself.

She swallowed heavily.

'Terry.'

She heard the relief in his voice. 'It *is* you.'

The line went quiet as each tried to think what to say.

'I want to see you, Maura.' Terry sounded unsure of himself. 'I mean, if you want to see me, of course.'

'I was just going home. To my house. I just got the message.'

'Can I come to your house, Maura?' His voice was pleading.

'I'll give you the address.' She could barely talk.

'I know the address. I'll meet you there soon!' His voice had a jubilant ring to it that made her heart lurch in her chest.

She laughed. The ice had broken into a thousand pieces.

'Of course. You're a policeman – you would know my address.'

'Naturally.' She could practically see his little lopsided grin, could hear it in his voice.

'See you soon then.' She replaced the receiver and shivered with delight. She was hungry again. Only this time it wasn't for food.

Terry Petherick was staring at the telephone in his hand. She had rung! He wasn't wrong. She still wanted him as much as he still wanted her! He picked up his car keys and jacket and literally ran from his flat. He leapt into his car, a Ford Escort, and began the journey to Rainham. To Maura's house.

He had found himself driving to Dean Street earlier that evening, hoping for a glimpse of Maura. That was all. He had experienced an all-consuming passion for weeks just to look at her. Ever since he had seen her the night of the bombing, it had been like stepping back through a doorway, into another world. There had been women over the years but never any who affected him like Maura Ryan.

Every warning bell in his body was clanging and jangling at this moment, but he did not care. All he was really sure of was the fact that he had to see her. Touch her. Feel her. Even knowing what she had done – that she had been an accessory to murder. The attraction that had been between them from the start was still there like a shining beacon. He put his foot on the accelerator and whizzed through the icy streets towards her and all that she promised. For once in his life he was acting on impulse, and he was loving every moment of it. He felt alive. Really alive. And it felt good.

Maura pulled into her drive and sat in the car for a few minutes. She could feel her own nervousness and savoured every second of it. She looked at the large house sitting in ghostly darkness and for the very first time was glad to be home . . . and glad that Carla was not there. She had never been with a man since Terry, had gradually suppressed all her feelings, both sexual and romantic, concentrating on her work and Carla. And now her senses were filling her up, overflowing from her body, like the bursting of a great dam.

She got out of her car and went into her house. Her daily woman, Mrs MacMullen, had been in and as usual had left the central heating on low. The house was warm and inviting. Maura ran up the stairs like a young schoolgirl getting ready for her first date. She threw off her clothes and stepped into the shower, scrubbing her body until it glowed pink.

When she finally heard Terry's car she was in her lounge in a white silk dressing gown, sipping a glass of red wine. As she heard his footsteps crunch on the gravelled driveway she felt an intense euphoria flood her body. He had come. He had really come for her. She went into her hall and opened the front door.

She noticed that he was breathing as heavily as she. And then, without a word spoken, she was being kissed. And it was all so natural, as it should have been. How it once had been. He was kissing her face, her eyes, her neck. Taking his hand, she led him slowly up the stairs and into her bedroom.

They faced one another in the soft light from bedside lamps. She stared deeply into his eyes and saw mirrored in them her own feelings of love and desire. She began to unbutton his shirt and as she pulled it from him saw the broad shoulders, the tightly muscled arms, and felt new again, as she had the first time they had made love. He opened his trousers and showed her he was hard.

242

She traced the outline of his erection with her fingers, softly and tantalisingly. She was feeling the woman heat between her legs and the tightening of her nipples. He was naked and she watched him, fascinated, as he stood before her, proud and strong. He opened the cord of her dressing gown and she stood, quivering with excitement and longing.

She saw his eyes roaming over her body and wanted him then, more than she had ever wanted anyone or anything in her life. He pushed her backwards gently on to the bed and kissed her body, little biting kisses that were hurtful and so erotic. He tasted the muskiness of her and felt the heady delight that he had thought was gone forever. He pushed her legs up to her shoulders until she was full open to him – like a ripe pink peach. She watched him enter her with one deep thrust, and she groaned like an animal. Together they moved in perfect unison.

She matched his strokes with hard thrusts of her hips against him. She could feel the mounting excitement as she reached her orgasm and heard herself moaning and panting, begging him to thrust deeper. She could feel the droplets of sweat from his body dripping on to hers and gripped him with her legs, drawing him inside her, deeper and deeper, until she thought that she would die of pleasure. Their slippery bodies thrashed wildly as they reached orgasm. She could feel his hand squeezing her breast so hard that she cried out.

Then they lay, spent and replete, their hearts thudding against each other's chests. They lay tangled together for long quiet minutes, savouring the familiar feel of one another after so long an absence. Finally Terry leant on his elbow and kissed her gently on her swollen lips, and she looked at his face – the face that had alternately haunted and drawn her for nearly nine years – and smiled.

'It's been so long.' Her voice was so low as to be virtually inaudible.

'Too long, Maura. Much too long.'

They lay together until their bodies became still and the passion that had encompassed them had drained away. He kissed her again, staring down at her as if he wanted to devour her. His eyes drank in every feature and his brain filed them away, never to be forgotten. And she did the same, lying there. They were both aware that it was only a temporary love affair. That in the cold light of day they would have to part, each going back to their different world which neither would ever be able to leave. But this was never said. What they had at this moment was enough for them. And if they had to part, they would at least have had this night.

Terry gathered her to him and locked her into his embrace. 'I never meant to hurt you, you know. I swear.'

Maura spoke softly. 'I know, Terry.' She should tell him about the baby now. It was the perfect opening. But she could not. She would never, ever tell him about it. A lone tear slipped from her eye as she looked at him and he licked it away with his tongue. She would not tell him about their child as he would not talk about what Michael had had done to him. It was like a silent agreement, an unspoken treaty. So they lay together, speaking the love words that came so naturally to their lips. And then they loved again. Not the wild thrashings of before but a long, slow, leisurely loving that left them both breathless and satiated. Then all too soon it was the morning and they could delay their parting no longer.

'Come on. I'll make you some breakfast.' She pulled on her dressing gown and went to the kitchen. The birds were singing in the early morning light and Maura wished that the day would never come. That they could keep the night forever. She heard him whistling as he showered and felt an urge to cry out. Against God. Against fate. And against injustice.

She took a loaf of bread from her freezer and made toast. She had just finished scrambling the eggs when he came into the kitchen, his hair still wet from the shower. She gave him a cup of coffee and placed his breakfast in front of him.

'You never cooked me breakfast before.'

'I was never allowed to stay out all night in those days.' She made her voice light.

He smiled. 'What are we going to do, Maura?' The words were like a physical blow. They both knew that there was nothing they could do.

She sat at the table opposite him.

'What happened last night was beautiful, Terry, but we must accept it for what it was – a beautiful interlude from our lives. Our real lives. Tomorrow is a new year . . . 1976 . . . and you will go back to your policing while I will go back to being Maura Ryan.' She smiled sadly. 'Please don't let's spoil it with might have beens and halfhearted promises. We live in different worlds, you and I. Worlds that can never be united.' Her voice broke.

Terry knew that she was right, and he loved her all the more for her honesty. Too much had happened over the years. And she was more of a woman in his eyes for what had just said than any so-called Earth Mother would ever be.

They ate breakfast together, both acutely aware of the sky gradually becoming lighter outside the kitchen window. They chatted about nothing, little inconsequential things that stopped them thinking or talking about the big things. The real things.

244

The real world. Finally Terry got up from his chair, and Maura knew that the parting had come.

'Can't we meet sometimes, Maura?'

She shook her head sadly. 'No, Terry. It's best we leave things as they are. There's no future for us.'

'Will you come to the door with me?' She could hear the tears in his voice. She shook her head.

'No. You go. I'll sit here. I don't want to see you driving away from me.'

'Oh, Maws.' He was kneeling in front of her, holding her so tight she could barely breathe. 'I can't go, Maura. I can't leave you like this.'

She kissed the top of his head. 'Go. Go on. Don't make this harder than it already is.' She cupped his face in her hands for the last time.

'I love you, Terry Petherick. God help me, I'll always love you.'

'I know. I love you too.'

She pushed him away from her. She had read so many times the phrase 'their hearts were breaking', and now she found out that it was true. Your heart could break and it was an intense physical pain that made you want to scream out, a deep roaring scream, from the depths of your body.

She sat at the table and it was as if her senses had been magnified a thousand million times. She heard his footfalls on the thick carpet. The sound of the front door closing behind him was like a deafening crash. And finally she heard his car start up. Then she listened to it driving away.

Away from her . . . and back to his real life.

It was over. The night was finished and real life had begun again. But she would carry the memory of it with her to her grave. She cried, a loud, noisy cry that was all the more wrenching because it sounded so lonely.

Terry drove home to his flat in Hampstead. He drove slowly, not in the reckless way he had driven the night before. Leaving Maura had been the hardest thing he had ever done in his life, but he knew that she was right. That she was stronger than him. Much stronger. And he guessed, correctly, that she was much lonelier. But whatever she was, he loved her.

Chapter Twenty-One

It was the third of January and Maura and Michael were driving to Lord Templeton's office. Maura still had the glow of lovemaking on her, despite the tears afterwards. In the last few days she had somehow resigned herself to being without Terry, to being without any man, though the thrill of the sexual encounter was still vivid in her mind and body. Michael was discussing what had happened between Maura and Janine.

'Calm down, Maws, for Christ's sake. After what happened to Benny, you can't blame her for getting a bit shirty. Janine's what's known as a shitter. And there's plenty of them about, believe me.'

'It's not that, Mickey. But the fact that Roy was a Ryan is what attracted her in the first place. She was after a bit of rough and then she came unstuck. Look at how she dumped Carla! Now Roy, who's turned out to be a bloody good provider, is in a bit of schtuck, she wants him to become a bloody bank clerk or something! It's laughable.'

'Then laugh! I know that our Roy would no more leave this firm than he would cut his own throat. Stick him back in the bookies, that should shut Madam up for a while.' He grinned. 'I wonder what she'll say when she finds our Roy wants us to be godparents? That should go down about as well as a pork chop in a synagogue!'

Maura laughed, a marsh bitter laugh.

'What a start to the New Year. Benny dead. Mother treating us as if we've contracted bubonic plague, the old man permanently pissed . . .'

'Stop talking crap, Maura.' Michael's voice was sharp as glass. 'What happened to Benny was an occupational hazard. It could have been any of us. You, me, any of us. That's the chance we take in our line of . . .'

He paused as if looking for a word. Maura finished the sentence for him.

'Business!'

He grinned. 'That's it, Maws! Business. All we can do now is go on from here. We can't bring Benny back no more than we could

Antney. Concentrate on Templeton. He's the goose that's gonna lay our golden eggs. Only he don't know that yet!' He laughed again.

'You were dead right about the docklands, I can see that now, Maws. He offered Dopolis the East End bait. What Lord Wily was after was the warehouses and the old Dockers' Mansions.

'I know this much, girl. He's gonna need muscle. Plenty of muscle. And we have that in abundance. That's our strength.'

She nodded absently.

'I'm telling you, Maura, 1976 is going to be *our* year.'

She looked out at the cold, dirty London streets and sighed. 'I hope so. God, I hope so.'

Lord Templeton stepped out of his limousine. His chauffeur held the door open for him and Templeton walked past him as if he was invisible, as he did every day. He walked with his confident stride up the flight of steps that led into the main reception area of his building in Park Lane. His liveried doorman saluted him and he acknowledged the man with a minute nod of his head. His personal secretary, David Manners, followed him, practically running to keep up. He had a detailed list of Templeton's appointments for the day.

Templeton strode purposefully into the large reception area and, just for a second, his step faltered. Standing beside his personal lift were Michael and Maura Ryan. Swallowing deeply, he glanced around him. The staff milling about were staring at him curiously. Pulling himself together, he plastered a broad smile on to his face and carried on walking to his lift.

He concentrated his attention on Maura. He was surprised at how lovely she was. She looked like a deb in her light beige Chanel suit with its black piping. Her hair, freshly washed, glistened in the artificial light. He took in everything about her from the kidskin boots to the silk scarf wrapped carelessly across her shoulders and held there with a gold and diamond tiger brooch. Against his will he was impressed. She was exquisite.

As for the man standing beside her, he was probably the most outstandingly handsome man Templeton was ever likely to see. Michael also was dressed in impeccable taste. Templeton felt that sickening feeling that precedes a fall from a high place. Never in all his life had he been intimidated. Now that he was experiencing it, he decided he did not like it one bit. He carried on walking towards them, and with every step that took him closer felt more scared, more nervous.

Maura smiled as he approached them and held out her hand. 'So pleased to meet you at last, Lord William. My brother and I have been so looking forward to it.' Her voice held no trace of its usual cockney accent.

Her words reassured Templeton slightly and he smiled back at her, showing perfect white teeth.

'Delighted, my dear. If I had known how lovely you were, I would have made sure we met much sooner.'

He turned his attention to Michael, amazed at just how big he was – almost a foot taller than himself. Michael shook his hand without speaking, his hard eyes telling Templeton exactly how the land lay.

His lift door opened and he ushered them both inside, waving David Manners away imperiously.

'I'll send for you, David, when I need you.'

Manners nodded. There was something funny going on here, he knew that much.

The old man who worked the lift gave Maura an appraising stare.

They made their brief journey in silence. Maura watched Templeton's face. She knew that he was frightened but had to admit to herself that for all that she liked the look of him. He was angular-looking: pointed nose, pointed cheekbones, and even pointed ears. He had a mass of sandy brown hair that, she guessed, was difficult to tame. It seemed to give him a slight air of vulnerability. He had very deep brown eyes, and thin sparse eyebrows like most sandy-haired people. It was his mouth that attracted her. It was not very big for a man, but it was strong. It could have been due to his very angular jawline. Whatever it was, she liked it. She only hoped they could all come out of this place today with a degree of accord.

The lift doors opened and they all stepped out into a wealth of mahogany. The walls were panelled, the only furniture a large mahogany desk and two leather-covered wing chairs. Behind the desk sat a young woman, the standard secretary to a rich man. She was very attractive in a subdued way. Maura could picture her unpinning her luxuriant black hair one day and turning into a femme fatale. She put her hand to her mouth to stop herself giggling. She had to try to control the weird things that kept invading her mind.

By the secretary's desk were two large double doors. Templeton opened these and led them into his office. Michael looked around him contemptuously. Like the room outside this also was a shrine to wood. Once more it had panelled walls, but in here they were adorned with a few well-chosen and, Michael guessed, very expensive sporting paintings. He was not aware that the largest, of a beautiful dark horse, was in fact a Stubbs. The floor was covered in the same deep grey carpet as the ante room. There was another, much larger mahogany desk. Along the right- and left-hand walls were two large Chesterfields, black and gleaming, as if just taken from their protective wrappings and never yet sat upon. In front of the desk were two more wing armchairs. Maura sat in one and Michael in the other.

Templeton went to the double doors and told his secretary to bring in some refreshments. He then walked nervously to his own chair behind the desk. As he reached it he stumbled and had to grab the desk to right himself. Eventually he sat down. His chair was much higher than the two opposite; an American designer had once told him that it would give him a psychological advantage. Obviously the designer had never met anyone like the Ryans. He put his hands together as if in prayer.

'What can I do for you?' He was embarrassed to find that his voice sounded cracked and high. It was Maura who answered him.

'I think you already know the answer to that, Lord William.' She made his name sound ridiculous. Her voice had hardened now they were alone and once again he was reminded of how danger-ous these people were. He was saved from answering by his secretary who came in wheeling a trolley, also mahogany. Michael was beginning to wonder if the man was a wood fetishist. The trolley held not only coffee and tea but also toast, muffins, jam and honey.

'Would you like me to serve, sir? The girl smiled, watching Michael from the corner of her eye.

'Just leave it, Marie.' Templeton's voice was brisk. The girl nodded and slowly left the room, shutting the double doors behind her.

Maura pulled off her kidskin gloves and placed them on the floor with her bag.

'Fancy a cuppa, Mickey?'

Michael nodded and Maura poured three cups of tea, as if they were at a tea party. She handed one to Michael who spoke for the first time, his voice as rough as concrete.

'Well, this is nice, I must say. My little brother Benny used to love a cup of Rosie in the mornings. Said it made him crap.' He looked directly at Templeton, causing the hairs on the back of his neck to rise.

'Crapped regular did our Benny. Seven o'clock every morning. Did he crap himself while he was being murdered? I understand you know all about it.' Michael's voice was matter-of-fact.

William Templeton felt sick. The cup of tea that Maura had handed him was rattling in its saucer. He was shaking from head to foot. Maura put down her own cup and, going to him, removed

250

the cup and saucer from his grasp.

'What do you want?'

Michael sipped his tea and said: 'What we want is a little bastard called Dopolis. I think that you know where we can find him. I want to question him personally about my brother's death.' He smiled at Templeton. 'The police are looking for Benny's murderer as well, you know. Why don't you give them a ring? Ask them about me, Michael Ryan. Ask them about my temper.' He was talking in a conversational way, and somehow it made his words more frightening. 'My temper's a legend in London, ain't it, Maws?' She nodded. 'I once rammed a Rolls-Royce because I thought the driver had given me a dirty look. Wrote off a brand new Merc doing it. But, you see, my temper is atrocious.' He leant towards Templeton. 'It's just like the wrath of God. Only in London, I *am* God.'

'I had nothing to do with your brother's death. I swear it!' Templeton was aware that he was babbling.

'Then you won't mind telling us where Dopolis is, will you?'

'I have no idea.'

Maura shook her head as if looking at a naughty child. 'I don't think you realise what you're dealing with here. We . . .' she gestured with her hand towards Michael '. . . are like terminal cancer. We'll get you in the end, so you might as well save yourself unnecessary grief. You've already made us very angry and that's dangerous. Now, I'll give you one last chance. Where can we find Dopolis?'

Templeton was rooted to his chair. His eyes darted around the room as if looking for some kind of divine intervention from behind the panelling. He had thought he was dealing with illiterate fools. But no. The so-called fools had tracked him down and cornered him on his own territory. All he could do now was extricate himself as best he could.

'He lives in Surrey.' He scribbled the address on to the pad in front of him and practically threw it across the table at Michael. Please God, he prayed, make them go away now. If you do this for me, I swear that I will be a good man from now on. Like many a man before him, he was praying as a last resort.

Michael picked up the scrap of paper and stood up. 'Right then, I'm off. I'll leave you in my sister's capable hands. She can explain to you all about the partnership.'

'Partnership?' Templeton was flabbergasted.

Michael laughed. 'Catches on quick, does old Willy. The partnership between us. Me, her, and lastly you.' He pointed towards Templeton. 'Oh, and before I forget, I'll be calling you Willy. Lord William's a bit too much of a gobful, ain't it? You, though, will call

251

me Mr Ryan. If – but only if, mind – I get to like you, I might let you call me Mickey.' He laughed again. 'Give you something to look forward to, won't it?

'There's just one last thing before I go. Don't get Harry Dash – that's flash to you – with my sister here. Whatever she says, you do it. Get that?'

Templeton stared at him.

Michael shouted: 'I said, GET IT?'

'Yes!'

'There's a good boy. Well, cheery bye, or whatever you big nobs say.'

Kissing Maura on the cheek, he left the room. Templeton stared at the doorway as if he had never seen it before.

Maura poured herself another cup of tea. 'Right then, shall we get down to business?'

She felt a bit sorry for the man in front of her. After her night with Terry and the hurt she felt at their parting, she found room in her heart for pity. She took a deep breath and started on what had long been her favourite subject: docklands.

'We know you were really after our properties in Tobacco Dock and similar areas. I happen to know you also have properties there. The idea is that we pool resources. I realise that you have more of an insider's knowledge of what's going on there. Between us we could sew that place up. Once the work starts, we can guarantee the labour and that there will be no delays of any kind. We "own" just about every major contractor in the South East. If push ever came to shove we could stop work there from ever beginning, and I know you wouldn't want that to happen. We're willing to let our brother's death go as far as you are concerned. Dopolis will pay for that. You can either come in with us or sink. It's your choice.'

She picked up her cup and drank her tea. William Templeton was dumbfounded. He was being threatened by a woman! And a working-class woman at that. And these yobs wanted to go into partnership with *him*! If it wasn't so scary he would laugh. He was all for cads and bounders – as long as one kept to one's own class. But to be associated with Michael Ryan! It was unbelievable.

Dopolis had turned out to be a bigger mistake than he had first thought. Now he would *have* to get involved with the Ryans, whether he liked it or not. His idea of getting the Greek to start a gang war seemed stupid now that he had met the real McCoy. He admitted to himself that he had been a damn' fool. His belief that the working class was a bunch of mindless dunderheads had proved fatally wrong. It seemed he was the dunderhead at this moment.

'Well, what's it to be? I haven't got all day.'

Templeton grimaced. 'I don't really seem to have much choice, do I?'

Maura smiled at him. A real smile that made her look very young and very pretty.

'Believe me, Lord William, when I say that you saw the nice side of Michael today. Unless you'd lived our kind of life, you could not hope for one minute to be able to understand us. I would ask you, though, to treat us with the same respect as you would any business associates. You will find that you deal mainly with me. I run the property side of our businesses. What I'm hoping to learn from you is the redevelopment business. It is my fervent wish that my family should find a good respectable outlet to channel money into.'

Grudgingly, Templeton admitted that he could like this girl. She was at least sincere. He shrugged his shoulders at the inevitable. He knew that he had to deal with the Ryans whether he liked it or not. There was no way out. He was caught up in a spider's web, and like the fly knew he would eventually give up struggling.

'The development business is not really respectable, Miss Ryan. In fact, it can be very dirty.'

Maura interrupted him, laughing.

'I think you misunderstand me, Lord William! What I mean by respectable is that, although it may be illegal and at times dirty, it is socially acceptable. Like adultery. If you want my honest opinion, I think you and your kind are the biggest bunch of hypocrites I have ever had the misfortune to come across.' She took a cigarette from the packet she had placed in front of her and lit it, blowing the smoke across the desk into his face.

'You frown on Mr Working Class for having a little flutter. Yet the Stock Exchange gambles daily with millions of pounds. Banks do it, and building societies. And let's face it, it's not even their money they're using. But there you are. The double standard prevails. One set of rules for the Hooray Henrys and another for Mr Joe Public. Well, let me tell you something. I may not have a family tree like yours, or be that articulate in my grammar, but there's one thing I *have* got going for me – I have money. Plenty of it. And with the kind of money I have, every door can be opened. Even the Royal Enclosure at Ascot. That's how we found you out. You broke the golden rule of villainy, Lord William. You let the world in on what you were doing. A fatal mistake.'

A light seemed to go on behind Templeton's eyes and Maura could not help grinning at him.

'Let me guess. You couldn't resist showing off to him, am I right? Well, that little faux pas on your part led us straight to your door. Whereas me and my brothers – Michael especially – our faces are slapped across the *News of the World* at least once a month, but they can't prove anything. It's all supposition. Now you,' she pointed at him with her cigarette, 'are going to be our Mr Legit. I want you to tell me exactly what's going to happen to the old docks.'

Templeton stared at Maura for a few seconds. He knew that all she had said was right.

'Maura . . . may I call you Maura?'

'Of course.'

'I think that you and I could do business together. I have a feeling we could even be friends.'

She smiled at him and breathed a sigh of relief. She made a conscious decision to prove to him that she was as good as, if not better than, anyone he had done business with before.

'Seeing as we have you by the bollocks, as my brother would term it, I don't see why we can't be friends. Now, about the docks.'

She was being deliberately crude. She wanted his friendship, but she also wanted his co-operation and until she was certain she had that, she would continue to remind him just who he was dealing with.

Templeton pressed the button of the intercom on his desk.

'Yes, sir?' The sweet voice of Marie crackled into the room.

'Hold all my calls and bring in some fresh tea.'

'But, sir! You have an appointment in ten minutes to see the Secretary of State for the Environment!'

'Then you'll just have to tell him that I am in an urgent meeting.' He cut off the connection.

Maura raised her eyebrows at him and he was amazed to hear himself laugh. He had taken rather a fancy to the girl. Opening a drawer in his desk, he brought out a folder. He opened it and took out some papers and a map. He passed this to Maura. While she studied it, Marie brought in some more tea and removed the large trolley. Her face was set in a frown. This time she banged the door shut behind her.

'Well, Maura, I will tell you all that I know. This,' he swept his hand across the papers in front of him, 'has been discussed behind closed doors for some time. As you so astutely pointed out, there's a lot of money to be made there. In 1967 the East India Dock closed. In '68 the London Docks. In '69 Katherine Dock, and in '70 Surrey Docks. All we are waiting for is the eventual closure of Millwall, and the Royal Victoria and Albert. That is when it will all start to happen.'

'So the other docks will eventually close?' Maura kept her voice neutral. In fact, she was flabbergasted.

'Oh, yes. Within the next five years. That's why no money's going in there. The more rundown and depressed the area gets, the more we can justify reclaiming the land. Job creation et cetera.' He smiled at her. 'I am afraid that we live in a world where the masses are spoonfed bullshit, if you will forgive the expression. The average man on the street buys the *Sun* to look at a pair of breasts. In reality, he's reading Tory propaganda. Whoever is in office at the time all this begins, be it Tory, Labour or, God help us, Screaming Lord Sutch, will be jumping on the bandwagon. Funding it, giving out grants. "We'll give you money to make money" . . . that's every government's policy. Personally, I think it will be the Conservatives, but I'm not worried either way. This has been sewn up for a long time. Now, drink your tea while it's hot and I'll explain to you more fully. I think you will find it fascinating.'

She and William Templeton smiled at one another. Maura shook her head slowly and said, 'And they have the nerve to call *us* villains!'

In 1976 the Docklands Joint Committee published the London Dockland Strategic Plan. The Ryans and Lord Templeton were on their way.

Book Three

THE DOWNFALL

It is a strange desire to seek power and to lose
liberty –

Francis Bacon, 1561–1626

What will you give me, and I will deliver him
unto you?
And they covenanted with him for thirty pieces
of silver –

Matthew, xxvi, 15

Chapter Twenty-Two

12 February 1985

Geoffrey Ryan parked outside Le Buxom. It was not yet nine o'clock in the morning. He picked up his briefcase from the passenger seat of his dark blue BMW, locked up his car and went into the club. The cleaners all greeted him. In 1980, a restaurant had been opened in what had been the basement. This meant that the club was open nearly twenty-four hours of the day. He went down there to discuss the day's menu with Peter Petrillo, the head chef, who had finished a ten-year stretch in Parkhurst then been given the job by Michael Ryan.

Geoffrey looked over the menu briefly and nodded his head, as he did every day. Then he ordered coffee and went up to his offices. He lit a cigarette and, settling himself into his chair, began his work for the day, going over the figures for the clubs and wine bars – a new acquisition of Maura's to cash in on the yuppie boom. When he opened a drawer to get his calculator, he saw it was missing: Michael had been in and taken it again. Putting his cigarette out, he pulled himself from his seat and made his way to Michael's office next door.

Although Geoffrey had the larger office, most of the business was done by Michael and Maura from the smaller office. He knew deep inside that they had given him the larger office to placate him. Also, the smaller office was always referred to as Michael's office when in reality it was Michael's and Maura's.

He frowned as he walked through the door. He never came in here unless he absolutely had to. The room was empty. He looked on the large desk for his calculator, moving papers and files haphazardly. As he turned away he noticed that the small filing cabinet was unlocked, the keys still in the lock but the top drawer slightly open. He shook his head. Walking to it he pushed the drawer shut and was about to lock it when he stopped dead. Biting his lip he pulled the drawer back open. This was the one place he and the others were barred from. Only Michael and Maura had access to it. Now by some twist of fate it was open to him and he was torn between a desire to know what was in there that was so private and fear that he'd be caught looking. He decided to take his chances. Checking the corridor outside, he shut the door quietly and went back to the filing cabinet. He pulled out one of the files and began to read it. After a few minutes he forget his fear of Michael and Maura, and took the file back to his office. A deep rage grew inside him as he realised just what he had stumbled across.

Maura and Leslie were in Brixton. They pulled up outside a block of flats. Leslie got out of the car and opened the door to let Maura out. Having locked the car, he followed her up the filthy stairs that led into the block of flats. They were low rise flats, only two storeys. Maura walked along the balcony until she came to No. 28. She knocked on the front door, which was opened by a little girl of about eight. The child was half caste and, Maura noticed, extremely thin and emaciated.

'We're looking for Jackie Traverna's house. Is this it?' Maura's voice was friendly and kind.

'Yeah. But she's in bed.'

'I think she will see me. Just take me to her, my love.' Maura's voice sounded false, even to her own ears. She had lost the knack of talking to children.

The child shrugged her skinny shoulders. As if to say, who cares? Maura followed her up a dark narrow hallway and into a small bedroom. The place was messy, the bedroom entirely taken up by a large double bed, though Maura guessed that when Jackie was on her feet she kept it clean and tidy. In the giant bed lay Jackie herself. Her coffee-coloured skin was shining with a film of sweat.

Maura gasped when she saw her. 'Leslie! Get in here.'

He ran in the room thinking that Maura had come across some kind of trouble.

'Fucking hell!' His voice was shocked.

In the bed lay Jackie, recognisable only by her wiry Afro hair. Her face was so swollen she looked as if she had been attacked by bees. On each of her cheeks was a large stripe which went from the corner of her mouth to rise up until it disappeared into her hairline. Jackie looked up with sad eyes.

'Maura.' Her voice was muffled.

'All right, Jackie. All right, mate. Who did this? Was it Rubens . . . Danny Rubens?'

Jackie nodded her head, fear in her eyes.

'Don't worry now. I'm going to see you're looked after.'

'Thanks. Can't . . . speak.' The woman could barely move.

'I know. I know. I'll be back later. All right?'

She smiled at Jackie, but inside she was fuming. 'Come on, Leslie. Get your arse in gear.'

Once they were back inside the car, Maura lit herself a cigarette and said, 'Pick up Lee and Garry. We're going to pay Rubens a little visit.'

Geoffrey had been reading the file for about an hour. He was still reading it when Michael came into his office. Geoffrey looked up at him, the hurt in his eyes almost a tangible thing. Michael saw the green folder and tried to play for time.

'Any more coffee going, Geoff?'

Geoffrey ignored him. Picking up the folder, he threw it across the desk.

'Thanks a lot, Bruv.' His voice was flat.

Michael sighed. 'For Christ's sake, Geoff. You're not my keeper, you know.'

Geoffrey lit another cigarette, his hands trembling.

'That's just it, though, ain't it, Mickey? I ain't nothing.'

'Look, Geoff, you know what they say. What you don't know, don't hurt you.'

Geoffrey pulled on his cigarette and let out the smoke through his nose, looking like a belligerent bull.

'You've mugged me off, ain't you?'

Mickey laughed. 'Come on, Geoff. I would have told you eventually. Why are you making such a big deal?'

Michael's voice was getting tight. He did not feel like all this today.

'I'll tell you why I'm making such a big deal, shall I? I've just read this crap.' He pointed to the green folder. 'And I realise just what I am in this firm. I run the clubs, sort of. I run the wine bars, sort of. I watch over the bookies and the cab ranks. While you and Maura – marvellous fucking Maura – do the *real* work.'

'Leave her out of this.' Michael's voice was hard and low.

Geoffrey stubbed out his cigarette. 'No, I won't leave her out of all this. She's the cause of it all. Since the day she came into this firm you've pushed me out.'

Geoffrey's voice was high and he knew it sounded hysterical, but he did not care. He had to get this thing sorted out, once and for all.

'You're talking crap and you know it, Geoffrey. Now give it a rest, for fuck's sake.'

Geoffrey began shouting, all caution gone now. 'No, I will not give it a rest! I read, by accident, that you are about to embark on the biggest gold robbery this country's ever known, and you have the nerve to stand there and tell me I would have been told eventually! And when was that gonna be? When it was in the papers or on the news? Just what kind of cunt do you take me for? What else has been going on behind my back, eh? Well, answer me then.'

Geoffrey had risen from his seat and stood in front of Michael who was a good three inches taller and at least two stone heavier. Both knew that if it came to blows, Michael would win hands down. Geoffrey did not care.

Michael tried once more to pacify him. 'Keep your voice down, Geoff. There's no need to let everyone know, is there?'

'I bet everyone *does* bloody know! Everyone except me, that is.' He prodded his chest. '*I've* stood by you through thick and thin, from day one. But since that fucking leech Maura came on the scene, I've been pushed out. It's been you and Maura . . . Maura and Michael . . . the dynamic duo. Batman and Robin's got nothing on you two. She was shagging an old Bill and yet you treat her like visiting royalty.'

Michael's hand went up to Geoffrey's throat. He slipped his other hand around his brother's neck and squeezed.

'Let's get the violins out, shall we? Geoffrey's little heart is broken! You ponce! You disgust me.'

He hurled Geoffrey away from him and went to the window, running his hands through his hair.

Turning back, he thrust out a finger. 'I'll tell you why Maura has taken your so-called place, shall I? Because she's got more bollocks than you will ever have! You've been like a bloody albatross hanging around my neck all my life. I've had to carry you ever since we were kids.' Michael wiped his hand across his face, agitated and annoyed. 'If you'd been left to your own devices, you'd have been banged up years ago. And *you're* jealous of your own bloody sister because she has what it takes. She sussed all this out.' He gestured around him wildly. 'You couldn't organise the proverbial piss up, mate. You could never have figured half of what she has. You fucking wind me up! You always have done.'

He pointed at Geoffrey again, his face contorted with temper. 'Shall I tell you something? You're working here because Maura suggested it. If it had been left to me, I'd have had Gerry Jackson running this show, mate. I'd have dumped you years ago. But, no, Maura said: "Family first." I swallowed, but deep down in my heart I didn't give a toss.

'Now if you don't like it, you can piss off. But I tell you this now. If you ever . . . ever . . . speak about her like that again, I'll bury you. Now do me a favour and fuck off before I really lose me rag.'

Geoffrey stared at Michael, dumbstruck. He could feel the waves of resentment coming out of every pore in Michael's body. He realised something he had known secretly for years, something he had never dared admit to himself before: he irritated Mickey. And yet he would have died for him. He was the only brother left who was not married or living with a girl. Even Michael had a regular boyfriend. He had lived his life for Michael.

He straightened himself up slowly and, picking up his jacket and car keys, walked from the office. As he came down the stairs into the foyer he realised that the cleaners had all stopped work. They had been listening to everything. He could feel his face burning with humiliation. He left the club and got into his car as if in a daze. That Michael could have spoken like that to him! He felt sick with the realisation of what had just happened. And with the fact that nothing could ever be the same between them again.

Maura and the three boys were at Danny Ruben's gaff, a terraced house in Tulse Hill. Lee banged on the front door hard. It was opened by a young girl who looked about seventeen. Though knowing Ruben's taste, Maura thought she was probably about fifteen, top whack.

'Is Danny about?' They pushed past the girl into the house.

'He ain't up yet. He don't get up before twelve.'

Garry smiled at her. 'Well, it'll be a nice change for him then, won't it?' They all began to walk up the stairs.

'Who is it, Estelle?' A deep brown voice bellowed the words down the stairs. The four walked in its direction.

Maura and her brothers noticed that the house was very well decorated and very clean. Inside Danny's bedroom, Maura smiled at him.

'Well, well. You are a big boy, aren't you?' Danny Rubens was lying in bed naked. He pulled the duvet over himself. He was still half stoned from the previous evening but alert enough to know he had invited big trouble to his house.

'Shut the door, Garry. We don't want everyone hearing Danny's screams.'

Danny's big black face was sweating and his eyes were like dark brown pools in his head. His head was shaved and Maura could see a vein pulsing, just below his right eyebrow. He was scared, very scared, and that was just what she wanted. Danny Rubens had taken to body building while doing a three-year stretch for

263

aggravated assault. He was enormous and that usually gave him the edge.

'What you want?'

Maura laughed. 'Cut the coon talk, Rubens, you've never been out of London in your life.'

Garry, Leslie and Lee guffawed at this. They knew how to play the game. Maura pulled the duvet from his body, leaving him naked and exposed.

'I'm here about a girl of mine – Jackie Traverna.'

'Ain't never heard of her.'

Maura opened her bag and lit one of her cigarettes. Every action was watched closely by Rubens. She puffed on her cigarette until the end glowed.

'I've been hearing stories about you, Rubens.' Maura pointed to her brothers. 'Hold him.'

Leslie and Lee went to the bed and, after a struggle, held Danny Rubens down on it. Maura gestured to Garry. 'Hold his legs open for me.'

She drew the cigarette smoke into her lungs and watched impassively as Rubens tried to fight his way out of the situation. Finally he was lying spreadeagled on the bed. 'Now I want you to tell me why you striped up one of my girls.'

Rubens was absolutely terrified. His eyes were stretched to their utmost, showing all the yellow whiteness.

'I tell you, sis, I ain't never done no harm to no black chick.'

Garry punched him in the face.

'If you ain't never heard of her, how do you know what colour she is?'

'I guessed, man. I guessed.'

'Oh, shut up, you black ponce.' This was Leslie. 'Let my sister speak.' His voice was slow and bored-sounding. Rubens thought he would wet himself with fright.

'I have heard, Mr Rubens,' Maura stressed the Mr, 'that you have some rather big ambitions. One being to become the Pimp Extraordinaire of the West End. I also hear that you are after some of my girls.'

She sat on the bed and opened her bag. Rubens was holding his head off the bed, straining his neck to see what was going on. He was naked and vulnerable and did not like it.

Maura took a snub-nosed .38 special from her handbag. Ruben's eyes were now like flying saucers.

'What you want with that!' He was nearly crying.

'My sister is going to blow your balls off, Danny. One by one.' Leslie's voice was jocular.

Maura held the gun against Ruben's genitals. He could feel the hard coldness of the steel against his skin. She rubbed it gently along the length of his penis and under his testicles. Rubbed it slowly, dreamily, as if she was enjoying it. Then she took another long drag of her cigarette. Rubens, who had been 'The Daddy' while he was in Durham jail, who had been working the streets nearly all his adult life and who could instil fear into most people, burst into tears. They ran from his eyes and down his face. Great bubbles of snot billowed out of his nose and his gigantic shoulders heaved.

'Please . . . don't shook my cock off!' He sounded like a small boy.

Garry, Leslie and Lee were laughing again.

Maura put her cigarette butt on Ruben's stomach. He felt the burning through his tears. Maura left the cigarette on his belly, so the embers would scorch the skin slowly and painfully. He was howling in pain.

'Where's your Stanley knife, Danny?' Maura's voice was soft and gentle, as if they were lovers on a picnic.

'I swear . . . I swear to you I ain't got no Stanley knife.'

'Pain is a terrible thing, isn't it? Jackie Traverna was in pain, Danny, she was in such terrible pain.' Her voice hardened. 'Now it's your turn.' She nodded at Leslie who took a Stanley knife from the pocket of his jacket. He held it glinting over the man's face.

'What's it to be, Danny boy? Cheek or cock? It's up to you. But make your mind up quickly or I might just do both.'

Danny was staring at Leslie's face and knew he was not joking. He saw, even through his fear and his tears, that he had met with a will much stronger than his own.

'Please, man. Please.' His voice was just a croaky whisper.

'Face it is then!' Leslie grinned and pulled the Stanley knife from Danny's eye down to his mouth. He cut deeply and confidently. The blood came out slowly, as if not sure what it wanted to do as the layers of skin gradually unfolded. By the time he had repeated the action on the other side of the man's face, the blood was pumping out with each of his heartbeats. They all stood up as if of one mind. As his hands were released, Danny brought them up to his face. When he took them away, his palms were stained with deep crimson blood.

He screamed loudly, painfully, like a hare caught in a trap.

'Don't ever get ambitious for anything or anyone that belongs to me, Danny. Next time you might not be so lucky.'

'Oh, God, I'm bleeding! Help me somebody!' The white satin sheets on his bed were slowly being dyed red.

'Come on, boys. We've got a lot of work to do.'

As they left the room the young girl Estelle ran inside. When they left the house, her screams were even louder than Danny's.

Geoffrey was sitting in his flat. He had poured himself a large Scotch and was sitting on the sofa remembering every detail of his life with Michael. One memory stood out like a shining beacon. He gulped his Scotch as he remembered a day almost forty years earlier.

He had been just coming up eight, Michael nearly ten. It was during the war, and their father had dropped them both through a hole in the remains of a bombed-out house. Mickey, as usual, had no fear. He just put his torch on and shone it around the debris-strewn cellar. The occupants of the house were lying around like lumps of bloody red meat. The stench had been unbearable. Geoffrey could still remember the way he'd felt that day, rooted to the spot with fear. His father's voice had been coming from above, urging them to hurry up. Looting bombed houses was a serious criminal offence.

Michael dragged the body of a little girl off a tin petty cash box. She had been blown across it in the blast. He then passed this up to their father and quickly began collecting up anything that was useful, edible or saleable. He had gone about his work silently and quickly, calling softly to Geoffrey to help him move the body of a man. He had known it was a man by the clothes. The face had completely gone.

Geoffrey had found it impossible to move. Michael had gone to him and punched him in the stomach, winding him, urging him to hurry up and help him. Between them they dragged the man's heavy body on to the floor. Geoffrey had been crying by this time. Michael had stripped the man of his wallet and watch. Then he had gone to the woman who had been grotesquely thrown to the floor. Her legs were wide open and her arms and neck lay in positions that would have been impossible had she been alive. Michael took her brooch and her wedding ring. Geoffrey had heard the crunching click of her bone as he had broken her bent finger to remove it. Then their father had pulled them both out of the hole. He could still feel the sting of his father's belt later that night as he had been strapped for 'being a baby'.

From that day on he had tried to emulate his brother. He had joined him in beating people, robbing the bombsites, everything. In all truth, Geoffrey admitted to himself, he had hated every minute of it. And it dawned on him now that Michael knew this, had always known it, and that's why he despised him. In Maura, Michael had found a kindred spirit. Another loner. Another

266

warped version of their father. He finished his glass of Scotch and sat back in his seat.

He couldn't join Mickey now, that much was obvious, but he would sure as hell beat him. And that bitch of a sister! He had the knowledge and he would sit and wait, and then one day he would use it. He saw once more the looks that had been on the cleaners' faces, and felt an urge to murder the pair of them.

Still, as his old dad used to say when they were small: 'Don't get mad. Get even.' That's just what he intended to do.

Maura and Michael were eating a late dinner in The Greek Revolution in Beauchamp Place. They had been discussing their day. They made a stunning pair. Even at thirty-five Maura was still as young-looking as ever. She dressed down, never wearing clothes that were in fashion but choosing plain and expensive classics, as only the very rich can. Her blonde hair was longer now, cut into a long bob. It hung just below her jawline, framing her finely boned face. With her lightness, and Michael's dark good looks, they were the perfect foil for one another.

Even in his fifties, Michael was still a very attractive man. He dressed conservatively but well, sticking as he had always done to greys and blacks. Occasionally he wore something he termed 'ostentatious', but those times were few and far between.

'Well, I think Geoffrey's probably over his tantrum by now.' Maura sounded worried.

'Quite frankly, Maws, I don't give a shit. He winds me up.'

Maura was quiet for a moment. She had felt the tension building up between them for months. It truly amazed her that Michael, who was usually so perceptive about everything, failed to notice what was in front of his eyes. Geoffrey was jealous of her and she knew it. But now he was also jealous of Michael, and she had a gut feeling that Geoffrey could turn out to be quite dangerous.

Michael wiped his pitta bread around the plate, picking up the last of the tsatsiki, and popped the bread into his mouth. 'So, tell me. What are you going to do for Jackie Traverna?'

'Oh, I don't know, Michael. The poor bitch is in a terrible state. Give her some money, I suppose.'

Michael laughed. 'You're like a fucking social worker! I'd better keep a close eye on you, girl. Next thing I know you'll be giving all our cash away to the starving millions!'

Maura smiled, knowing that Michael was deliberately steering the conversation away from Geoffrey.

'Before I forget, Maws. Willy Templeton wants in on the gold plan. I said yeah. What do you reckon?'

'Why not?' She shrugged. 'He seems to be in on everything else.' She picked up a prawn and pulled its head off. 'If that's what you want, Mickey. I'm easy.'

'He's doing a great job down at St Martin's Wharf. It's a funny thing, Maws, but having a lord on your side certainly helps matters along. Don't you think?'

His voice was cold and calculating.

'Of course it helps. It's like going to parties with famous people. Everyone's a starfucker at heart. Stars included. They love us because we're rough diamonds. Personally, I don't give a monkey's either way. I like Willy, though.'

And she did. She liked him very much and it was strange, because she knew that without him Benny would still be alive. Even knowing that, she still could not help liking and admiring him. He was what she had learned to term an 'educated villain'. Through William Templeton she had met many more like him – rich, educated men who pulled off brilliant scams. Scams that were never allowed to get into the newspapers or come to prosecution because the firms involved would lose their credibility on the Stock Market with disastrous economic and political results. Instead the wrongdoers were given enormous golden handshakes and a big party as a leaving present. And their pictures appeared in the papers with the sob story: 'Ill health brings the head of So and So corporation's career to an end.' 'I want to spend more time with my wife and family' was another favourite excuse. It was not only the big businessmen who were involved in these things, but politicians, judges . . . just about every profession had its fair share of con men. Gradually, through William Templeton,, Maura and Michael were finding out exactly who they were. And they were learning a whole new ballgame.

The waiter brought their main course, kleftiko, and refilled their wine glasses. When he left them, Maura spoke.

'I want an early start tomorrow. I've finally sorted out the last few wrinkles in the gold plan. If everything looks OK to you, we can begin to set it all up.'

'I'll drink to that, Maws.' Michael picked up his glass of Chablis. 'Cheers.'

They touched glasses. If you did not know them you would think they were planning a party, not the biggest bullion robbery England had ever known.

★ ★ ★

While they were sitting in the restaurant, Danny Rubens was lying in hospital. He had been sedated heavily, but one of the nurses was intrigued. Because, although he was in a deep, drug-induced sleep, his hand was still holding on tightly to his genitals.

Chapter Twenty-Three

14 February 1985

Maura knocked on the door of Geoffrey's flat. He lived not far from Michael in Knightsbridge. She had been there only twice before. Even though they had worked together and were brother and sister, they had an accepted and unspoken agreement: I don't like you, so keep your distance. Up till now Maura had respected this.

Geoffrey opened the door. He seemed surprised to see her standing there. He looked terrible. He had not shaved for a couple of days, and being so dark-haired now had dark stubble around his jaw. Maura was shocked to see that it was tinged with grey.

He and Michael had been so alike all their lives, Geoffrey was like a watered-down version of his brother. He looked great, he was handsome, but when people saw Michael they seemed to overlook Geoffrey afterwards. Today he looked old and ill and Maura felt sorry for him. The lines around his eyes, so sexy on Michael, made Geoffrey look jaded and debauched. His dark hair, normally washed and gleaming, was greasy and lank. She watched him look her over from head to toe. It was a sneering look as if she was so much dirt.

'And what do you want?' His voice was belligerent. His face was close to hers and she could smell the sourness of the vast amount of Scotch he had been consuming since his fight with Michael.

'May I come in?' Her voice was neutral.

He held the door open and watched her pass. For the first time in her life she was a bit frightened of him. He slammed the door shut behind her and walked into his lounge. Maura followed, unsure if she was doing the right thing. The room was in a state of chaos. The curtains were still pulled even though it was nearly lunchtime. She went to his oak bookcase and studied the titles for something to do. Her mind was trying to think of a way to defuse the situation.

Geoffrey pulled open the heavy curtains and the weak February sunshine lit the room. She carried on looking at the books, waiting for him to open the conversation. Give her some kind of inkling of

271

how to go about pacifying him over what had happened.

'Thinking of taking up reading? How about *Crime and Punishment*? You can borrow it if you like.' His voice was sarcastic.

She faced him.

'Why didn't you turn in for work yesterday?' She tried to sound ignorant of what had taken place between the two brothers, but as soon as she spoke knew she had said the wrong thing.

Geoffrey laughed.

'Are you telling me that Big Brother didn't tell you all about our little fight? Mickey even tells you when he gives his boyfriend one up the jacksey. I'm sure a good row with his brother would have been worth mentioning.'

Maura stared at Geoffrey for a few seconds before answering him. She decided to come clean with him. It was obvious that he was not going to make this easy.

'Look, Geoff, he did tell me about it. And he really is cut up about it. You took it too much to heart . . .'

Geoffrey sat in a chair and began to laugh at her.

'Oh, get stuffed, Maura. Cut up? He'd be more cut up if that mangy old dog of Benny's died. He don't give a toss about me, and from now on I ain't gonna give a toss about him.'

'But where will you work? What will you do?' She went to him and knelt in front of his chair.

'Oh, don't you worry, I'll still be working for you all.' He stressed the you. 'But I tell you now, and you can tell Mickey this if you like, I'll not be at his beck and call twenty-four hours a day. When I've done my stint of work I'm off. And I won't do any "heavy" work. If you or him want anyone roughed up or threatened, then you'll have to get one of the others to do it.'

'That's fair enough, Geoff. I was thinking, how about you take over the docklands? I think you and Willy would work well together, and me and Mickey . . . well, we have other irons in the fire.'

Geoffrey grinned, a horrible smelly grin that made her feel sick.

'So little sister has come to pour oil on troubled waters? You're offering me the docklands because you think that it will make me toe the line. Be a good boy.'

'No, Geoffrey. You could have had it before.'

He cut her off, his voice low and serious. 'Do you realise that I am over fifty years old? I have never married or even lived with a woman. I just worked that business with Michael. And then you came and you took it all from me. You inveigled your way into his pocket and you've been resident there ever since.' He was looking at her with a hatred that was tangible. Maura sat back on her heels and stared into a wrinkled, hate-filled face. In the grey sunlight he looked like a gargoyle come to life. But he had hurt her. Hurt and annoyed her.

'Do you know your trouble, Geoffrey? You don't know how to live a life. You act like a leech sucking everyone else's glory. You lived in Mickey's shadow, mate. You didn't have to, it was your own choice. You could have married if you'd wanted to, but you didn't. Not because of Michael, but because you knew deep in your boots that you weren't fit to mate with anyone. Mother called me and Michael neuters years ago, and maybe she was right, but I think that you're one as well.'

'You bitch! How dare you come here spouting your crap?'

Maura stood up and smoothed out the creases in her skirt. Slowly and deliberately, she leaned towards him. 'Just because you've read a few books don't make you Magnus fucking Magnusson you know. You're full of old shit, mate. You want to put down Herman Hesse and Tolstoy and go out of this flat and get yourself a bird. A real bird, not one of the high-heeled call girls you normally knock around with. A real woman, with a mind of her own.

'You make me sick, Geoff. You're always moaning about something. Everything in your life is analysed and picked over until you find a slight to *you* somewhere in it. Whether it's a chance remark or a frigging so-called conspiracy, like the folder you read the other day. You're paranoid, that's your trouble. Now if you want to come back to work tomorrow, go to the offices at St Martin's Wharf. If not, then that's up to you.'

She started to walk from the room. His voice stayed her. 'I hate you, Maura. I hate you so much I can taste it in my mouth. It's like gall. Mother said to me once you weren't like a normal woman. You didn't have the normal feelings any woman has. And now I know it's true. You even killed your own baby.'

She turned on him like a tiger. Her voice bitter, she said, 'That's Mother's opinion, is it? Well, next time you two are chatting about me ask her this. Ask her who held me down on the table that day when a dirty old man scraped my baby away. Ask her that. And while you're about it, ask her why she accepts money from Michael every week, yet won't even acknowledge his existence. Ask her why she drove poor Carla into marrying that bloody Malcolm. Why she kept her and never tried to reunite her with her mother. I know what everyone thinks about Janine but I'll tell you this much . . . once Mother got Carla into her house and had another little girl to dress up and take to mass, she would never *let* her go back home. You an' Mother are like two peas in a pod. You're both manipulators but neither of you could ever manipulate me or Michael. That's what gets up your noses!'

Before he could speak again she had left the flat, slamming the door behind her.

Geoffrey sat in the chair for a while, thinking. All his instincts told him to forget Maura and Michael forever. But his devious brain told him that if he did not work for them he could not gather his information. And he would gather it. And he would use it. He would swallow his pride and go into work in the morning. But he would be biding his time . . .

Maura drove to Jackie Traverna's house. She was fuming inside. Geoffrey was a pain in the neck. He always had been, and she had a feeling he always would be. She parked her Mercedes Sports outside Jackie's block of flats. Locking it carefully, she went up the small flight of stairs.

As she walked along the landing towards Jackie's flat she was aware of the attention she commanded. Women were standing on the landing chatting, children of all colours and creeds were playing both on the landing and on the concrete forecourt of the flats. Everywhere was the flaking paint and crumbling brickwork that denoted the conditions of poverty these people lived in. The women who were chatting looked at her burgundy Jasper Conran dress and quite obviously real fur coat, and were quiet and hostile. Maura had to turn her body sideways to pass them.

In their crumpled velour tracksuits and shapeless dresses they looked like old women, yet Maura could see from the tight skin on their faces that they were much younger than her. If her life had been different she could quite easily have been one of them. Then her mind rebelled against that thought.

No. She would never have allowed herself to look like these women. Most of them had given up hope at a very early age. No matter what had happened to her, she knew she would always have kept her self-respect.

Jackie's front door was ajar and she walked inside, hesitantly. If those women who had looked at her with naked envy knew that she carried a gun in her bag, they might have had different feelings.

'Jackie? Jackie love?' Her voice was soft. She heard a noise from the bedroom and went inside. Jackie was lying on the bed. Her face had lost some of its puffiness and she looked better. Not much better but better than she had on Maura's last visit.

'Oh, Maura . . .' Jackie tried to speak.

Maura sat on her bed. 'I just popped by to see you, Jackie. Shall I make you a cup of tea?'

Jackie's deep brown eyes opened in surprise. Maura Ryan

274

making her tea? It was like expecting the Queen to wash your kitchen floor.

Maura smiled at her, guessing her thoughts. She found the kitchen and made a pot of tea. The room was tiny but relatively tidy. She noticed that there was hardly anything in the cupboards. Leaving the tea to draw she walked back out on to the landing. The women were still there and Maura guessed that they had been discussing her arrival. She strode purposefully towards them.

'Do any of you happen to be friends with Jackie Traverna?'

A fat woman with long straggly brown hair answered her. 'I am. Why?' Her voice was hard and flat.

'I suppose you know that she's had an accident.'

The fat woman sighed loudly. 'I've been taking her Debbie to school for her. Why?'

'If I gave you the money, would you get her in some shopping?' Maura saw the women exchange looks. 'I'll pay you to do it, of course.'

The fat woman shrugged. 'All right.'

She followed Maura back into the flat. Maura was gratified at the friendly way in which she went into Jackie's room. Maura picked her bag up from where she had placed it on the bed. Opening it, she took out five twenty-pound notes. 'Do you have a freezer, Jackie?' The woman nodded her head.

'Good. There's a hundred pounds there and I want you to fill her freezer and cupboards up. I'll give you a score for your trouble. OK?'

The fat woman stared at the money in astonishment. Then she took it from Maura. She guessed from Maura's voice that she was not Social Services or Probation. When the woman went she would find out about her from Jackie.

When the neighbour was gone, Maura poured Jackie and herself out some tea. Taking it into the bedroom, she placed Jackie's cup into her hands. She had managed to pull herself up in the bed and Maura could see the purple bruises on her arms and shoulders. Damn Danny Rubens!

Opening her bag again, she lit two cigarettes and gave one to Jackie. Maura studied her face. She had about thirty stitches in each cheek and would carry the scars for the rest of her life. She pulled out a building society book and gave it to the woman.

'Inside there is five thousand pounds, Jackie. I want you to use it for a holiday or whatever. When you're feeling better I want you to take over the job of head girl at the Crackerjack, our new club.'

It took Maura a minute to realise that Jackie was crying. She took the tea from her and placed it on the floor by the bed. Then she put an arm around her shoulders.

'Hey . . . hey. Calm down, Jackie.'

She spoke with difficulty. 'You've been so good. I was so worried. I thought I'd end up at King's Cross with the pervies.'

Maura looked into her eyes. 'No way. You're a good girl, Jackie. And the head girl's job is a bloody good earner. You'll be fine. Absolutely fine.'

She picked Jackie's tea up from the floor and passed it to her. 'Now you drink this while I get you and me an ashtray!'

When the fat woman got back from shopping she was amazed to find the 'rich bird', as she had termed Maura in her head, washing the kitchen floor. When Maura left a little later she was sure she had pushed up Jackie Traverna's street credibility a hundredfold, and only wished Jackie had not had to go through all that pain and suffering to achieve it.

When Maura got to her own house a bunch of white roses had been left in the glass porch. Intrigued, she opened the card. It said: 'Happy Valentine's Day. Mickey.'

She smiled to herself, but deep inside a little voice was asking her why she never got flowers from any 'real' men. Men who were not related to her. Inside the front door was a pile of letters. Picking them up, she went through to her kitchen. She placed the roses on the draining board and flicked through the letters. Bills and circulars. Then she noticed a thick cream-coloured envelope. Opening it, she brought out a beautiful card. It had real velvet flowers on it, arranged in a basket made of gold thread. This was definitely not a Woolworth's special. She smiled. Michael again. She opened the card and nearly died of shock.

'Will you be my Valentine? Have Dinner with me tonight. 7.30 at the Savoy. Willy.'

For a few sweet seconds she felt that powerful excitement that a new love affair can bring. Then she glanced at her watch. It was past five now! She ran up the stairs to get ready. She was gonna knock his eyes out!

William Templeton sat at his table. He sneaked a glance at his watch. It was twenty to eight. She wasn't coming. He felt his heart sink. Maybe he should have rung her. Then she could have cold-shouldered him over the phone and that would have been the end of it. But he had seen that card in Harrods and had felt a foolish urge to buy it for her. He almost laughed. At his age? On the wrong side of fifty . . .

He had that terrible feeling people get when they have been stood up. That feeling that makes them think that everyone knows what's happened to them. That everyone is smiling at them behind their hands. He felt a shadow fall across him as he stared at the menu for the hundredth time and waved his hand imperiously.

'I'm not ready to order yet, thank you.'

'I should hope not. The least I'd expect is that you would wait for me to arrive!'

His eyes lifted and she was standing there, looking lovelier than he had ever seen her before. She had on a grey fitted dress of watered silk. As with all her clothes, it was perfectly plain. But with her breasts and slim waist, she did not need any of the frippery that most women wore. In her ears she had perfect pearl earrings and around her neck a small single strand of the same grade. Her pale white skin brought them to shining life. Her silky white-blonde hair looked immaculate, as always. William took pleasure in the admiring glances that were coming their way.

He stood up awkwardly. 'I thought you weren't going to come.'

Maura sat down and smiled at the waiter who held her chair.

'Well, I didn't get your card until after five o'clock so I had to rush a bit.'

'You look exquisite, my dear, like a very beautiful painting. Now then, some champagne, I think.' He smiled. 'Real champagne, not the dishwater that's served in your clubs!'

Maura laughed. Really laughed, for the first time in years. It felt good to be pursued. Wanted. And this man certainly wanted her . . . She relaxed back into her chair and let good feelings wash over her.

Chapter Twenty-Four

19 March 1985

'Where did you get the number plates from?' Michael was keyed up.

Leslie grinned. 'I got the numbers from a motorway service station car park. I had the actual plates made up by Jimmy Charlton. He owes us a favour.'

'Good. Are the Range Rovers ready to go? And the bikes?'

Leslie nodded. 'Yep. They've been serviced and valeted. They're as clean as a nun's knickers.'

Garry grinned. 'I've sorted out all the guns. They're cleaned and ready to go.'

'Good. Very good. You realise this is a big undertaking, don't you? This ain't like a normal blag. Every filth in the country is going to be looking for that gold. It will be the biggest chance of promotion since Ronnie Biggs had it on his toes.'

'Well, they ain't caught him yet.' Maura's voice was jocular. Everyone laughed except Mickey.

'There's still time for that. Whatever happens, don't get too cocky, lads. Just keep to the ground rules I laid down and we'll be OK.'

Maura stood up and looked around at her brothers' faces. 'What about the hole?'

'All done. Ready and waiting.' This from Lee.

'Then all that's left is to sort out the alibis. I'll leave that to you lot. Whatever it is, make sure it's tighter than a duck's behind. OK?'

Everyone nodded.

'See you in the morning then.' Michael smiled at the faces around him. 'Unless there's any questions?'

'I've got a question.'

'It would be you, wouldn't it, brain box?' Maura's voice was light.

The chances were that if Garry asked a question it would be a good one.

He adjusted his glasses. 'What happens to the filth?'

Michael and Maura had been half expecting someone to ask this.

Michael answered. 'I wasn't going to tell you till the morning. But as you ask . . .'

He paused for effect and swept his gaze around all his brothers.

'You waste them. Every one of them. The fewer people to identify us, the better.'

Roy coughed. 'What about the old Bill though, Mickey? They're in on it, ain't they?'

'Yep. Right up to their shitty little necks. All the more reason to get rid of them. People get jumpy.' He shrugged his shoulders as if to finish his sentence.

'Righty ho. Now who fancies a few pints?'

The four younger brothers all got up from their seats.

'No pissing it up tonight!' Michael's voice was stern. 'And, Garry, contact lenses tomorrow.'

'Don't worry, Mickey. Everything will be fine. As sweet as a nut.'

When the boys left, Maura turned to Michael. 'I ain't happy about knocking everyone off, Mickey.'

Michael sighed heavily. In his dark handmade suit and pristine white shirt he looked like a banker. Which was exactly the impression he wanted to create. In the small Portakabin they both looked out of place.

'Look, Maws, you can never leave anything to chance.' He went to her and put his arm around her shoulder, pulling her so close she could feel his breath fan her face. 'You just let me do all the worrying now. You've done your bit.'

'Once the killing starts, Mickey, we lose the protection of all our plants. You realise that, don't you?'

'Yeah, I realise that, Maws. But that Tory MP, the one soliciting in King's Cross . . . well, he's gonna be our scapegoat. The day after tomorrow the pictures we've got of him will be on their way to the gutter press. That should take most people's minds off the actual robbery for a while. Until the main shock wears off anyway.'

Maura was quiet and he took it as a sign of acquiescence. 'Come on, girl, let's get off home. We're all a bit jumpy.'

Driving home Maura was more than jumpy. She was positively terror-stricken. As she drove into her driveway she saw that all the lights were on and her heart lifted a little. Carla was here. She jumped out of the car with delight. That meant that little Joey was with her as well. She let herself into the house.

'Auntie Maura! Auntie Maura!' Four-year-old Joey ran towards her, his chubby arms outstretched.

Maura picked him up in a big hug.

'Hello, Tiger.'

She saw Carla watching them from the kitchen doorway. As always when she saw her she was overwhelmed with a feeling of love and affection. Carla looked like a young Janine, with her red-brown hair and slim figure, except Carla had something more – she had a womanly aura that Janine had never had.

'I've just made some dinner. You couldn't have timed it better.'

'What brought you here? I didn't expect you until the weekend. Not that I mind. You could move in if you wanted to, you know that.' Maura sounded almost her old self. She could kiss Carla for taking her mind off what was happening tomorrow.

Carla went quiet. Her face closed up in the way that Maura knew so well. Something wasn't right.

'What's happened?'

Carla ran her hands through her long hair in her old familiar gesture.

'Come and have dinner, Maws. I'll tell you while we eat.'

Maura followed her into the kitchen. She was frowning now. Joey was holding her tightly around the neck. In the kitchen she could smell a chicken casserole, and realised that she was in fact quite hungry. She sat at the large kitchen table and watched Carla while she worked. This was Carla all over. She would not tell Maura anything until she was good and ready. She guessed that the trouble was with Malcolm, Carla's husband. After Benny's death and Carla's rejection of Maura and Michael, they had not seen her for nearly a year. Then one day Maura had come home to find Carla sitting on her doorstep. She had had a big row with her Nana, as she called Maura's mother. Maura had immediately installed her back in her own room and all had been forgiven between them.

Then, six years ago, Carla had married Malcolm Spencer. He had been two years older than Carla at twenty-six, and for Maura at least it had been loathing on first sight. He was an architect, he was middle-class, and he was the most pompous ass that Maura had ever come across. But Carla had loved him, so she had swallowed her own reservations and countenanced the match. When Joey had been born she had nearly liked the man who was married to the most important girl in her life. She could see how pleased he was with his son and it had made him seem human somehow. Until the christening.

This had been a strained affair as her mother was there, naturally. Sarah had studiously ignored her eldest son and only daughter. That was bad enough, but then Malcolm had upset everyone there. Carla was holding the baby next to the font, everyone standing respectfully around. Carla had handed the infant to the priest and had lost her grip, only slightly. The priest had instantly taken a firm hold on the child and no harm was done. It was the kind of thing that in most families would have been considered an excuse for a joke. Brought up every now and then in family gatherings with a bit added on.

Instead, Malcolm had snatched the child from his wife, causing Carla to lose her own balance. Maura and all her brothers had stood tight-lipped until the service was finally over. There had been no enjoyment after that. Everyone had just stood patiently waiting for it to end. After the service, outside the church, there had been murder. Michael had told Malcolm in no uncertain terms that if he ever as much raised his voice to his niece, or dragged her over again, he would bury him underneath the new motorway currently being built.

Maura was sure that the incident had finally shown Malcolm what he had inadvertently married into. Since then there had been a strained truce between all parties concerned. Now here was Carla and little Joey and she would bet her last pound there was something seriously up.

She played with Joey, who had recently learnt to sing 'The Wheels on the Bus', until such time as Carla finished preparing the meal. Finally, they were all seated and eating the chicken casserole. Carla had also made duchesse potatoes and broccoli and Maura was enjoying it until Carla started telling her what had happened.

Carla and Joey were supposed to be going to the zoo with his playgroup. When Carla had driven him there, with a packed lunch and his mackintosh because the spring weather had been so uncertain, she had been told that one of the minibus drivers was ill so the trip had been cancelled. Joey was heartbroken and had refused to stay at the playgroup. So Carla had put him back in the car and instead of going to the zoo as planned, decided to take him home with her and catch up on some household chores. She guessed that Malcolm would not be too happy as he worked from home the days that Joey went to the playgroup, especially today as they were not due to come home until five o'clock.

When she had reached her house she had noticed a pink Fiesta in the drive. She had parked her own car outside on the road, thinking that someone from Malcolm's work had come round to see him. Getting Joey out of the car, she had gone around the side of the house and in the back door, reasoning that if she opened the porch door, and then the front door, she would more than likely disturb Malcolm and his guest. Inside the kitchen, she pulled off Joey's coat and wellingtons and made him a drink of orange. He sat at the table drinking it, for once quiet and still.

Putting on the kettle Carla decided to ask Malcolm and his

visitor if they wanted a cup of tea. She left the kitchen, crossed the large entrance hall and went to the door of the room that was Malcolm's office when he was home. She tapped on it and walked inside. Her mind registered the fact that the heavy brocade curtains were drawn. She had not noticed this from the front of the house as this room backed on to the rear garden. Although the room was quite dark she could see well enough. She could see that Malcolm was sitting on his office chair, and that sitting on top of him, with her blouse open exposing her breasts and her skirt pulled up to her waist, showing anyone who cared to look that she was knickerless, was Miss Bradley-Hume, Malcolm's secretary. They were unaware of her for a few seconds and Carla stood rooted to the spot watching the rise and fall of Miss Bradley-Hume's buttocks. Then Malcolm had put his head forward to kiss the woman and had seen Carla standing there. In his fright he stood upright, dropping the prim and proper Miss Bradley-Hume on to the floor. Carla was mainly aware of the fact that Miss Bradley-Hume had large, rather baggy breasts.

Then she had the woman's long mousy hair and was pulling her by it across the carpet. She could see the woman trying to free herself, clawing at Carla's hands that had her hair in a vice-like grip. Malcolm was staring at Carla absolutely shell shocked.

Giving Miss Bradley-Hume a hard kick in her stomach, she turned her attention to her husband. Seeing him standing as he was with his underpants and jeans (his designer jeans that he thought made him look so macho) around his ankles, she was finally convinced that she had married a complete and utter fool. His little skinny legs with their sparse hairs looked like a chicken's. She noticed that his member, which had never been that big to begin with, had now shrunk into a small wrinkled sausage and she had the urge to laugh. If only he could see himself! Mr Important!

Miss Bradley-Hume had picked herself up off the floor and retrieved her knickers, which were on the drawing board. She stood now, fully attired, in front of Carla.

'This is not what it looks like.' Her refined twang sent shivers of diabolical hatred through Carla's body.

'Get out of my house, you slut. You fucking filthy dirty slut!'

Miss Bradley-Hume's long horsey face dropped with shock. Carla laughed, her eyes wild.

'Oh, have I shocked you with a naughty word? Fuck . . . don't you like that word? Well, that's what you were doing, you upper-class whore. You were fucking my husband. Fucking, fucking, fucking . . .'

Malcolm shuffled across to her as quickly as his trousers would allow. She felt the stinging blow as he slapped her across the face.

Then she was calm. She watched Malcolm pull up his ridiculous jeans.

'Get out of *my* house now. Both of you.'

Miss Bradley-Hume went quickly. The change in Carla's voice was enough to send her running to her car. On her way out of the door she knocked Joey to the floor. His shocked crying penetrated Carla's rage. Going to him, she picked him up.

'All right, baby. It's nothing. Just a little accident, that's all.'

She turned back to her husband. 'I meant what I said, Malcolm. I want you out of *my* home.'

He tried to bluff his way out, his domineering personality coming to the fore.

'I will not leave this house. You're overwrought. I admit I've been a naughty boy . . .'

'Naughty boy!' Carla's voice was incredulous. 'You're a fucking cretin, Malcolm, that's what you are. And you're getting out of this house, or I'll get my uncles to move you for me!'

It was the first time she had ever threatened him with anything, let alone her uncles. Malcolm was aware that his hold over Carla was not as tight as usual. He tried a different tack.

'Will you stop using that F Word! You really are showing your working-class lineage today, aren't you?'

Carla was patting Joey's back. His sobs were quieting now as he listened to his parents' quarrel.

'I am going to Maura's, Malcolm, and when I get back from there in a few days I want you out.' Her words had a finality about them that frightened him.

'Oh, baby, I know what I've done is wrong. But she was asking for it.' His voice was wheedling. Cajoling. He needed her.

Carla laughed harshly. 'I should think she *was* asking for it. No one else but you would fuck something so ugly. Only you. We're finished, Malcolm. Finished.'

'What about Joey? I'm his father!' Malcolm was self-righteous now.

'If you do what I tell you, and get out of my life and *my* house, I may let you see him from time to time.' She was enjoying herself. Now that the initial shock had worn off, she realised that she finally had a bona fide reason to get rid of him.

'Carla, please. For all the love we've shared . . .'

'Drop dead, Malcolm.' Her voice was flat and hard. 'Come on, Joey, let's go to Auntie Maura's, shall we?'

She went from the room, across the large entrance hall and finally out of the house. Settling Joey into his car seat, she went back into the house and collected her bag and a few things. As she left for the last time Malcolm tried again.

'Please, Carla.' His voice was desperate now.

Standing on the driveway, she placed the middle finger of her right hand in the air then, gathering as much air into her lungs as possible, shouted at him: 'Rotate on it gently, arsehole!'

Then, getting into the car, she drove to Maura's.

Maura listened to Carla in amazement. She could not help picturing her dragging the woman across the carpet by her hair.

'Oh, Carla love, I'm so sorry. It must have been terrible.'

Carla smiled sheepishly.

'Stop spitting the meat out, Joey.' She looked back at Maura. 'Actually, Maws, I enjoyed every minute of it! I think I finally saw him as you all see him.'

'We've never seen him with his cacks down!'

Both women laughed. 'You know what I mean. He's a prat, Maws. A prize prat.'

Maura was serious. 'But you did love him, didn't you?'

Carla looked at little Joey. 'Yeah. I did love him in the beginning. But not any more.'

Maura carried on eating. The food was tasteless now. She was consumed with a feeling of hatred for Malcolm that made her want to go and kill him.

'Can you imagine Nana's face when she finds out I've left my lawful husband?'

Maura was cavalier. 'Oh, sod her, Carla. Let her think what she likes. You can stay here with me until we get you sorted out.'

Carla put her hand gently over Maura's.

'I know that. I'm like a bad penny, ain't I? Always turning up. My mum didn't want me. Nor my dad. And now even my husband's done the dirty on me. Maybe I do something wrong.'

'Don't be so silly!' Maura's voice was sharp. 'I'll tell you something, shall I? Once, a long time ago, I was in a similar state to you. I went to Marge's. Well, she said something that I'll never forget. She said that self-pity was a luxury none of us could afford. Those weren't her exact words, but that was what she meant. You must pick yourself up, brush yourself down . . .'

'And start all over again.' Carla sang the last sentence and they both laughed again.

'Yeah, well. That's about the strength of it.'

'In a funny way I feel free. Like I've been let out of prison after a long stretch.'

'That's good, Carla. Try to keep that feeling. It will help you over the next few weeks. And there's one other good thing. My mother won't ring you here so you can put off talking to her for as long as you want.'

285

Joey upset his beaker of milk and both women jumped up to get a cloth. Even though Carla's being there was because of trouble, Maura was glad to have her and Joey anyway. It took her mind off what was going to happen the next day. And she could not rule out the fact that it would give her a cast-iron alibi if, by any chance, the police did decide to interview her.

Chapter Twenty-Five

It was 4am on 20 March 1985. Maura and Michael were sitting in a Portakabin in a yard owned by Michael's friend, Jim Dickenson. Jim was an old lag. Throughout his life he had been put into prison for various offences, ranging from bank robbery (he got only eight years because his gun was not loaded) to extortion. He had tried to blackmail a high-powered executive who was a transvestite. On leaving jail he had approached Michael. They were friends from the Notting Hill days of Joe the Fish. He was a big powerful man and Michael had set him up in a plant hire business in Cranford. He had bought the business as a going concern and it had been put into Jim Dickenson's name. To all intents and purposes, Michael Ryan had nothing whatsoever to do with it.

The yard consisted of over four acres of land, surrounded by ten-foot fence panels and guarded by three Dobermans and a Rottweiler. This morning, though, it was empty of any life other than Michael and Maura. The dogs were shut into a pen kept especially for them. Their barking and howling was already getting on Maura's nerves.

Michael glanced at his watch. It was four minutes past the hour.

'Another ten minutes, Maws, and it will all be over.'

Maura lit yet another cigarette and tried to concentrate her mind on Carla and Joey.

Roy and Gerry were waiting at the roundabout on the Bath Road. Both were on 650cc Kawasaki motorbikes. They were dressed in black from head to foot. Gerry could feel the sweat pouring from his forehead. He was frightened, really frightened. He wished he had the guts just to start the engine and go . . . go anywhere away from here.

Roy was thinking about Janine, and Benny who was nearly ten. Where his wife had completely disowned Carla, she tried to possess the boy. He closed his eyes, trying to concentrate on the job in hand. If they went wrong now, that would be the end of them. Banged up good and proper. He felt the loose feeling in his bowels and hoped that he would not have to empty them at the roadside.

He reassured himself with the fact that this robbery had been planned down to the minutest detail. What he would not give for a fag! Just to be doing something other than waiting for the lights of the articulated lorry. He could sense the nervousness of Gerry Jackson and it made him feel worse. He breathed deeply, trying to control his heartbeats.

Garry, Leslie and Lee were in a dark blue Range Rover. All three were already wearing black balaclavas with just slits for eyeholes. Garry kept up a stream of low chatter. Leslie and Lee just grunted replies. All were nervous. Garry caressed the shotgun that he was holding. At four minutes past four they all started counting down.

These were just ten minutes until the off.

Davie Muldoon drove the container lorry with its cargo of gold towards Heathrow airport. His mind was miles away on an argument that he'd had with his wife the night before. She was a pain in the bloody neck. First she informs him that her mother's coming, yet again. Then she drops the real bombshell. She's pregnant again. Four bloody kids in five years.

She looked like something from a Hammer horror film already. She tipped the scales at just over sixteen stone! When he had first met her she had been eight stone with the best set of bristols he had ever seen. Nowadays, what with the rolls of fat and the stretch marks, it was like mounting Red Rum. But true to form she went by her old ruse. Attack was the best form of defence. Before he could comment on the fact that they could barely meet the mortgage payments as it was, without another baby to feed and clothe, she had started on about his drinking. Well, if she had a good look in the mirror she might get an inkling as to why he drank so much.

He needed at least eight pints of Hurlimans even to consider kissing the ugly bitch. He shook his head sadly as he drove along. He had been well and truly caught there. All his mates had warned him: 'Look at the mother and see the daughter, twenty years on.' He was well gutted.

The house looked like a council tip. She never cleaned up. Last night she had stood before him in all her glory. With her bleached yellow hair with the roots grown out nearly two inches she looked like a candidate for the black and white minstrel show. He grinned to himself. Her outsize nightdress had been stained with every-thing from baby puke to tea. Even her teeth were going rotten in her head. She said it was because of having the kids so quick, but he had already made a shrewd guess that not cleaning them was also a large contributory factor. The dirty bitch! He shuddered.

She was only twenty-four! What would she be like in another five years?

Joey Granger had been watching the changing expressions on his friend's face with fascination. He also had an idea what had put them there. He had met Davie's wife Leona only once and that had been enough. She had reminded him of a Rottweiler in drag. Poor old Davie, he had to be the most easy-going bloke in the world. Which was probably why she got away with so much. If she had been his wife he would have given her a good slap a long time ago.

'Light me a fag, Joey?' Davie's voice was soft.

'We're not really supposed to, you know.'

'Of course I know, but it's never stopped us before!'

Joey lit two cigarettes and passed one to Davie.

'I hate these big pulls, they make me nervous.'

Joey laughed lightly.

'Smoke your fag and calm down. There's more old Bill out there than on the Masonic Lodge's annual Beano!'

Davie smiled despite himself.

In front of the articulated lorry was a white Granada. Inside were Detective Inspector Tomlinson and three younger men, DS Milton, DC Johns and DC Llewelyn. DC Johns was what was commonly termed a chatterbox.

'So, sir, if no one knows that this gold is going to Heathrow, why so many police?' His voice was very young and very naïve and DI Tomlinson was sorry for him. Just for a second though. He had too much else on his mind.

'DC Johns?' His voice was stern.

'Yes, sir?'

'Shut your bloody trap for five minutes, and give your arse a chance!'

Llewelyn and Milton laughed softly. Johns sat silent and embarrassed. How were you to find out anything if you never asked? he reasoned.

Tomlinson was nervous, very nervous, and the younger men put it down to the seriousness of what they were doing. In fact, he was more aware of what was going on than they were or even than the Bank of England was. He had always had a passion for the horses. Over the last few years it had become an expensive passion. A passion that Michael Ryan had encouraged wholeheartedly. At this moment he could not make his mortgage payments, his car payments or, God help him, his maintenance. He was also into Michael Ryan for so much money he felt faint if he thought about the actual amount. It was his job to see that these three imbeciles bodged their job. Then he was home and dry, with all his debts paid.

The guns were still locked in the special armouries built into the dashboard in the front of the armrest in the back. He had the keys, and would take as long as he could before arming the three young cowboys in the car with him. He sneaked a look at his watch. Four minutes till the off. He was surprised to find that he was not even sweating.

Behind the articulated lorry was another unmarked car. This time it was a Sierra. A dirty brown-coloured Sierra 1600E.

Inside were DI Becton and another three young plainclothes, DS Bronte, DS Marker and WDC Williams. Becton was annoyed. He did not like the thought of a WDC in this thing at all. He also held the magic keys that would arm what were in effect little more than children. Becton, too, had to make sure that his end of the operation went wrong.

After twenty years in the police force he had finally been found out. He was married with three teenage children, a lovely wife Jeanette whom he honestly loved with all his heart, and a nice detached house in Chiswick, nearly paid for. He had only one problem and it was a big one. He had discovered many years ago that he had a penchant for very young boys. Up until now it had never interfered with what he termed his 'real life', his family and his career. Then a week ago he had been sent certain pictures of himself through the post in a plain brown envelope. There was no mistaking that it was him in the pictures. They were in glorious colour. They were also very explicit.

He had been standing in the hallway, clutching the pictures to his chest, when Jeanette had walked out there. She had looked as pretty as a picture in the early morning light, not at all like the mother of three teenaged children or like the wife of a sexual pervert, because when he had seen himself in those pictures he had realised exactly what he was. And the thought of her knowing and his children knowing had nearly brought on a heart attack.

He had telephoned the number enclosed with the picture and now sat in this car, with two young men and a lovely young lady, waiting to do something that would be a blot on their career files all their life. He glanced in the mirror and saw the meatwagon full of uniforms driving behind him. He looked at the clock on the dashboard of the Sierra. Three minutes to the off. He was trembling.

As the meatwagon passed them, Gerry and Roy started up their bikes. Gerry's took three good kicks before it roared into life.

They pulled their visors down on their helmets and nodded to one another, then they roared off behind the meatwagon. It was about two hundred yards from the roundabout. Inside the meatwagon were ten armed officers, most of them dozing. Only two were alert. One was the driver, DS Raymond Paine, and the other the controller of the radio, DS Martin Fuller. Both were unaware that they were going to be blown off the road within seconds. Outside the window, Paine could hear the dull drone of the police helicopter that was following them above. He yawned. He hated these special assignments.

Roy had already cocked his .357 Magnum. He drove parallel with the meatwagon and with one shot completely disabled the vehicle. The back tyre blew out with a ferocious bang that woke up all the sleeping officers. They woke up just in time to feel the van mounting the grass verge at the side of the road and then turn over twice before it finally came to rest on its right side, on the opposite side of the carriageway.

'Jesus Christ! Did you see that?'
    Up above in the helicopter Officer Watts and Officer Harper had seen in the dim light a bright blue flash.
    'Calling all units in the vicinity of the roundabout on the Bath Road. We have reason to believe a robbery is in progress . . .'

As the helicopter message came over the radio in Becton's car, WDC Williams answered the call. Becton and the two young men were already out of the car and going to the aid of their colleagues. WDC Williams was aware in the pandemonium that Becton had not unlocked the small arms cache. She punched the dashboard in frustration. There had been the definite sound of a shot, officers were undoubtedly injured, and they did not have so much as a lolly stick between them. It was pathetic!
    She picked up the radio handset and began to call for the fire brigade and ambulances.

DI Tomlinson had done his job properly. At least from the Ryans' point of view. As soon as the shot had been fired he had pulled the white Granada on to the side of the road. The articulated lorry had had to swerve to avoid him. It had wheezed to a stop, only to find its way immediately blocked by a Range Rover that seemed to appear from thin air.
    'It's a robbery!' DC Johns' voice was incredulous.
    Before they had even had time to answer him, two sawn-off shotguns had been pointed at the windows of the car. Within

seconds, the doors had been opened and they were all lying on the damp road with their hands handcuffed behind their backs.

Davie and Joey were sitting in the articulated lorry, dumbstruck. Then a big man in a black balaclava motioned with a large gun for them to open their doors. Before the trip they had been told not to open the specially constructed doors even if Jesus himself appeared and asked for a lift. This was all forgotten in their panic. They opened the doors and jumped from the cab.

Davie watched his lorry being driven away by two masked men.

Gerry, Leslie and Lee jumped into the Range Rover and as they screeched off saw that the police helicopter was hovering just above their heads. Leaning dangerously out of the front window, Garry, always the most adventurous of the boys, opened fire on it with his M16 rifle. He had brought it with him deliberately for this job. In the distance, on the M4, they could hear the wailing of the police and ambulance sirens. Garry's hair caught fire beneath his balaclava as the helicopter exploded. Leslie dragged him back inside the window, then helped him to put his hair out. They were laughing hysterically now. It was all over.

Back at the yard, Maura and Michael were in a state of nervous agitation. It was four-twenty-five. As if of one mind, they both left the Portakabin and stood in the yard. Just to the right of them was an enormous black hole. It was twenty-five feet deep and almost forty long. It had been dug vertically as if it was a sloping runway, which in effect it was. It was fifteen feet wide. Brother and sister walked across the gravel and opened the large iron gates.

'Mickey, I'm so scared.' Maura's voice was barely a croak.

'Ain't we all, darling?'

He smiled at her in the darkness. She could not see it but she could hear it in his voice.

Fifteen minutes later the articulated lorry drove through the gates followed by the Range Rover. The bikes had been left at the scene of the robbery.

Roy drove the lorry straight into the hole. Getting out, he and Gerry scrambled up the sloping floor.

On either side of the hole were gigantic mounds of dirt. The hole itself had been dug by a large drag line crane. It had taken nearly five hours.

Leslie, Lee, Garry and Roy all got into giant Caterpillar 'dozers. In less than an hour, they had filled the hole back in. The lorry was gone. It had disappeared off the face of the earth. It would sit under the ground for a few years until it was safe to try to shift the gold. Michael watched his brothers parking different types of plant over the burial place. It was covered with everything from dumper trucks, low loaders for cranes and the caterpillar 'dozers.

At the scene of the robbery, pandemonium was breaking out. Becton and Tomlinson were both receiving the sharp edge of Chief Superintendent Liversey's tongue. He was absolutely fuming.

'The bloody lorry has disappeared off the face of the earth. You two didn't even have the sense to arm your men!' He was spitting with temper as he spoke. 'How the hell am I supposed to explain this one away? That's what I'd like to know. If I didn't know better I'd think you were communists! You bloody fools!'

He was interrupted by an ambulanceman. 'Excuse me, sir, but there were no fatalities. I thought you would like to know. Only one major casualty and that was a gunshot wound. I gather that in the course of the van crashing, one of the men in the back inadvertently shot the fellow sitting opposite.'

'What about the helicopter pilots?'

'Burnt to death, I'm afraid.'

'Then how can you say there were no fatalities? You're all bloody fools!'

Liversey stomped away from the men. He knew this much – heads were going to roll over this and he had a feeling that his would be one of them. He would have been even more galled if he'd known that the articulated lorry that had been carrying nearly twenty million in gold bullion was buried, with the engine still hot, not two miles away.

At eight o'clock that morning, Jim Dickenson opened his yard. By eight-fifteen it was a hive of activity. He loved his plant hire firm. He loved Michael Ryan for letting him have it. By five that afternoon the newly filled-in hole was just part of the usual landscape. Not one of the men who worked there even guessed that they were walking and driving over twenty million pounds' worth of gold. Yet the robbery was to be their only topic of conversation for ages.

At six-fifteen, Maura and Michael were driving along the M4 back into London. Leslie and Garry had driven off earlier, as had Roy. Lee was to dump the Range Rover in Langley, Slough, where he had left his car. Everyone agreed it had been a good night's work. Gerry Jackson had left earlier than everyone else as he had to open the main betting shop in Wandsworth. After all, life had to go on.

Maura walked into her house in Rainham at nearly nine in the

293

morning. She was tired out. Little Joey was there to greet her and she kissed and cuddled him for a while before going up to bed. She noticed that Carla did not enquire where she had been all night. After a warm bath, she slipped naked into her bed. The coolness of the sheets was reassuring to her somehow. She had managed to talk Michael out of a killing spree, but he had still allowed Garry to shoot at the helicopter. She burrowed into her pillow. She had heard on the news that the men had been burnt to death. Both were married with children. The radio announcer's voice had been so matter-of-fact about it.

She turned over again in bed and attempted once more to get comfortable and empty her mind of all the bad things. She had too many bad things filed away. She heard Joey's joyful laughter float up the stairs and into her bedroom and the thought of the helicopter pilots' children rose up in front of her. They were small and helpless in her mind's eye. And faceless. Like her own baby which still wandered into her thinking sometimes, especially when she was done like now. The robbery itself bothered her not one iota. It was the killing. She did not think for a moment that what she had told Leslie to do to Danny Rubens counted. He was scum. He had cut up one of the girls who worked for them and he had paid the price. She could not look on the police as her brothers did, as the enemy. An omnipotent force that had to be thwarted at every turn. She did not really care about the police much, one way or the other.

Except for Terry Petherick . . . She sat up in bed and rearranged her pillows, sinking back into their coolness. If she started to think about him she would never get any sleep. She heard the bedroom door creak open.

'Are you asleep?'

Carla's voice was soft.

'No, love. Come on in.'

Carla walked into the bedroom with a glass of brandy. She went to Maura and put it on the bedside table. 'I thought you could possibly do with this. I left Joey watching a Postman Pat video, so I have a few minutes to myself.'

Maura sat up in the bed. She knew that Carla was offering her an opening, if she wanted to talk to her. And she did want to talk; she wanted to tell her how unhappy she was about all that had happened in the last twenty-four hours. But she couldn't. She picked up the glass of brandy and sipped it. Carla tried again.

'William Templeton rang last night. He wants you to call him as soon as you can. I forgot to tell you.'

'Thanks. I'll ring him later.'

'I was listening to the news just now. It seems that two of the policemen who were guarding some gold that got stolen were shot dead about half an hour ago. The police think that the raiders may have thought they could identify them.'

She watched Maura's face closely and was not surprised to see her blanch.

'A Vecton I think it was, and a Tomlinson.' Her voice trailed off as she watched Maura's features. Her aunt's mouth was moving but she seemed unable to speak.

Maura's mind was whirling. Not Vecton . . . Becton and Tomlinson. The two who were being blackmailed. She put the brandy on the bedside table and, pushing Carla away roughly, jumped out of the bed.

She practically ran to the wardrobes that covered one entire wall. They were mirrored and Maura could see the reflection of her breasts, bouncing as she ran to them. Pulling one of the doors open she started to dress herself, dragging the clothes on to her body in her haste. She pulled on a pair of jeans and a cashmere sweater, and then, pushing her bare feet into some leather moccasins, ran out of the room and down the stairs, Carla following her.

'For goodness' sake, Maura. What's up?' Carla's voice was troubled. She knew that Maura was upset over what she had said. She felt responsible.

'Nothing. I just have to see Michael, that's all.' She picked up her car keys and ran from the house to her car.

Carla went into the lounge where Joey was sitting in front of the television set, watching Postman Pat and Jess. She sat on the sofa and stared at the screen, wishing that she had kept her mouth shut.

Michael was asleep when he heard the pounding on his door. He immediately thought it was the police, and jumped out of his bed naked. Then he heard Maura calling through the letterbox.

'It's me. Let me in now!'

Thinking that something had happened he rushed to the front door and let her in. As he opened up she almost fell into his hall. Her hair was dishevelled, her face streaked with mascara. He shut the door quickly and tried to grasp hold of her. She pushed him away roughly.

'You bastard! You rotten stinking bastard!'

Michael's mouth dropped open with shock. 'What? What have I done?'

'You had those two policemen shot after you promised me . . .'

Michael yawned. 'Oh, is that all? I thought it was something important.'

His voice was low and full of sleep.

Maura stared at him in astonishment. Is that all? she thought.

That is the extent of his morality.

'I thought something had happened. Something terrible.' He walked into his bedroom and pulled on a dressing gown. She followed him and, as he turned to face her, tying the belt, launched herself at him, hair and nails flying. Her right hand dug into his face and she felt the skin tear as she scratched him deeply.

'You rotten bastard! You stinking lousy bastard!'

Within seconds he had grabbed her arms and thrown her on the bed. He held her there, with her arms pinned to her sides, while she fought him like a wildcat. Using every ounce of her strength she tried to get away from him, so she could carry on her fighting. She could hear herself spitting obscenities at him, all the bad things that she had carefully locked away over the years bubbling out of her body. Spewing out from between her lips. And still Michael held her down on the bed, his face placid and closed. Finally, after what seemed to Maura to be an eternity but was only about five minutes, the tears came. Hot gushing tears that soaked her face and hair in seconds with their salty residue. She felt the fight leave her body as if it had been exorcised.

Then Michael had her in his arms. He was stroking her hair and murmuring calming words and phrases. And Maura was aware that she was letting him. She needed him. His arms were circling her like steel bands and she knew she would forgive him anything. Had, in fact, already forgiven him for what he had done. It was herself, Maura Ryan, she would never forgive.

Michael held her until she was calm again and her crying just little hiccups. Then, pushing her away from him so he could see into her face, he spoke.

'Listen, Maws. Those police were on the take. One was a child molester. He hung around the train stations looking for little rent boys. Now I'm queer, Maws. Or gay, whatever you want to call it. But most gay men would no more touch them little boys than they would cut their own arms off. That's pervert country, Maws, where all the nice Mr Respectables in their city suits and briefcases get a quick blow job off some poor little bugger, before going home to the wife and kids and their dinner.' His voice was low and sure and hypnotic.

'As for the other one, he was more bent than a nine-bob note. His wife suffered because he was a violent wife-beater. And when he began to take his temper out on the kids, she went on the trot and divorced him. He still had an injunction order out on him, to stop him going around her house and belting her.' He watched her face for any sign that she was weakening. He did not like this Maura. A frightened, beaten Maura. She sniffed loudly and looked into his eyes.

'What . . . what . . . about the heli-helicopter pilots?' She still could not control the little heaving sobs.

'They were nothing to do with you, Maws. That was down to me and the others. All you did was help us plan it. Don't go to pieces on me, Maws. Not you. Think of them as you would a scumbag like Danny Rubens. It's Us and Them, girl, and up until now you've lived by that rule. Don't go soft on me now. You've run this firm with me for years. You've been the mainstay of it. But I could do without you, Maws, if you really wanted out.'

His soft voice had an underlying threat in it that did not go unnoticed. She swallowed deeply.

'I don't want out, Mickey.' And she didn't. It was all that she knew.

He smiled. One of his best smiles that seemed to light his face up from within.

'That's my girl.' He enfolded her in his arms again and she relaxed against him. Michael was right. In all the years she had worked for him and with him it had never seemed to bother her before. But deep, deep down in the bottom of her being she knew that the killing had always bothered her. She still woke up at nights with her body bathed in sweat, thinking about Sammy Goldbaum. She opened the little filing cabinet in her brain and once more filed all the bad things away. Until the next time she broke down.

Michael held her close and stared at the wall over her shoulder. Of all the things he had expected to come from the gold robbery, this was not one of them. He had only seen her like this once before, after Benny's death, when Sammy and Jonny had been put away. Well, he would do now what he had done then. Keep her by him. Watch over her. And hopefully snap her out of it. He kissed the top of her white-blonde head. He did love her. He loved her very much.

The Gold Bullion Robbery hit every front page, as did the killing of the policemen. Everyone was blamed from the IRA to an Italian terrorist organisation, the latter in the *Sun*'s leader, three days after the robbery. The *Guardian* called for a Government Inquiry into how such a top secret operation could have been leaked to a person or persons unknown.

The police kept a low profile. They had their suspicions as usual, but no solid evidence of any kind. Chief Superintendent Liversey was given early retirement, as were two prominent members of the board at the Bank of England. If the police had held an Internal Inquiry they might have been given to wonder how so many high-ranking officers could afford holidays in the Seychelles and the Bahamas.

The robbery was finally knocked off the front pages by a Member of Parliament. He had been secretly photographed propositioning a prostitute who worked King's Cross 'rough trade'. As usual the British public much preferred to read about a good sex scandal rather than a robbery with violence and murder. The *Daily Mirror* called for another Government Inquiry, this time into the sex lives of prominent Tory MPs. The particular MP involved remained a favourite of Michael Ryan's for some time.

Geoffrey Ryan wrote out all he had read about the robbery in the green folder. He then placed it with the file he was gathering on Maura and Michael. One day, though he did not know when that day would be, he would use it against them.

Chapter Twenty-Six

12 October 1986

Michael Ryan walked along the Embankment. He turned up his coat collar to try to warm himself. People were hurrying by. A man walked up behind him and fell into step with him.

'Mr Ryan, you're very late.' He had the soft Southern Irish drawl.

'I know. I was caught up in some last-minute work. You know how it is.'

The man, although a full head shorter than Michael, was very powerfully built. His small dark eyes continuously scanned the crowds of people as if on the look out for something or someone.

'We need to know if you can deliver, Mr Ryan. We have been waiting this last two weeks for word. That's why I arranged this meet today. Every Garda from Belfast to Liverpool is looking for me. It's only for yourself that I came out of me hiding.'

Michael took a deep breath. He was as good looking as ever and more than one woman gave him an admiring glance as they passed.

'Look, Mr O'Loughlin, these things take time. Especially now. As you just said yourself, everyone is looking for you, and the people you are likely to be dealing with as well. Christ Almighty, I'm taking as big a chance as you are! All I can tell you is what I have been telling you for days. I am doing the best that I can. Everything is shitting hot bricks at the moment.'

Patrick O'Loughlin's face hardened and he grabbed Michael's arm.

'Look here, Ryan, you have more than enough police and judges in your pocket. Rumour has it that you have more than your fair share of politicians as well. All I want is a few passports, that's all. Jesus knows, we have enough guns and Semtex to rearm the bloody British Army. But it's not guns or Semtex we're after these days. It's passports.'

'Give me another couple of days. I have a big job going on in St Martin's Wharf. I have Germans, Micks, the lot on it. I'll get you passports and perfect watertight covers. Now let's leave it there,

299

shall we? I'll be in touch in a few days. OK?'

'I don't seem to have much choice, do I?'

O'Loughlin nodded at Michael and, turning away from him, disappeared back into the crowd. As he walked away from Michael two men approached on either side of him. Too late he realised their intent. As his hand went inside his jacket for his weapon, he felt a gun being pushed into his side.

'If you try anything, Pat, I'll drop you here in the street.'

Then he was bundled into a waiting Daimler at the kerbside. As he was relieved of his gun one of the men spoke to him.

'You've been grassed, Pat, me old mate. Well and truly grassed.'

Pat O'Loughlin sat back in the seat with a show of careless indifference. Inside he was like a seething cauldron. He stared out at the passing buildings. Michael Ryan had double crossed him. Only he could have fingered him. Involuntarily he clenched his fists. Michael Ryan would pay.

Maura got out of bed still half asleep. The low buzzing of her alarm had woken her too early, or at least that was how it felt. She stood by her bed and stretched. Pulling on a robe she went downstairs to her kitchen, picking up her mail and the daily paper as she went through her hall.

She made a pot of tea and, lighting one of the sixty cigarettes she would smoke that day, unfolded the paper. Staring out at her from the front page of the *Daily Mail* was Patrick O'Loughlin. She studied the picture, stunned. Then she looked at the headlines: IRA KILLER ARRESTED. Forcing her mind to work, she read the story.

'Due to information received, Patrick O'Loughlin, wanted for the bombing of a military base in Surrey where four soldiers died, was picked up by the police as he walked on the Embankment yesterday. He is also an escaped prisoner. He was given four life sentences for sectarian killings in Belfast. The man he was seen with yesterday is still being sought by the police . . .'

Maura's mind was racing. O'Loughlin had met Mickey yesterday and any policeman worth his salt would have recognised Michael Ryan. The ones who were not in their pay tried to make their careers by nicking him. She pulled deeply on her cigarette, got up from her seat and went to the telephone on the kitchen wall. She rang Michael's number. It was answered almost immediately by his boyfriend.

'Get Mickey, now!'

'But he's in the shower . . .'

'Well, get him out then!' Her voice was harsh.

Richard Salter pursed his lips. He did not like Maura and she did not like him. Placing the receiver on the small coffee table he went into the bathroom. Michael waved him away, soap running down his body as he washed his hair.

'Mickey love, your sister's on the phone. She says she must speak to you now.'

Michael stood under the water for a couple of seconds to get rid of most of the soap. Then pulling a towel from the rail he put it around his waist, knocking Richard flying as he hurried out of the bathroom. He picked up the phone, dripping water everywhere.

'What is it, Maws?'

Richard watched as Michael's face changed from undisguised shock to seething rage. He ran back to the kitchen to finish making the breakfast. Whatever that sister of his was saying had certainly given Michael the hump! Still, he reflected as he scrambled eggs, at least *he* had not done anything wrong.

Ten minutes later, as he placed breakfast on the table, he heard the front door slam. Michael had gone without even kissing him goodbye! Richard sat at the table with his face set in a frown. Damn that bloody bitch! He looked at Michael's fluffy scrambled eggs and, smiling, picked it up and scraped it on to this own plate. Waste not, want not, that was his motto.

Michael got into his car, his mind working overtime. As he made his way through the busy morning traffic his rage subsided. Maura had said that they had to think this thing through calmly, and she was right. He had a niggling suspicion in the back of his mind about who had grassed him up. His face set into a hard frown. From what Maura had told him the paper had more or less said that whoever had been with O'Loughlin had been responsible for his being picked up. Joe Public didn't know who that was but the IRA did. And that could mean big trouble. He had been dealing with them for years.

He carried on driving out of London towards Essex. He could not understand why Maura lived in that great big house out in the sticks. He pulled into her drive and got out of the car. She already had the front door open. He kissed her on the cheek. She put her finger to her lips and he followed her through the house to her kitchen, where her daily woman, Mrs MacMullen, was pulling on her coat.

'You'll be paid for today, Mrs Mac, but I need the house to myself.'

'Oh, that's all right, lovie. I don't mind.' She smiled at the pair of them and walked out of the kitchen. They both stood silently until they heard the front door slam.

'She let herself in while I was in the shower. Sorry about that. Coffee?'

Michael nodded.

'Look, Maws, whoever fingered me was very close to home. The only ones who knew about the meet were me, you and Geoffrey.'

Maura shrugged, not taking in what he was saying. 'It could have been someone from O'Loughlin's end.'

Michael sat at the table. 'Why would one of the Micks want to set me up?'

She turned to face him. 'Well, it certainly wasn't me!' Her voice was cold.

'I know that, Princess. That leaves only one other person . . .'

When Maura realised what he was saying she began to shake her head in disbelief.

'No. Not Geoffrey. For Christ's sake, Mickey, he's our brother.'

She poured out the coffee with trembling hands.

'I think that Geoffrey has tucked me up, Maws. It's a gut feeling. He ain't been right for a long time now. Whoever grassed to the old Bill knew exactly where we were meeting, everything. I only knew an hour beforehand myself. You know I have the phones swept once a month. They're cleaner than the Russian Embassy's. No, whoever it was, was close to home. There's no doubt about that.'

'It could have come from O'Loughlin's end.' Her voice was sad. Even as she spoke she knew that Michael was right. She sat down heavily, as if very weary. 'So, Mickey, what are you going to do?'

He sipped his tea. 'What do you think? I can't let this go.'

Maura bit on her thumbnail. 'You don't know for sure yet, Mickey.'

'Listen, Maws, there's a few things that have been bothering me for a while. He asked to be put back into the clubs, didn't he? He didn't want to work with William any more. Right?'

Maura nodded her head slowly.

'Well, the takings were right down. I asked him about it and he said that all the clubs were in the same boat. Then I find out that the New Rockingham Club and the Pink Pussycat have nearly doubled their takings. So I know that he has his hand in the till. He was also seen with Old Billy Bootnose, a known nark. Richard saw them.'

Maura flapped her hand at him. 'I'm sorry, Mickey. For all Geoff's faults he ain't a grass. As for your Richard . . .'

Michael bellowed at her, 'Oh, Maws, grow up for fuck's sake! It's staring us in the face. Richard works in and around London, picking up garbage for the gossip columns. There ain't nothing that he don't know or can't find out. You might not like him but that don't alter the facts. Geoff is selling us out. Not just me. I bet you any money you like, it's you as well.'

'So what's the next step?' Her voice was small.

'Let's just say he won't be going home to dinner with that snot-nosed bird he's got himself.'

Maura gave Michael a level stare, then shook her head, 'No, Mickey. You can't! Not your own flesh and blood. For me, Mickey. For Mum. Don't do it.'

Michael placed his hand over her smaller soft one and squeezed it.

'I can't let this go, Maws.' His voice was quiet now. Final. Maura looked at him wildly, trying to think of a solution to the problem.

'Mickey, please. I'll sort this out.' She forced conviction into her voice. 'I'll get rid of him to another country. He can go to Spain, look after our holdings there. I'll sort it out with him, I swear. He'll toe the line. He must know that you've tumbled him. I'll be responsible for him.'

'All right. All right.' Michael's voice was annoyed. 'You've got twenty-four hours to get rid of him. If he's still around after that, then he's dead. You can tell him that from me. Now I have got to go and square it all with Kelly. You can bet your life they all think it was me fingered O'Loughlin.'

He stood up abruptly and Maura was reminded just how big and dangerous he could be. He kissed her on the forehead and left the house. She sat for a few minutes letting all he had said sink in. Then, lighting another cigarette, she went to the phone and called Geoffrey. Her heart was so heavy, she felt physically sick at the turn of events. If Geoffrey refused to leave the country he was a dead man.

Michael drove to Le Buxom. Although they had offices all over London, the club would always be his favourite place. He had built an empire from these tiny offices and always felt safe here. He had never enjoyed working on the building projects, always feeling more at home with the seedier businesses. To all intents and purposes they were legitimate, valid excuses for spending money. They paid tax, they paid VAT. But deep in Michael's heart it would always be the clubs, the betting offices and the robberies that were his forte. Unlike Maura, he had never lost touch with his poverty-stricken roots. He only had to close his eyes to see once more the cockroaches, the bare floors, and his mother's ever-swollen belly.

Michael wanted money that would astound the senses, money that would be a never ending pit to draw from. He wanted to be like the educated villains he had met through Templeton. He wanted to wear his riches like a cloak, he wanted to be able to buy anyone and anything that he desired. And with the gold heist and the docklands' holdings he would be able to do that. He knew that they had pulled off one of the biggest scams in the history of English crime. That the police were no nearer solving the case of the stolen gold than they were to solving the murders of Jack the Ripper. He had been secretly pleased with himself. Now Geoffrey was going to ruin that.

He had an insight into himself that would have amazed and confused his sister. He knew in his heart that Geoffrey was his Achilles heel. If he ever got caught or called in for questioning, he knew that it would be because of Geoffrey. None of the other boys would ever dream of trying to implicate him or Maura. But Geoffrey would.

In 1980 Garry had been identified at the scene of a robbery. He had appeared at the Old Bailey, accused of armed robbery. Michael had retained the best barrister in London, Douglas Denby QC. Garry had walked free, but Michael knew that if he could have been persuaded to chat to the police about his eldest brother, the boy would never even have had to go to court. Yet Michael had not been worried. He knew that even if Garry got fifteen years, he still would not open his mouth to anyone. Not so Geoffrey. Geoffrey reminded him of a snake, fooling its quarry into a false sense of security, before pouncing on it and destroying it. He had a viper in his camp and his sister could not see it. And the sad part was, Geoffrey wanted to destroy her more than he did Michael.

He parked his car. After carefully scanning the road for anything suspicious, he got out and went into the club. Gerry Jackson was there.

'Hello, Mickey!' Michael heard the pleasure in his friend's voice and was gratified. Gerry was wearing his toupee. On the night of the club bombing his hair had been burnt off and it had never grown back. During the day Gerry wore his hairpiece. He had also lost an ear, and part of his face and neck was still raised and mauve all these years later. Michael cared for Gerry as much as he did his younger brothers.

'All right, Gerry? Anyone been asking for me?' He kept his voice light.

Gerry shook his head.

'The Irish looks better. Is it a new one?' Gerry laughed at the reference to his wig. He was very good-natured despite his ferocious looks.

'Yeah. Cost me nearly two hundred quid. Real hair, see.' He took the toupee off his head and handed it to Michael who took it from him. He did not know what else to do.

'Yeah. It's lovely.' They both laughed together. For the first time in years Michael remembered them as children, playing together. Gerry's dad had been killed in the war and his mum had worked the Bayswater Road. She had brought up her six children on the proceeds of the game and National Assistance. She lived out in Enfield now, a respectable old lady who doted on her grandchildren.

Michael had a terrible feeling of foreboding as he stood with Gerry. He threw the wig back to his friend and, smiling, went up to the offices.

It took him a while to get through to Kelly. When he finally did he was not surprised to find that he was treated with the utmost suspicion.

'Look, Kelly, I was set up. I take oath on that.'

Kelly's thick Northern Irish accent crackled over the wire. 'Pat O'Loughlin was a bad man to cross, Ryan. Once they ship him back to the Maze he'll be back in the driving seat. You're a dead man.'

Kelly's voice was matter-of-fact, as if he was discussing the weather.

Michael was having difficulty in controlling his temper. The famous temper that could instil fear into the most hardened of criminals.

'I told you, it was a set up. What more do you want from me? I've been associated with your bloody organisation for nearly thirty years, mate. I was giving contributions before you was even born.'

If he told them about Geoffrey they would never trust him again, and then his brother would be dead and his mother would be heartbroken.

Kelly broke into his racing thoughts.

'We think, Mr Ryan, that you have done a deal. An hour ago Sean Murphy and Liam McNamara were picked up at another of your so-called safe houses. You're a dead man, Ryan.'

The phone went dead.

Michael sat staring at it in amazement. Murphy and McNamara! He put the phone back in its cradle. A cold sweat had broken out on his forehead. He got up from his chair and went to the drinks cabinet in the corner of the room. He poured himself a large brandy and drank it straight back. Geoffrey had done him up like a kipper. Well, he would wipe Geoffrey Ryan off the face of the earth. Sod Maura, and sod his bloody mother! He would get the word out that Geoffrey had grassed the Irishman up. That way, if the IRA got to him first, all well and good. If not, then Michael himself would blast the bastard through his guts. He could do without the Irish anyway. He phoned Maura's house. He had to let her know what was going on.

Templeton answered the phone.

'Willy?'

'Why, hello, Michael.' His voice was warm.

'Is Maws there?'

'No. She's gone to your mother's to see Geoffrey. Can I help? I said I would man the phones for her. I wanted to take her out to lunch, but you know your sister. Business first!' His tone was jocular and friendly.

Michael forced himself to laugh.

'If she comes back before I see her, will you give her a message for me? Tell her that I *must*, absolutely must, get rid of the employee we were discussing. Tell her that Kelly insisted. Got that?'

'Yes. Don't worry, I've written it down.'

'See you later then, Willy.'

''Bye, Mickey.'

So Maura had swallowed her pride and gone to their mother's house. Obviously that was where she'd tracked the little bastard down to. He must think he was safe there. The slag!

Michael pulled on his coat and left the club. It was now early afternoon and the traffic was thick. He finally drove into Lancaster Road, seething with anger. Geoffrey had tucked him up and Geoffrey would pay. He would try to get his brother to leave his mother's house, but if he wouldn't then he would drag the bastard out if need be. Fuck his mother! Fuck the lot of them! He wasn't going under for the toe rag. In his temper Michael did not notice the black Granada Scorpio that was parked opposite.

Maura had finally located Geoffrey at their mother's house. Garry had answered the telephone and she had told him not to say she had called. She had a feeling that if Geoffrey knew, he would try and get away. She had to see him before Michael did. She told Garry to keep him there until she arrived. She had parked her car in Bletchedon Street and walked around to her mother's house, in case Geoffrey had been scanning the road from the window. As she had walked up the familiar steps her heart had been hammering dangerously. She had not been to this house in over ten years. Not since the fight after Benny had been murdered. She shuddered. She did not want to see her mother and open all the old wounds, but she had to. She only hoped Geoffrey would realise that she was trying to help him.

She plucked up her courage and knocked on the door. She could hear the dull taps of her mother's shoes across the linoleum and guessed that she had come from the kitchen. The door opened and the two women came face to face for the first time in eleven years.

Maura was shocked at the sight before her. Her mother was nothing more than a fat little old lady. Her face was wrinkled up like a walnut and her hair, still in the scraped bun of old, was completely grey. Only the eyes were as she remembered them, alive with malice and triumph.

Maura realised her mother thought that she had come to beg some kind of forgiveness. Well, that was all right with her. She would play any kind of game she had to today. She knew, though, that seeing her mother meant nothing to her now.

'Hello, Mum.' She was amazed to find that her voice was normal.

Sarah's eyes swept her from head to foot. Maura was wearing a black trouser suit with a white cashmere jumper underneath. She could practically hear her mother counting up the cost in her head.

'What do you want?' Sarah's voice was flat. It was obvious to Maura that she was going to make it as hard as possible for her.

Maura walked into the house without being asked. She had to push past her mother, and was made aware of just how tiny she was.

'Is our Geoffrey here?'

As Maura spoke she walked through to the kitchen. Sarah followed her. Her mettle was up but she kept silent. There was something funny going on here. Geoffrey was like a scalded cat. Every time the phone rang or someone knocked, he nearly had a seizure. Well, she had a feeling that her daughter held the key to a mystery and for that reason, and that reason only, would stomach her presence in her house.

Maura entered the kitchen. Geoffrey and Garry were sitting at the kitchen table. Garry smiled at her, but Geoffrey looked as if he had been struck by a thunderbolt.

'Hello, Geoffrey.' She looked straight at him. The kitchen looked and felt familiar. It had not changed one iota in the last ten years.

'Can I speak to you? Alone, please.'

She saw Geoffrey's eyes go to his mother who was standing behind her. Maura nodded at Garry. Getting up from the table, he went to where his mother was standing.

'Come on, Muvver. Let's leave the lovebirds alone for a minute.'

Sarah pushed at him roughly. 'Get your bleeding hands off me! What's going on here?'

Maura turned to her mother and, grabbing her shoulders, bundled her none too gently out of the kitchen door.

'Let go of me, you bloody lanky bitch!'

'Garry, take her into the front room. Her statues are probably lonely.' Maura's voice was sarcastic. She looked closely into her

307

mother's face. 'Keep your nose out, Mum. It doesn't concern you.'

She shut the kitchen door firmly, blocking out her mother's raised voice. She could hear Garry trying to pacify her. Geoffrey was watching her warily. Maura could feel the fear emanating from him.

'Michael knows everything.'

Geoffrey dropped his gaze.

'Let's face it, Geoff, it wouldn't take long to sniff out something so putrid, would it? I've come to help you, though looking at you, I don't know why I bothered. You've got twenty-four hours to get out of the country.'

Geoffrey's head shot up. There was a peculiar light in his eyes, as scared as he was.

'I ain't going nowhere. You don't scare me.'

Maura laughed out loud. 'Oh, but I do. I scare you shitless, and so does Michael. And the mood I left him in, he'd scare the devil.'

As she spoke, she heard four loud bangs, then Geoffrey began to laugh hysterically.

Michael screeched to a halt outside his mother's house. Fiona Dalgleesh was walking her young son to the shops and was startled by the squealing of wheels. She grabbed her son's hand. Bloody lunatic drivers! She saw a large, good-looking man get out of the offending car. It was about fifteen feet away. Then, in the weak October sunshine, she saw a distinct gleam. She looked across the road to where a black car was parked and opened her eyes wide with shock. A man was sitting in the passenger seat of the car, and he had a gun! Without thinking she threw her son to the pavement and lay on top of him. A piercing cry escaped from her lips.

Michael got out of the car still seething with rage. He heard the girl scream and looked in her direction. He saw her throw herself on top of a little boy. It was the last thing he was to see. A moment later a bullet entered the side of his head and splattered his brains all over the pavement.

The girl saw him crumple and fall, a bewildered expression on his face. The man with the gun then got out of his car and shot the victim three more times. Even in her shock and fear, Fiona Dalgleesh knew that those shots were unnecessary. The big, good-looking man was already dead.

As the car drove away, the road became once more quiet and residential. Only Michael's blood, running along the pavement in crimson rivulets, showed that anything was wrong.

When Maura and Garry heard the shots they both rushed from the house. Sarah followed them. Geoffrey stayed in the kitchen alone.

Suddenly the street was full of people, emerging from all the houses like ghouls. Maura ran down the steps to the pavement. She raised Michael's head and cradled it in her arms, too shocked even to cry.

Geoffrey, her mother, her brothers . . . everything was wiped from her mind. When the police and ambulance arrived they had forcibly to pull Maura from her brother's body. Her white cashmere jumper was stained with blood and particles of brain and skull. Garry stood beside her, silent and shocked. Sarah had taken one look at her eldest son lying sprawled across her daughter's lap and walked back into her house. She felt nothing.

Maura and Garry were taken to hospital suffering from shock. Maura had to be sedated. The next morning she left the hospital with William Templeton. The newspapers were in attendance. All the nationals had pictures of Maura with Templeton's arms around her. She was aware, even in her grief, that he had burnt his boats for her and she was grateful to him. He took her to her house and kept the world away from her.

She refused to speak to anyone, not even Carla or Marge or her brothers. Roy took over the reins of the business and though nothing was ever said, all the brothers wondered what had happened with Geoffrey and why, as the eldest after Michael, he had not taken over the businesses himself.

Maura had three separate interviews with the police. She told each of them the same thing. She had no idea who had been behind her brother's murder.

But she did know and she concentrated all her energy into that fact. After two weeks of seclusion Maura felt ready to face the world again. She emerged from her grief, tougher and harder than ever before. She had hatred inside her now, a great big sour-smelling hatred. And she was going to use it to her advantage. Michael was dead, but the Ryans would go on. She owed him that much.

Chapter Twenty-Seven

Maura walked into the club at nine-thirty, exactly fourteen days after Michael was murdered. Gerry Jackson went to her and put his hand on her shoulder gently.

'If you need me, Maura, just call.'

She nodded at him and walked up the stairs into the offices. The music in the club was loud and harsh. She could hear the chatter of the customers and the clink of glasses above the din.

Roy was obviously shocked to see her.

'Maws?'

'I had to get back into the world, mate. Thanks for taking over everything. I promise you won't lose by it.'

He got up from the desk, embarrassed to be caught sitting in what had been Michael's seat.

Maura waved him back. 'You don't have to move, Roy.'

He sat down again. He was shocked at the change in her. She looked old. The years had piled on her in the short time since Mickey's death. She also had a steely glint in her eyes that had not been there before. If he did not know better he would think it was Michael come back in female form.

'I've kept everything going here as best I can, like. I know that's what Mickey would have wanted.'

Maura could hear the sadness and loss in his voice. Going to where he sat, she slipped her arms around his neck.

'I miss him, Roy. It's like a physical pain at times. As if a crucial part of me is missing.'

'I know, Maws. I know.' He held her hands in his own, surprised at the gentleness in her. 'We'll find out who set him up, Maws. Don't you worry, girl.'

She sighed. She knew exactly who had set him up. She straightened up, running her hands through her hair.

'What's been happening here?'

'Oh, nothing for you to worry about, Maws.' Although she could not see Roy's face, she knew that something was up by the sound of his voice. She walked around to face him and sat opposite him on the chair by the desk.

311

'What's up?' Her voice was hard.

'Look, I'll tell you about it another time. You're in no fit state . . .'

'Cut the crap, Roy. I'm a big girl now, in case you haven't noticed. I also run this firm. I have done for nearly twenty years.' Her voice softened at the look on his face. 'You have no need to try to protect me, Roy. I can do that myself.'

'We've had aggro out on the streets. Every firm with dreams of the big time has been showing its face.'

Maura sighed heavily.

'I should have guessed that the tomb robbers would be out in force.'

'Look, Maws, it's nothing I can't handle.'

She picked up the pack of Benson and Hedges from the desk and lit one.

'I want to know what's been going on, and I want to know NOW!'

Roy just sat staring at her. Maura knew that he wanted to help her, that he wanted to do what Michael would have done. But he would never be Michael in a million years. *She* was the nearest thing to Michael Ryan. In fact, she felt as if he had entered her body and was looking out of her eyes, so strongly did she feel his presence at this moment.

'Look, Roy, I need to get back to normal. I know you all loved him, but me and Mickey . . . it was special.' Her voice was low and charged with emotion.

Roy felt choked. He looked into her ravaged face, so skilfully made up, and knew that all that she said was true. Maura and Michael had been closer than any two people he had ever known. He spoke and his words had the effect of a bomb blast on her, so great was her rage when she heard them.

'A black crew have been muscling in on the hot dogs. Yardies. They swooped on three prime sites the night Mickey died.'

Maura's voice when she finally spoke was dripping with malevolence.

'Yardies? YARDIES? I ain't trashed at the Scotland Yardies so a bunch of bloody coons won't give me any grief. I'll sort the buggers out myself. Get Gerry from downstairs and get on the phone to the other boys. We're going to have a sort out on the street. Starting with the bloody "macaroons". Now tell me *everything* that's been going on since Mickey died.'

Roy began to speak, glad in his heart that Maura had come to take over the reins. He had not done a very good job, he knew. He had wanted to but had no idea how everything was run. Maura, Mickey and Geoffrey had always been the thinkers of the family.

The rest of the boys had been the heavies. He had been impressed with Maura's acumen in the past, now he was impressed by her dogged determination to sort out all the trouble that Michael's passing had created.

Barrington Dennison was thirty years old. He stood five foot ten and, as a body builder, his shoulders and arms were huge. His biceps measured over twenty-eight inches. Barrington Dennison was proud of his physique and proud to be black. His hair, which was grown into long, fat, spiralling dreadlocks, was tied in a pony tail with a piece of spearmint green leather. The leather was the same shade as his tracksuit.

He walked with a strutting cockiness away from his BMW car. In Brixton, where he was born, the letters stood for 'Black Man's Wheels'. His current girlfriend, an eighteen-year-old blonde, was sitting in the car, smoking a joint. She was waiting for Barrington to conclude his business.

Barrington was a Yardie. He told everyone who asked that he was one. He loved it. Within hours of the news of Michael Ryan's death hitting the streets, he had taken over three sites that he had been after for a long time, believing, as many people did, that with Michael's death the streets were once more open territory. He also dealt in grass and ecstasy. And lately crack.

He looked at his watch, a brand new Rolex. It was just on eleven-fifteen and time for a pull. A 'pull' was the term used for clearing the tills on the pitches. This was done every few hours. That way, if the pitch was robbed, whoever did it would not get too big a 'wallet'.

He was unaware as he walked towards the busy pitch that he was being watched.

Maura called to him: 'Are you Barrington Dennison?' Her voice was friendly and soft.

Barrington glanced in the direction of the voice and saw a good-looking white woman standing by a Mercedes Sports. He smiled at her and was pleased to see her smiling back. 'Yo, Momma. You wantin' me, baby?'

He walked over to her, his strut even more emphasised as he realised that all the people on the hot dog pitch were watching him. A rich white bitch could only do his street credibility good. He stood in front of her, pleased as punch that he was in full view of the people on his pitch. He watched her lick her lips.

He grinned at her, showing perfect white teeth.

I have something for you, Barrington.' Her voice was caressing. She was opening her bag, a large leather shoulderbag.

'Do I know you? You sure look familiar.' He stopped talking as

313

he saw her take a length of lead piping from the enormous white leather bag. He heard her laugh.

'I'm Maura Ryan, you big, fat, bastard.'

As his mind registered her words he was held from behind. He could feel himself being dragged on to the dirty pavement, and for a second wondered if he could still be seen. Then he was being held by two large white men, and suddenly he was frightened. It had all happened too fast for his brain to react. They had got him exactly where they wanted him. He could have wept.

He saw Maura Ryan raise the piping over her head and bring it down with considerable force on his knees. The piping was twelve inches long and three inches thick. It shattered his kneecaps. He screamed. Then he felt the piping come down again and shrieked again. White hot pain was flashing behind his eyes, coming in sickening waves. He felt the arms that held him loosen their grip. Then Maura was kneeling beside him. She pulled his head up by its dreadlocks and stared into his face.

'Don't ever get ambitions again, prick. Do you hear me? Next time I'll leave you in the same state I left Danny Rubens in. Michael Ryan is dead, but I am alive and kicking and don't you ever forget that. You pass the message on to your Yardie friends.'

Barrington nodded through his agony.

Maura and the men stood up and he watched through a haze of pain as they approached the pitch. It was deserted. The two young black boys working it had run off. They had no intentions of getting involved with that type of violence. Maura and Roy secured it and left.

As Maura went to her Mercedes she passed Barrington Dennison again. She looked at his twisted legs and pain-ravaged face, and felt herself begin to buzz with excitement. She had handled that exactly as Michael would have done. He would be proud of her!

When they arrived at the other pitches, they were already deserted. Bad news travels fast on the streets.

Barrington's girlfriend was so stoned she did not even realise that anything out of the ordinary had happened until the ambulance arrived. She had been too busy listening to Bob Marley singing 'Redemption Song'.

Back at the club, Maura and the boys discussed the measures they would have to take to re-establish their superiority in London. Within a week it was done. Maura had proved herself a shrewd woman and slipped on Michael's mantle easily. When she was sure she was firmly entrenched, she turned her attention to the Irish problem and her brother Geoffrey.

Kelly was waiting for Maura in a small bedsit in Kilburn. The owner of the house was a sympathiser. There were many of them in London.

Kelly heard a car drive into the deserted street and glanced at his watch. It was just after two-fifteen. This must be Maura Ryan. He got up from his seat and went to the window. Pulling back a grubby net curtain, he watched her as she locked up her car and walked into the house. The front door was already open. He could hear her soft steps on the stairs.

He carried on looking out of the window to make certain there was no one else about. He was still not sure exactly what kind of meet this was going to be. The death of Michael Ryan must have hit her badly; he knew himself how close they had been. For his own part, Kelly had always liked and respected Maura, and enjoyed doing business with her. In the IRA there was no discrimination; women were blooded along with the men. He had met women in the cause who were much, much harder and shrewder than many of the men. He knew women who would not think twice about blowing up a school bus or shooting a pregnant woman, something that most of the so-called hard men would baulk at. But above everything else he trusted Maura Ryan, and it was for that reason, and that reason only, that he had agreed to meet her tonight.

He turned from the window as she tapped lightly on the door of the room, and let her in.

'Hello, Kelly.' Her voice was neutral.

'Maura. Please take a seat.'

As always, he was courteous. It came naturally to him where women were concerned.

Maura sat on the tiny PVC sofa and took the glass of Bushmills that Kelly offered her. He sat opposite her and smiled. He was quick to notice in the light of the naked light bulb that she smiled with her mouth but not her eyes. She was obviously still grieving. As she opened her black bag to get her cigarettes, Kelly felt a small twinge of uneasiness. Maura sensed it.

'Don't worry, Kelly, this isn't revenge time. I know exactly what happened and I want to explain it to you.'

He picked up a book of matches from the small coffee table between them and lit her cigarette for her.

'Go ahead. I'm listening.'

Maura pulled on the cigarette and blew the smoke out through her nose.

Kelly grimaced. He could stomach many things from women, but smoking was not one of them.

315

Maura breathed in deeply. When she spoke her words were hesitant and sad.

'It wasn't Mickey who grassed up O'Loughlin and the others.'

'Well, who was it then?' His voice was brisk.

Maura took a gulp of the Bushmills, its peaty tang giving her courage.

'It was my brother Geoffrey.'

Kelly digested this bit of information.

'Mickey was good to you over the years.' Her voice was full of the pain of losing him.

'Listen, Maura.' Kelly's voice was gentle. 'There was one thing Michael could never understand. In London, the Ryans are big. You own the majority of the police force. You run the main clubs. Your businesses include gambling, drinking, sex, all the things that are big money spinners. You're also involved in the building and construction games. But, you see, to us and the likes of us, you're small fry really. We're an international organisation, known and feared all over the world. We're given money by Gadaffi, Baader Meinhof, the PLO. The list is endless. All we ever gave you was our trust. And that trust was broken.'

Maura was angry. 'For God's sake, Kelly, why do you think that I'm here tonight? I want to clear Michael's name. He'd been paying into your cause since 1960. He helped you over the years more than he had to. He hid people. Got arms, Semtex. He gathered information on Members of Parliament and members of the armed forces. People whom you then blew up and killed or maimed.'

Kelly interrupted her.

'I'm not disputing all that. Michael was a good business asset over the years. Holy Jesus, we never wanted to harm him but it was the logical step to take after what happened.

'What exactly do you want here tonight? Tell me that, Maura. Michael's death is done, over with. I'm sorry we got the wrong man though that can soon be remedied. But I think that you came here tonight to ask for something. Not just to tell me that your brother Geoffrey is for the chop.'

'What I want is us all back on our old footing.'

Kelly laughed. Really laughed.

'Sure, you're a funny lass. Three of our best men are on their way to the Maze and you want us to forget all about it! Are you demented, woman?' He laughed again, wiping his eyes with the back of his hand.

Maura lit another cigarette from the butt of the previous one. She looked solemn and annoyed.

'I'm glad to think that you had such a high regard for Michael.'

Her voice dripped sarcasm. 'That he was so indispensable to you. But you see, Kelly, Michael meant everything to me. Everything. His death was not a "logical step" in my eyes. It was a brutal killing that was unnecessary. If you had waited and let us inform you of the circumstances, it could have been avoided.'

Kelly was sorry for his laughter. In his first flush of joviality he had forgotten that he was talking about this woman's kin. In the IRA you had no allegiance to family or friends. Only to the cause.

'I'm sorry. Sorry to the heart for laughing. But you do understand what I was saying?' He looked into her sad white face and was sad himself. There were many women like her who had lost their loved ones to the cause. Husbands and sons who would never be coming home again, or were rotting in the bloody Maze. He tried again.

'You realise that Geoffrey is a dead man now, don't you?'

She nodded.

'Look, Maura, I'll tell you what I'll try to do, but I can't promise anything. I'll talk to a few people for you . . . explain the situation like . . . put them straight. The fact that you sacrificed Geoffrey should tell them that you're trying to re-establish your old footing. But that's all I can do. I can't personally guarantee anything. You must understand that.'

It was all she had expected. She had at least seen the back of Geoffrey. That was her main reason for coming here. She smiled at Kelly wistfully.

'Well, I for one won't hold a grudge. I remember when my brother Benny was murdered, Michael said it was an occupational hazard. He said it could have been any one of us, and he was right. It's the price we pay for the life we lead, I suppose.'

'It's the same with us, Maura. Sure, isn't that fecking Geoffrey the foolish one? Biting the hand that feeds him. Well, in a family the size of yours, there has to be one bad apple. It's the law of averages.'

Maura shrugged.

'I suppose so. Still, he won't be around much longer.'

Kelly smiled and poured them both out another drink.

'I can guarantee that. Now drink up. You look as if you need it.'

317

Chapter Twenty-Eight

November 1986

Michael's body was being lowered into the ground. It was a freezing cold day. A fine rain had been falling all morning and overhead dark clouds were gathering for the storm that would erupt later in the afternoon. Maura was not crying. Her eyes scanned the crowd of people; over a hundred had turned out for Michael's funeral. She noticed that the hostesses were out in force. Some of them had stopped working over twenty years previously but stood now with their younger counterparts, in their smart coats and brightly made-up faces, looking genuinely sad. It pleased Maura to see them there. They remembered the strong, vibrant Michael of his youth.

Her eyes wandered to Geoffrey who was standing to the right of the grave. Maura could see he was crying, tears streaming down his face. He stood beside their mother, who was stony-faced and dry-eyed. Maura felt an urge to walk around the open grave and throw him in on top of the brother he had helped to murder. If it had not been for him, no one need be here today. Michael would be in his office as he always was, bright and early, no matter what time he had got to bed the night before. She only hoped that wherever Michael was he would see Geoffrey's death. She smiled to herself. It was to be the typical IRA assassination for informers. Kneecapped first and then a single shot to the back of the head. Ten days after the funeral, Kelly had said.

Geoffrey raised his gaze from his brother's coffin and locked eyes with his sister. He thought for one moment that she was smiling at him and smiled back at her tremulously. Then, when she dropped her eyes, he realised that the breach with Maura would never be healed. Geoffrey knew that he had opened up a can of worms that was going to be the finish of him. All his years of planning and watching and listening had been to no avail. When he had set the ball rolling for Michael's death he had regretted it almost immediately. He would give his own life now to have him back.

Maura stared into the gaping hole. Michael was down there in a wooden box and he would never be coming home. She hated Geoffrey with a vengeance now. If she had let Michael finish him when he had wanted to, maybe it could all have been avoided. If someone had told her a month ago that she would be the instigator of one of her own brothers' deaths, she would have protested vehemently. Now she could not wait for it to happen.

She saw that people were watching Geoffrey pityingly as he cried and that only made her anger more intense. She was disgusted. She turned her face away and buried it in William Templeton's coat. He held her tightly to him, murmuring into her hair.

'It's all right. Everything will be all right.'

Sarah Ryan was watching her daughter. She noticed that Carla was as usual close by her. Sarah herself had Geoffrey on the left of her and her grandson Benny on her right. She reached out her arm and placed it across her grandson's shoulders. He shrugged her off. At almost eleven years of age he thought that he was too old to be cuddled, thought that he was a man. He wished he had been allowed to stand with his father and his uncles. He had loved his Uncle Michael, and although he did not know it, was the double of him as a child. He had the same features, expressions, everything. He also had the same quirk to his nature that Michael had had. Sarah and Janine both doted on him and did not realise that he was turning into a greater misogynist by the day.

Sarah concentrated on her only daughter. She wished that she was burying *her* today. As bad as Michael had been she had preferred him to her daughter. In Sarah's mind men were a violent breed. It was a fact of life. While women should be strong but never violent.

She'd watched women brawling in the street – 'old shawlies' as the olden day Irish women had been called. Her own mother had been known as the most argumentative woman in Shepherd's Bush. But Sarah could never condone her daughter's way of life. She could not see what should have been staring her in the face: that Michael and Maura were as one, twins born years apart. She could not see that her daughter had loved her brother wholly and desperately. She could not see that Maura had been slowly dying inside since she was sixteen and had experienced the pain of rejection by Terry Petherick and the agony of having her baby scraped from her body. That all the pain and hurt had had to come out at some time. In some way Sarah herself had pushed the memory of the abortion into the back of her mind. If she ever did think about it she soothed her own guilt by telling herself that a child from her daughter's body should never have been allowed to walk the earth.

★ ★ ★

320

Terry Petherick and two other policemen were sitting in an unmarked car by the funeral cortège, jotting down the names and car numbers of everyone at the funeral that they recognised or were unsure of. From another car a police photographer was taking photos. In spite of everything, all the policemen were impressed by the number of influential people who had turned up to pay their last respects. It showed them also that Michael Ryan had had a lot of pull to get such a turn out.

The Shakespeare Set, also known as the Dear and Dahling Brigade, were all there: so-called respectable actors and actresses who lived on the fringes of the London gangster scene. There was the usual smattering of over-the-hill models, hoping to get their faces into the nationals once more and then sell their 'my nights of love with gangland murderer' story to the *News of the World*. Even though Michael Ryan was the best-known shirtlifter in the South East! Even after his death the sycophants and hangers-on were still after a little bit of reflected glory.

Terry Petherick smiled to himself. He had noticed a few back-benchers looking solemn and nervous. I wonder how much they owe? he thought to himself, and carried on scanning the mourners. A good few boxers and sports promoters were there along with some big name gangsters from Liverpool and Birmingham. They had travelled down to show their faces and offer their condolences, and also to see how the land lay. Whether there would be an opening for them now. See if the Ryan family was as strong as before. Terry counted three QCs and two judges, one of whom had been drummed out of his profession because of a penchant for rent boys and child pornography. Quite a little cache, he mused. There were the usual blaggers, mainly small-time, in catalogue suits and nervous twitches, who would relive Michael's funeral for years as the highlight of their criminal career. Give them a bit of pull if they ever got banged up again.

Then Terry saw that the funeral was now over and people were making their way to their cars. That's when he saw Maura. He felt the familiar tightening in his guts that she caused whenever he laid eyes on her. She was as lovely as ever and he relived in his mind the last night they had spent together. He was still unmarried, and it was because of this tall, stately, and utterly unscrupulous woman. He wound down the window of the car and the damp cold whipped at his face. He knew that she had seen him.

Maura was walking towards her funeral car when she saw the face of the man she had alternately loved and hated watching her. William had his arm round her waist and felt her body stiffen. He held her tighter but she pulled away from him and walked to Terry's car.

321

'Bloody hell! They won't do nothing to us, will they?'

Terry could have laughed at the fear in the young PC's voice, but was too busy watching Maura approach him. She spoke and her husky voice sent his pulses racing.

'Hello, Terry. It's been a long time.'

'Hello, Maura. Too long.' They stared at each other as if devouring one another with their eyes. The policemen and William Templeton were well aware of the spark that was flaring between them.

'I'm sorry about your brother's death.'

As Terry spoke, Garry and Leslie came over to the car, accompanied by a drunken Lee. They were all incensed at the police and press being there. Outside the graveyard was a film crew who were recording all the famous people who had turned up. Michael dead was as newsworthy as he had been alive.

Garry leaned in at Terry's open window.

'Why don't you fuck off? Mickey's dead and you lot still won't leave him alone.'

Leslie and Lee stood aggressively behind him. The atmosphere was charged with malice.

'Leave it, Garry!' Maura's voice was clipped and as hard as steel.

He faced her angrily.

'They're plainclothes filth, Maws.'

'Just shut it. I won't have any aggravation today. Now get moving. People are beginning to stare at us.'

Her voice dripped ice and Garry, Leslie and Lee were non-plussed for a moment. Lee, who was well away, did not grasp the warning in her voice. He lurched towards the car, belching loudly.

'You wankers!'

Maura grabbed his arm. Her hand was like a steel band. She spoke through gritted teeth.

'Garry, you'd better take him away from me before I get really annoyed.' She shoved Lee towards Garry and Leslie. 'I'll deal with you lot later. Now, take him and get out of my sight.'

The two men took Lee away from the car hurriedly. Maura was watching the people around her. She knew that the confrontation had not gone unnoticed. She nodded her head to Terry and walked to her own car. She was fuming inside at Lee and Garry but her own brain was telling her that she had been a fool to stop and talk to Terry in the first place. But she could not help herself. Seeing him sitting there had brought it all back, the longing and the wanting that she had suppressed for nearly all her adult life.

Sarah had witnessed Maura's talk with the police and had taken a long hard look at Terry Petherick.

He sat in the car watching Maura walk away from him. The

322

other two policemen were terrified.

'I thought we was all gonners there, sir.'

Terry dragged his eyes from Maura's retreating back and looked at the younger man.

'No. You were quite safe, son. Even the Ryans wouldn't murder in broad daylight.'

His friend, DS Cranmer, walked over from the other police car. Opening the back door of Terry's Sierra, he got inside. 'I see your old bird stopped for a chat then?'

Terry laughed. 'Get stuffed, Cranmer.'

As Cranmer chatted on Terry was wondering if he would ever live it down. It was the first thing any new officer was told when he came to Vine Street. And the funny thing was, nearly all of them were impressed by it. He shook his head at the double standards in his world.

Maura reached her waiting car amid condolences and offers of help for the future. She noticed that William had disappeared somewhere in the crowd. When she finally stepped into her car Roy was waiting inside for her as she had asked him. She settled herself and tapped on the glass screen that separated them from the driver.

He spoke to her over a microphone.

'Yes, madam.'

'Could you please take me to the Bramley Arms? We will not be going back to the house just yet.'

The driver nodded and started up the limousine, leaving St Mary's RC cemetery behind. When they arrived at the Bramley Arms a few minutes later they got out of the car and went straight into the back bar.

On the table was a bottle of Remy Martin and two glasses. Maura slipped off her black coat and gloves. Sitting at the table, she poured out two stiff drinks.

Roy sat beside her. He accepted the proffered drink and waited for her to speak.

Maura gulped at the brandy. Getting out her ever-present cigarettes she lit one, drawing the smoke deep into her lungs. Roy noticed that her hands were trembling.

'Did you notice Anthony's and Benny's graves? They look tatty. Remind me to get on to the cemetery officials.'

Roy nodded at her. He could see that she was wound up to fever pitch.

Maura looked into Roy's open face. She realised how like Michael he looked. How all the boys looked like Michael. She felt an urge to cry. Really cry. She gulped at her drink again. Seeing

323

Terry had re-opened old wounds.

'I wanted to talk to you, Roy, as the next in line in age.'

He looked shocked. 'What about our Geoff?'

Maura took a deep breath and slowly and precisely told Roy everything, glad of something to take her mind off Terry Petherick. Glad to be able to share her problem with someone . . . to be planning ahead. When she finished telling him he was white-faced and tight-lipped.

'He tucked Mickey up? That's what you're telling me, ain't it?'

Maura nodded.

'I'll kill him, Maws! I'll kill the bastard!' He raised himself out of his seat as if he was going to do it immediately. Maura grabbed his arm.

'Don't worry. As I told you just now Kelly's going to sort it out. He owes Michael that much.'

Roy sat back in his seat and wiped his hand over his face. 'I knew that something wasn't right, Maws, but I could never find out what it was. To think that Geoffrey's been waiting and planning this for years. The dirty sod!'

'Well, the only people who know about it, Roy, are you and me. And it's got to stay that way. Especially now with Mickey dying. We're going to be in the frontline.'

Roy nodded slowly.

'Why did you never tell me this before?'

Maura sighed heavily. 'When Mickey was alive we thought we had it all under control. Geoff was working for us. The friction that had occurred over the years seemed to have died down. Oh, there's lots of reasons. I never wanted Geoffrey dead. Never. Not until Michael was murdered. Christ, I even tried to save him!' Her voice broke.

Roy poured out another stiff brandy and put the glass into her hands. She took a large swallow to steady her nerves.

'So what's going to happen with the businesses now?'

'Firstly I'm going to hand over the docklands to Willy and the accountants. Willy's a partner and he's trustworthy. Then I'm going to extend all our other operations. I'm going to try to get rid of the gold bullion as well. Michael and I had a contact in the Channel Islands. He can offload the majority of it. But I'll need a number two, Roy, and that's why I am asking you. What do you say?'

'You know the answer to that, Maws.' He took her hand gently in his. 'I'll do whatever you say. I know you're the brainy one. Janine's always calling me a thicko.' He grinned.

Maura was annoyed.

'Listen, Roy, you might not have a degree but you're cute

enough. Janine should watch her trap. She's got too bloody much of it.'

'Don't worry, Maws. She don't get it all her own way. She just thinks she does.' He raised his thick black eyebrows and smiled. Maura found herself smiling with him.

Roy picked up his glass. 'Well then, girl. Here's to us!'

'To the Ryans!'

They both drank deeply, then Maura stood up unsteadily. 'We'd better get to the wake. Good grief, I'm pissed!'

'On a day like today, Maws, it's the only way to be.'

They laughed softly together. Except Maura's laughter was tinged with hysteria.

Back at Michael's flat the atmosphere was tense. Michael's boy-friend Richard was red-eyed and nervous. He had taken the death badly. About forty people had been invited back to the flat, mostly family and close friends. When Maura and Roy arrived, the first person she saw was Gerry Jackson. She went to him, the brandy making her more open than she usually was.

'You'll miss him more than anyone, Gerry. You went back a long time.'

He nodded sadly.

'Yeah, Maws. I will. You know that me mum's here? She always liked Mickey. Say hello to her for me. It would mean a lot to her.'

'I will, Gerry. She's a good woman.'

'I remember once when we was all small . . . you weren't even born then . . . me and Mickey was only about twelve. Just after the war. Well, me mum was on the "bash" then, down the Bayswater Road. I'm not ashamed of it. She fed and clothed the lot of us from her earnings. Anyway, me and Mickey was out playing and this gang of older boys came into Kensington Gardens and started taunting me about me mum. They were about sixteen and I was scared, Maws. Bloody terrified! And then Mickey started to punch the biggest one. He went garrity. And the other boys, they were frightened, see. Because even then Michael had something about him that scared people.'

His voice was low and charged with emotion. 'Did you know that he sent my old mum a ton every Christmas? Never forgot her once. A nice card and a hundred quid. I loved that man, Maura. Loved the bones of him. Whatever people might say about him.'

Maura was touched by his devotion. 'He loved you, Gerry. I know he did.'

Gerry brought out a large white handkerchief and blew his nose. His scarred face and missing ear were more noticeable than usual.

'He loved *you*, Maws. Loved you to death.'

325

She felt the large ball of tears in her throat and hurriedly excused herself. She made her way to the kitchen and got herself a drink. The kitchen worktops were piled with alcohol of every kind. Michael's boyfriend followed her in there. Looking at his white face, Maura felt sorry for him. She had never liked Richard, had never liked any of Michael's boyfriends, but seeing the grief on the man's face, she was sorry for him.

'I'll miss him, Maura. I know that people frowned on us but we loved each other in our own way.' She could see the tears shining in his eyes and suddenly wanted to escape from the flat. Run away somewhere where Michael was unknown. She fought down the feeling of panic. She was drunk, that's what was wrong with her. From the lounge she heard her father's voice starting to sing.

She patted Richard's shoulder and walked back into the lounge, holding on to her glass of brandy tightly. Her father was singing an old Irish ballad and it sounded funny with his cockney accent. She leaned against the wall and listened to the words of 'The Wild Colonial Boy'.

Maura studied her father's shrunken form. Thanks to her mother's dominance, she had hardly seen him over the years, and, looking at him as he sang, she was suddenly lonely for him. For his cuddles and his kind words. Everyone in the packed room, full of cigarette smoke and perfume, stood silently while he sang an ode to his dead boys.

Maura, along with many people in that room, blinked away tears. She decided that Michael would have approved of his father singing. Would have enjoyed it, had he been here. She sipped at her drink.

When Benjamin finished singing everyone called for another and Maura's voice was the loudest. Drinking his beer and clearing his throat, Benjamin began singing once more.

> Down in the valley, the valley so blue,
> Hang your head over . . .

Maura listened to the sad words and felt the grief inside her gradually ebbing away.

> Send it by letter, send it by mail,
> Send it by care of the Birmingham jail . . .

She knew the songs back to front. They were songs that had been sung at countless funerals over the years. Then her Auntie Nellie, an old lady now, began to sing a song that had all the older people

326

joining in. It was an old Irish rebel song and it made Maura feel sick.

The people they were singing about had murdered the man they had all come to bury, if only they knew it.

> Oh, I am a merry ploughboy,
> And I plough the fields by day,
> But I'm leaving home tomorrow morn
> To join the IRA.

Maura looked at Geoffrey, standing by their mother, and knew by his face that he was thinking the same thing as herself. Well, the same people would be getting rid of him soon and she thanked God for it.

She swallowed back the rest of the brandy, then made a decision. She was going to get Willy Templeton and she was going to take him to her house. Then she was going to have mad and passionate sex. It was the only way, to her mind, to end a day like today.

She lurched away from the wall and went to find him.

Chapter Twenty-Nine

Maura had been teaching Roy the ropes slowly over the last few months, until now, in January, he was finally getting an understanding of all the different aspects of the businesses. She had handed the docklands over the William Templeton. All she had to do there now was turn up for monthly meetings. She had found herself concentrating more and more on the family businesses as time went on – the clubs, betting shops, and the newer borderline businesses, such as the Mortgage and Investment Corporation that Michael had set up in 1984. Today she was trying to explain all this to Roy, as she wanted him to come in and take a large amount of the donkey work from her.

'The rub is, Roy, we give mortgages through our own lending company. Now the company itself has no actual investors, so we sell our clients to other companies, such as the Bank of Kuwait, et cetera. It's pretty simple really. That way we make a quick profit, and if the client gets into difficulties with their payments, then *they* can foreclose. That way *we* never have to take anyone to court. It's all out of our hands.'

'Sounds simple enough.' Roy's voice was worried and Maura guessed that he had not really grasped what she was saying.

'It is. That's the beauty of it. We advertise in the local papers, offering everything from small personal loans to remortgages. You'd be surprised at the number of people out there who want to "unlock their capital", as the advertisers put it. We offer from five to a hundred grand, secured against their properties. Even bought council houses. Literally anything. Our main aim, though, is to get the first-time buyers. We're already renting office space with a series of estate agents. That way, when people see the property they want, we're there waiting for the poor buggers. It's a doddle, Roy. You'll soon pick it up, mate.'

Roy frowned as he listened to her speak.

'And this is legal, Maws?'

His voice was sceptical and she laughed. 'Yeah, it's legal, all right. Hard as that is to believe.'

'What if they can't afford the place they want?'

'That's easily remedied. You can borrow three times your earnings, so if a youngster comes in and he earns, say, twelve grand a year, for argument's sake, then the borrower will tell him to bring in some "moody" pay slips, say one for a week when he did a load of overtime, so it looks like he earns sixteen grand a year. So instead of giving him a mortgage for thirty-six grand he gets one for forty-eight grand. I know it sounds bent, but believe me, Roy, banks and building societies do it all the time.'

'I see.'

Maura lit a cigarette and continued. 'Now about the council estates. I've extended the areas for the tally men. And that's another misnomer. The way that the law works, you can lend people money providing they buy goods from you. You can't under any circumstances offer them money straight off. What the tally men do is, they knock on someone's door and then offer them a continental quilt set at, say, two quid a week. The quilt set costs a score so you know that you have five weeks to get them to borrow off you.

'After a few weeks, the tally man then offers them a loan of maybe fifty quid, to be paid back at a fiver a week. The person takes up the offer and they get the money on the spot. They then pay back eighty quid. A clear profit of thirty quid. I know it doesn't sound much like that, but when you consider we make about three thousand loans a week it soon mounts up. Then they're offered a ton. The tally man holds out the hundred pounds and nine times out of ten the temptation is too strong. They go for it.'

'But what if they can't afford to pay the money back, Maws?'

'Then we send the big boys round. Some of the larger council estates are into us for a small fortune. And before you ask, it's perfectly legal. Getting into debt is now socially acceptable. You want that TV or video, you get it on the never-never. Big stores offer credit, everyone offers credit, it's like a public service these days. Even the social security has jumped on the band wagon. They borrow money now as well!'

Roy grinned but his big moon face was bewildered by it all. 'Can I take these files home and study them?'

'Of course you can. The sooner you learn the better.'

He picked up the files and put them into his briefcase.

'The bloke from Jersey is just about ready to shift the gold.'

'Don't you think that it's a bit quick, Maws? Michael was looking at leaving it for five or six years.'

'Well, Michael ain't here now, is he? I make the decisions and I want shot of it. The bloke's popping over at the weekend. I want you at the meet with me, OK?'

'Sure, Maws. Whatever you say.'

She went to the coffee percolator and replenished their cups. Passing one to Roy, she smiled at him sadly.

'Have you seen anything of Mother?'

Roy sipped the lukewarm liquid and shrugged.

'She was pretty cut up about Geoffrey.'

'I guessed as much.'

'Why didn't you go to the funeral, Maws?'

'Because I'm not a hypocrite, that's why. I would have spat on his grave.'

'Have the old Bill been in touch?'

Maura shook her head vigorously, sending her hair rioting around her face.

'Not so much as a hello, kiss me arse or anything. And that's just how I like it!'

'But don't you think that's strange?'

'Not really. They know that we do business with the Irish. They probably think he double crossed them or something. To be honest, I don't give a damn. If they had anything they'd be battering the door down, but I'm too wily for the old Bill. I have more plants in the police stations in London than there are in the Royal Botanical Gardens! If they walked in here now they'd find nothing. Nothing that they could nick me for. Me and Mickey only ever made one mistake and that was Geoffrey. Only you and I know the score now. Without one of us talking they ain't got nothing. So relax.'

'Well, you ain't got any worries where I'm concerned.'

'I know that, Bruv. That's why I'm trusting you with all this.'

Roy smiled at her, pleased to be so well thought of.

'Right then, Roy.' Maura checked her watch. 'I've got a meet with a firm of 'blaggers" from Liverpool. I'd better get on me way. It's ten-thirty now. If I don't leave soon I'll catch the lunchtime traffic.'

Roy stood up and stretched. 'Okey doke. Sure you don't want me to come with you?'

'No, thanks. I've been dealing with this little firm for about eight years now. They're kosher. See you later, mate.'

Roy left the house and Maura lit herself another cigarette. Roy was working out all right. He couldn't express himself very well, but he was shrewd enough. He was getting the hang of everything. She had given Leslie the betting shops for a while. He was doing a good job. Garry and Lee were finally getting their act together. They had got a bit lairy after Michael's funeral but she had nipped that in the bud. All in all, considering what had happened, things were going quite well.

331

She finished her cigarette and got ready for the meet with Tommy Rifkind. It would be the first with him since Michael's death. He had come to the funeral to pay his respects, but now Maura had to deal with him alone. For a few seconds she wondered if it was all worth it. But as usual she pushed the thought away. The least she could do was carry on, for Michael's sake. He had built this little empire up from nothing, from being a bookie's runner at barely ten to a breaker in his teens. She owed her brother this. As she owed him everything. And if he was watching over her, as she sometimes fancied that he was, she hoped that he was pleased with how she was carrying on without him.

When Maura got to the club in Dean Street, Tommy Rifkind was already inside waiting for her. She showed him up to her office immediately. Like herself he was a busy person. He had his number two with him, Joss Campion, a six feet six inch rugby player with the ugliest face Maura had ever seen. Tommy, on the other hand, was five foot eight with a slim, lithe build. He also had the darkest brown eyes that Maura had ever seen on a light-skinned man. Michael had always said that he had a touch of the tarbrush in him. Inside the office the men sat down and Maura smiled at them.

'Sorry to keep you. Get yourselves comfortable and I'll organise some coffee.'

A little while later they were all drinking hot coffee laced with brandy, Tommy's favourite. Joss Campion had poured his into his saucer and after blowing on the hot liquid loudly was now slurping it from the saucer. He was completely unaware of all the noise he was making. Maura had to bite her lip as Tommy rolled his eyes at her.

'Joss, would you rather I put the saucer on the floor for you?'

Joss hung his enormous head like a child.

'Sorry.'

'I apologise, Maura. Joss's mother never quite managed to get him completely house trained, you see.'

She laughed. 'That's all right. My brother Benny was much the same.'

'I'm glad you understand. My wife won't have him in the house.' Tommy smiled. 'Well, Maura, down to business. I have a little proposition to put to you.' She nodded. 'I've acquired some information on a bank in South London. The pull from it will be around two hundred thousand. As usual we'll give you twenty per cent, on the usual terms.'

Maura licked her lips as she thought.

'How many cars would you want?'

'Two. One a high-powered vehicle, the other a nondescript Volvo estate. You know the type of thing, a family car.'

Maura nodded. 'OK. I'll put the word out on the street. I can supply "shooters" if you need them.' Tommy shook his head. 'In that case, all I'll need is the times and the date. And I do ask that you keep the violence to a minimum. It's not just you, Tommy. I tell all "blaggers" the same thing.'

He smiled.

'This will be as sweet as a nut, as you cockneys say. You'll be given the information seven days before the off.'

'Great. That was short and sweet!'

'I try to please. By the way, I'm so sorry about Geoffrey, Maura. So soon after Michael.' He opened his arms in a gesture of helplessness.

'Yeah, well. These things happen. I'm in full control now and nothing has changed really. I'll run the streets as they've always been run. I won't take any nonsense.'

Tommy was quite aware of the underlying threat and nodded as if he was answering a question.

'I respect that, Maura, and you have nothing to worry about from me and mine.'

She laughed heartily, but when she spoke, her voice was icy cold. 'I know.'

Tommy felt a prickle of fear on the back of his neck. In Liverpool he was the Daddy. What he said invariably went. He prided himself on not being frightened of any man, yet this tall, beautiful and intelligent woman sitting opposite scared the life out of him.

He had never wondered, like many people, why Maura was not married. There were rumours that she was a lesbian, but he knew different. It was simply that the man who would take her on, her and all that she entailed, had not been born yet.

He cleared his throat.

'Did you receive the wreaths I sent?'

'Yes. Michael would have appreciated it. He always liked you, Tommy.'

'I expect you miss him.'

'Oh, yeah, I miss him.' She stood up abruptly to let him know that the meeting was over. She held out her hand and he shook it gently.

'I'll be in touch then.'

'OK.'

Joss smiled at Maura as he left and she forced herself to smile back. When they had left the office she lit herself a cigarette and, opening the drawer in her desk, took out a photo of Michael and herself. They had been having a drink in the club downstairs and Leslie had snapped them laughing together. It turned out to be a beautiful photograph and she had had it enlarged. She sat staring at Michael's handsome face. Oh, she missed him all right. Desperately.

Sarah Ryan sat at her kitchen table sipping a cup of steaming hot tea. In front of her, spread out on the table, were the papers from a file she had found in Geoffrey's old bedroom. He must have hidden them there at some point before he died. She knew that she had been meant to find them. Written in them, in Geoffrey's large bold script, was all the information he had gathered about Michael and Maura over the years. As Sarah read them a seething rage gathered inside her. Now she knew why Geoffrey was dead. Four sons she had buried, Anthony when he was no more than a baby. What was she to do with the information in front of her? She could take it to the police now and get it over with, but it incriminated all her sons, both living and dead. She had heard through the grapevine that Roy was now Maura's number two, whatever that meant. Janine had told her all about it a few days ago. She sighed. If she did take this little lot to the police, the whole family would be put behind bars.

She picked up the papers and took them upstairs to her bedroom. She hid them in her wardrobe. She would leave it for a while until she had thought it all through.

She looked out of her bedroom window and down on to the street. She saw Margaret walking along with her mother. If only Maura had turned out like her, Sarah would be a happy woman. If only she had not met up with that bloody policeman, that Terry Petherick. If she had got herself pregnant by anyone else, it would all have blown over. Then a thought struck her. That's who she could take the papers to if the day ever came when she decided to make them known to someone. She smiled to herself nastily. That would keep it in the family, so to speak. If she was going to expose her daughter, then that's who she would expose her to!

She clasped her hands together in a gesture of prayer and whispered: 'Oh, Jesus in Heaven, in the Kingdom of goodness and light, help me to make the right decision.'

There was one thing that Sarah was sure of: Maura was capable of anything, even capable of hurting her own mother if she had to . . .

Janine was sitting drinking coffee with Roy. The years had not been kind to her. She looked much older than forty-eight and her face held a permanent frown. Benny Anthony burst into the kitchen.

'Hello, Dad!' He was surprised to find his father at home and it showed in his voice.

'Hello, son.' Roy's voice was warm. 'No school then?'

'Nah. There's a teachers' strike on.'

Janine butted in to their conversation.

'Get upstairs and do some of your homework. Your dad's busy.'

Benny's face dropped.

'Oh, Mum!' He was whining. 'I hardly ever see me dad.'

Janine's voice rose in a screech. 'You do what I tell you!'

Roy cut her off. 'For crying out loud, Janine! Keep your hair on.'

She leapt from her seat. 'Oh, that's right! Shout at me in front of Benny. Go on, Roy. Turn him into an animal like you and that stinking sister of yours.'

He sighed. 'You're beginning to sound like a broken record. Do you know that? The same old shit is dug up and pulled out, day after day.'

Janine was standing in front of him. Her face was a mask of hatred.

'You won't get your claws into him.' She pointed to where Benny was standing watching the fight between his parents. 'Oh, no. Not you or that whore of a sister of yours. She's already turned my Carla against me. I'll see you both dead first!' She ended on another screech.

'Calm yourself down, you dozy bitch. You're frightening the boy.'

Janine began to laugh.

'Me! Me frighten him? That's a laugh. His father's working for the biggest whoremonger and murderess in London and you accuse *me* of frightening the boy! Are you sleeping with her, Roy? I heard that Mickey was.'

He got up from his seat and slapped her across the kitchen. She fell to the floor, a large red mark already appearing on her face. She put her hand to her cheek silently, afraid now of a Roy she did not know.

'You stinking bitch! That's the last time you badmouth me or my family. Do you hear me? How the hell have I stood you all these years, with your miserable face and your slutty ways? Well, you've ballsed yourself right up now because I'm going. I'm gonna leave you to pickle in your own juices, Janine, and I'm taking the boy with me.

'As for our Carla . . . you dumped her, darling. You dumped her on me mother. So where you got your information from I don't know. And Carla left my mother's because my mother is like you. She wants to own people and Carla won't be owned. Neither will I from now on.'

Janine slowly pulled herself up from the floor.

'You'll take my son nowhere, Roy. I mean it. I'll go to the police . . . I swear it, Roy. I'll do for you.'

He stared at her, disgusted.

'You would and all, wouldn't you?' His voice was quiet.

'Yes, I would. You'll never turn my son into a Ryan. Not in a million years. I'd see you dead first.'

Roy picked up his briefcase and walked to his son. 'Don't worry. I'll be back to see you in a few days.'

Benny was crying and threw himself at his father. 'Oh, please don't go, Dad! Don't leave me here with Mum and Nanny Ryan. I hate them . . . I hate them!'

Roy pulled the boy close and looked at his wife. 'See what you've caused, you bitch. SEE WHAT YOU'VE CAUSED!'

Janine was staring at her son as if he had grown another head. Then, forcing herself to move, she went to him and tried to pull him from his father's arms.

'No, Dad. Please! Don't leave me here with her. I want to go with you. Please, Dad. Please don't leave me here.'

As Janine tried to pull her son away from his father, Roy turned and punched her as hard as he could in the face.

'Get your bloody hands off him!' Roy was shouting again.

Janine had been knocked backwards by the force of the blow, grabbing the edge of the kitchen table to save herself from falling. Her nose was bleeding profusely and she could feel her eye beginning to swell.

'Son.' Roy shook the hysterical boy. 'I promise you that I'm not going to go anywhere. I'm gonna stay.'

Janine opened her mouth and Roy pointed at her. 'One more word out of you and I'll commit a fucking murder. Yours! I'm staying here. This is MY house! Get it? I can't leave this boy here alone with you, he hates you as much as I do. You're nothing but a silly, vindictive bitch. You move to the spare room as from tonight, and if I ever get wind that you've tried to take this boy away from me, or this house, I'll bury you.

'I should have put a stop to your gallop years ago, with your sluttish ways and your delusions of grandeur. I'm sick to death of you! So now you know.'

Roy held his son tightly. He should have put his foot down years ago. Instead he had let her have it all her own way, just to keep the peace. Well, no more.

'Come on, son. We'll go and get a McDonald's, shall we?'

Roy knew that Benny lived for McDonald's. At this moment he would have given his son anything to stop the racking sobs that were shaking his body.

He put his arm across his son's shoulders and walked from the room. Janine's face hardened. If it took her the rest of her life she would get even with him for this.

In the car, Roy let Benny's sobs subside before he spoke to him.

'I'm sorry that I hit your mum, son. I lost me temper.'

'I ha . . . hate her. I hate . . . her and Nanny Ryan.'

Roy sighed. What a state of affairs! That would teach him to break his usual habits. He had gone home for a quick coffee and five minutes' peace. Instead he had opened up a complete hornets' nest. His son hated not only his mother but his grandmother as well.

Benny sniffed and wiped his nose on his sleeve. 'I do, Dad. They never leave me alone. You're never there so you don't see them. They're both at me all the time.'

'Well, I can promise you this much, son. I'll be there for you in the future.'

Benny tried to smile. 'When I grow up, I want to be just like you, Dad.'

Roy bit his lip. Good job Janine couldn't hear him. He grinned. 'We'll see, son. We'll see.'

Chapter Thirty

'I'm telling you, Sarah, that's what happened.' Janine wiped her eyes with the back of her hand. 'He walked out with little Benny and they didn't come in till late.'

'And Roy actually raised his hand to you?'

'Yeah. Look at my face. Then when they finally came in he said that if I didn't toe the line he would take Benny and move into Maura's.' Janine was crying again.

Sarah put her arm around her shoulders. 'He didn't mean it, love.'

Janine pushed her away. 'Oh yes he did! I know he did.' She put her face into her hands. 'I have to get my Benny away from him otherwise Maura will get her claws into him and that will be that. Benny already thinks that the sun shines out of her . . .'

'Listen, Janine. For all Maura's faults, and God knows there are many, she wouldn't harm the child.'

'Not now maybe. But in the years to come, she will. She'll have him in the family business. And I couldn't stand that, Sarah. Not my Benny. My baby. He's eleven now, but what about when he's seventeen or eighteen? That's not far away, is it? First he'll go on the protection rackets. Then she'll have him in the betting shops. Then the hostess clubs. Where will it all end? I don't want my son shot like yours. Can't you see that? I don't want to be taken to the morgue to identify my son's remains.'

'Calm yourself down, Janine, that's not going to happen.'

'How do you know? You've already buried four sons!'

Sarah was silent as she digested the logic of Janine's argument. And she had to admit to herself that the girl was right. If little Benny went the same way as his father and uncles . . . And aunt. Oh, yes, she mustn't forget his aunt . . . that is what would happen.

The other boys were all living with girls. Only Leslie had married his. They would all have children, the Lord willing, and what would be the end result? They would eventually take over where their fathers left off.

'Listen, Janine. I promise you now that that will never happen to Benny. Not if I have anything to do with it.'

She made another of her famous pots of tea and finally, after calming Janine down, sent her back to her own house. Alone, Sarah thought about what Janine had said. It was odds on that Benny would eventually go into the so-called 'business'. All the grandchildren would, unless Maura and the others were stopped.

Her husband had had control of the boys when they were younger. He had taught them how to lie, cheat and steal. How to be 'hard men'. Now look where it had got them. Four of her sons had been brutally murdered. Not a day went by but she thought of them all. Even Michael, as a small boy. In her mind's eye she saw him when he was a child, when Benjamin used to take him to the bombed-out houses.

She looked around her kitchen. It was nice. Nice and clean and modern. A far cry from the days of cockroaches and squalor, when they had coats on the bed to keep them warm and only a thin stew to fill up their ever-empty bellies. Oh, they had come a long way since then, and in her own fashion she had been proud of Michael's determination to lift himself out of the slums. Until the killing had started. When Anthony had died, she had died a little bit herself. And Benny's death, her lovely, good-natured Benny who was always in trouble of some kind but always laughing . . . his death had broken her more than any of them. Then Michael, then Geoffrey. She could never allow that to happen to any of her children again. Or her grandchildren.

She got up from the table and glanced at the clock. It was just on one. She had plenty of time. Benjamin was drinking in the Kensington Park Hotel and would not be back for hours. She went to the phone in her hall and dialled the number she had taken down after Michael's funeral. She had got the number from Directory Inquiries, and now she knew why. She had taken it down for just such an occasion as this. It was the number of Vine Street Police Station.

'Good afternoon, Vine Street.' The clipped impersonal voice crackled in her ears.

'Can I speak to Detective Inspector Terry Petherick, please?' Sarah's voice was quavery and nervous.

'Who's calling?'

'I . . . I would rather not say. I . . . I have some information for him.'

'Hold the line, madam, and I'll see if he can take your call.'

The line went silent, and Sarah was beginning to wonder if she was doing the right thing when a deep male voice asked how he could help her.

Terry Petherick was putting on his sports jacket, ready to go to lunch. His friend and colleague Cranmer called to him as he was leaving the office.

'Hang on, Tel. There's a call for you. Some woman. She won't leave her name.'

Cranmer held the phone out. Terry walked across the crowded office, his heart beating fast. Surely it could not be Maura? The sensible part of his brain pooh-poohed such an idea but the illogical part hoped and prayed that it was her.

'Hello, Petherick here.'

'This is Sarah Ryan.' The second name was barely audible.

'Who?'

'Maura Ryan's mother.'

It was a Ryan but not the one he wanted.

'What can I do for you?'

'I want to see you, in private like. I have some information. You must keep this secret, though. Some of your men are on my daughter's payroll.'

Terry frowned.

'That's a very serious allegation.'

Sarah swallowed deeply and closed her eyes.

'I have certain papers in my possession that I think you would be interested in.'

'I see. So you want to meet me, is that it?'

'Yes, that's it. But you mustn't let anyone know what you're doing. Believe me when I tell you these papers could incriminate a lot of people. Do you know Regent's Park?'

'Of course.'

'I'll meet you there Saturday. In the Zoological Gardens, outside the cafeteria, at three.' Sarah replaced the receiver before he could answer. She was sweating profusely.

Terry stared at the telephone.

'Who was it?'

'Mind your own business, Cranmer!' He tried to make his voice jocular. 'I'm off for my lunch. See you later.'

As Terry left the police station and went to his car he was intrigued. What could Sarah Ryan, the well-known matriarch of the Ryan family, want with him? He knew that Geoffrey Ryan's murder was not even really under investigation. How they managed to get away with all they did was a mystery in itself . . . or was it? He had often thought that one or two of his colleagues were on the take. Not just because they had plenty of money, though that was one sign, but because the Ryans always seemed to be one step ahead of the police. He knew from experience that knowing

341

someone was guilty was one thing, proving it a different thing altogether. He was sure that the Ryans had inside information. Well, he would know when he met Sarah Ryan . . .

If only he was meeting Maura! But she had come a long, long way since the last time they had met. She was into the Ryan businesses up to her pretty little neck. They were further apart now than ever before. The word on the street was that Maura had taken over from Mickey with all guns blazing.

Suddenly he was not very hungry. All he really wanted was something that he had tasted many years ago. Like Adam and Eve, he preferred forbidden fruit.

Sarah put down the telephone and went back to her kitchen. Her heart was beating a tattoo inside her body. She had started the ball rolling, and she was glad. She would end her daughter's reign of terror. As she set about making her husband a meal, she thought again about what Janine had said and hardened her resolve. She would sacrifice her sons and her daughter if it saved at least one person from being destroyed. And if little Benny was to be saved, then she was the only one to do it.

It wasn't until much later that she remembered that the reading of Michael's will was to take place the next day, Friday.

Sarah sat in the solicitor's office with her husband. She sat well away from her only daughter and four remaining sons, as if they carried a fatal disease.

The solicitor, Derek Hattersley, was more nervous than the people in front of him. He kept having to blow his nose. This was a very difficult will. In his experience each member of a family regarded himself as the rightful chief beneficiary. He cleared his throat and began to speak.

'I must tell you all beforehand that the bulk of Mr Ryan's estate goes to just one person. He had, however, made some very substantial bequests to you all.' He smiled, trying to bring a note of lightness to the occasion. The only person to smile back was Benjamin Ryan and Derek Hattersley was aware that the man was slightly drunk.

'I'll start then.' He cleared his throat again noisily and began to read. ' "I, Michael David Ryan, being of sound mind, leave everything I own, other than the few bequests I have detailed, to my sister, Maura Ryan." '

Derek Hattersley glanced around the assembled family and was surprised to find that not one person had changed expression. All were as blank-faced as they had been when they arrived. But he reminded himself that these people were also criminals. They would not be the type to show their emotions anyway. He took a deep breath. If they wanted to fight about it, they could do it amongst themselves. He would not get involved.

' "I leave her all my properties and holdings. I also leave her two thirds of the monies in my bank account. The rest is to be shared between my mother and father and my brothers. I leave twenty thousand pounds each to my niece Carla Ryan and my nephew Benjamin Anthony Ryan. This is to be put in trust for Benjamin Anthony until he is twenty-one. Carla Ryan may have access to her money immediately. I also leave fifteen thousand pounds to my great-nephew Joseph Michael Spencer, also to be held in trust until he is twenty-one, and twenty thousand pounds to Gerry Jackson my closest friend." ' Derek Hattersley blew his nose again and looked at the people in his office.

'Mr Ryan was adamant that the will be as short as possible and in his own words. He wrote the will himself and I drafted it for him. He also left two letters to be given out on this day. I have no knowledge whatsoever of their contents.' He relaxed, feeling he had extricated himself from any tricky situation that might arise. 'The letters are addressed to his mother and his sister.' He nodded at each woman as he spoke.

Still nobody said a word. Then Sarah asked in a shaky voice, 'Where's my letter?'

'I have it here, Mrs Ryan.' He passed the long white envelope to her, and Sarah stared at her dead son's small close-knit writing.

'I want my share of his money to go to the police widows' fund.'

Roy was stunned.

'You can't do that!'

'Oh yes I can, Roy Ryan. I want none of his blood money.' She picked up her handbag and, jerking her head at her husband to follow, left the office.

Derek Hattersley blew his nose again. It was now red and shiny. He passed Maura's letter to her and she thanked him politely.

'If you would be so kind as to sign some documents . . .'

'Certainly.' Maura smiled at him.

Twenty minutes later they all left the office.

'Well, that's that then, Maws. Mickey's last will and testament.'

'Yeah, Garry. It's the final parting, ain't it?'

Leslie put his arm around her. 'Cheer up, girl. Mickey wouldn't want you moping.'

Maura tried to laugh. Leslie trying to be tactful was not a very pretty sight.

'Let's all go and have a good drink!' This from Lee.

'Sounds good to me. What about you, Maws?'

'All right then, Roy. Let's go back to the club. There we can drink for free!'

Sarah and Benjamin were in the back of a black cab. Benjamin was annoyed.

'You've got too bloody much of it, Sarah. They're your own flesh and blood, yet thanks to you I hardly ever see them nowadays.'

She crossed her arms over her chest.

'You should think yourself lucky! They're nothing but bloody criminals. Mind you, that shouldn't worry you, should it?' Her voice was sarcastic. 'You're no better. I've been on this earth for seventy years, and I've spent over fifty of them years with you. Eighteen I was when you got me pregnant, Benjamin Ryan. Eighteen! And I stuck by you, no matter what you did. I stuck by you. And for what? What? To bring a crowd of bloody hooligans into the world, that's all.'

She looked out of the taxi window at the passing people, all living lives that did not touch hers.

Benjamin scowled, his leathery old face more wrinkled than usual.

'You make me laugh with all your "holy joeing". When you was eighteen, Sarah Ryan, you was what would be termed today "a right little raver"!'

'I was not!' Sarah's voice was incredulous.

The London cabbie was listening avidly to the old people in the back of his taxi and had difficulty in keeping his face straight.

'Were so!' Benjamin's voice had the truculent note that grated on Sarah's nerves.

'Oi, mate!'

'Yeah.' The cabbie's voice was full of laughter.

'Do you know the Bramley Arms?'

'You hum it, son, and I'll play it.'

Benjamin scowled deeply at the cabbie. 'None of your sauce. Just drop me off there. You can dump her where you like.' He pointed at Sarah with his thumb, leaving her silent and tight-lipped all the way back to Notting Hill.

Once back inside her house Sarah made herself a pot of tea. Taking it into the lounge, as she now called her front room, she poured herself out a cup. Then sitting in her chair by the fire, she opened Michael's letter. Trust Benjamin not to be interested in his eldest son's last communication. All he was interested in was the money the boy left. She began to read.

344

Dear Mum,

I am writing this letter to you because I feel that there are many things that have to be said. I know that my life was not what you wanted for me, but it was the path that I chose and I do not regret one day. The only regret I have is that I loved you, Mum, and it hurt me when we fell out with one another. I understood how you felt about Benny, as I loved him as well. If you are reading this then I am with him and Anthony, and gone from your world. I want you to know that I will miss you more than anyone.

I want to ask you something, Mum. I want you to look out for our Maura. She needs you. She always has done. Since that trouble with the policeman, she has been hurting inside. I know this is true, Mum, because I have watched her. I have done all that I can for her. I now ask you to try and take her back into the arms that held her as a baby. Maura needs her mother. Please tell Dad that I loved him very much.

I will always love you, Mum, no matter what.

Michael

Sarah felt the scalding tears behind her eyelids and squeezed her eyes tightly shut to block them out. The letter in front of her was from the old Michael, the young tearaway, not the hard, embittered, bloodthirsty man that he became. She saw him as he had been the night that Maura was born, tall and strong and with his whole life in front of him.

'Oh, God. Oh, son.' She put her hand to her mouth and held it there tightly. Now the tears did break through, like a damn bursting.

'My beautiful son. Oh, God help me, I loved him so much.'

In the club Maura and her brothers were getting drunk. Good and drunk. Maura could feel the first waves of euphoria coursing through her veins, knowing that it would soon turn to maudlin sentiment.

It was a 'Michael' day. He was in the forefront of everyone's mind. Gerry Jackson had joined them and Lee was acting as bartender. Sitting in the meat seats they all drank steadily and seriously, as if by the sheer act of getting drunk they would all feel the pain of Michael's death less.

'I can remember when Mickey was working for Joe the Fish. Handsome bleeder he was then and all.'

'That's a long time ago, Gerry.' Roy's voice was unsteady.

Gerry gulped at his gin and tonic. 'Your old mum used to be really hard up them days. Everyone was. All the birds was after him but he never spent his money on them. Took it straight home to his muvver. Do you know, Maura, that he bought your communion dress from the proceeds of a robbery?'

'No, Gerry.' She smiled at him, glad to be talking about her brother.

'Oh, yeah. I remember it as clear as day. Me and him ripped off a betting shop. He was a crafty sod! Even then he was streets ahead of everyone. Joe the Fish tried to keep him in line but he couldn't. He was "ducking and diving" all the time he worked for the old git.' Gerry's voice was hard now. 'I hated that old bastard.'

'Well, Mickey didn't, did he?' Leslie was well and truly drunk otherwise he would have chosen his words more carefully. 'Mickey was knocking him off, weren't he?'

Garry turned on him. 'Shut your bloody gob!'

'Well, Mickey was queer. Mickey was as queer as a nine-bob note. As for Joe the Fish . . . that's where he got the bloody nickname! From "queer as a fish" . . .'

Leslie didn't finish because Garry punched him in the face, knocking him off his chair.

'You just shut your bloody trap up!'

'All right. Calm down.' Lee tried to pour oil on troubled waters.

'Bollocks, you! You're always sticking up for him.' Garry was belligerent when he was sober. Drunk he would fight his own finger nails.

'Shut up.' Maura's voice was low. She could not get up the enthusiasm to stop the argument.

'Look, Garry, we're here to honour Michael's name. So sit down and wrap up. If you can't take your drink, you shouldn't get drunk.'

Roy's voice was stern and authoritative. Everyone stared at him in awe. Leslie pulled himself from the floor and slumped back into his seat. Maura, through her drink-hazed mind, realised that Roy had really begun to get confidence in himself. He would be a good number two.

'When you gonna read your letter, Maws?' This from Lee, trying to change the subject.

'When I feel up to it.' She got up from her seat and made her way out to the reception area. Picking up the phone, she rang Willy at his office on St Martin's Wharf. He answered himself, which was a godsend as Maura was aware that she was having difficulty forming her words.

'Ish that you, Willy?'

'Hello, Maura.' His tone was cool. She had been seeing him less and less since the night of Michael's funeral and he didn't like it one bit. In spite of himself he thought a lot of her and it galled

346

him that she could take him or leave him as the fancy took her.

'I'm pissed.'

'What do you want me for? I'm very busy . . .'

'I've just been to the reading of Michael's will and I'm lonely and depressed.' And drunk, she thought.

'Really? So you want to see me, I take it?'

'Yeah . . . What I need at this moment is a good hard shag!'

William smiled. She certainly had a way with words. But if he went running now she would just carry on using him. On the other hand, he had finished most of his business for today and she did sound lonely and desolate. He couldn't bring himself to say 'desperate' but that's what he really meant, and deep inside he wanted Maura on any terms.

'Where can I meet you?'

'Come and get me from the club. I'll be waiting for you.'

She replaced the receiver and went back to the meat seats. The men were all friends again, talking about Michael, each trying to outdo the others with funny anecdotes. Maura sat back in her seat and picked up her replenished glass. She raised it in a silent toast to her brother.

Her last thought before she passed out was that Michael would have approved of this drinking session in his honour. When William turned up an hour later he had practically to carry her to his car.

He took her home, silently annoyed at the condition she was in. She lay across the back seat of his car snoring softly, her large breasts straining against the thin silk blouse she was wearing. He had to admit that even drunk and dishevelled she was still the sexiest woman he had ever known.

Maura woke at eleven-thirty that evening with a violent headache. She noticed that she was naked in her own bed. Slowly the events of earlier in the day came into her mind. She turned over in bed and felt someone lying beside her. It was William. She could feel that her body had been roughly mauled and guessed that he had taken advantage of her drunken state. Well, she had asked for it really. She lifted herself up gently and felt the waves of sickness assail her. She stepped gingerly from the bed, placing one foot firmly on the floor before attempting to walk in the semi-darkness to the bathroom. She could hear William's loud snores coming from the bed.

In the bathroom she looked into the mirror above the wash basin. She looked terrible. Her make-up was all over her face and her eyes were more lined than usual. She looked old. Older than her thirty-six years. She washed her face, splashing the cold liquid

347

over her face and neck to try and bring some life back to her brain. Then she remembered the letter.

She pulled on an old bathrobe that was hanging behind the bathroom door and went down to the lounge. Her bag was on the coffee table where Willy had obviously left it. Picking it up, she turned on one of the lamps by her reading chair. She settled herself down with her feet tucked up underneath her, opened the bag and took out the white envelope. She stared at Michael's closely written script for a while before she carefully ripped open the envelope and took out a single page of writing.

Hello, Maws,

If you're reading this then I'm brown bread! [He had drawn a little smiley to let her know that it was a joke.] You will already know I have left everything to you. You deserve it. It amounts to well over a million pounds. The docklands will bring in much more eventually. You have it all now. Everything.

I am writing this letter as I wanted to tell you some things that I may never have told you while I lived.

Firstly, I am heartily sorry for what happened all those years ago. I know that you loved that old Bill with all your heart and I ballsed it all up for you. I have tried to repay you for that, Maura.

Secondly, I think that you should try and marry old Templeton. If you did you would become a lady. Though you always have been in my eyes.

I love you more than you would ever think. Don't end up like me, Maws, with no home life to speak of. I admit that is the price I pay for being a homosexual.

Thirdly, try and make it up with Mother. You were very close once, and I think that deep down you both miss one another. Try and heal the breach, that's all I ask of you.

Lastly, I don't trust our Geoffrey as far as I can chuck him. He's not kosher, Maws. Put our Roy in as your number two. He's got more savvy than people give him credit for. Also try and keep an eye on the old man. Whatever happens with Mother, you was always his favourite and I know from talking to the boys that he misses you very much.

Well, that's about it, my darling. Keep this letter private as I don't want everyone knowing that I am really as soft as shit! [Another smiley.]

Look after the boys for me, and look after yourself. There's a codicil to my will that I asked old Hattersley to keep private. I have left my flat and personal belongings to Richard. We

348

have a good relationship and I want to leave him provided for.

I also left fifty grand to Save the Children. That is not to be made public in any way. I have a feeling, Maws, that I will never make 'Old Bones', as Auntie Nellie used to say, so I write new letters every year to be on the safe side.

Look after yourself, Maws.

Your loving brother,

Michael

P.S. Hattersley is as bent as a two-bob clock. I have left some papers for you that he will be holding until you have read this letter. Go and see him on the sly. It's stocks, bonds and other papers. There's also the number of my Swiss bank. They will be notified on my death that you are the new executor.

Maura stared at the letter. Trust Michael to cover all his bets. Only he would leave letters that were updated every year. She looked at the date at the top. It was written on 5 August 1986, before all the trouble with Geoffrey. She sighed. Fifty grand to Save the Children. Her eyes were misty. When they had seen pictures of the starving children on the news he had not said a word about it. Yet it had moved him enough for him to leave them fifty grand. That was the kind of gesture he would make. The papers always had him as a shady, murdering villain, and that was just how he liked it.

He knew about Geoffrey, had always known. If only she had let Michael sack him when he had wanted to maybe all this would have been avoided. She closed her eyes to stop the tears. She had done enough crying and it would not bring him back.

She opened her eyes and saw William standing in the doorway.

'My dear girl, you look absolutely scrumptious.'

She put the letter into her bag and smiled at him, a hard cynical smile that did not reach her eyes. She let her gaze roam over his body.

'You took advantage of me earlier, didn't you?' Her voice was low and husky. He nodded. 'Well, now I'm going to take advantage of you!'

William laughed, trying to imitate a cockney accent. 'Does that mean I'm gonna get a good hard shag?'

Maura placed her bag on the floor and stood up. 'Only if you're a very good boy.'

As they went back to bed together Maura prayed that William would be enough to take her mind off her troubles. Even as she thought it she knew it wouldn't happen. There was only one person who could do that, and he was as far from her grasp as the Milky Way.

Chapter Thirty-One

Saturday was cold and bleak, with a flurry of snow in the air. While Maura and William were eating a leisurely late lunch together, Sarah was sitting on a bench waiting for Terry Petherick. He arrived just after three. He smiled at her as she sat stony-faced and silent. Looking at him, she was reminded that he had fathered her first grandchild and was made aware of just how beautiful that child would have been.

'Mrs Ryan?'

Sarah nodded and he sat down beside her.

'It's cold today, isn't it?'

She nodded again.

'Would you rather we went and got a cup of coffee? Had our little chat in the warm?'

Yes. That would be better. I'm frozen to the marrow.'

Terry took her arm and led her into the cafeteria. Sitting in the warm drinking a cup of hot sweet tea, Sarah was plagued by doubts. She knew that what she was about to do would cause no end of trouble, not only for Maura but all her children.

She took a deep breath. 'If I give you the information, could you make it easier on my sons?'

'The information is mostly about Maura, I take it?'

Sarah nodded her head.

'Well, I could try. It really depends on what kind of information you give to me.'

Looking at Sarah, Terry felt like a snake in the grass. She was an old woman. She was Maura's mother. If things had worked out differently, she could have been his mother-in-law. He sipped his coffee. Her sons had beaten him nearly to death. He wondered if she knew that.

'I know many things about my daughter. My son Geoffrey, he kept names, dates, papers, that sort of thing. Going back years. I think that it was Maura who had him . . .' Her voice trailed off.

'Is that why you wanted to see me?'

Sarah gazed deeply into his eyes.

'You knew my daughter before . . . Well, before she went into the business with Michael.'

'You know about that then?'

'I knew everything. Maura was pregnant.'

Terry's eyes opened wide.

'That's impossible!'

'No, son. She was pregnant all right. That's why Michael had you so badly beaten. I took her to a back-street abortionist. She nearly died from what that bastard did to her. She was ill for a long time. It was because of the abortion that they sterilised her.' Sarah had no idea why she was telling him all this. Perhaps in her own way she wanted to make some sort of allowance for her daughter's actions. Give him some of the blame.

'I never knew. I swear to you that I never knew.'

'Oh, I know that, son. Maura told me that herself. She had gone to your flat to tell you when you finished with her. By then Michael had found out about the two of you, and the rest's history.'

Terry was reeling. Maura pregnant by him!

Sarah sipped her tea and began to talk again. Telling him everything.

'She changed then. I'm not saying it was all your fault but when she came out of the hospital she was hard. As the years went on she seemed to get harder. As if she was taking all her hurt out on the world. Whatever she may be now, before that happened to her she was a good girl. A kind girl.'

'I don't know if this will make any difference, Mrs Ryan, but I loved her.'

'I believe you did.'

'I just can't take it all in. If I had known, I would have stood by her.'

Sarah shook her head.

'You wouldn't have, son. Michael would never have let you. Even if you had left the police force, he would have hated you until the day you died. That's why I wanted to see you. In a way you're caught up in this as well. I want my grandchildren to grow up away from the taint of the Ryan name. I want them to be factory workers, road sweepers, anything! Anything but villains.'

'I understand. But you must realise that once you start something like this, it can't be stopped. There'll be no going back.'

'I know that. I've made up me mind. My children have got to be put right. Only I can do that. I made them, now I must destroy them. It's simple really. I want your help. If needs be, I'll go in the witness box.'

'No! That won't be necessary.'

352

'Listen, you, if you're worried that something might happen to me – don't be. I'm seventy years old and in all those years I've never been frightened of anything that came out of me own body.'

Sarah opened her bag and took out the file of papers that Geoffrey had left. She handed them to Terry.

'These are all that Geoffrey left. My phone number is on the outside of the file. Get in touch whenever you need me. The only thing I ask is, please try and help my boys. I know they must go away but the main one you should be after is Maura.'

She got up from her chair. Holding out her hand, she shook his. Then, nodding at him, she left.

Terry sat alone, thinking about all that had been said. Maura pregnant with his baby. He saw her as she had been that first night they had made love. Her willingness to learn from him. Her trusting eyes and soft body. He felt the burning of tears in his throat. She had been so soft then. He realised that having an abortion must have destroyed her. She loved children, they had discussed them enough times. Then he thought of the last night he had spent with her. That coming together of adults. The frenzied thrashing of their bodies. The cool musky smell of her. And she had not told him even then about the baby.

Neither of them had married. Both were put on this earth for one another, and one another only. He knew that now. He put his head into his hands.

A voice broke into his thoughts. 'Are you all right?' A short dumpy waitress stood beside him.

'Yes, thank you.'

She looked concerned about him. 'You look terrible.'

Terry stood up and threw three pound coins on to the table.

'It's nothing. Just a bit of bad news, that's all.'

He walked out into the freezing air, putting the file that Sarah had given him under his arm. He would read it later. At the moment all he wanted to do was walk and think.

Maura and William had gone back to bed. They were snuggled up together. Maura smiled at him, her first real smile for days. At last she had found someone to care for her. And he did care for her, she knew that. She would put all the bad behind her and just concentrate on the good.

She was still quite young and Michael's letter had shown her that time could run out quickly. She thought fleetingly of Terry Petherick, as she always did when she was feeling solemn. Terry Petherick was standing in Regent's Park thinking about her at the same moment.

Both began to make plans. And although Maura did not know

it, both her plans and his would one day merge with explosive consequences.

Terry was in a quandary. A week had passed since Sarah had given him the papers. He had no doubt that what Geoffrey had recorded was true. The names and dates coincided perfectly. What was worrying him was that not only were most of his colleagues on Maura's payroll, but a few of the higher ups too. His Chief Inspector for one. Armed with all this information, he was not sure who to confide in. This wasn't a case of a few bent coppers. This was more a case of a few honest men against a veritable army of policemen on the take! Whatever happened, it would burst wide open not only his friends but the whole of London's police force.

He now had documented evidence that Maura and Michael Ryan were behind the bullion robbery of '85. Geoffrey Ryan had even procured the route map that had been used. Terry was in no doubt that it was probably full of prints. He even knew who was warehousing the gold. All well and good, except how in all honesty could he break this news without letting on that the police were also involved right up to their shitty little necks?

He could have cried. In the last seven days he had looked at his friends with new eyes. Had listened to their accounts of arrests made and known deep in his heart that they were deliberately looking the other way where the Ryans were concerned. No wonder Mickey and Maura had got away with so much. They owned not only Vine Street but West End Central as well. He couldn't believe it. They had 'tags' in Brixton, Kilburn, Barking. In fact, there was not one station where they didn't have an 'ear' on the payroll.

Now he, Terry Petherick, had all the information he needed to put them away. Even the full co-operation of their mother. And his hands were tied because when the Ryan ship finally went down it would take the police force with it. It was bloody laughable! As for this Templeton . . . he was up to his neck in skulduggery of one sort or another and his family connections had kept him out of jail for years! Terry wasn't up against a few big villains, he was up against the whole bloody establishment.

He picked up the phone on his desk and dialled the number of the Special Investigations team. He would give the lot over to them. Let them have the honour of sorting it all out. He was sick to the stomach with the lot of it.

While the phone rang he doodled on his pad. It wasn't till later in the day he saw that he had drawn a heart with a dagger in it.

Superintendent Marsh was sitting staring out at the city skyline. It was dark and the lights were shining like beacons across the Thames. He had been sitting like that for nearly three hours. The information that the young DI had brought in had completely destroyed his equilibrium. He had been waiting for something like this for ten years. Now it was dropped, literally, into his lap he wasn't sure exactly what to do with it. He was waiting for his superior, who thankfully was not on the bent list, to come and talk with him. If all this information was true, and he had a sneaking suspicion that it was, all hell would be let loose and the West End police would be running on a skeleton crew. He shook his head at the enormity of what he was about to unleash, the sad part being that DI Petherick had unwittingly dug his own grave. If this hit the tabloids, no one would work with him ever again. Policemen were like doctors. They never shit on their own, no matter who the patients might be.

Terry was called at home at midnight. He was told to get dressed and meet Marsh at twelve-forty-five. As he got in his car he realised that he had started something that would have repercussions for years to come. Maura Ryan would finally be put away, but he wasn't sure it was a fair price to pay for all the trouble it was going to cause. He was even less sure an hour later when he found out exactly what was to happen.

He was sitting in a small back room in a terraced house in Wimbledon. Superintendent Marsh had been talking steadily for nearly an hour. While Marsh paused to light his cigar, Terry jumped in.

'What you're trying to say is that the people in authority will be getting off scot free?'

Marsh inhaled smoke into his lungs and coughed. Holding his hand across his mouth, he tried to explain.

'Look, son, I know how it must seem. The thing is, some of these men have been with the force for twenty years. They will retire quietly . . .'

'And get their pensions and their early retirement bonuses!' Terry's voice was disgusted. 'I can't believe my ears, Marsh. I bring you evidence of corruption on a bigger scale than anyone could ever dream of and you have the gall to sit there and tell me that the majority will be walking away completely exonerated.'

Marsh nodded.

'I know how you feel, son.'

'No, you don't! You have no idea what I am feeling at this moment. I am bitter and disgusted. These people have been collecting money from known criminals for years and they are not going to be brought to account. Whereas the little fish like Dobin will be crucified for them.'

'Listen, son . . .'

'Stop calling me fucking SON!' Terry smashed his fist on to the table in front of him. 'We're creeping around in the middle of the night like burglars. I can't believe this is happening. You tell me that bent coppers are going to walk out of their jobs without even a slap on the wrist. We are carrying on like guilty criminals, meeting in dingy little houses in the middle of the night, and the actual scumbags that we're here on account of are walking away from it all. It's not bloody on, mate.'

'Listen, Petherick. If this hits the streets we're fucked. If you want it plain then I'll give it to you plain. Can you imagine the outrage this would cause if it ever hit the tabloids? Have you thought? Our street credibility would be lower than a fucking gas meter bandit's! Think about it. We'd never live this thing down. The only way we can even begin to sort this out is internally.

'They know that they've been collared. They're leaving the force. That's all that we can do! When you get older you'll realise the sense in what I'm saying. Else all the toe rags they've put away, the rapists, muggers, murderers, would be screaming for retrials as soon as their arresting officers were nicked. We're talking too many people to let this ever get out. I know that what they're getting seems a small price to pay for their misdeeds, but believe me the other way would cost us more.'

Terry was stunned.

'What about Maura Ryan? Or is she to walk away too?'

'Don't you worry about her, we have her bang to rights.'

'Of course, let's get our priorities right, shall we? Get the real villains. Well, let me tell you something, Marsh, I think that Maura Ryan, as bad as she and her family are, is as nothing compared to the filth you're letting off so lightly. In my book a bent copper is worse than any villain.'

Marsh walked around the table and put his hand on Terry's shoulder.

'I know . . . I feel the same. I'm following orders the same as you. But the sheer magnitude of what you found out is what's stopping us making this public. Can't you see that? The force would be crucified in hours. Top men in key jobs on the take? Come on, son. It's too much.'

Terry listened to Marsh and had to agree with what he was saying. It just seemed unfair to him that so many people would walk away without so much as a stain on their character when, by rights, they should have been made to take the consequences of their actions.

'I'm still not happy. Even if this does cause trouble, surely it would be worth it? Joe Public isn't as stupid as you seem to think. I for one would much rather see justice being done than take part in something that I know is wrong.'

Marsh puffed on his cigar. His shiny bald head had a fine layer of perspiration over it. This young man was beginning to get on his nerves. The last thing the force needed at this time was a cop as honest as this one. Terry Petherick wanted to stir up a hornets' nest, and there was no way he would ever be allowed to get away with it.

'Look, go home. Sleep on it. Once you've had a chance to think about this logically you'll see it from our perspective.'

Terry got up slowly from his chair and looked into Marsh's eyes.

'Now I know why we're nicknamed the "filth".'

When Terry had left, Marsh sat back down at the table. If only everything was as easy as Petherick seemed to think it was. The nice policeman gets the naughty villains. Only in this world, most of the police were villains! Marsh let out a long drawn-out sigh. It was his job to keep Petherick's mouth shut. And that was just what he intended to do.

Terry drove home in a temper. The streets were deserted and he had an urge to drive to Fleet Street and shout his mouth off about the lot of it. He knew he wouldn't, though. He hadn't come this far in his career to blow it now. He realised that for the second time in his life he'd had to make an important decision between the force and Maura Ryan. And that for the second time the force had won.

Chapter Thirty-Two

Janine put Roy's breakfast in front of him. He began to eat. She poured herself a cup of coffee, walked out of the kitchen into the lounge and laced it with vodka. As she turned from the drinks cabinet she jumped. Standing in the doorway watching her was Roy.

'I thought you were eating your breakfast.'

He finished chewing his mouthful of food and pointed to the cup Janine had in her hand.

'Bit early even for you, ain't it?'

Janine dropped her eyes. She felt herself blushing. 'It's my life, Roy . . .'

'Well, in future, if I ain't here, you get Benny a cab to school. I don't want you wrapping your car round a lamp post with my son in it. Pissed out of your nut!'

Janine's voice rose. 'I'm not pissed!'

Roy sniffed and wiped his nose with the back of his hand. 'Not yet. You just do what I tell you. Get it?'

Janine stared at him, her face twisted with anger.

Roy bellowed at her: 'I SAID . . . GET IT?'

'Yes. I get it. I'm not deaf, you know.'

'No, darlin', not deaf. Just half pissed as usual.'

Roy walked back to the kitchen to finish his breakfast. Standing on the bottom stair in the hall watching him was Benny.

'You dropping me off at school, Dad?'

Roy nodded.

'Great. Mum's driving is getting worse.'

'In future, son, you do not get in any car with your mother, right?'

Benny shrugged his shoulders.

'Suits me, Dad.'

Janine, listening to all they said, swallowed her coffee and vodka down in two gulps and refilled her cup. Sitting on the settee she sipped the neat spirit. Slowly the tears came. Roy had taken everything away from her over the years, her self-respect and now her child. The tears came, tears of self-pity. A little while later she heard them leave the house. Benny had not even bothered to say goodbye to her.

Roy and Maura were driving out to Essex. She had an appointment with a goldsmith, Lenny Isaacs. Roy pulled up at some traffic lights and looked across at her.

'You're in a good mood today, Maws.'

She smiled at him. 'Yeah, I am actually.'

'What's brought all this fun and laughter on?'

'Nothing, you cheeky bugger. You better go, the lights have changed!'

'Oh, shit!'

A van behind started blowing its horn.

'All right. All right, I'm going. So what's the secret then, Maws. A bloke?'

'Maybe.' Maura thought of William Templeton.

'It *is* a bloke!' Roy's voice showed his surprise.

'Listen, dickhead, I'm in a good mood because I just am. That's all.'

'Women's bloody logic amazes me!'

Maura laughed at him.

'Talking of women, what's the score with Janine?'

Roy scowled.

'I thought we were talking about women. Not the monster from the black lagoon.'

'Nasty, nasty.' Maura grinned.

'Listen, Maws, Janine is getting on my nerves. She drinks like a fish.'

'Janine? She was always a teetotaller.' Maura sounded sceptical.

'Not any more. The marriage is going down the pan. Correction, *is* down the pan. We haven't slept together for over four years. If it wasn't for Benny I'd have had it on me toes ages ago.'

'How long has she been drinking?'

'The last year or so, I think. But the last few months she's been drinking quite heavily.'

'She always was a funny bird. I never liked her, I admit that. But all the same, she is your wife.'

'I tell you now, Maws, if it wasn't for Mother I'd dump the bitch. But Mother thinks the sun shines out of her arse.'

'That's a fact. Well, Roy, you know your own mind. Myself, though, I'd get shot of her, whatever the old woman thinks. Let's face it, you're the one who's got to live with her, not Mother.'

Roy nodded.

'What's the score with this Isaacs bloke?'

'Apparently he knows the big boys in Jersey. Reckons he can get

360

rid of the gold over there, and gradually it will be put on the market again. That means that the market will be flooded and the price of gold will drop, but by then we'll have made a mint, if you'll excuse the pun, and some prat will be running all over Europe counting the gold reserves. Eventually some bright spark will suss out that the missing bullion is being sold legally and it will all be hushed up. As usual. So if you want to buy any gold in the next few years, stick to South African Krugerrands!'

Roy burst out laughing.

'You're bloody mad!'

'I know . . . I know. I'm happy mad, though, that makes a difference!'

'I hope this Isaacs bloke ain't going to waffle all day. Front wheels never seem to know when to shut up. Sammy Goldbaum used to chew my ears off!'

At the mention of Sammy's name Maura felt herself go cold. She hadn't thought about him for a long time.

'Here! You all right, girl? You've gone pale.'

Maura lit a cigarette.

'Yes, I'm OK. Just felt a bit funny for a second.'

Roy realised that he shouldn't have mentioned Sammy Goldbaum. He could have kicked himself.

'I tell you what, Maws, before we go on this meet, what do you say we find a nice little pub and have a bite to eat and a drink?'

Maura knew Roy was trying to make amends and smiled at him. 'That would be great.'

Terry Petherick was called in to see Marsh. He took the seat offered to him and waited silently for his boss to tell him what was going down.

Marsh lit himself a cigar, his only extravagance. Blowing smoke across his desk, he began: 'Have you thought over what we were talking about?'

Terry nodded.

'I take it you are more amenable today?'

Terry nodded again.

'Good . . . good. We've decided that the collaring of the Ryans will be given to you. I'm sure you already know that whoever gets them has his career made. Unless, of course, you get knobbled by them first.'

Terry stared at him. He could see nothing to laugh about.

'We know that you're as straight as a die, and in view of all the information you've gathered we feel it is only fair . . .'

Terry interrupted him.

'All right. Cut the crap. What exactly's going down?'

361

Marsh had an overwhelming urge to put his cigar out in Petherick's face. Who the hell did this little shit think he was? Instead he took a deep breath and tried to control his temper.

'Yesterday Maura and Roy Ryan had a meet with a goldsmith . . . Lenny Isaacs. I had her tailed. Obviously they're going to be shifting the bullion soon. That's when we're going to pounce. Once she's nicked for that we can pile on the other charges as and when we feel like it. As I told you the other night, we have her bang to rights. We swoop when they make the exchange. It's as simple as that.

'About the other business . . . the Complaints Investigation Bureau are dealing with it internally. We're not going to approach anyone until the Ryans have been collared. That way they won't get any warnings. You and I will be working together closely on this one. You mustn't mention it to anyone. I'll see you in a few days when I have more to tell you.'

'Sarah Ryan asked me if it was possible to get the boys lighter sentences?'

Marsh smiled nastily. 'Well, there's no harm in asking, I suppose.'

When Terry had left the office Marsh sat for a while smoking his cigar. It would not do to tell Petherick that none of the Ryans could be allowed to go to prison. The Ryans were going to be wiped out. They had bought themselves too many friends in the force to be allowed to live. They had to be shut up, and shut up permanently. As Petherick would be finding out all too soon . . .

Sarah was making Benjamin's dinner. He had come in from the pub and gone straight up to bed. Said he felt tired today. Sarah was annoyed. Felt drunk more like. As she was peeling the potatoes she heard a crash from above her head and looked up at the ceiling. Nothing. She listened again. Then putting down the potato peeler, made her way up the stairs to their bedroom.

Benjamin Ryan was lying on the floor clutching his chest. One look at his face, grey and drawn, told Sarah he was very ill. She went to him and tried to lift his head from the floor.

'Benjamin!'

He opened his eyes. Sarah noticed the blue tinge around his lips.

'It's me chest, Sar. Get me a doctor. I've gotta pain in me chest . . .'

Sarah ran down the stairs and phoned an ambulance. Then she rang Janine and told her to tell the boys what had happened. Slamming down the phone, she went back upstairs and sat on the floor with her husband until the ambulance arrived.

★ ★ ★

Sarah sat in the Cardiac Care Unit with her husband until he lost consciousness. She was praying over him all day. At seven in the evening Maura and Roy turned up, both pale and worried. Janine had not thought to try to contact the other boys. Roy took his tiny mother into his arms.

'What happened, Mum?' His voice was gentle.

'It was terrible. He collapsed in the bedroom. I found him on the floor.'

'Do they know what caused it?'

'Yes. He had a coronary. He's never been ill in his life.'

'We would have been here sooner but we was out all day. You should have rung one of the other boys, not Janine. They'll be here soon.'

He was going to murder that drunken bitch when he got home. His father ill in hospital and she'd left a message at the club for him to call! Not even telling Gerry Jackson what it was all about.

'I was too scared to call anyone. I didn't want to leave your father. Look at him. He looks terrible.'

She sounded so old that Maura and Roy were suddenly reminded of the fact that their parents could die soon. That their father could be dying now.

Roy sat his mother in the chair by the bed then looked at his father's wasted body.

'I'm going to find a doctor. Maws. Look after Muvver. I'll find out what's going on.'

Maura automatically put her arm around the woman she had hardly spoken to for years. Both forgot their animosity in the light of Benjamin's illness. They were just a mother and daughter, united in their grief.

'Everything will be all right, Mum . . . I promise you.'

Sarah held Maura's hand in her own.

'Oh, Maws, he's so ill. What will I do without him?'

'Don't you worry, Mum, he'll be all right.' Maura's voice sounded much more confident than she felt.

Leslie, Garry and Lee turned up a little while later. All were sober, looking worried about their father.

Maura and Sarah stood by Benjamin's bed, the two women supporting each other as best they could. It was too soon after Michael's and Geoffrey's deaths to face another one. Though they had all treated Benjamin with scant respect and only haphazard affection over the years, now he lay ill they were all reminded of the fact that he was their father. Even a bad parent was entitled to respect on his death bed.

Carla rushed into the hospital at ten-thirty. Her long red-brown hair was blown all over the place and she had on an old coat. Even untidy, she looked lovely. She went straight to Roy. Her father held her while she cried. She was the living image of Janine, and for a second he remembered the vital woman he had married.

'How's Grandad Ryan? I was out all day with Joey. I only got the message when I came home.'

'He's very ill, Carla. But they think he could pull through.'

'Come on, Carla. Sit here beside me.'

Garry's voice was soft. Carla was like the family mascot. She sat down in the chair and he gave her a cup of coffee. Inside the room Maura and Sarah stood either side of Benjamin's bed. At ten-forty-two he opened his eyes and looked at them.

'Me two best girls. I suppose I've missed the pub?'

Looking at their anxious faces, he tried to grin.

Sarah and Maura laughed through their tears.

'Yes, Dad, you missed the pub.'

'Remember what I've always said . . . when I die, I want me ashes put in the Bramley Arms.' He closed his eyes.

Maura and Sarah finished the sentence for him: 'So you'll always be there for opening time.'

It was a saying of his they had heard all their lives.

'That's it, girls. I think I'll have another sleep now.'

He closed his eyes. When he was asleep the two women hugged one another.

'I reckon he'll be all right now, Mum.'

The nurse who was in the room and heard the exchange smiled at them.

'Why don't you all get home and get some rest? He's stable now.'

'Come on, Mum. I'll run you home.'

'No, I can't stay in that house on me own. I've never spent a night there alone since before the war.'

Maura could hear the fear in her mother's voice. 'I'll stay there with you. Don't worry. Come on, let's get you home.'

Both women kissed Benjamin and left the room.

Maura drove Sarah home a little later, amazed at the way events had brought them together as Michael had wanted.

'Sleep in my bed with me, Maws.'

'All right then, Mum.' They went up to the bedroom, both quiet and sad.

As they undressed they were both aware of the truce that had been drawn up between them. Maura knew that for the first time in years her mother needed her. She was sorry that it had taken her father's near death to achieve it.

Sarah got into her bed and watched Maura folding her clothes.

She looked at her daughter's unblemished body and beautiful profile. She would have been a fit mate for that Terry Petherick. He was one of the few men she had seen who towered over her daughter. Maura took off her bra and Sarah looked at her large firm breasts and pulled her eyes away quickly, feeling that spark of jealousy many women feel when they see their daughters' strong, taut bodies. Maura slipped into the bed beside her mother, feeling strange at the turn of events. She had rung William earlier and told him what had happened, and that she was staying the night with her mother. She knew he was miffed as he wanted her with him. They were now a real couple, making plans with each other. She had decided to give herself to him as he wanted her too. Seriously and for always.

'I'm frightened, Maws.' Sarah's voice sounded hopelessly old and tired. Maura patted her hand.

'He'll be fine, Mum.'

'I was eighteen when I married your father. My father, God rest him, had gone around to Ben's house and given him the hiding of his life. Then he had arranged the wedding. That was over fifty years ago now. And Michael had been that child. My first born son. 1935 that was. Then I had child after child. Your father. He used to joke that he only had to walk past me to get pregnant. You were me last one. Me daughter for me old age. I never really loved your father, you know, but when you spend all that time with someone, it's hard to imagine being without them. Even when they're a waster, like your father.'

'I can understand that, Mum. It's a long time.'

'It's good of you to stay with me, Maws. I know we haven't exactly seen eye to eye.'

'Look, forget that, Mum,' Maura interrupted her mother. 'We're together now. That's all that matters. That's what families are all about. Pulling together in the bad times and sharing the good.'

Not that we ever did that, Maura thought to herself.

Sarah stared into Maura's face. In the light of the bedside lamps, she looked very young and Sarah was reminded that she was the tool that was going to destroy her daughter. Whatever happened she was going to have to do that. Maura smiled at her sadly.

'Do you remember when I was a kid and I used to sleep with you when the old man was in prison? We used to have chats. That's what you always used to call them . . . chats. I wish we could turn the clock back to those days. Be like we were then.'

'So do I. But nothing can ever be the same as it was.' Sarah sounded as if she was holding back tears and Maura assumed they were for her father. She never dreamt they could be for her.

365

'I wish I had kept my baby, Mum. I still think about it sometimes.' Maura's voice was wistful.

'I wish you'd kept it and all. I wish I'd never taken you to that flat in Peckham.'

'That's all water under the bridge now, Mum. I went of my own accord.'

'No, Maws, it was me. I was scared that you'd be tied to someone you didn't love, like I was. Then, when I met Terry . . .'

'You met him? When?' Maura's voice was sharp, and Sarah realised her mistake.

'Oh, it was at the funeral. Michael's funeral. I spoke to him there.'

Maura relaxed. 'Oh, then. Yeah, our Garry had a go at him.'

Sarah swallowed deeply.

'I know. I was watching. Along with many other people.'

They were quiet for a while, both occupied with their own thoughts. Then Maura spoke softly.

'Look, Mum, let's just concentrate on getting me dad out of hospital and back home. Everything else is done. Over with.'

She nearly told her mother about William Templeton but stopped herself. She knew that her mother didn't really like him.

'Mum?' Maura's voice was quiet.

'Yes.'

'You don't regret having all us kids, do you?' Suddenly it was important that she knew the answer.

Sarah was silent for a while before answering.

'Of course not, Maws.'

As she spoke, she asked God to forgive her for lying.

Chapter Thirty-Three

February 1987

Leslie and Garry were collecting the protection money. As they pulled up outside a Greek restaurant in Ilford, Garry noticed a blue Granada parked a few cars away from them.

'Les . . . see that blue Granny? I'm sure it's been following us.'

Leslie looked at the car.

'I haven't noticed it.'

Garry got out and walked to the Granada. He tapped on the window. As it opened he leant down and looked into the car.

'What you doin' here?'

The blond man inside looked puzzled.

'I beg your pardon?'

'I said . . . what you doin' here?'

'I've come to have a meal in the restaurant. Why?'

'Nothing.'

Garry walked away from the car, still not sure what was going on. He got back in his own car beside Leslie.

'Let's sit here a minute and see if that bloke goes in the restaurant.' Sure enough, the man got out of his car and locked it up. Then he went into the restaurant.

'You wait here, Les.'

'OK.'

Garry went into the restaurant. The man from the Granada was studying a menu. Leslie walked through to the kitchen, picked up the envelope with the 'rent' in and walked back out again. As he passed the man's table he said, 'Have a nice meal.'

The blond man watched him leave. After a quick moussaka and a brandy, he paid his bill and left. He drove to the nearest phone box. He had to let Marsh know that Garry Ryan had tumbled him.

Maura and William were visiting Benjamin. He had been home from the hospital for ten days and was not taking kindly to his new regime. Not drinking, no smoking, no fats.

'Seems bloody silly living if you can't enjoy yourself.'

William smiled.

367

'Really, Mr Ryan, once you get used to the changes they won't seem so bad.'

'I dunno about that. It's easy for you to say, ain't it? You ain't been told you can't enjoy yourself no more.'

William shook his head. Benjamin Ryan was not only ignorant but stubborn. He had absolutely refused to conform to any advice that the doctors had given him.

'Nuffink but a load of bleeding foreigners. Can't understand half of wot they're waffling about. Bloody macaroons, eye ties and sodding krauts telling *me* wot to do!'

Maura laughed.

'Oh, Dad, Doctor Hummelbrunner isn't German. He's Austrian.'

'All the bleeding same if you asks me.'

'Leave him, Maura. I'll make sure he follows the doctor's orders. Now shut your trap, Benjamin Ryan, when we've got visitors. Would you like another cup of tea, Lord William?'

'I really wish you wouldn't call me that, Mrs Ryan. Willy will be quite adequate.'

Sarah smiled uneasily. She didn't like having a lord in her house. It made her uncomfortable. Where her daughter was concerned, there seemed to be nothing but trouble. Sarah had read about this Templeton in Geoffrey's papers. He was a villain. Only in Sarah's eyes he was worse than her children, because he had been given a good start in life which was more than her brood had ever had. It wasn't right . . .

Sarah was beginning to regret her newfound friendship with her daughter. She should have kept it as it was. Kept her away from the house. The trouble being she was the apple of her father's eye. She waited every day for that Petherick to call her about the papers she had given him and up till now she had heard nothing. She was beginning to wonder if she had done the right thing.

'You all right, Mum?'

Sarah looked at Maura.

'Tired, Maws, that's all. I think you two had better make a move in a minute. I want to settle your father for a nap.'

'Okey doke. I've got to meet Leslie and Garry anyway.'

William Templeton got up and placed his cup and saucer on the coffee table.

Maura went to the bed that had been put in the lounge and kissed her father goodbye.

'Take it easy, Dad, and do what Mum tells you.'

'I will, girl. See you tomorrow then.'

'Goodbye, Mr Ryan.'

'Tata, son. See you again.' He winked at William. 'Bring me a medicinal brandy next time.'

'Oh, Dad. Give it a rest, will you!'

When Maura and William had left Sarah settled Benjamin for his nap. 'Our Maura's done well for herself there, Sar. Looks like he's got a couple of bob.'

'Well, money isn't everything and I don't think our Maura's exactly hard up.'

Benjamin caught hold of her hand. 'I never give you much, did I, gel?'

She looked into his rheumy eyes.

'Well, you did your best. Now try and get yourself off to sleep. I'll call you at nine o'clock for your tablets and we'll watch a bit of telly. How's that?'

'All right, love.'

Sarah collected the used cups together and carried them out to the kitchen. As she filled the sink with hot water she looked around her, remembering the cockroaches, the empty bellies, and the years of hardship she had experienced within these walls. And she remembered Maura with her long blond hair flying behind her as she played out in the street . . . Leslie's permanently running nose. 'Silversleeves' the others had called him . . . She could almost hear Mickey's voice floating up from the basement . . .

She turned off the tap and began to wash up. In her mind's eye she could see Geoffrey on the day Maura had made her first Holy Communion. Geoffrey had been so proud of her. All the boys had been scrubbed up and taken to the church. Garry and Lee had been irritating her all that morning. Geoffrey had thumped the pair of them. She had felt so proud of them that day. She had walked, head high, with her nine children all clean and shining.

She smiled to herself. If only you had an idea what was in store for your children! All those years ago she had thought Maura would grow up, marry, and give her grandchildren. Instead, she had grown up and done the complete opposite. First thing in the morning she would phone that Petherick and see what was going on. If she had to wait much longer she'd have a heart attack herself! Once Maura was arrested she would be able to breathe freely. Whatever happened, she had to get her away from the boys. Benjamin's heart attack had shown her that they weren't getting any younger. If she was to sort her family out before she herself died, she had to do it now.

Maura and William were in Le Buxom by ten o'clock. Gerry Jackson had been in the act of throwing out a prominent Member of Parliament who had a penchant for trying to dance with the strippers when Roy had arrived. Recognising the man, Roy had taken him down to the restaurant to try to sober him up before the place got packed. He left him with one of the waitresses and went back into the club.

'That old bastard gets worse, Gerry.'

He nodded.

'He gets on my bloody nerves. He'll be on telly tomorrow or the next day telling everyone to listen to their consciences and vote for the Tory Party.'

'Mickey had the right idea, you know. He used to keep records on all the prominent citizens and use them to his advantage.'

'Yeah, I know. The West End's full of bloody Arabs at the moment. That'll cause hag, it always does. They won't go near the black birds and so the blondes will be "going case" two or three times a night, which means permanent bitching. By the way, that coon Rubber was in here earlier, selling coke. I slung him out but I thought I'd let you know. All the hostesses are as high as kites.'

'Thanks for telling me, Ger. That's all we need. Well, keep your eye on them. I don't want them fighting with the punters. They can do what they like to one another.'

Roy went back up to the offices to see Maura.

'All right, Roy?'

'Yeah, not too bad. We've got the Right Honourable Dickhead in again tonight and that bloody Rubber's been in and sold the hostesses coke. Other than that, everything's fine!'

Maura laughed.

'Send Leslie round to have a word with him. I heard through the grapevine he got a good hiding outside the Pink Pussycat last week for selling bad stuff. Tell Leslie to make it plain that this is his last warning. I don't want this place raided for drugs.'

'Okey doke. Leslie and Garry are due in shortly anyway. Actually, Garry rang in earlier. Reckons he was being followed by a bloke in a blue Granada.'

Maura rolled her eyes to the ceiling and took a deep breath. 'I don't believe him! He is so paranoid it's a joke!'

William Templeton looked at her, puzzled. 'What do you mean?'

'Oh, Will, it would take all night to explain it.'

Roy started to chuckle.

'He thinks that he's being followed all the time. We all wind him up about it. He's really paranoid.'

'Has he always been like this?'

'Since he was a kid. He told me once that when he gets really wound up he hears voices!' Roy laughed.

'Good God!'

Maura put her hand over her mouth to stifle her giggles. 'No, not God . . . more like the devil!'

370

William smiled but in fact he was disturbed.

'What did you say to him?'

'Not a lot, Maws, just the usual. That I'd phone around the Bill shops and see if they had any information. I'll tell him later it was just a mistake on his part.'

'Good. Humour him. That's the best way.'

'If you want to shoot off, Maws, I'll pick up the rents. I'm staying on here for a while anyway.'

'Thanks, Roy. That would be great. Once Les has been sent to sort out Rubber, would you ask him to pick up some parcels for me? The addresses are on this piece of paper.

'We're meeting Isaacs again on Sunday night to complete the deal, so I want you, the boys and Gerry Jackson with me. Tooled up. Sawn-offs, not handguns. OK?'

'What time?'

'We'll meet here at about five-thirty. Right then, Will, let's get going.'

He stood up.

'Would you like to go out to eat?'

'Why not?'

'See you's later then.'

When Maura and William left, Roy started going through the papers. Sunday was two days away, and he was going to wish that he had listened to Garry's story. Although none of them knew it, the net was closing.

Lenny Isaacs was sitting in his hotel room, shaking like a leaf. Terry Petherick and Superintendent Marsh were sitting opposite him.

'I swear on my mother's grave, I don't know what you're talking about!'

Terry flicked the ash from his cigarette onto the carpet.

'Listen, Lenny, we know everything. We know about the gold, about the robbery, and we also know about you. So why don't you save yourself some trouble and just tell us what we want to hear?'

Lenny was biting his lip. His short stubby fingers were trembling and he was trying as hard as he could to stop himself crying.

Marsh looked at him pityingly.

'I can promise you, Lenny, that the Ryans will not know where we got our information from. All we want to know is when the meet will be. We'll do the rest.'

'I'm sorry. I know nothing. I'm over here on holiday.'

Terry lost his temper.

'Cut the crap, Isaacs! You're over here to buy illegal gold. How about we pull you in now? Leak your name to the papers. Say that

371

you're helping us with our enquiries. Then leave you on remand in funky Brixton where you can sit and wait for the Ryans to waste you!'

Lenny paled.

'You wouldn't do that to me!'

Terry smiled.

'Just try us and see.'

Lenny looked down at his hands. Terry could see his shiny pate through his thinning hair.

'It's on Sunday. We all meet on Sunday. You realise that I'm a dead man?'

Marsh stopped chewing his thumbnail and said, 'We'll see about that, Lenny. Don't worry. Now tell us nice and slowly what's supposed to be going down.'

Lenny cleared his throat and took a sip of his wine. 'We're meeting at a place called Fenn Farm.'

'We know all about Fenn Farm. What we're more interested in is times.'

'Seven-thirty on Sunday evening.'

Terry looked at Marsh.

'That only gives us thirty-six hours.'

'Don't worry, Petherick. We'll be more than ready for them.'

Lenny Isaacs wiped a stray tear from his eye. Maura Ryan would have his nuts for this. He was already dead.

Maura had just put a chicken in the oven and was preparing the vegetables for Sunday lunch. She wanted to eat at twelve so she and William could have the afternoon free. When she had finished scraping the carrots, the telephone rang. It was Margaret.

'Hello, Marge.' Maura's voice was warm.

'Hiya! I thought I'd give you a quick ring and see how you was getting on.'

'Terrific. I was just starting the dinner actually.'

Margaret's voice was incredulous. 'Maura Ryan cooking! Now I've heard everything!'

'Ha, ha, Marge!'

'This William must be some guy. If he can domesticate you, he must be the business.'

'He has not domesticated me . . . I often cook.'

'Pull the other one, Maws, it plays "Hard Day's Night"! Seriously, I'm just pleased you're so happy. It's about time.'

'Oh, Marge, it's great! I wish to God I'd got myself in a relationship years ago. I don't think I'm in love exactly . . . but I just want to be with him all the time. In fact, I *am* with him all the time.'

372

'I can remember when me and Den were like that!'

'Come off it, Marge, you and Den are still like lovebirds. You two even embarrass your own kids with all your kissing and cuddling.'

'Don't talk to me about my kids . . .'

Margaret's voice was sad.

'Why, what's happened?'

'It's Penny. She's got herself a bloke.'

'What's wrong with that? You can't keep them tied to your apron strings forever.'

'It's not that, Maws. He's a bloody Sikh.'

'You're joking!'

'I wish I was. He even wears a turban. Mind you, I had to laugh. Little Dennis saw them together in the High Street and went up and asked him when his head was gonna get better. That's how we found out. Penny and him had a big fight about it and when I tried to sort it all out, Dennis dropped the bombshell.'

Maura was laughing so hard she had an ache in her ribs.

'I wish *I* could see the funny side of it all.'

'You bloody hypocrite, Marge! You're the one who brought them up with liberal ideas. Everyone's the same, no matter what colour they are or what religion. Now poor old Penny's got herself a coloured bloke, you're doing your nut!'

'Well, I never thought they'd want to go out with one, did I?'

Maura was still chuckling.

'What's big Den got to say?'

'Oh, him! He's about as much good as an ashtray on a motorbike. "Leave her alone, Marge. Let her find her own way . . ." I said, "You won't be saying that when she's walking round with a red spot on her forehead and a gold lamé sari." '

'Oh, Marge, stop it. You're making me guts ache. Can you see her in a sari with all that ginger hair of hers?'

'Oh, I don't know what to do.'

'Well, if you want my advice, I wouldn't protest too much. Remember what we were like at that age. The more people try and tell you what to do, the more you're inclined to go against them!'

'Yeah. I've thought of that.'

'Let her get it out of her system.'

Maura heard William get out of bed. 'I've gotta go, Marge. I'll try and get over to you tomorrow. Say about lunchtime, how's that?'

'All right, Maws. I'll make us a nice quiche.'

'How about a curry? You'd better start practising Indian cookery.'

'Piss off, Maura!'

'And you! 'Bye, Marge.'

Maura put the phone down and leant against the wall, laughing. Poor old Marge!

'What are you laughing about?'

Maura went to William and kissed him.

'I'll tell you all about it later. I've started the dinner, we're eating early today. I thought we could go out this afternoon for a walk or something. I have to leave at four to meet Roy and the others.'

William looked down into Maura's bright blue eyes.

'Tell you what. Scrub the walk, we'll go back to bed. How's that?'

Maura kissed his mouth hard.

'I was kinda hoping you'd say that!'

Terry and Marsh were in the Special Operations room at Scotland Yard, going over the final details with a hand-picked bunch of men. Marsh had recruited them from the SPG. All had licences to use firearms.

'So we swoop at precisely seven-forty-five. That gives them fifteen minutes to negotiate with Isaacs. We've put a man with him so he doesn't lose his nerve. He'll introduce him to Maura Ryan as his partner. You all understand what you are to do?'

All the men nodded.

'Good.'

Terry stood up and faced them.

'The main aim is to bring the Ryans in. All of them. This is going to be one of the biggest busts this country has ever seen. Nothing is to go wrong. You only fire if it is absolutely necessary and then you aim only to wound if possible.'

The men nodded and looked at one another. Unknown to Terry they had all been told to open fire immediately they entered the barn. Not one person was to be allowed to leave that place alive, Lennie Isaacs included. No one knew why this young DI was being kept in the dark. They were just following orders.

4.00

Sarah was sitting with Benjamin watching a Doris Day film on TV. She was trying to knit and finding it increasingly difficult to concentrate. She had left message after message for that young man Petherick and he had not been in touch. She was worried that one of the people who worked for Maura had found out what she had done. If Maura knew she would kill her, she knew that. For all her talk of never being frightened of anything that came out of her own body, she was increasingly nervous. Today for some reason she had had a terrible feeling of foreboding. It had been weighing down on her like a lump of concrete in her breast since she had got out of bed this morning. She put her knitting down and rubbed her eyes.

'How about a nice cuppa, Sar?'

Benjamin spoke without taking his eyes off the television. Sarah stood up, glad of something to do. She made her way out to her kitchen and put the kettle on. She had been going to visit the boys' graves today. Mainly Anthony's, Benny's and Geoffrey's, she only ever paid Mickey's a flying visit. But for some reason she did not want to leave the house.

As she set about making the tea, a deep coldness came over her and she had to sit down at the kitchen table. She had only felt like this twice in her life before and that was when Benny had died and Geoffrey had gone missing. She had had a feeling similar to this the day the police had reported to her Geoffrey's body had been found. She closed her eyes to blot out the picture of him in the mortuary. He had been shot in the back of the head and the bullet had come out just under his jawline. He had had a surprised expression on his face. Now she had that feeling again. She was convinced that something was going to happen today. Something bad.

When she finally took the tray of tea in to Benjamin he was asleep. She turned the sound down on the TV and sat and drank her own tea. Waiting for a knock on the door or the phone to ring.

4.30

Maura was driving to Le Buxom to meet the boys. She had not felt so happy for a long time. William had tried to persuade her to let Roy deal with the business today and she had been very tempted to stay in bed with him. After all these years she was finally having a relationship with a man, and loving every second of it. She only wished she had let herself go before now. She found herself smiling at complete strangers at traffic lights and laughed to herself. If this was love she was enjoying every moment of it. She decided that she would pass more of the business over to Roy. He was doing so well now. She wished he could get rid of Janine but knew that concern for Benny kept him with her.

She could understand that. If she had become a mother she knew she would have done anything for the good of her children. She wished again she had kept her baby. It would have been grown up now with a life of its own.

She pushed the thought from her mind. She was happy today and nothing was going to interfere with that! She turned her thoughts to Marge, determined that nothing was going to spoil her happiness. All she wanted to do was get the meet over and get back to William.

She was humming a little tune as she pulled into Dean Street.

4.45

Lenny Isaacs had dosed himself up with brandy. The policeman assigned to keep him from bolting was Detective Sergeant Paul Johnson. He had been given his orders two hours ago. Once the shooting started he was to push his gun into Isaacs' side and blast him. There was something definitely fishy about all this but as his old dad used to say: 'Ours is not to reason why.' If it got him a promotion he didn't give a toss. The likes of Lenny Isaacs were scum anyway. He'd be doing a public service.

Lenny sat in the barn. It was freezing and he shoved his hands into the pocket of his sheepskin. He was praying for the first time in thirty years. DS Johnson sat opposite staring at him. Lenny wished to Christ the copper wasn't such a big bastard. He would have tried to make an escape. The trouble was he had never been the hero type. More the 'I'll scratch your back' class of villain. He hadn't slept all night and had been jittery all day. Maura Ryan, whether she was nicked or not, would make sure he disappeared. Oh, God in heaven, help him, for fuck's sake!

376

Chapter Thirty-Four

4.50

Fenn Farm was derelict. It had not been worked for years. Maura had bought it for a song at an auction a few years previously and was going to sell it eventually, subject to planning permission for a housing estate. Green belt land was not classed as sacrosanct any more. If you had the money and the contacts you could build just about anywhere you wanted to. Arable land that was worth only a few hundred pounds an acre could become, overnight, prime building land worth millions. This was the Thatcher era, when anything that was commercially viable and cost the government nothing was encouraged wholeheartedly. Even building estates on old power stations was acceptable, provided you filled the land in with plenty of concrete first. Then the people who bought the houses were given lists of trees they could plant, trees with very shallow roots that would not disturb the sludge and radioactive waste lying beneath the houses. It was a developer's dream, and Maura Ryan had had the foresight to cash in when land was still at nominal prices. The days when the working-class men dreamt of winning fifty thousand pounds on the pools were long over. You could not buy a flat for that amount now, let alone live for the rest of your life on it. England was the epitome of the consumer society.

Today Terry Petherick was watching from the sidelines as the farm was being set up ready for the arrival of the Ryans. Everywhere he looked there were men with high velocity rifles, all taking up position in and around the barn. The light was fast fading, and Terry was reminded of an old World War Two movie, seeing the men dressed in black spiriting around with faces covered in camouflage make up and guns glinting in the half-light. He fingered his own gun and prayed that he would not have to use it. Especially not on Maura Ryan.

He was sitting on an oil drum watching the activity around him when a man standing near him answered a call on his walkie talkie. Terry had not been issued with one and until this moment had not thought it strange. When he heard what was being said on the man's radio, it became crystal clear to him just why he had been overlooked in that department.

The voice crackled over the radio and into Terry's brain. 'Remember, not one Ryan is to leave the farm alive. You cut them down as they arrive.'

'Understood. Over and out.'

The man began to walk towards the barn door, and Terry realised through his reeling thoughts that the man had not noticed him. In the twilight and with the camouflage make up he was indistinguishable. He sat for a while on the oil drum, letting what he had heard sink in.

Maura and her brothers were going to die. They were being led here, to this farm, like lambs to the slaughter. And it was his fault. He had taken the files to his superiors and then had listened to their excuses as to why none of the judges and policemen on the Ryans' payroll would be brought to justice. Now it was revealed to him with shocking clarity why the Ryans had to die. While they held knowledge that could rock the country, they were dead men. And women. He must not forget Maura, the mastermind behind it all. It was she who was the biggest target: Maura who was the fly in an otherwise perfect ointment. He could have kicked himself. Here he was, with his ideals about justice – good and bad, law and order – and there was no such thing. Not in this country, or indeed the world.

He looked at his watch. The luminous dial showed that it was just five o'clock. Looking around him surreptitiously, he began to move slowly towards one of the last remaining cars outside the farm. He was praying that the keys were still in it.

He slipped behind the wheel of the Sierra Estate and felt a surge of thankfulness that was almost sexual. The keys were in the ignition. He swallowed deeply, feeling the momentary hesitation that always precedes an act of wrong doing. Only what he was doing was not wrong. He had sworn an oath to uphold the law in this country, and as far as he was concerned that was just what he was doing. Stopping the wanton murder of a whole family. No matter what they had done, nothing warranted what was to happen at this farm tonight. He had two hours before the Ryans were supposed to arrive and he would try to stop them if it was the last thing he did.

He started the car up and drove cautiously away from the farm house and the barn. He drove as if he was supposed to be driving the car away, neither too fast nor too slow. He remembered that on their way to the farm today he had seen a phone box in the lane about a hundred yards from the farm's exit. He drove there, his breath barely entering his lungs in his state of nervous tension. If somebody tried to stop him, he would use his gun. Whatever happened, Maura Ryan was not going to die, not in a barn on a cold February evening, mown down like a dog.

5.05

'Right then. Is everyone happy with what they are to do?'

Roy, Leslie, Garry and Lee nodded at Maura.

'Good. We'll have a quick coffee and then make tracks. It'll take over an hour to get there.'

'I still think we're being watched.' Garry's voice was low.

Maura sighed.

'Oh, for Christ's sake, Gal. If we were being watched, one of our plants would have let us know before now. You're so paranoid lately.'

'I'm telling you now, that bloke I saw in the blue Granny was definitely waiting for us.'

'Give it a rest, Garry. You're like an old woman sometimes.'

Garry looked at Roy. 'Well, when we're all fucking nicked, don't say I never warned you.'

Lee laughed, then said in a girlish voice, 'All right then, Garry. I promise you with all my heart.'

Garry looked at him, frowning.

'I'm glad you think it's funny. I hope you find it as amusing when you're sitting in Parkhurst or Durham doing a twelve stretch.'

Leslie pulled on his cigarette.

'Only twelve years? I'd have thought we warranted at least a thirty.' He looked at Lee. 'Remind me to nail someone's leg to a table. We can't have the Krays outdoing us at the last moment.'

Everyone laughed but Garry would not be silenced.

'Yeah. And the Krays are still inside, remember that. In fact if you –' he pointed at Leslie viciously – 'get put on the "Island", you might get banged in a cell with one of them. Reggie, that is.'

Lee grinned.

'Not you though, Garry, you'll be put in Broadmoor with Ronnie. That's where all the nutters go.'

'Oh, shut up, for Christ's sake. No one's going anywhere.' Maura was getting annoyed.

Garry flicked his hair from his eyes. 'Well, there's one thing I can guarantee. You won't be in Cookham Wood with the other long-timers like Hindley. You'll be top security, girl. We'll all be A grade. Like terrorists.'

Before Maura could retort, Lee spoke. His voice was soft as silk. 'Have you been reading that book again? *How to Win Friends and Influence People*?'

Everyone laughed.

'Oh, piss off, the lot of you! The last book you's read was *Fluff and Nip*.'

Then the phone rang and Maura picked it up, chuckling as she did so.

Terry went into the phone box and dialled directory enquiries. He asked them for the number of Le Buxom. When they gave it to him, he dialled the operator for a reverse charge call. He did not have a single coin on him. He stood in the cold with bated breath as the operator tried to connect him. Le Buxom was the only place he could think of where someone would know the whereabouts of Maura Ryan.

He was literally praying as he heard the distant clicking and whirring of the telephone exchange.

Maura picked up the phone. 'Hello?' Her voice was calm and happy.

'I have a reverse charge call from a call box in Essex. Will you accept the charges?'

The operator's clipped tones were bored and efficient.

Who on earth could be ringing her from a call box? Maura racked her brains.

'Of course.'

'You're through, caller.'

'Hello, can I speak to Maura Ryan?'

She felt her heart stop in her chest. She would know that voice anywhere. All around her the boys were good-naturedly ragging Garry as they drank their coffee. In Maura's head there was only one sound: Terry Petherick's voice.

'Is there anyone there?' He sounded desperate. 'I must speak to Maura Ryan or someone who can contact her.'

'This is Maura Ryan.' She was amazed at how calm her voice sounded.

'Maura, this is Terry . . . Terry Petherick. Please don't put the phone down.'

'What do you want?' Even as she spoke so normally she could feel the almost adolescent longing and excitement he had always created in her.

'You mustn't go near Fenn Farm. The Special Investigations Branch are waiting for you. They're armed and ready.'

'What!' The sound of her voice silenced her brothers. They all looked at her.

'I know it sounds crazy, but believe me, Maura, you're in big trouble. We know everything about you. Everything.' He stressed the last word.

380

'But how?' She sounded very young in panic.

'Look, can we meet? I can't stand here explaining it all. They're looking for me . . . or will be when they realise I've gone.'

'What are you talking about?' Maura's voice was scared.

'Look, Maura, is there anywhere we can meet? It must be somewhere the police don't know about. Have you a secret hideaway?'

Maura was thinking out loud. 'Marge's house . . . Carla's . . .' Then it struck her. 'Do you know Mickey's old place?'

'Yes. I know it.'

'I'll meet you there.'

'OK.' Terry put the phone down and went to the car.

'What's happened, Maws?'

'You were right, Garry. The old Bill have tumbled us. Isaacs must have grassed.'

Garry stood up from his seat and threw his coffee cup at the wall.

'I knew it! I bloody knew it! You wouldn't listen, would you?'

'Calm down. Calm down. Shouting and hollering ain't gonna help us.'

Roy looked at his sister.

'What's the score?'

'I'm not sure yet. I want you all to lie low for a while. I'm meeting somebody who knows what's going on. Fenn Farm is well and truly out of the question. I'll be at Mickey's old flat. I want you all to ring in there from wherever you decide to go. All right?'

'Who was that on the dog and bone?'

'Just a friend, Les. A good friend.'

'Well, I'm off to Muvver's. Who wants to come?'

Leslie nodded at Lee. 'I'll go with you. At least she'll guarantee some decent grub with an alibi.'

'Well, wherever you all go, don't forget to ring me at Michael's.'

'What about Richard? He might not like you just turning up at his drum.'

Maura picked up her bag and scowled at Lee.

'Fuck Richard!'

'No, thanks. He's not my type.'

Maura laughed despite herself. 'Come on, you lot. Let's get a move on.'

Richard was asleep in bed with a Filipino man he'd picked up the night before. They had only emerged from the bedroom once to have some sandwiches before they went back to bed for another session. Richard was cuddling into the man's back when he heard the hammering on his front door. He hoped it was not that bitch

Denzil again. Since Michael had died he had practically haunted him. Richard's most oft repeated statement was: 'Straight I may not be . . . choosy I most definitely am!' And he had not sunk as low as Denzil. Not yet anyway.

He walked naked into the hallway.

'Who is it?' His voice was high and cracked.

'It's me. Maura Ryan.'

'Oh!' Richard opened the front door and let her in. Since Michael's death he had added a mortice lock to the door which was why Maura's key was not enough to gain her access.

'I never expected you!'

Maura could hear the surprise in his voice.

'Well, you've got me, Richy baby. Until I say otherwise.'

She walked into the lounge and threw her bag on the sofa. Going to the drinks cabinet, she poured herself a large Remy Martin.

Richard was in a quandary. He most definitely did not want Maura Ryan in his flat. And it *was* his flat. Michael had left it to him. But he was not brave enough to ask her to leave. He just stood in the doorway watching her. She was wearing a deep red trouser suit that perfectly complemented her white-blonde hair. Her large breasts were just covered by a white silk shirt. Richard could see that she was braless. He had envied her her breasts from the first time they had met. He had also been jealous of the way Michael worshipped her. The fact that he knew she did not like him had not helped matters very much either.

He heard a stirring in the bedroom and felt faint with fright. He had completely forgotten about his Filipino friend! He saw Maura's puzzled expression and tried to smile.

'It's a friend of mine.' As he spoke the man came out of the bedroom and Maura could not help but stare at him. He was tiny and slim, like most Filipinos, but he had the largest organ Maura had ever seen in her life. It was like a baseball bat. She made a conscious effort not to let her mouth fall open with shock.

'This is my friend, his name's Weykok.' Richard's voice trailed off as Maura began to guffaw with laughter.

'Well, it would be, wouldn't it?'

Weykok stood with his thin bony shoulders pulled back, as if trying to emphasise his enormous member. He seemed to enjoy the stir that he was creating. Richard turned to him and bundled him back into the bedroom. Maura sat on the sofa laughing her head off. She had needed something to lighten the situation and it had come in the shape of a man called Weykok.

Richard came back into the lounge; he was wearing a silk dressing-gown. 'He's leaving now.'

As he spoke the little man came into the room, fully dressed. He held out a tiny hand.

'Money, please.'

Maura saw Richard flush. Enjoying herself, she said innocently, 'Does he charge by the inch or the centimetre? After all, we're in the common market now.'

She started to laugh again and Weykok laughed with her good-naturedly. Maura went to her bag and opened it.

'Have him on me, Richard. How much?'

Weykok seemed to understand this as he said politely, 'Eighty-five pounds, madam, please.'

Maura pulled out two fifty-pound notes and gave them to him, saying, 'Keep the change.'

The little man bowed to her, and after a mumbled conversation with Richard in the hallway, left the flat.

'Well, Richard, I'm afraid I'll be invading your space for a while. Let's try and get on, shall we?' Her voice was friendly.

'Are you in some kind of trouble, Maura?' Richard was serious.

'Sort of.'

'In that case I'll do all I can to help. Not for you but for Michael. I know that's what he would have wanted me to do.'

He said the words simply and with an innate sincerity that made her feel guilty for her earlier jokes at his expense. She was reminded that she needed him. Needed him badly.

'Someone will be coming here soon to see me.'

She saw his face fall and hastily reassured him. 'Don't worry, Richard, there'll be no violence or anything like that.'

She saw him relax and for a second felt sorry for him. She sat back down on the sofa and patted the seat beside her.

'Come and sit here, Richard. We need to talk.'

Terry Petherick was in Dagenham. He parked the car he was using in the car park of the Ship and Shovel public house. Leaving it there, he went out on to the A13 and flagged down a passing mini cab.

'Bloody hell! You in the TA?'

As Terry sat beside the minicab driver, he remembered that he was still blacked up.

'Yes, actually. I've been on manoeuvres and my car broke down.'

'Oh, I see.' The man's voice was gravelly as if he needed to clear his throat. 'Where you want droppin' off?'

'Could you take me to Knightsbridge, please?'

'Yeah. Course, I was in the TA, you know. Went to Germany once . . .'

Terry closed his eyes. This was all he needed, a 'weekend warrior' for a cab driver.

Maura was chatting to Richard, trying to make friends with him. She knew that she needed him, desperately. She could not help noticing that all around the room were pictures of Michael and Richard, laughing and with their arms around one another. It was only Richard's association with her brother, and his fear of her, that was keeping him from throwing her out, she knew that.

'I needed somewhere to meet someone important. Where no one would think of looking for me. I know this is a cheek, Richard, but it was the only place I could think of.'

He shrugged.

'Well, it's yours for as long as you want to use it. Now, can I make you something? Tea? Coffee?'

Maura smiled. 'Coffee would be great.'

She looked at the large cuckoo clock on the wall. It was nearly a quarter to seven. She bit her lip. Where was Terry?

Roy was sitting at home with little Benny. He was nervous and worried. He would ring in to Maura at seven. Give her a chance to sort herself out. He looked at Janine. She was lying on the couch half drunk. He suddenly felt a tightening sensation in his bowels. For the first time in years he was scared.

Sarah was watching the three boys surreptitiously. They had all turned up together to visit their father, but they were not right somehow. They were all taut as bowstrings, as if waiting for something to happen. Garry got out of his chair.

'Can I use your phone, Mum?'

'Of course you can.'

He went out into the hallway and rang Maura. While he was doing it, Leslie and Lee kept Sarah in the front room chatting. Both were nervous under the plaster gaze of the holy family and the various saints that stood around the room. It seemed every time they visited her a new statue had been added to the collection.

Sarah sat with them while they chatted to her and Benjamin, but still had the bad feeling in her side. The dragging feeling that seemed to be increasing as the day wore on.

At six-thirty Marsh realised that Terry Petherick had gone missing. Busy as he was getting everything set up, he had not given him a thought till then. Although Terry did not know it, he was going to be silenced along with the Ryans. Oh, they would not kill him. Not unless they had to . . . He was going to be named as the person who had shot Maura Ryan on her entry into the barn.

Now Marsh knew that somehow Terry had cottoned on to what was going to happen and had driven one of the unmarked cars out of the farmyard. He was fuming. There had been two cars outside, both to be driven away before the Ryans were due to arrive. In the commotion, as everyone got ready and set up the barn for the meeting, Terry had just got into one of them and driven off. God knew where. Personally Marsh hoped it was not to the newspapers. While Maura Ryan was alive and kicking they dared not touch her. She could open her mouth about things that would smash open the Metropolitan Police force and West Midlands Serious Crime Squad, and she also knew things about docklands and other prime areas of development that could bring down the government. He shivered. She had them literally by the bollocks.

Now there was another thing that he knew for definite. Maura Ryan was not coming anywhere near this barn or even this county. Terry Petherick had jumped fences today. In either camp, whether it was the police's or the Ryans', Petherick was a dangerous man.

Terry knocked on the door of Michael's flat and Maura let him in almost immediately. They stood in the hallway staring at one another for long moments, both drinking in the other as if they were dying of thirst.

Maura was the first to speak.

'Come through, Terry.'

He followed her into the lounge.

'This is Richard, an old friend of my brother Michael's. He lives here now.'

Terry held out his hand and Richard shook it.

'I'll make some more coffee, shall I?'

'I could certainly do with some.'

Richard smiled at Terry and went to the kitchen.

'Sit down.'

They sat on the sofa together, nearly touching, and Maura felt the heady sensation of being close to him for the first in years. She savoured it for a few moments to try to commit it to memory. Terry was doing exactly the same.

Finally Maura spoke. 'So, what's going on?'

'You're not going to like what I have to tell you, Maura.'

'I know that, Terry. But I still have to know the score.'

He took a deep breath.

'Your brother Geoffrey kept a file on you and Michael.' He watched her large blue eyes open wider. 'When he died it came into your mother's possession. It had details of the gold bullion robbery, even the route map – which incidentally had your prints all over it. It had the names of every high-ranking official in the government, police and law courts, how much you paid them and what you paid them for. Maura, it had everything.'

She was absolutely dumbstruck.

'Your mother rang me and asked me to meet her. I did.' He swallowed deeply. 'She gave the file to me and I passed it on to the SIB.'

Maura shook her head in disbelief. 'The Special Investigations Branch? I see.' Her voice was small. 'So between my mother and yourself, I was well and truly . . .'

'No, Maura. No. I know how it sounds but we wanted to help you.'

Even as he spoke he knew it sounded lame.

'Come off it, Terry! I'm not as daft as you seem to think. You and my mother wanted me put away. Neither of you thought about all the so-called "goody two-shoes" wankers on my payroll. It never occurred to either of you that *they* were abusing *their* positions. Oh, no! You two just wanted me sent down, out of harm's way. Well, let me tell you something. If it hadn't have been me and Michael buying them bastards off it would have been someone else. This bloody country is rotten to the core, mate. Everything has its price, whether it's a small backhander to get a bit of planning permission or a large donation to the appropriate political party for a development. Like docklands . . .'

'I know now that what you're saying is right.'

'Oh, shut up! Shut up!' Maura was shouting now and Richard was listening to everything that was being said.

'You was always an idealist, Terry . . . like some sort of bloody knight errant. Always wanted to get the bad guys, didn't you? Well, let me ask you something. What's happening to the people we've been buying off? I bet they aren't being given a twelve-gun send-off, are they? Are they? Of course not. They'll walk away as they always have done with an OBE or a golden handshake. No one must ever know that Sir Godly Goodly, who just happened to go to Cambridge with most of the other scum from the higher echelons of British Society, is on the fucking take!'

Her mouth was flecked with spittle and she ran her hand through her hair in agitation. 'Why aren't they after the real criminals? The rich and pampered criminals. Why must we take the fall for them? You answer me that.'

Terry stared at her, knowing that all she said was true. He was aware from the day that Marsh had told him what was going to happen to the men on Maura's payroll, that it was unfair. That the Ryans were going to carry the can for them so that Joe Public never knew what was really going on. He felt a fool. He had betrayed her. After all he had done to her in the past, he had

386

betrayed her again because he'd thought that what he was doing was right. And now he knew that there was no such thing as 'right' and 'wrong' any more. Was it right that judges could sit on a bench and put away men for being a danger to society at large and then acquit other men who were a much bigger danger, just because they were being paid to do so? Was it right for the top police who were financing their gambling or other hobbies to be retired when in reality they should be doing time? No, it was wrong. Maura Ryan was a criminal but she had never pretended to be anything else. She did not shield herself with the mantle of a good education and a law degree. If what she did was wrong, at least she did it without pretending to benefit the nation.

Richard walked into the room with a tray of coffee and sandwiches. He placed it on the coffee table and spoke. 'I couldn't help hearing your conversation.'

Maura and Terry both looked at him as if they didn't know who he was. They'd forgotten him.

'I work for the papers. You know that, Maura. From what I've just heard, I think that while you have access to journalists you're safe as houses.' He looked from one to the other. 'Think about it. Maura knows all the people who are on her payroll. While you're alive, Maura, the police dare not touch you.'

'They were going to kill them all. Every one of them. At Fenn Farm tonight.' Terry's voice was flat.

'If you'll forgive me, I guessed as much for myself. What you must do, Maura, is leave the country. Go somewhere where they can't get to you.'

'They would!'

'No, let me finish. You must write down everything you know about the people who are on your payroll then you must leave it with someone, to be opened only on your death. That way you will live a very long time, believe me.'

Maura and Terry stared at him. As fantastic as it sounded, it held the ring of truth.

'I know plenty of journos who'd commit murder for a story like this. It's got everything a journalist needs.'

'He's got a point, you know.' Terry's voice was excited.

Richard spoke again. 'Honestly, Maura, I know what I'm talking about. Look at Profumo. Christ, that still gets dragged up every so often. People like to think that the rich people who run big businesses and the people in government are in cahoots with shadier people. It makes them feel better about their own lives. There's nothing the British like more than to tear someone apart, preferably someone they created or voted in in the first place. The gutter press makes its money doing it, whether it's the Westland affair, the Profumo scandal or a judge who's into pornography. As long as it's someone with plenty of money or a high profile, the British Public loves it.'

The more Richard spoke, the more sense he made to Maura.

'But where could I go?'

'Anywhere you wanted to, really. While you're alive and kicking and able to open your mouth, you and your brothers are as safe as houses.'

She slumped back on to the settee. 'Let me think about it. I can't concentrate . . .'

'Drink your coffee and have a sandwich. We'll think of something, don't you worry.'

Maura was beginning to understand what Michael had seen in Richard. He wasn't just a pretty face.

Chapter Thirty-Five

Marsh was worried. Very worried. It seemed that Maura Ryan had gone on the missing list. From information he had received, it seemed the only person at her house was William Templeton. Lord Templeton. Three of her brothers were at their mother's and the other brother, Roy, was at his own house in Chigwell. Maura Ryan had not appeared at any of her clubs or other businesses. He had put a call out to watch for her car but didn't hold out much hope there. He was dealing with a dangerous lady, a woman with the means of destroying numerous people, himself included. And to top it all, she now had the championship of Terry Petherick!

He sighed and lit one of his cigars, looking up as the door of his office opened.

It was Superintendent Ackland of the Special Investigations Branch. Ackland was notorious in the force for his violent and disruptive personality. He was one of those men who should by rights have chosen a life of crime. Brought up in the Gorbals, he had an animal cunning and an empathy with the criminal mind that was out of place in the world of the police. Or so Marsh had thought until he had read the names of seemingly respectable men on Maura Ryan's payroll.

Like many Scotsmen, James Ackland was quite small, with a muscular body and the high forehead and erratic hair of his ancestors. He had tiny blue eyes that seemed to be permanently on the move, darting around his head as if he was frightened that by the act of relaxing his gaze he would miss something important. Even after twenty years in London, his Scottish accent was as pronounced as ever.

'You've read the files, I take it?' Marsh's voice was low.

'Aye. I have that.' Ackland laughed. 'Well, there's one thing for sure . . . she's a canny lass. The way I see it, there's not a lot we can do to her. Or her family, come to that.'

His face seemed to straighten, as if wiped clean with a black-board rubber. 'But I'll think of something. Though myself, I think the people on the take should be brought to book. But you know and I know they won't be.'

Marsh nodded and puffed on his cigar.

Ackland picked his rather bulbous nose, making Marsh feel sick.

'The only way out is to annihilate the bitch. Usual code of conduct, of course. We find her, then we have what the papers euphemistically call a "shoot out". It's odds on that she's carrying a firearm. Christ, man, from what I read in the file, I wouldn't be surprised if she was carrying a tactical nuclear missile!'

His voice was jocular again. 'I don't like covering up for people, especially people who should know better, but there you are. We're all under orders.'

Ackland helped himself from the bottle of Famous Grouse that Marsh had on his desk, pouring the dregs from a coffee cup into a waste paper basket and filling it nearly full.

'We have to find her first.' Marsh's voice sounded as if that would be an impossible task.

Ackland sniffed. 'No one can hide forever, Marsh.'

Maura was writing furiously. She was making a document which, if it got into the wrong hands, would bring the country to its knees. Her brain was working overtime, remembering every little detail she could about the people she had dealt with. Unknown to her there were people named in her account who had not appeared in Geoffrey's. She was concentrating on the 'biggies', as Richard had called the cabinet ministers and the Bank officials. She also listed every large developer and industry chairman who had at one time or another dealt with either herself or Michael.

Terry watched her as she worked, reading each page as she finished it and realising with each word just how corrupt and evil the establishment had become.

William Templeton was worried. Very worried. Like Marsh he was wondering where on earth Maura had got to. He glanced at his watch. It was nearly two in the morning and still no word. He looked around Maura's lounge at the family pictures that abounded. On top of the television cabinet were photographs of Carla. From a small child to a grown woman, her life was lovingly documented. On the occasional tables were photos of Maura and her brothers, mainly Michael.

He got up from his chair and went to the kitchen to make himself yet another coffee. As he poured hot water over the coffee granules there was a knock on the door. Banging the kettle down on the worktop he answered it, his heart in his mouth.

A man was standing outside the porch. He was holding a police badge in his hand. Slowly, William opened the door.

'Sorry to disturb you at this time of night, sir.' The man had a pronounced Scottish accent. 'I am Superintendent Ackland of the Special Investigations Branch. Could I please talk to you for a moment?'

The man smiled and William saw that he had tobacco-stained teeth. He held the door open and gestured for the man to come inside.

Please God, don't let her be dead. William was convinced that it was bad news of some kind. It was not until Ackland told him that he was going to be arrested and charged with certain offences, including conspiracy to murder and armed robbery, that he realised just how bad.

'Do you realise who I am?' His voice was outraged.

'Aye, I do. But you see, Lord William, I couldn't care less if you were the Prince Regent himself. If you don't do what I tell you, I'll drag you to the police station so fast you'll burn a hole in the pavement! Outside this house is an army of policemen, with guns, just waiting for a word from me. You're going to be the bait that tempts the big fish. The big fish being Maura Ryan.'

'I have no idea where she is.'

'Maybe not, but it's odds on you'll be able to find out. Now, shall we have a nice cup of tea and a chat?'

Ackland's voice was friendly and for some reason this worried William more than anything.

Maura was in deep trouble and he guessed that he was going to be asked to double cross her. This Scottish lout had as good as already said that. What was worrying William was the fact that, as much as he cared about Maura, his own skin would always come first. It always had.

At two-thirty Maura took a rest from her writing to have a cup of coffee. Richard had produced a photocopier that he kept for when he worked from home. He was busy in the bedroom copying all that Maura had written so far. Richard had wanted to be a 'real' journalist all his adult life. He realised that in his hands he had the scoop of the century and that he could never use it. As he read what Maura had written his eyes goggled. He would bet his last pound that the Secretary of State for the Environment was probably sitting at home and sweating like a pig. He must have been told all that was going on. The same could be said for the Home Secretary.

As he read, Richard had the beginnings of a plan forming in his mind.

In the lounge Terry and Maura drank their coffee in silence.

'What do you think the outcome will be?' she asked.

391

Terry shook his head.

'I really don't know, Maura. I feel responsible for it all.'

'That's not surprising, is it? Considering you are! You and my mother.' Her voice was bitter.

'I don't blame you for being upset with me but I am trying to help you now. Surely that says something?' Terry was desperate to reassure her of his backing.

'You're trying to help me now because the people that you worked for . . . the people that you revered and tried to emulate . . . turned out to be more bent than I am. *That's* why you're trying to help now. You said yourself that you knew before you even went to Fenn Farm that the so-called "biggies" who were on the take would walk. I don't need you, Terry Petherick. I never needed you.'

'You did need me once, Maura.' His voice was quiet and earnest.

She lit a cigarette and looked into his face.

'Oh, yeah? And when was that?'

'When you were pregnant. When you had the abortion. When you were lying in hospital desperately ill. Your mother told me all about it.'

He sounded calm and caring.

Maura snorted. 'So, mouth almighty told you that as well, did she? What else did she tell you? Did she tell you that she once accused me of sleeping with Michael? Did she tell you that? Did she tell you that for all our faults, real and imagined, she took the money that was sent to her every week?' She was quiet for a few seconds. Then, her voice low, she spoke again.

'I never needed you then, Terry, so don't flatter yourself. I was young and naïve and the only mistake I made, as I see it, was getting involved with someone like you. Even then you wanted to change the world. Michael told me what happened to you. We had enough plants in the force, even then. You were pulled over the carpet for your association with Michael Ryan's sister and you dumped me. You had a choice, me or the force, and your precious police force won. Then, when my mother gave you Geoffrey's papers, you couldn't wait to run to your superiors with them. Terry Petherick, the Vine Street Marvel, uncovers the biggest case of corruption this century. Only you didn't realise then that what you actually had was something the government and the police would rather hush up than expose. You struck out, mate.'

'I've lost everything. My job . . .'

'Oh, sod your job!' Maura was shouting. 'I don't give a toss about you or your stupid job!'

'Whatever you think now, Maura, I loved you. But we were so

392

young then. What about the night we spent together after Benny died? You told me then that you still loved me.' He pointed at her. 'You told me to go the next morning. It was your decision.'

He felt an urge to weep. He had inadvertently brought her nothing but grief from the day they met.

'I sent you away because I wanted to.'

'Oh no you didn't! I won't have you saying that. You sent me away because you were in too deep with Michael. It was for that reason and that reason only.'

Maura watched his handsome face and admitted the truth of what he was saying to herself.

'Shall I tell you something? Shall I tell you the real truth of my life?'

'Yes. Please tell me.'

'When I met you in 1966, I felt something I had never felt before. Or since.' She stared at a spot on the carpet, afraid to look at his face. 'I wanted you so badly I could taste it. Do you remember when you told me you were a policeman? I nearly had a heart attack!'

She laughed softly. 'I sneaked around for months to meet you, lying to my mother and father and my brothers. Then, when I got pregnant and went to your flat to tell you, you finished with me. I had that baby scraped out of me by a dirty little Paki. I can still smell that flat sometimes. I can still see the baby lying in the bottom of a washing up bowl. Perfectly formed and dead.

'And do you know what the ironic part of it is? I never wanted to be anything other than a wife and mother. I know that the feminists would crucify me if they heard me speaking like this but it was all I ever wanted: a husband, a home, and children. A houseful of children. Then when I had the abortion and it went wrong, I came out of the hospital and all that had been taken away from me. I had nothing to give to a husband or a lover. I was empty inside. I nearly died, you know. And for a long time that's exactly what I prayed for. Then I had the idea of working for Michael. He never really wanted me to work in the family business but I forced him. I knew that he felt responsible for what had happened to me and I used that to get the ice cream and hot dogs from him. After that, I gradually took over from poor Geoffrey.

'If I hadn't gone into the business then, Geoffrey and Michael would have stayed together as a team. Though Michael never really had a lot of time for him, I must admit that. And somehow, all that happened over the years built up and built up . . . until this. I'm the most wanted woman in England now and all I ever wanted was to be Mrs Average. That child would be twenty-one now. Grown up and going out into the world. Instead it was flushed down a toilet in a multi-storey tower block in Peckham, and I'm being hunted by armed police . . .'

Her voice trailed away and Terry knew that silent tears were falling from her eyes. For the first time he realised just how much he had really hurt this woman. He asked himself for the hundredth time since Mrs Ryan had told him about the abortion, whether he would have stayed with her had he known. And being an honest person he knew that he could not answer that question so many years later. All he was sure of was that he had wrecked Maura's life. That she had always been inside him somewhere, like a piece of a puzzle that was gradually being put together.

He put an arm around her hesitantly, afraid that she would push him away, but she didn't. Instead she held on to him tightly, pulling his body against her own as if trying to crawl under his skin. And he held her while she cried and was not surprised to feel his own tears fall as they both healed a breach that spanned twenty years.

Richard had heard what had been said and being a tactful person coughed loudly before he went into the lounge. Maura and Terry pulled away from one another and Richard acted as if he could not see they were both very upset. Instead he smiled brightly and sat on the floor in front of them.

'I have the most amazing idea. I think that you'll love it.'

Maura wiped her eyes, grateful for the intervention. He was going up more in her estimation with every hour that passed.

'What is it?'

'I've been reading what you've written down and I think that you have more than enough to do a deal.'

'What kind of deal?' Maura's voice was more alert now.

'I think that if our friend here . . .' he pointed at Terry . . . 'goes to see his superiors with a copy of what you have written, and tells them that there are numerous other copies in the hands of unscrupulous people, then they'll be more than ready to come across.'

'They'll never do a deal.'

'How can you be so sure, Terry? I think that the Secretary of State for the Environment will have the last say on what happens. After all, there are some pretty heavy heads on the chopping block.'

'But who will we give the copies to?'

'Let me worry about that, Maura.'

'I know one person who would be glad to help us.'

'And who's that?'

Maura looked at Terry. 'Patrick Kelly.'

'What, the IRA man?' Terry's voice was shocked.

'Yeah. He's an old friend of mine. We go back years. Plus he owes me one.' She thought of Michael as she spoke.

'Wouldn't he use it, though?'

'Only to his own advantage. The British Government are in closer contact with the Irish than people think. They trade information with each other when necessary. The government know who the real leaders behind Sinn Fein are. Gerry Adams is just the media go-between. The real leaders are never mentioned.'

'Rich and important men, I suppose?'

'No, Terry, not all of them. I know that the IRA get a bad press but the majority of them are fighting for a cause that they believe in. Like any society they have all sorts, from the lower end of the scale to the top of it. Kelly is at the top of the scale and I know I can trust him.'

'So that's one person. Can you think of any more?' Richard was loving every second of this now. It was the most exciting night of his life. For the first time he was involved in something that was really important, and even though he would never be able to boast about it, he would know inside that he had been a part of it. Had helped to mastermind it.

Maura frowned. 'The only other person I can think of is Derek Lane.'

'But no one knows where he is.' Terry's voice was puzzled.

Maura couldn't help laughing. 'Terry, Derek Lane and people like him are easy to find if you have the right connections. Michael and I were in partnership with him out in Spain. He owns the monopoly on the timeshares out there. I have the full partnership with him now that Michael's dead. I could fly out to Marbella and explain the situation to him.'

Terry was flabbergasted. Even though he knew that Maura and Michael were heavyweights as far as the British gangland scene were concerned, he never dreamt for a second that they were in league with people like Derek Lane. Yet he should have guessed. After all, they were birds of a feather really. Derek Lane had gone on the trot in 1977 and not been seen or heard from since. He was wanted for countless murders and other serious crimes. He had been the Birmingham equivalent of Michael Ryan, only unlike Michael had not tried to work within the law as well as outside it. In the end England had got too hot for him and he had disappeared.

'Well, that's two good people. They'll do for the moment. Now then, Terry, are you willing to be negotiator? Will you go and see Marsh?' It was the least he could do for Maura.

'Yes. I'll go.'

Richard smiled.

'Good! Now all we have to do is work out what terms we want and everything will be underway.'

Maura laughed softly. 'You're really enjoying this, aren't you, Richard?'

He nodded his head at her. 'Yes, actually, I am. Now who wants more coffee?'

Roy heard the phone ring through a fitful sleep. He sat up in the chair, not sure for a moment exactly where he was. He looked at the clock on the mantelpiece. Four-fifteen. The television showed an old black and white film. He dragged himself over to the phone.

'Yeah?'

'Roy? Roy Ryan?'

The clipped voice was familiar.

'Yeah. Who's this?'

'It's Jackson. DI Jackson.'

'Well, what do you want?' Roy had never liked Jackson.

'William Templeton was brought in earlier and he's shouting his mouth off about your sister and other things. I thought you ought to know.'

The line went dead and Roy stared at it for a few moments, letting the words sink in. Then he dialled Michael's flat.

Maura answered.

'Maws? I just had a call from Jackson. Willy's been nicked and he's telling them anything they want to know.'

'OK, Roy. Thanks.'

'What's happening, Maws?'

'At the moment you're as safe as you possibly can be. After eight o'clock this morning, everything will be fine, I promise you.'

'But what . . .'

'Roy, I'm sorry, mate, but I have to go. Get some sleep. I promise that you'll be fine. Tell the other boys for me.' She put the phone down, leaving Roy for the second time in five minutes with a dead phone in his hand.

'They've dragged in William Templeton.' Maura's voice was flat. She had hardly thought about him since the trouble had started and yet, not twenty-four hours ago, she had been making love to him.

'Does he know much?' Terry was concerned.

'No. Nothing that they don't already know. If I know Willy, he'll be trying to save his own neck. They must have picked him up from my house.'

396

'Well, let's forget him then and concentrate on what the terms are going to be. We haven't got long now.' Maura stretched and both men watched the rise and fall of her breasts. She yawned loudly.

'Right. Where were we?'

Chapter Thirty-Six

Marsh and Ackland were already sick to death of William Templeton and the Home Secretary had been on the phone twice in the last hour. Like everyone else he wanted this 'little business', as he put it, cleared up once and for all. Marsh had wondered fleetingly whether the Home Secretary had been up all night as well, because by the annoyed note in his voice Marsh got the impression that the man was tired. Sick and tired, by the sounds of it. As they all were.

The phone on his desk rang and he answered it.

'What!' He had lost any remnants of civility at about four in the morning. Now, at eight-fifteen, he had had just about enough.

'Detective Inspector Petherick is here to see you, sir. I told him that you were not to be disturbed but he insisted that you would see him.'

The WPC's voice was petrified. She had already been bawled out twice by Marsh already, and she had only come on duty at seven o'clock.

'Send him up, girl! Send the bugger up!'

Marsh slammed the phone into its cradle.

'It's Petherick . . . the little scumbag!'

William Templeton stared at the two policemen. Marsh snapped at him, 'Go into the other office, you. And keep your mouth shut!'

William walked through the connecting door and sat down. He was tired and hungry and scared. From what he could gather, they knew all about him and his royal connections were not going to help him at all. He sat in the uncomfortable chair and put his head in his hands.

Terry walked into Marsh's office with his head held high and a confident stride. Under his arm was a blue cardboard folder. He could feel Ackland measuring him up.

'Well, well, well . . . if it isn't the laughing policeman.' Marsh's voice dripped sarcasm.

Terry sat in the chair vacated by Templeton.

'It seems to me that I'm the only policeman in England who

399

actually has something to laugh at. I know for a fact that you don't.'

Marsh screwed up his eyes. This was not the man he had seen previously. This was a man with a secret, an important secret, and one who knew how to use it.

'What happened to you? Where did you go?'

Terry looked at Ackland.

'I can't tell you that. What I can tell you is, Maura Ryan is willing to do a deal.'

'A what?' Marsh's voice bounced off the plasterboard walls.

'A deal.' Terry threw the folder on to the desk. 'In there is information. More than was in Geoffrey Ryan's file, I might add. There are copies of this information with numerous different people. I am here to talk business with you, gentlemen. And the Home Secretary, if he hasn't already been informed.'

Terry relaxed into his chair. He was enjoying this which was the last thing he'd expected. He watched Ackland pick up the file and flick through the papers.

'And what kind of a deal were you looking for?' Ackland's voice was resigned, as if he had expected something like this.

'Maura Ryan wants to be left alone. She and her brothers. She wants to keep her holdings in docklands, which are perfectly legal, and to run her clubs as before.'

'And what will she give us in return?'

Terry smiled at Ackland. 'In return she won't open her mouth about any of this.' He pointed to the file that Ackland was holding. 'And she will return the gold bullion that went missing in eighty-five. She also gives you her word that she will only deal with legitimate operations in all her future business investments.'

'And you honestly think she'll get away with this?' Marsh was practically foaming at the mouth.

Terry nodded. 'Yeah, I do.'

'Your career is finished, my boy!'

Terry laughed. 'Oh, shut up, Marsh, for God's sake. You sound like something from "Dixon of Dock Green". This whole place . . .' he waved his arm '. . . is rotten, mate. Rotten to the bloody core. Of course my career is over. It was over before it began. Because if you read those files carefully, Maura's and Geoffrey's, the only people to get any kind of real promotion were those on the bloody take!'

Ackland sighed.

'So you know where Maura Ryan is, I take it?'

'Yeah, I know. And I'll never tell you, so you'd better think again if you're going to try and kick it out of me.'

Terry stood up. 'I'm warning you both now. Copies of those

files have been faxed to two other countries. They were sent hours ago to reliable people. If so much as one hair of Maura Ryan's head is harmed they go straight to the tabloids. The Ryans own a bit more than you think. They own journalists and newspaper editors, with more than a few television newspeople thrown in. Not just in England but in the States and in Europe. Maura Ryan is willing to retire gracefully and just carry on with her legitimate holdings. Think about it carefully, gentlemen. She is not a woman to cross, believe me.'

Ackland raised his hand to silence Marsh who looked as if he was going to have a coronary at any moment.

'I'll have to speak to my superiors before anything can be decided.'

'Fair enough.' Terry glanced at his watch. 'I'll be in contact in four hours. At twelve-thirty.'

'You won't get away with this, Petherick. I'll get you personally.' Marsh's voice dripped with venom.

Terry leant on the desk, both palms flat, and looked into Marsh's sharp-featured face.

'You'll get me, will you? Funny how you don't want to get the others, the ones on the take. The big developers and the MPs and the Chief Super that you work for. Does he know that he's been tumbled yet? That his holidays in Kenya and the Maldives are over? That his little scams have all been found out? Does he know that the Ryans even have the name of the prostitute he visits every Wednesday night? The one who ties him up and spanks him?

'Don't say you're getting me, Marsh! Go and get some real villains for once in your life.'

Terry straightened his back and stared defiantly at the silent and grim-faced man before him. 'One last thing. Would you tell the Chief Super that I have a bit of news that might interest him?'

'What's that?' Marsh spat the words out.

'Tell him that the girl he sees every Wednesday, Samantha Golding, was diagnosed as having Aids. Tell him the Ryans even knew that before him. Before any of you. And don't you dare act the outraged policeman with me! You were willing to take part in the murder of an entire family. If you had done you would have kidded yourself it was for your country. Well, you know and I know it would not have been. It would just have saved a load of fat bastards' arses. If you loved your country so much you should have pissed off to the Falklands, Marsh. And from what's in that file,' he pointed to the folder Ackland was holding, 'that was another complete cover up and shambles!

'Now, I'm leaving. I'll be back in touch at half-past twelve.'

He stormed out of the office, leaving a white-faced Marsh and a quiet and subdued Ackland.

'You asked for that, Marsh. I have to take my hat off to the man. What he said was true.'

Marsh was in such a monumental temper he forgot his fear of Ackland. He picked up his cigar and said, 'Oh, fuck off, you Scottish turd!'

In the office next door William Templeton began to laugh.

Terry did not go back to Michael's flat. It had been arranged that he would go back to his own place, in case he was followed.

He drove there on a high. At least he had told Marsh exactly what he thought of him. Inside his flat he made himself some coffee and sat reading the paper. He had lost the urge to sleep, was in the state of overtiredness that seems to make a person more alert and mentally agile.

He sat at the table and thought about Maura. Nothing he did would get her out of his mind for even five minutes. Once again the words on the page in front of him were replaced by a vision of her face. She was flying to Marbella today. Although he had told Marsh that the file had been faxed through to two different countries, it was not true. Maura was going to take copies to the people concerned herself. She was flying to Marbella at five-thirty from Gatwick.

He sipped his coffee. He had lost everything now. His job, his way of life. And he had sacrificed it all for Maura Ryan. He looked around his kitchen, and then, as if he had been jolted from his chair, went to the phone. He knew what he had to do.

Sarah was enjoying having the three boys home. The feeling of foreboding that had plagued her the whole day before lifted off her as she cooked breakfast for them. She prepared what had long been known in the family as a 'Benny Special': two eggs, five slices of bacon, black pudding, tomatoes, beans, mushrooms, and even fried liver sausage, along with huge amounts of toast and a good strong pot of tea to wash it down with. She had felt sorry for Benjamin, eating his poached egg while they wolfed down his favourite meal, but consoled herself with the fact that he would thank her for it one day.

Just after breakfast the phone rang and Garry ran to answer it. Sarah was not sure what was said but the boys all looked a lot happier. She left them all in the kitchen while she gave Benjamin a blanket bath. He still couldn't get out of bed.

As she washed her husband's face, he grabbed her arm gently. 'All right, Sar?'

'Yeah, why?' She looked at him, puzzled.

'You're enjoying having the boys home again, ain't you?'

She smiled. 'Yeah. I miss them all.'

'I never gave you much, did I, girl? Except the back of my hand. It makes you think, you know, being stuck in bed.'

Sarah looked down at her husband's rapidly wasting body. Just for a split second she saw the eighteen-year-old boy who had whistled at her one bright summer evening in 1934. He had been tall, dark and handsome, wearing a bowler hat that night which had somehow set him apart from his contemporaries. Sarah felt an enormous lump in her throat for the man he had been.

'I know I never tell you very often, Sar, but you was always my girl. You know that, don't you? I always loved you.'

She nodded at him. It was one of those rare moments that occur in everyone's life. One of those times when there really isn't anything to say.

Ackland had spoken to the Home Secretary at length, and was now waiting for Terry Petherick to ring through to his office. Marsh had already left, as had William Templeton. Whereas Marsh had been disgusted by the turn of events, Templeton had been relieved – though Ackland was quick to guess that Templeton knew he had lost Maura Ryan's friendship.

He sighed heavily as he waited for Terry to call. The file that Petherick had left was, even at this moment, winging its way across London to be studied and talked over with the Secretary of State for the Environment amongst others. Ackland, unlike Marsh, knew when he was beaten and deep in his heart was glad that Maura Ryan had eventually outwitted them. His own conscience said to him: Why should she be a scapegoat for the real criminals?

He was glad when the phone finally rang. Lack of sleep was catching up with him.

Maura picked up the phone at twelve-forty. It was Terry and she knew even before he spoke what had happened. She could feel his euphoria coming over the telephone line.

'They've agreed! Agreed to everything!'

'Oh, thank God!'

Maura took her first really deep breath for what seemed like days.

'They didn't argue about any of it?'

'No, Maws, not a thing. It's perfectly acceptable. Tell Richard he did a good job. We all did a good job.'

'What about my brothers?'

'Fine. Everything's Hunkydory.'

'Thanks for all your help, Terry. I promise you won't lose by it.' Maura's voice was humble and sounded strange to Terry's ears.

'So you're off to warmer climes then?'

'Yeah. I suppose we won't see each other again.'

'Well . . . you never know what's going to happen, do you? I'd better let you go. You have a lot to do before you fly out.'

'Goodbye then, Terry. And thanks again.'

'You're welcome.' His voice was soft. 'Goodbye, Maura.'

He put down the phone and Maura stood in Michael's flat feeling more desolate and alone than she had ever done before. She had beaten the police and the establishment and yet she felt nothing. Nothing except an overwhelming loneliness.

Richard came into the room.

'We won then?' He sounded happy.

'Yeah. We won.'

He was sad to hear Maura's flat and broken voice. 'You'd better get a move on, you know. You have to be at Gatwick by three-thirty.'

'I know.'

Richard put his arm around her. She was much taller than him and he had to look up into her face.

'Michael used to say to me when I was down: "Ricky, remember that today is the first day of the rest of your life." I know it's an old cliché, but it's also a very true one.'

'Oh, Richard. What would I have done without you?'

She kissed him full on the mouth then said, 'I'd better phone Roy, tell him the good news.'

Maura sat on the Monarch Flight to Gibraltar. It was five-twenty-nine and the plane was due to take off at any time. She was sitting in a window seat. The seat next to her was unoccupied and she was glad – she was not up to making conversation with strangers. Plus she was shattered. She had been awake for nearly twenty-eight hours.

She closed her eyes, willing the plane to take of. Terry Petherick came straight to mind . . . She admitted to herself that she still had all the old feelings for him. The feelings that had assailed her on and off for over twenty years. When she had spoken to him on the telephone and he had said goodbye, she had felt as if her heart had been ripped from her chest. What was it about the man? Why did he make her feel like this? Even when she had learned that William, who was supposed to love her, had been willing to trade her to the police, she had not felt the intensity of feeling as when she had heard that single word from Terry: 'Goodbye'.

When she had told him the night before about the baby and

what had happened, she had hoped, deep down, that it would bring them closer together. And it had, for a little while. But only for a little while. She supposed he thought that by doing the negotiating for her with the police he had repaid any debt that he owed her. She bit her lip.

In the seat in front of her were two little boys, both excited to be going on holiday. The bigger of the two, a boy of about ten with light brown hair and mischievous brown eyes, kept looking through the gap in the seats at her. As they jumped around in excitement Maura knew that she would not have a lot of peace on the flight.

She closed her eyes tighter, willing the plane to take off so she could at least have a cigarette. She felt someone sit down in the seat beside her and pretended she was asleep. She was too overwrought to start making small talk with anyone.

'Maura Ryan, I arrest you.'

Her eyes flew open and she looked at the man beside her, dumbstruck.

'But . . . but . . .' Her voice was locked inside her throat.

'I hope you're pleased to see me?' Terry's voice was deep and husky. He was smiling that little lopsided grin that had captured her heart so many years before.

'But I don't understand. When I spoke to you . . .'

'I was still trying to get on this flight then. They held the place for me, you know. One of the last perks of being a policeman. My final abuse of my position.'

He smiled at her again. 'I don't know if you want me, Maura. But I want you more than ever. I think deep in my heart I've always known that one day I would come and claim you as my own.'

She was still staring at him in absolute amazement. Terry was frightened now. If she pushed him away this time it would be for good and he did not think he could live with that.

The plane began to taxi down the runway, building up speed. As its nose left the tarmac, Maura smiled at him.

'Oh, Terry. I'm so glad you came. So very, very glad.'

He kissed her then, a long lingering kiss that was witnessed by the two boys in the seat in front. It was their giggling that broke them apart.

'Do you mind?' Terry's voice was jocular and the two little faces disappeared from sight.

He looked at Maura's radiant face and thanked God she still wanted him.

'So you're arresting me, are you?' Her voice was full of love.

He nodded at her, drinking in every feature and contour of her face.

405

'Yes, I'm arresting you . . . and I'm afraid that you're going to get a life sentence. The whole of it to be spent with me.'

Maura looked at him seriously. 'I'll still be running the clubs and . . .'

Terry put his finger to her lips.

'I don't care, Maura. All I want from now on is you.'

They smiled at one another as the plane gradually flew higher into the sky.

Twenty-five years of DANGEROUS LADY

An interview with Martina Cole

What was it like to get a deal?

I remember when my agent, Darley, called me with the news. He was auctioning the book and I was supposed to have lunch with lots of different publishers. At the time I thought that happened to everyone – I didn't know how rare it actually was. My first meeting was with Headline in their then offices on Great Titchfield Street which were so winding – it felt like Middle Earth! I was really nervous, but it was absolutely amazing. I got home early evening and Darley rang and said, 'Headline's made a pre-emptive offer of £150,000 to call off the auction.' And I said to him, 'Are you sure you've rung the right person?' At the time that was a record-breaking advance for an unknown author. I just couldn't believe it. It was a watershed moment for me – life changing – and it was absolutely fantastic. And after twenty-five years I'm still with Headline. I still have the same publisher, agent and publicist, and I feel incredibly lucky.

Twenty-five years on, why do you think fans keep coming back to Maura Ryan being a favourite? Why is Maura such an appealing and enduring character?

In a lot of ways, I think *Dangerous Lady* was an 'anti-book'. I wrote it in the early eighties – ten years before it was published – and most women in books at the time were only really famous if they were fashion models or particularly beautiful. I wanted to put a woman in a man's world, and the underworld of Notting Hill seemed a perfect fit for me then. I think the secret of Maura Ryan is that she's such a strong character. She's not classically beautiful either – for some reason everyone always mentions the

407

fact she has such big feet! But she's a nice girl whose circumstances turn her into a powerful woman. So, it's a case of dynamics. I think what people like about this book – about all my books, in fact – is that the woman starts off with a regular life, and then things happen to her which means she drastically has to change the way she lives – and thinks. Maura changes her whole life.

It's also significant that Maura and the whole Ryan family's story was already set in the past. Even if you read it now, twenty-five years on, you are reading about an era – the fifties, sixties, seventies... I give birth to characters and I bring them up. Maura's story is multigenerational which I think appeals to a lot of readers, and, of course, it continues in *Maura's Game*. People can come to Maura at any time. It doesn't matter if you first read *Dangerous Lady* twenty-five years ago or if you pick it up next week because I write about the whole progress of a person's life, which is why I think Maura still resonates with fans and continues to have relevance today.

What is it like being Martina Cole 'Queen of Crime' vs Martina Cole 'Debut Breakthrough Author'?

It really hadn't occurred to me that it was twenty-five years since I published *Dangerous Lady* as it still feels like just a decade ago. You forget how quickly time does go. But I've got to say it's been a fantastic ride. I think the only difference twenty-five years on is that I'm not as nervous as I used to be about beginning a new book. I always used to wonder, 'Do I even have anything to write about? Will my next one be as good?' I think all authors try to do better each time. I've always written for me, never for a specific audience. *Dangerous Lady* was very much a novel for me. I'm writing my twenty-fourth book now, and I'm starting to feel that maybe I'm finally getting there. I know what I'm doing.